U.S. LAND AND NATURAL RESOURCES POLICY

History | Debates | State Data | Maps | Primary Documents

Second Edition

Mark Grossman and Gary C. Bryner

Grey House
Publishing

PUBLISHER: Leslie Mackenzie
EDITORIAL DIRECTOR: Laura Mars
EDITORIAL ASSISTANT: Diana Delgado
PRODUCTION MANAGER: Kristen Thatcher
MARKETING DIRECTOR: Jessica Moody

AUTHOR: Gary C. Bryner, First Edition
Mark Grossman and
Gary C. Bryner, Second Edition
COPYEDITOR: Marquerite Duffy
COMPOSITION: NPC, Inc.

Grey House Publishing, Inc.
4919 Route 22
Amenia, NY 12501
518.789.8700 FAX 845.373.6390
www.greyhouse.com
e-mail: books@greyhouse.com

Publisher's Cataloging-In-Publication Data
(Prepared by The Donohue Group, Inc.)

Grossman, Mark.
    U.S. land and natural resources policy : history, debates, on-going issues & primary documents / Mark Grossman. — 2nd ed.

    p. : ill. ; cm.

    First ed.: U.S. land and natural resources policy : a public issues handbook / Gary C. Bryner. Westport, Conn. : Greenwood Press, 1998.

    Includes bibliographical references and index.
    ISBN: 978-1-59237-684-1

    1. Public lands—Government policy—United States. 2. Natural resources--Government policy—United States. 3. Public lands—United States—Management. 4. Natural resources—United States—Management. 5. Land use—Government policy—United States. I. Bryner, Gary C., 1951- U.S. land and natural resources policy. II. Title.

HD216 .G76 2011
333.1/0973

Contents

List of Figures & Maps

List of Tables

Preface

This work, the product of many hands and many hours of work, was originally written by the late Gary C. Bryner. Before his death in 2010, he had hoped to update the work, but his illness prevented it. In taking over this task, I made substantive changes to the original volume, but its intended audience, those interested in the history and application of land resource law, remains the same.

While this work is not a complete history of natural resource law, it nevertheless covers areas not found in the first edition, or in works of a similar nature. Whereas the first edition covered the years up until 1998, this second edition brings this specific field of study into the 21st century, examining the records of the Clinton and George W. Bush administrations, and the early years of the administration of President Barack Obama, as current law and policy was changed or accepted. Further, a backward look examines what else may have shaped natural resource law in this country.

I found a wealth of government reports that examine land, water, energy, and other areas of policy that are barely referred to in other works dealing with these issues. Graphs and other information from these reports are included in this edition, intended to give the reader a more comprehensive and detailed examination of the subject.

This second edition covers decisions on both sides of the issues, from increasing energy mining and drilling in the wake of high oil prices, and the BP oil spill, in 2010, to global warming and the controversy that became ClimateGate. This work is designed to help average citizens reach their own conclusions about the role of government agencies at all levels, specifically concerning policies that impact the American people in all walks of life.

The United States has a rich and diverse collection of resources, a bounty that is perhaps unmatched in any other nation in the world. From land, to energy, to soil, to mining, to minerals, to the air we breathe and the water we drink, to animals on land, in water and air, there have been movements throughout history to conserve all of these resources at one time or another. And conserve we must. At the same time, however, we need to consider the effects of both over-utilizing and under-utilizing these resources. There needs to be a balance. This work, designed to help find that balance, is not based on ideology but on facts and on science.

From the start of the nation, how we treat the land and our other natural resources has been at the forefront of the government's public policy goals. This work attempts to give that history and much more. As we enter the second decade of the 21st century, policies, both new and old, will have to be based on scientific fact. This work is designed to present those facts in a clear, balanced voice.

Mark Grossman
Scottsdale, Arizona

Introduction

The first edition of *U.S. Land and Natural Resources Policy* was published in 1998 by Greenwood Press. Much has happened in the land policy arena in the 14 years since, including the untimely death of Professor Gary C. Bryner, former Director of the Public Policy Program at Brigham Young University and of the Natural Resource Law Center at the University of Colorado, and also author of the first edition.

Praise for the first edition:

". . . Bryner's handbook . . .is an important contribution to understanding and debating these crucial issues including environmental conditions, problems, trends, major laws and regulations, policy-making structures and political context. The strengths and weaknesses of alternative positions are informative to readers and focus their opinions . . . the purpose is to bring together the relevant data and to outline the major issues that are at the heart of the debate over public lands . . . Anyone concerned with the future, especially policy makers and environmental studies students, will find this book a valuable resource and reference."

American Reference Books Annual

New to this Edition

We are grateful to reference book author Mark Grossman (*The Encyclopedia of Political Corruption; Encyclopedia of the U.S. Cabinet; Speakers of the House of Representatives* and others) for authoring this second edition. This new edition not only brings the topic into the 21st century, but also includes a number of significant new elements, including 33

Primary Documents, extensive state and national data with ranking tables and hundreds of colorful maps, detailed listings for the Department of the Interior and related industry resources, Chronology, List of Public Acts & Laws, and Glossary. This expanded material helps to provide not only an historical look back, but also an informative call to action, whatever side of the land policy debate you sit on.

Content Details

Chapters 1-10

The body of this second edition, with 14 years of new data and 15 additional figures, provides:

- Overview of the politics of public lands, and the tension between preservation and consumptive use;

- History and evolution of public lands;

- Major provisions of federal public lands and natural resource laws, including descriptions of relevant federal departments, agencies and bureaus;

- Key issues, specifically, endangered species, forests, grazing, mining, energy, water, parks and wilderness;

- Ongoing debate about public lands and natural resources.

Primary Documents

Thirty-three Primary Documents are reprinted here, and include current articles, debates, historical court cases and more. They are arranged by the book's 10 specific chapters, and are designed to provide users with deeper insight into the topics discussed. Some of the longer documents have been excerpted, but most are reprinted in their entirety, and all include a brief introduction by the author to help put the document into context. They span more than 160 years of U.S. land policy, from George Perkins Marsh's address in 1847 to the Agricultural Society of Rutland County, Vermont, to *American Electric Power v. the State of Connecticut* in 2011.

State Data & Maps

Each state profile begins with a table of 31 specific data points that help define the state in relation to land designations, land use, natural resources, national parks and landmarks, and more. This table is followed by an informative narrative from the Energy Information Administration that summarizes the state's energy situation with specifics about resources, consumption, petroleum, natural gas, coal, electricity, and renewables. There are three 4-color maps for each state: Populated Places and Roads; Federal Lands and Indian Reservations; and a Satellite view that shows the landscape with relief shading that enhances the terrain.

National Data, Maps & Rankings

This data table gives national statistics for the 31 state data points, and is followed by ten 4-color maps, that visually illustrates the amount and location of public land in the United

States, specifically Federal Lands and Indian Reservations, Bureau of Land Management Lands, Department of Defense Lands, Fish and Wildlife Lands, Forest Service Lands, and others.

Following the maps are 31 ranking tables that rank each topic by state, from most to least. Which state has the most Federal land? The most Conservation Reserve Program acres? The most National Parks? The most barrels of Crude Oil Reserves? These tables make it easy to find the answers and compare states to each other.

Department of the Interior

This new section gives detailed information about this Federal department, which manages and maintains America's public lands. It starts with an organizational chart, followed by detailed profiles of important DOI agencies and their regional offices, including key executives.

Industry Resources

These 129 pages of associations, publications, databases and trade shows provide not only current contact information, but also key executives, founding year, frequency and circulation of periodicals, and number of trade show exhibits and attendees. The 1,354 listings in this section give readers the opportunity to further research the issues of land use, natural resources, and conservation, and an entry index for this section makes it easy to find exactly what you are looking for.

Appendices

1. **Chronology** starts in 1787, when Congress enacted the Northwest Ordinance, authorizing the government to sell up to 640 acres to the highest bidder for $1 an acre, and ends with several 2011 court cases dealing with the use of federal land and resources. This document illustrates, at a glance, when major changes in U.S. land policy occurred, and includes the publication of Rachel Carson's significant environmental work, *Silent Spring*, in 1962.

2. **U.S. Land Acts and Laws** includes the major legislation affecting land and natural resource policy since 1903, when President Theodore Roosevelt established the Pelican Island Reservation in Florida as a preserve and breeding ground for native birds.

3. **Glossary** has 200 terms that help define various types of land designations, land use, and natural resources, from ACEC (Area of Critical Environment Concern) to WSA (Wilderness Study Area).

This edition's **Bibliography** is categorized into Books and Articles, US Government Documents, US Government Reports & Speeches, Other Reports, and Dissertations & Thesis. A helpful **Index** ends this completely revised and expanded second edition.

1

Natural Resources and Public Lands Policies

From the 1970s on, the focus on federal public lands and natural resources policy has been on all of the United States, each one with a separate culture of land (public and private), animals, wildlife, natural resources, and other areas under the care and responsibility of the U.S. Department of the Interior and other government agencies. While many of the western states have been increasingly under the microscope regarding the ability of the U.S. government to seize or put aside lands for the public good, or, as some see it, to invade the sacred trust of landowners with the land they themselves own and take care of, all of the states of the union have been, in one way or another, under the policy of the government about how the lands and their natural resources are managed. As the first decade of the twenty-first century ends, this debate has not only not gone away, but it has intensified, what with the recent U.S. Supreme Court decision in *Kelo v. City of New London* (545 U.S. 469 {2005}, which gave states and other localities the right to seize land from private owners to the public for whatever reason. This work, updated from a first edition done in 1998, aims to fill in the gaps of the policies of federal, state, and local governments concerning the fair use of public lands and natural resource policies as we head into the second decade of the twenty-first century.

This examination, not just of federal public lands and natural resource policy, is expanded from the original work to now include state and local policy as well. Also, any focus also has to look not just at the federal lands in what is the western United States but the entire nation as a whole, where federal policy encompasses a wide swath of lands in each state. While one side in the argument over federal policy calls such intervention protectionist of land, natural resources, wildlife, and additional areas of concern, others, from a wide range of interests, have resisted and deplored what they see as excessive federal intervention, not just in public lands policy but in the ownership, maintenance, and running of private lands and resources.

From the earliest days of the American republic, the federal government has had a varying interest in the maintenance of the public lands. Throughout most of the nineteenth century, the federal government, mostly through congressional legislation, encouraged people to "head West" and utilize land and resources to the best of their abilities. Despite this, it was not until 1849 that a federal Department of the Interior (DOI) was established as a cabinet-level agency. At the same time, the natural growth of the population through immigration, travel, homesteading, and industry pushed people into areas that before had been mostly left alone or had been trotted upon only by Native American tribes. Trade and business exploded in intensity as the century moved along, so that by its end, historian Frederick Jackson Turner wrote that "[t]he existence of an area of free land, its continuous recession, and the advance of American settlement westward explain American development."

A history of land policy in all 50 states is unfeasible; this edition will focus exclusively on the eleven states that are considered the western United States, encompassing some 370 million acres of federal land, from the plains to the grasslands, inclusive of hills and mountains, all rich in resources such as minerals, timber, and wildlife. From the start of the American nation, this area has held a fascination in the American psyche, from books to plays to movies. Governmental policy, most notably from Congress, encouraged persons sturdy enough to head to the region to take charge of the land, use it to its maximum, and make it a part of a burgeoning American nation. Motivated by newspaperman John B. L. Soule and his words in an 1851 editorial in the *Terre Haute Express* to "go west, young man" (words attributed erroneously to New York Tribune editor Horace Greeley), tens of thousands of hearty people decided to do just that and settled in lands that appeared, at first, to be wholly uninhabited. On these same lands, however, for untold millennium prior, were peoples labeled as "American Indians," a hodgepodge of tribes of natives who would fight to the bitter end to preserve the West and their lives there. The desire of one people to take lands seemingly owned by another people led to fighting, massacres on both sides, and, finally, action from the U.S. military. By the end of the nineteenth century, the "Indian problem" had been cured by seizing the millions of acres of lands that these natives had once lived on in seeming freedom. In

1849, Congress established a Department of the Interior to oversee all matters of land resources and other policy regarding internal land matters. California soon became the focus of more emigration when gold was found by prospector James Marshall near the mill of his friend, John A. Sutter, setting off the "gold rush" that fostered more homesteaders to head westward.

By the 1870s, unrestrained growth and expansion forced Congress to reconsider the "encouragement" it had been providing for many years by offering people free land if they lived and cultivated it for a period of five years. In 1872, Congress enacted the General Mining Act of 1872, which gave the Congress oversight over the mining of such minerals as gold, silver, copper, platinum, and other resources. Just a few years earlier, a new idea swept the nation of preserving a portion of the lands as federal property for the protection of the resources and the species of wildlife on them. Starting in 1864, with the publication of George Perkins Marsh's "Man and Nature; or, Physical Geography as Modified by Human Action," an awareness of the responsibility of people to preserve or conserve the environment grew, opening the way for what was called the *Conservation movement*. It was not until 1879, when Congress appropriated money for the creation of the Geological Survey and for a Public Land Commission. Slowly at first, but then gathering speed, opposition to the preservation of such lands, especially in the West, became smaller and smaller. Even today, more than a century after these initial arguments, there remains a debate over how much land and resources should be preserved, and whether or not the government should be in the business of preservation at all. As the author of the first edition of this work first noted in 1998,

> *Two issues help provide the context for the policy discussions that follow. First, the West is in the middle of a major transformation that began several decades ago and has important implications for public lands and natural resource policy. Some observers argue that there really are two Wests, the old and the new, and they represent incompatible views about what the West should become. Second, public lands policy clashes with the individualism and libertarian values Americans hold dear. The idea of preserving public lands for the needs of current and future generations is a tenuous one in American public philosophy and its commitment to the pursuit of self-interest.*

THE CHANGING AMERICAN WEST

If you want to see something stay the same, don't look towards the American west for such consistency. Even from the time of Theodore Roosevelt in the first years of the twentieth century, arguments over the role of government in the land policy debate in the West continue unabated, and came about anew with each new administration in power in Washington, D.C. There have been drastic changes in land and natural resource policy over the last two decades, from the years of the administration of President Bill Clinton (1993-2001) to that of President George W. Bush (2001-09), to that of President Barack Obama (2009-). During that time, there have been four Secretaries of the Interior, all of different political stripes: Under Clinton was Bruce Babbitt (1993-2001), under Bush was Gale Ann Norton (2001-06) and Dirk Kempthorne (2006-09), and under Obama is Ken Salazar (2009-). While all four approach land and resource policy in drastically different ways, they all have one thing in common: all come from western states — Babbitt was a former Governor (1978-87) of Arizona; Norton was an Attorney General of Colorado (1991-99); Kempthorne was a U.S. Senator from (1993-99) and the Governor (1999-2006) of the state of Idaho; and Salazar was the Attorney General (1999-2005) and a U.S. Senator (2005-09) from Colorado. Under Babbitt, the Clinton administration began a systematic change to the way the U.S. government handled land policy, initiating a major effort to revise public land policies that had been in use for decades and had remained basically unchanged since the early years of the twentieth century. Although Clinton had Democrat majorities in Congress seemingly able to enact his measures into law, resistance came not just from Republicans but from Democrats from western states where their idea of government intervention was not the same as Clinton's. Unable to get his program completely through the Congress, Clinton used his Department of the Interior — through Babbitt — and the executive pen of the presidency to make changes. The largest — and most controversial — came in 1996, when he invoked the Antiquities Act of 1906 to establish, through an executive order, the Grand Staircase-Escalante National Monument in southern Utah, one of the largest set-asides of land from private hands to public control in U.S. history. John Heilprin of the Associated Press wrote in 2002, "As dominant as the 1.9 million-acre monument is in southern Utah, Grand Staircase-Escalante casts an even larger shadow over the debate on [the] use of federal lands. It is a prototype for other vast land monuments being planned and, to Western Republicans, a symbol of federal intrusion." [1] Ironically, when George W. Bush succeeded Clinton in the White House in January 2001, the new Secretary of the Interior, Gale Norton, announced that Bush would not overturn any of Clinton's designations of setting aside lands for public use, promising only to "adjust the boundaries" and to "alter the rules" which oversaw any use of resources on the lands. In fact, Bush set aside nearly 200,000 square miles of the Pacific Ocean controlled by the United States as underseas monuments. [2] In 2009, a secret Department of the Interior memo stated that President Barack Obama intended to use his power of executive orders to set aside millions of acres of land across the western United States, putting them out of the reach of forestry, mining, energy developments, and ranching. [3] Only when western Democrats in both houses of Congress, conscious of the impact such policies could have on their re-election chances, raised objections, was the plan put on the shelf.

As Clinton, and Bush, and Obama have seen, while there is wide support for environmental protection, there is also deep and sustained opposition to the government taking land for public use, especially in the West. The economic, social, and environmental changes such set-asides have created, and will continue to create, have yet to be adequately examined by any side of the argument. As the need for the increased use of natural resources, most notably energy such as oil and natural gas, expands due to the high costs of imported gasoline, this debate will continue to gain steam and pit environmentalists against those who advocate the "wise use" of the lands. Although some have warned that those opposed to government intrusion would resort to violence, none has been seen as of this writing; in fact, it is some radical environmentalists who have destroyed private and public property that they felt was being used in a misguided way. This "ecoterrorism" was considered, during the first decade of the twenty-first century, as the worst domestic threat to the nation, and second only in totality to the external threat from Islamic terrorism. In 2002, in congressional testimony, James Jarboe, Domestic Terrorism section chief of the Counterterrorism Division of the FBI, told Congress that the agency estimated that two groups, the Animal Liberation Front (ALF) and the Earth Liberation Front (ELF) "have committed more than 600 criminal acts in the United States since 1996, resulting in damages in excess of 43 million dollars." [4]

The lands of the United States offer incredible bounties, be they natural resources taken from the earth, or for their grand vistas and views of unimagined beauty. For more than 200 years, people have taken to all forms of transportation to head West, to farm the land, to dig for gold, to explore the richness of this region, unseen anywhere else in the world. It has attracted diverse figures, and diverse opinions. In 1908, Scotsman John Muir, who had seen the Hetch-Hetchy Valley in California and would remain in love with it until his dying breath, wrote to J. Horace McFarland, the President of the American Civic Association,

> *Timber and water are universal wants, and of course the Government is aware that no scheme of management of the public domain failing to provide for them can possibly be maintained. But, however abundantly supplied from legitimate sources, every national park is besieged by thieves and robbers and beggars with all sorts of plans and pleas for possession of some coveted treasure of water, timber, pasture, rights of way, etc. Nothing dollarable is safe, however guarded. Thus the Yosemite Park, the beauty glory of California and the nation, nature's own mountain wonderland, has been attacked by spoilers ever since it was established, and this strife I suppose must go on as part of the eternal battle between right and wrong.* [5]

Until the last few decades, people came to the West primarily for the natural resources that the lands contained. They left the urban comforts, refinements, and amenities for the pursuit of wealth and independence. Migrants to the late twentieth-century West now come to escape urban crime, pollution, and decay and seek solitude and recreation. The clashes in values could not be more striking. Neither the newcomer nor the longtime residents are monolithic. Some immigrants are as fearful of a strong federal government as are those who have worked public lands for generations. Some preservationists have been working to protect wild lands from development for decades, joined by others who have recently moved to the West. There are also tourists who found their nirvana and decided to stay; and, for others, there is the simple lure of the mystique of the West itself. The mountains, the scenery, the beauty of the entire region: all of it plays a role in highlighting life in there. But there are also business opportunities: Before the huge economic crisis that swept the United States and much of the world in the last years of the first decade of the twenty-first century, the Great Basin states, composed of the states of the West including parts of Arizona, California, Idaho, Oregon, Utah, and Wyoming, jutting into Mexico itself, saw more economic growth from the 1970s onward than any other part of the United States. Although long out of date, a 1991 article in *The New York Times* stated that from 1980 to 1990, job growth grew some 56.1 percent in Nevada, 41.2 percent in Arizona, 31.0 percent in Utah, and 26.2 percent in New Mexico; in the United States as a whole, jobs grew by 22.0 percent. Population grew during the same decade by 50.7 percent in Nevada, 35.3 percent in Arizona, 18.3 percent in Utah, and 16.8 percent in New Mexico. [6] A 2005 report from the St. Louis, Missouri, Federal Reserve, noted that some of the greatest rates of job growth from 1980 to 2000 came from such places as Las Vegas, Nevada, the Phoenix-Mesa area in central Arizona, and Boise City, Idaho. [7]

The economic crisis that consumed much of the world from late 2007 until well into the next decade, and which continues as of this writing, changed the outlook for job performance across the spectrum in the United States. Whereas economic booms in the American West came from the search for natural resources — gold, oil, etc. — this does not appear to be the shape things are taking to lead the nation out of this specific economic crisis. Tourism appears to be a leading way states and localities can expand their economic opportunities for their populations. The collapse of the manufacturing and housing sectors during the crisis have also put a major crack in the ability of western states to raise needed funds for their growing budget deficits.

POLICY CHANGES

At the same time that the states are going through these economic troubles, they also have to contend with more and more mandates from Washington, D.C., most notably during the years starting with the administration of President Barack Obama. Whereas the administration of President George W. Bush (2001-09) put more of an emphasis in job creation and less on environmental protection or land set-asides, the Obama administration overturned many rules instituted by the Bush administration and has made states put more money into the preservation of natural resources rather than immediate job growth. Faced with diminishing budget income during the economic crisis, these states, especially in the western part of the country (and, most notably, Nevada and Arizona, to name two), have settled on massive cuts in state spending to offset the calls to raise taxes to make up for the shortfalls. In addition, the housing collapse has left these states, again with Nevada and Arizona being among the worst hit, less money from property taxes than before. So, having seen the massive expansion of towns and cities in the 1990s and 2000s via construction and suburban growth, these states are now battling whether or not to preserve the wilderness or try to make different economic choices.

But the fight for both sides does not necessarily pit Democrats vs. Republicans: For many Democrats from western states, their support comes from ranchers, miners, and others who want to see less regulation from Washington and more local control over natural resources. Senator Max Baucus, Democrat of Montana, explained that nearly his entire state's economy is based on this kind of industry: "It's true that values are changing in the West. But in Montana, it's timber, it's mining, it's agriculture, it's livestock. That's the economy."

In the first decade of the twenty-first century, the preservation of so-called "old-growth forests" was one of the most contentious in the West. Following a number of forest fires that allegedly could have been less damaging because environmental regulations disallowed any cutting or thinning of dead trees from protected old growth forests, the debate raged whether or not such thinning — called the *wildland/urban interface* — should be allowed. Another split came when the U.S. government stepped in to protect the habitat of the spotted owl, specifically in Oregon, which covered areas where mills cut down trees: again, should the emphasis been on jobs or protecting the wilderness and the beauty of its habitat? Senator Ben Nighthorse Campbell of Colorado, a Democrat who switched to the Republican Party in 1995, looked at both sides of this debate, and said of Secretary of the Interior Bruce Babbitt's push for more environmental regulation: "He's not supposed to be advocating the destruction of all these western jobs any more than [Ronald Reagan's Secretary of the Interior] Jim Watt should have been advocating the destruction of the environment." [8] Unfortunately, Campbell didn't notice that both sides of the debate are set in concrete regarding their platforms, and that there appears to be little room for compromise. As well, the back-and-forth of regulations seem to rise and fall depending on which administration is in power in Washington, D.C. For every person who condemned Babbitt, there were equal voices against George W. Bush's environmental policies, who slammed his two Secretaries of the Interior, Gale Norton and Dirk Kempthorne. As well, there is now equal angst against the policies of current (as of this writing) Secretary of the Interior Ken Salazar, including those angered by department inaction following the horrendous BP oil spill in the Gulf of Mexico in 2010.

For instance, in January 2010 Salazar announced that he was changing the regulations of the Bureau of Land Management (BLM) regarding the leasing of federal land for oil and gas drilling, reversing Bush administration policy. [9] In March 2010, after an internal DOI memo showed that the Obama administration would move forward on a series of land designations in every western state, even if there was widespread opposition in Congress, Senator John Barrasso, Republican of Wyoming and chairman of the Senate Western Caucus, wrote to Salazar to protest the administration's "land-grab strategy" in eleven western states. "Expansion of federal land holdings and authority is an unsustainable policy," Barrasso wrote, representing eight Senators, all Republicans, from western states. "The bureaus of the Department of the Interior are already overloaded with acreage and responsibility. The BLM faces budget shortfalls annually, and the National Park Service (NPS) faces a maintenance backlog on its existing facilities of over 9 billion dollars. Policy makers must focus on making responsible investments on behalf of the American taxpayer. With that priority in mind, there is no basis for expanding acreage and creating new management requirements for federal land across the West." He added, "The Senate Western Caucus opposes the recently released Department of the Interior strategy for land designation and acquisition. Unilateral action will not be successful in the West. Western communities have a long, successful history of land stewardship. We urge the Department to defer to local land use decision-making and grassroots conservation efforts." [10]

At the same time that there have been changes to specific laws governing the land, there have been angry and sometimes violent reactions to them. During the Clinton administration, militia members, especially in the Northwest, fought the government over water and land rights. One Nevadan said at the time, "We don't know what to do but to fight. If we can't use the land, we can't exist." [11] Later, during the Bush administration, such groups as Earth First! used such actions that earned them the term "domestic terrorists," even after the Islamic terrorist attacks on the United States on 11 September 2001, including bombing radio towers and burning down car dealerships, causing millions of dollars of damage.

The tensions surrounding public lands and natural resources are only natural, as both sides of the ideological debate try to win over converts or merely have their policies put in place no matter the cost. By 2010, such arguments reached a fevered pitch, as anger with the Obama administration over unfunded mandates led to the growth of the so-called "Tea Party" movement. In the 2008 election, Obama won several western states, most notably Colorado, by espousing moderate policies; by 2010, however, through massive government spending and a continued rise in unemployment, many who had backed Obama conceded that any chances of a repeat of winning western votes was rapidly draining away. Whether or not that translates into changes regarding land and water policy to placate the opposition to the administration remains to be seen as of this writing. What has become apparent is that moderates who try to weave a middle path are rapidly becoming extinct from the political landscape.

The first generation of laws and regulations aimed specifically at land and water policies triggered a backlash against the federal government, most notably in the western states. The effectiveness of these laws and regulations, as well as the additional ones that may be needed as new matters and issues present themselves, will depend to a great extent on how well policy makers are able to respond to the arguments raised by opponents of federal public lands policies, and balance these concerns with the imperatives of effective policymaking.

THE FIGHT OVER PUBLIC LANDS

The idea of public lands, areas held in common by all Americans, conflicts with the idea of individualism and opportunity that in the past have compelled these lands to be free for the taking. Until the passage of environmental laws in the late 1960s and early 1970s, federal land officials saw their role as facilitating resource development; as protective policies were instituted, westerners began to chafe at the restraints. The Sagebrush Rebellion began in the 1970s as an effort by wealthy ranchers and others in the West to gain control of public lands. The movement had proponents in government in the 1980s, particularly Interior Secretary James Watt. The movement was reinvigorated in the early 1990s as the Wise Use and County Supremacy movements garnered attentions. Between 1991 and 1995, fifty-nine western counties passed ordinances that claim authority to supercede federal environmental and land use laws and regulations. Organizations like the Mountain States Legal Foundation (MSLF), headquartered in Lakewood, Colorado, and the Individual Rights Foundation have led the legal fight against federal lands and the imposition of federal laws upon the states. By 1995, thirty-four counties in Nevada, California, Idaho, New Mexico, and Oregon had passed ordinances challenging federal control of local lands, and, by the end of the decade, it had risen to sixty counties. **[12]** This movement is known by some as the "County Supremacy Movement." In perhaps the strongest move to protest laws mandated by Washington, in 1994 Dick Carver, a Nevada rancher and commissioner in Nye County, Nevada, which was almost completely controlled by the federal government, got on a bulldozer and openly plowed a road into a protected forest in violation of the U.S. Forest Service. Carver became a local hero; in the meantime, across the West, federal agents carrying out these mandates were targeted for violence.

Determined to end the County Supremacy Movement, the Clinton Department of Justice filed two lawsuits: in the first, *Boundary Backpackers v. Boundary County* (913 P.2d 1141 {1996}), the Idaho state Supreme Court invalidated a 1991 Boundary County ordnance, which required all state and local agencies to conform to its specific land-use laws. In the second case, *United States v. Nye County* (920 F.Supp. 1108 {1996}), a district judge struck down as unconstitutional two 1993 Nye County resolutions stating that the county, and not the state or U.S. government, owned all public lands and areas. While the Clinton administration may have won these two cases, the wins were phyrric victories, as the anger from the legal defeats carried over to the Democrats losing seats across the West in the 1990s, and, in 2000, cost them the White House. **[13]**

THE FIGHT OVER PRIVATE LANDS

No issue has been more contentious, especially in the last several years, than the interests of private property rights vs. the preservation of natural lands, natural resources, and wildlife. Prior to 2005, there were few major cases that dealt with the taking of private land by government, although the issue is dealt with clearly in the so-called "Takings

Clause" of the Fifth Amendment to the U.S. Constitution. But it was a little-discussed U.S. Supreme Court case decided by the high court in 2005 that changed takings law completely. In 2000, the city of New London, Connecticut, approved a measure that allowed to literally seize private land if it was in the "public interest" and could create jobs or add to the economy. New London was, and continues to be, a severely economically depressed city, and, in the words of the Connecticut state Supreme Court, the measure passed by the city was "projected to create in excess of 1,000 jobs, to increase tax and other revenues, and to revitalize an economically distressed city, including its downtown and waterfront areas." The key words of the measure were "public use": if a city believed that private property could be better used by the public, it would be allowed to "take" the property, only allowing for the "fair compensation" given to the owner. The owner, however, had no way to resist being forced to sell their property. One of the people affected by the new law, Susette Kelo, sued when the city desired to take her home for the waterfront project even though she did not want to sell. Kelo sued the city, and by 2005 the case had been appealed up to the U.S. Supreme Court.

On 23 June 2005, the Court held, 5-4, that the city did have the right to take land it deemed "in the public interest." Writing for a badly-split court, Justice John Paul Stevens explained that "[t]wo polar propositions are perfectly clear. On the one hand, it has long been accepted that the sovereign may not take the property of A for the sole purpose of transferring it to another private party B, even though A is paid just compensation. On the other hand, it is equally clear that a State may transfer property from one private party to another if future "use by the public" is the purpose of the taking; the condemnation of land for a railroad with common-carrier duties is a familiar example." He added,

> In affirming the City's authority to take petitioners' properties, we do not minimize the hardship that condemnations may entail, notwithstanding the payment of just compensation. We emphasize that nothing in our opinion precludes any State from placing further restrictions on its exercise of the takings power. Indeed, many States already impose "public use" requirements that are stricter than the federal baseline. Some of these requirements have been established as a matter of state constitutional law, while others are expressed in state eminent domain statutes that carefully limit the grounds upon which takings may be exercised. As the submissions of the parties and their amici [brief] make clear, the necessity and wisdom of using eminent domain to promote economic development are certainly matters of legitimate public debate.24 This Court's authority, however, extends only to determining whether the City's proposed condemnations are for a "public use" within the meaning of the Fifth Amendment to the Federal Constitution. [14]

Although *Kelo* had little to do with the discussion over private vs. public lands, it has been used by both sides in their attempts to either gain additional property for public lands or to raise funds to frustrate these efforts.

ANGER FROM THE RIGHT IN THE 1990S AND ANGER FROM THE LEFT IN THE 2000S

During the eight years of the Clinton administration (1993-2001), the rise of anger from the right side of the political arena was unmatched in recent American history, centered almost completely over administration land and natural resource policy, as well as the rights of persons to own guns. While the second issue is of no importance to this work, the first is what galvanized public opposition to nearly all Clinton initiatives during the eight years of his two terms. In some cases, the anger turned to violence, with some federal agents being targeted with guns and bombs.

In 2000, Texas Governor George W. Bush was elected the 43rd President, and he had made it one of the parts of his platform that if elected he would seek to undo, or change to a major degree, Clinton land and natural resources policy. To this end, he named Gale Norton as his Secretary of the Interior. Norton, a former state Attorney General in Colorado (1991-99), had also served as Associate Solicitor of the Department of the Interior. Her career, however, began in 1979 when she served as a member of the Mountain States Legal Foundation (MSLF), a conservative-leaning think tank that fights for individual and private land rights against the government. Depending again on which side of the political aisle one came from, Norton was either a defender of individual property rights or a destroyer of the environment. During her tenure, she clashed with such groups as the Wilderness Society, the Sierra Club, and the Natural Resources Defense Council for her views and the way in which she conducted the business of the department she was the first woman to serve as head of. During the tenure of Norton and her successor, it was Bush administration policy to open federal lands to the mining of coal, oil, and natural gas for an ever-expanding American market; some 30% of all U.S. energy comes in one form or another from federal lands. Norton even pushed to open the Arctic National Wildlife Refuge in Alaska for oil and gas exploration, but the U.S. Senate blocked the proposal. When she resigned in 2006, the *Houston Chronicle* called her tenure a "mixed legacy," lauded by industry and those favoring private land rights but attacked by environmentalists. [15]

Norton's successor, Dirk Kempthorne, had served as a U.S. Senator (1993-99) and Governor (1999-06) of Idaho, his native state, and as such, like Norton, brought the conservative side of the land policy argument to the Department of the Interior. Again, as with Norton, conservation interest groups denounced Kempthorne's tenure as being violation of several laws, including the Endangered Species Act. [16] The same groups that opposed Norton and Kempthorne angled to have one of their own named to the department when Democrat Barack Obama was elected President in 2008. Obama named Senator Ken Salazar of Colorado, who, according to some environmentalists, had a spotty record because of his support for drilling and mining on public lands. [17] Whereas Salazar pledged when nominated to undo a Bush policy of regulating greenhouse gas emissions through the Endangered Species Act, in May 2009 Salazar surprised environmental groups when he decided to let the policy stand. One environmental group, The Defenders of Wildlife, angrily called Salazar's decision "illegal" and threatened to sue the administration in court. [18]

So, despite the change in administrations, anger from all sides continued to be exhibited against government policy, particularly in the area of environmental decision making.

INCREASED REGULATION: GOOD OR BAD?

Since 1845, the U.S. government has had the absolute right under the laws of Congress to have full control and power over the public lands in the country. This mandate comes from the U.S. Supreme Court, which in 1845 decided on the constitutionality of congressional law in *Pollard's Lessee v. Hagen* (3 Howard {44 US} 21). It held that that the "property clause," located in Article IV, Section 3, clause 2 of the U.S. Constitution, and which states that "The Congress shall have Power to dispose of and make all needful Rules and Regulations respecting the Territory or other Property belonging to the United States; and nothing in this Constitution shall be so construed as to Prejudice any Claims of the United States, or of any particular State," was absolute. Justice John McKinley wrote that the property clause "authorized the passage of all laws necessary to secure the rights of the United States to the public lands, and to provide for their sale, and to protect them from taxation." [19]

Since this little-remembered but landmark decision, the U.S. government has had the command of sectioning off areas of the nation under the aegis of protection as public lands. And with these decisions come the proper regulation of these lands, i.e., allowing limited mining, drilling, gas, oil, and other resource exploration as well as hiking, boating, or other forms of motorized navigation. The amount of regulation shifts with the change of administration; some administrations allow less regulation, while others have more. The balance is always a shifting one, normally between who is in power in Washington and whose support they wish to have, be it from conservation and/or environmental groups, or industry and other similar groups. Yes, the balance is always a shifting one, indeed.

For instance, in 2002, the issue of the governmental regulation of navigable waterways came forward when Rep. James Oberstar, Democrat of Minnesota, pushed to have an amendment added to the Clean Water Act (CWA) of 1972, which would give Congress the power to regulate all "navigable" waterways in the United States, which Oberstar said was the original intent of Congress when the CWA was first enacted. Oberstar's amendment came about after the U.S. Supreme Court, in *Solid Waste Agency of Northern Cook County v. Army Corps of Engineers* (531 US 159 {2001}), held that provisions of the CWA did not extend to intrastate waters, which it could not consider "navigable." Holding for a 5-4 court, Chief Justice William H. Rehnquist wrote that "The term 'navigable' has at least the import of showing us what Congress had in mind as its authority for enacting the CWA: its traditional jurisdiction over waters that were or had been navigable in fact or which could reasonably be so made." Rehnquist then added, "We thus decline respondents' invitation to take what they see as the next ineluctable step [[0085]]: holding that isolated ponds, some only seasonal, wholly located within two Illinois counties, fall under §404(a)'s definition of "navigable waters" because they serve as habitat for migratory birds." [20] Oberstar denounced the decision; he introduced the amendment, but it could not get enough support in Congress. As of this writing, in 2011, Oberstar continues to try to get his amendment an up or down vote in the U.S. House of Representatives, with little success.

The question regarding Obsertar's action is thus: can the government regulate all bodies of water in the country, regardless of their size, and where they might be located? And since a piece of water would be protected, would not the land that embraces it also be protected as well? What would such regulations mean for private property rights?

This entire debate is just another of the arguments over public land policy: is the regulation of public — and even private — lands a good thing or a bad thing? According to the libertarian think tank the Cato Institute, in 2010 the U.S. Forest Service, the Bureau of Land Management, the National Park Service, and the U.S. Fish and Wildlife Service have control of and manage some 630 million acres of public lands in the United States; this represents approximately 28% of all of the land in the nation as a whole. While the Cato Institute points out that such management sets aside land to be properly preserved for present and future generations, it also states that federal land management costs government entities — including federal, state, and local — approximately $7 billion a year. [21] These costs are coming at a time when the U.S. government is heavily in debt. The question then arises: Could more be done to lower these costs, or could some public lands be sold or used to a degree so that costs could be recouped?

The issue of how to use the lands "properly" — again, depending on who is being asked — is not a new one. In 1908, in writing about mining rights in the public domain, Colorado attorneys R.S. Morrison and Emilio De Soto wrote, "Practically all of the Pacific slope and the land east of the mountains to the Missouri River was then [in 1849, at the time of the California gold rush] public domain. The vast ore bodies of the Comstock [Lode], the wealth of Alder Gulch, the veins and placers of Pike's Peak, and of [the] countless intermediate mineral localities were all appropriated and their values extracted under the protection of this form of local self-government for many years, with no paternal interference by the National Legislature." [22]

CONSERVATION TRUSTS AND COMMUNITY LAND TRUSTS

Some conservation groups have decided to use a system of land purchases to establish trusts to preserve private lands in perpetuity. While some private landowners voluntarily deed or will their lands to these trusts, other tracts of land, be they in important wildlife or natural resource areas, are purchased by private groups who then hold the land and preserve it. In a sense, this middle ground pleases both those who do not wish to see government "take" lands from owners, while still allowing the lands to be preserved from mining or drilling or whatever use it may be destined for. It is the ultimate NGO — nongovernmental organization. Authors Sally Fairfax and Darla Guenzler wrote in 2001, "For more than a century, bequests of land and funds for environmental protection have been common, but in recent decades the trusts used to address conservation issues and resolve environmental disputes have diversified and grown significantly." [23] Although terribly outdated (in a 1996 article), author Tom Peterson wrote, "There are essentially two types of land trusts: conservation trusts, which acquire and protect open space and agricultural land; and community land trusts (CLTs), which tend to focus more on housing and community development." Still, the concept of just what a land trust is has not changed; in fact, it has grown in popularity. [24] These trusts work with limited government intervention at best; at the same time, however, they apply all government-mandated regulations to the way the land is preserved.

"Wise Use" vs. Preservation

As the United States enters the second decade of the twenty-first century, the fights that have been fought over land and natural resources, particularly in the American West, continue unabated. The fight over whether or not to give priority to jobs and private property, exemplified in the "Wise Use" movement, or to the preservation of natural resources and the biodiversity of the land seems not to be one in which a middle ground can be found. Whether or not that remains to be true is up to those who make policy, be it in Washington, D.C. or elsewhere.

The chapters that follow focus on the economic necessities that drive increased usage of the lands and their resources, as well as ecological considerations that guide policymaking for public lands and natural resources. What kind of balance can be achieved, if any, will be discussed and examined. In the end, both sides want to make sure that future generations enjoy the land and the air and water as past generations have. How that will be done is the true question for all.

NOTES:

[1] Heilprin, John, "Utah Monument Casts Big Shadow Over Land Policy," *The Sunday Free Lance-Star* [Fredericksburg, Virginia], 21 July 2002, A1.

[2] "Bush Creates World's Largest Set of Marine Sanctuaries," *Science Now*, 5 January 2009, online at http://news.sciencemag.org/sciencenow/2009/01/05-01.html.

[3] "Attachment 4. Prospective Conservation Designation: National Monument Designations Under the Antiquities Act," internal memo, undated, courtesy of The Hill, online at http://thehill.com/images/stories/blogs/antiquitiesdocument.pdf.

[4] "The Threat of Eco-Terrorism," testimony of James F. Jarboe, Domestic Terrorism Section Chief, Counterterrorism Division, FBI, Before the House Resources Committee, Subcommittee on Forests and Forest Health February 12, 2002, online at http://www.fbi.gov/congress/congress02/jarboe021202.htm.

[5] John Muir to J. Horace McFarland, 14 May 1908, in Muir, "The Hetch-Hetchy Valley: A National Question," *American Forestry*, XVI:5 (May 1910), 263.

[6] Johnson, Dirk, "Far from an Arid Economy, Desert States Thrive," *The New York Times*, 13 May 1991, A1.

[7] Wheeler, Christopher H., "Employment Growth in America: Exploring Where Good Jobs Grow," research report of the Federal Reserve Bank of St. Louis, July 2005, 6.

[8] Rasband, James R., "The Rise of Urban Archipelagoes in the American West: A New Reservation Policy?," *Environmental Law Review*, XXXI:1 (Winter 2001), 3-4.

[9] "Public Gets Say on Drilling," *Western Citizen*, 7 January 2010, online at http://www.westerncitizen.com/tag/ken-salazar/.

[10] "Washington Land Grab Unwelcome in West," press release of the office of Senator John Barrasso (R-WY), 2 March 2010, online at http://barrasso.senate.gov/public/index.cfm?FuseAction=PressOffice. PressReleases&ContentRecord_id=24d4890a-0494-c686-7c4a-df31887403ea&Region_id=&Issue_id=.

[11] Seymour Martin Lipset, " American Exceptionalism: A Double-Edge Sword" (New York: W.W. Norton, 1996), 19.

[12] Schneider, Keith, "When the Bad Guy Is Seen as the One in the Green Hat," *The New York Times*, 16 February 1992, 3.

[13] See Scheberle, Denise, "Federalism and Environmental Policy: Trust and the Politics of Implementation" (Washington, D.C.: Georgetown University Press, 2004).

[14] *Kelo et al. v. City of New London* (545 U.S. 469{2005}.

[15] "Norton"s Mixed Legacy. Resigning U.S. Secretary of the Interior Lauded by Industry but Despised by Environmentalists," *The Houston Chronicle*, 15 March 2006, online at http://www.chron.com/disp/story.mpl/editorial/3726671.html.

[16] "Kempthorne, Dirk," biography courtesy of the "Biographical Directory of the United States Congress," online at http://bioguide.congress.gov/scripts/biodisplay.pl?index=k000088.

[17] Broder, John M., "Environmentalists Wary of Obama's Interior Pick," *The New York Times*, 17 December 2008, A1.

[18] Tankersley, Jim, "Obama Administration Won't Reverse Bush Ruling on Polar Bears," *Los Angeles Times*, 9 May 2009, online at http://articles.latimes.com/2009/may/09/nation/na-polar-bear9.

[19] See McKinley's decision in *Pollard's Lessee v. Hagan* (3 Howard {44 US} 21 {1845}.

[20] See the decision of the majority in *Solid Waste Agency of Northern Cook County v. Army Corps of Engineers* (531 US 159 {2001}.

[21] Statistics on land use in "The Cato Handbook for Policymakers" (Washington, D.C.: The Cato Institute, 2009), 249.

[22] Morrison, R.S.; and Emilio De Soto, "Mining Rights on the Public Domain: Lode and Placer Claims. Tunnels, Mill Sites and Water Rights. Statutes, Decisions, Forms and Land Office Procedure for Prospectors, Attorneys, Surveyors, and Mining Companies" (Denver, Colorado: The Smith-Brooks Printing Company, 1908), 3.

[23] Fairfax, Sally K. and Darla Guenzler, "Conservation Trusts" (Lawrence: University of Kansas Press, 2001).

[24] Peterson, Tom, "Community Land Trusts: An Introduce," Planner's Web: *The Planning Commissioners Journal*, XXIII (Summer 1996), online at http://www.plannersweb.com/articles/pet112.html.

2

The Evolution of Public Lands Policy

Since the first people headed to certain western parts of the Americas to find treasure, be it gold or other precious metal or item, the land has been seen as a place to take, capture, and control. Gold miners saw it for the bounty of precious metal that could be extracted from it; oil producers saw it for the substance that could be taken from its depths to power the American economic engine; farmers and others saw it as a place to grow their crops, and harvest the natural bounty of the earth; homesteaders saw it as a place to place a stake in the American dream and own something of their very own if they stayed and worked the land for a period of years. And although each one of these groups saw the land for its intrinsic value, they also saw it for its value as a renewable resource: the farmer who lets his fields lay fallow so he won't overwork the land; the homesteader who wants to build a home or a business on land so that it will work in harmony for years to come; gold miners and others looking for treasure wanting to make sure that lands were preserved for future generations. And while many of these people wished to use the land is a wise and educated way, others desired to utilize the land as a place for quick profits and then throw the land away, polluting or destroying the resource that earned them their keep. Yet some believe that it has only been in the last few decades that a movement arose to preserve the land; instead, such a movement has been around since America was first declared as a nation.

PUBLIC LANDS AS NATURAL RESOURCES

When the nation was first formed in the last decades of the eighteenth century, the term "public lands" referred to all lands west of the 13 original colonies, and U.S. government was most anxious to sell them and to make them work for the new country in one form or another, either through the usage of natural resources or as places for future development as homesteads. And, as new lands were gained through treaties or purchase or conquest, the role of the government in distributing them intensified. For instance, under the Northwest Ordinance of 1787, the U.S. government was authorized to sell up to 640 acres of land to the highest bidder, at a minimum price of $1 dollar per acre. Although the ordnance was ratified as a way to form towns and cities in the new areas of what is now the American upper midwestern states (Ohio, Michigan, Wisconsin, etc.) — for instance, the first township established under its principles was Marietta, Ohio — it became the driving force in settling the American West to the shores of California. [1] According to the U.S. Department of Agriculture, while most land in the United States was once publicly owned, in 2010, some 60%, mostly farmland, is privately held. From just before the time of the passage of the Northwest Ordinance, starting in 1781, until 1976, when the homestead laws were repealed by the passage of the Federal Land Policy and Management Act of 21 October 1976 (90 Stat. 2743; Public Law 94-579), a total of 287.5 million acres were granted or sold to homesteaders; an additional 303.5 million acres were disposed of through what the Bureau of Land Management calls "methods not classified elsewhere," making a total of 591 million acres of public lands disposed of during that period. [2] An additional 224.9 million acres was land granted in support of common schools, reclamation of swampland, the construction of railroads, for the support of miscellaneous institutions, and other purposes. Land was also granted to the states to be given to railroad corporations, given away to veterans as military bounties and bonuses, sold under timber and stone laws, granted or sold under timber culture laws, or sold under desert land laws. In total, which also includes land given to the state of Alaska as well as conveyances granted to Native Americans, the total acreage given away or granted by the U.S. government is approximately 1,285,780 million acres. [3]

The acts, which allowed the government to give these lands away or grant them to various parties, include the Pre-emption act of 1841, which allowed for the settlement of lands taken from Native Americans after they were forcibly removed from their native lands, and the Homestead Act of 1862, which offered 160 acres of land to anyone who remained on it and worked it for a period of five years. As well, the government sought to preserve those lands that it did have control of; starting in 1872, with the setting aside of land for Yellowstone National Park in California, this role has continued up to this very day. Presidents from Theodore Roosevelt to Bill Clinton and George W. Bush set aside millions of acres of federal land for national forests, preserves, or other national land monuments that cannot be sold, although some of the lands can be used for the drilling of oil and the digging of minerals, the harvesting of timber, or to have the lands utilized for the grazing of cattle. The tug-of-law between those in the "Wise Use" movement and environmentalists is whether or not these lands should even be used at all, and to what degree they should be used. It is a battle that has gone on for more than a century, and will continue to go on.

The western states have been treated much differently than the eastern states; in the American West, states had to give up a major portion of their acreage to federal control in order to be admitted to the Union. Since their admission, these states have battled federal control of the lands, both in Congress and the courts. Dissatisfaction with the federal management of the public lands, especially in the 1920s, led to the first major movement that called for the ceding of lands, and federal control, to the states, to use as they wished. During the administration of President Franklin D. Roosevelt (1933-45), however, more federal control was pushed onto the western states, most notably through the passage of the Taylor Grazing Act of 1934, which changed the system of grazing from open-range grazing to one strictly controlled by the federal government. According to the Bureau of Land Management, "Under the Taylor Grazing Act, the first grazing district to be established was Wyoming Grazing District Number 1 on March 23, 1935. Secretary of the Interior Harold Ickes created a Division of Grazing within the Department to administer the grazing districts; this division later became the U.S. Grazing Service and was headquartered in Salt Lake City. In 1946, as a result of a government reorganization by the Truman Administration, the Grazing Service was merged with the General Land Office to become the Bureau of Land Management." [4] In 1949, Anderson-Mansfield Reforestation and Revegetation Act of 1949 (Public Law 81-348), enacted by Congress, established a new public lands system and authorized millions of dollars of federal lands for improvements to range grazing.

Other laws enacted by Congress facilitated the harvesting of what were believed at one time to be boundless natural resources. The General Mining Law of 1872, now codified at 30 USC 22-24, authorized and governed the prospecting and mining for hardrock materials, such as gold and silver, on public lands, and provided that all valuable mineral deposits belong to the United States, both surveyed and unsurveyed, were to be free and open to exploration and purchase by American citizens. The act further provided that all lands on which such minerals were to be found would be open to occupation and purchase by U.S. citizens, at a cost of $2.50 per acre. [5] In 1970, the U.S. Congress reinforced the regulations in the 1872 by passing the Mining and Minerals Policy Act of 1970, which declared that it was the "continuing policy" of the United States government to

> foster and encourage private enterprise in: the development of economically sound and stable domestic mining, minerals, metal and mineral reclamation industries; the orderly and economic development of domestic mineral resources, reserves, and reclamation of metals and minerals to assure satisfaction of industrial, security and environmental needs; mining, mineral and metallurgical research, including the use and recycling of scrap to promote the wise and efficient use of our natural and reclaimable resources; the study and development

of methods for the disposal, control and reclamation of mineral waste products, and the reclamation of mined land, so as to lessen adverse impacts of mineral extraction and processing on the physical environment that may result from mining or mineral activities.

For some reason, however, the 1872 act and its progeny do not cover coal resources, and since that time those who mine for coal must pay a royalty on the value of the coal that they bring out of the ground.

While Congress was allowing unlimited harvesting of minerals from public lands, they were working to protect forests. In 1891, the Forest Reserve Act was enacted; it replaced the Timber Culture Act of 1873, and allowed the President to set aside public lands marked by either timber or forest land for protection from public use. President Theodore Roosevelt used the presidential pen more than any president up to that time to set aside millions of acres into protected habitants, national parks, and the like. Congress also enacted laws that protected historical sites and migratory birds, leading up to the creation of the National Park Service in 1916. Although environmentalists won victory after victory to place public lands out of the reach of landowners and those looking to mine for natural resources, by the time of American entry into the First World War the argument had changed to one where the nation now needed those materials for the war effort. During the administration of President Warren G. Harding, the pendulum swung back the other way when the Interior Department, led by Secretary Albert B. Fall, sold off public lands to cronies for campaign donations and other payments, leading to the Teapot Dome scandal. It was during the 1930s that Franklin D. Roosevelt again followed the conservation pattern and set aside lands from private use, although this again was tempered by American entry into the Second World War and the need again rose for the mining of natural resources on public lands.

The rise of the modern environmental movement, particularly in the 1960s, forced Congress to establish a system for the protection of all types of public lands. Led by the publication of three important environmental works — Marjory Stoneman Douglas' "The Everglades: River of Grass" (1947), Robert Porter Allen's "On the Trail of Vanishing Birds" (1957), and Rachel Carson's "Silent Spring" (1962) — Congress set out to pass a series of landmark legislation that addressed all areas of environmental concerns. Per our interest here regarding land policy, the enactment of the Wilderness Act on 3 September 1964 established the National Wilderness Preservation Program. Throughout the 1960s and into the 1970s, Congress enacted a series of laws to protect natural resources but, at the same time, to make sure that their usage for commercial development was sustained. For instance, the Multiple Use Sustained Yield Act of 1960 and the Classification and Multiple Use Act of 1964 gave explicit recognition to the theory that public lands were only to be used for timber harvesting or cattle grazing. The Federal Land Policy and Management Act of 1976 sought to broaden the interests involved in the management of public lands, but also continued to favor increased resource development. The era ended on 2 December 1980, when Congress enacted the Alaska National Interest Lands Conservation Act, which deposited some 97 million acres of formerly private or unused lands in national refuges in Alaska; as well, 25 rivers in the state were listed as protected, and an additional 56 million acres were placed into the category of protected wilderness.

ARGUMENT OVER THE PUBLIC LANDS

Starting with the Carter administration in the 1970s, the arguments for the "wise use" of natural resources, coupled with a strong movement to exert states' rights over the continued intrusion of the federal government into such areas as the distribution of land, particularly in the western states, gave rise to the "Sagebrush Rebellion," a series of nonviolent uprisings, mostly from elected officials in and out of courts, challenging the federal government's right to set aside large swaths of public lands. This rebellion, coupled with a bad economy and a sense of weakness in international affairs, led to Carter's electoral defeat in 1980 and the election of former California Governor Ronald Reagan. [6] Reagan, a westerner, hitched his wagon to the frustrations of those involved in the "Sagebrush Rebellion" and, once in office, applied more of a "hands-off" approach to the takings of land, especially in the western states. Reagan found that his policies were popular, and it was during his administration, and that of his successor, George H.W. Bush, that the Department of the Interior used fewer regulations to limit the size and scope of land set-asides as well as the implementation of environmental laws. At the same time, Congress was loathe to enact more environmental laws at a time when the American economy needed to be given priority over the protection of natural resources.

By the time of the election of Arkansas Governor Bill Clinton to the presidency in 1992, environmentalists were demanding a change in the way the federal government worked with regarding environmental policy, including with land policy in the West. Senator Dale Bumpers, Democrat of Arkansas, sponsored a series of bills during the 1980s to change mining laws to get users of the public lands to pay more in royalties to the federal government, but his legislation never made it out of the Energy and Natural Resources Committee in the U.S. Senate. In 1992, the U.S. House of Representatives debated the passage of a new mining law, but its sponsors could not bring their bills to the floor before the session ended. The previous year, the House enacted a law that increased grazing fees on western lands, but western Senators in the U.S. Senate, both Republican and Democrat, blocked the measure and it never came up for a vote. Democrats in the House tried to add provisions to increase fees on grazing, mining, and timber harvests on federal land by attaching them to appropriations bills for the Department of the Interior, but western Senators blocked them in the Senate. [7]

The election of Bill Clinton in 1992 changed all of this, most notably with the nomination and confirmation of Bruce Babbitt, a former Governor of Arizona, to be the Secretary of the Interior. Environmentalists who had been shut out of decision making in the Department of the Interior were now named to high-ranking and other offices in that department, as well as the Environmental Protection Agency (EPA) and other federal offices dealing with the environment. Almost from the start of his tenure, Babbitt infuriated westerners from both parties, particularly in the U.S. Senate, by stating that the "new West" would no longer be dominated by ranchers, miners, and loggers, but by "urban dwellers" who wished to conserve all of the public lands. Babbit and the Clinton administration proposed sweeping changes in public lands policies, including raising grazing fees, imposing first-time royalties on hardrock mining and timber sales in national forests, and other changes that had been the cause of the Sagebrush Rebellion just 15 years earlier. These changes were attacked by western politicians from both parties, particularly Democrats, who had made inroads with voters in the American West for the first time in many years and were competing with Republicans for seats once off limits to their party. As well, these changes directly impacted states in the American West that Clinton had won in 1992 and were vital to his future electoral success as well as his party's. One of his biggest challengers to such changes was Max Baucus, Democrat of Montana, who wanted some reforms but called into question the administration's changes. When other Democrats left the changes in budget resolutions, Baucus and other western Democrats went to Clinton, who offered to remove them in exchange for support for his other budgetary matters, one of his bigger priorities. Environmentalists, who had backed the reforms and thought that Clinton was on their side, condemned the administration for caving in to the demands of western Senators, although Clinton placated them by pledging to initiate the changes through administrative actions, specifically through dictates done by the Secretary of the Interior. In October 1993, an administration initiative to add grazing fee hikes and new grazing directives to the Interior Department appropriations bill failed when the Senate could not end a filibuster by Republicans and western Democrats. Although the Clinton administration later dropped these initiatives at the time, some western Senators denounced the attempt as part of a "war on the West." [8]

Despite the Clinton administration's continued push for changes in environmental laws, the opposition from Republicans and western Democrats blocked most of the major changes in the U.S. Senate. At the same time, Clinton and Babbitt came under withering criticism from environmentalists, who felt that their support for Clinton in 1992 had been sacrificed in exchange for other matters Clinton felt were more important, like budget matters. The Wise Use movement, again gaining strength in the American West, saw Clinton and Babbitt as their enemy, calling Babbitt the "perfect Darth Vader" to demonize and oppose. Clinton, threatened by declining polls, saw his support in western states, seen as vital to his re-election efforts in 1996, fall precipitously, and he and Babbitt backed off those changes to land policy law that evoked the most opposition, especially in the few western states that Clinton had won in 1992. At the same time, Clinton continued to anger his opponents, while buying himself little support among those who worked to get him elected in the first place. [9]

Concentrating on different areas of environmental policy, Clinton and his administration focused on those areas where both sides could gain something: For instance, in 1993 an agreement was brokered between farmers of sugar cane in Florida and federal officials to change the way that sugar cane was treated with water, runoff that was laden with phosphorus that were damaging the wildlife in the Everglades National Park. Although an agreement was reached, further steps were promised, including asking for a tax on sugar to pay for conservation programs. In November 1996, Florida voters rejected a ballot initiative that would have added a 1 cent tax to each pound of raw sugar grown in the Everglades region.

However, unable to accept a challenge to his ability to change western land policy, in 1994 Secretary Babbitt initiated "Rangeland Reform '94," which would force through mining, grazing, and other changes in the western states, although Babbitt did agree to bring westerners aboard and give more input to department policymaking. This attempt to find some middle ground earned Babbit enmity from both sides, as westerners denounced his proposed changes, and environmentalists criticized them for not going far enough. In an attempt to get new grazing initiatives into place, he tried to form grazing advisory boards that would be composed of both ranchers and conservationists. Yet he was continually criticized by his allies for any compromises, including timber cuts in the Northwest's old-growth forests, pollution of the Everglades by the sugar industry, endangered species in southern California, and grazing reform. By the end of 1994, the only real substantial change that Clinton had brought to land policy were the creation of two national parks in California — Death Valley National Park and Joshua Tree National Park — and the establishment of a protected area in the Mojave Desert. Thus, despite having control of the White House and dominating majorities in both houses of Congress, in effect Clinton and Babbitt had done little in their first two years to change much in the way of land policy. In the 1994 midterm elections, many Democrats, especially in the western states, ran against the Clinton administration and touted their opposition to the administration's "anti-Western" policies. Although many Democrats had stood side-by-side with anti-environmentalist elements in these western states, members of the "Wise Use" movement as well as Republicans and Independents came out to vote against any Democrat seen as too close to the administration. The Republicans drafted their ideas for changes in Congress in their "Contract with America," in which they promised to "roll back government regulations and create jobs."

On election night, the GOP won 52 seats, many in western states, to take control of the U.S. House of Representatives for the first time in five decades. Many blamed the Clinton administration's land policies for the wide swath of defeats of Democrats, but in fact it was a combination of an unsteady economy, a belief that Clinton wanted to outlaw guns that many felt were protected by the Second Amendment, and the land policy issue that were the causes behind the losses at the polls. Democrats who had served for years in Congress went down to defeat in one of the worst first midterm elections for any sitting President in many years.

Clinton, the day after the election, took the blame for his party's electoral debacle. In fact, the forces that took down Clinton's party had been in place for many decades: the growth of private property, especially in western states, had given people the idea that they could own a slice of the American dream, and they saw the poor economy, coupled with the Clinton-Babbitt reforms, as a threat to that way of life.

Now in actual control of the House of Representatives, and in operative control of the entire Congress with the aid of Democrats who opposed the administration on some issues, the Republicans attacked the Clinton policies on land policy, and attached to nearly every bill dealing with environmental or land policy provisions that gave priority to private property or to the rights of industry over environmentalists on public lands. With the GOP in firm control of almost all arms of congressional policy, any attempt to change land policy laws and regulations was dead.

One of the central pieces of legislation promised by the GOP if given control of Congress was the Job Creation and Wage Enhancement Act, introduced almost immediately as soon as the party gained control of the House. Although the legislation did not specifically mention the environment or conservation matters directly, it did include provisions to change administrative law and the rule-making process for major rules, increase opportunities for regulated industries to help shape the provisions, ensure that only relatively serious risks are regulated, require a demonstration that the benefits resulting from these regulations costs exceed the cost of compliance with them and that the regulation proposed is the most costeffective option, create a regulatory moratorium on the issuance of new regulations until the regulatory reform agenda is enacted, establish a regulatory "budget" that places a cap on compliance costs to be imposed on industry, change the way federal programs are funded, so that unfunded federal mandates require additional votes by Congress, require federal agencies to compensate property owners for loss in property values resulting from environmental regulation, and increase procedural protections for those subject to regulatory inspections and enforcement such as a right to have counsel present during inspections and legal actions that can be taken against regulatory officials. The Republicans also proposed new rules shifting regulatory authority from the federal government to the states, while at the same time giving Congress the power to review and to overturn proposed administration regulations by enacting a joint resolution of disapproval that would be subject to presidential veto; holding "correction days" to take up proposals for legislation to eliminate existing federal rules that are considered "obnoxious or burdensome to state or local governments" to be proposed by a congressional task force that would identify possible regulations, confer with the relevant committees, and (if there was broad support) bring them to the House floor for an up-or-down two-thirds majority vote; and creating a "regulatory burden commission" to propose legislation on an industry-by-industry basis. **[10]**

Starting in 1996, and continuing for the remainder of the decade, growth in federal spending was curtailed, and with it came calls for less money to be spent on environmental regulations that many saw as impacting job creation. Historians Michael Kraft and Norman Vigorous wrote in 1997, "Deep cuts in federal agency budgets in 1996 and the heightened anti-environmental rhetoric and political backlash - in the states as well as in Congress - plainly indicate that environmental policy is at an important crossroads. Future achievements are critically dependent on understanding the new anti-environmental movements within and outside of government, improving our knowledge of the diversity of environmental risks we face, and devising effective policy actions that are broadly acceptable to the American public." **[11]**

At the same time, the Republicans, who held onto control of Congress in 1996, 1998, and 2000 — eventually losing it in 2006 — enacted conservation and land policy on three distinct tracks: first, it sought to restructure the process by which federal agencies issued regulations by requiring the cost-benefit analysis of the regulations, allowing industry and/or impacted groups to challenge the costs of imposing the regulations on their specific land or industry; second, through the legislative process, it changed each individual environmental or land policy law to that affecting a specific endangered species but not to its habitat unless that needed protection as well, and laid out a system of compensation of owners of private property merely harmed by the government for such habitat preservation for 20% of their property's value, and forced the government to purchase the land outright if the land value was impacted by more than 50%. Further, while the GOP did allow for the increase of grazing fees, they would be moderate compared to the Clinton administration, and would go up at a slower rate; it also extended the life of grazing permits. Laws dealing with timber cutting and mining were also enacted. Third, the Congress utilized the budget process to expedite what it saw as reform in the land policy area: Republicans threatened to cut the Interior Department budget by two-thirds if it did not close small national parks that did not draw a large number of visitors, while also restricting access to such major parks as Yellowstone and the Grand Canyon, among others. To close a huge budget gap, the House Appropriations Committee called for the Bureau of Land Management to hand over all lands within their borders to the states, which would expand mining, logging, and grazing, while also allowing states to take control of and operate — and also pocket the proceeds from — national parks. Among the bills that were enacted by both houses of Congress that sought to have economic concerns addressed before the environment were the Unfunded Mandates Reform Act of 1995 and the Small Business Regulatory Enforcement Fairness Act of 1996. Republicans estimated that if the federal government opened for oil and gas exploration the 1.5 million acres in the Arctic National Wildlife Refuge (ANWR) in Alaska, it could raise some $1.3 billion in revenue just from oil leases. However, Clinton did not budge on many of these initiatives, and although Congress did not tackle any major federal wetlands policy during the six years that Clinton dealt with a GOP-controlled Congress, he himself made changes through administrative regulations enacted inside his administration.

In a 2001 report done for the John F. Kennedy School of Government in Massachusetts on environmental policy during the Clinton administration, Sheila Cavanaugh, Robert W. Hahn, and Robert Stavins explained, "One of the most visible natural resource policy developments of the 1990s was the Clinton Administration's designation of more than 20 new national monuments and expansion of three existing national monuments, under the 1906 Antiquities Act. The designations and expansions gave monument status to almost 6 million acres of Federal public lands, restricting uses relative to prior designations. Clinton also created the largest protected area in U.S. history, the 84 million-acre Northwest Hawaiian Islands Coral Reef Ecosystem Reserve. During the 1990s, the Congress created one new national monument of 272,000 acres, and one national preserve (the Mojave Desert) of 1.6 million acres. Taken together, Clinton's national monument designations constitute the largest withdrawal of U.S. Federal lands from commercial activity since President Jimmy Carter withdrew 56 million acres of Alaskan lands in 1978. All but one of Clinton's designations were declared in the final year of his presidency, from January 2000 to January 2001. The unilateral, final-hour nature of the declarations raised scores of objections from Western legislators and property-rights activists. The efficiency and cost-effectiveness aspects of these declarations have not been assessed; unlike rules issued by regulatory agencies, Presidential actions under the 1906 Antiquities Act are not subject to benefit-cost analysis requirements. The economic costs and benefits of many of these monument declarations are likely to be quite large and merit further study. [12]

Despite his earlier poor approval ratings and the repudiation of his party in the 1994 election, Clinton won a second term in 1996. For much of this second term, Clinton worked with the GOP in Congress on finding budget reconciliation, although historians like to describe the era in harsher and more stark terms. Perhaps, however, the one area that Clinton butted heads with the majority party in Congress came over environmental policy, which he compromised on but not to the extent that Republicans demanded. [13] According to all histories of the Clinton administration, he spent the latter part of his presidency quietly changing regulations rather than try to take on the Congress on each individual bill that it passed.

In 2000, Gov. George W. Bush of Texas, son of former President George H.W. Bush, was narrowly elected the 43rd President over Vice President Al Gore in one of the closest presidential elections in American history. He intended, and announced during his presidential campaign, that he would drastically change the way that the Clinton administration had emphasized environmental and land policy law; Bush said that he would favor business and private property over conservation wherever the two ideals clashed. To this end, he nominated Gale Norton, the former Attorney General of the state of Colorado and a member of the Mountain States Legal Foundation, a pro-business and pro-private property law firm located in Lakewood, Colorado, as his Secretary of the Interior. Bush also tapped a series of persons for other high governmental posts who had long ties to business, including Mark Rey, a former Vice President of the American Forest and Paper Association and a former staffer for the Senate Energy and Natural Resources Committee, to serve as Undersecretary of Agriculture.

In one of his first moves in office, Bush placed a 60-day "stay" on all federal rules enacted but not yet in effect on 20 January 2001, his first day in office. One of the rules put into place in the last days of the Clinton administration was to ban cars and trucks from roads in national parks; on 4 May 2001, Bush announced that he would allow the rule to go into effect, but that he would make changes to it. Six interested parties — including timber and other companies, off-road enthusiasts, livestock companies, members of the Kootenai tribe of Indians, and three states (Alaska, Idaho, and Utah) — sued the administration in court to force Bush to overturn the rule altogether. To avoid litigation, Bush eventually repealed the Clinton rule and allowed road-building and land development as well. In 2005, 20 environmental groups sued in San Francisco to get the rule reinstated. (In 2007 a federal judge overturned the rule change, and the 9th Circuit Court of Appeals upheld the decision, which remained when Bush left office in January 2009.) [14] Charles Davis, in a paper from 2008 that examined Bush administration policy and how it differed from Clinton administration policy, wrote that from the beginning Bush gave hope to many in the "Wise Use" and other pro-private property movements that he would be on their side; to that same argument, environmentalists feared the change in administration. Davis explained, "The Public Lands Council (PLC) and other organizations representing commodity interests were hopeful that the new Administration would overturn or alter Clinton era regulations that members considered to be overly biased in favor of environmental and conservation constituencies. Their policy prayers were soon answered by a host of regulatory and other administrative initiatives aimed at reducing or eliminating governmental restrictions on the production of rangeland, mineral, and timber resources. Opposition to these proposals from environmental groups such as the NRDC stems from the belief that these changes would collectively serve to reduce incentives to comply with resource conservation policies. All policy actors were aware that programmatic changes stemming from regulatory shifts might be significant but short term since they could eventually be trumped by the differing policy priorities of a subsequent Administration, federal court decisions, and Congressional policy riders." [15]

In 2005, Bush pushed to get Congress to enact the Healthy Forest Restoration Act, which required federal agencies to reduce the risk of fire in national parks by thinning out underbrush and dead trees; opponents accused the administration of merely selling off national forests to industry. In 2008, after years of litigation, Bush opened lands near the two national monuments opened by President Clinton in 1999 to oil and gas leases. According to Felicity Barringer, "Many in the state, where resentment of the federal government runs deep, remain angry about the Clinton administration's decision in 1999 to set aside for protection three million acres deemed to have 'wilderness qualities.' The state sued; in 2003, the Bush administration settled and removed protections from those acres." [16]

In 2008, Senator Barack Obama, Democrat of Illinois, ran on a platform that he would drastically change the direction of the country; one of his appeals was that he would usher in a new era of environmentalism and conservation, enacted through congressional laws and regulations. Once in office, Obama did just what he said he would do, signing a number of laws and executive orders that changed the fabric of how the federal government responded to the environmental movement. Erin Kelly, writing in *The Arizona Republic* in November 2009, explained, "Obama has begun a dramatic reversal in Western land-use policy that already has had a major impact in Arizona. In a sharp departure from the Bush administration, the Obama team has halted new uranium-mining claims near the Grand Canyon, proposed new preserves for wild mustangs and funded the expansion of the Petrified Forest National Park.

Obama also signed into law the Omnibus Public Lands Management Act of 2009 that protected thousands of miles of scenic, historic and recreational trails, including the 807-mile Arizona National Scenic Trail from the state line with Mexico to the Utah border. The sweeping bill designated more than 2 million acres as wilderness area - nearly as much protected land as President George W. Bush created in two terms in office." [17]

As of this writing, Obama has been in office for less than 3 years, so the complete impact of the congressional laws and regulations enacted by his administration have yet to be fully examined.

NOTES:

[1] The full text of the Northwest Ordinance of 1787 can be found online at http://avalon.law.yale.edu/18th_century/nworder.asp.

[2] "Disposition of the Public Domain, 1781-2009," courtesy of the Bureau of Land Management, online at http://www.blm.gov/public_land_statistics/pls09/pls1-2_09.pdf.

[3] Ibid.

[4] "Fact Sheet on the BLM's Management of Livestock Grazing," courtesy of the Bureau of Land Management, August 2009, online at http://www.blm.gov/wo/st/en/prog/grazing.html.

[5] "Mining Law of 1872," courtesy of the University of New Mexico, online at http://wildlifelaw.unm.edu/fedbook/mining72.html.

[6] Graf, William L., "Wilderness Preservation and the Sagebrush Rebellions" (Savage, Maryland: Rowman & Littlefield, 1990).

[7] Taylor, Andrew, "President Will Not Use Budget to Rewrite Land-Use Laws," *Congressional Quarterly Weekly Report* (3 April 1993), 833-34.

[8] Kriz, Margaret, Kriz, "Turf Wars," National Journal, (22 May 1993), 1232-35.

[9] Berke, Richard L., "Clinton Backs Off from Policy Shift on Federal Lands," *The New York Times*, 30 March 1993, A1; online at http://www.nytimes.com/1993/03/31/us/clinton-backs-off-from-policy-shift-on-federal-lands.html. See also Lehmann, Scott, "Privatizing Public Lands" (New York: Oxford University Press, 1995).

[10] Riebsame, William E., "Ending the Range Wars," *Environment* (May 1996), 4- 9, 27-29.

[11] Kraft, Michael E.; and Norman J. Vig, "Environmental Policy from the 1970s to the 1990s: An Overview," in Michael E. Kraft and Norman J. Vig, eds., "Environmental Policy in the 1990s" (Washington, D.C.: CQ Press, 1997), 2.

[12] Cavanaugh, Sheila; Robert W. Hahn, and Robert Stavins, "National Environmental Policy During the Clinton Years," report for the Center for Business and Government, the John F. Kennedy School of Government, Harvard University, Cambridge, Massachusetts, 28 June 2001, online at http://www.hks.harvard.edu/fs/rstavins/Papers/Clinton_Env't_Policy_Working_Paper_1.pdf; see 25-26.

[13] See Martin R. Lee, "Enviromental Protection Issues in the 106th Congress," *CRS Issue Brief for Congress*, 11 September 2000, online at http://ncseonline.org/nle/crsreports/legislative/leg-34.cfm.

[14] Egelko, Bob, "Groups Sue to Preserve Roadless Areas in National Forests; Claimants Support Clinton-era Rules Overturned by Bush," *The San Francisco Chronicle* October 2005, online at http://articles.sfgate.com/2005-10-07/news/17397270_1_roadless-areas-national-forests-forest-service.

[15] See Davis, Charles, "Regulating Public Lands under the George W. Bush Administration," paper presented at the annual meeting of the Western Political Science Association, 20 March 2008, online at http://www.allacademic.com/meta/p_mla_apa_research_citation/2/3/7/8/4/p237849_index.html; see 5-6.

[16] Barringer, Felicity, "U.S. to Open Public Land Near Parks for Drilling," *The New York Times*, 7 November 2008, A13.

[17] Kelly, Erin, "Obama Moves Quickly to Preserve the West," *The Arizona Republic*, 5 November 2009, online at http://www.azcentral.com/news/articles/2009/11/05/20091105az-enviro1105.html#ixzz0qYcbhXbe.

3

Overview of Land Set Asides Withdrawals and Policies

The U.S. government's policies dealing with lands, both public and private, as well as resources on these lands, are diffuse and fragmented, owing to decades of competing interests forming legislation and differing administrations adding their policy measures to the mix. This mélange of laws has led to battles within and without the government, sometimes with differing agencies, over which policies take precedent. The early government calls to go forth and develop the lands, harvest its resources, and establish population centers in areas with few inhabitants have competed in the last 70 years with pushes to regulate the development, to manage the resources, and to set aside public and private lands by the government. The changes to federal law, particularly in the last four decades since the 1960s, have forced a shift in the way the federal government deals with land policy. With changes in administrations, the amount of government intervention ranges from hands-off and little regulation to deep involvement in the way lands are managed. This policy shift has posed a difficult challenge to federal and state agencies as they attempt to balance the competing interests of conserving and preserving the environment and the rights of those who wish to utilize the lands, both public and private. Although this is not strictly an issue for the western states, it impacts these areas more than any other in the United States.

THE ACTIONS OF THE U.S. GOVERNMENT IN LAND SET-ASIDES

The battle between those who wish to preserve the lands and those who wish to use it has been long, hard, and controversial. According to the federal government, the United States has set aside more lands as public lands than any other nation in the history of the world, with approximately 27.7 percent, or some 643.2 million acres (of the total of 2.27 billion acres of total land in the United States), held in trust by the federal government and overseen or managed by several federal agencies, including the National Park Service (NPS), the Bureau of Land Management (BLM), the Fish and Wildlife Service (FWS), the United States Forest Service (USFS), and the Bureau of Reclamation (BOR), among others; the BLM and the Forest Service are the largest "landowners." Excluding Alaska, there are 400 million acres held in the so-called "lower 48" states, approximately 21% of its land; Alaska has 250 million acres, or 62.4%, held as public land. However, this is not the largest set-aside: Nevada, with 58 million acres, or 82.9%, is the most government-controlled state. California has 43.7 million acres, or 43.6% of the state, held by the government.

There are five major classifications of the public lands: they range from governmental declarations that either allow for limited resource development to those that ban any development whatsoever. Rangelands do allow limited grazing of livestock, national forests do allow limited amounts of timber to be taken for commercial use, and some other public lands allow for the taking of some natural resources; these designations are known as "multiple use." Exceptions are national parks, and national wilderness lands, which are both off limits to all but only limited recreational use, and even these uses are closely regulated.

Table 1: Federal Land Acres, Controlled by a U.S. Federal Agency, 2007

(in millions of acres, and in millions of U.S. dollars)

Agency	Acres Controlled	Land Management Appropriations
Bureau of Land Management	258	$996
U.S. Forest Service	193	$4,129
National Park Service	84	$2,181
Fish & Wildlife Service	96	$398
Minerals Management Service [1]	---	$80
Totals:	631	$7,784

[1] The Minerals Management Service [MMS], an agency inside the Department of the Interior, was abolished in 2010 following the sinking of an oil rig in the Gulf of Mexico and the subsequent finding that the service had had little if any oversight over deepwater drilling off the coast of the United States. It was recreated into two agencies, whose exact duties and perameters have yet to be fully explored as of this writing in July 2010.

Source: "2009 Budget Justification for the U.S. Forest Service" (Washington, D.C.: Government Printing Office, 2008), D2-D4; "2009 Budget Justification for the Fish & Wildlife Service" (Washington, D.C.: Government Printing Office, 2008), RF-4, RM-11; "2009 Budget Justification for the Bureau of Land Management" (Washington, D.C.: Government Printing Office, 2008), I-11; "2009 Budget Justification for the Minerals Management Service" (Washington, D.C.: Government Printing Office, 2008), 45.

In addition to the areas mentioned in Table 1 that have been set aside, there are other areas that have been set aside by the federal government; these include national memorials, heritage corridors, historic reserves, historic sites, international parks, and scientific reserves, the latter of which are not part of the National Park System but receive financial and technical assistance from the Park Service. According to the Bureau of Land Management, their land holdings account for 40% of all coal production in the country, 11% of all natural gas production, and 5% of all oil production. As well, 48% of the geothermal energy comes from these lands, as well as 15% of wind power capacity. [1]

WITHDRAWALS OF LAND PRIOR TO THE WILDERNESS ACT OF 1964

From 1872, the U.S. government began a systematic withdrawal of lands from the private preserves of the nation to control by the government itself. The first law under which a true withdrawal took place was the establishment of Yellowstone National Park. And although this was the first, it was several years before additional lands were withdrawn. The first major push to remove lands to public control came under Theodore Roosevelt, whose power came through both Executive Orders and the passage of the Organic Act of 1897 (16 USC 473) and the Antiquities Act of 1906 (16 USC 88, 431-33). Additional lands were removed through the Taylor Grazing Act of 1934 (43 USC 315 et. seq.) and the Alaska Native Claims Settlement Act of 1971 (43 USC 1601 et. seq.)

According to an analysis by the Congressional Research Service, an arm of the U.S. Congress, currently, there are four types of withdrawal: First, there are instances where Congress has the sole authority to withdraw or reserve public lands. For example, creating National Parks and wilderness areas and in some cases national wildlife refuges can only be done by an act of Congress. Second, the executive branch has used power delegated to it by Congress under the previously mentioned Antiquities Act of 1906 and the Pickett Act of 1910. Third, Congress may withdraw specific resources such as when oil, gas, coal, and like minerals were removed from the General Mining Law of 1872. Lastly, there is the "general congressiona" withdrawal, which allows lands to be removed from potential development pending "final disposition." [2]

The Pickett Act of 1910 was eventually overridden by the enactment of the Federal Land Policy and Management Act of 1976 (FLPMA), which made the policies regarding the withdrawal of land more strict and more streamlined.

THE WILDERNESS ACT OF 1964 AND SUBSEQUENT LAWS

A map of the areas managed by the Bureau of Land Management show that most, if not all, of these lands are in the westernmost states, with six states — Nevada, Arizona, New Mexico, Colorado, Wyoming, and Alaska — having the most land managed by the governmental agency.

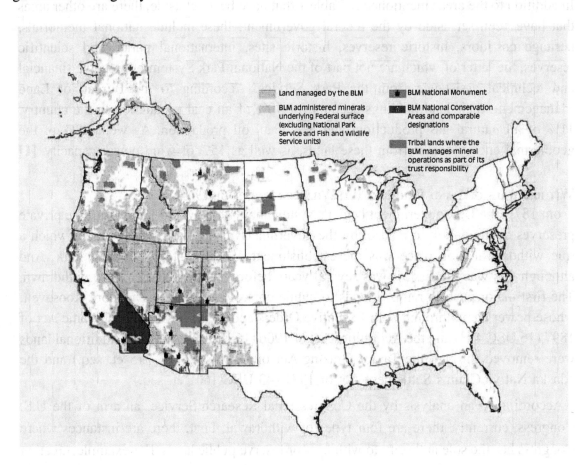

Many of the lands managed by the U.S. government comes from the Wilderness Act of 1964; this legislation established the National Wilderness Preservation System, which set aside to Congress the right to designate wilderness areas, and, according to the U.S. government, "directed the Secretaries of Agriculture and of the Interior to review certain lands for their wilderness potential." The act initially established a system of 54 wilderness areas with a total of 9 million acres of land. In its legislative language, the act defined "wilderness" as:

> *A wilderness, in contrast with those areas where man and his works dominate the landscape, is hereby recognized as an area where the earth and its community of life are untrammeled by man, where man himself is a visitor who does not remain. An area of wilderness is further defined to mean...an area of undeveloped Federal land retaining its primeval character and influence, without permanent improvements or human habitation, which is protected and managed so as to preserve its natural conditions and which (1) generally appears to have been affected primarily by the forces of nature, with the imprint of man's work substantially*

unnoticeable; (2) has outstanding opportunities for solitude or a primitive and unconfined type of recreation; (3) has at least five thousand acres of land or is of sufficient size as to make practicable its preservation and use in an unimpaired condition; and (4) may also contain ecological, geological, orother features of scientific, educational, scenic, or historical value. [3]

In 1968, four years after the act was enacted, Congress expanded the Wilderness System. The latest numbers, from 2005, show that there are 649 separate wilderness areas, in 44 states across the Union, encompassing some 105 million acres. [4]

Table 2: Additions to the National Wilderness Preservation System

Congress	Number of Laws[a]	Number of States	Number of Areas New (Additions)		Acres Designated[b]
88th	1	13	54	(0)	9,139,721
89th	0	0	0	(0)	0
90th	5	4	5	(1)	794,550
91st	3	12	25	(0)	305,619
92nd	9	7	8	(1)	912,439
93rd	5	22	35	(0)	1,264,594
94th	6	21	35	(0)	2,142,486
95th	7	18	28	(5)	4,555,496
96th	6	10	70	(11)	60,799,111
97th	5	5	7	(0)	83,261
98th	21	21	177	(49)	8,576,450
99th	4	4	11	(2)	97,393
100th	7	8	22	(4)	1,988,509
101st	5	5	68	(3)	1,759,479
102nd	2	2	6	(4)	424,590
103rd	2	2	79	(14)	8,272,699
104th	1	2	1	(2)	29,420
105th	1	1	0	(1)	160
106th	8	6	18	(1)	1,086,490
107th	5	5	18	(13)	441,520
108th	1	1	14	(0)	768,294
Total	104	44	681	(111)	106,255,809

[a] Excludes laws with minor boundary and acreage adjustments (less than 10 acres of net change)

[b] Column total differs from this figure, because of acreage revisions

From that initial 1964 act, Congress expanded its powers to include wilderness and other areas under the aegis of federal control. The first major act, as well as the largest up to that time, was the Alaska National Interest Lands Conservation Act, or ANILCA, enacted by the 96th Congress in 1980. ANILCA set aside some 56.4 million acres in Alaska to be designated as wilderness. [5] Another action was taken by the Forest Service in 1977. That year, the agency established a review, known as the Roadless Area Review and Evaluation (RARE II) [6], of some 62 million acres, all part of the mandate established by Congress by the Forest and Rangeland Renewable Resources Planning Act of 1974 (RPA) [7] and the National Forest Management Act of 1976 (NFMA) [8]. The final report for RARE II was not issued until 1979; it called on Congress to add an additional 15 million acres to the Wilderness System; 11 million current acres were to be studied further, and 36 million acres could be allowed to be used for resource extraction and other uses, including recreation and tourism. In 1980, after Congress enacted these changes, the state of California sued the Department of Agriculture, in which the Forest Service was housed, to halt the non-wilderness uses of the wilderness lands. [9] A lower district court in California sided with the state in 1980, and the 9th Circuit Court of Appeals in San Francisco upheld in part and overturned in part the lower court's decision in 1982, setting aside the entire RARE II review. [10]

Although the narrative seems to remain that under Ronald Reagan that environmental policies suffered, in fact during his administration, most notably during the Ninety-eighth Congress (1983-85), when 21 separate wilderness statutes were enacted, encompassing land set-asides in 21 different states, more lands and acreage were set aside than by any other Congress or President since the Wilderness Act had been passed in 1964. In addition, under Republican Presidents, the boundaries of how Wilderness Act lands could be used has been expanded. For instance, the original act prohibited any commercial activities, as well as the construction of any roads or structures on the lands. The legislative language of this section of the act states,

> Except as specifically provided for in this Act, and subject to existing private rights, there shall be no commercial enterprise and no permanent road within any wilderness area designated by this Act and, except as necessary to meet minimum requirements for the administration of the area for the purpose of this Act (including measures required in emergencies involving the health and safety of persons within the area), there shall be no temporary road, no use of motor vehicles, motorized equipment or motorboats, no landing of aircraft, no other form of mechanical transport, and no structure or installation within any such area.

At the same time, however, the act did have a loophole that allowed mineral mining, as long as the mining was done with the preservation of the wilderness in mind. As well, mining and other mining techniques were also continued for a period of 20 years, until 1983, unless that then-future Congress allowed for their extension.

Despite this language, which gave the authority to allow for permits to be issued by the Secretary of Agriculture, no such leases were issued until 1981. That year, when Reagan became President, James Watt was named as Secretary of the Interior, and he stepped in and issued permits for mining to go forward. Congress, led by Democrats, objected, and in the appropriations for FY (fiscal year) 1983 and FY 1984 enacted a moratorium on leases for wilderness lands mining. [11] However, the Congress retained the loophole that allowed for those mineral and/or mining leases that existed on or prior to 31 December 1983 to be retained, and that the Secretary of Agriculture could institute "reasonable regulations" for the usage of such lands. [12]

Major Federal Agencies That Control Public Lands

According to the U.S. government, there are four major agencies that deal with the public lands, spread out among the width and breadth of the federal government. The largest of these is the Bureau of Land Management (BLM), located in the Department of the Interior. According to the Bureau of Land Management's "accomplishments" brochure published in December 2009, "BLM Alaska manages more than 78.5 million acres of public lands. Some smaller parcels of land are scattered across the State's interior and south-central region. Larger stretches of public lands span the mountain ranges, forested hills, and arctic tundra of far western and northern Alaska." [13]

Founded in 1946 by the merging of the U.S. Grazing Service and the General Land Office (GLO), the Bureau of Land Management controls, according to its own Web site, 253,366,500 acres of land across the entire United States; as well, it also manages some 700 million acres of lands that have mineral resources, all of which encompass federal, state, and even private land holdings.

As shown in Table 1, while the Bureau of Land Management controls the most public lands in the United States, just behind it is the U.S. Forest Service (USFS). This agency controls the entire forest system on the public lands in all 50 states, U.S. territories, and other lands under the control of the U.S. government. The national forest system includes 159 forests and nineteen grasslands in forty-four states, Puerto Rico, and the U.S. Virgin Islands, which are managed to ensure sustainable yield (harvested no faster than it is replaced) and multiple use (logging, mining, oil and gas exploration, grazing, farming, hunting, recreation, and conservation of plants and animals, soils, and watersheds), managed by the U.S. Forest Service. Logging is the chief economic use of the lands, although recreation is the greatest source of revenue. Some Forest Service lands have been set aside as wilderness areas. While the BLM is in the Department of the Interior, the USFS is in the Department of Agriculture. A BLM study, completed in 2000 [14], noted that of the approximately 700 million acres of federal subsurface minerals under the agency's jurisdiction in 2000, approximately 165 million acres have been withdrawn from mineral entry, leasing, and sale, subject to valid existing subsurface mineral rights. Lands in the National Park System (except National Recreation Areas), Wilderness Preservation System, and the Arctic National Wildlife Refuge (ANWR) are among those that are statutorily withdrawn. Also of the 700 million acres, mineral development on another 182 million acres was subject to the approval of the surface management agency, and must not be in conflict with land designations and plans, according to the BLM. Wildlife refuges (except ANWR), wilderness study areas, and roadless areas are examples of lands in this category, although many other wildlife refuges also are withdrawn from leasing. [15]

Just behind the USFS is the National Park Service (NPS). Established in 1916, its mission was to "conserve the scenery and the natural and historic objects and the wild life [sic] [in national parks] and to provide for the enjoyment of the same in such a manner and by such means to leave them unimpaired for the enjoyment of future generations." However, as noted, public lands had been withdrawn starting in 1872, when Congress established Yellowstone National Park in California, and for the next 44 years their care and upkeep was under the direction of the USFS. The mission of the NPS as set in 1916 and that of the USFS were not in synch: the USFS's mission was that "all the resources of the forest reserves are for use and where conflicting interests exist the issue will be resolved based on the greatest good for the greatest number of people in the long run." As shown with Table 1, the NPS controls some 84 million acres of land, fourth of the major federal agencies (the Fish & Wildlife Service controls more). The NPS controls the entire national park system.

Another important federal agency with control over land and other natural resources is the U.S. Fish & Wildlife Service (USFWS). In 1871, Congress established the U.S. Commission of Fisheries (CoF), the first federal agency to deal with the issues surrounding water resources and fish hatcheries. The joint resolution of the Congress created the commission "for the protection and preservation of the food fishes of the Coast of the United States." The Congress found in the legislation that "it is asserted that the most valuable food fishes of the coast and the lakes of the United States are rapidly diminishing in number, to the public injury, and so as to materially to affect the interests of trade and commerce," leading to the passage of the legislation. President Ulysses S Grant named the first commissioner, Spencer Fullerton Baird (1823-1887), a leading scientist who was an expert in natural history. Baird would remain as the first commissioner until his death in 1887, but during his tenure he worked at Woods Hole, Massachusetts, where he helped to found the Marine Biology Laboratory there. [16]

According to its current mission statement, "The mission of the U.S. Fish and Wildlife Service...is to conserve, protect, and enhance fish and wildlife, and their habitats for the continuing benefit of the American people. USFWS activities include, but are not limited to: enforcing the federal Endangered Species Act; acquiring wetlands, fishery habitats, and other lands for restoration and preservation; insuring compliance with the National

Environmental Policy Act; managing National Wildlife Refuges and National Fish Hatcheries; and reviewing and commenting on all water resource projects." [17] The agency itself states that "The National Wildlife Refuge System now comprises more than 520 units in all 50 states, American Samoa, Puerto Rico, the Virgin Islands, the Johnson Atoll, Midway Atoll and several other Pacific Islands. Refuges now encompass over 93 million acres of valuable wildlife habitat." In addition, "included in this total are nearly 1.9 million acres of wetlands in the prairie pothole region of the north-central United States. These wetlands are known as 'waterfowl production areas,' and have Federal protection through fee acquisition or easements. This vital habitat, together with the wetlands of the Canadian prairies and Alaska, provides the key production areas where the bulk of North America's waterfowl nest and rear their young." [18]

PUBLIC LANDS AGENCIES

Perhaps the most important public land agency in the United States is the Department of the Interior, one of the departments of the President's cabinet, established in 1849 as the Home Department (as opposed to the Department of State, which handled external affairs). Included in the original department structure were the General Land Office, the Office of Indian Affairs; the Pension Office, and the U.S. Patent Office, were later added to the department's responsibilities. [19] In 2000, in a history of the President's cabinet, Mark Grossman wrote of the Department of the Interior,

> In the years following its establishment, the Congress added new agencies to the Interior department's responsibilities. In 1867, it established a "department" of Education (actually more of a bureau), and, six years later, transferred authority over territorial matters from the State Department to Interior. In 1879 the Geological Survey was created, in 1916 President Woodrow Wilson created the National Park Service to oversee all national parks in the United States, and, in 1940, a bureau which existed in the Department of Commerce, the Bureau of Fisheries, and one in Agriculture, the Bureau of Biological Survey, were both transferred to Interior, consolidated, and named the Fish and Wildlife Service. Other agencies which were part of the department were moved around: the establishment of the Department of Justice in 1870 allowed the movement of Interior's jurisdiction over district attorneys, marshals, and court officers (including so-called "Indian courts" in Indian territories) to that new department. As well, jurisdiction over labor was given completely to the new Department of Labor (not at that time a cabinet-level department when it was initially formed in 1888), and, in 1903, the Census Bureau was made a part of the Department of Commerce and Labor. [20]

In 1950, following the recommendations of a government panel headed up by former President Herbert Hoover, the administration of President Harry S Truman reorganized the entire government, and in the Department of the Interior its mission strictly became that as the custodian of the national lands and resources. However, although this and further reorganizations of the government made sure to include all of the relevant agencies with this mission in the department, nevertheless the responsibility for some of the oversight is spread around, to the Department of Agriculture and even the Department of Homeland Security.

According to its Web site, the Department of the Interior's responsibilities are as follows: fostering sound use of our land and water resources; assessing and protecting our fish, wildlife, and biological diversity; preserving the environmental and cultural values of our national parks and historical places; and providing for the enjoyment of life through outdoor recreation." The department also "assesses our mineral resources and works to ensure that their development is in the best interests of all our people by encouraging stewardship and citizen participation in their care." Finally, the department "has a major responsibility for American Indian reservation communities and for people who live in island territories under United States administration." In its mission statement, the department states, "The U.S. Department of the Interior protects and manages the Nation's natural resources and cultural heritage; provides scientific and other information about those resources; and honors its trust responsibilities or special commitments to American Indians, Alaska Natives, and affiliated Island Communities. [21]

One of the recent important missions of the department is the responsibility over those lands held in trust for Native Americans. An Office of the Special Trustee (OST) was established by the American Indian Trust Fund Management Reform Act of 1994 (Public Law 103-412), which, the department states, "was created to improve the accountability and management of Indian funds held in trust by the federal government. As trustee, DOI has the primary fiduciary responsibility to manage both tribal trust funds and Individual Indian Money (IIM) accounts." According to the department and the OST, "The Indian trust consists of 55 million surface acres and 57 million acres of subsurface minerals estates held in trust by the United States for American Indian, Indian tribes, and Alaska Natives. Over 11 million acres belong to individual Indians and nearly 44 million acres are held in trust for Indian tribes. On these lands, the Department manages over 100,000 leases. It also manages approximately $3.5 billion in trust funds. For fiscal year 2009, funds from leases, use permits, land sales and income from financial assets, totaling approximately $298 million, were collected for about 384,000 open IIM accounts. Approximately $566 million was collected in fiscal year 2009 for about 2,700 tribal accounts (for over 250 tribes)." [22] As of November 2009, "There are currently 153,950 individual Indian allotments and more than 4.5 million fractionated interests." [23]

OVERVIEW OF MAJOR PUBLIC LANDS AND NATURAL RESOURCE LAWS

PUBLIC LAND LAWS

The General Mining Law of 1872. Enacted in the years after the California gold rush, the act, also known as the National Mining Act or the Stewart Act, was passed to exert federal control over mining resources. Authored by Senator William Morris Stewart, Democrat of Nevada [24], the 1872 action is not a stand-alone piece of legislation, but is rather an amendment to the 1862 Homestead Act. A history of the 1872 action noted that "[t]he 1872 amendment included a flaw by asserting that the prospector who claimed the highest point of an ore body had the right to follow it underground. This inspired a great deal of legal action as contesting interests fought over which claim included this critical part of the deposit. Critics also maintained the 1872 amendment failed to overturn the 1866 assertion that local mining practice was a form of common law. Stewart believed, however, that mining district regulations adopted before 1866 should remain in force because overturning them would create chaos throughout the West." [25] Over the years, there have been various attempts to either amend the law or to do away with it altogether, in an effort to exert more federal control over mining lands and resources. A 1920 amendment removed gas and oil supplies so that the U.S. government could charge royalties for them. In 1988, however, Congress finally changed the fee schedule; according to a Congressional report on the 1988 legislation, "Beginning January 3, 1989, a fee of $250 per patent application plus $50 per claim within each application has been required. If the patent application is approved, the claimant may purchase surface and mineral rights at a rate of $2.50 per acre for placer claims and $5 per acre for lode claims. A placer deposit is an alluvial deposit of valuable minerals usually in sand or gravel; a lode or vein deposit is of a valuable mineral consisting of quartz or other rock in place with definite boundaries. A placer claim is usually limited to 20 acres but a lode claim may be slightly greater than 20 acres. These per-acre fees were substantial when the Mining Law was enacted — claimed land and minerals now far exceed these amounts in value." [26]

Federal Land Policy Management Act (FLPMA) of 1976 (Public Law 94-579). The act established overall public management and policy objectives for federal lands and required resource management plans by both the U.S. Forest Service and the Bureau of Land Management, governed the sale and acquisition of public lands, provided for public participation in public lands policy making, authorized the Interior Department to regulate grazing, and ordered the BLM to identify wilderness study areas and make recommendations concerning the creation of new wilderness areas. According to a report on the legislation, "The FLPMA, as amended, is the Bureau of Land Management 'organic act' that establishes the agency's multiple-use mandate to serve present and future generations." [27] Eleanor Schwartz, in a 1979 law review article outlining the history of the legislation, explained that the act "was a relatively simple document. The proposed legislation would have repealed several hundred outdated and duplicative laws, provided

BLM with broad policy guidelines and management tools, and given BLM disposal and enforcement authority. However, by the time the Federal Land Policy and Management Act (FLPMA) was passed in 1976, it had become a lengthy, complex document, much more than an organic act. In addition to broad management guidelines and authority, FLPMA provides legislative direction to numerous specific interests and areas of management." [28]

In its findings headlining the legislation, Congress found that, among other matters:

(1) the public lands be retained in Federal ownership, unless as a result of the land use planning procedure provided for in this Act, it is determined that disposal of a particular parcel will serve the national interest;

(2) the national interest will be best realized if the public lands and their resources are periodically and systematically inventoried and their present and future use is projected through a land use planning process coordinated with other Federal and State planning efforts;

(3) public lands not previously designated for any specific use and all existing classifications of public lands that were effected by executive action or statute before the date of enactment of this Act be reviewed in accordance with the provisions of this Act. [29]

Public Rangelands Improvement Act (PRA) of 1978 (43 U.S.C. 1901-08). According to the act, it established "a national policy and commitment to improve the conditions on public rangelands, require[d] a national inventory and consistent federal management policies, and provide[d] funds for range improvement projects." It also amended the Wild Free-Roaming Horses and Burros Act and the Federal Land Policy and Management Act of 1976. Congress found in the declaration of policy that "vast segments of the public rangelands are producing less than their potential for livestock, wildlife habitat, recreation, forage, and water and soil conservation benefits, and for that reason are in an unsatisfactory condition," that "such rangelands will remain in an unsatisfactory condition and some areas may decline further under present levels of, and funding for, management," that "unsatisfactory conditions on public rangelands present a high risk of soil loss, desertification, and a resultant underproductivity for large acreages of the public lands, contribute significantly to unacceptable levels of siltation and salinity in major western watersheds including the Colorado River; negatively impact the quality and availability of scarce western water supplies; threaten important and frequently critical fish and wildlife habitat; prevent expansion of the forage resource and resulting benefits to livestock and wildlife production; increase surface runoff and flood danger; reduce the value of such lands for recreational and esthetic purposes; and may ultimately lead to unpredictable and undesirable long-term local and regional climatic and economic changes," and, through this legislation, "conditions can be addressed and corrected by an intensive public rangelands maintenance, management, and improvement program involving significant increases in levels of rangeland management and improvement funding for multiple-use values." One controversial part of the act stated, "to prevent economic disruption and harm to the western livestock industry, it is in the public interest to charge a fee for livestock grazing permits and leases on the public lands which is based on a formula reflecting annual changes in the costs of production." This fee was condemned in the western portion of the United States as doing harm to the livestock industry. [30] According to the U.S. Department of the Interior, the 1978 act was the last in a long line of legislation dealing with public land grazing issues: "Laws that apply to the BLM's management of public lands grazing include the Taylor Grazing Act of 1934, the National Environmental Policy Act of 1969, the Endangered Species Act of 1973, the Federal Land Policy and Management Act of 1976, and the Public Rangelands Improvement Act of 1978." [31]

Multiple-Use Sustained-Yield Act of 1960 (Public Law 86-517). This legislation set the congressional intent that "the national forests are established and shall be administered for outdoor recreation, range, timber, watershed, and wildlife and fish purposes." The act was a supplement to the congressional action that established the foundation for national forests on 4 June 1897 (16 USC 475). It authorized the Secretary of Agriculture to "develop and administer the renewable surface resources of the national forests for multiple use and sustained yield of the various products and services obtained from these areas. The Secretary must give appropriate consideration to the relative values of the resources of particular areas. The Act authorizes the Secretary to cooperate with interested state and local governmental agencies and others in developing and managing the national forests."

Forest and Rangeland Renewable Resources Planning Act of 1974 (Public Law 93-378). This action, approved on 17 August 1974, was enacted "to serve the national interest, the renewable resource program must be based on a comprehensive assessment of present and anticipated uses, demand for, and supply of renewable resources from the Nation's public and private forests and rangelands, through analysis of environmental and economic impacts, coordination of multiple use and sustained yield opportunities as provided in the Multiple-Use Sustained-Yield Act of 1960."

National Forest Management Act of 1976 (90 Stat. 2949). This legislation amended the Forest and Rangeland Renewable Resources Planning Act of 1974; in it, Congress found that "the public interest is served by the Forest Service, Department of Agriculture, in cooperation with other agencies, assessing the Nation's renewable resources, and developing and preparing a national renewable resource and program, which is periodically reviewed and updated." Further, "to serve the national interest, the renewable resource program must be based on a comprehensive assessment of present and anticipated uses, demand for, and supply of renewable resources from the Nation's public and private forests and rangelands, through analysis of environmental and economic impacts, coordination of multiple use and sustained yield opportunities as provided in the Multiple-Use, Sustained-Yield Act of 1960, and public participation in the development of the program."

ATOMIC ENERGY AND ENERGY CONSERVATION

Low-Level Radioactive Waste Policy Act (42 USC 2021b). This 1980 legislation, known as LLRWPA, gave the individual states until 1 January 1986 to complete plans for the disposal of commercially-generated low-level radioactive waste (LLRW), giving the states incentives to form alliances or groups to develop and construct disposal and/or containment facilities. In 1985, when Congress realized that most states could not meet the 1 January 1986 deadline, it amended the 1980 act to give the states more time, extending the period of compliance until the end of 1992.

Atomic Energy Act of 1954 (42 USC 2011 et. seq.). This legislation, coming during the middle years of the Cold War between the United States and the Soviet Union, this is considered the leading congressional legislation on atomic energy. The Nuclear Regulatory Commission (NRC) says of the legislation,

> *This Act is the fundamental U.S. law on both the civilian and the military uses of nuclear materials. On the civilian side, it provides for both the development and the regulation of the uses of nuclear materials and facilities in the United States, declaring the policy that "the development, use, and control of atomic energy shall be directed so as to promote world peace, improve the general welfare, increase the standard of living, and strengthen free competition in private enterprise." The Act requires that civilian uses of nuclear materials and facilities be licensed, and it empowers the NRC to establish by rule or order, and to enforce, such standards to govern these uses as "the Commission may deem necessary or desirable in order to protect health and safety and minimize danger to life or property." Commission action under the Act must conform to the Act's procedural requirements, which provide an opportunity for hearings and Federal judicial review in many instances.* [32]

In 1974, the Energy Reorganization Act (Public Law 93-438) replaced the Atomic Energy Commission (AEC) with the Nuclear Regulatory Commission (NRC).

Energy Reorganization Act of 1974 (Public Law 93-438; 88 Stat. 1233; 42 USC 5801 et. seq.). Under this congressional legislation, the energy functions of the U.S. government were established in one, encompassing agency, the Federal Energy Administration; as well, and as noted above, the Atomic Energy Commission (AEC) was succeeded by the Nuclear Regulatory Commission (NRC). In the findings of the legislation, Congress "declares that the general welfare and the common defense and security require effective action to develop, and increase the efficiency and reliability of use of, all energy sources to meet the needs of present and future generations, to increase the productivity of the national economy and strengthen its position in regard to international trade, to make the Nation self-sufficient in energy, to advance the goals of restoring, protecting, and enhancing environmental quality, and to assure public health and safety." In order to accomplish these goals, this legislation was needed, according to its organic act. "The Congress finds that, to best achieve these objectives, improve Government operations, and assure the coordinated and effective development of all energy sources, it is necessary to establish an Energy Research and Development Administration to bring together and direct Federal activities relating to research and development on the various sources of energy, to increase the efficiency and reliability in the use of energy, and to carry out the performance of other functions, including but not limited to the Atomic Energy Commission's military and production." Three years later, in 1977, the Congress established the U.S. Department of Energy as a full-level cabinet department.

Energy Policy and Conservation Act (EPCA) of 1975 (Public Law 94-163). This legislation came at a time of growing concern over the conservation of energy. The U.S. Senate Committee on Energy & Natural Resources reports on their site, "President Ford in his January 1975 State of the Union Message outlined a comprehensive set of legislative proposals also built around the theme of energy independence. The struggle which ensued to enact the first major energy law of the 1970's culminated in the signing of the Energy Policy and Conservation Act [EPCA] in December of 1975, which included authorization of the Strategic Petroleum Reserve." **[33]** The important portions of this legislation included increasing oil production through price incentives, trying to cut domestic oil prices in the United States to the 15 May 1973 price of $1.35 a barrel, authorized the establishment of the Strategic Petroleum Reserve to store up to 1 billion barrels of oil to be held in case of a national emergency, and authorized Corporate Average Fuel Economy (CAFE) standards for automobiles sold in the United States to increase fuel standards and conserve fuel. These standards were set for an average of 18 mpg for passenger vehicles (light trucks have different standards) in 1978, rising to 27.5 mpg by 1985. In 2011, that rate is set to hit 30.2 mpg. **[34]**

Energy Conservation and Production Act of 1976 (42 USC 6801). In this act, according to the congressional findings, "The Congress finds that improvement in electric utility rate design has great potential for reducing the cost of electric utility services to consumers and current and projected shortages of capital, and for encouraging energy conservation and better use of existing electrical generating facilities." Thus, through the act, "[i]t is the purpose of this subchapter to require the Secretary to develop proposals for improvement of electric utility rate design and transmit such proposals to Congress; to fund electric utility rate demonstration projects; to intervene or participate, upon request, in the proceedings of utility regulatory commissions; and to provide financial assistance to State offices of consumer services to facilitate presentation of consumer interests before such commissions." **[35]**

WATER

The Clean Water Act (CWA) of 1948 (Public Law 80-845). Officially known as the Federal Water Pollution Control Act (FWPCA), this legislation was enacted to deal with the growing post-WWII water pollution problem in the United States. Prior to this act, the only major action dealing with water pollution was the Refuse Act, which was a part of the Rivers and Harbors Appropriations Act of 1899; so, when the FWPCA was enacted, nearly half a century had passed since Congress had dealt with the problem. In the legislation, the Congress found that in "consequence of the benefits resulting to the public health and welfare by the abatement of stream pollution, it is...the policy of Congress to recognize, preserve, and protect the primary responsibilities and rights of the States in controlling water pollution, to support and aid technical research to devise and perfect methods of treatment of industrial wastes which are not susceptible to known effective methods of treatment, and to provide Federal technical services to State and interstate agencies and to industries, and financial aid to State and interstate agencies and to municipalities, in the formulation and execution of their stream pollution abatement programs." Amendments were made to the law by Congress in 1965 and 1972. [36]

Safe Drinking Water Act (SDWA) of 1974 (42 USC 300 et. seq.). According to the Environmental Protection Agency (EPA),

> The Safe Drinking Water Act (SDWA) was established to protect the quality of drinking water in the U.S. This law focuses on all waters actually or potentially designed for drinking use, whether from above ground or underground sources. The Act authorizes EPA to establish minimum standards to protect tap water and requires all owners or operators of public water systems to comply with these primary (health-related) standards. The 1996 amendments to SDWA require that EPA consider a detailed risk and cost assessment, and best available peer-reviewed science, when developing these standards. State governments, which can be approved to implement these rules for EPA, also encourage attainment of secondary standards (nuisance-related). Under the Act, EPA also establishes minimum standards for state programs to protect underground sources of drinking water from endangerment by underground injection of fluids. [37]

The SDWA authorizes the EPA to issue national primary drinking water standards that set maximum levels of specified contaminants in drinking water; regulates underground injection through EPA standards; and provides technical assistance and grants. Congress reauthorized the Safe Drinking Water Act in 1996. The new law creates a $1 billion/year state revolving fund (SRF) for communities to improve drinking water facilities; up to 15 percent of a state's allocation can be used to protect source waters. Under the 1986 law, the EPA was required to issue standards for twenty-five contaminants every three years; the bill requires the EPA to issue, within eighteen months of passage and then every five years, a list of contaminants subject to regulation; the agency must issue a standard for at least five contaminants on the list within three and one-half years; the agency is to use cost-benefit analysis and risk assessments in formulating standards. States are given discretion in several areas: They can exempt, on an interim basis, water systems serving fewer than 10,000 people from monitoring requirements, for example, and grant variances and exemptions from federal requirements for systems serving fewer than 3,300 people.

COASTAL PROTECTION

Coastal Zone Management Act (CZMA) of 1972 (Public Law 92-583, 16 USC 1451-56). This was one of the first major laws to cover the protection of coastal zones. Signed into law by President Richard M. Nixon on 27 October 1972 and amended eight times since, Congress found in the law's mission statement that "[t]here is a national interest in the effective management, beneficial use, protection, and development of the coastal zone." It held that [t]he coastal zone is rich in a variety of natural, commercial, recreational, ecological, industrial, and esthetic resources of immediate and potential value to the present and future well-being of the Nation," and that "[t]he increasing and competing demands upon the lands and waters of our coastal zone occasioned by population growth and economic development, including requirements for industry, commerce, residential development, recreation, extraction of mineral resources and fossil fuels, transportation and navigation, waste disposal, and harvesting of fish, shellfish, and other living marine resources, have resulted in the loss of living marine resources, wildlife, nutrient-rich areas, permanent and adverse changes to ecological systems, decreasing open space for public use, and shoreline erosion." [38]

Coastal Barrier Resources Act (CBRA) of 1982 (Public Law 97-348). This legislation was enacted to establish certain coastal lands, notably barrier islands, in the Coastal Barrier Resources System (CBRS). The act was supplemented by the Great Lakes Coastal Barrier Act of 1988 (102 Stat. 4713) and the Coastal Barrier Improvement Act (CBIA) of 1990 (Public Law 101-591; 104 Stat. 2931). [39]

MARINE PROTECTION

The Marine Protection, Research, and Sanctuaries Act (MPRSA) of 1972 (Public Law 92-532). Also known as The Ocean Dumping Act, this legislation prohibits the dumping of materials into the oceans that would, as the Environmental Protection Agency states, "would unreasonably degrade or endanger human health or the marine environment." [40] The legislation allows for licenses to be issued to allow for dumping if the government accedes to it.

Magnuson Fisheries Management and Conservation Act (Public Law 94-265). Better known as the Magnuson-Stevens Fishery Conservation and Management Act of 1976, or MFMCA, this landmark legislation established protections for fish supplies inside a zone of 200 miles around the United States. Congress found that "[t]he fish off the coasts of the United States, the highly migratory species of the high seas, the species which dwell on or in the Continental Shelf appertaining to the United States, and the anadromous species which spawn in United States rivers or estuaries, constitute valuable and renewable natural resources. These fishery resources contribute to the food supply, economy, and health of the Nation and provide recreational opportunities." According to a congressional report on the act, "The enactment of the Fishery Conservation and Management Act in 1976 (later renamed the Magnuson Fishery Conservation and Management Act after the late Senator Warren G. Magnuson) ushered in a new era of federal marine fishery management. The **MFMCA** was signed into law on April 13, 1976, after several years of debate. On March 1, 1977, marine fishery resources within 200 miles of all U.S. coasts came under federal jurisdiction, and an entirely new multifaceted regional management system began allocating fishing rights, with priority given to domestic enterprise. Primary federal management authority was vested in the National Marine Fisheries Service (NMFS) within the National Oceanic and Atmospheric Administration (NOAA) of the Department of Commerce. The 200-mile fishery conservation zone was superseded by an Exclusive Economic Zone (EEZ), proclaimed by President Reagan on March 10, 1983." [41] On 12 January 2007, President George W. Bush signed the 2006 reauthorization of the MFMCA which, according to NOAA's National Marine Fisheries Service (NMFS), "is ground-breaking in several respects: it mandates the use of annual catch limits and accountability measures to end overfishing, provides for widespread market-based fishery management through limited access privilege programs, and calls for increased international coopera-tion." [42]

GENERAL ENVIROMENTAL LAWS
National Environmental Policy Act (NEPA) of 1969 (Public Law 91-190). This legislation was the first to create an environmental policy board inside the federal administration. According to the title of the legislation, it was "[a]n Act to establish a national policy for the environment, to provide for the establishment of a Council on Environmental Quality, and for other purposes." In its mission statement, Congress held that,

> *recognizing the profound impact of man's activity on the interrelations of all components of the natural environment, particularly the profound influences of population growth, high-density urbanization, industrial expansion, resource exploitation, and new and expand-ing technological advances and recognizing further the critical importance of restoring and maintaining environmental quality to the overall welfare and development of man, declares that it is the continuing policy of the Federal Government, in cooperation with State and local governments, and other concerned public and private organizations, to use all practicable means and measures, including financial and technical assistance, in a manner calculated to foster and promote the general welfare, to create and maintain conditions under which man and nature can exist in productive harmony, and fulfill the social, economic, and other requirements of present and future generations of Americans.* [43]

According to the White House, where the Council on Environmental Quality (CEQ) still remains as one of the myriad of enviromental advisors to the President, "The Council on Environmental Quality (CEQ) coordinates Federal environmental efforts and works closely with agencies and other White House offices in the development of environmental policies and initiatives. CEQ was established within the Executive Office of the President by Congress as part of the National Environmental Policy Act of 1969 (NEPA) and additional responsibilities were provided by the Environmental Quality Improvement Act of 1970." [44]

Comprehensive Environmental Response, Compensation, and Liability Act (CERCLA) of 1980 (Public Law 96-510; 94 Stat. 2767). Few followers of the number of environmental laws passed by the U.S. Congress know of this law by its true legislative name; it is far better known as "The Superfund Law." By 1980, a number of hazardous waste sites dating back to the 1950s were becoming a toxic menace to various communities around the nation. The largest, and worst, was at Love Canal in New York State. With no law with which to cause a cleanup of these sites (the Resource Conservation and Recovery Act (RCRA) of 1976 oversaw only active hazardous sites; CERCLA addressed those sites that had been abandoned), Congress enacted this specific legislation, which, as the Environmental Protection Agency notes, "created a tax on the chemical and petroleum industries and provided broad Federal authority to respond directly to releases or threatened releases of hazardous substances that may endanger public health or the environment. Over five years, $1.6 billion was collected and the tax went to a trust fund for cleaning up abandoned or uncontrolled hazardous waste sites." The legislation also: "established prohibitions and requirements concerning closed and abandoned hazardous waste sites; provided for liability of persons responsible for releases of hazardous waste at these sites; and established a trust fund to provide for cleanup when no responsible party could be identified." [45]

Emergency Planning and Community Right to Know Act (EPCRA) of 1986 (88 Stat. 2156). This legislation is known better as the Superfund Amendments and Authorization Act (SARA) of 1986, or SARA Title III, enacted as a separate, stand-alone piece of legislation that would nevertheless work hand-in-hand with the law known as CERCLA, which established the Superfund in 1980. The Environmental Protection Agency (EPA) calls this specific law "a statute designed to improve community access to information about chemical hazards and to facilitate the development of chemical emergency response plans by state/tribe and local governments. EPCRA required the establishment of state/tribe emergency response commissions (SERCs/TERCs), responsible for coordinating certain emergency response activities and for appointing local emergency planning committees (LEPCs)." [46] The 1986 law requires certain manufacturers to report to the states and EPA the volume of each of some 300 chemicals and twenty chemical categories they release each year into the environment. The inventory requirement applies only to manufacturing facilities with at least ten employees that manufacture more than 25,000 pounds or use more than 10,000 pounds of any chemical included in the inventory. The reporting requirements apply to chemicals that are either released into the environment or transported off-site for subsequent treatment, storage, or disposal. Facilities are also required to submit information concerning their efforts to reduce the production of wastes and recycle. The EPA publishes an annual Toxics Release Inventory based on the data. Other sections regulate accidental release of toxics and require plant and community emergency planning.

Air Pollution Control Act (APCA) of 1955 (Public Law 84-159; 69 Stat. 322). This was the first federal legislation dealing with air pollution. Better known as the Clean Air Act, it marked a turning point that showed that the U.S. Congress had to address the growing pollution problem in the air in the United States. According to the Environmental Protection Agency (EPA), "this Act provided funds for federal research in air pollution. The Clean Air Act of 1963 was the first federal legislation regarding air pollution control. It established a federal program within the U.S. Public Health Service and authorized research into techniques for monitoring and controlling air pollution. In 1967, the Air Quality Act was enacted in order to expand federal government activities. In accordance with this law, enforcement proceedings were initiated in areas subject to interstate air pollution transport. As part of these proceedings, the federal government for the first time conducted extensive ambient monitoring studies and stationary source inspections." The act has been amended, first by the Clean Air Act of 1970, then by the Clean Air Act Amendments of 1977 and 1990. [47]

ASSESSING PUBLIC LANDS AGENCIES AND POLICIES

From the first moves by the U.S. government to ameliorate the impact of man on the environment, there have been criticisms of the laws Congress has enacted, from both sides: Enviromentalists feel that the laws have not gone far enough, while those industies and persons involved in using the lands in one way or another believe that the Congress and administrations have done too much to protect the lands and resources of the country while threatening the property rights of the people. Thus, it has been a political battle to fully implement environmental laws. The problems with implementation of environmental laws are not limited to shortcomings of federal agencies; they are ultimately rooted in the statutes they administer. Some laws include very specific and detailed mandates for implementing agencies. The specific problems with each major policy are addressed in the chapters that follow. Before moving to those discussions, however, it is important to review the broader criticisms of environmental, natural resource, and public lands policy as they provide the general context for assessments of specific programs, agencies, and laws.

From both sides comes an almost identical criticism: that those who implement the environmental laws do not closely examine the costs of such legislation. For instance, environmentalists state that cost is not possible to consider when the environment is under the threat from pollution and waste and development. On the other hand, those who wish to use the lands claim that the government and those whom implement the laws do not consider the costs to the economy and to private individuals when enacting such legislation. To this end, the changes in administration in Washington or in states has done little to appease either side; whichever party or idea is in power, the other side calls their moves extreme and denounces them. Both sides also agree that federal laws are sometimes hard to implement because they are centralized in Washington, D.C. and not in the states or the areas where they have the most impact. There is wide agreement that the federal government's "one size fits all" approach has largely failed, but it is impossible to change this, what with the ever-expanding power of the federal government, especially in the areas of land resources and usage, and the refusal of federal officials to allow local citizens and politicians to take control of their own laws and resources.

No matter whether private property rights or the land and its resources are being protected, critics continue to denounce either excessive or short-sighted legislation. Critics of regulation have also focused on bureaucratic, administrative problems that are characteristic of large, complex agencies. The implementation of environmental and natural resource laws is particularly problematic because of the breadth of agencies' jurisdiction, scientific uncertainties concerning the causes and consequences of pollution, the political and ideological conflict in which agencies have become intertwined, and the interaction of federal and state regulatory and management efforts. Advocates of private property rights argue that federal natural resources and environmental laws have failed to give sufficient protection to those rights and call for the expansion of property rights and common-law protections as an alternative to traditional bureaucratic policy. Representatives of regulated industries regularly raise concerns with the inflexibility given them under regulatory requirements, the uncertainty that comes from a ponderous regulatory process, and the short timelines given them to comply with mandates. They often blame regulators (and congressional staff members) for failing to have some minimum manufacturing experience to help guide them as they impose restrictions on industrial activity. They seek more cooperative interaction with regulators so that environmental improvements can be achieved in ways that still permit firms to satisfy financial and other objectives.

In 1993, the National Performance Review, a top-to-bottom study of the entire U.S. government by Vice President Al Gore, found that it failed to serve as a model of responsible environmental behavior but has contributed much to the nation's environmental problems. Environmental management is "divided among numerous federal agencies with inconsistent mandates and conflicting jurisdictions that follow bureaucratic, not ecological, boundaries." As a result, the report noted, "the government spends far too little time focused on the health of whole ecosystems."

In the years since the report's release in 1993, little has changed in the way of the implementation of existing legislation and/or the passage of new legislation. Whether or not through a lack of clarity or a refusal to see the other side, both political parties, as well as the entrenched bureaucracy refuses to change any of its dictates or models for what should happen in the hinterlands. A Department of the Interior during the George W. Bush administration that pushes for unlimited oil exploration during the first decade of the twenty-first century may have led to the BP oil spill in the Gulf of Mexico in 2010; however, a refusal by the Obama administration in 2010 to allow any existing oil drilling in the gulf cost some 100,000 jobs in the area. One swing to one side begets another swing to another side, and in the end the residents and animals of the Gulf of Mexico paid through destroyed resources and lost jobs. Whether or not a new way can be found, which takes into account both sides of the argument, both sides of what is best for everyone in a fight over the environment and land rights, is what will be seen as the success or failure of the legislation enacted to help in one way or another.

NOTES:

[1] "BLM General Brochure," undated, courtesy of the Bureau of Land Management, online at http://www.blm.gov/pgdata/etc/medialib/blm/wo/Communications_Directorate/general_publications/general.Par.46489.File.dat/HighResBLMbro.pdf.

[2] Humphries, Marc, "Oil and Gas Exploration and Development on Public Lands," *CRS Report for Congress* (Washington, D.C.: Congressional Research Service, 26 March 2004), 22.

[3] Act of 3 September 1964: 78 Stat. 890, Public Law 88-577.

[4] Gorte, Ross W., "Wilderness: Overview and Statistics," CRS [*Congressional Research Service*] Report for Congress, 18 March 2005, overview.

[5] Act of 2 December 1980: 94 Stat. 2371, Public Law 96-487.

[6] The first RARE review, in 1970, was halted when a federal lawsuit claimed that it violated the National Environmental Policy Act of 1969 (NEPA), which was actually enacted by Congress in 1970. See Act of 1 January 1970, 88 Stat. 852, Public Law 91-190. Thus, the 1977 review is known as RARE II.

[7] Act of 17 August 1974: 88 Stat. 476, Public Law 93-378.

[8] Act of 22 October 1976: 90 Stat. 2949, Public Law 94-588.

[9] See *California v. Bergland*, 483 F.Supp. 465 (Eastern District of California, 1980), and *Block v. California*, F. 2d 753 (U.S. Court of Appeals for the Ninth Circuit, 1982).

[10] In 1980, when the lawsuit was first begun, Secretary of Agriculture John Bergland was the defendant; when the suit was appealed to the appeals court, Jimmy Carter had lost the presidency to Ronald Reagan, and Bergland had been succeeded by John Block, hence the change of names on the suit.

[11] Watt's decision occurred based on his belief that although the Forest Service is in the Department of Agriculture, mining and mineral land claims are controlled by the Bureau of Land Management, which was a part of the Department of the Interior.

[12] Mathews, Olen Paul; Amy Haak, and Kathryn Toffenetti, "Mining and Wilderness: Incompatible Uses or Justifiable Compromise?" *Environment*, XXVII (April 1985), 12-17, 30-36.

[13] Bureau of Land Management, "Information Resources Management: Activities and Accomplishments: December 2009" (Washington, D.C.: Government Printing Office, 2009), 19.

[14] Chiang, Sie Long, "Public Lands, Onshore Federal and Indian Minerals in Lands of the U.S., Responsibilities of the BLM," Report of the Department of the Interior/Bureau of Land Management, 1 December 2000.

[15] Quoted in Humphries, Marc, "Oil and Gas Exploration and Development on Public Lands," *CRS Report for Congress* (Washington, D.C.: Congressional Research Service, 26 March 2004), 6.

[16] Biography of Baird courtesy of Dickinson University, online at http://chronicles.dickinson.edu/encyclo/b/ed_bairdSF.html; see also his official biography at the National Oceanic & Atmospheric Administration (NOAA), online at http://www.history.noaa.gov/giants/baird.html.

[17] "U.S. Fish & Wildlife Service," courtesy of ceres.ca.gov, online at http://ceres.ca.gov/wetlands/agencies/usfws.html.

[18] "History of the U.S. Fish & Wildlife Service National Wildlife Refuge System," courtesy of The Encyclopedia of Earth, online at http://www.eoearth.org/article/History_of_the_U.S._Fish_and_Wildlife_Service_National_Wildlife_Refuge_System#Approaching_the_Centennial_.281997_and_on.29.

[19] Forness, Norman Olaf, "The Origins and Early History of the United States Department of the Interior" (Master's thesis, Pennsylvania State University, 1964).

[20] Grossman, Mark, "Encyclopedia of the United States Cabinet: 1789-2010" (New York: Grey House Publishing; two volumes, 2010).

[21] "DOI Mission [Statement]," courtesy of the U.S. Department of the Interior, online at http://www.doi.gov/archive/secretary/mission.html.

[22] "American Indian Trust Fund Management Reform Act of 1994," courtesy of the Library of Congress, Washington, D.C., online at http://thomas.loc.gov/cgi-bin/bdquery/ z?d103:HR04833:L&summ2=m&.

[23] "Office of the Special Trustee for American Indians," courtesy of the U.S. Department of the Interior, online at http://www.doi.gov/ost/about_ost/history.html.

[24] "William Stewart," biography courtesy of Online Nevada, online at http://www.onlinenevada.org/William_Stewart.

[25] "National Mining Act of 1872," courtesy of Online Nevada, online at http://www.onlinenevada.org/national_mining_act_of_1872.

[26] Humphries, Marc, "Mining on Federal Lands: Hardrock Materials," *CRS Report for Congress*, 30 April 2008, CRS-2.

[27] "The Federal Land Policy and Management Act of 1976, As Amended" (U.S. Department of the Interior Bureau of Land Management and Office of the Solicitor, October 2001), inside front cover.

[28] Schwartz, Eleanor, "A Capsule Examination of the Legislative History of the Federal Land Policy and Management Act (FLPMA) of 1976," Arizona Law Review, 21 (1979), 285.

[29] Declaration of Policy for the act, section 101, at 43 USC 1701.

[30] Text of the act at 43 USC 1901 et. seq., online at http://uscode.house.gov/download/pls/43C37.txt.

[31] "Fact Sheet on the BLM's Management of Livestock Grazing," July 2010, courtesy of the U.S. Department of the Interior, online at http://www.blm.gov/wo/st/en/prog/grazing.html.

[32] U.S. Nuclear Regulatory Commission (NRC), "Over Governing Legislation," online at http://www.nrc.gov/about-nrc/governing-laws.html#aea-1954.

[33] "About the Committee," courtesy of the United States Senate Committee on Energy & Natural Resources, online at http://energy.senate.gov/public/index.cfm?FuseAction=About.History.

[34] "Energy Policy and Conservation Act of 1975," courtesy of the U.S. Energy Information Administration, online at http://www.eia.doe.gov/pub/oil_gas/petroleum/analysis_publications/chronology/ petroleumchronology2000.htm#T_4_.

[35] Congressional findings in the 1976 act courtesy of Findlaw, online at http://codes.lp.findlaw.com/uscode/42/81/I/6801.

[36] "Digest of Federal Resource Laws of Interest to the U.S. Fish and Wildlife Service," courtesy of the U.S. Fish & Wildlife Service, online at http://www.fws.gov/laws/lawsdigest/fwatrpo.html.

[37] "Safe Drinking Water Act," courtesy of the Environmental Protection Agency, online at http://www.epa.gov/ogwdw/sdwa/.

[38] "Coastal Zone Management Act of 1972," courtesy of the National Park Service, online at http://www.nps.gov/history/local-law/fhpl_cstlzonemngmt.pdf [PDF file].

[39] "Digest of Federal Resource Laws of Interest to the U.S. Fish & Wildlife Service," online at http://www.fws.gov/laws/lawsdigest/coasbar.html.

[40] "Marine Protection, Research and Sanctuaries Act," courtesy of the Environmental Protection Agency, online at http://www.epa.gov/history/topics/mprsa/index.htm.

[41] Buck, Eugene H., "Magnuson Fishery Conservation and Management Act Reauthorization," *CRS Report for Congress*, 4 December 1996, 3.

[42] "Magnuson-Stevens Fishery Conservation and Management Act Reauthorized," courtesy of the National Oceanic and Atmospheric Administration (NOAA), online at http://www.nmfs.noaa.gov/msa2007/index.html.

[43] "The National Environmental Policy Act of 1969, as amended," courtesy of the U.S. Department of Energy, online at http://ceq.hss.doe.gov/nepa/regs/nepa/nepaeqia.htm.

[44] "The Council on Environmental Quality — About," courtesy of the White House, online at http://www.whitehouse.gov/administration/eop/ceq/about.

[45] "CERCLA Overview," courtesy of the Environmental Protection Agency (EPA), online at http://www.epa.gov/superfund/policy/cercla.htm.

[46] "Emergency Planning and Community Right-to-Know Act," courtesy of the Environmental Protection Agency (EPA), online at http://www.epa.gov/agriculture/lcra.html.

[47] "History of the Clean Air Act," courtesy of the Environmental Protection Agency (EPA), online at http://www.epa.gov/air/caa/caa_history.html.

4

Biodiversity and the Preservation of
Endangered Species

THE POLICY FRAMEWORK

The first laws that were instituted in the United States to protect wildlife were based mainly on English laws that, like their later brethren, were enacted to protect wildlife, at least to a limited degree. These first laws had the main purpose of limiting the amount of hunting specimens that wealthy hunters could bag. By the middle of the eighteenth century, the states, rather than the federal government, were providing protection to wildlife species under threat; this started first with fish populations in the areas of water that could be protected. The first land laws began in 1868, when the federal government did ban the hunting of fur-bearing animals in the territory of Alaska, and, 26 years later, halted all hunting in the Yellowstone National Park in California. By the start of the twentieth century, however, the wholesale slaughter of birds, with their colorful feathers, for ladies' hats and other garments, gave rise to a call for the ending of the practice.

The Bird and Game Act of 1900

One of the most important laws up to that time dealing with ending the trafficking of wildlife products — from birds and other animals — was then enacted in response to the call to end the mass murder of birds: the Lacey Act (now codified at 16 USC 701), passed by Congress on 25 May 1900, "provide[d] authority to the Secretary of the Interior to designate injurious wildlife and ensure the humane treatment of wildlife shipped to the United States. Further, it prohibits the importation, exportation, transportation, sale, or purchase of fish and wildlife taken or possessed in violation of State, Federal, Indian tribal, and foreign laws. The Amendments strengthen and improve the enforcement of Federal wildlife laws and improve Federal assistance to the States and foreign governments in the enforcement of their wildlife laws. Also, the Act provides an important tool in the effort to gain control of smuggling and trade in illegally taken fish and wildlife." [1] Sponsored by Rep. John Fletcher Lacey (1841-1913), Republican of Iowa, the act was the first of its kind. Lacey, a Civil War veteran and attorney, was elected to the U.S. House of Representatives in 1888 and had a long and distinguished political career in which he spent protecting land resources and wildlife. [2] According to historian Rebecca Conard, "During his first term [in office], Lacey secured passage of...the Yellowstone Park Protection Act, which empowered the Interior Department to protect the park's natural resources from human destruction. Lacey would wield his greatest influence in Congress as chair of the House Committee on Public Lands (1894-1906). A strong advocate of federal responsibility for resource conservation in the public domain, Lacey championed the establishment of game preserves in Yellowstone and other public lands, including Alaska, the Grand Canyon, and the Olympic Range; worked to establish bison breeding grounds in Yellowstone and the Wichita Forest Reserve (Oklahoma); and advocated scientific management of forest reserves and preservation of scenic wonders." [3] Lacey's sponsorship of the 1900 Bird and Game Act — called the Lacey Act in his honor — was the first real attempt by the U.S. government to end the grotesque slaughter of birds for their feathers, which were used in ladies' hats.

What followed from the U.S. Congress and the U.S. government was a series of important laws and other actions that focused protections on wildlife in four separate areas: migratory and game birds, wild horses and burros, marine animals, and endangered species across the spectrum of the animal kingdom.

Three years after Congress enacted the Lacey Act, with his Executive Order of 14 March 1903, President Theodore Roosevelt established the National Wildlife Refuge (NWR) System, with the first National Wildlife Refuge on Pelican Island, Florida, where brown pelicans and wood storks, among other birds, were threatened with extinction. Before he left office in March 1909, Roosevelt had created a total of 51 refuges. At the time of this writing, in 2011, the NWR system "has grown to more than 150 million acres, 553 national wildlife refuges and other units of the Refuge System, plus 38 wetland management districts," according to the U.S. Fish & Wildlife Service.

Yet while Roosevelt and other leaders were trying to protect animals in the wild, other wildlife, particularly in zoos, were dying out. This became most evident in 1914, when the last passenger pigeon, named Martha, died in a zoo in Cincinnati. Whereas just a century earlier millions of these birds had flown across the skies, by 1910 they had been hunted to the edge of extinction, and within four years after that the last of its species, a female, was gone.

The death of the last passenger pigeon gave rise to further legislative protections. Among these acts was the Migratory Bird Act of 1918 (40 Stat. 755), which limited the hunting of migratory birds while also outlawing the taking of their eggs or the destruction of their nests. The Bald Eagle Protection Act of 1940 (54 Stat. 250), according to the Fish & Wildlife Service, "provide[d] for the protection of the bald eagle (the national emblem) and the golden eagle by prohibiting, except under certain specified conditions, the taking, possession and commerce of such birds." [4] Amendments added to the act in 1972 "increased penalties for violating provisions of the Act or regulations issued pursuant thereto and strengthened other enforcement measures." [5] The Wild Free-Roaming Horses and Burros Act of 1971 (Public Law 92-195) came about as Congress found "that wild free-roaming horses and burros shall be protected from capture, branding, harassment, or death; and to accomplish this they are to be considered in the area where presently found, as an integral part of the natural system of the public lands." [6] The Marine Mammal Protection Act (MMPA) of 1972, according to the U.S. Fish & Wildlife Service, "established a Federal responsibility to conserve marine mammals with management vested in the Department of Interior for sea otter, walrus, polar bear, dugong, and manatee. The Department of Commerce is responsible for cetaceans and pinnipeds, other than the walrus." Further, adds the agency, "[w]ith certain specified exceptions, the Act establishe[d] a moratorium on the taking and importation of marine mammals as well as products taken from them, and establishes procedures for waiving the moratorium and transferring management responsibility to the States." [7] The MMPA had one exception: allowing Arctic and Pacific Coast peoples to kill marine animals as part of their culture.

Although all of these acts were important steps in the drive to end the senseless slaughter of various animals, perhaps the most important legislative action was the passage of the Endangered Species Preservation Act (Public Law 89-669) in 1966. This act, which remains to this day one of the leading environmental laws concerning animals, required the Secretary of the Interior to develop a plan to conserve, protect, restore, and propagate selected species of native fish and wildlife that the Secretary found were "threatened with extinction." Although the legislation did have problems — it was provided with inadequate funding, as well as allowing the preservation of species only when considered "practicable and consistent" with the "primary purposes of the federal agencies," nevertheless it was a landmark move regarding the protection of animal species. A years after the law was signed, Secretary of the Interior Stewart Udall announced that he was using the law to add 77 mammals, birds, reptiles, amphibians, fish, and other wildlife considered threatened or endangered to the list held by the department. Congress amended the law in 1969; these improvements expanded the protections given to additional species, including those threatened with worldwide, and not just American, extinction; expanded these protections to animals other than fish and wildlife; and prohibited the importation of endangered and threatened species into the United States. The administration of President Richard M. Nixon told Congress that the original law and its amended update were insufficient to protect endangered species, and requested that tougher amendments be ratified. Thus, the Endangered Species Act of 1973 took these recommendations into consideration and expanded the original law, covering all members of the animal kingdom and calling on all federal agencies to protect both the animals and their habitat. [8] The act was further amended in 1988, when Congress expanded it to include recovery and monitoring activities. In 1990, Senator James McClure, Republican of Idaho, established a plan to reintroduce wolves back into the ecosystem in his state. Although it took five years to gain federal support for his plan, in 1995 the first wolves were released by the Fish & Wildlife Service. Two years later, the agency announced that the reintroduction was "exceeding all expectations." Although this was one of the clear successes of the law, perhaps its greatest impact came on 7 July 1997, when the Fish & Wildlife Service announced that it was removing the American bald eagle, once considered to be on the way to being wiped out, from the Endangered Species List. In 2009, in another successful conclusion, the wolves reintroduced to Idaho and then Montana were also removed from the Endangered Species List.

THE ENDANGERED SPECIES ACT EXPANDS PROTECTION OF WILDLIFE & HABITAT

From its inception in 1966 as the Endangered Species Protection Act, Congress was pushed to improve the law. In 1973 it enacted the Endangered Species Act (ESA) (Public Law 93-205). This legislation, and with the inclusion of amended forms of the law, is the basis for all animals and wildlife and habitat protection to current times. The act, according to the Environmental Protection Agency, "provides a program for the conservation of threatened and endangered plants and animals and the habitats in which they are found. The lead federal agencies for implementing ESA are the U.S. Fish and Wildlife Service (FWS) and the U.S. National Oceanic and Atmospheric Administration (NOAA) Fisheries Service. The FWS maintains a worldwide list of endangered species. Species include birds, insects, fish, reptiles, mammals, crustaceans, flowers, grasses, and trees." Further, states the agency, "The law requires federal agencies, in consultation with the U.S. Fish and Wildlife Service and/or the NOAA Fisheries Service, to ensure that actions they authorize, fund, or carry out are not likely to jeopardize the continued existence of any listed species or result in the destruction or adverse modification of designated critical habitat of such species. The law also prohibits any action that causes a 'taking' of any listed species of endangered fish or wildlife. Likewise, import, export, interstate, and foreign commerce of listed species are all generally prohibited." [9] The law gives any "interested person" the right to petition the Secretary of the Interior to list a species they believe is either endangered or threatened; the Secretary then has 90 days to determine whether or not the petition has sufficient scientific and other evidence to merit such a listing. If such action is merited, the determination is passed to the other agencies involved, such as the Fish & Wildlife Service, for additional hearings and follow-up; further, there is an investigation if the animal or animals or wildlife area deserves partial or full protection. This process can be lengthy; however, once completed, that animal or wildlife or habitat is then listed as an endangered or threatened species, with five separate criteria for their listing:

1. The animal or wildlife is threatened by destruction of their habitat;
2. The animal or wildlife or habitat is threatened by commercial, recreational, scientific, or other purposes;
3. The animal or wildlife is threatened due to illness or predation;
4. The animal or wildlife does not have existing law protecting it adequately;
5. Other natural or man-made factors affect the animal's or wildlife's existence.

Figure 1: Listing of Petitions for Inclusion on the Endangered Species Act List, 1974-91

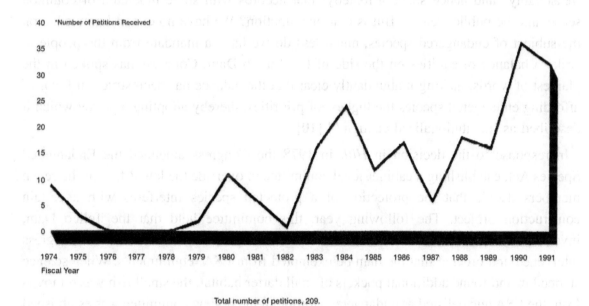

Total number of petitions, 209.

Figure 2: Facts About the Endangered Species Act (following page)

Definition of "Species"
According to the act, a "species" includes species, subspecies, and, for vertebrates only, "distinct population segments (DPSs)." Pacific salmon are listed as "evolutionarily significant units (ESUs)," which are essentially equivalent to DPSs for the purpose of the ESA. [11]

Types of Listing Status for Animals or Plants:

Endangered

Threatened

Emergency Listing (Threatened)

Emergency Listing (Endangered)

Experimental Population (Essential)

Experimental Population (Nonessential)

Similarity of Appearance (Endangered)

Similarity of Appearance (Threatened)

The courts have given some latitude to the government in the controlling of how the ESA is utilized and interpreted; for instance, in *Tennessee Valley Authority v. Hill* (437 US 153 {1978}), the U.S. Supreme Court held that Section 7 of the act found that Congress intended to stop any construction project that may be found to jeopardize an animal or wildlife or a habitat, in this case halting the construction of a dam in the TVA system to protect the endangered snail darter, a small fish. Speaking for the Court, Chief Justice Warren Burger wrote, "Here we are urged to view the Endangered Species Act 'reasonably,' and hence shape a remedy 'that accords with some modicum of common sense and the public weal.' ...But is that our function? We have no expert knowledge on the subject of endangered species, much less do we have a mandate from the people to strike a balance of equities on the side of the Tellico Dam. Congress has spoken in the plainest of words, making it abundantly clear that the balance has been struck in favor of affording endangered species the highest of priorities, thereby adopting a policy which it described as 'institutionalized caution.'" [10]

In response to the decision in *Hill,* in 1978 the Congress amended the Endangered Species Act, establishing a cabinet-level committee to override the law if five of the seven members decide that the protection of a protected species interferes with a certain construction project. The following year, this committee held that the Telico Dam, involved in the *Hill* decision, should be halted to save the snail darter; however, Congress intervened and ordered that the dam be exempted from ESA requirements. When science stepped in and found additional pockets of snail darter habitat, the small fish was removed from the ESA and delisted as endangered. Although the review committee was established to make such decisions, in the years since its inception it has only been called on to make decisions in only a handful of cases. One of these instances came in 1991, when timber sales on Bureau of Land Management lands in Oregon threatened the spotted owl. When the U.S. Forest Service demanded that certain areas of timber land be set aside for the owl, environmentalists sued the Service for failing to set aside all of the lands in question, and timber companies sued to open all of the lands for timber harvesting. In 1992, the review committee held that the land sales be exempted from the ESA requirements, although it decided this for only one-fourth of all of the land permits that the Forest Service had once offered. Although the review committee's decision was final, it did not appease either side, and the issue continues to be a controversial one in Oregon to this day.

Figure 3: Breakdown of Listed Species by Biological Classification under the Endangered Species Act, 1991

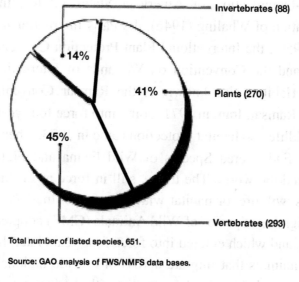

Total number of listed species, 651.

Source: GAO analysis of FWS/NMFS data bases.

Figure 4: Listed Species under the Endangered Species Act Found in the 11 Western States, 2009

Other Legislation and Actions

There have been other pieces of congressional action outside of those mentioned previously, but more importantly world conventions have moved to protect endangered species. These include the Convention for the Preservation and Protection of Fur Seals (1911), the Washington Convention on Nature Protection and Wild Life Preservation in the Western Hemisphere-Organization of American States (1940), the International Convention for the Regulation of Whaling (1946), the Paris International Convention for the Protection of Birds (1950), the International Plant Protection Convention (1951), the Antarctic Treaty (1959), and the Convention on Wetlands of International Importance Especially as Waterfowl Habitat, also known as the Ramsar Convention after being adopted at a conference in Ramsar, Iran, in 1971, going into force four years later. Perhaps the nadir of animal and wildlife and habitat protection came in 1973, when the Convention on International Trade in Endangered Species of Wild Fauna and Flora (CITES) was signed by 80 nations around the world. The treaty, still in force as of this writing, seeks to ban all trade in animals, wildlife, or habitat without permits. In 1979, the Convention on the Conservation of Migratory Species of Wild Animals (CMS) adopted in Bonn, West Germany (now Germany), and which entered into force four years later, laid out a plan to conserve species of wild animals that migrate across or outside national boundaries by restricting harvests, conserving habitat, and controlling other adverse factors.

More Court Decisions

Although few U.S. congressional actions have occurred since the passage of the original Endangered Species Protection Act in 1966, there have been some laws, both American and international, which have addressed the problem of wildlife and their habitat. In 1962, Rachel Carson's landmark work, *"Silent Spring,"* highlighted the threat of chemicals, particularly pesticides, on wildlife as well as people, and led to the banning of DDT (chlorodiphenyltrichloroethane), a synthetic pesticide, which was found to cause birth defects in humans and animals and cause the eggs of animals to be weakened, which led to the deaths of the animals before they could be born. In 1972, after hearings, the Environmental Protection Agency banned the further use of DDT, and, on 31 December 1972, that ban went into effect. There have been studies that the use of DDT may have some positive effects, mainly in ending the scourge of malaria; in fact, in countries where DDT use was ended, malaria incidents and deaths exploded. As of this writing, however, there has been no move by the U.S. government to even reconsider the DDT ban.

In addition to legislative action, American courts have stepped in to either uphold or demonstrate the constitutionality of the Endangered Species Act and other environmental legislation. The 1994 decision by the U.S. Supreme Court in *Dolan v. City of Tigard, Oregon* (512 US 687 {1994}), although not an environmental case, held that a city or other entity could not take certain lands from landowners or homeowners when the entity's requirements conflicted with a person's rights under the Fifth Amendment of the U.S. Constitution. The following year, the U.S. Supreme Court, in a landmark but little-noticed case, *Babbitt v. Sweet Home Chapter of Communities for a Greater Oregon* (515 US 687 {1995}), held that Fish & Wildlife Service regulations that use the term "harm" to include destroying or modifying habitats that result in the taking or killing of the species in the habitat were constitutional. The plaintiffs, according to the decision, were small landowners and logging companies in Oregon that asked Secretary of the Interior Bruce Babbitt, who oversaw the Fish & Wildlife Service, to allow them to take forest products or utilize the land even if it caused harm or destruction to habitats of endangered species, and then sued the Secretary when the agency refusing to allow the takings. [12]

Two years after *Babbitt*, the same court decided perhaps the most important ESA case: *Bennett et. al. v. Spear et. al.* (520 US 154 {1997}). In this case, the court examined the section of the act that required the Secretary of the Interior to specify animal species that are "threatened" or "endangered" and designate their "critical habitat." After the Bureau of Reclamation notified the Fish & Wildlife Service that the operation of the Klamath Irrigation Project in Oregon could affect two endangered species of fish, the FWS issued a Biological Opinion (BO), which stated that the project jeopardized the fish's habitat.The Bureau was told that it had to operate the project with minimum standards of water height. Upon this determination the plaintiffs, who were irrigation districts due to get water from the project and led by Brad Bennett, sued the FWS director, Michael Spear, and others in the service. The U.S. Circuit Court for the Ninth Circuit dismissed the plaintiffs' suit, alleging that they had no standing in the matter. However, on 19 March 1997, Justice Antonin Scalia spoke for a unanimous court in holding that the plaintiffs indeed have standing to sue. Scalia explained, "The Court of Appeals erred in affirming the District Court's dismissal of petitioners' claims for lack of jurisdiction. Petitioners' complaint alleges facts sufficient to meet the requirements of Article III standing, and none of their ESA claims is precluded by the zone of interests test. Petitioners' §1533 claim is reviewable under the ESA's citizen suit provision, and petitioners' remaining claims are reviewable under the APA [Administrative Procedure Act]." [13]

Lower courts have also narrowed, although not substantially, the range of options governmental entities have under the ESA. For instance, in *Arizona Cattle Growers Association v. United States Fish and Wildlife Service* (273 F3d 1229 {9th Circuit Court of Appeals}, 2001), the 9th Circuit held that while the evidentiary bar that the Fish & Wildlife Service must use to list an animal, wildlife, or habitat is rather low, nevertheless it must at least clear that bar; while issuing permits under Section 10(a) of the Act, the court held that that the FWS "must demonstrate that a species is or could be in an area before regulating it, and must establish the causal connection between the land use being regulated and harm to the species in question." [14] In *National Association of Home*

Builders v. Defenders of Wildlife (127 S. Ct. 1258 {2007}), the U.S. Supreme Court held that the Court of Appeals for the Ninth Circuit erred when it held that Section 7(a)(2) of the Endangered Species Act constituted "an independent source of authority for federal agencies," ruling by a 5-4 decision (authored by Justice Samuel Alito) that under the Clean Water Act, the Environmental Protection Agency did not need to utilize Section 7(a)(2) and make a determination that certain construction impacted endangered species. A Congressional Research Service report from 2010 stated that "under Section 7 of ESA, if federal agency actions (or actions of a nonfederal party that require an agency's approval, permit, or funding) may affect a listed species, the agency must ensure that those actions are 'not likely to jeopardize the continued existence' of any endangered or threatened species, nor to destroy or adversely modify CH [critical habitat]. This does not apply in those instances where a law requires a federal agency to take only certain specific actions in order to satisfy the law," as found in the *National Association of Home Builders* decision. [15]

THE DEBATE OVER PROTECTING ENDANGERED SPECIES

Since Congress enacted the Lacey Act in 1900 and Theodore Roosevelt stepped forward to protect migratory birds in 1903 through the establishment of the National Wildlife Refuge System, there has been a debate over how far government — be it federal, state, or local — should go to protect those animals, wildlife, and plants and their habitats it considers threatened or endangered. As of this writing in mid-2011, there are approximately 1,950 total species listed under the Endangered Species Act (ESA); of these, 1,375 are found entirely or in part in the United States, while the remainder are foreign species that fall under the aegis of the act.

At the same time, however, many interests believe that government intrusion into the protection of wildlie and their habitats actually makes things worse for the affected wildlife. Opponents of the Endangered Species Act include hunters, fishermen, timber and mining interests, and those who stand for land ownership, all of whom have argued that the act hinders economic development and impacts not just wildlife and habitat but also people in the area. They argue that fishing and hunting license fees are used to increase land purchases for habitat protection and to fund government efforts to provide assistance to the habitats.

Although there are no recent reports, the only references to the costs of the ESA and its implementation came in 1987 and 1992, respectively. The first showed that of 3,200 consultations, listings of endangered species only impacted 68 total construction projects, with none of these being stopped entirely. [16] In 1992, the Government Accounting Office (GAO) [17] reported during a House committee hearing that between 1987 and 1991, 89% of all consultations for ESA listings were resolved through the hearing and other processes (16,161 out of a total of 18,211 consultations). Of the 2,050 consultations that did go forward, 91% were found not to harm any species or habitat. Of the remaining 9% (181), 87%, or 158, found alternative construction sites that allowed the project under consideration to go ahead. Thus, at the end, during this 5-year span, only 23 consultations were resolved with the construction project having to be halted to preserve the species or the habitat. **[18]** According to the National Oceanic and Atmospheric Administration, which administers fisheries that protect endangered and threatened fish species,

> *Although occasional extinction of species is natural, extinctions are currently occurring at a rate that is unprecedented in human history. Each plant, animal, and their physical environment is part of an ecosystem and part of a much more complex web of life. Because of this, the extinction of a single species can cause a series of negative events to occur that affect many other species. Endangered species also serve as "sentinel" species to indicate larger ecological problems that could affect the functioning of the ecosystem and likely humans as well. As importantly, species diversity is part of the natural legacy we leave for future generations. The wide variety of species on land and in our oceans has provided inspiration, beauty, solace, food, livelihood, medicines and other products for previous generations. The ESA is a mechanism to help guide conservation efforts, and to remind us that our children deserve the opportunity to enjoy the same natural world we experience.*
> **[19]**

The debate over a comprehensive environmental policy was ramped up in 1995, when Republicans took control of the U.S. House of Representatives for the first time in over 40 years. One of their stated goals was the amendment of the Endangered Species Act to account for landowners and businesses impacted by the law. When the party took control of the House in January 1995, party leaders established the Endangered Species Task Force, which held hearings on the impact of the law and what kind of legislation could be drafted to amend it. In September 1995, Representatives Don Young (R-Alaska) and Richard Pombo (R-California) introduced a reform bill, which would allow states and landowners more imput into how ESA listings would be made and considered, while also reimbursing landowners and others not just for takings to preserve wildlife and habitats but also for the loss of land value when an ESA determination is made that impacts them. The bill was approved by the House Resources Committee in October, but when a national backlash began that made the party look as though it were attacking the environment, House leaders did not bring it up for a vote. With this in mind, two moderate Republicans, Jim Saxton of New Jersey and Wayne Gilchrest of Maryland worked on a bill that looked less harsh in 1996, but because 1996 was an election year, the bill did not come up for a vote. In fact, even after Bill Clinton left office in 2001, Republicans in the majority of both houses of Congress could not get enough support even amongst their own to get amendments to the act through the legislature. Many Democrats, however, sided with them; in 2003, Rep. Dennis Cardoza (D-California) introduced the Critical Habitat Reform Act, which would shorten the time between when a species is listed on the Endangered Species Act List to the time that a recovery act is put into place. Again, this act did not pass the Congress, and the ESA remains a bitterly contested piece of legislation that one side wants to make stronger while the other side wishes to change.

BIODIVERSITY AND ENDANGERED SPECIES

Biodiversity is defined by the *Oxford English Dictionary* as "the variety of life in the world or in a particular habitat or ecosystem." The Convention of Biological Diversity, signed at Rio de Janiero, Brazil, in 1992, defined it as "the variability among living organisms from all sources including terrestrial, marine and other aquatic ecosystems and the ecological complexes of which they are a part...[including diversity within species, between species and of ecosystems." [20] To this end, legislation like the Endangered Species Act set out to reinforce biodiversity in the world around us with the ultimate goal of keeping intact as many habitats for animals and other wildlife as possible. Unfortunately, even with governments all over the world setting wide-ranging resources aside to protect the world's biodiversity, the loss of animals and wildlife and the encroachment of man on habitats, coupled with pollution, hunting, and poaching of animals and other wildlife continues at a rapid pace. Even as this is being written, there is loss to habitat; the rate of species loss cannot be estimated, with scientists and others arguing over how the measure exact numbers. We may look back in the coming decades and see the death of Martha the Passenger Pigeon in 1914 not as a unique moment but as one snapshot among many.

Lecturer James Maclaurin and Professor Kim Sterelny wrote in 2008, "[I]f we accept that biodiversity is important, and if we accept that there is more to biodiversity than species number, we must be able to answer the following questions: What is biodiversity and how do we measure it?...The concept of biodiversity was coined at the intersection of science, applied science, and politics. Moreover, though most who talk about biodiversity think that there is something important at it, there are very different rationales for its preservation. Thus, some have argued that biodiversity ought to be conserved because it is a feature of the natural world that people enjoy and find useful. It is what conservation ethicists call 'demand values.'" [21] Others, most notably Edward Osbourne Wilson (1929-), who was the first to write about the issue, have issued more dire warnings; in his work "The Gaia Atlas of Planet Management," he penned, "The worst thing that can happen during the 1980s is not energy depletion, economic collapse, limited nuclear war, or conquest by a totalitarian government. As terrible as these catastrophes would be for us, they can be repaired within a few generations. The one process ongoing in the 1980s that will take millions of years to correct is the loss of genetic and species diversity by the destruction of natural habitats. This is the folly that our descendents are least likely to forgive us." He continued, "Species extinction is now accelerating and will reach ruinous propositions during the next twenty years. No one is sure of the number of living species of plants and animals, including such smaller forms as mosses, insects, and minnows, but estimates range from between five and ten million. A conservative estimate of the current extinction rate is one thousand species a year, mostly due to the accelerating destruction of tropical forests and other key habitats." **[22]**

THE ROLE OF THE DEBATE OVER DIVERSITY AND THE ENDANGERED SPECIES ACT

The debate over the Endangered Species Act has primarily focused on the impact of the law on human development and property use. But from a biological perspective, the agenda is much broader and much more important. Protecting biodiversity produces economic, medical, recreational, scientific, ecological, and aesthetic benefits. It reminds humans of their stewardship over the earth as its most powerful species and its opportunity to protect the place of each species as a unique part of the biosphere we inhabit. Each species can contribute to our understanding of how life evolves and is preserved and to the functioning of ecosystems. Wildlife is a source of beauty, joy, and wonder.

There are opportunities for compromise, but the preservation of biodiversity is itself a tremendously important public policy goal. It is not simply one of several goals that should be balanced but is essential in ensuring our survival. The fate of the human species on earth is intricately intertwined with the fate of those who make up the biosphere.

There is some opportunity for common ground, and it does need to be found — from both sides of the debate. Congressional reformers' interest in revising the ESA in order to permit priority setting focuses attention on the need for more research about the role of biodiversity in the ecosystem. Since we are not doing a very good job of protecting endangered species, there are opportunities to fashion agreements around more effective measures. At the same time, the economic impact of protecting species must be examined, if only to make sure that while efforts are made to protect species and habitat that those people or businesses that are affected by governmental decisions must be either compensated or assisted in some way to avoid continuing anger and resentment over the issue as a whole. But the business side of the equation needs to agree that preserving species and habitat must be something that all strive to accomplish. We need each side to come together as closely as possible; a true agreement of the minds may be impossible, but if both sides could put aside their differences and look at the large picture — the salvation of the planet and its resources without doing harm to others that inhabit the planet as well — there would be some measure of acceptance and agreement that today seems so far away. Broadening the focus of our attention from individual species to broader habitats and ecosystems is essential. But reorienting the law in that direction will require a great deal of trust and good faith on the part of all parties and a strong commitment to the idea of preserving biodiversity while also protecting the lives of all who live on the planet. The political conflicts surrounding the Endangered Species Act and other environmental and like-minded legislation reflect a recognition that the economic

states involved in protecting species and their habitats are extremely high, but the
ecological issues at stake are just as profound.

NOTES:

[1] See the text of the act at 16 USC 701.

[2] For information on Lacey and his work to save bird species, see Mary Annette Gallagher, "John F. Lacey: A Study in Organizational Politics" (Ph.D. dissertation, University of Arizona, 1970).

[3] Conard, Rebecca, "Lacey, John Fletcher" in David Hudson, Marvin Bergman, & Loren Horton, "The Biographical Dictionary of Iowa" (Iowa City: University of Iowa Press, 2008), 297-98.

[4] "Digest of Federal Resource Laws of Interest to the U.S. Fish & Wildlife Service: Bald Eagle Protection Act of 1940," courtesy of the U.S. Fish & Wildlife Service, online at http://www.fws.gov/laws/lawsdigest/baldegl.html.

[5] ibid.

[6] "The Wild Free-Roaming Horses and Burros Act of 1971," courtesy of the Bureau of Land Management, online at http://www.blm.gov/pgdata/etc/medialib/blm/wo/Planning_and_Renewable_Resources/wild_horses_and_burros/sale_authority.Par.69801.File.dat/whbact_1971.pdf.

[7] "Marine Mammal Protection Act of 1972," courtesy of the U.S. Fish & Wildlife Service, online at http://www.fws.gov/laws/lawsdigest/marmam.html.

[8] "The History of the Endangered Species Act," courtesy of The Thoreau Institute, online at http://www.ti.org/ESAHistory.html.

[9] "Summary of the Endangered Species Act," courtesy of the Environmental Protection Agency, online at http://www.epa.gov/lawsregs/laws/esa.html.

[10] *Tennessee Valley Authority v. Hill* (437 US 153 {1978}).

[11] "Endangered Species Act," courtesy of the National Oceanic and Atmospheric Administration, online at http://www.nmfs.noaa.gov/pr/laws/esa/.

[12] *Babbitt v. Sweet Home Chapter of Communities for a Greater Oregon* (515 US 687 {1995}).

[13] *Bennett et. al. v. Spear et. al.* (520 US 154 {1997}

[14] Buck, Eugene H., et al., "The Endangered Species Act (ESA) and the 111th Congress: Conflicting Values and Difficult Choices" (Congressional Research Service Report 7-5700 {23 July 2010}, 14.

[15] See text of *National Association of Home Builders v. Defenders of Wildlife* (127 S. Ct. 1258 {2007}); see also Buck, Eugene H., et al., "The Endangered Species Act (ESA) and the 111th Congress: Conflicting Values and Difficult Choices" (Congressional Research Service Report 7-5700 (23 July 2010), 4.

[16] General Accounting Office, "Endangered Species: Limited Effect of Consultation Requirements on Western Water Projects" (GAO/RCED-87-78) (March 1987), 2-3.

[17] The General Accounting Office was later renamed the General Accountability Office.

[18] General Accounting Office, "Endangered Species Act: Types and Number of Implementing Actions" (GAO/CED-92-131BR) (May 1992), 30.

[19] Statistics on the Endangered Species Act courtesy of the National Oceanic and Atmospheric Administration, online at http://www.nmfs.noaa.gov/pr/pdfs/esa_factsheet.pdf.

[20] Spicer, John I., "World Issues Today: Biodiversity" (New York: The Rosen Publishing Group, Inc., 2009), 8.

[21] Maclaurin, James; and Kim Sterelny, "What is Biodiversity?" (Chicago: The University of Chicago Press, 2008), 2, 5.

[22] Wilson, Edward O., "Nature Revealed: Selected Writings, 1949-2006" (Baltimore: The Johns Hopkins University Press, 2006), 618.

5

National Forests and Timber Policy

THE POLICY FRAMEWORK

From the period even before it became a country, the United States has had a broad supply of timber and timber products, utilized to build houses and other items that aided in the growth of the nation. Although some argue that the supplies — and thus the overall amount of timber — in the nation has gone down over the years, studies show that there is more timber now, in the first decade of the twenty-first century, than at any time in the nation's history. The goal of keeping the rich timber lands of the nation protected while utilizing it for products, has been an overarching one of the federal, state, and local government structure. The goal of national forest policy has been to allow for the quantitative harvesting of as much timber as is necessary to meet the needs of both this country and overseas markets. Congressional policy has been aimed towards this goal.

In 1873, the U.S. government first reacted to the initial calls to protect the nation's timber lands, when the American Association for the Advacement of Science called upon the Congress to enact policies designed to protect all timber supplies. Three years later, after a small ride was placed inside one piece of legislation authorizing the spending of $2,000 to appoint a "special forestry agent" inside the U.S. government [1], the administration of President Ulysses S Grant established, inside the U.S. Department of

Agriculture, created the U.S. Forest Service, naming Franklin Benjamin Hough as the first U.S. forester. There was no assurance that the position would be permanent: in fact, Hough was named by Frederick Watts, who was serving as the Commissioner, and not Secretary of Agriculture, as that "cabinet post" was also merely an office. According to the inventory list for his papers at the New York State Library, "Hough traveled widely to compile his official 1877 Report on Forestry. Congress ordered the publication of 25,000 copies of the 650-page volume. In 1881, the Division of Forestry was created within the Department of Agriculture, with Hough appointed as its first chief. In 1882 he published a handbook entitled "*Elements of Forestry.*" Many of his observations were published in a periodical which he established, called the *American Journal of Forestry*. The subject had not, however, received sufficient attention in this country to secure support of such a journal, and it was suspended after the completion of the first volume. Through the influence of Hough, forestry associations were formed, and the system, adopted in many states, of planting trees on Arbor Day." [2] In 1883, an argument with Commissioner of Agriculture George B. Loring led to Hough's demotion, and, later that year, Congregational minister and former Vice President of the American Forestry Association Nathaniel Hilyer Egleston was named as the head of the Division of Forestry. Historians have blasted the selection and the replacement of Hough as rank politics. Little of Egleton's work is remembered; his 1884 work, "*Handbook of Tree-Planting; or, Why to Plant, Where to Plant, What to Plant, How to Plant,*" may be his best-known accomplishment. [3]

By the end of the nineteenth century, it was decided that government intervention was needed to protect forestry reserves across the country. In response, the Congress enacted the General Revision Act (26 Stat. 1103), better known as the Creative Act of 1891, a piece of legislation that authorized the President of the United States to set aside those public lands where forestry areas were considered to be endangered as forestry reserves. [4] Six years later, Congress enacted the Organic Administration Act of 1897 (30 Stat. 34) on 4 June 1897; according to the U.S. Forest Service, "The Act provides that no national forest may be established except to improve and protect the forest, or to secure favorable conditions of water flows, and to furnish a continuous supply of timber. The Act is not intended to authorize the inclusion within national forests of lands that are more valuable for mineral or agricultural purposes." [5]

In 1896, Republican William McKinley was elected President of the United States; in defiance of this change in administrations, President Grover Cleveland, before leaving office on 4 March 1897, doubled the size of national forest reserves from 20 to 40 million acres. Historian Douglas Hillman Strong wrote, "Westerners...rose in bitter protest against this new government encroachment on what they considered to be their domain. A compromise in 1897 included an amendment that provided the Secretary of the Interior with broad authority to regulate the occupancy and use of the reserves. This amendment opened the door for the economic use of government forests and for a professional forest service; in short, it provided the legal basis for federal management of national forests." **[6]**

Although a compromise was reached, Cleveland's action locked up forests in South Dakota and Montana that had been the source of timber for two major mining companies. Nevertheless, with the change to the law in 1897 through the Organic Administration Act of 1897, the door had been opened for the federal administration of the forestry reserves of the nation, although allowing limited amounts of harvesting and use of the lands and timber. The change, however, to federal law would now be permanent.

Just eight years later, Congress strengthened the 1897 legislation. Under the so-called "Transfer Act" of 1905 (33 Stat. 628), the control of the reserves of timber were moved from Interior back to the Department of Agriculture, now under the aegis of the U.S. Forest Service. He then named his good friend Gifford Pinchot, an advocate for the federal administration of forestry reserves, as the head of the new service. Under this act, as well as the 1891 act, Roosevelt during his administration (1901-09) withdrew some 235 million acres of public lands and set them aside as national forests; in 1907 he created 21 national forests alone. In total, from 1903 until he left office in March 1909, he established 150 national forests. **[7]**

Roosevelt's goal was to transform wild, natural lands into "cultivated" forests, managed for their maximum sustainable yield. In his autobiography, published in 1913, Roosevelt explained his reasoning as to the hectic pace of setting aside lands for national parks, forests, and other preserves:

> *"While the Agricultural Appropriation Bill was passing through the Senate, in 1907, Senator Fulton* **[8]***, of Oregon, secured an amendment providing that the President could not set aside any additional National Forests in the six Northwestern States. This meant retaining some sixteen million of acres to be exploited by land grabbers and by the representatives of the great special interests, at the expense of the public interest. But for four years the Forest Service had been gathering field notes as to what forests ought to be set aside in these States, and so was prepared to act. It was equally undesirable to veto the whole agricultural bill, and to sign it with this amendment effective. Accordingly, a plan to create the necessary National Forest in these States before the Agricultural Bill could be passed and signed was laid before me by Mr. Pinchot. I approved it. The necessary papers were immediately prepared. I signed the last proclamation a couple of days before by my signature, the bill became law; and when the friends of the special interests in the Senate got their amendment through and woke up, they discovered that sixteen million acres of timberland had been saved for the people by putting them in the National Forests before the land grabbers could get at them.*
>
> *The opponents of the Forest Service turned handsprings in their wrath; and dire were their threats against the Executive; but the threats could not be carried out, and were really only a tribute to the efficiency of our action.* **[9]**

The 1891 and 1905 acts led down a path of the protection of forests unforeseen in American history. Subsequent Forest Service employees, including Aldo Leopold and Robert Marshall, helped direct the agency to protecting some 13 million acres by the 1930s as wilderness areas off limits for private use. But in the years during the Second World War and after, when the need for wood products increased, the government had to lessen its regulation of timber areas, allowing for sales of timber in national forests to rise; according to an article by Paul Raeburn on the U.S. Forest Service in 1994, "Timber harvests swelled from 2.1 billion board feet in 1941 to 12.1 billion board feet in 1966. As a result, many wood-products companies and rural communities grew dependent on the national forests for timber supplies and jobs." [10]

From the end of WWII until 1960, the Congress stayed out of regulating timber supplies. In that year, however, Congress enacted the Multiple Use-Sustained Yield Act of 1960 (74 Stat. 215), also known as MUSYA. The impact of this legislation, according to the U.S. Forest Service, "was to ensure that all possible uses and benefits of the national forests and grasslands would be treated equally. The 'multiple uses' included outdoor recreation, range, timber, watershed, and wildlife and fish in such combinations that they would best meet and serve human needs." [11] This legislation again tried to tip the balance away from business interests and a growing economy to protection of timber supplies. In 1974, the Congress, in enacting the Forest and Rangeland Renewable Resources Planning Act (RPA) (88 Stat. 476), which required the U.S. Forest Service (USFS) to engage in long-term planning for the sustained use of timber lands, assess the resources under its care every 10 years, and require management plans for each separate unit and update them every fifteen years.

In 1976, Congress moved to address the continued use of forestry reserves on public lands when it enacted The National Forest Management Act (NFMA) (Public Law 94-588). This action, an update to the Forest and Rangeland Renewable Resources Planning Act of 1974, came in response to the so-called "Monongahela Decision." In 1973, the Federal District Court for the Northern District of West Virginia struck down the authority of the U.S. Forest Service to sell timber from the Monongahela National Forest in the Allegheny Mountains in West Virginia. The decision came after local residents, grouped together as the Izaak Walton League, sued Secretary of Agriculture Earl Butz to halt any additional USFS contracts being sold for timber in that national forest. The judge held that the USFS could only sell dead timber from the national forests. Congress, forced to deal with the issue, enacted The National Forest Management Act, which found that timber in national forests must be considered as renewable resources, able to be sold by the government. In the findings of the legislation, the Congress held that "it is in the public interest for the Forest Service to assess the nation's public and private renewable resources and develop a national renewable resource program; to serve the national interest, the development of the renewable resource program must include a thorough analysis of environmental and economic impacts, coordination of multiple-use and sustained-yield, and public participation; the Forest Service has the responsibility and opportunity to assure a national natural resource conservation posture that will meet our citizens' needs in perpetuity; the knowledge derived from coordinated public and private research programs will promote a sound technical and ecological base for the effective management, use and protection of the nation's renewable resources." **[12]** However, the NFMA imposes several restrictions on sales of Forest Service timber and lumber harvesting: the service, for instance, is prohibited from allowing logging on lands that are "not suited for timber production, considering physical, economic, and other pertinent conditions."

The NFMA was the first federal law to address the issue of biodiversity, as it required the Forest Service, for the first time, to promote that program when establishing plans for timber sales, even if limits imposed due to biodiversity caused harm to timber sales.

PRESIDENTIAL TIMBER POLICY, 1993-2001

Until 1993, the Forest Service's main goal was to allow timber sales with some limits on the harvesting of trees based on several criteria, most notably the impact of harvesting on the environment. In 1993, however, the incoming Clinton administration changed the entire Forest Service policy from one of strict timber management to one dealing more with land management. The change had actually begun four years before: in 1989, federal judge William Dwyer ruled against logging in old-growth forests in the Northwestern United States; he upheld his decision in 1991. Thus, in 1993, when Clinton entered office, his administration decided to build upon the Dwyer ruling to protect the northern spotted owl and he held a Forest Conference in Portland, Oregon, in the center of the old-growth territory, to formulate a new policy. From this parley came the orders from the administration to develop a program of "scientifically sound, ecologically credible, and legally responsible" plans which would end the controversy over the spotted owl once and for all. In 1994, despite widespread opposition from the people in the area, the administration developed the so-called Northwest Forest Plan, which called for a system of old-growth reserves, setting aside wide swaths of timber that the community needed for timber sales. The decision, although ecologically sound, sounded the death knell for the Northwest forest timber and logging community, and led to a deep recession which, to this day, has still not abated.

Opposition to the plan from Congress grew, particularly after the Republicans won control of both houses in the 1994 midterm elections. In 1995, Congress ordered the Forest Service to allow for the logging of dead or diseased and dying trees in the northwest area, and a suspension of all environmental laws during a 16-month emergency period. Jack Ward Thomas, a biologist who had been named by Clinton to head the Forest Service — the first of his field to run the agency — resigned in 1996 because he was caught in a full-on civil war between Congress and the administration. He was replaced by Mike Dombeck, also a biologist, who was soon caught in the same battle with Congress that his predecessor had been. In 1998, four western Senators, all Republicans, wrote to Dombeck, "Since you seem bent on producing fewer and fewer results from the National Forests at rapidly increasing costs, many will press Congress to seriously consider the option to simply move to custodial management of our National Forests in order to stem the flow of unjustifiable investments. That will mean the Agency will have to operate with significantly reduced budgets and with far fewer employees." Dombeck also drew controversy when a year into his tenure, he proposed a moratorium on all new roads into most national forest areas where there were no roads; at the same time, he called for a halt to all sales of timber from roadless areas in Idaho, Oregon, Washington State, and other western states. Although he got support from administration allies, western interests, both in the Republican and Democrat parties, barraged him for his decisions. [13] The rule was eventually put into place, and it took the succeeding Bush administration more than four years to get it overturned; it was allowed to sunset on 5 May 2005. In January 2001, as he prepared to leave office, Clinton enacted the Roadless Area Conservation Rule, which banned road construction and/or logging in 58.5 million acres of national forest lands that were mostly undeveloped. The rule was challenged in court; the administration of George W. Bush decided not to defend it, and in 2005 it initiated the State Petitions Rule, which allowed states to decide on the management of these lands. In August 2009, the 9th Circuit Court of Appeals in San Francisco struck down the State Petitions Rule, reinstating the nearly-decade old Roadless Area Conservation Rule except for the Tongass National Forest in Alaska and for all of Idaho, which had developed its own plan for its national forests. The decision had been expected, especially since May 2009, when Secretary of Agriculture Thomas Vilsack said that no logging permit would be allowed in a national forest without his personal approval. [14]

In a 2003 report, three environmentalists who supported Clinton's policies wrote, "The Administration proposed initiatives to reduce subsidies for private resource extraction on public lands, but Congress was not receptive. The Administration did, however, shift U.S. Forest Service priorities away from timber production to resource protection, placing some 60 million acres of Federal forests off-limits to road building. President Clinton also designated more than 20 new national monuments, thereby restricting the use of 6 million additional acres of Federal lands." [15] Working closely with Secretary of the Interior Bruce Babbitt, a former Governor of Arizona, and Carol Browner, the administrator of the Environmental Protection Agency, Clinton used all of the tools of the federal government. For instance, he designated or expanded 22 national monuments, from establishing the Grand Staircase-Escalante National Monument in Utah in 1996, to expanding Governor's Island National Monument in New York on his final day in office to 172 total acres. At the tail end of Clinton's administration, after the 2000 election in which his party lost both the White House and the Congress, Clinton decided to continue setting aside land, angering his most vocal opponents. During both of his terms in office, Clinton set aside more than three million acres, or 1.25 million hectares) of land into wilderness or national monuments, ranking him alongside Theodore Roosevelt as the president to have set aside the most land for public areas.

Figure 5: States with Roadless Forest Lands, 2005

Alaska	--	14,779,000 acres
Idaho	--	9,322,000 acres
Montana	--	6,397,000 acres
Colorado	--	4,433,000 acres
California	--	4,416,000 acres
Utah	--	4,013,000 acres
Wyoming	--	3,257,000 acres
Nevada	--	3,186,000 acres
Washington	--	2,015,000 acres
Oregon	--	1,965,000 acres
New Mexico	--	1,597,000 acres
Arizona	--	1,174,000 acres

PRESIDENTIAL TIMBER POLICY, 2001-09

When former Texas Governor George W. Bush entered the presidency in 2001, he brought with him an almost completely different land-use policy from that of the outgoing Clinton administration. Whereas Clinton had almost universally ignored the wishes of business, land, and other interests in the areas affected by governmental regulation, Bush did a 180° change, embracing the beliefs and tenets of these local interests and ignoring the national — and, in many cases, state and local — environmental groups and movements. On 20 January 2001, on his first day in office, Bush's first act was to set aside all of the regulations that the Clinton administration had put into place, waiting until their impact on Bush's own administration could be assessed. Eventually, utilizing his majorities in Congress, as well as implementing new policies through the Department of the Interior, Bush was able to change, although not overturn, much of what Clinton had done. However, courts across the country heard challenges to the new administration's policies regarding timber from environmental groups, and, in most cases, stayed the governmental actions. Because of the slowness of the courts, these suits ran out the clock on two complete terms while Bush was in office; by 2009, when Bush left office, most of his program to reshape timber and land policy had been stopped in the courts. In the areas where Bush was able to change Clinton policy, namely making public areas free for road construction and timber harvesting, when Bush left office the new administration of President Barack Obama went about redoing these policies back to where they had been when Bush took office in 2001. When Bush first took office, a federal district court held that the federal government must protect a land mass of some 58 million acres of forest land from roads, logging, and any type of development. The Bush administration challenged this rule, to no effect. It is known as the Roadless Area Conservation Rule. In May 2005, after years of examining ways to comply with the rule but also allow limited development and road construction, the administration announced that it would allow states to submit to the U.S. Department of Agriculture a comprehensive management plan for the Forest Service to allow road construction in the individual states. In 2007, after the new plan was challenged by environmental groups, a federal district court held the Bush plan to be unconstitutional, and ordered that the 2001 Roadless Area Conservation Rule be reinstated. When Bush left office, the plan was effectively dead.

Presidential Timber Policy, 2009-

The new administration of President Barack Obama, through Secretary of the Interior Ken Salazar of Colorado, reverted almost completely back to the policies of the Clinton administration from 2001. Secretary of Agriculture Tom Vilsack, a former Governor of Iowa, announced in 2009 a moratorium on all logging and road construction in national forest areas. In April 2010, Vilsack renewed the moratorium for an additional year. As of this writing, it appears that the 2001 Roadless Area Conservation Rule will be the federal government's policy for the near future.

Case Law

Almost since the beginning of the country's founding, the courts in the United States have tried to fashion a remedy for the increasing role of the U.S. government in land and forestry matters. For instance, as early as 1839, the U.S. Supreme Court, in *Wilcox v. Jackson* (38 US {13 Peters} 498 {1839}, held that "appropriation of land by the government is nothing more or less than setting it apart for some particular use. In the case before the Court, there has been an appropriation of the land not only in fact but in law, for a military post, for an Indian agency, and for the erection of a lighthouse." The decision found that a man who had applied for a land title and took possession of the land "acquired no title to the land by his entry, and that the right of the United States to the land was not divested or affected by the entry at the land office" where the title had been entered. [16] However, it was not until the end of the nineteenth century, and into the twentieth, that the U.S. Supreme Court, specifically, began to deal with issues of land that eventually related to forestry matters. Although not a forestry case, the court held in *United States v. Rio Grande Dam & Irrigation Co.* (174 US 690 {1899}) that "in the absence of specific authority from Congress[,] a State cannot by its legislation destroy the right of the United States, as the owner of lands bordering on a stream, to the continued flow of its waters; so far at least as may be necessary for the beneficial uses of the government property." [17] Although this specific decision dealt with waters and water rights, nevertheless the courts would use this same line of thinking in forestry cases. However, the Court held in *Kansas v. Colorado* (206 US 46 {1907}) that a state had the power to "determine for itself whether the common law rule in respect to riparian rights or that doctrine which obtains in the arid West of appropriation of waters for the purposes of irrigation shall control," and that Congress "cannot enforce either rule upon any State." [18]

The Court upheld the so-called "Rio Grande rule" the following year in *Winters v. United States* (207 US 564 {1908}), when it decided that "[t]he power of the Government to reserve the waters and exempt them from appropriation under the state laws is not denied, and could not be." [19]

Perhaps the leading modern case regarding timber and public lands is *United States v. New Mexico* (438 US 696 {1978}. In this case, the Court held that when the Gila National Forest in southwest New Mexico was set aside, the U.S. government allowed water to be taken out of the Rio Mimbres River "only where necessary to preserve the timber in the forest or to secure favorable water flows," and not for other reasons, including, as Justice William Rehnquist wrote, "for aesthetic, recreational, wildlife preservation, and stockwatering purposes." The Court examined several pieces of congressional legislation, including the Multiple Use-Sustained Yield Act of 1960 (74 Stat. 215). The case specifically outlined the strict measures that the government could set aside lands for, and could only add to those purposes through specific congressional legislation. [20]

The Debate over U.S. Forestry Policy

In the ensuing years since the 1970s, it appears that forestry policy has become a political football, with Republican administrations wanting to open public lands for limited development and/or usage, and Democratic administrations wanting to close off these areas completely from any use whatsoever. Neither side sees the arguments of those that they oppose, and in doing so we are left with endless rounds of litigation and stalling by one group or another until a change in administration comes about. It is a recipe for gridlock, not solutions.

One side of the policy divide believes that forests have intrinsic values as diverse ecosystems as well as instrumental environmental values such as stabilizing climates and serving as watersheds, and that human activity within them should be limited, and at best avoided at all costs. The other side sees a similar idea: that forests and their timber have an intrinsic value, but to allow all of that timber to merely grow and then rot without something coming from it is a loss to the nation and to the community. Those in this camp believe that "public" lands should be open to the public, and that means roads and other navigable areas inside the forests themselves. Because these two sides represent such divergent views, at complete loggerheads with each other, the Forest Service, as well as other parts of the federal, state, and local governments, as well as other policy makers, face a daunting challenge trying to come up with policies that can meet the tests of the populace as well as the courts.

Let us examine the second side of this argument: that forests, and their timber, represent a resource that with some basic limits should be utilized to the benefit of the community and the nation.

The chief way to harvest timber is through logging. Private companies have for years battled the Forest Service to allow the agency some rein in harvesting old-growth forests, or trees that are extremely old. This not only strips the forests of trees that are older and in many cases dying, allowing new trees to grow, but it fuels the local economy through jobs and services relating to the industry. Environmentalists argue that such commercial usage disrupts the ecosystem, and causes land erosion, stream pollution, and damage to fish and aquatic life. The Forest Service, whose goal is to protect the forests, is also in the business of selling off old-growth forest timber. Its congressional mandate, upheld by congresses for many years, is to sell off timber and use the proceeds for its own budget, including giving localities a portion — up to 25% - of this take. The service has a Timber Sale Program Information Reporting System (TSPIRS), a reporting system that gives out information on the costs of timber harvesting as well as the sales figures and other information. [21]

According to a 2007 GAO report on timber sales,

> The Forest Service's timber sales-related activities are funded by a variety of appropriations. Within the Service's appropriations, there are several programs (or "budget line items") directly or indirectly related to timber sales. For the Forest Products Program, which is responsible for most timber sales-related activity, the Forest Service received about $277.6 million of its $1.5 billion national forest system appropriation in fiscal year 2006. However, the Forest Products Program is not limited to timber sales; some expenditures within the program are associated with other products, such as mushrooms and decorative grasses and foliage. The Service issues permits that allow individuals to gather such products from the forests, whether for personal use or for sale. Conversely, not all timber sales-related expenditures are included in the Forest Products Program. Certain timber sales' planning expenses, for example, might be borne by other programs–including vegetation and watershed management or wildlife and fish management–if the primary purpose of the sale is to improve vegetative conditions or wildlife habitat rather than to provide commercial timber.

The report added that aside from congressional appropriations and sales of timber, "[t]he Forest Service also uses various other funds to pay for timber sales-related activities, including (1) the Knutson-Vandenberg Trust Fund, (2) the Salvage Sale Fund, (3) the Brush Disposal Fund, (4) the Timber Sales Pipeline Restoration Fund, and (5) stewardship contracting revenue." [22]

The possibilities regarding Forest Service timber sales is essential to the agency: in a 1998 Congressional Research Service (CRS) report, it was stated that "The federal government owns about 20% of U.S. timberlands, concentrated in the [W]est, and about 30% of U.S. timber inventory (and 44% of the softwood inventory). Declines in federal harvests in recent years, and legislation to end federal harvests, have led to concerns about the impacts on forest health and on the economy. The national impacts appear to be relatively modest, but local and regional effects could be substantial." [23]

A study of government reports, by the Congressional Research Service (CRS) or the Government Accountability Office (GAO), show that few reports have been generated in the last decade on the work of the Forest Service or the Bureau of Land Management (BLM) regarding timber harvesting; thus, numbers utilized here are woefully out of date with no way to get more recent figures. A 1998 CRS report stated, "The importance of national forest timber has debated at length for many years. The Forest Service defines 'timberland' as land capable of producing 20 cubic feet of industrial wood per acre annually. In 1992, there were nearly 490 million acres of timberland in the United States, nearly 22% of the total land area. Another 247 million acres (11%) were identified as other forest land lands either less productive than the standard (such as interior Alaska) or reserved (withdrawn from potential timber harvesting by administrative or legislative action, such as wilderness designation)." [24]

Table 3: U.S. Timberlands by Landowner and Region, 1992

	National Forests	Other Public	Wood Industry	Nonind. Private	Total
North	9.545	20.761	16 198	111.294	157.799
South	11.544	8.948	39.025	139.782	199.309
Rocky Mtns.	36.402	5.987	2.918	17.322	62.628
Pacific Coast	27.160	11.137	12.314	19.209	69.819
Total	**84.661**	**46.833**	**70.455**	**287.606**	**489.555**

Source: Gorte, Ross, "Federal Timber Harvests: Implications for U.S. Timber Supply" (Congressional Research Service report 98-233 {1998}), 2.

The clash between those who wish to protect all facets of timber and the land surrounding it, and those who want to utilize, to some extent, these valuable assets of nature, has been long and it has been bitter, fought in the political realm as well as the courts. For decades, since the 1930s, the debate over a potential balance between some resource protection and sales of either timber, or minerals, or other parts of federally-owned lands, has continued to dog both presidential administrations and congresses led by both political parties. And when a plan is settled on — be it limited sales of natural resources, or complete protection of these resources — a subsequent administration or Congress undoes the plan and changes it to their liking. And, with control over some 53 million acres of forest land, the Bureau of Land Management, an agency inside the U.S. Department of the Interior, has been in the center of the controversy. At odds with environmentalists, the BLM continues to allow timber to be sold from these lands. In 2003, the Government Accountability Office (GAO) found, after being asked by Congress to investigate BLM timber sales, that "the volume of timber offered for sale has declined substantially since fiscal year 1990." The investigators found that "[f]rom 1990 to 2002, the volume of timber offered for sale by BLM declined about 74 percent. Declines were experienced for each of the timber's components — sawtimber (trees or logs suitable for conversion into lumber) and other wood products (small logs used to make firewood, posts, and poles). Consequently, in 2002, the proportion of sawtimber in the total volume offered for sale was less than it was in 1990." [25]

Figure 6: BLM Public Domain Timber Offered for Sale by Type, Fiscal Years 1990-2002

Source: Government Accountability Office, "Volume of Timber Offered for Sale Has Declined Substantially Since Fiscal Year 1990" (GAO Report 03-615, 2003), 5.

Figure 7: Proportion of BLM Public Domain Timber Offered for Sale by Type, Fiscal Years 1990-2002

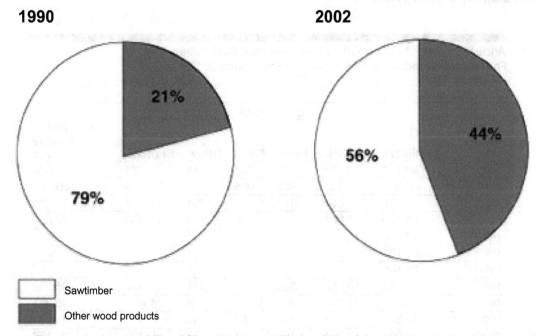

Source: Government Accountability Office, "Volume of Timber Offered for Sale Has Declined Substantially Since Fiscal Year 1990" (GAO Report 03-615, 2003), 6.

Table 4: Public Domain Forest & Woodland Acres by Bureau of Land Management State Office, 2003

Public Domain Forest and Woodland Acres by BLM State Office			
Acres in thousands			
BLM state office	Forests	Woodlands	Total
Alaska[a]	5,297	22,982	28,279
Arizona	20	1,054	1,074
California	204	2,004	2,208
Colorado	1,069	3,041	4,110
Eastern States	0	30	30
Idaho	512	380	892
Montana	783	27	810
Nevada	5	6,269	6,274
New Mexico	44	941	985
Oregon (excludes western Oregon)	194	847	1,041
Utah	338	5,735	6,073
Wyoming	474	530	1,004
Total	8,940	43,840	52,780

Source: Government Accountability Office, "Volume of Timber Offered for Sale Has Declined Substantially Since Fiscal Year 1990" (GAO Report 03-615, 2003), 15.

Table 5: Annual Volume of Timber Offered for Sale from BLM Public Domain Forests and Woodlands, Fiscal Years 1990-2002

Annual Volume of Timber Offered for Sale from BLM Public Domain Forests and Woodlands, Fiscal Years 1990 through 2002							
Board feet in thousands							
		Other wood products					Total timber volume offered
Fiscal year	Sawtimber	Cords[a]	Posts	Poles	Other[b]	Subtotal	
1990[c]	80,116	19,227	1,733	254	14	21,228	101,344
1991	86,395	18,941	465	615	7	20,028	106,423
1992	59,161	16,691	457	1,756	234	19,138	78,299
1993	28,150	18,351	571	566	14	19,502	47,652
1994[d]	13,672	d	d	d	d	d	d
1995[d]	61,128	d	d	d	d	d	d
1996[d]	25,168	d	d	d	d	d	d
1997	21,148	10,502	335	2,776	471	14,084	35,232
1998[e]	15,635	12,353	388	1,807	78	14,626	30,261
1999[fg]	12,523	7,804	468	483	95	8,850	21,373
2000[f]	12,327	8,584	454	207	585	9,830	22,157
2001[f]	17,233	8,609	683	130	65	9,487	26,720
2002[f]	14,427	10,463	679	303	27	11,472	25,899

Source: Government Accountability Office, "Volume of Timber Offered for Sale Has Declined Substantially Since Fiscal Year 1990" (GAO Report 03-615, 2003), 16.

In 1968, William R. Bentley wrote, "Controversy concerning Forest Service timber sales indicates [the] need for a reconsideration of policy objectives and procedures. There have been conflicts regarding many details of the sales and related procedures but the basic cause is the relationship between federal timber and private industrial development. Distinctly new alternatives for selling public timber may be possible within the coming decade, however, which would alter this relationship." [26]

Because of a number of environmental laws enacted by Congress, the Forest Service (FS) and the Bureau of Land Management (BLM) must move carefully regarding timber sales on public lands. While some pieces of pieces of legislation allow sales of timber, others do not. For instance, the Federal Land Policy and Management Act of 1976 (Public Law 94-579) specifies that "[t]he Secretary [of the Interior] is authorized to provide for the acquisition, construction and maintenance of roads within or near public lands in locations and according to specifications that permit maximum economy in harvesting timber while also meeting requirements for protection, development and management of the lands for utilization of their other resources." [27] However, other laws specifically put the onus on the government to stop or prevent timber cutting and sales — these laws include the Clean Water Act of 1972 (86 Stat. 816) [28] and the Endangered Species Act of 1973 (87 Stat. 884).

However, due to lawsuits by environmentalists and others, the rate of timber being sold by the government agencies responsible for their sales has declined rapidly. For instance, from 1990 until 2002, the volume of timber sold by the BLM declined some 74%. At the same time, declines were seen in the areas of each of the timber's components: sawtimber (trees or logs suitable for conversion into lumber) and other wood products (small logs used to make firewood, posts, and poles). Thus, by 2002, the proportion of timber, and sawtimber, offered for sale by both the FS and the BLM was less than it had been just 12 years earlier. Another reason for this decline is the implementation by the government of so-called Forest plans, which set aside large tracts of forested land on public lands until government agencies can come up with plans for their use; unfortunately, these agencies are in the middle of a political fight between those who wish to preserve all of the lands and those who wish to use all of the lands, and these forest plans never come about, or take years to fashion and implement, frustrating both sides of the argument. Initially projected to cost some $100 million and last just five years by the Clinton administration, in fact the forest plans took more than a decade and cost upwards of $2 billion, far more than the government would have realized had the lands been utilized from the first. Some plans were obsolete before they were released and were not updated. Public participation opportunities were limited. The process did produce useful inventories of forestlands, but that information has not always been made available or communicated effectively. The laws and regulations are inconsistent, and the agency lacks the resources to comply with all of them. As a result, managers must choose which requirements to comply with and which ones to ignore. When business and other groups challenged the validity of the forest plans, federal courts held that they must defer to the Forest Service based on that agency's "judgment and expertise." For instance, in *Sierra Club v. Espy* (38 F.3d 792 {5th Circuit Court of Appeals, 1994}), the Appeals court held environmental groups suing the government must defer to the judgment of the Forest Service. In citing a case from Arkansas in 1994, the *Espy* court found that "[t]he agency's judgment in assessing issues requiring a high level of technical expertise, such as diversity, must...be accorded the considerable respect that matters within the agency's expertise deserve." [29] *Espy* is not an uncommon decision: Federal courts have generally given the Forest Service great discretion to balance the relevant factors when signing timber contracts and have deferred to agency expertise in harvesting methods, protection of old-growth forests, and fostering biodiversity.

Both sides of the environmental argument have criticized the Forest Service and their planning efforts as impeding their specific goals for the area that is targeted. In numerous congressional hearings, industry groups and environmental groups charge that the FS or the BLM is either siding wholly with one side or another, which cannot be possible. Charges also flew that the government agencies spent years, and millions of dollars, to formulate plans that were never put into practice. For instance, in 1996 the American Forest and Paper Association, during a congressional hearing, charges that the Forest Service had used up 19 years, and had spent more than $250 million, to prepare some 123 resource management plans (RMPs) but had failed completely to implement the plans once they had been completed. These industry groups also argue that the agencies expand their oversight without congressional approval, examining not just the impact of timber harvesting on the timber supplies themselves but on the watershed, the ecology as a whole, and even biodiversity. They also charged that the Clinton administration had authorized the sale of a certain amount of timber and yet had sold far less: in FY 1995, some 7.6 million board feet of timber was to be sold, but only 4 billion board feet actually was allowed to be cut; and, further, than in FY 1996 the administration requested that only 3.6 million board feet be cut and sold. Critics of Clinton's plans argued that the Forest Service's regulation implementing the statutory provision mandating protection of the diversity of plant and animal communities, permits injunctions that effectively shut down forests and provide for more protection of species than does the Endangered Species Act. The idea of ecosystem management, they argued, was ill defined and gave managers the opportunity to override long-standing statutory and administrative declarations aimed at promoting timber cuts. Administrative and judicial appeals of timber sales have become almost automatic, further delaying cuts.

Industry officials blame Congress for permitting attorneys bringing these challenges to be reimbursed under the Equal Access to Justice Act, for failing to provide narrow standing requirements, and for not providing deadlines for bringing administrative or judicial challenges. **[30]** At the same time, environmental groups faulted the Clinton, and the Bush, administrations for pushing a progrowth agenda as far as old-growth forests were concerned. During Bush's two terms, an unprecedented wave of lawsuits from environmental and other groups bottled much of the Bush administration's forestry plans up in the courts. Ironically, Rep. Peter DeFazio of Oregon, a liberal, has been at the forefront of trying to change the forestry plans for the area he represents in Congress. His Web site notes that "[s]ince the mid-1990s, DeFazio has urged the Clinton, Bush, and Obama administrations to revise the Northwest Forest Plan to protect old growth and provide sustainable jobs. DeFazio also continues to work on an alternative forest plan that would provide a predictable supply of timber to mills and rural communities, protect remaining old growth, and create family-wage jobs in the Pacific Northwest."

One answer to this situation may be the granting by the Forest Service and the Bureau of Land Management of stewardship contracts. In 2008, a Government Accountability Office report stated,

> Recent severe wildland fire seasons have focused attention on the state of the nation's forests. Many of these forests have become dense with small, tightly spaced trees and thick brush, which — combined with drought, wind, insect damage, and other adverse conditions — have fueled extensive wildland fires in recent years. In response, both the Department of Agriculture's Forest Service and the Department of the Interior's Bureau of Land Management (BLM) have placed substantial emphasis on thinning forests and rangelands to help reduce the buildup of potentially hazardous fuels. The Forest Service and BLM, which together manage a total of about 450 million acres of federal land, have frequently cited the importance of one too–stewardship contracting — in their efforts to reduce hazardous fuels and restore forest health. This tool was designed to help the agencies conduct land management projects — such as thinning forests, installing culverts, harvesting timber, and the like — more efficiently, by allowing them to use any of several innovative contracting approaches. For example, through stewardship contracting, the agencies can trade goods — such as timber–for fuel reduction or forest restoration services that the agencies would otherwise pay for with appropriated dollars. **[31]**

The Western Governors Association (WGA), a group of governors from 19 western U.S. states and three American territories, have come out wholly against continued declining sales of timber as being economically devastating to the region. In 2008, they drafted a resolution to Congress calling on the body to reauthorize the Secure Rural Schools and Community Self-Determination Act of 2000 (Public Law 106-393). This act, according to the WGA, "provided for federal and non-federal wildfire mitigation, habitat improvement, watershed restoration, road maintenance, recreational improvement activities, as well as search and rescue response. Through citizen-involved Resource Advisory Committees, there is significant improvement in the collaborative approach to managing public and private forestlands." In 2008, Congress extended the funding for the program for three additional years, but in 2011 all funding will end. **[32]** At the same time, the WGA has offered seven principles for public land management, particularly in the states that they have jurisdiction over:

1. Laws, policies, and management decisions must be based on sound resource stewardship that provides resource sustainability and protection to meet the diverse needs of present and future generations.

2. Management of public lands should promote stability and predictability in the production of goods and services and sustainability of resources on the public lands. At the same time, management must be sufficiently flexible to adapt to changing social, economic, and ecological conditions.

3. Federal administration of the public land laws should provide incentives for sustained management and encourage efficiency.

4. The role of public involvement in the management of public lands should be meaningful, collaborative, and timely.

5. The diversity and significance of natural resources must be acknowledged in land management decisions.

6. When value is created by the use of the public lands and their resources, federal managers should be enabled to recover an appropriate amount of that value.

7. Federal budgets, incentives for federal managers, and incentives for good stewardship to users of the federal lands should support these goals.

THE FOREST SERVICE: THE FUTURE

Starting in 1990, the Forest Service began ending its program of timber sales, to the consternation of many industry groups. As noted previously, by 1996 the amount of timber being sold from public lands had fallen some 85%, and while the program has not been completely phased out, it is now at its lowest levels ever as of this writing in 2011. Changes came in 2000, following a devastating fire that burned hundreds of homes in Los Alamos, New Mexico. When it was discovered that the fire had begun because of poor planning by the Forest Service in allowing old growth forest to die and not be removed, Congress gave the service a large increase in its budget, starting with a 38% rise in FY 2001, to remove timber that causes fires. According to the conservative Cato Institute, "[f]ire expenditures have grown from about 10 percent of the Forest Service budget in the early 1990s to more than 40 percent today." [33] However, under the Bush administration, there was an increase in the amount of timber from public lands being cut and sold: In 2001, for instance, this amounted to 2 billion board feet. The Forest Service, however, has moved towards spending more and more of its funding on either preparing for, or reacting to, forest fires. Since the agency's mission "changed," the U.S. Congress has had little oversight over its spending, and has given it a virtual "blank check" for its funding.

At the same time that the U.S. government has scaled back its plans for the harvesting of timber products, the industrial need for such products has grown — and American corporations have gone overseas, where environmental regulations are less stringent, to get the timber supplies that they need. The aforementioned sawtimber, whole logs, and other timber supplies are made into a myriad of products utilized by the American people on a grand scale: among these are paper, paperboard, paneling and roofing materials, and other products are now being manufactured overseas, to the detriment of American jobs and the American economy. It requires approximately 1.8 acres of timberland to fulfill the timber needs of each American, with one acre producing, on average, 44 cubic feet of raw wood products.

What is the future of timber harvesting in the United States, and of the role played by the Forest Service? Despite warning from environmentalists that timber reserves in the United States are under constant threat from industry, in fact today there are more trees in the United States than there were when the nation was founded in 1776. Strict congressional and other regulations will always limit how much timber can be harvested, but lawsuits by environmentalists and others have limited that even more.

At the same time, the role of the forests in the health of the area they inhabit and the surrounding area is pretty clear: They help nourish the diversity of life on which all living things are dependent, help maintain soil fertility, recycle nutrients, produce oxygen and absorb carbon dioxide, filter water, and provide new products for medicine and agriculture. Old-growth forests are particularly important in promoting biodiversity, but most of the nation's old-growth forests have been cut down. Only small pockets remain, plus one large area in the Pacific Northwest and Alaska. In the 1990s, scientists working on the Clinton administration's forest plan for Oregon and Washington concluded that "old-growth forests in the Pacific Northwest may be unique ecosystems that developed under climatic and disturbance regimes that may never be duplicated." While some old-growth forests can regenerate over centuries, their loss will result in the extinction of some species. [34]

What comes next is anyone's guess. In an economy as of this writing mired deep in recession, the issue of jobs — especially in severely economically depressed areas where jobs relating to timber have vanished — will take precedence. But in the clash between those who wish to have unlimited development of timber and other resources, and those who want no development whatsoever, there has to be a balance somewhere, and no one has come forward in years with a viable alternative or a middle ground. What needs to be found is a route in which industry can have a chance to cultivate resources, but a check put on them so that there is not sustained or permanent damage done to the environment or to the forested areas. The Forest Service, or the Bureau of Land Management, should lead in this area, but, again, government either sides with one side or the other, depending on the political leanings of the party in control of either the executive branch or the Congress or both. Ultimately, it will be the administration and the Congress that the

American people elect that will make the final verdict on what becomes of the forests and what lies within them. They will decide, as will the courts, whether or not to allow some, all, or no logging or the utilization of its resources, and whether, as some believe, that the primary value and importance of the nation's national forests lie in their role as the sustainers of biodiversity and environmental quality, placing trees and timber harvesting as a subordinate, or secondary, goal.

NOTES:

[1] 19 Stat. 143, at 167. See also Ise, John, "The United States Forest Policy" (New Haven: Yale University Press, 1920).

[2] Franklin Benjamin Hough Papers inventory, courtesy of The New York State Library, online at http://www.nysl.nysed.gov/msscfa/sc7009.htm.

[3] Egleston, Nathaniel H., "Handbook of Tree-Planting; or, Why to Plant, Where to Plant, What to Plant, How to Plant" (New York: D. Appleton, 1884).

[4] Later codified at 16 USC 471, the act was repealed in 1976.

[5] "Forest Service Organic Administration Act of 1897," courtesy of the New Mexico Center for Wildlife Law, online at http://wildlifelaw.unm.edu/fedbook/fsact.html.

[6] Strong, Douglas Hillman, "Dreamers & Defenders: American Conservationists" (Lincoln: The University of Nebraska Press, 1988), 66.

[7] U.S. Department of Agriculture, Forest Service, Division The Lands Staff, "Establishment and Modification of National Forest Boundaries: A Chronological Record, 1891-1996" (Washington, D.C.: Government Printing Office, 1996), 3-25.

[8] Senator Charles William Fulton (1853-1918), Republican of Oregon.

[9] Roosevelt, Theodore, "Theodore Roosevelt: An Autobiography" (New York: Macmillan, 1913), 419.

[10] Raeburn, Paul, "Can This Man Save Our Forests? Now Led by a Scientist, the Forest Service Explores new Strategies for Managing Public Lands," *Popular Science*, CCXXXXIV:6 (June 1994), 84.

[11] "USDA Forest Service: The First Century," with information on the Multiple Use-Sustained Yield Act of 1960, online at http://www.foresthistory.org/ASPNET/Publications/first_century/sec7.htm.

[12] "National Forest Management Act of 1976," findings and policy, courtesy of the New Mexico Center for Wildlife Law, online at http://wildlifelaw.unm.edu/fedbook/nfma.html.

[13] Anderson, H. Michael, "Reshaping National Forest Policy," *Issues in Science and Technology* (Fall 1999), online at http://www.issues.org/16.1/anderson.htm.

[14] Preusch, Matthew, "Court Strikes Down 2005 Change to Forest Roadless Rule," 5 August 2009, online at http://www.oregonlive.com/environment/index.ssf/2009/08/court_strikes_down_2005_change.html.

[15] Hahn, Robert W.; Sheila M. Olmstead, and Robert N. Stavins, "Environmental Regulation During the 1990s: A Retrospective Analysis," a Report of the American Enterprise Institute-Brookings Institute Joint Center for Regulatory Studies (27 January 2003), 2.

[16] *Wilcox v. Jackson* (38 US {13 Peters} 498 {1839}), at 498-99.

[17] *United States v. Rio Grande Dam & Irrigation Co.* (174 US 690 {1899}), at 703.

[18] *Kansas v. Colorado* (206 US 46 {1907}), at 94, 95.

[19] *Winters v. United States* (207 US 564 {1908}), at 577. See also Ranquist, Harold A., "The Winters Doctrine and How It Grew: Federal Reservation of Rights to the Use of Water," *Brigham Young University Law Review*, III (1975), 639-724.

[20] See *United States v. New Mexico* (438 US 696 {1978}). See also Fairfax, Sally K., and Dan Tarlock, "No Water for the Woods: A Critical Analysis of *United States v. New Mexico*," *Idaho Law Review*, XV (1979), 509-54.

[21] Recent (1996-99) TSPIRS reports can be found at http://www.fs.fed.us/forestmanagement/reports/tspirs/index.shtml.

[22] For information on timber sales, see Government Accountability Office, "Federal Timber Sales: Forest Service Could Improve Efficiency of Sales Management by Maintaining More Detailed Data," GAO Report 07-764, June 2007.

[23] Gorte, Ross W., "Federal Timber Harvests: Implications for [the] U.S. Timber Supply," *CRS Report for Congress*, 10 March 1998, 1.

[24] Gorte, Ross, "Federal Timber Harvests: Implications for U.S. Timber Supply" (Congressional Research Service report 98-233 {1998}), 1.

[25] Government Accountability Office, "Volume of Timber Offered for Sale Has Declined Substantially Since Fiscal Year 1990" (GAO Report 03-615, 2003), ii.

[26] Bentley, William R., "Forest Service Timber Sales: A Preliminary Evaluation of Policy Alternatives," *Land Economics*, XXXXIV:2 (May 1968), 205.

[27] See the Federal Land Policy and Management Act of 1976 (Public Law 94-579), courtesy of the New Mexico Center for Wildlife Law, online at http://wildlifelaw.unm.edu/fedbook/flpma.html.

[28] Officially known as the Federal Water Pollution Control Amendments of 1972.

[29] See *Sierra Club v. Espy* (38 F.3d 792 {5th Circuit Court of Appeals, 1994}), quoting *Sierra Club v. Robertson* (810 F.Supp. 1021, 1028 (Western District of Ark, 1992), affirmed in part, vacated in part on other grounds, 28 F.3d 753 (8th Circuit Court of Appeals,1994).

[30] "Forest Management," courtesy of the office of Rep. Peter DeFazio, online at http://www.defazio.house.gov/index.php?option=com_content&view=article&id=617:natural-resources&catid=45.

[31] Government Accountability Office, "Federal Land Management: Use of Stewardship Contracting Is Increasing, but Agencies Could Benefit from Better Strategies" (GAO Report 09-23, November 2008), 1.

[32] "Western Governors' Association, Policy Resolution 10-6: Secure Rural Schools and Community Self-Determination Act," courtesy of the Western Governors Association, online at http://www.westgov.org/index.php?option=com_joomdoc&task=doc_details&gid=1266&Itemid=85.

[33] Randal O'Toole, "The Forest Service," a report by the Cato Institute, August 2009, online at http://www.downsizinggovernment.org/agriculture/forest-service.

[34] Anderson, H. Michael, "Reforming National-Forest Policy," *Issues in Science and Technology*, X (Winter 1993-94), 42-43.

6

Grazing and Public Lands

THE POLICY FRAMEWORK

According to a 1991 Government Accountability Office (GAO) report, the Bureau of Land Management (BLM) "administers livestock grazing on about 170 million acres of federal rangeland in 16 western states. To administer the grazing activity, the land is divided into about 22,000 separate grazing areas known as *allotments*. Annually, 3.6 million head of domestic livestock graze on BLM'S allotments. Much of the rangeland on which livestock grazing is permitted is fragile and can be seriously damaged by misuse. When more livestock than the land can support are continually allowed to graze on the public rangeland, the result can be damage to, and even permanent loss of, range resources." [1]

From the start of the nation's history, the U.S. government, through various means, encouraged settlers to head westward and to settle the areas that soon became the states of first the Midwest and then the entire western United States. The push to develop the resources of these areas, tame wilderness, and make the lands work for the new settlers in building up the wealth of the nation was one of the key reasons for the ability of the nation to grow. Perhaps the most important piece of federal legislation that came about to drive forward this policy was the Homestead Act of 1862. Through this legislation, people were able to lay claim to 160 acres of land, although many received parcels of up to 320 and perhaps even as much as 640 acres. However, one had to remain on the land for a period of five years, ranching to make the land economically feasible to remain on, and with the American West being as dry as it was at the time, many of the settlers selected lands near public land areas and relied on the open range to graze cattle and to get water to feed their animals and crops. Competition for these lands soon erupted into range wars between factions who used violence to gain control over the lands. At the same time, overgrazing in many areas damaged streams and other waterways, destroying natural vegetation that led to the growth of sagebrush and other nonnative plants to take hold, producing near desert conditions throughout many states.

By the early 1930s, years of such abuse, unregulated by either the federal or state governments, led to such events as the Dust Bowl in Oklahoma and other states, destroying a way of life for untold numbers of people. To try to alleviate the situation, Congress then enacted the Taylor Grazing Act of 1934 (P.L. 73-482). This action authorized the Secretary of the Interior to "to establish grazing districts of vacant, unappropriated, and unreserved land from any parts of the public domain, excluding Alaska, which are not national forests, parks and monuments, Indian reservations, railroad grant lands, or revested Coos Bay Wagon Road grant lands, and which are valuable chiefly for grazing and raising forage crops. Whenever grazing districts are established, the Secretary shall grant adjacent landowners, upon application, rights-of-way over the lands for stock-driving purposes to provide access to marketing facilities or to lands not within the district but owned by the person with stock-grazing rights." [2] The act also established a Division of Grazing inside the Department of the Interior to work with such entities as the General Land Office to establish grazing districts, a system of payments for land use, and grazing fees. It established a system of fees based on Animal Unit Months (AUMs) Authorized the amount of forage land required to feed a cow and her calf and a horse or five goats or sheep for a month. The fee initiated in 1934 was five cents per AUM. This was a radical departure from past grazing policy, both state and federal. To implement the policy, in 1946 Congress merged two existing agencies to form the Bureau of Land Management.

The Taylor Act was a landmark in more ways than the fact that it passed in the midst of the Depression; it had future implications as well as the ones that occurred when it first passed Congress. Historians Michael Borman and Douglas E. Johnson wrote in 1990, "Through the mid-1960s emphasis was placed on stabilization of the rangeland livestock industry and dependent communities as a management objective. Equity considerations in public rangeland management and development worked to the advantage of local interests and traditional users, i.e., those holding grazing permits." [3]

Although the first edition of this work stated that about one-third of the total land area in the United States is classified as rangeland, one statistic, that being that 52% of this land is privately owned, with 43% in federal hands, could not substantiated. Historian Walter H. Schacht, writing in the 2004 work "Encyclopedia of the Great Plains," stated with more up-to-date figures that rangeland "is the dominant land type in the Great Plains, comprising about 50 percent of the total land area [of that section]." What Schacht does note is that aggressive congressional and other action, including by private parties, starting with the aforementioned Taylor Act, helped to rescue these lands from complete destruction; in 2004, he explained, "only 6 percent of the rangeland in the Northern Great Plains is classified in poor condition, although 25 per cent in the Southern Great Plains is in the poor category." [4]

At the same time that the Bureau of Land Management has control over the rangelands of the United States, the U.S. Department of Agriculture Forest Service (FS) also manages some 120 million acres of publicly-owned rangelands in the nation. In a 2006 report, "National Report on Efforts to Mitigate Desertification in the Western United States," it was stated that "USDA programs influence the use and management of other Federal and 414 million acres of nonfederal rangeland supplying livestock forage, water, recreation, wildlife and fish habitat and cover, as well as minerals and archeological, historical, and cultural amenities. USDA emphasizes cooperation and coordination among Federal, State, and local agencies; private organizations and institutions; and individuals in planning and executing sustainable rangeland programs." [5]

Table 6: Grazing Fees from 1981 to 2008 (dollars per AUM)

1981.........$2.31	1991.........$1.97	2001.....................$1.35
1982........$1.86	1992.........$1.92	2002..................$1.43
1983........$1.40	1993.........$1.86	2003..................$1.35
1984........$1.37	1994.........$1.98	2004..................$1.43
1985........$1.35	1995.........$1.61	2005..................$1.79
1986........$1.35	1996.........$1.35	2006..................$1.56
1987........$1.35	1997.........$1.35	2007..................$1.35
1988........$1.54	1998.........$1.35	2008..................$1.35
1989........$1.86	1999.........$1.35	
1990........$1.81	2000........$1.35	

Source: Vincent, Carol Hardy, "Grazing Fees: An Overview and Current Issues" (Report of the Congressional Research Service, 10 March 2008), CRS-3.

According to the Bureau of Land Management, the agency, "which administers about 245 million acres of public lands, manages livestock grazing on 157 million acres of those lands, as guided by Federal law. The terms and conditions for grazing on BLM-managed lands (such as stipulations on forage use and season of use) are set forth in the permits and leases issued by the Bureau to public land ranchers.

The BLM administers nearly 18,000 permits and leases held by ranchers who graze their livestock, mostly cattle and sheep, at least part of the year on more than 21,000 allotments under BLM management. Permits and leases generally cover a 10-year period and are renewable if the BLM determines that the terms and conditions of the expiring permit or lease are being met. The amount of grazing that takes place each year on BLM-managed lands can be affected by such factors as drought, wildfire, and market conditions. In managing livestock grazing on public rangelands, the BLM's overall objective is to ensure the long-term health and productivity of these lands and to create multiple environmental benefits that result from healthy watersheds. The Bureau administers public land ranching in accordance with the Taylor Grazing Act of 1934, and in so doing provides livestock-based economic opportunities in rural communities while contributing to the West's, and America's, social fabric and identity. Together, public lands and the adjacent private ranches maintain open spaces in the fast-growing West, provide habitat for wildlife, offer a myriad of recreational opportunities for public land users, and help preserve the character of the rural West." [6]

Figure 8. Distribution of Forest Service Grazing Fees

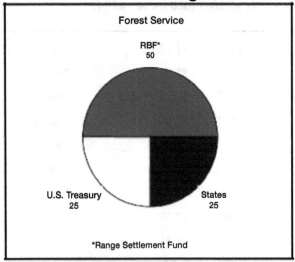

Source: Vincent, Carol Hardy, "Grazing Fees: An Overview and Current Issues" (Report of the Congressional Research Service, 10 March 2008), CRS-4.

Congressional legislation has dictated the role of the federal government in land management and grazing policy. Following the Taylor Act in 1934, Congress enacted a series of measures that worked at the edges of grazing policy: these included such pieces of legislation as The Bankhead-Jones Farm Tenant Act of 1937 (Public Law 75-210), which "direct[ed] the Secretary of Agriculture to develop a program of land conservation and utilization to correct maladjustments in land use and thus assist such things as control of soil erosion, reforestation, preservation or natural resources and protection of fish and wildlife." More important, but little noticed, was the Granger-Thye Act of 1950 (Public Law 81-478), which "authorize[d] the Forest Service to issue grazing permits and use grazing receipts for range improvements; [and] provide[d] direction on the establishment of local grazing advisory boards and other purposes." The National Environmental Policy Act of 1969 (Act of 1 January 1970, Public Law 91-190), better known as as NEPA, opened the way for Congress to demand that the Bureau of Land Management and other government agencies must prepare environmental studies, known as Environmental Impact Statements (EISs) before grazing permits can be issued. In a leading case involving the law, *Natural Resources Defense Council, Inc. v. Morton* (388 F. Supp. 829 {District of Columbia Circuit, 1974}), 527 F.2d 1386 (D.C. Circuit of Appeals), certiorari denied (427 U.S. 913 {1976}), the environmental group the Natural Resources Defense Council sued Rogers Clark Ballard Morton, the Secretary of the Interior, for not properly preparing EISs for western states with regard to grazing permits. The district court in the District of Columbia held — to be upheld on appeal — that the Bureau of Land Management could not fulfill its duties under NEPA by issuing a single EIS for the entire grazing permit program, which covered 11 western states, ordering the agency to provide an EIS for each of the 52 districts where such permits had to be issued. The court, in its decision, stated, "The term 'actions' refers not only to actions taken by federal agencies, but also to decisions made by the agencies, such as the decision to grant a license, which allow another party to take an action affecting the environment." **[7]** Under the Endangered Species Act of 1973 (16 U.S.C. 1531, et seq.), the Congress also placed limits on grazing in habitats that supported threatened or endangered species.

Figure 9. Distribution of BLM Grazing Fees: Section 3

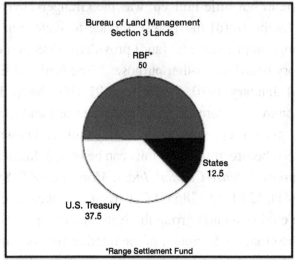

Figure 10. Distribution of BLM Grazing Fees: Section 15

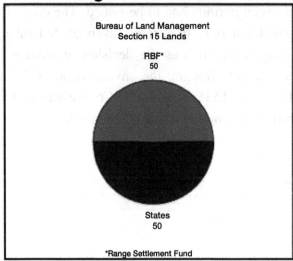

Source for Figures 9 and 10: Vincent, Carol Hardy, "Grazing Fees: An Overview and Current Issues" (Report of the Congressional Research Service, 10 March 2008), CRS-4.

Additional legislation has impacted grazing, especially in the western states. The Federal Land Policy Management Act of 1976 (Public Law 94-579), also known as FLPMA, gave the BLM new powers to control grazing, improve rangeland health, and manage public lands for multiple uses, specifically in response to a congressional finding which led to the law's passage. In Title IV of the legislation, Congress found that "a substantial amount of the Federal range lands is deteriorating in quality, and that installation of additional range improvements could arrest much of the continuing deterioration and could lead to substantial betterment of forage conditions with resulting benefits to wildlife, watershed protection, and livestock production." It mandated

> that 50 per centum or $10,000,000 per annum, whichever is greater [Public Law 95-514, 1978] of all moneys received by the United States as fees for grazing domestic livestock on public lands (other than from ceded Indian lands) under the Taylor Grazing Act and on lands in National Forests in the sixteen [Public Law 95-514, 1978] contiguous Western States under the provisions of this section shall be credited to a separate account in the Treasury, one-half of which is authorized to be appropriated and made available for use in the district, region, or national forest from which such moneys were derived, as the respective Secretary may direct after consultation with district, regional, or national forest user representatives, for the purpose of on-the-ground range rehabilitation, protection, and improvements on such lands, and the remaining one-half shall be used for on-the-ground range rehabilitation, protection, and improvements as the Secretary concerned directs. **[8]**

FLPMA is considered, as the Bureau of Land Management states, "the organic act that establishes the agency's multiple-use mandate to serve present and future generations." **[9]** In 1978, the U.S. Senate Committee on Energy and Natural Resources published a lengthy legislative history of the act, in which the-then committee chairman, Senator Henry Jackson, Democrat of Washington State, wrote,

> The Federal Land Policy and Management Act of 1976 represents a landmark achievement in the management of the public lands of the United States. For the first time in the long history of the public lands, one law provides comprehensive authority and guidelines for the administration and protection of the Federal lands and their resources under the jurisdiction of the Bureau of Land Management. This law enunciates a Federal policy of retention of these lands for multiple use management and repeals many obsolete public land laws which heretofore hindered effective land use planning for and management of public lands. The policies contained in the Federal Land Policy and Management Act will shape the future development and conservation of a valuable national asset, our public lands. **[10]**

Two years after the passage of FLPMA, Congress enacted the Public Rangelands Improvement Act of 1978 (Public Law 95-514), better known as PRIA. In it, the Congress found that "vast segments of the public rangelands [were in] an unsatisfactory condition." Thus, this law expressly targeted grazing and its uses to improve or harm the land once that was done.

The legislation "requires that public lands be managed in a manner that will protect the quality of scientific, scenic, historical, ecological, environmental, air and atmospheric, water resource, and archeological values; that, where appropriate, will preserve and protect certain public lands in their natural condition; that will provide food and habitat for fish and wildlife and domestic animals; and that will provide for outdoor recreation and human occupancy and use. It also states that the United States shall receive fair market value of the use of the public lands and their resources unless otherwise provided for by law." [11] According to the Bureau of Land Management, the law established a set price for grazing fees. Noted the agency, "The Federal grazing fee, which applies to Federal lands in 16 Western states on public lands managed by the BLM and the U.S. Forest Service, is adjusted annually and is calculated by using a formula originally set by Congress in the Public Rangelands Improvement Act of 1978. Under this formula, as modified and extended by a presidential Executive Order issued in 1986, the grazing fee cannot fall below $1.35 per animal unit month (AUM); also, any fee increase or decrease cannot exceed 25 percent of the previous year's level. (An AUM is the amount of forage needed to sustain one cow and her calf, one horse, or five sheep or goats for a month.) The grazing fee for 2010 is $1.35 per AUM, the same level as it was in 2009." [12]

Table 7: Public Lands under Exclusive Jurisdiction of BLM, FY 2009

State	2008 Grand Total /a/ Acres	2009 Acquisitions Increase /b/ Acres	2009 Restorations Increase /c/ Acres	2009 Total Increase /d/ Acres	2009 Disposal Decrease /e/ Acres	2009 Withdrawn Reserved Decrease /f/ Acres	2009 Total Decrease /g/ Acres	2009 Net Change /h/ Acres	2009 Inventory /i/ Acres	2009 Grand Total /j/ Acres
Alabama	3,523	0	0	0	0	0	0	0	0	3,523
Alaska	78,512,482	0	0	0	3,682,360	0	3,682,360	(3,682,360)	0	74,830,122
Arizona	12,201,794	1,540	0	1,540	0	0	0	1,540	0	12,203,334
Arkansas	6,078	0	0	0	0	0	0	0	0	6,078
California	15,281,882	17,687	0	17,687	1,118	0	1,118	16,569	0	15,298,451
Colorado	8,349,000	236	0	236	961	0	961	(725)	(2,230)	8,346,045
Florida	3,134	0	0	0	0	0	0	0	0	3,134
Idaho	11,608,909	7,765	0	7,765	4,183	2,970	7,153	612	0	11,609,521
Illinois	0	0	0	0	0	0	0	0	0	0
Indiana	0	0	0	0	0	0	0	0	0	0
Iowa	0	0	0	0	0	0	0	0	0	0
Kansas	0	0	0	0	0	0	0	0	0	0
Louisiana	16,474	0	0	0	0	0	0	0	0	16,474
Maryland	548	0	0	0	0	0	0	0	0	548
Michigan	0	0	0	0	0	0	0	0	0	0
Minnesota	1,447	0	0	0	0	0	0	0	0	1,447
Mississippi	241	0	0	0	0	0	0	0	0	241
Missouri	0	0	0	0	0	0	0	0	0	0
Montana	7,967,413	0	0	0	0	0	0	0	0	7,967,413
Nebraska	6,354	0	0	0	0	0	0	0	0	6,354
Nevada	47,808,114	0	0	0	1,376	0	1,376	(1,376)	0	47,806,738
New Mexico	13,463,356	15,836	0	15,836	2,190	20	2,210	13,626	0	13,476,982

State	2008 Grand Total [a] Acres	2009 Acquisitions Increase [b] Acres	2009 Restorations Increase [c] Acres	2009 Total Increase [d] Acres	2009 Disposal Decrease [e] Acres	2009 Withdrawn Reserved Decrease [f] Acres	2009 Total Decrease [g] Acres	2009 Net Change [h] Acres	2009 Inventory [i] Acres	2009 Grand Total [j] Acres
North Dakota	58,841	0	0	0	0	0	0	0	0	58,841
Ohio	0	0	0	0	0	0	0	0	0	0
Oklahoma	1,975	0	0	0	0	0	0	0	0	1,975
Oregon	16,132,741	1,154	0	1,154	2,021	0	2,021	(867)	1,919	16,133,793
South Dakota	274,437	0	0	0	0	0	0	0	0	274,437
Texas	11,731	0	0	0	0	0	0	0	102	11,833
Utah	22,856,673	3,041	0	3,041	1,344	2,215	3,559	(518)	0	22,856,155
Virginia	805	0	0	0	0	0	0	0	0	805
Washington	428,676	1,564	0	1,564	0	0	0	1,564	(1)	430,239
Wisconsin	2,366	0	0	0	0	0	0	0	0	2,366
Wyoming	18,367,506	7	0	7	7	0	0	7	0	18,367,513
Total	**253,366,500**	**48,830**	**0**	**48,830**	**3,695,553**	**5,205**	**3,700,758**	**(3,651,928)**	**(210)**	**249,714,362**

Note: "Public lands under exclusive jurisdiction of the Bureau of Land Management (BLM)" are those lands and interest in lands owned by the United States and administered by the Secretary of the Interior through the Bureau of Land Management, without regard to how the United States acquired ownership, except (1) lands located on the outer continental shelf, and (2) lands held for the benefit of Indians, Aleuts, and Eskimos (Section 103 (e) of the Federal Land Policy and Management Act of October 21, 1976, as amended (Public Law 94-579; 90 Stat. 2743; 43 U.S.C. 1701).

/a/   Grand Total Fiscal Year 2008: Acreage data from the Fiscal Year 2008 edition of *Public Land Statistics*.

/b/   Acquisitions (Increase): Lands obtained by the BLM through purchase, donation, condemnation, gift, or exchange.

/c/   Withdrawn-reserved lands administered by another Federal agency that have been restored to the BLM's jurisdiction (Increase). These lands were withdrawn or reserved for specific public purposes by an Executive Order, Secretarial Order, Act of Congress, or Public Land Order; removed from the jurisdiction of the BLM; and placed under the jurisdiction of another Federal agency. The appropriate action has been taken and these lands have now been returned to the jurisdiction of the BLM.

/d/ (Total Increase): Total acres added to the BLM's jurisdiction (sum of "/b/" and "/c/").

/e/ Disposals (Decrease): Lands that have been disposed of by the BLM under various public land laws. Disposal may be by a patent (deed) or an Act of Congress.

/f/ Withdrawn-reserved lands administered by another Federal agency (Decrease): Lands which have been withdrawn or reserved and designated for a specific public purpose by an Executive Order, Secretarial Order, Act of Congress, or Public Land Order and removed from the jurisdiction of the BLM and placed under the jurisdiction of another Federal agency. The lands will remain under the jurisdiction of another Federal agency until the appropriate action has been taken to return the lands to the jurisdiction of the BLM.

/g/ (Total Decrease): Total acres removed from the BLM's jurisdiction (sum of "/e/" and "/f/").

/h/ (Net Change): Plus or minus () change from Fiscal Year 2008 to Fiscal Year 2009 (difference between "Total Increase /d/" and "Total Decrease /g/"). Negative numbers in this column are displayed in parentheses.

/i/ The following States conducted an inventory of the lands that resulted in an increase or decrease in acreage as follows: Colorado (-2,330 acres); Oregon (+1,919 acres); Texas (+102 acres); and Washington (-1 acre).

/j/ Grand Total Acres Fiscal Year 2009: Consists of (1) Vacant Lands (both outside and within grazing districts) that are not withdrawn, reserved, appropriated, or set aside for a specific or designated purpose, and opened to some or all of the public land laws. The lands are not covered by any non-Federal right or claim other than permits, leases, rights-of-way, and unopened mining claims; (2) Land Utilization (LU) Project Lands, purchased by the Federal Government and administered under Title III of the Bankhead-Jones Farm Tenant Act and subsequently transferred by various Executive Orders between 1949 and 1960 from jurisdiction of the U.S. Department of Agriculture to the U.S. Department of the Interior, now administered by the Bureau of Land Management; and (3) Withdrawn-Reserved Lands that have been segregated from the operation of some or all of the public land laws and designated for specific purposes (e.g., BLM-managed monuments, wilderness, public water reserves, special designated areas, etc.).

Table 8: Summary of Authorized Use of Grazing Lease (Section 15) Lands, FY 2009

Administrative State	Cattle, Yearlings, & Bison	Horses & Burros	Sheep & Goats	Authorization Count /a/
Number of Authorizations				
Arizona	314	10	3	320
California	217	10	20	241
Colorado	342	15	39	366
Idaho	344	24	22	370
Montana	1,454	45	78	1,514
Nevada	9	0	0	9
New Mexico	693	28	26	706
Oregon	570	18	6	585
Utah /b/	0	0	0	0
Wyoming	1,478	139	150	1,552
Total	**5,421**	**289**	**344**	**5,663**
Animal Unit Months Authorized /c/				
Arizona	113,152	529	797	114,478
California	60,005	353	4,594	64,952
Colorado	30,911	496	4,458	35,865
Idaho	26,008	358	3,276	29,642
Montana	194,427	796	12,556	207,779
Nevada	10,861	0	0	10,861
New Mexico	172,433	692	31,652	204,777
Oregon	59,385	470	1,455	61,310
Utah /b/	0	0	0	0
Wyoming	375,225	5,591	35,718	416,534
Total /d/	**1,042,407**	**9,285**	**94,506**	**1,146,198**

/a/   This is a count of authorizations, regardless of livestock kind. Some lessees run more than one kind of livestock and thus may be represented in more than one livestock column. However, they are counted only once in this column.

/b/   There are no Section 15 lands in Utah.

/c/   These animal unit months (AUMs) were calculated for grazing authorized on bills that were due during Fiscal Year 2009 (October 2008—September 2009).

/d/   Totals do not include authorized nonuse.

Source: The BLM Rangeland Administration System (RAS).

Table 9: Grazing Permits in Force on Grazing Lease (Sec 15) Lands, FY 2009

Administrative State /a/	Number	Active AUMs /b/	Suspended AUMs /c/
Arizona	401	489,855	100,055
California	253	238,491	117,130
Colorado	1,126	571,521	109,664
Idaho	1,459	1,319,614	202,763
Montana	2,732	1,124,017	22,861
Nevada	623	2,045,274	537,129
New Mexico	1,502	1,635,115	85,512
Oregon	760	963,603	132,871
Utah	1,460	1,206,695	317,434
Wyoming	1,116	1,472,481	362,214
Total	**11,432**	**11,066,666**	**1,987,633**

Geographic State /a/	Number	Active AUMs /b/	Suspended AUMs /c/
Arizona	402	489,872	100,074
California	228	175,874	80,886
Colorado	1,132	572,603	109,664
Idaho	1,458	1,318,892	202,763
Montana	2,732	1,124,017	22,861
Nebraska	0	0	0
Nevada	648	2,105,753	573,373
New Mexico	1,502	1,635,115	85,512
North Dakota	0	0	0
Oklahoma	0	0	0
Oregon	760	963,603	132,871
South Dakota	0	0	0
Utah	1,455	1,208,575	317,466
Washington	0	0	0
Wyoming	1,115	1,472,362	362,163
Total	**11,432**	**11,066,666**	**1,987,633**

/a/ Administrative State boundaries differ from geographic State boundaries. For example: California BLM administers some lands within the State of Nevada, and Montana BLM administers all BLM public lands in North Dakota and South Dakota.

/b/ Active animal unit months (AUMs): AUMs that *could* be authorized on public lands; these totals differ from AUM totals shown in the previous tables, which are AUMs authorized for use.

/c/ Suspended AUMs on public lands are not shown in previous tables because they are not authorized for use.

Source: The BLM Rangeland Administration System (RAS).

Rangeland Policy in the 1990s

During the 1990s, the Clinton administration (1993-2001) initiated a series of regulations aimed at changing the way the federal government impacted grazing and other environmental policies, especially in the western states. Clinton's election in 1992, and his nomination of former Arizona Governor Bruce Babbitt, a strict environmentalist, as his Secretary of the Interior, set off a wild battle between ranchers, local officials, and the federal government. Even Democrats in Congress, especially from western states, stood strongly against the administration's policies concerning land. Then-Rep. Mike Synar, a liberal Democrat from Oklahoma, nevertheless called the movement for changing grazing fees an experiment that was a failure. He noted, "Taxpayers are losing 80 cents of every dollar that we use in this Federal program. In fact, the grazing fee...has gone down from $1.98 per AUM to $1.86. That is because of the problem with the formula, as Ralph pointed out. That formula, which was developed in 1978, was an experiment to put in place basically a political compromise, and what we have learned since that date is that that experiment was a failure. As a result, what we are seeing is that grazing fees are going in the opposite direction, the $1.86. That is at the same time when the price of beef, the demand for grass, private land lease rates for all comparable lands, have all increased. So that shows you how idiotic the formula is." [13] However, the move to reform the grazing fee system met with opposition in the U.S. Senate, and from 1990 to 1992, before Clinton took over the presidency, all reform bills were killed in the upper body. On the backs of the hearing that Synar had conducted, the Clinton administration, in 1993, proposed raising the grazing fee from the-then $1.92 per AUM to $5.00 per AUM. U.S. Senators from western states objected to the measure, and when Clinton got pushback among even Democrats he quietly dropped the provision from his 1993 stimulus package. Instead, in August 1993, the administration proposed raising the grazing fee gradually to $4.28 per AUM over a period of three years, along with a package of reforms that would compensate ranchers for improvements they made to public lands and reduce the use of pesticides on the public lands. One of the strongest voices against these reforms was U.S. Senator Pete Domenici, Republican of New Mexico, who led a filibuster to kill the program from passing in the U.S. Senate. In 1994, Secretary Babbitt held a series of meetings across the American West where again he called for the increase in grazing fees. His program, dubbed "Rangeland Reform '94," called for the establishment of Resource Advisory Councils, or RACs, composed of ranchers, environmentalists, and others involved in policymaking in the American West, and the raising of the grazing fee immediately to $3.68 per AUM, among other reforms. While the new policy had support in Congress, western representatives and Senators opposed it. In 1995, Domenici introduced, with Rep. Wes Cooley, Republican of Oregon, the Public Grazing Act of 1995, later to become the Public Rangelands Management Act of 1996. The Senate version would have placed grazing policy from the BLM and the USFS under one piece of legislation, lengthened grazing permits from 10 to 12 years, removed national grasslands from the National Forest System (NFS), and offered ranchers more control over the management of the lands on which they grazed. A similar bill was introduced in the U.S. House in April 1996, but a coalition of liberal Democrats and moderate Republicans voted the bill down; an attempt to attach the bill to the Omnibus Parks bill, covering funding for national parks, was met with a veto threat from the President, and it, too, was stripped out. In the end, nothing came from Congress regarding the reform of grazing policy during the remainder of the Clinton administration.

Instead, in November 1996, soon after Clinton won a second four-year term as President, Secretary Bruce Babbitt issued a series of findings that were called "Standards and Guidelines for Grazing Administration," better known as "Standards," codified at 61 Federal Register [FR] 59834-35. Section 4100 covers grazing and grazing issues. In it, the Department of the Interior specifically noted:

The current regulations at 43 CFR Sec. 4180.2 require the BLM State Director to develop State or regional standards and guidelines. These standards and guidelines are being developed at the State or regional level, in consultation with affected RACs to reflect local resource conditions and management practices. The standards and guidelines will reflect properly functioning conditions, or those conditions which must be met to ensure sustainability and healthy productive ecosystems and outline best management practices to achieve standards. They will provide the basis for evaluation of rangeland health and subsequent corrective actions. The regulations further provide that in the event State or regional standards and guidelines are not completed and in effect by February 12, 1997, fallback standards and guidelines described in the regulations will go into effect.

This revision of 43 CFR Sec. 4180.2(f) gives the Secretary discretion to postpone the implementation of the fallback standards and guidelines for up to 6 months. The Department is making this change because it has become apparent that development of State or regional standards and guidelines might, in some instances, require longer than the 18-month period provided in the regulation.

The discretion to grant up to a 6 month extension will ensure that BLM State Directors, working with RACs and the public, will have adequate time to develop appropriate State or regional standards and guidelines. In adopting, this final rule, the Department considered the benefits of efficient rangeland administration, effective public participation, and possible impacts resulting from a minor delay. The Department has concluded that 6 months is an appropriate maximum period of extension. Postponing implementation of the fallback standards and guidelines will enhance the efficient administration and promote the long-term health of public rangelands for two primary reasons. First, where locally developed standards and guidelines are nearly complete, implementation of the more general fallback standards and guidelines on a short-term interim basis would be likely to create confusion and increased administrative costs. Second, postponing implementation of the fallback measures will allow the Department to achieve its commitment to improving public land management through a collaborative process that utilizes RAC recommendations, local public input, and consideration of State or regional public rangelands issues. The Department has concluded that the final rule will not have a significant impact on the environment since postponement of the fallback standards and guidelines would be for a limited period of no more than 6 months. Furthermore, the Department does not anticipate that every BLM State Director would need a postponement.

In determining whether to grant a postponement, the Secretary will evaluate whether the requested postponement will promote administrative efficiencies and long-term rangeland health. Factors relevant to this evaluation will include, among others, when the State or regional standards and guidelines are scheduled for completion and whether the delay would promote the efficient administration, use, and protection of the public rangelands. **[14]**

In addition to these regulations, the Clinton administration issued a program called "Fundamentals of Rangeland Health," also known as "Fundamentals," which set a series of standards for all BLM offices across the United States, particularly in the western states. **[15]** The standards are laid out in 43 CFR [Code of Federal Regulations], Section 4180.1:

"The authorized officer shall take appropriate action under subparts 4110, 4120, 4130, and 4160 of this part as soon as practicable but not later than the start of the next grazing year upon determining that existing grazing management needs to be modified to ensure that the following conditions exist.

(a) Watersheds are in, or are making significant progress toward, properly functioning physical condition, including their upland, riparian-wetland, and aquatic components; soil and plant conditions support infiltration, soil moisture storage, and the release of water that are in balance with climate and landform and maintain or improve water quality, water quantity, and timing and duration of flow.

(b) Ecological processes, including the hydrologic cycle, nutrient cycle, and energy flow, are maintained, or there is significant progress toward their attainment, in order to support healthy biotic populations and communities.

(c) Water quality complies with State water quality standards and achieves, or is making significant progress toward achieving, established BLM management objectives such as meeting wildlife needs.

(d) Habitats are, or are making significant progress toward being, restored or maintained for Federal threatened and endangered species, Federal Proposed, Category 1 and 2 Federal candidate and other special status species. **[16]**

To fight these regulations from taking effect, the proranching group The Public Lands Council sued Babbitt and the U.S. Department of the Interior. A district court held for the Secretary of the Interior, and, on appeal, the U.S. Court of Appeals for the 10th Circuit upheld the ruling. The case was appealed to the U.S. Supreme Court, which granted certiorari. Argued on 1 March 2000, a decision was handed down on 15 May of that same year. Holding for a unanimous Court, Justice Stephen Breyer ruled that under the Taylor Act of 1934, such regulations could be enacted specifically by the Secretary of the Interior without additional authority from Congress. Breyer explained, "grants the Secretary of the Interior authority to divide the public rangelands into grazing districts, to specify the amount of grazing permitted in each district," and to issue grazing leases or permits to "settlers, residents, and other stock owners," 43 U.S.C. § 315 315a, 315b; gives preference with respect to permits to "landowners engaged in the livestock business, bona fide occupants or settlers, or owners of water or water rights," §315b; and specifies that grazing privileges "shall be adequately safeguarded," but that the creation of a grazing district or the issuance of a permit does not create "any right, title, interest, or estate in or to the lands," Ibid. Since 1938, conditions placed on grazing permits have reflected the grazing privileges' leasehold nature, and the grazing regulations in effect have preserved the Secretary's authority to (1) cancel a permit under certain circumstances, (2) reclassify and withdraw land from grazing to devote it to a more valuable or suitable use, and (3) suspend animal unit months (AUMs) of grazing privileges in the event of range depletion." [17]

RANGELAND POLICY IN THE FIRST DECADE OF THE TWENTY-FIRST CENTURY

The administration of President George W. Bush (2001-09) got the most grief from the environmental community over what it said were Bush's alleged laxity in enforcing environmental and other laws, or even reforming them. When it comes to grazing, few sources give critical analysis over the pros and cons of Bush's policies, with most merely decrying his administration's overall environmental record, which was opposed by most major environmental groups. [18] However, Bush was also criticized by those groups that oppose environmental groups, namely free market organizations who thought that Bush, more than any other modern president, would undo the regulations imposed by government on drilling, mining, and grazing. J.R. Pegg wrote in January 2003 that these groups were giving Bush low marks for his first two years in office. "The administration...has endorsed the concept of willing buyer/willing seller trades of grazing permits, but has not moved forward even though a willing trade is ready to proceed," Pegg wrote. "With private funding, the Grand Canyon Trust and grazing permit holders in Utah have struck a deal to reduce or retire grazing on some 300,000 acres in or around the Grand Staircase-Escalante National Monument." [19]

Soon after this criticism, in December 2003, the Bush administration laid out new regulations for the use, by grazing, of the more than 160 million acres of public land managed by the BLM, which the administration stated would "protect the health of rangelands." However, in 2005, a federal court halted these regulations from being implemented, and for the remainder of his time as President Bush was unable to get any further grazing regulations enacted. Victoria Sutton, writing in the Western New England Law Review in 2003, explained that Bush was more of a realist when it came to environmental policy than his critics gave him credit for:

> The Bush Administration has made significant efforts toward implementing regulatory mechanisms and has learned from successes and failures in the grand experiment of federal environmental regulation. The command-and-control regulatory approaches of the 1970s have been useful for the job for which they were created, but they were administratively unwieldy and enforcement was spotty. The public information and corporate image mechanisms of the federal environmental statutes of the 1980s were also effective for the jobs at hand, but their effectiveness is limited. The next generation of regulatory mechanisms must be a combination of incentives that have proven to be successful in the past. Such

mechanisms and trading in emissions allowances are such a device. The Bush Administration has made the bold step of pushing us into the next generation of regulatory mechanisms, with the promise of the successes we need in environmental protection. [20]

Rangeland Policy in the Obama Administration

As this is written, Barack Obama has been President for little more than two years, but in that time has made barely a ripple when it comes to grazing policy. In January 2011, however, it angered environmentalists when the administration rejected a proposal from these same groups to raise grazing fees on public lands. In letters to these groups, the Bureau of Land Management and the U.S. Forest Service said that "other priorities" prevented the agencies from pursuing either additional rules regarding grazing, or time to raise the current grazing fees. The action came in response to a lawsuit filed against the Obama administration in 2010 by several environmental groups seeking specifically to raise grazing fees. When told of the decision, these groups dismissed the action with anger and astonishment. [21] However, except for this single instance, no major policy regarding grazing has come out of the White House since Obama took over the presidency in January 2009.

The Policy Debate

There has been, and will continue to be, a tug-of-war between ranchers and environmentalists and government bureaucrats and others wishing to either tighten or loosen grazing policy, especially in the western states. While those wishing for more government regulation defend the policies of the Bureau of Land Management (BLM) and/or the U.S. Forest Service, conservatives and ranchers have long opposed even the most basic policies of these and other government agencies. In the 1970s, a "revolt" against what some westerners saw as drastic federal intrusion into their lives, particularly with regards to land and grazing policy, led to what has been dubbed "The Sagebrush Rebellion." The movement lasted until the 1980s, when those in the movement felt that the administration of President Ronald Reagan lessened the burden of such federal regulations. Rising up at nearly the same time, a group of similar-thinking individuals formed the Wise Use movement, calling for the government to allow the "wise use" of resources on the land, including allowing unlimited grazing. These groups an others also tried, but failed, to get Congress to transfer the BLM and the U.S. Forest Service control over public lands in the states to state control. Even today, some 30+ years after these initial battlelines were first drawn, the tension between those who wish to use the lands, for whatever reason, and those who wish to preserve them, continues. Whether the argument is over lands being used at all, or whether or not they should be protected, or used only in regulated ways, these arguments still dominate talk in Congress and in the western states.

There is evidence on both sides to make for a debate worth having. There is evidence that the wise use of the lands, be it for grazing as discussed in this chapter, allows the lands to become more fertile. Others, however, argue that grazing destroys natural grasses and places imbalances in the ecosystem. Some environmentalists believe that once natural grasses are destroyed, the potential for desertification grows, one of the arguments they use to counter the usage of any grazing lands. However, as noted in the first edition of this work, rangeland grasses can be a renewable resource, since their roots are generally deep, and, if animals are allowed to graze only on the tops of the grass the resources can be utilized over and over. It is what happens when overgrazing occurs — when too many animals are allowed to graze for too long in one specific area — that the resources become damaged and unsustainability occurs.

Getting back to the original argument — grazing and its impact on the environment — always takes a sideline into the cost of grazing fees and permits. The Congress has authorized the federal government, either through the U.S. Forest Service or the Bureau of Land Management, to collect fees for grazing since 1906. According to one report from the Congressional Research Service, in 2009 "fees are charged for grazing on approximately 160 million acres of BLM land and 95 million acres of FS land basically under a fee formula established in the Public Rangelands Improvement Act of 1978 (PRIA) and continued administratively." Further, "On BLM rangelands, in FY2006, there were 15,799 operators authorized to graze livestock, and they held 17,880 grazing permits and leases. Under these permits and leases, a maximum of 12,634,580 animal unit months (AUMs) of grazing could have been authorized for use. Instead, 7,536,412 AUMs were used. The remainder were not used due to resource protection needs, forage depletion caused by drought or fire, and economic and other factors. BLM defines an AUM, for fee purposes, as a month's use and occupancy of the range by one animal unit, which includes one yearling, one cow and her calf, one horse, or 5 sheep or goats. On FS [Forest Service] rangelands, in FY2005 (most recent available), there were 7,039 livestock operators authorized to graze stock." The report added, "The BLM and FS are charging a grazing fee of $1.35 per AUM from March 1, 2008, through February 28, 2009. This is the lowest fee that can be charged. It is generally lower than fees charged for grazing on other federal lands as well as on state and private lands. A study by the Government Accountability Office (GAO) found that other federal agencies charged $0.29 to $112.50 per AUM in FY2004. While the BLM and FS use a formula to set the grazing fee (see "The Fee Formula" below), most agencies charge a fee based on competitive methods or a market price for forage. Some seek to recover the costs of their grazing programs. State and private landowners generally seek market value for grazing, with state fees ranging from $1.35 to $80 per AUM and private fees from $8 to $23 per AUM.2 The average monthly lease rate for grazing on private lands in 11 western states in 2006 was $15.10 per head." [22]

Information Station: Federal Grazing Fees

Under the Public Rangeland Improvement Act of 1978 (PRIA) (Public Law 95-514), fees for grazing were established in 1978, and modified in 1986. Since the passage of the act, the Bureau of Land Management (BLM) and the US Forest Service (FS) act in concert at the start of each calendar year to announce the specific grazing fee per cow for that specific year only. For instance, in 2011, the Obama administration announced that the PRIA grazing fee for that year would be $1.35 per Animal Unit Month Authorized (AUM) for lands administered by the BLM and the FS. The 2011 fee was the same as that for 2010.

The BLM charges per AUM; the FS charges per Head Month (HM) — both are fees for the use of the public lands by one cow and her calf, one horse, or five sheep or goats for a single calendar month. The fee is done by a formula contained in the 1978 act, continued through an Executive Order signed by Ronald Reagan in 1986; by law, the fee cannot fall below $1.35 per AUM or HM per year. The fees becomes effective each 1 March. On average, the BLM issues some 18,000 grazing permits per year, while the FS issues some 8,000 for the same period.

Source: "BLM and Forest Service Announce 2011 Grazing Fee," *Bureau of Land Management News Release*, 31 January 2011, online at http://www.blm.gov/wo/st/en/info/newsroom/2011/january/NR_01_31_2011.html.]

In 2010, the BLM reported that the agency administered nearly 18,000 grazing permits and leases held by ranchers; according to the agency, "Permits and leases generally cover a 10-year period and are renewable if the BLM determines that the terms and conditions of the expiring permit or lease are being met. The amount of grazing that takes place each year on BLM-managed lands can be affected by such factors as drought, wildfire, and market conditions." [23]

Robert H. Nelson, a professor of environmental policy at the School of Public Affairs of the University of Maryland, wrote in 1997 of the "economic value" of federal grazing policy and what moves could be made to make the policies of the agencies charged with handling grazing, namely the BLM and the U.S. Forest Service, more budget-conscious. He explained, "[T]he federal rangelands have low economic value in grazing use. It takes at least fifteen acres of standard Bureau of Land Management ("BLM") land to support the grazing of one cow (and often a calf) for one month. As shown by market trades that have long occurred among ranchers, it would require an average of only about $2.50 to $2.60 per acre to buy out a BLM grazing permit. At these prices, many environmental groups have sufficient resources to buy out rancher permits covering significant acreages of federal grazing lands, including the lands of most environmental interest." [24] In fact, in March 2009, President Barack Obama signed the Omnibus Public Land Management Act of 2009, which established a program of retiring grazing permits while allowing private interests to compensate the ranchers for the costs of the permits. The legislation, however, only authorized the permit retirement to occur over 2 million total acres in and around Oregon's Cascade-Siskiyou National Monument as well as six new wilderness areas in Idaho's Owyhee Canyonlands; these lands were the first ones targeted because ranchers had found the grounds there to be tough to graze on.

To sum up, the debate still rages over the role of the federal government in setting grazing and environmental policy, especially in the western states, as well as what should be done about the cost of grazing fees and grazing as a whole. Politicians who argue against subsidies do not realize at the same time that low grazing fees are a form of subsidy; at the same time, it is unknown what the raising of grazing fees would do to the market and to jobs and the economies of the western states where they take up a large degree of influence, both economic and political. And this issue does not adhere to strict party lines: Many western Democrats are shy about taking on ranching and grazing interests, while some eastern and other Republicans or Independents may find that they desire an end to subsidizing grazing operations in other states with taxpayer funds. So, the arguments are not as cut and dry and clear as other modern political controversies are. Nevertheless, it will take a meeting of the minds to find a solution to this problem, with both sides giving ground to find a middle way that allows public lands to be utilized while at the same time making sure that environmental damage is held to a minimum. It will not be an easy road to reach.

NOTES:

[1] "Rangeland Management: Comparison of Rangeland Condition," Report to the Chairman, Subcommittee on National Parks and Public Lands, Committee on Interior and Insular Affairs, House of Representatives (July 1991), 2.

[2] "Taylor Grazing Act," courtesy of the Federal Wildlife and Related Laws Handbook, from the New Mexico Center for Wildlife Law at the University of New Mexico School of Law, Albuquerque, New Mexico, online at http://wildlifelaw.unm.edu/fedbook/taylorgr.html.

[3] Borman, Michael M., and Douglas E. Johnson, "Evolution of Grazing and Land Tenure Policies on Public Lands," *Rangelands*, XII:4 (August 1990), 203-06.

[4] Schacht, Walter H., "Range Management" in David J. Wishart, ed., "Encyclopedia of the Great Plains" (Lincoln: University of Nebraska Press, 2004), 49.

[5] "National Report on Efforts to Mitigate Desertification in the Western United States: The First United States Report on Activities Relevant to the United Nations Convention to Combat Desertification" (2006) (online at http://www.unccd.int/cop/reports/otheraffected/national/2006/united_states_of_america-eng.pdf), 14.

[6] "Fact Sheet on the BLM's Management of Livestock Grazing," courtesy of the Bureau of Land Management, July 2010, online at http://www.blm.gov/wo/st/en/prog/grazing.html.

[7] *Natural Resources Defense Council, Inc. v. Morton* (388 F. Supp. 829 {District of Columbia Circuit, 1974}), 527 F.2d 1386 (D.C. Circuit of Appeals), Certiorari denied (427 U.S. 913 {1976}).

[8] "The Federal Land Policy and Management Act of 1976, As Amended" (a publication of the U.S. Department of the Interior, Bureau of Land Management, and the Office of the Solicitor, Washington, D.C., October 2001), 30.

[9] Ibid., introduction.

[10] Quoted in Schwartz, Eleanor R., "A Capsule Examination of the Legislative History of the Federal Land Policy and Management Act of 1976," *Arizona Law Review*, XXI (1979), 285-95. See also Clawson, Marion, "The Federal Land Policy and Management Act of 1976 in a Broad Historical Perspective," *Arizona Law Review*, XXI (1979), 585.

[11] "Rangelands: Laws, Regulations, and Policies," handbook courtesy of the U.S. Department of Agriculture, U.S. Forest Service, August 2010, online at http://www.fs.fed.us/rangelands/whoweare/lawsregs.shtml.

[12] "Fact Sheet on the BLM's Management of Livestock Grazing," courtesy of the Bureau of Land Management, July 2010, online at http://www.blm.gov/wo/st/en/prog/grazing.html.

[13] Synar comments, in "Grazing Management Reform: Hearing before the Subcommittee on National Parks, Forests, and Public Lands of the Committee on Natural Resources, House of Representatives, One Hundred Third Congress, First Session, on H.R. 1602, to Reform the Management of Grazing on the Public Range Lands, [and] H.R. 643, to Raise Grazing Fees on Public Lands, and For Other Purposes" (Washington, D.C.: U.S. Government Printing Office, 1993), 26-27.

[14] "Standards and Guidelines for Grazing Administration," Department of the Interior, Bureau of Land Management, 43 CFR [Code of Federal Regulations], codified at 61 Federal Register 59834-35.

[15] "Fundamentals of Rangeland Health," courtesy of the Bureau of Land Management, online at http://www.blm.gov/ut/st/en/prog/grazing/fundamentals_of_rangeland.print.html.

[16] See Pendery, Bruce M., "Reforming Livestock Grazing on the Public Domain: Ecosystem Management-Based Standards and Guidelines Blaze a New Path for Range Management," *Environmental Law*, XXVII (1997), 513.

[17] See *Public Lands Council v. Babbitt* (529 US 728 {2000}). See also Baldwin, Pamela, "Federal Grazing Regulations: Public Lands Council v. Babbitt," *CRS Report for Congress*, 20 November 2003.

[18] There is widespread belief that the Bush administration was bad for environmental policy; however, see Sutton, Victoria, "The George W. Bush Administration and the Environment," *Western New England Law Review*, XXV (2003), 221-42, where she argues that Bush's administration made "significant efforts" to regulate environmental policy in seven distinct areas of environmental protection; for the opposite view, see Donahue, Debra L., "Western Grazing: The Capture of Grass, Ground, and Government," *Environmental Law*, XXXV (2005), 721-806.

[19] Pegg, J.R., "Bush Supporters Unhappy with Environmental Policy," *Environment News Service*, 22 January 2003, online at http://www.ens-newswire.com/ens/jan2003/2003-01-22-10.html.

[20] See Sutton, Victoria, "The George W. Bush Administration and the Environment," *Western New England Law Review*, XXV (2003), 241. See also Vincent, Carol Hardy, "Grazing Regulations: Changes by the Bureau of Land Management," *CRS Report for Congress*, 22 November 2006.

[21] Taylor, Phil. "Obama Administration Denies Petition to Raise Grazing Fees on Public Lands," *The New York Times*, 19 January 2011, online at http://www.nytimes.com/gwire/2011/01/19/19greenwire-obama-admin-denies-petition-to-raise-grazing-f-43764.html.

[22] See Vincent, Carol Hardy, "Grazing Fees: An Overview and Current Issues" (Report of the Congressional Research Service, 10 March 2008), CRS-2.

[23] "Fact Sheet on the BLM's Management of Livestock Grazing," courtesy of the Bureau of Land Management, July 2010, online at http://www.blm.gov/wo/st/en/prog/grazing.html.

[24] Nelson, Robert H., "How to Reform Grazing Policy: Creating Forage Rights on Federal Rangelands," *Fordham Environmental Law Journal*, VIII (1996-97), 651-52.

7

Mining and Energy

THE POLICY FRAMEWORK

One of the most important usages of federal land comes with the extraction of minerals and energy to power the nation's energy needs in one form or another; this includes natural gas, coal, and petroleum, as well as oil shale and tar sands. And while standard energy sources are covered by federal agencies, others are as well, including renewable resources such as wind, solar, and others, including geothermal and biomass.

The first congressional legislative action dealing with a mineral resource came in 1864, when Congress enacted The Coal Act of 1864 (16 Stat. 456). Enacted on 1 July 1864, the legislation was titled "An Act for the Disposal of Coal Lands and of Town Property in the Public Domain." [1] The legislation stated that "where any tracts embracing coal beds or coal fields constituting portions of the public domain, and which as mines are excluded from the Preemption act of Eighteen Hundred and Forty One and which under past legislation are not liable to ordinary private entry, it shall and may be lawful for the President to cause such tracts in suitable legal subdivisions to be offered at public sale to the highest bidder after public notice of not less than three months at a minimum price of twenty dollars per acre and any lands not thus disposed of shall thereafter be liable to private entry at said minimum." In 1887, in the decision for *Colorado Coal and Iron Company v. United States* (123 US 307), the U.S. Supreme Court said, "In the case of *Mullan v US* {118 US 271}, after referring to the Acts of Congress above recited, the court speaking of the Act of July 1, 1864, says on page 277:

> This is clearly a legislative declaration that "known" coal lands were mineral lands within the meaning of that term as used in statutes regulating the public lands, unless a contrary intention of Congress was clearly manifested. Whatever doubt there may be as to the effect of this declaration on past transactions, it is clear that after it was made coal lands were to be treated as mineral lands. That the land now in dispute was known as coal land at the time it was selected no one can doubt It had been worked as a mine for many years before and it had upon its surface all the appliances necessary for reaching taking out and delivering the coal That Barnard knew what it was when he asked for its location for his use is absolutely certain because he was one of the agents of the coal company at the time and undoubtedly acted in its behalf in all that he did. If Mullan and Avery were ignorant of the fact when they acquired their respective interests in the property it was because they willfully shut their eyes to what was going on around them and purposely kept themselves in ignorance of notorious facts. But the evidence satisfies us entirely that they were not ignorant. [2]

The mining of coal was regulated by the states until 1872, when Congress, desiring to pass an all-encompassing action dealing with the mining of all minerals, enacted the General Mining Act of 1872. The reasons for the enactment of this law were twofold: Congress wanted to encourage the settlement of land in the newly-established states in the American West; at the same time, it wanted additional control over the mining of minerals such as silver, gold, copper, platinum, and uranium, as well as natural gas, oil, and other energy sources on federal lands (ironically, coal was not included in the list of minerals covered under the act). Under the law, individuals (usually prospectors) or companies mining on the lands in question have the right to stake a claim on public domain land without the need to pay royalties for the specific minerals mined to the federal government, paying only an annual claim fee. The miner may decide to patent the claim to gain title of the claimed lands and extracted minerals by paying a patent application fee plus US$2.50 to $5 per acre after patent approval. In a 2008 report on mining on federal lands, the Congressional Research Service stated, "Mining of hardrock minerals on federal lands is governed primarily by the General Mining Law of 1872. The law grants free access to individuals and corporations to prospect for minerals in public domain lands, and allows them, upon making a discovery, to stake (or "locate") a claim on that deposit. A claim gives the holder the right to develop the minerals and may be "patented" to convey full title to the claimant. A continuing issue is whether this law should be reformed, and if so, how to balance mineral development with competing land uses." [3] However, although the act allows for permanent claims to be patented, according to the U.S. government, only a small number of claims are ever patented; from 1867 through 2006, the recent year for which numbers exist as of this writing, only about 3.4 million total acres have ever been patented, which, according to the U.S. government, represents only about 1.5% of all of the public lands patented, with the remainder coming from homestead patents, grants from states, railroad grants, and other non-mineral public land legislation enacted by Congress.

The 1872 act has been perhaps the most successful congressional legislation in American history to open the lands of the western United States to settlement and usage. In that 2008 report, the Congressional Research Service noted,

> *The 1872 Mining Law was one of the primary forces behind the development of mineral resources in the West, along with the industries and services that supported mineral production. Major hardrock minerals developed in the West include copper, silver, gold, lead, zinc, molybdenum, and uranium. During the 19th century, major mining districts for silver and gold were developed under the Mining Law in Colorado, California, Idaho, and Nevada. Early in the 20th century, there were major developments of porphyry copper in Arizona. Large molybdenum and tungsten deposits in Colorado were also developed. The Mining Law continues to provide the structure for much of the western mineral development on public domain lands. Western mining, although not as extensive as it once was, is still a major economic activity, and a high percentage of hardrock mining is on public lands.* [4]

Since the 1872 act, Congress has enacted a series of amendments, all separate pieces of legislation, which have changed the way the nation reacts to the mining of minerals on public lands. Six years after the 1872 act, Congress enacted the Timber and Stone Act (20 Stat. 89), which allowed for the private purchase of government lands with minable minerals on it. However, after the 1878 action, Congress did not act on the issue for four decades.

Although the 1872 act was a landmark for its overachieving in consolidating almost all minerals under its aegis, Congress did spend the next four decades chipping away at it, removing lands and minerals from its regulation. It was not until the passage of the Mineral Leasing Act of 1920 (61 Stat. 913) that the first major legislation relating to minerals on public lands was enacted, fully addressing this growing problem. According to the act, it authorizes and governs "[the] leasing of public lands for developing deposits of coal, phosphates, oil, gas, and other hydrocarbons and sodium." The act made "deposits of coal, phosphate, sodium, potassium, oil, oil shale, gilsonite (including all vein-type solid hydrocarbons) or gas, and lands containing U.S.-owned deposits, subject to disposition under the Act." It also applied "to deposits of coal, phosphate, sodium, oil, oil shale, gilsonite or gas in U.S. lands that have been or may be disposed of under laws reserving the deposits to the U.S." [5] According to the U.S. government in a 2008 Congressional Research Service report, "Development of oil, gas, and coal on BLM and FS lands (and other federal lands) is governed primarily by the Mineral Leasing Act of 1920 (30 U.S.C. § 181).

Leasing on BLM lands goes through a multi-step approval process. If the minerals are located on FS lands, the FS must perform a leasing analysis and approve leasing decisions for specific lands before the BLM may lease minerals." [6] The Council on Foreign Relations, in discussing "essential documents" of the U.S. Congress, said of this legislation, "This act was designed to 'promote the mining of coal, phosphate, oil, oil shale, gas and sodium on the public domain.' Following oil shortages after WWI, Congress passed this legislation; the U.S. Geological Survey states, 'Under the terms of that act, mineral lands were to be leased by competitive bidding, and royalties and other income were to be divided between the Federal Government and the States. The Survey's responsibility for classification of mineral lands was again changed; its major task became the determination of the known geological structure of producing oil or gas fields within which oil and gas leases would be issued. Congress then for the first time appropriated funds for the classification of public lands, which in turn were allotted to the field branches.'" [7]

The next major legislation dealing with mining was the Mining Materials Act of 1947 (30 USC 601, et. seq.), which authorized the Secretaries of the Interior and Agriculture to "dispose of mineral materials, specifically including, but not limited to, common varieties of sand, stone, gravel, pumice, pumicite, cinders, clay, and petrified wood, in lands under their respective jurisdiction, if such disposal is not otherwise authorized by law." As one source noted, "The act also authorize[d] [the] disposal of minerals found on lands which have been withdrawn in aid of the function of the federal agency other than the DOI [Department of the Interior], or a state, county, municipality, water district, or other local-government-subdivision or agency, with the consent of such federal department or agency or such state or local government unit." [8]

The enactment of the Multiple Mineral Use Act of 1954 (68 Stat. 708) was the impetus

> to amend the mineral leasing laws and the mining laws to provide for multiple mineral development of the same tracts of public lands." The third section of that act, now codified at 30 USC 12, states that: "Known to be valuable for minerals subject to disposition under the mineral leasing laws, shall be effective to the same extent in all respects as if such lands at the time of location, and at all times thereafter, had not been so included or covered or known: Provided, however, That, in order to be entitled to the benefits of this act, the owner of any such mining claim located prior to January 1, 1953, must have posted and filed for record, within the time allowed by the provisions of the Act of August 12, 1953 (67 Stat. 539) [not later than December 10, 1953.] an amended notice of location as to such mining claim, stating that such notice was filed pursuant to the provisions of said Act of August 12, 1953, and for the purpose of obtaining the benefits thereof... [9]

Since the 1954 act, only two major pieces of legislation have addressed mineral usage and mining on public lands: the first was the Multiple Surface Use Mining Act of 1955 (61 Stat. 681), which, according to several sources, "withdrew common varieties [of minerals] from mineral entry," and the Federal Land Policy and Management Act of 1976, which while an all-encompassing law (and has been discussed at length elsewhere in this work), in part redefines claim recording procedures and provided for the abandonment of the lands specified if the specific procedures laid out by the legislation were not followed. In the 1955 act, "Congress [acted] to curtail nonmining use of the surface of mining claims. The Act provides that any mining claim located after July 23, 1955, 'shall not be used, prior to [the] issuance of [a] patent, for any purposes other than prospecting, mining or processing operations and uses reasonably incident thereto.'" **[10]**

THE USE OF PUBLIC LANDS: THE CONTINUING CONTROVERSY

The conservative Heritage Foundation, a think tank in Washington, D.C., reported in 2011, "The federal government owns about 650 million acres of land, nearly a third of the total land in the United States. The government also holds title to millions of subsurface acres teeming with valuable resources. Although some land and subsurface mineral holdings are being used for defense, national parks, or energy production (albeit inefficiently), a large portion is not being used for any purpose. Furthermore, federal agencies spend billions every year to 'manage' these lands (doing a poor job, at that), and still continue to spend money on acquiring even more." The group claimed that if the U.S. government sold off just the unused lands it was holding, it would earn some $1.5 *trillion*, or $1,500 billion dollars, which is the U.S. budget deficit for FY 2011. **[11]** This tremendous amount of property contains a staggering amount of energy and mineral resources that are either being underused or just not being utilized at all and going to waste. A 2006 report for the Bureau of Land Management found, according to the Congressional Research Service, "that 51% of the estimated oil and 27% of the estimated natural gas on the 99 million acres of federal land inventoried (about 15% of all federal lands) are off-limits to leasing." **[12]** Since the 1970s, and particularly during the Clinton (1993-2001) and Obama (2009-13) administrations, the role of environmentalists to have these lands sealed off from any major usage of the energy and minerals has led the way in making these lands off limits to miners and to corporations willing to harvest the energy for the needs of the nation. At the same time, however, because the Congress has failed to either update or reform the 1872 General Mining Law, the harvesting of gold, silver, and copper resources has gone on with few negligible returns to the U.S. Treasury or to local agencies. The costs of using these lands for these purposes is lower than one would imagine: It costs nothing to lodge a patent for public land, or if one purchases private land, although there is an expense of approximately $500 for an "assessment' to prepare the land for mining, a cost of $100 a year to develop the claim, and a small fee of $2.50 per acre for placer deposits or $5 an acre for lodes. Once an individual or corporation lays claim to the lands for these purposes, they own the land, and it can only be taken away if they abandon it.

The Bureau of Land Management regulates mining on lands under its jurisdiction; section 302(b) of the Federal Land Policy and Management Act (FLPMA) of 1976 (43 USC 1761) directs the Secretary of the Interior, "by regulation or otherwise, [to] take any action necessary to prevent unnecessary or undue degradation of the lands." However, the Congress inserted into the 1976 act specific language, which stated that "nothing in [the act] shall in any way amend the Mining Law of 1872 or impair the rights of any locators of claims under that Act, including, but not limited to, rights of ingress and egress." In 1980, BLM issued regulations that set standards for the protection of surface and other mining resources on certain unpatented mining claims from the adverse effects of mining operations. Mining specialist Bruce Kennedy wrote in 1990, "Of most interest [in the 1980 regulations] to the operator of a surface mine is the requirement that operations be preceded by submission and approval of a plan of operations where the disturbance level will exceed 2.02 ha [hectares] (5 acres) per annum. Such a plan will also be required in special areas such as areas designated as a part of the National Wilderness Preservation System and administered by the Bureau of Land Management, areas withdrawn from operation of the mining laws in which valid existing rights are being exercised, and designated areas of critical environmental concern." [13] Mines that disturb less than 2.02 ha or five acres need only require that notice be given to the BLM of its location and the extent of the mining activity, and the declaration of a statement promising to complete the reclamation of disturbed areas.

The BLM has implementing regulations pertaining to the development of mining claims, which include three levels of review:

- Casual use—for which no notification or approval is necessary;

- Notice level—for cumulative annual disturbances that total less than five acres. Operators must notify BLM officials (and commit to reclamation), but no approval is required. Consultation may be required if access routes are to be constructed; and

- Approval level—for disturbances exceeding 5 acres in a calendar year or any disturbance in certain specified areas (wilderness areas, wild and scenic rivers, critical habitat, areas of the California Desert Conservation Area). Operators must obtain BLM approval (within specified time frames) of a plan of operations for such disturbances. [14]

Determining what materials are defined as a mineral has been an important part of mining law development and implementation: If materials on public lands are simply defined as minerals, then private interests can mine them, patent or buy the land, and pay no royalties. Courts have ruled that water drilled on federal lands, peat and organic soil, fossils of prehistoric animals, radon gas, silt or drilling mud, quartzite, and stalactites, stalagmites, and other natural "curiosities" are not defined as minerals. Legal and policy questions have also arisen over when the provisions of the law apply and when miners can claim legal protection. The Mining Law has been interpreted to give some protection to prospectors before mines are actually discovered, and the lands are patented. Miners prospecting in good faith are protected from claim jumpers. But no claim can actually be made until the discovery of the vein or load. Claims can also extend beyond the sidelines of a claim in order to follow a vein or lode. But since veins often intersect and rarely match the irregular claims indicated on the surface of the land, conflicts among claim holders concerning the extension of their claims underground have spawned thousands of court decisions.

Through the enactment of laws, regulations and court decisions, the U.S. government has put into place a series of steps miners must follow to mine properly. Some state reclamation laws also oversee mining to protect air, water, and even cultural resources. Because improper mining operations can harm groundwater tables, regulations require permits through the Clean Water Act and the Safe Drinking Water Act. Some portions of the National Environmental Policy Act (NEPA) apply to mining. Through all of these measures, environmental impact statements (EISs) and environmental assessments (EAs) must be done.

Fossil Fuels

A thorough discussion of American energy policy, and the government's role in it, is well beyond the scope of this book. However, the development of energy resources on the public lands is an important element of public lands policy, and deserves some mention and discussion here.

Under the Mineral Leasing Act of 1920, discussed earlier in this chapter, the government has control over "[the] leasing of public lands for developing deposits of coal, phosphates, oil, gas, and other hydrocarbons and sodium." The act made "deposits of coal, phosphate, sodium, potassium, oil, oil shale, gilsonite (including all vein-type solid hydrocarbons) or gas, and lands containing U.S.-owned deposits, subject to disposition under the Act." It also applied "to deposits of coal, phosphate, sodium, oil, oil shale, gilsonite or gas in U.S. lands that have been or may be disposed of under laws reserving the deposits to the U.S." Unlike hardrock mining, the operations for oil and gas drilling, either on land or in waters under the jurisdiction of the United States, must receive permissions from the specific federal agencies before exploration can even begin. Agencies usually have discretion to approve or reject applications and are empowered to regulate exploration and development efforts. Royalties are charged on all resources developed from federal lands. All offshore oil and gas leasing is done through competitive bidding; onshore leasing must also begin competitively, but if no bids are received, noncompetitive bids are permitted. The Web site geology.com notes, "In most cases, oil and gas rights are leased. The lessee is usually uncertain if oil or gas will be found so they generally prefer to pay a small amount for a lease rather than pay a larger amount to purchase. A lease gives the lessee a right to test the property by drilling and other methods. If drilling discovers oil or gas of marketable quantity and quality it may be produced directly from the exploratory well." A "signing bonus" must be paid; after that, there are fees and royalties that must also be submitted. The site continues, "In addition to a signing bonus, most lease agreements require the lessee to pay the owner a share of the value of produced oil or gas. The customary royalty percentage is 12.5 percent or 1/8 of the value of the oil or gas at the wellhead. Some states have laws that require the owner be paid a minimum royalty (often 12.5 percent). However, owners who have highly desirable properties and highly developed negotiating skills can sometimes get 15 percent, 20 percent, 25 percent or more. When oil or natural gas is produced the royalty payments can greatly exceed the amounts paid as a signing bonus." [15]

Coal

Although coal plays a large role in the economies of states like West Virginia, overall it involves only a tiny amount of federal land as an overall portion of the coal harvest from American lands altogether. There are several pieces of congressional legislation that control all government action and regulation over coal harvesting and production. In addition to the aforementioned action, the Mineral Leasing Act of 1920 (as amended later), the second most important, but little-known, action, is the Mineral Leasing Act for Acquired Lands of 1947 (30 USC 351-59). According to the BLM, "The Mineral Leasing Act of 1920, as amended, and the Mineral Leasing Act for Acquired Lands of 1947, as amended, give the BLM responsibility for coal leasing on approximately 570 million acres of the 700 million acres of mineral estate that is owned by the Federal Government, where coal development is permissible. The surface estate of these lands could be controlled by the BLM, United States Forest Service, private landowners, state landowners, or other Federal agencies. The BLM works to ensure that the development of coal resources is done in an environmentally sound manner and is in the best interests of the Nation." [16]

The most recent controlling law that dominates all government regulation over coal harvesting and production is the Surface Mining Control and Reclamation Act (Public Law 95-87) of 1977, also known as SMCRA, which "establishes a program for the regulation of surface mining activities and the reclamation of coal-mined fields, under the administration of the Office of Surface Mining, Reclamation and Enforcement (OSMRE) in the U.S. Department of the Interior," according to the U.S. Fish & Wildlife Service. [17] According to the legislation's statement of purpose, the act was enacted to

> establish a nationwide program to protect society and the environment from the adverse effects of surface coal mining operations; assure that the rights of surface landowners and other persons with a legal interest in the land or appurtenances thereto are fully protected from such operations; assure that surface mining operations are not conducted where reclamation as required by this Act is not feasible; assure that surface coal mining operations are so conducted as to protect the environment; assure that adequate procedures are undertaken to reclaim surface areas as contemporaneously as possible with the surface coal mining operations; assure that the coal supply essential to the Nation's energy requirements, and to its economic and social well-being is provided and strike a balance between protection of the environment and agricultural productivity and the Nation's need for coal as an essential source of energy; assist the States in developing and implementing a program to achieve the purposes of this Act. [18]

The legislation "sets forth minimum uniform requirements for all coal surface mining on Federal and State lands, including exploration activities and the surface effects of underground mining. Mine operators are required to minimize disturbances and adverse impact on fish, wildlife and related environmental values and achieve enhancement of such resources where practicable. Restoration of land and water resources is ranked as a priority in reclamation planning." [19]

Table 10: Fossil Fuel Production on Federally Administered Lands

Year	Crude Oil & Lease Condensate			Natural Gas Plant Liquids			Natural Gas			Coal			Fossil Fuels	
	Million Barrels	Quadrillion Btu	Percent of U.S. Total	Million Barrels	Quadrillion Btu	Percent of U.S. Total	Trillion Cubic Feet	Quadrillion Btu	Percent of U.S. Total	Million Short Tons	Quadrillion Btu	Percent of U.S. Total	Quadrillion Btu	Percent of U.S. Total
Calendar-Year Data														
1949	95.2	0.55	5.2	4.4	0.02	2.8	0.15	0.15	2.8	9.5	0.24	2.0	0.98	3.3
1950	105.9	0.61	5.4	4.4	0.02	2.4	0.14	0.15	2.4	7.7	0.19	1.4	0.98	3.0
1951	117.3	0.68	5.2	5.3	0.02	2.6	0.17	0.18	2.4	9.3	0.23	1.6	1.12	3.1
1952	118.7	0.69	5.2	5.5	0.02	2.5	0.25	0.25	3.2	8.7	0.22	1.7	1.19	3.4
1953	136.9	0.79	5.8	5.7	0.03	2.4	0.29	0.30	3.6	7.5	0.19	1.5	1.31	3.7
1954	146.5	0.85	6.3	6.1	0.03	2.4	0.39	0.40	4.6	7.4	0.19	1.8	1.46	4.3
1955	159.5	0.92	6.4	6.0	0.03	2.1	0.43	0.45	4.8	5.9	0.15	1.2	1.55	4.1
1956	174.1	1.01	6.7	6.4	0.03	2.2	0.49	0.51	5.1	5.8	0.15	1.1	1.69	4.3
1957	189.4	1.10	7.2	6.6	0.03	2.2	0.62	0.64	6.1	5.7	0.14	1.1	1.91	4.8
1958	216.8	1.26	8.9	8.0	0.04	2.7	0.69	0.71	6.5	5.3	0.13	1.2	2.13	5.7
1959	258.2	1.50	10.0	9.5	0.04	3.0	0.83	0.86	7.2	4.9	0.12	1.1	2.52	6.5
1960	277.3	1.61	10.8	11.6	0.05	3.4	0.95	0.98	7.8	5.2	0.13	1.2	2.77	6.9
1961	297.3	1.72	11.3	13.5	0.06	3.7	1.03	1.06	8.1	5.2	0.13	1.2	2.97	7.4
1962	321.7	1.87	12.0	15.3	0.07	4.1	1.18	1.22	8.9	5.8	0.14	1.3	3.29	7.9
1963	342.8	1.99	12.5	16.0	0.07	4.0	1.37	1.41	9.7	5.4	0.14	1.1	3.60	8.2
1964	356.0	2.07	12.8	15.5	0.07	3.7	1.51	1.55	10.2	7.1	0.18	1.4	3.86	8.4
1965	378.6	2.20	13.3	14.3	0.06	3.2	1.56	1.61	10.2	8.2	0.20	1.6	4.07	8.6
1966	426.7	2.47	14.1	15.2	0.06	3.2	2.02	2.09	12.3	8.3	0.20	1.5	4.83	9.7
1967	472.6	2.74	14.7	20.1	0.09	3.9	2.41	2.48	13.8	9.5	0.23	1.7	5.54	10.5
1968	523.7	3.04	15.7	13.7	0.06	2.5	2.61	2.69	14.1	9.1	0.22	1.6	6.01	11.1
1969	563.8	3.27	16.7	19.9	0.08	3.4	3.05	3.14	15.4	10.1	0.25	1.8	6.74	12.0
1970	605.6	3.51	17.2	40.6	0.17	6.7	3.56	3.67	16.9	12.0	0.29	2.0	7.64	12.9
1971	648.9	3.76	18.8	54.0	0.22	8.7	3.95	4.08	18.3	17.3	0.41	3.1	8.47	14.6
1972	630.5	3.66	18.2	56.7	0.23	8.9	4.17	4.28	19.3	19.0	0.44	3.1	8.61	14.6
1973	604.3	3.51	18.0	54.9	0.22	8.7	4.37	4.46	20.1	24.2	0.57	4.1	8.75	15.0
1974	570.2	3.31	17.8	61.9	0.25	10.1	4.75	4.87	22.9	32.1	0.74	5.3	9.16	16.3
1975	531.5	3.08	17.4	59.7	0.24	10.0	4.57	4.67	23.8	43.6	1.00	6.7	8.99	16.4
1976	525.7	3.05	17.7	57.2	0.23	9.7	4.81	4.91	25.2	86.4	1.98	12.6	10.16	18.6
1977	535.0	3.10	17.8	57.4	0.23	9.7	4.94	5.04	25.8	74.8	1.69	10.7	10.06	18.3
1978	523.6	3.04	16.5	25.9	0.10	4.5	5.60	5.71	29.3	79.2	1.76	11.8	10.61	19.3
1979	519.8	3.01	16.7	11.9	0.05	2.1	5.93	6.05	30.1	84.9	1.91	10.9	11.02	19.0
1980	510.4	2.96	16.2	10.5	0.04	1.8	5.85	6.01	30.2	92.9	2.08	11.2	11.09	18.8
1981	529.3	3.07	16.9	12.3	0.05	2.1	6.15	6.31	32.1	138.8	3.10	16.8	12.53	21.4
1982	552.3	3.20	17.5	15.0	0.06	2.7	5.97	6.14	33.5	130.0	2.89	15.5	12.29	21.4
1983	568.8	3.30	17.9	14.0	0.05	2.5	5.17	5.33	32.1	124.3	2.74	15.9	11.43	21.0
1984	595.8	3.46	18.3	25.4	0.10	4.3	5.88	6.07	33.7	136.3	3.00	15.2	12.62	21.4
1985	628.3	3.64	19.2	26.6	0.10	4.5	5.24	5.41	31.8	194.6	4.04	20.9	13.19	22.9
1986	608.4	3.53	19.2	23.3	0.09	4.1	4.87	5.01	30.3	189.7	4.16	21.3	12.79	22.6
1987	577.3	3.35	18.9	23.7	0.09	4.1	5.56	5.73	33.4	195.2	4.28	21.2	13.45	23.5
1988	516.3	2.99	17.3	37.0	0.14	6.2	5.45	5.61	31.9	225.4	4.92	23.7	13.67	23.6
1989	488.9	2.84	17.6	45.1	0.17	8.0	5.32	5.49	30.7	236.3	5.14	24.1	13.64	23.7
1990	515.9	2.99	19.2	50.9	0.19	8.9	6.55	6.74	36.8	280.6	6.12	27.2	16.05	27.4
1991	491.0	2.85	18.1	72.7	0.28	12.0	5.99	6.17	33.8	285.1	6.18	28.5	15.47	26.7
1992	529.1	3.07	20.2	70.7	0.27	11.4	6.25	6.43	35.0	266.7	5.78	26.6	15.55	27.0
1993	529.3	3.07	21.2	64.4	0.24	10.2	6.56	6.74	36.3	285.7	6.12	30.0	16.17	29.0
1994	527.7	3.06	21.7	60.0	0.23	9.5	6.78	6.97	36.0	321.4	6.88	30.9	17.14	29.5
1995	567.4	3.29	23.7	74.0	0.28	11.5	6.78	6.96	36.4	376.9	8.04	36.2	18.56	32.3
1996	596.5	3.46	25.2	71.2	0.27	10.6	7.31	7.50	38.8	354.5	7.56	33.0	18.79	32.2
1997	632.8	3.67	26.9	74.7	0.28	11.3	7.43	7.62	39.3	362.6	7.72	33.0	19.29	32.8
1998	606.3	3.52	26.6	60.3	0.23	9.4	7.06	7.27	37.1	371.1	7.95	33.0	18.97	32.0
1999	628.9	3.65	29.3	66.5	0.25	9.9	7.24	7.44	38.4	414.5	8.73	37.4	20.07	34.8
2000	689.2	4.00	32.3	88.9	0.33	12.7	7.14	7.32	37.2	440.2	9.27	40.7	20.92	36.5
Fiscal-Year Data														
2001	676.5	3.92	32.0	93.0	0.35	14.0	6.98	7.17	35.7	425.4	8.87	38.1	20.31	34.9
2002	647.8	3.76	30.5	106.5	0.40	15.2	6.78	6.96	35.4	507.8	10.51	45.7	21.63	37.6
2003	422.6	2.45	20.4	101.0	0.38	16.0	6.01	6.17	31.5	446.7	9.18	41.3	18.18	32.4
2004	356.4	2.07	17.7	110.7	0.41	16.8	7.38	7.58	39.4	551.1	11.27	49.7	21.32	38.1
2005	439.9	2.55	22.7	96.6	0.36	14.8	6.70	6.88	36.6	431.0	8.78	37.8	18.57	33.4
2006	502.1	2.91	27.4	84.1	0.31	13.7	4.96	5.10	27.4	466.2	9.47	40.1	17.80	32.3
2007	584.7	3.39	31.5	94.5	0.35	14.7	5.73	5.90	30.1	467.5	9.51	40.4	19.15	34.0
2008	476.6	2.76	26.1	101.3	0.38	15.2	4.96	5.09	24.6	506.1	10.24	43.3	18.48	32.2
2009	544.3	3.16	28.8	87.3	0.32	13.1	6.60	6.77	31.7	490.6	9.83	43.8	20.08	35.1

SMCRA has been controversial since its passage; during the 1980s, the administration of President Ronald Reagan tried to lessen its requirements on coal companies to increase coal production and decrease the amount of foreign oil being shipped into the country, but a series of court decisions diminished the administration's ability and it was only through budget cuts by Congress that change was attempted. Based on allegations from environmentalists that the U.S. government did not collect enough money from leasing the lands where coal could be found, Congress enacted two laws, the Federal Coal Leasing Amendments Act of 1976, also known as FCLAA (Public Law 95-554), now codified as section 2(a)(2)(A) of the Mineral Leasing Act of 1920, and the Federal Land Policy and Management Act of 1976 (Public Law 94-579). The former action "forbids the issuance of any new Federal onshore mineral leases to any person or company that owns a Federal coal lease that is not producing coal in commercial quantities and has been held for 10 or more years." The latter legislation required the development of coal leases and mandated a system of payments based on "fair-market values," and required leaseholders to develop their leases and not simply hold them for speculative purposes.

Figure 11: Oil and Gas

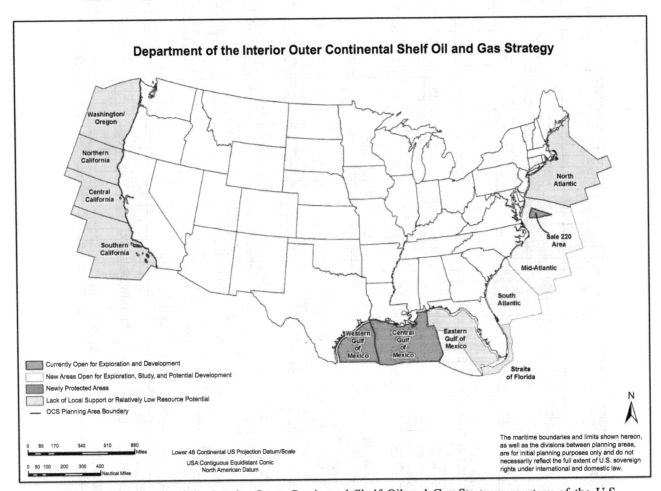

Source: Department of the Interior Outer Continental Shelf Oil and Gas Strategy, courtesy of the U.S. Department of the Interior, online at http://www.eoearth.org/files/144901_145000/144911/ ocs_lower48_states_strategy.jpg.

Although there has been decades of denunciations from various American leaders to find new or alternative sources of energy to fuel the American economy, several of these same leaders have done their utmost to hinder oil and gas production here in the United States.

The federal government first began to regulate natural gas prices in 1938, with the enactment of the Natural Gas Act (Public Law 75-688), also known as the NGA, which, with the passage of the Federal Power Act of 1935, regulated the interstate activities of electric and natural gas companies. The 1938 act also authorized the Federal Power Commission, established in the 1935 legislation, to not only regulate natural gas supplies and pricing, but also led to the regulation of wellhead prices. The 1938 act appears to be the only action by Congress in this area of concern until the 1970s. At that time, shortages in domestic supplies of natural gas and international pressures (including the 1979-81 Iranian hostage crisis) led to severe spikes in the price of natural gas. In response, Congress enacted the Natural Gas Policy Act (NGPA) of 1978 (Public Law 95-621), which loosened strict government regulation over natural gas to encourage additional domestic drilling, leading to the full deregulation by 1985; however, Congress kept strict regulation over natural gas drilled prior to the passage of the act. The action had the desired effect, and by the early 1980s, natural gas production was up. Additional moves came in 1989, when Congress voted to end regulations over wellhead pricing. By 1993, all price controls over wellhead gas were lifted, and prices declined and domestic production surged.

In 1981, after years of little exploration, President Ronald Reagan came into office and, working with his Secretary of the Interior, James Watt, proposed to double the rate of oil, natural gas, and other mineral leases. The U.S. House of Representatives, held by Democrats, blocked these changes through legislation. Six years later, however, even the Democrats in the House realized that there needed to be a change in the way the government leased lands for oil and gas exploration: In 1987, it enacted the Federal Onshore Oil and Gas Leasing Reform Act (30 USC 181 et. seq.), also known as FOOGLRA, which, according to the Natural Resources Law Center, "granted the USDA Forest Service the authority to make decisions and implement regulations concerning the leasing of public domain minerals on National Forest System lands containing oil and gas. The Act changed the analysis process from responsive to proactive. The BLM administers the lease but the Forest Service has more direct involvement in the leasing process for lands it administers. The Act also established a requirement that all public lands that are available for oil and gas leasing be offered first by competitive leasing." [20] In Congressional testimony, the act's implementation was discussed in 1989. James Duffus III, the director of the Resources, Community, and Economic Development Division of the Government Accountability Office, said, "The act authorized the BLM to conduct lease sales to test procedures while regulations were being developed. Overall, BLM implemented the Reform Act well, including conducting test sales and issuing, within the legislatively required time frame, final regulations that conform with the act. The results of BLM's test sales showed substantial increases in the percentage of land leased competitively as well as in per-acre revenues." [21]

Table 11: U.S. Offshore Crude Oil Production, 2004-2009

U.S. Offshore Crude Oil Production, 2004-2009
(millions of barrels per day)

	Federal Offshore	State Offshore
2004	1.528	0.356
2005	1.355	0.358
2006	1.371	0.331
2007	1.344	0.312
2008	1.218	0.280
2009	1.584	0.269

Source: The Energy Information Administration, available at http://www.eia.doe.gov.

Recent moves to end the moratorium on drilling off the U.S. coast have ended with opposition in Congress or from the federal administration. In 2005, Congress enacted the Energy Policy Act of 2005, which granted the Department of the Interior "the jurisdiction over renewable energy projects and over projects proposing alternate uses of existing OCS platforms."

Table 12: U.S. Natural Gas Consumption, 2004-2009

U.S. Natural Gas Consumption, 2004-2009
(trillion cubic feet)

	Delivered to Consumers	Total Consumption
2004	20.725	22.388
2005	20.315	22.010
2006	19.958	21.685
2007	21.249	23.097
2008	21.354	23.266
2009	20.935	22.844

Source: Energy Information Administration, available at http://www.eia.doe.gov/oil_gas/natural_gas/info_glance/ natural_gas.html.

In February 2010, the National Association of Regulatory Utility Commissioners released a report showing that the United States had more oil and natural gas reserves on federal land than previously thought: It found that federal acreage onshore and offshore holds more than 2,000 trillion cubic feet of natural gas (about 75 years worth of current domestic consumption) and 229 billion barrels of oil (about 50 years worth). [22] As oil prices rose to record levels in 2008, and now again as of this writing in 2011 with instability in the Middle East the main cause, questions again rise why the United States is not utilizing its oil and natural gas resources, specifically in the Outer Continental Shelf (OCS) area. In 2007, the U.S. Department of Energy found "technically recoverable undiscovered resources in the lower 48 OCS increase to 59 billion barrels of oil and 288 trillion cubic feet of natural gas, as compared with the reference case levels of 41 billion barrels and 210 trillion cubic feet." [23]

The discussion in the last several years, as energy sources have been needed to increase due to restrictions placed by the U.S. government on oil and other drilling (particularly following the 2010 BP disaster), has turned to the use of hydraulic fracturing. Also known as fracking, this technique is described as pressurized fluid forcing fractures in rock layers in order to release petroleum, natural gas or other substances. However, there is controversy over the technique, and some environmentalists believe that fracking harms the environment. In December 2011, the Environmental Protection Agency (EPA) stated for the first time that fracking could be the cause for groundwater pollution after such contamination was found near a fracking site in Wyoming. [36] Further study will prove if such concerns are warranted. There have been some small moves to encourage additional drilling; in the late 1990s, the Federal Energy Regulatory Commission (FERC) looked at ways of streamlining the approval process for drilling new wells for oil and natural gas. During the administration of President George W. Bush (2001-09), attempts were made to open the Arctic National Wildlife Refuge (ANWR) in Alaska to oil and natural gas development, but the administration was stifled by liberal opposition in Congress and by environmental groups.

Table 13: OCS Natural Gas Resource Estimates

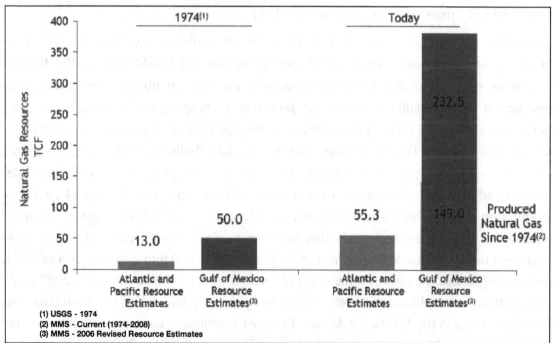

Source: OCS Natural Gas Resource Estimates, online at http://www.eoearth.org/article/U.S._offshore_oil_and_gas_resources:_prospects_and_processes?topic=50363.

Nuclear Energy

Always controversial, the usage of nuclear energy remains a potential answer for many of America's domestic energy needs but remains out of reach as opposition from environmental groups continues, despite overwhelming support from the American people (for instance, in March 2010, a Gallup poll showed that 62% backed the use of nuclear power, while 33% opposed it). [24] Congress has been unable to come to a consensus as to allowing additional nuclear plants to be constructed, leaving the nation further and further behind the rest of the world when it comes to this technology.

As of 2011, the recent date for figures available, there are 104 operating reactors in the United States, according to the Nuclear Regulatory Commission (NRC); these include 69 pressurized water reactors and 35 boiling water reactors.

The accident at the Three Mile Island facility in Pennsylvania in March 1979, as well as that at the Chernobyl plant in the Ukraine in April 1986 has made the world leery of nuclear power, leading many to resist its continued usage and especially its expansion. One of the few places in the world that has gotten over this fear is France. According to recent (2007) figures, France derives some 570 kWh (kilowatt hours) from its 58 nuclear power plants spread around the country, all operated by Electricite de France (EdF); thus, France derives some 75% of its total electricity output from nuclear energy. While it produces 570 billion kWh, it consumes only 447 billion kWh, and it exports all of the additional capacity, making France the world's largest net exporter of electricity, and gaining some €3 billion per year in revenues from these sales. Further, France is now constructing its first Generation III reactor and is planning a second; the country gets 17% of its electricity from recycled nuclear fuel. [25]

American nuclear policy began following the dropping of the atomic bomb over Hiroshima and Nagasaki, Japan, which ended the Second World War in the Pacific. Nuclear energy then took a two-track approach: government policy went towards the construction and oversight over nuclear power as a weapon, while private and other interests funded actual power plants. The first nuclear reactor to produce electricity was the National Reactor Testing Station (NRTS) at Idaho Falls (now the Idaho National Laboratory), founded in 1949; two years later it was actively producing electricity. Under the aegis of the Atomic Energy Commission (AEC), now the Nuclear Regulatory Commission (NRC), this and other plants, including the plant at Shippingport, Pennsylvania, were actively promoting civilian uses for nuclear power. Additional legislation came from the U.S. Atomic Energy Act of 1946 and the U.S. Atomic Energy Act of 1954, which strengthened the agency's handling of nuclear power. The authors of a 2007 study on nuclear power applications wrote, "After the apparently successful commercialization of nuclear power in the 1960s, the Atomic Energy Commission anticipated that more than 1,000 reactors would be operating in the United States by the year 2000." This was all a pipe dream; they add that by the 1970s, orders had slowed considerably [26] — and fights from environmental groups, and the film, *The China Syndrome*, based on faked science, causes the population to turn against nuclear power.

With only a few exceptions, today nearly all of the nuclear power plants in the United States are privately owned, with oversight by the NRC. In 2011, despite the fight by certain interests to limit or even end nuclear power in the United States, the usage of nuclear power has made the United States the world's largest producer of such power. Starting in 1953, the U.S. government laid out plans to construct, over the next three decades, more than 250 nuclear power plants which, had they been completed, would have made the United States one of the most energy-efficient and energy-independent in the world; however, nearly half — 120 plants — were canceled due to various causes, and more than 10% of the rest, nearly 30 plants, were prematurely shut down during construction and never completed, again for various reasons. [27]

Legislation regarding nuclear power has been few and far between; in the last three decades, there has been, at best, sporadic congressional action. In 1982, the Nuclear Waste Policy Act of 1982 (Public Law 97-425) was enacted to give increased government oversight over the waste that comes from the creation of nuclear energy. One source noted about the legislation, "[The] United States Congress passed the Nuclear Waste Policy Act of 1982 primarily to encourage development of repositories for the disposal of high-level radioactive waste and spent nuclear fuel. The act established the Office of Civilian Radioactive Waste Management within the U.S. Department of Energy (DOE) to handle such repositories. The Office had the responsibility of building, operating, and monitoring these geologically-mined repositories. It was also charged with developing a transportation system connecting the nuclear power plants and repositories to guarantee the safe transport of nuclear waste." [28] A congressional reconciliation act passed in 1987 ordered the Department of Energy to investigate whether Yucca Mountain, in Nevada, would be a suitable depository for such nuclear waste. Although it set a 10-year period of study, the report on Yucca Mountain did not come in until 2010. By then, Senator Harry Reid (D-NV) was the Senate Majority Leader, and he refused to allow a vote in the U.S. Senate on allowing the construction of a facility at Yucca Mountain to proceed. In 1992, the Energy Policy Act of 1992 (Public Law 102-486), also known as EPACT92, amended the National Energy Conservation Policy Act (NECPA) and established energy management goals, including those involving nuclear energy. One of the more recent congressional actions was the enactment of the Energy Policy Act of 2005 (Public Law 109-58), also known as EPACT. This legislation provided for what a Congressional Research Service (CRS) report called "significant incentives for new commercial reactors" to be built in the United States; these included "production tax credits, loan guarantees, insurance against regulatory delays, and extension of the Price-Anderson Act nuclear liability system." Due to this act, by 2009 plans for 31 new reactors were announced. [29]

However, in 2009, the administration of George W. Bush, friendly to the nuclear power industry, left office, and that of Barack Obama came in; Obama, leaning more towards environmental groups, backed off allowing these additional plants to go ahead with their plans for construction, and by 2011, as of this writing, the entire industry is in flux, with no signs ahead that any of the plants will be allowed to be built any time in the near future. Further, in the Obama administration's FY 2010 budget, the Department of Energy's proposed nuclear waste repository at Yucca Mountain, Nevada, was ended altogether, with a "blue ribbon panel" being considered to develop alternative programs for waste disposal. More than two years later, as of this writing, the members of this panel have yet to be named, much less come forward with a proposal to replace the Yucca Mountain facility. Under the Bush administration, a program called Nuclear Power 2010, to encourage the construction of new facilities, was funded by Congress; however, in the FY 2010 budget, the Obama administration cut funding from $177.5 million in FY 2009 to $20 million in FY 2010 and finally cutting the program altogether in FY 2011.

As of this writing, there is only one new nuclear power plant being constructed in America; that of the Watts Barr I plant in Tennessee, ordered in 1970, begun in 1973, and slated to be completed by 2012. Aside from this one, it is possible that we may not see a new nuclear plant built in the United States for years and years.

THE DEBATE OVER ENERGY AND MINERAL POLICY
Mining Reform

The push to reform mineral and energy laws in the United States has been next to impossible to find a consensus for. Industries desiring additional mining and drilling have demanded lesser regulations; environmental groups and their allies have pushed for even stricter controls on such mining and drilling. For many years, advocates of reforming the General Mining Law have attempted to "bring the law into the modern age," although western interests joined with mining interests have opposed them. [30] However, the usual clash between western and mining interests and environmental groups arose, and even modest reforms were dashed in a haze of partisanship. As of this writing, more than 20 years of moves by members of Congress of both parties, in congresses run by both parties under presidents of both parties have failed to find common ground, and the 1872 law remains the operating legislation for mining in this country.

Mining was at one time a major component of the economies of the western states, but with the passage of time and the invention of new technologies, the industry has melded into the background. However, according to one source, the numbers of those affected by the mining industry are far greater than the pure numbers of people employed in the industry itself. According to Geoffrey G. Snow and Allan P. Juhas, writing in 2002, mining employment in the United States, including employment in finished mineral products to the point of first sale, dropped from a high of 1.2 million people in 1920 to less than 500,000 at the end of the twentieth century. This precipitious drop accounted for a loss that went from 4.2% of the workforce in 1920 to .4% in 2002. **[31]** In states like Alaska, however, mining does continue to occupy a significant, albeit shrinking, portion of the local economy: In 2002, Professor Thomas M. Power of the University of Montana at Missoula wrote, "Metal mining is directly responsible for only about one-half of one percent of Alaskan jobs and personal income: about 2,000 of Alaska's 400,000 jobs and $87 million of Alaska's $18.6 billion of personal income in the year 2000. Even after applying any reasonable 'multiplier' to these numbers, metal mining would continue to provide only a small sliver of total Alaskan jobs and income." **[32]** According to a 2008 Congressional Research Service report,

> *Most of the current mining activity and mineral claims under the Mining Law are in Nevada, Arizona, California, Montana, and Wyoming. As of the end of FY2005, approximately 35% of mining claims were in Nevada alone and another nearly 35% were in the other four states. According to the Bureau of Land Management, the number of active claims declined from about 1.2 million claims in FY1989 to 294,678 for FY1993. Many claims were dropped as a result of provisions of law charging a $100-per-claim annual maintenance fee. The number of active claims subsequently rose to 324,651 in FY1997, reflecting the relative strength of the gold and copper industries. The number of active claims fell to a low of 207,757 for FY2001, reflecting a decline in the gold and copper industries and, according to the BLM, changes in public land policy that significantly lengthened the time necessary to get permission to mine. Active claims stood at 207,241 in FY2005.* **[33]**

Prior to the BP oil spill in the Gulf of Mexico, all mineral mining and leasing was handled by the Minerals Management Service (MMS), headquartered in the Department of the Interior. According to the FY 2007 report by the department, the MMS "administrators over 8,200 active mineral leases on almost 40 million OCS [Outer Continental Shelf] acres; oversees 15 percent of the natural gas and 25 percent of oil produced domestically; [and] collects, accounts for, substantiates, and disburses revenues, including approximately $15 billion in FY 2006 and $12 billion in FY 2007, associated with mineral production from leased Federal and Indian land." **[34]**

Two of the minerals that have gained in value are gold and silver. In 2000, gold stood at $264 per ounce; as this is written, in March 2011, it has risen above $1,400 per ounce. Silver has had a likewise, but not as steep, climb: in 2000 it sold for $5.44 per ounce; in 2011, it had reached a high of $29.54 an ounce. It is for these reasons that gold and silver mining, whether on public or private lands, make the potential of reform of the mining laws, particularly the 1872 General Mining Law, more remote than ever.

ENERGY POLICY

For years, politicians have argued over the right mix of technologies to make the United States more independent from the rest of the world for its own energy. Nuclear power, wind power, green energy — all have been tried, and all have been opposed for various reasons. In the 2008 election, the argument over whether the nation, in the midst of spiking gas prices, should explore even more gave rise to the cry "drill, baby, drill." When gas prices receded within a year, even these calls were halted. In 2011, however, as instability in Middle Eastern nations, including such oil-producing countries as Egypt and Libya, drove world oil prices upwards towards new highs, calls once again rose demanding that drilling be increased. The British Petroleum (BP) oil spill in the Gulf of Mexico in 2010 led the Obama administration to put a halt to all old and new drilling contracts in that waterway, as well as calling for a complete moratorium on all drilling off of the coasts of the United States. Such a nearsighted policy created instant job losses in the oil drilling and associated industries, which worsened with the continuing economic downturn that had begun in 2008. Obama's move was not the first, nor will it be the last, time that a presidential administration grappled with the issue of energy policy and how to make it work without angering one side or both sides of the political aisle. Early in his presidency, Bill Clinton proposed the levying of a broad tax on all forms of energy to boost federal revenues to cut the federal budget deficit. The proposed tax, called a BTU (short for British Thermal Unit, a measure of energy) Tax, would have raised fees and taxes on a wide range of energy supplies, including gasoline, electricity, coal, and others that are used by people and industries to power their homes and the workplace. However, because of a bipartisan group of Senators from energy-producing states who blocked the measure, it never became law. The Clinton administration did add a 4.3 cent-a-gallon tax on gasoline, inserted into its deficit reduction plan. In 1996, when Clinton ran for a second term, and gas prices reached new limits, Republicans called for the repeal of the gas tax, which Clinton refused; instead, he ordered the release of 12 million barrels of oil from the Strategic Oil Reserve (SOR). According to the U.S. Department of Energy, "the Strategic Petroleum Reserve is a U.S. Government complex of four sites with deep underground storage caverns created in salt domes along the Texas and Louisiana Gulf Coasts. The caverns have a capacity of 727 million barrels and store emergency supplies of crude oil owned by the U.S. Government." [35]

As of 30 November 2010, the current update per that government department, there were 292.5 million barrels of so-called "sweet crude" and 434 million barrels of so-called "sour crude," making a total, at that exact period, of 726.5 million barrels of oil held in reserve. According to the U.S. Government's Energy Information Administration, the United States consumes about 400 million gallons, or 1.51 billion liters, of gasoline every day, which equals about 20 million barrels of oil every day. Thus, Clinton's ordering of the release of 12 million barrels would not be enough to aid the entire United States consumption of oil for one single day; further, even if the SOR were used until it were empty, in a vain attempt to keep oil prices low, its 726 million barrels of oil would last 36.3 days in total. In 2000, on the edge of another presidential election, Clinton did release oil from the SOR; a Cato Institute study of its effects showed that it did nothing to lower the price of gas.

During the administration of President George W. Bush (2001-09), attempts were made by the administration to open up areas of drilling, most notably in the Alaska National Wildlife Refuge (ANWR) in northern Alaska; Democrats in both houses of Congress succeeded in blocking this initiative. Further attempts to open drilling areas in the Outer Continental Shelf (OCS) areas off the coasts of the United States also were dashed by Congress and by local officials in states such as Florida and California. When the Obama administration (2009-) came into office, the new president directed his Secretary of the Interior to cancel all 70+ drilling permits for the Gulf of Mexico; in 2010, after the BP oil disaster, the administration imposed a moratorium on all new drilling leases, even though a federal judge in New Orleans held such a move to be unconstitutional. Nevertheless, when the administration refused to even admit that the judge had a say over whether or not a moratorium could be imposed, the judge held the administration in civil contempt. As of March 2011, the original order and the contempt citation had both been ignored by the administration.

In the wake of violent uprisings against regimes in the Middle East, the price of oil rose precipitously, and, once again, the American consumer saw an increase in the price being paid at the pump for a gallon of gasoline. Options to drill more or to utilize differing forms of energy were ruled out by the administration, which considered a possible gas tax to fund infrastructure construction, and a potential release of oil reserves from the SOR. Such small and tiny moves will, in the end, do little to combat the price of oil or to make America self-sufficient from foreign oil. Whether or not this administration, or a future administration, can grapple both with the politics and the decision-making behind moving the country in the right direction is yet to be seen as of this writing. But a close look at what has become 30+ years of energy decision-making shows little promise that either side in the policy debate will do anything more than posture and postulate and refuse to do anything but argue. And in the end, the American consumer, both present and future, will suffer for this ignorance.

NOTES:

[1] For the complete language of the act, see George P. Sanger, ed., "By Authority of Congress. The Statutes at Large, Treaties, and Proclamations, of the United States of America. From December 1863, to December 1865. Arranged in Chronological Order and Carefully Collated with the Originals in Washington. With References to the Matter of Each Act and to the Subsequent Acts on the Same Subject. Edited by George P. Sanger, Counsellor at Law" (Boston: Little, Brown, and Company, 1866), XIII:343-44.

[2] *Colorado Coal and Iron Company v. United States* (123 US 307 {1887}), at 326-27.

[3] Humphries, Marc, "Mining on Federal Lands: Hardrock Minerals," *CRS Report for Congress*, 30 April 2008, ii.

[4] Ibid., CRS-2.

[5] "Mineral Leasing Act of 1920," in "Federal Wildlife and Related Laws Handbook," courtesy of the New Mexico Center for Wildlife Law, the University of New Mexico School of Law, online at http://wildlifelaw.unm.edu/fedbook/minerall.html.

[6] Gorte, Ross W., Carol Hardy Vincent, and Marc Humphries, "Federal Lands Managed by the Bureau of Land Management (BLM) and the Forest Service (FS): Issues for the 110th Congress," *CRS Report for Congress*, 9 May 2008, CRS-3.

[7] "Essential Documents: Mineral Leasing Act of 1920," Courtesy of the Council on Foreign Relations, 14 February 2011, online at http://www.cfr.org/united-states/mineral-leasing-act-1920/p24121.

[8] Hartman, Howard L., A.B. Cummins and I.A. Given, "SME Mining Engineering Handbook" (Littleton, Colorado: Society for Mining, Metallurgy, and Exploration, Inc.; two volumes, 1992), I:153.

[9] See the act at 30 USC 12.

[10] "SME Mining Engineering Handbook," I:155.

[11] "[The] Federal government Could Reduce [Its] Debt by $1.5 Trillion with a Sale of Unneeded Assets," *The Foundry*, a Heritage Foundation blog, 17 February 2011, online at http://blog.heritage.org/?p=52659.

[12] Gorte, Vincent, and Humphries, "Federal Lands Managed by the Bureau of Land Management (BLM) and the Forest Service (FS): Issues for the 110th Congress," *CRS Report for Congress*, 9 May 2008, CRS-3.

[13] Kennedy, Bruce A., "Surface Mining" (Littleton, Colorado: Society for Mining, Metallurgy, and Exploration, Inc., 1990), 281.

[14] "Technical Document: Background for NEPA Reviewers: Non-Coal Mining Operations" (Washington, D.C.: U.S. Environmental Protection Agency, December 1994), 1-8.

[15] "Oil and Gas Rights," courtesy of Geology.com, online at http://geology.com/articles/mineral-rights.shtml.

[16] "Coal Operations" and "Federal Coal Leasing," courtesy of the Bureau of Land Management, online at http://www.blm.gov/wo/st/en/prog/energy/coal_and_non-energy.html.

[17] "Digest of Federal Resource Laws of Interest to the U.S. Fish & Wildlife Service: Surface Mining Control and Reclamation Act," courtesy of the U.S. Fish & Wildlife Service, online at http://www.fws.gov/laws/lawsdigest/surfmin.html.

[18] "Public Law 95-87: Surface Mining Control and Reclamation Act of 1977," handbook courtesy of the Office of Surface Mining, Reclamation and Enforcement (OSMRE), 23 July 2010, 3.

[19] "Digest of Federal Resource Laws of Interest to the U.S. Fish & Wildlife Service: Surface Mining Control and Reclamation Act," courtesy of the U.S. Fish & Wildlife Service, online at http://www.fws.gov/laws/lawsdigest/surfmin.html.

[20] Committee on Onshore Oil and Gas Leasing, Board on Earth Sciences and Resources, Commission on Physical Sciences, Mathematics, and Resources, the National Research Council, "Land Use Planning and Oil and Gas Leasing on Onshore Federal Lands" (Washington, D.C.: National Academy Press, 1989); "Federal Laws: Federal Oil and Gas Statutes," courtesy of the Intermountain Oil and Gas BMP Project, online at http://www.oilandgasbmps.org/laws/federal_law.php.

[21] "Statement of James Duffus III" in "Implementation of the Federal Onshore Oil and Gas Leasing Reform Act of 1987: Testimony," Government Accountability Office, 28 September 1989, 9.

[22] Helman, Christopher, "Study: Fed Lands Hold Oil and Gas Bonanza," *Forbes Magazine Blogs*, 15 February 2010, online at http://blogs.forbes.com/energysource/2010/02/15/study-fed-lands-hold-oil-and-gas-bonanza/.

[23] "Impacts of Increased Access to Oil and Natural Gas Resources in the Lower 48 Federal Outer Continental Shelf," report of the U.S. Energy Information Administration (USEIA), 2007, online at http://www.eia.gov/oiaf/aeo/otheranalysis/ongr.html.

[24] "U.S. Support for Nuclear Power Climbs to New High of 62%," Gallup poll, 22 March 2010, online at http://www.gallup.com/poll/126827/support-nuclear-power-climbs-new-high.aspx.

[25] Information on France's nuclear power industry and figures from the World Nuclear Association, 21 January 2011, online at http://www.world-nuclear.org/info/inf40.html.

[26] Facts and figures on plants cancelled or not completed in Parker, Larry, and Mark Holt, "Nuclear Power: Outlook for New U.S. Reactors," *CRS Report for Congress*, 9 March 2007, CRS-3, courtesy of the Federation of American Scientists, online at http://www.fas.org/sgp/crs/misc/RL33442.pdf.

[27] Ibid., CRS-3.

[28] "Nuclear Waste Policy Act of 1982, United States," *Encyclopedia of the Earth*, 28 August 2008, online at http://www.eoearth.org/article/Nuclear_Waste_Policy_Act_of_1982,_United_States.

[29] Holt, Mark, "Nuclear Energy Policy," *CRS Report for Congress*, 10 December 2009, i.

[30] For a short look at attempts at reform during the 1990s, see Scott Fitzgerald Murray, "Civic Virtue and Public Policy: Discerning the Particulars of Reforming the General Mining Law of 1872" (Master of Arts thesis, University of Nevada at Las Vegas, 1997), 45-60.

[31] Snow, Geoffrey G.; and Allan P. Juhas, "Trends and Forces in Mining and Mineral Exploration," *Society of Economic Geology*, Special Publication 9 (2002), 7, quoted in "History of Mineral Policy in the United States," *Encyclopedia of the Earth*, 1 May 2008, online at http://www.eoearth.org/article/History_of_mineral_policy_in_the_United_States?topic=49464.

[32] Power, Thomas Michael, "The Role of Metal Mining in the Alaska Economy," report prepared for the Southeast Alaska Conservation Council and the Northern Alaska Environmental Center (2002), online at http://wman-info.org/resources/technicalreports/The%2520Role%2520of%2520Metal%2520Mining%2520in%2520the%2520Alaska%2520Economy.doc&rct=j&q=Mining%20of%20metals%20provides%20only%20about%20one-tenth%20of%201%20percent%20of%20the%20jobs%20in%20the%20twelve%20western%20states.%20&ei=d8FuTf7KH4rUtQPV2LTaCw&usg=AFQjC, 1.

[33] Humphries, Marc, "Mining on Federal Lands: Hardrock Materials," *CRS Report for Congress*, 30 April 2008, online at http://assets.opencrs.com/rpts/RL33908_20080430.pdf, CRS-2.

[34] U.S. Department of the Interior, "Stewardship for America with Integrity and Excellence: U.S. Department of the Interior Annual Performance and Accountability Report: FY 2007 Highlights" (Washington, D.C.: Government Printing Office, 2007), 4.

[35] "The Strategic Petroleum Reserve - Quick Facts and Frequently Asked Questions," courtesy of the U.S. Department of Energy, undated, online at http://fossil.energy.gov/programs/reserves/spr/spr-facts.html.

[36] Gruver, Mead, "EPA: Fracking May Cause Groundwater Pollution," USA Today, 8 December 2011, online at http://www.usatoday.com/money/industries/energy/environment/story/2011-12-08/epa-fracking-pollution/51745004/1.

8

Water Resources

THE FUNDAMENTALS OF WATER

Water plays a vital role in all of our lives — we need it to live through various bodily sources, we use it to drink, to bathe, to wash our cars and our homes and our streets. The importance of water can never be underestimated.

At the same time, water is a fragile resource. Although it covers approximately 70.8% of earth's surface, some 75% of that water is saltwater, and a total of 99% of all the water on the planet is completely unusable by humans for consumption; only 3% of all water is freshwater, and of the total amount of water on the planet only 1% is used by humans and animals.

Figure 12: Distribution of Earth's Water

Distribution of Earth's Water

Source: Igor Shiklomanov's chapter "World fresh water resources" in Peter H. Gleick (editor), 1993, Water in Crisis: A Guide to the World's Fresh Water Resources.

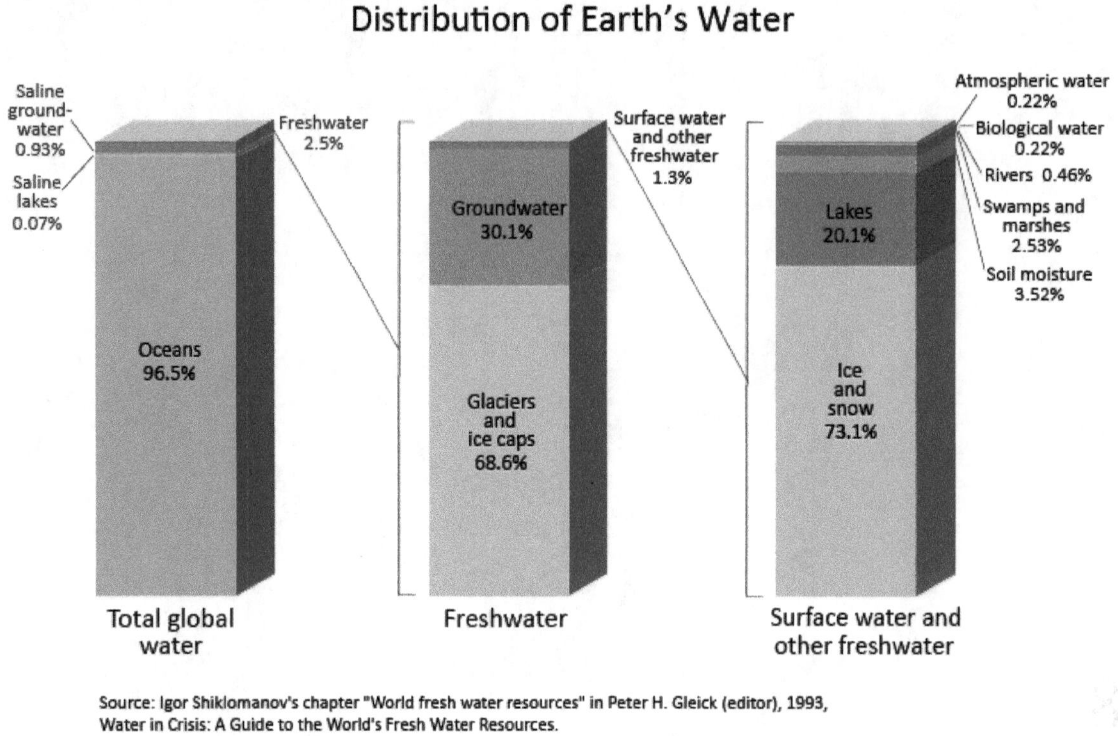

The increasing usage of water challenges resources and government policy: how to protect these resources while at the same time making them accessible to the general public and other sources? The average American for instance, uses, on average, about 80-100 gallons of water per day, for a various number of activities, for instance:

Activity	Water used (on average)
Shower	15-30 gallons (57-114 liters)
Brushing teeth (water running)	1-2 gallons (3.75-7.51 liters)
Shaving (water running)	10-15 gallons (38-57 liters)
Washing dishes by hand	20 gallons (75 liters)
Washing dishes in dishwasher	9-12 gallons (34-45 liters)
Flushing toilet	5-7 gallons (19-26 liters)

These numbers are just for personal usage; the average American uses another 600 gallons in manufacturing, and up to 800 gallons per person in the development of agriculture; however, averaged over all people, it equals approximately 80-120 gallons. [1]

Most of the water that people drink in the United States comes either from local sources, such as aquifers or pumps, or even streams and lakes or even wetlands, or bottled water.

While the latter is cleansed of impurities and chemicals that could be harmful, the other water sources do have some degree of chemical residue or mineral residue from nature. Bottled water ironically comes from municipal sources as other forms of drinking water except that it goes through a series of cleanings before being bottled. Aquifers are continually refreshed and restored by precipitation. According to the U.S. Geological Survey, "The principal water-yielding aquifers of North America can be grouped into five types: unconsolidated and semiconsolidated sand and gravel aquifers, sandstone aquifers, carbonate-rock aquifers, aquifers in interbedded sandstone and carbonate rocks, and aquifers in igneous and metamorphic rocks." [2] In 2003, the U.S. Geological Survey identified 62 principal aquifers in the United States.

Figure 13: Locations and Names of the Principal Aquifers

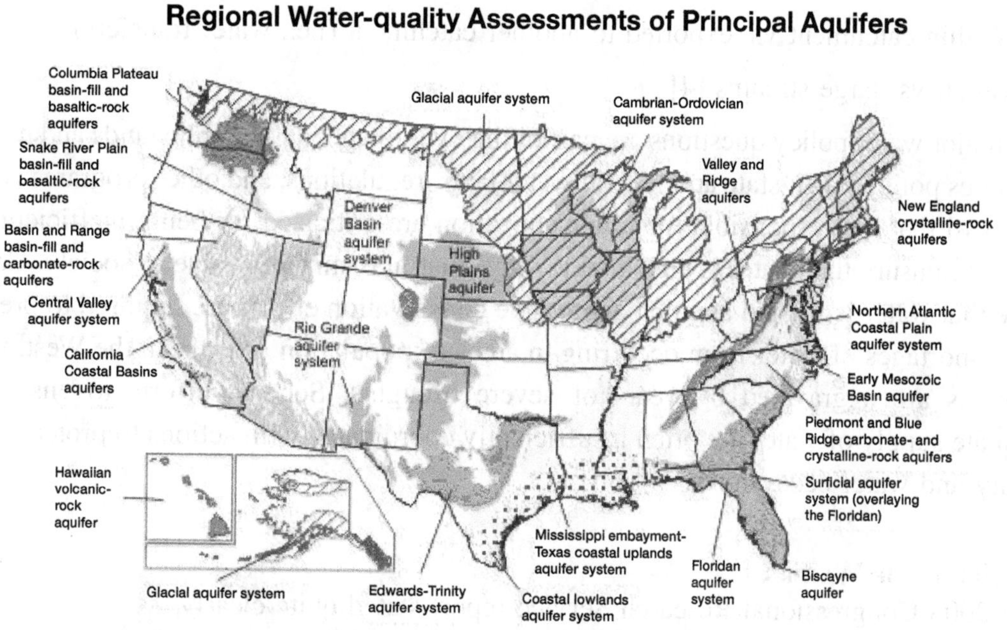

Regional Water-quality Assessments of Principal Aquifers

Source: U.S. Geological Survey, online at http://water.usgs.gov/nawqa/studies/praq/.

According to the Environmental Protection Agency (EPA),

Like extent, condition is influenced by both natural sources and human activities. Some groundwater has high levels of naturally occurring dissolved solids (salinity), or metals such as arsenic that can be present as a result of natural rock formations. Land use can affect the condition of groundwater; for example, pesticides, fertilizers, and other chemicals applied to the land can leach into groundwater, while waste from livestock and other animals can contribute contaminants such as nutrients, organic matter, and pathogens. Shallow and unconfined aquifers are particularly susceptible to this type of contamination. In addition, landfills may leach metals, solvents, and other contaminants into ground water (particularly older landfills that do not have liners and leachate collection systems). Mining operations can mobilize toxic metals, acidic compounds, and other substances that can impact the condition of groundwater. Finally, chemical or biological contaminants may enter aquifers as a result of unintentional releases, including chemical spills on land, leaks from storage tanks, sewers or septic systems, and unplugged abandoned wells that allow a direct route of entry for contaminants. [3]

The agency also notes that the withdrawal of water has direct effects on the environment. These effects depend on several factors, which include:

Where the water comes from:

1. Surface water vs. groundwater

2. Within catchment vs. imported from another catchment (i.e., water transfers)

3. Direct intake from channel vs. from water supply reservoir

4. Small vs. large streams

Where the water goes:

1. Within catchment vs. exported to another catchment (i.e., water transfers)

2. Small vs. large streams [4]

Two major water policy questions are part of the overall agenda of public lands and natural resources policy. First, state and federal water laws, regulations, and other programs across the board that are responsible for water allocation are criticized for being inefficient, for failing to ensure that water is allocated in ways that maximize its value to society. Critics argue that water is wasted and that aggressive conservation efforts are required to prevent major shortages of water from occurring in areas of population growth. In the West, these problems are aggravated by years of severe droughts. Second, efforts to ensure an adequate supply of water are often insufficiently coordinated with actions to protect water quality and water ecosystems.

The Supply of Water

As a 2008 Congressional Research Service report stated quite clearly,

> *[e]nsuring the security of the nations' drinking water supplies poses a substantial challenge, partly because the number of water systems is very large and also because the responsibility for protecting drinking water safety is shared among federal, state and local governments and utilities. Nationwide, there are some 158,000 public water systems, and these systems range greatly in size, serving from as few as 25 persons to more than 1 million persons. Roughly 53,000 of all public water systems are community water systems (CWSs) that serve the same residences year-round. These 53,000 systems provide water to approximately 282 million people. Nearly 400 community systems serve more than 100,000 people and provide water to nearly half of the total population served. Because water supplies support many uses (from drinking water to fire suppression), their disruption could have significant impacts.* [5]

The jurisdiction over water supplies and allocation is convoluted in 2011, to say the least, and it appears to grow more complicated with each passing year. For instance, the authority for water allocation belongs, per the U.S. Constitution, to the states themselves, and they have all established state agencies to oversee this process. At the same, however, more than 35 separate agencies in 10 federal cabinet departments, as well as 7 independent agencies and additional organizations, all have a say over water programs, how they are carried out, and congressional mandates for their usage. The two leading U.S. government agencies with responsibilities over water are the Bureau of Reclamation (BOR), an agency inside the U.S. Department of the Interior, which "manages scarce water resources in the semiarid western United States," and the U.S. Army Corps of Engineers (USACE), which "works with both engineering and environmental matters. The Corps' responsibilities include designing and constructing flood control systems, such as navigation locks and dams, beach nourishment projects, environmental regulation, ecosystem restoration and engineering services." **[6]** Let us examine these two important agencies.

THE BUREAU OF RECLAMATION

The Bureau of Reclamation (Reclamation) is responsible for the construction of most of the large irrigation and water resources infrastructure in the West. Reclamation manages water resource facilities in 17 western states with an original development cost of over $20 billion. Reclamation is over 100 years old, and many of its facilities now have an average age of over 50 years. This aging infrastructure requires increased maintenance and replacement efforts and expenditures. **[7]** Among the projects constructed in the western United States by the Bureau of Reclamation include, as of 2008, 471 dams and dikes that create 348 reservoirs with a total storage capacity of some 245 million acre-feet of water. (According to the Congressional Research Service, "one acre-foot is the amount of water required to cover an area of one acre to a depth of one foot" — in short, some 325,851 gallons.) **[8]**

The Bureau of Reclamation was established in 1902 by President Theodore Roosevelt as the United States Reclamation Service (USRC), initially placed under the jurisdiction of the U.S. Geological Survey (USGS) with a director of its own, in this case being Charles D. Walcott. The agency was created "to implement the Reclamation Act of 1902, which authorzed the construction of water works to provide water for irrigation in arid western states." **[9]** Better known as the Newlands Act, after its congressional sponsor, Senator Francis G. Newlands of Nevada, this legislation will be discussed later in this chapter. Five years after it was created, on 9 March 1907, the agency was changed as an independent bureau inside the U.S. Department of the Interior. This condition remained constant until 20 June 1923, when the agency was renamed the Bureau of Reclamation, with David W. Davis named as the agency's first commissioner. Since 1923, the Bureau of Reclamation has remained as an independent agency inside the Department of the Interior, where it remains to this day. **[10]** During its heyday, the bureau constructed such projects as the Hoover Dam in the Boulder Canyon between Nevada and Arizona, as well as the Grand Teton Dam and other well-known irrigation projects. In the later 1980s, a major reorganization of the entire bureau began as funding for projects considered and authorized in the 1960s during Lyndon Baines Johnson's "Great Society" came to an end. The reorganization, which ended in 1994 after six years, cut the budget of the agency substantially and staff levels were also trimmed to historic lows. But the overarching goal of the service remains: the reclamation of irrigable land in the western United States.

As of 2011, the agency is the largest wholesaler of water in the United States, responsible for bringing water to more than 31 million people. The bureau's water projects also provide one out of five farmers (140,000) in the western states with irrigation water for a total of some 10 million acres of farmland that, in total, produce some 60% of the nation's vegetables and 25% of its fruits and nuts. The Bureau is also the second largest producer of hydroelectric power in the western United States, managing 58 power plants that produce enough electricity to serve 6 million homes.

In addition to water reclamation, the bureau also operates several programs for households, farms, businesses, Native American tribes, and other interested parties, to demonstrate a number of initiatives dealing with reclamation. For instance, these include dam safety, established in 1978 in the wake of the Teton Dam disaster near Newdale, Idaho, on 5 June 1976, which left 14 people dead; a drought program, which authorizes the bureau to establish programs to minimize or mitigate drought and the damage that it causes; the establishment of a Fisheries and Wildlife Resources Group, which brings together fish experts, wildlife biologists, environmental specialists, and other experts to conduct field and other experiments to demonstrate the impact of irrigation, reclamation, and drought have on fish and wildlife populations in affected areas; the establishment of a Flood Hydrology and Meteorology Group, which establishes criteria for the examination of potential flooding and dam failure where the Bureau of Reclamation has control over such dams; and the establishment of a Hydropower Technical Services Group, which offers expertise to the bureau's engineers in the areas of safety and failure mitigation with regards to hydroelectric plants and dams, and, in the case of such a failure, can provide for expert analysis of why the failure occurred and how to avoid a similar failure in the future. [11]

In 2002, in another Congressional Research Service report, it was noted that

"Today, the Bureau operates nearly 350 storage reservoirs and approximately 250 diversion dams — including some of the largest dams in the world, such as Hoover Dam on the Colorado River and Grand Coulee Dam on the Columbia River. In total, the Bureau's projects provide water to approximately 9 million acres of farmland and nearly 31 million people in 17 western states. The Bureau also operates 58 power plants." [12]

THE U.S. ARMY CORPS OF ENGINEERS

Although many people have heard of the U.S. Army Corps of Engineers (USACE), its actual role and the decisions it makes, and the impact it has on the environment and environmental and land policy in the United States is barely understood. Christopher Klyza, writing in 2002, explained,

> [t]hroughout the nineteenth century the federal government undertook a number of natural resources policy initiatives. During this "state of courts and parties," the federal state needed some administrative presence to help it supply public goods within the development-oriented distributive politics. The United States Army was called upon to play this role in water projects and scientific geography. Toward the end of the century, the Army's natural resources management mission changed. As a new American state was being built, one in which regulatory politics played a more significant role, the Army served an important function in providing patchwork administrative capacity, demonstrated by its administration of national parks and forest reserves. [13]

Strangely, the USACE is housed as an independent agency not in the U.S. Department of the Interior, or in the U.S. Department of Agriculture, but in the U.S. Department of Defense...it employs some 35,000 people (exact statistics are hard to come by), and is responsible for more water projects and water construction projects than any government or nongovernmental agency in the entire world. The agency has a storied history, which harkens back to the immediate foundations of the American nation. According to the agency,

> George Washington appointed the first engineer officers of the Army on June 16, 1775, during the American Revolution, and engineers have served in combat in all subsequent American wars. The Army established the Corps of Engineers as a separate, permanent branch on March 16, 1802, and gave the engineers responsibility for founding and operating the U.S. Military Academy at West Point. Since then the U.S. Army Corps of Engineers has responded to changing defense requirements and played an integral part in the development of the country. Throughout the 19th century, the Corps built coastal fortifications, surveyed roads and canals, eliminated navigational hazards, explored and mapped the Western frontier, and constructed buildings and monuments in the Nation's capital. [14]

Since its founding, however, the USACE's chief mission has been the construction of national infrastructure — most notably, water projects and other construction projects dealing with water, including dredging channels for shipping, constructing hydroelectric dams across untamed rivers to provide rural and other areas with cheap or low-cost electricity, and building levees and other measures to ward off flooding.

Since the 1980s, a strange coalition of environmentalists and conservative budget cutters on the national stage have joined together to oppose any further funding for the Corps; environmentalists oppose the corps because they believe that their vast projects over the years have harmed the environment, most notably wetlands and pristine water vistas; conservatives, on the other hand, have tired of what they consider "pork barrel" spending for costly projects with few tangible results for the cost. It was not until the administration of President George W. Bush that an effort was made not in Congress but in the administration itself to cut funding for the Corps. However, another coalition of liberals who support funding for agency projects and conservatives who wish to "bring the pork back home to their constituents" got together and held back any attempt to cut agency funding.

As one source noted, "the Army Corps of Engineers led the way in developing the West; they explored, surveyed, and mapped the land, built forts and roads, and later assisted in building the transcontinental railway. The corps later specialized in improving harbours and inland waterways and constructing dams and levees." [15]

THE POLICY FRAMEWORK

The action of legislation dealing with water irrigation and reclamation is a little more than a century old. The controversy first arose, albeit in a roundabout way, in 1899, when the U.S. Supreme Court decided the case of *United States v. Rio Grande Dam & Irrigation Co.* (174 US 690 {1899}). Wells A. Hutchins, in a history of water rights law in the western states from 1971, explained, "The bill was brought by the United States to restrian construction of a dam across the Rio Grande and appropriation of the stream waters for purposes of irrigation, the result of which would seriously obstruct the navigability of the entire river below the dam. The United States Supreme Court reversed the judgment of the Territorial Supreme Court, which had held that the river was not navigable within the limits of the Territory of New Mexico and that the United States therefore had no jurisdiction over the stream." [16] The Court, through the unanimous opinion delivered by Justice David Josiah Brewer, noted, "The power of the general government to secure the uninterrupted navigability of all navigable streams within the limits of the United States is within the jurisdiction of the general government over interstate commerce and its natural water highways."

Congress had already enacted a law in 1886 dealing with water: the River and Harbor Act of 1886 (24 Stat. 310). Up until that time, according to one source, "there [was] no federal authority to regulate activities associated with the nation's river systems, so individuals and businesses [we]re free to build bridges and establish tolls that obstruct navigation. As a result, Congress passe[d] the Rivers and Harbors Act in 1886 that [gave]the federal government authority to take action to improve navigation on the nation's rivers." [17] In 1899, fearing that the courts could strike the law down because of the vagueness of what an "obstruction" could be classified as, Congress enacted a similar law, this time codified as the Rivers and Harbors Act of 1899 (30 Stat. 1151); this legislation clearly delineated what the Congress meant by an "obstruction." One source notes, "The Act prohibit[ed] the construction of any bridge, dam, dike, or causeway over or in navigable waterways of the U.S. without Congressional approval. Structures authorized by state legislatures [might] be built if the affected navigable waters are completely within one state, provided the plan is first approved by the Chief of Engineers [of the U.S. Army Corps of Engineers] and the Secretary of the Army. The Act also prohibit[ed] the building of wharfs, piers, jetties, and other structures without approval." [18] In 1959, the U.S. Supreme Court, in *United States v. Republic Steel Corp.* (362 US 482 {1959}), decided what constituted an "obstruction" to a navigable waterway. In the decision, the court heard arguments that "respondents [Republic Steel Corp.], who operate mills for the production of iron and related products, had, without first obtaining permits from the Chief of Engineers of the Army providing conditions for their removal, discharged through sewers into a navigable river of the United States industrial waste solids which, on settling out, had substantially reduced the depth of the channel; and it enjoined them from continuing to do so and ordered them to restore the depth of the channel by removing the deposits." The Supreme Court held, unanimously, that "the deposit of industrial solids in the river by respondents created an "obstruction" to the "navigable capacity" of the river forbidden by § 10 of the Rivers and Harbors Act of 1899; they were discharges forbidden by, and not exempt under, § 13; and the District Court was authorized to grant injunctive relief." [19]

After the 1899 act was passed, it would be nearly 50 years before Congress once again enacted a major piece of legislation dealing with water regulation, although a little-remembered piece of legislation was enacted in this period. In 1920, the Congress enacted the Federal Water Power Act (41 Stat. 1063), which established the Federal Power Commission, whose mission was to control hydroelectric dam construction on all navigable rivers across the United States. The administration of President Woodrow Wilson pushed for the law, which for the first time regulated private electric utilities in an attempt to lower energy costs.

In 1948, passage of the Federal Water Pollution Control Act (Public Law 80-845) or the FWPCA, better known as the Clean Water Act (and not to be confused with the CWA enacted in the 1960s), dealt with the issue of pollution in water used for drinking or other purposes. Fedcenter.gov, a clearinghouse of information on federal laws, said,

> *Originally this Act authorized the Surgeon General of the Public Health Service, in cooperation with other Federal, state and local entities, to prepare comprehensive programs for eliminating or reducing the pollution of interstate waters and tributaries and improving the sanitary condition of surface and underground waters. The original statute also authorized the Federal Works Administrator to assist states, municipalities, and interstate agencies in constructing treatment plants to prevent discharges of inadequately treated sewage and other wastes into interstate waters or tributaries. Since 1948, the original statute has been amended extensively either to authorize additional water quality programs, standards and procedures to govern allowable discharges, funding for construction grants or general program funding. Amendments in other years provided for continued authority to conduct program activities or administrative changes to related activities.* [20]

After passage of the 1948 act, there would be another lull of 17 years before Congress once again examined water issues. The Federal Water Quality Act (Public Law 89-234, 79

Stat. 903), or FWQA, enacted on 2 October 1965, and its subsequent amendments which became law in 1977, for the first time involved the U.S. government in specifically pushing for clean water standards across the country. Since the passage of the 1948 act, Congress concluded that that action did not have the legislative "teeth" it was supposed to have, and set about to enact a law that did have major enforcement regulations. Thus the Congress established, in the mission statement of the 1965 act, what the act's process was being set up to do:

"An Act to amend the Federal Water Pollution Control Act [of 1948] to establish a Federal Water Pollution Control Administration, to provide grants for research and development, to increase grants for construction of sewage treatment works, to require establishment of water quality criteria, and for other purposes." In Section six of the act, subsection (a), Congress displayed the authorization for enforcement of the act:

> *The Secretary is authorized to make grants to any State, municipality, or intermunicipal or interstate agency for the purpose of assisting in the development of any project which will demonstrate a new or improved method of controlling the discharge into any waters of untreated or inadequately treated sewage or other waste from sewers which carry storm water or both storm water and sewage or other wastes, and for the purpose of reports, plans, and specifications in connection therewith. The Secretary is authorized to provide for the conduct of research and demonstrations relating to new or improved methods of controlling the discharge into any waters of untreated or inadequately treated sewage or other waste from sewers which carry storm water or both storm water and sewage or other wastes, by contract with public or private agencies and institutions and with individuals without regard to sections 3648 and 3709 of the Revised Statutes, except that not to exceed 25 per centum of the total amount appropriated under authority of this section for any fiscal year may be expended under authority of this sentence during such fiscal year.* [21]

The legislation also established the Federal Water Pollution Control Administration (FWPCA) in the Department of Health, Education, and Welfare (HEW) (which itself was later broken up into the Department of Health and Human Services and the Department of Education). FWPCA was composed of the Division of Water Supply and Pollution Control, the Public Health Service, and the Federal Security Agency. On 10 May 1966, as part of a governmental reorganization plan, the administration's responsibilities were moved to the Department of the Interior. In 1970, with passage by Congress of the Water Quality Improvement Act of 1970 (84 Stat. 113), the entire FWPCA was abolished. [22]

A year after the passage of the 1965 act, Congress revisited the subject of clean water when it enacted the Clean Waters Restoration Act (Public Law 89-753), which is rarely spoken about even in works on clean water issues. In discussing the range of social and other legislation enacted by the U.S. Congress in 1966, at the height of Lyndon Baines Johnson's "Great Society" mandate of governmental programs enacted across a wide swath of American life, Chester James Antieau wrote, "By the Clear Water Restoration Act of 1966, federal funds were to made available for the construction of sewage treatment plants." [23] The Environmental Protection Agency adds, "The Clean Water Restoration Act of 1966 imposed a $100 per day fine on a polluter who failed to submit a required report." [24]

Following passage of this law, Congress hesitated for several years to pass any additional legislation dealing with water issues, although, in 1969, it did enact the National Environmental Policy Act (Public Law 91-190), which has been discussed in early chapters, and, in 1970, the Water Quality Improvement Act (Public Law 91-224), also known as WQIA. Historians Albert J. Verheij, Michael Faure, and Tom vanden Borre wrote in 2007, "A very important step forward was taken by the Federal Water Quality Improvement Act (WQIA) of 1970. The regime of this Act became the model for subsequent oil pollution laws and there are remarkable similarities between the WQIA and the Oil Pollution Act of 1990. The WQIA and the subsequent Clean Water Act of 1977 merit separate attention." They added that passage of the 1970 law set into place a harsh set of rules governing liability for oil spills and pollution. "The liability regime under this Act was strict," they explain. "The responsible party could only exempt himself from liability in case of: an act of war, an act of God, negligence on the part of the U.S. government, or an act or omission (either negligent or not) of a third party...Only clean-up costs were compensable under the WQIA. Liability was limited to $100 per gross ton or $14 million, whichever is less except when the oil was caused by the wilful misconduct or wilful negligence of the responsible party." [25]

The next major piece of legislation were the Federal Water Pollution Control Amendments of 1972 (Public Law 92-500), better known as the Clean Water Act. The Fish & Wildlife Service said of this action that it "stipulated broad national objectives to restore and maintain the chemical, physical, and biological integrity of the Nation's waters...[p]rovisions included a requirement that the Federal Power Commission not grant a license for a hydroelectric power project to regulate streamflow for the purpose of water quality unless certain conditions are satisfied." Further, the agency explained, "the amendments significantly expanded provisions related to pollutant discharges. These included requirements that limitations be determined for point sources which are consistent with State water quality standards, procedures for State issuance of water quality standards, development of guidelines to identify and evaluate the extent of nonpoint source pollution, water quality inventory requirements, as well as development of toxic and pretreatment effluent standards." Established in this law was the National Pollutant Discharge Elimination System (NPDES), which allowed the EPA to issue discharge permits for sewage. Under Section 403 of the act, guidelines were laid out for the EPA to grant such discharge permits. Finally, in Section 404 was the authorization of the U.S. Army Corps of Engineers to issue permits for the discharge of withdrawn, dredged, or other filler material into specifically listed navigable waters at specified dumping sites, which the

EPA could rule out based on the disposal site's "adverse effect" on municipal water supplies, animals habitats, or other uses. [26]

Two years later, Congress enacted the Safe Drinking Water Act (Public Law 93-523) (SDWA). This is the chief federal legislation that mandates safe drinking water in the United States; its coverage is to all public water supplies in the entire nation to be covered by strict federal standards for drinking water. Prior to its passage, federal mandates for the entire nation were spotty at best. The first standards had been issued by the United States Public Health Service in 1914, and these remained the norm until the creation of the Environmental Protection Agency in 1970. However, these standards only applied to water supplies that were provided by interstate carriers — for instance, planes and ships directly involved in interstate commerce — while states had had their own patchwork of regulations. Under the SDWA, public water supplies were defined as those involved in publically- or privately-owned water delivery, serving at least 15 connections or 25 customers on a yearly basis. The act gave the EPA the authority to issue specific drinking water regulations first to protect the health of those who use the supplies and second to protect the economic and/or aesthetic qualities of the water. Under these regulations, the EPA was given the authority to regulate any contaminants that might harm or affect the health of people, compounds which are used during water treatment that could become contaminants, and treatment options which were used by the states to make water fit and of good quality to drink. The act also allowed the EPA to grant waivers to states where specific water treatment programs that had been approved were already in place, and to allow these states to administer their own drinking water standards. [27]

A sidenote here: Congress made periodic inspections of how the SDWA was being worked out. In 1983, the EPA initiated a process to revise and update its drinking water regulations. Three years later, however, the Congress found that the EPA had not accomplished its mission under the original 1974 act, so it enacted SWDA amendments that year. These amendments required the EPA to lay out specific standards for nine specific contaminants within one year, for 40 more within two years, 34 more after three years, and, finally, 25 additional contaminants by 1991; at the same time, it would also have to issue new rules, within 18 months, for the injection of certain waste products below the surface of the ground that could inpact a water source.

After the passage of the SDWA in 1974, Congress enacted a series of additional protections for water usage prior to the 1986 amendments: these include the Toxic Substances Control Act of 1976 (Public Law 94-469) and the Clean Water Act of 1977 (Public Law 95-217). After the 1986 amendments, added to the roster of legislation were the Water Quality Act of 1987 (Public Law 100-4) and the Safe Drinking Water Act Amendments of 1996 (Public Law 104-182). [28]

Recent attempts to go beyond the strictures of the prior actions with regard to water quality have gone nowhere in Congress; the most recent legislative action was in 2009, when several members introduced the Clean Water Restoration Act of 2009. Its introduction was done in reaction to two recent U.S. Supreme Court decisions: *Solid Waste Agency of Northern Cook County v. United States Army Corps of Engineers (531 U.S. 159 {2001}) and Rapanos v. United States* (547 U.S. 715 {2006}). In the 2001 case, the court held that section 404(a) of the Clean Water Act (CWA), now codified at 33 CFR (Code of Federal Regulations) section 1362(7), which gives the US Army Corps of Engineers the right to issue permits allowing the discharge of dredged or fill materials into "navigable waters," was given beyond congressional authority to regulate intrastate waters, and struck down the regulations. In the second case, petitioner John A. Rapanos backfilled wetlands on a parcel of land he had purchased in Michigan; when the U.S. Army Corps of Engineers informed him that he needed a permit because the lands and wetlands were considered "waters of the United States," Rapanos sued, starting a legal challenge that lasted for some 12 years. Finally, in June 2006, the U.S. Supreme Court held 5-4 that the lands that Rapanos wanted to develop could not be considered "waters of the United States" and thus could not be considered to be under the rules of the U.S. Army Corps of Engineers. Writing for the majority, Justice Antonin Scalia explained, "'The waters of the United States' include only relatively permanent, standing or flowing bodies of water. The definition refers to water as found in 'streams,' 'oceans,' 'rivers,' 'lakes,' and 'bodies' of water 'forming geographical features.' All of these terms connote continuously present, fixed bodies of water, as opposed to ordinarily dry channels through which water occasionally or intermittently flows. Even the least substantial of the definition's terms, namely 'streams,' connotes a continuous flow of water in a permanent channel — especially when used in company with other terms such as 'rivers,' 'lakes,' and 'oceans.' None of these terms encompasses transitory puddles or ephemeral flows of water."

In 2009, Democrats in Congress sought to overturn the court in these two decisions by introducing the Clean Water Restoration Act. According to their own description, "[i]t would amend the Clean Water Act (CWA), to 'clarify the jurisdiction of the United States' and establish the CWA's application to U.S. waters, including interstate wetlands, tributaries, territorial seas, 'intrastate lakes, rivers, streams (including intermittent streams), mudflats, sandflats, wetlands, sloughs, prairie potholes, wet meadows, playa lakes, or natural ponds." Additionally, "[t]he measure amends the Federal Water Pollution Control Act in order to clarify the jurisdiction of the U.S. federal government in dealing with water pollution. To allow the jurisdiction to unambiguously extend to all waters in the U.S., it replaces the existing term 'navigable waters' with 'waters of the United States,' which means 'all waters subject to the ebb and flow of the tide, the territorial seas, and all interstate and intrastate waters and their tributaries, including lakes, rivers, streams (including intermittent streams), mudflats, sandflats, wetlands, sloughs, prairie potholes, wet meadows, playa lakes, natural ponds, and all impoundments of the foregoing, to the fullest extent that these waters, or activities affecting these waters." [29]

Despite growing support for their cause, and the ability of having majorities in both houses of Congress and the White House in Democrat hands, the bill failed to get out of committee in either house and eventually died.

Figure 14: The Clean Water Act: Water Quality in Assessed U.S. Rivers and Streams

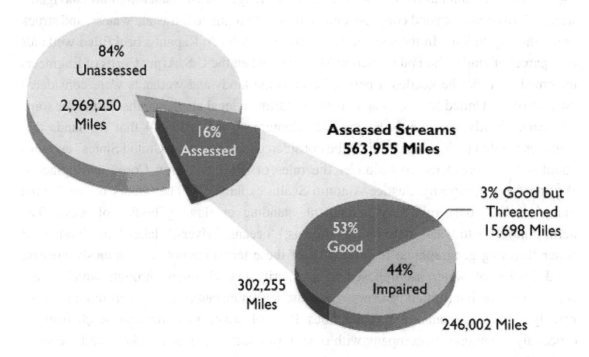

Source: "EPA — Water Quality in Assessed U.S. Rivers and Streams," courtesy of Environmental Protection Agency, online at http://www.intellectualtakeout.org/library/water/clean-water-act/chart-graph/epa-water-quality-assessed-us-rivers-and-streams.

THE POLICY DEBATE

Consistent threats of drought or the ruination of water tables have caused unending worry about the future of safe and easy-to-find water supplies in the United States and around the world. Currently, usage in the United States are rapidly stripping all available supplies of fresh drinking water in the country. According to the U.S. Geological Survey from 2005 (the last year that complete figures could be found as of this writing):

> Estimates of water use in the United States indicate that about 410 billion gallons per day (Bgal/d) were withdrawn in 2005...[t]his total is slightly less than the estimate for 2000, and about 5 percent less than total withdrawals in the peak year of 1980. Freshwater withdrawals in 2005 were 349 Bgal/d, or 85 percent of the total freshwater and saline-water withdrawals. Fresh groundwater withdrawals of 79.6 Bgal/day in 2005 were about 5 percent less than in 2000, and fresh surface-water withdrawals of 270 Bgal/day were about the same

as in 2000. Withdrawals for thermoelectric-power generation and irrigation, the two largest uses of water, have stabilized or decreased since 1980. Withdrawals for public-supply and domestic uses have increased steadily since estimates began. **[30]**

Figure 15: Total Withdrawals of Water in the United States by State, 2005

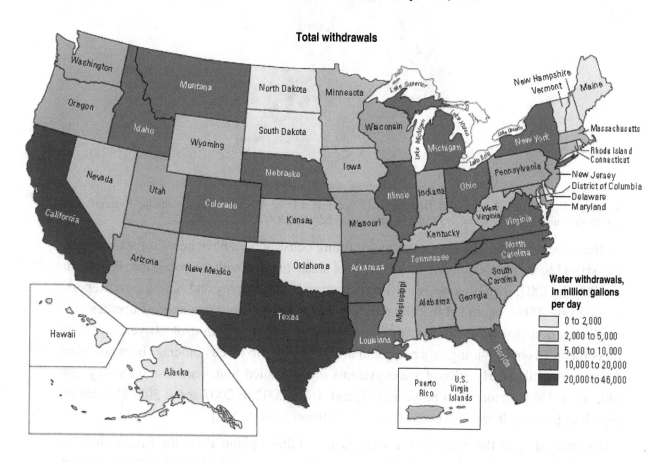

Source: Kenny, Joan F.; and Nancy L. Barber, Susan S. Hutson, Kristin S. Linsey, John K. Lovelace, and Molly A. Maupin, "Estimated Use of Water in the United States in 2005" (Washington, D.C.: U.S. Department of the Interior, U.S. Geological Survey, 2009), 33.

At this time, some 85% of the U.S. population receives its water from either a private or public source of water, with the remainder coming from domestic wells. Of the withdrawals of water, surface sources account for about 79% of that supply. In 2009, the period for these statistics, there were about 153,000 privately- and publicly-owned water systems that provide water for human use and consumption; and, of these, approximately 34%, or 52,000, are what are considered community water systems, or CWSs. In total, only 8% of CWSs provide water to 82% of the entire American population. On average, CWSs deliver an average of 119,000 gallons per year to each specific residential connection. **[31]**

Figure 16: Percentage of Water Withdrawals by Source

Percentage of Water
Withdrawals by Source[1]

Surface
(saline)
1 5%

Ground
(fresh)
20%

Surface
(fresh)
64%

Ground
(saline)
<1%

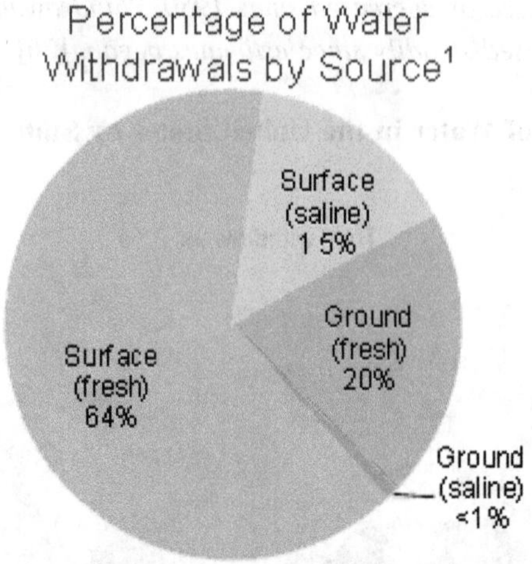

[1] 96% of saline withdrawals were for thermoelectric use.

Source: "U.S. Water Supply and Distribution," courtesy of the Center for Sustainable Systems, the University of Michigan, online at http://css.snre.umich.edu/css_doc/CSS05-17.pdf, 1.

At the same time, construction, or plans for future construction, have been impacted by the massive U.S. budget deficit and the inability of states to cope with the recession that began in 2008. In 2007, the Drinking Water Infrastructure Needs Survey and Assessment Report, released in 2009, concluded that the nation's water delivery systems needed updates and modernization that would cost some $334.8 billion over the period of 20 years, just to meet the needs of providing safe and clean drinking water to its customers. The report also found that while nearly 80% of water systems in the United States are less than 40 years old, some 4% are more than 80 years old, and, from 2002 to 2007 some 50,000 miles of pipe had been replaced at a cost of some $4 billion dollars. **[32]**

However, despite the water projects in place and those planned for the future, there is a growing gap between the supply of water and its usage, and addressing the increased needs of the American public and anticipated shortages in the near and distant future will be a major policy challenge in the states and in the nation as a whole.

The following graph (Figure 17) showcases this growing demand, showing the growth in water use from 1950 to 2000:

Figure 17: Trends in Water Use, 1950-2000

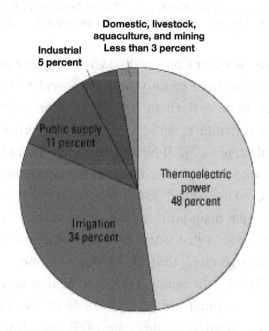

Source: "Trends in Water Use, 1950-2000," courtesy of nationalatlas.gov, online at http://www.nationalatlas.gov/articles/water/a_wateruse.html.

Figure 18: Estimated Use of Water in the United States in 2000

Further, here is a breakdown of the specific uses of water in the United States, by type:

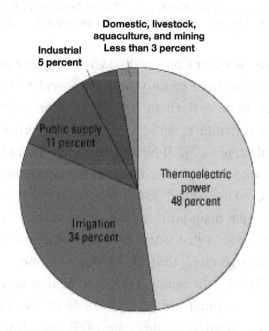

Source: "Estimated Use of Water in the United States in 2000," courtesy of the U.S. Geological Survey, 15 December 2005, online at http://pubs.usgs.gov/fs/2005/3051/.

In the western United States, agriculture accounts for the largest single use of water; the following graph shows the top 10 western states for usage, with their total use and irrigation water use:

Table 14: Water Availability for the Western States—Key Scientific Challenges

Total water use (per capita) for the top 10 States in the United States with total water use and irrigation water use.

[Data from Hutson and others, 2004]

State	Per capita total water withdrawals, in gallons per day	Total water use, in millions of gallons per day	Irrigation water use, in millions of gallons per day
Idaho	15,100	19,500	17,100
Wyoming	10,000	4,940	4,500
Montana	9,190	8,290	7,950
Nebraska	7,140	12,200	8,790
Arkansas	4,080	10,900	7,910
Colorado	2,930	12,600	11,400
West Virginia	2,840	5,150	0
Kansas	2,460	6,610	3,710
Louisiana	2,330	10,400	1,020
Alabama	2,240	9,990	43

Source: Anderson, Mark T., and Lloyd H. Woosley, Jr., "Water Availability for the Western States — Key Scientific Challenges" (Reston, Virginia: U.S. Department of the Interior, U.S. Geological Survey, 2005), 27.

According to the Agricultural Water Conservation Clearinghouse at Ft. Collins, Colorado, "These values vary somewhat from country to country and from the less developed to more developed countries. In general, about 70% of the water withdrawn from freshwater sources globally supports agriculture, while about 20% supports industrial activities and 10% is used for municipal supplies." [33] According to The Sierra Club, an environmental group, "Fifty percent of the nation's population, and 100 percent in virtually all rural areas, rely on groundwater for drinking water." [34] Specifically then, states the Massachusetts Institute of Technology, "[t]he main problem with groundwater in the Western Northern American Region of the world is that water is being withdrawn from aquifers at a rate much greater than the recharge rate." [35] This problem is more acute in Texas, where, according to the state of Texas, "the massive Ogallala aquifer accounts for 90 percent of the total water in all the Texas aquifers. In the mid-to-late 1980s 11 million acre-feet a year was being withdrawn from aquifers in the state of Texas. However, only 5.3 million acre-feet a year replenished the aquifers." **[36]** Despite the gloom and doom, predictions that by 2000 or 2010 that severe water shortages would plague specifically the western states proved to be wrong.

One issue of much controversy is that of water subsidies by the federal government and the states. Critics contend that these subsidies assist wealthy farms and so-called "agribusiness" corporations rather than the small family farms they were initially intended to help. An examination of federal reports on the issue of water subsidies unfortunately shows that a major study of the issue has not been done since 1994 — and 17+ years later, those figures are now woefully out-of-date. In 1994, Mark Kanazawa wrote, "Water pricing subsidies and restrictions on water transfers are integral features of federal water supply policies in the western United States. Critics claim that these features discourage efficient use of water. However, current analyses ignore an important feature of federal water supply contracts: entitlement ceilings. This paper analyzes the implications of entitlement ceilings for federal water policies and several proposals for policy reform, including eliminating transfer restrictions, reducing pricing subsidies, and imposing groundwater pump taxes. Analysts may overstate both the efficiency losses resulting from Bureau policies and the amount of water that would be freed up from agriculture if the proposed policy reforms were instituted." **[37]** Federal water subsidies, subsidies for the development of hydroelectric power, crop subsidies, constraints on the transfer of water rights, and other policies have distorted markets and resulted in inefficient allocation and use of scarce water. Recipients of water generated by reclamation projects in the West have rarely met the reimbursements schedules outlined in federal laws.

California provides an interesting case study of the impact of water subsidies and the role of agribusiness in California's water dilemma. For instance, in 2000, the last year as of this writing that figures are available, 22% of the nation's entire supply of irrigation water was used in California alone. Water in California is controlled by two major state water projects: The Central Valley Project (CVP), and the State Water Project (SWP). The first was established in 1933 under Franklin D. Roosevelt's New Deal economic program; the second was created by California Governor Pat Brown in 1960. According to the California Department of Water Resources, "Today the Central Valley Project, operated by the U.S. Bureau of Reclamation, is one of the world's largest water storage and transport systems. Its 22 reservoirs have a combined storage of 11 million acre-feet, of which 7 million acre-feet is delivered in an average year. In comparison, the SWP's 20 major reservoirs can hold 5.8 million acre-feet, with annual deliveries averaging up to 3 million acre-feet." **[38]** The State Water Project, as that agency states, "is a water storage and delivery system of reservoirs, aqueducts, powerplants and pumping plants. Its main purpose is to store water and distribute it to 29 urban and agricultural water suppliers in Northern California, the San Francisco Bay Area, the San Joaquin Valley, the Central Coast, and Southern California. Of the contracted water supply, 70 percent goes to urban users and 30 percent goes to agricultural users. The Project makes deliveries to two-thirds of California's population. It is maintained and operated by the California Department of Water Resources." [39] Although the goal was to create new farms and, by extension, new jobs, prices for water continue to rise while the output from these farms continues to go down or to stagnate. At the same time, the cost of producing these crops continues to go up, while the cost of the water goes up. In 2008, a report by the Pacific Institute noted, "California produces a diverse array of agricultural commodities that can be grouped into four major crop types: field crops (including hay and pastureland); vegetables; orchards; and vineyards. There is significant variation among each in terms of resource use and economic value. Field crops, for example, currently account for 56% of total irrigated acreage. Field crops use 63% of the applied water but generate only 17% of California's crop revenue. Vegetables, however, produce substantially more revenue per unit of land water: vegetables account for only 16% of the irrigated acreage but use 10% of the applied water and generate 39% of California's crop revenue." [40] But California is not the state with the largest amount of irrigated land for crops: that honor belongs to Nebraska. According to one group, "As of 2007, Nebraska had the most irrigated land at 8.5 million acres. California was second at just over 8 million acres. Texas was third at 5 million acres, followed by Arkansas at 4.4 million. Idaho and Colorado have approximately 3 million each. The only states within the southeast with over a million acres in irrigation are Florida with about 2.2 million and Georgia with about 1.2 million acres. Utah has over 1.3 million acres in irrigation and the states of South Dakota, Michigan, North Carolina and Hawaii have over 100 thousand acres in irrigation but less than half a million." [41]

A 1997 Government Accounting Office (now the Government Accountability Office) report looked at the costs associated with federal irrigation projects, especially in the American West, and how the Bureau of Reclamation, the main U.S. government agency overseeing such projects, was in charge of their overall costs and cost overruns. "Since 1902, the federal government has helped finance and build water projects, mainly to reclaim arid land in the West. Initially, those projects were often small and built almost solely to provide irrigation. Over the years, however, new projects have grown more ambitious and today they provide a host of benefits in addition to irrigation, including municipal and industrial water supply, hydroelectric power, recreation, and flood control. The Bureau of Reclamation and the U.S. Army Corps of Engineers build most federal water projects. Although the Corps operates nationwide, the Bureau's activities are limited to 17 western states," the report noted. [42]

The system that has been set up for the allocation of water subsidized by the federal and/or state governments discourages water conservation; users continue to withdraw the amount allocated to them, even if they do not need it, and in most cases it goes to waste — if they do not use the amount given to them, their allotment will be reduced. If farmers or any form of agribusiness were to be given credit for selling or leasing their excess water, incentives for conservation would be increased. Instead, the water is just wasted. And in the midst of potential water shortages that may or may not occur in the future, such waste makes the entire situation worse than it could be.

Water Conservation

As is true in energy and other fields, conservation and the wise use of resources is the ultimate solution to water shortages no matter where they occur. The system of subsidies and tax rebates to farmers has exacerbated the water problem, although ending these is politically unfeasible in an age when every political group has its portions of the federal and state budgets that it refuses to touch. Investments in dams and other sources to produce cheap energy, starting with the Tennessee Valley Authority (TVA) in the 1930s, have caused drought and disruptions to fish stocks in the specific water streams.

Conservation, however, is not enough. But attempts by the federal government to establish funding mechanisms to clean up underground water storage tanks that leak, funded through a tax on certain fuels, raised less money than what was needed and in the end did not accomplish what it was aimed to do. Further, mandates from Congress for tighter and tighter standards for water cleanliness by the Environmental Protection Agency, despite being considered far lower than is humanly possible, have an additional cost — estimates are that under these mandates, local municipalities will spend upwards of $500 billion to comply with these standards, and that estimate was before the Obama administration came into office in 2009. Bryan Flowers wrote, in 2004,

> There are many advanced techniques and devices to help conserve water, such as greywater reuse, rainwater collection, water-conserving landscaping and irrigation practices, the installation of low-flow fixtures and appliances, and proper swimming pool maintenance. Water users can also conserve water through some common-sense strategies in the home. These are known as "Wise Water Use" methods and include taking shorter showers, taking baths instead of showers, running only full loads of laundry and dishes, and being prompt in repairing leaky plumbing. Methods undertaken by the water supplier often include the aforementioned water use restrictions, vigilant water metering, and increased awareness of water distribution system maintenance needs. [43]

At the same time, much of the water consumed specifically in the western United States comes from the Bureau of Reclamation. Marcia Weinberg, writing in 1987, explained that "[t]he Bureau of Reclamation is the largest supplier of irrigation water in the United States. Over 150,000 farms in the 17 western states received water from the bureau annually. Its water irrigates roughly 10 million acres — about half of all cropland irrigated by surface water in the West." [44] Bureau water is provided at greatly subsidized prices, as beneficiaries usually reimburse the government for only a fraction of the total costs of constructing the reclamation facilities. As a result, much of the water is used for relatively low-value crops, such as alfalfa for cattle grazing, while high-value crop farmers cannot find sufficient water. Worse yet, some Bureau of Reclamation water subsidies are used to grow crops that the Agriculture Department pays farmers in the East not to grow. In most places, water supplied by federal projects is sold at only a small fraction of its real cost. In a time when the federal government is running historic deficits that are threatening to destabilize the entire American economy in the future, the elimination of such subsidies and programs does more than just make sense. Alas, as stated previously, too many hands feeding at the trough of federal payments make any attempt to end these programs fail.

Water Quality

Water pollution comes in a variety of forms — and, most importantly, it impacts all forms of life across the entire environmental spectrum. The National Institutes of Health, quoting the Environmental Protection Agency, noted, "Many different pollutants can harm our rivers, streams, lakes and oceans. The three most common are soil, nutrients and bacteria. Rain washes soil into streams and rivers. The soil can kill tiny animals and fish eggs. It can clog the gills of fish and block light so plants die. Nutrients, often from fertilizers, cause problems in lakes, ponds and reservoirs. Nitrogen and phosphorus make algae grow and can turn water green. Bacteria, often from sewage spills, can pollute fresh or salt water." [45] The U.S. Geological Survey Office of Water Quality (USGSOWQ) has as its specific mission to "collect, analyze, and interpret water-quality data; engage in field and laboratory research and methods development; [and] work with local, State, and Federal agencies and the citizenry to identify and understand environmental issues and concerns." [46] As far as human beings are concerned, bacteria and viruses in drinking and other water comes from human and animal wastes; a May 2002 report by the Government Accounting Office (now the Government Accountability Office) stated that a majority of states at that time reported finding MTBE, or methyl tertiary butyl ether, in groundwater, after it had leached from underground storage tanks of fuel and gasoline. [47] Additional contaminants in drinking and other water include organic materials that have decomposed and threaten both human, animal, and plant life, inorganic plant materials such as nitrates and phosphates, acids, salts, and toxic metals that cause the growth of algae that cuts off the supply of oxygen to water supplies. Additional substances such as oil, pesticide runoff, detergents, and plastics (in solid or liquid form) all add to the materials that cause water to become polluted. Their use, most notably by humans, cause a variety of diseases, including cancer.

Table 15: Pollutants Commonly Found in Stormwater and Their Forms

Pollutant Category	Specific Measures
Solids	Settleable solids Total suspended solids (TSS) Turbidity (NTU)
Oxygen-demanding material	Biochemical oxygen demand (BOD) Chemical oxygen demand (COD) Organic matter (OM) Total organic carbon (TOC)
Phosphorus (P)	Total phosphorus (TP) Soluble reactive phosphorus (SRP) Biologically available phosphorus (BAP)
Nitrogen (N)	Total nitrogen (TN) Total Kjeldahl nitrogen (TKN) Nitrate+nitrite-nitrogen (N03+N02-N) Ammonia-nitrogen (NH3-N)
Metals	Copper (Cu), lead (Pb), zinc (Zn), cadmium (Cd), arsenic (As), nickel (Ni), chromium (Cr), mercury (Hg), selenium (Se), silver (Ag)
Pathogens	Fecal coliform bacteria (FC) Enterococcus bacteria (EC) Total coliform bacteria (TC) Viruses
Petroleum hydrocarbons	Oil and grease (OG) Total petroleum hydrocarbons (TPH)
Synthetic organics	Polynuclear aromatic hydrocarbons (PAH) Pesticides and herbicides Polychlorobiphenals (PCB)

As explained by Table 15, many pollutants enter the environment through storm water. Further, pollution enters the environment through specific, or point, sources, such as pipes, ditches, and sewers connected to plants and other facilities, abandoned mines, and the transportation of oil. So-called nonpoint sources, those sources of pollution not traced to one specific site but to an overall slice of the environment (i.e., agricultural sources), include sediment, inorganic fertilizer, manure, and dissolved salts. These nonpoint sources account for some 64% of all pollutants in streams and other similar bodies of water; they account for 57% of the pollution entering lakes. As a total, pollutants in storm water accounts for some 33% of contamination in lakes and estuaries.

One of the pollutants that enters the water table, be it above ground or underground, is pesticides. The Federal Insecticide, Fungicide, and Rodenticide Act (FIFRA) (Public Law 75-717) governs how the EPA oversees pesticide use in the United States — and, by extension, what happens when such pesticides enter the environment, particularly the water system. A 2007 CRS report stated,

FIFRA is a regulatory statute governing the licensing, distribution, sale, and use of pesticides, including insecticides, fungicides, rodenticides, and other designated classes of chemicals. Its objective is to protect human health and the environment from unreasonable adverse effects of pesticides. To that end, it establishes a nationally uniform pesticide labeling system requiring the registration of all pesticides and herbicides sold in the United States, and requiring users to comply with conditions of use included on the national label. A FIFRA label encompasses the terms on which a chemical is registered, and its requirements become part of FIFRA's regulatory scheme. In registering the chemical, EPA makes a finding that the chemical "when used in accordance with widespread and commonly recognized practice...will not generally cause unreasonable adverse effects on the environment." [48]

Another point of pollutants is animal waste, usually from animals farms; under the Clean Water Act, there are regulations on such large facilities known as confined animal feeding operations (CAFOs). A 2000 CRS report explained that CAFOs

are specifically defined in the CWA as "point sources" rather than "nonpoint sources." CAFOs are treated in a similar manner to other industrial sources of pollution, such as factories and municipal sewage treatment plants, and are subject to the Act's prohibition against discharging pollutants into waters of the United States without a permit. In 1974 and 1976, EPA issued regulations defining the term CAFO for purposes of permit requirements (40 CFR §122.23) and effluent limitation guidelines specifying limits on pollutant discharges from feedlots (40 CFR Part 412). Discharge permits, issued by EPA or qualified states (43 states have been delegated this responsibility), implement the Part 412 requirements for individual facilities. [49]

Other pollutants have come under either congressional and/or Environmental Protection Agency scrutiny.

Regulating water pollution has had mixed results. Nonpoint sources of pollution have been very difficult to identify and regulate. Flowing streams can recover naturally from limited levels of some forms of pollution, and depending on the levels of pollution and the size, flow, temperature, and pH level, regulation may not be needed in a few cases. Federal funding of wastewater facilities in the United States has stabilized water quality, although no examinations of their overall effect have been done. Some highly polluted rivers, such as Ohio's Cuyahoga, have been cleaned up. But there continues to be a pattern of water quality issues across the nation that government seems unable to clean up, leaving the issue to state and local officials to deal with.

Lake — and other large water body — pollution is more difficult to address in some ways, because the stratified layers of most lakes, the lack of dilution of pollutants from water movement, and the lack of replenishment of oxygen from water flow cause pollutants to remain in lakes much longer than in rivers. Some lakes undergo eutrophication, which the U.S. Geological Survey defines as "[t]he process by which a body of water acquires a high concentration of nutrients, especially phosphates and nitrates. These typically promote excessive growth of algae. As the algae die and decompose, high levels of organic matter and the decomposing organisms deplete the water of available oxygen, causing the death of other organisms, such as fish. Eutrophication is a natural, slow-aging process for a water body, but human activity greatly speeds up the process." **[50]** As nutrients accumulate from urban and agricultural runoff, oxygen levels in the water are reduced, and fish and other aquatic life are killed off. Lake pollution threatens drinking water supplies, fishing industries, recreational use, and other values. One Web site source estimated that "[a]utomobiles and coal-burning power plants are serious contributors to eutrophication, sometimes accounting for as much as 40 percent or 50 percent of the nitrogen in a body of water or coastal ocean area." **[51]**

A 2003 study on the eutrophication of the lakes in urban centers came to two conclusions: that there was no firm proof that these specific water masses suffered from a higher rate of eutrophication than any other water body, and, that uban centers by themselves did not cause specific water bodies to become eutropic. The study, by scientists Daniel E. Schindler, Danielle Smith, research scientist Jonathan Frodge, researcher Mark D. Scheuerell, and graduate student Jonathan W. Moore, stated,

> Whether lakes in urban centers or lakes along the urban fringe suffer more from eutrophication remains unanswered. Lakes in urban centers may be more eutrophic because they have higher densities of humans and associated human impacts...If so, then we would predict that lake eutrophication would be correlated with shoreline residential development. Alternatively, lakes along the urban fringe could be more eutrophic due to pollution from nonpoint sources such as septic systems or other sources that are not controlled by infrastructure or regulations..., which may not be directly proportional to local shoreline population levels....Patterns of eutrophication along urban-rural gradients have not been described in previous studies. Increased levels of eutrophication have been attributed to urbanization by some studies...However, there have been instances of human lakeshore development that did not lead to eutrophication...Other cases of eutrophication have been attributed to agricultural pollution..., which would be more likely to be an important factor along the urban-rural fringe. **[52]**

One of the chief threats to large bodies of water, particularly near urban centers or coastal areas, is that of untreated sewage and other untreated wastes being dumped directly into these waters. The history of how this problem came about is one more example of government trying to do one thing and having the complete opposite occur instead. In the 1970s, following the passage of the Clean Water Act, untold billions of dollars were spent by the U.S. government to construct a nationwide system of treatment plants for the raw sewage being up to that time dumped into the nation's waterways. When completed, some 16,000 treatment centers had been built, and cities removed sludge and other impurities from water. But, as historian Rose George wrote in 2009, "cleaning sewage more efficiently meant removing more dirt. In other words, the Clean Water Act increased the amount of sludge being produced, which was mostly dumped at sea. Farmers like sludge because it has nutrients, but the same nitrogen and phosphorous can feed and breed algae that suck out water's dissolved oxygen content, leaving it lifeless. Sewage can suffocate the sea. After too many toxic shellfish beds and algal blooms, Congress passed the...Ocean Dumping Ban Act. This gave industry four years to come up with an alternative to ocean dumping. "[53]

Under the Ocean Dumping Ban Act of 1988 (also known as ODBA) (Public Law 100-688), it became:

> *unlawful for any person to dump, or transport for the purpose of dumping, sewage sludge or industrial waste into ocean waters after December 31, 1991; [p]rohibits, after the 270th day after enactment, any person from dumping, or transporting for the purpose of dumping, sewage sludge or industrial waste into ocean waters unless the person: (1) enters into a compliance or enforcement agreement (which includes a plan negotiated by the dumper, the State, and EPA for terminating dumping as well as a schedule which EPA believes will result in the termination of the dumping), and (2) obtains a permit issued by EPA under authority of sec. 102 of the Marine Protection, Research, and Sanctuaries Act (MPRSA); [and] [p]rovides for the payment of special fees for dumping and any penalties incurred by a dumper to be deposited into certain funds for use in finding alternatives to ocean dumping.*
> **[54]**

According to one Web site, "Four federal agencies have responsibilities under the Ocean Dumping Act: EPA, the U.S. Army Corps of Engineers, the National Oceanic and Atmospheric Administration (NOAA), and the U.S. Coast Guard. EPA has primary authority for regulating ocean disposal of all substances except dredged spoils, which are under the authority of the Corps of Engineers. NOAA is responsible for long-range research on the effects of human-induced changes to the marine environment, while EPA is authorized to carry out research and demonstration activities related to phasing out sewage sludge and industrial waste dumping. The Coast Guard is charged with maintaining surveillance of ocean dumping." [55] According to a Congressional Research Service report on the 1988 legislation,

> *The Act authorizes EPA to assess civil penalties of not more than $50,000 for each violation of a permit or permit requirement, taking into account such factors as gravity of the violation, prior variations, and demonstrations of good faith; however, no penalty can be assessed until after notice and opportunity for a hearing. Criminal penalties (including seizure and forfeiture of vessels) for knowing violations of the Act also are authorized. In addition, the Act authorizes penalties for ocean dumping of medical wastes (civil penalties up to $125,000 for each violation and criminal penalties up to $250,000, 5 years in prison, or both). The Coast Guard is directed to conduct surveillance and other appropriate enforcement activities to prevent unlawful transportation of material for dumping, or unlawful dumping. Like many other federal environmental laws, the Ocean Dumping Act allows individuals to bring a citizen suit in U.S. district court against any person, including the United States, for violation of a permit or other prohibition, limitation, or criterion issued under title I of the Act.* **[56]**

The ODBA of 1988 is actually an amendment of The Marine Protection, Research and Sanctuaries Act (MPRSA) of 1972 (Public Law 92-532). It is not too hard to stress the importance of sewage treatment systems to the environmental health of a city or town or the people, animals, and plants that live in its atmosphere. Congressional Research Service historian Claudia Copeland, whose reports document the history of government intervention to mandate clean water laws and actions, wrote, "Properly designed, sized, and maintained combined sewers can be an acceptable part of a city's water pollution control infrastructure. However, combined sewer overflow (CSO) occurs when the capacity of the collection and treatment system is exceeded due to high volumes of rainwater or snowmelt, and the excess volume is diverted and discharged directly into receiving waters, bypassing the sewage treatment plants. Often the excess flow that contains raw sewage, industrial wastes, and stormwater is discharged untreated. Many combined sewer systems are found in coastal areas where recreational areas, fish habitat and shellfish beds may be contaminated by the discharges." [57]

Two additional areas of concern include groundwater contamination by pollution and the protection of wetlands from contamination. According to the Groundwater Foundation, "Fifty percent of the United States population depends on groundwater for daily drinking water." Additionally, groundwater accounts for some 20% of all of the water used, for various reasons, in the United States, with some 65% of that going for agriculture; incredibly, approximately 30% of this entire subset of water use comes from one source: the High Plains aquifer in the midwestern United States, starting in South Dakota and heading south until it reaches Texas. [58]

In 1996, the Environmental Protection Agency reported that "over 80 percent of the most serious hazardous waste sites in the U.S. have adversely impacted the quality of nearby groundwater (the water present underground in tiny spaces in rocks and soil). Just as the groundwater cleanup process is complex, so are the issues behind the methods and techniques EPA uses to determine the best approach for each site. This brochure explains some of the approaches EPA uses to clean up groundwater contamination and, most importantly, offers information on how citizens can help reduce and prevent groundwater contamination." [59] Superfund, the program established by the Congress in 1980 to clean up such contaminated sites, has overall been a horrendous failure and has led to massive spending by government instead of the companies that left the contamination in the first place. Thus, the fight to have clean groundwater without additional government appropriations goes on.

As mentioned, the second area of concern is the protection of wetlands from pollution and other contaminants. The Environmental Protection Agency reports that "[i]mproper development or excessive pollutant loads can damage wetlands. The degraded wetlands can no longer provide water quality benefits and become significant sources of NSP , or "nonpoint source pollution," which is diffuse sources, and is carried by rainfall or snow water melting and moving across and under the ground.

Excessive amounts of decaying wetlands vegetation, for example, can increase biochemical oxygen demand, making habitat unsuitable for fish and other aquatic life. Degraded wetlands also release stored nutrients and other chemicals into surface water and groundwater." [60]

However, even if there is pollution inserted into the wetlands, there appears to be good news. In 2009, scientists Robert H. Kadlec and Scott Wallace, in an update of their 1995 work on wetlands and pollution, wrote,

> Because wetlands have a higher rate of biological activity than most ecosystems, they can transform many of the common pollutants that occur in conventional wastewaters into harmless byproducts or essential nutrients that can be used for additional biological productivity. These transformations are accomplished by virtue of the wetland's land area, with its inherent natural environmental senergies of sun, wind, soil, plants, and animals. These pollutant transformations can be obtained for the relatively low clost of earthwork, piping, pumping, and a few structures. Wetlands are one of the least expensive treatment systems to operation and maintain. Because of the natural environmental energies at work in a wetland treatment system, minimal fossil fuel energy and chemicals are typically necessary to meet treatment obectives. [61]

So, we sum up the "fundamentals" of water: We cannot live without it, we must maintain its cleanliness in stocks that we utilize for all sorts of human, animal, and plant activity; and, at the same time, we are inundated with challenges to continuing human activity while maintaining clean water areas, such as large lakes and the oceans. A lengthy history of congressional and other legislation has aided in the maintainence of clean waters, but they can only go so far without additional solutions, such as the cooperation of industry and state and local officials. Drought is another problem that must be addressed, and, from recent government studies, the time for addressing this issue may be sooner rather than later. Yes, there are challenges, but there appears to be little incentive to allow private industry and private groups and even large agricultural farms to adhere to a free market standard that could open up areas of concern, while calling on government in its strict sense of oversight rather than as master. Whatever the answer, it must come in such a way that humans are not harmed by dirty water, and our environment is not fouled by the same substance. Water is too important to destroy. That is a conclusion that no one disputes.

NOTES:

[1] "Water Q&A: Water Use at Home," courtesy of the U.S. Geological Survey, online at http://ga.water.usgs.gov/edu/qahome.html.

[2] "Sandstone Aquifers," courtesy of the U.S. Geological Survey, online at http://water.usgs.gov/ogw/aquiferbasics/sandstone.html.

[3] "What are the trends in extent and condition of ground water and their effects on human health and the environment?" courtesy of the Environmental Protection Agency, online at http://cfpub.epa.gov/eroe/index.cfm?fuseaction=list.listBySubTopic&ch=47&s=201.

[4] "Water Withdrawals & Transfers," courtesy of the Environmental Protection Agency, online at http://www.epa.gov/caddis/ssr_urb_hyd3.html.

[5] Tiemann, Mary, "Safeguarding the Nation's Drinking Water: EPA and Congressional Actions," *CRS Report for Congress*, 30 January 2008, CRS-1.

[6] "Bureau of Reclamation," courtesy of Allgov.com, online at http://www.allgov.com/Agency/Bureau_of_Reclamation, and "U.S. Army Corps of Engineers," courtesy of Allgov.com, online at http://www.allgov.com/agency/US_Army_Corps_of_Engineers.

[7] Lane, Nic, "The Bureau of Reclamation's Aging Infrastructure," *CRS Report for Congress*, 30 April 2008, preface.

[8] Gorte, Russ, "Federal Sales of Natural Resources: Pricing and Allocation," *CRS Report for Congress* (98-980), 11 December 1998, CRS-6.

[9] Copeland, Claudia, et. al., "Federally Supported Water Supply and Wastewater Treatment Programs," *CRS Report for Congress*, 15 June 2009, Summary.

[10] "Name and Status Changes: U.S. Reclamation Service/Bureau of Reclamation Through 1945," in Rowley, William D., "The Bureau of Reclamation: Origins and Growth to 1945, Volume I" (Washington, D.C.: U.S. Department of the Interior, Bureau of Reclamation, 2006), 425.

[11] "Bureau of Reclamation," courtesy of Allgov.com, online at http://www.allgov.com/Agency/Bureau_of_Reclamation.

[12] Cody, Betsy A., "Western Water Resource Issues," *CRS Report for Congress*, 25 October 2002, CRS-2.

[13] Klyza, Christopher McGrory, "The United States Army, Natural Resources, and Political Development in the Nineteenth Century," *Polity*, XXXV:1 (Autumn 2002), 1-28.

[14] "The U.S. Army Corps of Engineers: A Brief History," courtesy of the U.S. Army Corps of Engineers, online at http://www.usace.army.mil/History/Documents/Brief/index.html. See also Walker, Paul K., "Engineers of Independence: A Documentary History of the Army Engineers in the American Revolution, 1775 1783" (Washington, D.C.: Historical Division, U.S. Army Corps of Engineers, 1981).

[15] "Military Engineering," courtesy of History.com, online at http://www.history.com/topics/military-engineering.

[16] Hutchins, Wells A., Harold H. Ellis and J. Peter DeBraal, "Water Rights Laws in the Nineteen Western States" (Washington, D.C.: U.S. Department of Agriculture; three volumes, 1971; reprint, Clark, New Jersey: The Lawbook Exchange, Ltd.; three volumes, 2004), I:108.

[17] "Of Time and the River: Federal Water Pollution Legislation," courtesy of Of Time and the River, online at http://www.oftimeandtheriver.org/resources/misc/fwpl.htm.

[18] "Rivers and Harbors Act of 1899," courtesy of the New Mexico Center for Wildlife Law, online at http://wildlifelaw.unm.edu/fedbook/rivers89.html.

[19] Text of the decision, in *United States v. Republic Steel Corp.* (362 US 482 {1959}), at 482.

[20] "Federal Water Pollution Control Act (Clean Water Act) of 1948," courtesy of Fedcenter.gov, online at http://www.fedcenter.gov/Bookmarks/index.cfm?id=2431.

[21] Language from the act, at the introduction, and, in a separate section, at Section 6.

[22] From "Records of the Federal Water Pollution Control Administration," online at http://www.archives.gov/research/guide-fed-records/groups/382.html.

[23] Antieau, Chester James, "Our Two Centuries of Law and Life, 1775-1975: The Work of the Supreme Court and the Impact of both Congress and Presidents" (Buffalo, New York: Fred B. Rothman Publications, of William S. Hein & Co., 2001), 188.

[24] Environmental Protection Agency, "EPA: History: Water," courtesy of the EPA, online at http://www.epa.gov/history/topics/fwpca/05.htm.

[25] Faure, Michael, Albert J. Verheij, and Tom vanden Borre, eds., "Shifts in Compensation for Environmental Damage" (New York: SpringerWein, 2007), 163.

[26] "Federal Water Pollution Control Act (Clean Water Act), courtesy of "The Digest of Federal Resource Laws of Interest to the U.S. Fish & Wildlife Service," courtesy of the Fish & Wildlife Service, online at http://www.fws.gov/laws/lawsdigest/fwatrpo.html.

[27] Tiemann, Mary, "Safe Drinking Water Act Amendments of 1996: Overview of P.L. 104-182," *CRS Report for Congress*, 8 February 1999.

[28] For in-depth examinations of these specific acts, see the following sources: Ingram, Colin, "The Drinking Water Book: A Complete Guide to Safe Drinking Water" (Berkeley, California: Ten Speed Press, 1991); Lewis, Scott A., "The Sierra Club Guide to Safe Drinking Water" (San Francisco, California: Sierra Club Books, 1996), and The National Research Council, "Setting Priorities for Drinking Water Contaminants" (Washington, DC: National Academy Press, 1999).

[29] "Overview: Clean Water Restoration Act of 2009," courtesy of Clean Water Action, online at http://www.cleanwateraction.org/mediakit/overview-clean-water-restoration-act-2009.

[30] "Estimated Use of Water in the United States in 2005," courtesy of the U.S. Geological Survey, online at http://pubs.usgs.gov/circ/1344/.

[31] All facts and figures in this section come from "U.S. Water Supply and Distribution," courtesy of the Center for Sustainable Systems, the University of Michigan, online at http://css.snre.umich.edu/css_doc/CSS05-17.pdf.

[32] Environmental Protection Agency, "Drinking Water Infrastructure Needs Survey and Assessment: Fourth Report to Congress" (Washington, D.C.: U.S. Department of the Interior, Environmental Protection Agency, Office of Water, 2009), 7, online at http://www.epa.gov/safewater/needssurvey/pdfs/2007/report_needssurvey_2007.pdf.

[33] "FAQs: Water Supply, Sources, & Agricultural Use," courtesy of the Agricultural Water Conservation Clearinghouse, online at http://agwaterconservation.colostate.edu/ FAQs_WATER%20SUPPLYSOURCESAGRICULTURALUSE.aspx.

[34] "Leaking Underground Storage Tanks: A Threat to Public Health & Environment," report of the Sierra Club, 2005, online at http://www.csu.edu/CERC/documents/LUSTThreattoPublicHealth.pdf.

[35] "Mission 2012: Clean Water," report of the Massachusetts Institute of Technology, online at http://web.mit.edu/12.000/www/m2012/finalwebsite/problem/groundwater.shtml.

[36] "Underground Water," at the Handbook of Texas Online, courtesy of the Texas State Historical Association, online at http://www.tshaonline.org/handbook/online/articles/gru01.

[37] Kanazawa, Mark T., "Water Subsidies, Water Transfers, and Economic Efficiency," *Contemporary Economic Policy*, XII:2 (1994), 112-22.

[38] "California State Water Project and the Central Valley Project," courtesy of the California Department of Water Resources, online at http://www.water.ca.gov/swp/cvp.cfm.

[39] "California State Water Project Overview" courtesy of the California Department of Water Resources, online at http://www.water.ca.gov/swp/index.cfm.

[40] Cooley, Heather; Juliet Christian-Smith, and Peter H. Gleick, "More with Less: Agricultural Water Conservation and Efficiency in California: A Special Focus on the Delta" (Oakland, California: The Pacific Institute, September 2008), 12.

[41] "FAQs: Water Supply, Sources, & Agricultural Use," courtesy of the Agricultural Water Conservation Clearinghouse, online at
http://agwaterconservation.colostate.edu/FAQs_WATER%20SUPPLYSOURCESAGRICULTURALUSE.aspx.

[42] U.S. General Accounting Office, "Bureau of Reclamation: Reclamation Law and the Allocation of Construction Costs for Federal Water Projects" (Washington, D.C.: Government Printing Office, 1997), 1.

[43] Flowers, Bryan, "Domestic Water Conservation: Greywater, Rainwater and Other Innovations," *Cambridge Discovery Guides*, February 2004, online at
http://www.csa.com/discoveryguides/water/overview.php.

[44] Weinberg, Marcia, "Water Use Conflicts in the West: Implications of Reforming the Bureau of Reclamation's Water Supply Policies" (Washington, D.C.: Congressional Budget Office, 1997), 11.

[45] "Water Pollution," courtesy of the National Institutes of Health, undated, online at
http://www.nlm.nih.gov/medlineplus/waterpollution.html.

[46] "USGS Water Quality," courtesy of the U.S. Geological Survey, online at
http://water.usgs.gov/owq/.

[47] See "Environmental Protection: MTBE Contamination From Underground Storage Tanks" (Washington, D.C.: U.S. General Accounting Office, 21 May 2002).

[48] Copeland, Claudia, "Pesticide Use and Water Quality: Are the Laws Complementary or in Conflict?" *CRS Report for Congress*, 14 June 2007, CRS-2.

[49] Copeland, Claudia, "Water Quality Initiatives and Agriculture," *CRS Report for Congress*, 20 December 2000, CRS-9.

[50] "Eutrophication," courtesy of the U.S. Geological Survey, 12 October 2010, online at
http://toxics.usgs.gov/definitions/eutrophication.html.

[51] "Ocean Issue Briefs," courtesy of SeaWeb, online at
http://www.seaweb.org/resources/briefings/nutrient.php.

[52] Moore, Jonathan W.; Daniel E. Schindler, Mark D. Scheuerell, Danielle Smith and Jonathan Frodge, "Lake Eutrophication at the Urban Fringe, Seattle Region, U.S. ," *Ambio*, XXXII:1 (February 2003), 13-18.

[53] George, Rose, "The Big Necessity: The Unmentionable World of Human Waste nd Why It Matters" (New York: Macmillan, 2009), unpaginated.

[54] "Ocean Dumping Ban Act of 1988," courtesy of the Environmental Protection Agency, 31 March 2011, online at http://www.epa.gov/history/topics/mprsa/02.htm.

[55] "Ocean Dumping Act, United States," *Encyclopedia of the Earth*, 22 December 2006, online at http://www.eoearth.org/article/Ocean_Dumping_Act,_United_States#gen5.

[56] Copeland, Claudia, "Ocean Dumping Act: A Summary of the Law," *CRS Report for Congress*, 22 January 1999, CRS-3.

[57] Copeland, Claudia, "Water Quality: Implemented the Clean Water Act," *CRS Report for Congress*, 12 December 2006, CRS-12-13.

[58] "Groundwater Contamination Concerns," courtesy of The Groundwater Foundation, online at http://www.groundwater.org/gi/contaminationconcerns.html.

[59] "Ground Water Cleanup at Superfund Sites," December 1996, online at http://www.epa.gov/superfund/health/conmedia/gwdocs/brochure.htm.

[60] "Managing Wetlands to Control Nonpoint Source Pollution," report by the Environmental Protection Agency, undated, online at http://water.epa.gov/polwaste/nps/outreach/point11.cfm.

[61] Kadlec, Robert H.; and Scott D. Wallace, "Treatment Wetlands" (Boca Raton, Florida: CRC Press, 2009), 4.

9

National Parks and Wilderness

THE POLICY FRAMEWORK

According to the National Park Service, "Frederick Law Olmsted (1822-1903) is recognized as the founder of American landscape architecture and the nation's foremost parkmaker. Olmsted moved his home to suburban Boston in 1883 and established the world's first full-scale professional office for the practice of landscape design. During the next century, his sons and successors perpetuated Olmsted's design ideals, philosophy, and influence." [1] He was instrumental in putting together the coalition and plans that formulated Central Park in the middle of New York City. *Garden and Forest Magazine* memorialized him upon his death in 1903, stating that because of his work "millions of people now unborn will find rest and refreshment in the contemplation of smiling landscapes which he has made." [2] His son, Frederick Law Olmsted, Jr., was a key member in the group which helped to found the National Park Service in 1916. That agency, according to its organic or organizing act, "was charged with promoting and regulating parks in ways that would conserve the scenery and the natural and historic objects and the wild life therein and to provide for the enjoyment of the same in such manner and by such means as will leave them unimpaired for the enjoyment of future generations." [3]

For generations, it has become the goal of the American people to preserve the wilderness and areas of natural beauty; how that would or could be done has been a matter of controversy and specification. A number of people, concerned over how certain areas would be protected, spoke out in an effort to move those in power to safeguard these places in the wilderness. One of these people was George Catlin, an artist whose images of Native Americans have become landmarks for their beauty and authenticity. Seeing not just the people but the land they lived on, he wrote that both needed to be safeguarded:

> And what a splendid contemplation too, when one (who has travelled these realms, and duly appreciate them) imagines them as they might in future be seen, (by some great protecting policy of government) preserved in their pristine beauty and wildness, in a magnificent park, where the world could see for ages to come, the native Indian in his classic attire, galloping his wild horse, with sinewy bow, and shield and lance, amid the fleeting herds of elks and buffaloes. What a beautiful and thrilling specimen for America to preserve and hold up to the view of her refined citizens and the world, in future ages! A nation's Park, containing man and beast, in all the wild and freshness of their nature's beauty!
> I would ask no other monument to my memory, nor any other enrolment of my name amongst the famous dead, than the reputation of having been the founder of such an institution.
> Such scenes might easily have been preserved, and still could be cherished on the great plains of the West, without detriment to the country or its border; for the tracts of country on which the buffaloes have assembled, are uniformly sterile, and of no available use to cultivating man. [4]

But Catlin's proposal, coming in the 1830s, when "Manifest Destiny," the unofficial plan of the U.S. government to move as far west as the continent would allow, was impractical at best and impossible at worst. Additional people, such as Henry David Thoreau, called for a national policy for the protections of certain lands, but these calls, too, were ignored.

William Cullen Bryant, the famed editor of the *New York Evening Post*, came up with the idea of a national park, but rather of localized parks. He published such a proposal in his paper on 3 July 1844, but the idea was shelved for several years until a viable plan could be found. In 1851, land in central New York City was purchased, and the layout of a large municipal park was drawn up by famed architect Frederick Law Olmsted. Olmsted had just returned from Europe, where he had made a thorough investigation of public parks large and small there. Although Olmsted was integral in aiding in the architecture and ultimate construction of what would become New York's Central Park, in 1863 he was removed, for various political reasons, as the superintendent of the park project. Instead, he was invited out West by General John Charles Frémont to manage Frémont's Mariposa estate. Once in California, Olmsted was able to see for the first time the area that would become Yellowstone National Park. But, in 1863, Yellowstone was merely an unprotected wilderness. It would take years, and lobbying by many dedicated individuals, to realize the goal of making it a national park.

But it was Olmsted's work to bring recognition to what is known as the Yosemite Valley, which was the driving force that changed the movement to designate national parks.

Although Olmsted's manifesto calling for the protection of Yosemite was suppressed for political reasons, a bill doing just that was introduced in the U.S. Senate by Senator John Conness, Republican of California, which culminated in the passage on 30 June 1864 by Congress of "an Act authorizing a grant to the State of California of the 'Yo-Semite Valley' [sic] and of the land embracing the Mariposa Big Tree Grove." [5] Yosemite had first been viewed by white men in March 1851; four years later, James Mason Hutchings led the first group of tourists to what is known as that park's Inspiration Point. But it was not until 1869, when a then little-known Scottish traveler named John Muir first arrived in Yosemite to work for Hutchings and construct a saw-mill. In the years to come, Muir would become Yosemite's greatest champion.

The key moment in the history of national parks came on 1 March 1872, when President Ulysses S Grant signed into law the act that created, in the northwestern corner of what was then the Wyoming Territory, into Yellowstone National Park, the nation's first. Yellowstone was not just a park — after all, by itself it is larger than the entire land mass of the states of Rhode Island and Delaware combined — but was the first true set-aside of land to be protected forever from sale or development.

Fourteen years after Yellowstone was designated as a national park, the U.S. Army was dispatched there, and assigned to the park specifically to protect it. This came after a hotel inside the park went bankrupt; the corporation that handled the affairs of the park was reorganized as the Yellowstone Park Association. In 1892, President Benjamin Harrison established the Casa Grande Ruins as a national park in Arizona. But the focus remained on the western United States in general, and Yellowstone in particular. Western railroad companies advertised the park as part of their attractions to urge easterners to head west to see the natural beauty of the region. The belief that additional areas needed protecting spurred Congress to set aside the Sequoia and General Grant National Parks in California.

However, the need for a central government authority became clearer in the years to come. In 1906, President Theodore Roosevelt signed into law the Antiquities Act (Public Law 59-209, 34 Stat. 225), the first specific act of Congress to protect archaelogical and other natural resources. Historians Sherry Hutt, Caroline M. Blanco, and Ole Varmer wrote, "In the late nineteenth century, with the cessation of wars between the United States and the Indian tribes, and the opening of vast territories through the expansion of the railroads, pristine archaelogical sites in the West became accessible to vandals, commercial looters, and anyone with a curiosity about the past. As a result, the public felt that its heritage was in danger of being lost, and agitated for Congressional action to address this issue. Finally, on 8 June 1906, the Antiquities Act was enacted." [6] Most importantly, the legislation authorized presidents to enunciate their belief in setting aside these places as federal lands and offer them the protection as natural and historic monuments. Roosevelt, an ardent outdoorsman, became the first President, whether in office or out, to actually visit these parks; one photograph shows him standing with John Muir during a trip to Yosemite in 1903. It was during this trip that Muir convinced Roosevelt to preserve Yosemite.

Speaking at the Grand Canyon in Arizona that same year, Roosevelt said, "I hope you will not have a building of any kind, not a summer cottage, a hotel, or anything else, to mar the wonderful grandeur, sublimity, the great loneliness and beauty of the cañon," using the Spanish word for canyon. Using Muir's push to preserve these areas of unspeakable beauty, Roosevelt took full advantage of the Antiquities Act, creating with the use of a men 18 total national parks and national monuments, including Devil's Tower in Wyoming (seen with great effect in the 1977 film, *Close Encounters of the Third Kind)*, Montezuma Castle in Arizona, the Muir Woods and the Yosemite Valley in California, and the Gila (pronounced "hee-la") Cliff Dwelling in New Mexico. When Roosevelt left office in March 1909, he had effectively doubled the acreage of all of the national parks during his $7\frac{1}{2}$ years in office.

By 1915, the U.S. government decided that a central federal agency was needed to oversee the administration and protection of all of the national parks and monuments. Using the blueprint drawn up by conservationist Stephen Tyng Mather, a descendant of some of America's earliest settlers (including Cotton Mather), in 1916 the U.S. Congress enacted the National Park Service Organic Act, establishing the National Park Service as the official agency to oversee the running of the-then 36 national parks branching out across the nation. Three years later, the eastern United States saw the establishment of its first national park, Lafayette (later renamed Acadia) National Park in Maine. In 1926, Congress established the Great Smoky Mountains National Park in Tennessee and North Carolina. As the National Park Service states, this park, which contains over 800 miles of hiking trails, "is renowned for its diversity of plant and animal life, the beauty of its ancient mountains, and the quality of its remnants of Southern Appalachian mountain culture." Great Smoky Mountains National Park is the most visited national park in the United States. [7]

Most lands protected within the National Park System (NPS) are designated through an act of Congress. These laws may provide detailed management mandates or may give the NPS broad discretion under the National Park Service Act enacted in 1916. Other designations are made by the president. The designation of preserved lands has not been consistent, primarily because they have been designated by different authorities and during different periods of time. National parks are the flagship of the system. A national park is generally defined as "a large, spectacular natural place having a wide variety of attributes, at times including significant historic assets." Hunting and consumptive activities are not permitted in parks; Congress has created a new classification, national preserves, in order to permit hunting and other activities in areas that have the characteristics of parks. National preserves include areas where hunting, oil and gas exploration, and other activities prohibited in national parks are allowed, although with strict rules governing them. As of this writing in mid-2011, there are 18 national preserves across the entire United States, 10 of which are located in Alaska alone.

Figure 19: Listing of National Preserves in the National Park Service System

---

Aniakchak National Monument and Preserve
Location: The Aleutian Mountains, Alaska
Size: 137,176 acres (monument) and 465,603 acres (preserve)

Bering Land Bridge National Preserve
Location: On the Seward Peninsula, Alaska
Size: 2.7 million acres

Big Cypress National Preserve
Location: Southern Florida, across Collier, Monroe, and Miami-Dade Counties
Size: 720,566 acres

Big Thicket National Preserve
Location: It comprises 9 land units and 6 water corridors in eastern Texas.
Size: 97,168 acres

Craters of the Moon National Monument and Preserve
Location: South-cental Idaho.
Size: 410,000 acres (park) and 304,727 acres (preserve)

Denali National Park and Preserve
Location: Around the Toklat River in Alaska, it includes the 20,320-foot Mount McKinley, the highest mountain in North America.
Size: 6,075,107 acres

Gates of the Arctic National Park and Preserve
Location: Along the Brooks Range in Alaska, near the Arctic Circle.
Size: 8,472,506 acres

Glacier Bay National Park and Preserve
Location: West of the Alaskan capital, Juneau, in southeastern Alaska, it inclues Mount Fairweather, the highest peak in southeast Alaska.
Size: 3,224,840 acres

Great Sand Dunes National Park and Preserve
Location: Northeast of Alamosa, Colorado, in the Sangre de Cristo Mountains. A new added section, known as "The Baca," was purchased in 2004 and added to the preserve.
Size: 107,452 acres (park) and 41,686 acres (preserve).

Katmai National Park and Preserve
Location: On the Alaskan peninsula across from Kodiak Island.
Size: 3,674,530 acres (national park), 418,699 acres (national preserve)

Lake Clark National Park and Preserve
Location: Located on the Cook Inlet southwest of Anchorage and east of Crescent Lake in southern Alaska; it has two active volcanoes, Iliamna and Redoubt.
Size: 4,030,025 acres

Little River Canyon National Preserve
Location: The Little River Canyon region of northeastern Alabama.
Size: 13,633 acres

Mojave National Preserve
Location: This preserve encompasses the entire Mojave region of California. It was established by Congress on 31 October 1994 by passage of the California Desert Protection Act.
Size: 1,534,819 acres

Noatak National Preserve
Location: Northeastern Alaska, in the Brooks Range, covering the area of the Noatak River.
Size: 6,569,904 acres

Tallgrass Prairie National Preserve
Location: Northeast of Wichita, Kansas, this preserve protects the rare tallgrass prairie ecosystem in the central United States, of which 400,000 square miles once existed.
Size: 10,894 acres

Timucuan Ecological and Historical Preserve
Location: Just east of Jacksonville, Florida, this preserve protects the estuaries of Florida's Saint Johns and Nassau Rivers.
Size: 46,287 acres

Wrangell-St. Elias National Park and Preserve
Location: The largest preserve in the National Park Service system, this park and preserve in southeastern Alaska is where the Chugach, Wrangell, and St. Elias mountain ranges come together, and includes Mount St. Elias as well as a series of rare glaciers.
Size: 8,323,148 acres (park) and 4,852,753 acres (preserve)

Yukon-Charley Rivers National Preserve
Location: Located along the Canadian border in east-central Alaska, the preserve embraces only 115 miles of the 1,800 mile-long Yukon River but also takes in the entire Charley River basin.
Size: 2,525,512 acres

Source: National Preserves, information courtesy of the National Park Service.

Another category of places to be protected under the aegis of the National Park Service are National Historic Sites (NHSs) or National Historic Landmarks (NHLs). According to the National Park Service,

> *National Historic Landmarks are nationally significant historic places designated by the Secretary of the Interior because they possess exceptional value or quality in illustrating or interpreting the heritage of the United States. Today, fewer than 2,500 historic places bear this national distinction. Working with citizens throughout the nation, the National Historic Landmarks Program draws upon the expertise of National Park Service staff who work to nominate new landmarks and provide assistance to existing landmarks. National Historic Landmarks are exceptional places. They form a common bond between all Americans. While there are many historic places across the nation, only a small number have meaning to all Americans — these we call our National Historic Landmarks.* **[8]**

The National Park Service also protects National Battlefields; in 1890, the Chickamauga and Chattanooga National Military Park was established, but in 1958 the National Park Service recommended that all battlefield designations be cited as National Battlefields, but the original names for some of the fields remain as they were first designated. As of 2011, there are 11 National Battlefields in the National Park System, including Gettysburg in Pennsylvania and Andersonville in Georgia.

Another designation are National Recreation Areas, or NRAs, which, according to the National Park Service, preserve recreation areas centered around reservoirs or near urban centers. The first National Recreation Area was the Boulder Dam Recreation Area, established in 1936 and later renamed the Lake Mead National Recreation Area.

Another designation is a National Lakeshore; these were first established in 1953, when a National Seashore (the designation has since been changed to Lakeshore) was created at Cape Hatteras in North Carolina. The first official area designated as a National Lakeshore was the Indiana Dune National Lakeshore in 1966; the last, in 1975, was Canaveral, into north-central Florida. All such areas with this designation must be established not by a President but only through an act of Congress. As of 2011, there are 10 protected areas with this specific designation, all managed by the National Park Service.

In addition to these designations, there are National Rivers, first begun in 1964 with the Ozark National Scenic Riverways in Missouri, and National Parkways, started with the George Washington Memorial Parkway, mostly in Virginia with a small section in Washington, D.C., which was established in 1930.

Finally, the last designated protected area covered by the National Park Service are National Scenic Trails. The first, the 2,100-mile long Appalachian National Trail, was created after passage of the National Trails System Act of 1968 (Public Law 90-543). This trail extends from Maine in the north to Georgia in the south. As of 2011, there are 11 separate trails in the National Scenic Trail system.

In all of these cases, the specific legislation that allows either the President, or Congress, or some other entity, to establish a protected area gives the authority great discretion in making and implementing policy, but only when it comes to allowing for the limited use of natural resources (oil, water, etc.) or the usage of the specific areas for tourism or other activities. But when it comes to areas that are set aside for total protection, it is then that the agency handling the implementation of the policy, namely the National Park Service, has very little wiggle room in which to change the mandate under which the protected area was set aside. Even when the National Park Service is not the agency in control of the area, again there is very little discretion allowed as to how far the agency can go to open the protected lands. The Bureau of Land Management (BLM), located in the Department of the Interior, manages, as of 2008, between 253 million and 258 surface acres [9] of public land, most in 12 western states including Alaska. Additionally, according to the agency's own Web site, it controls another 700 million acres [10] of below-ground mineral stocks which can be found throughout the entire United States. All of these acres are managed through a series of laws, most notably — and most comprehensively — is the Federal Land Policy and Management Act (FLPMA). [11] In addition, while the National Park Service manages the wilderness areas across the United States, the Bureau of Land Management controls the subsurface minerals. In 2009, Congress enacted the Omnibus Public Land Management Act (Public Law 111-11), which designated an additional 900,000 acres of wilderness areas in eight states, adjusting and increasing their boundaries.

Figure 20: National Wilderness Areas Changed by The Omnibus Public Land Management Act of 2009

Wild Monongahela Wilderness, West Virginia

Mt. Hood Wilderness, Oregon

Copper Salmon Wilderness, Oregon

Cascade-Siskiyou National Monument, Oregon

Owyhee Public Land Management, Owyhee County, Idaho

Sabinoso Wilderness, New Mexico

Pictured Rocks National Lakeshore Wilderness

Oregon Badlands Wilderness, Deschutes and Crook Counties, Oregon

Spring Basin Wilderness, Oregon

Eastern Sierra and Northern San Gabriel Wilderness, California

Riverside County Wilderness, California

Sequoia and Kings Canyon National Parks Wilderness, California

Rocky Mountain National Park Wilderness, Colorado

Washington County, Utah [*]

[*] Includes the Beaver Dam Wash National Conservation Area, the Canaan Mountain Wilderness, the Northeastern Washington County Wilderness, the Northwestern County Wilderness, and the Red Cliffs National Conservation Area.

Source: "Text of The Omnibus Public Land Management Act of 2009," courtesy of Thomas, the legislative arm of the Library of Congress, Washington, D.C., online at http://thomas.loc.gov/cgi-bin/bdquery/z?d111:H.R.146.

All of these lands managed by the Bureau of Land Management are under the aegis of the National Landscape Conservation System. In the 2012 budget request for the U.S. Department of the Interior, it was said of this system,

> *Some of the most ecologically pristine and biophysically significant landscapes managed by BLM are those in its National Landscape Conservation System (NLCS). The mission of the NLCS is to conserve, protect, and restore nationally significant landscapes recognized for their outstanding cultural, ecological, and scientific values. The NLCS, which totals over 27 million acres, is comprised of specific geographic areas of BLM-administered public lands designated by Acts of Congress or Presidential proclamations to be specially managed on a landscape level to enhance their conservation value while allowing for appropriate multiple uses. Units of the NLCS include red-rock deserts, rugged ocean coastlines, deep river canyons, and broad Alaskan tundra. Many serve as outdoor scientific laboratories where significant cultural and paleontological discoveries are commonly made, yet are just minutes from major metropolitan areas. The NLCS areas include 37 National Monuments and National Conservation Areas and similar designations, 223 Wilderness Areas, 545 Wilderness Study Areas, 69 Wild and Scenic Rivers (totaling 2,416 miles), and 16 National Scenic and Historic Trails (totaling over 6,000 miles).* **[12]**

Four federal agencies manage lands under the Wilderness Act of 1964, the landmark act through which wilderness areas, as well as the entire National Wilderness Preservation System, is set up. These agencies also control separate blocks of land: for instance, the National Park Service controls 44 million wilderness acres, the U.S. Forest Service controls 36 million wilderness acres, the U.S. Fish & Wildlife Service manages 21 million wilderness acres, and, finally, the Bureau of Land Management manages only 9 million wilderness acres. While the Wilderness Act, when enacted in 1964, began with just 9 million total acres in its initial creation of 54 wilderness areas in 13 states, in 2009 that number was at 109.5 million acres throughout the entire wilderness system, in 757 areas in 44 states and Puerto Rico. The congressional enactment of the Alaska National Interest Lands Conservation Act (ANILCA) (Public Law 96-487) added more than 56 million acres of wilderness, all in the nation's 49th state, to the wilderness system.

THE POLICY DEBATE

A History of Wilderness Legislation in the U.S. Congress

The designation of Yosemite and Yellowstone was not the end of such designations; instead, it was merely the beginning. In 1911, Congress enacted the Weeks Act (36 Stat. 961), to "examine, locate and recommend for purchase...such lands within the watersheds of navigable streams as...may be necessary to the regulation of flow of navigable streams." The act set aside $9 million to buy six million acres of land in the eastern United States to create national forests, but in fact some of the money was used for land in the western United States as well. The act was modified and amended by the Clarke-McNary Act of 1924.

Years after the federal government set aside parks and monuments as protected areas, some noted Americans, among them the writer Aldo Leopold, called for the protection of additional lands. A member of the U.S. Forest Service from 1909, he rose to become a ranger and supervisor in New Mexico, and saw wonders and sights he felt needed protection outside of the mandates of the national parks and monuments. In 1924, he took a position with the Forest Products Laboratory in Madison, Wisconsin, but before he left the Forest Service he convinced his superiors to set aside some 500,000 acres of New Mexico's Gila National Forest as a protected wilderness area. It was the first such area of this new designation, and the first of many under the aegis of the Forest Service. Leopold left the Forest Products Laboratory in 1933, and two years later, joining with other noted conservations, formed the Wilderness Society, considered today the leading advocate for the protection of wilderness areas. In 1980, Congress established the Aldo Leopold Wilderness directly to the east of the Gila National Forest, located in western New Mexico. As of 2011, this area has 202,016 acres, while the Gila National Forest, next to it, now has 3.3 million acres.

Since that first designation in 1924, the Forest Service began to designate wilderness areas, so that by the 1960s the amount of acreage had grown to over 14.6 million acres in total. It was time for congressional legislation to give full backing to these designations. One of the major legislative attempts came in 1960 with the passage of the Multiple Use and Sustained Yield Act (MUSYA) (Public Law 86-517). According to the New Mexico Center for Wildlife Law at the University of New Mexico School of Law, "This Act declares that the purposes of the national forest include outdoor recreation, range, timber, watershed and fish and wildlife. The Act directs the Secretary of Agriculture to administer national forest renewable surface resources for multiple use and sustained yield." In its policy declaration in the act, Congress found "that national forests are established and administered for outdoor recreation, range, timber, watershed, and fish and wildlife purposes. This Act is intended to supplement these purposes. The Act does not affect the jurisdiction or responsibilities of the states, the use or administration of the mineral resources of national forest lands, or the use or administration of federal lands not within the national forests." Through the act, it defined "multiple use" as "the management of all the renewable surface resources of the national forests to meet the needs of the American people," and "sustained yield" as "[the] achievement and maintenance of a high-level regular output of the renewable resources of the national forest without impairment of the land's productivity." **[13]**

In 1964, the Congress enacted what is considered the "granddaddy" of wilderness legislation: the Wilderness Act of 1964 (Public Law 88-577). This action "secure[d] for the American people of present and future generations the benefits of an enduring resource of wilderness." The law established the National Wilderness Preservation System (NWPS), composed specifically of lands in the federal land system, "for the use and enjoyment of the American people in such a manner as will leave them unimpaired for future use and enjoyment as wilderness." The Wilderness Society states, "The Wilderness Act established the NWPS to include all designated Wilderness. It now totals more than 109 million acres in 662 Wilderness Areas." **[14]** The Wilderness Act defines a wilderness as:

> *an area where the earth and its community of life are untrammeled by man, where man himself is a visitor who does not remain. An area of wilderness is further defined to mean in this Act an area of undeveloped Federal land retaining its primeval character and influence, without permanent improvements or human habitation, which is protected and managed so as to preserve its natural conditions and which (1) generally appears to have been affected primarily by the forces of nature, with the imprint of man's work substantially unnoticeable; (2) has outstanding opportunities for solitude or a primitive and unconfined type of recreation; (3) has at least five thousand acres of land or is of sufficient size as to make practicable its preservation and use in an unimpaired condition, and (4) may also contain ecological, geological, or other features of scientific, educational, scenic, or historical value.*

"The act requires relevant government agencies to give priority to "recreational, scenic, scientific, educational, conservation, and historical use" and mandates that "there shall be no commercial enterprise and no permanent road...[and] no temporary road, no use of motor vehicles, motorized equipment or motorboats, no landing of aircraft, no other form of mechanized transport, and no structure or installation within any such area."

These vehicles can be used, but only for administering the areas being protected and for human health and safety reasons (i.e., the need to move a person or persons quickly because of an accident in the area).

The Wilderness Act of 1964 initially set aside some 9.1 million acres of land as wilderness, and the Congress ordered the Secretary of Agriculture, as the immediate superior of the U.S. Forest Service, to look into the inclusion of new areas in the Wilderness system. It required both officers, of the Forest Service and the Department of Agriculture, to spend the next 10 years to review lands eligible for wilderness designation and to make such recommendations to the President, although such designations, for wilderness areas only, can only be made through an act of Congress and not through the President.

To comply with portions of the 1964 law that oversaw the banning of drilling for minerals and the prohibition of building roads, in 1971 the Forest Service began its Roadless Area Review and Evaluation (RARE). Better known as RARE I, it made a survey of 56 million acres of Forest Service land. However, critics condemned the review for failing to examine national forests, grasslands, and roadless areas that were less than 5,000 acres in size. The Forest Service abandoned RARE I, and, in 1977, opened RARE II, a second attempt to conduct a proper review of the system. After two years, RARE II had canvassed some 62 million acres in 38 states and Puerto Rico. This second evaluation proposed an additional 15.4 million acres, including nearly 10 million acres in the Continental United States, to be set aside and designated as wilderness, called for an additional 10.6 million acres be studied further, and that 36 million total acres be opened for limited logging, mining, and other uses.

At a Senate hearing in 1978, Zane G. Smith, then the director of Recreation Management for the Forest Service, told the U.S. Senate Committee on Energy and Natural Resources:

"This RARE II is a special planning effort. I want to emphasize that. It is within the contex of our land management planning that has been ongoing in the National Forest System and within the general guidelines of the RPA program [under the The Forest and Rangeland Renewable Resources Planning Act (RPA) of 1974 {Public Law 93-378}] and assessment prepared in 1975, and that will be updated in 1980. The RARE II project's purpose, of course, is to accelerate the resolution of as many of the roadless properties of the National Forests as possible, acknowledging that we are not satisfied with the speed with which we are able to do that job through our regular unit planning process at the National Forest level." [15]

Speaking of the law that was spoken about in this small clip, we turn to the Forest and Rangeland Renewable Resources Planning Act (RPA) of 1974. According to the U.S. Department of Agriculture, this law "requires the Secretary of Agriculture to conduct an assessment of the Nation's renewable resources every 10 years." The law has several specific areas that it mandated, and among them are:

- an analysis of present and anticipated uses, demand for, and supply of the renewable resources, with consideration of the international resource situation, and an emphasis of pertinent supply and demand and price relationship trends;
- an inventory...of present and potential renewable resources, and an evaluation of opportunities for improving their yield of tangible and intangible services;
- a description of Forest Service programs and responsibilities; and

- a discussion of important policy considerations, laws, regulations, and other factors expected to influence and affect significantly the use, ownership, and management of forest, range, and other associated lands. [16]

Two years after the passage of the RPA Act, Congress enacted the Federal Land Policy and Management Act (FLPMA) of 1976 (Public Law 94-579). Passed "[t]o establish public land policy; to establish guidelines for its administration; to provide for the management, protection, development, and enhancement of the public lands," this legislation was enacted, as Congress wrote in the "declaration of policy," that

> the public lands be retained in Federal ownership, unless as a result of the land use planning procedure provided for in this Act, it is determined that disposal of a particular parcel will serve the national interest; [that] the national interest will be best realized if the public lands and their resources are periodically and systematically inventoried and their present and future use is projected through a land use planning process coordinated with other Federal and State planning efforts; [and that] public lands not previously designated for any specific use and all existing classifications of public lands that were effected by executive action or statute before the date of enactment of this Act be reviewed in accordance with the provisions of this Act. [17]

The act ordered the Bureau of Land Management to review all roadless areas greater than 5,000 within the agency's jurisdiction for possible wilderness declaration and designation, and to complete the process by 1991, 15 years in the future at that time. However, by 1980, the BLM had reviewed some 174 million acres in the western United States, and stated that 24 million additional acres in 936 areas could be classified as wilderness. In 1991, as the date for final reports under FLPMA came due, the total for all of the new land recommendations and designations was 9.8 million acres in 330 differing areas. Going along with lage amounts of the recommendations, the administration of President George H.W. Bush recommended to Congress in 1992 that 9.1 million acres in 302 areas, all in western states, get wilderness designations.

Most of these wilderness designations have been in western states, and are in many ways unpopular in those areas. The designations add to the federal control of the public lands, sectioning off large tracts of states from any private land ownership or land usage. While overall only 4% of the United States is designated as wilderness, nevertheless some states, particularly in the West, are almost wholly publicly owned — for instance, as of 2004, 84% of the entire state of Nevada is owned by the federal government; in other states in the West, smaller but still significant numbers come up: in Arizona, it is 48.1%; in California, it is 45.3%; in Oregon it is 53.1%; and in Utah it is 57.4%. This has led to increased protection for millions of acres of land that would not come under this designation; but, at the same time, it has increased anger and frustration among the people of these specific states at their inability to use the lands of their states for increased jobs and resources. Opposition to additional land set-asides continues to grow.

This opposition, especially in western states, came to a head in 1980 when Congress considered setting aside record amounts of land in Alaska for preservation and protection. Usually, when such designations are made, they are with unanimous or near unanimous support from the national legislators from that specific state; however, in this case, Alaska, represented in the House by a single member of Congress, Rep. Don Young, Republican, and in the Senate by Senators Ted Stevens (Republican) and Mike Gravel (Democrat), saw unanimity in *opposition* to the passage of what would become the Alaska National Interest Lands Conservation Act (ANILCA). Signed into law by Jimmy Carter in 1980, this act established 13 new national parks, 16 new national wildlife refuges, and two new national forests, setting aside an additional 56.7 million acres of land in Alaska with a wilderness designation, tripling the size of the National Wilderness System in the United States. The largest wilderness area in the entire system, the Wrangell-St. Elias Wilderness Area in Alaska, was established by ANILCA. And although Congress had been pushed to try to open some of the land covered by ANILCA, most notably in the 1.5 million acre Arctic National Wildlife Refuge (ANWR) to limited oil and gas exploration, Democrats and some Republicans in Congress stymied all attempts to do this.

Figure 21: Wilderness Legislation in Congress since the Passage of the Wilderness Act, 1964, by Congress

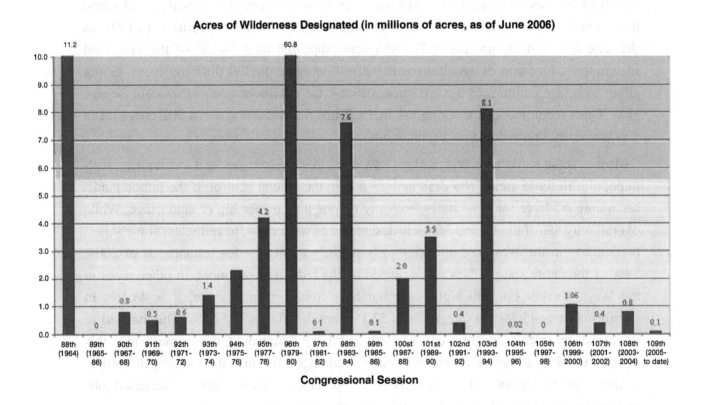

Source: Courtesy of Wilderness.org, online at http://wilderness.org/content/timeline-wilderness-history-and-conservation.

After the passage of ANILCA, there was no major congressional legislation enacted for nearly 15 years, although Congress did continue to set aside various tracts and parcels of land through specific set-asides in the states. But these were small, and individual in scope. In 1994 came the passage of the California Desert Protection Act (Public Law 103-433). Simply subtitled "a bill to designate certain lands in the California desert as wilderness, [and] to establish Death Valley, Joshua Tree and Mojave National Parks," this legislation, according to the National Park Service, sought to protect areas specific to the southeastern area of southern California. The NPS stated that "Congress made various findings about the need to enlarge and protect Death Valley National Monument, established in 1933 and 1937. The Act abolishe[d] the monument and incorporate[d] its lands into a new Death Valley National Park to be administered as part of the National Park System. Grazing of domestic livestock is permitted to continue at no more than the current level. The Act require[d] the Secretary of the Interior to establish a Death Valley National Park Advisory Commission to advise the Secretary on the development and implementation of a comprehensive management plan for the park. [18]

Two years after the passage of this legislation, Congress moved to create additional national parks and other areas of protection. It enacted the Omnibus Parks and Public Lands Management Act (OPPLMA) of 1996 (Public Law 104-333), which was an amalgamation of various pieces of legislation all rolled into one large bill. In short, this act established protections for numerous areas across the nation, and included the following:

The Aleutian World War II National Historic Areas Act of 1996

The American Battlefield Protection Act of 1996

The Bisti/De-Na-Zin Wilderness Expansion and Fossil Forest Protection Act

The Father Aull Site Transfer Act of 1996

The Hudson River Valley National Heritage Area Act of 1996

The Kenai Natives Association Equity Act Amendments of 1996

The National Coal Heritage Area Act of 1996

The Ohio & Erie Canal National Heritage Corridor Act of 1996

The Revolutionary War and War of 1812 Historic Preservation Study Act of 1996

The Shenandoah Valley Battlefields National Historic District and Commission Act of 1996

The South Carolina National Heritage Corridor Act of 1996

The Steel Industry American Heritage Area Act of 1996

The Tallgrass Prairie National Preserve Act of 1996

Although he usually opposed creating national parks and wilderness areas inside his native Alaska, this bill was introduced in the U.S. House of Representatives by Rep. Don Young, Republican of Alaska. [19]

A year after that law was enacted, Congress passed the National Wildlife Refuge System Improvement Act (NWRSIA) of 1997 (Public Law 105-57; 11 Stat. 1255). Enacted specifically to amend the National Wildlife System Administration Act of 1968, this law was aimed at the over 92 million acres in 509 individual areas in the National Wildlife Refuge System as of 1997. In this law, Congress, according to the U.S. Fish & Wildlife Service, "gave guidance to the Secretary of the Interior for the overall management of the Refuge System." The main points of the act established:

- a strong and singular wildlife conservation Mission for the Refuge System;
- a requirement that the Secretary of the Interior maintain the biological integrity, diversity, and environmental health of the Refuge System;
- a new process for determining compatible uses on refuges;
- a recognition that wildlife-dependent recreational uses involving hunting, fishing, wildlife observation and photography, and environmental education and interpretation, when determined to be compatible, are legitimate and appropriate public uses of the Refuge System;
- that these compatible wildlife-dependent recreational uses are the priority general public uses of the Refuge System; and
- a requirement for preparing a comprehensive conservation plan for each refuge. [20]

The 1997 act was the last major piece of wilderness and wilderness-related legislation to come out of Congress up until the present, in mid-2011. And while there have been minor moves — legislation to set aside small or medium tracts of land as new wilderness areas, or to add to previously established ones — these have been few and are not noted here. Whether or not, during the current period of tough fiscal and poor economic times, that Congress will once again work to pass major legislation regarding wilderness, is anyone's guess.

A HISTORY OF WILDERNESS DECISIONS IN THE COURTS

In the Wilderness Act of 1964, Congress defined "wilderness" thusly:

> Wilderness" is further defined as an area of undeveloped Federal land retaining its primeval character and influence, without permanent improvements or human habitation, which is protected and managed so as to preserve its natural conditions and which (1) generally appears to have been affected primarily by the forces of nature, with the imprint of man's work substantially unnoticeable; (2) has outstanding opportunities for solitude or a primitive and unconfined type of recreation; (3) has at least five thousand acres of land or is of sufficient size as to make practicable its preservation and use in an unimpaired condition; and (4) may also contain ecological, geological, or other features of scientific, educational, scenic, or historical value.

Despite the intent of Congress to establish national parks, wilderness areas, and other areas of protection, litigation to protect or to end protection for these areas has been a mainstay in America's courts for many years. The Web site Wilderness.net noted, "The list of wilderness case law is not extensive..." [21] Nevertheless, an examination of court decisions, large and small, dealing with the attempt by government to define just what is "wilderness" and who may control it, goes back nearly to the roots of the United States itself. The first major "land" case deals very little with true land law, but it does start the argument over what the government may do with certain lands. In *Johnson and Graham's Lessee v. M'Intosh* (8 Wheaton 543 {1823}), U.S. Supreme Court Chief Justice John Marshall wrote that lands inhabited by Native Americans could be seized by the United States, which enjoyed what he called "preeminent sovereignty" over all lands in the nation. He explained,

> The title by conquest is acquired and maintained by force. The conqueror prescribes its limits. Humanity, however, acting on public opinion, has established, as a general rule, that the conquered shall not be wantonly oppressed, and that their condition shall remain as eligible as is compatible with the objects of the conquest. Most usually, they are incorporated with the victorious nation, and become subjects or citizens of the government with which they are connected. The new and old members of the society mingle with each other; the distinction between them is grandually lost, and they make one people. Where this incorporation is practicable, humanity demands, and a wise policy requires, that the rights of the conquered to property should remain unimpaired; that the new subjects should be governed as equitably as the old, and that confidence in their security should gradually banish the painful sense of being separated from their ancient connexions, and united by force to strangers.
>
> When the conquest is complete, and the conquered inhabitants can be blended with the conquerors, or safely governed as a distinct people, public opinion, which not even the conqueror can disregard, imposes these restraints upon him; and he cannot neglect them without injury to his fame, and hazard to his power.
>
> But the tribes of Indians inhabiting this country were fierce savages, whose occupation was war, and whose subsistence was drawn chiefly from the forest. To leave them in possession of their country, was to leave the country a wilderness; to govern them as a distinct people, was impossible, because they were as brave and as high spirited as they were fierce, and were ready to repel by arms every attempt on their independence. [22]

Perhaps the next most important case to come before the U.S. Supreme Court, both in importance as well as chronologically, is *Tee-Hit-Ton Indians v. United States* (348 U.S. 272, 75 S.Ct. 313, 99 L.Ed. 314 {1955}). This case dealt with one simple issue: Could the Tee-Hit-Ton, a clan of Native Tlingits from Alaska, receive compensation from the federal government after being prohibited from cutting timber on their ancestral lands in and around the Tongass National Forest in Alaska? A trial in a district court, followed by an appeal to to the U.S. Court of Claims, led to the case being heard by the Supreme Court. On 7 February 1955, Justice Stanley F. Reed, writing for a unanimous court, held that since Congress did not explicitly grant the Tee-Hit-Tons a permanent right to their lands but had merely given them permission to occupy and live on it, the tribe had no right to cut timber on lands now belonging to the national forest. As Chief Justice Marshall had written in *Johnson v. M'Intosh* in 1823, now, 132 years later, Justice Reed reiterated the theory of "preeminent sovereignty" — that the U.S. government could seize lands, even those belonging to Native peoples, and could do with them as Congress so desired and intended. Reed wrote that the earlier cited case from 1823 "confirmed the practice of two hundred years of American history that discovery gave an exclusive right to extinguish the Indian title of occupancy, either by purchase or by conquest." Reed then concluded,

"Every American schoolboy knows that the savage tribes of this continent were deprived of their ancestral ranges by force and that, even when the Indians ceded millions of acres by treaty in return for blankets, food and trinkets, it was not a sale but the conquerors' will that deprived them of their land." [23]

While the court has not overturned the rulings in *Johnson v. M'Intosh* or *Tee-Hit-Ton* as far as the rights of native peoples to use the lands they live and work on despite being federal lands, there has been an onrush of litigation, against all of the agencies involved in the decision-making process for land management. The authors of a study on the lawsuits filed against the U.S. Forest Service from 1989 to 2002 explain,

> *The land management decisions of the USDA Forest Service have been challenged and appealed frequently in federal court, and the agency believes such litigation constrains its professional expertise and frustrates effective forest management. This study provides the first complete picture of Forest Service land management litigation. Previous litigation studies limited their examination to published cases and did not analyze final case outcomes. We document the characteristics and final outcomes of 729 Forest Service management cases filed in federal court from 1989 to 2002. The Forest Service won 57.6% of cases, lost 21.3% of cases, and settled 17.6% of cases. It won 73% of the 575 cases decided by federal judges. Plaintiffs seeking less resource use lost more than half the cases they initiated, and plaintiffs seeking greater resource use lost more than two of every three cases they initiated. Most litigation (1) was for less resource use, (2) was based on the National Environmental Policy Act, and (3) challenged logging projects.* [24]

A study of more recent cases demonstrates this trend; however, it also shows that the various groups involved in the land management debate continue to file lawsuits. In a case that dealt with the powers of the Secretary of the Interior under the Federal Land Policy and Management Act of 1976, the U.S. Supreme Court held in *Norton v. Southern Utah Wilderness Alliance* (542 US 55, 124 S.Ct. 2373, 159 L.Ed.2d 137 {2004}) that Secretary of the Interior Gale Norton, under powers granted to her office by the act as well as others, had the right to designate certain wilderness lands in Utah as "wilderness study areas" (WSAs), which enjoy special protections until Congress acts to create a national wilderness area or other congressionally-mandated area of protection. However, under the WSA for the specific land in Utah, Norton allowed off-road vehicles to use the lands until Congress acted. The Southern Utah Wilderness Alliance (SUWA) and other environmental groups (under the banner of "et. al.") sued Norton to force her to stop allowing the use of off-road vehicles. A district court in Utah dismissed the groups' lawsuit, but on appeal the U.S. Court of Appeals for the 10th Circuit reversed. Norton then sued to the U.S. Supreme Court, which granted certiorari to hear the appeal. On 14 June 2004, a unanimous court struck down the 10th Circuit's decision. Writing for the 9-0 decision, Justice Antonin Scalia wrote that while section 1782 of FLPMA directed the Secretary of the Interior to "manage [WSAs]...so as not to impair the[ir] suitability for preservation as wilderness," "it leaves BLM discretion to decide how to achieve that object." [25] The most recent case as of this writing, decided in early 2011, is *The Wilderness Society v. Kane County* (U.S. Court of Appeals for the 10th Circuit, 11 January 2011). The majority of this appeals court held that the Wilderness Society and other environmental groups lacked what the court called "prudential standing" to sue Kane County, Utah, challenging a local governmental decision to assert its right to right-of-way access to federal lands managed by the Bureau of Land Management and the National Park Service. [26]

THE FUTURE OF WILDERNESS AND LAND MANAGEMENT

In 1984, Congress passed the Utah Wilderness Act (Public Law 98-428), which established wilderness areas in twelve separate areas inside Utah, including the Wasatch-Cache National Forest, the Ashley National Forest, and the Manti-LaSal National Forest, among others. More importantly, the legislation specifically stated that future lands could be considered as well for wilderness protection. In the next decade and a half, various environmental groups advocated for additional lands to be added to protective status. In Congress, members of the Utah congressional delegation introduced competing bills: Rep. Wayne Owens (D) asked for 5.4 million acres to be set aside, while Rep. James Hansen (R) asked for 1.4 million acres. Over the next few years, battles ranged over how much additional land should be protected. Owens ran for the Senate in 1992 but was defeated. The Republicans in the Utah House delegation refused to back the 5.4 million acre designation; in fact, Rep. Bill Orton (D) backed a proposal for even smaller tracts than 1.4 million additional acres to be set aside. With the Republicans taking control of both the House of Representatives and the Senate in 1994, Hansen became, in the next Congress, the chairman of the House Committee on Public Lands Subcommittee. Although Hansen's bill won the support of Utah's two U.S. Senators, Orrin Hatch (R) and Bob Bennett (R), it could not win enough votes in either house of Congress, and was pulled from consideration in 1995. The following year, an omnibus package of land protection measures was passed by Congress, but when Republicans inserted the Hansen Utah language, Democrats in the U.S. Senate filibustered the bill until those provisions were removed. This stripped-down act was signed into law in September 1996 by President Bill Clinton.

The Clinton administration was deep into the middle of the Utah lands controversy. In a congressional hearing in April 1996, Secretary of the Interior Bruce Babbitt stated that at least five million additional acres of land in Utah should be set aside, positioning the administration completely against the interests and wishes of the state and their congressional delegation. Although BLM should have considered a new environmental impact statement (EIS) to see whether Hansen or Babbitt was right, it never did. On 18 September 1996, as he was in the middle of his re-election campaign, Clinton signed an executive order setting aside 1.7 million acres in southern Utah as the Grand Staircase-Escalante National Monument. Citing his authority under the Antiquities Act of 1906, which allows a President to designate lands or objects "of historic or scientific interest," Clinton created the monument with one swipe of a pen. Outrage broke out across the American West, especially in Utah, where Clinton and Secretary Babbitt were hung in effigy. Although anger eventually subsided, what Senator Hatch called the Democrats' "war on the West" eventually hurt the Democratic Party with independent voters and even conservative Democrats.

Unfortunately, Democrats have yet to fully understand that such set-asides can only work if they are supported by the local populace as well as the specific state's congressional delegation. Again, in 2009, this argument arose when President Barack Obama signed the Omnibus Public Land Management Act of 2009 (Public Law 111-11) into law — this legislation designated 52 new wilderness areas and added acreage to 26 existing areas, a total addition to the NWPS of over 2 million acres. In many of these places, there was intense local opposition to these land set-asides, all of which was ignored by the federal government.

THE FUTURE

The future of the National Park Service and National Parks and wilderness areas is a matter of extreme interest. In 2016, the NPS will celebrate its 100th anniversary, but as that date approaches there are challenges great and small to the agency. In 2006, in celebration of the agency's 90th birthday, then-Secretary of the Interior Dirk Kempthorne, speaking at Yellowstone National Park, said, "National parks preserve majestic natural wonders. They keep watch over battlefields hallowed by red badges of courage. They keep culture alive at sites dedicated to the performing arts, poetry and music. Parks offer recreation and discovery through spectacular backcountry hiking and climbing. They honor great leaders like Thomas Jefferson, Abraham Lincoln, Frederick Douglass, Chief Joseph, John Muir, Eleanor Roosevelt and Martin Luther King, Jr. As havens of enjoyment, recreation, learning and personal renewal, national parks must endure." [27]

What is the future of national parks, of the national wildlife refuge system, of wilderness areas in the United States? In 2001, the Pinchot Institute for Conservation in Milford, Pennsylvania, penned a report for the U.S. Forest Service, the Bureau of Land

Management, the U.S. Fish & Wildlife Service, the National Park Service, and the U.S. Geological Survey, entitled, "Ensuring the Stewardship of the National Wilderness Preservation System." In the report's executive summary, the group recommended "a need to forge an integrated and collaborative system across the four wilderness management agencies. Given the importance of wilderness as part of a land use spectrum, its historical, scientific, recreational, philosophical, and spiritual significance, and the lack of a truly systematic approach to protecting and managing Wilderness, the report offers an agenda and specific recommendations to the Secretaries of Agriculture and Interior, the officials designated in the Wilderness Act as primarily responsible for guaranteeing an enduring resource of wilderness." [28]

In 2008, the Congressional Research Service, in a report on the statistics behind the National Wilderness Preservation System (NWPS), stated, "Since the Wilderness Act created the National Wilderness Preservation System in 1964, Congress has enacted 115 additional laws designating new wilderness areas or adding to existing ones...The Wilderness System now contains 708 wilderness areas with more than 107 million acres in 44 states, managed by the four federal land management agencies...The agencies have recommended additional lands be added to the Wilderness System; these lands are generally managed to protect their wilderness character while Congress considers adding them to the Wilderness System. Additional lands are being studied by the agencies, to determine if they should be added to the System." [29] Whether or not the NWPS is expanded, or which lands will be added to the system, and whether or not those additions are done with local approval — or disapproval — are questions that will be answered in the coming years. In the meantime, the Wilderness Act is, as of this writing, nearing its 50th birthday. It began with 9 million acres of land in 54 wilderness areas when enacted; siunce then, Congress has added 107 million acres to its system, making a total of 708 wilderness areas across 44 states, nearly 1/6th of the 623 million total acres of federal land managed by the four federal agencies established to manage these lands. In total, the U.S. government owns 29% of all of the land in the United States; 17% of all federal land, and nearly 5% of all of the land in the country, has been designated as wilderness. The state with the most federal control, Alaska, has 53% of all of the wilderness areas in the nation; 16% of the entire state's land mass has been designated as wilderness. In contrast, just 3% of all land in the United States outside of the 49th state is designated as wilderness.

The Wilderness Act, and subsequent legislation, has settled the argument over whether or not such lands should be protected. The debate now is whether or not such lands should be open to off-road vehicles, to mining and drilling and other similar activities. The future of the wilderness, of national parks, of the protection of such lands, may boil down to which side is willing to give a little to continue to get the protections they claim they want.

NOTES:

[1] "Frederick Law Olmsted," courtesy of the National Park Service, online at http://www.nps.gov/frla/index.htm.

[2] See Beveridge, Charles E.; and Paul Rocheleau (David Larkin, ed.), "Frederick Law Olmsted: Designing the American Landscape" (New York: Rizzoli, 1995).

[3] "Appendix A: Frederick Law Olmsted, Jr., and the National Park Service Organic Act of 1916," in Allen, David Grayson, "The Olmsted National Historic Site and the Growth of Historic Landscape Preservation" (Lebanon, New Hampshire: Northeastern University Press, 2007), 251.

[4] See Catlin, George, "Letters and Notes on the Manners, Customs, and Condition of the North American Indians. Written During Eight Years' Travel Amongst the Wildest Tribes of Indians in North America" (Philadelphia: Willis P. Hazard; two volumes, 1857), I:397.

[5] Act of 30 June 1864 (13 Stat. 325). For the full text of the act, see Muir, John, "The Yosemite" (New York: The Century Company, 1912), 263.

[6] Hutt, Sherry; Caroline M. Blanco, and Ole Varmer, "Heritage Resources Law: Protecting the Archaelogical and Cultural Environment" (New York: John Wiley & Sons for The National Trust for Historic Preservation, 1999), 182.

[7] "Great Smoky Mountains National Park," courtesy of the National Park Service, online at http://www.nps.gov/grsm/index.htm.

[8] "National Historic Landmarks," courtesy of the National Park Service, online at http://www.nps.gov/nhl/whatis.htm.

[9] There are differing statistics, all coming from the Bureau of Land Management. For instance, in the Public Land Statistics for FY 2008, it states that as of the end of that fiscal year, the agency controlled 253 million surface acres; however, on the agency's Web site, with information dated 2008, it uses the 258 million acres number; see http://www.blm.gov/public_land_statistics/pls08/pls1-4_08.pdf; see also http://www.blm.gov/es/st/en/info/about_blm.html.

[10] This number is also in dispute; although, according to the BLM's own Web site, this is the number that is given: see http://www.blm.gov/es/st/en/info/about_blm.html.

[11] "What is the Bureau of Land Management?" courtesy of the Bureau of Land Management, online at http://www.blm.gov/or/faq/index.php.

[12] "General Statement [of Principles]," in "The United States Department of the Interior: Budget Justifications and Performance Information, Fiscal Year 2012. Bureau of Land Management" (Washington, D.C.: Bureau of Land Management, Department of the Interior, 2011), I-2.

[13] "Multiple-Use Sustained-Yield Act of 1960," courtesy of the New Mexico Center for Wildlife Law at the University of New Mexico School of Law, online at http://wildlifelaw.unm.edu/fedbook/multiu.html.

[14] "What is Wilderness?" courtesy of the Wilderness Society, online at http://wilderness.org/content/what-wilderness.

[15] United States Senate, Committee on Energy and Natural Resources, "Roadless Area Review and Evaluation (RARE II), Printed at the Request of Henry M. Jackson, Chairman, Committee on Energy and Natural Resources, United States Senate" (Washington, D.C.: U.S. Government Printing Office; two volumes, 1978), I:6.

[16] "Resources Planning Act," courtesy of the U.S. Department of Agriculture, online at http://nrs.fs.fed.us/fia/topics/rpa/.

[17] Text of the act in U.S. Department of the Interior, Bureau of Land Management, "Federal Land Policy and Management Act of 1976, As Amended. Compiled by the U.S. Department of the Interior, Bureau of Land Management and Office of the Solicitor" (Washington, D.C.: Government Printing Office, October 2001), 1.

[18] "California Desert Protection Act," courtesy of the National Park Service, online at http://www.nps.gov/jotr/parkmgmt/caldesprotect.htm.

[19] See "H.R. 4236: Omnibus Parks and Public Lands Management Act of 1996," courtesy of Govtrack.us, online at http://www.govtrack.us/congress/bill.xpd?bill=h104-4236.

[20] "National Wildlife Refuge System Improvement Act of 1997," courtesy of the U.S. Fish & Wildlife Service, 19 August 2009, online at http://www.fws.gov/refuges/policiesandbudget/HR1420_index.html.

[21] "The Wilderness Stewardship Reference System," courtesy of Wilderness.net, online at http://leopold.wilderness.net/wsrs/index.cfm?fuse=WSRS&sec=sources.

[22] Marshall opinion in *Johnson and Graham's Lessee v. M'Intosh* (8 Wheat. 543 {1823}), at 590-91.

[23] See the text of *Tee-Hit-Ton Indians v. United States* (348 U.S. 272, 75 S.Ct. 313, 99 L.Ed. 314 {1955}). See also a discussion of this case as well as *Johnson v. M'Intosh* in Reeves, Donna Marie, "U.S. Culture and the Politics of Wilderness" (Ph.D. dissertation, University of Colorado, 2008).

[24] Keele, Denise M.; Robert W. Malmsheimer, Donald W. Floyd, and Jerome E. Perez, "Forest Service Land Management Litigation 1989-2002," *Journal of Forestry*, CIV:4 (June 2006), 196-202.

[25] See the text of the decision in *Norton v. Southern Utah Wilderness Alliance* (542 US 55, 124 S.Ct. 2373, 159 L.Ed.2d 137 2004}), which is only about a page in length.

[26] See *The Wilderness Society v. Kane County* (U.S. Court of Appeals for the 10th Circuit, No 08-4090, 11 January 2011).

[27] "The Future of America's National Parks: Celebrating the 90th Anniversary and Looking Forward to the Centennial an Beyond," National Park Service News Release, 25 August 2006, courtesy of the National Park Service, online at http://home.nps.gov/applications/release/print.cfm?id=683.

[28] Pinchot Institute for Conservation, "Ensuring the Stewardship of the National Wilderness Preservation System: A Report to the USDA Forest Service, Bureau of Land Management, U.S. Fish & Wildlife Service, National Park Service, [and] U.S. Geological Survey" (Milford, Pennsylvania: Pinchot Institute for Conservation, September 2001), i.

[29] Gorte, Ross W., "Wilderness: Overview and Statistics," *CRS Report for Congress*, 10 March 2008, CRS-4.

10

The Debate about Public Lands and Natural Resources

The debate over public lands, how they should be protected (or not protected), and natural resource policy, is infused with any unknown number of paradoxes. Perhaps the most important is that mainstream media, politicians, and environmental groups all argue that in the last 40+ years, environmental legislation has made the air cleaner, the water cleaner, the environment as a whole far better than it was just a few decades ago. On the other hand, these same groups and politicians and media outlets claim that additional legislation is needed because the air is not clean, the water is not clean, and the environment will become spoiled if this legislation is not enacted sooner rather than later. Scare tactics of "children will drink dirty water" or "people will breathe dirty air" are used time and time again, even as these same groups congratulate themselves and their movement for pushing for clean water and air for nearly half a century. It is impossible to argue that there has not been major progress towards undoing damage to the environment, while claiming that additional progress would mean that things would return to how they once were. Criticisms of these tactics and the groups and politicians who make them are becoming louder and louder, especially as the alleged threat of "global warming" and "climate change" has proven to be little more than wishful thinking at best. Science and predictions of a worldwide crisis have been shown to be patently false or, worse yet, falsified by scientists with a vested interest in making the "climate change" argument work for them.

At the same time, protections for certain lands and species and habitats are a must — and the debate centers now on how much to protect rather than whether to protect at all. Policies, both national and local, are constantly being examined and reformed to react to changes in the habitats, to specific species, or to economic conditions. Warnings about impending doom from alleged environmental damage have turned out to be overblown: in 2005, the United Nations predicted that by 2011 there would be some 50 million "climate refugees" fleeing from areas inundated by rising waters caused by "climate change." By the time the report stated these events would happen, not only could the agency that wrote the report not find any "climate refugees," but it found that the areas it predicted would be underwater were in fact above water, with *increasing*, rather than decreasing, populations. A similar thing happened in 1992. Henry W. Kendall (1926-1999), a former chairman of the board of directors of the Union of Concerned Scientists (UCS) and a Nobel laureate (he shared the 1990 Nobel for Physics), penned a "World Scientists' Warning to Humanity," a manifesto that claimed that continued human interaction with the environment would cause disaster on earth, and that drastic changes had to be made, and made quickly. In the manifesto's opening, Kendall wrote, "Human beings and the natural world are on a collision course." He added, "Human activities inflict harsh and often irreversible damage on the environment and on critical resources. If not checked, many of our current practices put at serious risk the future that we wish for human society and the plant and animal kingdoms, and may so alter the living world that it will be unable to sustain life in the manner that we know. Fundamental changes are urgent if we are to avoid the collision our present course will bring about." Kendall then circulated the document, and it was eventually signed by 1,670 scientists around the world, including a majority, at that time, of Nobel Prize laureates.

The 1992 report also pointed to a series of environmental indicators and what the authors saw as potential areas for disaster:

> *The Atmosphere: Stratospheric ozone depletion threatens us with enhanced ultraviolet radiation at the earth's surface, which can be damaging or lethal to many life forms. Air pollution near ground level, and acid precipitation, are already causing widespread injury to humans, forests, and crops.*

> *Water Resources: Heedless exploitation of depletable groundwater supplies endangers food production and other essential human systems. Heavy demands on the world's surface waters have resulted in serious shortages in some 80 countries, containing 40% of the world's population. Pollution of rivers, lakes, and groundwater further limits the supply.*

> *Oceans: Destructive pressure on the oceans is severe, particularly in the coastal regions which produce most of the world's food fish. The total marine catch is now at or above the estimated maximum sustainable yield. Some fisheries have already shown signs of collapse.*

Rivers carrying heavy burdens of eroded soil into the seas also carry industrial, municipal, agricultural, and livestock waste - some of it toxic.

Soil: Loss of soil productivity, which is causing extensive Land abandonment, is a widespread byproduct of current practices in agriculture and animal husbandry. Since 1945, 11% of the earth's vegetated surface has been degraded — an area larger than India and China combined — and per capita food production in many parts of the world is decreasing.

Forests: Tropical rain forests, as well as tropical and temperate dry forests, are being destroyed rapidly. At present rates, some critical forest types will be gone in a few years and most of the tropical rain forest will be gone before the end of the next century. With them will go large numbers of plant and animal species.

Living Species: The irreversible loss of species, which by 2100 may reach one third of all species now living, is especially serious. We are losing the potential they hold for providing medicinal and other benefits, and the contribution that genetic diversity of life forms gives to the robustness of the world's biological systems and to the astonishing beauty of the earth itself. [1]

The UCS was a firm backer of the 1992 global conference held in Kyoto, Japan, which enacted a series of measures that world governments would have to abide by to end the threat of "climate change," then called "global warming." Although the administration of President Bill Clinton was a prime supporter of the Kyoto Protocols, in 1999 the U.S. Senate told Clinton in a 99-0 vote that the treaty signed in 1992 would never pass that legislative body, and it was never resent for any additional votes.

In 1997, the UCS followed up its 1992 document with another, "World Scientists Call For Action," demanding that governments around the world sign the Kyoto Protocols. The 1997 document stated, "A broad consensus among the world's climatologists is that there is now 'a discernible human influence on global climate...'" and demanded that governments institute "legally binding commitments to reduce industrial nations' emissions of heat-trapping gases." Again, large numbers of scientists around the world signed the document, including a large group of Nobel laureates.

In 2007, concerned that the UCS was pushing U.S. governmental policy without any challenge to their facts, the conservative think tank the Capital Research Center published a study by three so-called "climate change skeptics," Myron Ebell, Iain Murray, and Ivan Osorio, which blasted the UCS and accused the group of waging "a jihad against climate skeptics." [2]

In November 2009, the so-called "ClimateGate" scandal exploded. Computer experts who hacked into the computers of the Climate Research Unit at the University of East Anglia in the United Kingdom found a series of some 1,000 e-mails between scientists at the university privately covering up and even eliminating scientific data that seemed to raise doubts about climate change and its role in world temperatures. Although an investigation — which many "climate change skeptics" denounced as a cover-up of the cover-up — cleared the university and its head, Phil Jones, of any wrongdoing, skeptics of the school and the science continued to lambast Jones for the e-mails. One of these people, blogger James Delingpole of the *Daily Telegraph* of London, continued his campaign to denounce Jones. Jones became upset at Delingpole's campaign against him, and in a move many criticized, Jones complained about Delingpole to the UK Press Complaints Commission, an independent body that has no close relative in the United States, where free speech, and with it the right to oppose someone's ideas, are paramount. The fact that Jones taught at a university, where free speech is usually heralded above all other values, was noted by Jones' admirers and critics alike. After holding hearings, the commission concluded that Delingpole's criticisms of Jones, and by extension the entire "ClimateGate" scandal, were wholly allowed within the realm of British law. In their final report, the commission summarized Jones', and his colleagues', complaints against Delingpole: "In particular, the complainants were concerned that the blog posts described Professor Phil Jones as 'disgraced, FOI [Freedom of Information Act]-breaching, email-deleting, [and] scientific-method abusing'."

Although the commission found that Delingpole had used words to describe Jones which tended to accuse him of acts of which he had been cleared, i.e., deleting certain e-mails or abusing the scientific standard, nevertheless the panel held that Delingpole was within his rights: "The Commission was satisfied that readers would be aware that the comments therein represented the columnist's own robust views of the matters in question...The Commission has previously ruled [in the case of *North v. The Guardian*] that [i]n the realm of blogging (especially in cases touching upon controversial topics such as climate change), there is likely to be strong and fervent disagreement, with writers making use of emotive terms and strident rhetoric. This is a necessary consequence of free speech. The Commission felt that it should be slow to intervene in this, unless there is evidence of factual inaccuracy or misleading statement." Since it found none, it ruled in Delingpole's favor.

However, we have gone far afield here, diving into the realm over the controversy over the controversy over the "ClimateGate" scandal; but this ending chapter is, and should not, be about whether or not "climate change" is real, or invented, or could be proven wrong or right. This is a summing up — of where we have been, and where we may go, in the future when it comes to the issue of land rights and the use of natural and other resources.

As the peoples of the Earth enter the second decade of the twenty-first century, the regular issues over the protection of resources, whatever they may be, and how to do it with as little impact on the economic well-being of a nation, have expanded into how those resources can be used for the future. The use of fossil fuels has powered world economies for over a century, and the debate is now over what kind of governmental impact should be had on "green" options — wind, solar, electric — even though these potential options are perhaps decades away from seeing their full impact, and what their cost may be and how well they may replace, or can only supplement, fossil fuels, is also argued. There is no argument anymore over whether or not we should have clean water or clean air acts; the movement has come full circle into whether *cleaner* water, or *cleaner* air, can be had when there is some question as to the cost of getting to these places, and whether or not the ability to get to them makes much difference in the environment. For instance, cleaning up smog from the air is a notable and laudable goal, and clean air acts by Congress have made those important targets ones that we as a nation all feel must be met. But if the air is 95% cleaner than before, and it takes literally hundreds of billions of dollars, or untold numbers of jobs, to get the additional 5% cleaner, is it worth it? And if scientific studies show that that last 5% is so prohibitively expensive to gain, is that also worth it? What is the "cutoff" when human health and economic health collide, where one must win while the other loses?

This is the debate that has shaped economic policy, not just in the United States, but around the world, for the past forty years. As populations expand, and more human interaction — and intrusion — into the environment occur, the role of government, and of peoples with a definite interest in making their environment safe to live in, has taken a leading role. As well, the role of biodiversity in the environment is also part of the debate. While the risk of the extinction of species becomes more pressing, protections from all quarters have grown. The risks to certain species has led to the formation of a "Noah's ark": a collection of seeds, and DNA, and other remnants of earthly species, is being collected at the University of Bath in the United Kingdom. Known as "The Biodiversity Lab," this collection is aimed at saving species even after they may be extinct.

The arguments over the extinction of nonanimal species needs clear and reasoned thinking. The debate over the amount of old-growth forest remaining in the United States is one example. Even when all sides — antigrowth and progrowth — in the debate agree to the definition of just what is to be considered as "old-growth forest," they still argue over just how much remains. The National Commission on Science for Sustainable Forestry (NCSSF), formed in 2001, met in 2005 and 2006 and shaped a report, "Beyond Old Growth: Older Forests in a Changing World," which examined the debate over just what is "old-growth" forest and took a look at how much there was remaining in the United States. In the preface of the report, the members of the commission stated their definition of what "old-growth forest" entailed:

> *To many it describes a forest that has grown for centuries without human disturbance and now is a stand of massive, towering trees with jumbles of large decaying tree trunks; deep shade pierced by shafts of sunlight; and dense patches of herbs, shrubs, and saplings that may conceal rare species. Such a forest is as awe-inspiring as it is biologically rich. It may contain the largest trees, the oldest trees, the most at-risk forest species, and the largest accumulation of carbon per acre of any forest type on earth." They added, "This image accurately depicts many old-growth forests, but it doesn't fit all or even most of them. The basic definition of old growth is simply a forest that is dominated by big, old trees, both live*

and dead, standing and fallen, and that usually contains many other smaller trees. The individual trees are irregularly distributed over the land, and their diverse sizes give rise to a layered appearance. Most true old-growth forests give an overwhelming impression of diversity instead of uniformity. [3]

Although this definition was not completed until 2007, it was agreed to in 1991. In that year, the U.S. Forest Service and the Wilderness Society released separate reports detailing what it considered the amount of "old-growth forests" remaining in the United States. Despite their general agreement over what constituted this kind of forest, the Forest Service concluded that there were, in 1991, 4.3 million acres of old-growth forest remaining in the United States. However, the Wilderness Society reported that there were only 2 million acres. Upon opening their commission, the NCSSF took up both groups' studies and concluded that the Forest Service had overcalculated the amount of forest and the Wilderness Society had undercalculated the amount, coming up with a number, in 2007, of 3.5 million total acres. The NCSSF also stated that if they expanded their definition of such forests to include older forest with trees of minimum diameters and canopies that were both simple and complex, that the number could rise substantially. And while some regions had considerably less growth — the southwestern United States, for instance, has just 425 old growth sites, according to a 1993 examination — overall the NCSSF said that the outlook for old-growth forest was clean and bright. But, again, these sites do need protection. That much is agreed to across the spectrum of thinking.

In this work we have taken close examinations of all facets of the resource debate — from policymaking to lawmaking to cases in the courts and other avenues of investigation. All of these resources, from our water to our air to the ground below us and the sky above us, play some role in our lives on a daily basis. From making sure that the air and water are clean to recycling to preserving the natural resources to using them wisely, we have looked at how there can be a moderate course taken with respect to all of these resources. Despite what either side may try to do in their zeal to protect their interests, in the end some meeting of the minds must come together to find solutions to the problems that plague the planet. But there must be that moderation; otherwise, we will all continue to find ourselves spending more time fighting over how to keep the planet clean and healthy or be able to house, feed, and clothe the growing numbers who join the human race rather than finding ways to solve those problems. One side must admit that clean air and clean water and saving the resources from overuse is a good way to keep the environment healthy; on the other hand, the other side must admit that predictions of doom and gloom from "climate change" or the growing world population have not come to fruition and new solutions must be found.

Just as man has adapted to his environment around him (no disrespect to women here), the environment has adapted itself around man. In the 1930s, it was rare to see people live into their 80s or 90s, when the world population was at 1 or 2 billion; now, at 6 billion and climbing, people are seeing their 110th birthday and beyond, and they are no longer considered outside the realm of what is normal. New ways of growing food have led to less but not an eradication of hunger. And while we have found new and safer ways of using building materials to construct tall and other buildings, disasters such as the earthquake and tsunami that hit Japan in March 2011, and the earthquakes that struck Haiti in 2010 and New Zealand in early 2011 continue to plague the human race. Regardless of environmental policy, war also remains a scourge, drastically lowering the quality of life for people it impacts.

To sum up, it will take a daring and prudent approach to find solutions to the way forward concerning environmental policy, in this nation and others. One place to look may be the Cuyahoga River. Once a dumping ground for oil, gas, and other chemicals, in 1969 the body of water, which is key to the city of Cleveland, Ohio, burst into flames. The disaster, coming as it did at the end of the 1960s, spurred on the then-moribund environmental movement, culminating in the passage of the Clean Water Act in 1972. In 2009, on the fire's 40th anniversary, Karen Schaefer of WKSU Radio wrote, "Where vacuum boats once sucked up oil spills, boating clubs now enjoy an evening rowing on the river. The Cuyahoga is so much cleaner, state officials have applied to take parts of it off a list of the most polluted Great Lakes waterways." [4] The Cuyahoga experience is a key argument that even rivers and other bodies of water so horribly polluted that they would normally be written off and abandoned can in fact be cleaned up. Perhaps not all sites can make the comeback that the Cuyahoga did, but it is a fantastic message for those who consider a polluted area to be ruined forever.

Is the solution then to set aside certain lands from all facets of development? Set-asides, be they by private individuals or by local, state, or even the federal government, takes land out of the system forever and blocks its sale. Ironically, it is in Scottsdale, Arizona, this author's hometown, that leads the entire nation in setting aside land for parks and preserve areas: in 2010, the total was 15,172 acres across the entire city, or 64.5 acres per 1,000 residents, triple the area density for cities the size of Scottsdale. [5] Easements and other ways to cut through the set-asides are usually private-public partnerships allowing certain people a right-of-way to land that has been set aside. Whether or not this is a prudent way to protect land and resources on that land is another argument for another time: After all, if people legally own land and wish to use it as they see fit, that is their right. If they wish to honor these agreements with easements, allowing viewing or crossing by certain people, again, that is their right. Landownership has a storied legacy in this country, and among the "rights" and "wants" of peoples who have come here for generations was the wish to own a piece of land to call their own. No other country in the world has such a desire in their DNA as does the United States.

At the same time, though, there should be a concerted effort by both sides of the resource argument to find a common ground allowing for the careful extraction of certain resources, be there minerals, or oil, or other matters, without disturbing or even harming the land. A small piece of personal property being put aside is one thing; for government to take tens or hundreds of millions of acres and put them out of the reach of being exploited for the economic health of the nation is wrong and should be addressed. But instead the argument gets bogged down to who wants to "kill" the land, or who wants people to "be ripped off" for resources on that land. Is there no middle ground, no common American identity that can be called upon to settle these arguments? As of now, there is not. There is demonization — and there is no progress. Windmills and electric cars sound nice, but windmills cannot power a car and electric cars will not be a solution for 95% of the American people, even if they weren't decades away from being economically feasible. $5 a gallon gas — perhaps even as high as $6 or $7 a gallon — has a way of pushing people to demand more drilling.

Much of this work focuses on the West: the lore, the pull of its storied habitats and stunning views and way of life that continues, even as of this writing, to drive people to listen to those words mouthed by journalist John B.L. Soule, and popularized by Horace Greeley in the mid-nineteenth century: "Go West, young man." The romance, the sheer vision of "America" found in the lands, mountains, and hills of the West continue to lure generations of people from all areas of the United States and the world. Although the stories are now tempered with reality, this was not always so: From the start of the nation, the vision of "Manifest Destiny," that the people could continue to move west until the ocean was reached, was the overriding policy concern. Men with little education but a spirit of hard work packed their lives and sometimes their families and headed to areas where there were few if any amenities. Untamed wilderness, harsh weather, Native Americans seeing their ancestral lands being besieged, all stood before these men of alleged iron will who sought to impose their way of life on the land. In most cases, the land imposed its will on the men. This concept was first discussed, at least in considerable length, by journalist John L. Sullivan, in an article in the *United States Democratic Review* in 1839, in which he stated that the United States was becoming "the nation of progress, of individual freedom, of universal enfranchisement." He argued for a government policy, for a policy of the American people, that exercised this view westward. He wrote, "We must onward to the fulfillment of our mission—to the entire development of the principle of our organization—freedom of conscience, freedom of person, freedom of trade and business pursuits, universality of freedom and equality. This is our high destiny." [6]

In 1893, historian Frederick Jackson Turner delivered his masterful discussion of the movement west in a paper read at the American Historical Association's annual meeting that year in Chicago, held at the same time as the World's Fair in that same city. Titled "The Significance of the Frontier in American History," Turner's paper, which has since become more myth than reality, has opened a debate that still encapsulates parts of the historical community in the United States: What is the "frontier," and what role did westward migration play in the settling of the West? Turner argued that as people moved westward, they encountered a series of challenges, based on the land, the weather, the overall environment, which they then had to abandon well-known and proven "European" solutions and instead invent new ones, ideas which Turner credits as being wholly "American." Through these challenges, the people who moved west promoted a system of self-reliance and hard work unseen in other cultures, particularly from the European cultures that most of these people had come from in one way or another. Controversially, however, Turner argued that by the end of the nineteenth century, when he wrote his paper, "the West" was in effect gone — the movement of people west had caused unavoidable environmental ruin, of pollution, of the destruction of wetlands and habitats. Turner then argued that new sources of products, from wood to other timber products, to minerals from mines, to energy from gas and oil, had to be found, or else the West would continue to suffer a rapid decline in environmental standards. [7]

Turner's 1893 paper, now nearly 120 years old as of this writing, is not only controversial to this day, but has spawned a movement of "pro-Turnerians" and "anti-Turnerians" who argue the pros and cons of his thesis and whether or not the passage of time has proven him right. Ray Allen Billington wrote in 1963 that Turner was frustrated that he never wrote more. "But always he failed," Billington explained. "The result was tragedy: Turner's was a life of repeated frustrations, of gnawing doubts of his own ability, of a recurring sense of failure. His last words as he lay on his deathbed were of regret that he had done no more." [8]

Despite this, Turner's writing on the West was comprehensive. William Cronon, writing in 1987, explained, "According to Turner, the West was a place where easterners and Europeans experiences a return to a time before civilization when the energies of the race were young. Once the descent to the primitive was complete, frontier communities underwent a revolution which recapitulated the development of civilization itself, tracing the path from hunter to trader to farmer to town. In that process of descent and reevolution — as the frontier successively emerged and vanished — a special American character was forged, marked by fierce individualism, pragmatism, and egalitarianism. Thus, fundamentally transformed as a people, Americans built their commitment to democracy, escaped the perils of class conflict, and overran a continent." [9]

Aldo Leopold, who wrote of a "land ethic" in his 1949 work "A Sand County Almanac," explained,

> *All ethics so far evolved rest upon a single premise: that the individual is a member of a community of interdependent parts. His instincts prompt him to compete for his place in that community, but his ethics prompt him also to co-operate (perhaps in order that there may be a place to compete for). The land ethic simply enlarges the boundaries of the community to*

include soils, waters, plants, and animals, or collectively: the land. This sounds simple: do we not already sing our love for and obligation to the land of the free and the home of the brave? Yes, but just what and whom do we love? Certainly not the soil, which we are sending helter-skelter downriver. Certainly not the waters, which we assume have no function except to turn turbines, float barges, and carry off sewage. Certainly not the plants, of which we exterminate whole communities without batting an eye. Certainly not the animals, of which we have already extirpated many of the largest and most beautiful species. A land ethic of course cannot prevent the alteration, management, and use of these "resources," but it does afirm their right to continued existence, and, at least in spots, their continued existence in a natural state. In short, a land ethic changes the role of Homo sapiens from conqueror of the landcommunity to plain member and citizen of it. It implies respect for his fellow-members, and also respect for the community as such. **[10]**

In my 1994 work on the history of the conservation movement of the late nineteenth and early twentieth centuries and the modern environmental movement, I wrote, "The movement to conserve the environment stretches back the years even before the founding of the Republic. Scientists like John and William Bartram, John Bradbury, and Thomas Nuttall were doing work in the environmental field in the 17th and 18th centuries. As early as 1799, Congress was passing laws to protect the nation's timber reserves for use by the military. In 1828, one Henry M. Brackenridge was planting acorns to grow trees to be used by the navy to build ships." **[11]**

Little has changed when it comes to environmental protection in the period covered by that work...the names have changed, the Congresses have changed, the laws have changed and have become stricter and more imposing. But at the same time there has become an almost universal belief that the environment needs protection — be it federal, state, or local, or, usually, a combination of the three. As the amount of resources diminishes, and the population of the planet increases, the question about how to use the earth's resources in a better way will take precedence over no usage at all. The time for that debate is fast approaching.

NOTES:

[1] "World Scientists' Warning to Humanity," courtesy of deoxy.org, online at http://deoxy.org/sciwarn.htm.

[2] Ebell, Myron, Iain Murray, and Ivan Osorio, "Union of Concerned Scientists: Its Jihad against Climate Skeptics," report of the Capital Research Group, March 2007.

[3] National Commission on Science for Sustainable Forestry (NCSSF), "Beyond Old Growth: Older Forests in a Changing World. A Synthesis of Findings from Five Regional Workshops" (2007), 5-6.

[4] Schaefer, Karen, "Comeback of the Cuyahoga River; On the 40th Anniversary of Clean-Up, the Once-Burning River Rebounds," WKSU Radio, 22 June 2009, online at http://www.wksu.org/news/story/23583.

[5] Corbett, Peter, "Scottsdale is national leader in land set aside for parks, preserve," *AZCentral.com*, 24 September 2010, online at http://www.azcentral.com/news/articles/2010/09/24/20100924scottsdale-national-leader-parks-preserve.html.

[6] Sullivan, John L., "The Great Nation of Futurity," *The United States Democratic Review*, VI:23 (November 1839), 426-30.

[7] Handley, William Ross, "The Literary West: Imagining America from Turner to Fitzgerald" (Ph.D. dissertation, University of California, Los Angeles, 1997). See also Vierling, Ronald, "The New Western Mythology: A Study of Frederick Jackson Turner's Frontier Thesis, its Origins and Relationship to American Thought and Literary Themes" (Master's thesis, University of Wyoming, 1972), and Costello, Philip Paul, "Frederick Jackson Turner Frontier Historian" (Master's thesis, Southern Connecticut State University, 1960).

[8] Billington, Ray Allen, "Why Some Historians Rarely Write History: A Case Study of Frederick Jackson Turner," *The Mississippi Valley Historical Review*, L:1 (June 1963), 3-27.

[9] Cronon, William, "Revisiting the Vanishing Frontier: The Legacy of Frederick Jackson Turner," *The Western Historical Quarterly*, XVIII:2 (April 1987), 157-76.

[10] "Leopold's Land Ethic," courtesy of the Aldo Leopold Foundation, Baraboo, Wisconsin, online at http://www.aldoleopold.org/about/LandEthic.pdf.

[11] Grossman, Mark, "The ABC-Clio Companion to the Environmental Movement" (Santa Barbara, California: ABC-Clio, 1994), xii.

U. S. Land and Natural Resources Policy
Primary Documents

The following documents are arranged by chapter they are most relevant to.

"Yellowstone National Park," *The Kansas City Star*, 3 July 1890

This newspaper story was one of the first which heralded the myriad wonders yet to be completely seen in the newly-established Yellowstone National Park in the scenic American West.

YELLOWSTONE NATIONAL PARK

———————

The Wonderland of America, as Seen by an Explorer

———————

Corresponded by Kate Field in Washington.

In 1872 congress [sic] set aside a piece of land in the heart of the Rocky mountains [sic], to be devoted to the pleasures of the people forever, retaining control on the name of the government. The reservation is situated in three states, the greater part in Northwestern Wyoming and Southeastern Idaho. It also embraces a small part on Montana—in all 3,600 square miles.

The first white person known to have visited this part of the country was a man named Carter, who was led there in his search for gold in 1807. On this return he told is such wonderful things he had seen that he was set down as crazy. He repeated his stories until public curiosity was so much aroused that the government sent Prof. [Frederick V.] Hayden to examine that region. He not only corroborated Carter's amazing stories, but added much to them. In 1870 Governor [Henry D.] Washburn went through the same part of the country, thoroughly exploring it. On his report of the natural wonders he found congress [sic] took the action which gave the people this great pleasure ground.

The park is surrounded but mountains capped all year with snow. In winter the snow storms and blizzards are something fearful. The few adventurous people who have gone there that time of the year have been able to live through the forty degrees below zero which prevailed at night by campfire as near as they could get to the boiling springs. At other times the climate is lovely, and many delicate flowers abound—phlox, fragrant violets, primroses, lark, spurs, harebells, columbines, daisies, water lilies and many other varieties grow wild in luxuriant masses. Of trees the black [unreadable] is the most numerous, often found 150 feet high. The others trees that make up the dense forest are balsam, white pine, willow and maple.

One half the park is forest, through which wander foxes, buffalo, mink, California lions, deet, antelope, big horn sheep, elk, bear and many other wild animals, the streams swarm with otter and beaver, while geese, snipe, cranes, swans, seal, plover, pelicans, herons, gulls, [unreadable], hawks, ravens and eagles and all kinds of ducks are among the feathered natives of the park. The game is strictly preserved, and visitors are not permitted to carry firearms with them.

The tribe of Indians who originally inhabited this region were called Sheepeaters. They lived almost solely on the flesh and clothed themselves in the skins of the big horn sheep. They were small of stature, and lived in caves, which may still be seen among the hills. They are said to have been a harmless race, their only weapons being bows and arrows with hatchers and knives formed of the volcanic glass found on the spot. No Indians are now permitted to enter the reservation, as they would make sad havoc among the animals gathered there.

The average elevation of the park, independent of mountains, is 7000 feet above the sea. Mount Washington is the highest point, measuring 7000 feet from base to peak. On clear day the naked eye can see a distance of 150 miles. Three of the largest rivers in the country too have their source here—the Yellowstone, three of the forks of the Missouri and the Snake river [sic].

Of course, no one is allowed to settle in the park but tourists may camp out in it for the summer. The reservation is under control of the Secretary of the Interior. A superintendent lives here, having under him a [unreadable] of game keepers and government police. Gangs of workmen are employed under army engineers, and two companies of United States cavalry take charge of the premises.

A hotel has been built for the accommodation of tourists, and stages start from it daily, making the rounds of the park and showing their passengers all the interesting sights. The marvels nearest the hotel are the mammoth hot springs, covering two hundred acres of sloping ground. Athey are terraced springs, flowing into the Gardiner river [sic] one thousand feet below. Five hundred feet from the springs the water is clear, cool and perfectly tasteless. The springs are themselves building [unreadable] of circular pools in beautiful stalctite basins, formed by the chemical substances they contain. Some are red, many by oxide of iron, some yellow from sulphur, some are bordered by frills of green showing arsenic, some have scalloped frill-like borders; others have borders like beadwork, others again have a fret work of great regularity as if made by some artistic hand. All go to make up a terrace like a flight of steps two hundred feet high and five hundred feet broad. The water in some is boiling but, charges with iron, soda, magnesia and sulphur. The chemical properties of each spring are distinctive. There is one column of carbonite of lime over forty feet high and measuring fifteen feet at the base, formed by one of the springs in the past ages.

The next great sight is the middle falls of the Gardiner river [sic]. The river flows through a canyon 1000 feet below you. The canyon at the top is 500 feet wide, and narrows toward the bottom and the river has an unbroken fall of 100 feet.

The latest waterfall in the park is called the Lower Fall. It is 100 feet wide, making one leap of 100 feet.

The Grand Canyon of the Yellowstone River [sic] is 200 miles long and the sides blaze with color produced by first, lightning, rain and sunshine acting on the chemicals in the rock. What is called the Obsidian cliffs are about twelve miles from the hotel. They are formed of volcanic glass. They are about 200 feet high from Beaver Lake and 1000 feet in length. The color of the glass is dark green and glistens but is opaque. There is a glass carriage road at the base of the cliffs a quarter of a mile long. It was built by making large fires and when the glass was heated dashing water on it. The glass crumbled, and in time has made a good road bed. Beaver Lake is half a mile wide by two miles long. There are over thirty dams in it having falts [sic] of from three to six feet, and all formed by a colony of beavers. The lake near the shore is covered with [unreadable] flowers. Close to the cliffs is a cool, shady spot and pasture land, with clear stream of water flowing through it. This is called Willow park [sic].

Twenty miles from the hotel is the Norris Geyser basin. In places the ground will tremble under you as you walk, and is so hit you cannot keep your hand on it. The basin is dotted with springs, some bubbling hot, others cool, each spring as different from the others in color as in temperature. The largest spring is fifty feet across and of an emerald green color; the others are all smaller and yellow, red, white and pink. The water is forced from some of the springs in a column more than 200 feet high several times a day. Near here is the Monarch geyser, throwing a triple stream of water 110 feet high once in every twenty-four hours, the spout lasting fifteen minutes.

One of the greatest curiosities in the park is the Gibbon Paint Pot Basis, being a collection of some 500-mud springs. They are of all sizes. The mud has become piled up about the springs and each spring shoots from a mound called a pot.

The largest geyser in the world is in the park, known as the Excelsior. It comes from a pit 270 feet in diameter in the solid rock. The spring plays at irregular intervals, throwing a stream of water sixty feet in diameter, a hundred feet into the air, freighted with all kinds of dirt and stones, the latter often weighing a hundred pounds.

A frightful spot, some five acres in area, is called Hell's Half Acre. The soil in places is boiling hot, and it seems so thin as to be thin as to be dangerous to walk over. Persons stepping on the thinnest parts have sunk almost out of sight before they could be rescued by those at their side.

A peculiar spring is Old Faithful, which once an hour, as regular as clock work, sends forth a large body of water. All other geysers are irregular in their habits but Old Faithful has never been known to let an hour pass without showing what he could do.

In times long past two thirds of the park was a lake fully 2500 square miles in extent, and about 9000 feet above the sea. Now the lake has only 150 square miles of surface, and of course is much lower than formerly. It is surrounded by high hills, well wooded, part of the shore is a mass of volcanic material, shining in the sun as if it were a bed of gems and so brilliant that it is called [unreadable]. The lake is well stocked with fish.

Source: "Yellowstone National Park," *The Kansas City Star*, 3 July 1890, 5.

John Muir Writes About the Hetch-Hetchy Valley, *The Yosemite,* 1912

This excerpt about the Hetch-Hetchy Valley is from the first edition of John Muir's The Yosemite, *published in 1912. Muir often expressed his strong opinions about use of Yosemite Park and the Hetch-Hetchy Valley, especially the proposed dam that was being considered for the valley to help with the region's supply of water and light. After years of debate, the dam was completed in 1923.*

Yosemite is so wonderful that we are apt to regard it as an exceptional creation, the only valley of its kind in the world; but Nature is not so poor as to have only one of anything. Several other yosemites have been discovered in the Sierra that occupy the same relative positions on the Range and were formed by the same forces in the same kind of granite. One of these, the Hetch Hetchy Valley, is in the Yosemite National Park about twenty miles from Yosemite and is easily accessible to all sorts of travelers by a road and trail that leaves the Big Oak Flat road at Bronson Meadows a few miles below Crane Flat, and to mountaineers by way of Yosemite Creek basin and the head of the middle fork of the Tuolumne.

It is said to have been discovered by Joseph Screech, a hunter, in 1850, a year before the discovery of the great Yosemite. After my first visit to it in the autumn of 1871, I have always called it the "Tuolumne Yosemite," for it is a wonderfully exact counterpart of the Merced Yosemite, not only in its sublime rocks and waterfalls but in the gardens, groves and meadows of its flowery park-like floor. The floor of Yosemite is about 4000 feet above the sea; the Hetch Hetchy floor about 3700 feet. And as the Merced River flows through Yosemite, so does the Tuolumne through Hetch Hetchy. The walls of both are of gray granite, rise abruptly from the floor, are sculptured in the same style and in both every rock is a glacier monument.

Standing boldly out from the south wall is a strikingly picturesque rock called by the Indians, Kolana, the outermost of a group 2300 feet high, corresponding with the Cathedral Rocks of Yosemite both in relative position and form. On the opposite side of the Valley, facing Kolana, there is a counterpart of the El Capitan that rises sheer and plain to a height of 1800 feet, and over its massive brow flows a stream which makes the most graceful fall I have ever seen. From the edge of the cliff to the top of an earthquake talus it is perfectly free in the air for a thousand feet before it is broken into cascades among talus boulders. It is in all its glory in June, when the snow is melting fast, but fades and vanishes toward the end of summer. The only fall I know with which it may fairly be compared is the Yosemite Bridal Veil; but it excels even that favorite fall both in height and airy-fairy beauty and behavior. Lowlanders are apt to suppose that mountain streams in their wild career over cliffs lose control of themselves and tumble in a noisy chaos of mist and spray. On the contrary, on no part of their travels are they more harmonious and self-controlled. Imagine yourself in Hetch Hetchy on a sunny day in June, standing waist-deep in grass and flowers (as I have often stood), while the great pines sway dreamily with scarcely perceptible motion. Looking northward across the Valley you see a plain, gray granite cliff rising abruptly out of the gardens and groves to a height of 1800 feet, and in front of it Tueeulala's silvery scarf burning with irised sun-fire. In the first white outburst at the head there is abundance of visible energy, but it is speedily hushed and concealed in divine repose, and its tranquil progress to the base of the cliff is like that of a downy feather in a still room. Now observe the fineness and marvelous distinctness of the various sun-illumined fabrics into which the water is woven; they sift and float from form to form down the face of that grand gray rock in so leisurely and unconfused a manner that you can examine their texture, and patterns and tones of color as you would a piece of embroidery held in the hand. Toward the top of the fall you see groups of booming, comet-like masses, their solid, white heads separate, their tails like combed silk interlacing among delicate gray and purple shadows, ever forming and dissolving, worn out by friction in their rush through the air. Most of these vanish a few hundred feet below the summit, changing to varied forms of cloud-like drapery. Near the bottom the width of the fall has increased from about twenty-five feet to a hundred feet. Here it is composed of yet finer tissues, and is still without a trace of disorder—air, water and sunlight woven into stuff that spirits might wear.

So fine a fall might well seem sufficient to glorify any valley; but here, as in Yosemite, Nature seems in nowise moderate, for a short distance to the eastward of Tueeulala booms and thunders the great Hetch Hetchy Fall, Wapama, so near that you have both of them in full view from the same standpoint. It is the counterpart of the Yosemite Fall, but has a much greater volume of water, is about 1700 feet in height, and appears to be nearly vertical, though considerably inclined, and is dashed into huge outbounding bosses of foam on projecting shelves and knobs. No two falls could be more unlike—Tueeulala out in the open sunshine descending like thistledown; Wapama in a jagged, shadowy gorge roaring and thundering, pounding its way like an earthquake avalanche.

Besides this glorious pair there is a broad, massive fall on the main river a short distance above the head of the Valley. Its position is something like that of the Vernal in Yosemite, and its roar as it plunges into a surging trout-pool may be heard a long way, though it is only about twenty feet high. On Rancheria Creek, a large stream, corresponding in position with the Yosemite Tenaya Creek, there is a chain of cascades joined here and there with swift flashing plumes like the one between the Vernal and Nevada Falls, making magnificent shows as they go their glacier-sculptured way, sliding, leaping, hurrahing, covered with crisp clashing spray made glorious with sifting sunshine. And besides all these a few small streams come over the walls at wide intervals, leaping from ledge to ledge with birdlike song and watering many a hidden cliff-garden and fernery, but they are too unshowy to be noticed in so grand a place.

The correspondence between the Hetch Hetchy walls in their trends, sculpture, physical structure, and general arrangement of the main rock-masses and those of the Yosemite Valley has excited the wondering admiration of every observer. We have seen that the El Capitan and Cathedral rocks occupy the same relative positions In both valleys; so also do their Yosemite points and North Domes. Again, that part of the Yosemite north wall immediately to the east of the Yosemite Fall has two horizontal benches, about 500 and 1500 feet above the floor, timbered with golden-cup oak. Two benches similarly situated and timbered occur on the same relative portion of the Hetch Hetchy north wall, to the east of Wapama Fall, and on no other. The Yosemite is bounded at the head by the great Half Dome. Hetch Hetchy is bounded in the same way though its head rock is incomparably less wonderful and sublime in form.

The floor of the Valley is about three and a half miles long, and from a fourth to half a mile wide. The lower portion is mostly a level meadow about a mile long, with the trees restricted to the sides and the river banks, and partially separated from the main, upper, forested portion by a low bar of glacier-polished granite across which the river breaks in rapids.

The principal trees are the yellow and sugar pines, digger pine, incense cedar, Douglas spruce, silver fir, the California and golden-cup oaks, balsam cottonwood, Nuttall's flowering dogwood, alder, maple, laurel, tumion, etc. The most abundant and influential are the great yellow or silver pines like those of Yosemite, the tallest over two hundred feet in height, and the oaks assembled in magnificent groves with massive rugged trunks four to six feet in diameter, and broad, shady, wide-spreading heads. The shrubs forming conspicuous flowery clumps and tangles are manzanita, azalea, spiræa, brier-rose, several species of ceanothus, calycanthus, philadelphus, wild cherry, etc.; with abundance of showy and fragrant herbaceous plants growing about them or out in the open in beds by themselves—lilies, Mariposa tulips, brodiaeas, orchids, iris, spraguea, draperia, collomia, collinsia, castilleja, nemophila, larkspur, columbine, goldenrods, sunflowers, mints of many species, honeysuckle, etc. Many fine ferns dwell here also, especially the beautiful and interesting rock-ferns—pellaea, and cheilanthes of several species—fringing and rosetting dry rock-piles and ledges; woodwardia and asplenium on damp spots with fronds six or seven feet high; the delicate maiden-hair in mossy nooks by the falls, and the sturdy, broad-shouldered pteris covering nearly all the dry ground beneath the oaks and pines.

It appears, therefore, that Hetch Hetchy Valley, far from being a plain, common, rock-bound meadow, as many who have not seen it seem to suppose, is a grand landscape garden, one of Nature's rarest and most precious mountain temples. As in Yosemite, the sublime rocks of its walls seem to glow with life, whether leaning back in repose or standing erect in thoughtful attitudes, giving welcome to storms and calms alike, their brows in the sky, their feet set in the groves and gay flowery meadows, while birds, bees, and butterflies help the river and waterfalls to stir all the air into music—things frail and fleeting and types of permanence meeting here and blending, just as they do in Yosemite, to draw her lovers into close and confiding communion with her.

Sad to say, this most precious and sublime feature of the Yosemite National Park, one of the greatest of all our natural resources for the uplifting joy and peace and health of the people, is in danger of being dammed and made into a reservoir to help supply San Francisco with water and light, thus flooding it from wall to wall and burying its gardens and groves one or two hundred feet deep. This grossly destructive commercial scheme has long been planned and urged (though water as pure and abundant can be got from outside of the people's park, in a dozen different places), because of the comparative cheapness of the dam and of the territory which it is sought to divert from the great uses to which it was dedicated in the Act of 1890 establishing the Yosemite National Park.

The making of gardens and parks goes on with civilization all over the world, and they increase both in size and number as their value is recognized. Everybody needs beauty as well as bread, places to play in and pray in, where Nature may heal and cheer and give strength to body and soul alike. This natural beauty-hunger is made manifest in the little window-sill gardens of the poor, though perhaps only a geranium slip in a broken cup, as well as in the carefully tended rose and lily gardens of the rich, the thousands of spacious city parks and botanical gardens, and in our magnificent National parks—the Yellowstone, Yosemite, Sequoia, etc.—Nature's sublime wonderlands, the admiration and joy of the world. Nevertheless, like anything else worth while, from the very beginning, however well guarded, they have always been subject to attack by despoiling gainseekers and mischief-makers of every degree from Satan to Senators, eagerly trying to make everything immediately and selfishly commercial, with schemes disguised in smug-smiling philanthropy, industriously, shampiously crying, "Conservation, conservation, panutilization," that man and beast may be fed and the dear Nation made great. Thus long ago a few enterprising merchants utilized the Jerusalem temple as a place of business instead of a place of prayer, changing money, buying and selling cattle and sheep and doves; and earlier still, the first forest reservation, including only one tree, was likewise despoiled. Ever since the establishment of the Yosemite National Park, strife has been going on around its borders and I suppose this will go on as part of the universal battle between right and wrong, however much its boundaries may be shorn, or its wild beauty destroyed.

The first application to the Government by the San Francisco Supervisors for the commercial use of Lake Eleanor and the Hetch Hetchy Valley was made in 1903, and on December 22nd of that year it was denied by the Secretary of the Interior, Mr. Hitchcock, who truthfully said:

Presumably the Yosemite National Park was created such by law because within its boundaries, inclusive alike of its beautiful small lakes, like Eleanor, and its majestic wonders, like Hetch Hetchy and Yosemite Valley. It is the aggregation of such natural scenic features that makes the Yosemite Park a wonderland which the Congress of the United States sought by law to reserve for all coming time as nearly as practicable in the condition fashioned by the hand of the Creator—a worthy object of national pride and a source of healthful pleasure and rest for the thousands of people who may annually sojourn there during the heated months.

In 1907 when Mr. Garfield became Secretary of the Interior the application was renewed and granted; but under his successor, Mr. Fisher, the matter has been referred to a Commission, which as this volume goes to press still has it under consideration.

The most delightful and wonderful camp grounds in the Park are its three great valleys—Yosemite, Hetch Hetchy, and Upper Tuolumne; and they are also the most important places with reference to their positions relative to the other great features—the Merced and Tuolumne Cañons, and the High Sierra peaks and glaciers, etc., at the head of the rivers. The main part of the Tuolumne Valley is a spacious flowery lawn four or five miles long, surrounded by magnificent snowy mountains, slightly separated from other beautiful meadows, which together make a series about twelve miles in length, the highest reaching to the feet of Mount Dana, Mount Gibbs, Mount Lyell and Mount McClure. It is about 8500 feet above the sea, and forms the grand central High Sierra camp ground from which excursions are made to the noble mountains, domes, glaciers, etc.; across the Range to the Mono Lake and volcanoes and down the Tuolumne Cañon to Hetch Hetchy. Should Hetch Hetchy be submerged for a reservoir, as proposed, not only would it be utterly destroyed, but the sublime cañon way to the heart of the High Sierra would be hopelessly blocked and the great camping ground, as the watershed of a city drinking system, virtually would be closed to the public. So far as I have learned, few of all the thousands who have seen the park and seek rest and peace in it are in favor of this outrageous scheme.

One of my later visits to the Valley was made in the autumn of 1907 with the late William Keith, the artist. The leaf-colors were then ripe, and the great godlike rocks in repose seemed to glow with life. The artist, under their spell, wandered day after day along the river and through the groves and gardens, studying the wonderful scenery; and, after making about forty sketches, declared with enthusiasm that although its walls were less sublime in height, in picturesque beauty and charm Hetch Hetchy surpassed even Yosemite.

That any one would try to destroy such a place seems incredible; but sad experience shows that there are people good enough and bad enough for anything. The proponents of the dam scheme bring forward a lot of bad arguments to prove that the only righteous thing to do with the people's parks is to destroy them bit by bit as they are able. Their arguments are curiously like those of the devil, devised for the destruction of the first garden—so much of the very best Eden fruit going to waste; so much of the best Tuolumne water and Tuolumne scenery going to waste. Few of their statements are even partly true, and all are misleading.

Thus, Hetch Hetchy, they say, is a "low-lying meadow." On the contrary, it is a high-lying natural landscape garden, as the photographic illustrations show.

"It is a common minor feature, like thousands of others." On the contrary it is a very uncommon feature; after Yosemite, the rarest and in many ways the most important in the National Park.

"Damming and submerging it 175 feet deep would enhance its beauty by forming a crystal-clear lake." Landscape gardens, places of recreation and worship, are never made beautiful by destroying and burying them. The beautiful sham lake, forsooth, should be only an eyesore, a dismal blot on the landscape, like many others to be seen in the Sierra. For, instead of keeping it at the same level all the year, allowing Nature centuries of time to make new shores, it would, of course, be full only a month or two in the spring, when the snow is melting fast; then it would be gradually drained, exposing the slimy sides of the basin and shallower parts of the bottom, with the gathered drift and waste, death and decay of the upper basins, caught here instead of being swept on to decent natural burial along the banks of the river or in the sea. Thus the Hetch Hetchy dam-lake would be only a rough imitation of a natural lake for a few of the spring months, an open sepulcher for the others.

"Hetch Hetchy water is the purest of all to be found in the Sierra, unpolluted, and forever unpollutable." On the contrary, excepting that of the Merced below Yosemite, it is less pure than that of most of the other Sierra streams, because of the sewerage of camp grounds draining into it, especially of the Big Tuolumne Meadows camp ground, occupied by hundreds of tourists and mountaineers, with their animals, for months every summer, soon to be followed by thousands from all the world.

These temple destroyers, devotees of ravaging commercialism, seem to have a perfect contempt for Nature, and, instead of lifting their eyes to the God of the mountains, lift them to the Almighty Dollar.

Dam Hetch Hetchy! As well dam for water-tanks the people's cathedrals and churches, for no holier temple has ever been consecrated by the heart of man.

Source: "The Yosemite" (New York: The Century Co., 1912), 249-62.

"Public Gets Say on Drilling,"
Western Citizen, 7 January 2010 by Sabrina Shankman

The following article demonstrates the change in drilling policy that occurred when the Obama administration came into office in January 2009.

Interior Secretary Ken Salazar has changed the procedures the Bureau of Land Management must follow before leasing federal land for oil and gas drilling, sending a message that the Department of the Interior aims to reverse some energy policies of the Bush administration.

"The previous Administration's 'anywhere, anyhow' policy on oil and gas development ran afoul of communities, carved up the landscape, and fueled costly conflicts that created uncertainty for investors and industry," Salazar said in a news release. The BLM, which is part of the Department of the Interior, regulates oil and gas on the 256 million acres of federal land it manages.

The reformed policy, which Salazar announced earlier today, will require more detailed reviews before leases are issued, will allow for more public involvement in developing master leasing and development plans, and will shift the focus of new drilling toward areas already being developed. The reforms also create an Energy Reform Team to identify and implement the reforms.

In the past, BLM has used categorical exclusions to approve leases, allowing leases to be rubber-stamped based on existing environmental analysis rather than relying on new reviews. Based on today's announcement, BLM will no longer be allowed to use those exclusions in cases of "extraordinary circumstances"—meaning drilling that could impact protected species, historic or cultural resources, or human health and safety.

"Restoring balance to an agency that was out of whack for years is a good move," said Amy Mall, a senior policy analyst with the Natural Resources Defense Council. "It means [the BLM is] not just going to lease a parcel because the industry wants it."

She added that while the announcement is a positive one, it remains to be seen whether the reforms will be adequately implemented.

Source: http://www.westerncitizen.com/1826/public-gets-more-say-on-drilling/

"Washington Land Grab Unwelcome in West," from the office of Senator John Barrasso (R-WY), 2 March 2010

In 2010, prior to the Republican take-over of the US House of Representatives and the near takeover of the US Senate, western Senators from both parties argued against the Obama administration's land policies. This press release comes from the Senate Western Caucus (SWC) and its chairman, Senator John Barrasso (R-WY).

"THIS STRATEGY IS A FUNDAMENTALLY FLAWED APPROACH TO MANAGING PUBLIC LANDS, AND IMPLEMENTING IT WOULD BREAK TRUST WITH THE PEOPLE OF THE WEST."

March 2, 2010

WASHINGTON, DC—Today, Senate Western Caucus (SWC) Chairman John Barrasso (R-Wyo.) and caucus members sent a letter to Secretary of the Interior Ken Salazar in opposition to the Department of the Interior's (DOI) land grab strategy affecting eleven western states.

A leaked DOI document outlines a strategy to use the Antiquities Act to enact presidential designations of 17 National Monuments in Utah, Montana, New Mexico, Nevada, California, Arizona, Oregon, Colorado, Wyoming, Alaska and Washington and to acquire approximately $4 billion of private land in Nevada, California, Utah, Colorado, Montana, Idaho, Wyoming and Oregon.

The SWC letter calls on Secretary Salazar to abandon one-size-fits-all policies for public and private lands in the West.

The text of the letter follows:

March 2, 2010

The Honorable Ken Salazar
Secretary of the Interior
1349 C Street Northwest
Washington, DC 20004

Dear Secretary Salazar;

As members of the Senate Western Caucus, we write in opposition to a recently released document from the Department of the Interior detailing a strategy to overhaul public and private lands in the West. The document outlines plans for presidential monument designations and land acquisition in 12 western states. Implementing this strategy would break trust with the people of the West.

Americans enjoy a variety of benefits from our public lands, but many westerners rely on public lands for their very livelihoods. For that reason, Congress has ensured that public land management decisions are made in a process that is both public and transparent. Pursuing the strategy outlined in the released documents would threaten western livelihoods and violate the multiple use management framework that is relied upon in western communities. Americans should never live in fear that the stroke of a pen in Washington could forever change their lives.

Land management is most successful when built from local consensus and stakeholder involvement. Grassroots conservation efforts are succeeding in communities across the West. In contrast, top-down land management directives from Washington are recipes for failure. Presidential designations often engender local strife and a loss of public trust. Conflicts over jurisdiction and private property rights continue to plague national monuments designated by the Clinton Administration. Embracing these failed methods would foster resentment in western communities and eliminate the potential for collaborative conservation efforts.

Expansion of federal land holdings and authority is an unsustainable policy. The bureaus of the Department of the Interior are already overloaded with acreage and responsibility. The Bureau of Land Management faces budget shortfalls annually, and the National Park Service faces a maintenance backlog on its existing facilities of over 9 billion dollars. Policy makers must focus on making responsible investments on behalf of the American taxpayer. With that priority in mind, there is no basis for expanding acreage and creating new management requirements for federal land across the West.

The Senate Western Caucus opposes the recently released Department of the Interior strategy for land designation and acquisition. Unilateral action will not be successful in the West. Western communities have a long, successful history of land stewardship. We urge the Department to defer to local land use decision-making and grassroots conservation efforts.

The following Senators participated in the letter:

Senator John Barrasso (R-WY)
Senator Orrin Hatch (R-UT)
Senator Jon Kyl (R-AZ)
Senator Mike Enzi (R-WY)
Senator Bob Bennett (R-UT)
Senator John Ensign (R-NV)
Senator Mike Johanns (R-NE)

Source: http://barrasso.senate.gov/public/index.cfm?FuseAction=PressOffice.SenateWesternCaucus&Content Record_id=24d4890a-0494-c686-7c4a-df31887403ea&Region_id=&Issue_id=

"Repeal Timber Land Law," *Morning Oregonian* [Portland], 4 December 1908

This article highlights opposition to governmental environmental laws. Senator Knute Nelson of Minnesota called for an end to the Timber and Stone Act (1878), in which Congress authorized public lands in the states of California, Nevada, Oregon, and Washington State to be sold in plots of 160 acres at $2.50 an acre, provided the land was wooded and "unfit for civilization." By 1902, large timber companies had taken advantage of the law by purchasing large tracts of land. In 1909, President Theodore Roosevelt's National Conservation Commission called for the repeal of the 1878 act. For years, however, Western Democrats refused to allow a vote on any repeal. By 1923, the act had allowed the sale of some twelve million acres of public land to private owners. Finally, on 1 August 1955, Congress voted to repeal the act after nearly 77 years on the books.

REPEAL TIMBER LAND LAW

Nelson Voices Demand in Conservation Meeting.

Havoc Wrought in Western Forests by Speculators Who Buy Cheap and Sell Dear.

WASHINGTON, Dec. 2.—The necessity for repeal of the timber and stone act, under which, it was asserted, millions of acres of public land had been taken up by land speculators at low figures and sold later at phenomenal advances, was emphasized at the night session of the National Conservation Commission by Senator Knute Nelson, of Minnesota.

Mr. Nelson's declaration that he wanted to see that law off the statute books stirred up a lively conversation. Among those who took part were Senators Flint, Smoot and Dixon, Representative Shirley and ex-Governors Blanchard and Pardee.

Commission Fred Dennett, of the General Land Office, was the principal speaker and his remarks, dwelling upon the havoc wrought in the forests of the West by land speculators under the existing act, sounded the keynote for the views which were then voiced later and which, it is declared, probably will have weight in the recommendations the Commission will make to President Roosevelt.

Mr. Dennett spoke of the wild latitude given the speculators under the timber and stone act, by which 160 acres may be bought at $2.50 per acre and sold probably as high as $50. The Government, he said, was powerless at this time to prevent this traffic during the operation of the act.

Mr. Dennett stated that during the past year nearly 2,000,000 acres of land had been taken up, according to entries on the record.

Source: "Repeal Timber Land Law," *Morning Oregonian* [Portland], 4 December 1908, 4.

"Present Land Laws Are Not Adapted to Present Needs": Special Message of President William Howard Taft to Congress, 14 January 1910, *Morning Oregonian* [Portland], 15 January 1910

The following is excerpted from President Taft's special message on conservation of natural resources sent to Congress, January 15, 1910.

PRESENT LAND LAWS ARE NOT ADAPTED TO PRESENT NEEDS, PRESIDENT DECLARES

———————

Reappraisement According to Use is Urged—Irrigation Will Work Wonders—
Forests Must be Preserved. Waterways Important as Rate Regulators, Taft Says in Message.

———————

To the Senate and House of Representatives:

In my annual message I reserved the subject of the conservation of our natural resources for discussion in a special message from as follows:

"In several departments there is presented the necessity for legislation looking to the further conservation of our natural resources and the subject is one of such importance as to require a more detailed and extensive discussion than can be entered upon in this communication. For this reason I shall take an early opportunity to send a special message to the Congress on the subject of the improvement of our waterways and on the reclamation and irrigation of arid, semi-arid and swamp lands; upon the preservation of our forests and the reforesting of suitable areas; upon the reclassification of the public domain a view of separating from agricultural settlement mineral, coal and phosphate lands and sites belonging to the Government bordering on streams suitable for the utilization of water power."

In 1860 we had a public domain of 1,033,911,288 acres. We have now 731,354,081 acres, confined largely to the mountain ranges and the arid and semi-arid plains. We have in addition 368,035,975 acres of land in Alaska.

Lax Methods Aided Frauds.

The public lands were, during the earliest administrations, treated as a National asset for the liquidation of public debt and a source of reward for our soldiers and sailors. Later on they were donated in large amounts in aid of the construction of wagon roads and railways in order to open up regions in the West then almost inaccessible.

The principal land statutes were enacted more than a quarter of a century ago. The homestead act, the pre-emption and timber culture act, the coal land and the mining acts were among these. The rapid disposition of the public lands under the early statutes and the lax methods of distribution prevailing, due, I think, to belief that these lands should rapidly pass into private ownership, gave rise to the impression that the public domain was legitimate prey for the unscrupulous, and that it was not contrary to good morals to circumvent lands laws. This prodigal manner of disposition resulted in the passing of large areas of valuable lands and many of our natural resources into the hands of persons who felt little or no responsibility for promoting the National welfare through their development.

The truth is that title to millions of acres of public lands was fraudulently obtained, and that the right to recover a large part of such lands for the Government long since ceased by reason of statutes of limitation.

People Deeply Concerned.

There has developed in recent years a deep concern in the public mind respecting the preservation and proper use of our natural resources. This has been particularly directed toward the conservation of resources of the public domain. The problem is how to save and how to utilize, how to conserve and still to develop, for no sane person can contend that that is of the common good, that nature's blessings are only for unborn generations.

Among the most noteworthy reforms initiated by my distinguished predecessor were the vigorous prosecution of land frauds and the bringing to public attention of the necessity for preserving the remaining public domain from further spoliation, for the maintenance and extension of our forest resources and for the enactment of laws amending the obsolete statutes so as to retain Government control over that part of the public domain on which there are valuable deposits of coal, oil and phosphate, and in addition thereto to preserve control, under conditions favorable to the public, or lands along the streams in which the fall of water can be made to generate power to be transmitted in the form of electricity many miles to the points of its use, known as "water power" sites.

Investigations into violations of public land laws and prosecution of land frauds have been vigorously continued under my administration, as has been the withdrawal of coal lands for classification and valuation and the temporary withholding of power sites. Since March 4, 1909, temporary withdrawals of power sites had been made on 102 streams and these withdrawals therefore cover 229 percent more streams than were covered by the withdrawals made prior to that date.

The present statutes, except so far as they dispose of precious metals and purely agricultural lands, are not adapted to carry out the modern view of the best disposition of public lands to private ownership, under conditions offering, on the one hand, sufficient inducement to private capital to take them over for proper development with restrictive conditions, and, on the other, which shall secure to the public that character of control which will prevent a monopoly or a misuse of the lands or their products.

Statutes Are Antiquated.

One of the most pressing needs in the matter of public land reform is that lands should be classified according to their principal value or use. This ought to be done by that department whose force is best adapte to that work. It should be done by the Interior Department through the Geological Survey. Much of the confusion, fraud and contention which has existed in the pat has arisen from the lack of an official and determinative classification of the public lands and their contents.

It is now proposed to dispose of agricultural lands as such, and at the same time to reserve for other disposition the treasure of coal, oil, asphaltum, natural gas and phosphate contained therein. This may be best accomplished by separating the right to mine from the title to the surface, giving the necessary use of so much of the latter as may be required for the extraction of the deposits. The surfce might be disposed of as agricultural land under the general agricultural statute, while the coal or other mineral could be disposed of by lease on a royalty basis, with provisions requiring a certain amount of development each year; and in order to prevent the use and possession of such lands with others of similar character, which seems to constitute a monopoly forbidden by law, the lease should contain suitable provision subjecting to forfeiture the interests of persons participating in such monopoly. Such law should apply to Alaska aa to the United States.

Phosphates Will Foster Greed.

The extent of the values of phosphate is hardly realized, at what the need that there will be for it as the years roll on, and the necessity for fertilizing the land shall be calm more acute, this will be a product which will probably attract the greed of monopolists.

With respect to the public land which lies along the streams offering opportunity to convert water power into transmissible electricity, another important phase of the public question is presented. There are valuable water power sites through all public land states. Opinion is held that the transfer of sovereignty from the Federal Government to territorial governments, as they become states, included water power in rivers except that owned by riparian proprietors. I do not think it necessary to go into a discussion of this somewhat mooted question of law. It seems to me sufficient to say that the man who owns and controls the land along the stream from which the power is to be converted and transmitted owns land to which is indispensable to the conversion and use of that power. I cannot conceive how the power in streams, flowing through public lands, can be made available at all except by using the land itself as the site for the construction of the plant by which the power is generated and converted, and securing a right of way thereover for transmission lines. Under these conditions, if the Government owns the adjacent lands—indeed, if the Government is the riparian owner—it may control the use of water power by imposing proper conditions on the disposition of land necessary in the creation and utilization of water power.

[...]

Soil Must Be Conserved.

Their productive power should have the attention of our scientists that we may conserve the new soils, improve the old soils, drain wet soils, ditch swamp soils, levee river overflow soils, grow trees on thin soils, pasture hillside soils, rotate crops on all soils, discover method for cropping dry land soils, find grasses and legumes for all soils, feed grain and millfeeds on the farms where they originate, that the soils from which they come may be enriched.

The act by which, in semi-arid parts of the public domain, the area of the homestead has been enlarged from 160 to 320 acres, has resulted most beneficially in the extension of dry-farming and the demonstration which has been made of the possibility, through a variation in the character and mode of culture, of raising substantial crops without the presence of such a supply of water as has been heretofore thought to be necessary for agriculture.

But there are millions of acres of completely arid land in the public domain, which, by the establishment of reservoirs for the storing of water and the irrigation of the lands, may be made much more fruitful and productive than the best lands in a climate where the moisture comes from the clouds. Congress recognized the importance of this method of artificial distribution of water on the arid lands by the passage of the reclamation act. The proceeds of the public lands creates a fund to build the works needed to store and furnish necessary water, and it was left to the Secretary of the Interior to determine what projects should be selected among those suggested, and to direct the reclamation service, with the funds at hand, and through the engineers in the departments employ labor to construct the works.

No one can visit the far West and the country of arid and semi-arid lands without being convinced that this is one of the most important methods of conservation of our natural resources that the Government has entered upon. It would appear that over 30 projects have been undertaken and that a few of them are likely to be unsuccessful because of the lack of water or for other reasons, but generally the work which has been done had been well done and many important engineering problems have been met and solved.

Source: "Present Land Laws Are Not Adapted to Present Needs, President Declares," *Morning Oregonian* [Portland], 15 January 1910, 5.

"Groups Sue to Preserve Roadless Areas in National Forests: Claimants Support Clinton-era Rules Overturned by Bush," *The San Francisco Chronicle,* October 2005 by Bob Egelko

The fight of the Bush administration to end some of the environmental policies of the Clinton administration was frustrated by the courts. This article illustrates how environmentalists used friendly courts to halt changes in policies regarding roads in national forests.

Major environmental groups sued the Bush administration Thursday over its repeal of a Clinton administration ban on road-building and development in vast pristine areas of U.S. national forests.

The suit in San Francisco federal court by 20 organizations, including the Wilderness Society, the Sierra Club and Greenpeace, follows a suit filed Aug. 30 by California and three other states. Both challenge the government's decision in May that potentially opened some of the forests' 58.5 million roadless acres to logging and mining trucks and off-road vehicles.

"By failing to protect these critical roadless lands, the (U.S.) Forest Service erodes the public's clean-water resource and pushes a whole variety of valued fish and wildlife species toward the point where they may require endangered species listings," said Chris Frissell of the Pacific Rivers Council, one of the plaintiff groups.

Roadless areas occupy nearly one-third of the national forests and are some of the nation's last remaining untouched terrain, treasured by hikers and conservationists. Nearly all of the areas are in 12 Western states, including California. President Bill Clinton ordered the road-building ban just before leaving office in 2001 over timber industry objections.

The Bush administration rescinded the ban this year and gave states until late next year to propose roadless protections within their borders, while leaving the final decision up to the federal government. Some governors have indicated they will seek to open forest land to road-building, but Gov. Arnold Schwarzenegger has said he wants the 4.1 million roadless acres in California national forests to remain as they are.

Forest Service regional spokesman Mark Mathes said Thursday the agency, mindful of Schwarzenegger's stance and the public's concern for the environment, had no plans to build roads in California roadless areas.

Those areas are mostly steep, with unstable soil, and are not suitable for roads, Mathes said. Also, he said, California national forests have virtually no underlying oil or gas reserves, a motivation for road-building in other states.

The suit accused the Forest Service of ignoring its own scientific evidence of likely harm to water and wildlife habitat, of flouting a legal mandate to consult with government biologists about the impacts on wildlife, and of violating the agency's legal duty "to provide for the health, diversity, and productivity of the nation's forests and grasslands." The suit seeks restoration of the 2001 roadless rule.

A timber industry group criticized the environmentalists' action. Chris West, vice president of the American Forest Resource Council, told the Associated Press that the suit was "a sad case of the abuse of courts for political ends" and that road construction would help prevent forest fires.

Source: http://articles.sfgate.com/2005-10-07/news/17397270_1_roadless-areas-national-forests-forest-service.

"History of the U.S. Fish and Wildlife Service National Wildlife Refuge System," courtesy of *The Encyclopedia of Earth, The Early Years (1864–1920)*

The article is a synopsis of the early years of the US Fish & Wildlife Service and the National Wildlife Refuge System, established by President Theodore Roosevelt in 1903.

By Executive Order of March 14, 1903, President Theodore Roosevelt established Pelican Island National Wildlife Refuge, along Florida's central Atlantic coast, as the first unit of the present National Wildlife Refuge System. It is misleading, however, to conclude that this was the genesis of wildlife sanctuaries in the United States.

There is no clear documentation of just when the concept of protecting wildlife through habitat preservation was born, but as long ago as the mid-1800's, diaries of early western explorers, pictorial records and reports from journalists and speakers familiar with the West brought a public realization that the unrestricted slaughter of wildlife for food, fashion and commerce was systematically destroying an irreplaceable national heritage.

The first Federal action aimed in part at protecting wildlife resources on a designated area appears to be an Act of Congress on June 30, 1864, that transferred the Yosemite Valley from the public domain to the State of California. One of the terms of the transfer was that State authorities "shall provide against the wanton destruction of the fish and game found within the said reservation and against their capture and destruction for purposes of merchandise or profit."

Yosemite Valley was later returned to the Federal government. In 1872, Yellowstone National Park was established, primarily to protect the area's hot springs and geysers, but again, the "wanton destruction" of wildlife was forbidden. Establishment as a national park did not, however, produce the desired wildlife protection effect until passage of the Yellowstone Park Protection Act of 1894.

The earliest effort to set aside an area of Federally-owned land specifically for wildlife occurred in 1868 when President Ulysses S. Grant took action to protect the Pribilof Islands in Alaska as a reserve for the northern fur seal. In 1869, the Congress formally enacted legislation for this purpose. These remote islands in the Bering Sea were the site of the world's largest rookery of this commercially valuable animal, and the Federal government was prompted in its action primarily due to interest in obtaining revenue from the management of the fur resource. Fundamentally, this action marked a formal recognition of the need to protect and manage wildlife resources for their renewable values.

Under provisions of the Forest Reservation Creation Act of March 3, 1881, President Benjamin Harrison created by an Executive Order the Afognak Island Forest and Fish Culture Reserve in Alaska, "including its adjacent bays and rocks and territorial waters, including among others the sea lion and sea otter islands." The action showed, in its executive history, that wildlife concerns were a paramount element in the proposal. However, possibly because of the emphasis on forest and fish resource protection, the value of this area as a wildlife refuge often escapes deserved recognition. This order also established the first reservation for fish.

As a result of an increasing awareness of the importance of fish and wildlife resources, in 1871 the Federal Office of Commissioner of Fisheries and in 1886 the Division of Economic Ornithology and Mammalogy (Department of Agriculture) were established to gain better information about the

Nation's fish and wildlife resources. From studies performed by these agencies it became evident that the resources were in jeopardy and conservation, sportsmen's and scientific organizations began to lobby the Congress.

One such organization was the Boone and Crockett Club, founded in 1887 by a group of leading explorers, writers, scientists and political leaders, including Theodore Roosevelt. Roosevelt's activities during the 1880's and 1890's placed him in the mainstream of events concerning the plight of fish and wildlife and other natural resources from coast to coast. He was acquainted with resource management needs and with the many individuals, organizations and agencies that were in the forefront of efforts to stem the losses. Thus, when he became President in 1901, he was singularly well-suited to the task of natural resource protection.

By the turn of the century the nation had witnessed the near extinction of the bison, increasing devastation of wading bird populations by plume hunters in Florida, and severe reductions in the populations of other once abundant forms of wildlife such as the passenger pigeon. Public support increased for more vigorous actions on the part of the government to reverse this downward slide.

In Florida, in an effort to control plume hunting, the American Ornithologists Union and the National Association of Audubon Societies (now the National Audubon Society) persuaded the State Legislature to pass a model non-game bird protection law in 1901. These organizations then employed wardens to protect rookeries, in effect establishing colonial bird sanctuaries.

Such public concern, combined with the conservation-minded President Roosevelt, resulted in the initial Federal land specifically set aside for a non-marketable form of wildlife (the brown pelican) when 3-acre Pelican Island was proclaimed a Federal Bird Reservation in 1903. Thus, it is said to be the first bona fide "refuge." The first warden employed by the government at Pelican Island, Paul Kroegel, was an Audubon warden whose salary was $1 a month.

Following the modest trend begun with Pelican Island, many other islands and parcels of land and water were quickly dedicated for the protection of various species of colonial nesting birds that were being destroyed for their plumes and other feathers. Such refuge areas included Breton, Louisiana (1904), Passage Key, Florida (1905), Shell Keys, Louisiana (1907), and Key West, Florida (1908).

The need for sound management of these reservations or refuges had become apparent as the knowledge of preservation and conservation requirements grew. In 1905, the Bureau of Biological Survey was established in the Department of Agriculture, replacing the old Division of Economic Ornithology and Mammalogy, with responsibility for new reservations and "set-aside" areas.

During this period of time, on the Pacific coast sea bird populations were declining due to their extensive exploitation for eggs, feathers and guano. In response to this growing bird resource threat, Federal reserve status was granted to Quillayute Needles, Washington in 1907 and to Farallon Islands, California and areas of the Hawaiian Islands in 1909. Establishment of Lower Klamath, California in 1908 then marked the beginning of the practice of creating wildlife refuges on Bureau of Reclamation reservoirs. Seventeen such western "overlay" refuges were established on one day alone in 1909 by Executive Order 1032 of February 25. By the end of his administration in 1909, Roosevelt had issued a total of 51 Executive Orders that established wildlife reservations in 17 states and three territories.

Congress also had continued to respond to the public mood recognized by Roosevelt in establishing the Wichita Mountains Forest and Game Preserve in 1905, the National Bison Range in 1908, and the National Elk Refuge in 1912. The latter was the first unit of the present system to be referred to as a "refuge." The Izaak Walton League had initiated establishment of the National Elk Refuge by purchasing lands which they then donated to the government as a nucleus for the refuge. At the time it was said that elk were so plentiful that they were killed for their prized teeth alone, which brought as much as $1,500 a pair. Then in 1913, some 2.7 million acres were set aside in one action by President William Howard Taft when the vast Aleutian Island chain was added to the system.

The Federal government first exerted authority over migratory birds by legislation, the Migratory Bird Act, enacted in 1913 to protect migratory bird species. An interesting historical footnote is that this landmark legislation was attached as a rider to an agricultural appropriation bill and signed unknowingly by outgoing President Taft. Subsequently, the Migratory Bird Treaty was concluded between the United States and Great Britain (for Canada) in 1916. This treaty, implemented by Congress in 1918, created an even larger role for the Federal government in managing migratory birds.

Organization and Growth (1921–1955)

The Migratory Bird Treaty Act of 1918 provided for regulations to control the taking of migratory species. Implementation of this Act did result in increased populations for a time. However, it soon became clear that effective management of the resource would require increased efforts to protect habitat. Refuges, established primarily by Executive Order, were still for the most part too few and too small to ensure the future of such wide-ranging migratory species as waterfowl and shore birds.

The first refuge acquisitions specifically for management of waterfowl came about with the Acts establishing the Upper Mississippi River Wild Life and Fish Refuge in 1924 (again through impetus provided by the Izaak Walton League) and the Bear River Migratory Bird Refuge in 1928. Prior to this, the initial attempts to provide for the systematic acquisition of new lands for refuges had begun in 1921. A bill was introduced in Congress that would establish a "Refuge System," a Migratory Bird Refuge Commission, and a one-dollar Federal hunting stamp.

The bill was rejected four times during the next eight years. Finally, in 1929, it became law under the Migratory Bird Conservation Act, but only after it was stripped of any provisions for refuge hunting areas and a Federal hunting stamp. The costs for managing and expanding the system were to be funded by Congressional appropriations. Despite these shortcomings, this Act provided the authority under which the National Wildlife Refuge System grew in the years that followed.

A major stimulus for the Refuge System came in 1934 with the passage of the Migratory Bird Hunting and Conservation Stamp Act (known as the Duck Stamp Act). The Act's later amendments increased the price of the stamp providing a continuing source of revenue for acquisition of migratory bird habitat. They also authorized that a part of a refuge's area could be opened to waterfowl hunting (now set at 40 percent by the NWRS Administration Act of 1966).

Of equal importance in 1934 was the appointment by President Franklin D. Roosevelt of a special "blue ribbon" committee, consisting of Jay Norwood "Ding" Darling, Chairman, and Thomas Beck and Aldo Leopold to study and advise him on waterfowl needs. This dynamic trio alerted the Nation, as no other group had done before, to the crisis facing the waterfowl resource as a result of drought, over-harvest and habitat destruction. They also campaigned vigorously for the funds to combat these problems. Then, in 1935 "Ding" Darling was appointed head of the Bureau of Biological Survey and brought with him a dynamic and energetic young midwesterner, J. Clark Salyer II, to manage the fledgling refuge program.

For the next 31 years, until his death in 1966, Salyer was the primary driving force in selecting new refuge areas and campaigning for their acquisition, in defending their integrity, in protecting the wildlife which they harbored, and in seeing that refuges were administered and managed to best serve the wildlife resource. Theodore Roosevelt, "Ding" Darling and others had a profound influence on the development of the Refuge System, but Salyer was unquestionably the "father" of the system. The imprints of his involvement remain to this day.

The year 1934 also saw the passage of the Fish and Wildlife Coordination Act. This Act, amended several times between 1934 and 1965, authorizes most Federal water resource agencies to acquire lands associated with water use projects as mitigation and enhancement of fish and wildlife. The Act further provides for the management of these lands by the U.S. Fish and Wildlife Service or State wildlife agencies.

Two other important developments during these years were the Migratory Bird and Mammal Treaty with Mexico in 1936 and the Lea Act of 1948. The latter legislation served to greatly increase the acquisition of waterfowl habitat in California. The Bankhead-Jones Farm Tenant Act, passed in 1937, was the authority used for establishing a number of wildlife refuges across the country. Under this Act, certain lands acquired by the Resettlement Administration were designated by Executive Order for management as refuges. Refuges acquired under this authority include Carolina Sandhills in South Carolina, Piedmont in Georgia, Noxubee in Mississippi, and Necedah in Wisconsin.

For several decades the Bureau of Biological Survey had remained in the Department of Agriculture and the Bureau (formerly Commission) of Fisheries in the Department of Commerce. In 1939 both bureaus were transferred to the Department of the Interior through an Executive Branch reorganization.

They were merged to form the Fish and Wildlife Service in 1940. Then in 1956, two bureaus were formed under the U. S. Fish and Wildlife Service-the Bureau of Sport Fisheries and Wildlife (which included the Division of Wildlife Refuges) and the Bureau of Commercial Fisheries. Subsequently, the Bureau of Commercial Fisheries was transferred in 1970 to the Department of Commerce and became the National Marine Fisheries Service, while the Fish and Wildlife Service still remains a bureau of the Department of the Interior.

New Directions, New Opportunities (1956–1996)

The Fish and Wildlife Act of 1956 established a comprehensive national fish and wildlife policy and broadened the authority for acquisition and development of refuges. The funds necessary to implement this authority, however, were not immediately forthcoming. Without increased funding, land acquisition during the 1950's could not keep pace with the high rate of drainage (primarily due to intensive agricultural development) of waterfowl breeding habitat in the prairie pothole country.

To remedy this situation, Congress passed an amendment to the Duck Stamp Act in 1958 which authorized the Waterfowl Production Area (WPA) program. To fund the WPA program and accelerate the wetland preservation effort, Congress also passed the Wetlands Loan Act of 1961. As later amended, this Act authorized a loan of $200 million to be spent over a period of 23 years and to be repaid from duck stamp revenues.

Recognizing new public demands for recreational activities after World War II, Congress passed the Refuge Recreation Act of 1962. This Act authorized the recreational use of refuges when such uses did not interfere with the area's primary purposes and when sufficient funds were available to conduct recreational activities. The Act also clarified the appropriateness of public use on refuges, encouraged efforts to provide wildlife-oriented recreation, interpretation and environmental education activities, and required that such uses be compatible with the purposes for which the lands were acquired.

Perhaps the law of greatest significance to wildlife refuges since the Migratory Bird Conservation Act of 1929 has been the National Wildlife Refuge System Administration Act of 1966. The Act provided guidelines and directives for administration and management of all areas in the system including "wildlife refuges, areas for the protection and conservation of fish and wildlife that are threatened with extinction, wildlife ranges, game ranges, wildlife management areas, and waterfowl production areas."

In addition, the 1966 law established the standard of "compatibility," requiring that uses of refuge lands must be determined to be compatible with the purposes for which individual refuges were established. This standard was later strengthened and clarified in the National Wildlife Refuge System Improvement Act of 1997.

The Endangered Species Act of 1973 also redirected management emphasis on some refuges. It is considered the world's foremost law protecting species faced with extinction. This Act has provided extensive means of protection for endangered species (including penalties for harming endangered animals, review and compliance obligations for various Federal agency programs, and the listing of species eligible for protection). Over 25 new refuges have been added to the NWRS under this authority including Attwater Prairie Chicken, Texas, Mississippi Sandhill Crane, Mississippi, Columbian White-tailed Deer, Washington, and Crocodile Lake, Florida.

The Alaska Native Claims Settlement Act of 1971 (ANCSA), an outgrowth of the Alaska Statehood Act, is a law of enormous importance to the National Wildlife Refuge System. Among numerous other provisions, it authorized the addition of immense acreages of highly productive, internationally significant wildlife lands to the NWRS. Further far-reaching resource protection measures for Alaska were mandated by Congress in the passage on December 2, 1980, of the Alaska National Interest Lands Conservation Act (ANILCA). The Act added nine new refuges, expanded seven existing refuges and added 53.7 million acres to the NWRS. This Act alone nearly tripled the acreage of lands encompassed in the Refuge System.

Approaching the Centennial (1997 and on)

In 1997, Congress provided much-needed organic legislation with the passage of the National Wildlife Refuge System Improvement Act. This legislation amended the National Wildlife Refuge System Administration Act of 1966 and provided significant new guidance for the management of the Refuge System. It provided a new statutory mission statement and directed that the Refuge System be managed as a national system of lands and waters devoted to conserving wildlife and maintaining biological integrity of ecosystems. The law also clarified management priorities by declaring that certain wildlife-dependent recreational uses are appropriate activities on refuges, strengthened the compatibility determination process, and required the Service to undertake comprehensive conservation planning for each refuge.

From the earliest years national wildlife refuges have played a major role in the evolution of resource conservation in the United States. The National Wildlife Refuge System now comprises more than 520 units in all 50 states, American Samoa, Puerto Rico, the Virgin Islands, the Johnson Atoll, Midway Atoll and several other Pacific Islands. Refuges now encompass over 93 million acres of valuable wildlife habitat.

Included in this total are nearly 1.9 million acres of wetlands in the prairie pothole region of the north-central United States. These wetlands are known as "waterfowl production areas," and have Federal protection through fee acquisition or easements. This vital habitat, together with the wetlands of the Canadian prairies and Alaska, provides the key production areas where the bulk of North America's waterfowl nest and rear their young.

Wilderness designation also helps protect diverse refuge areas including islands, lakes, forests, deserts, and mountains. Currently, 20.6 million acres of refuge lands have been designated as wilderness under provisions of the Wilderness Act of 1964. The Act states that these Congressionally-designated areas "... shall be administered for the use and enjoyment of the American people in such a manner as will leave them unimpaired for future use and enjoyment as wilderness."

The history of the Refuge System is the history of farsighted actions, untiring efforts, and generous donations from untold numbers of dedicated individuals from both government and private sectors. These individuals have recognized that our wildlife resources are an invaluable national heritage. They have collectively pressed for their protection and won, often against conflicting interests. As we approach the Refuge System's Centennial in 2003, it is a good time to reflect upon the collective efforts of these dedicated people in creating what is regarded as the largest and most outstanding wildlife conservation program in the world-the National Wildlife Refuge System.

Source: http://www.eoearth.org/article/History_of_the_U.S._Fish_and_Wildlife_Service_National_Wildlife_Refuge_System#Approaching_the_Centennial_.281997_and_on.29.

"Fact Sheet on the BLM's Management of Livestock Grazing," July 2010, courtesy of the U.S. Department of the Interior

The use of public lands to graze livestock animals began about the time of the US Civil War and has continued to today. Overgrazing and fees charged mark the controversies over this use of public lands since the practice began. This report, from the Bureau of Land Management in July 2010, lays out the agency's mandate over these lands, their usage, and the system of permits and fees imposed on those who utilize the lands for grazing.

Grazing on Public Lands

The Bureau of Land Management, which administers about 245 million acres of public lands, manages livestock grazing on 157 million acres of those lands, as guided by Federal law. The terms and conditions for grazing on BLM-managed lands (such as stipulations on forage use and season of use) are set forth in the permits and leases issued by the Bureau to public land ranchers.

The BLM administers nearly 18,000 permits and leases held by ranchers who graze their livestock, mostly cattle and sheep, at least part of the year on more than 21,000 allotments under BLM management. Permits and leases generally cover a 10-year period and are renewable if the BLM determines that the terms and conditions of the expiring permit or lease are being met. The amount of grazing that takes place each year on BLM-managed lands can be affected by such factors as drought, wildfire, and market conditions.

In managing livestock grazing on public rangelands, the BLM's overall objective is to ensure the long-term health and productivity of these lands and to create multiple environmental benefits that result from healthy watersheds. The Bureau administers public land ranching in accordance with the Taylor Grazing Act of 1934, and in so doing provides livestock-based economic opportunities in rural communities while contributing to the West's, and America's, social fabric and identity. Together, public lands and the adjacent private ranches maintain open spaces in the fast-growing West, provide habitat for wildlife, offer a myriad of recreational opportunities for public land users, and help preserve the character of the rural West.

A Brief History of Public Lands Grazing

During the era of homesteading, Western public rangelands were often overgrazed because of policies designed to promote the settlement of the West and a lack of understanding of these arid ecosystems. In response to requests from Western ranchers, Congress passed the Taylor Grazing Act of 1934 (named after Rep. Edward Taylor of Colorado), which led to the creation of grazing districts in which grazing use was apportioned and regulated. Under the Taylor Grazing Act, the first grazing district to be established was Wyoming Grazing District Number 1 on March 23, 1935. Secretary of the Interior Harold Ickes created a Division of Grazing within the Department to administer the grazing districts; this division later became the U.S. Grazing Service and was headquartered in Salt Lake City. In 1946, as a result of a government reorganization by the Truman Administration, the Grazing Service was merged with the General Land Office to become the Bureau of Land Management.

The unregulated grazing that took place before enactment of the Taylor Grazing Act caused unintended damage to soil, plants, streams, and springs. As a result, grazing management was initially designed to increase productivity and reduce soil erosion by controlling grazing through both fencing and water projects and by conducting forage surveys to balance forage demands with the land's productivity ("carrying capacity").

These initial improvements in livestock management, which arrested the degradation of public rangelands while improving watersheds, were appropriate for the times. But by the 1960s and 1970s, public appreciation for public lands and expectations for their management rose to a new level, as made clear by congressional passage of such laws as the National Environmental Policy Act of 1969, the Endangered Species Act of 1973, and the Federal Land Policy and Management Act of 1976. Consequently, the BLM moved from managing grazing in general to better management or protection of specific rangeland resources, such as riparian areas, threatened and endangered species, sensitive plant species, and cultural or historical objects. Consistent with this enhanced role, the Bureau developed or modified the terms and conditions of grazing permits and leases and implemented new range improvement projects to address these specific resource issues, promoting continued improvement of public rangeland conditions.

Current Management of Public Lands Grazing

Today the BLM manages livestock grazing in a manner aimed at achieving and maintaining public land health. To achieve desired conditions, the agency uses rangeland health standards and guidelines, which the BLM developed in the 1990s with input from citizen-based Resource Advisory Councils across the West. Standards describe specific conditions needed for public land health, such as the presence of streambank vegetation and adequate canopy and ground cover. Guidelines are the management techniques designed to achieve or maintain healthy public lands, as defined by the standards. These techniques include such methods as seed dissemination and periodic rest or deferment from grazing in specific allotments during critical growth periods.

Legal Mandates relating to Public Lands Grazing

Laws that apply to the BLM's management of public lands grazing include the Taylor Grazing Act of 1934, the National Environmental Policy Act of 1969, the Endangered Species Act of 1973, the Federal Land Policy and Management Act of 1976, and the Public Rangelands Improvement Act of 1978.

Federal Grazing Fee

The Federal grazing fee, which applies to Federal lands in 16 Western states on public lands managed by the BLM and the U.S. Forest Service, is adjusted annually and is calculated by using a formula originally set by Congress in the Public Rangelands Improvement Act of 1978. Under this formula, as modified and extended by a presidential Executive Order issued in 1986, the grazing fee cannot fall below $1.35 per animal unit month (AUM); also, any fee increase or decrease cannot exceed 25 percent of the previous year's level. (An AUM is the amount of forage needed to sustain one cow and her calf, one horse, or five sheep or goats for a month.) The grazing fee for 2011 is $1.35 per AUM, the same level as it was in 2010.

The Federal grazing fee is computed by using a 1966 base value of $1.23 per AUM for livestock grazing on public lands in Western states. The figure is then adjusted each year according to three factors - current private grazing land lease rates, beef cattle prices, and the cost of livestock production. In effect, the fee rises, falls, or stays the same based on market conditions, with livestock operators paying more when conditions are better and less when conditions have declined.

Number of Livestock on BLM-managed Lands

The Bureau does not make an annual national "count" of the livestock that graze on BLM-managed lands because the actual number of livestock grazing on public lands on any single day varies throughout the year and livestock are often moved from one grazing allotment to another. So an aggregate head count would provide very little information on overall livestock use. Instead, the BLM compiles information on the number of AUMs used each year, which takes into account both the number of livestock and the amount of time they spend on public lands. (For the definition of an AUM, see previous section.) Over time there has been a gradual decrease in the amount of grazing that takes place on BLM-managed land, and that trend continues today. Grazing use on public lands has declined from 18.2 million AUMs in 1954 to 8.2 million AUMs in 2010. In most years, the actual use of forage is less than the amount authorized because forage amounts and demands depend on several factors, such as drought, wildfire, and market conditions, as noted earlier regarding annual public land grazing levels.

Grazing Permit System

Any U.S. citizen or validly licensed business can apply for a BLM grazing permit or lease. To do so, one must either:

buy or control private property (known as "base property") that has been legally recognized by the Bureau as having preference for the use of public land grazing privileges,

or acquire property that has the capability to serve as base property and then apply to the BLM to transfer the preference for grazing privileges from an existing base property to the acquired property (which would become the new "base property").

The first alternative happens when base property (a private ranch) is sold or leased to a new individual or business; the buyer or lessee then applies to the BLM for the use of grazing privileges associated with that property. The second alternative would happen when a rancher wants to transfer existing public land grazing privileges to another party while keeping the private ranch property. Before buying or leasing ranch property, it is advisable to contact the BLM Field Office that administers grazing in the area of the base property. The BLM has information on the status of the grazing privileges attached to the base property, including the terms and conditions of the associated grazing permit or lease that authorizes the use of those privileges and other important information. All applicants for grazing permits or leases must meet the qualifications for public land grazing privileges that are specified in the BLM's grazing regulations.

The Role of Livestock Grazing on Public Lands Today

Grazing, which was one of the earliest uses of public lands when the West was settled, continues to be an important use of those same lands today. Livestock grazing now competes with more uses than it did in the past, as other industries and the general public look to the public lands as sources of both conventional and renewable energy and as places for outdoor recreational opportunities, including off-highway vehicle use. Among the key issues that face public land managers today are global climate change, severe wildfires, invasive plant species, and dramatic population increases, including the associated rural residential development that is occurring throughout the West.

Livestock grazing can result in impacts on public land resources, but well-managed grazing provides numerous environmental benefits as well. For example, while livestock grazing can lead to increases in some invasive species, well-managed grazing can be used to manage vegetation. Intensively managed "targeted" grazing can control some invasive plant species or reduce the fuels that contribute to severe wildfires. Besides providing such traditional products as meat and fiber, well-managed rangelands and other private ranch lands support healthy watersheds, carbon sequestration, recreational opportunities, and wildlife habitat. Livestock grazing on public lands helps maintain the private ranches that, in turn, preserve the open spaces that have helped write the West's history and will continue to shape this region's character in the years to come.

Source: http://www.blm.gov/wo/st/en/prog/grazing.html.

Remarks of Rep. John F. Lacey on The Lacey Act, *The Congressional Record*, 30 April 1900

Rep. John Fletcher Lacey (1841-1913), Republican of Iowa, introduced The Lacey Act in 1900 after years of extreme abuse against wildlife in the United States. Reports of the mass slaughter of animals for their skins, or, as Lacey tried to fix, of birds for their feathers for ladies' hats, led Congress to pass this act, which was signed into law by President William McKinley on 25 May 1900. Speaking in the debate with Lacey in the excerpted section below is Rep. James Mann, Republican of Illinois, who later rose to become House Minority Leader. On 22 May 2008, as the 100th anniversary of the act neared, Congress enacted an amendment to the original law, passed as The Food, Conservation, and Energy Act of 2008, which expanded the protections afforded to a wider and broader range of plants and animals not covered in the original act. For further study on the topic, see Mary Annette Gallagher, "John F. Lacey: A Study in Organizational Politics" (Ph.D. dissertation, University of Arizona, 1970), *and Robert S. Anderson, "The Lacey Act: America's Premier Weapon in the Fight Against Unlawful Wildlife Trafficking,"* Public Land Law Review, 16 (1995), 27-89.

Mr. LACEY. Mr. Chairman, this bill is one that has attracted a good deal of interest in various sections of the country. Horticulturists, agriculturists, and lovers of birds everywhere, and also the League of American Sportsmen, and others interested in game and the protection of game all over the United States have been strongly enlisted in its support.

Briefly, the bill provides for a few purposes only. First, it authorizes the Secretary of Agriculture to utilize his Department for the reintroduction of birds that have become locally extinct or are becoming so in some parts of the United States. There are some kinds of insectivorous birds and some kinds of game birds, that heretofore were abundant in many localities, which have become very scarce indeed, and in some localities entirely exterminated. The wild pigeon, formerly in this country in flocks of millions, has entirely disappeared from the face of the earth. Some hopeful enthusiasts have claimed that the pigeon would again be heard from in South America, but there seems to be no well-grounded basis for this hope. In some localities certain kinds of grouse have almost entirely disappeared. This bill gives the Secretary of Agriculture power to aid in the reintroduction, which, I think, will prove a useful adjunct to the action of the States, which have undertaken the preservation of the native wild birds.

Now, the next purpose in the bill is to allow the Secretary of Agriculture to control the importation of foreign wild birds and foreign wild animals. If this law had been in force at the time the mistake made in the introduction of the English sparrow we should have been spared from the pestilential existence of that "rat of the air," that vermin of the atmosphere. But some gentlemen who thought they knew better than anybody else what the country needed saw fit to import these little pests, and they have done much toward driving the native wild bird life out of the States. This bill provides that the Secretary may prevent the importation of the fruit bat, the flying fox, the English sparrow, the starling, and other birds of that kind, which, in his discretion, he may regard as detrimental.

The necessity for a provision of this kind is obvious. The mongoose, a miserable, murderous animals that was introduced for the purpose of killing snakes in Jamaica—by the way, one member of the House asked me the other day was kind of a bird the mongoose was [Laughter]—the mongoose has proved a nuisance and a pest worse than the serpent that it kills. It drove the rats in Jamaica to the trees, and the rat now there has become an arboreal animal. The rat still exists and keeps out of the way of the mongoose. But the birds of the island have been almost destroyed by this imported pest. Now, a proper control on the part of the Secretary of Agriculture would prevent the importation of injurious foreign animals. Some gentlemen in California have suggested the propriety of introducing the fruit bat or the flying fox there, and this bill would prevent their importation. They would prove as great a nuisance as the English rabbits in Australia and the Scotch thistle in Canada. Some patriotic son of Scotland wanted to to see if the thistle would grow in Canada. He tried it, and there is no dispute about it now. It grows in Canada.

There is compensation in the distribution of plants, birds, and animals by the God of nature. Man's attempt to change and interfere often leads to serious results. The French pink was introduced as a flower in Oregon, and it has spread throughout the wheat fields and become an injury to agriculture. The English yard plantain has become a great evil in New Zealand.

Rabbits were introduced in Australia, and today the most persistent efforts are necessary to keep them within endurable limits. The Russian thistle is spreading with great rapidity in the Dakotas, and though this plant has finally proven to have some value for forage, yet the people of the Northwest would be glad if that plant had never found a footing in that region.

It is important that the introduction of foreign wild birds and animals should be under competent legal supervision, and this bill will accomplish that result.

Mr. MANN. Would it interrupt the gentleman if I asked a question right here?

Mr. LACEY. I would rather state the outlines of this bill and then yield upon any point in the bill. The next proposition in the bill, and that is the vital one of all, is to prohibit interstate commerce in birds and wild game—that is, insectivorous, useful birds, and wild game birds, and wild game of any kind killed in violation of local laws. Take the State of Georgia, that has enacted most rigid laws for the protection of insectivorous birds and game birds. Trappers go there and catch the quail, net or trap them in violation of the local law, pack them in barrels or boxes and ship them to other markets in the United States. It is done secretly. The result is that the market houses in other States have been utilized as places in which to dispose of these birds and animals killed in violation of the laws of the State. Game wardens of the various States have long desired some legislation of this kind by which they can stop the nefarious traffic in birds and game killed in defiance of their State laws.

Take the State which I have the honor in part to represent—the State of Iowa. A few years ago it was filled with prairie chickens; quails were abundant. A careful protection of the quail has recently resulted in an increase of those beautiful birds; but the shipment of prairie chickens has been going on until they have well-nigh become extinct. This bill if enacted into law would enable the local authorities to prevent the transportation of these birds. Is perfectly evident however that such law might be abused unless suitably guarded. Persons might make use of it for the purpose of blackmailing the carriers. Therefore a provision has been inserted in this bill by which carriers will not be held responsible for the shipment unless they have knowingly carried the forbidden articles. But the shipper can not plead ignorance, and when complaint is made against the carrier, he will transfer the responsibility of the crime to the shipper, and the result will be that the whole traffic can be broken up.

As to insectivorous birds, I saw an article going the rounds of the newspapers the other day purporting to give an interview between my friend from Illinois [Mr. CANNON] and myself. Whilst the interview was not stated with entire accuracy, the general facts are true, and I will repeat it now as an illustration of one of the features of this bill.

When this bill was up in the House before on a motion to suspend the rules, my friend from Illinois [Mann] raised the question of "no quorum." Two-thirds of the House were in favor of passing the bill, but there was not a quorum present; and the gentlemen from Illinois raised that point and prevented further consideration to the bill...

[...]

Objection was made to this bill upon the theory that it was a purely sentimental measure and intended merely to strike at bird millinery. Not so. It is true, Mr. Chairman, that there is some sentiment in the bill: and it is a proper, a legitimate, sentiment. The love of birds is something that ought to be taught in every school. Their protection is something that ought to be inculcated in the mind of every boy and girl.

Source: Remarks of Rep. John F. Lacey and others, in "Congressional Record: Containing The Proceedings and Debates of the Fifty-Sixth Congress, First Session. Volume XXXIII" (Washington, D.C.: Government Printing Office, 1900), 4871-75.

"Roosevelt's Land Policy," *The Kansas City Star*, 25 October 1907

Theodore Roosevelt, who served as President from 1901 to 1909, was the first conservationist President. In his eight short years, he set aside more land for national parks, refuges, and other protective areas than all of his predecessors combined. This article illuminates his land policies as they were seen by his contemporaries.

ROOSEVELT'S LAND POLICY

Conservation of Resources The President's Purpose.

Would Save Public Forests, Grazing Lands and Coal Fields for the People's Use—Forests Frightfully Wasted—Startling Statistics

---

Excerpted from Frederick W. Ford in Boston Transcript.

It is perhaps not too much to say that the future millions of Americans will remember Theodore Roosevelt with greatest gratitude for his saving for them and for their use these natural rights—the soil, the woods and the waters with which this country is so richly dowered.

Briefly stated, the President's policy is:

(1) To conserve the national forests for the use of the people.

(2) To furnish homes for the farmer in the desert by reclaiming the soil through irrigation.

(3) To maintain unimpaired the public ranges for the grazing of live stock.

(4) To retain control by the government of the public coal lands, to the end that the people may be insured of their proper use.

(5) To place a homesteader on every plot of stable land, whether that plot be on a national forest, a public range or among the mineral lands.

There is no flaw in the logic of the theory which the President is working out, but there is, nevertheless, a tremendous amount of opposition, direct and indirect, to his course. This comes from selfish and corrupt interests which in the past have looted the public domain right and left, and from a public that had stood by and profited indirectly and perhaps persuaded itself that it was not a very grave offense to rob the government. So powerful is this opposition that it makes itself felt in the halls of Congress, and [the] last session of that body tried to head off the President in his effort to protect the people and it is understood that the fight will be renewed this winter. We have cut and slashed our great forests in the most wasteful manner, forgetting that there was any limit to our resources, and made barren wastes of great areas of country. The stern logic of events, however, finally brought to the attention of the thoughtful the absolute peril that confronted us. Then forestry, which had been practiced in other countries for hundreds of years, was invoked to prevent the utter destruction of our standing timber.

Annual Output of Forest Products.

Lumber consumption has increased more rapidly than production. From 1880 to 1900 the population increase was 52 percent and the lumber cut increase was 94 percent. The United States is now using 400 board feet of lumber per capita, while the average for Europe is just 60 feet per capita.

Since 1880—twenty-six years—the lumber cut has aggregated 706,712,000,000 board feet.

The present estimated stumpage of the United States is a trillion board feet. We are consuming this at the rate of exceeding 20 billion cubic feet per year. To produce this quantity of wood without impacting our forests of 700 million acres they must make an annual increment of thirty cubic feet per acre. Under present conditions the average annual increment is probably less than ten cubic feet per acre. This means that each year's cut at the present rate takes the growth of more than three years. If there were no annual increase these figures would mean that our forest would disappear in twenty of thirty years but there is an annual increment even under present wasteful methods of about 33 percent of the yearly cut, which would give our forests a life of forty or fifty years. Under scientific management, however, it would be possible to make our forests yield the necessary annual increment of 30 cubic feet per acre to meet the present demand; indeed, forestry experts claim that this figure could be exceeded and the forest made to meet the larger demand of an increased population.

Practical forestry does not forbid the cutting of trees; it rather treats them as a crop to be cultivated and harvested when ripe, care being taken to do it without waste, and makes simple provision for reproduction. It is only when the ripe wood is harvested properly that the forests attain to their highest usefulness. A forest lumbered in usual way is harvested at an enormous cost to the forest itself. The young growth for the present and the future is injured or killed, the uncared for slash provokes and feeds fires, and the productive capacity of the forest land often times is destroyed for scores of years to come. On the other hand, proper methods of forestry not only maintain but also increase the capital value of forestland, the crop is harvested more completely, although less rapidly, the way is prepared for reproduction and the young growth is protected, and the danger of forest fires is minimized. To be able to do this intelligently, a full knowledge of the life of trees must be obtained in order that it might be possible to co-operate with nature in bringing about the desired results.

Forests Conserve Rainfall.

Forests properly handled not only furnish a continuous and undiminishing supply of wood but they also protect the soil and act as a natural reservoir, insuring a constant supply of water for rivers. The tremendous importance to the country of the conservation of the forests for wood alone already has been shown in figures. No figures are possible to show the incalculable value of the forests in conserving the water supply. Strip the forests from the hills and valleys of the very Western states, where the greatest opposition has been shown to the President's land policy, and many of the streams that now furnish water for reclaiming the desert lands would dry up. Others would be torrents during the wet season, and perhaps not even trickling rivulets during the dry season. Forests conserve rainfall, preventing drought within their confines during rainless periods. The litter which covers the floor of a forest saves the water which would otherwise be lost; the water thus retained finds its way by seepage to the sources of springs and streams and thus maintains their steady flow. Deforestation and drainage cause a rapid flow, and the immediate result is freshers and floods, and the final result is drought during long continued rainless periods.

How the Water is Saved.

Rainfall escapes from the ground upon which it falls in five ways—through evaporation, transpiration, surface runoff, seepage runoff and deep seepage. By evaporation is meant the moisture which passes into the atmosphere in the form of vapor from water and soil surfaces, and from objects resting upon such surfaces, including vegetation. Transpiration is that portion of the rainfall which sinks into the soil and which is later taken up by the vegetation through the roots and given off to the atmosphere through the stems and foliage. To this latter should be added, although not actually a part of it, the comparatively small amount of moisture taken up by the vegetation, but which through chemical change becomes a part of the organic vegetable structure, by surface or superficial runoff is meant that portion of the precipitation which, from the time of falling until its exit from the drainage basin, passes over the surface without gaining access to the soil. On the other hand, by seepage runoff is meant that portion of the rainfall which sinks into the earth, but which later reappears on the surface at lower elevations, and with the surface runoff escapes from the drainage basin in the streams. By deep seepage is meant that portion of the precipitation which sinks into the soil, but to such depths that it does not reappear later on the surf of the drainage basin. Evaporation and transpiration are frequently classes together as evaporation.

Penalty of Reforestation.

Stream flow consists of both surface runoff and seepage runoff. Although these two cannot be separately determined, total runoff admits of accurate measurement. Surface runoff may be considered as flood water, while seepage runoff is that portion of the drainage which gives the streams a sustained flow. It is evident that any factor which decreases the surface or superficial runoff and increases the seepage runoff is of the utmost importance in regulating the flow of the streams. Again, forests, by checking the velocity of the wind and covering the mineral soil with a thick layer of dead leaves and other forest litter, effectively prevent soil transportation by both wind and water. On high elevations, where streams generally have their birth, the influence of the forest in this respect is of the utmost importance. So great is this influence that it exerts a marked effect upon topography. In mountainous regions particularly the repeated destruction of forests permits the soil formed by the decomposition of the rocks at the sources of streams to be transported to lower elevations, with a consequent slow change in the details of the landscape. Such regions, if unforested, are apt to have precipitous slopes and scanty soil on the higher elevations. In that case there is no adequate medium to absorb the rain, and it flows over the surface. On the other hand, if such refions are well wooded the slopes are less precipitous, and a considerable depth of soil usually covers the broad summits. As a result, the rain water is absorbed, the surface flow is reduced to a minimum and a steady supply of water is furnished to the streams.

Ten years ago Prof. Shaler estimated that in the upland regions of the states south of Pennsylvania 3,000 square miles of soil had been destroyed as the result of forest denudation, and that the destruction was then proceeding at the rate of 100,000 square miles of fertile soil per year. This enormous loss of fertility by soil wash can be prevented by forestry and the regulation of grazing, the destruction of forest plants by overgrazing, and accompanied by a loss of surface soil through erosion, as is the case with forest destruction.

Source: "Roosevelt's Land Policy," *The Kansas City Star*, 25 October 1907, 2.

Tennessee Valley Authority v. Hiram G. Hill, Jr., et al. (437 U.S. 153 {1978})

Starting in the early 1970s, the effort to construct a dam on the Tellico River in Tennessee led to a series of court cases that culminated in the landmark Tennessee Valley Authority v. Hill, which, 30 years later, still echoes across the landscape of environmental law, and gave rise to powers under the Endangered Species Act (ESA) unforeseen at the time. As one law article noted, "a majority of the [US Supreme] Court proclaimed that the ESA was intended [to halt and reverse the trend toward species extinction, whatever the cost]" and backed up those and other bold words by preventing a nearly completed federal dam from impounding its reservoir because doing so would eliminate the only known (at the time) habitat of a small fish, the now infamous snail darter. To this day, Hill remains actively discussed in judicial opinions.

Mr. Chief Justice BURGER delivered the opinion of the Court.

The questions presented in this case are (a) whether the Endangered Species Act of 1973 requires a court to enjoin the operation of a virtually completed federal dam-which had been authorized prior to 1973-when, pursuant to authority vested in him by Congress, the Secretary of the Interior has determined that operation of the dam would eradicate an endangered species; and (b) whether continued congressional appropriations for the dam after 1973 constituted an implied repeal of the Endangered Species Act, at least as to the particular dam.

I

The Little Tennessee River originates in the mountains of northern Georgia and flows through the national forest lands of North Carolina into Tennessee, where it converges with the Big Tennessee River near Knoxville. The lower 33 miles of the Little Tennessee takes the river's clear, free-flowing waters through an area of great natural beauty. Among other environmental amenities, this stretch of river is said to contain abundant trout. Considerable historical importance attaches to the areas immediately adjacent to this portion of the Little Tennessee's banks. To the south of the river's edge lies Fort Loudon, established in 1756 as England's southwestern outpost in the French and Indian War. Nearby are also the ancient sites of several native American villages, the archeological stores of which are to a large extent unexplored.[1] These include the Cherokee towns of Echota and Tennase, the former being the sacred capital of the Cherokee Nation as early as the 16th century and the latter providing the linguistic basis from which the State of Tennessee derives its name.[2]

In this area of the Little Tennessee River the Tennessee Valley Authority, a wholly owned public corporation o the United States, began constructing the Tellico Dam and Reservoir Project in 1967, shortly after Congress appropriated initial funds for its development.[3] Tellico is a multipurpose regional development project designed principally to stimulate shoreline development, generate sufficient electric current to heat 20,000 homes,[4] and provide flatwater recreation and flood control, as well as improve economic conditions in "an area characterized by underutilization of human resources and outmigration of young people." Hearings on Public Works for Power and Energy Research Appropriation Bill, 1977, before a Subcommittee of the House Committee on Appropriations, 94th Cong., 2d Sess., pt. 5, p. 261 (1976). Of particular relevance to this case is one aspect of the project, a dam which TVA determined to place on the Little Tennessee, a short distance from where the river's waters meet with the Big Tennessee. When fully operational, the dam would impound water covering some 16,500 acres-much of which represents valuable and productive farmland-thereby converting the river's shallow, fast-flowing waters into a deep reservoir over 30 miles in length.

The Tellico Dam has never opened, however, despite the fact that construction has been virtually completed and the dam is essentially ready for operation. Although Congress has appropriated monies for Tellico every year since 1967, progress was delayed, and ultimately stopped, by a tangle of lawsuits and administrative proceedings. After unsuccessfully urging TVA to consider alternatives to damming the Little Tennessee, local citizens and national conservation groups brought suit in the District Court, claiming that the project did not conform to the requirements of the National Environmental Policy Act of 1969 (NEPA), 83 Stat. 852, 42 U.S.C. § 4321 et seq. After finding TVA to be in violation of NEPA, the District Court enjoined the dam's completion pending the filing of an appropriate environmental impact statement. *Environmental Defense Fund v. TVA,* 339 F.Supp. 806 (ED Tenn.), aff'd, 468 F.2d 1164 (CA6 1972). The injunction remained in effect until late 1973, when the District Court concluded that TVA's final environmental impact statement for Tellico was in compliance with the law. *Environmental Defense Fund v. TVA,* 371 F.Supp. 1004 (ED Tenn.1973), aff'd, 492 F.2d 466 (CA6 1974).[5]

A few months prior to the District Court's decision dissolving the NEPA injunction, a discovery was made in the waters of the Little Tennessee which would profoundly affect the Tellico Project. Exploring the area around Coytee Springs, which is about seven miles from the mouth of the river, a University of Tennessee ichthyologist, Dr. David A. Etnier, found a previously unknown species of perch, the snail darter, or *Percina (Imostoma) tanasi.*[6] This three-inch, tannish-colored fish, whose numbers are estimated to be in the range of 10,000 to 15,000, would soon engage the attention of environmentalists, the TVA, the Department of the Interior, the Congress of the United States, and ultimately the federal courts, as a new and additional basis to halt construction of the dam.

Until recently the finding of a new species of animal life would hardly generate a cause celebre. This is particularly so in the case of darters, of which there are approximately 130 known species, 8 to 10 of these having been identified only in the last five years.[7] The moving force behind the snail darter's sudden fame came some four months after its discovery, when the Congress passed the Endangered Species Act of 1973 (Act), 87 Stat. 884, 16 U.S.C. § 1531 et seq. (1976 ed.). This legislation, among other things, authorizes the Secretary of the Interior to declare species of animal life "endangered"[8] and to identify the "critical habitat"[9] of these creatures. When a species or its habitat is so listed, the following portion of the Act-relevant here-becomes effective:

"The Secretary [of the Interior] shall review other programs administered by him and utilize such programs in furtherance of the purposes of this chapter. All other Federal departments and agencies shall, in consultation with and with the assistance of the Secretary, utilize their authorities in furtherance of the purposes of this chapter by carrying out programs for the conservation of endangered species and threatened species listed pursuant to section 1533 of this title and *by taking such action necessary to insure t at actions authorized, funded, or carried out by them do not jeopardize the continued existence of such endangered species and threatened species or result in the destruction or modification of habitat of such species* which is determined by the Secretary, after consultation as appropriate with the affected States, to be critical." 16 U.S.C. § 1536 (1976 ed.) (emphasis added).

In January 1975, the respondents in this case[10] and others petitioned the Secretary of the Interior[11] to list the snail darter as an endangered species. After receiving comments form various interested parties, including TVA and the State of Tennessee, the Secretary formally listed the snail darter as an endangered species on October 8, 1975. 40 Fed.Reg. 47505-47506; see 50 C.F.R. § 17.11(i) (1976). In so acting, it was noted that "the snail darter is a living entity which is genetically distinct and reproductively isolated from other fishes." 40 Fed.Reg. 47505. More important for the purposes of this case, the Secretary determined that the snail darter apparently lives only in that portion of the Little Tennessee River which would be completely inundated by the reservoir created as a consequence of the Tellico Dam's completion. Id., at 47506.[12]

The Secretary went on to explain the significance of the dam to the habitat of the snail darter:

"[T]he snail darter occurs only in the swifter portions of shoals over clean gravel substrate in cool, low-turbidity water. Food of the snail darter is almost exclusively snails which require a clean gravel substrate for their survival. *The proposed impoundment of water behind the proposed Tellico Dam would result in total destruction of the snail darter's habitat." Ibid.* (emphasis added).

Subsequent to this determination, the Secretary declared the area of the Little Tennessee which would be affected by the Tellico Dam to be the "critical habitat" of the snail darter. 41 Fed.Reg. 13926-13928 (1976) (to be certified as 50 CFR § 17.81). Using these determinations as a predicate, and notwithstanding the near completion of the dam, the Secretary declared that pursuant to § 7 of the Act, "all Federal agencies must take such action as is necessary to insure that actions authorized, funded, or carried out by them do not result in the destruction or modification of this critical habitat area." 41 Fed.Reg. 13928 (1976) (to be codified as 50 CFR § 17.81(b)). This notice, of course, was pointedly directed at TVA and clearly aimed at halt ng completion or operation of the dam.

During the pendency of these administrative actions, other developments of relevance to the snail darter issue were transpiring. Communication was occurring between the Department of the Interior's Fish and Wildlife Service and TVA with a view toward settling the issue informally. These negotiations were to no avail, however, since TVA consistently took the position that the only available alternative was to attempt relocating the snail darter population to another suitable location. To this end, TVA conducted a search of alternative sites which might sustain the fish, culminating in the experimental transplantation of a number of snail darters to the nearby Hiwassee River. However, the Secretary of the Interior was not satisfied with the results of these efforts, finding that TVA had presented "little evidence that they have carefully studied the Hiwassee to determine whether or not" there were "biological and other factors in this river that [would] negate a successful transplant."[13] 40 Fed.Reg. 47506 (1975).

Meanwhile, Congress had also become involved in the fate of the snail darter. Appearing before a Subcommittee of the House Committee on Appropriations in April 1975-some seven months before the snail darter was listed as endangered-TVA representatives described the discovery of the fish and the relevance of the Endangered Species Act to the Tellico Project. Hearings on Public Works for Water and Power Development and Energy Research Appropriation Bill, 1976, before a Subcommittee of the House Committee on Appropriations, 94th Cong., 1st Sess., pt. 7, pp. 466-467 (1975); Hearings on H.R. 8122, Public Works for Water and Power Development and Energy Research Appropriations for Fiscal Year 1976, before a Subcommittee of the Senate Committee on Appropriations, 94th Cong., 1st Sess., pt. 4, pp. 3775 3777 (1975). At that time TVA presented a position which it would advance in successive forums thereafter, namely, that the Act did not prohibit the completion of a project authorized, funded, and substantially constructed before the Act was passed. TVA also described its efforts to transplant the snail darter, but contended that the dam should be finished regardless of the experiment's success. Thereafter, the House Committee on Appropriations, in its June 20, 1975, Report, stated the following in the course of recommending that an additional $29 million be appropriated for Tellico:

"The *Committee* directs that the project, for which an environmental impact statement has been completed and provided the Committee, should be completed as promptly as possible . . . ." H.R.Rep.No.94-319, p. 76 (1975). (Emphasis added.)

Congress then approved the TVA general budget, which contained funds for continued construction of the Tellico Project.[14] In December 1975, one month after the snail darter was declared an endangered species, the President signed the bill into law. Public Works for Water and Power Development and Energy Research Appropriation Act, 1976, 89 Stat. 1035, 1047.

In February 1976, pursuant to § 11(g) of the Endangered Species Act, 87 Stat. 900, 16 U.S.C. § 1540(g) (1976 ed.),[15] respondents filed the case now under review, seeking to enjoin completion of the dam and impoundment of the reservoir on the ground that those actions would violate the Act by directly causing the extinction of the species *Percina (Imostoma) tanasi*. The District Court denied respondents' request for a preliminary injunction and set the matter for trial. Shortly thereafter the House and Senate held appropriations hearings which would include discussions of the Tellico budget. At these hearings, TVA Chairman Wagner reiterated the agency's position that the Act did not apply to a project which was over 50% finished by the time the Act became effective and some 70% to 80% complete when the snail darter was officially listed as endangered. It also notified the Committees of the recently filed lawsuit's status and reported that TVA's efforts to transplant the snail darter had "been very encouraging." Hearings on Public Works for Water and Power Development and Energy Research & Appropriation Bill, 1977, before a Subcommittee of the House Committee on Appropriations, 94th Cong., 2d Sess., pt. 5, pp. 261-262 (1976); Hearings on Public Works for Water and Power Development and Energy Research Appropriations for Fiscal Year 1977, before a Subcommittee of the Senate Committee on Appropriations, 94th Cong., 2d Sess., pt. 4, pp. 3096-3099 (1976).

Trial was held in the District Court on April 29 and 30, 1976, and on May 25, 1976, the court entered its memorandum opinion and order denying respondents their requested relief and dismissing the complaint. The District Court found that closure of the dam and the consequent impoundment of the reservoir would "result in the adverse modification, if not complete destruction, of the snail darter's critical habitat,"[16] making it "highly probable" that "the continued existence of the snail darter" would be "jeopardize[d]." 419 F.Supp. 753, 757 (ED Tenn.). Despite these findings, the District Court declined to embrace the plaintiffs' position on the merits: that once a federal project was shown to jeopardize an endangered species, a court of equity is compelled to issue an injunction restraining violation of the Endangered Species Act.

In reaching this result, the District Court stressed that the entire project was then about 80% complete and, based on available evidence, "there [were] no alternatives to impoundment of the reservoir, short of scrapping the entire project." *Id.*, at 758. The District Court also found that if the Tellico Project was permanently enjoined, "[s]ome $53 million would be lost in nonrecoverable obligations," *id.*, at 759, meaning that a large portion of the $78 million already expended would be wasted. The court also noted that the Endangered Species Act of 1973 was passed some seven years after construction on the dam commenced and that Congress had continued appropriations for

Tellico, with full awareness of the snail darter problem. Assessing these various factors, the District Court concluded:

"At some point in time a federal project becomes so near completion and so incapable of modification that a court of equity should not apply a statute enacted long after inception of the project to produce an unreasonable result. . . . Where there has been an irreversible and irretrievable commitment of resources by Congress to a project over a span of almost a decade, the Court should proceed with a great deal of circumspection." *Id.,* at 760.

To accept the plaintiffs' position, the District Court argued, would inexorably lead to what it characterized as the absurd result of requiring "a court to halt impoundment of water behind a fully completed dam if an endangered species were discovered in the river on the day before such impoundment was scheduled to take place. We cannot conceive that Congress intended such a result." *Id.,* at 763.

Less than a month after the District Court decision, the Senate and House Appropriations Committees recommended the full budget request of $9 million for continued work on Tellico. See S.Rep.No.94-960, p. 96 (1976); H.R.Rep.No.94-1223, p. 83 (1976). In its Report accompanying the appropriations bill, the Senate Committee stated:

"During subcommittee hearings, TVA was questioned about the relationship between the Tellico project's completion and the November 1975 listing of the snail darter (a small 3-inch fish which was discovered in 1973) as an endangered species under the Endangered Species Act. TVA informed the Committee that it was continuing its efforts to preserve the darter, while working towards the scheduled 1977 completion date. TVA repeated its view that the Endangered Species Act did not prevent the completion of the Tellico project, which has been under construction for nearly a decade. The subcommittee brought this matter, as well as the recent U. S. District Court's decision upholding TVA's decision to complete the project, to the attention of the full Committee. *The Committee does not view* the Endangered Species Act as prohibiting the completion of the Tellico project at its advanced stage and directs that this project be completed as promptly as possible in the public interest." S.Rep.No.94-960, *supra,* at 96. (Emphasis added.)

On June 29, 1976, both Houses of Congress passed TVA's general budget, which included funds for Tellico; the President signed the bill on July 12, 1976. Public Works for Water and Power Development and Energy Research Appropriation Act, 1977, 90 Stat. 889, 899.

Thereafter, in the Court of Appeals, respondents argued that the District Court had abused its discretion by not issuing an injunction in the face of "a blatant statutory violation." *Hill v. TVA,* 549 F.2d 1064, 1069 (CA6 1977). The Court of Appeals agreed, and on January 31, 1977, it reversed, remanding "with instructions that a permanent injunction issue halting all activities incident to the Tellico Project which may destroy or modify the critical habitat of the snail darter." *Id.,* at 1075. The Court of Appeals directed that the injunction "remain in effect until Congress, by appropriate legislation, exempts Tellico from compliance with the Act or the snail darter has been deleted from the list of endan ered species or its critical habitat materially redefined." *Ibid.*

The Court of Appeals accepted the District Court's finding that closure of the dam would result in the known population of snail darters being "significantly reduced if not completely extirpated." *Id.,* at 1069. TVA, in fact, had conceded as much in the Court of Appeals, but argued that "closure of the Tellico Dam, as the last stage of a ten-year project, falls outside the legitimate purview of the Act if it is rationally construed." *Id.,* at 1070. Disagreeing, the Court of Appeals held that the record revealed a prima facie violation of § 7 of the Act, namely that TVA had failed to take "such action . . . necessary to insure" that its "actions" did not jeopardize the snail darter or its critical habitat.

The reviewing court thus rejected TVA's contention that the word "actions" in § 7 of the Act was not intended by Congress to encompass the terminal phases of ongoing projects. Not only could the court find no "positive reinforcement" for TVA's argument in the Act's legislative history, but also such an interpretation was seen as being "inimical to . . . its objectives." 549 F.2d, at 1070. By was of illustration, that court pointed out that "the detrimental impact of a project upon an endangered species may not always be clearly perceived before construction is well underway." *Id.,* at 1071. Given such a likelihood, the Court of Appeals was of the opinion that TVA's position would require the District Court, sitting as a chancellor, to balance the worth of an endangered species against the value of an ongoing public works measure, a result which the appellate court was not willing to accept. Emphasizing the limits on judicial power in this setting, the court stated:

"Current project status cannot be translated into a workable standard of judicial review. Whether a dam is 50% or 90% completed is irrelevant in calculating the social and scientific costs attributable to the disappearance of a unique form of life. Courts are ill-equipped to calculate how many dollars must be invested before the value of a dam exceeds that of the endangered species. Our responsibility under § 1540(g)(1)(A) is merely to preserve the status quo where endangered species are threatened, thereby guaranteeing the legislative or executive branches sufficient opportunity to grapple with the alternatives." *Ibid.*

As far as the Court of Appeals was concerned, it made no difference that Congress had repeatedly approved appropriations for Tellico, referring to such legislative approval as an "advisory opinio[n]" concerning the proper application of an existing statute. In that court's view, the only relevant legislation was the Act itself, "[t]he meaning and spirit" of which was "clear on its face." *Id.,* at 1072.

Turning to the question of an appropriate remedy, the Court of Appeals ruled that the District Court had erred by not issuing an injunction. While recognizing the irretrievable loss of millions of dollars of public funds which would accompany injunctive relief, the court nonetheless decided that the Act explicitly commanded precisely that result:

"It is conceivable that the welfare of an endangered species may weigh more heavily upon the public conscience, as expressed by the final will of Congress, than the writeoff of those millions of dollars already expended for Tellico in excess of its present salvageable value." *Id.,* at 1074.

Following the issuance of the permanent injunction, members of TVA's Board of Directors appeared before Subcommittees of the House and Senate Appropriations Committees to testify in support of continued appropriations for Tellico. The Subcommittees were apprised of all aspects of Tellico's status, including the Court of Appeals' decision. TVA reported that the dam stood "ready for the gates to be closed and the reservoir filled," Hearings on Public Works for Water and Power D velopment and Energy Research Appropriation Bill, 1978, before a Subcommittee of the House Committee on Appropriations, 95th Cong., 1st Sess., pt. 4, p. 234 (1977), and requested funds for completion of certain ancillary parts of the project, such as public use areas, roads, and bridges. As to the snail darter itself, TVA commented optimistically on its transplantation efforts, expressing the opinion that the relocated fish were "doing well and ha[d] reproduced." *Id.,* at 235, 261-262.

Both Appropriations Committees subsequently recommended the full amount requested for completion of the Tellico Project. In its June 2, 1977, Report, the House Appropriations Committee stated:

"It is *the Committee's view* that the Endangered Species Act was not intended to halt projects such as these in their advanced stage of completion, and [the Committee] strongly recommends that these projects not be stopped because of misuse of the Act." H.R.Rep.No.95 379, p. 104. (Emphasis added.)

As a solution to the problem, the House Committee advised that TVA should cooperate with the Department of the Interior "to relocate the endangered species to another suitable habitat so as to permit the project to proceed as rapidly as possible." *Id.,* at 11. Toward this end, the Committee recommended a special appropriation of $2 million to facilitate relocation of the snail darter and other endangered species which threatened to delay or stop TVA projects. Much the same occurred on the Senate side, with its Appropriations Committee recommending both the amount requested to complete Tellico and the special appropriation for transplantation of endangered species. Reporting to the Senate on these measures, the Appropriations Committee took a particularly strong stand on the snail darter issue:

"This *committee has not viewed* the Endangered Species Act as preventing the completion and use of these projects which were well under way at the time the affected species were listed as endangered. If the act has such an effect which is contrary to *the Committee's understanding* of the intent of Congress in enacting the Endangered Species Act, funds should be appropriated to allow these projects to be completed and their benefits realized in the public interest, the Endangered Species Act notwithstanding." S.Rep.No.95-301, p. 99 (1977). (Emphasis added.)

TVA's budget, including funds for completion of Tellico and relocation of the snail darter, passed both Houses of Congress and was signed into law on August 7, 1977. Public Works for Water and Power Development and Energy Research Appropriation Act, 1978, 91 Stat. 797.

We granted certiorari, 434 U.S. 954, 98 S.Ct. 478, 54 L.Ed.2d 312 (1977), to review the judgment of the Court of Appeals.

II

We begin with the premise that operation of the Tellico Dam will either eradicate the known population of snail darters or destroy their critical habitat. Petitioner does not now seriously dispute this fact.[17] In any event, under § 4(a)(1) of the Act, 87 Stat. 886, 16 U.S.C. § 1533(a)(1) (1976 ed.), the Secretary of the Interior is vested with exclusive authority to determine whether a species such as the snail darter is "endangered" or "threatened" and to ascertain the factors which have led to such a precarious existence. By § 4(d) Congress has authorized-indeed commanded-the Secretary to "issue such regulations as he deems necessary and advisable to provide for the conservation of such species." 16 U.S.C. § 1533(d) (1976 ed.). As we have seen, the Secretary promulgated regulations which declared the snail darter an endangered species whose critical habitat would be destroyed by creation of the Tellico Dam. Doubtless petitioner would prefer not to have these regulations on the books, but there is no suggestion that the Secretary exceeded his authority or abused his discretion in issuing the regulations. Indeed, no judicial review of the Secretary's determinations has ever been sought and hence the validity of his actions are not open to review in this Court.

Starting from the above premise, two questions are presented: (a) Would TVA be in violation of the Act if it completed and operated the Tellico Dam as planned? (b) If TVA's actions would offend the Act, is an injunction the appropriate remedy for the violation? For the reasons stated hereinafter, we hold that both questions must be answered in the affirmative.

(A)

It may seem curious to some that the survival of a relatively small number of three-inch fish among all the countless millions of species extant would require the permanent halting of a virtually completed dam for which Congress has expended more than $100 million. The paradox is not minimized by the fact that Congress continued to appropriate large sums of public money for the project, even after congressional Appropriations Committees were apprised of its apparent impact upon the survival of the snail darter. We conclude, however, that the explicit provisions of the Endangered Species Act require precisely that result.

One would be hard pressed to find a statutory provision whose terms were any plainer than those in § 7 of the Endangered Species Act. Its very words affirmatively command all federal agencies "to *insure* that actions *authorized, funded, or carried out* by them do not *jeopardize* the continued existence" of an endangered species or "*result* in the destruction or modification of habitat of such species . . . ." 16 U.S.C. § 1536 (1976 ed.). (Emphasis added.) This language admits of no exception. Nonetheless, petitioner urges, as do the dissenters, that the Act cannot reasonably be interpreted as applying to a federal project which was well under way when Congress passed the Endangered Species Act of 1973. To sustain that position, however, we would be forced to ignore the ordinary meaning of plain language. It has not been shown, for example, how TVA can close the gates of the Tellico Dam without "carrying out" an action that has been "authorized" and "funded" by a federal agency. Nor can we understand how such action will *"insure "* that the snail darter's habitat is not disrupted.[18] Accepting the Secretary's determinations, as we must, it is clear that TVA's proposed operation of the dam will have precisely the opposite effect, namely the *eradication* of an endangered species.

Concededly, this view of the Act will produce results requiring the sacrifice of the anticipated benefits of the project and of many millions of dollars in public funds.[19] But examination of the language, history, and structure of the legislation under review here indicates beyond doubt that Congress intended endangered species to be afforded the highest of priorities.

When Congress passed the Act in 1973, it was not legislating on a clean slate. The first major congressional concern for the preservation of the endangered species had come with passage of the Endangered Species Act of 1966, 80 Stat. 926, repealed, 87 Stat. 903.[20] In that legislation Congress gave the Secretary power to identify "the names of the species of native fish and wildlife found to be threatened with extinction," § 1(c), 80 Stat. 926, as well as authorization to purchase land for the conservation, protection, restoration, and propagation of "selected species" of "native fish and wildlife" threatened with extinction. §§ 2(a)-(c), 80 Stat. 926-927. Declaring the preservation of endangered species a national policy, the 1966 Act directed all federal agencies both to protect these species and *"insofar as is practicable and consistent with the[ir] primary purposes,"* § 1(b), 80

Stat. 926, "preserve the habitats of such threatened species on lands under their jurisdiction." *Ibid.* (Emphasis added.) The 1966 statute was not a sweeping prohibition on the taking of endangered species, however, except on federal lands, § 4(c), 80 Stat. 928, and even in those federal areas the Secretary was authorized to allow the hunting and fishing of endangered species. § 4(d)(1), 80 Stat. 928.

In 1969 Congress enacted the Endangered Species Conservation Act, 83 Stat. 275, repealed, 87 Stat. 903, which continued the provisions of the 1966 Act while at the same time broadening federal involvement in the preservation of endangered species. Under the 1969 legislation, the Secretary was empowered to list species "threatened with worldwide extinction," § 3(a), 83 Stat. 275; in addition, the importation of any species so recognized into the United State was prohibited. § 2, 83 Stat. 275. An indirect approach to the taking of endangered species was also adopted in the Conservation Act by way of a ban on the transportation and sale of wildlife taken in violation of any federal, state, or foreign law. §§ 7(a) (b), 83 Stat. 279.[21]

Despite the fact that the 1966 and 1969 legislation represented "the most comprehensive of its type to be enacted by any nation"[22] up to that time, Congress was soon persuaded that a more expansive approach was needed if the newly declared national policy of preserving endangered species was to be realized. By 1973, when Congress held hearings on what would later become the Endangered Species Act of 1973, it was informed that species were still being lost at the rate of about one per year, 1973 House Hearings 306 (statement of Stephen R. Seater, for Defenders of Wildlife), and "the pace of disappearance of species" appeared to be "accelerating." H.R.Rep.No.93-412, p. 4 (1973). Moreover, Congress was also told that the primary cause of this trend was something other than the normal process of natural selection:

"[M]an and his technology has *[sic]* continued at any ever-increasing rate to disrupt the natural ecosystem. This has resulted in a dramatic rise in the number and severity of the threats faced by the world's wildlife. The truth in this is apparent when one realizes that half of the recorded extinctions of mammals over the past 2,000 years have occurred in the most recent 50-year period." 1973 House Hearings 202 (statement of Assistant Secretary of the Interior).

That Congress did not view these developments lightly was stressed by one commentator:

"The dominant theme pervading all Congressional discussion of the proposed [Endangered Species Act of 1973] was the overriding need *to devote whatever effort and resources were necessary* to avoid further diminution of national and worldwide wildlife resources. Much of the testimony at the hearings and much debate was devoted to the biological problem of extinction. Senators and Congressmen uniformly deplored the irreplaceable loss to aesthetics, science, ecology, and the national heritage should more species disappear." Coggins, Conserving Wildlife Resources: An Overview of the Endangered Species Act of 1973, 51 N.D.L.Rev. 315, 321 (1975). (Emphasis added.)

The legislative proceedings in 1973 are, in fact, replete with expressions of concern over the risk that might lie in the loss of *any* endangered species.[23] Typifying these sentiments is the Report of the House Committee on Merchant Marine and Fisheries on H.R. 37, a bill which contained the essential features of the subsequently enacted Act of 1973; in explaining the need for the legislation, the Report stated:

"As we homogenize the habitats in which these plants and animals evolved, and as we increase the pressure for products that they are in a position to supply (usually unwillingly) we threaten their-and our own-genetic heritage.

"The value of this genetic heritage is, quite literally, incalculable.

* * * * *

"From the most narrow possible point of view, *it is in the best interests of mankind to minimize the losses of genetic variations.* The reason is simple: they are potential resources. They are keys to puzzles which we cannot solve, and may provide answers to questions which we have not yet learned to ask.

"To take a homely, but apt, example: one of the critical chemicals in the regulation of ovulations in humans was found in a common plant. Once discovered, and analyzed, humans could duplicate it synthetically, but had it never existed-or had it been driven out of existence before we knew its potentialities-we would never have tried to synthesize it in the first place.

"Who knows, or can say, what potential cures for cancer or other scourges, present or future, may lie locked up in the structures of plants which may yet be undiscovered, much less analyzed? . . . Sheer self-interest impels us to be cautious.

"The institutionalization of that caution lies at the heart of H.R. 37 . . . .." H.R.Rep.No.93-412, pp. 4-5 (1973). (Emphasis added.)

As the examples cited here demonstrate, Congress was concerned about the unknown uses that endangered species might have and about the *unforeseeable* place such creatures may have in the chain of life on this planet.

In shaping legislation to deal with the problem thus presented, Congress started from the finding that "[t]he two major causes of extinction are hunting and destruction of natural habitat." S.Rep.No.93-307, p. 2 (1973) U.S.Code Cong & Admin.News 1973, pp. 2989, 2990. Of these twin threats, Congress was informed that the greatest was destruction of natural habitats; see 1973 House Hearings 236 (statement of Associate Deputy Chief for National Forest System, Dept. of Agriculture); *id.,* at 241 (statement of Director of Mich. Dept. of Natural Resources); id., at 306 (statement of Stephen R. Seater, Defenders of Wildlife); Lachenmeier, The Endangered Species Act of 1973: Preservation or Pandemonium?, 5 Environ. Law 29, 31 (1974). Witnesses recommended, amo ng other things, that Congress require all land-managing agencies "to avoid damaging critical habitat for endangered species and to take positive steps to improve such habitat." 1973 House Hearings 241 (statement of Director of Mich. Dept. of Natural Resources). Virtually every bill introduced in Congress during the 1973 session responded to this concern by incorporating language similar, if not identical, to that found in the present § 7 of the Act.[24] These provisions were designed, in the words of an administration witness, "for the first time [to] *prohibit* [a] federal agency from taking action which does jeopardize the status of endangered species," Hearings on S. 1592 and S. 1983 before the Subcommittee on Environment of the Senate Committee on Commerce, 93d Cong., 1st Sess., 68 (1973) (statement of Deputy Assistant Secretary of the Interior) (emphasis added); furthermore, the proposed bills would *"direc[t]* all . . . Federal agencies to utilize their authorities for carrying out programs *for the protection* of endangered animals." 1973 House Hearings 205 (statement of Assistant Secretary of the Interior). (Emphasis added.)

As it was finally passed, the Endangered Species Act of 1973 represented the most comprehensive legislation for the preservation of endangered species ever enacted by any nation. Its stated purposes were "to provide a means whereby the ecosystems upon which endangered species and threatened species depend may be conserved," and "to provide a program for the conservation of such . . . species . . . ." 16 U.S.C. § 1531(b) (1976 ed.). In furtherance of these goals, Congress expressly stated in § 2(c) that "all Federal departments and agencies *shall* seek to *conserve endangered species* and threatened species . . . ." 16 U.S.C. § 1531(c) (1976 ed.). (Emphasis added.) Lest there be any ambiguity as to the meaning of this statutory directive, the Act specifically defined "conserve" as meaning *"to use and the use of all methods and procedures which are necessary to bring any endangered species or threatened species* to the point at which the measures provided pursuant to this chapter are no longer necessary." § 1532(2). (Emphasis added.) Aside from § 7, other provisions indicated the seriousness with which Congress viewed this issue: Virtually all dealings with endangered species, including taking, possession, transportation, and sale, were prohibited, 16 U.S.C. § 1538 (1976 ed.), except in extremely narrow circumstances, see § 1539(b). The Secretary was also given extensive power to develop regulations and programs for the preservation of endangered and threatened species.[25] § 1533(d). Citizen involvement was encouraged by the Act, with provisions allowing interested persons to petition the Secretary to list a species as endangered or threatened, § 1533(c)(2), see n. 11, *supra,* and bring civil suits in United States district courts to force compliance with any provision of the Act, §§ 1540(c) and (g).

Section 7 of the Act, which of course is relied upon by respondents in this case, provides a particularly good gauge of congressional intent. As we have seen, this provision had its genesis in the Endangered Species Act of 1966, but that legislation qualified the obligation of federal agencies by stating that they should seek to preserve endangered species only *"insofar as is practicable and consistent with the[ir] primary purposes . . . ."* Likewise, every bill introduced in 1973 contained a qualification similar to that found in the earlier statutes.[26] Exemplary of these was the administration bill, H.R. 4758, which in § 2(b) would direct federal agencies to use their authorities to further the ends of the Act *"insofar as is practicable and consistent with the[ir] primary purposes . . . ."* (Emphasis added.) Explaining the idea behind this language, an administration spokesman told Congress that it "would further signal to all . . . agencies of the Government that this is the *first priority, consistent with their primary objectives."* 1973 House Hearings 213 (statement of Deputy Assistant Secretary of the Interior). (Emphasis added.) This type of language did not go unnoticed by those advocating strong endangered species legislation. A representative of the Sierra Club, for example, attacked the use of the phrase "consistent with the primary purpose" in proposed H.R. 4758, cautioning that the qualification "could be construed to be a declaration of congressional policy that other agency purposes are necessarily more important than protection of endangered species and would always prevail if conflict were to occur." 1973 House Hearings 335 (statement of the chairman of the Sierra Club's National Wildlife Committee); see *id.,* at 251 (statement for the National Audubon Society).

What is very significant in this sequence is that the final version of the 1973 Act carefully omitted all of the reservations described above. In the bill which the Senate initially approved (S. 1983), however, the version of the current § 7 merely required federal agencies to "carry out such programs as are practicable for the protection of species listed . . . ."[27] S. 1983, § 7(a). (Emphasis added.) By way of contrast, the bill that originally passed the House, H.R. 37, contained a provision which was essentially a mirror image of the subsequently passed § 7— indeed all phrases which might have qualified an agency's responsibilities had been omitted from the bill.[28] In explaining the expected impact of this provision in H.R. 37 on federal agencies, the House Committee's Report states:

"This subsection *requires* the Secretary and the heads of all other Federal departments and agencies to use their authorities in order to carry out programs for the protection of endangered species, and it further *requires* that those agencies take *the necessary action* that will *not jeopardize* the continuing existence of endangered species or result in the destruction of critical habitat of those species." H.R.Rep.No.93-412, p. 14 (1973). (Emphasis added.)

Resolution of this difference in statutory language, as well as other variations between the House and Senate bills, was the task of a Conference Committee. See 119 Cong.Rec. 30174 30175, 31183 (1973). The Conference Report, H.R. Conf.Rep. No. 93-740 (1973), U.S.Code Cong. & Admin.News 1973, p. 2989, basically adopted the Senate bill, S. 1983; but the conferees rejected the Senate version of § 7 and adopted the stringent, mandatory language in H.R. 37. While the Conference Report made no specific reference to this choice of provisions, the House manager of the bill, Representative Dingell, provided an interpretation of what the Conference bill would require, making it clear that the mandatory provisions of § 7 were not casually or inadvertently included:

"[Section 7] substantially amplifie[s] the obligation of [federal agencies] to take steps within their power to carry out the purposes of this act. A recent article . . . illustrates the problem which might occur absent this new language in the bill. It appears that the whooping cranes of this country, perhaps the best known of our endangered species, are being threatened by Air Force bombing activities along the gulf coast of Texas. Under existing law, the Secretary of Defense has some discretion as to whether or not he will take the necessary action to see that this threat disappears . . . . [O]nce the bill is enacted, [the Secretary of Defense] *would be required to take the proper steps. . . .*

"Another example . . . [has] to do with the continental population of grizzly bears which may or may not be endangered, but which is surely threatened. . . . Once this bill is enacted, the appropriate Secretary, whether of Interior, Agriculture or whatever, *will have to take action* to see that this situation is not permitted to worsen, and that these bears are not driven to extinction. The purposes of the bill included the conservation of the species and of the ecosystems upon which they depend, and *every agency of government is committed* to see that those purposes are carried out. . . . [T]he agencies of Government can no longer plead that they can do nothing about it. *They can, and they must. The law is clear."* 119 Cong.Rec. 42913 (1973). (Emphasis added.)

It is against this legislative background[29] that we must measure TVA's claim that the Act was not intended to stop operation of a project which, like Tellico Dam, was near completion when an endangered species was discovered in its path. While there is no discussion in the legislative history of precisely this problem, the totality of congressional action makes it abundantly clear that the result we reach today is wholly in accord with both the words of the statute and the intent of Congress. The plain intent of Congress in enacting this statute was to halt and reverse the trend toward species extinction, whatever the cost. This is reflected not only in the stated policies of the Act, but in literally every section of the statute. All persons, including federal agencies, are specifically instructed not to "take" endangered species, meaning that no one is "to harass, harm,[30] pursue, hunt, shoot, wound, kill, trap, capture, or collect" such life forms. 16 U.S.C. §§ 1532(14), 1538(a)(1)(B) (1976 ed.). Agencies in particular are directed by §§ 2(c) and 3(2) of the Act to "use . . . all methods and procedures which are necessary" to preserve endangered species. 16 U.S.C. §§ 1531(c), 1532(2) (emphasis added) (1976 ed.). In addition, the legislative history undergirding § 7 reveals an explicit congressional decision to require agencies to afford first priority to the declared national policy of saving endangered species. The pointed omission of the type of qualifying language previously included in endangered species legislation reveals a conscious decision by Congress to give endangered species priority over the "primary missions" of federal agencies.

It is not for us to speculate, much less act, on whether Congress would have altered it stance had the specific events of this case been anticipated. In any event, we discern no hint in the deliberations of Congress relating to the 1973 Act that would compel a different result than we reach here.[31]

Indeed, the repeated expressions of congressional concern over what it saw as the potentially enormous danger presented by the eradication of *any* endangered species suggest how the balance would have been struck had the issue been presented to Congress in 1973.

Furthermore, it is clear Congress foresaw that § 7 would, on occasion, require agencies to alter ongoing projects in order to fulfill the goals of the Act.[32] Congressman Dingell's discussion of Air Force practice bombing, for instance, obviously pinpoints a particular activity—intimately related to the national defense—which a major federal department would be obliged to alter in deference to the strictures of § 7. A similar example is provided by the House Committee Report:

"Under the authority of [§ 7], the Director of the Park Service would e required *to conform the practices of his agency* to the need for protecting the rapidly dwindling stock of grizzly bears within Yellowstone Park. These bears, which may be endangered, and are undeniably threatened, should at least be protected by supplying them with carcasses from excess elk within the park, *by curtailing the destruction of habitat by clearcutting National Forests surrounding the Park,* and by preventing hunting until their numbers have recovered sufficiently to withstand these pressures." H.R.Rep.No.93-412, p. 14 (1973). (Emphasis added.)

One might dispute the applicability of these examples to the Tellico Dam by saying that in this case the burden on the public through the loss of millions of unrecoverable dollars would greatly outweigh the loss of the snail darter.[33] But neither the Endangered Species Act nor Art. III of the Constitution provides federal courts with authority to make such fine utilitarian calculations. On the contrary, the plain language of the Act, buttressed by its legislative history, shows clearly that Congress viewed the value of endangered species as "incalculable." Quite obviously, it would be difficult for a court to balance the loss of a sum certain-even $100 million against a congressionally declared "incalculable" value, even assuming we had the power to engage in such a weighing process, which we emphatically do not.

In passing the Endangered Species Act of 1973, Congress was also aware of certain instances in which exceptions to the statute's broad sweep would be necessary. Thus, § 10, 16 U.S.C. § 1539 (1976 ed.), creates a number of limited "hardship exemptions," none of which would even remotely apply to the Tellico Project. In fact, there are no exemptions in the Endangered Species Act for federal agencies, meaning that under the maxim *expressio unius est exclusio alterius,* we must presume that these were the only "hardship cases" Congress intended to exempt. *National Railroad Passenger Corp. v. National Assn. of Railroad Passengers,* 414 U.S. 453, 458, 94 S.Ct. 690, 693, 38 L.Ed.2d 646 (1974).[34]

Notwithstanding Congress' expression of intent in 1973, we are urged to find that the continuing appropriations for Tellico Dam constitute an implied repeal of the 1973 Act, at least insofar as it applies to the Tellico Project. In support of this view, TVA points to the statements found in various House and Senate Appropriations Committees' Reports; as described in Part I, supra, those Reports generally reflected the attitude of the *Committees* either that the Act did not apply to Tellico or that the dam should be completed regardless of the provisions of the Act. Since we are unwilling to assume that these latter Committee statements constituted advice to ignore the provisions of a duly enacted law, we assume that these Committees believed that the Act simply was not applicable in this situation. But even under this interpretation of the Committees' actions, we are unable to conclude that the Act has been in any respect amended or repealed.

There is nothing in the appropriations measures, as passed, which states that the Tellico Project was to be completed irrespective of the requirements of the Endangered Species Act.

These appropriations, in fact, represented relatively minor components of the lump-sum amounts for the *entire* TVA budget.[35] To find a repeal of the Endangered Species Act under these circumstances would surely do violence to the " 'cardinal rule . . . that repeals by implication are not favored.' " *Morton v. Mancari,* 417 U.S. 535, 549, 94 S.Ct. 2474, 2482, 41 L.Ed.2d 290 (1974), quoting *Posadas v. National City Bank,* 296 U.S. 497, 503, 56 S.Ct. 349, 352, 80 L.Ed. 351 (1936). In *Posadas* this Court held, in no uncertain terms, that "the intention of the legislature to repeal must be clear and manifest." *Ibid.* See *Georgia v. Pennsylvania R. Co.,* 324 U.S. 439, 456-457, 65 S.Ct. 716, 725-726, 89 L.Ed. 1051 (1945) ("Only a clear repugnancy between the old . . . and the new [law] results in the former giving way . . ."); *United States v. Borden Co.,* 308 U.S. 188, 198-199, 60 S.Ct. 182, 188, 84 L.Ed. 181 (1939) ("[I]ntention of the legislature to repeal 'must be clear and manifest.' . . . '[A] positive repugnancy [between the old and the new laws]' "); *Wood v. United States,* 16 Pet. 342, 363, 10 L.Ed. 987 (1842) ("[T]here must be a positive repugnancy . . ."). In practical terms, this "cardinal rule" means that "[i]n the absence of some affirmative showing of an intention to repeal, the only permissible justification for a repeal by implication is when the earlier and later statutes are irreconcilable." *Mancari, supra,* 417 U.S., at 550, 94 S.Ct., at 2482.

The doctrine disfavoring repeals by implication "applies with full vigor when . . . the subsequent legislation is an *appropriations* measure." *Committee for Nuclear Responsibility v. Seaborg,* 149 U.S.App.D.C. 380, 382, 463 F.2d 783, 785 (1971) (emphasis added); *Environmental Defense Fund v. Froehlke,* 473 F.2d 346, 355 (CA8 1972). This is perhaps an understatement since it would be more accurate to say that the policy applies with even *greater* force when the claimed repeal rests solely on an Appropriations Act. We recognize that both substantive enactments and appropriations measures are "Acts of Congress," but the latter have the limited and specific purpose of providing funds for authorized programs. When voting on appropriations measures, legislators are entitled to operate under the assumption that the funds will be devoted to purposes which are lawful and not for any purpose forbidden. Without such an assurance, every appropriations measure would be pregnant with prospects of altering substantive legislation, repealing by implication any prior statute which might prohibit the expenditure. Not only would this lead to the absurd result of requiring Members to review exhaustively the background of every authorization before voting on an appropriation, but it would flout the very rules the Congress carefully adopted to avoid this need. House Rule XXI(2), for instance, specifically provides:

"No appropriation shall be reported in any general appropriation bill, or be in order as an amendment thereto, for any expenditure not previously authorized by law, unless in continuation of appropriations for such public works as are already in progress. *Nor shall any provision in any such bill or amendment thereto changing existing law be in order.*" (Emphasis added.)

See also Standing Rules of the Senate, Rule 16.4. Thus, to sustain petitioner's position, we would be obliged to assume that Congress meant to repeal *pro tanto* § 7 of the Act by means of a procedure expressly prohibited under the rules of Congress.

Perhaps mindful of the fact that it is "swimming upstream" against a strong current of well-established precedent, TVA argues for an exception to the rule against implied repealers in a circumstance where, as here, Appropriations Committees have expressly stated their "understanding" that the earlier legislation would not prohibit the proposed expenditure. We cannot accept such a proposition. Expressions of committees dealing with requests for appropriations cannot be equated with statutes enacted by Congress, particularly not in the circumstances presented by this case. First, the Appropriations Committees had no jurisdiction over the subject of endangered species, much less did they conduct the type of extensive hearings which preceded passage of the earlier Endangered Species Acts, especially the 1973 Act. We venture to suggest that the House Committee on Merchant Marine and Fisheries and the Senate Committee on Commerce would be somewhat surprised to learn that their careful work on the substantive legislation had been undone by the simple—and brief—insertion of some inconsistent language in Appropriations Committees' Reports.

Second, there is no indication that Congress as a whole was aware of TVA's position, although the Appropriations Committees apparently agreed with petitioner's views. Only recently *SEC v. Sloan,* 436 U.S. 103, 98 S.Ct. 1702, 56 L.Ed.2d 148 (1978), we declined to presume general congressional acquiescence in a 34-year-old practice of the Securities and Exchange Commission, despite the fact that the Senate Committee *having jurisdiction over the Commission's activities* had long expressed approval of the practice. Mr. Justice REHNQUIST, speaking for the Court, observed that we should be "extremely hesitant to presume general congressional awareness of the Commission's construction based only upon a few isolated statements in the thousands of pages of legislative documents." *Id.,* at 121, 98 S.Ct., at 1713. A fortiori, we should not assume that petitioner's views—and the Appropriations Committees' acceptance of them—were any better known, especially when the TVA is not the agency with primary responsibility for administering the Endangered Species Act.

Quite apart from the foregoing factors, we would still be unable to find that in this case "the earlier and later statutes are irreconcilable," *Mancari,* 417 U.S., at 551, 94 S.Ct., at 2483; here it is entirely possible "to regard each as effective." Id., at 550, 94 S.Ct., at 2482. The starting point in this analysis must be the legislative proceedings leading to the 1977 appropriations since the earlier funding of the dam occurred prior to the listing of the snail darter as an endangered species. In all successive years, TVA confidently reported to the Appropriations Committees that efforts to transplant the snail darter appeared to be successful; this surely gave those Committees some basis for the impression that there was no direct conflict between the Tellico Project and the Endangered Species Act. Indeed, the special appropriation for 1978 of $2 million for transplantation of endangered species supports the view that the Committees saw such relocation as the means whereby collision between Tellico and the Endangered Species Act could be avoided. It should also be noted that the Reports issued by the Senate and House Appropriations Committees in 1976 came within a month of the District Court's decision in this case, which hardly could have given the Members cause for concern over the possible applicability of the Act. This leaves only the 1978 appropriations, the Reports for which issued after the Court of Appeals' decision now before us. At that point very little remained to be accomplished on the project; the Committees understandably advised TVA to cooperate with the Department of the Interior "to relocate the endangered species to another suitable habitat so as to permit the project to proceed as rapidly as possible." H.R.Rep.No.95-379, p. 11 (1977). It is true that the Committees repeated their earlier expressed "view" that the Act did not prevent completion of the Tellico Project. Considering these statements in context, however, it is evident that they " 'represent only the personal views of these legislators,' " and "however explicit, [they] cannot serve to change the legislative intent of Congress expressed before the Act's passage." *Regional Rail Reorganization Act Cases,* 419 U.S. 102, 132, 95 S.Ct. 335, 353, 42 L.Ed.2d 320 (1974).

(B)

Having determined that there is an irreconcilable conflict between operation of the Tellico Dam and the explicit provisions of § 7 of the Endangered Species Act, we must now consider what remedy, if any, is appropriate. It is correct, of course, that a federal judge sitting as a chancellor is not mechanically obligated to grant an injunction for every violation of law. This Court made plain *Hecht Co. v. Bowles,* 321 U.S. 321, 329, 64 S.Ct. 587, 591, 88 L.Ed. 754 (1944), that "[a] grant of *jurisdiction* to issue compliance orders hardly suggests an absolute duty to do so under any and all circumstances." As a general matter it may be said that "[s]ince all or almost all equitable remedies are discretionary, the balancing of equities and hardships is appropriate in almost any case as a guide to the chancellor's discretion." D. Dobbs, Remedies 52 (1973). Thus, in *Hecht Co.* the Court refused to grant an injunction when it appeared from the District Court findings that "the issuance of an injunction would have 'no effect by way of insuring better compliance in the future' and would [have been] 'unjust' to [the] petitioner and not 'in the public interest.' " 321 U.S., at 326, 64 S.Ct., at 590.

But these principles take a court only so far. Our system of government is, after all, a tripartite one, with each branch having certain defined functions delegated to it by the Constitution. While "[i]t is emphatically the province and duty of the judicial department to say what the law is," *Marbury v. Madison,* 1 Cranch 137, 177, 2 L.Ed. 60 (1803), it is equally—and emphatically—the exclusive province of the Congress not only to formulate legislative policies and mandate programs and projects, but also to establish their relative priority for the Nation. Once Congress, exercising its delegated powers, has decided the order of priorities in a given area, it is for the Executive to administer the laws and for the courts to enforce them when enforcement is sought.

Here we are urged to view the Endangered Species Act "reasonably," and hence shape a remedy "that accords with some modicum of common sense and the public weal." *Post,* at 196. But is that our function? We have no expert knowledge on the subject of endangered species, much less do we have a mandate from the people to strike a balance of equities on the side of the Tellico Dam. Congress has spoken in the plainest of words, making it abundantly clear that the balance has been struck in favor of affording endangered species the highest of priorities, thereby adopting a policy which it described as "institutionalized caution."

Our individual appraisal of the wisdom or unwisdom of a particular course consciously selected by the Congress is to be put aside in the process of interpreting a statute. Once the meaning of an enactment is discerned and its constitutionality determined, the judicial process comes to an end. We do not sit as a committee of review, nor are we vested with the power of veto. The lines ascribed to Sir Thomas More by Robert Bolt are not without relevance here:

"The law, Roper, the law. I know what's legal, not what's right. And I'll stick to what's legal. . . . I'm *not* God. The currents and eddies of right and wrong, which you find such plain-sailing, I can't navigate, I'm no voyager. But in the thickets of the law, oh there I'm a forester. . . . What would you do? Cut a great road through the law to get after the Devil? . . . And when the last law was down, and the Devil turned round on you-where would you hide, Roper, the laws all being flat? . . . This country's planted thick with laws from coast to coast—Man's laws, not God's—and if you cut them down . . . d'you really think you could stand upright in the winds that would blow then? . . . Yes, I'd give the Devil benefit of law, for my own safety's sake." R. Bolt, A Man for All Seasons, Act I, p. 147 (Three Plays, Heinemann ed. 1967).

We agree with the Court of Appeals that in our constitutional system the commitment to the separation of powers is too fundamental for us to pre-empt congressional action by judicially decreeing what accords with "common sense and the public weal." Our Constitution vests such responsibilities in the political branches.

Affirmed.

Source: http://scholar.google.com/scholar_case?case=11603759272819987617&q=437+U.S.+153&hl=en&as_sdt=2,10 (footnotes included)

Lacey Act/Gibson Guitar Controversy: Raid at Gibson Strikes Sour Note, 21 September 2011, by Kris Maher

In 2011, a controversy arose over the seizing of wood from India imported into the United States by the Gibson Guitar Company. The US Department of Justice allegedly acted because they claimed that the wood was violative of the Lacey Act of 1906; however, as demonstrated in this article, it appeared that other companies which also imported the same wood, but had contributed to the Obama campaign for President, had avoided being targeted by the Department of Justice.

A Justice Department raid at a famous guitar maker is prompting inquiries from Congress, a call to amend the act that prompted the raid and fresh debate about the impact of federal regulation on jobs.

On Tuesday, Republican lawmakers demanded more details from the Justice Department and Interior Department regarding the August raid at Gibson Guitar Corp., in which agents seized ebony suspected of being illegally imported from India.

"Why did they send armed agents into Gibson's facilities," asked Rep. Marsha Blackburn (R., Tenn.), a member of the House Committee on Energy and Commerce. In a statement, she said she couldn't understand why the administration "felt the need to act like a bunch of cowboys," when a letter or phone call could outline concerns that Gibson had violated the Lacey Act. The Lacey Act makes it illegal to import plants or wildlife obtained in violation of the laws in the U.S. or other countries.

Chris Tollefson, a spokesman for the Fish & Wildlife Service, part of the Interior Department, declined to comment on the Gibson investigation. He said the agency's enforcement is focused on companies that buy large quantities of wood products and won't focus on individual consumers or musicians.

"We are following the law as it was established by Congress," Mr. Tollefson said.

A Justice Department spokesman declined to comment.

As lawmakers were calling for more details into the raid, business and industry leaders offered varied views on whether the Lacey Act should be upheld or amended. Gibson Chief Executive Henry Juszkiewicz said in an interview Tuesday that he has hired a law firm to help craft a bill to amend the Lacey Act and is looking for sponsors in Congress.

Mr. Juszkiewicz said he wants clearer guidelines regarding "due care" to certify that wood imports are legal and for the law to apply only to importers and manufacturers, and not to retailers and consumers.

More broadly, he said he wants a mechanism to arbitrate grievances if there is "overreach" by federal agencies conducting investigations. Mr. Juszkiewicz estimated the government's raids have cost Gibson roughly $1 million in seized products and production disruptions as the company switched to alternate materials. The Nashville, Tenn., company is a big user of ebony and other scarce woods.

"Suppose the government is wrong, which I would say it is," he said. "They just incurred millions of dollars of damage for us and there are no consequences for that."

Other officials from the wood-products industry defended the Lacey Act, saying it has preserved U.S. jobs in timber, furniture and retail sectors and helped boost U.S. exports of wood products to foreign buyers who want assurance that the goods don't contain illegally forested material.

"This very much is a bill that has helped save domestic jobs in the hardwood industry," said Jameson French, CEO of Northland Forest Products Inc., in a conference call with representatives from the National Hardwood Lumber Association, the Environmental Investigation Agency, a non-profit that tracks illegal logging, and the United Steelworkers labor union.

In 2008, the 111-year-old Lacey Act, originally passed to protect wildlife, was amended to cover wood and plant materials to help prevent illegal logging and deforestation in areas including the border between Russia and China, and to protect U.S producers from low-priced illegally sourced wood. The amendments were passed by Congress with bipartisan support, with the backing of the timber and wood products industries, environmentalists and labor, and were signed into law by President George W. Bush.

Rep. Earl Blumenauer (D., Ore.), an original supporter of the amendments, called the recent controversy over the Lacey Act "painfully overblown."

"The record is absolutely clear. If we have these provisions and they're enforced, it creates jobs in this country," he said.

Some industry groups, including the National Retail Federation, are concerned about compliance costs, given the multitude of products, including lipstick, that contain wood composites or small amounts of plant material might require verification that it complied with foreign law.

"The concern is that they impose huge compliance costs on the business community," said Erik Autor, international trade counsel for the federation. He said retailers could also have inventory seized if regulators believe it contained illegally sourced material.

The Agriculture Department is working on additional rules regarding enforcement of the act and trying to determine what types of products would have to be certified as legally imported by companies, including big-box retailers.

Source: http://online.wsj.com/article/SB10001424053111903374004576583091410412376.html

Address delivered before the Agricultural Society of Rutland County, 30 September 1847 by George Perkins Marsh

In 1847, Rep. George Perkins Marsh (1801-1882) made the following comments before the Agricultural Society of Rutland County, Vermont, in which he stated that man was doing destructive damage to the environment—the first time such a claim was made. Marsh said that deforestation, more than anything, was contributing to the degradation of the American environment. One of Marsh's contemporaries, George Barrell Emerson, a cousin of the famed writer Ralph Waldo Emerson, used Marsh's insights in an update of his own 1846 work, "A Report on the Trees and Shrubs Growing Naturally in the Forests of Massachusetts. Published Agreeably to an Order of the Legislature, by the Commissioners on the Zoological and Botanical Survey of the State" (Boston: Dutton and Wentworth, State Printers, 1846). Marsh's own address was published in pamphlet form in 1847, excerpts from which are reprinted below. Marsh, who would go on to write one of the seminal works on the 19th century conservation movement, "Man and Nature" (1864), revised it and republished it a decade later as "Man and Nature: The Earth as Modified by Human Action" (1874).

America offers the first example of the struggle between civilized man and barbarous uncultivated nature. In all other primitive history, the hero of the scene is a savage, the theatre a wilderness, and the earth has been subdued in the same proportion, and by the same slow process, that man has been civilized. In North America, on the contrary, the full energies of advanced European civilization, stimulated by its artificial wants and guided by its accumulated intelligence, were brought to bear at once on a desert continent, and it has been but the work a day to win empires from the wilderness, and to establish relations of government and commerce between points as distant as the rising and the setting sun. This marvellous change, which has converted unproductive wastes into fertile fields, and filled with light and life, the dark and silent recesses of our aboriginal forests and mountains, has been accomplished through the instrumentality of those arts, whose triumphs your are this day met to celebrate, and your country is the field, where the stimulus of necessity has spurned them on to their most glorious achievements. But besides the new life and vigor infused into these arts, by the necessity of creating food and shelter and clothing for a swarming emigration and a rapidly multiplying progeny, the peculiar character of the soil and of the indigenous products of America has introduced most important modifications into the objects and processes of all of them, by offering to European industry new plants for cultivation, and new and more abundant materials for artificial elaboration. At the same time, American husbandry and mechanical art are totally different in their objects, character, and processes from what they would be, were they conversant only with the indigenous products of our native soil. To exemplify; America has given to the Eastern Hemisphere maize, tobacco, the potatoe, the batata, the pine-apple, the turkey, and more lately the alpaca, not to mention innumerable flowering plants, as well as other vegetables of less economical importance, or the tribute which her peltry, her forests, her fisheries, and her mines of gems and the precious metals have paid to European cupidity; she has received in return wheat, rye, other cerealia, new varieties of the cotton plant, flax, hemp, rice, the sugar-cane, coffee, our orchard fruits, kitchen and medicinal roots, pulse and herbs, the silkworm, the honey-bee, the swine, the goat, the sheep, the horse and the ox. By these interchanges, the industry of both continents has been modified and assimilated, and it is a curious fact, that the greater proportion of properly agricultural American labor is devoted to the growth of vegetable products of transatlantic origin, while the workshops and the maritime commerce of Europe find one of their principal sources of employment in the conversion the or carriage of vegetable substances either indigenous to, or most advantageously grown in the soil of America. The colonization of a new continent under such remarkable circumstances could not fail to give a powerful impulse to the productive arts; and their increased economical, commercial and financial importance has invested them with an interest in the eyes of statesmen, and a prominence as objects especially to be cherished, in every well regulated scheme of political economy, which they had never before attained, and the social position of those who are engaged in them has been elevated accordingly. Further, there are certain features of our institutions and our primary legislation, which have contributed not a little to raise and improve the condition of those who pursue the industrial arts, and especially of those devoted to agricultural occupations. The most important of these is the rejection of feudal tenures to lands, and the creation of pure allodial estates—a title scarcely known to the common law, and which makes every man the absolute irresponsible owner of his own land, subject neither to services, wardships, pents, tithes, reliefs forfeiture, nor any manner of burden or restraint upon alienation by sale, inheritance or devise, or upon the cultivation of his soil for such purposes, or by such course of husbandry, as he may deem expedient. Another of these new features is the abolition of the law of primogeniture, and the equal distribution of all the estate of intestates, whether real or personal between the representatives in equal degree, without distinction of age or sex. The effect of this system together with the low price of lands, has been to make almost every person, who lives to years of maturity, an absolute proprietor of the soil, or in other words one of the landed mobility of the republic, for the notion of hereditary nobility in Europe was founded on the right of inheriting real estate, they who owned the soil of a particular country being considered as its rightful lords and governors, because, by concert among themselves, they could lawfully exclude all others from the right of possession, or ever of commorancy, upon any portion of its territory. Our laws do not indeed restrict political franchises to those alone, who are seized of real estate, but as a majority of those who are of the legal age for the exercise of those franchises are landholders, the proprietors of the soil are in fact here, as in most civilized governments, the real rulers of the land. The mechanic arts too, have been relieved from the burden of long apprenticeships, and other legal obstacles to their free exercise, and every species of productive industry is among us as free and unrestricted as the winds of heaven. The result of all this has been, that the arts of production as well as of conversion, in our time, and especially in our land, have proved a source of thrift to those who pursue them, of physical and financial strength to the commonwealth, and of general benefit to society, in a degree of which history gives no previous example, and they need only a wise, liberal and stable policy on the part of our government, to be a most important agent, in elevating us to as high a pitch of power and prosperity, as has as yet been attained by any nation under heaven.

Source: Marsh, George Perkins, "Address delivered before the Agricultural Society of Rutland County, by George Perkins Marsh, Sept. 30, 1847" (Rutland, Vermont: Printed at the Herald Office, 1848), 2-5.

"Reshaping National Forest Policy,"
Issues in Science and Technology, **Fall 1999 by Michael H. Anderson**

Forest Service Chief Michael Dombeck brought a new and controversial outlook to the service when he was nominated by President Bill Clinton in 1993. This article from that period shows the controversy surrounding Dombeck's tenure.

Chief Mike Dombeck is steering the Forest Service in a fundamentally different direction.

During his two and a half years as chief of the U.S. Forest Service, Mike Dombeck has received considerable attention and praise from some unlikely sources. On June 15 this year, for instance, the American Sportfishing Association gave Dombeck its "Man of the Year" award. Two days earlier, the New York Times Magazine featured Dombeck as "the environmental man of the hour," calling him "the most aggressive conservationist to head the Forest Service in at least half a century."

Dombeck has also drawn plenty of criticism, especially from the timber industry and members of Congress who want more trees cut in the 192-million-acre National Forest System. Last year, angered by Dombeck's conservation initiatives, four western Republicans who chair the Senate and House committees and subcommittees that oversee the Forest Service threatened to slash the agency's budget. They wrote to Dombeck, "Since you seem bent on producing fewer and fewer results from the National Forests at rapidly increasing costs, many will press Congress to seriously consider the option to simply move to custodial management of our National Forests in order to stem the flow of unjustifiable investments. That will mean the Agency will have to operate with significantly reduced budgets and with far fewer employees."

Based on his performance to date, Dombeck is clearly determined to change how the Forest Service operates. He has a vision of the future of the national forests that is fundamentally at odds with the long-standing utilitarian orientation of most of his predecessors. Dombeck wants the Forest Service to focus on protecting roadless areas, repairing damaged watersheds, improving recreation opportunities, identifying new wilderness areas, and restoring forest health through prescribed fire.

Although Dombeck's conservation-oriented agenda seems to resonate well with the U.S. public, it remains to be seen how successful he will be in achieving his goals. To succeed, he must overcome inertial or hostile forces within the Forest Service and Congress, while continuing to build public support by taking advantage of opportunities to implement his conservation vision.

An Historic Shift

Dombeck's policies and performance signify an historic transformation of the Forest Service and national forest management. Since the national forests were first established a century ago, they have been managed principally for utilitarian objectives. The first chief of the Forest Service, Gifford Pinchot, emphasized in a famous 1905 directive that "all the resources of the [national forests] are for use, and this use must be brought about in a prompt and businesslike manner." After World War II, the Forest Service began in earnest to sell timber and build logging access roads. For the next 40 years, the national forests were systematically logged at a rate of about 1 million acres per year. The Forest Service's annual timber output of 11 billion board feet in the late 1980s represented 12 percent of the United States' total harvest. By the early 1990s, there were 370,000 miles of roads in the national forests.

During the postwar timber-production era of the Forest Service, concerns about the environmental impacts of logging and road building on the national forests steadily increased. During the 1970s and 1980s, Forest Service biologists such as Jerry Franklin and Jack Ward Thomas became alarmed at the loss of biological diversity and wildlife habitat resulting from logging old-growth forests. Aquatic scientists from federal and state agencies and the American Fisheries Society presented evidence of serious damage to streams and fish habitats caused by logging roads. At the same time, environmental organizations stepped up their efforts to reform national forest policy by lobbying Congress to reduce appropriations for timber sales and roads, criticizing the Forest Service in the press, and filing lawsuits and petitions to protect endangered species.

The confluence of science and environmental advocacy proved to be the downfall of the Forest Service's timber-oriented policy. Change came first and most dramatically in the Pacific Northwest, when federal judge William Dwyer in 1989 and again in 1991 halted logging of old-growth forests in order to prevent extinction of the northern spotted owl. In 1993, President Clinton held a Forest Conference in Portland, Oregon, and directed a team of scientists, including Franklin and Thomas, to develop a "scientifically sound, ecologically credible, and legally responsible" plan to end the stalemate over the owl. A year later, the Clinton administration adopted the scientists' Northwest Forest Plan, which established a system of old-growth reserves and greatly expanded stream buffers. Similar court challenges, scientific studies, and management plans occurred in other regions during the early 1990s.

The uproar over the spotted owl and the collapse of the Northwest timber program caused the Forest Service to modify its traditional multiple-use policy. In 1992, Chief Dale Robertson announced that the agency was adopting "ecosystem management" as its operating philosophy, emphasizing the value of all forest resources and the need to take an ecological approach to land management. The appointment of biologist Jack Ward Thomas as chief in 1994—the first time the Forest Service had ever been headed by anyone other than a forester or road engineer—presaged further changes in the Forest Service.

Meanwhile, Congress was unable to agree on legislative remedies to the Forest Service's problems. The only significant national forest legislation enacted during this period of turmoil was the temporary "salvage rider" in 1995. That law directed the Forest Service to increase salvage logging of dead or diseased trees in the national forests and exempted salvage sales from all environmental laws during a 16-month "emergency" period. Congress also compelled the agency to complete timber sales in the Northwest that had been suspended or canceled due to endangered species conflicts.

The salvage rider threw gasoline on the flames of controversy over national forest management. Chief Thomas's efforts to achieve positive science-based change were largely sidetracked by the thankless task of attempting to comply with the salvage rider. Thomas resigned in frustration in 1996, warning that the Forest Service's survival was threatened by "demonization and politicization."

Fish Expert with a Land Ethic

Dombeck took over as chief less than a month after the salvage rider expired. With a Ph.D. in fisheries biology, Dombeck has brought a perspective and agenda to the Forest Service that are very different from those of past chiefs. He has made it clear that watershed protection and restoration, not timber production, will be the agency's top priority.

What sets Dombeck apart as a visionary leader, though, is not his scientific expertise but his philosophical beliefs and his desire to put his beliefs into action. The land ethic of fellow Wisconsinite Aldo Leopold is at the root of Dombeck's policies and motivations. He first read Leopold's land conservation essays in A Sand County Almanac while attending graduate school. Dombeck now considers it to be "one of the most influential books about the relationship of people to their lands and waters," and he often quotes from Leopold in his speeches and memoranda.

In his first appearance before Congress on February 25, 1997, Dombeck made it clear that he would be guided by the land ethic. The paramount goal of the Forest Service under his leadership would be "maintaining and restoring the health, diversity, and productivity of the land." What really caught the attention of conservationists, though, were Dombeck's remarks regarding management of "controversial" areas. Citing the recommendations of a forest health report commissioned by Oregon Governor John Kitzhaber, Dombeck stated, "Until we rebuild [public] trust and strengthen those relationships, it is simply common sense that we avoid riparian, old growth, and roadless areas."

The Damaging Effects of Roads

Roadless area management has long been a lightning rod of controversy in the national forests. Roadless areas cover approximately 50 to 60 million acres, or about 25 to 30 percent of all land in the national forests, and another 35 million acres are congressionally designated wilderness. The rest of the national forests contain some 380,000 miles of roads, mostly built to access timber to be cut for sale. During the 1990s, Congress became increasingly reluctant to fund additional road construction because of public opposition to subsidized logging of public lands. In the summer of 1997, the U.S. House of Representatives came within one vote of slashing the Forest Service's road construction budget. Numerous Forest Service research studies shed new light on the ecological values of roadless areas and the damaging effects of roads on water quality, fish habitat, and biological diversity.

Still, many observers were shocked when in January 1998, barely a year after starting his job, Dombeck proposed a moratorium on new roads in most national forest roadless areas. The moratorium was to be an 18-month "time out" while the Forest Service developed a comprehensive plan to deal with its road system. Although the roads moratorium would not officially take effect until early 1999, the Forest Service soon halted work on several controversial sales of timber from roadless areas in Washington, Oregon, Idaho, and elsewhere. The moratorium catapulted Dombeck into the public spotlight, bringing editorial acclaim from New York to Los Angeles, along with harsh criticism in congressional oversight hearings.

The big question for Dombeck and the Clinton administration is what will happen once the roadless area moratorium expires in September 2000. There is substantial public and political support for permanent administrative protection of the roadless areas. Recent public opinion polls indicate that more than two-thirds of registered voters favor a long-term policy that protects roadless areas from road building and logging. In July 1999, 168 members of Congress signed a letter urging the administration to adopt such a policy.

One possible approach for Dombeck is to deal with the roadless areas through the agency's overall road management strategy and local forest planning process. This may be the preferred tactic among Dombeck's more conservative advisors, since it could leave considerable discretion and flexibility to agency managers to determine what level of protection is appropriate for particular roadless areas. However, it would leave the fate of the roadless areas very much in doubt, while ensuring continued controversy over the issue.

A better alternative is simply to establish a long-term policy that protects all national forest roadless areas from road building, logging, and other ecologically damaging activities. Under this scenario, the Forest Service would prepare a programmatic environmental impact statement for a nationwide roadless area management policy that would be adopted through federal regulation. This approach may engender more controversy in the short term, but it would provide much stronger protection for the roadless areas and resolve a major controversy in the national forests.

The roadless area issue gives Dombeck and the administration an historic opportunity to conserve 60 million acres of America's finest public lands. Dombeck should follow up on his roadless area moratorium with a long-term protection policy for roadless areas.

Water Comes First

Shortly after the roadless area moratorium announcement in early 1998, Dombeck laid out his broad goals and priorities for the national forests in A Natural Resource Agenda for the 21st Century. The agenda included four key areas: watershed health, sustainable forest management, forest roads, and recreation. Among the four, Dombeck made it clear that maintaining and restoring healthy watersheds was to be the agency's first priority.

According to Dombeck, water is "the most valuable and least appreciated resource the National Forest System provides." Indeed, more than 60 million people in 3,400 communities and 33 states obtain their drinking water from national forest lands. A University of California study of national forests in the Sierra Nevada mountains found that water was far more valuable than any other commodity resource. Dombeck's view that watershed protection is the Forest Service's most important duty is widely shared among the public. An opinion survey conducted by the University of Idaho in 1995 found that residents in the interior Pacific Northwest consider watershed protection to be the most important use of federal lands.

If the Forest Service does indeed give watersheds top billing in the coming years, that will be a major shift in the agency's priorities. Although watershed protection was the main reason why national forests were originally established a century ago, it has played a minor role more recently. As Dombeck observed in a speech to the Outdoor Writers Association of America, "Over the past 50 years, the watershed purpose of the Forest Service has not been a co-equal partner with providing other resource uses such as timber production. In fact, watershed purposes were sometimes viewed as a 'constraint' to timber management." Numerous scientific assessments have documented serious widespread impairment of watershed functions and aquatic habitats caused by the cumulative effects of logging, road building, grazing, mining, and other uses.

Forest Service watershed management should be guided by the principle of "protect the best and restore the rest." Because roadless areas typically provide the ecological anchors for the healthiest watersheds, adopting a strong, long-term, roadless area policy is probably the single most important action the agency can take to protect high-quality watersheds. The next step will be to identify other relatively undisturbed watersheds with high ecological integrity to create the basis for a system of watershed conservation reserves.

Actively restoring the integrity of degraded watersheds throughout the national forests will likely be an expensive long-term undertaking. The essential starting point is to conduct interagency scientific assessments of multiple watersheds in order to determine causes of degradation, identify restoration needs, and prioritize potential restoration areas and activities. Effective restoration often will require the cooperation of other landowners in a watershed. Once a restoration plan is developed, the Forest Service will have to look to Congress, state governments, and others for funding.

The revision of forest plans could provide a good vehicle to achieve Dombeck's watershed goals. Dombeck has repeatedly stated that watershed health and restoration will be the "overriding priorities" of all future forest plans. Current plans, which were adopted during the mid-1980s, generally give top billing to timber production and short shrift to watershed protection. This fall, the Forest Service expects to propose new regulations to guide the plan revisions. Dombeck should take advantage of this opportunity to ensure that the planning regulations fully reflect his policy direction and priorities regarding watersheds and that the new plans do more than just update the old timber-based plans.

Designating Wilderness Areas

In May 1999, Dombeck traveled to New Mexico to commemorate the 75th anniversary of the Gila Wilderness, which was established through the efforts of Aldo Leopold while he was a young assistant district forester in Albuquerque. Dombeck said that the Wilderness Act of 1964 was his "personal favorite. It has a soul, an essence of hope, a simplicity and sense of connection." Dombeck pledged that "wilderness will now enjoy a higher profile in national office issues."

Presently, there are 34.7 million acres of congressionally designated wilderness areas in the national forests, or 18 percent of the National Forest System. The Forest Service has recommended wilderness designation for another 6.1 million acres. Because of congressional and administrative inaction, very little national forest wilderness has been designated or recommended since the mid-1980s, but Dombeck wants to change that. "The responsibility of the Forest Service is to identify those areas that are suitable for wilderness designation. We must take this responsibility seriously. For those forests undergoing forest plan revisions, I'll say this: our wilderness portfolio must embody a broader array of lands—from prairie to old growth."

To his credit, Dombeck has begun to follow through on his wilderness objectives. Internally, he has formed a wilderness advisory group of Forest Service staff from all regions to improve training, public awareness, and funding of wilderness management. He has also taken the initiative in convening an interagency wilderness policy council to develop a common vision and management approaches regarding wilderness.

A significant test of Dombeck's sincerity regarding future wilderness will come in his decisions on pending administrative appeals of four revised forest plans in Colorado and South Dakota. The four national forests contain a total of 1,388,000 acres of roadless areas, of which conservationists support 806,000 acres for wilderness designation. However, the revised forest plans recommend wilderness for only 8,551 acres—less than one percent of the roadless areas. The chief can show his agency and the public that he is serious about expanding the wilderness system by remanding these forest plans and insisting that they include adequate consideration and recommendation of new wilderness areas.

Recreational Uses

Dombeck sees a bright future for the national forests and local economies in satisfying Americans' insatiable appetite for quality recreation experiences. National forests receive more recreational use than any other federal land system, including national parks. Recreation in the national forests has grown steadily from 560 million recreational visits in 1980 to 860 million by 1996. The Forest Service estimates that national forest recreation contributes $97.8 billion to the economy, compared to just $3.5 billion from timber.

However, Dombeck has cautioned that the Forest Service will not allow continued growth in recreational use to compromise the health of the land. In February this year, Dombeck explained the essence of the recreation strategy he wants the agency to pursue: "Most Americans value public lands for the sense of open space, wildness and naturalness they provide, clean air and water, and wildlife and fish. Other uses, whether they are ski developments, mountain biking trails, or off-road vehicles have a place in our multiple use framework. But that place is reached only after we ensure that such activities do not, and will not, impair the productive capacity of the land."

Off-road vehicles (ORVs) are an especially serious problem that Dombeck needs to address. Conflicts between nonmotorized recreationists (hikers, horse riders, and cross-country skiers) and motorized users (motorcyclers and snowmobilers) have escalated in recent years. The development of three- and four-wheeled all-terrain vehicles, along with larger and more powerful snowmobiles, has allowed ORV users to expand their cross-country routes and to scale steeper slopes. Ecological consequences include disruption of remote habitat for elk, wolverine, wolves, and other solitude-loving species, as well as soil erosion and stream siltation. Yet the Forest Service has generally shied away from cracking down on destructive ORV use. Indeed, in 1990 the agency relaxed its rules to accommodate larger ORVs on trails.

One way for Dombeck to deal firmly with the ORV issue is to adopt a regulation that national forest lands will be closed to ORV use except on designated routes. ORVs should be permitted only where the Forest Service can demonstrate that ORV use will do no harm to the natural values, wildlife, ecosystem function, and quality of experience for other recreationists. The chief clearly has the authority to institute such a policy under executive orders on ORVs issued in the 1970s.

The Need for Institutional Reform

Perhaps Dombeck's biggest challenge is to reorient an agency whose traditions, organizational culture, and incentives system favor commercial exploitation of national forest resources. For most of the past 50 years, the Forest Service's foremost priority and source of funding has been logging and road building. During the 1990s, the Forest Service has sold only one-third as much timber as it did in the 1980s and 1970s, while recreation use has steadily grown in numbers and value. Yet many of the agency's 30,000 employees still view the national forests primarily as a warehouse of timber and other commodities.

The Forest Service urgently needs a strong leader who is able to inspire the staff and communicate a favorable image to the public. For the past decade, the Forest Service has been buffeted by demands for reform and reductions in budgets and personnel. The number of agency employees fell by 15 percent between 1993 and 1997, largely in response to the decline in timber sales. Yet the public's expectations and the agency's workload have grown in other areas such as recreation management, watershed analysis, and wildlife monitoring, creating serious problems of overwork and burnout. Consequently, even Forest Service staff who are philosophically supportive of Dombeck's agenda worry about the potential for additional "unfunded mandates" from their leader. They are watching—some hopefully, others skeptically—to see if Dombeck can deliver the personnel and funding necessary to carry out his agenda.

Dombeck has shown that he is willing to make significant personnel changes to move out the old guard in the agency. In his first two years as chief, he replaced all six deputy chiefs and seven of the nine regional foresters. He has made a concerted effort to bring more women, ethnic minorities, and biologists into leadership roles. The Timber Management division has been renamed the Forest Ecosystems division. Now he needs to take the time to go to the national forests to visit and meet with the rangers and specialists who are responsible for carrying out his agenda. Dombeck has been remarkably successful at communicating with the media and the public and gaining support from diverse interest groups. But he needs to do a better job of connecting with and inspiring his field staff.

Dombeck has also taken on the complex task of reforming the Forest Service's timber-based system of incentives. During the agency's big logging era, agency managers were rated principally on the basis of how successful they were in "getting out the cut": the quantity of timber that was assigned annually to each region, national forest, and ranger district. On his first day as chief, Dombeck announced that every forest supervisor would have new performance measures for forest health, water quality, endangered species habitat, and other indicators of healthy ecosystems.

Far more daunting is the need to reform the agency's financial incentives. A large chunk of the Forest Service's annual budget is funded by a variety of trust funds and special accounts that rely exclusively on revenue from timber sales. Dombeck summed up the problem as follows at a meeting of Forest Service officials in fall 1998. "For many years, the Forest Service operated under a basic formula. The more trees we harvested, the more revenue we could bring into the organization, and the more people we could hire.

Not surprisingly, the management activities that have primarily benefited from timber revenues are logging and other resource utilization activities. An analysis of the Forest Service budget between 1980 and 1997 by Wilderness Society economist Carolyn Alkire shows that nearly half of the agency's expenditures for resource-use activities has been funded through trust funds and special accounts. In contrast, virtually all funds for resource-protection activities, such as soil and wilderness management, have come from annual appropriations, which are subject to the vagaries of congressional priorities and whims.

Although clearly recognizing the problem of financial incentives, Dombeck has had little success in solving it thus far. He has proposed some administrative reforms, such as limiting the kinds of logging activities for which the salvage timber sale trust fund can be used. However, significant reform of the Forest Service's internal financial incentives will depend on the willingness of Congress to appropriate more money for nontimber management activities.

Dombeck could force the administration and Congress to address the incentives issue by proposing an annual budget for the coming fiscal year that is entirely funded through appropriations. Dispensing with the traditional security of trust funds and special accounts would doubtless meet resistance from those in the agency who have benefited from off-budget financing. Still, bold action is appropriate and essential to eliminate a solidly entrenched incentive system that is blocking Dombeck's efforts to achieve ecological sustainability in the national forests.

Dombeck's second major challenge is to convince Congress to alter funding priorities from commodity extraction to environmental restoration. The timber industry has traditionally had considerable sway over the agency's appropriations, and the recent decline in timber production from the national forests has happened in spite of continued generous funding of the timber program. However, Congress has become increasingly skeptical of appropriating money for new timber access roads, partly because of the realization that new roads will add to the Forest Service's $8.5 billion backlog in road maintenance. In July 1999, the House voted for the first time to eliminate all funding for new timber access roads.

Congress has also shown somewhat greater interest in funding restoration-oriented management. For example, funding for fire prevention activities such as prescribed burning and thinning of small trees has increased dramatically. This year's Senate appropriations bill includes a new line item requested by the administration for forest ecosystem restoration and improvement. On the other hand, the Senate appropriations committee gave the Forest Service more money than it requested for timber sales, stating that "the Committee will continue to reject Administration requests designed to promote the downward spiral of the timber sales program."

Probably the best hope for constructive congressional action in the short term is legislation to reform the system of national forest payments to counties. Since the early 1900s, the Forest Service has returned 25 percent of its receipts from timber sales and other management activities to county governments for roads and schools. As a consequence of the decline in logging on national forests, county payments have dropped substantially in recent years, prompting affected county officials to request congressional help. Legislation has been introduced that would restore county payments to historical levels, irrespective of timber sale receipts.

Environmentalists and the Clinton administration want to enact legislation that will permanently decouple county payments from Forest Service revenues. Decoupling would stabilize payments and eliminate the incentive for rural county and school officials to promote more logging. The timber industry and some county officials want to retain the link between logging and schools in order to maintain pressure on the Forest Service and to avoid reliance on annual congressional appropriations. However, the legislation could avoid the appropriations process and ensure stable funding by establishing a guaranteed entitlement trust fund in the Treasury, much as Congress did in 1993 to stabilize payments to counties in the Pacific Northwest affected by declining timber revenues.

Guided by a scientific perspective and a land ethic philosophy, Chief Dombeck has brought new priorities to the Forest Service. He has succeeded in communicating an ecologically sound vision for the national forests and a sense of purpose for his beleaguered agency. He has begun to build different, more broadly based constituencies and receive widespread public support for his policies. Dombeck still faces considerable obstacles to achieving his vision within the Forest Service and in Congress. But by remaining true to his values and taking advantage of key opportunities to gain public support, he may go down in history as one of America's greatest conservationists.

Source: http://www.issues.org/16.1/anderson.html.

"Court Strikes Down 2005 Change to Forest Roadless Rule," 5 August 2009 by Matthew Preusch

The Bush administration (2001-09) attempted to change a series of environmental rules put into place by the Clinton administration (1993-2001). This article illustrates how, after Bush left office, courts continued to rule against the changes, some originally put into place in 2001.

A federal court Wednesday reinstated protection for tens of millions of acres of federal forests in Oregon and across the West.

But the ruling from the 9th Circuit Court of Appeals does not end the uncertainty of the long-debated "roadless rule" for national forests.

The Roadless Area Conservation Rule, put forward in 2001 by the Clinton administration, banned road construction or logging in 58.5 million acres of largely undeveloped forest lands, nearly a third of the total area managed by the Forest Service.

Almost immediately, the rule was challenged in court. The Bush administration chose not to defend it and in 2005 replaced it with the State Petitions Rule, which left it to the states to decide which roadless areas in their boundaries should be protected.

And the last decade has seen competing suits and appeals by states, ATV users, the timber industry, and environmental group, leading to a series of often contradictory rulings from federal courts.

On Wednesday, a panel of three judges determined the Bush rule illegal, and the judges reinstated the Clinton era rule except in the Tongass National Forest in Alaska and in Idaho, which created its own plan for its roadless forests.

"The Forest Service's use of a categorical exemption to repeal the nationwide protections of the Roadless Rule and to invite States to pursue varying rules for roadless area management was unreasonable," said the ruling, which upheld a lower court's decision.

The Forest Service, the judges said, failed to comply with national environmental laws and wrongly asserted that the change to the roadless rule wouldn't affect endangered species or their habitat.

"This is the final word forever on the validity of the Bush repeal," said Kristen Boyles, an attorney for Earthjustice who argued the case.

But it's not the final word on roadless forests.

Environmental groups are appealing a Wyoming district court judge's decision from last year repealing the Clinton roadless rule.

"We're really in a state of limbo here until we get this whole thing sorted out," said Tom Partin, executive director of the American Forest Resource Council, whose members rely on logs from federal forests.

Oregon was among those states that sued the federal government to keep the roadless rule in place, and today Gov. Ted Kulongoski praised the ruling.

"I hope that after years of litigation, the new administration allows this ruling to stand so we can end the courtroom battles and instead focus our efforts on working together to both protect our remaining wild areas as well as develop more comprehensive forest management policies that support our timber industry while protecting our environment," Kulongoski said in a statement.

The Obama administration hasn't said yet whether it will defend the Clinton rule in the Wyoming court battle.

"We are actively exploring this positive development and how it intersects with the various roadless discussions taking place around the country," said Jay Jensen, Deputy Under Secretary for Natural Resources and Environment in the Department of Agriculture.

In May, Secretary of Agriculture Tom Vilsack said any project proposed in roadless forests would have to get his personal approval.

Right now there is one such potential project in Oregon, a forest thinning proposal in the Umpqua National Forest near Diamond Lake.

About 900 acres of that project would be in inventoried roadless forests, according to the group Oregon Wild.

"What the Forest Service is proposing on the doorstep of Crater Lake National Park is harmful, unnecessary, and illegal," said Oregon Wild's Doug Heiken in a statement. "The ruling today backs that up."

Source: http://www.oregonlive.com/environment/index.ssf/2009/08/court_strikes_down_2005_change.html.

"The Forest Service," The Cato Institute, August 2009 by Randal O'Toole

This work gives a concise early history of the US Forest Service.

Origins

Congress established a Division of Forestry in the Department of Agriculture in 1881. [1] The division focused on research and the provision of information; it did not actively manage forest lands. The agency's name was later changed to the Bureau of Forestry.

The Forest Reserve Act (also known as the Creative Act) of 1891 allowed presidents to set aside forest reserves out of public lands by executive order. Those reserves were managed by the Department of the Interior. By 1897, 40 million acres had been set aside.

The Federal Forest Transfer Act of 1905, signed into law by President Theodore Roosevelt, moved control of the forest reserves from the Department of the Interior to the Department of Agriculture's Bureau of Forestry, which was renamed the Forest Service. The new Forest Service grew quickly - by 1908, it had 1,500 employees and controlled 150 million acres of land. [2]

The Weeks Act of 1911 was an important early law that expanded the powers of the Forest Service. The law authorized federal subsidies to the states for forest fire prevention, and it allowed the Forest Service to purchase private lands for the creation of national forests.

The Forest Service was heavily influenced by its charismatic first chief, Gifford Pinchot, a close friend of Roosevelt's. Pinchot was a progressive who believed that professional forest managers employed by the government could manage forests better than private owners. He made no secret of the fact that his eventual goal was for the Forest Service to gain authority over all public and private forest lands in the nation, a goal that was the policy of the agency until 1953.

Pinchot and others also believed that the nation was about to experience a timber famine that could be relieved only by huge investments in forest management. The reality turned out to be far different. U.S. timber consumption peaked in 1910 as the use of wood for fuel declined and as wood products manufacturers greatly increased the amount of useful wood they produced from each log.

Because of the continued availability of private supplies, Forest Service lands accounted for just two percent of the nation's lumber supply by the early 1940s. [3] The "national wood famine" that the Forest Service had predicted never happened. [4] Indeed, the United States had a glut of wood on the market from the time the Forest Service was created through at least the 1980s.

Despite its flawed projections, the Forest Service was one of the most popular agencies in government in the 1950s. "No one can deny that the Forest Service is one of Uncle Sam's soundest and most businesslike investments," gushed Newsweek in 1952. "It is the only major government branch showing a cash profit." [5] The magazine also lauded the agency's contribution to the value of recreation, wildlife management, timber stands, and pure and abundant water. The Newsweek issue, which featured Smokey the Bear on its cover, ascribed the agency's success to decentralized management.

Incentives to Cut

The popularity of the Forest Service did not last. Incentives built into the agency's budget by well-intentioned but poorly conceived laws effectively rewarded forest managers for losing money on environmentally questionable practices. [6] At the same time, managers were penalized for earning a positive return for following environmentally sound practices.

Congress gave the Forest Service funding to arrange timber sales, but it directed the agency to fund reforestation and other post-sale activities out of the timber receipts. Agency managers soon learned to maximize timber sales in order to fund an array of programs. The budgetary system created perverse incentives. Because extra funds could be spent on restoration, the more damage timber sales created the larger were the budgets that managers got to control. Every level of the agency's hierarchy had a stake in the below-cost timber sale program because as much as a third of the funds went for agency overhead.

Forest Service cutting practices were also problematic. At the time of the 1952 Newsweek story, most national forest timber was managed using selection cutting: individual trees were cut when they were mature, leaving behind beautiful stands of younger trees. When done right, a selection cut forest is hard to distinguish from wilderness.

Clearcutting, in which all trees on 20 to 100 acres or more are cut regardless of maturity, imposes higher reforestation and rehabilitation costs. But since agency managers got to keep those costs out of timber receipts, they had an incentive to clearcut even when other cutting techniques were more compatible with recreation and other uses. From a timber industry point of view, clearcutting sometimes makes sense. But when considering recreation, wildlife, and watershed, it was often devastating. The cash profits of the 1950s also vanished, and by the 1980s the Forest Service was losing billions of dollars a year on the timber program and other activities.

By 1970, the Forest Service was cutting almost four times as much timber as it did in 1952, almost all of it clearcut. The resulting controversies over both clearcutting and the large amount of timber being cut rocked the agency and led to lawsuits, congressional hearings, and tree-sitting protests. Ironically, agency leaders responded to the controversies by becoming more centralized in their management, which only made the Forest Service more vulnerable to criticism.

In 1976, Congress tried to resolve Forest Service problems by instituting a comprehensive forest planning process. But the resulting plans proved to be a costly mistake: the agency spent more than a billion dollars planning the national forests, but the plans were often based on fabricated data, and they did not resolve any debates.

The Forest Service's legacy of poor management continues today. A 2003 report by the Government Accountability Office concluded: "Historically, the Forest Service has not been able to provide Congress or the public with a clear understanding of what the Forest Service's 30,000 employees accomplish with the approximately $5 billion the agency receives each year. Since 1990, the GAO has reported seven times on performance accountability weaknesses at the Forest Service." [7] The agency's financial operations were on the GAO's "high-risk" list for waste between 1999 and 2005. [8]

The timber program continues to be subject to inefficiency and scandal. The Washington Post reported in 2004 that a large area of the Tongass National Forest in Alaska was clearcut and the trees left to rot because of inept planning by the Forest Service. [9] U.S. taxpayers lost millions of dollars in Tongass. The agency's costs of selling timber from Tongass have substantially exceeded fees collected from timber companies. In 1992, a quirk in timber sale contracts even caused the Forest Service to pay timber companies $14 million to cut Tongass timber, which was a cost to taxpayers on top of the $40 million that the agency spent to manage the timber. [10]

Nonetheless, big changes have come to the agency despite its poor planning and management. Starting in 1990, a new generation of national forest managers began to wind down the agency's timber program. Within six years, timber sales had fallen by 85 percent, and they remain at fairly low levels today. This relieved the controversies about overcutting, but it led many to wonder where the agency would shift its focus after timber: Recreation? Wildlife management?

Fires Are the New Cash Cow

The answer came in 2000, when a fire burned more than a billion dollars worth of homes in Los Alamos, New Mexico. Congress responded by giving the Forest Service a whopping 38 percent increase in its 2001 budget, mostly for fire activities. Total national forest fire expenditures have more than quadrupled in the last 15 years. [11] Fire expenditures have grown from about 10 percent of the Forest Service budget in the early 1990s to more than 40 percent today.

Much of this money is being spent reducing hazardous fuels within the forests. Far more is spent preparing for and suppressing fires. Yet much of the spending on fire activities is as questionable as the Forest Service's earlier timber programs. National forest fire problems are not as bad as the Forest Service claims; hazardous fuels are only a major issue on about 15 percent of federal lands in the West.

Forest managers have known for decades that some fires should be allowed to burn for the good of forest ecosystems. But from the beginning, Congress has given a virtual blank check to the Forest Service for fire suppression activities, and much of the spending has been of dubious value. The agency has made poor management decisions regarding prescribed burnings over many decades. [12]

Agency leaders are taking advantage of Congress's willingness to throw money at the fire issue. With an increasingly large share of the Forest Service bureaucracy dependent on the extra funding that comes around each fire season, the agency blindly puts out almost all fires. Even people within the Forest Service fear that the agency's traditional commitment to conservation is being lost in an orgy of spending on fire-related activities. [13]

Reform Options

Today, the Forest Service controls 193 million acres of land, has a budget of $5 billion, and employs more than 30,000 workers. [14] The Forest Service is in need of serious reforms. The services provided by the agency should be restructured to reduce taxpayer costs and to improve forest management practices.

One option is for Congress to allow the agency to charge fair market value for recreation and other uses of Forest Service land. That would probably raise enough revenue to cover all of the agency's costs. Taxpayers would save about $5 billion annually if the Forest Service was shifted to a self-funding structure.

If Forest Service activities were self-funded, it would force the agency to be more efficient in its operations and more responsive to forest land users. Self-funding would create incentives for the agency to decentralize its operations, allowing managers to respond to local conditions instead of being controlled by top-down plans from Washington.

Another reform step would be to revive federalism by eliminating federal forest subsidies to the states and turning portions of the national forests over to the states. Other activities could be privatized. It might be possible, for example, for some national forests to buy private insurance, as Oregon did until recently.

Some experts have proposed full privatization of the national forests. [15] Alternately, the national forests could be structured as independent trusts that would be owned by the federal government, but managed by a board of directors and funded out of forest-related receipts. The trusts would have special obligations to promote conservation, while still producing many valuable resources.

For decades, the Forest Service has been plagued by mismanagement and subject to perverse and damaging incentives. In the coming years, policymakers should focus on the goal of reforming the Forest Service to reduce taxpayer costs, while improving the sound and ecological management of forest lands.

Source: http://www.downsizinggovernment.org/agriculture/forest-service.

NOTES:

[1] A discussion of Forest Service history is available at www.foresthistory.org/research/ usfscoll/index.html. See also U.S. Department of Agriculture, "Centennial Mini-Histories of the Forest Service," Report FS-518, 1992, www.fs.fed.us/global/wsnew/fs_history.htm.

[2] U.S. Department of Agriculture, "Centennial Mini-Histories of the Forest Service," Report FS-518, 1992, Chapter 15.

[3] U.S. Department of Agriculture, "Centennial Mini-Histories of the Forest Service," Report FS-518, 1992, Chapter 10.

[4] U.S. Department of Agriculture, "Centennial Mini-Histories of the Forest Service," Report FS-518, 1992, Chapter 10.

[5] Newsweek, "Fabulous Bear, Famous Service Fight Annual Billion-Dollar Fire," June 2, 1952, 50-54.

[6] For background on Forest Service policies, see Randal O'Toole, Reforming the Forest Service (Covelo, CA: Island Press, 1988).

[7] Government Accountability Office, "Forest Service: Little Progress on Performance Accountability Likely Unless Management Addresses Key Challenges," GAO-03-503, May 2003, 1.

[8] Government Accountability Office, "High-Risk Series: An Update," GAO-05-207, January 2005.

[9] Blaine Harden, "Reopening Forest Areas Stirs Debate in Alaska," The Washington Post, August 1, 2004, A3.

[10] Randal O'Toole, "The $64 Million Question: How Taxpayers Pay Pulpmills to Clearcut the Tongass National Forest" (Bandon, Oregon: Thoreau Institute, 1993), ii.

[11] Randal O'Toole, "The Perfect Firestorm: Bringing Forest Service Wildfire Costs under Control," Cato Institute Policy Analysis no. 591, April 30, 2007. And see U.S. Department of Agriculture, Forest Service, "Overview of the President's FY2008 Budget," 3, http://www.fs.fed.us/publications/budget-2008/fy2008-forest-service-budget-overview.pdf.

[12] Randal O'Toole, "The Perfect Firestorm: Bringing Forest Service Wildfire Costs under Control," Cato Institute Policy Analysis no. 591, April 30, 2007.

[13] Randal O'Toole, "The Perfect Firestorm: Bringing Forest Service Wildfire Costs under Control," Cato Institute Policy Analysis no. 591, April 30, 2007.

[14] U.S. Department of Agriculture, Forest Service, "Overview of the President's FY2008 Budget," http://www.fs.fed.us/publications/budget-2008/fy2008-forest-service-budget-overview.pdf.

[15] Robert H. Nelson, "A Burning Issue: A Case for Abolishing the U.S. Forest Service" (Lanham: Maryland: Rowman and Littlefield, 2000).

"Bush Supporters Unhappy with Environmental Policy,"
Environment News Service, 22 January 2003 by J. R. Pegg

George W. Bush came into office promising his supporters to change the environmental policies of the Clinton administration (1993-2001), but was frustrated by Congress and the courts to change these rules. In this article, one of Bush's supporters demonstrates their dissatisfaction with Bush's administration for not doing enough to overturn Clinton policies.

WASHINGTON, DC, January 22, 2003 (ENS)—A free market environmental think tank with close ties to the Bush administration is disappointed with the President's environmental policy, but not for reasons often cited by other environmental groups. The Political Economy Research Center (PERC) gives the Bush administration low marks because it has not aggressively moved forward with environmental policies that are based on free market principles.

Environmental policies can work better and be more cost effective, according PERC, when they rely on market based incentives, private initiatives and voluntary action. But the Bush administration has failed to apply these free market principles to its environmental policy, a new report from PERC finds, and has thereby ignored the rights of property owners and the benefits of decentralizing many environmental protections and regulations.

"President [George W.] Bush's administration is moving away from the principles of free market environmentalism, when we thought he would be moving toward it," said Bruce Yandle, PERC senior associate and director of the project. "We are disappointed."

In its new report, PERC graded the Bush administration for policies related to 16 environmental issues and gave it an overall midterm grade of C–.

The report criticized the Bush administration for its enactment of stricter arsenic standards for drinking water, its signing of a United Nations treaty banning persistent organic pollutants such as DDT, and its support of continued subsidies for fishing and farming interests.

But policies that have received sharp criticism from many environmental groups, including the administration's decision to withdraw U.S. support for the Kyoto Protocol, its changes to the Clean Air Act's New Source Review, and its support for genetically modified crops, were all praised by PERC in the report.

Overall, the Montana based think tank's report finds that President Bush has not seized a range of opportunities to shift the environmental debate and policy to include the free market principles the organization is still convinced the President holds dear.

Free market environmentalism is based on these principles, PERC says.

- Private property rights encourage stewardship of resources.
- Government subsidies often degrade the environment.
- Market incentives spur individuals to conserve resources and protect environmental quality.
- Polluters should be liable for the harm they cause others

In 1999, Yandle and PERC Executive Director Terry Anderson were part of a team that advised then Governor Bush on environmental policies in preparation for his presidential campaign. The low grades on this report, Anderson explained, indicate that the President is not following the advice given by that team or the free market environmental policies they support.

"Much of this report suggests that this administration has emphasized the wrong things," Anderson said, adding that the administration needs to do a better job in communicating with the public about its environmental policies.

"Over and over I see an administration emphasizing what everybody expects from a Republican administration with regulatory rollbacks and the like," Anderson said. "This is frustrating because it really does have some good ideas on incentives, but it doesn't emphasize them."

Public land management is the area where PERC expected the most improvement, Yandle said, but little was accomplished "except rhetorically." The Bush administration received a C- for its policies on public land management.

Lack of action earned a C- for policies impacting grazing on public lands and left Anderson frustrated with the Bush administration's lack of commitment to free market environmentalism.

The administration, Anderson said, has endorsed the concept of willing buyer/willing seller trades of grazing permits, but has not moved forward even though a willing trade is ready to proceed. With private funding, the Grand Canyon Trust and grazing permit holders in Utah have struck a deal to reduce or retire grazing on some 300,000 acres in or around the Grand Staircase-Escalante National Monument.

This would effectively protect the lands from future grazing through market based incentives, something the administration readily supports. But the Bureau of Land Management and the Bush administration are delaying final approval.

"Just tell the ranchers who are raising the red flag that this is one we are doing and that they need to live with it," Anderson said. "It is willing buyer, willing seller. Let it go."

The recent unveiling by the Environment Protection Agency (EPA) of a water trading policy, which will allow the trading of pollution credits for watersheds, was "one of the few bright spots," Yandle said. This policy protects water through a system of local control and market trading, he explained, two pillars of free market environmentalism's foundation.

The water trading policy, although supported by a few environmental groups, has been criticized by others as incomplete and in possible violation of the Clean Water Act.

Anderson readily admits that PERC's report is different than some done by environmental groups, even though the grades may look similar.

One example of this is PERC's grade of C for the Bush administration's global climate change policy. Many environmentalists have criticized the administration for its withdrawal from the Kyoto Protocol, but this is the only area of global climate change policy viewed favorably by the PERC report.

"The administration did get high marks for recognizing that the Kyoto Protocol is fatally flawed and would do nothing to address the problems that global warming theories express," said David Riggs, author of the section on global climate change and executive director of GreenWatch at the Capital Research Center.

But Riggs lowered the administration's grade because it is pursuing some voluntary domestic programs to reduce greenhouse gas emissions.

"These domestic programs will set the stage for mandatory controls on fossil fuel use, harming the economy and reducing freedom unnecessarily," Riggs said. "The Bush administration skipped over that very important point of whether or not we should control and reduce greenhouse gas emissions."

The worst grades came for the policies on regulation of lead releases, air quality regulation, drinking water and arsenic, ocean fisheries and persistent organic pollution. Regulation of lead releases received an F; the other four all received a D in the report.

On lead release regulation, the report finds that the Bush administration went forward with a rule written by the previous administration that requires companies that use 100 pounds or more of lead a year to report to the EPA about their transfers or releases of this material. According to PERC, the science behind the rule is weak, the health benefits unclear, and the costs to small businesses too high to merit the regulation.

The only air quality regulation that received favorable marks was the Bush administration's reform of the Clean Water Act's New Source Review. Many environmental groups have argued that these reforms will allow for increased air pollution, but according to the PERC report, the reforms "will likely reduce the costs of complying with environmental regulations while, at worst, having no effect on air quality."

Anderson said that despite his disappointment with the first two years, he sees signs that the Bush administration and others are beginning to embrace the merits of free market environmentalism. He cited the recent decision by the Interior Secretary Gale Norton to cut California's annual share of the Colorado River by some 13 percent and the potential that states upstream will be able to sell their excess water supplies.

"The administration could improve its grade by promoting legislation that allows recipients of federal water to sell it to higher valued uses and that requires all beneficiaries to pay the full cost of water they receive," Anderson wrote in the report.

"These are not the ideas of a bunch of kooky economists out in Montana or Clemson or within the beltway," Anderson told ENS. "They are ideas that are being more and more embraced by environmental groups."

Source: http://www.ens-newswire.com/ens/jan2003/2003-01-22-10.html.

United Nations Report on Efforts to Mitigate Desertification in the Western United States, 2006

In 2006, the United Nations requested developed countries to prepare reports on each nation's work to end or mitigate rapid desertification occurring around the world. This was the first American report (although no follow-up has occurred as of this writing), and focuses on the US government's efforts to try to halt or even reverse the process of desertification, particularly in the western United States. The following summary is excerpted from this report.

EXECUTIVE SUMMARY

Desertification has historically been a problem and remains a concern across a large portion of the western United States. Desertification has been a problem on rangelands and lower elevation forests and woodlands due to unsustainable practices such as overgrazing, particularly during drought conditions. Improved management and restoration has decreased the amount of degraded land in this region. However, the amount of land still requiring improvement is unknown since there is not a current assessment of land condition due to multiple ownership and management entities. Several national efforts (Sustainable Resources Roundtable and the Heinz Center Report) are underway to correct this deficiency.

The federal government manages 39% of the land susceptible to desertification in the western U.S. Federal lands are managed for sustainability, although agency missions may vary due to different policies and laws. These federal lands provide renewable energy sources, clean water, habitat and ecosystem protection, and economic and recreational opportunities for the public. The remaining 61% of the land in the western U.S. is owned or managed by private individuals or companies and state governments. Private lands provide the majority of the agricultural products in the western U.S. Federal and state governments seek to help private producers ranch and farm efficiently and to use technologies that reduce soil loss and that maximize the efficient use of water and other resources. Government agencies and non-government centers provide research capabilities to improve the sustainability of agricultural and rangeland and forest ecosystems.

Drought is a common phenomenon on western rangelands and can heighten the risk of land degradation and other hazards such as fire. The federal government has a national policy in place to coordinate responses to drought and to seek to minimize its impact. This policy stresses a proactive approach to resolving drought issues in a collaborative setting. Numerous resources are available on the web to assist managers and the public with dealing with drought planning and mitigation.

Even though the lands in the western U.S. are diverse and management entities are numerous, federal, state and other institutions continue to make a concerted effort to maintain the sustainability of all lands and to minimize desertification impacts, including the restoration of degraded lands.

INTRODUCTION

The United States (U.S.) ratified the United Nations Convention to Combat Desertification (UNCCD) in November 2000 and has been a major contributor of funds and technical expertise as a developed country to affected developing countries (see U.S. AID component of this report). The United States is also an affected country under the Convention given the large portion of the Western United States that meets the U.N.'s criteria for potential for desertification.

This report satisfies the U.N. request for developed countries to prepare a National Report on efforts to mitigate desertification. This is the first National Report prepared by the U.S. on this subject and focuses on the U.S. Government efforts to reverse desertification in the western U.S. The scope of the report will be increased in future updates to reflect more of the activities of State governments and private entities in this effort.

Historical Perspective on Desertification in the United States

A number of factors were historically responsible for the early land degradation and subsequent desertification of lands in the western U.S. Livestock grazing, largely unregulated from the mid-1880s until the 1930s, caused major damage to forests and rangelands. Natural vegetation was lost and the resulting increase in bare soil increased soil erosion (Figure 1).

Figure 1. Uncontrolled livestock grazing in Southern Idaho in the early 1900's resulted in loss of productivity and increased soil erosion.

The U.S. Government took action to reduce this degradation/desertification with the establishment of forest reserves (Forest Reserve Act of 1891) and the Department of Agriculture's U.S. Forest Service (http://www.fs.fed.us/) in 1905.

The vast majority of lands not in private ownership in the West were rangelands, first regulated by the U.S. Grazing Service, established with the passage of the Taylor Grazing Act of 1934, enacted in part to "stop injury to the public grazing lands by preventing overgrazing and soil deterioration,..." The U. S. Department of the Interior's (DOI) Bureau of Land Management (BLM) now manages the majority of the federal rangelands in the western U.S. (http://www.blm.gov).

Congress established Yellowstone National Park in 1872, which was the first reservation of wild lands for recreational purposes under the direct management of the Federal government. A system of wildlife reserves was also established starting in 1903 that are now managed by DOI's Fish and Wildlife Service. These early activities by Congress were taken to reverse the desertification of the American West by properly managing commodity uses (including timber harvesting, livestock use, and mining) of the land and preserving unique landscapes and wildlife habitat.

Desertification on agricultural lands east of the Rocky Mountains was first recognized as a national problem with the Great Drought of the 1930s (e.g., Dust Bowl) which stimulated early recognition of the results of land abuse and loss of soil and vegetation (Figure 2). This drought shaped American policy on dealing with desertification and society as a whole. The Dust Bowl caused a large, influential migration from the southern Great Plains to California and forever changed agricultural policy on the Great Plains. At its height in July 1934, nearly two-thirds of the nation was considered to be in a severe to extreme drought. Congress acted by establishing the Soil Erosion Service in 1933 to assist land owners in implementing proper soil and agricultural practices. In 1935, this agency was transferred to the Department of Agriculture from Interior and renamed the Soil Conservation Service. In 1994 it became the Natural Resources Conservation Service, with a similar mission of assisting private land owners in implementing sound agricultural practices.

In the 1930's, Congress also established the predecessor agency to USDA's Farm Service Agency. Its purpose was, among other things, to work with U.S. farmers and ranchers to preserve natural resources under the Agricultural Conservation Program in order to promote the conservation of private land.

Figure 2. Farm in the Great Plains abandoned during the Dust Bowl.

Improvements in range, forestry, and agricultural practices have resulted in a marked improvement in land health since the 1930's. Even with these improvements, there were still concerns about desertified lands in the Western U.S., as evidenced by two reports prepared in the 1980's. Sheridan (1981) expressed concern about the magnitude of desertified lands and the loss of biological and economic productivity. Sabadell et al. (1982) prepared an assessment of conditions in the western U.S. for the BLM as part of the U.N.'s initial meetings on desertification. This report concluded that a better understanding of the desertification processes and impacts in the western U.S. would lead to more desertification mitigation and better conditions of all resources.

Since the 1980's, management of rangelands and croplands has continued to improve and the overall area of degraded land has decreased (McClure 1998). However, desertification is still a problem in certain parts of the western U.S., especially when inappropriate management activities are combined with drought conditions. Unfortunately, no assessments of ecological condition or economic impacts of desertification have been consistently carried out so the degree of improvement is difficult to quantify.

What is Desertification and How Does it Apply to the United States?

The U.N. Convention to Combat Desertification defines desertification and related terms as:

Desertification: Land degradation in arid, semi-arid, and dry subhumid areas resulting from various factors, including climatic variations and human activities.

Land degradation: The reduction or loss, in arid, semi-arid, and dry subhumid areas, of the biological and economic productivity and complexity of rain-fed cropland, irrigated cropland, or range, pasture, forests and woodlands, resulting from land uses or from a process or combination of processes, including processes arising from human activities and habitation patterns, such as:
    1) Soil erosion caused by wind or water.
    2) Deterioration of the physical, chemical, and biological or economic properties of soil.
    3) Long-term loss of natural vegetation.

Arid, semi-arid, and dry subhumid areas: Areas other than polar and subpolar regions, in which the ratio of annual precipitation to potential evapotranspiration falls within the range from 0/05 to 0.65.

The area within the U.S. that meets the arid, semi-arid, and dry subhumid includes the 17 western states. The Great Plains are the lands east of the Rocky Mountains where agriculture is a predominant use of the land while the land between the major Western mountain ranges are more adapted to livestock grazing, recreational use and extractive industries.

"Obama Administration Denies Petition to Raise Grazing Fees on Public Lands," *The New York Times*, 19 January 2011 by Phil Taylor

Just like the supporters of President George W. Bush (2001–2009) were unhappy with his inability to go around the Congress and the courts to undo the environmental policies of his predecessor, supporters of the Obama administration (2009–) were unhappy when a promised increase in grazing fees on public lands wasn't fulfilled. This article illustrates Obama's decision.

The Obama administration yesterday rejected a proposal to raise grazing fees on public lands, a decision that suggests ranchers will continue to be charged below-market prices to graze cattle on federal rangelands.

The Bureau of Land Management and Forest Service in separate letters yesterday to environmental groups said other priorities prevent them from pursuing new rules to revise the current grazing fee.

Both agencies also said they disagreed with the groups' legal arguments in a 2005 petition challenging the legality of the current fee structure.

Joel Holtrop, deputy chief of the National Forest System, said the agency is pursuing separate rulemakings to revise its forest planning rule and respond to Colorado's roadless proposal, each of which have drained agency resources.

Moreover, roughly 4,000 grazing allotments on Forest Service property are in need of environmental analyses that will help determine the best management of rangeland resources, Holtrop said in the letter.

"This major effort will require focused agency range management technical expertise and funding and is not expected to be completed for several years," he said.

A recent order from a U.S. District Court in Montana also requires the Forest Service to prepare an environmental impact statement in order to continue applying aerial chemical fire retardants to fight wildfires, Holtrop said.

"Given these and other significant agency priorities, I am reluctant to burden the agency's limited resources by initiating an additional major rulemaking endeavor at the present time," he said.

BLM Director Bob Abbey in his letter to the groups said his agency was working to implement proposed orders aimed at reducing the venting of natural gas, revising coal management regulations, updating standards for oil and gas measurement and securing oil and gas production facilities.

"These initiatives represent major undertakings for the BLM and involve significant investments of limited agency resources and staff time," Abbey wrote.

Abbey added that he had discussed the fee structure with "numerous" lawmakers on Capitol Hill and that none of them had requested a change to the grazing fees.

Unwelcome News for Enviros

The government's response was prompted by a lawsuit filed last summer by the Center for Biological Diversity, Western Watersheds Project, WildEarth Guardians, Great Old Broads for Wilderness and Oregon Natural Desert Association seeking to raise grazing fees and require agencies to re-evaluate the effects of grazing on public lands.

Ranchers currently pay the federal government $1.35 a month to graze one cow and her calf—several times lower than the cost of grazing on private lands.

The federal government's grazing program cost taxpayers $115 million in fiscal 2004, according to a Government Accountability Office report. The report also found that BLM's and Forest Service's fees decreased by 40 percent from 1980 to 2004, while grazing fees charged by private ranchers increased by 78 percent for the same period.

Conservationists also contend that grazing damages wildlife habitats, water quality, scenic views and native vegetation.

"Subsidizing the livestock industry at the cost of species, ecosystems and taxpayers is plainly bad public-lands policy," said Taylor McKinnon, public lands campaigns director for CBD. "Today's choice to continue that policy is both a disappointment and a blight on the Obama administration's environmental record."

The GAO report found that if the purpose of the grazing fee were to recover expenditures, BLM and the Forest Service would have to charge $7.64 and $12.26 per "animal unit month," several times higher than the current $1.35.

"Given the massive budget shortfalls our country faces, we can no longer afford to subsidize a small group of ranchers to graze public lands at public expense," said Mark Salvo, director of the Sagebrush Sea Campaign for WildEarth Guardians. "As long as grazing is permitted on public lands, it's only fair that public lands ranchers pay for the cost of their activity."

The groups said they will consider additional litigation in response to the agencies' decision not to increase the fees.

The groups recently reached a "tentative settlement" with the Interior and Agriculture departments that awaits final approval by Justice Department officials, according to the filing in the U.S. District Court for the District of Columbia.

Greta Anderson, Arizona director for Western Watersheds Project, said the settlement will likely still be filed but that the government's response was less than they had hoped.

The government's 2011 fee is expected to be announced at the end of the month.

Source: http://www.nytimes.com/gwire/2011/01/19/19greenwire-obama-admin-denies-petition-to-raise-grazing-f-43764.html.

"Study: Fed Lands Hold Oil and Gas Bonanza,"
Forbes Magazine Blogs, 15 February 2010 by Christopher Helman

While the arguments go on as to whether or not to utilize foreign sources of energy, this article demonstrates that the United States could wean itself off foreign energy, using the vast supplies of energy inside the country.

The United States has more oil and gas reserves on federally owned lands than previously thought. Federal acreage onshore and offshore holds more than 2,000 trillion cubic feet of natural gas (about 75 years worth of current domestic consumption) and 229 billion barrels of oil (about 50 years worth).

So says a study released Monday by the National Association of Regulatory Utility Commissioners. Data gathering and number crunching for the two-year study was done by Science Applications International Corporation (SAIC), a big government contractor, with input from academics and oil companies like Shell, BP, Marathon Energy.

Previous government estimates, using the same methodology, identified 1750 tcf of gas and 186 billion barrels of oil. The increase is due largely to improvements in finding and recovering oil and gas. Any way you look at it, those reserves are more than those controlled by most OPEC nations.

What's more, the report states that some 285 trillion cubic feet of gas and 46 billion barrels of oil are on certain federal lands still off limits to oil and gas drilling (such as more than 6 billion barrels in the Alaska National Wildlife Refuge). Congress in 2008 removed restrictions on some promising areas, like the offshore Outer Continental Shelf, but the Department of Interior hasn't yet determined whether to lease sections of the OCS to development.

This might spur action. The report states that continuing to keep promising lands off limits will mean foregoing $2.36 trillion in cumulative gross domestic product between now and 2030.

The reports conclusions are no surprise, seeing as most of the parties that worked on the report are in favor of throwing open all restricted acreage to development. In the executive summary, they state that the effect of maintaining this moratoria would be to "reduce real consumption levels; decrease gross domestic product; increase dependence on foreign oil and natural gas imports; increase payments to exporting nations; decrease real industrial shipments; elevate energy costs; decrease employment levels; decrease household income; and, produce a mix of negative and positive environmental effects."

It's hard to argue with any of that. Sure, environmentalists will insist that more drilling in the U.S. will just continue our addiction to fossil fuels and will dirty up the air and water. Yet it doesn't make much sense to hand over $300 billion a year to foreign oil producers when there's still so much oil left in the U.S. Offshore oil drilling techniques perfected over 30 years in the Gulf of Mexico and along the continental shelf of Norway can be deployed along the U.S. coasts with minimal environmental impact.

These oil and gas fields will be produced eventually. There might not be much pressure to drill now, with plentiful oil on world markets and reasonable prices. But if the Peak Oilers are right that a supply crunch will usher in $500 a barrel prices within a decade, then those federal lands better get drilled soon.

A reasonable position that could get bipartisan traction (when pigs fly): open certain federal lands to drilling on two conditions: 1. That oil companies adhere to higher environmental standards than anywhere else in the world, and 2. that before they they put up an "environmental bond" before they start drilling (say $100 million per lease block) to cover any spills and to fund the eventual plugging and abandonment of wells.

Source: http://blogs.forbes.com/energysource/2010/02/15/study-fed-lands-hold-oil-and-gas-bonanza/.

"U.S. Support for Nuclear Power Climbs to New High of 62%," Gallup poll, 22 March 2010 by Jeffrey M. Jones

Prior to the Japanese tsunami in early 2011, which led to a near-meltdown of a nuclear power plant, support for the use of nuclear energy inside the United States was growing, as demonstrated by this article on recent polling numbers.

U.S. Support for Nuclear Power Climbs to New High of 62%

Twenty-Eight Percent Strongly Favor Its Use

PRINCETON, NJ—Americans' support for the use of nuclear power has inched up to 62%, establishing a new high.

A majority of Americans have typically favored using nuclear power to provide electricity for the United States since Gallup began asking about this topic in 1994. Support has edged up in the last two years, eclipsing 60% this year for the first time. In addition, 28% of Americans now say they "strongly favor" nuclear power, also the highest Gallup has measured since the question was first asked in 1994.

This year's results, from a March 4-7 Gallup poll, came after President Obama announced federal government loan guarantees to build the first nuclear power plants in the United States in three decades.

Obama's support for nuclear power apparently hasn't done much to change how Democrats view the issue, as a slim majority of 51% favor it, virtually unchanged from last year. Most of the increased support for nuclear energy over the past three years has come among Republicans and Republican-leaning independents, who have consistently been more likely than Democrats and Democratic leaders to favor the use of nuclear energy.

Last year, Gallup documented a significant increase in support for nuclear power, and that upward trend has continued this year. Although President Obama has announced his support for increased use of nuclear power, Republicans remain significantly more supportive than Democrats.

Source: http://www.gallup.com/poll/126827/support-nuclear-power-climbs-new-high.aspx.

"Americans Support Offshore Drilling, but Washington Wavers," *The New York Times*, 17 June 2011 by John M. Broder

After the BP oil spill in 2010, high gas prices led overwhelming numbers of voters, especially in a time of economic recession, to call for more drilling. Despite public opinion, the Obama administration did little to try to get new oil leases pushed through, and even shut down oil drilling in the Gulf of Mexico. This story demonstrates the power of economy over environment.

Americans Support Offshore Drilling, but Washington Wavers

The last year and a half has brought a rapid sequence of reversals in the Obama administration's policy toward oil and gas exploration on public lands and in United States waters.

Since the beginning of 2010, Washington has caromed from a restrictive approach to drilling to a permissive policy closely mirroring that of the Bush administration to a near-total shutdown of offshore drilling after the Deepwater Horizon blowout in the Gulf of Mexico. After that fatal accident, the administration decreed a deepwater drilling moratorium, lifted it six months later, then took five more months before beginning to issue drilling permits.

Throughout that time, the American public's attitudes toward domestic oil and gas development have been remarkably consistent: Americans are in favor of it, though Democrats and those on the coasts are much less likely than Republicans and those in the South and Southwest to be supportive.

National support for offshore drilling and for domestic oil and gas development generally dipped for a time after the BP disaster—from a strong majority to a bare majority—but quickly rebounded.

A Gallup poll taken immediately after the gulf spill showed that 50 percent of Americans supported offshore drilling while 46 percent opposed it. By March of this year, public support had risen to 60 percent versus 37 percent.

The administration's offshore drilling policy, like its fervor for domestic production more generally, has gone through rapid changes. In March 2010, President Obama announced that the United States would make vast tracts of the Gulf of Mexico and the Atlantic and Arctic oceans available for leasing by oil and gas companies. After the BP spill began on April 20, 2010, he declared those areas off-limits for at least five years. Then, last month, the president announced that he would permit accelerated development in Alaska, the gulf and along parts of the Atlantic coast.

Administration officials defend the policy changes as reasonable responses to changed circumstances.

Mr. Obama came to office as a proponent of increased domestic oil and gas development, as part of a broader strategy to reduce oil imports. Accordingly, they said, he took steps to accelerate development. He then imposed a sharp cutback after the BP disaster to give regulators and oil companies time to put new safeguards in place.

After the president was satisfied that drilling could resume safely, and in response to public anxiety about high fuel costs, he shifted back to a more pro-development stance, the aides said.

"These spikes in gas prices are often temporary," Mr. Obama said on May 14 in a radio and Internet address, "and while there are no quick fixes to the problem, there are a few steps we should take that make good sense."

The public's support for offshore drilling has tracked changes in the price of gasoline. When gas prices were near record highs in the summer of 2008 and again this spring, support for domestic drilling was highest.

Conversely, unease about the effects of offshore drilling peaked after the BP accident, which killed 11 rig workers and spewed nearly five million barrels of crude into the gulf.

"News of that incident has faded, possibly lessening Americans' resistance to coastal area drilling," Gallup said when releasing its poll in March that showed 60 percent of Americans supportive.

The poll found that 49 percent of Americans favor opening the Arctic National Wildlife Refuge for oil exploration, a step the Obama administration strongly opposes. That is the highest level of support for drilling in the Arctic refuge since Gallup first asked the question in 2002.

The nationwide poll of 1,021 adults was conducted by telephone in early March.

"Timing is everything," said Jack N. Gerard, president of the American Petroleum Institute, the industry's most prominent lobbying group in Washington. "As the price of gasoline has increased, public attention has turned once again to the question of energy. When they hear their elected officials continue to resist development of American resources, they are appalled."

The Gallup survey found that men are more likely than women to support drilling offshore and in Alaska and support is much higher among Republicans than Democrats. It also found regional variations, with the strongest backing for aggressive oil exploration in the South and the most significant opposition along the East and West Coasts.

And while the public appears to support exploiting domestic oil and gas resources, there is also skepticism about the economic and environmental costs of America's continued reliance on oil. A New York Times/CBS News poll taken in March asked how important it was for the United States to develop an alternative to oil as a major source of energy. Fully 94 percent of respondents said it was very or somewhat important to do so.

The Times/CBS News poll was conducted by telephone with 1,266 adults nationwide.

Daniel J. Weiss, a senior fellow in Washington at the Center for American Progress, said that while the public tends to support more domestic oil and gas drilling, they see it as only one egg in a basket of policies to lower energy costs, reduce dependence on foreign oil and clean up the environment.

"Americans generally support an all-of-the-above strategy," Mr. Weiss said. "They say, 'Let's have more offshore drilling, but also higher mileage standards for our cars and trucks. Let's crack down on the speculators and invest in electric cars, natural gas trucks and biofuels.'"

Mr. Gerard said that Mr. Obama's sporadic and reluctant support for increased domestic production was largely politically driven and not part of a comprehensive energy strategy. But he praised the president for at least appearing responsive to public opinion in calling for more American oil and gas.

"Until the economy gets back on track, until the unemployment rate comes down, and with the price of energy high, I think you'll see the president focus more and more on the supply side," he said. "And as pressure continues to mount as we get closer to Election Day, I think you'll see more of that."

Source: *The New York Times,* 17 June 2011

"Reclamation of the Arid Region," *Forestry & Irrigation Magazine,* November 1902 by George H. Maxwell

The following was excerpted from an address delivered by Maxwell before the Executive Committee of the Omaha Commercial Club on 14 October 1902.

The people of this whole country, and especially the western half of the United States, are thoroughly aroused to the gigantic possibilities of national benefit which would flow from the reclamation and settlement of the arid region under a national irrigation policy. But there are comparatively few who realize that many things must yet be done to accomplish that result. The national irrigation act merely brought us to the thresh hold of the problem. It opened the door just far enough to see the vast benefits that lie beyond if we can get the door thrown wide open, so that the people of this generation may enter and enjoy them. Mere appropriations from Congress will not solve the question, no matter how large they may be. We must not only get larger appropriations, but we must put down a foundation of public sentiment on which to build which will insure an enduring structure.

In the first place the commercial and manufacturing interests of the country, who will benefit just in proportion as the whole people benefit, and who have no local or personal selfish interests to subserve, must be permanently organized throughout the whole United States to carry on a great educational propaganda to awaken the people to a continuing realization of the vast importance of this problem and to maintain an active and right public sentiment with reference to every phase of it.

[...]

Obstacles To Be Overcome.

We have had to contend against wrong theories emanating from the west from the beginning of this movement. We have fought our way over them, one at a time, inch by inch and step by step, until we have finally overcome most of them. First, we had to defeat State Cession; then we had to defeat the State Leasing Bill; then we had to defeat the State Engineer's Bill. All of these turned the control of the reclamation of Uncle Sam's farm over to the state politicians. All of these measures were either advocated or approved at one time or another by Elwood Mead, the irrigation expert in charge of the irrigation investigations of the office of experiment stations of the Department of Agriculture.

But the ghost of State Control, like that of Banquo, will not down. Mr. Mead, ever since he has held that office, has used the influence which it gives him to try and induce the adoption in every western state of a code of water laws providing for an administrative system similar to that of Wyoming, where the water is distributed by a corps of state ditch tenders appointed by state officials.

Such a system as this is the very thing that should not be created where it does not already exist. It puts the control of the distribution of the waters of a state in the hands of a great political irrigation machine controlled by state politicians, and raises innumerable possibilities of complications between the state and national governments in carrying into actual operation the National Irrigation Act.

[...]

What States Should Do.

There are things that the states ought to do, but those things are not the adoption of complicated codes of water laws. The states should establish a few simple fundamental principles by constitutional amendment and judicial decision. It cannot be done by statutory enactment.

Every state should adopt a constitutional amendment to the effect that the right to the use of water for irrigation vests in the user and becomes appurtenant to the land irrigated, and that beneficial use is the basis the measure and the limit of all rights to water.

In every state in addition to this constitutional amendment, decisions should be had in the supreme court of the state establishing this to be the law, and also establishing the doctrine that this same rule of beneficial use applies to the rights of a riparian owner as well as to the right of an appropriator. It is the law of our entire arid region, when correctly interpreted, and should be clearly so declared by our courts, that a riparian owner cannot prevent by injunction a diversion from the stream above him, unless it interferes with some beneficial use of the water then being made by the riparian owner.

It should also be established by our courts clearly and beyond question that the right of a riparian owner to use water to irrigate land to produce crops, as we understand the meaning of the term irrigation in the arid region, is not a common-law right, but one growing out of the necessities of this arid country, and that the riparian owner's right to the use of water for irrigation arises from necessity and is based on and limited by use. It is not perfected until the water has been actually used, and therefore if an appropriator perfects a right by use on the stream below the riparian owner before the riparian owner uses the water, the right of the lower appropriator becomes a vested right which the upper riparian owner must respect, and the riparian owner cannot afterward take the water away from the lower prior appropriator.

These are matters which must be adjudicated by our courts, who have jurisdiction to determine not only what the rights of riparian owners now are, but to find what they have been in the past. If these rights are thus limited by judicial decision, the decision is not an interference with any vested right. It is merely a determination of what that right is and has been and fixes its limitations.

Source: Maxwell, George H., "Reclamation of the Arid Region," *Forestry & Irrigation*, VIII:11 (November 1902), 444-47, from The Papers of George Hebard Maxwell (1860-1946), 1897-1955, Folder "Maxwell Biography. Collection of Articles Shedding Light on His Life and Work. 1902-1935," courtesy of The Arizona Department of Library, Archives and Public Records, Phoenix, Arizona.

"Oil Slick Fire Damages 2 River Spans," *The Cleveland Plain Dealer*, 23 June 1969

During the 1950s and 1960s, Cleveland allowed massive dumping of chemicals and other wastes into the Cuyahoga River. Finally, in June 1969, the river literally exploded into flames, and although the degree of the catastrophe remains controversial, the anger it caused led to the passage of numerous congressional laws, and gave birth to what is considered the modern environmental movement. This article reports on that fire, which is considered to have launched the modern environmental movement.

Oil Slick Fire Damages 2 River Spans

A burning oil slick floating on the Cuyahoga River caused $50,000 damage to two key railroad trestles at the foot of Campbell Road Hill S.E. about noon yesterday, closing one to traffic.

Ballalion 7 Fire chief Bernard E. Campbell said the fire was reported at 11:56 a.m. and was under control by 12:20 p.m. The burning slick floated under the wooden bridges and set them on fire. Cause of the blaze was undetermined, said Campbell.

A fireboat battled the flames on the water while units from three battalions brought the fire on the trestles under control. Campbell said a bridge belonging to Norfolk and Western Railway Co. sustained $45,000 damage, closing both of its tracks.

The other, one-track trestle is open. The fire did $5,000 damage to the timbers of this Newburgh & South Shore Railroad Co. crossing.

Flames climbed as high as five stories, said Campbell.

Campbell pointed out a fireboat patrols the Cuyahoga River daily checking for oil slicks and clearing them away. He said waterfront industries are responsible, dumping oil wastes into the river rather than reclaiming them.

Source: "Oil Slick Fire Damages 2 River Spans," *The Cleveland Plain Dealer*, 23 June 1969, C1.

"Scientists Look for Lingering Damage from BP Oil Spill,"
The Orlando Sentinel, 25 May 2011 by Kevin Spear

Following the disastrous BP oil spill in the Gulf of Mexico in 2010, scientists continue to test the waters to see what continuing impact, if any, the oil spill has on the environment, as well on area wildlife. This article summarizes that effort.

Florida scientists are meeting this week to look at the effects of the BP oil spill in the Gulf of Mexico

ORLANDO, Fla.—If dolphins could turn out for a roll call, biologist Graham Worthy would have a much easier task determining the survivors, victims and overall harmful effects of the massive oil spill last spring and summer in the Gulf of Mexico.

But because that isn't possible, Worthy and dozens of other Florida scientists meeting Wednesday and Thursday at the University of Central Florida have been forced to probe bits and pieces of evidence in the wake of the nearly three-month spill from an offshore well drilled by oil company BP.

Their general and early consensus: A significant measure of luck was on the Gulf's side last year, in that the crude oil could have been much more poisonous and the currents could have carried a lot more of it to Florida's shores.

The spill began April 20 under mile-deep waters nearly 50 miles south of Louisiana and spread slowly before reaching Panhandle beaches in early June.

The scientists, whose efforts are being coordinated by the Florida Institute of Oceanography with a $10 million grant from BP, said Wednesday that they are most worried that some degree of ecological collapse is taking shape in ways they don't yet have the knowledge or tools to measure or predict.

Signs of some serious trouble were presented on the first day of the meeting, including observations of new, predatory species that are capable of inflicting damage on coral and sponge ecosystems.

David Hollander, professor of chemical oceanography at the University of South Florida, said water samples collected in pressure-holding containers at great depths were found to contain dissolved "benzene, toluene and xylene, all of these extraordinarily toxic and carcinogenic compounds."

And William Patterson, marine fisheries ecologist at the University of West Florida, said there have been widespread reports along the Panhandle coast of popular fish, such as red snapper, having large areas of rot, missing fins, strange colors, lesions, parasites that cause bulging growths, and extensive loss of scales.

"Not only are these being reported by fishermen, contrary to reports about scientists not seeing them, we are seeing them. And we are also getting them on video," Patterson said.

The scientists said much investigation remains to be done to determine the potential consequences of those and other findings.

For Worthy, a University of Central Florida professor who will give his presentation Thursday, getting a better understanding of the fate of dolphins has meant returning to a familiar research destination: Choctawhatchee Bay, which lies just inland from the coastal cities of Fort Walton Beach and Destin.

Choctawhatchee Bay is one of the few places along Florida's coast where scientists had identified and monitored bottlenose dolphins for at least several years before the spill occurred.

Since the BP spill, Worthy and students have collected nearly 40,000 photos of dolphins' dorsal fins, which have distinctive and unique features, collected a limited number of dolphin skin biopsies and netted tons of small fish that the dolphins there feed on.

With those photos, Worthy will conduct a painstaking review to see which dolphins observed before the spill are no longer in Choctawhatchee Bay. But that assessment is only for waters in and near Choctawhatchee Bay and not the vastly larger Gulf of Mexico.

"People ask, 'How many dolphins died and how many do we have today?'" Worthy said. "We may be able get assessments of how many dolphins we have today. But in general, we couldn't tell you how many dolphins are gone because we don't know how many there were before the spill."

During the past several months, hundreds of newborn and aborted dolphins have been found dead along the coasts of Louisiana and Mississippi. Scientists think cold weather may have been a factor, as well as the possibility that dolphins there are in poor health because of exposure to oil.

There hasn't been a significant die-off of dolphins in Choctawhatchee Bay. But Worthy's fear is that the fish that dolphins eat—mullet, sea trout and others—were hard hit by the oil spill during spawning.

If significant numbers of young fish were wiped out, then dolphins may be faced with a shortage of food in coming years, he said.

"People are saying, 'There's no oil on the beach, there's none floating around, everything looks good. So what was the big deal? Why was everybody worried about this spill?'" Worthy said.

"I have a feeling these impacts are going to take a little while to come to the surface, so to speak. Three to five years wouldn't be unreasonable."

Source: [http://www.orlandosentinel.com/news/environment/gulf-of-mexico-oil-spill/os-gulf-spill-research-dolphins-20110525,0,891324.story]

State Policies for Groundwater Withdrawals from "Mission 2012: Clean Water," from Massachusetts Institute of Technology

Presently, policies regarding groundwater are implemented on a state by state basis, and are highly variable. Some set specific depletion caps, others only say that water must go to "beneficial uses." Many but not all states require permits for drilling and producing from wells; generally, wells for domestic purposes do not require a permit and go primarily unregulated. Outlined below is each state's current approach to groundwater management.

Colorado

In Colorado, one must obtain a permit to use groundwater. Water permits are considered property rights and can be bought and sold independently of the land upon which the well rests. The governing body for groundwater issues is The Colorado Ground Water Commission. This commission is in charge of issuing and changing water permits. In addition, the Colorado Ground Water Commission divided the groundwater in Colorado into two districts: the Northern High Plains Designated Basin and the Southern High Plains Designated Basin. These districts can put additional rules regarding groundwater management into place; however they cannot issue permits. Only the Colorado Ground Water Commission can issue or change permits.

Since 1990 permits have been issued with the policy that no permit will be issued for a new well if it is projected that that well will deplete the aquifer within a 3-mile radius by 40% within 100 years. Also, since 1967 new large-capacity well permits will not be issued if they are closer than 0.5 miles from an existing large-capacity well drawing from the same aquifer. To change a permit "requires that the well be limited to the average annual historical consumptive use and proof that no material injury will occur to other vested water rights" (McGuire et al, 2000, 37). Changing permits is difficult because most new proposals fail the less than 40% depletion in 100 years criteria mentioned above. (McGuire et al, 2000, 37)

Kansas

In Kansas, anyone with a permit or a vested right can use groundwater for nondomestic purposes. A vested right means that that well had been pumping water since June 28, 1945 and therefore has a right to continue pumping; however, water pumping for domestic purposes is not regulated by permits. In all cases, a landowner must "use the water for beneficial purposes" (McGuire et al, 2000, 39).

The governing bodies for groundwater in Kansas are the five Groundwater-Management Districts. These districts are in charge of regulating nondomestic water use and they can propose regulations that do not conflict with state law. Of these governing bodies some follow the idea of "safe yield" and others follow the idea of "allowable depletion". "Safe yield" is the concept that total groundwater withdrawal in their district must be a certain percentage of the aquifer recharge in that radius. "Allowable depletion" is the concept that total groundwater withdrawal in their district must not deplete the aquifer in that radius by more than a specific amount in a specific time (McGuire et al, 2000, 39).

Nebraska

In Nebraska, one has the right to use "a reasonable amount of the ground water under their land for beneficial use on that land"(McGuire et al, 2000, 40). The Nebraska Department of Natural Resources (NDNR) is in charge of groundwater withdrawals. The NDNR is divided into 23 Natural Resource Districts (NRDs) which each have the authority to manage groundwater use. Each NRD must have a ground-water-management-plan, approved by the NDNR, which outlines what they will do to manage depletion and quality concerns in their area. NRDs are also in charge of distributing well permits, which are required for all wells constructed after September 1993 except for those "used exclusively for domestic purposes and for test holes and dewatering wells used for less than 90 days" (McGuire et al, 2000, 40). In areas where there is not NDNR governance, residents follow the Nebraska correlative rights doctrine that states that residents must share when groundwater supplies are limiting (McGuire et al, 2000, 40).

New Mexico

In New Mexico, water rights are based on the prior appropriation doctrine. There are six groundwater basins all governed by the State Engineer. The State Engineer has the authority to grant permits. In general, the State Engineer approves most permits for domestic use. For nondomestic use, however, the State Engineer will approve permits only if these 4 criteria are met: "(1) no objections are filed, (2) unappropriated water exists in the basin, (3) no infringement on the water rights of prior appropriators occurs, and (4) it is not detrimental to the public welfare or the water conservation goals of the State" (McGuire et al, 2000, 41). The State Engineer determines the validity of criteria 2 by monitoring the groundwater levels 9 to 25 miles around a proposed well site. If water levels decrease by 2.5 feet in one year then the well does not receive a permit. In addition, water rights are bought and sold independently of the land upon which the well sits. As long as the State Engineer approves, water rights can be sold for out-of-state use (McGuire et al, 2000, 41).

Oklahoma

Oklahoma management policy is based on the reasonable use doctrine. Licenses, granted by the Oklahoma Water Resources Board (OWRB), are needed to withdraw water from the aquifer. The amount of water withdrawn is determined by the OWRB and varies from region to region. This amount is determined by the maximum amount of water that can be withdrawn and still secure the availability of water at least 20 years from the time of the license; hence, the specific amount of water is uniquely calculated for each region. This amount is adjusted yearly when each license holder must check in with the OWRB and report how much water they pumped and set limits for the amount of water allowed for the next year. (McGuire et al, 2000, 42).

South Dakota

South Dakota's water resources are managed by the South Dakota Department of Environment and Natural Resources (SDDENR). The Water Management Board (WMB), a group of citizens, works with the SDDENR to manage groundwater. South Dakota law says that all water is a public resource. However, water can be withdrawn once a permit has been approved. The state also sets a specified amount of water that can be withdrawn. Generally, the amount of water withdrawn does not exceed the natural recharge rate. All permits, other than irrigation permits, can be transferred to out-of-state. Most of the groundwater is found below the Rosebud Indian Reservation land. Hence, these tribes have pre-dominant control over the use and development of the groundwater (McGuire et al, 2000, 43).

Wyoming

Wyoming management policy is based on prior appropriation. Wyoming law mandates that all natural waters are property of the state. Permits are given out to users, given that beneficial use is demonstrated. There is no specific limit on the amount of water that can be withdrawn. If the user would like to change any aspect of the permit, the user must first appeal to the state. No permits are needed if the out-of-state transfer is less than 1,000 acre-feet per year (McGuire et al, 2000, 45).

Texas

Texas regards groundwater that is still in the aquifer as a public resource. However, once the groundwater is withdrawn, it is specific to the landowner. Groundwater can be sold to other locations, including out-of-state. No landowner can purposefully withdrawal groundwater for "malicious reasons or to willfully waste the water". Groundwater in the Groundwater Conservation District can regulate the withdrawal, by regulating the permits. No permits are needed for wells that withdrawal less than 25,000 gallons per day or for domestic/livestock wells (McGuire et al, 2000, 44).

California

In California, there are currently three types of water rights that are given out. There are riparian rights, appropriative rights, pueblo rights. The water itself is considered the property of the State, however the water right entitles the user to withdraw water from the source for beneficial use. Water rights are considered as property and hence can be sold and transferred between individuals and/or parties. Riparian rights are generally senior to other rights and are incurred by owning property that borders a water body, such as streams, lakes or ponds. Riparian rights allow the owner to use the water from such sources for beneficial uses without any permits. On the other hand, appropriative rights are designated for surface water being used for beneficial uses. One must file an application, in order to acquire appropriative rights. Pueblo rights apply to both surface and subsurface water source and the entire watershed. Hence, the amount of available water for beneficial use, under pueblo rights, increases with population and urban growth. In California, groundwater provides 30% of the water source. However, there are no current permit application procedures for groundwater use. California only mandates that all owners of land above the aquifer share the right to the "reasonable use" of the aquifer (Water Rights Fact Sheet, 2001).

Oregon

Groundwater in Oregon is considered property of the state and one must obtain a permit to pump groundwater. One will not be granted a permit if the proposed well will interfere with existing wells or surface water use. Oregon declares an area a Critical Groundwater Area if the depletion rate exceeds the recharge rate; currently there are six such areas. Within these areas groundwater use is restricted and certain users have priority, regardless of when their pump was established (Water Rights Fact Sheet, 2001).

Idaho

To pump groundwater in Idaho one must obtain a permit. Permits are granted if pumping water from the proposed pump will not adversely affect existing water rights and if there is enough water underground to support it. The only exception to this is pumps used exclusively for domestic purposes. Domestic purposes are defined as single family homes, camps, livestock, and irrigation of up to half of an acre of land (Water Rights Fact Sheet, 2001).

Utah

In order to use groundwater in Utah, one must obtain a permit from the State Engineer. Utah is divided into groundwater areas and each area determines who will obtain a permit differently. Drilling wells is also regulated by the state. If a well is greater than 30 ft deep then a licensed Utah well driller must build it. The state Engineer is in charge of overseeing the well drilling process (Water Rights Fact Sheet, 2001).

Montana

In Montana one must obtain a permit from the Division of the Montana Department of Natural Resources and Conservation (DNRC) in order to use groundwater. Permits are not required for wells using less than 35 gal/min and wells that do not exceed 10 acre-ft per year. Within the state of Montana, the DNRC can declare a region a Controlled Groundwater Area if depletion rates are, or are expected to, exceed the recharge rate, if there are disputes regarding water rights, or if there is too much groundwater contamination. Currently, there are nine such areas in Montana (Water Rights Fact Sheet, 2001).

Nevada

Groundwater in Nevada is treated as public property and must be used for beneficial purposes. One must receive a permit to pump groundwater unless the water is used for domestic purposes or the owner has vested rights (pumping started prior to March 22, 1913). The State Engineer is in charge of distributing water rights. It is generally their policy to limit withdrawals to the annual recharge rate; however, more water can be extracted if there is an assured source of recharge. Recently, temporary permits have been created in the Las Vegas Artesian Basin and the Colorado River Basin. These permits can be recalled when Colorado River water is obtainable (Water Rights Fact Sheet, 2001).

Arizona

Groundwater rights in Arizona are managed by the Arizona Department of Water Resources (ADWR). In general, water can be pumped from the ground without permits, as long as it is used reasonably and the owner gives a notice of intent to ADWR. However, regions within Arizona can be designated as Irrigation Non-Expansion Areas (INAs) or Active Management Areas (AMAs). INAs have more regulation than non INAs, and IMAs have the most regulation. Within AMAs groundwater pumping requires a permit. The only cases within AMAs that groundwater use does not require a permit is for "grandfathered groundwater rightsÉmunicipal water providers, private water companies,Éirrigation districts, [and]Ésmall domestic wells" (Water Rights Fact Sheet,

2001). Exceptions may be granted for these categories. Grandfathered rights are historical rights based on pumping five years before the region was deemed an AMA. However, in general, permits are required within AMA regions.

Source: Mission 2012, Clean Water, Massachusetts Institute of Technology

"What is Wilderness?" courtesy of the Wilderness Society

What is wilderness? The Wilderness Society answers the question in this online story.

What is Wilderness?

Wilderness provides so much more than a place to camp or fish or hunt. Wilderness clears our air and filters our water. Wilderness provides essential habitat for wildlife, including endangered species. And wilderness is a natural retreat from the stress of our everyday lives.

So what is Wilderness? When we talk about Wilderness, we're referring to a legal definition laid out in the Wilderness Act of 1964. In short, Wilderness is designated by Congress on federal public lands—National Parks, Forests, and Wildlife Refuges, and Bureau of Land Management lands—and is the highest form of protection for federal lands. No roads or permanent structures are allowed in Wilderness, nor activities like logging, mining, or most vehicular traffic.

Since passage of the Wilderness Act, more than 109 million acres of public lands have been designated as Wilderness, less than five percent of the entire United States. But as much as 200 million additional acres of federal public lands may be suitable for Wilderness, and so we and others continue the fight to win Wilderness designation for those lands—because once an area falls victim to roads or other destructive activity, that land is no longer eligible for Wilderness designation.

National Wilderness Preservation System (NWPS)

The Wilderness Act established the NWPS to include all designated Wilderness. It now totals more than 109 million acres in 662 Wilderness Areas. Read more about the NWPS.

Wilderness Designation

Federal land management agencies—National Park Service, National Fish & Wildlife Service, Bureau of Land Management, U.S. Forest Service, and occasionally others—are required to recommend to Congress lands they believe qualify for wilderness designation on a state-by-state basis. Congress then decides which areas to designate. In many cases, Congress has designated more lands for wilderness than federal land management agencies recommended.

The Wilderness Act of 1964 directed the Forest Service, National Park Service, and the Fish and Wildlife Service to survey their roadless lands for possible wilderness designation. The Act requires that wilderness areas be "administered for the use and enjoyment of the American people in such a manner as will leave them unimpaired for future use and enjoyment as wilderness."

The Wilderness Act protects Congressionally-designated wilderness areas from roads, dams, or other permanent structures; from timber cutting and the operation of motorized vehicles and equipment; and, since 1984, from new mining claims and mineral leasing.

Two other laws require wilderness reviews on national lands: the Federal Land Policy and Management Act of 1976 (FLPMA) directed the Bureau of Land Management to inventory its roadless lands for wilderness protection; and the Alaska Lands Act of 1980 also called for wilderness reviews.

Mining operations and livestock grazing are permitted to continue in wilderness areas where such operations existed prior to an area's designation. Hunting and fishing are also allowed in wilderness areas (except in national parks), as are a wide range of other non-mechanized recreation, scientific, and outdoor activities.

The Importance of Wilderness

Wilderness offers people solitude, inspiration, natural quiet, a place to get away. At the same time, designated wilderness protects biodiversity, the web of life.

Of 261 basic ecosystem types in the U.S., 157 are represented in the wilderness system. Without these large, complex areas of preserved landscape, species protection would be virtually impossible and our understanding of how natural systems work would be reduced to childish speculation.

Designated wilderness protects ecological values vital to all of us:

- Wilderness areas protect watersheds that provide drinking water to many cities and rural communities.
- Wilderness serves as critical habitat for wildlife threatened by extinction.
- Wilderness helps filter and improve the quality of our air.
- Wilderness areas maintain gene pools that help to protect biodiversity—the "web of life," and provide natural laboratories for research.
- Wilderness helps meet the nation's increasing demand for outdoor recreation: hiking, hunting, fishing, bird watching, canoeing, camping, and many other activities.
- Wilderness is a haven from the pressures of our fast-paced, industrialized society, providing places where we can seek relief from the noise, haste, and crowds that too often confine us.

The Future of Wilderness

More than 109 million acres of our national lands now have wilderness protection. That's under five percent of the total U.S. land base—and just two percent of the U.S. land base outside of Alaska. The Wilderness Society believes there are many more acres of federal public lands that should be protected as Wilderness, much of it in Alaska, including the coastal plain of the Arctic National Wildlife Refuge.

Other key areas for protection are found in the canyons of southern Utah and southeastern Oregon, ancient forests of the Pacific Northwest, Great Smoky Mountains National Park, Southern Appalachian national forests, Greater Yellowstone ecosystem, northern Rocky Mountains in Idaho and Montana, Florida's marine ecosystem, Colorado's Canyon Country, and others.

27. "The Future of America's National Parks: Celebrating the 90th Anniversary and Looking Forward to the Centennial an Beyond," National Park Service News Release, 25 August 2006, courtesy of the National Park Service, online at http://home.nps.gov/applications/release/print.cfm?id=683.

The National Park Service website page with this information is now down and may be gone forever.

[—]. The Antiquities Act.

The American Antiquities Act of 1906

[34 Stat. 225]

Be it enacted by the Senate and House of Representatives of the United States of America in Congress assembled, That any person who shall appropriate, excavate, injure, or destroy any historic or prehistoric ruin or monument, or any object of antiquity, situated on lands owned or controlled by the Government of the United States, without the permission of the Secretary of the Department of the Government having jurisdiction over the lands on which said antiquities are situated, shall, upon conviction, be fined in a sum of not more than five hundred dollars or be imprisoned for a period of not more than ninety days, or shall suffer both fine and imprisonment, in the discretion of the court.

Sec. 2. That the President of the United States is hereby authorized, in his discretion, to declare by public proclamation historic landmarks, historic and prehistoric structures, and other objects of historic or scientific interest that are situated upon the lands owned or controlled by the Government of the United States to be national monuments, and may reserve as a part thereof parcels of land, the limits of which in all cases shall be confined to the smallest area compatible with proper care and management of the objects to be protected: Provided, That when such objects are situated upon a tract covered by a bona fied unperfected claim or held in private ownership, the tract, or so much thereof as may be necessary for the proper care and management of the object, may be relinquished to the Government, and the Secretary of the Interior is hereby authorized to accept the relinquishment of such tracts in behalf of the Government of the United States.

Sec. 3. That permits for the examination of ruins, the excavation of archaeological sites, and the gathering of objects of antiquity upon the lands under their respective jurisdictions may be granted by the Secretaries of the Interior, Agriculture, and War to institutions which the may deem properly qualified to conduct such examination, excavation, or gathering, subject to such rules and regulation as they may prescribe: Provided, That the examinations, excavations, and gatherings are undertaken for the benefit of reputable museums, universities, colleges, or other recognized scientific or educational institutions, with a view to increasing the knowledge of such objects, and that the gatherings shall be made for permanent preservation in public museums.

Sec. 4. That the Secretaries of the Departments aforesaid shall make and publish from time to time uniform rules and regulations for the purpose of carrying out the provisions of this Act.

Approved, June 8, 1906

Source: http://wilderness.org/content/what-wilderness.

Norton, Secretary of the Interior, et al., v. Southern Utah Wilderness Alliance, et al. (542 US 55 {2004})

The Bureau of Land Management (BLM), an Interior Department agency, manages the Utah land at issue here under the Federal Land Policy and Management Act of 1976 (FLPMA). Pursuant to 43 U. S. C. §1782, the Secretary of the Interior has identified certain federal lands as "wilderness study areas" (WSAs) and recommended some of these as suitable for wilderness designation. Land designated as wilderness by Act of Congress enjoys special protection; until Congress acts, the Secretary must "manage [WSAs]...so as not to impair the[ir] suitability for preservation as wilderness." In addition, each WSA or other area is managed "in accordance with" a land use plan, a BLM document which generally describes, for a particular area, allowable uses, goals for the land's future condition, and next steps. Respondents Southern Utah Wilderness Alliance and others (collectively SUWA) sought declaratory and injunctive relief against Secretary of the Interior Gale Norton for BLM's failure to act to protect Utah public lands from environmental damage caused by off-road vehicles (ORVs), asserting three claims relevant here, and contending that they could sue under the Administrative Procedure Act (APA) to "compel agency action unlawfully withheld or unreasonably delayed." A district court found for the SUWA, and the US Court of Appeals for the Tenth Circuit upheld the decision. The US Supreme Court heard the case, and handed down its decision on 14 June 2004. Justice Antonin Scalia spoke for a unanimous court is holding that even if BLM had failed to upheld the law, such failure was not remediable under the APA. The following are excerpts from that decision.

Justice Scalia delivered the opinion of the Court.

In this case, we must decide whether the authority of a federal court under the Administrative Procedure Act (APA) to "compel agency action unlawfully withheld or unreasonably delayed," 5 U. S. C. §706(1), extends to the review of the United States Bureau of Land Management's stewardship of public lands under certain statutory provisions and its own planning documents.

[...]

Of course not all uses are compatible. Congress made the judgment that some lands should be set aside as wilderness at the expense of commercial and recreational uses. A pre-FLPMA enactment, the Wilderness Act of 1964, 78 Stat. 890, provides that designated wilderness areas, subject to certain exceptions, "shall [have] no commercial enterprise and no permanent road," no motorized vehicles, and no manmade structures. 16 U. S. C. §1133(c). The designation of a wilderness area can be made only by Act of Congress.

"The Great Nation of Futurity,"
The United States Demographic Review, **1839 by John L. O'Sullivan**

This article is an essay on Manifest Destiny—the belief that the American people, particularly those in the integrated eastern states, had a right to continue westward until halted by the ocean: to colonize, to utilize, to expand the nation to its outer edges. O'Sullivan (1813-1895), was a writer and columnist who actually coined the term "Manifest Destiny" in 1845.

THE GREAT NATION OF FUTURITY.

The American people having derived their origin from many other nations, and the Declaration of National Independence being entirely based on the great principle of human equality, these facts demonstrate at once our disconnected position as regards any other nation; that we have, in reality, but little connection with the past history of any of them, and still less with all antiquity, its glories, or its crimes. On the contrary, our national birth was the beginning of a new history, the formation and progress of an untried political system, which separates us from the past and connects us with the future only; and so far as regards the entire development of the natural rights of man, in moral, political, and national life, we may confidently assume that our country is destined to be *the great nation* of futurity.

It is so destined, because the principle upon which a nation is organized fixes its destiny, and that of equality is perfect, is universal. It presides in all the operations of the physical world, and it is also the conscious law of the soul—the self-evident dictate of morality, which accurately defines the duty of man to man, and consequently man's rights as man. Besides, the truthful annals of any nation furnish abundant evidence, that its happiness, its greatness, its duration, were always proportionate to the democratic equality in its system of government.

How many nations have had their decline and fall, because the equal rights of the minority were trampled on by the despotism of the majority; or the interests of the many sacrificed to the aristocracy of the few; or the rights and interests of all given up to the monarchy of one? These three kinds of government have figured so frequently and so largely in the ages that have passed away, that their history, through all time to come, can only furnish a resemblance. Like causes produce like effects, and the true philosopher of history will easily discern the principle of equality, or of privilege, working out its inevitable result. The first is regenerative, because it is natural and right; the latter is destructive to society, because it is unnatural and wrong.

What friend of human liberty, civilization, and refinement, can cast his view over the past history of the monarchies and aristocracies of antiquity, and not deplore that they ever existed ?   What philanthropist can contemplate the oppressions, the cruelties, and injustice inflicted by them on the masses of mankind, and not turn with moral horror from the retrospect ?

America is destined for better deeds.   It is our unparalleled glory that we have no reminiscences of battle fields, but in defence of humanity, of the oppressed of all nations, of the rights of conscience, the rights of personal enfranchisement.   Our annals describe no scenes of horrid carnage, where men were led on by hundreds of thousands to slay one another, dupes and victims to emperors, kings, nobles, demons in the human form called heroes.   We have had patriots to defend our homes, our liberties, but no aspirants to crowns or thrones; nor have the American people ever suffered themselves to be led on by wicked ambition to depopulate the land, to spread desolation far and wide, that a human being might be placed on a seat of supremacy.

We have no interest in the scenes of antiquity, only as lessons of avoidance of nearly all their examples.   The expansive future is our arena, and for our history.   We are entering on its untrodden space, with the truths of God in our minds, beneficent objects in our hearts, and with a clear conscience unsullied by the past.   We are the nation of human progress, and who will, what can, set limits to our onward march?   Providence is with us, and no earthly power can.   We point to the everlasting truth on the first page of our national declaration, and we proclaim to the millions of other lands, that "the gates of hell"—the powers of aristocracy and monarchy—"shall not prevail against it."

The far-reaching, the boundless future will be the era of American greatness.   In its magnificent domain of space and time, the nation of many nations is destined to manifest to mankind the excellence of divine principles; to establish on earth the noblest temple ever dedicated to the worship of the Most High—the Sacred and the True.   Its floor shall be a hemisphere—its roof the firmament of the star-studded heavens, and its congregation an Union of many Republics, comprising hundreds of happy millions, calling, owning no man master, but governed by God's natural and moral law of equality, the law of brotherhood—of " peace and good will amongst men."

But although the mighty constituent truth upon which our social and political system is founded will assuredly work out the glorious destiny herein shadowed forth, yet there are many untoward circumstances to retard our progress, to procrastinate the entire fruition of the greatest good to the human race.   There is a tendency to imitativeness, prevailing amongst our professional and literary men, subversive of originality of thought, and wholly unfavorable to progress.   Being in early life devoted to the study of the laws, institutions, and antiquities of other nations, they are far behind the mind and movement of the age in which they live : so much so, that the spirit of improvement, as well as of enfranchisement, exists chiefly in the great masses—the agricultural and mechanical population.

This propensity to imitate foreign nations is absurd and injurious. It is absurd, for we have never yet drawn on our mental resources that we have not found them ample and of unsurpassed excellence; witness our constitutions of government, where we had no foreign ones to imitate. It is injurious, for never have we followed foreign examples in legislation; witness our laws, our charters of monopoly, that we did not inflict evil on ourselves, subverting common right, in violation of common sense and common justice. The halls of legislation and the courts of law in a Republic are necessarily the public schools of the adult population. If, in these institutions, foreign precedents are legislated, and foreign decisions adjudged over again, is it to be wondered at that an imitative propensity predominates amongst professional and business men. Taught to look abroad for the highest standards of law, judicial wisdom, and literary excellence, the native sense is subjugated to a most obsequious idolatry of the tastes, sentiments, and prejudices of Europe. Hence our legislation, jurisprudence, literature, are more reflective of foreign aristocracy than of American democracy.

European governments have plunged themselves in debt, designating burthens on the people "national blessings." Our State Legislatures, humbly imitating their pernicious example, have pawned, bonded the property, labor, and credit of their constituents to the subjects of monarchy. It is by our own labor, and with our own materials, that our internal improvements are constructed, but our British-law-trained legislators have enacted that we shall be in debt for them, paying interest, but never to become owners. With various climates, soils, natural resources, and products, beyond any other country, and producing more real capital annually than any other sixteen millions of people on earth, we are, nevertheless, borrowers, paying tribute to the money powers of Europe.

Our business men have also conned the lesson of example, and devoted themselves body and mind to the promotion of foreign interests. If States can steep themselves in debt, with any propriety in times of peace, why may not merchants import merchandise on credit? If the one can bond the labor and property of generations yet unborn, why may not the other contract debts against the yearly crops and daily labor of their contemporary fellow citizens?

And our literature!—Oh, when will it breathe the spirit of our republican institutions? When will it be imbued with the God-like aspiration of intellectual freedom—the elevating principle of equality? When will it assert *its* national independence, and speak the soul—the heart of the American people? Why cannot our literati comprehend the matchless sublimity of our position amongst the nations of the world —our high destiny—and cease bending the knee to foreign idolatry, false tastes, false doctrines, false principles? When will they be inspired by the magnificent scenery of our own world, imbibe the fresh enthusiasm of a new heaven and a new earth, and soar upon the expanded wings of truth and liberty? Is not nature as original—her truths as captivating—her aspectsas various, as lovely, as grand—her Promethean fire as glowing in this, our Western hemisphere, as in that of the East? And above all, is not our private life as morally beautiful and good—is not our public life as politically right, as indicative of the brightest prospects of humanity, and therefore as inspiring of the highest conceptions? Why, then, do our authors aim at no higher degree of merit, than a successful imitation of English writers of celebrity?

But with all the retrograde tendencies of our laws, our judicature, our colleges, our literature, still they are compelled to follow the mighty impulse of the age; they are carried onward by the increasing tide of progress; and though they cast many a longing look behind, they cannot stay the glorious movement of the masses, nor induce them to venerate the rubbish, the prejudices, the superstitions of other times and other lands, the theocracy of priests, the divine right of kings, the aristocracy of blood, the metaphysics of colleges, the irrational stuff of law libraries. Already the brightest hopes of philanthropy, the most enlarged speculations of true philosophy, are inspired by the indications perceptible amongst the mechanical and agricultural population. There, with predominating influence, beats the vigorous national heart of America, propelling the onward march of the multitude, propagating and extending, through the present and the future, the powerful purpose of soul, which, in the seventeenth century, sought a refuge among savages, and reared in the wilderness the sacred altars of intellectual freedom. This was the seed that produced individual equality, and political liberty, as its natural fruit; and this is our true nationality. American patriotism is not of soil; we are not aborigines, nor of ancestry, for we are of all nations; but it is essentially personal enfranchisement, for "where liberty dwells," said Franklin, the sage of the Revolution, "there is my country."

Such is our distinguishing characteristic, our popular instinct, and never yet has any public functionary stood forth for the rights of conscience against any, or all, sects desirous of predominating over such right, that he was not sustained by the people. And when a venerated patriot of the Revolution appealed to his fellow-citizens against the overshadowing power of a monarch institution, they came in their strength, and the moneyed despot was brought low. Corporate powers and privileges shrink to nothing when brought in conflict against the rights of individuals. Hence it is that our professional, literary, or commercial aristocracy, have no faith in the virtue, intelligence or capability of the people. The latter have never responded to their exotic sentiments, nor promoted their views of a strong government irresponsible to the popular majority, to the will of the masses.

Yes, we are the nation of progress, of individual freedom, of universal enfranchisement. Equality of rights is the cynosure of our union of States, the grand exemplar of the correlative equality of individuals; and while truth sheds its effulgence, we cannot retrograde, without dissolving the one and subverting the other. We must onward to the fulfilment of our mission—to the entire development of the principle of our organization—freedom of conscience, freedom of person, freedom of trade and business pursuits, universality of freedom and equality. This is our high destiny, and in nature's eternal, inevitable decree of cause and effect we must accomplish it. All this will be our future history, to establish on earth the moral dignity and salvation of man—the immutable truth and beneficence of God. For this blessed mission to the nations of the world, which are shut out from the life-giving light of truth, has America been chosen; and her high example shall smite unto death the tyranny of kings, hierarchs, and oligarchs, and carry the glad tidings of peace and good will where myriads now endure an existence scarcely more enviable than that of beasts of the field. Who, then, can doubt that our country is destined to be *the great nation* of futurity?

WILLIAM LEGGETT.

BY WILLIAM CULLEN BRYANT.

The earth may ring, from shore to shore,
  With echoes of a glorious name,
But he whose loss our tears deplore,
  Has left behind him more than fame.

For when the death-frost came to lie
  Upon that warm and mighty heart,
And quench that bold and friendly eye,
  His spirit did not all depart.

The words of fire, that from his pen
  Were flung upon the lucid page,
Still move, still shake the hearts of men,
  Amid a cold and coward age.

His love of Truth, too warm, too strong,
  For hope or fear to chain or chill,
His hate of tyranny and wrong,
  Burn in the breasts he kindled still.

Massachusetts v. Environmental Protection Agency (549 U.S. 497 {2007})

Massachusetts joined several other states to ask the Environmental Protection Agency (EPA) to rule that carbon dioxide and other "greenhouse gases" were harmful to man and the environment and that they should be regulated. The agency turned down the request, holding that it did not have proper authorization from Congress to make such a decision, and that even if it did have such authorization it needed to conduct scientific surveys on whether "greenhouse gases" were in fact harmful. Massachusetts and the other states sued the agency in the US Court of Appeals for the District of Columbia Circuit, which ruled for the EPA. The states then appealed to the US Supreme Court, which heard the case. On 2 April 2007, a 5-4 court (decision excerpted below) held that the EPA did have such authority to regulate greenhouse gases based on the Clean Air Act and its amendments, and that the agency could avoid making such a ruling only if it investigated "whether greenhouse gas emissions contribute to climate change." On 7 December 2009, the EPA, under the authority of the Obama administration, changed agency policy and ruled that it could regulate greenhouse gases.

[Justice John Paul Stevens wrote the majority opinion.]

"The alternative basis for EPA's decision—that even if it does have statutory authority to regulate greenhouse gases, it would be unwise to do so at this time—rests on reasoning divorced from the statutory text. While the statute does condition the exercise of EPA's authority on its formation of a "judgment," ...that judgment must relate to whether an air pollutant "cause[s], or contribute[s] to, air pollution which may reasonably be anticipated to endanger public health or welfare." ...Put another way, the use of the word "judgment" is not a roving license to ignore the statutory text. It is but a direction to exercise discretion within defined statutory limits. If EPA makes a finding of endangerment, the Clean Air Act requires the agency to regulate emissions of the deleterious pollutant from new motor vehicles. EPA no doubt has significant latitude as to the manner, timing, content, and coordination of its regulations with those of other agencies. But once EPA has responded to a petition for rulemaking, its reasons for action or inaction must conform to the authorizing statute. Under the clear terms of the Clean Air Act, EPA can avoid taking further action only if it determines that greenhouse gases do not contribute to climate change or if it provides some reasonable explanation as to why it cannot or will not exercise its discretion to determine whether they do. To the extent that this constrains agency discretion to pursue other priorities of the Administrator or the President, this is the congressional design.

[...]

"In short, EPA has offered no reasoned explanation for its refusal to decide whether greenhouse gases cause or contribute to climate change. Its action was therefore "arbitrary, capricious,...or otherwise not in accordance with law." We need not and do not reach the question whether on remand EPA must make an endangerment finding, or whether policy concerns can inform EPA's actions in the event that it makes such a finding...We hold only that EPA must ground its reasons for action or inaction in the statute."

American Electric Power Co., Inc., et. al., v. Connecticut
(564 U.S. ___ {U.S. Supreme Court}, 2011)

The U.S. Supreme Court decision came down just as this work was going to press; as a decision involving the Environmental Protection Agency and how it operates within the law, it was included. At this time, the case does not yet have a proper citation in the decisions of the US Supreme Court, except that it will appear in volume 564 of the U.S. Reports.

According to The Scotus Blog, which covers the U.S. Supreme Court and its decisions, "The Court then held that the Clean Air Act and EPA's implementation of the Act displace any federal common-law right to seek abatement of carbon dioxide emissions from fossil-fuel fired power plants. If EPA does not set emissions limits for a particular pollutant or source of pollution, States and private parties may petition for a rulemaking on the matter, and EPA's response will be reviewable in federal court. Thus, the Court ruled that the Act itself provides a means to seek limits on emissions of carbon dioxide from domestic power plants—the same relief the plaintiffs seek by invoking federal common law."

Justice Ruth Bader Ginsburg wrote the unanimous opinion for the Court, which was an 8-0 decision because Justice Sonia Sotomayor did not take part.

"In Massachusetts v. EPA, 549 U. S. 497, this Court held that the Clean Air Act authorizes federal regulation of emissions of carbon dioxide and other greenhouse gases, and that the Environmental Protection Agency (EPA) had misread that Act when it denied a rulemaking petition seeking controls on greenhouse gas emissions from new motor vehicles. In response, EPA commenced a rulemaking under §111 of the Act...to set limits on greenhouse gas emissions from new, modified, and existing fossil-fuel fired power plants. Pursuant to a settlement finalized in March 2011, EPA has committed to issuing a final rule by May 2012. The lawsuits considered here began well before EPA initiated efforts to regulate greenhouse gases. Two groups of plaintiffs, respondents here, filed separate complaints in a Federal District Court against the same five major electric power companies, petitionershere. One group of plaintiffs included eight States and New York City; the second joined three nonprofit land trusts. According to the complaint, the defendants are the largest emitters of carbon dioxide in the Nation. By contributing to global warming, the plaintiffs asserted, the defendants' emissions substantially and unreasonably interfered with public rights, in violation of the federal common law of interstate nuisance, or, in the alternative, of state tort law."

[...]

"Legislative displacement of federal common law does not require the "same sort of evidence of a clear and manifest [congressional] purpose" demanded for preemption of state law...Rather, the test is simply whether the statute "speak[s] directly to [the] question" at issue...Here, Massachusetts made plain that emissions of carbon dioxide qualify as air pollution subject to regulation under the Clean Air Act...And it is equally plain that the Act 'speaks directly' to emissions of carbon dioxide from the defendants' plants. The Act directs EPA to establish emissions standards for categories of stationary sources that, "in [the Administrator's] judgment," "caus[e], or contribut[e] significantly to, air pollution which may reasonably be anticipated to endanger public health or welfare.'...Once EPA lists a category, it must establish performance standards for emission of pollutants from new or modified sources within that category...and, most relevant here, must regulate existing sources within the same category...The Act also provides multiple avenues for enforcement. If EPA does not set emissions limits for a particular pollutant or source of pollution, States and private parties may petition for a rulemaking on the matter, and EPA's response will be reviewable in federal court. See §7607(b)(1).The Act itself thus provides a means to seek limits on emissions of carbon dioxide from domestic power plants—the same relief the plaintiffs seek by invoking federal common law. There is no room for a parallel track."

"The Court rejects the plaintiffs' argument, and the Second Circuit's holding, that federal common law is not displaced until EP Aactually exercises its regulatory authority by setting emissions standards for the defendants' plants. The relevant question for displacement purposes is "whether the field has been occupied, not whether it has been occupied in a particular manner.'.The Clean Air Act is no less an exercise of the Legislature's 'considered judgment' concerning air pollution regulation because it permits emissions until EPA acts. The critical point is that Congress delegated to EPA the decision whether and how to regulate carbondioxide emissions from power plants; the delegation displaces federal common law. If the plaintiffs in this case are dissatisfied with the outcome of EPA's forthcoming rulemaking, their recourse is to seek Court of Appeals review, and, ultimately, to petition for certiorari.

"The Act's prescribed order of decision making—first by the expert agency, and then by federal judges—is yet another reason to resist setting emissions standards by judicial decree under federal tort law.The appropriate amount of regulation in a particular greenhouse gas producing sector requires informed assessment of competing interests. The Clean Air Act entrusts such complex balancing to EPA in the first instance, in combination with state regulators. The expert agency is surely better equipped to do the job than federal judges, who lack the scientific, economic, and technological resources an agency can utilize in coping with issues of this order. The plaintiffs' proposal to have federal judges determine, in the first instance, what amount of carbondioxide emissions is 'unreasonable' and what level of reduction is necessary cannot be reconciled with Congress' scheme.

"The plaintiffs also sought relief under state nuisance law. The Second Circuit did not reach those claims because it held that federal common law governed. In light of the holding here that the Clean Air Act displaces federal common law, the availability vel non of a state lawsuit depends, inter alia, on the preemptive effect of the federal Act. Because none of the parties have briefed preemption or otherwise addressed the availability of a claim under state nuisance law, the matter is left for consideration on remand."

Source: *ScotusBlog*, online at http://www.scotusblog.com/case-files/cases/american-electric-power-co-inc-v-connecticut-2/.

Natural Resources Defense Council and The Sierra Club v. Jackson (US Circuit Court of Appeals for the Seventh Circuit, 2011)

In 2002, the Environmental Protection Agency enacted a series of rules dealing with power companies and industrial plants that pollute. In 2005, several environmental groups challenged the rules in court, but the US Court of Appeals for the District of Columbia Circuit held that such rules were "rational" and consistent with the Clean Air Act. In 2009, the Bush administration, which promulgated the 2002 rules, left office, replaced by the more-environmentally friendly Obama administration. However, the EPA retained the 2002 rules. Again, a number of environmental groups, including the Natural Resources Defense Council (NRDC) and The Sierra Club sued the new EPA administrator, Lisa P. Jackson, to get the rules overturned. In June 2011, the US Circuit Court of Appeals for the Seventh Circuit held there was no legal basis to the groups' claims, and they dismissed their lawsuit. The following is an excerpt from that 7th Circuit opinion, authored by Chief Judge Frank Easterbrook.

"Two sections of the Clean Air Act provide that neither national nor state officials may make any changes that cause air quality to deteriorate in parts of the country that have yet to attain the required standard.

"In 2002 the Environmental Protection Agency changed the rules that determine when polluters need permits in order to modify existing facilities—and, if they need permits, what restrictions they carry...These new rules were challenged as violations of §§ 7410(l) and 7515, among other statutes, but the D.C. Circuit concluded that the new rules are rational and consistent with the Act...Along the way, the court deemed unr ipe an argument that the agency's new approach actually would lead to more emissions...The EPA's models project that the new approach will have neutral or beneficial effects on aggregate emissions; whether that is true, or instead backsliding occurs, depends on data rather than lawyers' arguments, the court stated.

[...]

"Petitioners say that the EPA should have allowed another round of comments after responding to their comments on the Wisconsin plan. That's not how rulemaking works. An agency publishes draft rules; private parties comment; the agency analyzes the comments and adopts a rule, making revisions as needed. Unless the revisions materially change the text, adding features that the commentators could not have anticipated, there's no need for another round of public comments...In other words, the public gets to comment on the proposed rules, not on the agency's response to earlier public comments. The EPA did not make any material change to Wisconsin's proposed implementation plan, so there was no need for another round of comments.

"Petitioners contend that Wisconsin's plan contains a technical error in its definition of 'major modification.' This was not pointed out to the EPA during the rulemaking and so has not been preserved for judicial review. Complainants must exhaust their administrative remedies."

State Data and Maps

Each state profile in this section begins with a chart of information that is significant to the state's land and natural resources. It provides 31 pieces of data, including the total acres of land and water, and how much of that is federal land, either owned, leased, national forest or wilderness. This chart also gives the state's number of national landmarks and parks, acres in conservation programs, plus quantities of energy resources—oil, gas and coal. The Glossary on page 883 gives helpful definitions for many terms used throughout this book. Additional definitions, specifically relevant to the state profiles, include:

- National Forest – land managed by the National Forest Service.

- National Wilderness – area of undeveloped federal land retaining its primeval character and influence, without permanent improvement or human habitation.

- National Natural Landmark – area that offers a best known example of a natural region's characteristic biotic or geologic features, including land or water communities, landforms, geological features, habitats of native species, or fossil evidence of the development of life on earth.

- Archeological Sites in National Parks – a site that contains objects of antiquity or cultural value relating to history or prehistory that warrant special protection.

- Conservation Reserve Program – a cost-share and rental payment program that encourages farmers to convert highly erodible cropland to vegetative cover.

- Land and Water Conservation Fund Grants – provides funds for the acquisition of land and water for recreation and the protection of national natural treasures in the form of parks and protected forest and wildlife areas.

Following the chart are three 4-color maps for each state that provide a visual understanding of the state's populated areas, federal and Indian lands, and the natural landscape as viewed from a satellite's camera.

Alabama

Topic	Value	Time Period
Total Surface Area (acres)	33,423,800	2007
Land	32,133,700	2007
Federal Land	997,900	2007
Owned	194,917	FY 2009
Leased	185,547	FY 2009
Otherwise Managed	1,215	FY 2009
National Forest	670,000	September 2006
National Wilderness	41,367	October 2011
Non-Federal Land, Developed	2,942,900	2007
Non-Federal Land, Rural	28,192,900	2007
Water	1,290,100	2007
National Natural Landmarks	7	December 2010
National Historic Landmarks	36	December 2010
National Register of Historic Places	1,239	December 2010
National Parks	7	December 2010
Visitors to National Parks	781,550	2010
Historic Places Documented by the National Park Service	1,229	December 2010
Archeological Sites in National Parks	223	December 2010
Threatened and Endangered Species in National Parks	15	December 2010
Economic Benefit from National Park Tourism (dollars)	18,781,000	2009
Conservation Reserve Program (acres)	361,053	October 2011
Land and Water Conservation Fund Grants (dollars)	63,927,462	Since 1965
Historic Preservation Grants (dollars)	31,160,393	2010
Community Conservation and Recreation Projects	24	Since 1987
Federal Acres Transferred for Local Parks and Recreation	4,073	Since 1948
Crude Petroleum Production (millions of barrels)	7	2010
Crude Oil Proved Reserves (millions of barrels)	37	2009
Natural Gas Reserves (billions of cubic feet)	2,871	2009
Natural Gas Liquid Reserves (millions of barrels)	106	2008
Natural Gas Marketed Production (billions of cubic feet)	236	2009
Coal Reserves (millions of short tons)	4,074	2009

Sources: U.S. Department of the Interior, National Park Service, State Profiles, December 2010; United States Department of Agriculture, Natural Resources Conservation Service, 2007 National Resources Inventory; U.S. General Services Administration, Federal Real Property Council, FY 2009 Federal Real Property Report, September 2010; University of Montana, www.wilderness.net; U.S. Department of Agriculture, Farm Services Agency, Conservation Reserve Program, October 2011; U.S Census Bureau, 2012 Statistical Abstract of the United States

Alabama Energy Overview and Analysis

Quick Facts

- Although it produces substantial amounts of coal, Alabama relies on deliveries from other States to meet roughly half of State demand.
- Alabama produces natural gas largely from wells offshore in the Gulf of Mexico and from coalbed methane deposits, found primarily in the Black Warrior Basin and the Cahaba Coal Field.
- With numerous dams along the Alabama and Coosa Rivers, Alabama is one of the largest hydroelectric power-producing States east of the Rocky Mountains.
- Alabama's soil is well suited for growing switchgrass, making the State a potential site for the installation of bioenergy plants.
- Alabama is a top producer of energy from wood resources and contains one of the world's largest solid biofuel plants, designed to produce 520,000 metric tons of wood pellets each year.

Analysis

Resources and Consumption

Alabama is rich in energy resources. The State has considerable conventional and unconventional natural gas reserves, substantial deposits of coal, and numerous rivers capable of hydroelectric generation. Several regions of Alabama are well suited for growing switchgrass, making the State a potential site for the installation of bioenergy plants. With a strong manufacturing base in paper products, chemicals, and textiles, Alabama's industrial sector leads State energy consumption, accounting for nearly one-half of total energy use.

Petroleum

Alabama produces a small amount of crude oil from reserves located in the Black Warrior Basin in the north and the Gulf Coast in the south. Although production has been in decline since the early 1990s, new onshore drilling activity has occurred in recent years. To increase production from aging fields, producers have repaired old wells and applied new technology. One petroleum refinery is located near the Port of Mobile, a second is located in Tuscaloosa on the Black Warrior River, and a third is located in Atmore in the southern part of the State. Petroleum products made at Alabama's refineries are delivered to local and regional markets and shipped via pipeline to States in the Northeast. Alabama markets receive additional finished petroleum products from Texas and Louisiana through the Colonial and Plantation pipelines. Per capita petroleum consumption in Alabama is about average compared to other States.

Natural Gas

Alabama's annual natural gas production accounts for more than 1 percent of total U.S. output. More than one-half of this production typically comes from onshore wells, and about two-fifths come from coalbed methane deposits (unconventional natural gas found trapped within coal seams) in the Black Warrior Basin and the Cahaba Coal Field. As with oil production, Alabama's natural gas production is in decline and does not satisfy State demand, about four-fifths of which is from industrial users and electric power generators. Consequently,

Alabama purchases additional supplies of natural gas transported by pipeline mainly from the Gulf of Mexico, Louisiana, and Texas. The Southeast Supply Header pipeline, transporting natural gas from the Perryville Hub in Texas to southern Alabama, came on-line in September 2008. This pipeline has a capacity of 1 billion cubic feet per day and is intended to give Alabama consumers an alternative to offshore supply, which may be vulnerable to weather-related disruptions.

Coal, Electricity, and Renewables

Alabama ranks among the top 10 States in electricity generation. Coal is the dominant fuel for electric power generation, typically accounting for more than one-half of the electricity produced within the State. Alabama produces large amounts of coal in the northern part of the State. Industrial plants and coke plants consume a larger share of the State's output than in most other States. Additional coal, largely used for electricity generation, is shipped in from other States, primarily Wyoming, Kentucky, and West Virginia. Alabama is a major nuclear power generator; its two nuclear power plants produce about one-fourth of the electricity generated in the State. The State's nuclear power capacity expanded in mid-2007 when the Tennessee Valley Authority (TVA) restarted a nuclear reactor at its Browns Ferry plant that had been idle since 1985. With more than two dozen hydroelectric dams, located mainly along the Alabama and Coosa Rivers, Alabama is one of the top producers of hydroelectric power east of the Rocky Mountains. Hydroelectric power typically supplies at least 5 percent of State electricity generation. Alabama ranks among the top States in net summer capacity for generation from wood and wood waste. The State also contains one of the world's largest solid biofuel plants, designed to produce 520,000 metric tons of wood pellets each year, the majority of which is shipped to Europe.

Due to high demand from the industrial and residential sectors, Alabama's total electricity consumption is high when compared to other States. Alabama's per capita consumption of residential electricity is one of the highest in the country due to high air-conditioning demand during the hot summer months and the widespread use of electricity for home heating during the generally mild winter months. However, despite high total and per capita electricity demand, Alabama electricity production exceeds consumption and the State exports large amounts of electricity to neighboring States via several high-voltage interstate transmission lines.

Source: U.S. Energy Information Administration, October 2009

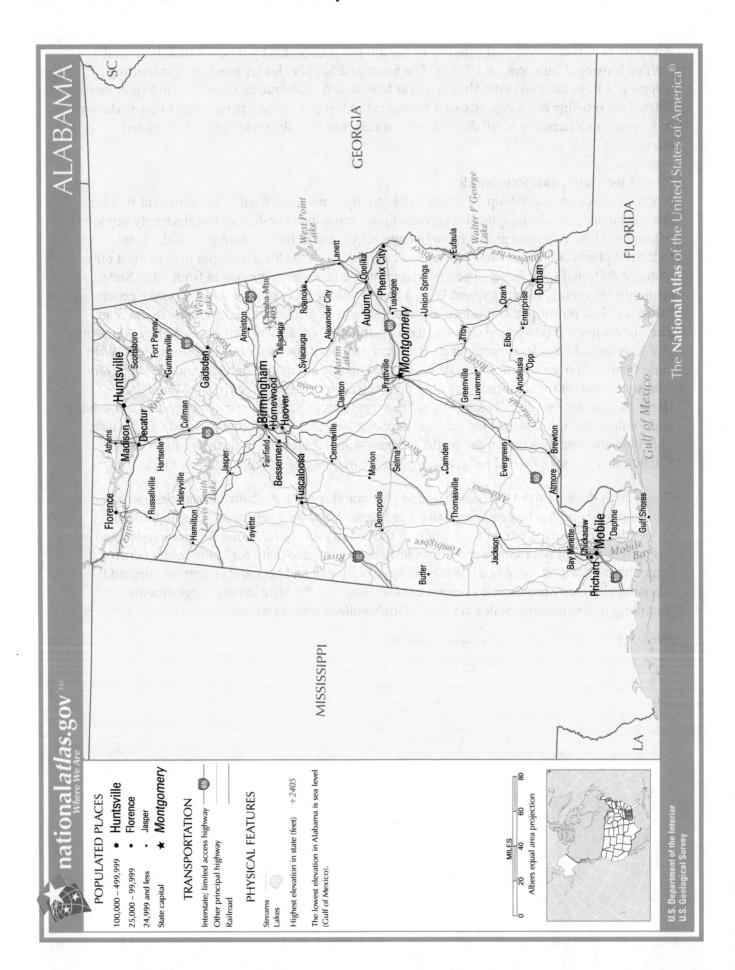

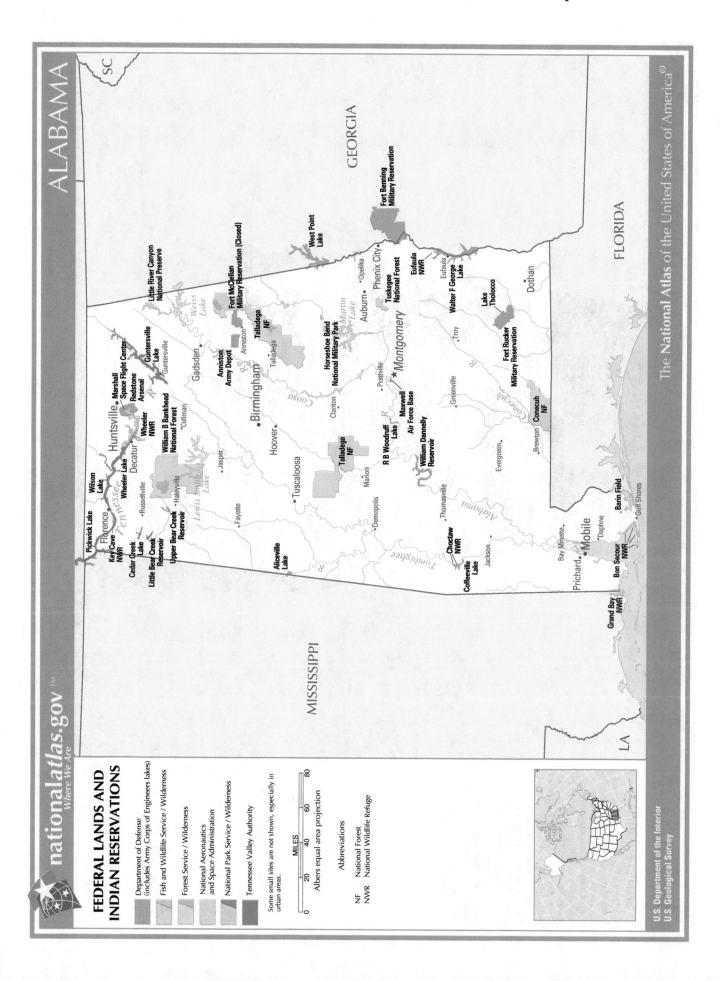

ALABAMA

nationalatlas.gov™
Where We Are

FEDERAL LANDS AND INDIAN RESERVATIONS

Department of Defense
(includes Army Corps of Engineers lakes)

Fish and Wildlife Service / Wilderness

Forest Service / Wilderness

National Aeronautics
and Space Administration

National Park Service / Wilderness

Tennessee Valley Authority

Some small sites are not shown, especially in
urban areas.

MILES

0   20   40   60   80

Albers equal area projection

Abbreviations

NF   National Forest
NWR   National Wildlife Refuge

U.S. Department of the Interior
U.S. Geological Survey

The National Atlas of the United States of America®

SC

GEORGIA

FLORIDA

MISSISSIPPI

LA

Little River Canyon
National Preserve

West Point
Lake

Fort Benning
Military Reservation

Fort McClellan
Military Reservation (Closed)

Phenix City

Tuskegee
National Forest

Eufaula
NWR

Eufaula

Opelika

Weiss
Lake

Talladega
NF

Anniston

Talladega

Auburn

Martin
Lake

Walter F George
Lake

Lake
Tholocco

Dothan

Guntersville
Lake

Marshall
Space Flight Center

Redstone
Arsenal

Guntersville

Gadsden

Anniston
Army Depot

Horseshoe Bend
National Military Park

Troy

Fort Rucker
Military Reservation

Huntsville

Wheeler
NWR

William B Bankhead
National Forest

Cullman

Birmingham

Montgomery

Maxwell
Air Force Base

Greenville

Conecuh
NF

Wilson
Lake

Wheeler Lake

Decatur

Russellville

Hoover

Coosa

Prattville

Clanton

R B Woodruff
Lake

William Dannelly
Reservoir

Brewton

Evergreen

Pickwick Lake

Florence

Key Cave
NWR

Cedar Creek
Lake

Little Bear Creek
Reservoir

Upper Bear Creek
Reservoir

Haleyville

Jasper

Tuscaloosa

Talladega
NF

Marion

Demopolis

Alabama

Thomasville

Tennessee

Lewis Smith
Lake

Fayette

Aliceville
Lake

Tombigbee

Choctaw
NWR

Coffeeville
Lake

Jackson

Bay Minette

Prichard

Mobile

Daphne

Barin Field

Gulf Shores

Bon Secour
NWR

Grand Bay
NWR

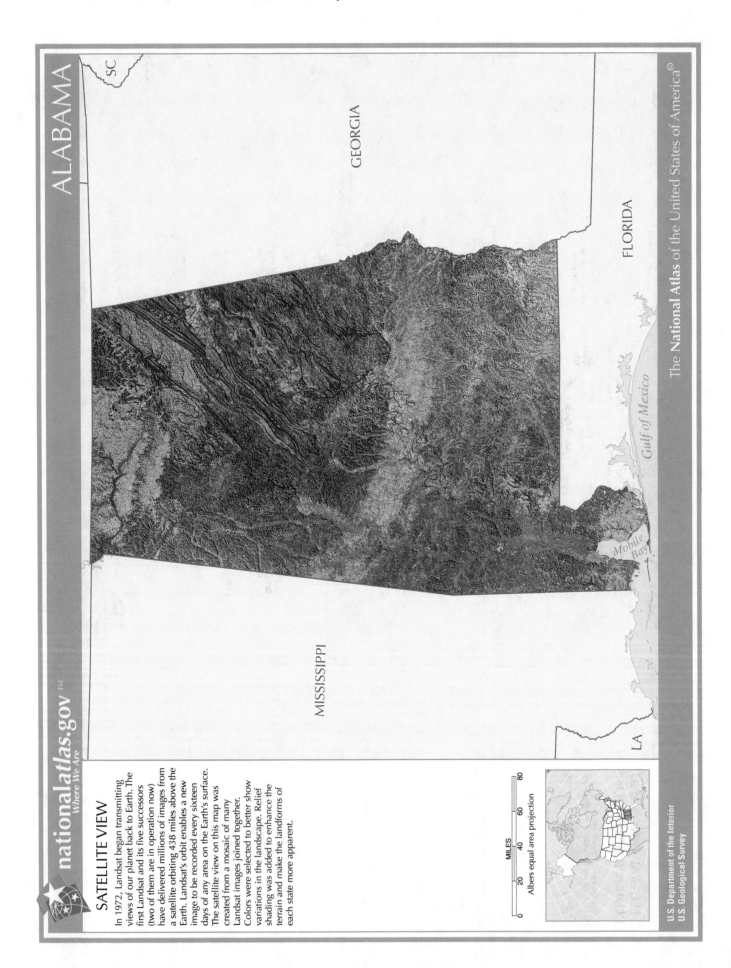

ALABAMA

nationalatlas.gov™
Where We Are

SC

GEORGIA

FLORIDA

MISSISSIPPI

LA

Gulf of Mexico

Mobile Bay

The **National Atlas** of the United States of America©

SATELLITE VIEW

In 1972, Landsat began transmitting views of our planet back to Earth. The first Landsat and its five successors (two of them are in operation now) have delivered millions of images from a satellite orbiting 438 miles above the Earth. Landsat's orbit enables a new image to be recorded every sixteen days of any area on the Earth's surface. The satellite view on this map was created from a mosaic of many Landsat images joined together. Colors were selected to better show variations in the landscape. Relief shading was added to enhance the terrain and make the landforms of each state more apparent.

MILES

0   20   40   60   80

Albers equal area projection

U.S. Department of the Interior
U.S. Geological Survey

Alaska

Topic	Value	Time Period
Total Surface Area (acres)	Not Available	2007
Land	Not Available	2007
Federal Land	Not Available	2007
Owned	1,782,622	FY 2009
Leased	14,900	FY 2009
Otherwise Managed	46,413	FY 2009
National Forest	21,956,000	September 2006
National Wilderness	57,425,910	October 2011
Non-Federal Land, Developed	Not Available	2007
Non-Federal Land, Rural	Not Available	2007
Water	Not Available	2007
National Natural Landmarks	16	December 2010
National Historic Landmarks	49	December 2010
National Register of Historic Places	410	December 2010
National Parks	23	December 2010
Visitors to National Parks	2,274,843	2010
Historic Places Documented by the National Park Service	516	December 2010
Archeological Sites in National Parks	4,539	December 2010
Threatened and Endangered Species in National Parks	8	December 2010
Economic Benefit from National Park Tourism (dollars)	216,224,000	2009
Conservation Reserve Program (acres)	19,007	October 2011
Land and Water Conservation Fund Grants (dollars)	33,609,258	Since 1965
Historic Preservation Grants (dollars)	22,289,153	2010
Community Conservation and Recreation Projects	80	Since 1987
Federal Acres Transferred for Local Parks and Recreation	266	Since 1948
Crude Petroleum Production (millions of barrels)	219	2010
Crude Oil Proved Reserves (millions of barrels)	3,566	2009
Natural Gas Reserves (billions of cubic feet)	9,101	2009
Natural Gas Liquid Reserves (millions of barrels)	312	2008
Natural Gas Marketed Production (billions of cubic feet)	397	2009
Coal Reserves (millions of short tons)	6,102	2009

Sources: U.S. Department of the Interior, National Park Service, State Profiles, December 2010; United States Department of Agriculture, Natural Resources Conservation Service, 2007 National Resources Inventory; U.S. General Services Administration, Federal Real Property Council, FY 2009 Federal Real Property Report, September 2010; University of Montana, www.wilderness.net; U.S. Department of Agriculture, Farm Services Agency, Conservation Reserve Program, October 2011; U.S Census Bureau, 2012 Statistical Abstract of the United States

Alaska Energy Overview and Analysis

Quick Facts

- Excluding Federal offshore production, Alaska ranks second in the Nation in crude oil production.
- Prudhoe Bay on Alaska's North Slope is the highest yielding oil field in the United States, producing approximately 264,000 barrels per day.
- The Trans-Alaska Pipeline transports crude oil from the frozen North Slope to the warm-water Port of Valdez, on Alaska's southern coast.
- Alaska has six oil refineries, most of which are "topping" plants.
- Alaska's electricity infrastructure differs from the lower 48 States in that most consumers are not linked to large interconnected grids through transmission and distribution lines. Rural communities rely primarily on diesel electric generators for power.
- Plans are being discussed to develop two small nuclear facilities to help meet electricity demand in Alaska.

Analysis

Resources and Consumption

Alaska has vast energy resources with major oil and gas reserves found in the Alaska North Slope (ANS) and Cook Inlet basins. The ANS contains 14 of the 100 largest oil fields in the United States, and five of the 100 largest natural gas fields. The North Slope's Prudhoe Bay field is the largest oil field in the country, producing an average of 264,000 barrels per day. Substantial coal deposits are found in Alaska's bituminous, subbituminous, and lignite coal basins. Alaska's numerous rivers offer some of the highest hydroelectric power potential in the Nation, and large swaths of the Alaskan coastline offer wind and geothermal energy potential. The oil and gas industry dominates the Alaskan economy, and production activities drive State energy demand. Although Alaska has a low absolute energy demand compared to the U.S. average, its per capita energy consumption is the highest in the country - more than three times the U.S. average.

Petroleum

Alaska is the second-ranked oil-producing State after Texas, when output from the Federal Outer Continental Shelf (OCS) is excluded from the State totals. Nearly all of Alaska's oil production takes place on the North Slope. The Trans-Alaska Pipeline System (TAPS) transports crude oil from the frozen North Slope to the warm-water Port of Valdez, on Alaska's southern coast. The pipeline has a maximum daily throughput of over 2 million barrels per day, but actual throughput has been less than 1 million barrels per day since 2003. From Valdez, tankers ship the ANS crude oil primarily to refineries along the West Coast. Those refineries are designed to process the intermediate, sour (high-sulfur) crude oil from the ANS. Alaskan crude oil production has been in decline since 1988, when output peaked at over 2 million barrels per day. However, experts believe that large oil and gas reserves in the State remain untapped, and some have called for the Federal government to open more public lands, including the Arctic National Wildlife Refuge, for oil exploration and drilling.

Demand for finished petroleum products in Alaska is low. Although Alaska has six refineries, most of them are "topping" plants that strip away lighter products from the TAPS heavy crude oil stream for internal refinery use. State motor gasoline demand is primarily met by refineries in Kenai and near Fairbanks. By a wide margin, Alaska has the highest per-capita jet fuel consumption in the United States.

Due to harsh weather conditions that persist throughout most of the year, Alaska's oil infrastructure is particularly vulnerable to weather-related accidents and disruptions. The worst accident occurred in March 1989, when the tank vessel Exxon Valdez struck Bligh Reef and spilled 260,000 barrels of oil into the Prince William Sound.

Natural Gas

Alaska has substantial marketed natural gas production, most of which takes place in the Cook Inlet, where output is in decline. Although large volumes of natural gas are extracted during oil production on the ANS, this supply has no way of reaching consumption markets and is subsequently pumped back into the ground for repressurization or used as lease fuel to operate equipment at oil production facilities. It has not been considered commercially feasible to build a natural gas pipeline linking ANS natural gas with markets in the Lower 48 States, although two separate consortia have filed project applications with the State of Alaska.

Most of Alaska's marketed natural gas is consumed at the production site as lease fuel or plant fuel. Only about one-fourth of Alaska's marketed natural gas production is delivered to customers. Of these customers, the electric power sector is the largest. Since Alaskan natural gas is abundant and cheap, the State has attracted a petrochemicals industry that produces ammonia and urea fertilizer. In addition, the Kenai liquefied natural gas (LNG) terminal in the Cook Inlet exports LNG, primarily to Japan. Kenai is the only LNG export terminal in the United States.

Coal, Electricity, and Renewables

Alaska's electricity infrastructure differs from that of the lower 48 States because most Alaskan consumers are not linked to large, interconnected grids through transmission and distribution lines. An interconnected grid exists in the populated areas from Fairbanks to south of Anchorage; however, that grid is isolated from those in Canada and the 48 contiguous States. Rural communities rely on their own power sources, almost exclusively using diesel electric generators.

Natural Gas fuels almost three-fifths of Alaska's electricity generation, and hydroelectric power supplies about one-fifth. Petroleum and coal each account for approximately one-tenth of net electricity generation. While Alaska does not currently produce energy from nuclear sources, plans are being considered for small nuclear reactors near Fairbanks and in Galena, a village on the Yukon River. More than 50 hydroelectric power plants supply Alaskan communities, and three of those plants are among the ten largest generators in the State. Alaska's renewable energy sources also include a 200-kilowatt geothermal plant at Chena Hot Springs and 14 small wind energy projects with a total of about 3 megawatts of capacity. Alaskans also operate one of the Nation's largest fuel cell systems, in Anchorage, and the world's largest battery storage system.

Source: U.S. Energy Information Administration, October 2009

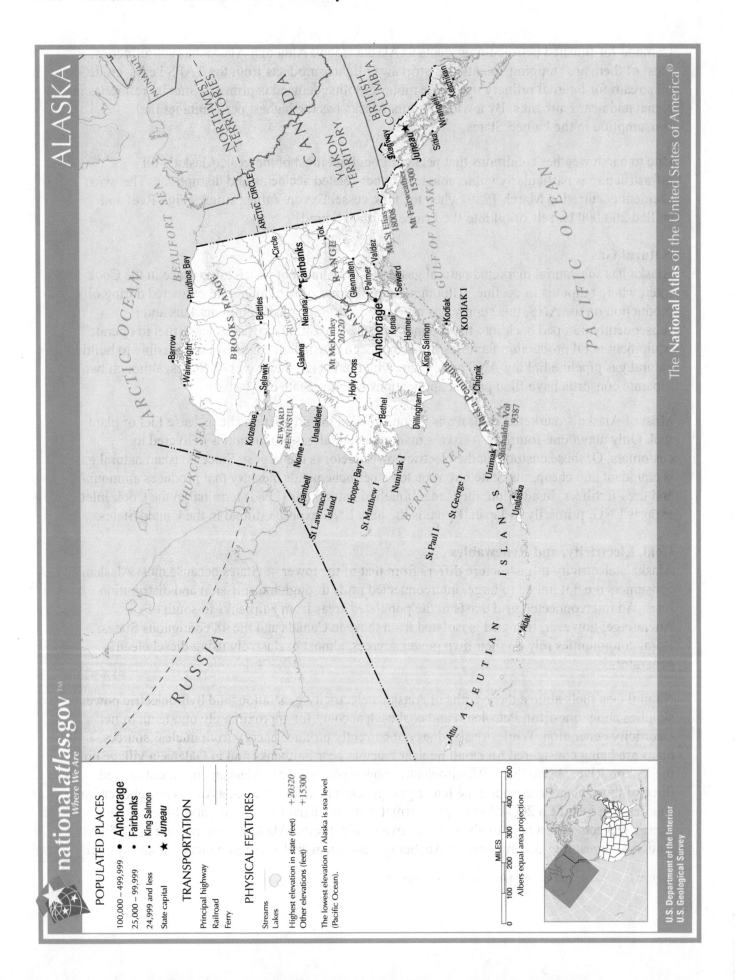

ALASKA

nationalatlas.gov™
Where We Are

POPULATED PLACES

100,000 – 499,999   ● **Anchorage**
25,000 – 99,999   ● Fairbanks
24,999 and less   • King Salmon
State capital   ★ *Juneau*

TRANSPORTATION

Principal highway
Railroad
Ferry

PHYSICAL FEATURES

Streams
Lakes
Highest elevation in state (feet)   +20320
Other elevations (feet)   +15300
The lowest elevation in Alaska is sea level
(Pacific Ocean).

MILES
0   100 200 300 400 500
Albers equal area projection

U.S. Department of the Interior
U.S. Geological Survey

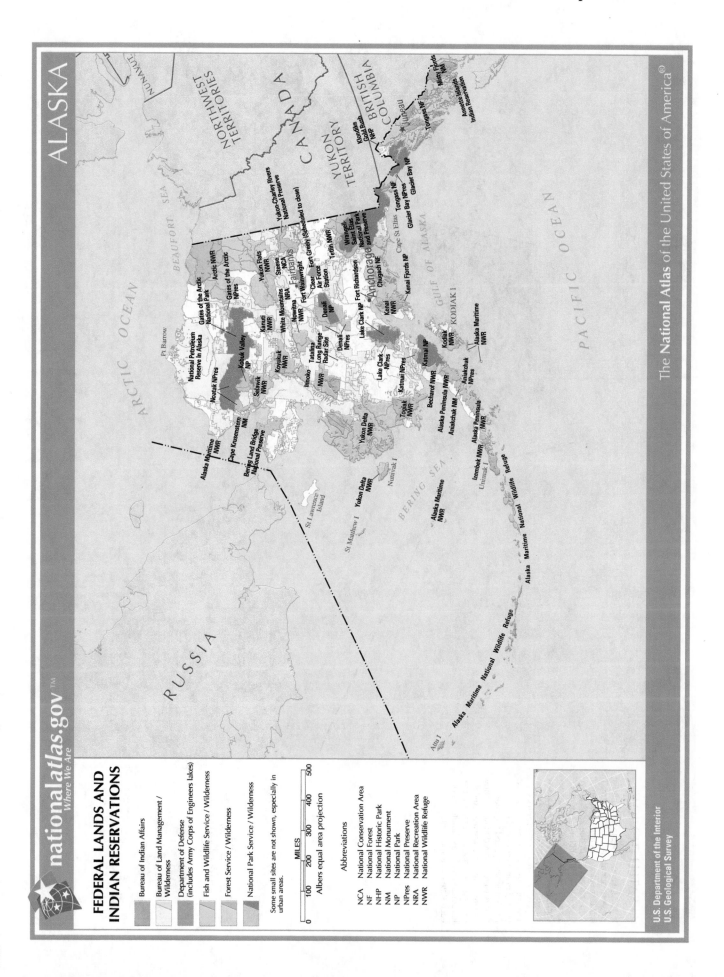

ALASKA

nationalatlas.gov™
Where We Are

FEDERAL LANDS AND INDIAN RESERVATIONS

Bureau of Indian Affairs

Bureau of Land Management / Wilderness

Department of Defense (includes Army Corps of Engineers lakes)

Fish and Wildlife Service / Wilderness

Forest Service / Wilderness

National Park Service / Wilderness

Some small sites are not shown, especially in urban areas.

MILES

0   100   200   300   400   500

Albers equal area projection

Abbreviations

NCA	National Conservation Area
NF	National Forest
NHP	National Historic Park
NM	National Monument
NP	National Park
NPres	National Preserve
NRA	National Recreation Area
NWR	National Wildlife Refuge

The **National Atlas** of the United States of America®

U.S. Department of the Interior
U.S. Geological Survey

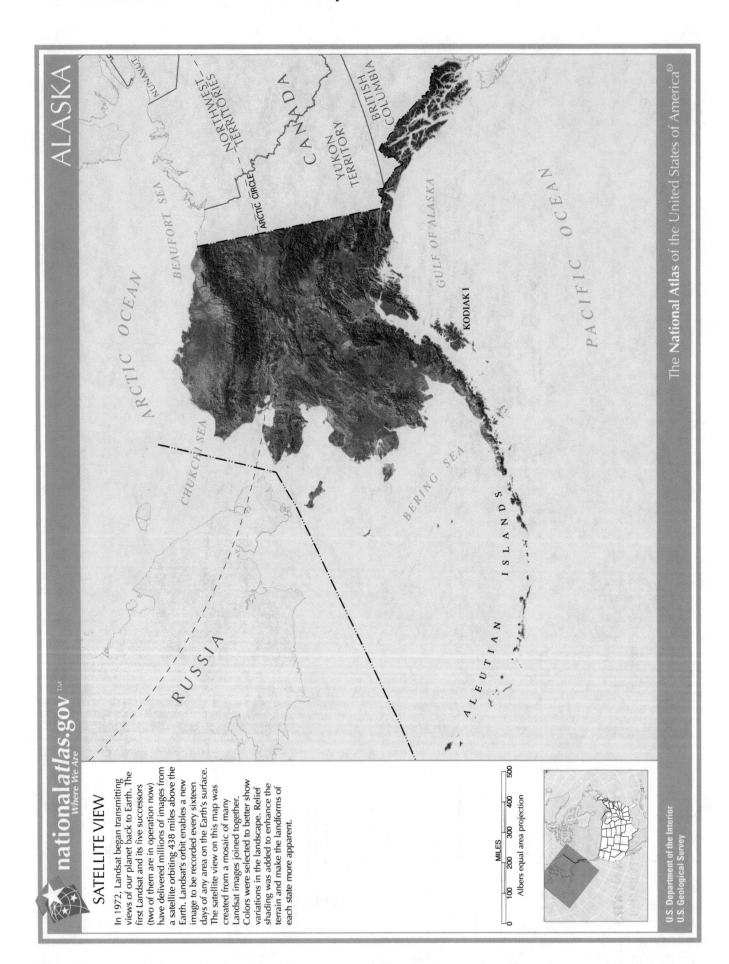

ALASKA

nationalatlas.gov™
Where We Are

SATELLITE VIEW

In 1972, Landsat began transmitting views of our planet back to Earth. The first Landsat and its five successors (two of them are in operation now) have delivered millions of images from a satellite orbiting 438 miles above the Earth. Landsat's orbit enables a new image to be recorded every sixteen days of any area on the Earth's surface. The satellite view on this map was created from a mosaic of many Landsat images joined together. Colors were selected to better show variations in the landscape. Relief shading was added to enhance the terrain and make the landforms of each state more apparent.

MILES
0   100   200   300   400   500

Albers equal area projection

U.S. Department of the Interior
U.S. Geological Survey

The **National Atlas** of the United States of America®

NUNAVUT

NORTHWEST TERRITORIES

CANADA

BRITISH COLUMBIA

YUKON TERRITORY

ARCTIC CIRCLE

BEAUFORT SEA

ARCTIC OCEAN

CHUKCHI SEA

RUSSIA

BERING SEA

ALEUTIAN ISLANDS

GULF OF ALASKA

KODIAK I

PACIFIC OCEAN

Arizona

Topic	Value	Time Period
Total Surface Area (acres)	72,964,400	2007
Land	72,774,700	2007
Federal Land	30,426,200	2007
Owned	3,993,434	FY 2009
Leased	37,151	FY 2009
Otherwise Managed	687	FY 2009
National Forest	11,265,000	September 2006
National Wilderness	4,529,613	October 2011
Non-Federal Land, Developed	2,006,200	2007
Non-Federal Land, Rural	40,342,300	2007
Water	189,700	2007
National Natural Landmarks	9	December 2010
National Historic Landmarks	41	December 2010
National Register of Historic Places	1,362	December 2010
National Parks	22	December 2010
Visitors to National Parks	10,546,150	2010
Historic Places Documented by the National Park Service	537	December 2010
Archeological Sites in National Parks	10,999	December 2010
Threatened and Endangered Species in National Parks	32	December 2010
Economic Benefit from National Park Tourism (dollars)	659,180,000	2009
Conservation Reserve Program (acres)	Not Available	October 2011
Land and Water Conservation Fund Grants (dollars)	58,531,701	Since 1965
Historic Preservation Grants (dollars)	21,112,060	2010
Community Conservation and Recreation Projects	55	Since 1987
Federal Acres Transferred for Local Parks and Recreation	794	Since 1948
Crude Petroleum Production (millions of barrels)	Not Available	2010
Crude Oil Proved Reserves (millions of barrels)	Not Available	2009
Natural Gas Reserves (billions of cubic feet)	Not Available	2009
Natural Gas Liquid Reserves (millions of barrels)	Not Available	2008
Natural Gas Marketed Production (billions of cubic feet)	Not Available	2009
Coal Reserves (millions of short tons)	Not Available	2009

Sources: U.S. Department of the Interior, National Park Service, State Profiles, December 2010; United States Department of Agriculture, Natural Resources Conservation Service, 2007 National Resources Inventory; U.S. General Services Administration, Federal Real Property Council, FY 2009 Federal Real Property Report, September 2010; University of Montana, www.wilderness.net; U.S. Department of Agriculture, Farm Services Agency, Conservation Reserve Program, October 2011; U.S Census Bureau, 2012 Statistical Abstract of the United States

Arizona Energy Overview and Analysis

Quick Facts

- Arizona's Palo Verde nuclear power plant is the largest nuclear plant and has the second-highest rated capacity of any power plants in the United States.
- Arizona exports large amounts of electricity to neighboring States, particularly to markets in Southern California.
- Arizona's large desert areas offer some of the highest solar power potential in the country.
- Substantial coal production takes place in the Black Mesa Basin in northeast Arizona.
- Arizona's first refinery is expected to be fully operational in 2012. Once completed, it could be the first in the United States specifically designed to produce clean petroleum fuels such as CARB3 (California Air Resources Board fuel specification), Arizona Clean Burning Gasoline, and ultra-low sulfur gasoline.

Analysis

Resources and Consumption

Arizona has substantial coal deposits but few other fossil fuel resources. The coal deposits are concentrated in the Black Mesa Basin in the northeast part of the State. Arizona has one nuclear power plant and extensive solar energy potential. Its large desert areas offer some of the highest solar power potential in the country, and the Colorado River is a tremendous source of hydropower. While Arizona ranks near the middle of the States in total energy consumption, per capita energy consumption is low, and the State economy is not energy intensive. The transportation sector is the leading energy-consuming sector in the State.

Petroleum

Arizona's crude oil production is minimal. Arizona currently has no refineries and receives its petroleum product supply via two pipelines, one from southern California and the other from El Paso, Texas. In summer 2003, the line from El Paso ruptured, causing spillage of petroleum products, and the section of the line between Tucson and Phoenix had to be shut down. Even though the line was repaired in less than one month, the accident caused shortages at Phoenix area motor gasoline fueling stations.

A new refinery in Yuma County, Arizona, about 100 miles southwest of Phoenix, was initially proposed for completion by 2010. However, it was delayed because the Quechan tribe expressed concerns about disturbing cultural artifacts and the Mexican government refused to supply the refinery with crude oil. The refinery was reapproved in 2008 for a location in Mohawk Valley, 4 miles east of the proposed Yuma location, and is now expected to be fully operational by 2012. The refinery is planning to receive its crude supplies from Alberta oil sands that will be shipped by barge to Mexico and shipped by pipeline to Arizona. The facility will have a capacity to refine 163,000 barrels per day of crude oil and produce 6.3 million gallons per day of petroleum clean fuels such as CARB3 (California Air Resources Board fuel specification), Arizona Clean Burning Gasoline, ultra-low sulfur gasoline, as well as other petroleum products. This new facility will be Arizona's first refinery and could be the first refinery in the United States specifically designed to produce clean petroleum fuels.

An oxygenated motor gasoline blend is used in the Tucson area during the winter and in Maricopa County (Phoenix) year-round. Arizona also requires the use of a motor gasoline blend with low volatility in the area just south of Phoenix.

Natural Gas
The electric power sector dominates natural gas consumption in Arizona, consuming roughly three-fourths of State supply. Winters are generally mild and almost two-fifths of Arizona households rely on natural gas as their primary energy source for home heating. Arizona relies on interstate and international deliveries to meet most of its natural gas demand. Arizona is part of the transportation corridor for shipping gas from production areas in Texas and the Rocky Mountains to the southern California region via several major natural gas pipelines. Arizona has recently begun construction on a new natural gas-fired power plant in Coolidge, southeast of Phoenix, which is expected to be completed by 2011.

Coal, Electricity, and Renewables
Arizona's coal production takes place primarily in the Black Mesa Basin and large volumes of coal move in and out of the State via rail. More than one-third of the coal produced in Arizona is delivered to coal-fired generators in Nevada. The remaining two-thirds, along with coal supplies transported primarily from New Mexico, are consumed at power plants in the State.

Coal-fired plants supply almost two-fifths of Arizona's demand for electricity. Natural gas-fired plants and nuclear power supply most of the remainder. Arizona's sole nuclear power plant, the 3-unit Palo Verde plant, provides about one-fourth of the State's total electricity generation. Palo Verde is the Nation's largest nuclear plant and has the second-highest rated capacity of any power plant in the United States. The Glen Canyon and Hoover dams, both located on the Colorado River in northern Arizona, provide hydroelectric power. Although Arizona is a leader in the Nation in solar power potential, its solar-powered generation facilities are small and the State has not yet developed its solar resource on a large scale. In February 2006, Arizona adopted a renewable portfolio standard that requires electric utilities to generate 15 percent of their energy from renewable resources by 2025.

More than one-half of Arizona households rely on electricity as their primary energy source for home heating.

Source: U.S. Energy Information Administration, October 2009

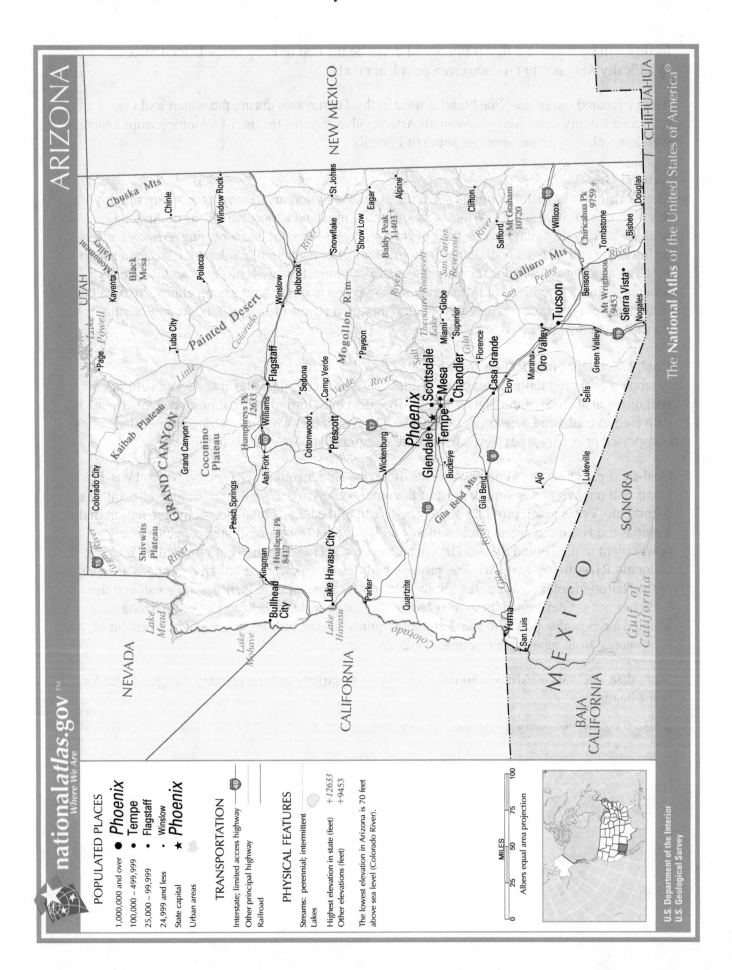

ARIZONA

nationalatlas.gov™
Where We Are

POPULATED PLACES

● **Phoenix**   1,000,000 and over
● Tempe   100,000 – 499,999
• Flagstaff   25,000 – 99,999
• Winslow   24,999 and less
★ **Phoenix**   State capital
Urban areas

TRANSPORTATION

Interstate; limited access highway
Other principal highway
Railroad

PHYSICAL FEATURES

Streams: perennial; intermittent
Lakes
Highest elevation in state (feet)   +12633
Other elevations (feet)   +9453

The lowest elevation in Arizona is 70 feet above sea level (Colorado River).

MILES
0   25   50   75   100
Albers equal area projection

U.S. Department of the Interior
U.S. Geological Survey

The **National Atlas** of the United States of America©

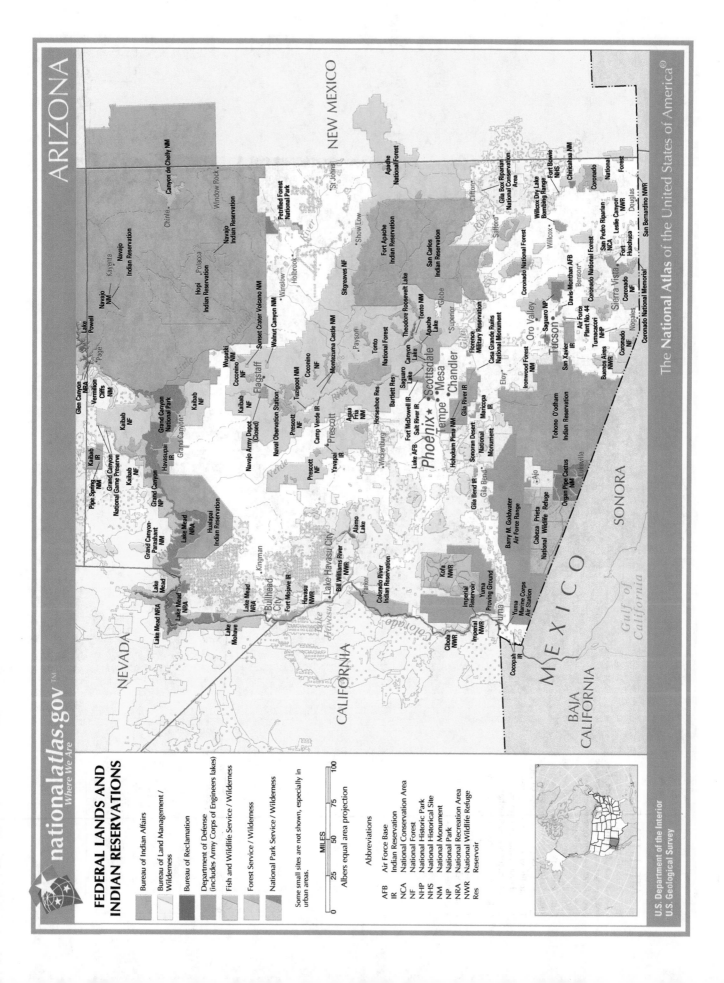

**FEDERAL LANDS AND
INDIAN RESERVATIONS**

Bureau of Indian Affairs

Bureau of Land Management /
Wilderness

Bureau of Reclamation

Department of Defense
(includes Army Corps of Engineers lakes)

Fish and Wildlife Service / Wilderness

Forest Service / Wilderness

National Park Service / Wilderness

Some small sites are not shown, especially in
urban areas.

MILES

0   25   50   75   100

Albers equal area projection

Abbreviations

AFB   Air Force Base
IR   Indian Reservation
NCA   National Conservation Area
NF   National Forest
NHP   National Historical Park
NHS   National Historical Site
NM   National Monument
NP   National Park
NRA   National Recreation Area
NWR   National Wildlife Refuge
Res   Reservoir

U.S. Department of the Interior
U.S. Geological Survey

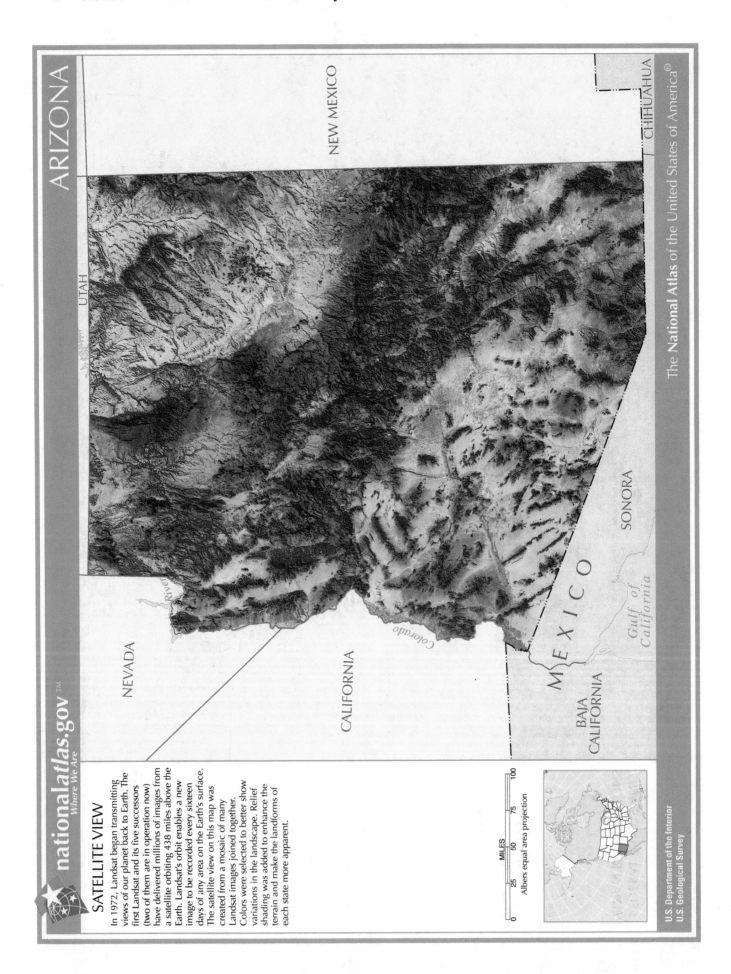

ARIZONA

nationalatlas.gov ™
Where We Are

SATELLITE VIEW

In 1972, Landsat began transmitting views of our planet back to Earth. The first Landsat and its five successors (two of them are in operation now) have delivered millions of images from a satellite orbiting 438 miles above the Earth. Landsat's orbit enables a new image to be recorded every sixteen days of any area on the Earth's surface. The satellite view on this map was created from a mosaic of many Landsat images joined together. Colors were selected to better show variations in the landscape. Relief shading was added to enhance the terrain and make the landforms of each state more apparent.

UTAH

NEVADA

CALIFORNIA

River

Colorado

NEW MEXICO

CHIHUAHUA

M E X I C O

SONORA

BAJA CALIFORNIA

Gulf of California

The **National Atlas** of the United States of America®

MILES

0   25   50   75   100

Albers equal area projection

U.S. Department of the Interior
U.S. Geological Survey

Arkansas

Topic	Value	Time Period
Total Surface Area (acres)	34,036,900	2007
Land	33,134,800	2007
Federal Land	3,104,200	2007
Owned	621,732	FY 2009
Leased	2,420	FY 2009
Otherwise Managed	33,208	FY 2009
National Forest	2,599,000	September 2006
National Wilderness	153,655	October 2011
Non-Federal Land, Developed	1,809,300	2007
Non-Federal Land, Rural	28,221,300	2007
Water	902,100	2007
National Natural Landmarks	5	December 2010
National Historic Landmarks	16	December 2010
National Register of Historic Places	2,514	December 2010
National Parks	7	December 2010
Visitors to National Parks	3,125,664	2010
Historic Places Documented by the National Park Service	161	December 2010
Archeological Sites in National Parks	710	December 2010
Threatened and Endangered Species in National Parks	6	December 2010
Economic Benefit from National Park Tourism (dollars)	129,498,000	2009
Conservation Reserve Program (acres)	248,740	October 2011
Land and Water Conservation Fund Grants (dollars)	48,121,617	Since 1965
Historic Preservation Grants (dollars)	26,415,983	2010
Community Conservation and Recreation Projects	13	Since 1987
Federal Acres Transferred for Local Parks and Recreation	852	Since 1948
Crude Petroleum Production (millions of barrels)	6	2010
Crude Oil Proved Reserves (millions of barrels)	28	2009
Natural Gas Reserves (billions of cubic feet)	10,869	2009
Natural Gas Liquid Reserves (millions of barrels)	2	2008
Natural Gas Marketed Production (billions of cubic feet)	680	2009
Coal Reserves (millions of short tons)	416	2009

Sources: U.S. Department of the Interior, National Park Service, State Profiles, December 2010; United States Department of Agriculture, Natural Resources Conservation Service, 2007 National Resources Inventory; U.S. General Services Administration, Federal Real Property Council, FY 2009 Federal Real Property Report, September 2010; University of Montana, www.wilderness.net; U.S. Department of Agriculture, Farm Services Agency, Conservation Reserve Program, October 2011; U.S Census Bureau, 2012 Statistical Abstract of the United States

Arkansas Energy Overview and Analysis

Quick Facts

- Coal-fired plants in Arkansas supply about one-half of State electricity demand and rely entirely on coal deliveries via railcar from Wyoming.
- Arkansas natural gas production accounts for about 1 percent of U.S. output.
- Companies are beginning to extract small amounts of natural gas from coalbed methane deposits in the Arkoma basin.
- Arkansas is one of the few States in the Nation that allow the use of conventional motor gasoline statewide.

Analysis

Resources and Consumption

Arkansas has moderate energy resources. Substantial natural gas reserves are found in the Arkoma basin in western Arkansas and in the Gulf Coastal Plain in the south. Smaller oil reserves and coal deposits are also found in those regions. Several river basins, including the Lower Arkansas River, offer hydroelectric power potential. Areas of the State are also suitable for wind, wood, and wood waste power generation. Per capita energy use is high due in part to an energy-intensive industrial sector, which leads State energy consumption.

Petroleum

Arkansas extracts small amounts of crude oil mostly from stripper wells (wells that produce less than 10 barrels per day) in the southern part of the Gulf Coastal Plain of south Arkansas. Arkansas has two refineries located in the same region. Petroleum products are delivered to consuming regions by barge via the Arkansas and Mississippi Rivers. The TEPPCO pipeline also supplies petroleum products from Texas and Louisiana. Arkansas is one of the few States in the Nation that allow the statewide use of conventional motor gasoline. (Most States require the use of special fuel blends in non-attainment areas due to air-quality considerations.)

Natural Gas

Arkansas natural gas production typically accounts for about 1 percent of annual U.S. output. Most of the State's natural gas production takes place in the Arkoma basin, although several wells also operate in the Gulf Costal Plain. In addition to conventional production, small amounts of natural gas have been extracted from coalbed methane deposits in the Arkoma basin since 2001, with a cumulative production of about 10 Bcf.

Several major natural gas pipelines from Texas, Louisiana, and Oklahoma pass through the State on the way to markets in the Midwest and Northeast. In addition, two new pipeline projects will soon be able to transport gas extracted from newly productive wells in Texas, Louisiana, and Arkansas. The recently completed 500-mile Midcontinent Express Pipeline passes through Texas and Arkansas, and the 187-mile Fayetteville Express Pipeline passes through Arkansas and is expected to be complete in late 2010 or early 2011.

Although it is still the leading sector in the State, the Arkansas industrial sector's natural gas consumption has declined in recent years. Until 2001, the industrial sector accounted for more than one-half of the State's natural gas consumption but this share had fallen to two-fifths by 2007. Almost one-half of Arkansas households use natural gas as their primary energy source for home heating.

Coal, Electricity, and Renewables

Coal and nuclear power are the dominant energy sources used for electricity generation in Arkansas, although natural gas and hydroelectric power are also important. Coal-fired power plants account for about one-half of the electricity produced within the State, and these plants rely entirely on coal deliveries from Wyoming. The State's only nuclear plant, the dual-unit Arkansas Nuclear One Plant in Russellville, typically generates more than one-fourth of the total electricity generated in the State. Hydroelectric power plants in the White River Basin in the north, along the Arkansas River in central Arkansas, and in the Ouachita River Basin in the south also contribute to electricity supply. About one-third of Arkansas households use electricity as their primary energy source for home heating. Arkansas has adopted several policies to encourage renewable energy and energy efficiency including green building standards for State facilities.

Source: U.S. Energy Information Administration, October 2009

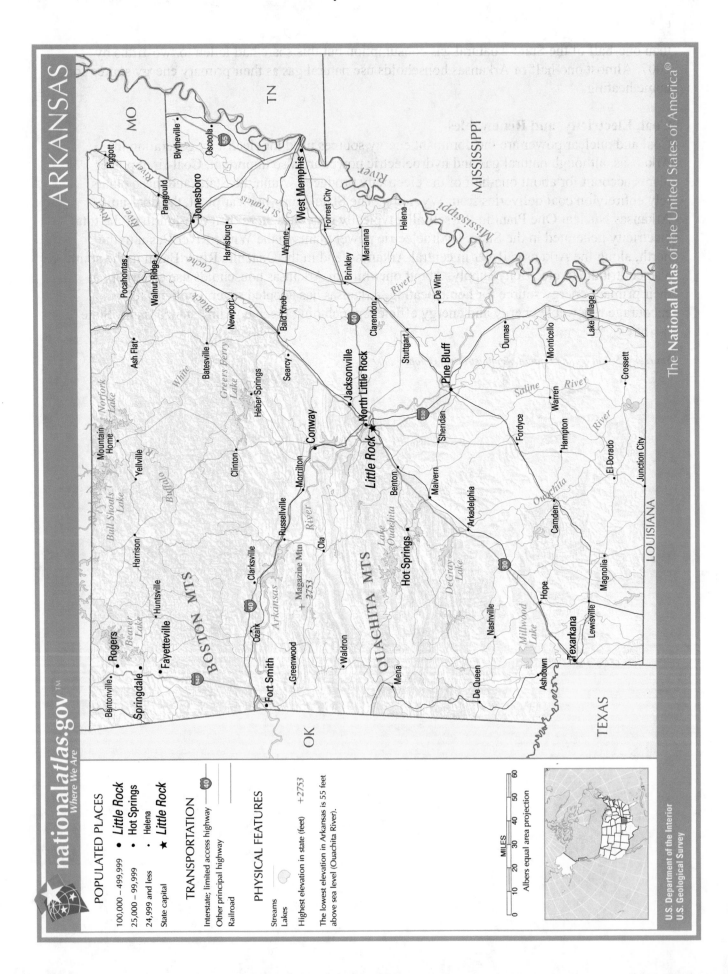

ARKANSAS

TN

MO

MISSISSIPPI

LOUISIANA

TEXAS

OK

The **National Atlas** of the United States of America©

nationalatlas.gov ™
Where We Are

POPULATED PLACES

100,000 – 499,999   ● *Little Rock*
25,000 – 99,999   ● Hot Springs
24,999 and less   Helena
State capital   ★ *Little Rock*

TRANSPORTATION

Interstate; limited access highway ——40——
Other principal highway
Railroad

PHYSICAL FEATURES

Streams
Lakes
Highest elevation in state (feet)   +2753

The lowest elevation in Arkansas is 55 feet
above sea level (Ouachita River).

MILES
0   10   20   30   40   50   60

Albers equal area projection

U.S. Department of the Interior
U.S. Geological Survey

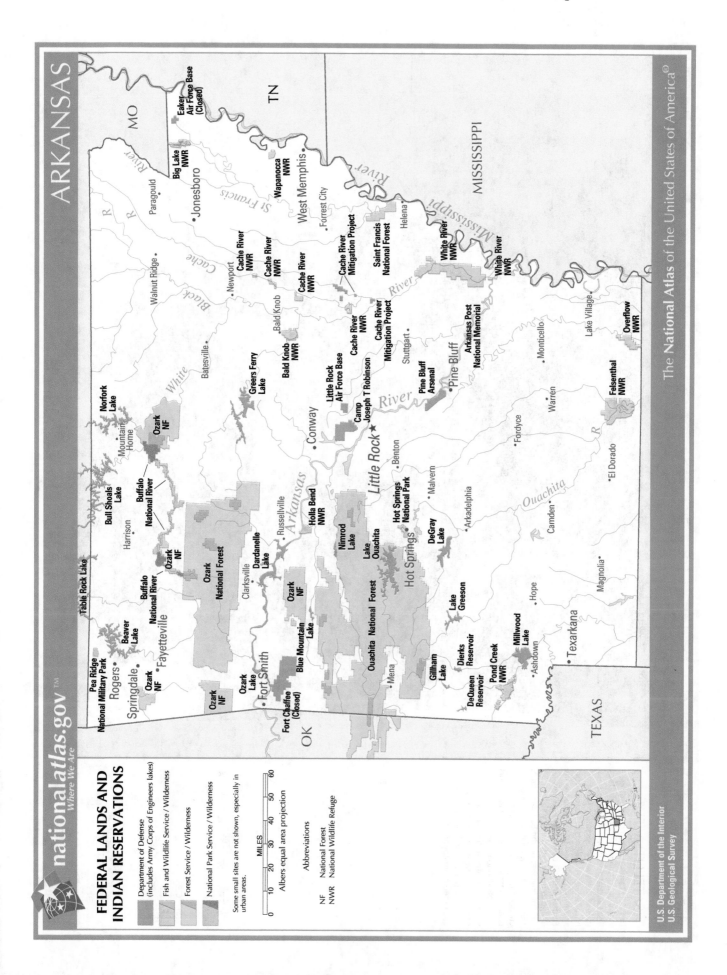

ARKANSAS

nationalatlas.gov™
Where We Are

FEDERAL LANDS AND INDIAN RESERVATIONS

Department of Defense
(includes Army Corps of Engineers lakes)

Fish and Wildlife Service / Wilderness

Forest Service / Wilderness

National Park Service / Wilderness

Some small sites are not shown, especially in urban areas.

MILES
0 10 20 30 40 50 60
Albers equal area projection

Abbreviations

NF   National Forest
NWR National Wildlife Refuge

The National Atlas of the United States of America®

U.S. Department of the Interior
U.S. Geological Survey

MO

TN

Eaker
Air Force Base
(Closed)

Big Lake
NWR

Paragould

Jonesboro

Wapanocca
NWR

West Memphis

St Francis

River

MISSISSIPPI

Walnut Ridge

Cache

Black

R

R

River

Newport

Cache River
NWR

Cache River
NWR

Cache River
NWR

Cache River
Mitigation Project

Saint Francis
National Forest

Helena

White River
NWR

White River
NWR

Forrest City

Bald Knob

Cache River
NWR

Cache River
Mitigation Project

River

Stuttgart

Arkansas Post
National Memorial

Lake Village

Overflow
NWR

Batesville

Greers Ferry
Lake

Bald Knob
NWR

Little Rock
Air Force Base

Camp
Joseph T Robinson

Pine Bluff
Arsenal

Pine Bluff

Monticello

Felsenthal
NWR

Norfork
Lake

White

Ozark
NF

Buffalo
National River

Conway

Little Rock ★

River

Hot Springs
National Park

Malvern

Warren

Fordyce

El Dorado

Mountain
Home

Bull Shoals
Lake

Harrison

Ozark
NF

Ozark
NF

Buffalo
National River

Ozark
National Forest

Clarksville

Dardanelle
Lake

Russellville

Arkansas

Holla Bend
NWR

Nimrod
Lake

Lake
Ouachita

Hot Springs

Benton

DeGray
Lake

Arkadelphia

Ouachita

Camden

Magnolia

R

Table Rock Lake

Pea Ridge
National Military Park

Rogers

Springdale

Beaver
Lake

Ozark
NF

Fayetteville

Ozark
Lake

Ozark
NF

Fort Smith

Ozark
NF

Blue Mountain
Lake

Fort Chaffee
(Closed)

OK

Ouachita National Forest

Mena

Gillham
Lake

DeQueen
Reservoir

Dierks
Reservoir

Pond Creek
NWR

Lake
Greeson

Millwood
Lake

Ashdown

Hope

Texarkana

TEXAS

ARKANSAS

MO

TN

MISSISSIPPI

Mississippi River

LOUISIANA

TEXAS

OK

nationalatlas.gov ™
Where We Are

SATELLITE VIEW

In 1972, Landsat began transmitting views of our planet back to Earth. The first Landsat and its five successors (two of them are in operation now) have delivered millions of images from a satellite orbiting 438 miles above the Earth. Landsat's orbit enables a new image to be recorded every sixteen days of any area on the Earth's surface. The satellite view on this map was created from a mosaic of many Landsat images joined together. Colors were selected to better show variations in the landscape. Relief shading was added to enhance the terrain and make the landforms of each state more apparent.

MILES

0 10 20 30 40 50 60

Albers equal area projection

The **National Atlas** of the United States of America ®

U.S. Department of the Interior
U.S. Geological Survey

California

Topic	Value	Time Period
Total Surface Area (acres)	101,510,200	2007
Land	99,635,300	2007
Federal Land	46,639,000	2007
Owned	4,537,255	FY 2009
Leased	11,807	FY 2009
Otherwise Managed	7,414	FY 2009
National Forest	20,822,000	September 2006
National Wilderness	14,982,645	October 2011
Non-Federal Land, Developed	6,173,800	2007
Non-Federal Land, Rural	46,822,500	2007
Water	1,874,900	2007
National Natural Landmarks	35	December 2010
National Historic Landmarks	138	December 2010
National Register of Historic Places	2,479	December 2010
National Parks	25	December 2010
Visitors to National Parks	34,915,676	2010
Historic Places Documented by the National Park Service	3,310	December 2010
Archeological Sites in National Parks	9,261	December 2010
Threatened and Endangered Species in National Parks	99	December 2010
Economic Benefit from National Park Tourism (dollars)	1,054,833,000	2009
Conservation Reserve Program (acres)	108,870	October 2011
Land and Water Conservation Fund Grants (dollars)	287,823,890	Since 1965
Historic Preservation Grants (dollars)	46,667,855	2010
Community Conservation and Recreation Projects	153	Since 1987
Federal Acres Transferred for Local Parks and Recreation	13,816	Since 1948
Crude Petroleum Production (millions of barrels)	204	2010
Crude Oil Proved Reserves (millions of barrels)	2,835	2009
Natural Gas Reserves (billions of cubic feet)	2,773	2009
Natural Gas Liquid Reserves (millions of barrels)	113	2008
Natural Gas Marketed Production (billions of cubic feet)	277	2009
Coal Reserves (millions of short tons)	Not Available	2009

Sources: U.S. Department of the Interior, National Park Service, State Profiles, December 2010; United States Department of Agriculture, Natural Resources Conservation Service, 2007 National Resources Inventory; U.S. General Services Administration, Federal Real Property Council, FY 2009 Federal Real Property Report, September 2010; University of Montana, www.wilderness.net; U.S. Department of Agriculture, Farm Services Agency, Conservation Reserve Program, October 2011; U.S Census Bureau, 2012 Statistical Abstract of the United States

California Energy Overview and Analysis

Quick Facts

- California ranks third in the Nation in refining capacity and its refineries are among the most sophisticated in the world.
- California's per capita energy consumption is low, in part due to mild weather that reduces energy demand for heating and cooling.
- California leads the Nation in electricity generation from nonhydroelectric renewable energy sources, including geothermal power, wind power, fuel wood, landfill gas, and solar power. California is also a leading generator of hydroelectric power.
- California imports more electricity from other States than any other State.
- In 2000 and 2001, California suffered an energy crisis characterized by electricity price instability and four major blackouts affecting millions of customers.
- Two solar power plants are proposed for central California, covering 12.5 square miles and generating as much as 800 megawatts of power.

Analysis

Resources and Consumption

California is rich in both conventional and renewable energy resources. It has large crude oil and substantial natural gas deposits in six geological basins, located in the Central Valley and along the Pacific coast. Most of those reserves are concentrated in the southern San Joaquin Basin. Seventeen of the Nation's 100 largest oil fields are located in California, including the Belridge South oil field, the third largest oil field in the contiguous United States. In addition, Federal assessments indicate that large undiscovered deposits of recoverable oil and gas lie offshore in the federally administered Outer Continental Shelf (OCS), which in 2008 was reopened for potential oil and gas leasing. California's renewable energy potential is extensive. The State's hydroelectric power potential ranks second in the Nation behind Washington State, and substantial geothermal and wind power resources are found along the coastal mountain ranges and the eastern border with Nevada. High solar energy potential is found in southeastern California's sunny deserts.

California is the most populous State in the Nation and its total energy demand is second only to Texas. Although California is a leader in the energy-intensive chemical, forest products, glass, and petroleum industries, the State has one of the lowest per capita energy consumption rates in the country. The California government's energy-efficiency programs have contributed to the low per capita energy consumption. Driven by high demand from California's many motorists, major airports, and military bases, the transportation sector is the State's largest energy consumer. More motor vehicles are registered in California than any other State, and worker commute times are among the longest in the country.

Petroleum

California is one of the top producers of crude oil in the Nation, with output accounting for more than one-tenth of total U.S. production. Drilling operations are concentrated primarily in Kern County and the Los Angeles basin, although substantial production also takes place offshore in both State and Federal waters. Concerns regarding the cumulative impacts of offshore oil and gas development, combined with a number of major marine oil spills throughout the world in recent years, have led to a permanent moratorium on offshore oil and gas leasing in California waters. However, development on existing State leases is not affected and may still occur within offshore areas leased prior to the effective date of the moratorium. A moratorium on oil and gas leasing in Federal OCS waters expired in 2008.

A network of crude oil pipelines connects production areas to refining centers in the Los Angeles area, the San Francisco Bay area, and the Central Valley. California refiners also process large volumes of Alaskan and foreign crude oil received at ports in Los Angeles, Long Beach, and the Bay Area. Crude oil production in California and Alaska is in decline and California refineries have become increasingly dependent on foreign imports. Led by Saudi Arabia, Iraq, and Ecuador, foreign suppliers now provide more than two-fifths of the crude oil refined in California; however, California's dependence on foreign oil remains less than the national average.

California ranks third in the United States in petroleum refining capacity and accounts for more than one-tenth of total U.S. capacity. California's largest refineries are highly sophisticated and are capable of processing a wide variety of crude oil types and are designed to yield a high percentage of light products like motor gasoline. To meet strict Federal and State environmental regulations, California refineries are configured to produce cleaner fuels, including reformulated motor gasoline and low-sulfur diesel.

Most California motorists are required to use a special motor gasoline blend called California Clean Burning Gasoline (CA CBG). In the ozone non-attainment areas of Imperial County and the Los Angeles metropolitan area, motorists are required to use California Oxygenated Clean Burning Gasoline. There are five ethanol production plants in central and southern California, but most of California's ethanol supply is transported by rail from corn-based producers in the Midwest. Some supply is also imported from abroad.

Due to the relative isolation and specific requirements of the California fuel market, California motorists are particularly vulnerable to short-term spikes in the price of motor gasoline. No pipelines connect California to other major U.S. refining centers, and California refineries often operate at near maximum capacity due to high demand for petroleum products. When an unplanned refinery outage occurs, replacement supplies must be brought in via marine tanker. Locating and transporting this replacement gasoline (which must conform to the State's strict fuel requirements) can take from two to six weeks.

Natural Gas
California natural gas production typically accounts for less than 2 percent of total U.S. production and satisfies less than one-fifth of State demand. Production takes place in basins located in northern and southern California, as well as offshore in the Pacific Ocean. As with crude oil production, California natural gas production is in decline. However, State supply has remained relatively stable due to increases in net receipts from pipelines that supply California with natural gas produced in the Rocky Mountains, the Southwest, and western Canada. California markets are served by two key natural gas trading centers - the Golden Gate Center in northern California and the California Energy Hub in southern California - and the State has a

dozen natural gas storage facilities that help stabilize supply. In part to help meet California's demand for natural gas, an offshore LNG import terminal in southern California has been proposed to the Maritime Administration and the U.S. Coast Guard. If approved, this terminal could import up to 1.4 billion cubic feet of natural gas per day. Two additional potential southern Californian LNG import facility sites have been identified by project sponsors.

Coal, Electricity, and Renewables

Natural gas-fired power plants typically account for about one-half of State electricity generation. California is one of the largest hydroelectric power producers in the United States, and with adequate rainfall, hydroelectric power typically accounts for close to one-fifth of State electricity generation. California's two nuclear power plants account for about 17 percent of total generation. Due to strict emission laws, only a few small coal-fired power plants operate in California.

California leads the Nation in electricity generation from nonhydroelectric renewable energy sources. California generates electricity using wind, geothermal, solar, fuel wood, and municipal solid waste/landfill gas resources. California is the top producer of geothermal energy in the Nation with over 2,500 megawatts of capacity. A facility known as "The Geysers," located in the Mayacamas Mountains north of San Francisco, is the largest complex of geothermal power plants in the world, with more than 700 megawatts of installed capacity. California is also a leading producer of wind energy and holds nearly 10 percent of the Nation's capacity. The world's largest solar power facility operates in California's Mojave Desert. Two new solar power plants have been proposed for central California, and would cover 12.5 square miles and generate as much as 800 megawatts of power. Both plants still require numerous permits, but if approved, they would generate more than 12 times as much electricity as the Mojave Desert plant. To further boost renewable energy use, California's Energy Action Plan includes incentives that encourage Californians to install solar power systems on their rooftops.

Due to high electricity demand, California imports more electricity than any other State. States in the Pacific Northwest deliver power to California markets primarily from hydroelectric sources, while States in the Desert Southwest deliver power primarily from coal-fired sources. Hydroelectric power comes to California primarily through the Western USA interconnection, which runs from northern Oregon to southern California. The system, also known as the Pacific Intertie, is the largest single electricity transmission program in the United States. Although the Pacific Intertie was originally designed to transmit electricity south during California's peak summer demand season, flow is sometimes reversed overnight and has occasionally been reversed during periods of reduced hydroelectric generation in the Northwest. California restricts the use of coal-fired generation within its boundaries. However, the Los Angeles Department of Water and Power (LADWP) operates the coal-fired Intermountain power plant in Utah, which delivers almost all of its output to LADWP and other California municipal utilities. A recent California law forbids utilities from entering into long-term contracts with conventional coal-fired power producers. Intermountain's existing contracts with southern California cities are set to expire in 2027.

In 2000 and 2001, California suffered an energy crisis characterized by electricity price instability and four major blackouts and caused by a supply and demand imbalance. Multiple factors contributed to this imbalance, including: a heavy dependence on out-of-State electricity providers, drought conditions in the northwest that reduced hydroelectric power generation, a rupture on a major natural gas pipeline supplying California power plants, strong economic growth leading to increased electricity demand in western States, an increase in unplanned power plant outages, and unusually high temperatures that increased electricity demand for air-conditioning and other cooling uses. Following the energy crisis, the California State government created an Energy Action Plan designed to eliminate outages and excessive price spikes. To achieve these goals, the plan calls for optimizing energy conservation, building sufficient new generation facilities, upgrading and expanding the electricity transmission and distribution infrastructure, and ensuring that generation facilities can quickly come online when needed.

In 2006, California amended its renewable portfolio standard to require investor-owned utilities, electric service providers, small and multi-jurisdictional utilities, and community choice aggregators to provide at least 20 percent of retail sales from renewable sources by the end of 2010 and 33 percent by the end of 2020. California has also adopted other policies to promote energy efficiency and renewable energy, including energy standards for public buildings, power source disclosure requirements for utilities, and net metering.

Source: U.S. Energy Information Administration, October 2009

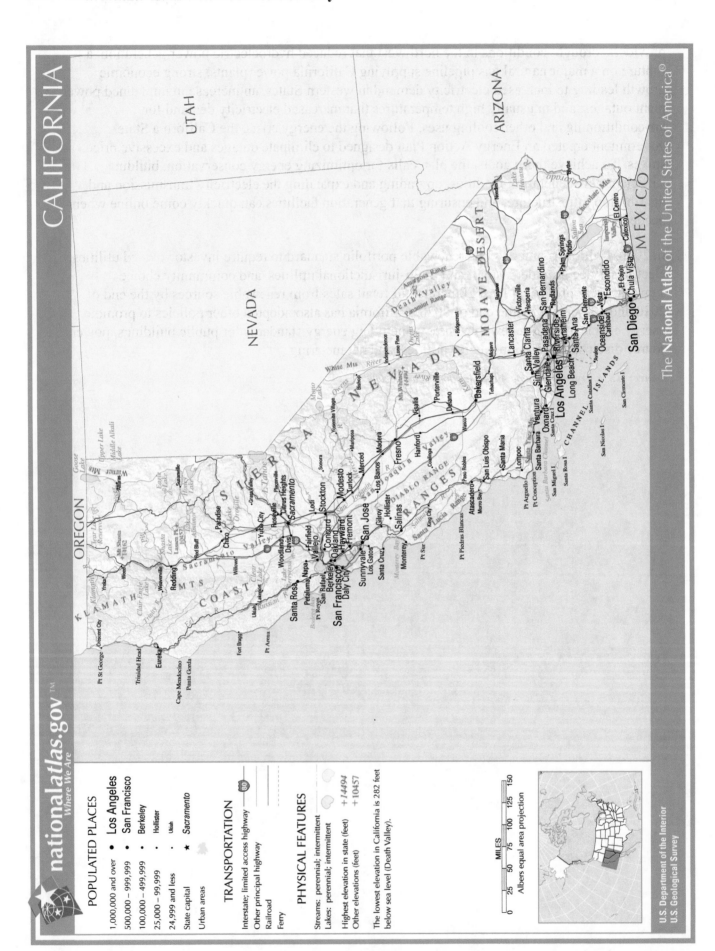

CALIFORNIA

nationalatlas.gov™
Where We Are

POPULATED PLACES

● Los Angeles — 1,000,000 and over
● San Francisco — 500,000 – 999,999
● Berkeley — 100,000 – 499,999
● Hollister — 25,000 – 99,999
· Ukiah — 24,999 and less
★ *Sacramento* — State capital
    Urban areas

TRANSPORTATION

Interstate; limited access highway
Other principal highway
Railroad
Ferry

PHYSICAL FEATURES

Streams: perennial; intermittent
Lakes: perennial; intermittent

+14494 Highest elevation in state (feet)
+10457 Other elevations (feet)

The lowest elevation in California is 282 feet
below sea level (Death Valley).

MILES
0 25 50 75 100 125 150
Albers equal area projection

U.S. Department of the Interior
U.S. Geological Survey

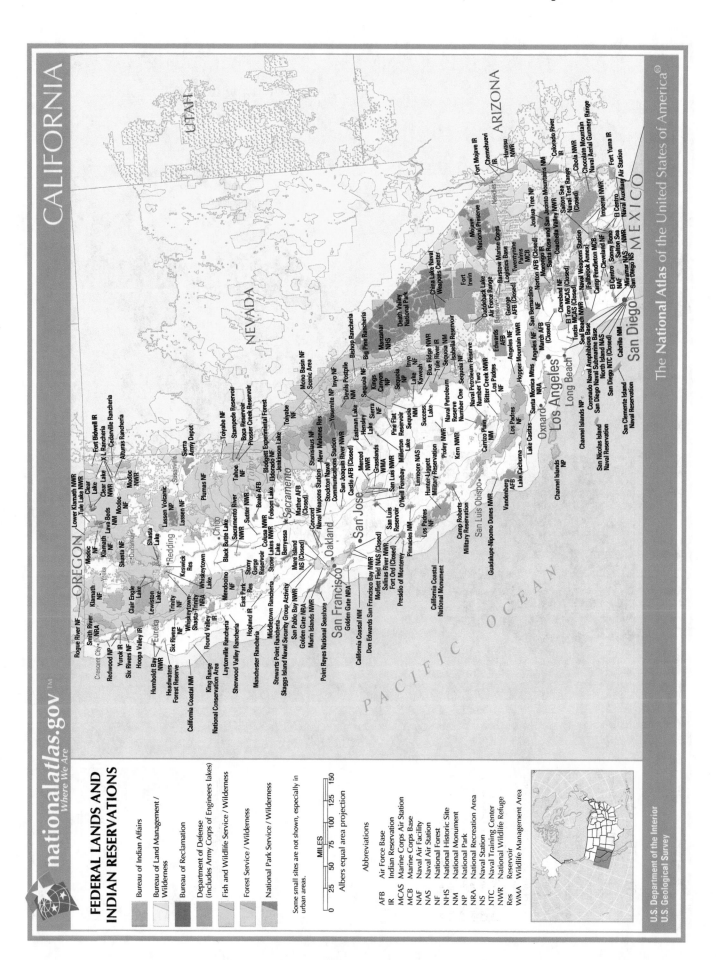

CALIFORNIA

nationalatlas.gov™
Where We Are

FEDERAL LANDS AND INDIAN RESERVATIONS

Bureau of Indian Affairs

Bureau of Land Management / Wilderness

Bureau of Reclamation

Department of Defense
(includes Army Corps of Engineers lakes)

Fish and Wildlife Service / Wilderness

Forest Service / Wilderness

National Park Service / Wilderness

Some small sites are not shown, especially in urban areas.

MILES
0   25   50   75   100   125   150

Albers equal area projection

Abbreviations

AFB	Air Force Base
IR	Indian Reservation
MCAS	Marine Corps Air Station
MCB	Marine Corps Base
NAF	Naval Air Facility
NAS	Naval Air Station
NF	National Forest
NHS	National Historic Site
NM	National Monument
NP	National Park
NRA	National Recreation Area
NS	Naval Station
NTC	Naval Training Center
NWR	National Wildlife Refuge
Res	Reservoir
WMA	Wildlife Management Area

The National Atlas of the United States of America®

U.S. Department of the Interior
U.S. Geological Survey

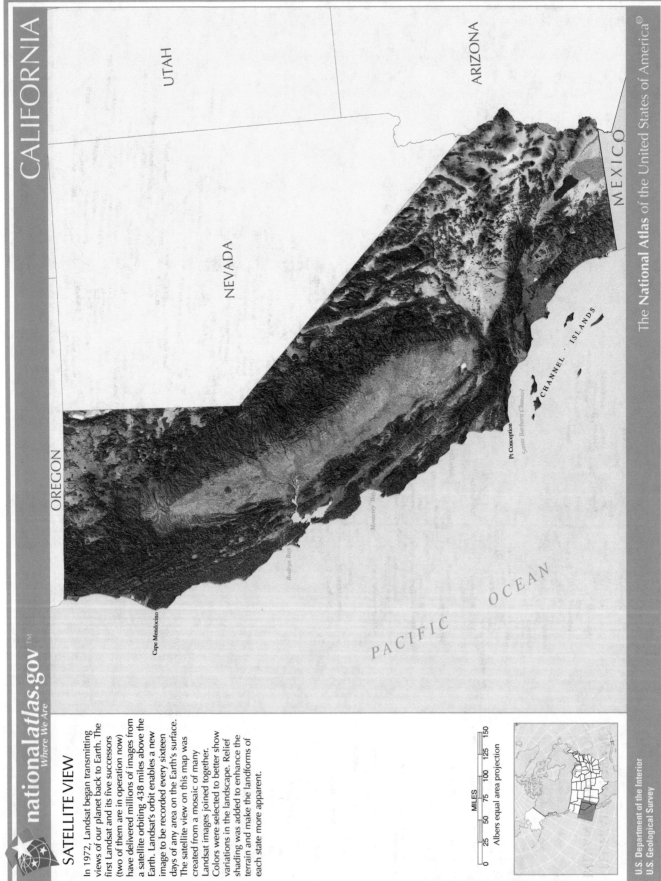

CALIFORNIA

nationalatlas.gov™
Where We Are

The **National Atlas** of the United States of America®

UTAH

ARIZONA

NEVADA

MEXICO

OREGON

CHANNEL · ISLANDS

Santa Barbara Channel

Pt Conception

Monterey Bay

Bodega Bay

Cape Mendocino

PACIFIC   OCEAN

SATELLITE VIEW

In 1972, Landsat began transmitting views of our planet back to Earth. The first Landsat and its five successors (two of them are in operation now) have delivered millions of images from a satellite orbiting 438 miles above the Earth. Landsat's orbit enables a new image to be recorded every sixteen days of any area on the Earth's surface. The satellite view on this map was created from a mosaic of many Landsat images joined together. Colors were selected to better show variations in the landscape. Relief shading was added to enhance the terrain and make the landforms of each state more apparent.

MILES

0   25   50   75   100   125   150

Albers equal area projection

U.S. Department of the Interior
U.S. Geological Survey

Colorado

Topic	Value	Time Period
Total Surface Area (acres)	66,624,500	2007
Land	66,292,400	2007
Federal Land	23,796,900	2007
Owned	819,789	FY 2009
Leased	37,324	FY 2009
Otherwise Managed	89	FY 2009
National Forest	14,521,000	September 2006
National Wilderness	3,700,148	October 2011
Non-Federal Land, Developed	1,934,300	2007
Non-Federal Land, Rural	40,561,200	2007
Water	332,100	2007
National Natural Landmarks	12	December 2010
National Historic Landmarks	21	December 2010
National Register of Historic Places	1,400	December 2010
National Parks	13	December 2010
Visitors to National Parks	5,635,307	2010
Historic Places Documented by the National Park Service	881	December 2010
Archeological Sites in National Parks	6,767	December 2010
Threatened and Endangered Species in National Parks	13	December 2010
Economic Benefit from National Park Tourism (dollars)	336,956,000	2009
Conservation Reserve Program (acres)	2,160,890	October 2011
Land and Water Conservation Fund Grants (dollars)	59,060,399	Since 1965
Historic Preservation Grants (dollars)	25,910,178	2010
Community Conservation and Recreation Projects	64	Since 1987
Federal Acres Transferred for Local Parks and Recreation	3,014	Since 1948
Crude Petroleum Production (millions of barrels)	26	2010
Crude Oil Proved Reserves (millions of barrels)	279	2009
Natural Gas Reserves (billions of cubic feet)	23,058	2009
Natural Gas Liquid Reserves (millions of barrels)	716	2008
Natural Gas Marketed Production (billions of cubic feet)	1,499	2009
Coal Reserves (millions of short tons)	15,981	2009

Sources: *U.S. Department of the Interior, National Park Service, State Profiles, December 2010; United States Department of Agriculture, Natural Resources Conservation Service, 2007 National Resources Inventory; U.S. General Services Administration, Federal Real Property Council, FY 2009 Federal Real Property Report, September 2010; University of Montana, www.wilderness.net; U.S. Department of Agriculture, Farm Services Agency, Conservation Reserve Program, October 2011; U.S Census Bureau, 2012 Statistical Abstract of the United States*

Colorado Energy Overview and Analysis

Quick Facts

- Ten of the Nation's 100 largest natural gas fields and three of its 100 largest oil fields are found in Colorado.
- Colorado is responsible for more than one-fourth of all coalbed methane produced in the United States. Coalbed methane output accounts for about one-half of Colorado's natural gas production.
- The Rockies Express Pipeline, which began service in May 2008, helps move Colorado's rapidly increasing natural gas production to markets in the Midwest.
- Colorado's oil shale deposits hold an estimated 1 trillion barrels of oil - nearly as much oil as the entire world's proven oil reserves. However, oil production from those deposits remains speculative.
- A proposed biomass plant in Vail would use thousands of trees that were recently killed by pine beetles as its feedstock.

Analysis

Resources and Consumption

Colorado has substantial conventional fossil fuel and renewable energy resources. The State contains several fossil fuel-rich basins, including the Sand Walsh, Piceance, Paradox, and San Juan basins in the west, and the Denver and Raton basins in the east. Ten of the Nation's 100 largest natural gas fields and three of its 100 largest oil fields are found in Colorado. Substantial deposits of bituminous, subbituminous, and lignite coal are also found in the State.

Colorado's high Rocky Mountain ridges offer wind power potential, and geologic activity in the mountain areas provides potential for geothermal power development. Major rivers flowing from the Rocky Mountains offer hydroelectric power resources. Corn grown in the flat eastern part of the State offers potential resources for ethanol production. The Colorado economy is not energy intensive. The transportation and industrial sectors are the leading energy-consuming sectors in the State.

Petroleum

Colorado oil production typically accounts for around 1 percent of the U.S. total. Most production takes place in the Denver and Piceance basins. Crude oil output serves Colorado's two refineries in Commerce City north of Denver. Several petroleum product pipelines from Wyoming, Texas, and Oklahoma help supply the Colorado market. The Denver/Boulder and Ft. Collins areas use oxygenated motor gasoline; the rest of the State uses conventional motor gasoline. Although the Denver metropolitan area was the first area in the Nation to require the use of motor gasoline blended with ethanol to reduce carbon monoxide emissions, the State is relatively new to large-scale ethanol production. Colorado produces ethanol mostly from corn at small facilities in the northeastern part of the State. Colorado's smallest ethanol production plant is co-located with the Coors brewery in Golden and uses waste beer to produce ethanol for fuel consumption. Using waste beer to produce ethanol lowers the emissions of volatile organic compounds from the Coors brewery significantly.

Although its proven crude oil reserves account for only about 1 percent of the U.S. total, Colorado has enormous deposits of oil shale rock, known as marlstone, which can be converted into crude oil through destructive distillation. The Green River Formation, a group of basins in Colorado, Wyoming, and Utah, holds the largest known oil shale deposits in the world. Colorado's oil shale deposits, concentrated in the Piceance Basin in the western part of the State, hold an estimated 1 trillion barrels of oil - as much oil as the entire world's proven oil reserves. Although this natural resource holds tremendous promise, oil shale development remains speculative and faces several major obstacles involving technological feasibility, economic viability, resource ownership, and environmental considerations. While pilot oil shale projects have been undertaken in the area, there are no plans for the construction of commercial oil shale production facilities in Colorado.

Natural Gas

Colorado is a top natural gas-producing State. Conventional and unconventional output from several Colorado basins typically accounts for more than 5 percent of U.S. natural gas production. Coalbed methane (unconventional natural gas produced from coal seams) accounts for over forty percent of Colorado's natural gas production, and almost thirty percent of all coalbed methane produced in the United States. Coalbed methane production is active in the San Juan and Raton Basins, and further development is possible in northwest Colorado's Piceance Basin, which holds the second-largest proved reserves in the Nation.

Natural Gas consumption by the electric power sector has been increasing since 2003, with a dramatic increase in 2007 putting the sector second only to the residential as the leading natural gas-consuming sector in Colorado. About three-fourths of Colorado households use natural gas as their primary energy source for home heating, one of the highest shares in the Nation.

Colorado uses only about two-fifths of its natural gas production. The remainder is transported to markets in the West and Midwest. Colorado is part of the transportation corridor for shipping gas from the Rocky Mountain supply region to the Midwest and West markets. Colorado's natural gas production is growing, and construction of a new pipeline was recently completed to help move the rapidly increasing output to the Midwest. The new system, known as the Rockies Express Pipeline, originates in the Piceance Basin and extends from Colorado to Audrain County, Missouri with completion of an extension to Clarington, Ohio targeted for the fall of 2009.

Coal, Electricity, and Renewables

Coal- and natural gas-fired power plants dominate electricity generation in Colorado. Coal-fired plants account for over seven-tenths of the State's generation and natural gas-fired plants account for close to one-fourth. Colorado produces coal from both underground and surface mines, primarily in its western basins, and large quantities of coal are shipped into and out of the State by rail. Colorado uses about one-fourth of its coal output and transports the remainder to markets throughout the United States. Colorado also brings in coal, primarily from Wyoming, to supplement local production.

Hydroelectric and wind power facilities account for most of the State's renewable electricity generation. However, much of Colorado's substantial renewable energy potential remains to be developed, and the State currently ranks relatively low in renewable energy generation. In

August 2009, a proposal was made for a biomass plant to be located in Vail that would use the thousands of trees that were recently killed by pine beetles to create a new sustainable source of energy. The proposed plant would reduce carbon emissions and forest fires in addition to creating a reliable source of energy that is likely to last at least ten years. A feasibility study is planned to look at environmental issues and the ability to obtain a sustainable supply of trees. In March 2007, a new renewable portfolio standard was adopted by Colorado that requires large investor-owned utilities to produce 20 percent of their energy from renewable sources by 2020.

Less than one-fifth of Colorado households use electricity as their main energy source for home heating.

Source: *U.S. Energy Information Administration, October 2009*

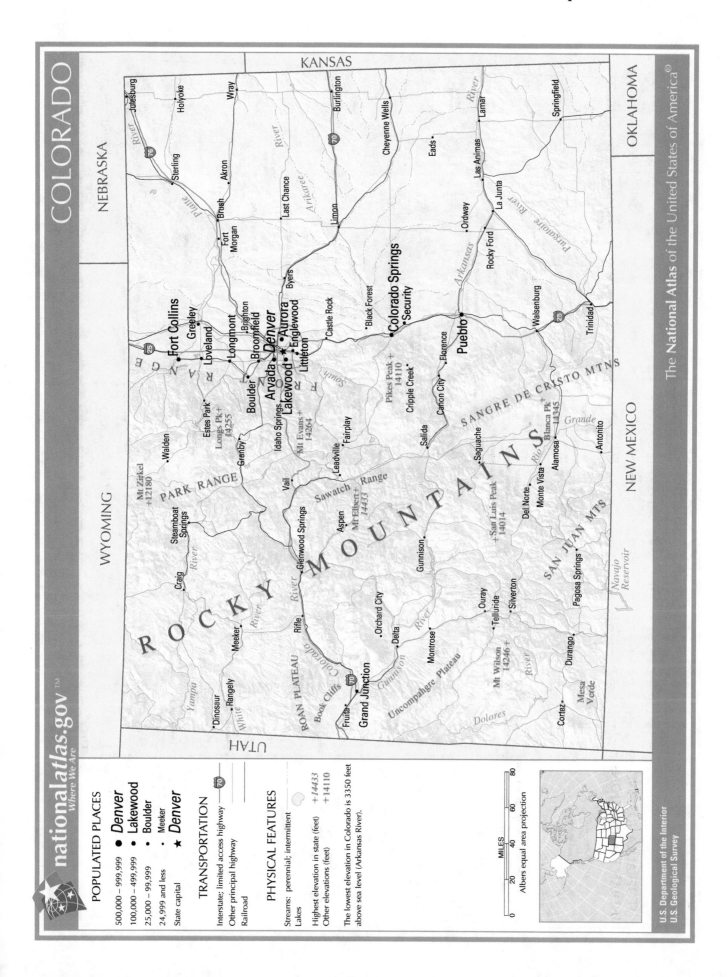

COLORADO

nationalatlas.gov ™
Where We Are

POPULATED PLACES

500,000 – 999,999 ● **Denver**
100,000 – 499,999 ● Lakewood
25,000 – 99,999 • Boulder
24,999 and less · Meeker
State capital ★ **Denver**

TRANSPORTATION

Interstate; limited access highway 🛣70
Other principal highway
Railroad

PHYSICAL FEATURES

Streams: perennial; intermittent
Lakes
Highest elevation in state (feet) +*14433*
Other elevations (feet) +14110

The lowest elevation in Colorado is 3350 feet above sea level (Arkansas River).

MILES
0 20 40 60 80
Albers equal area projection

U.S. Department of the Interior
U.S. Geological Survey

The **National Atlas** of the United States of America®

KANSAS

NEBRASKA

WYOMING

UTAH

OKLAHOMA

NEW MEXICO

Julesburg
Holyoke
Wray
Sterling
Akron
Brush
Fort Morgan
Last Chance
Limon
Burlington
Cheyenne Wells
Eads
Springfield
Lamar
Las Animas
La Junta
Ordway
Rocky Ford
Walsenburg
Trinidad

Fort Collins
Greeley
Loveland
Longmont
Brighton
Broomfield
Boulder
Denver
Aurora
Englewood
Arvada
Lakewood
Littleton
Byers
Castle Rock
Black Forest
Colorado Springs
Security
Pueblo
Florence
Canon City
Cripple Creek
Pikes Peak +14110
Salida
Saguache
Blanca Pk +14345
Alamosa
Monte Vista
Del Norte
Antonito
San Luis Peak +14014

Estes Park
Longs Pk +14255
Walden
Granby
Idaho Springs
Mt Evans +14264
Fairplay
Leadville
Vail
Mt Zirkel +12180
Steamboat Springs
Craig
Meeker
Rifle
Glenwood Springs
Aspen
Mt Elbert +14433
Gunnison
Sawatch Range
Leadville
SANGRE DE CRISTO MTNS
Rio Grande
SAN JUAN MTS
Pagosa Springs
Navajo Reservoir
Durango
Silverton
Ouray
Telluride
Mt Wilson +14246
Montrose
Orchard City
Delta
Grand Junction
Fruita
Book Cliffs
ROAN PLATEAU
Dinosaur
Rangely
Uncompahgre Plateau
Mesa Verde
Cortez

PARK RANGE
ROCKY MOUNTAINS
FRONT RANGE

Platte River
Arikaree River
Arkansas River
Purgatoire River
South Platte
Yampa River
White River
Colorado River
Gunnison River
Dolores River
Navajo Reservoir

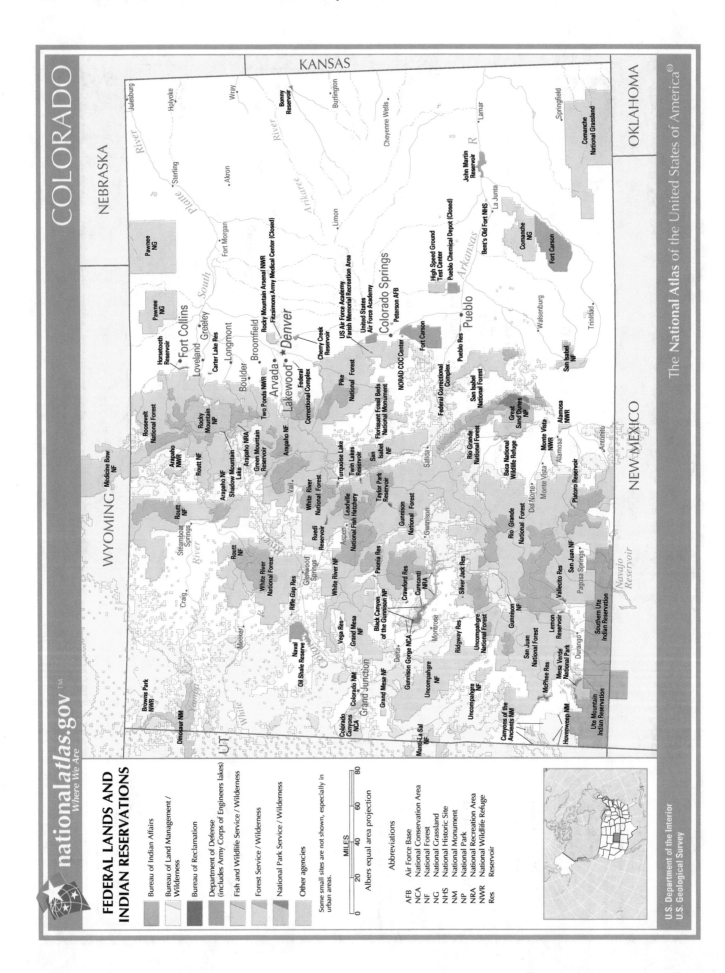

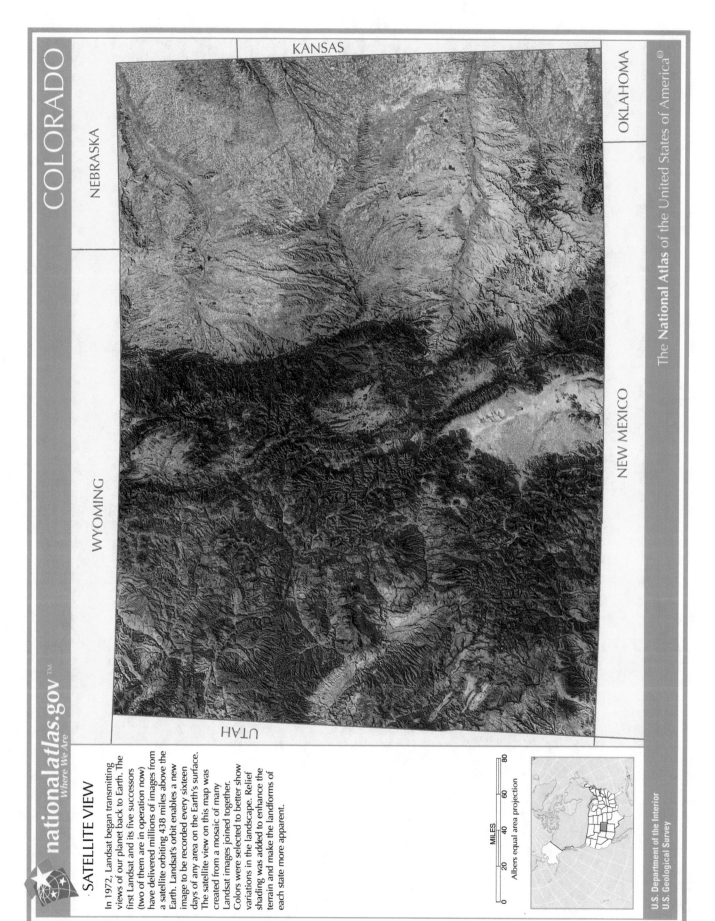

COLORADO

nationalatlas.gov™
Where We Are

SATELLITE VIEW

In 1972, Landsat began transmitting views of our planet back to Earth. The first Landsat and its five successors (two of them are in operation now) have delivered millions of images from a satellite orbiting 438 miles above the Earth. Landsat's orbit enables a new image to be recorded every sixteen days of any area on the Earth's surface. The satellite view on this map was created from a mosaic of many Landsat images joined together. Colors were selected to better show variations in the landscape. Relief shading was added to enhance the terrain and make the landforms of each state more apparent.

KANSAS

NEBRASKA

OKLAHOMA

NEW MEXICO

WYOMING

UTAH

MILES

0   20   40   60   80

Albers equal area projection

U.S. Department of the Interior
U.S. Geological Survey

The **National Atlas** of the United States of America®

Connecticut

Topic	Value	Time Period
Total Surface Area (acres)	3,194,700	2007
Land	3,066,100	2007
Federal Land	14,500	2007
Owned	9,277	FY 2009
Leased	858	FY 2009
Otherwise Managed	2,342	FY 2009
National Forest	24,000	September 2006
National Wilderness	0	October 2011
Non-Federal Land, Developed	1,051,600	2007
Non-Federal Land, Rural	2,000,000	2007
Water	128,600	2007
National Natural Landmarks	8	December 2010
National Historic Landmarks	60	December 2010
National Register of Historic Places	1,552	December 2010
National Parks	2	December 2010
Visitors to National Parks	19,313	2010
Historic Places Documented by the National Park Service	637	December 2010
Archeological Sites in National Parks	10	December 2010
Threatened and Endangered Species in National Parks	0	December 2010
Economic Benefit from National Park Tourism (dollars)	1,130,000	2009
Conservation Reserve Program (acres)	151	October 2011
Land and Water Conservation Fund Grants (dollars)	63,407,882	Since 1965
Historic Preservation Grants (dollars)	24,951,043	2010
Community Conservation and Recreation Projects	39	Since 1987
Federal Acres Transferred for Local Parks and Recreation	297	Since 1948
Crude Petroleum Production (millions of barrels)	Not Available	2010
Crude Oil Proved Reserves (millions of barrels)	Not Available	2009
Natural Gas Reserves (billions of cubic feet)	Not Available	2009
Natural Gas Liquid Reserves (millions of barrels)	Not Available	2008
Natural Gas Marketed Production (billions of cubic feet)	Not Available	2009
Coal Reserves (millions of short tons)	Not Available	2009

Sources: U.S. Department of the Interior, National Park Service, State Profiles, December 2010; United States Department of Agriculture, Natural Resources Conservation Service, 2007 National Resources Inventory; U.S. General Services Administration, Federal Real Property Council, FY 2009 Federal Real Property Report, September 2010; University of Montana, www.wilderness.net; U.S. Department of Agriculture, Farm Services Agency, Conservation Reserve Program, October 2011; U.S Census Bureau, 2012 Statistical Abstract of the United States

Connecticut Energy Overview and Analysis

Quick Facts

- Two of the Nation's three Northeast Home Heating Oil Reserve sites, intended to cushion the effects of disruptions in the supply of home heating oil, are located in Groton and New Haven.
- The 2,037-megawatt Millstone nuclear power plant is the State's highest-capacity power plant.
- Connecticut is one of the few States that require the statewide use of reformulated motor gasoline blended with ethanol.
- In 2008, Connecticut ranked in the top-ten States for solar power capacity within the United States.

Analysis

Resources and Consumption

Connecticut has no fossil fuel reserves but does have minor renewable energy resources, including wind power potential and fuelwood resources in the northern part of the State. Connecticut's economy is not energy intensive, and industry is the State's smallest energy-consuming sector. The residential and transportation sectors lead State energy consumption.

Petroleum

Connecticut receives petroleum products at the coastal ports of New Haven, New London, and Bridgeport, and the Connecticut River is an important inland water route for petroleum product barges supplying central Connecticut. In addition, a small-capacity product pipeline originating in New Haven supplies Hartford before terminating in central Massachusetts. Connecticut is one of a handful of States that require the statewide use of reformulated motor gasoline blended with ethanol.

Connecticut, along with much of the U.S. Northeast, is vulnerable to distillate fuel oil shortages and price spikes during winter months due to high demand for home heating. About one-half of Connecticut households use fuel oil as their primary energy source for home heating. In January and February 2000, distillate fuel oil prices in the Northeast rose sharply when extreme winter weather increased demand unexpectedly and hindered the delivery of new supply, as frozen rivers and high winds slowed the docking and unloading of barges and tankers. In July 2000, in order to reduce the risk of future shortages, the President directed the U.S. Department of Energy to establish the Northeast Heating Oil Reserve. The Reserve gives Northeast consumers adequate supplies for about 10 days, the time required for ships to carry heating oil from the Gulf of Mexico to New York Harbor. One of the Reserve sites, with an inventory of 750 thousand barrels, is located in New Haven while another, with an inventory of 250 thousand barrels, is located in Groton. The Reserve's third storage facility is located in Perth Amboy, New Jersey.

Natural Gas

In Connecticut, natural gas is used mostly for electricity generation and residential home heating. Connecticut receives its natural gas supply from production areas in the U.S. Gulf Coast region and Canada, and from natural gas storage sites in the Appalachian Basin region, which includes parts of New York, Pennsylvania, and Ohio. The gas is supplied by pipelines entering the State from New York and Massachusetts. Connecticut ships almost one-third of its natural gas supplies to Rhode Island. Like other New England States, Connecticut has no natural gas storage sites and must rely on the Appalachian Basin storage capacity to supply peak demand in winter.

Coal, Electricity, and Renewables

For many years, nuclear power from Waterford's Millstone nuclear plant accounted for more than one-half of Connecticut's electricity production. However, nuclear power lost some of its dominance in the late 1990s when one of Millstone's three reactors was permanently taken offline. In recent years, natural gas-fired electricity production has grown rapidly, and natural gas is now Connecticut's second leading generation fuel, typically accounting for more than one-fourth of net generation. As in other New England States, the growing use of natural gas in Connecticut's power industry has been driven by the benefits of the lower emission levels of natural gas compared with other fossil fuels and the ease of siting new natural gas-fired power plants. In addition to nuclear power and natural gas, Connecticut also produces electricity from coal, petroleum, and renewable energy sources including landfill gas, municipal solid waste, hydroelectric power, and solar radiation. In 2008, Connecticut ranked in the top-ten States for solar power capacity within the United States. In June 2007, Connecticut adopted a renewable portfolio standard that requires 27 percent of the State's electricity to be generated from renewable sources by 2020.

Connecticut's residential electricity use is below the national average, in part because demand for air-conditioning is low during the typically mild summer months and electricity is not widely used as a primary energy source for home heating in winter.

Source: U.S. Energy Information Administration, October 2009

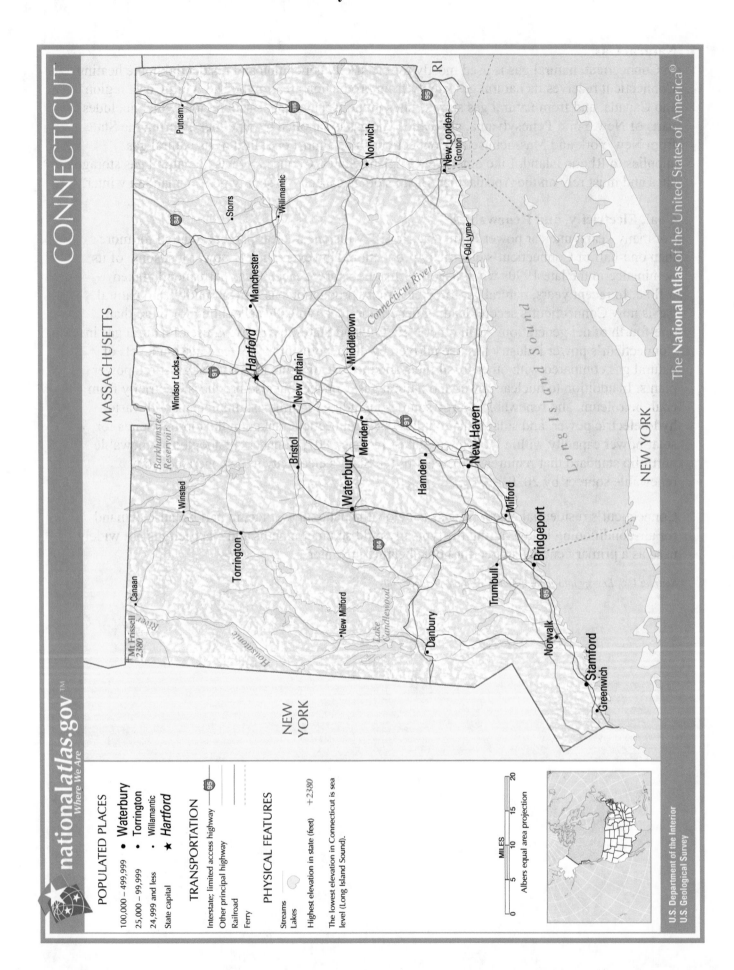

CONNECTICUT

nationalatlas.gov ™
Where We Are

POPULATED PLACES

100,000 – 499,999   ● Waterbury
25,000 – 99,999   ● Torrington
24,999 and less   • Willamantic
State capital   ★ *Hartford*

TRANSPORTATION

Interstate; limited access highway —— 95
Other principal highway
Railroad
Ferry

PHYSICAL FEATURES

Streams
Lakes
Highest elevation in state (feet)   +2380

The lowest elevation in Connecticut is sea
level (Long Island Sound).

MILES
0   5   10   15   20
Albers equal area projection

U.S. Department of the Interior
U.S. Geological Survey

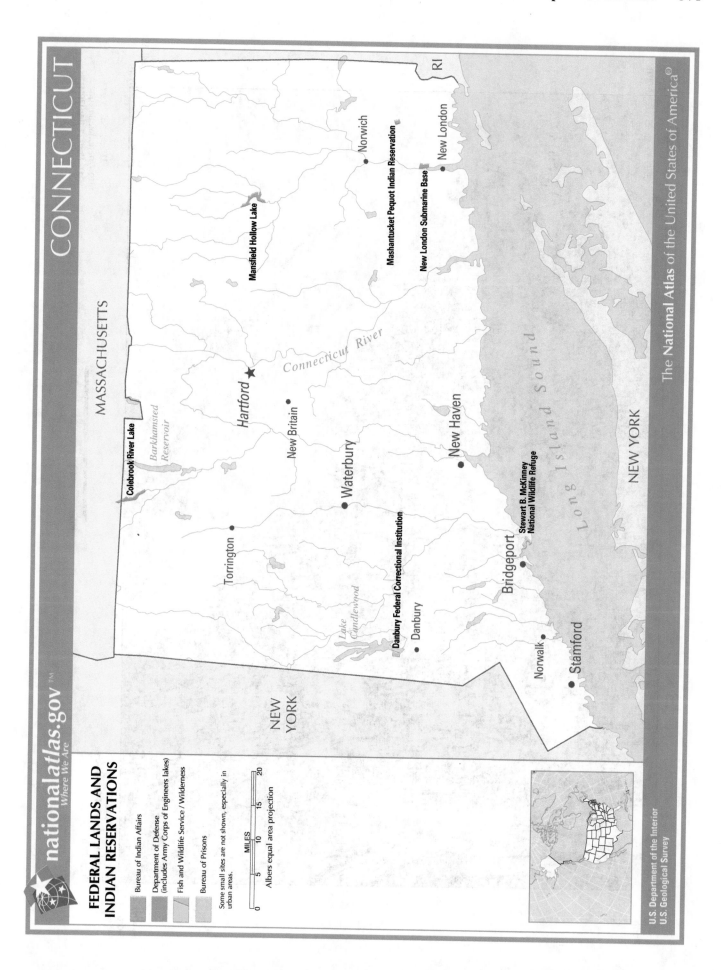

CONNECTICUT

nationalatlas.gov™
Where We Are

**FEDERAL LANDS AND
INDIAN RESERVATIONS**

Bureau of Indian Affairs

Department of Defense
(includes Army Corps of Engineers lakes)

Fish and Wildlife Service / Wilderness

Bureau of Prisons

Some small sites are not shown, especially in
urban areas.

MILES
0   5   10   15   20
Albers equal area projection

U.S. Department of the Interior
U.S. Geological Survey

The **National Atlas** of the United States of America®

MASSACHUSETTS

RI

NEW YORK

NEW
YORK

Colebrook River Lake

Barkhamsted
Reservoir

Mansfield Hollow Lake

Norwich

Mashantucket Pequot Indian Reservation

New London Submarine Base

New London

Connecticut River

Hartford

New Britain

Waterbury

Torrington

New Haven

Lake
Candlewood

Danbury Federal Correctional Institution

Danbury

Bridgeport

Stewart B. McKinney
National Wildlife Refuge

Norwalk

Stamford

Long Island Sound

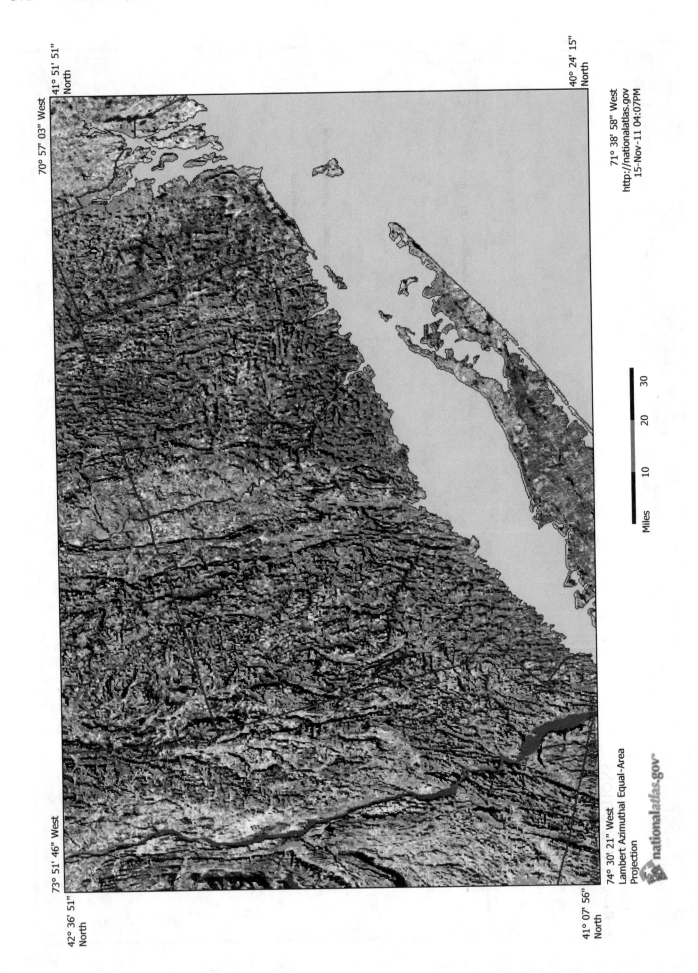

41° 51' 51"
North

70° 57' 03" West

40° 24' 15"
North

71° 38' 58" West
http://nationalatlas.gov
15-Nov-11 04:07PM

73° 51' 46" West

42° 36' 51"
North

74° 30' 21" West
Lambert Azimuthal Equal-Area
Projection

41° 07' 56"
North

Miles   10   20   30

nationalatlas.gov

Delaware

Topic	Value	Time Period
Total Surface Area (acres)	1,533,500	2007
Land	1,243,300	2007
Federal Land	31,000	2007
Owned	11,711	FY 2009
Leased	198	FY 2009
Otherwise Managed	205	FY 2009
National Forest	0	September 2006
National Wilderness	0	October 2011
Non-Federal Land, Developed	280,100	2007
Non-Federal Land, Rural	932,200	2007
Water	290,200	2007
National Natural Landmarks	0	December 2010
National Historic Landmarks	12	December 2010
National Register of Historic Places	681	December 2010
National Parks	0	December 2010
Visitors to National Parks	0	2010
Historic Places Documented by the National Park Service	390	December 2010
Archeological Sites in National Parks	0	December 2010
Threatened and Endangered Species in National Parks	0	December 2010
Economic Benefit from National Park Tourism (dollars)	0	2009
Conservation Reserve Program (acres)	6,721	October 2011
Land and Water Conservation Fund Grants (dollars)	35,989,038	Since 1965
Historic Preservation Grants (dollars)	17,775,495	2010
Community Conservation and Recreation Projects	16	Since 1987
Federal Acres Transferred for Local Parks and Recreation	2,394	Since 1948
Crude Petroleum Production (millions of barrels)	Not Available	2010
Crude Oil Proved Reserves (millions of barrels)	Not Available	2009
Natural Gas Reserves (billions of cubic feet)	Not Available	2009
Natural Gas Liquid Reserves (millions of barrels)	Not Available	2008
Natural Gas Marketed Production (billions of cubic feet)	Not Available	2009
Coal Reserves (millions of short tons)	Not Available	2009

Sources: *U.S. Department of the Interior, National Park Service, State Profiles, December 2010; United States Department of Agriculture, Natural Resources Conservation Service, 2007 National Resources Inventory; U.S. General Services Administration, Federal Real Property Council, FY 2009 Federal Real Property Report, September 2010; University of Montana, www.wilderness.net; U.S. Department of Agriculture, Farm Services Agency, Conservation Reserve Program, October 2011; U.S Census Bureau, 2012 Statistical Abstract of the United States*

Delaware Energy Overview and Analysis

Quick Facts

- The Delaware City petroleum refinery supplies petroleum products to regional markets.
- Delaware is one of the few States that require the statewide use of reformulated motor gasoline blended with ethanol.
- Delaware produces no natural gas; two interstate natural gas pipeline systems supply the State.
- The State's largest consumer of energy is the industrial sector, in part due to several energy-intensive industries, including petroleum refining, chemical production, and other manufacturing.
- The Department of the Interior approved the construction of two meteorological towers off the coast of New Jersey and Rehoboth Beach, Delaware, that will help map weather patterns for determining the location of an offshore wind farm.

Analysis

Resources and Consumption

Delaware has few energy resources aside from wind power potential, which is located onshore and offshore along the Atlantic Coast and in the Delaware Bay. Delaware's population and total energy consumption are among the lowest in the Nation. The State's largest consumer of energy is the industrial sector, in part because of several energy-intensive industries, including petroleum refining, chemical production, and other manufacturing. Despite these industries, however, Delaware's overall energy intensity is among the lowest in the Nation.

Petroleum

Delaware has a single medium-sized refinery in Delaware City. Since the State has no crude oil production, the refinery relies on crude oil supplies delivered via the Delaware River. The Delaware City refinery supplies petroleum products to regional markets. Additional petroleum products are supplied to Delaware via shipments received at ports in the Wilmington area and along the Delaware River. Delaware requires the use of reformulated motor gasoline blended with ethanol throughout the State. About one-fifth of Delaware households use fuel oil as their primary energy source for home heating.

Natural Gas

Delaware produces no natural gas and its total natural gas consumption is low. Eastern Shore Natural Gas is the predominant of the two interstate natural gas pipeline systems that supply the State. Delaware's industry and electricity generating facilities are the largest consumers of natural gas in the State, followed closely by the residential sector. More than one-third of Delaware households use natural gas for home heating.

Coal, Electricity, and Renewables

Delaware's electricity generation capacity is among the lowest in the Nation. In recent years, coal-fired power plants have accounted for about three-fifths of electricity generation within the

State, natural gas-fired plants have accounted for about one-fifth, and petroleum-fired plants have accounted for about one-tenth. Delaware receives its coal supplies primarily by rail from West Virginia, Kentucky, Colorado, and Virginia. More than one-fourth of Delaware households use electricity as their primary energy source for home heating.

Delaware currently produces minimal renewable energy, but plans to increase renewable energy generation are in development. In May 2009, the U.S. Department of the Interior approved Bluewater Wind to build two meteorological towers off the coasts of New Jersey and Rehoboth Beach, Delaware, that will allow the company to map weather patterns for determining the location of an offshore wind farm. In July 2007, Delaware expanded its renewable portfolio standard to require that 2 percent of the state's electricity be generated from solar photovoltaic sources in addition to 18 percent from other renewable sources by 2019.

Source: U.S. Energy Information Administration, October 2009

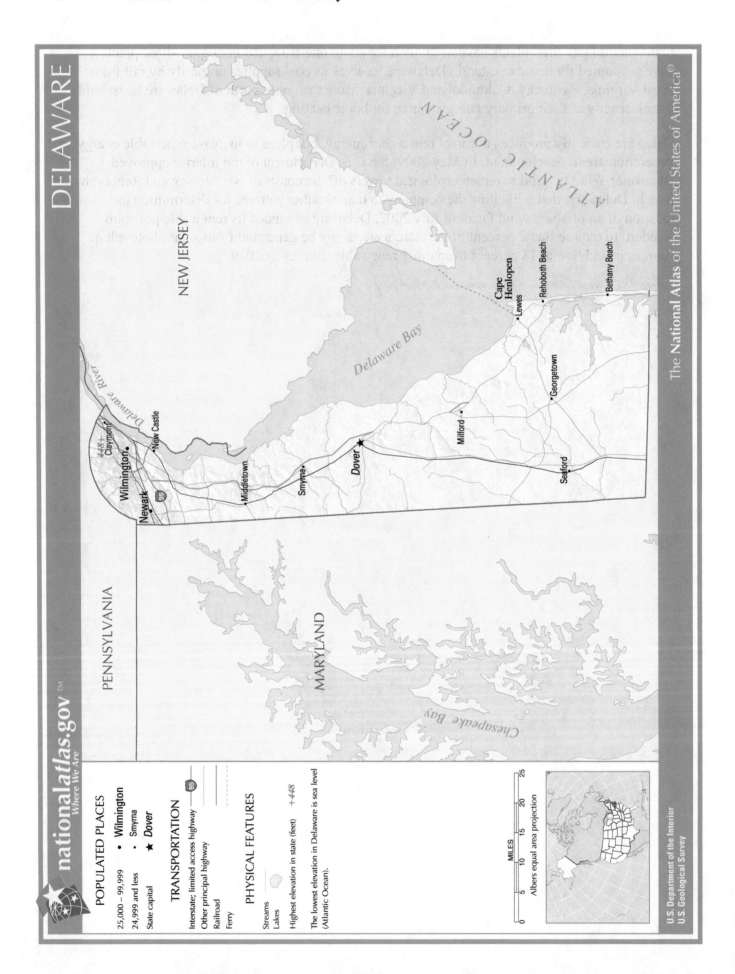

DELAWARE

nationalatlas.gov™
Where We Are

POPULATED PLACES

25,000 – 99,999   ● Wilmington
24,999 and less   ● Smyrna
State capital   ★ Dover

TRANSPORTATION

Interstate; limited access highway ——95——
Other principal highway ————
Railroad ————
Ferry · · · · · · ·

PHYSICAL FEATURES

Streams
Lakes
Highest elevation in state (feet)   +448

The lowest elevation in Delaware is sea level
(Atlantic Ocean).

MILES
0   5   10   15   20   25
Albers equal area projection

U.S. Department of the Interior
U.S. Geological Survey

The **National Atlas** of the United States of America®

NEW JERSEY

PENNSYLVANIA

MARYLAND

ATLANTIC OCEAN

Delaware Bay

Chesapeake Bay

Delaware River

Wilmington
Claymont
448+
New Castle
Newark
95
Middletown
Smyrna
Dover ★
Milford
Georgetown
Seaford
Lewes
Cape Henlopen
Rehoboth Beach
Bethany Beach

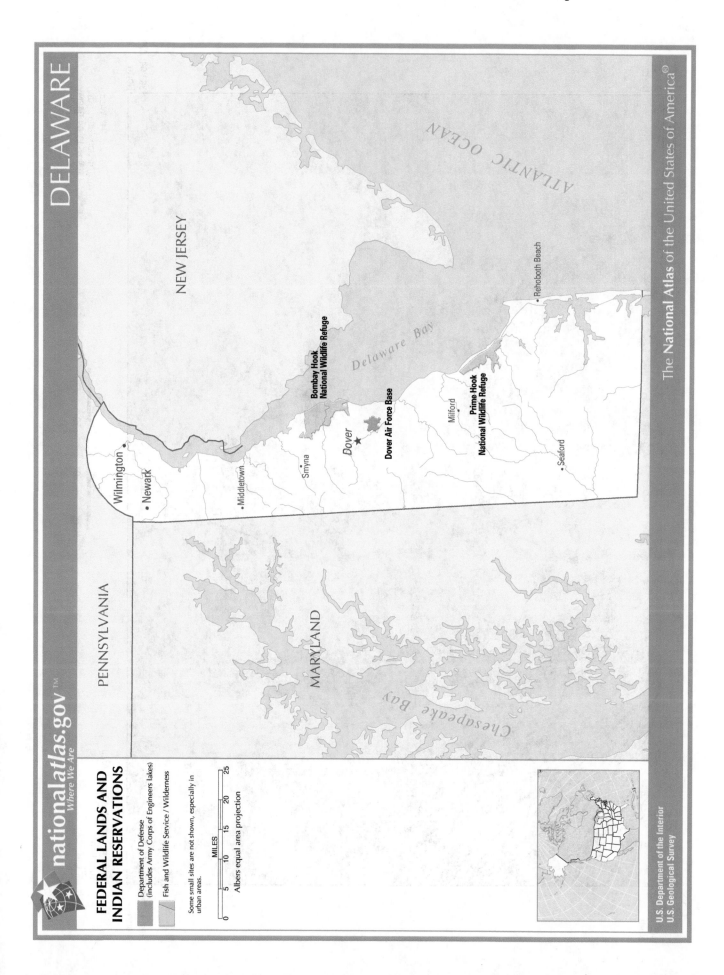

DELAWARE

nationalatlas.gov ™
Where We Are

**FEDERAL LANDS AND
INDIAN RESERVATIONS**

Department of Defense
(includes Army Corps of Engineers lakes)

Fish and Wildlife Service / Wilderness

Some small sites are not shown, especially in
urban areas.

MILES
0   5   10   15   20   25

Albers equal area projection

The **National Atlas** of the United States of America ®

U.S. Department of the Interior
U.S. Geological Survey

PENNSYLVANIA

NEW JERSEY

MARYLAND

Chesapeake Bay

ATLANTIC OCEAN

Delaware Bay

Wilmington
• Newark

Middletown

Smyrna

Dover
★

Dover Air Force Base

Bombay Hook
National Wildlife Refuge

Milford

Prime Hook
National Wildlife Refuge

Seaford

• Rehoboth Beach

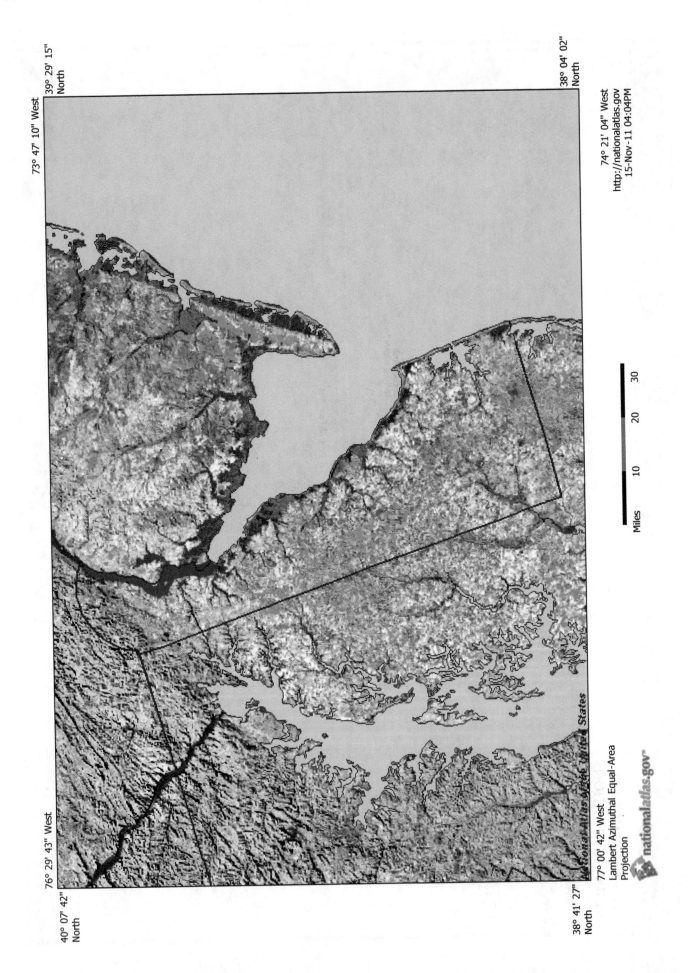

77° 00' 42" West
Lambert Azimuthal Equal-Area
Projection

74° 21' 04" West
http://nationalatlas.gov
15-Nov-11 04:04PM

Miles   10   20   30

nationalatlas.gov™

73° 47' 10" West
39° 29' 15"
North

38° 04' 02"
North

76° 29' 43" West
40° 07' 42"
North

38° 41' 27"
North

District of Columbia

Topic	Value	Time Period
Total Surface Area (acres)	Not Available	2007
Land	Not Available	2007
Federal Land	Not Available	2007
Owned	4,645	FY 2009
Leased	62	FY 2009
Otherwise Managed	10	FY 2009
National Forest	0	September 2006
National Wilderness	0	October 2011
Non-Federal Land, Developed	Not Available	2007
Non-Federal Land, Rural	Not Available	2007
Water	Not Available	2007
National Natural Landmarks	0	December 2010
National Historic Landmarks	74	December 2010
National Register of Historic Places	516	December 2010
National Parks	22	December 2010
Visitors to National Parks	33,140,005	2010
Historic Places Documented by the National Park Service	996	December 2010
Archeological Sites in National Parks	149	December 2010
Threatened and Endangered Species in National Parks	5	December 2010
Economic Benefit from National Park Tourism (dollars)	966,189,000	2009
Conservation Reserve Program (acres)	Not Available	October 2011
Land and Water Conservation Fund Grants (dollars)	14,425,124	Since 1965
Historic Preservation Grants (dollars)	24,785,473	2010
Community Conservation and Recreation Projects	13	Since 1987
Federal Acres Transferred for Local Parks and Recreation	0	Since 1948
Crude Petroleum Production (millions of barrels)	Not Available	2010
Crude Oil Proved Reserves (millions of barrels)	Not Available	2009
Natural Gas Reserves (billions of cubic feet)	Not Available	2009
Natural Gas Liquid Reserves (millions of barrels)	Not Available	2008
Natural Gas Marketed Production (billions of cubic feet)	Not Available	2009
Coal Reserves (millions of short tons)	Not Available	2009

Sources: U.S. Department of the Interior, National Park Service, State Profiles, December 2010; United States Department of Agriculture, Natural Resources Conservation Service, 2007 National Resources Inventory; U.S. General Services Administration, Federal Real Property Council, FY 2009 Federal Real Property Report, September 2010; University of Montana, www.wilderness.net; U.S. Department of Agriculture, Farm Services Agency, Conservation Reserve Program, October 2011; U.S Census Bureau, 2012 Statistical Abstract of the United States

District of Columbia Energy Overview and Analysis

Quick Facts

- Electricity generating facilities in the District of Columbia consist of the Benning and Buzzard Point power plants, both of which are fueled by distillate fuel oil.
- The overall average price of energy in the District of Columbia is among the highest in the United States largely because it has the highest natural gas prices and the second highest motor gasoline prices in the contiguous United States.
- Nearly two-thirds of all D.C. households rely on natural gas for home heating.
- The Washington D.C. Metropolitan Area joined the U.S. Department of Energy's Clean Cities Program in 1993, and alternative-fuel vehicles, as well as several alternative-fuel stations, currently operate in the District of Columbia.
- In 2005, the District adopted a renewable portfolio standard that requires utilities to provide 20 percent of retail electricity sales from renewable sources by 2020.

Analysis

Resources and Consumption

The District of Columbia has few energy resources. About two-thirds of energy consumption comes from the commercial sector. The overall average price of energy in the District of Columbia is among the highest in the United States largely because it has the highest natural gas prices and the second highest motor gasoline prices in the contiguous United States.

Petroleum

The District of Columbia requires district-wide use of reformulated motor gasoline blended with ethanol. The District relies on petroleum products supplied by pipeline.

Natural Gas

Most natural gas in the District of Columbia is consumed by the commercial sector. The residential sector is another important natural gas consumer, as nearly two-thirds of the homes in the District are heated by natural gas. The District receives its natural gas via Virginia and Maryland; the majority of the area's natural gas is supplied by a major pipeline originating in the Gulf Region.

Coal, Electricity, and Renewables

The District of Columbia has two distillate fuel oil-fired power plants, Benning and Buzzard Point. Both plants are more than 35 years old, and for many years now have been used primarily as peaking plants, operating only a few hours per year during times of highest electricity demand. Both are scheduled to be shut down in 2012. The coal-fired Capitol Power Plant, which began generating electricity in 1910, now provides steam for heating and chilled water for cooling the Capitol, the House and Senate office buildings, the Supreme Court building, and other buildings within the Capitol Complex. Most of the electricity consumed in the District of Columbia comes from adjacent States. The price of electricity to residential consumers is lower than the price to commercial consumers, whereas the U.S. average price is higher to residential consumers than to commercial consumers.

In 1993, the Washington D.C. Metropolitan Area joined the Clean Cities program. The program consists of 90 coalitions whose objectives are to promote alternative fuel use, reduce petroleum consumption, and promote measures such as idle reduction and alternative-fueled vehicles including hybrid electric vehicles. In 2005, the District adopted a renewable portfolio standard that requires utilities to provide 20 percent of retail electricity sales from renewable sources by 2020.

Source: U.S. Energy Information Administration, October 2009

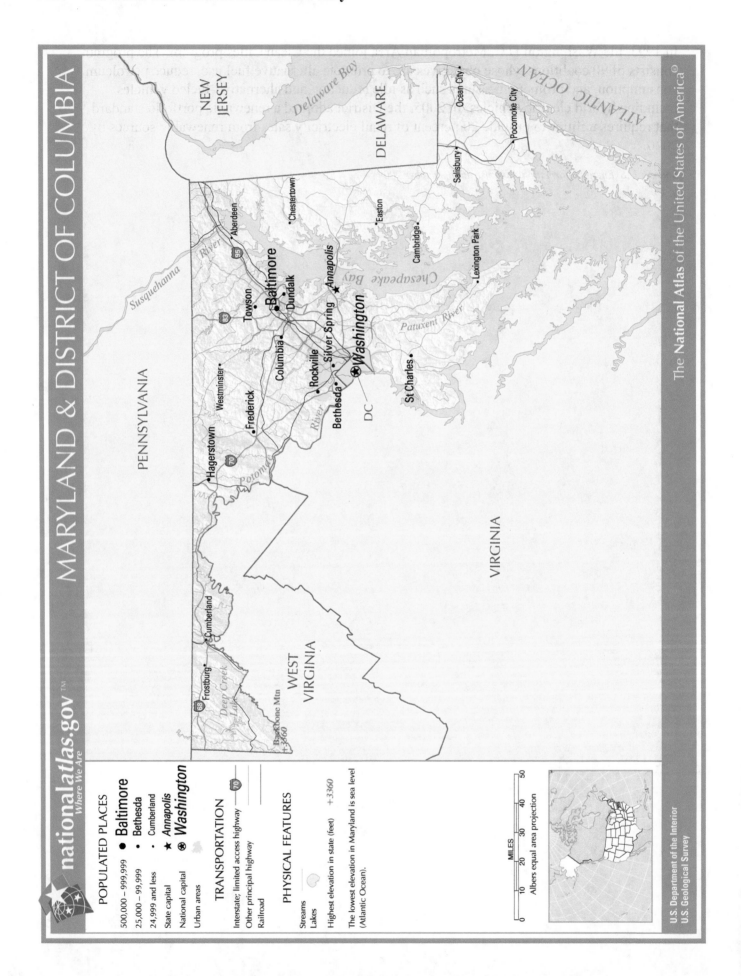

MARYLAND & DISTRICT OF COLUMBIA

nationalatlas.gov™
Where We Are

The **National Atlas** of the United States of America®

POPULATED PLACES

● **Baltimore**   500,000 – 999,999
● **Bethesda**   25,000 – 99,999
· Cumberland   24,999 and less
★ **Annapolis**   State capital
⊛ **Washington**   National capital
Urban areas

TRANSPORTATION

Interstate; limited access highway
Other principal highway
Railroad

PHYSICAL FEATURES

Streams
Lakes
+3360   Highest elevation in state (feet)

The lowest elevation in Maryland is sea level (Atlantic Ocean).

MILES
0 10 20 30 40 50
Albers equal area projection

U.S. Department of the Interior
U.S. Geological Survey

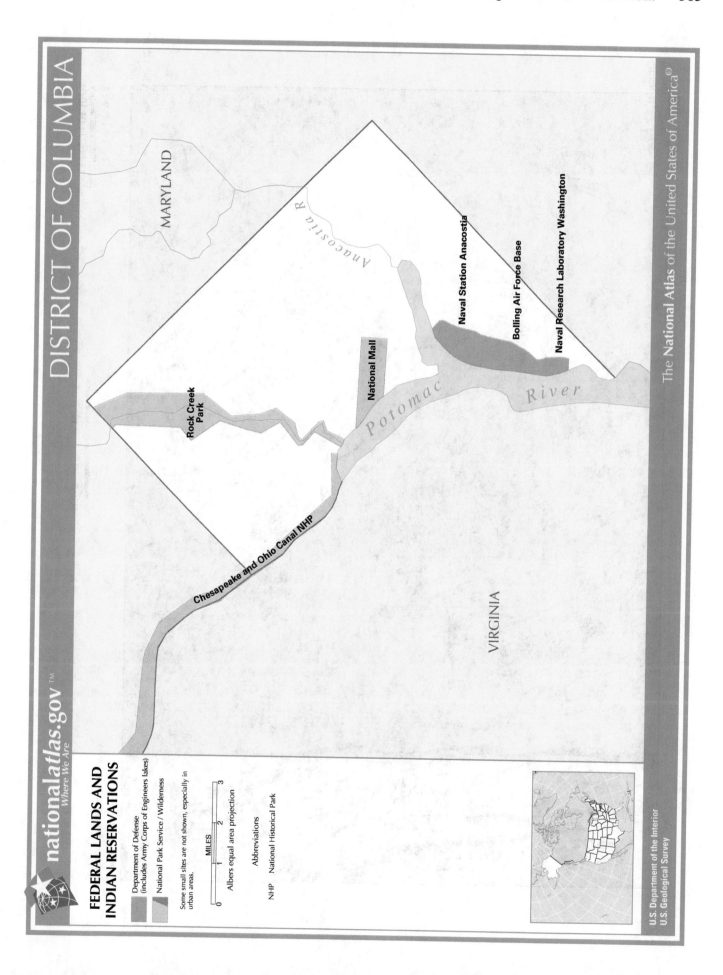

DISTRICT OF COLUMBIA

nationalatlas.gov™
Where We Are

FEDERAL LANDS AND INDIAN RESERVATIONS

Department of Defense
(includes Army Corps of Engineers lakes)

National Park Service / Wilderness

Some small sites are not shown, especially in urban areas.

MILES

0   1   2   3

Albers equal area projection

Abbreviations

NHP   National Historical Park

MARYLAND

Anacostia R

Rock Creek Park

National Mall

Naval Station Anacostia

Bolling Air Force Base

Naval Research Laboratory Washington

Potomac   River

Chesapeake and Ohio Canal NHP

VIRGINIA

The National Atlas of the United States of America®

U.S. Department of the Interior
U.S. Geological Survey

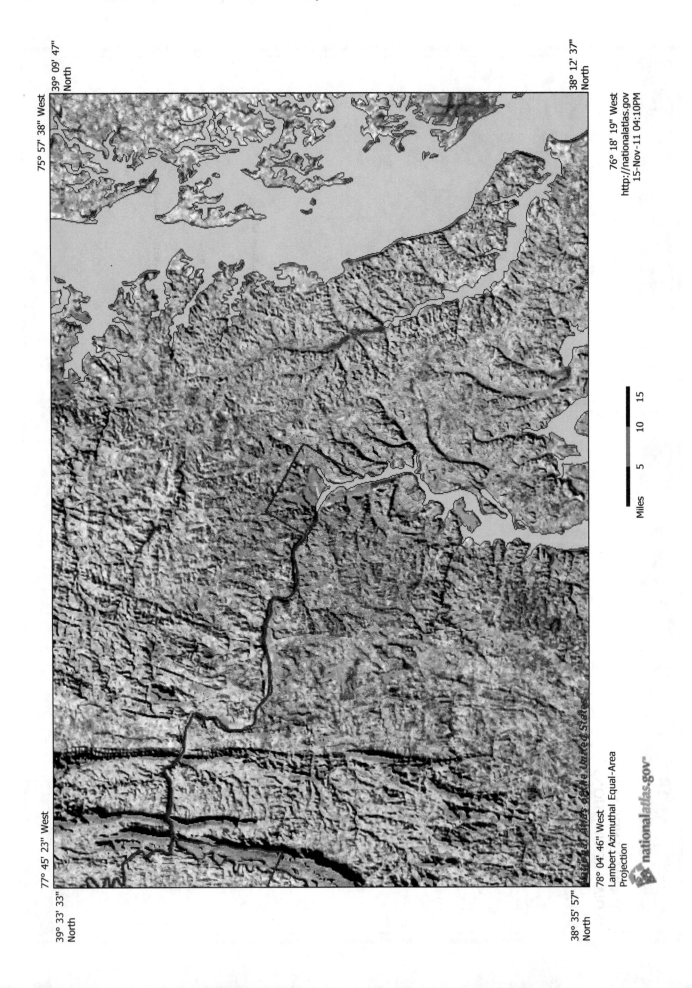

Florida

Topic	Value	Time Period
Total Surface Area (acres)	37,533,700	2007
Land	34,400,100	2007
Federal Land	3,784,200	2007
Owned	802,079	FY 2009
Leased	6,280	FY 2009
Otherwise Managed	87,841	FY 2009
National Forest	1,176,000	September 2006
National Wilderness	1,422,247	October 2011
Non-Federal Land, Developed	5,515,200	2007
Non-Federal Land, Rural	25,100,700	2007
Water	3,133,600	2007
National Natural Landmarks	18	December 2010
National Historic Landmarks	42	December 2010
National Register of Historic Places	1,619	December 2010
National Parks	11	December 2010
Visitors to National Parks	9,222,981	2010
Historic Places Documented by the National Park Service	557	December 2010
Archeological Sites in National Parks	1,116	December 2010
Threatened and Endangered Species in National Parks	54	December 2010
Economic Benefit from National Park Tourism (dollars)	552,809,000	2009
Conservation Reserve Program (acres)	51,993	October 2011
Land and Water Conservation Fund Grants (dollars)	128,772,261	Since 1965
Historic Preservation Grants (dollars)	31,077,920	2010
Community Conservation and Recreation Projects	46	Since 1987
Federal Acres Transferred for Local Parks and Recreation	12,061	Since 1948
Crude Petroleum Production (millions of barrels)	2	2010
Crude Oil Proved Reserves (millions of barrels)	9	2009
Natural Gas Reserves (billions of cubic feet)	7	2009
Natural Gas Liquid Reserves (millions of barrels)	0	2008
Natural Gas Marketed Production (billions of cubic feet)	0	2009
Coal Reserves (millions of short tons)	Not Available	2009

Sources: U.S. Department of the Interior, National Park Service, State Profiles, December 2010; United States Department of Agriculture, Natural Resources Conservation Service, 2007 National Resources Inventory; U.S. General Services Administration, Federal Real Property Council, FY 2009 Federal Real Property Report, September 2010; University of Montana, www.wilderness.net; U.S. Department of Agriculture, Farm Services Agency, Conservation Reserve Program, October 2011; U.S Census Bureau, 2012 Statistical Abstract of the United States

Florida Energy Overview and Analysis

Quick Facts

- Florida's per capita residential electricity demand is among the highest in the country, due in part to high air-conditioning use during the hot summer months and the widespread use of electricity for home heating during the winter months.
- Geologists believe there may be large oil and gas deposits in the Federal Outer Continental Shelf off of Florida's western coast.
- Florida is a leading producer of oranges and a planned facility that would make 4 million gallons of ethanol from citrus waste would become the world's first producer of ethanol from that feedstock.
- More petroleum-fired electricity is generated in Florida than in any other State.
- Hurricanes and severe storms from the Atlantic Ocean put Florida at risk for massive power outages during the storm season.

Analysis

Resources and Consumption

Florida has minor oil and gas reserves and few other energy resources. However, geologists believe that large deposits of oil and gas may be found in the federally administered Outer Continental Shelf (OCS) off Florida's western coast. Congressional and Presidential moratoria prohibiting energy development in most of the OCS were lifted in 2008,but a separate Act banning energy development within 100-125 miles of Florida remains in effect until 2022.

Although Florida has few renewable energy resources, researchers are looking for ways to produce ethanol using citrus peel waste from Florida's juice-processing industry. A planned facility in Hendry County is expected to produce 4 million gallons per year of ethanol from citrus waste; the facility would be the first ethanol plant in the world to use that feedstock. The plant, which would be located near the center of the State's sugar cane industry, is planning to experiment with sugar cane feedstock as well.

Due to its large population, Florida's total energy consumption is among the highest in the country. However, due to relatively low energy use by the industrial sector, per capita energy consumption is among the lowest in the country. Florida's transportation and residential sectors lead State energy demand.

Petroleum

Most of Florida's minor crude oil production comes from fields in the northwestern Panhandle, but the State also produces some crude oil from smaller fields in the south. Although companies have explored for oil and gas in the Federal OCS south of Panama City, exploration activity has been dormant since 1995, when a litigation settlement returned 73 oil and gas leases in this area to the Federal Government. Florida has no oil refineries and relies on petroleum products delivered by tanker and barge to marine terminals near the State's major coastal cities. Due in part to Florida's tourist industry, demand for petroleum-based transportation fuels (motor gasoline and jet fuel) is among the highest in the United States. Traffic at the international airports in Miami and Orlando is among the heaviest in the country.

Natural Gas

Florida receives most of its natural gas supply from the Gulf Coast Region via two major interstate pipelines: the Florida Gas Transmission line, which runs from Texas through the Florida Panhandle to Miami, and the Gulfstream pipeline, an underwater link from Mississippi and Alabama to central Florida. With the completion of the Cypress Pipeline in May 2007, the Jacksonville area has also begun receiving supplies from the liquefied natural gas (LNG) import terminal at Elba Island, Georgia. Florida's natural gas consumption is high and has grown rapidly in recent years, due primarily to increasing demand from the electric power sector, which dominates State natural gas use. To help meet Florida's growing demand for natural gas, companies have proposed building new LNG import terminals in the Federal waters off Florida's Atlantic and Gulf coasts and on the nearby islands of the Bahamas that would be connected via underwater pipeline to Florida's existing natural gas pipeline system.

Coal, Electricity, and Renewables

Electricity generation in Florida is among the highest in the United States. Natural gas and coal are the leading fuels for electricity production, typically accounting for about 40 percent and 30 percent of net generation, respectively. Nuclear and petroleum-fired power plants account for much of the remaining electricity production within the State. Florida has more petroleum-fired electricity generation than any other State. Florida also a leading producer of electricity from municipal solid waste and landfill gas, although generation from those sources contributes only minimally to the electricity grid. There are no coal mines in Florida and coal-fired power plants rely on supplies delivered by railroad and barge, mostly from Kentucky, Illinois, and West Virginia.

Florida's per capita residential electricity demand is among the highest in the country, due in part to high air-conditioning use during the hot summer months and the widespread use of electricity for home heating during the winter months. Despite high demand from the residential and commercial sectors, total per capita electricity consumption in Florida is not high, because industrial electricity use is relatively low. About nine-tenths of Florida households use electricity as their main energy source for home heating.

While the State does not have a renewable portfolio standard, Florida did adopt energy standards that require major facility projects in the State to be constructed to high energy efficiency standards in order to reduce energy use. In addition, utilities in Florida are required to disclose their fuel sources and adopt net metering to credit customers' utility bills for electricity they provide to the grid from renewable sources.

Source: U.S. Energy Information Administration, October 2009

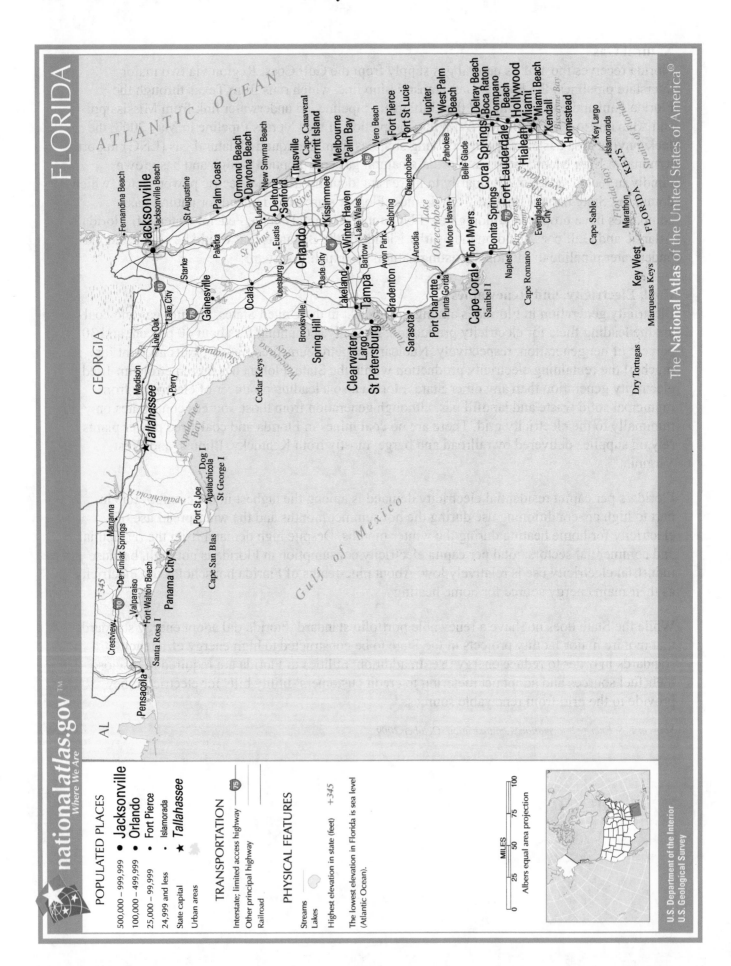

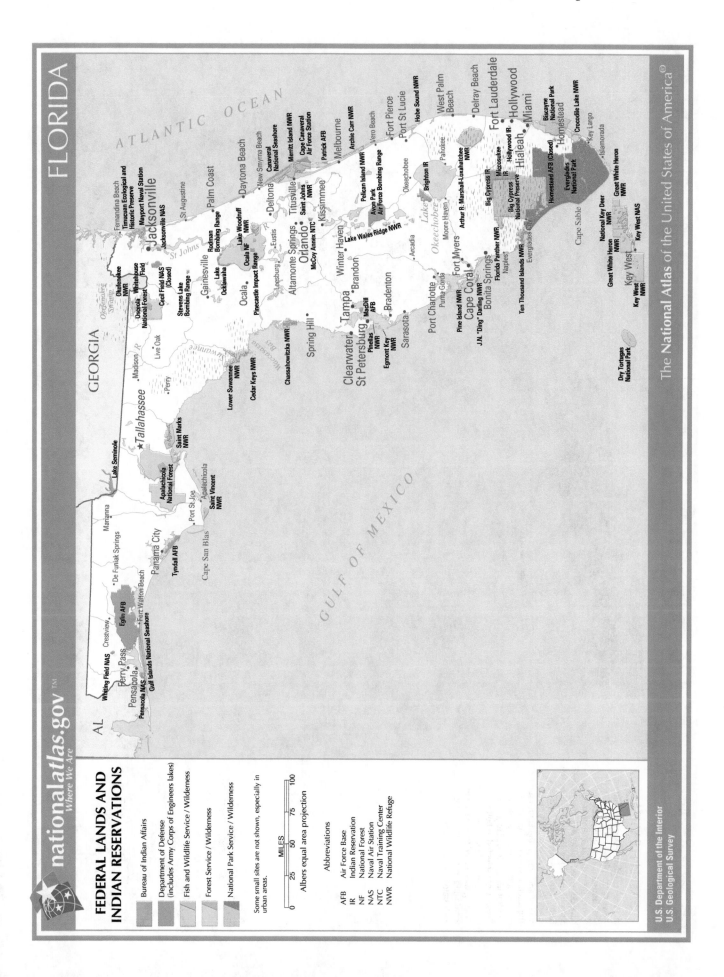

U.S. Department of the Interior
U.S. Geological Survey

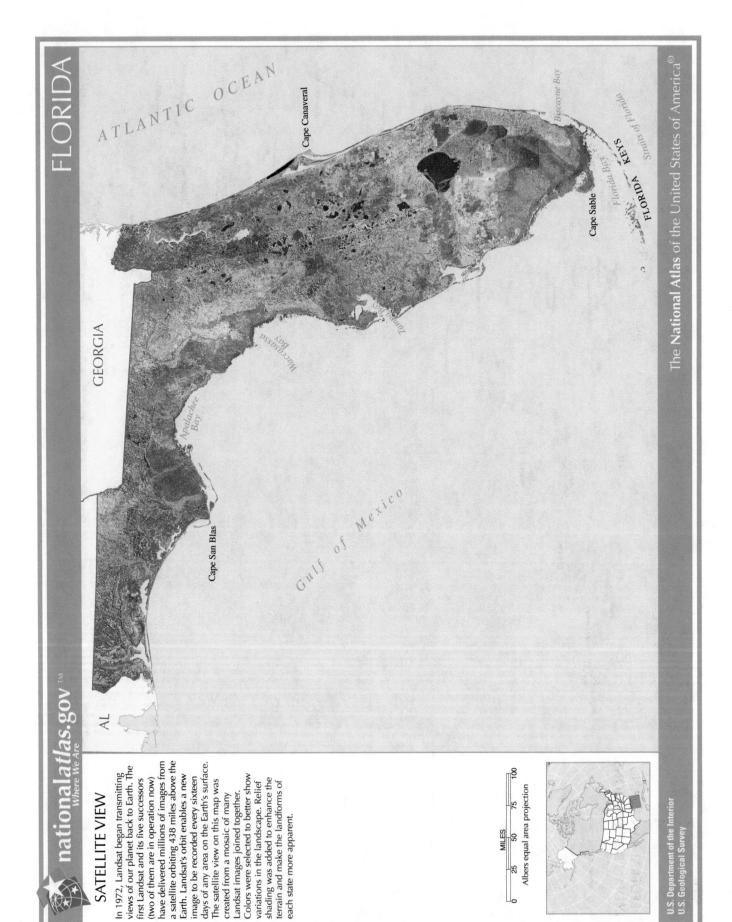

FLORIDA

nationalatlas.gov™
Where We Are

SATELLITE VIEW

In 1972, Landsat began transmitting views of our planet back to Earth. The first Landsat and its five successors (two of them are in operation now) have delivered millions of images from a satellite orbiting 438 miles above the Earth. Landsat's orbit enables a new image to be recorded every sixteen days of any area on the Earth's surface. The satellite view on this map was created from a mosaic of many Landsat images joined together. Colors were selected to better show variations in the landscape. Relief shading was added to enhance the terrain and make the landforms of each state more apparent.

ATLANTIC OCEAN

Cape Canaveral

Biscayne Bay

Straits of Florida

FLORIDA KEYS

Florida Bay

Cape Sable

FLORIDA

GEORGIA

Apalachee Bay

Waccasassa Bay

Tampa Bay

Gulf of Mexico

Cape San Blas

AL

MILES
0   25   50   75   100

Albers equal area projection

The **National Atlas** of the United States of America®

U.S. Department of the Interior
U.S. Geological Survey

Georgia

Topic	Value	Time Period
Total Surface Area (acres)	37,740,500	2007
Land	36,681,200	2007
Federal Land	2,124,000	2007
Owned	974,375	FY 2009
Leased	6,569	FY 2009
Otherwise Managed	808	FY 2009
National Forest	867,000	September 2006
National Wilderness	486,530	October 2011
Non-Federal Land, Developed	4,639,900	2007
Non-Federal Land, Rural	29,917,300	2007
Water	1,059,300	2007
National Natural Landmarks	10	December 2010
National Historic Landmarks	48	December 2010
National Register of Historic Places	2,040	December 2010
National Parks	11	December 2010
Visitors to National Parks	6,776,556	2010
Historic Places Documented by the National Park Service	920	December 2010
Archeological Sites in National Parks	297	December 2010
Threatened and Endangered Species in National Parks	20	December 2010
Economic Benefit from National Park Tourism (dollars)	199,024,000	2009
Conservation Reserve Program (acres)	315,213	October 2011
Land and Water Conservation Fund Grants (dollars)	81,455,120	Since 1965
Historic Preservation Grants (dollars)	32,149,564	2010
Community Conservation and Recreation Projects	41	Since 1987
Federal Acres Transferred for Local Parks and Recreation	3,617	Since 1948
Crude Petroleum Production (millions of barrels)	Not Available	2010
Crude Oil Proved Reserves (millions of barrels)	Not Available	2009
Natural Gas Reserves (billions of cubic feet)	Not Available	2009
Natural Gas Liquid Reserves (millions of barrels)	Not Available	2008
Natural Gas Marketed Production (billions of cubic feet)	Not Available	2009
Coal Reserves (millions of short tons)	Not Available	2009

Sources: *U.S. Department of the Interior, National Park Service, State Profiles, December 2010; United States Department of Agriculture, Natural Resources Conservation Service, 2007 National Resources Inventory; U.S. General Services Administration, Federal Real Property Council, FY 2009 Federal Real Property Report, September 2010; University of Montana, www.wilderness.net; U.S. Department of Agriculture, Farm Services Agency, Conservation Reserve Program, October 2011; U.S Census Bureau, 2012 Statistical Abstract of the United States*

Georgia Energy Overview and Analysis

Quick Facts

- The Elba Island liquefied natural gas (LNG) terminal near Savannah is one of nine existing LNG import sites in the United States and an expansion of this facility is expected to be complete by sometime in 2010.
- Coal is the primary fuel for electricity generation in Georgia.
- Georgia's two nuclear power plants typically account for about one-fourth of the State's electricity generation.
- The industrial sector is the largest energy-consuming sector in the State, in part because Georgia is a leader in the energy-intensive wood and paper products industry.
- Georgia's electricity generation and consumption are among the highest in the Nation.
- Georgia is one of the Nation's top producers of electricity from wood and wood waste.

Analysis

Resources and Consumption

Georgia has no fossil fuel resources but does have substantial hydroelectric power resources located in several river basins. The largest energy-consuming sectors in the State are the transportation and industrial sectors. Industrial consumption is high, in part because Georgia is a leader in the energy-intensive wood and paper products industry.

Petroleum

Georgia receives petroleum products at the Port of Savannah and through the Colonial and Plantation pipelines, which run through the State from Texas and Louisiana. The Dixie Pipeline, also originating in the Gulf Coast region, supplies the State's propane needs.

Natural Gas

Georgia purchases its natural gas from other States and from abroad, including Trinidad and Tobago and Egypt. The State receives large amounts of natural gas on a net basis and then delivers over two-thirds of those receipts to South Carolina. En route to major Northeast markets, minimal amounts of Georgia's natural gas go to Florida and Tennessee. Several interstate pipeline systems, including systems operated by the Southern Natural Gas Company and Transcontinental Gas Pipeline Company, supply Georgia from the Gulf Coast. Georgia also imports international supplies at a liquefied natural gas (LNG) terminal located on Elba Island, at the mouth of the Savannah River. The Elba Island facility, which is one of nine existing LNG import sites in the United States, receives LNG by tanker from Trinidad and Tobago. An expansion of this facility has been approved by the Federal Energy Regulatory Commission and is expected to be completed sometime in 2010.

The industrial, electric power, and residential sectors are Georgia's largest consumers of natural gas. Nearly one-half of all Georgia households use natural gas as their main energy source for home heating.

Coal, Electricity, and Renewables

Georgia's electricity generation and consumption are among the highest in the United States. Coal and nuclear power dominate electricity generation in Georgia, with coal typically supplying about half of electricity output and nuclear supplying about one-fourth. There is no coal production in Georgia, and the State burns coal supplied mostly from Wyoming, Kentucky, and Virginia. Georgia's two nuclear plants, both located in the eastern part of the State, make it a major producer of nuclear power. Georgia is also one of the top hydroelectric power producers east of the Rocky Mountains and one of the Nation's top producers of power from wood and wood waste, with just over 9 percent of the Nation's capacity. While Georgia does not have a renewable portfolio standard, the State adopted a net metering policy to credit customers' utility bills for electricity they provide to the grid generated from renewable sources.

Source: U.S. Energy Information Administration, October 2009

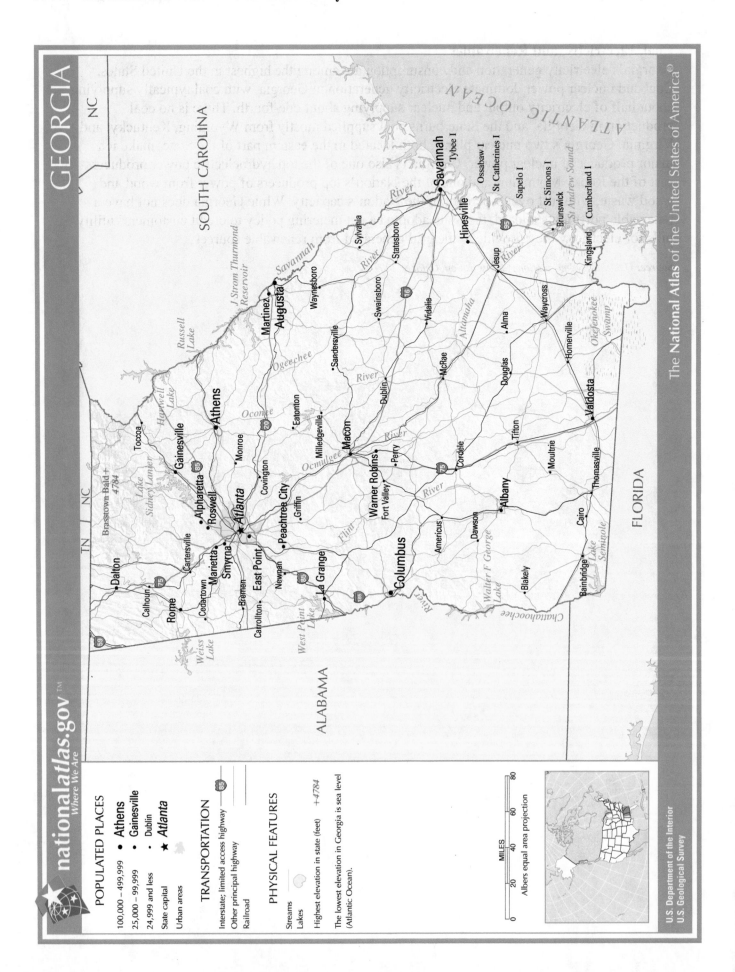

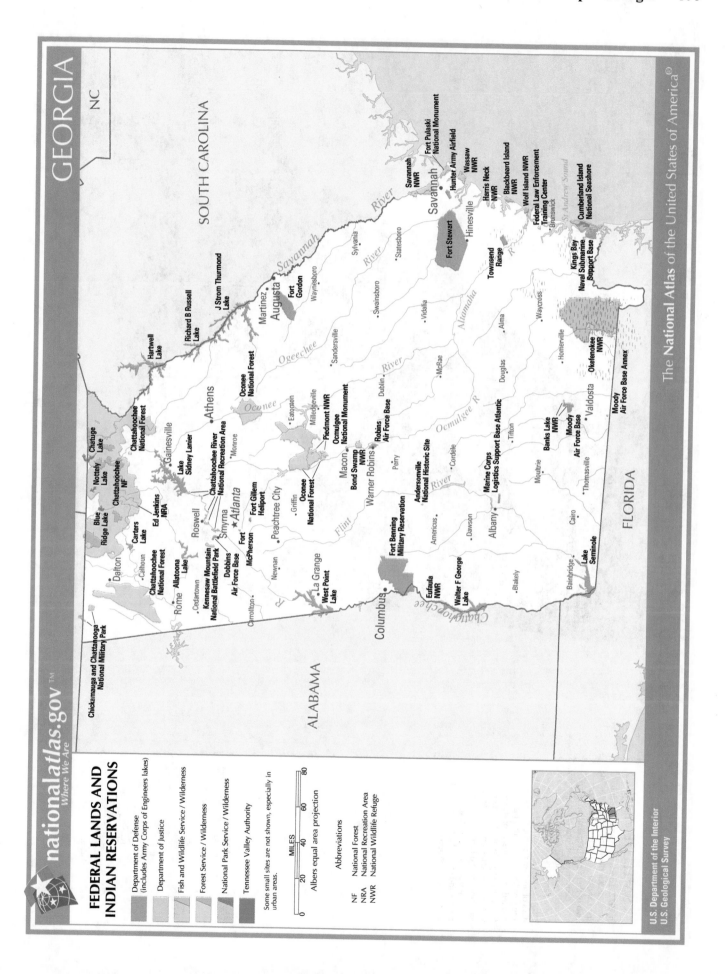

GEORGIA

nationalatlas.gov™
Where We Are

FEDERAL LANDS AND
INDIAN RESERVATIONS

Department of Defense
(includes Army Corps of Engineers lakes)

Department of Justice

Fish and Wildlife Service / Wilderness

Forest Service / Wilderness

National Park Service / Wilderness

Tennessee Valley Authority

Some small sites are not shown, especially in
urban areas.

MILES

0   20   40   60   80

Albers equal area projection

Abbreviations

NF   National Forest
NRA   National Recreation Area
NWR   National Wildlife Refuge

The National Atlas of the United States of America®

U.S. Department of the Interior
U.S. Geological Survey

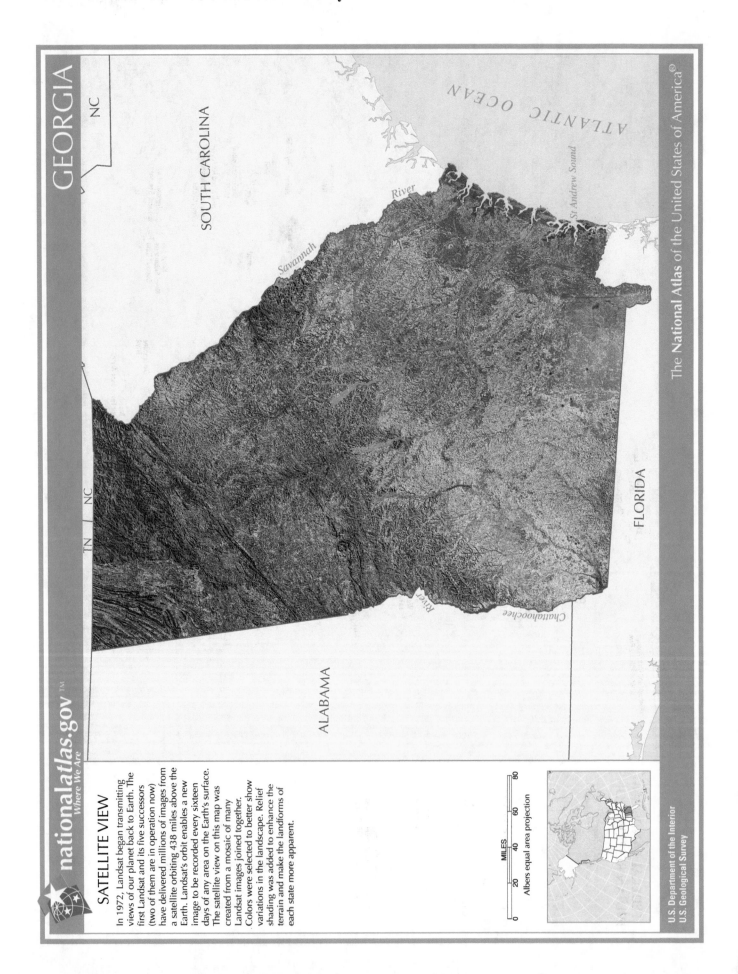

GEORGIA

NC

SOUTH CAROLINA

ATLANTIC OCEAN

St Andrew Sound

Savannah River

TN | NC

ALABAMA

Chattahoochee River

FLORIDA

nationalatlas.gov ™
Where We Are

SATELLITE VIEW

In 1972, Landsat began transmitting views of our planet back to Earth. The first Landsat and its five successors (two of them are in operation now) have delivered millions of images from a satellite orbiting 438 miles above the Earth. Landsat's orbit enables a new image to be recorded every sixteen days of any area on the Earth's surface. The satellite view on this map was created from a mosaic of many Landsat images joined together. Colors were selected to better show variations in the landscape. Relief shading was added to enhance the terrain and make the landforms of each state more apparent.

MILES
0 20 40 60 80
Albers equal area projection

U.S. Department of the Interior
U.S. Geological Survey

The **National Atlas** of the United States of America®

Hawaii

Topic	Value	Time Period
Total Surface Area (acres)	Not Available	2007
Land	Not Available	2007
Federal Land	Not Available	2007
Owned	178,192	FY 2009
Leased	55,811	FY 2009
Otherwise Managed	1,035	FY 2009
National Forest	1,000	September 2006
National Wilderness	155,509	October 2011
Non-Federal Land, Developed	Not Available	2007
Non-Federal Land, Rural	Not Available	2007
Water	Not Available	2007
National Natural Landmarks	7	December 2010
National Historic Landmarks	33	December 2010
National Register of Historic Places	325	December 2010
National Parks	7	December 2010
Visitors to National Parks	4,493,123	2010
Historic Places Documented by the National Park Service	807	December 2010
Archeological Sites in National Parks	1,388	December 2010
Threatened and Endangered Species in National Parks	89	December 2010
Economic Benefit from National Park Tourism (dollars)	222,157,000	2009
Conservation Reserve Program (acres)	490	October 2011
Land and Water Conservation Fund Grants (dollars)	38,308,514	Since 1965
Historic Preservation Grants (dollars)	14,917,599	2010
Community Conservation and Recreation Projects	29	Since 1987
Federal Acres Transferred for Local Parks and Recreation	364	Since 1948
Crude Petroleum Production (millions of barrels)	Not Available	2010
Crude Oil Proved Reserves (millions of barrels)	Not Available	2009
Natural Gas Reserves (billions of cubic feet)	Not Available	2009
Natural Gas Liquid Reserves (millions of barrels)	Not Available	2008
Natural Gas Marketed Production (billions of cubic feet)	Not Available	2009
Coal Reserves (millions of short tons)	Not Available	2009

Sources: U.S. Department of the Interior, National Park Service, State Profiles, December 2010; United States Department of Agriculture, Natural Resources Conservation Service, 2007 National Resources Inventory; U.S. General Services Administration, Federal Real Property Council, FY 2009 Federal Real Property Report, September 2010; University of Montana, www.wilderness.net; U.S. Department of Agriculture, Farm Services Agency, Conservation Reserve Program, October 2011; U.S Census Bureau, 2012 Statistical Abstract of the United States

Hawaii Energy Overview and Analysis

Quick Facts

- Petroleum provides nearly nine-tenths of all the energy consumed in Hawaii.
- The transportation sector leads energy demand in Hawaii, due in large part to heavy jet fuel use by military installations and commercial airlines.
- Petroleum-fired power plants supply more than three-fourths of Hawaii's electricity generation.
- Due to the mild tropical climate, most households do not require energy for home heating.
- A planned wave-to-energy project could supply up to 2.7 megawatts of electricity to Hawaii by the end of 2011.

Analysis

Resources and Consumption

Because Hawaii is isolated from the U.S. mainland, its energy infrastructure and consumption are unique among the States. Hawaii depends heavily on imported fossil fuels to meet energy demand. Close to nine-tenths of Hawaii's energy comes from petroleum. Hawaii uses small amounts of coal and very little natural gas. Hawaii's main industry is tourism, and the State economy is not energy intensive. Per capita energy consumption in Hawaii is among the lowest in the Nation. Due in large part to heavy jet-fuel use by military installations and commercial airlines, the transportation sector is the leading energy-consuming sector, accounting for over one-half of the State's total energy consumption.

Petroleum

Hawaii's two refineries depend on crude oil shipped from Alaska and imported from foreign countries. The refineries, located near Honolulu on the island of Oahu, supply petroleum products to local markets. Hawaii has no major pipelines, and its ports are crucial for the distribution of petroleum products to the State's many islands. Hawaiian consumption of most petroleum products is among the lowest in the country, but jet fuel is a notable exception. Due to heavy use by military installations and commercial airlines, jet fuel makes up a larger share of total petroleum consumption than it does in any other State except Alaska. Hawaii requires the statewide use of oxygenated motor gasoline.

Natural Gas

Although Hawaiian natural gas consumption is the lowest in the country, the State has the distinction of being one of three States that produce synthetic natural gas. Hawaii's synthetic natural gas plant, which is located in Oahu, converts a refinery byproduct stream into a commercially viable synthetic natural gas. Studies have been undertaken to assess the feasibility of establishing a liquefied natural gas (LNG) import facility on the islands. The commercial sector, which includes hotels and restaurants, accounts for over three-fifths of the natural gas consumed in Hawaii. The residential sector accounts for less than one-fifth of consumption, in part because very few Hawaiians rely on natural gas as their primary fuel for home heating. Natural gas is also used for cooking, water heating, drying, and lighting.

Coal, Electricity, and Renewables

Petroleum-fired power plants supply more than three-fourths of Hawaii's electricity generation. Generation from coal and several renewable sources supply the remainder of the State's electricity generation. Hawaii ranks among the top ten solar-producing States and produces energy from other renewable sources such as hydroelectricity, geothermal, landfill gas, and other biomass. Hawaii is one of eight States with geothermal power generation and ranks third among them. State electricity demand is among the lowest in the country. More than one-third of all Hawaiian households use electricity as their primary energy source for home heating. Due to the mild tropical climate, most households do not use any energy for home heating.

Because Hawaii has some of the most powerful waves per square meter in the world, numerous wave energy projects are being proposed and implemented off the State's coasts. The Office of Naval Research is currently monitoring a 40-kilowatt experimental buoy that drives an electrical generator from energy generated from the bobbing motion of the waves. Floating platforms are also planned less than a mile off the northeast coast of Maui that would provide up to 2.7 megawatts of electricity derived from air driven through turbines from the rising and falling of sea swells. These wave-to-electricity systems could be operational by the end of 2011. In June 2009, Hawaii extended its renewable electricity portfolio standard to require utilities to generate 10 percent of their net electricity sales from renewable sources by the end of 2010, increasing to 40 percent by 2030.

Source: U.S. Energy Information Administration, October 2009

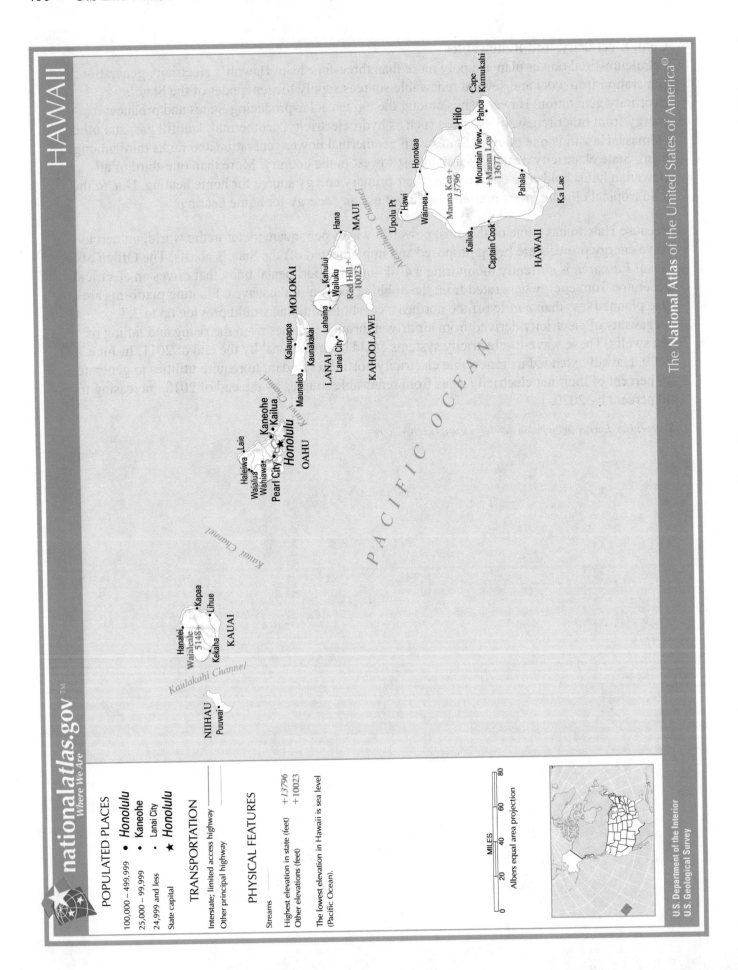

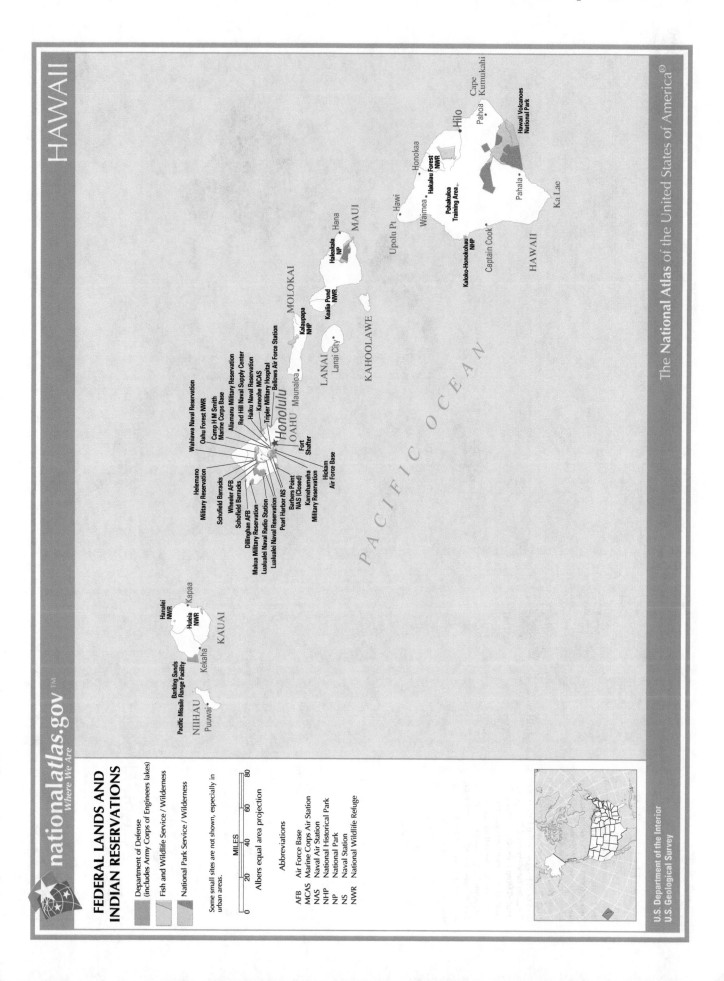

HAWAII

nationalatlas.gov ™
Where We Are

FEDERAL LANDS AND INDIAN RESERVATIONS

Department of Defense
(includes Army Corps of Engineers lakes)

Fish and Wildlife Service / Wilderness

National Park Service / Wilderness

Some small sites are not shown, especially in urban areas.

MILES

0   20   40   60   80

Albers equal area projection

Abbreviations

AFB	Air Force Base
MCAS	Marine Corps Air Station
NAS	Naval Air Station
NHP	National Historical Park
NP	National Park
NS	Naval Station
NWR	National Wildlife Refuge

U.S. Department of the Interior
U.S. Geological Survey

The **National Atlas** of the United States of America ®

PACIFIC OCEAN

NIIHAU
Puuwai

KAUAI
Kapaa
Kekaha
Barking Sands
Pacific Missile Range Facility
Hanalei NWR
Huleia NWR

OAHU
Honolulu
Wahiawa Naval Reservation
Oahu Forest NWR
Camp H M Smith Marine Corps Base
Aliamanu Military Reservation
Red Hill Naval Supply Center
Haiku Naval Reservation
Kaneohe MCAS
Tripler Military Hospital
Bellows Air Force Station
Helemano Military Reservation
Schofield Barracks
Schofield Barracks
Wheeler AFB
Dillingham AFB
Makua Military Reservation
Lualualei Naval Radio Station
Lualualei Naval Reservation
Pearl Harbor NS
Barbers Point NAS (Closed)
Kamehameha Military Reservation
Fort Shafter
Hickam Air Force Base
Maunaloa

MOLOKAI
Kalaupapa NHP
Kealia Pond NWR

LANAI
Lanai City

KAHOOLAWE

MAUI
Hana
Haleakala NP

HAWAII
Upolu Pt
Hawi
Waimea
Honokaa
Honokaa
Hilo
Pahoa
Cape Kumukahi
Hakalau Forest NWR
Hawaii Volcanoes National Park
Pohakuloa Training Area
Pahala
Kaloko-Honokohau NHP
Captain Cook
Ka Lae

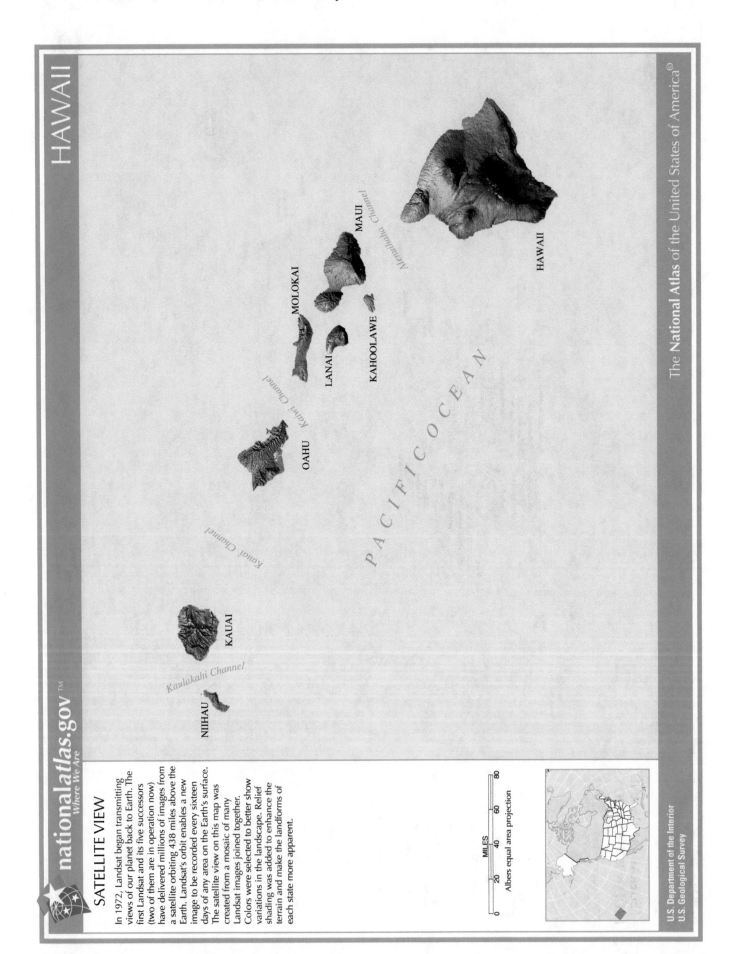

HAWAII

nationalatlas.gov ™
Where We Are

SATELLITE VIEW

In 1972, Landsat began transmitting
views of our planet back to Earth. The
first Landsat and its five successors
(two of them are in operation now)
have delivered millions of images from
a satellite orbiting 438 miles above the
Earth. Landsat's orbit enables a new
image to be recorded every sixteen
days of any area on the Earth's surface.
The satellite view on this map was
created from a mosaic of many
Landsat images joined together.
Colors were selected to better show
variations in the landscape. Relief
shading was added to enhance the
terrain and make the landforms of
each state more apparent.

NIIHAU

Kaulakahi Channel

KAUAI

Kauai Channel

OAHU

Kaiwi Channel

MOLOKAI

LANAI

MAUI

KAHOOLAWE

Alenuihaha Channel

HAWAII

PACIFIC OCEAN

MILES
0   20   40   60   80
Albers equal area projection

The **National Atlas** of the United States of America®

U.S. Department of the Interior
U.S. Geological Survey

Idaho

Topic	Value	Time Period
Total Surface Area (acres)	53,487,500	2007
Land	52,929,900	2007
Federal Land	33,563,300	2007
Owned	916,725	FY 2009
Leased	11,998	FY 2009
Otherwise Managed	196,143	FY 2009
National Forest	20,465,000	September 2006
National Wilderness	4,522,717	October 2011
Non-Federal Land, Developed	907,300	2007
Non-Federal Land, Rural	18,459,300	2007
Water	557,600	2007
National Natural Landmarks	11	December 2010
National Historic Landmarks	Not Available	December 2010
National Register of Historic Places	1,016	December 2010
National Parks	7	December 2010
Visitors to National Parks	530,977	2010
Historic Places Documented by the National Park Service	367	December 2010
Archeological Sites in National Parks	105	December 2010
Threatened and Endangered Species in National Parks	8	December 2010
Economic Benefit from National Park Tourism (dollars)	17,952,000	2009
Conservation Reserve Program (acres)	646,391	October 2011
Land and Water Conservation Fund Grants (dollars)	38,699,925	Since 1965
Historic Preservation Grants (dollars)	18,717,254	2010
Community Conservation and Recreation Projects	32	Since 1987
Federal Acres Transferred for Local Parks and Recreation	2,915	Since 1948
Crude Petroleum Production (millions of barrels)	Not Available	2010
Crude Oil Proved Reserves (millions of barrels)	Not Available	2009
Natural Gas Reserves (billions of cubic feet)	Not Available	2009
Natural Gas Liquid Reserves (millions of barrels)	Not Available	2008
Natural Gas Marketed Production (billions of cubic feet)	Not Available	2009
Coal Reserves (millions of short tons)	Not Available	2009

Sources: *U.S. Department of the Interior, National Park Service, State Profiles, December 2010; United States Department of Agriculture, Natural Resources Conservation Service, 2007 National Resources Inventory; U.S. General Services Administration, Federal Real Property Council, FY 2009 Federal Real Property Report, September 2010; University of Montana, www.wilderness.net; U.S. Department of Agriculture, Farm Services Agency, Conservation Reserve Program, October 2011; U.S Census Bureau, 2012 Statistical Abstract of the United States*

Idaho Energy Overview and Analysis

Quick Facts

- Hydroelectric power plants supply roughly four-fifths of Idaho's electricity generation.
- The Hells Canyon Complex on the Snake River is the largest privately owned hydroelectric power complex in the Nation.
- In March 2006, Idaho established a 2-year moratorium on licensing or processing proposals for new coal-fired power plants; all subsequent proposals have been rejected.
- Idaho is one of the few States that uses conventional motor gasoline statewide.

Analysis

Resources and Consumption

Idaho is rich in renewable energy resources but has few fossil fuel reserves. The Snake River and several smaller river basins offer Idaho some of the greatest hydroelectric power resources in the Nation. Idaho's geologically active mountain areas have substantial geothermal and wind power potential. The State economy is energy-intensive, and energy-consuming industries include mining, forest products, and transportation equipment. Although Idaho's total energy consumption is low when compared with other States, the total population is also low, and, as a result, per capita energy consumption is close to the national average.

Petroleum

Idaho markets receive petroleum product supply from refineries in Montana and Utah via two petroleum product pipelines. Total petroleum consumption is low. Idaho is one of the few States that uses conventional motor gasoline statewide. (Most States require the use of specific gasoline blends in non-attainment areas due to air-quality considerations.)

Natural Gas

The industrial and residential sectors are Idaho's largest natural gas-consuming sectors. Close to one-half of households in Idaho use natural gas as their primary energy source for home heating. Idaho is part of the transportation corridor for shipping natural gas from Canada to the West and Midwest markets via two natural gas pipeline systems. The Gas Transmission Northwest Co. pipeline system from Alberta enters the U.S. at Idaho's Kingsgate Center on the border with Canada before flowing south to California markets. The smaller Northwest Pipeline system supplies Idaho with gas from Canada via Washington State and if necessary, from Wyoming via Utah taking advantage of the pipeline's bi-directional capabilities.

Coal, Electricity, and Renewables

Hydroelectric power plants dominate Idaho electricity generation, supplying roughly four-fifths of the State's production. Natural gas-fired power plants provide over one-tenth of the State's production, while coal- and wood-fired generation and wind turbines supply the remainder. Six of Idaho's 10 largest generating facilities run on hydroelectric power. Idaho also has dozens of privately owned hydroelectric power projects, including the 450-megawatt Hells Canyon Complex on the Snake River, the largest privately owned hydroelectric power complex in the Nation. In March 2006, the Idaho State legislature passed a 2-year moratorium on licensing or processing proposals for new coal-fired power plants. Although the moratorium has since expired, all subsequent proposals for new coal-fired power plants have been rejected. A nuclear plant has been proposed in Elmore County, just south of Boise, that would be the State's first commercial nuclear plant and would power all of Idaho, as well as provide an opportunity to sell electricity to other states. Several high voltage transmission lines connect Idaho to other western power grids, enabling large interstate electricity transfers, and Idaho currently purchases large amounts of electricity from neighboring States to meet demand. About one-third of Idaho households use electricity as their primary energy source for home heating.

Source: *U.S. Energy Information Administration, October 2009*

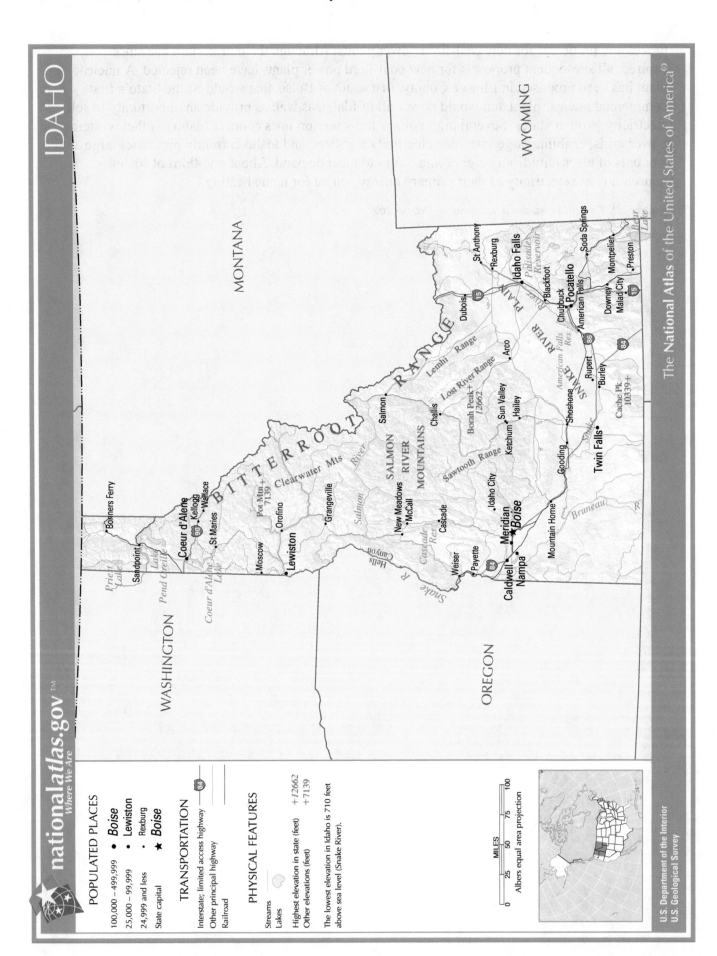

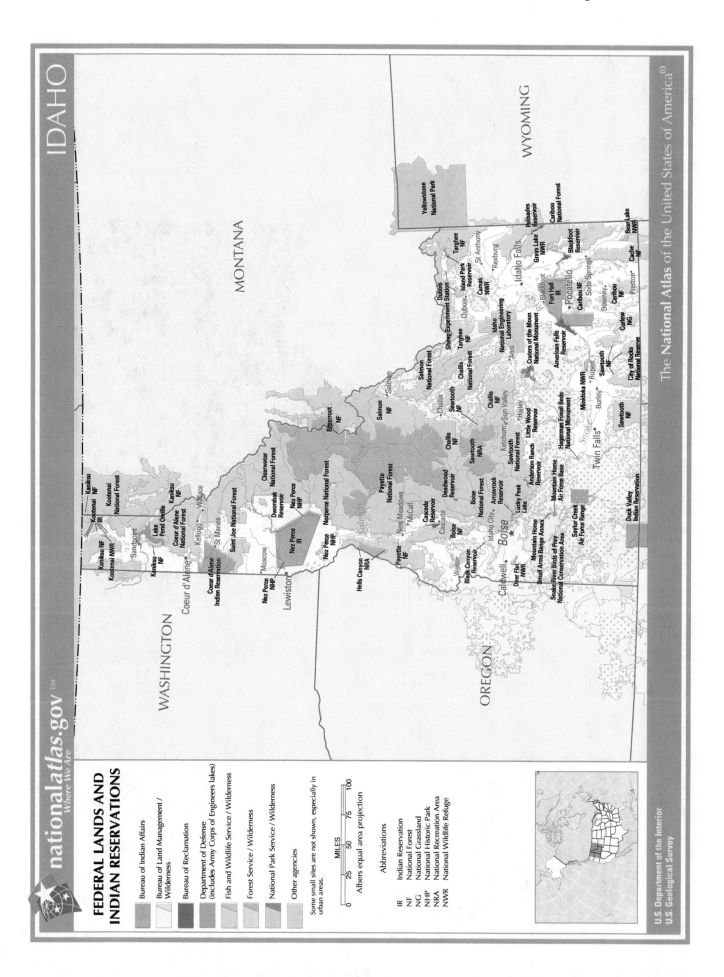

IDAHO

nationalatlas.gov™
Where We Are

**FEDERAL LANDS AND
INDIAN RESERVATIONS**

Bureau of Indian Affairs

Bureau of Land Management /
Wilderness

Bureau of Reclamation

Department of Defense
(includes Army Corps of Engineers lakes)

Fish and Wildlife Service / Wilderness

Forest Service / Wilderness

National Park Service / Wilderness

Other agencies

Some small sites are not shown, especially in
urban areas.

MILES
0   25   50   75   100
Albers equal area projection

Abbreviations

IR   Indian Reservation
NF   National Forest
NG   National Grassland
NHP   National Historic Park
NRA   National Recreation Area
NWR   National Wildlife Refuge

The *National Atlas of the United States of America*®

U.S. Department of the Interior
U.S. Geological Survey

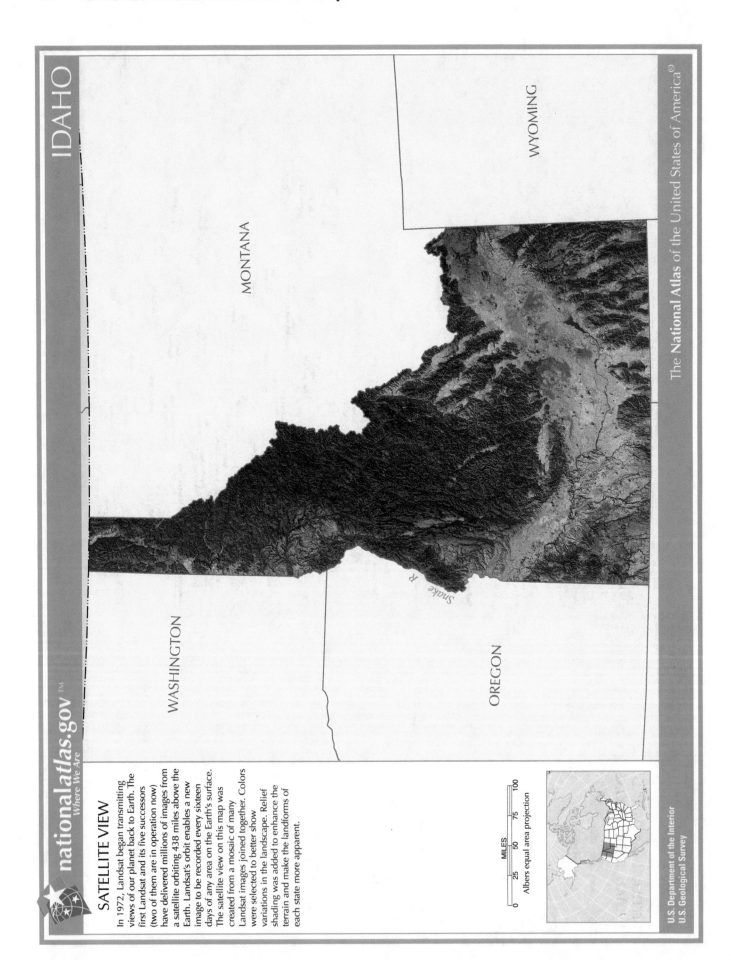

IDAHO

nationalatlas.gov™
Where We Are

SATELLITE VIEW

In 1972, Landsat began transmitting views of our planet back to Earth. The first Landsat and its five successors (two of them are in operation now) have delivered millions of images from a satellite orbiting 438 miles above the Earth. Landsat's orbit enables a new image to be recorded every sixteen days of any area on the Earth's surface. The satellite view on this map was created from a mosaic of many Landsat images joined together. Colors were selected to better show variations in the landscape. Relief shading was added to enhance the terrain and make the landforms of each state more apparent.

WASHINGTON

MONTANA

OREGON

Snake R.

WYOMING

MILES
0   25   50   75   100
Albers equal area projection

U.S. Department of the Interior
U.S. Geological Survey

The **National Atlas** of the United States of America®

Illinois

Topic	Value	Time Period
Total Surface Area (acres)	36,058,700	2007
Land	35,326,200	2007
Federal Land	491,100	2007
Owned	221,650	FY 2009
Leased	3,797	FY 2009
Otherwise Managed	6,002	FY 2009
National Forest	298,000	September 2006
National Wilderness	32,113	October 2011
Non-Federal Land, Developed	3,383,300	2007
Non-Federal Land, Rural	31,451,800	2007
Water	732,500	2007
National Natural Landmarks	18	December 2010
National Historic Landmarks	85	December 2010
National Register of Historic Places	1,715	December 2010
National Parks	1	December 2010
Visitors to National Parks	354,125	2010
Historic Places Documented by the National Park Service	926	December 2010
Archeological Sites in National Parks	19	December 2010
Threatened and Endangered Species in National Parks	0	December 2010
Economic Benefit from National Park Tourism (dollars)	23,166,000	2009
Conservation Reserve Program (acres)	1,024,409	October 2011
Land and Water Conservation Fund Grants (dollars)	155,159,737	Since 1965
Historic Preservation Grants (dollars)	28,315,736	2010
Community Conservation and Recreation Projects	57	Since 1987
Federal Acres Transferred for Local Parks and Recreation	5,059	Since 1948
Crude Petroleum Production (millions of barrels)	9	2010
Crude Oil Proved Reserves (millions of barrels)	66	2009
Natural Gas Reserves (billions of cubic feet)	Not Available	2009
Natural Gas Liquid Reserves (millions of barrels)	Not Available	2008
Natural Gas Marketed Production (billions of cubic feet)	1	2009
Coal Reserves (millions of short tons)	104,222	2009

Sources: U.S. Department of the Interior, National Park Service, State Profiles, December 2010; United States Department of Agriculture, Natural Resources Conservation Service, 2007 National Resources Inventory; U.S. General Services Administration, Federal Real Property Council, FY 2009 Federal Real Property Report, September 2010; University of Montana, www.wilderness.net; U.S. Department of Agriculture, Farm Services Agency, Conservation Reserve Program, October 2011; U.S Census Bureau, 2012 Statistical Abstract of the United States

Illinois Energy Overview and Analysis

Quick Facts

- A central location and well-developed infrastructure make Illinois a key transportation hub for crude oil and natural gas moving throughout North America.
- Illinois typically accounts for roughly one-tenth of total nuclear-powered electricity generation in the United States.
- Illinois leads the Midwest in refining capacity.
- Illinois is one of the top producers of ethanol in the Nation.

Analysis

Resources and Consumption

Illinois estimated recoverable coal reserves rank third in the United States, behind Montana and Wyoming. Coal deposits, as well as smaller deposits of oil and gas, are concentrated in the Illinois Basin, which underlies much of the southern and eastern parts of the State. In addition to fossil fuel reserves, Illinois has high ethanol potential as its production of corn, which is the primary feedstock for U.S. ethanol production, ranks second in the country behind Iowa. Illinois is one of the Nation's top energy-consuming States, primarily due to its large population and high demand from the industrial sector, which includes the energy-intensive aluminum, chemicals, metal casting, petroleum refining, and steel industries.

Petroleum

Illinois is a major crude oil refining State, leading the Midwest in refining capacity. The State has four refineries: two located near Chicago; one in the Illinois suburbs of St. Louis, Missouri; and one in Robinson, near the border with Indiana. Until about 1970, Illinois was among the top oil-producing States, but crude oil production today is minor. Illinois refineries rely on crude oil received mostly from Canada and the U.S. Gulf Coast. Illinois is an important transportation hub for crude oil moving throughout North America, as several major pipeline systems terminate in the State, including the Capline Pipeline system from Louisiana and the Lakehead Pipeline and Express/Platte Pipeline systems from Alberta, Canada.

U.S. imports of heavy crude oil produced from oil sands in Alberta, Canada, have increased rapidly in recent years. Alberta's oil exports to the Midwest have increased so much that they have saturated the regional market, and some pipeline systems that once pumped crude oil north from the Gulf Coast to Illinois refineries have reversed flow to supply growing Canadian imports to Gulf Coast markets.

The Illinois suburbs of St. Louis, Missouri, are required to use motor gasoline specially blended to reduce emissions that contribute to ozone formation during the summer months. The Chicago metropolitan area is required to use reformulated gasoline blended with ethanol to reduce emissions of smog-forming and toxic pollutants. Illinois ranks among the top States in ethanol production capacity, as more than a dozen active and under-construction ethanol plants convert the State's abundant corn resources. The State ranks second behind Minnesota in the number of E85 (an alternative fuel composed of 85 percent ethanol and 15 percent gasoline) fueling stations, with approximately 200. In addition to serving the Chicago market, Illinois ships much of its ethanol output to other markets throughout the country.

Natural Gas

Although Illinois has very little indigenous natural gas production, the State is a major transportation hub for natural gas supply moving through North America. Major natural gas pipeline systems from the U.S. Gulf Coast, U.S. midcontinent regions, and western Canada converge at the Chicago Hub and the ANR Joliet Hub. From there, natural gas is transported to consumption markets in the Midwest and Northeast. In June 2009, a section of the eastern leg of the Rockies Express Pipeline system from Colorado and Wyoming began delivering additional natural gas supply to Illinois. To meet peak demand during the winter, Illinois stores natural gas in natural aquifers and depleted oil or natural gas reservoirs. Underground natural gas storage capacity in Illinois is second only to that of Michigan. The residential sector leads natural gas demand in Illinois, with more than four-fifths of Illinois households relying on the fuel as their primary energy source for home heating.

Coal, Electricity, and Renewables

Although the State's estimated recoverable coal reserves represent more than one-tenth of the U.S. total, only a small fraction of those reserves are located at producing mines. Illinois does not rank among the Nation's top coal producers, due in part to unfavorable geologic conditions and surface development, such as towns and roads, and in part to the fact that Illinois high-sulfur coal is less attractive to electric utilities than low-sulfur western coals. Illinois delivers more than one-half of its coal output to other States, including Indiana, Tennessee, Florida, and Missouri. Illinois also receives coal from other States, particularly Wyoming, and uses that coal to generate electricity.

Illinois is one of the top electricity-generating States in the Nation and a leading net exporter of electricity to other States. Coal and nuclear account for over 95 percent of the electricity generated in Illinois, with an even split between the two fuels. With 11 operating reactors at six nuclear power plants, Illinois ranks first among the States in nuclear generation, and generates more than one-tenth of all the nuclear power in the United States. The growth of the Illinois nuclear industry is due largely to State government initiatives, which began encouraging nuclear power development in the 1950s. The eventual outgrowth of this active interest in nuclear power was the construction of the first privately built commercial nuclear power plant, Dresden 1, which received its operating permit on September 28, 1959. Just over one-tenth of Illinois households use electricity as their primary energy source for home heating.

In August 2007, Illinois adopted a statewide renewable energy standard requiring the State's utilities to produce at least 25 percent of their power from renewable sources by 2025. Seventy-five percent of the electricity used to meet the renewable standard must come from wind; other eligible sources include solar, biomass, and existing hydroelectric power. The law also includes an energy efficiency portfolio standard that requires utilities to implement cost-effective energy efficiency measures to reduce electric usage by 2 percent of demand by 2015.

Source: U.S. Energy Information Administration, October 2009

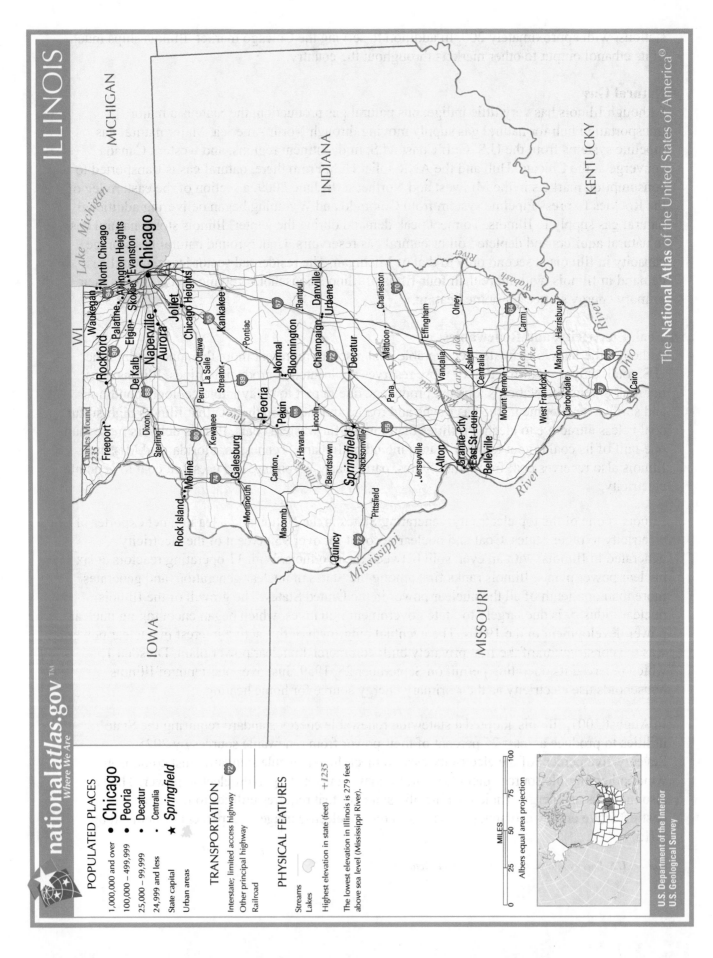

ILLINOIS

MICHIGAN

Lake Michigan

WI

INDIANA

KENTUCKY

IOWA

MISSOURI

Waukegan
North Chicago
Palatine · Arlington Heights
Elgin · Skokie · Evanston
Chicago
Rockford
De Kalb
Naperville
Aurora   Joliet
Chicago Heights
Ottawa   Kankakee
La Salle
Pontiac
Streator
Peru
Kewanee
Peoria   Bloomington
Pekin   Normal
Canton
Havana
Lincoln
Beardstown
Springfield
Jacksonville
Pittsfield

Freeport
Charles Mound
1235
Dixon
Sterling
Rock Island
Moline
Galesburg
Monmouth
Macomb
Quincy

Rantoul   Danville
Champaign   Urbana
Decatur
Pana
Jerseyville
Alton
Granite City
East St.Louis
Belleville

Charleston
Effingham
Mattoon
Vandalia
Salem
Centralia
Mount Vernon
West Frankfort
Carbondale
Cairo

Olney
Carmi
Harrisburg
Marion

Wabash River
Rend Lake
Carlyle Lake
Ohio River
Mississippi River
Illinois River

nationalatlas.gov™
Where We Are

POPULATED PLACES

1,000,000 and over   ● Chicago
100,000 – 499,999   ● Peoria
25,000 – 99,999   ● Decatur
24,999 and less   · Centralia
State capital   ★ Springfield
Urban areas

TRANSPORTATION

Interstate; limited access highway ——⓽⓶
Other principal highway
Railroad

PHYSICAL FEATURES

Streams
Lakes
Highest elevation in state (feet)   +1235

The lowest elevation in Illinois is 279 feet
above sea level (Mississippi River).

MILES
0   25   50   75   100
Albers equal area projection

The **National Atlas** of the United States of America®

U.S. Department of the Interior
U.S. Geological Survey

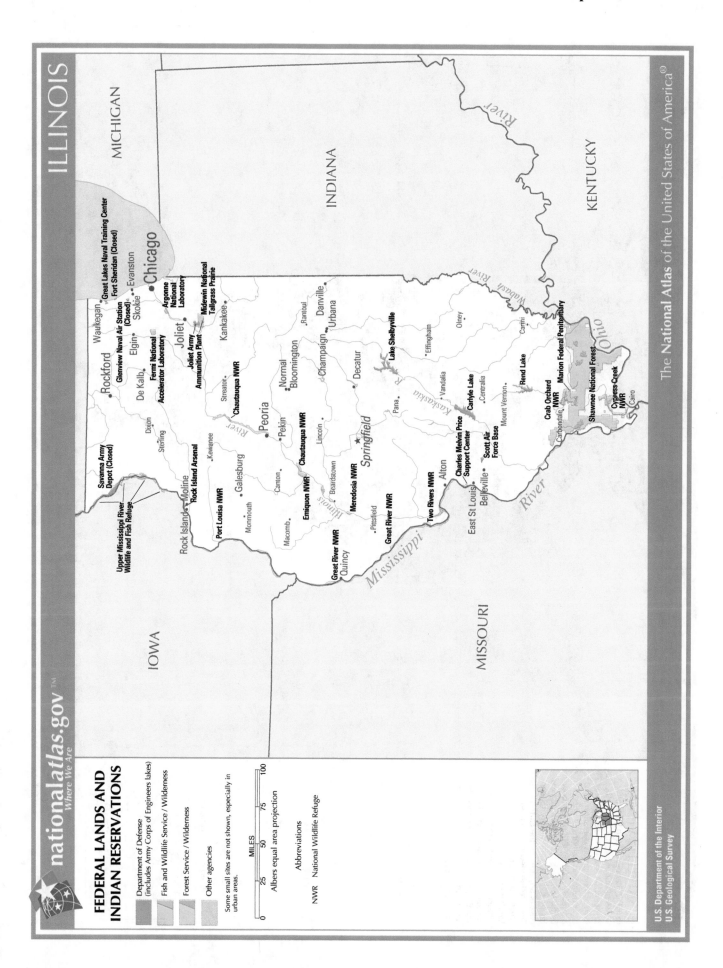

ILLINOIS

MICHIGAN

INDIANA

KENTUCKY

IOWA

MISSOURI

The National Atlas of the United States of America ®

nationalatlas.gov ™
Where We Are

FEDERAL LANDS AND INDIAN RESERVATIONS

Department of Defense
(includes Army Corps of Engineers lakes)

Fish and Wildlife Service / Wilderness

Forest Service / Wilderness

Other agencies

Some small sites are not shown, especially in urban areas.

MILES

0   25   50   75   100

Albers equal area projection

Abbreviations

NWR   National Wildlife Refuge

U.S. Department of the Interior
U.S. Geological Survey

Chicago

Evanston
Skokie

Great Lakes Naval Training Center
Fort Sheridan (Closed)
Glenview Naval Air Station (Closed)

Argonne National Laboratory
Midewin National Tallgrass Prairie

Waukegan

Rockford

Elgin

De Kalb

Fermi National Accelerator Laboratory

Joliet

Joliet Army Ammunition Plant

Kankakee

Dixon

Sterling

Streator

Chautauqua NWR

Peoria

Normal
Bloomington

Pekin

Chautauqua NWR

Lincoln

Danville

Rantoul

Urbana

Champaign

Decatur

Springfield

Lake Shelbyville

Effingham

Olney

Carmi

Rock Island
Moline

Savanna Army Depot (Closed)

Upper Mississippi River Wildlife and Fish Refuge

Rock Island Arsenal

Port Louisa NWR

Galesburg

Kewanee

Canton

Monmouth

Macomb

Emiquon NWR

Meredosia NWR

Great River NWR

Quincy

Beardstown

Pittsfield

Two Rivers NWR

Great River NWR

Alton

Pana

Vandalia

Centralia

Mount Vernon

Charles Melvin Price Support Center

Scott Air Force Base

Carlyle Lake

Rend Lake

Crab Orchard NWR

Marion Federal Penitentiary

Shawnee National Forest

Cypress Creek NWR

Carbondale

Cairo

East St Louis

Belleville

Ohio River

Wabash River

Kaskaskia

Mississippi River

Illinois River

Ohio

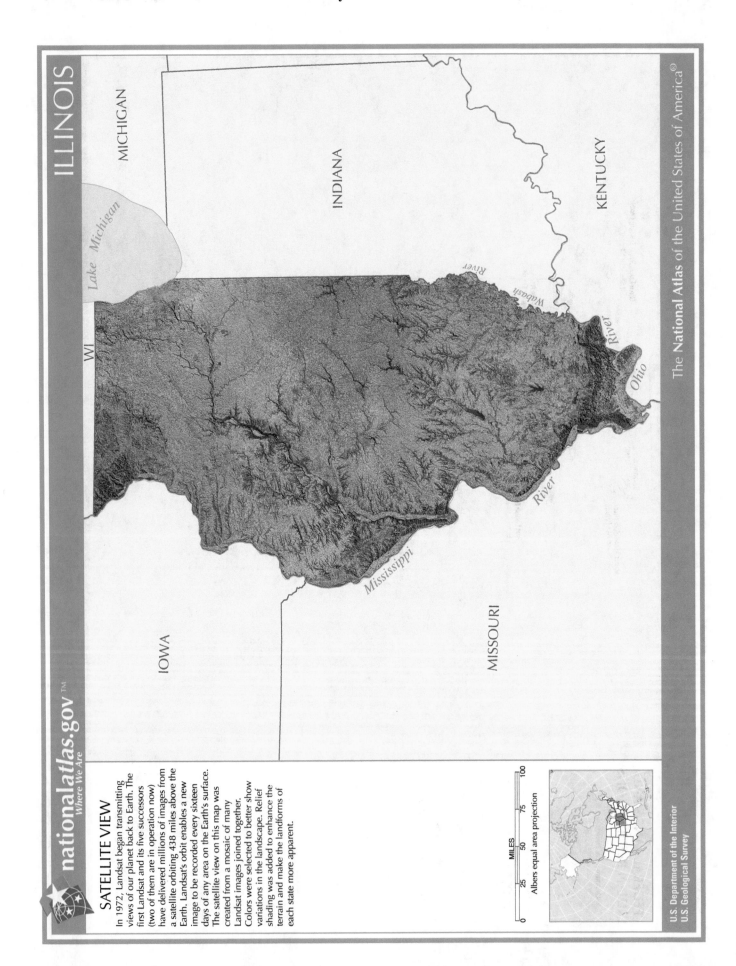

ILLINOIS

MICHIGAN

INDIANA

KENTUCKY

Lake Michigan

WI

IOWA

MISSOURI

Mississippi River

Wabash River

Ohio River

nationalatlas.gov ™
Where We Are

SATELLITE VIEW

In 1972, Landsat began transmitting views of our planet back to Earth. The first Landsat and its five successors (two of them are in operation now) have delivered millions of images from a satellite orbiting 438 miles above the Earth. Landsat's orbit enables a new image to be recorded every sixteen days of any area on the Earth's surface. The satellite view on this map was created from a mosaic of many Landsat images joined together. Colors were selected to better show variations in the landscape. Relief shading was added to enhance the terrain and make the landforms of each state more apparent.

MILES
0   25   50   75   100

Albers equal area projection

The National Atlas of the United States of America ®

U.S. Department of the Interior
U.S. Geological Survey

Indiana

Topic	Value	Time Period
Total Surface Area (acres)	23,158,400	2007
Land	22,785,300	2007
Federal Land	472,400	2007
Owned	239,808	FY 2009
Leased	1,071	FY 2009
Otherwise Managed	1,603	FY 2009
National Forest	203,000	September 2006
National Wilderness	12,463	October 2011
Non-Federal Land, Developed	2,446,000	2007
Non-Federal Land, Rural	19,866,900	2007
Water	373,100	2007
National Natural Landmarks	30	December 2010
National Historic Landmarks	37	December 2010
National Register of Historic Places	1,716	December 2010
National Parks	3	December 2010
Visitors to National Parks	2,395,485	2010
Historic Places Documented by the National Park Service	447	December 2010
Archeological Sites in National Parks	199	December 2010
Threatened and Endangered Species in National Parks	6	December 2010
Economic Benefit from National Park Tourism (dollars)	51,232,000	2009
Conservation Reserve Program (acres)	277,609	October 2011
Land and Water Conservation Fund Grants (dollars)	83,729,854	Since 1965
Historic Preservation Grants (dollars)	20,764,490	2010
Community Conservation and Recreation Projects	41	Since 1987
Federal Acres Transferred for Local Parks and Recreation	12,521	Since 1948
Crude Petroleum Production (millions of barrels)	2	2010
Crude Oil Proved Reserves (millions of barrels)	8	2009
Natural Gas Reserves (billions of cubic feet)	Not Available	2009
Natural Gas Liquid Reserves (millions of barrels)	Not Available	2008
Natural Gas Marketed Production (billions of cubic feet)	5	2009
Coal Reserves (millions of short tons)	9,271	2009

Sources: *U.S. Department of the Interior, National Park Service, State Profiles, December 2010; United States Department of Agriculture, Natural Resources Conservation Service, 2007 National Resources Inventory; U.S. General Services Administration, Federal Real Property Council, FY 2009 Federal Real Property Report, September 2010; University of Montana, www.wilderness.net; U.S. Department of Agriculture, Farm Services Agency, Conservation Reserve Program, October 2011; U.S Census Bureau, 2012 Statistical Abstract of the United States*

Indiana Energy Overview and Analysis

Quick Facts

- The BP Products refinery in Whiting has the largest processing capacity of any refinery outside of the Gulf Coast region.
- Almost all of Indiana's electricity generation is fueled by coal.
- As one of the Nation's top corn-producing States, Indiana has major ethanol production potential.
- Indiana's industrial sector, including aluminum, chemicals, glass, metal casting, and steel, contributes to the State's high total and per capita energy consumption.
- Indiana's first utility-scale wind project was installed in 2008 in Benton County, in the northwestern part of the State.

Analysis

Resources and Consumption

Indiana has moderate coal reserves in the Illinois basin in the southwestern part of the State but relatively few other energy resources. As one of the Nation's top corn-producing States, it has major ethanol production potential. Driven by an energy-intensive industrial sector, Indiana's total and per capita energy consumption are both high. Energy-intensive industries in the State include aluminum, chemicals, glass, metal casting, and steel.

Petroleum

Most of Indiana's oil-refining capacity is located at the BP Products oil refinery in Whiting, just east of Chicago. The Whiting plant has the largest processing capacity of any refinery outside of the Gulf Coast region. Crude oil is produced in southwestern Indiana, but output is minimal, and the Whiting refinery relies heavily on supply from the Gulf Coast region. In September 2006, BP announced plans to invest $3 billion to reconfigure the refinery to process Canadian heavy crude oil, which is increasingly brought to the U.S. Midwest by pipeline from Alberta, where production from oilsands is expanding rapidly. The smaller Countrymark Cooperative refinery in Mount Vernon produces motor and heating fuels for farm, commercial, and residential use, as well as a high grade of diesel fuel used by farmers.

Indiana's total petroleum consumption is high, and the State is one of the top consumers of distillate fuels, including diesel, in the country. Conventional motor gasoline is used throughout most of Indiana. However, reformulated motor gasoline blended with ethanol is required in the northwestern corner of the State, and gasoline formulated to reduce emissions that contribute to ozone formation is required near the southeastern border adjacent to Louisville, Kentucky. Indiana currently has two ethanol plants with several more under construction.

Natural Gas

Although output has expanded in recent years, Indiana's natural gas production remains minimal, and the State's demand is met by deliveries from several major pipelines that carry natural gas from the U.S. Gulf Coast and western Canada. Natural gas consumption is increasing in Indiana and is being met in part by the Rockies Express Pipeline. In June 2009, a section of the eastern leg of the Rockies Express Pipeline system from Colorado and Wyoming began delivering additional natural gas supply to Indiana. Indiana's industrial sector uses about half of the natural gas consumed in the State. The residential sector is the next largest consumer; nearly two-thirds of Indiana households use natural gas as their primary energy source for home heating.

Coal, Electricity, and Renewables
Indiana is a moderate producer of coal. Relatively small coal mines are concentrated in the Illinois basin region of southwestern Indiana. Although their combined output typically amounts to roughly 3 percent of total U.S. coal production, these mines supply only about half of State demand. The remainder is brought in by railcar and river barge primarily from Wyoming, West Virginia, and Illinois. Coal is primarily used in Indiana for electricity generation, although large amounts are also used by the industrial sector. Indiana is a leader in the use of coal in coke plants, which serve the State's steel industry.

Almost all of Indiana's electricity generation is fueled by coal. Natural gas, the next leading fuel for electricity generation in the State, typically supplies less than 5 percent of the market. Although electricity generated from renewable fuels continues to constitute a very small share of Indiana's total generation, production rose dramatically in 2008 when the State's first utility-scale wind project was installed in Benton County. Indiana is a net exporter of electricity, as it produces significantly more than it consumes. Households in Indiana use less electricity than the typical American household, due in part to a heavy reliance on natural gas for home heating during the typically cold winters. Less than one-fourth of Indiana households rely on electricity as their main source of energy for home heating.

Indiana does not have a renewable or alternative energy portfolio standard. However, the State did adopt net metering rules in 2004 for small solar, wind, and hydroelectric projects.

Source: U.S. Energy Information Administration, October 2009

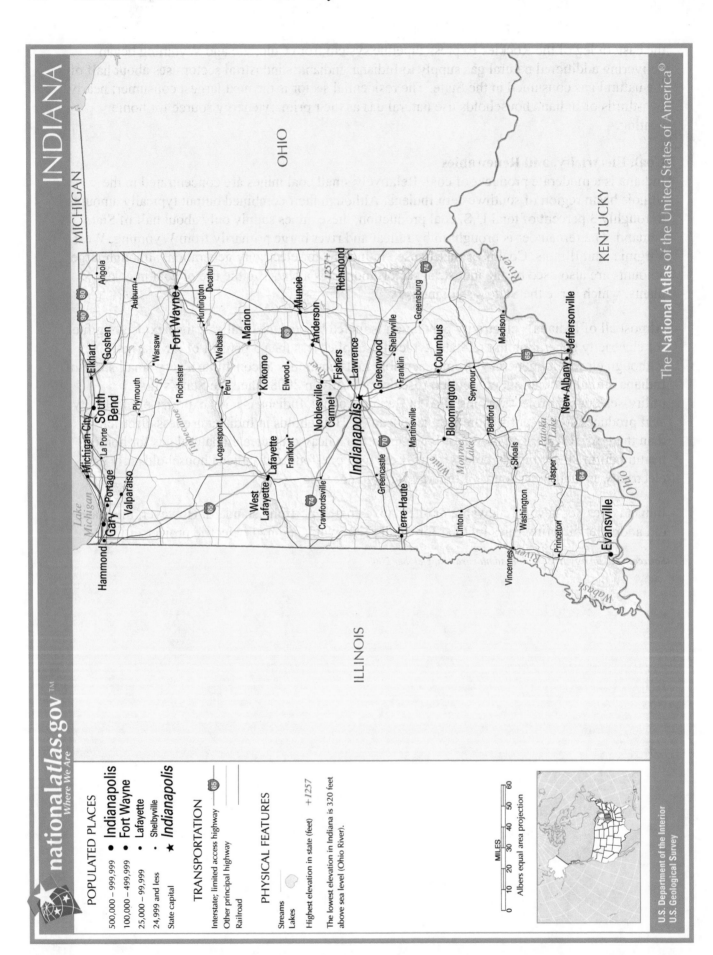

INDIANA

nationalatlas.gov™
Where We Are

POPULATED PLACES

- 500,000 – 999,999 ● Indianapolis
- 100,000 – 499,999 ● Fort Wayne
- 25,000 – 99,999 ● Lafayette
- 24,999 and less • Shelbyville
- State capital ★ *Indianapolis*

TRANSPORTATION

- Interstate; limited access highway [65]
- Other principal highway
- Railroad

PHYSICAL FEATURES

- Streams
- Lakes
- Highest elevation in state (feet) +1257

The lowest elevation in Indiana is 320 feet above sea level (Ohio River).

MILES
0 10 20 30 40 50 60
Albers equal area projection

U.S. Department of the Interior
U.S. Geological Survey

The **National Atlas** of the United States of America®

MICHIGAN

OHIO

KENTUCKY

ILLINOIS

Lake Michigan

Angola
Michigan City
La Porte
Elkhart
Goshen
South Bend
Hammond
Gary
Portage
Valparaiso
Auburn
Decatur
Huntington
Fort Wayne
Warsaw
Plymouth
Rochester
Wabash
Marion
Peru
Kokomo
Logansport
Lafayette
West Lafayette
Frankfort
Muncie
Anderson
Elwood
Noblesville
Fishers
Carmel
Lawrence
Indianapolis
Greenwood
Franklin
Shelbyville
Richmond
Greensburg
Columbus
Madison
Crawfordsville
Greencastle
Terre Haute
Martinsville
Bloomington
Seymour
Bedford
Shoals
Jasper
Jeffersonville
New Albany
Linton
Washington
Princeton
Vincennes
Evansville

Monroe Lake
Patoka Lake
White River
Ohio River
Wabash
Tippecanoe

+1257

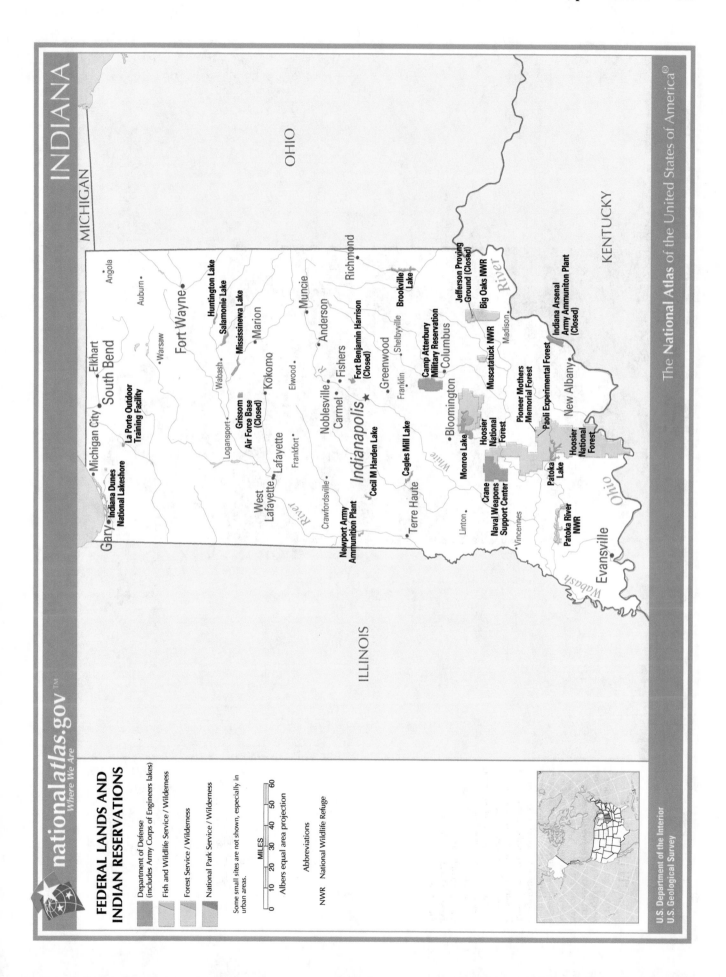

nationalatlas.gov™
Where We Are

FEDERAL LANDS AND INDIAN RESERVATIONS

Department of Defense
(includes Army Corps of Engineers lakes)

Fish and Wildlife Service / Wilderness

Forest Service / Wilderness

National Park Service / Wilderness

Some small sites are not shown, especially in urban areas.

MILES

0 10 20 30 40 50 60

Albers equal area projection

Abbreviations

NWR   National Wildlife Refuge

INDIANA

MICHIGAN

OHIO

ILLINOIS

KENTUCKY

The National Atlas of the United States of America®

U.S. Department of the Interior
U.S. Geological Survey

Angola

Auburn

Fort Wayne

Michigan City

Elkhart

South Bend

Gary

Indiana Dunes
National Lakeshore

La Porte Outdoor
Training Facility

Warsaw

Huntington Lake

Salamonie Lake

Mississinewa Lake

Marion

Muncie

Anderson

Richmond

Wabash

Logansport

Grissom
Air Force Base
(Closed)

Kokomo

Elwood

Lafayette

West
Lafayette

Frankfort

Crawfordsville

Noblesville

Carmel

Fishers

Fort Benjamin Harrison
(Closed)

Greenwood

Shelbyville

Franklin

Brookville
Lake

Jefferson Proving
Ground (Closed)

Big Oaks NWR

Indiana Arsenal
Army Ammuniton Plant
(Closed)

Camp Atterbury
Military Reservation

Columbus

Muscatatuck NWR

Madison

Pioneer Mothers
Memorial Forest

Paoli Experimental Forest

New Albany

Indianapolis

Cecil M Harden Lake

Cagles Mill Lake

Terre Haute

Bloomington

Monroe Lake

Hoosier
National
Forest

Crane
Naval Weapons
Support Center

Patoka
Lake

Hoosier
National
Forest

Linton

Vincennes

Patoka River
NWR

Evansville

Newport Army
Ammunition Plant

River

White

Ohio

Wabash

River

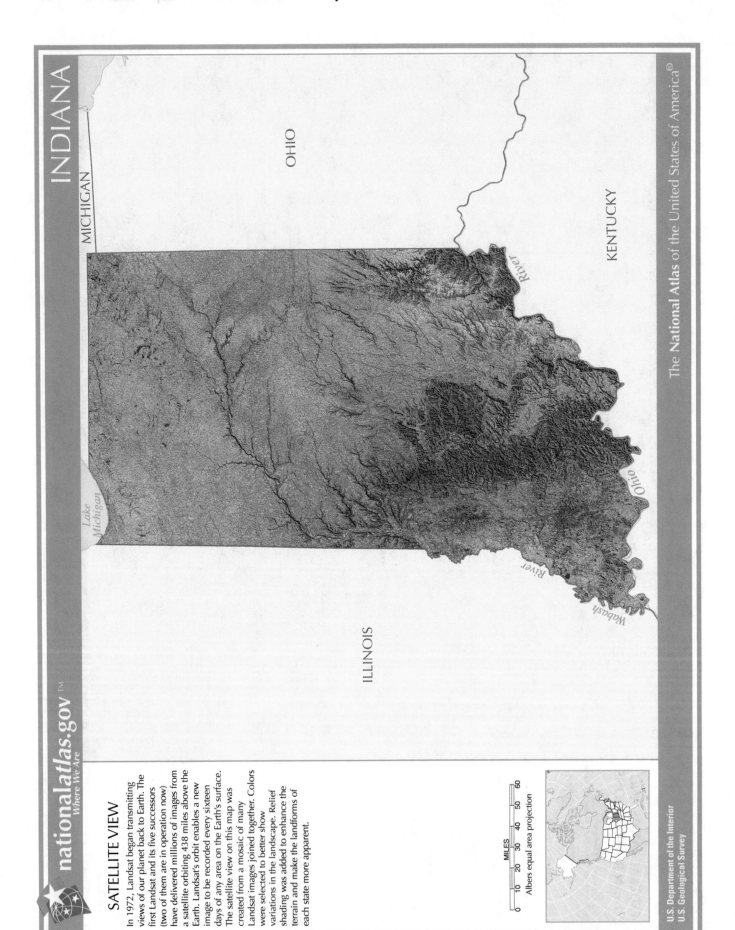

INDIANA

MICHIGAN

OHIO

KENTUCKY

ILLINOIS

Lake Michigan

Ohio River

Wabash River

River

nationalatlas.gov ™
Where We Are

SATELLITE VIEW

In 1972, Landsat began transmitting views of our planet back to Earth. The first Landsat and its five successors (two of them are in operation now) have delivered millions of images from a satellite orbiting 438 miles above the Earth. Landsat's orbit enables a new image to be recorded every sixteen days of any area on the Earth's surface. The satellite view on this map was created from a mosaic of many Landsat images joined together. Colors were selected to better show variations in the landscape. Relief shading was added to enhance the terrain and make the landforms of each state more apparent.

MILES
0   10   20   30   40   50   60
Albers equal area projection

The **National Atlas** of the United States of America ®

U.S. Department of the Interior
U.S. Geological Survey

Iowa

Topic	Value	Time Period
Total Surface Area (acres)	36,016,500	2007
Land	35,530,600	2007
Federal Land	172,400	2007
Owned	225,630	FY 2009
Leased	1,536	FY 2009
Otherwise Managed	2,689	FY 2009
National Forest	0	September 2006
National Wilderness	0	October 2011
Non-Federal Land, Developed	1,892,300	2007
Non-Federal Land, Rural	33,465,900	2007
Water	485,900	2007
National Natural Landmarks	7	December 2010
National Historic Landmarks	24	December 2010
National Register of Historic Places	2,142	December 2010
National Parks	2	December 2010
Visitors to National Parks	222,295	2010
Historic Places Documented by the National Park Service	480	December 2010
Archeological Sites in National Parks	77	December 2010
Threatened and Endangered Species in National Parks	4	December 2010
Economic Benefit from National Park Tourism (dollars)	11,494,000	2009
Conservation Reserve Program (acres)	1,656,057	October 2011
Land and Water Conservation Fund Grants (dollars)	54,145,208	Since 1965
Historic Preservation Grants (dollars)	24,473,390	2010
Community Conservation and Recreation Projects	43	Since 1987
Federal Acres Transferred for Local Parks and Recreation	889	Since 1948
Crude Petroleum Production (millions of barrels)	Not Available	2010
Crude Oil Proved Reserves (millions of barrels)	Not Available	2009
Natural Gas Reserves (billions of cubic feet)	Not Available	2009
Natural Gas Liquid Reserves (millions of barrels)	Not Available	2008
Natural Gas Marketed Production (billions of cubic feet)	Not Available	2009
Coal Reserves (millions of short tons)	2,189	2009

Sources: U.S. Department of the Interior, National Park Service, State Profiles, December 2010; United States Department of Agriculture, Natural Resources Conservation Service, 2007 National Resources Inventory; U.S. General Services Administration, Federal Real Property Council, FY 2009 Federal Real Property Report, September 2010; University of Montana, www.wilderness.net; U.S. Department of Agriculture, Farm Services Agency, Conservation Reserve Program, October 2011; U.S Census Bureau, 2012 Statistical Abstract of the United States

Iowa Energy Overview and Analysis

Quick Facts

- Iowa is the largest producer of ethanol in the United States.
- Heavy use of liquefied petroleum gases (LPG) for agriculture and residential heating contribute to Iowa's disproportionately high consumption of LPG.
- Iowa is a leading State in electricity generation from wind turbines.

Analysis

Resources and Consumption

Iowa has few conventional fossil energy resources but is rich in renewable energy potential. Iowa leads the Nation in production of both corn and ethanol made from corn. The wind power potential harnessed in northwest Iowa places the State among the leading wind producers. The industrial sector leads State energy consumption. Iowa's population is low and its economy is relatively energy intensive, resulting in high per-capita energy consumption.

Petroleum

Iowa relies on petroleum products brought in by pipeline from other States. Total petroleum consumption in Iowa is low and is led by the transportation sector. The State ranks disproportionately high in LPG consumption, due to the heavy use for agricultural purposes and for residential heating.

Iowa grows the most corn of any State in the Nation, and is also the leading producer of ethanol, accounting for approximately one-fourth of the Nation's ethanol supply. Iowa produces over double the ethanol volume of Illinois, the next highest producing State. Iowa has over three dozen operating ethanol plants, with one under construction and several planned expansions to existing plants. Although Iowa's ethanol production is high, consumption is low, in part because Iowa is one of the few States in the Nation that allow the statewide use of conventional motor gasoline. (Most States require the use of specific gasoline blends in non-attainment areas due to air-quality considerations.) Iowa delivers much of its ethanol to U.S. fuel markets that require motor gasoline blended with ethanol. Currently, ethanol must be transported by tanker, truck, or rail but a proposed 1,800-mile pipeline, if built, could deliver ethanol from South Dakota, Iowa, Minnesota, Illinois, Indiana, and Ohio to distribution terminals in the northeastern U.S.

Natural Gas

Natural gas, which supplies nearly one-fifth of the State's energy demand, reaches Iowa through pipelines from Canada via Minnesota and from the Texas and Oklahoma panhandle area that extend to other Midwestern U.S. consumption markets. Iowa ships over three-fourths of the natural gas it receives to Illinois. About two-thirds of Iowa's households use natural gas as their primary home heating fuel. Natural gas is also used to generate a small amount of electricity and to make fertilizer products such as anhydrous ammonia.

Coal, Electricity, and Renewables

Electricity generation and consumption in Iowa are relatively low, and coal-fired plants produce about three fourths of the electricity generated in the State. Due largely to air-quality concerns, approximately nine-tenths of the coal used in Iowa is low-sulfur coal brought in by rail from Wyoming. The State's one nuclear plant, Duane Arnold, is located just northwest of Cedar Rapids and generates roughly one-tenth of the State's electricity. Since 2004, electricity generated from natural gas has increased from less than 2 percent to 6 percent of total generation in Iowa. Wind turbines, primarily located in northwest and north-central Iowa, place Iowa among the leading States in wind power generation, and have helped to increase the share of the State's electricity generated from wind from under 3 percent in 2004 to 6 percent in 2007.

In 1983, Iowa passed the Iowa Alternative Energy Production Law, which requires the State's two investor-owned utilities to generate a total of 105 megawatts of their electricity from renewable-energy sources.

Source: U.S. Energy Information Administration, October 2009

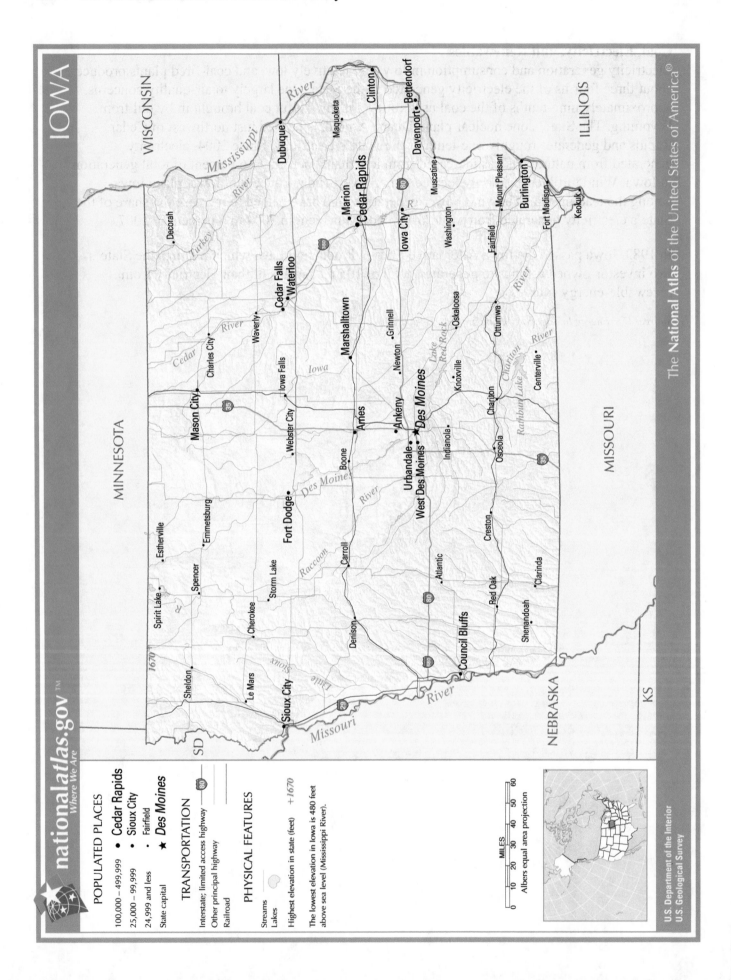

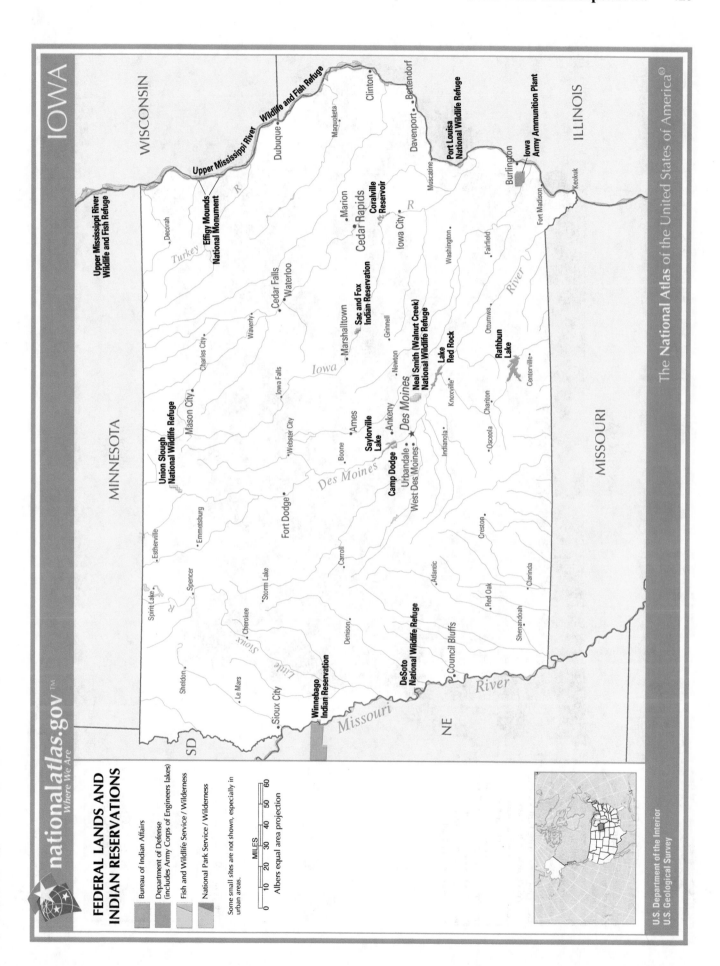

IOWA

WISCONSIN

Upper Mississippi River Wildlife and Fish Refuge

Upper Mississippi River Wildlife and Fish Refuge

Clinton

Davenport • Bettendorf

Port Louisa National Wildlife Refuge

Iowa Army Ammunition Plant

ILLINOIS

Dubuque

Maquoketa

Muscatine

Burlington

Keokuk

Fort Madison

Decorah

Effigy Mounds National Monument

Turkey R

Marion

Cedar Rapids

Coralville Reservoir

Cedar R

Iowa City

Washington

Fairfield

Cedar Falls

Waterloo

Sac and Fox Indian Reservation

Grinnell

Neal Smith (Walnut Creek) National Wildlife Refuge

Lake Red Rock

Rathbun Lake

Ottumwa

Centerville

Charles City

Waverly

Marshalltown

Iowa

Iowa Falls

Newton

Des Moines

Knoxville

Chariton

Osceola

MINNESOTA

Union Slough National Wildlife Refuge

Mason City

Webster City

Ames

Saylorville Lake

Ankeny

Camp Dodge

Urbandale

West Des Moines

Indianola

Boone

Des Moines

Emmetsburg

Estherville

Fort Dodge

Carroll

Atlantic

Creston

Clarinda

Spencer

Storm Lake

Red Oak

Shenandoah

Spirit Lake

Cherokee

Denison

DeSoto National Wildlife Refuge

Council Bluffs

River

Sheldon

Le Mars

Sioux City

Winnebago Indian Reservation

Missouri

SD

NE

MISSOURI

Little Sioux R

WISCONSIN

R

The National Atlas of the United States of America®

U.S. Department of the Interior
U.S. Geological Survey

nationalatlas.gov ™
Where We Are

FEDERAL LANDS AND INDIAN RESERVATIONS

Bureau of Indian Affairs

Department of Defense (includes Army Corps of Engineers lakes)

Fish and Wildlife Service / Wilderness

National Park Service / Wilderness

Some small sites are not shown, especially in urban areas.

MILES

0 10 20 30 40 50 60

Albers equal area projection

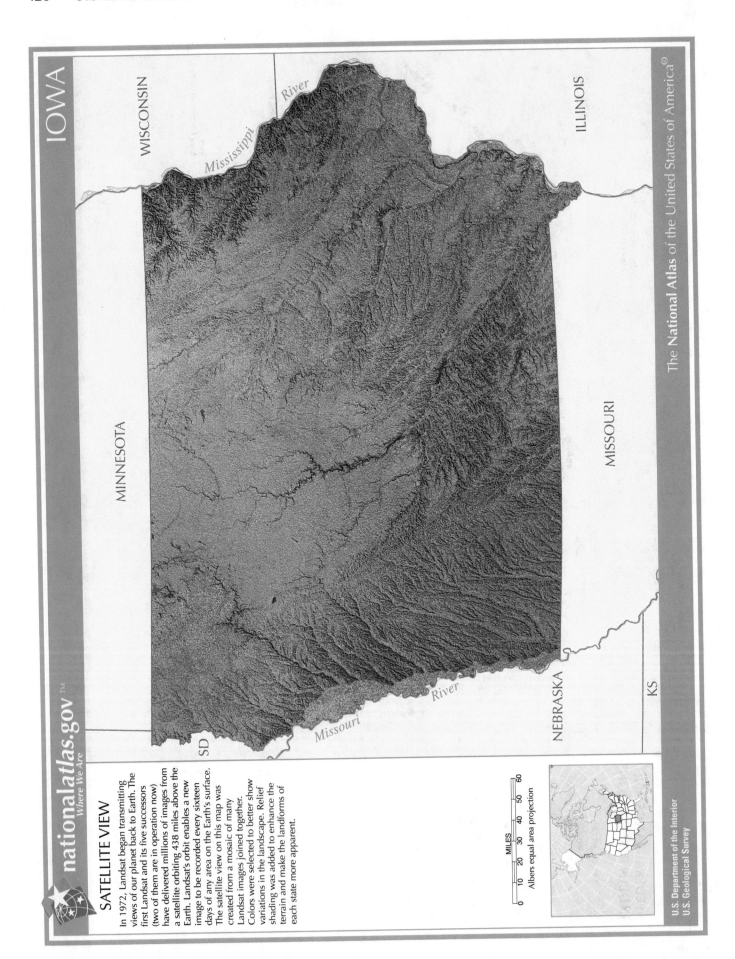

IOWA

nationalatlas.gov ™
Where We Are

SATELLITE VIEW

In 1972, Landsat began transmitting
views of our planet back to Earth. The
first Landsat and its five successors
(two of them are in operation now)
have delivered millions of images from
a satellite orbiting 438 miles above the
Earth. Landsat's orbit enables a new
image to be recorded every sixteen
days of any area on the Earth's surface.
The satellite view on this map was
created from a mosaic of many
Landsat images joined together.
Colors were selected to better show
variations in the landscape. Relief
shading was added to enhance the
terrain and make the landforms of
each state more apparent.

WISCONSIN

MINNESOTA

SD

Mississippi River

ILLINOIS

MISSOURI

NEBRASKA

KS

Missouri River

The National Atlas of the United States of America ®

U.S. Department of the Interior
U.S. Geological Survey

MILES
0   10   20   30   40   50   60

Albers equal area projection

Kansas

Topic	Value	Time Period
Total Surface Area (acres)	52,660,800	2007
Land	52,106,400	2007
Federal Land	504,000	2007
Owned	605,202	FY 2009
Leased	15,932	FY 2009
Otherwise Managed	324	FY 2009
National Forest	108,000	September 2006
National Wilderness	0	October 2011
Non-Federal Land, Developed	2,095,700	2007
Non-Federal Land, Rural	49,506,700	2007
Water	554,400	2007
National Natural Landmarks	5	December 2010
National Historic Landmarks	23	December 2010
National Register of Historic Places	1,233	December 2010
National Parks	5	December 2010
Visitors to National Parks	100,361	2010
Historic Places Documented by the National Park Service	205	December 2010
Archeological Sites in National Parks	21	December 2010
Threatened and Endangered Species in National Parks	2	December 2010
Economic Benefit from National Park Tourism (dollars)	4,337,000	2009
Conservation Reserve Program (acres)	2,536,321	October 2011
Land and Water Conservation Fund Grants (dollars)	50,383,110	Since 1965
Historic Preservation Grants (dollars)	16,253,023	2010
Community Conservation and Recreation Projects	12	Since 1987
Federal Acres Transferred for Local Parks and Recreation	899	Since 1948
Crude Petroleum Production (millions of barrels)	40	2010
Crude Oil Proved Reserves (millions of barrels)	259	2009
Natural Gas Reserves (billions of cubic feet)	3,279	2009
Natural Gas Liquid Reserves (millions of barrels)	181	2008
Natural Gas Marketed Production (billions of cubic feet)	354	2009
Coal Reserves (millions of short tons)	971	2009

Sources: *U.S. Department of the Interior, National Park Service, State Profiles, December 2010; United States Department of Agriculture, Natural Resources Conservation Service, 2007 National Resources Inventory; U.S. General Services Administration, Federal Real Property Council, FY 2009 Federal Real Property Report, September 2010; University of Montana, www.wilderness.net; U.S. Department of Agriculture, Farm Services Agency, Conservation Reserve Program, October 2011; U.S Census Bureau, 2012 Statistical Abstract of the United States*

Kansas Energy Overview and Analysis

Quick Facts

- Kansas ranks among the top 10 States in crude oil production.
- The Anadarko Shelf in southwestern Kansas contains the Hugoton Gas Area, one of the top producing natural gas fields in the United States.
- The Mid-Continent Center, located in Wichita, is a key natural gas supply hub that merges production from several States in the region before piping it east toward major consumption markets.
- Natural gas production from coalbed methane is rapidly expanding in the Cherokee Platform, where reserves have become economically recoverable.
- While Kansas ranks among the top ten wind-producing States in the Nation, renewable energy generation contributes only minimally to the State's electricity supply.

Analysis

Resources and Consumption

Kansas has substantial fossil fuel reserves found in several basins, mostly in the south of the State. The Hugoton Gas Area, in southwestern Kansas, is the fifth largest natural gas field in the United States. Minor reserves of bituminous coal are found in the Cherokee basin in the southeastern corner of the State. In addition to fossil fuel resources, the State's flat plains offer some of the highest wind power potential in the country, and its cornfields offer a major feedstock for ethanol production. The industrial sector leads Kansas's energy consumption.

Petroleum

Kansas is one of the top 10 oil-producing States in the Nation and is a substantial oil-refining State, as well. Crude oil production, which typically represents 2 percent of total U.S. production, takes place throughout the State. A network of pipelines delivers crude oil to the State's three refineries, which account for approximately 2 percent of the Nation's crude oil refining capacity. Kansas's total petroleum product consumption is commensurate with its population, even though use of liquefied petroleum gases (LPG) is disproportionately large While Kansas does not require that motor gasoline sold in the State be blended with ethanol, it does produce a substantial amount of ethanol at several production plants.

Natural Gas

Kansas produces substantial quantities of natural gas, and its infrastructure serves as a transportation hub for supplies moving throughout the country. Natural gas wells and pipelines are concentrated in the Anadarko Shelf in southwest Kansas. Kansas consumes about 85 percent of its natural gas output and transports most of the remainder to Nebraska and Missouri through several major transmission pipelines. Natural gas is also supplied to Kansas by pipelines entering the State from Oklahoma and Colorado. The Mid-Continent Center, located in Wichita, is a key natural gas supply hub that merges production from several States in the region before piping it east toward major consumption markets. Although Kansas's conventional natural gas production has declined by almost a quarter since 2001, the State holds untapped reserves of coalbed methane in its southeastern coal-producing region. Natural gas production from this unconventional resource is rapidly expanding in the Cherokee Platform, where reserves have become economically recoverable. Kansas's active industrial sector consumes over one-half of the natural gas used in the State. Nearly three-fourths of Kansas households use natural gas as their primary energy source for home heating.

Coal, Electricity, and Renewables

Coal-fired power plants supply about three-fourths of the Kansas electricity market, and the single-unit Wolf Creek nuclear plant in Burlington supplies almost all of the remainder. Kansas has two small coal mines in the east. Almost all of the coal used in Kansas's power plants is shipped by railcar from other States, and over four-fifths of this coal comes from Wyoming. Kansas produces a substantial amount of wind energy, ranking among the top ten wind-producing States in the Nation. However, total renewable energy production contributes only minimally to Kansas's electricity supply, providing less than 3 percent of the State's total electricity production. Less than one-fifth of Kansas households rely on electricity as their primary energy source for home heating. In May 2009, Kansas adopted a renewable portfolio standard that requires utilities to acquire one-tenth of their energy from renewable sources by 2011 and one-fifth by 2020.

Source: U.S. Energy Information Administration, October 2009

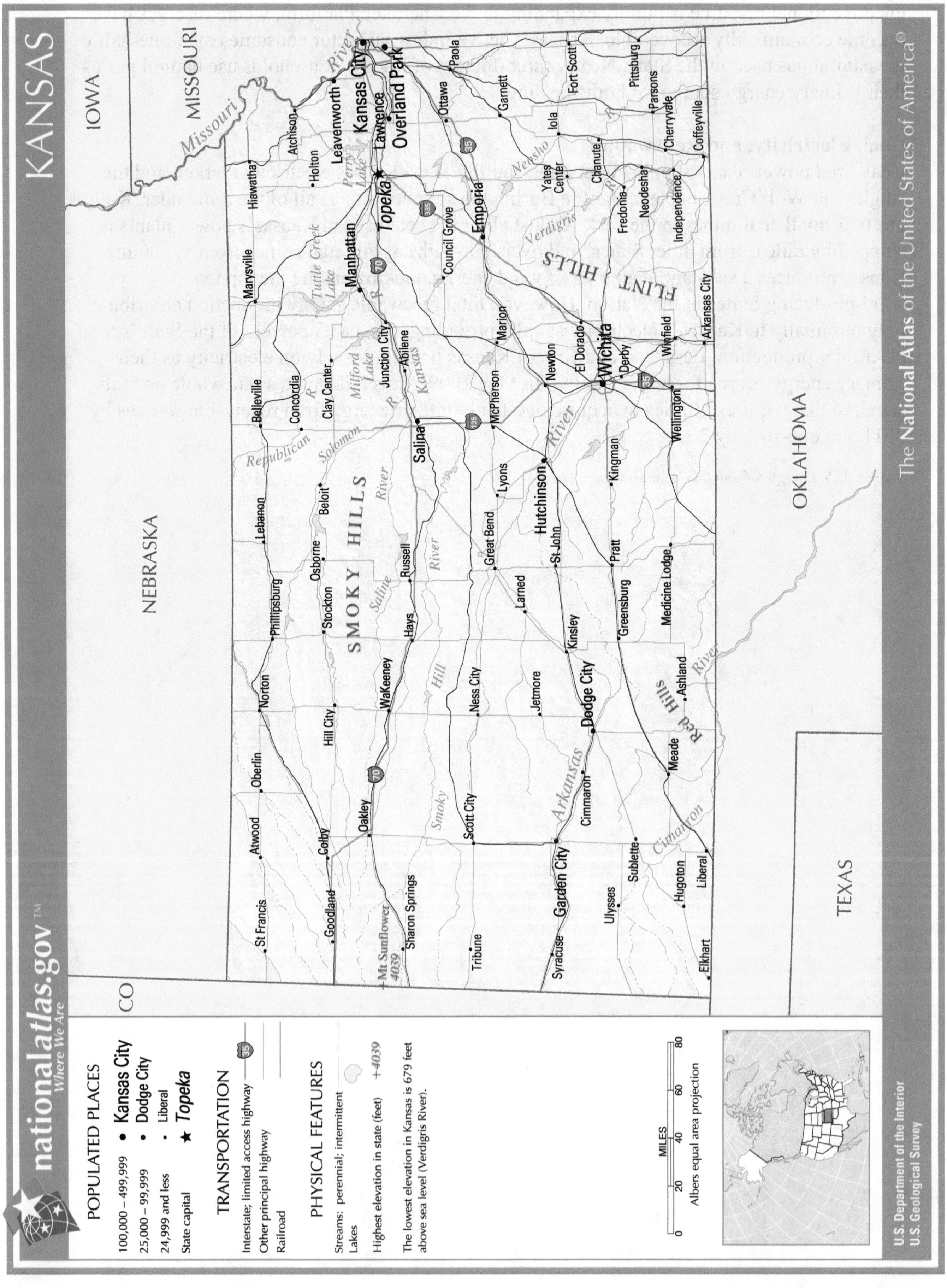

KANSAS
The National Atlas of the United States of America®
nationalatlas.gov™
Where We Are
POPULATED PLACES
100,000 – 499,999 • Kansas City
25,000 – 99,999 • Dodge City
24,999 and less · Liberal
State capital ★ Topeka
TRANSPORTATION
Interstate; limited access highway
Other principal highway
Railroad
PHYSICAL FEATURES
Streams: perennial; intermittent
Lakes
Highest elevation in state (feet) +4039
The lowest elevation in Kansas is 679 feet above sea level (Verdigris River).
MILES
0 20 40 60 80
Albers equal area projection
U.S. Department of the Interior
U.S. Geological Survey
NEBRASKA
IOWA
MISSOURI
OKLAHOMA
TEXAS
CO
SMOKY HILLS
FLINT HILLS
Red Hills
Mt Sunflower 4039
Kansas City
Overland Park
Topeka
Wichita
Lawrence
Leavenworth
Atchison
Manhattan
Junction City
Salina
Hutchinson
Emporia
Dodge City
Garden City
Liberal
Hays
Great Bend
McPherson
Newton
El Dorado
Derby
Winfield
Arkansas City
Wellington
Coffeyville
Independence
Parsons
Pittsburg
Fort Scott
Chanute
Iola
Ottawa
Paola
Garnett
Goodland
Colby
Oakley
WaKeeney
Norton
Phillipsburg
Concordia
Abilene
Pratt
Kingman
Meade
Elkhart
Ulysses
Hugoton
Scott City
Ness City
Syracuse
Tribune
Sharon Springs
St Francis
Missouri River
Arkansas River
Cimarron River
Republican River
Solomon River
Smoky Hill River
Saline River
Verdigris
Neosho

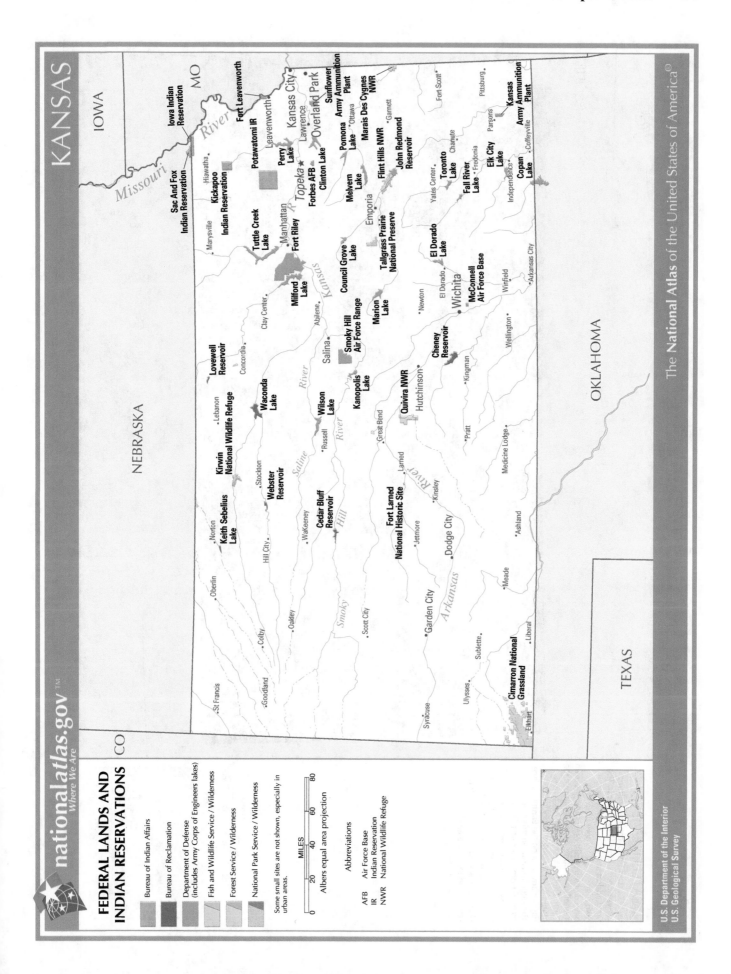

nationalatlas.gov™
Where We Are

FEDERAL LANDS AND INDIAN RESERVATIONS

Bureau of Indian Affairs

Bureau of Reclamation

Department of Defense
(includes Army Corps of Engineers lakes)

Fish and Wildlife Service / Wilderness

Forest Service / Wilderness

National Park Service / Wilderness

Some small sites are not shown, especially in urban areas.

MILES
0   20   40   60   80

Albers equal area projection

Abbreviations

AFB   Air Force Base
IR   Indian Reservation
NWR   National Wildlife Refuge

The **National Atlas** of the United States of America©

U.S. Department of the Interior
U.S. Geological Survey

KANSAS

IOWA

MO

NEBRASKA

CO

OKLAHOMA

TEXAS

Missouri

Iowa Indian Reservation

Sac And Fox Indian Reservation

Kickapoo Indian Reservation

Potawatomi IR

Fort Leavenworth

Leavenworth

Kansas City

Overland Park

Sunflower Army Ammunition Plant

Pomona Lake

Marais Des Cygnes NWR

Kansas Army Ammunition Plant

Hiawatha

Marysville

Tuttle Creek Lake

Perry Lake

Lawrence

Topeka ★

Forbes AFB

Clinton Lake

Melvern Lake

Flint Hills NWR

John Redmond Reservoir

Ottawa

Garnett

Fort Scott

Pittsburg

Coffeyville

Copan Lake

Elk City Lake

Parsons

Fredonia

Independence

Arkansas City

Winfield

Fall River Lake

Toronto Lake

Yates Center

Chanute

El Dorado Lake

El Dorado

Wichita

McConnell Air Force Base

Newton

Emporia

Tallgrass Prairie National Preserve

Council Grove Lake

Smoky Hill Air Force Range

Marion Lake

Manhattan

Fort Riley

Milford Lake

Clay Center

Abilene

Salina

Kanopolis Lake

Wilson Lake

Quivira NWR

Hutchinson

Cheney Reservoir

Kingman

Wellington

Medicine Lodge

Great Bend

Russell

Lovewell Reservoir

Concordia

Waconda Lake

Lebanon

Kirwin National Wildlife Refuge

Stockton

Webster Reservoir

Hill City

Norton

Keith Sebelius Lake

Oberlin

St Francis

Goodland

Colby

Oakley

WaKeeney

Cedar Bluff Reservoir

Fort Larned National Historic Site

Larned

Kinsley

Jetmore

Dodge City

Garden City

Scott City

Meade

Ashland

Liberal

Sublette

Ulysses

Syracuse

Cimarron National Grassland

Elkhart

Pratt

River

Kansas R

Saline River

Smoky Hill River

Arkansas River

Smoky

Missouri River

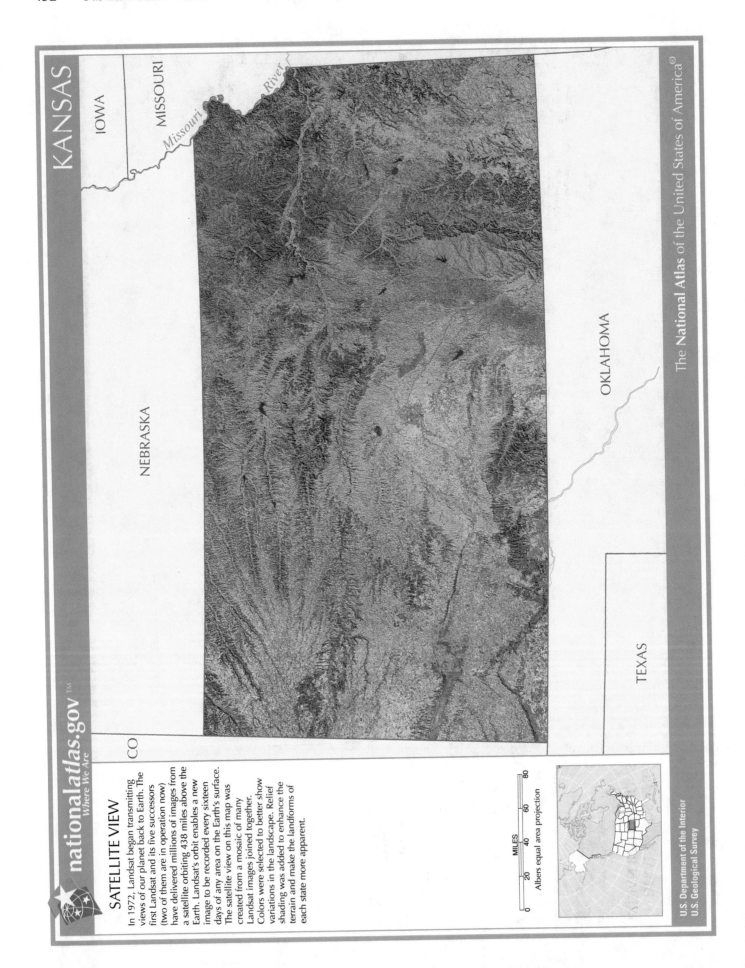

KANSAS

nationalatlas.gov™
Where We Are

SATELLITE VIEW

In 1972, Landsat began transmitting views of our planet back to Earth. The first Landsat and its five successors (two of them are in operation now) have delivered millions of images from a satellite orbiting 438 miles above the Earth. Landsat's orbit enables a new image to be recorded every sixteen days of any area on the Earth's surface. The satellite view on this map was created from a mosaic of many Landsat images joined together. Colors were selected to better show variations in the landscape. Relief shading was added to enhance the terrain and make the landforms of each state more apparent.

IOWA

MISSOURI

Missouri River

NEBRASKA

CO

OKLAHOMA

TEXAS

The **National Atlas** of the United States of America®

MILES
0   20   40   60   80
Albers equal area projection

U.S. Department of the Interior
U.S. Geological Survey

Kentucky

Topic	Value	Time Period
Total Surface Area (acres)	25,863,400	2007
Land	25,232,500	2007
Federal Land	1,295,400	2007
Owned	532,573	FY 2009
Leased	1,472	FY 2009
Otherwise Managed	13,493	FY 2009
National Forest	814,000	September 2006
National Wilderness	18,132	October 2011
Non-Federal Land, Developed	2,093,100	2007
Non-Federal Land, Rural	21,844,000	2007
Water	630,900	2007
National Natural Landmarks	7	December 2010
National Historic Landmarks	30	December 2010
National Register of Historic Places	3,296	December 2010
National Parks	4	December 2010
Visitors to National Parks	1,797,894	2010
Historic Places Documented by the National Park Service	400	December 2010
Archeological Sites in National Parks	1,581	December 2010
Threatened and Endangered Species in National Parks	27	December 2010
Economic Benefit from National Park Tourism (dollars)	76,593,000	2009
Conservation Reserve Program (acres)	335,167	October 2011
Land and Water Conservation Fund Grants (dollars)	58,728,074	Since 1965
Historic Preservation Grants (dollars)	34,033,765	2010
Community Conservation and Recreation Projects	24	Since 1987
Federal Acres Transferred for Local Parks and Recreation	7,498	Since 1948
Crude Petroleum Production (millions of barrels)	3	2010
Crude Oil Proved Reserves (millions of barrels)	20	2009
Natural Gas Reserves (billions of cubic feet)	2,782	2009
Natural Gas Liquid Reserves (millions of barrels)	100	2008
Natural Gas Marketed Production (billions of cubic feet)	113	2009
Coal Reserves (millions of short tons)	29,234	2009

Sources: U.S. Department of the Interior, National Park Service, State Profiles, December 2010; United States Department of Agriculture, Natural Resources Conservation Service, 2007 National Resources Inventory; U.S. General Services Administration, Federal Real Property Council, FY 2009 Federal Real Property Report, September 2010; University of Montana, www.wilderness.net; U.S. Department of Agriculture, Farm Services Agency, Conservation Reserve Program, October 2011; U.S Census Bureau, 2012 Statistical Abstract of the United States

Kentucky Energy Overview and Analysis

Quick Facts

- Kentucky ranks third in the Nation in coal production. It accounts for about one-tenth of U.S. coal production and nearly one-fourth of U.S. production east of the Mississippi River.
- Nearly one-third of all the coal mines in the Nation are found in Kentucky.
- Coal-fired plants typically generate more than nine-tenths of the electricity produced in Kentucky.
- The majority of Kentucky's natural gas is supplied by pipeline from the Gulf Coast.

Analysis

Resources and Consumption

Kentucky has major coal deposits in the eastern Central Appalachian Basin and in the western Illinois Basin. Those basins also hold minor reserves of oil and gas. The Tennessee and Cumberland Rivers in the Ohio River Basin provide hydroelectric power potential. Kentucky's per capita energy consumption is among the highest in the Nation, and the industrial sector leads State energy demand. The State is a leader in the energy-intensive aluminum industry.

Petroleum

Kentucky has minor crude oil production but is host to two refineries, located in Catlettsburg and Somerset. The Catlettsburg refinery is the larger of the two and receives crude oil supply from the Gulf Coast via the Capline Pipeline. The much smaller Somerset refinery processes crude oil produced regionally in Kentucky, Tennessee, and West Virginia. In addition to deliveries from these refineries, Kentucky also receives petroleum product shipments by pipeline and river barge. Kentucky's total petroleum consumption is high relative to its population. The Louisville metropolitan area and the Kentucky suburbs of Cincinnati require reformulated motor gasoline blended with ethanol. Kentucky has two ethanol plants that help supply those areas.

Natural Gas

Kentucky's natural gas production, much of which comes from the Big Sandy field in the eastern part of the State, typically accounts for less than 1 percent of total U.S. natural gas production. The majority of Kentucky's natural gas is supplied by pipeline from the Gulf Coast. Industry is Kentucky's largest natural gas-consuming sector, accounting for about one-half of total natural gas consumption in the State. More than two-fifths of Kentucky households use natural gas as their primary fuel for home heating.

Coal, Electricity, and Renewables

Kentucky is the third largest coal-producing State, after Wyoming and West Virginia. It accounts for roughly one-tenth of total U.S. coal production and nearly one-fourth of U.S. coal production east of the Mississippi River. Although all Kentucky coal is bituminous, its sulfur content varies across the State. Coal produced in the Central Appalachian Basin is low in sulfur, while coal produced in the Illinois Basin is high in sulfur. Nearly one-third of all the coal mines in the Nation are found in Kentucky, more than in any other State. Kentucky has both surface and underground coal mines. Large volumes of coal move into and out of Kentucky by railcar and river barge. Kentucky delivers approximately three fourths of State coal production to more than two dozen States, most of which are on the East Coast and in the Midwest. Nearly 95 percent of the coal used in Kentucky is burned for electricity generation, and most of the remainder is used in industrial and coke plants.

Coal-fired power plants typically account for more than nine-tenths of the electricity produced in Kentucky, making it one of the most coal-dependent States in the Nation. The remaining electricity generation within the State is mostly provided by petroleum-fired and hydroelectric power plants.

Kentucky's per capita consumption of residential electricity is among the highest in the United States. More than two-fifths of Kentucky households use electricity as their primary energy source for home heating.

Source: U.S. Energy Information Administration, October 2009

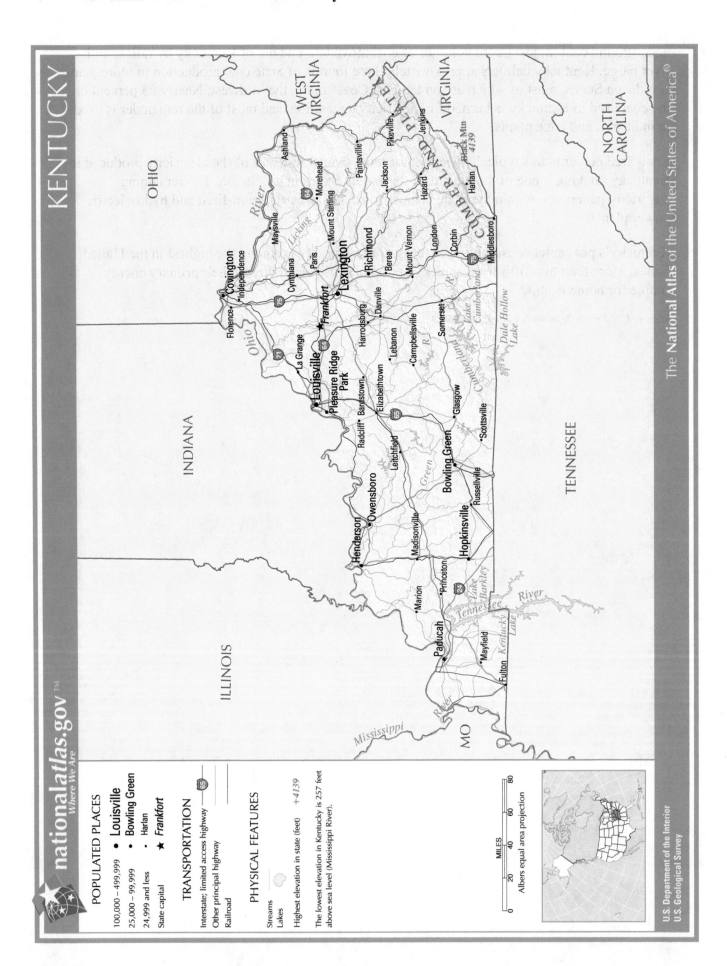

KENTUCKY

nationalatlas.gov™
Where We Are

POPULATED PLACES

100,000 – 499,999   ● Louisville
25,000 – 99,999   ● Bowling Green
24,999 and less   • Harlan
State capital   ★ *Frankfort*

TRANSPORTATION

Interstate; limited access highway
Other principal highway
Railroad

PHYSICAL FEATURES

Streams
Lakes
Highest elevation in state (feet)   +4139

The lowest elevation in Kentucky is 257 feet
above sea level (Mississippi River).

MILES
0   20   40   60   80
Albers equal area projection

U.S. Department of the Interior
U.S. Geological Survey

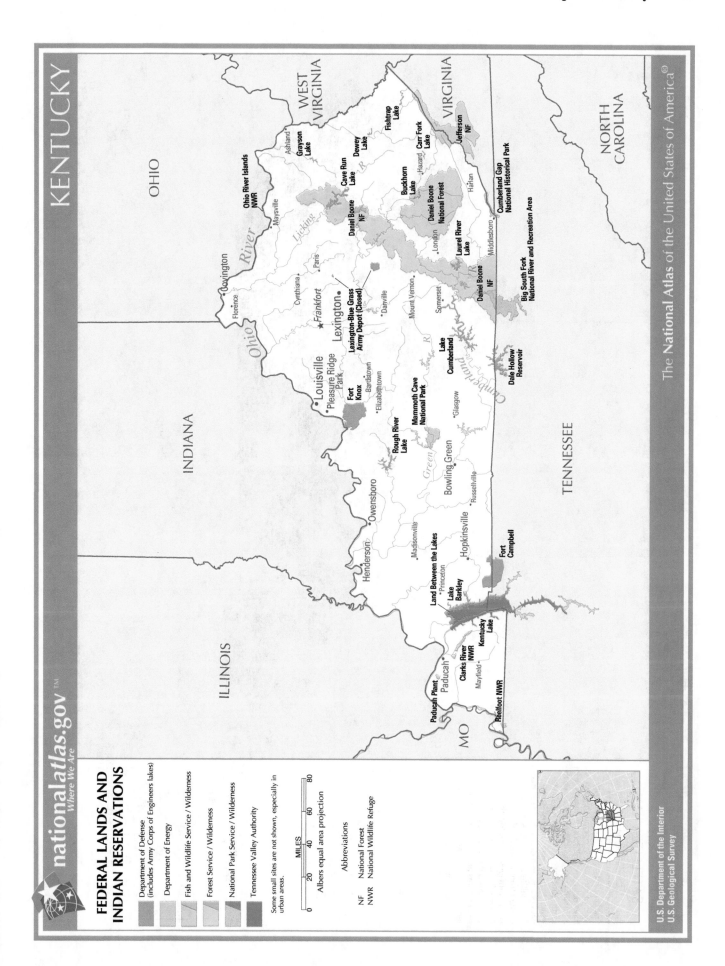

KENTUCKY

nationalatlas.gov™
Where We Are

FEDERAL LANDS AND INDIAN RESERVATIONS

Department of Defense
(includes Army Corps of Engineers lakes)

Department of Energy

Fish and Wildlife Service / Wilderness

Forest Service / Wilderness

National Park Service / Wilderness

Tennessee Valley Authority

Some small sites are not shown, especially in urban areas.

MILES
0   20   40   60   80

Albers equal area projection

Abbreviations

NF   National Forest
NWR   National Wildlife Refuge

The **National Atlas** of the United States of America®

U.S. Department of the Interior
U.S. Geological Survey

OHIO

WEST VIRGINIA

VIRGINIA

NORTH CAROLINA

INDIANA

ILLINOIS

TENNESSEE

MO

Ohio River Islands NWR

Ashland

Grayson Lake

Dewey Lake

Fishtrap Lake

Carr Fork Lake

Jefferson NF

Maysville

Cave Run Lake

Buckhorn Lake

Hazard

Daniel Boone National Forest

Cumberland Gap National Historical Park

Licking

River

Cynthiana

Paris

Daniel Boone NF

Harlan

Laurel River Lake

Middlesboro

London

Daniel Boone NF

Big South Fork National River and Recreation Area

Covington

Florence

Frankfort

Lexington

Lexington-Blue Grass Army Depot (Closed)

Danville

Mount Vernon

Somerset

Ohio

Louisville

Pleasure Ridge Park

Bardstown

Fort Knox

Elizabethtown

Lake Cumberland

Dale Hollow Reservoir

Mammoth Cave National Park

Glasgow

Rough River Lake

Owensboro

Bowling Green

Russellville

Green

Henderson

Madisonville

Hopkinsville

Land Between the Lakes

Princeton

Fort Campbell

Paducah Plant

Paducah

Clarks River NWR

Mayfield

Lake Barkley

Kentucky Lake

Reelfoot NWR

Cumberland

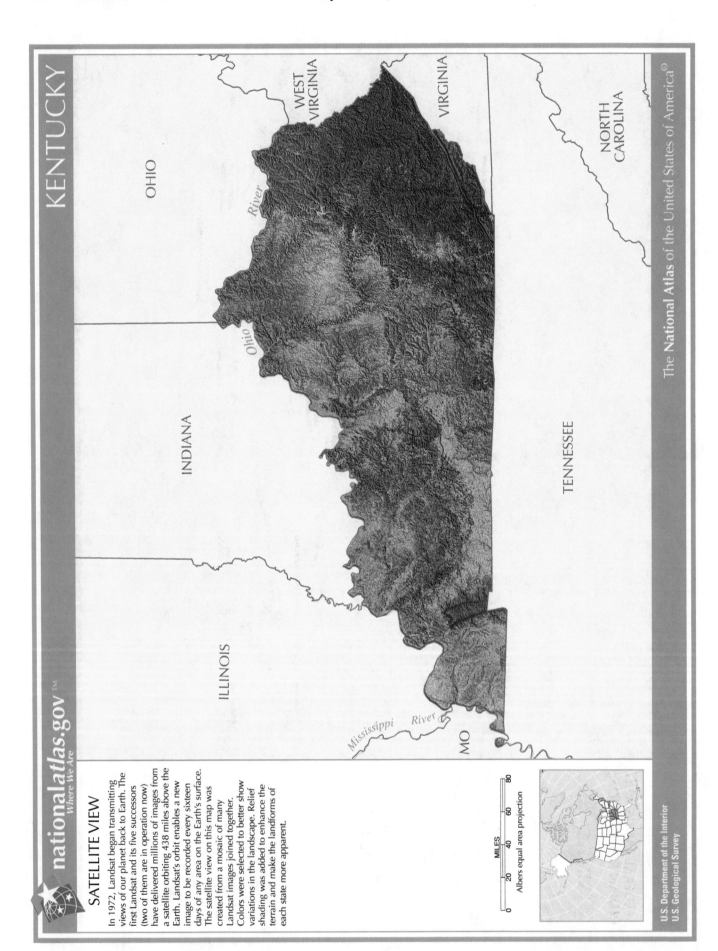

KENTUCKY

SATELLITE VIEW

In 1972, Landsat began transmitting views of our planet back to Earth. The first Landsat and its five successors (two of them are in operation now) have delivered millions of images from a satellite orbiting 438 miles above the Earth. Landsat's orbit enables a new image to be recorded every sixteen days of any area on the Earth's surface. The satellite view on this map was created from a mosaic of many Landsat images joined together. Colors were selected to better show variations in the landscape. Relief shading was added to enhance the terrain and make the landforms of each state more apparent.

OHIO

WEST VIRGINIA

VIRGINIA

NORTH CAROLINA

River

Ohio

INDIANA

TENNESSEE

ILLINOIS

Mississippi   River

MO

MILES

0   20   40   60   80

Albers equal area projection

**U.S. Department of the Interior
U.S. Geological Survey**

The **National Atlas** of the United States of America©

Louisiana

Topic	Value	Time Period
Total Surface Area (acres)	31,376,800	2007
Land	27,452,600	2007
Federal Land	1,310,000	2007
Owned	248,416	FY 2009
Leased	6,348	FY 2009
Otherwise Managed	31,614	FY 2009
National Forest	604,000	September 2006
National Wilderness	17,025	October 2011
Non-Federal Land, Developed	1,862,800	2007
Non-Federal Land, Rural	24,279,800	2007
Water	3,924,200	2007
National Natural Landmarks	0	December 2010
National Historic Landmarks	53	December 2010
National Register of Historic Places	1,346	December 2010
National Parks	5	December 2010
Visitors to National Parks	496,329	2010
Historic Places Documented by the National Park Service	597	December 2010
Archeological Sites in National Parks	90	December 2010
Threatened and Endangered Species in National Parks	3	December 2010
Economic Benefit from National Park Tourism (dollars)	19,869,000	2009
Conservation Reserve Program (acres)	324,938	October 2011
Land and Water Conservation Fund Grants (dollars)	70,723,303	Since 1965
Historic Preservation Grants (dollars)	24,563,495	2010
Community Conservation and Recreation Projects	36	Since 1987
Federal Acres Transferred for Local Parks and Recreation	1,125	Since 1948
Crude Petroleum Production (millions of barrels)	67	2010
Crude Oil Proved Reserves (millions of barrels)	370	2009
Natural Gas Reserves (billions of cubic feet)	20,688	2009
Natural Gas Liquid Reserves (millions of barrels)	300	2008
Natural Gas Marketed Production (billions of cubic feet)	1,549	2009
Coal Reserves (millions of short tons)	Not Available	2009

Sources: *U.S. Department of the Interior, National Park Service, State Profiles, December 2010; United States Department of Agriculture, Natural Resources Conservation Service, 2007 National Resources Inventory; U.S. General Services Administration, Federal Real Property Council, FY 2009 Federal Real Property Report, September 2010; University of Montana, www.wilderness.net; U.S. Department of Agriculture, Farm Services Agency, Conservation Reserve Program, October 2011; U.S Census Bureau, 2012 Statistical Abstract of the United States*

Louisiana Energy Overview and Analysis

Quick Facts

- Louisiana ranks fourth among the States in crude oil production, behind Texas, Alaska, and California (excluding Federal offshore areas, which produce more than any single State).
- The Louisiana Offshore Oil Port (LOOP) is the only port in the United States capable of accommodating deepdraft tankers.
- Two of the U.S. Strategic Petroleum Reserve's four storage facilities are located in Louisiana.
- The Henry Hub is the largest centralized point for natural gas spot and futures trading in the United States, providing access to major markets throughout the country.
- The liquefied natural gas (LNG) import terminal at Sabine is the largest of nine existing LNG import sites in the United States.

Analysis

Resources and Consumption

Louisiana is rich in crude oil and natural gas. Oil and gas deposits are found in abundance both onshore and offshore in State-owned waters. However, the vast majority of Louisiana's crude oil reserves and a large share of its natural gas reserves are found offshore in the Louisiana section of the federally administered Outer Continental Shelf (OCS) in the Gulf of Mexico. The Gulf of Mexico OCS is the largest U.S. oil-producing region, and the Louisiana section, which contains many of the Nation's largest oil fields, holds more than nine-tenths of the crude oil reserves in that region. Including its federally administered reserves, Louisiana's crude oil reserves account for nearly one-fifth of total U.S. oil reserves, and its natural gas reserves account for nearly one-tenth of the U.S. total. Louisiana's fossil fuel resources also include minor deposits of lignite coal, located in the northeastern part of the State.

Louisiana has substantial bioenergy potential in comparison with other States due to its productive agriculture and forestry industries. In particular, fuelwood potential is high in the forested areas of northern Louisiana.Driven largely by its industrial sector, which includes the energy-intensive chemical manufacturing and petroleum refining industries, Louisiana's total and per capita energy consumption rank among the highest in the Nation. Louisiana's industrial energy consumption is second only to that of Texas.

Petroleum

Louisiana is the country's top crude oil producer when production from its section of the federally administered Outer Continental Shelf (OCS) is included. When that production is excluded, Louisiana ranks fourth in the Nation behind Texas, Alaska, and California. Commercial oil production began in Louisiana in the early 20th century, soon after the discovery of the Spindle Top oil field in neighboring Texas. Louisiana's onshore production increased until about 1970, when it peaked at more than 1.35 million barrels per day. Output quickly declined thereafter and has fallen to a little more than one-tenth of the 1970 peak in recent years.

Although drilling had taken place in the lakes, marshes, and bayous of Louisiana since the 1920s, it was not until after World War II that offshore workers, including many returning veterans, began applying new skills and technologies to overcome the challenges of producing oil from beneath the ocean floor. A historical milestone for Louisiana's offshore industry occurred in 1947, when Kerr McGee completed the world's first offshore well out of sight of land. Although Louisiana's State offshore oil production peaked in 1970, the same year as onshore production, Louisiana's production in the federal OCS continued to expand into the 21st century as new offshore technologies allowed companies to access reserves in deeper, more remote areas of the Gulf. Louisiana's OCS production reached a peak in 2002, but experts believe that large new oil deposits remain to be discovered in deepwater areas, and future exploration and production is promising. Louisiana's offshore petroleum industry was dealt a serious blow in 2005 when hurricanes Katrina and Rita damaged offshore oil platforms and curbed production for several months. In 2008, hurricanes Gustav and Ike also caused damage offshore and forced refining and production shutdowns.

Louisiana is also a major importer of crude oil from around the world, typically bringing in about one-fifth of all foreign crude oil processed in the United States. The State receives petroleum supplies at several ports, including the Louisiana Offshore Oil Port (LOOP), the only port in the United States capable of accommodating deepdraft tankers. The LOOP, which began receiving foreign crude oil in 1981 after domestic U.S. production peaked in the 1970s, can import up to 1.2 million barrels per day and is connected through a network of crude oil pipelines to about one-half of U.S. refining capacity. Associated with LOOP are Clovelly Dome, a 40-million-barrel salt cavern storage facility, and the Capline pipeline, which is the largest pipeline system delivering crude oil from the Gulf Coast to the Midwest. Because Louisiana's infrastructure provides multiple connections to the Nation's commercial oil transport network, the U.S. Department of Energy chose the State as a site for two of the Strategic Petroleum Reserve's four storage facilities. The two facilities are located in salt caverns in Bayou Choctaw and West Hackberry.

State crude oil production and imports that are not sent to other States are processed at Louisiana's 16 operating refineries, clustered mostly along the Lower Mississippi River and in the Lake Charles area. With a refining capacity of more than 2.5 million barrels per day, Louisiana produces more petroleum products than any State but Texas. Many of Louisiana's refineries are sophisticated facilities that use additional refining processes beyond simple distillation to yield a larger quantity of lighter, higher value products, such as gasoline. Because of this "downstream" capability, Louisiana refineries often process a wide variety of crude oil types from around the world, including heavier, lower value varieties.

About three-fourths of Louisiana's refined petroleum products are sent to other States for consumption. The Plantation Pipeline, originating near Baton Rouge, supplies much of the South with motor gasoline and distillate fuel. Other major product pipeline systems passing through the State include the Colonial, Centennial, and TEPPCO systems. Petroleum products that are not shipped to other States primarily feed Louisiana's industrial sector, which includes one of the largest petrochemical industries in the Nation. Consequently, Louisiana's total and per capita consumption of petroleum products are among the highest the Nation.

Natural Gas

Louisiana is one of the top natural gas-producing States in the country. Including output from the Louisiana Outer Continental Shelf (OCS), Louisiana ranks second in the Nation in natural gas production. Excluding OCS production, Louisiana ranks fifth. About three-fifths of the State's natural gas production typically takes place in the OCS, although substantial production takes place in the northern and southern parts of the State, as well as offshore in State waters. Louisiana's offshore natural gas platforms were damaged by hurricanes Katrina and Rita in 2005, and production was curbed for several months afterward. In 2008, hurricanes Gustav and Ike also caused damage offshore and forced production shutdowns.

Driven by its industrial sector, Louisiana's natural gas consumption is high, ranking third among the States. Nearly one-half of Louisiana households use natural gas as their primary energy source for home heating. In order to accommodate the State's high demand for natural gas, a new pipeline project has been proposed. The 180-mile Tiger Pipeline would extend from Carthage, Texas, to Perryville, Louisiana, and be complete in 2011.

Louisiana plays an essential role in the movement of natural gas from the U.S. Gulf Coast region to markets throughout the country. Despite high demand from State consumers, Louisiana delivers most of its natural gas production to other States via a vast network of interstate pipelines. Over half of the natural gas that is supplied to Louisiana enters the State via pipelines from Texas. The State also receives, stores, and re-ships natural gas supplies from numerous international sources, including Nigeria, Algeria, and Trinidad and Tobago. Louisiana has four natural gas marketing centers, including the Henry Hub, the most active and publicized natural gas market center in North America. The Henry Hub connects nine interstate and four intrastate pipelines, providing access to markets in the Midwest, Northeast, Southeast, and Gulf Coast. Almost half of all U.S. wellhead production either occurs near the Henry Hub or passes close to the Henry Hub as it moves to downstream markets. The Henry Hub is the delivery point for New York Mercantile Exchange (NYMEX) natural gas futures contracts.

Louisiana has 15 natural gas storage facilities and its storage capacity is among the highest in the Nation. These storage facilities, located in depleted fields and salt caverns, allow Louisiana to store its natural gas production during the summer when national demand is typically low, and quickly ramp up delivery during the winter months when markets across the country require greater volumes of natural gas to meet their home heating needs. Due to the growing use of natural gas for electricity generation in the United States, Louisiana has occasionally withdrawn natural gas from storage during the summer months to help meet peak electricity demand for air-conditioning use.

Louisiana's natural gas production history largely mirrors the State's crude oil timeline, with State production peaking in 1970 and OCS production peaking shortly after the turn of the century. To offset the decline in Louisiana's natural gas supply, which is in demand throughout the country, the State began to supplement indigenous production with foreign imports of liquefied natural gas (LNG). Louisiana contains one offshore and three onshore LNG import terminals, more than any other State in the Nation. Louisiana's first LNG import terminal, located in Lake Charles, came online in 1981 and is the second largest LNG import site in the United States. The largest LNG terminal is located in Sabine, Louisiana, which opened in 2008 and can import up to 2.6 billion cubic feet per day. In addition, several new LNG import facilities along the Louisiana coast have been approved for construction.

Coal, Electricity, and Renewables

Natural gas is Louisiana's leading fuel for electric generation, typically accounting for nearly one-half of electricity produced within the State. Coal, Louisiana's second leading generation fuel, typically accounts for about one-fourth of State electricity production. Louisiana has two coal mines in the northwestern part of the State, which supply lignite coal to the nearby Dolet Hills power plant. Louisiana's remaining coal-fired power plants are supplied with subbituminous coal, almost exclusively from Wyoming. Louisiana's two single-reactor nuclear power plants, both located along the Lower Mississippi River, typically account for almost one-fifth of State generation. Louisiana has some hydroelectric generation but very little electricity production from other renewable energy sources. Wood and wood waste energy sources currently provide Louisiana with about 3 percent of its total electricity production. Louisiana has policies and incentives in place to encourage the use of renewable sources, including energy standards for public buildings.

Louisiana's per capita residential electricity consumption is high, due in part to high demand for air-conditioning during the hot summer months and the widespread use of electricity as the primary energy source for home heating.

Source: U.S. Energy Information Administration, October 2009

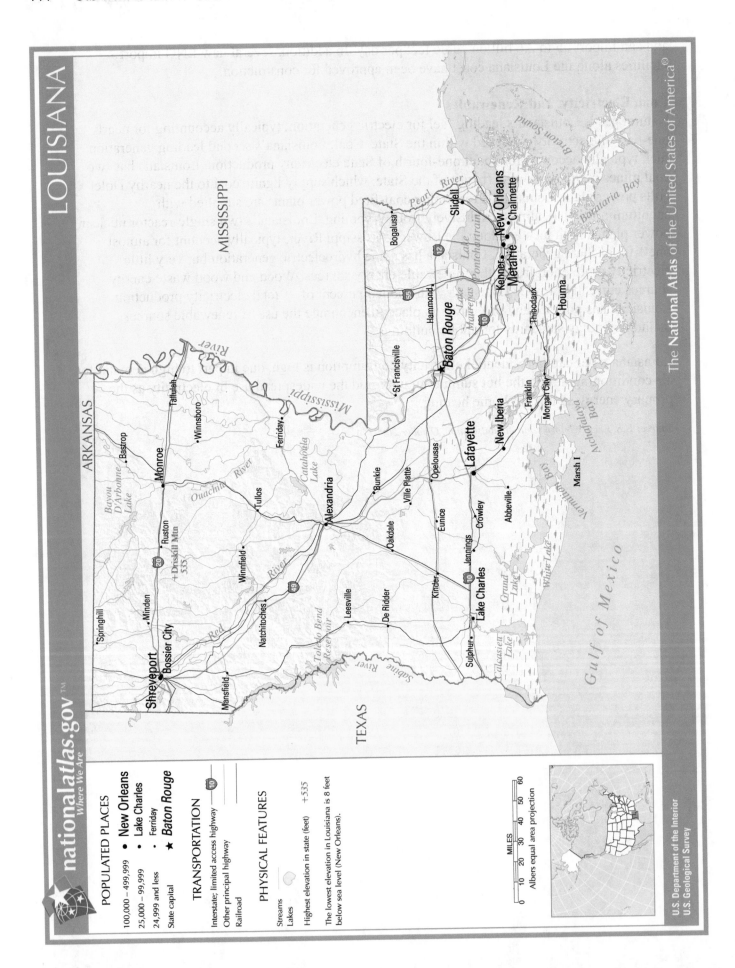

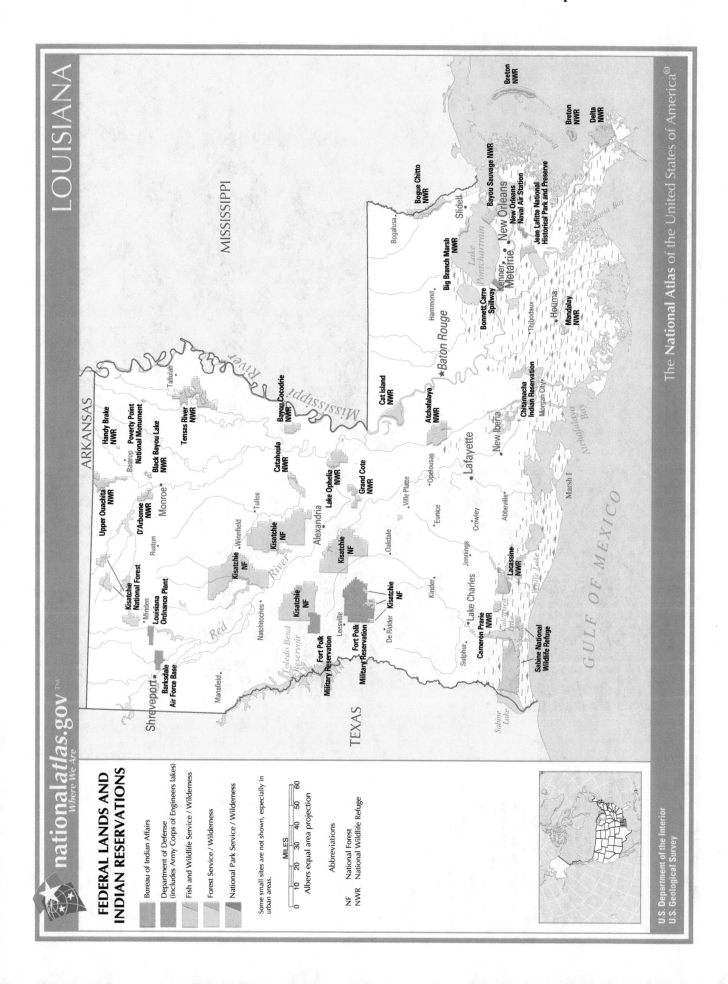

LOUISIANA

nationalatlas.gov™
Where We Are

FEDERAL LANDS AND INDIAN RESERVATIONS

Bureau of Indian Affairs

Department of Defense
(includes Army Corps of Engineers lakes)

Fish and Wildlife Service / Wilderness

Forest Service / Wilderness

National Park Service / Wilderness

Some small sites are not shown, especially in urban areas.

MILES
0 10 20 30 40 50 60
Albers equal area projection

Abbreviations

NF   National Forest
NWR   National Wildlife Refuge

U.S. Department of the Interior
U.S. Geological Survey

The **National Atlas** of the United States of America®

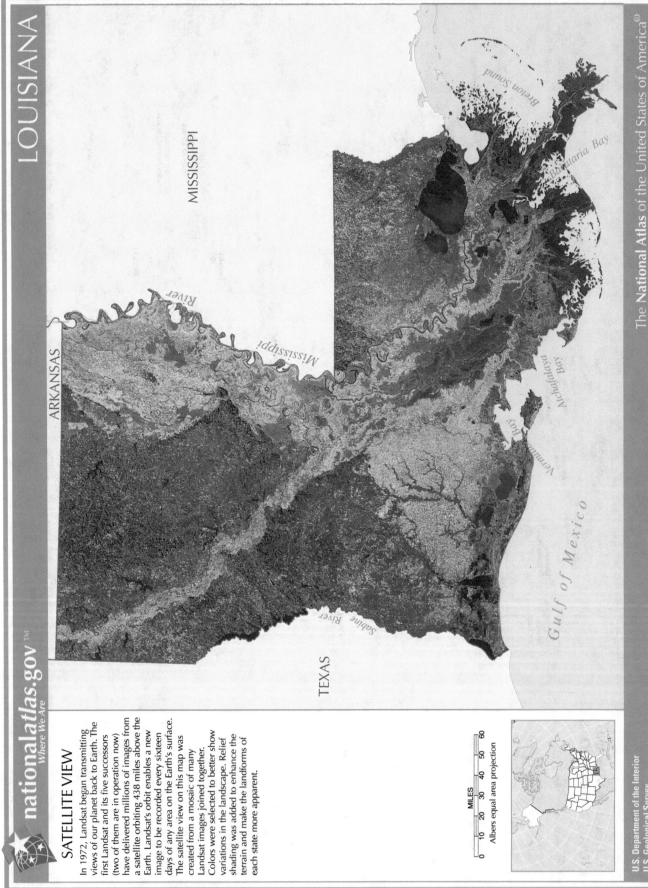

LOUISIANA

SATELLITE VIEW

In 1972, Landsat began transmitting views of our planet back to Earth. The first Landsat and its five successors (two of them are in operation now) have delivered millions of images from a satellite orbiting 438 miles above the Earth. Landsat's orbit enables a new image to be recorded every sixteen days of any area on the Earth's surface. The satellite view on this map was created from a mosaic of many Landsat images joined together. Colors were selected to better show variations in the landscape. Relief shading was added to enhance the terrain and make the landforms of each state more apparent.

ARKANSAS

MISSISSIPPI

TEXAS

Mississippi River

Sabine River

Gulf of Mexico

Vermilion Bay

Atchafalaya Bay

Barataria Bay

Breton Sound

MILES
0   10   20   30   40   50   60
Albers equal area projection

U.S. Department of the Interior
U.S. Geological Survey

The **National Atlas** of the United States of America ®

Maine

Topic	Value	Time Period
Total Surface Area (acres)	20,966,200	2007
Land	19,709,600	2007
Federal Land	207,200	2007
Owned	25,148	FY 2009
Leased	4,606	FY 2009
Otherwise Managed	722,198	FY 2009
National Forest	54,000	September 2006
National Wilderness	18,625	October 2011
Non-Federal Land, Developed	851,100	2007
Non-Federal Land, Rural	18,651,300	2007
Water	1,256,600	2007
National Natural Landmarks	14	December 2010
National Historic Landmarks	41	December 2010
National Register of Historic Places	1,540	December 2010
National Parks	3	December 2010
Visitors to National Parks	2,504,208	2010
Historic Places Documented by the National Park Service	331	December 2010
Archeological Sites in National Parks	204	December 2010
Threatened and Endangered Species in National Parks	2	December 2010
Economic Benefit from National Park Tourism (dollars)	159,106,000	2009
Conservation Reserve Program (acres)	13,573	October 2011
Land and Water Conservation Fund Grants (dollars)	40,472,779	Since 1965
Historic Preservation Grants (dollars)	18,087,441	2010
Community Conservation and Recreation Projects	72	Since 1987
Federal Acres Transferred for Local Parks and Recreation	273	Since 1948
Crude Petroleum Production (millions of barrels)	Not Available	2010
Crude Oil Proved Reserves (millions of barrels)	Not Available	2009
Natural Gas Reserves (billions of cubic feet)	Not Available	2009
Natural Gas Liquid Reserves (millions of barrels)	Not Available	2008
Natural Gas Marketed Production (billions of cubic feet)	Not Available	2009
Coal Reserves (millions of short tons)	Not Available	2009

Sources: *U.S. Department of the Interior, National Park Service, State Profiles, December 2010; United States Department of Agriculture, Natural Resources Conservation Service, 2007 National Resources Inventory; U.S. General Services Administration, Federal Real Property Council, FY 2009 Federal Real Property Report, September 2010; University of Montana, www.wilderness.net; U.S. Department of Agriculture, Farm Services Agency, Conservation Reserve Program, October 2011; U.S Census Bureau, 2012 Statistical Abstract of the United States*

Maine Energy Overview and Analysis

Quick Facts

- The Port of Portland receives crude oil shipments, which it then sends via pipeline to refineries in Quebec and Ontario.
- About three-quarters of Maine's households - the highest share in the Nation - use fuel oil for home heating.
- Maine generates a larger share of its electricity from nonhydroelectric renewable resources than any other State.
- Maine is the only New England State in which industry is the leading energy-consuming sector.
- Maine has the highest wood and wood waste power generation capacity in the United States.

Analysis

Resources and Consumption

Maine has no fossil fuel reserves but has substantial renewable energy potential. The State's numerous rivers, forests, and windy areas provide the potential for hydroelectric, wood-fired, and wind-powered generation. Due to its energy-intensive forest products industry, Maine is the only New England State in which industry is the leading energy-consuming sector.

Petroleum

Coastal ports, including Portland, Searsport, and Calais, receive petroleum products from abroad. Although Maine has no refining capacity, the Port of Portland receives crude oil shipments that it then sends via pipeline to refineries in Quebec and Ontario. Maine's per capita petroleum consumption is high due to the widespread use of fuel oil for home heating during the long, cold winters. About four-fifths of Maine households use fuel oil as their primary energy source for home heating, a higher share than in any other State.

Maine, along with much of the U.S. Northeast, is vulnerable to distillate fuel oil shortages and price spikes during winter months. In January and February 2000, distillate fuel oil prices rose sharply when extreme winter weather increased demand unexpectedly and hindered the arrival of new supply, as frozen rivers and high winds slowed the docking and unloading of barges and tankers. In July 2000, in order to reduce the risk of future shortages, the President directed the U.S. Department of Energy to establish the Northeast Heating Oil Reserve. The Reserve gives Northeast consumers adequate supplies for about 10 days, the time required for ships to carry heating oil from the Gulf of Mexico to New York Harbor. The Reserve's storage terminals are located in Perth Amboy, New Jersey, and Groton and New Haven, Connecticut.

Natural Gas

Maine's per capita natural gas consumption is low and supply is used primarily for electricity generation. Maine receives its natural gas by pipeline mostly from Canada, and ships over one-half of its natural gas receipts to the Boston area via New Hampshire. With the expansion of the Maritimes and Northeast Pipeline and completion of a new LNG facility in New Brunswick, Canada, Maine has increased its supply capabilities to the Northeast markets.

Coal, Electricity, and Renewables

Maine's net electricity generation is among the lowest in the United States. As in several other New England States, natural gas has become the dominant fuel for power generation in Maine; it has accounted for at least 40 percent of generation since 2001. Renewable sources, mainly wood and wood waste and hydroelectric, account for almost half of Maine's net electricity generation. Maine is one of the top U.S. producers of electricity from wood and wood waste. Nonhydroelectric renewable energy sources (including wood and wood waste) account for a larger share of net electricity generation (about one-quarter) in Maine than in any other State. Maine's residential electricity use is low compared with the rest of the Nation, in part because demand for air-conditioning is low during the cool summer months and because few households use electricity as their primary energy source for home heating. In September 1999, Maine's Public Utilities Commission adopted a renewable portfolio standard requiring that at least 30 percent of retail electricity sales come from renewable sources. In June 2006, Maine adopted another renewable portfolio goal to increase renewable energy capacity by 10 percent between September 1, 2005 and 2017. Renewable sources that are used to satisfy the State's new capacity requirement cannot be used to satisfy the Public Utilities Commission's portfolio requirement. Maine made its renewable capacity goal a mandatory target in 2007.

Source: U.S. Energy Information Administration, October 2009

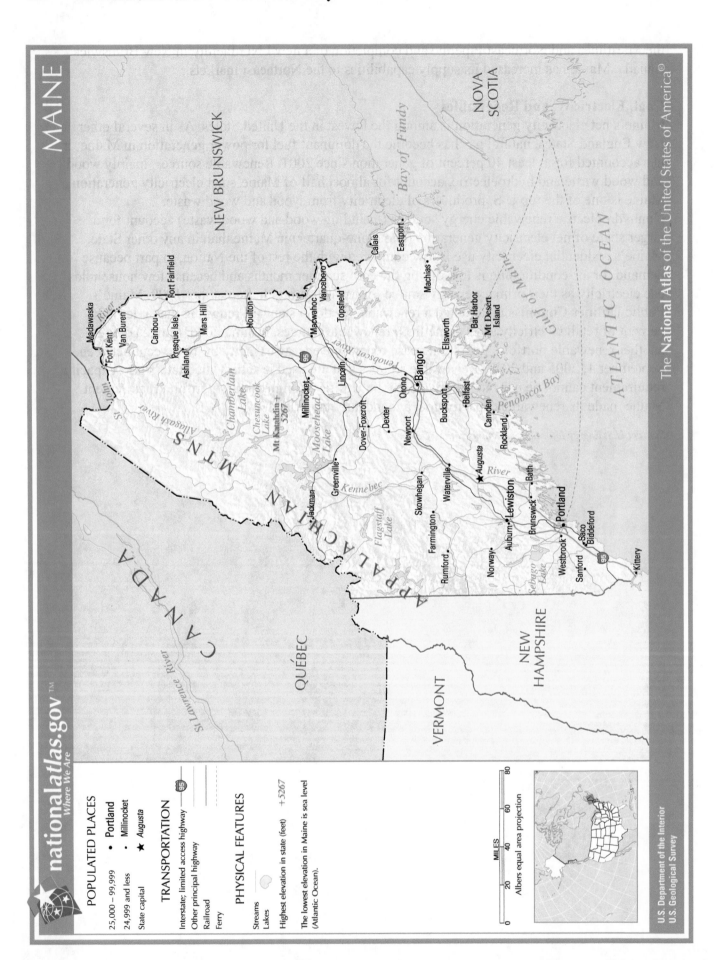

MAINE

MAINE

NEW BRUNSWICK

NOVA SCOTIA

Bay of Fundy

ATLANTIC OCEAN

Gulf of Maine

Madawaska
Fort Kent
Van Buren
Fort Fairfield
Caribou
Presque Isle
Mars Hill
Ashland
Houlton

St. John River

Calais
Eastport
Vanceboro
Macwahoc
Topsfield
Machias

Bar Harbor
Mt Desert
Island
Ellsworth

Chamberlain Lake
Chesuncook Lake
Mt Katahdin + 5267
Millinocket
Moosehead Lake

Penobscot River

Lincoln
Orono
Bangor
Belfast
Bucksport
Penobscot Bay

APPALACHIAN MTNS

Allagash River

Dover-Foxcroft
Dexter
Newport
Camden
Rockland

Greenville
Jackman
Kennebec
Skowhegan
Waterville
Augusta
River
Bath
Brunswick

Flagstaff Lake
Farmington
Rumford
Norway
Auburn
Lewiston
Westbrook
Portland
Saco
Biddeford

Sebago Lake
Sanford
Kittery

CANADA

St Lawrence River

QUÉBEC

VERMONT

NEW HAMPSHIRE

nationalatlas.gov™
Where We Are

The **National Atlas** of the United States of America®

POPULATED PLACES

25,000 – 99,999   ● Portland
24,999 and less   ● Millinocket
State capital   ★ Augusta

TRANSPORTATION

Interstate; limited access highway ——[95]——
Other principal highway
Railroad
Ferry

PHYSICAL FEATURES

Streams
Lakes
Highest elevation in state (feet)   + 5267

The lowest elevation in Maine is sea level
(Atlantic Ocean).

MILES
0   20   40   60   80
Albers equal area projection

U.S. Department of the Interior
U.S. Geological Survey

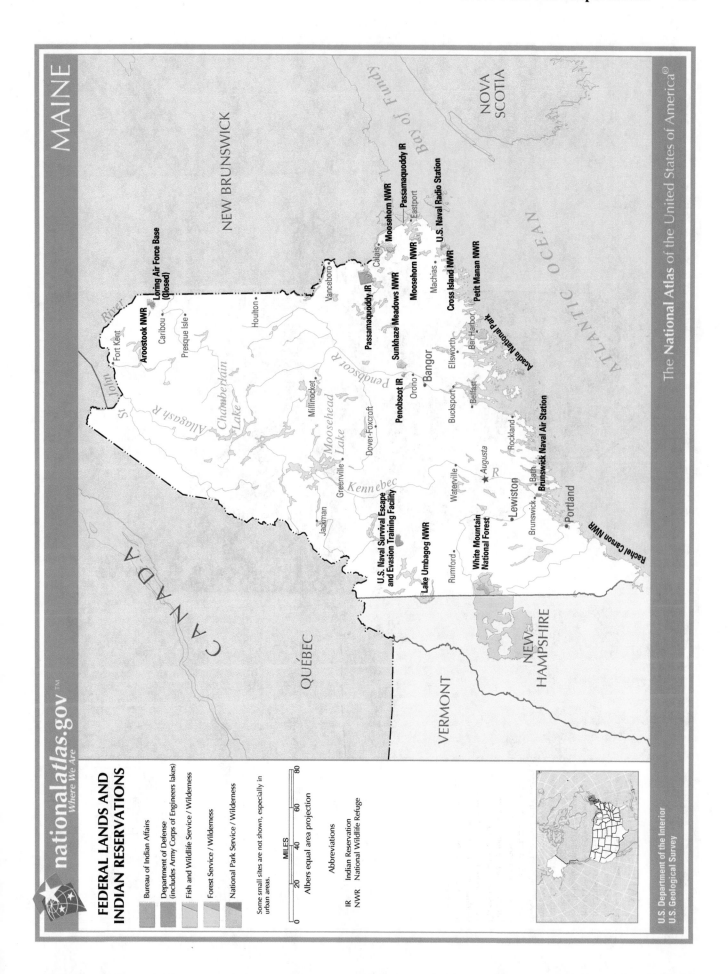

MAINE

nationalatlas.gov™
Where We Are

FEDERAL LANDS AND INDIAN RESERVATIONS

Bureau of Indian Affairs

Department of Defense
(includes Army Corps of Engineers lakes)

Fish and Wildlife Service / Wilderness

Forest Service / Wilderness

National Park Service / Wilderness

Some small sites are not shown, especially in urban areas.

MILES

0   20   40   60   80

Albers equal area projection

Abbreviations

IR   Indian Reservation
NWR   National Wildlife Refuge

NEW BRUNSWICK

NOVA SCOTIA

Bay of Fundy

ATLANTIC OCEAN

The **National Atlas** of the United States of America®

CANADA

QUÉBEC

VERMONT

NEW HAMPSHIRE

St. John River

Fort Kent

Allagash R.

Chamberlain Lake

Caribou

Presque Isle

Loring Air Force Base
(Closed)

Aroostook NWR

Houlton

Vanceboro

Calais

Passamaquoddy IR

Passamaquoddy IR

Moosehorn NWR

Moosehorn NWR

Eastport

Passamaquoddy IR

U.S. Naval Radio Station

Machias

Moosehorn NWR

Sunkhaze Meadows NWR

Cross Island NWR

Petit Manan NWR

Millinocket

Penobscot R.

Moosehead Lake

Dover-Foxcroft

Penobscot IR

Orono

Bangor

Ellsworth

Bar Harbor

Acadia National Park

Greenville

Kennebec

Belfast

Bucksport

Jackman

U.S. Naval Survival Escape
and Evasion Training Facility

Lake Umbagog NWR

Waterville

Rockland

White Mountain
National Forest

Augusta

R

Brunswick Naval Air Station

Rumford

Lewiston

Bath

Brunswick

Portland

Rachel Carson NWR

U.S. Department of the Interior
U.S. Geological Survey

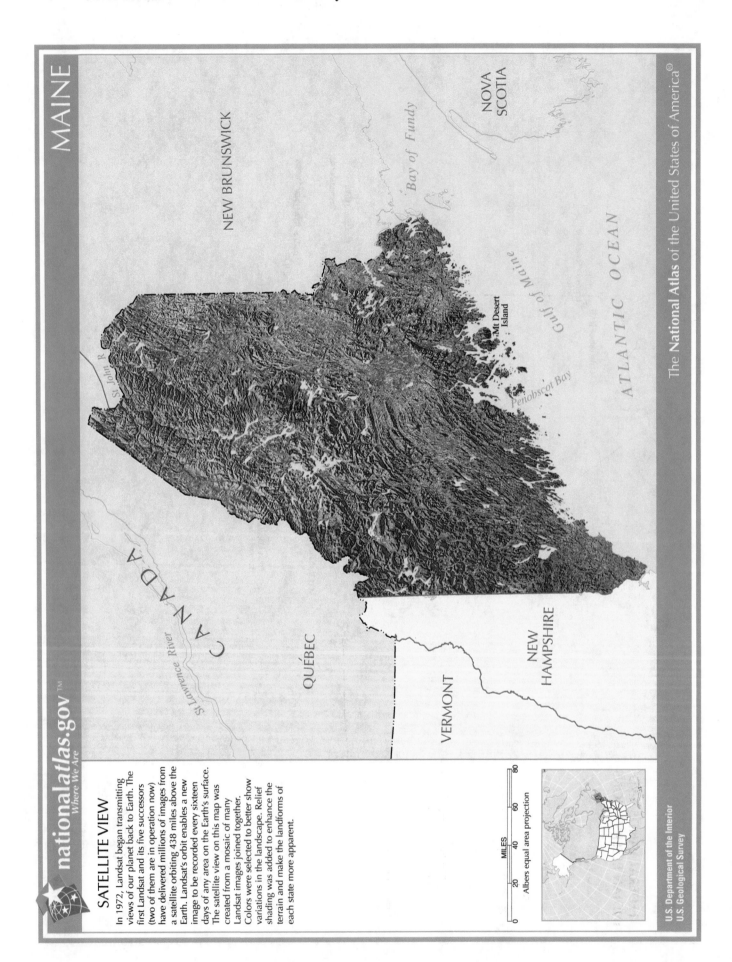

MAINE

MAINE

SATELLITE VIEW

In 1972, Landsat began transmitting views of our planet back to Earth. The first Landsat and its five successors (two of them are in operation now) have delivered millions of images from a satellite orbiting 438 miles above the Earth. Landsat's orbit enables a new image to be recorded every sixteen days of any area on the Earth's surface. The satellite view on this map was created from a mosaic of many Landsat images joined together. Colors were selected to better show variations in the landscape. Relief shading was added to enhance the terrain and make the landforms of each state more apparent.

NEW BRUNSWICK

Bay of Fundy

NOVA SCOTIA

St. John R.

CANADA

St. Lawrence River

QUÉBEC

VERMONT

NEW HAMPSHIRE

Mt Desert Island

Gulf of Maine

Penobscot Bay

ATLANTIC OCEAN

The **National Atlas** of the United States of America®

MILES

0   20   40   60   80

Albers equal area projection

U.S. Department of the Interior
U.S. Geological Survey

Maryland

Topic	Value	Time Period
Total Surface Area (acres)	7,869,900	2007
Land	6,208,300	2007
Federal Land	168,900	2007
Owned	125,613	FY 2009
Leased	1,024	FY 2009
Otherwise Managed	2,280	FY 2009
National Forest	0	September 2006
National Wilderness	0	October 2011
Non-Federal Land, Developed	1,496,700	2007
Non-Federal Land, Rural	4,542,700	2007
Water	1,661,600	2007
National Natural Landmarks	6	December 2010
National Historic Landmarks	71	December 2010
National Register of Historic Places	1,496	December 2010
National Parks	16	December 2010
Visitors to National Parks	3,541,570	2010
Historic Places Documented by the National Park Service	1,572	December 2010
Archeological Sites in National Parks	581	December 2010
Threatened and Endangered Species in National Parks	12	December 2010
Economic Benefit from National Park Tourism (dollars)	155,549,000	2009
Conservation Reserve Program (acres)	76,955	October 2011
Land and Water Conservation Fund Grants (dollars)	78,414,087	Since 1965
Historic Preservation Grants (dollars)	35,077,169	2010
Community Conservation and Recreation Projects	74	Since 1987
Federal Acres Transferred for Local Parks and Recreation	1,513	Since 1948
Crude Petroleum Production (millions of barrels)	Not Available	2010
Crude Oil Proved Reserves (millions of barrels)	Not Available	2009
Natural Gas Reserves (billions of cubic feet)	Not Available	2009
Natural Gas Liquid Reserves (millions of barrels)	Not Available	2008
Natural Gas Marketed Production (billions of cubic feet)	Not Available	2009
Coal Reserves (millions of short tons)	623	2009

Sources: U.S. Department of the Interior, National Park Service, State Profiles, December 2010; United States Department of Agriculture, Natural Resources Conservation Service, 2007 National Resources Inventory; U.S. General Services Administration, Federal Real Property Council, FY 2009 Federal Real Property Report, September 2010; University of Montana, www.wilderness.net; U.S. Department of Agriculture, Farm Services Agency, Conservation Reserve Program, October 2011; U.S Census Bureau, 2012 Statistical Abstract of the United States

Maryland Energy Overview and Analysis

Quick Facts

- Converted natural gas from Maryland's Cove Point liquefied natural gas (LNG) import facility is distributed throughout the Mid-Atlantic and Northeast.
- The Federal Energy Regulation Commission has approved a second LNG terminal to be located in Baltimore County.
- Maryland produces small amounts of coal in the Appalachian Mountains in the western part of the State.
- Maryland requires motor gasoline blended with ethanol across the center of the State, including the Baltimore area and the metropolitan area adjacent to Washington, DC.
- The State's only nuclear plant, the dual-unit Calvert Cliffs facility, supplies more than one-fourth of the electricity generated in the State.

Analysis

Resources and Consumption

Maryland has few energy resources. Minor coal reserves are found in the Appalachian Mountains in western Maryland. Wind power potential is found in the Chesapeake Bay, off the Atlantic Coast, and in the Appalachian Mountains. The Susquehanna River in the north is a source of hydroelectric power. Maryland's economy is not energy-intensive, and per capita energy consumption is low.

Petroleum

Maryland relies on petroleum product deliveries from other States and abroad. The Colonial Pipeline from the Gulf Coast region supplies Maryland markets as it passes through the State on the way to major Northeast population centers. The Port of Baltimore receives petroleum products delivered via the Chesapeake Bay. Maryland requires motor gasoline blended with ethanol across the center of the State, including the Baltimore area and the metropolitan area adjacent to Washington, DC.

Natural Gas

Several major pipelines from the Gulf Coast region supply natural gas to Maryland markets. One of nine U.S. liquefied natural gas (LNG) import facilities is located at Cove Point on the Chesapeake Bay's western shore. The Cove Point terminal receives its LNG supply from Trinidad and Tobago, Egypt, and Norway. The converted natural gas is distributed throughout the Mid-Atlantic and Northeast. Maryland's residential and commercial sectors dominate State natural gas consumption. Nearly one-half of Maryland households use natural gas for home heating.

Coal, Electricity, and Renewables

Maryland's coal-fired power plants typically supply more than one-half of the electricity generation within the State. Power from the State's only nuclear plant, the dual-unit Calvert Cliffs facility, typically supplies more than one-fourth of generation, and petroleum- and natural gas-fired plants supply much of the remainder. Maryland is a minor producer of coal with supplies in the West; most of the State's coal-fired power plants burn coal shipped from West Virginia and Pennsylvania. The Conowingo hydroelectric plant on the Susquehanna River, one of Maryland's largest generation facilities, provides almost all of the State's hydroelectricity. More than one-third of Maryland households use electricity as their main source of energy for home heating.

In April 2008, Maryland accelerated its existing renewable portfolio standard to require that renewable energy sources generate 20 percent of the State's electricity by 2022, with 2 percent of that from solar sources.

Source: U.S. Energy Information Administration, October 2009

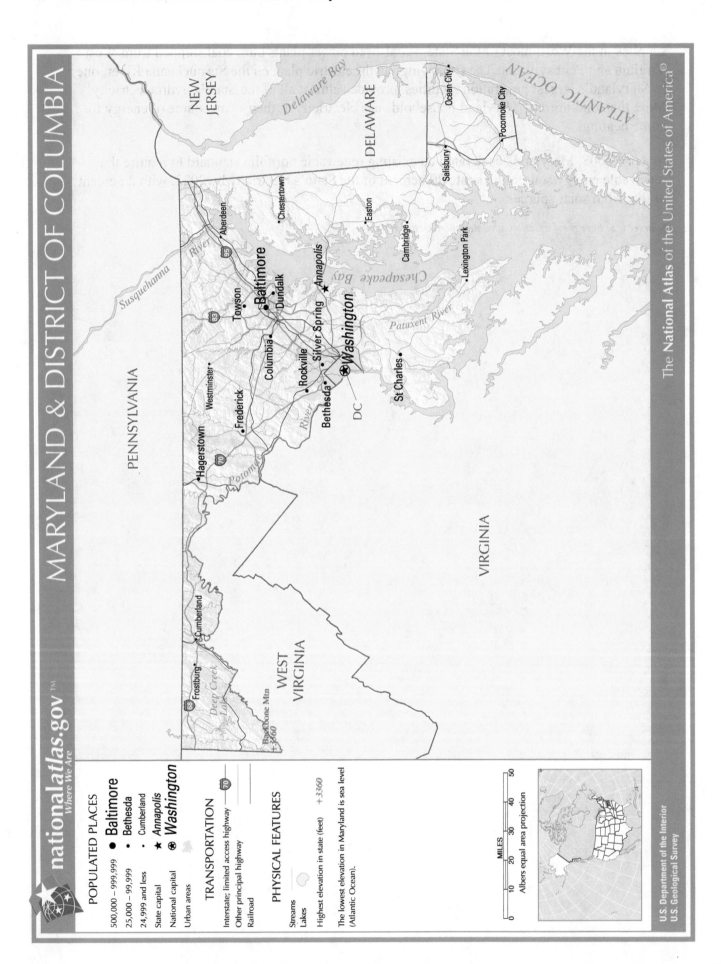

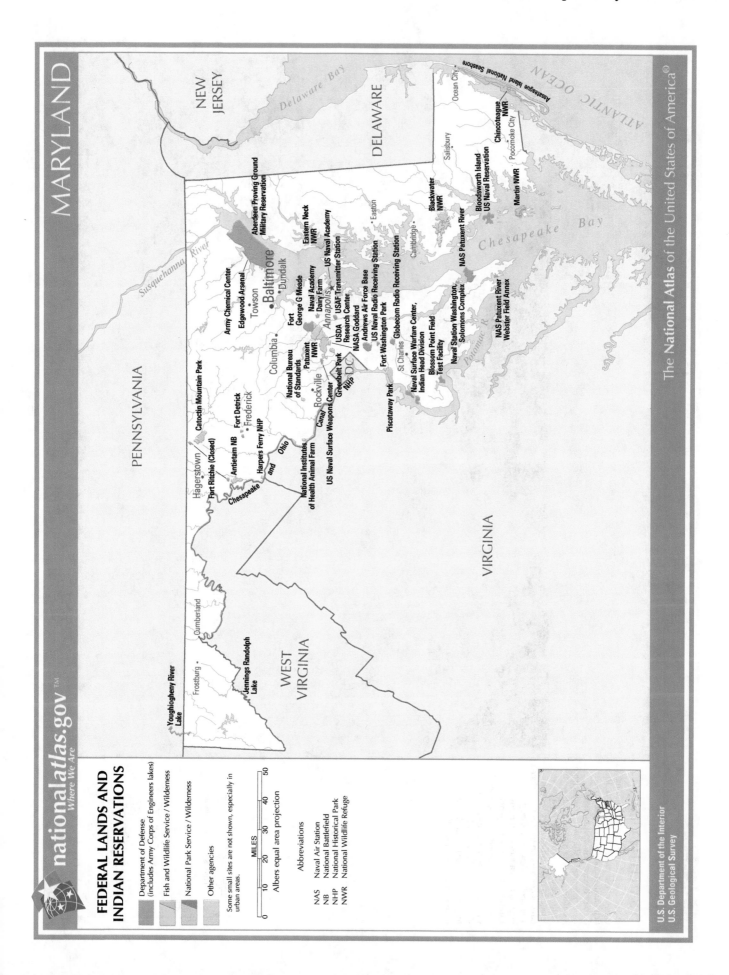

MARYLAND

nationalatlas.gov™
Where We Are

FEDERAL LANDS AND INDIAN RESERVATIONS

Department of Defense
(includes Army Corps of Engineers lakes)

Fish and Wildlife Service / Wilderness

National Park Service / Wilderness

Other agencies

Some small sites are not shown, especially in urban areas.

MILES

0   10   20   30   40   50

Albers equal area projection

Abbreviations

NAS   Naval Air Station
NB   National Battlefield
NHP   National Historical Park
NWR   National Wildlife Refuge

The National Atlas of the United States of America®

U.S. Department of the Interior
U.S. Geological Survey

Map labels

NEW JERSEY
PENNSYLVANIA
WEST VIRGINIA
VIRGINIA
DELAWARE

Delaware Bay
Chesapeake Bay
ATLANTIC OCEAN
Susquehanna River
Potomac R.

Frostburg
Cumberland
Hagerstown
Frederick
Towson
Baltimore
Dundalk
Columbia
Rockville
Annapolis
Easton
Cambridge
Salisbury
Ocean City
Pocomoke City
St Charles

Youghiogheny River Lake
Jennings Randolph Lake
Catoctin Mountain Park
Fort Ritchie (Closed)
Antietam NB
Harpers Ferry NHP
Chesapeake and Ohio Canal
Fort Detrick
National Institutes of Health Animal Farm
US Naval Surface Weapons Center
National Bureau of Standards
Army Chemical Center
Edgewood Arsenal
Aberdeen Proving Ground Military Reservation
Eastern Neck NWR
Fort George G Meade
Naval Academy Dairy Farm
USAF Transmitter Station
US Naval Academy
USDA Research Center
NASA Goddard
Greenbelt Park
Patuxent NWR
Andrews Air Force Base
US Naval Radio Receiving Station
Globecom Radio Receiving Station
Piscataway Park
Fort Washington Park
Naval Surface Warfare Center, Indian Head Division
Blossom Point Field Test Facility
Naval Station Washington, Solomons Complex
NAS Patuxent River
NAS Patuxent River Webster Field Annex
Blackwater NWR
Bloodsworth Island US Naval Reservation
Martin NWR
Chincoteague NWR
Assateague Island National Seashore

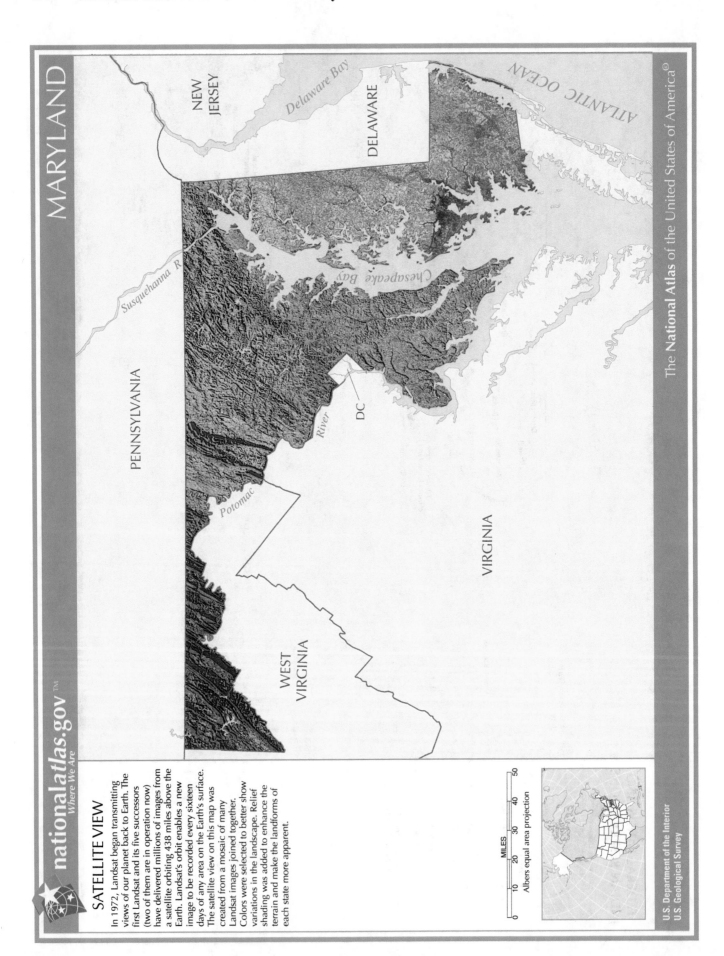

MARYLAND

nationalatlas.gov™
Where We Are

SATELLITE VIEW

In 1972, Landsat began transmitting views of our planet back to Earth. The first Landsat and its five successors (two of them are in operation now) have delivered millions of images from a satellite orbiting 438 miles above the Earth. Landsat's orbit enables a new image to be recorded every sixteen days of any area on the Earth's surface. The satellite view on this map was created from a mosaic of many Landsat images joined together. Colors were selected to better show variations in the landscape. Relief shading was added to enhance the terrain and make the landforms of each state more apparent.

NEW JERSEY

Delaware Bay

DELAWARE

ATLANTIC OCEAN

Susquehanna R.

Chesapeake Bay

PENNSYLVANIA

DC

River

Potomac

VIRGINIA

WEST VIRGINIA

MILES

0   10   20   30   40   50

Albers equal area projection

The **National Atlas** of the United States of America®

U.S. Department of the Interior
U.S. Geological Survey

Massachusetts

Topic	Value	Time Period
Total Surface Area (acres)	5,339,000	2007
Land	4,972,400	2007
Federal Land	97,100	2007
Owned	57,888	FY 2009
Leased	23,119	FY 2009
Otherwise Managed	831	FY 2009
National Forest	0	September 2006
National Wilderness	3,244	October 2011
Non-Federal Land, Developed	1,716,400	2007
Non-Federal Land, Rural	3,158,900	2007
Water	366,600	2007
National Natural Landmarks	11	December 2010
National Historic Landmarks	185	December 2010
National Register of Historic Places	4,161	December 2010
National Parks	15	December 2010
Visitors to National Parks	9,913,501	2010
Historic Places Documented by the National Park Service	1,629	December 2010
Archeological Sites in National Parks	440	December 2010
Threatened and Endangered Species in National Parks	11	December 2010
Economic Benefit from National Park Tourism (dollars)	384,992,000	2009
Conservation Reserve Program (acres)	10	October 2011
Land and Water Conservation Fund Grants (dollars)	97,519,236	Since 1965
Historic Preservation Grants (dollars)	42,037,690	2010
Community Conservation and Recreation Projects	54	Since 1987
Federal Acres Transferred for Local Parks and Recreation	6,781	Since 1948
Crude Petroleum Production (millions of barrels)	Not Available	2010
Crude Oil Proved Reserves (millions of barrels)	Not Available	2009
Natural Gas Reserves (billions of cubic feet)	Not Available	2009
Natural Gas Liquid Reserves (millions of barrels)	Not Available	2008
Natural Gas Marketed Production (billions of cubic feet)	Not Available	2009
Coal Reserves (millions of short tons)	Not Available	2009

Sources: *U.S. Department of the Interior, National Park Service, State Profiles, December 2010; United States Department of Agriculture, Natural Resources Conservation Service, 2007 National Resources Inventory; U.S. General Services Administration, Federal Real Property Council, FY 2009 Federal Real Property Report, September 2010; University of Montana, www.wilderness.net; U.S. Department of Agriculture, Farm Services Agency, Conservation Reserve Program, October 2011; U.S Census Bureau, 2012 Statistical Abstract of the United States*

Massachusetts Energy Overview and Analysis

Quick Facts

- With the start-up of a second offshore liquefied natural gas (LNG) import facility in March 2010, Massachusetts now has three LNG import terminals that serve markets in the Northeast. The third terminal is an onshore facility located in Everett.
- Massachusetts is one of the few States that require the statewide use of reformulated motor gasoline blended with ethanol.
- Massachusetts is a leading source of electricity generated from landfill gas and municipal solid waste.
- Massachusetts is the only New England State that relies significantly on coal-fired power plants, with coal accounting for one-fourth of electricity generation.
- A proposed 420-megawatt wind power project in Nantucket Sound could become the Nation's first offshore wind farm.
- Massachusetts received $25 million in 2009 from the U.S. Department of Energy for the development of the Nation's first large commercial-scale Wind Technology Testing Center, which will be able to test blades longer than 50 meters.

Analysis

Resources and Consumption

Massachusetts has no fossil fuel reserves but does possess substantial renewable energy resources. The State's Atlantic coast in the east and the Berkshire Mountains in the west offer considerable wind power potential, and much of the State is covered in dense forest, offering potential fuel wood resources. Massachusetts is one of the most densely populated States in the Nation. Per capita energy consumption is low and the Massachusetts economy is one of the least energy-intensive in the Nation. The transportation and residential sectors lead State energy consumption.

Petroleum

Petroleum products are shipped into Massachusetts by barge, primarily to the Boston Harbor. In addition, two small-capacity product pipelines run from ports in Connecticut and Rhode Island to Springfield, Massachusetts. Massachusetts is one of a handful of States that require the statewide use of reformulated motor gasoline blended with ethanol.

Massachusetts, along with much of the U.S. Northeast, is vulnerable to distillate fuel oil shortages and price spikes during winter months due to high demand for home heating. Nearly two-fifths of Massachusetts households use fuel oil as their primary energy source for home heating. In January and February 2000, distillate fuel oil prices in the Northeast rose sharply when extreme winter weather increased demand unexpectedly and hindered the delivery of new supply, as frozen rivers and high winds slowed the docking and unloading of barges and tankers. In July 2000, in order to reduce the risk of future shortages, the President directed the U.S. Department of Energy to establish the Northeast Heating Oil Reserve. The Reserve gives Northeast consumers adequate supplies for about 10 days, the time required for ships to carry heating oil from the Gulf of Mexico to New York Harbor. The Reserve's storage terminals are located in Perth Amboy, New Jersey, and Groton and New Haven, Connecticut.

Natural Gas

Electric power generators and the residential sector are the leading consumers of natural gas in Massachusetts. More than two-fifths of Massachusetts households use natural gas as their primary energy source for home heating. The State's natural gas is supplied by pipeline from production areas in the U.S. Gulf Coast and Canada, from natural gas storage sites in the Appalachian Basin region, which includes parts of New York, Pennsylvania, and Ohio, and from other international sources, including Trinidad. The gas is supplied by pipelines entering the State from New York, Rhode Island, and New Hampshire. Like other New England States, Massachusetts has no natural gas storage sites and must rely on the Appalachian Basin storage capacity to supply peak demand in winter. Massachusetts also imports some of its natural gas from overseas via liquefied natural gas (LNG) import terminals near Boston. The onshore Everett facility and 2 offshore facilities are 3 of 10 existing LNG import terminals in the United States.

Coal, Electricity, and Renewables

Before the mid-1990s, petroleum-fired power plants led electricity production in Massachusetts. However, this source has declined steadily since 1991, as State power producers have reduced use of petroleum in favor of cleaner-burning natural gas. As in other New England States, this switch has been driven by the benefits of the lower emission levels of natural gas compared with other fossil fuels and the ease of siting new natural gas-fired power plants. Today, natural gas-fired power plants are the State's leading power producers, accounting for over half of net generation. Coal, transported largely from Colorado and West Virginia, is the State's second leading generation fuel, typically accounting for about one-fourth of net electricity production. The Pilgrim nuclear power plant located in Plymouth on Cape Cod Bay also contributes to the Massachusetts grid.

Residential electricity use is lower in Massachusetts than the national average, in part because demand for air-conditioning is minimal during the mild summer months, and because few households use electricity as their primary energy source for home heating.

Although renewable energy makes only a small contribution to net electricity generation, Massachusetts has several hydroelectric facilities and is one of the Nation's major producers of electricity from landfill gas and municipal solid waste. In July 2008, Massachusetts adopted a renewable portfolio standard requiring renewable energy to account for 15 percent of total electricity generation by 2020 and 25 percent by 2030. Regulations covering the leasing, siting, permitting, and building of wind turbines and other renewable energy sources in Federal waters could allow a proposed 420-megawatt wind power project to be built in Nantucket Sound, to become the Nation's first offshore wind farm. However, the high-profile project faces significant opposition from area landowners. In May 2009, the U.S. Department of Energy awarded Massachusetts $25 million in funding to accelerate development of the State's Wind Technology Testing Center that will test commercial-sized wind turbine blades to help reduce cost, improve technical advancements, and speed deployment of the next generation of wind turbine blades into the marketplace. This center will be the first commercial large-blade test facility in the United States able to test blades longer than 50 meters.

Source: U.S. Energy Information Administration, October 2009

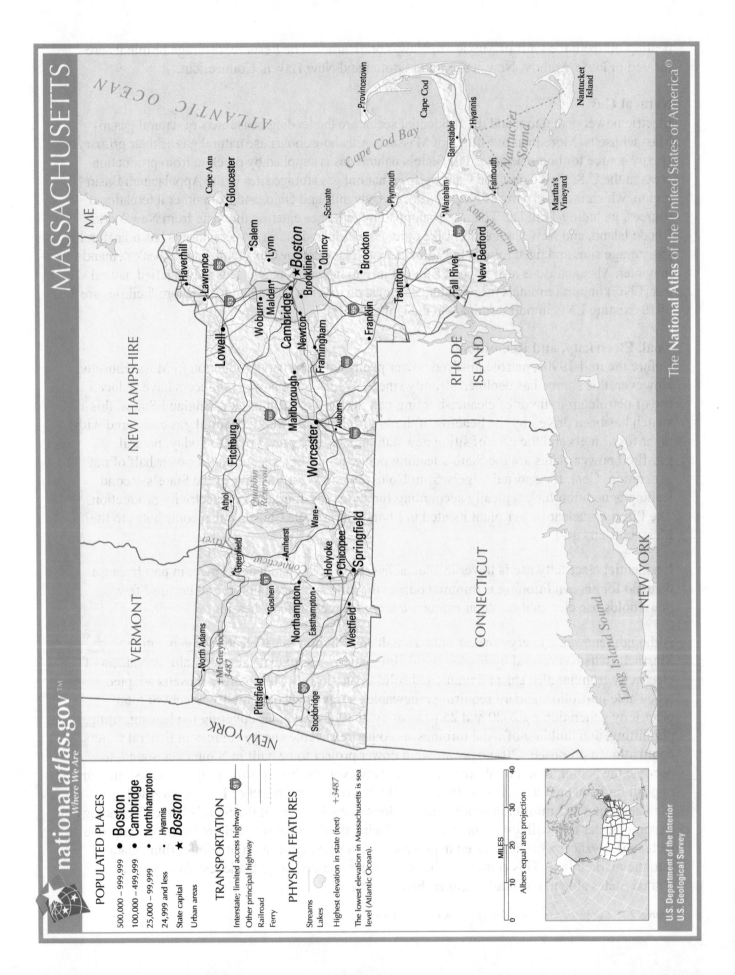

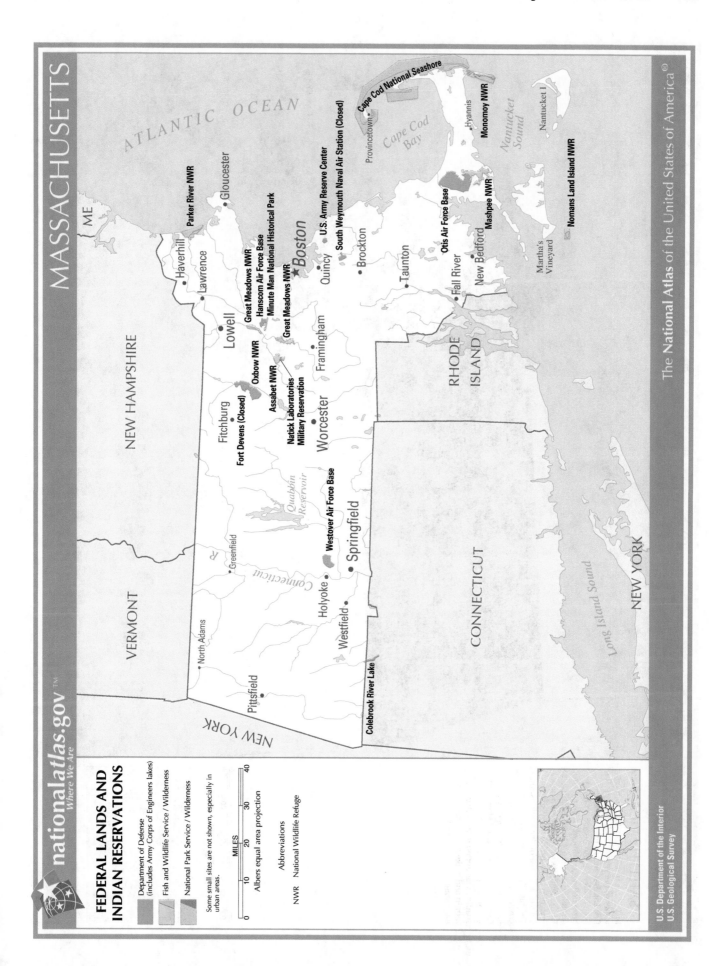

MASSACHUSETTS

nationalatlas.gov™
Where We Are

**FEDERAL LANDS AND
INDIAN RESERVATIONS**

Department of Defense
(includes Army Corps of Engineers lakes)

Fish and Wildlife Service / Wilderness

National Park Service / Wilderness

Some small sites are not shown, especially in
urban areas.

MILES
0 10 20 30 40
Albers equal area projection

Abbreviations

NWR   National Wildlife Refuge

The National Atlas of the United States of America ®

U.S. Department of the Interior
U.S. Geological Survey

ATLANTIC OCEAN

ME

NEW HAMPSHIRE

VERMONT

NEW YORK

RHODE
ISLAND

CONNECTICUT

NEW YORK

Cape Cod National Seashore

Cape Cod
Bay

Nantucket Sound

Nantucket I

Monomoy NWR

Hyannis

Provincetown

Nomans Land Island NWR

Martha's
Vineyard

Parker River NWR

Gloucester

Haverhill

Lawrence

Lowell

Fitchburg

Fort Devens (Closed)

Oxbow NWR

Assabet NWR

Natick Laboratories
Military Reservation

Worcester

Framingham

Great Meadows NWR
Hanscom Air Force Base
Minute Man National Historical Park

Great Meadows NWR

★ Boston

U.S. Army Reserve Center

South Weymouth Naval Air Station (Closed)

Quincy

Brockton

Taunton

Otis Air Force Base

Fall River

New Bedford

Mashpee NWR

Quabbin
Reservoir

Westover Air Force Base

Springfield

Holyoke

Westfield

Greenfield

North Adams

Pittsfield

Colebrook River Lake

Connecticut

Long Island Sound

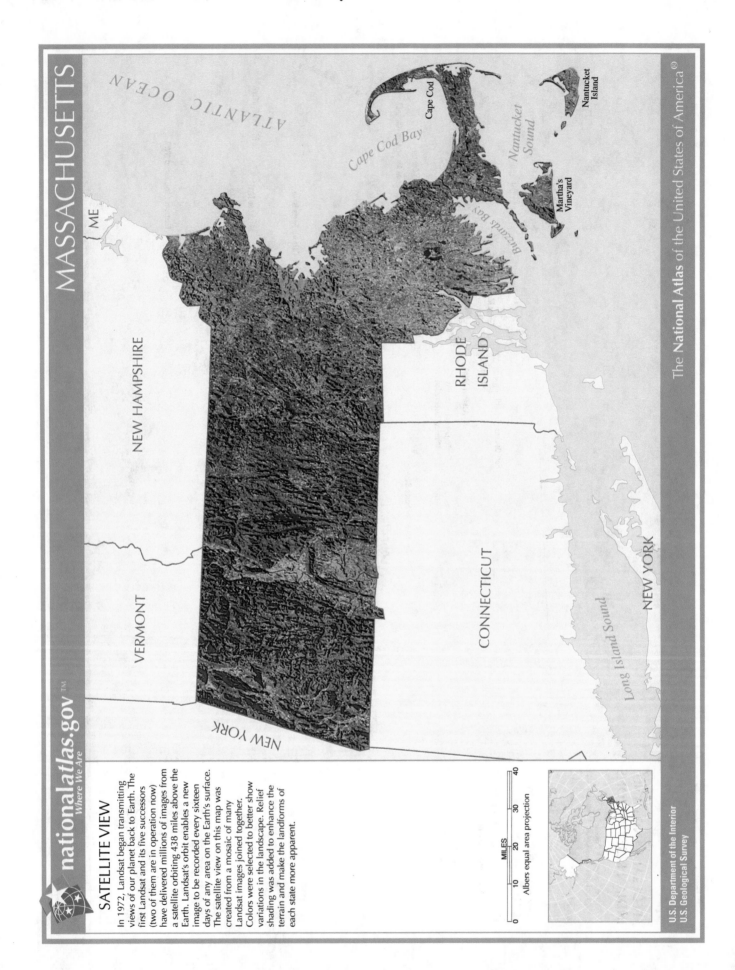

MASSACHUSETTS

ATLANTIC OCEAN

ME

NEW HAMPSHIRE

VERMONT

NEW YORK

Cape Cod Bay

Cape Cod

Nantucket
Sound

Nantucket
Island

Martha's
Vineyard

Buzzards Bay

RHODE
ISLAND

CONNECTICUT

Long Island Sound

NEW YORK

nationalatlas.gov™
Where We Are

SATELLITE VIEW

In 1972, Landsat began transmitting
views of our planet back to Earth. The
first Landsat and its five successors
(two of them are in operation now)
have delivered millions of images from
a satellite orbiting 438 miles above the
Earth. Landsat's orbit enables a new
image to be recorded every sixteen
days of any area on the Earth's surface.
The satellite view on this map was
created from a mosaic of many
Landsat images joined together.
Colors were selected to better show
variations in the landscape. Relief
shading was added to enhance the
terrain and make the landforms of
each state more apparent.

MILES

0   10   20   30   40

Albers equal area projection

U.S. Department of the Interior
U.S. Geological Survey

The **National Atlas** of the United States of America ®

Michigan

Topic	Value	Time Period
Total Surface Area (acres)	37,349,200	2007
Land	36,228,400	2007
Federal Land	3,273,600	2007
Owned	21,357	FY 2009
Leased	8,381	FY 2009
Otherwise Managed	147,351	FY 2009
National Forest	2,876,000	September 2006
National Wilderness	258,596	October 2011
Non-Federal Land, Developed	4,227,600	2007
Non-Federal Land, Rural	28,727,200	2007
Water	1,120,800	2007
National Natural Landmarks	12	December 2010
National Historic Landmarks	34	December 2010
National Register of Historic Places	1,759	December 2010
National Parks	5	December 2010
Visitors to National Parks	1,796,006	2010
Historic Places Documented by the National Park Service	622	December 2010
Archeological Sites in National Parks	433	December 2010
Threatened and Endangered Species in National Parks	5	December 2010
Economic Benefit from National Park Tourism (dollars)	124,132,000	2009
Conservation Reserve Program (acres)	222,370	October 2011
Land and Water Conservation Fund Grants (dollars)	128,032,310	Since 1965
Historic Preservation Grants (dollars)	28,956,082	2010
Community Conservation and Recreation Projects	60	Since 1987
Federal Acres Transferred for Local Parks and Recreation	4,499	Since 1948
Crude Petroleum Production (millions of barrels)	7	2010
Crude Oil Proved Reserves (millions of barrels)	33	2009
Natural Gas Reserves (billions of cubic feet)	2,763	2009
Natural Gas Liquid Reserves (millions of barrels)	62	2008
Natural Gas Marketed Production (billions of cubic feet)	154	2009
Coal Reserves (millions of short tons)	Not Available	2009

Sources: U.S. Department of the Interior, National Park Service, State Profiles, December 2010; United States Department of Agriculture, Natural Resources Conservation Service, 2007 National Resources Inventory; U.S. General Services Administration, Federal Real Property Council, FY 2009 Federal Real Property Report, September 2010; University of Montana, www.wilderness.net; U.S. Department of Agriculture, Farm Services Agency, Conservation Reserve Program, October 2011; U.S Census Bureau, 2012 Statistical Abstract of the United States

Michigan Energy Overview and Analysis

Quick Facts

- Michigan has more natural gas reserves than any other State in the Great Lakes region.
- The Antrim natural gas fields, in the northern Lower Peninsula, are among the largest in the Nation.
- Michigan has the most underground natural gas storage capacity of any State in the Nation and supplies natural gas to neighboring States during high-demand winter months.
- Michigan is a substantial generator of electricity from wood and wood waste.
- Natural gas heats roughly four-fifths of Michigan homes.
- Two renewable energy technology manufacturers plan to transform an abandoned automobile factory in Wixom to the Nation's largest renewable energy park, producing solar panels and large-scale batteries to store power for the electric grid.

Analysis

Resources and Consumption

Michigan has substantial natural gas reserves - more than any other State in the Great Lakes region - but is relatively limited in other energy resources. The State's Antrim natural gas fields in the northern portion of the Lower Peninsula are among the largest in the United States. Michigan has some renewable energy potential, particularly from wood and wood waste in the northern portion of the State, wind energy potential near the Great Lakes shoreline and in the Thumb region of the State, and corn grown in southern Michigan. Michigan's total energy consumption is high due in part to its large population, northern climate, and active industrial sector. Energy-intensive activities in the State include durable goods manufacturing such as the automotive, glass, and metal-casting industries.

Petroleum

Michigan has some crude oil production from small wells scattered across the Lower Peninsula and a 102,000-barrel-per-day refinery in Detroit. Two major crude oil pipelines from western Canada, both part of the Lakehead Pipeline System, enter Michigan from the northwest and southwest and supply both Michigan and eastern Canada. Several petroleum product pipeline systems supply Michigan consumption markets, including the Wolverine Pipeline system, which runs from Chicago area refineries to the Detroit area. Michigan's consumption of petroleum products, particularly liquefied petroleum gases (LPG), is high. Michigan has the largest residential LPG market in the Nation, and the State ranks in the top ten in the use of LPG as an alternative vehicle fuel. Although Michigan does not require the use of motor gasoline blended with ethanol as many States do, the Detroit area requires the use of gasoline blended to reduce evaporative emissions that contribute to ozone formation. As a major corn producer, Michigan also has substantial ethanol production capacity.

Natural Gas

Natural gas production in Michigan is substantial and supplies over three-tenths of State demand. Natural gas wells are concentrated in the Antrim fields in the northern portion of the Lower

Peninsula. Several major pipelines, including the Vector Pipeline from Illinois and the ANR Pipeline from the Gulf of Mexico, Louisiana, and the panhandles of Texas and Oklahoma, satisfy the remainder of the State's natural gas demand as they cross Michigan on the way to markets in the U.S. Northeast and eastern Canada. With over one-tenth of U.S. capacity, Michigan has the most underground natural gas storage capacity in the Nation and supplies natural gas to neighboring States during high-demand winter months. Driven largely by the residential sector, Michigan's natural gas consumption is high. Nearly four-fifths of Michigan households use natural gas as their primary energy source for home heating.

Coal, Electricity, and Renewables

Coal dominates electricity generation in Michigan, supplying nearly three-fifths of the market. Most of the State's coal is supplied by Wyoming and Montana and transported by rail to the western end of Lake Superior and then by ship to power plants largely located along the Great Lakes shorelines. Michigan also obtains coal, principally by rail, from eastern sources, including West Virginia, Kentucky, and Pennsylvania. Michigan's three nuclear power plants supply more than one-fourth of the State's electricity generation, while natural gas fuels much of the remainder. Michigan is a substantial generator of electricity from wood and wood waste, with many small hydroelectric plants and several plants that generate electricity using methane recovered from landfills and anaerobic digesters. Overall, however, renewable power generation contributes only minimally to the State electricity grid. Electricity generation in Michigan is high, but per capita residential electricity use in Michigan is lower than the national average, in part due to low demand for air-conditioning during the mild summers and a reliance on natural gas for home heating. Less than one-tenth of Michigan households rely on electricity as their primary source of energy for home heating. Michigan currently has several ethanol and biodiesel production plants in operation.

Michigan adopted an Integrated Renewable Portfolio Standard (RPS) of 10 percent by 2015. Utilities can meet part of the standard by adopting emission reduction technologies at power plants fired by conventional fuels. Additionally, the State allows for the authorization of up to 15 Renewable Energy Renaissance Zones, which offer tax incentives to promote the development of renewable energy facilities. In September 2009, two renewable energy technology manufacturers bought an abandoned automobile factory in Wixom, Michigan. By the fall of 2011, this factory is slated to become the largest renewable energy park in the Nation, producing solar panels and large-scale batteries to store power for the electric grid.

Source: U.S. Energy Information Administration, October 2009

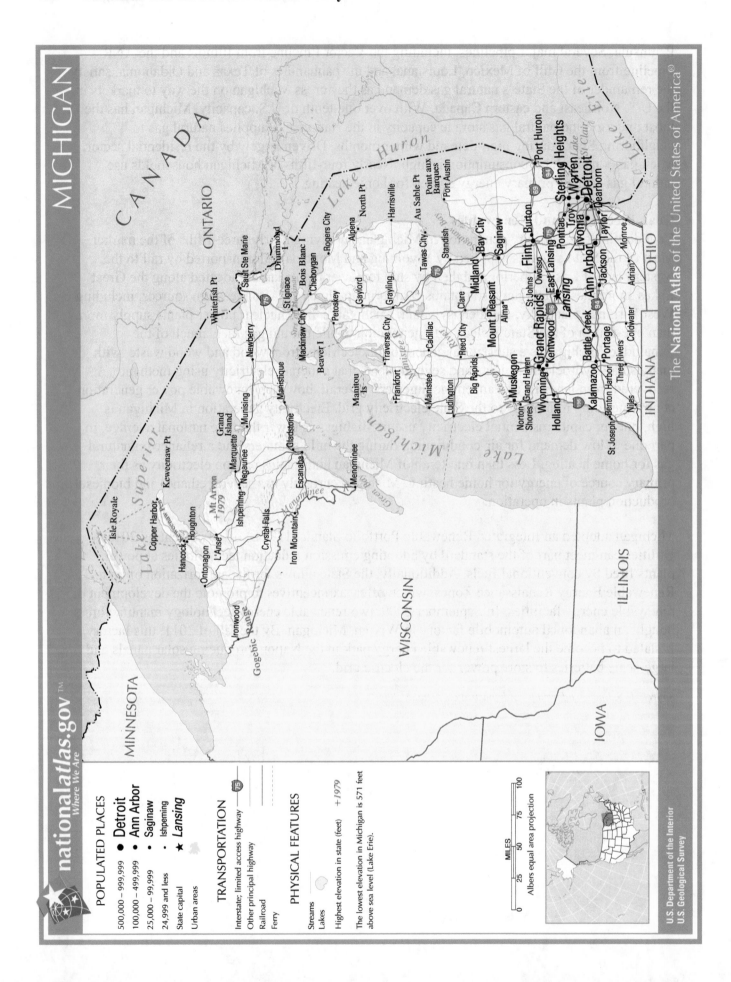

U.S. Department of the Interior
U.S. Geological Survey

The **National Atlas** of the United States of America®

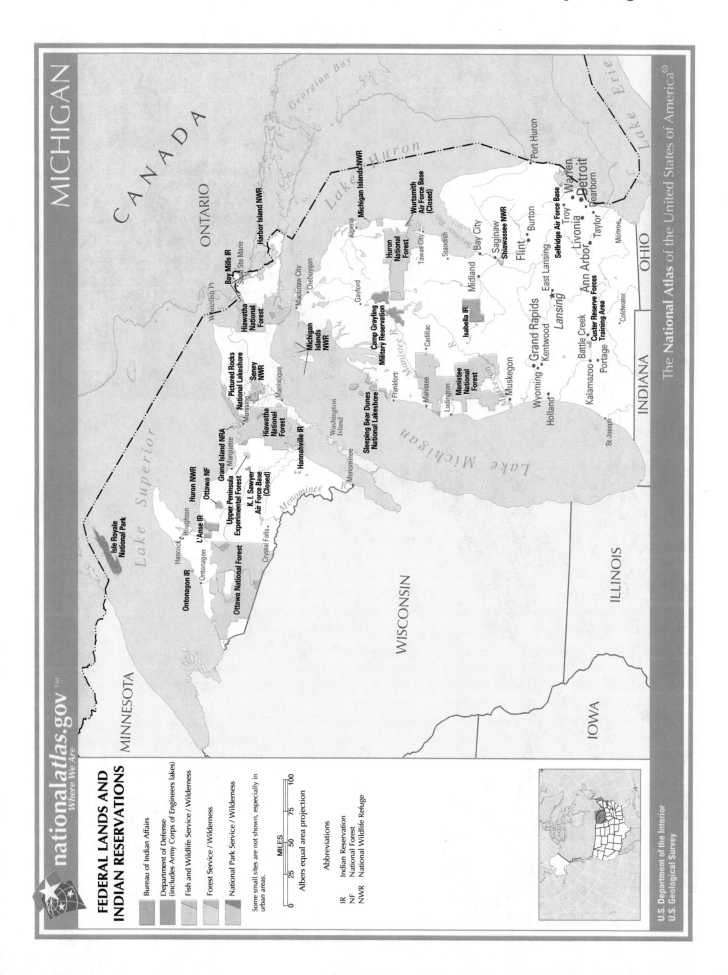

MICHIGAN

nationalatlas.gov™
Where We Are

**FEDERAL LANDS AND
INDIAN RESERVATIONS**

Bureau of Indian Affairs

Department of Defense
(includes Army Corps of Engineers lakes)

Fish and Wildlife Service / Wilderness

Forest Service / Wilderness

National Park Service / Wilderness

Some small sites are not shown, especially in
urban areas.

MILES

0   25   50   75   100

Albers equal area projection

Abbreviations

IR   Indian Reservation
NF   National Forest
NWR   National Wildlife Refuge

CANADA

ONTARIO

Georgian Bay

Lake Huron

Lake Superior

Lake Michigan

Lake Erie

MINNESOTA

WISCONSIN

IOWA

ILLINOIS

INDIANA

OHIO

Isle Royale
National Park

Ontonagon IR

Huron NWR

Ottawa NF

Grand Island NRA

Ottawa National Forest

L'Anse IR

Upper Peninsula
Experimental Forest

K. I. Sawyer
Air Force Base
(Closed)

Hannahville IR

Crystal Falls

Houghton

Hancock

Ontonagon

Marquette

Whitefish Pt

Sault Ste Marie

Bay Mills IR

Hiawatha
National
Forest

Harbor Island NWR

Pictured Rocks
National Lakeshore

Seney
NWR

Munising

Manistique

Hiawatha
National
Forest

Michigan
Islands
NWR

Washington
Island

Menominee

Sleeping Bear Dunes
National Lakeshore

Frankfort

Manistee

Ludington

Manistee
National
Forest

Mackinaw City

Cheboygan

Gaylord

Cadillac

Alpena

Huron
National
Forest

Tawas City

Standish

Bay City

Midland

Saginaw

Isabella IR

Camp Grayling
Military Reservation

Michigan Islands NWR

Wurtsmith
Air Force Base
(Closed)

Saginaw Bay

Shiawassee NWR

Flint

Burton

East Lansing

Lansing

Grand Rapids

Kentwood

Wyoming

Holland

Muskegon

Battle Creek

Kalamazoo

Custer Reserve Forces
Portage Training Area

St Joseph

Coldwater

Selfridge Air Force Base

Warren

Detroit

Dearborn

Troy

Livonia

Ann Arbor

Taylor

Monroe

Port Huron

The **National Atlas** of the United States of America®

U.S. Department of the Interior
U.S. Geological Survey

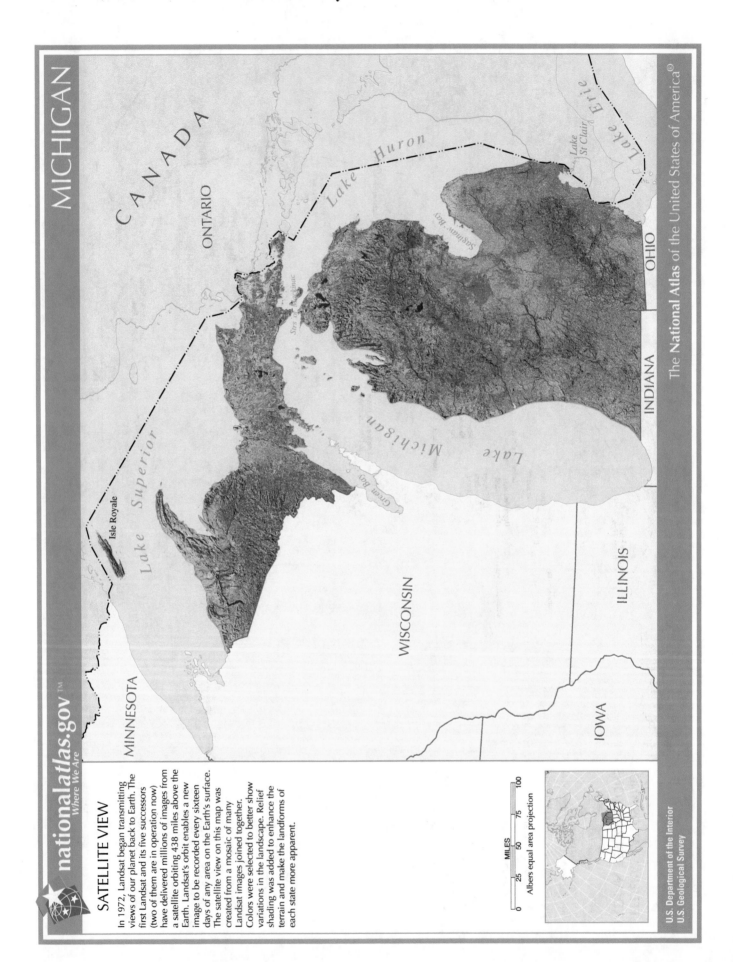

nationalatlas.gov™
Where We Are

MICHIGAN

SATELLITE VIEW

In 1972, Landsat began transmitting views of our planet back to Earth. The first Landsat and its five successors (two of them are in operation now) have delivered millions of images from a satellite orbiting 438 miles above the Earth. Landsat's orbit enables a new image to be recorded every sixteen days of any area on the Earth's surface. The satellite view on this map was created from a mosaic of many Landsat images joined together. Colors were selected to better show variations in the landscape. Relief shading was added to enhance the terrain and make the landforms of each state more apparent.

CANADA

ONTARIO

Lake Huron

Lake St Clair

Lake Erie

Saginaw Bay

Isle Royale

Lake Superior

Strs of Mac....

Lake Michigan

Green Bay

MINNESOTA

WISCONSIN

ILLINOIS

IOWA

INDIANA

OHIO

MILES
0   25   50   75   100
Albers equal area projection

U.S. Department of the Interior
U.S. Geological Survey

The **National Atlas** of the United States of America©

Minnesota

Topic	Value	Time Period
Total Surface Area (acres)	54,009,900	2007
Land	50,865,000	2007
Federal Land	3,336,100	2007
Owned	40,345	FY 2009
Leased	5,578	FY 2009
Otherwise Managed	54,457	FY 2009
National Forest	2,842,000	September 2006
National Wilderness	816,267	October 2011
Non-Federal Land, Developed	2,395,200	2007
Non-Federal Land, Rural	45,133,700	2007
Water	3,144,900	2007
National Natural Landmarks	8	December 2010
National Historic Landmarks	23	December 2010
National Register of Historic Places	1,592	December 2010
National Parks	5	December 2010
Visitors to National Parks	540,195	2010
Historic Places Documented by the National Park Service	562	December 2010
Archeological Sites in National Parks	508	December 2010
Threatened and Endangered Species in National Parks	6	December 2010
Economic Benefit from National Park Tourism (dollars)	27,990,000	2009
Conservation Reserve Program (acres)	1,558,423	October 2011
Land and Water Conservation Fund Grants (dollars)	70,412,569	Since 1965
Historic Preservation Grants (dollars)	26,388,433	2010
Community Conservation and Recreation Projects	58	Since 1987
Federal Acres Transferred for Local Parks and Recreation	508	Since 1948
Crude Petroleum Production (millions of barrels)	Not Available	2010
Crude Oil Proved Reserves (millions of barrels)	Not Available	2009
Natural Gas Reserves (billions of cubic feet)	Not Available	2009
Natural Gas Liquid Reserves (millions of barrels)	Not Available	2008
Natural Gas Marketed Production (billions of cubic feet)	Not Available	2009
Coal Reserves (millions of short tons)	Not Available	2009

Sources: U.S. Department of the Interior, National Park Service, State Profiles, December 2010; United States Department of Agriculture, Natural Resources Conservation Service, 2007 National Resources Inventory; U.S. General Services Administration, Federal Real Property Council, FY 2009 Federal Real Property Report, September 2010; University of Montana, www.wilderness.net; U.S. Department of Agriculture, Farm Services Agency, Conservation Reserve Program, October 2011; U.S Census Bureau, 2012 Statistical Abstract of the United States

Minnesota Energy Overview and Analysis

Quick Facts

- Minnesota is a leading producer of ethanol and has over a dozen ethanol production plants primarily in the southern half of the State.
- Minnesota is one of the few States that require the statewide use of oxygenated motor gasoline blended with 10 percent ethanol.
- Minnesota is a major producer of wind power.
- Over two-thirds of Minnesota households use natural gas as their primary heating fuel during the State's long, cold winters.
- Two nuclear power plants near the Twin Cities generate nearly one-fourth of the electricity produced in the State.

Analysis

Resources and Consumption

Minnesota has no fossil fuel resources, but the western part of the State has wind energy potential, and cornfields in the south and west provide feedstock for ethanol production. Minnesota's population and total energy consumption place the State in the middle of national rankings. The industrial and transportation sectors lead State energy demand.

Petroleum

Minnesota has two oil refineries in the Minneapolis-St. Paul area for processing crude oil that comes primarily from Canada. Several pipeline systems bring the crude to Minnesota, including the Lakehead Pipeline System from Canada that passes through northern Minnesota on its way to other markets in the U.S. Midwest. In an effort to keep pace with growing State demand for petroleum products, Minnesota recently completed construction on a new, 300-mile pipeline to carry additional Canadian crude oil to the State's refineries. Plans for two additional oil pipelines, running from northwestern Minnesota to Superior, Wisconsin, were recently approved by the Minnesota Public Utilities Commission.

Since 1992, Minnesota has had a robust program in place to support ethanol production and consumption. Minnesota is one of the few States that require the statewide use of oxygenated motor gasoline blended with 10 percent ethanol. Minnesota also offers incentives to encourage the adoption of E85 - a mixture of 85 percent ethanol with 15 percent motor gasoline - throughout the State and now has more E85 refueling stations than any other State. Minnesota is among the Nation's top producers of ethanol, with over a dozen corn-based production plants located primarily in the southern part of the State and additional facilities under construction.

Natural Gas

The residential sector is Minnesota's largest natural gas consumer, accounting for over one-third of State consumption. Over two-thirds of Minnesota households use natural gas as their primary heating fuel during the State's long, cold winters. Natural gas is mostly supplied by pipelines entering the State from Canada and from North and South Dakota. The State ships over four-fifths of the natural gas it receives to Iowa and Wisconsin, on the way to other markets in the U.S. Midwest.

Coal, Electricity, and Renewables

Coal-fired power plants typically account for roughly three-fifths of Minnesota's electricity generation. Minnesota receives most of its coal supply by rail from Montana and Wyoming. Two nuclear plants near the Twin Cities typically account for nearly one-fourth of the State's electricity production. Recent legislation permits the Prairie Island Plant to store additional nuclear waste onsite, extending the plant's operation through 2014. After receiving approval from the U.S. Nuclear Regulatory Commission for license renewal in 2006, the smaller Monticello nuclear plant is now licensed through September 2030.

Minnesota has numerous wind farms, particularly in the southwest, and is a major producer of wind power. Wind contributes nearly 5 percent of Minnesota's electricity production. The State generates electricity from other renewable sources, as well, including hydroelectric dams, municipal solid waste, landfill gas, and wood waste, which together contribute minimally to the State's total electricity production.

In February 2007, Minnesota adopted a renewable portfolio standard that requires one-fourth of Minnesota's power to come from renewable sources by 2025. The mandate also requires Xcel Energy, the provider of about one-half of the State's electricity, to have one-third of its total power come from renewable sources by 2020.

Source: U.S. Energy Information Administration, October 2009

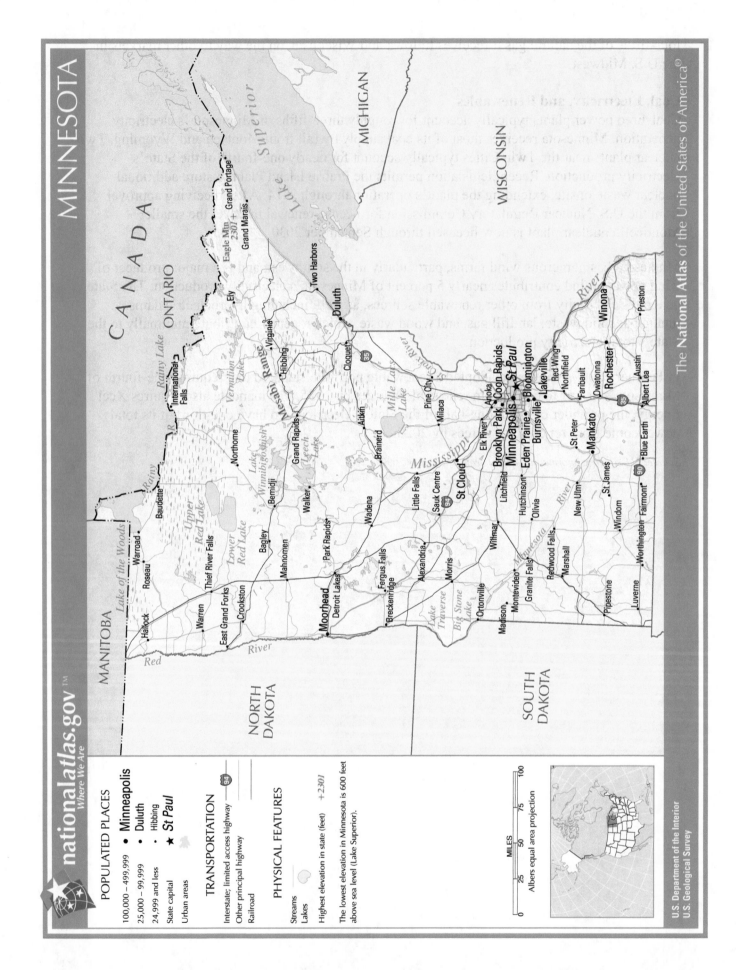

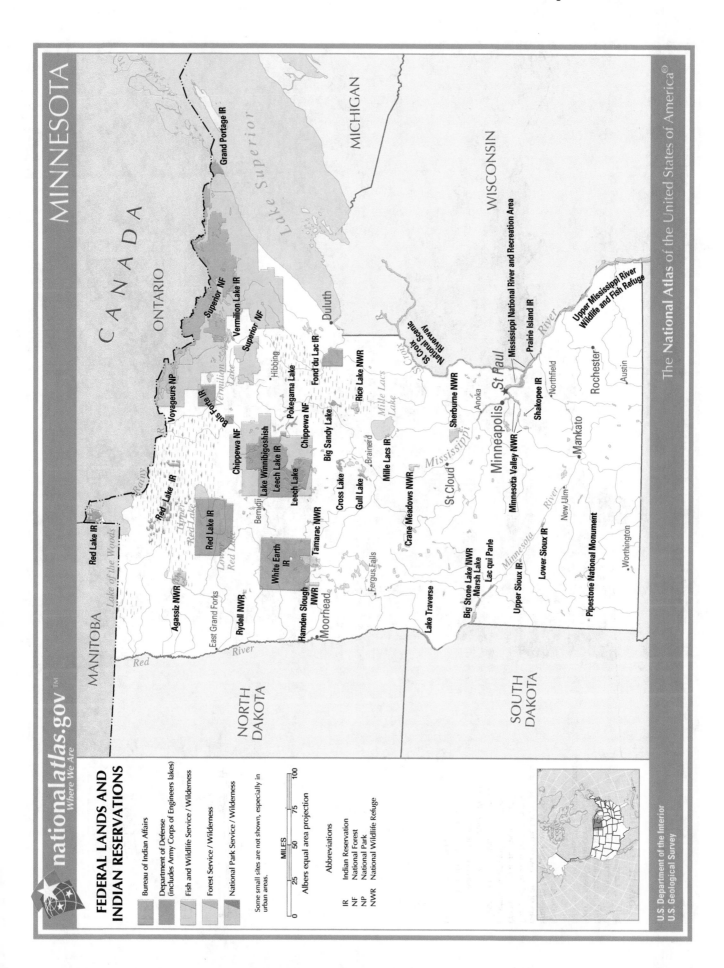

nationalatlas.gov ™
Where We Are

FEDERAL LANDS AND INDIAN RESERVATIONS

Bureau of Indian Affairs

Department of Defense
(includes Army Corps of Engineers lakes)

Fish and Wildlife Service / Wilderness

Forest Service / Wilderness

National Park Service / Wilderness

Some small sites are not shown, especially in urban areas.

MILES

0   25   50   75   100

Albers equal area projection

Abbreviations

IR   Indian Reservation
NF   National Forest
NP   National Park
NWR   National Wildlife Refuge

MINNESOTA

The National Atlas of the United States of America®

U.S. Department of the Interior
U.S. Geological Survey

CANADA

MANITOBA

ONTARIO

Lake Superior

MICHIGAN

WISCONSIN

NORTH DAKOTA

SOUTH DAKOTA

Grand Portage IR

Superior NF

Vermilion Lake IR

Superior NF

Voyageurs NP

Bois Forte IR

Vermilion Lake

Red Lake IR

Red Lake

Upper Red Lake

Lower Red Lake

Turtle River

Rainy

Lake of the Woods

Red Lake IR

Agassiz NWR

Rydell NWR

Hamden Slough NWR

White Earth IR

Tamarac NWR

Chippewa NF

Lake Winnibigoshish

Leech Lake IR

Leech Lake

Chippewa NF

Pokegama Lake

Big Sandy Lake

Cross Lake

Gull Lake

Fond du Lac IR

Rice Lake NWR

Mille Lacs IR

Mille Lacs Lake

Hibbing

Bemidji

Duluth

Brainerd

Fergus Falls

East Grand Forks

Moorhead

Lake Traverse

Big Stone Lake NWR

Marsh Lake

Lac qui Parle

Upper Sioux IR

Lower Sioux IR

Pipestone National Monument

Worthington

Crane Meadows NWR

Sherburne NWR

St Cloud

Minneapolis

St Paul

Anoka

Minnesota Valley NWR

Shakopee IR

Prairie Island IR

Mississippi National River and Recreation Area

Upper Mississippi River Wildlife and Fish Refuge

St Croix National Scenic Riverway

New Ulm

Mankato

Northfield

Rochester

Austin

Mississippi

Minnesota River

Red River

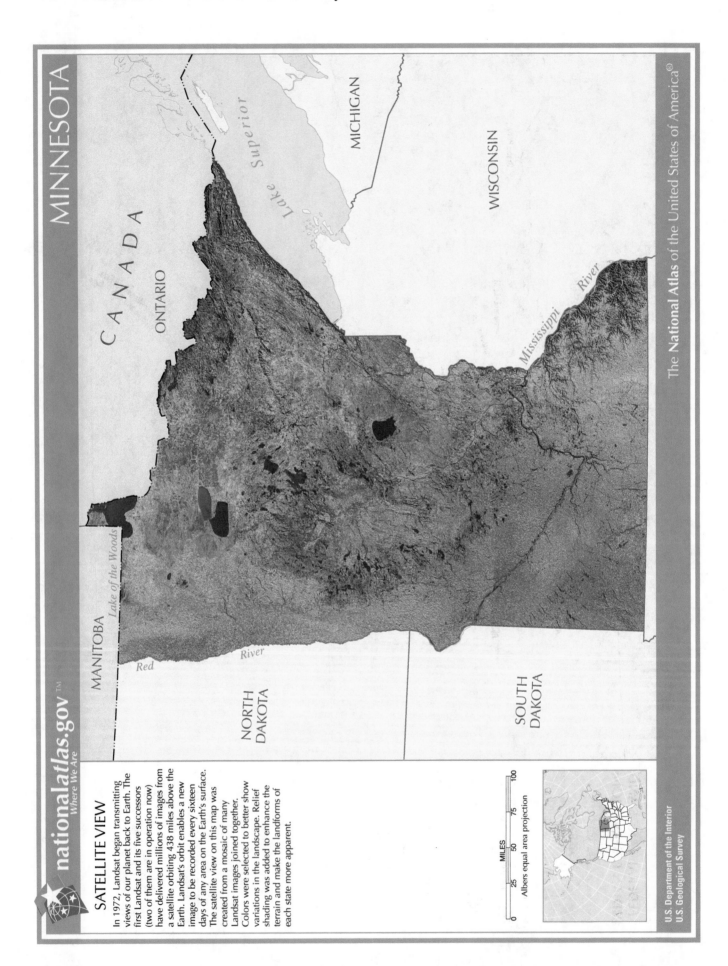

MINNESOTA

nationalatlas.gov ™
Where We Are

SATELLITE VIEW

In 1972, Landsat began transmitting views of our planet back to Earth. The first Landsat and its five successors (two of them are in operation now) have delivered millions of images from a satellite orbiting 438 miles above the Earth. Landsat's orbit enables a new image to be recorded every sixteen days of any area on the Earth's surface. The satellite view on this map was created from a mosaic of many Landsat images joined together. Colors were selected to better show variations in the landscape. Relief shading was added to enhance the terrain and make the landforms of each state more apparent.

CANADA

ONTARIO

Lake Superior

MICHIGAN

WISCONSIN

Mississippi River

MANITOBA

Lake of the Woods

Red   River

NORTH DAKOTA

SOUTH DAKOTA

MILES
0   25   50   75   100

Albers equal area projection

U.S. Department of the Interior
U.S. Geological Survey

The **National Atlas** of the United States of America®

Mississippi

Topic	Value	Time Period
Total Surface Area (acres)	30,527,300	2007
Land	29,637,400	2007
Federal Land	1,794,800	2007
Owned	523,633	FY 2009
Leased	5,127	FY 2009
Otherwise Managed	132,785	FY 2009
National Forest	1,174,000	September 2006
National Wilderness	10,126	October 2011
Non-Federal Land, Developed	1,811,900	2007
Non-Federal Land, Rural	26,030,700	2007
Water	889,900	2007
National Natural Landmarks	5	December 2010
National Historic Landmarks	39	December 2010
National Register of Historic Places	1,334	December 2010
National Parks	8	December 2010
Visitors to National Parks	6,588,026	2010
Historic Places Documented by the National Park Service	339	December 2010
Archeological Sites in National Parks	239	December 2010
Threatened and Endangered Species in National Parks	22	December 2010
Economic Benefit from National Park Tourism (dollars)	76,254,000	2009
Conservation Reserve Program (acres)	827,191	October 2011
Land and Water Conservation Fund Grants (dollars)	46,678,810	Since 1965
Historic Preservation Grants (dollars)	25,587,829	2010
Community Conservation and Recreation Projects	25	Since 1987
Federal Acres Transferred for Local Parks and Recreation	800	Since 1948
Crude Petroleum Production (millions of barrels)	24	2010
Crude Oil Proved Reserves (millions of barrels)	244	2009
Natural Gas Reserves (billions of cubic feet)	917	2009
Natural Gas Liquid Reserves (millions of barrels)	9	2008
Natural Gas Marketed Production (billions of cubic feet)	88	2009
Coal Reserves (millions of short tons)	Not Available	2009

Sources: *U.S. Department of the Interior, National Park Service, State Profiles, December 2010; United States Department of Agriculture, Natural Resources Conservation Service, 2007 National Resources Inventory; U.S. General Services Administration, Federal Real Property Council, FY 2009 Federal Real Property Report, September 2010; University of Montana, www.wilderness.net; U.S. Department of Agriculture, Farm Services Agency, Conservation Reserve Program, October 2011; U.S Census Bureau, 2012 Statistical Abstract of the United States*

Mississippi Energy Overview and Analysis

Quick Facts

- Mississippi produces oil and gas but not enough to meet high in-State demand.
- A single reactor at the Grand Gulf Nuclear Power Station supplies nearly one-fourth of the electricity generated within the State.
- A major propane supply hub is located at Hattiesburg, Mississippi, where the Dixie Pipeline has a network of terminals and storage facilities.
- Two liquefied natural gas (LNG) import terminals have been proposed near Pascagoula, Mississippi, one of which is currently under construction.
- Mississippi is one of the few States that allow the use of conventional motor gasoline statewide.

Analysis

Resources and Consumption
Although Mississippi is not as rich in energy as neighboring Louisiana, the State has substantial energy resources. Oil and gas fields are found primarily in the southern half of the State. In recent years, new deposits have been discovered in the Black Warrior Basin in the north, and onshore and offshore along the Gulf Coast. Geologists believe that further exploration of those areas could reveal important new oil and gas reserves. Although Mississippi's economy traditionally relied on agriculture, manufacturing has now become the State's largest industry. The industrial and transportation sectors dominate State energy use and per capita energy consumption is high.

Petroleum
Mississippi produces a small amount of crude oil, mostly from wells in the southern half of the State. Mississippi has three oil refineries, which together account for about 2 percent of total U.S. refining capacity. Mississippi's largest refinery, located along the Gulf Coast in Pascagoula, processes crude oil imported by marine tanker from Central and South America. The Pascagoula refinery supplies fuel to markets in the South and Southeast, using marine shipments and connections to the Colonial and Plantation pipelines. Mississippi is one of the few States in the Nation that allow the statewide use of conventional motor gasoline. (Most States require the use of specific gasoline blends in non-attainment areas due to air-quality considerations.)

A major propane supply hub is located in Hattiesburg, Mississippi, where the Dixie Pipeline has a network of terminals and storage facilities. Nearly one in five Mississippi households use liquefied petroleum gases (LPG) as their primary home heating fuel, compared with fewer than one in 10 households nationwide.

In January 2007, the U.S. Department of Energy (DOE) chose a group of salt domes in Richton, Mississippi, as a new storage site for the Strategic Petroleum Reserve. The new facility, with a capacity of 160 million barrels, is designed to cushion the effects of potential crude oil supply disruptions. DOE chose this site in part because its inland location makes it less vulnerable to hurricanes.

Hurricane vulnerability is an issue for Mississippi's oil and gas infrastructure, much of which is located along the Gulf Coast. In 2005, Hurricane Katrina caused major damage to the Pascagoula refinery, and power outages in Mississippi affected a Plantation Pipeline pump station, ultimately forcing the line to shut down and causing fuel supply problems throughout the southeastern United States.

Natural Gas

Mississippi's natural gas production is minimal, accounting for less than 1 percent of total U.S output. In recent years, new wells have been completed at the Mariner Field along the Gulf Coast and at the Maben Field in the Black Warrior Basin. Despite new completions, Mississippi's marketed natural gas production has fallen drastically since 2003, when the State's natural gas wells began producing increasing volumes of non-hydrocarbon gases, such as carbon dioxide, helium, hydrogen sulfide, and nitrogen.

Mississippi's natural gas processing industry has expanded in recent years to serve growing offshore supplies brought in from the federally administered Outer Continental Shelf (OCS). Mississippi has one of the largest natural gas processing plants in the United States, in Pascagoula, which expanded capacity in 2000 in order to accept natural gas production transported by pipeline from the OCS.

Due primarily to demand from electricity generators and the industrial sector, Mississippi's per capita natural gas consumption is high. To meet demand, Mississippi purchases more than one-half of its natural gas from neighboring States. Mississippi will soon begin importing international supplies, as two liquefied natural gas (LNG) import terminals have been approved near Pascagoula, with one of those terminals currently under construction.

Coal, Electricity, and Renewables

Mississippi's electric power production is low given its high per capita consumption, and as a result, the State imports electricity from neighboring States in order to satisfy consumer demand. Coal and natural gas are Mississippi's leading generation fuels, each typically accounting for more than one-third of electricity produced within the State. Mississippi's only coal mine, located in Choctaw County, supplies lignite coal to a 440-megawatt mine-mouth power plant that uses clean-coal technology. Mississippi's other coal-fired power plants are fueled by coal shipped primarily from Colorado, Kentucky, and Illinois. Nuclear power is the third most important fuel for electricity generation in Mississippi, typically accounting for almost one-fourth of the electricity produced in the State. A single large reactor at the Grand Gulf Nuclear Power Station provides all of Mississippi's nuclear power. Mississippi also produces a small amount of electricity from a wood-fired power plant in the eastern part of the State.

Mississippi's residential per capita electricity use is high, due in part to high air-conditioning demand during the hot summer months and the widespread use of electricity for home heating during the generally mild winter months.

Source: U.S. Energy Information Administration, October 2009

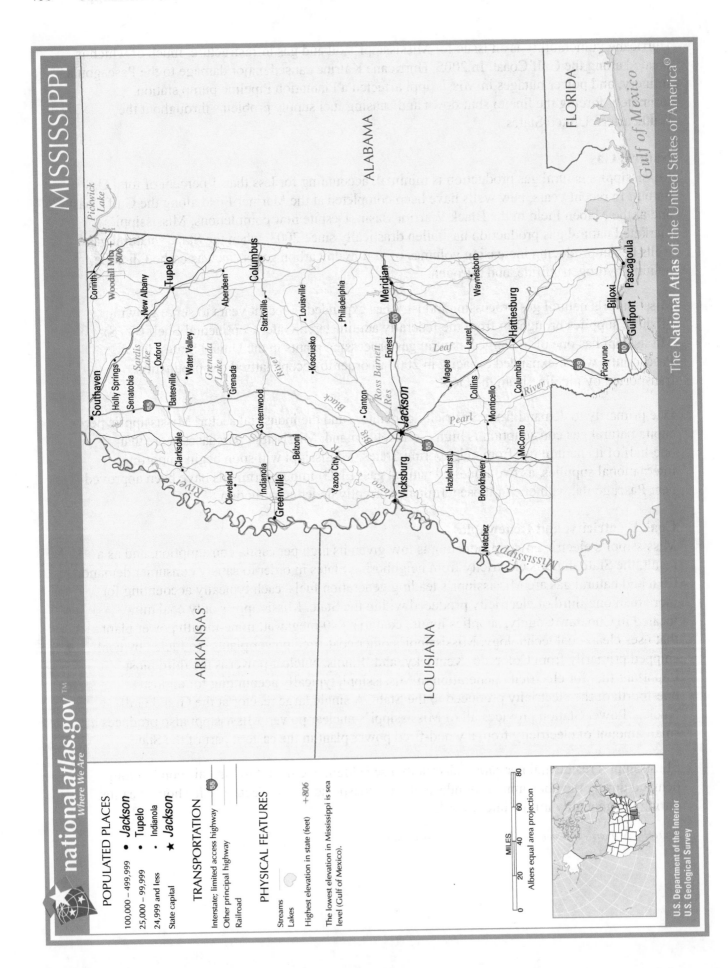

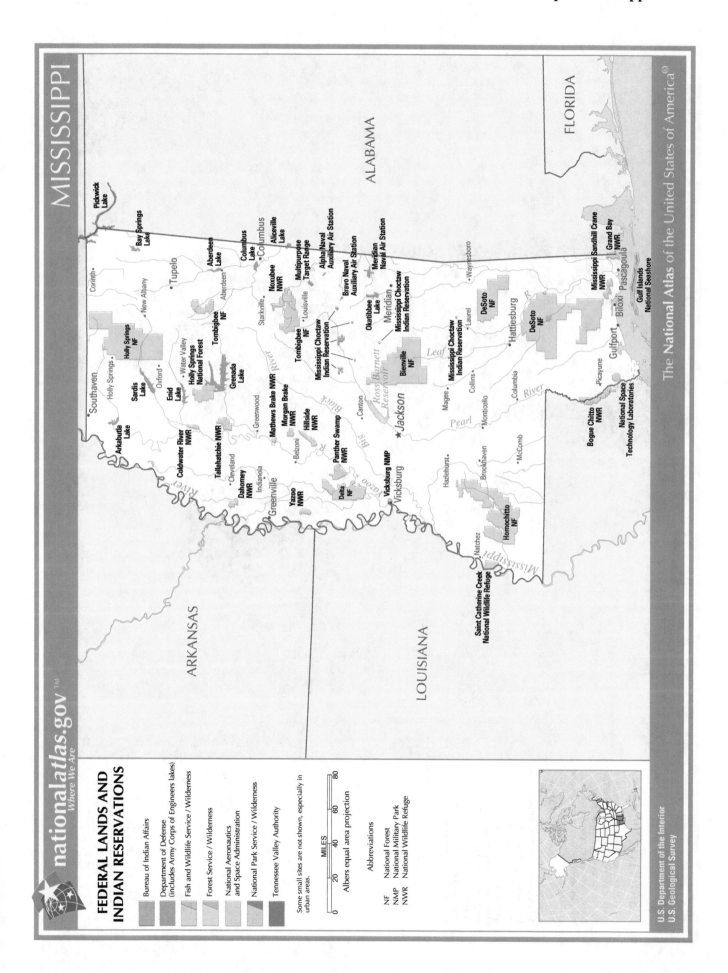

MISSISSIPPI

nationalatlas.gov™
Where We Are

**FEDERAL LANDS AND
INDIAN RESERVATIONS**

Bureau of Indian Affairs

Department of Defense
(includes Army Corps of Engineers lakes)

Fish and Wildlife Service / Wilderness

Forest Service / Wilderness

National Aeronautics
and Space Administration

National Park Service / Wilderness

Tennessee Valley Authority

Some small sites are not shown, especially in
urban areas.

MILES

0   20   40   60   80

Albers equal area projection

Abbreviations

NF   National Forest
NMP   National Military Park
NWR   National Wildlife Refuge

U.S. Department of the Interior
U.S. Geological Survey

The **National Atlas** of the United States of America®

ARKANSAS

LOUISIANA

ALABAMA

FLORIDA

Pickwick
Lake

Bay Springs
Lake

Corinth

New Albany

Tupelo

Southaven

Holly Springs

Holly Springs
NF

Oxford

Water Valley

Sardis
Lake

Enid
Lake

Holly Springs
National Forest

Arkabutla
Lake

Coldwater River
NWR

Grenada
Lake

Tombigbee
NF

Aberdeen
Lake

Aberdeen

Columbus
Lake

Columbus

Aliceville
Lake

Noxubee
NWR

Multipurpose
Target Range

Starkville

Louisville

Tombigbee
NF

Alpha/Naval
Auxiliary Air Station

Bravo Naval
Auxiliary Air Station

Meridian
Naval Air Station

Meridian

Okatibbee
Lake

Mississippi Choctaw
Indian Reservation

Mississippi Choctaw
Indian Reservation

Mississippi Choctaw
Indian Reservation

Greenwood

Tallahatchie NWR

Cleveland

Indianola

Dahomey
NWR

Greenville

Yazoo
NWR

Belzoni

Morgan Brake
NWR

Mathews Brake NWR

Hillside
NWR

Panther Swamp
NWR

Delta
NF

Vicksburg NMP

Vicksburg

Canton

Big Black

Yazoo

Ross Barnett
Reservoir

Jackson

Pearl

Bienville
NF

Leaf

Laurel

Hattiesburg

DeSoto
NF

DeSoto
NF

Collins

Magee

Monticello

Columbia

Waynesboro

Mississippi Sandhill Crane
NWR

Grand Bay
NWR

Biloxi Pascagoula

Gulfport

Gulf Islands
National Seashore

Picayune

Bogue Chitto
NWR

National Space
Technology Laboratories

Hazlehurst

Brookhaven

McComb

Homochitto
NF

Natchez

Saint Catherine Creek
National Wildlife Refuge

Mississippi River

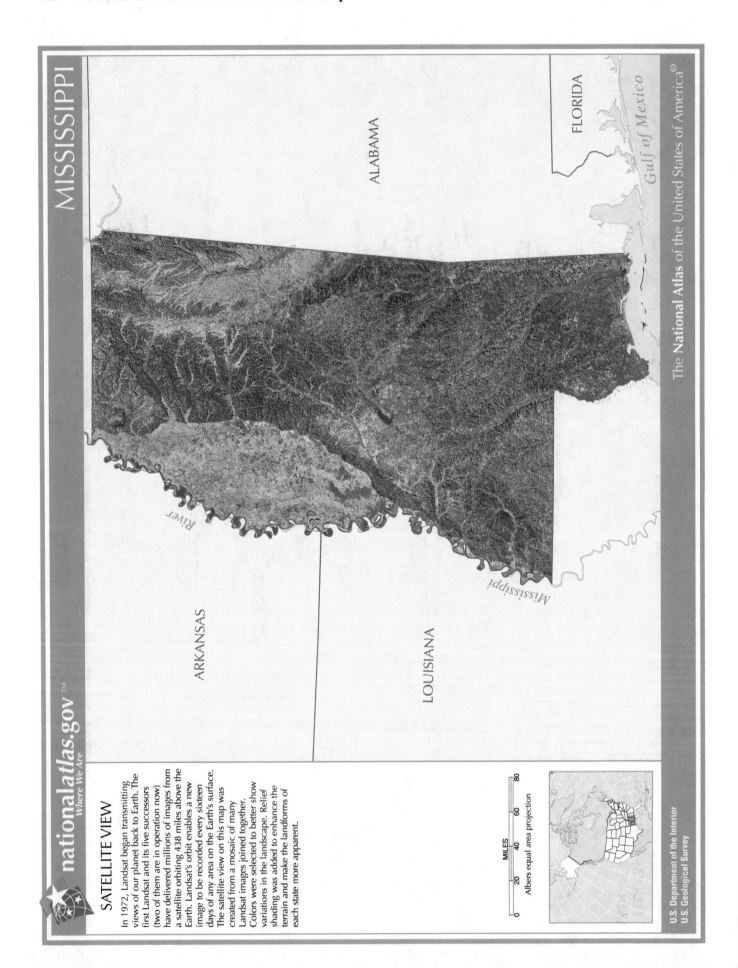

MISSISSIPPI

nationalatlas.gov ™
Where We Are

SATELLITE VIEW

In 1972, Landsat began transmitting
views of our planet back to Earth. The
first Landsat and its five successors
(two of them are in operation now)
have delivered millions of images from
a satellite orbiting 438 miles above the
Earth. Landsat's orbit enables a new
image to be recorded every sixteen
days of any area on the Earth's surface.
The satellite view on this map was
created from a mosaic of many
Landsat images joined together.
Colors were selected to better show
variations in the landscape. Relief
shading was added to enhance the
terrain and make the landforms of
each state more apparent.

MILES
0   20   40   60   80
Albers equal area projection

U.S. Department of the Interior
U.S. Geological Survey

The **National Atlas** of the United States of America®

ARKANSAS

LOUISIANA

River

Mississippi

ALABAMA

FLORIDA

Gulf of Mexico

Missouri

Topic	Value	Time Period
Total Surface Area (acres)	44,613,900	2007
Land	43,747,600	2007
Federal Land	1,919,400	2007
Owned	585,879	FY 2009
Leased	2,541	FY 2009
Otherwise Managed	6,704	FY 2009
National Forest	14,923,000	September 2006
National Wilderness	71,849	October 2011
Non-Federal Land, Developed	2,931,500	2007
Non-Federal Land, Rural	38,896,700	2007
Water	866,300	2007
National Natural Landmarks	16	December 2010
National Historic Landmarks	37	December 2010
National Register of Historic Places	2,082	December 2010
National Parks	6	December 2010
Visitors to National Parks	4,140,544	2010
Historic Places Documented by the National Park Service	1,341	December 2010
Archeological Sites in National Parks	530	December 2010
Threatened and Endangered Species in National Parks	6	December 2010
Economic Benefit from National Park Tourism (dollars)	142,684,000	2009
Conservation Reserve Program (acres)	1,294,005	October 2011
Land and Water Conservation Fund Grants (dollars)	83,944,170	Since 1965
Historic Preservation Grants (dollars)	27,475,484	2010
Community Conservation and Recreation Projects	40	Since 1987
Federal Acres Transferred for Local Parks and Recreation	4,133	Since 1948
Crude Petroleum Production (millions of barrels)	Not Available	2010
Crude Oil Proved Reserves (millions of barrels)	Not Available	2009
Natural Gas Reserves (billions of cubic feet)	Not Available	2009
Natural Gas Liquid Reserves (millions of barrels)	Not Available	2008
Natural Gas Marketed Production (billions of cubic feet)	Not Available	2009
Coal Reserves (millions of short tons)	5,988	2009

Sources: U.S. Department of the Interior, National Park Service, State Profiles, December 2010; United States Department of Agriculture, Natural Resources Conservation Service, 2007 National Resources Inventory; U.S. General Services Administration, Federal Real Property Council, FY 2009 Federal Real Property Report, September 2010; University of Montana, www.wilderness.net; U.S. Department of Agriculture, Farm Services Agency, Conservation Reserve Program, October 2011; U.S Census Bureau, 2012 Statistical Abstract of the United States

Missouri Energy Overview and Analysis

Quick Facts

- Missouri was the first State west of the Mississippi River to produce coal commercially, although output today is minimal.
- The western leg of the Rockies Express natural gas pipeline passes near Kansas City before terminating in northeast Missouri.
- Coal is the dominant fuel for electricity generation in Missouri and typically supplies more than four-fifths of the electricity market.

Analysis

Resources and Consumption

Missouri has substantial nuclear capacity, minimal coal and crude oil reserves, and few other major energy resources. Coal deposits are located in the northwestern Forest City basin. Missouri's overall energy consumption is about average among the U.S. States, in line with its population. Missouri's economy is not energy intensive, and the transportation and residential sectors lead State energy consumption.

Petroleum

Although Missouri has no refineries, several major crude oil pipelines pass through the State on their way to refining centers elsewhere in the Midwest. Missouri receives its petroleum products from several pipelines that originate in the Gulf Coast region. The Mississippi and Missouri Rivers also provide important transportation routes for petroleum products moving via barge. Missouri's petroleum product consumption is commensurate with its population, even though the use of liquefied petroleum gases (LPG) is disproportionately high. While the majority of the State now uses oxygenated gasoline, the St. Louis metropolitan area requires reformulated motor gasoline blended with ethanol, and the Kansas City area requires the use of a gasoline specially blended to reduce emissions that contribute to ozone formation. The State has several plants that produce ethanol from corn.

Natural Gas

The residential sector accounts for nearly two-fifths of the State's natural gas consumption, with nearly three-fifths of Missouri households using natural gas as their primary energy source for home heating. The industrial and commercial sectors each account for just under one-fourth of the State's natural gas consumption.

Natural Gas is supplied by several major pipelines entering the State from Kansas, Arkansas, Nebraska, and Oklahoma. Missouri ships over 80 percent of the natural gas it receives to Illinois and Iowa on its way to other markets in the Midwest and Northeast. A new pipeline, in service as of May 2008, brings additional natural gas supply to the State: the 713-mile western leg of the Rockies Express Pipeline originates in Colorado and passes near Kansas City before terminating in the northeastern portion of the State. Missouri is one of only three States that produce synthetic natural gas.

Coal, Electricity, and Renewables

Coal is the dominant fuel for electricity production in Missouri and typically supplies more than four-fifths of the electricity market. Missouri was the first State west of the Mississippi River to produce coal commercially, but production today is minimal. The vast majority of the coal used in Missouri is brought in from other States, and over nine-tenths of this coal is transported via railcar from Wyoming. The single-reactor Callaway nuclear plant in Fulton supplies much of the State's non-coal electricity. Approximately 3 percent of Missouri's electricity is generated from renewable sources, and the majority of that is from hydroelectricity generation. One-fourth of Missouri households rely on electricity as their primary energy source for home heating.

In November 2008, Missouri adopted a renewable portfolio standard that requires investor-owned utilities to increase their use of renewable sources to 2 percent of total electricity generation by 2011, 5 percent by 2014, 10 percent by 2018, and 15 percent by 2021.

Source: U.S. Energy Information Administration, October 2009

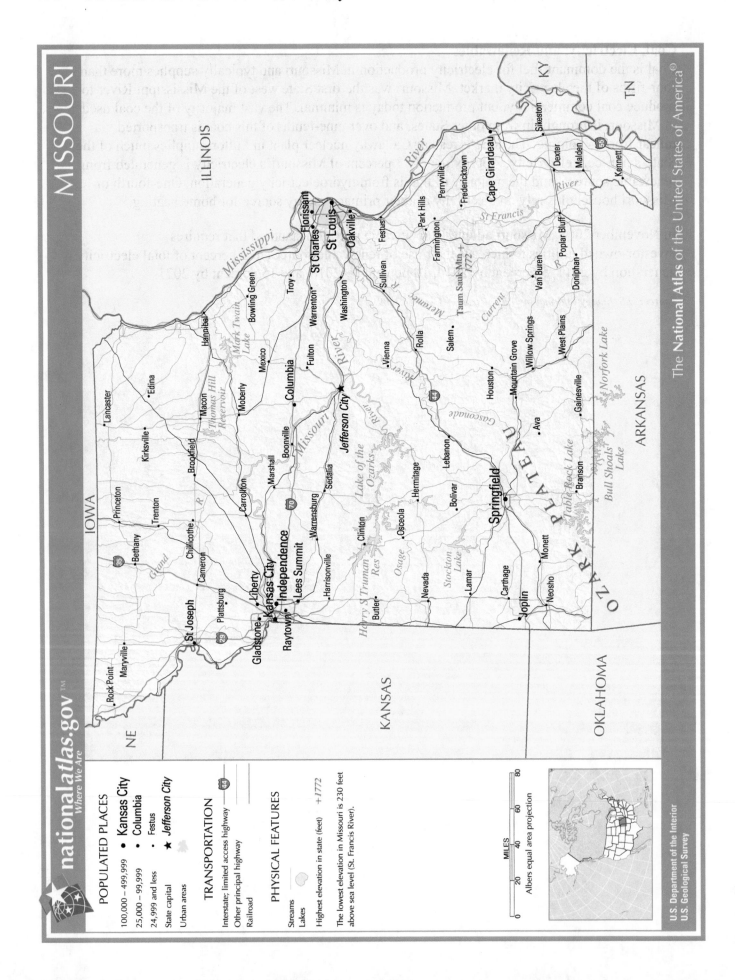

MISSOURI

nationalatlas.gov™
Where We Are

POPULATED PLACES

100,000 – 499,999   ● **Kansas City**
25,000 – 99,999   ● Columbia
24,999 and less   • Festus
State capital   ★ *Jefferson City*
Urban areas

TRANSPORTATION

Interstate; limited access highway
Other principal highway
Railroad

PHYSICAL FEATURES

Streams
Lakes
Highest elevation in state (feet)   +1772

The lowest elevation in Missouri is 230 feet
above sea level (St. Francis River).

MILES
0   20   40   60   80

Albers equal area projection

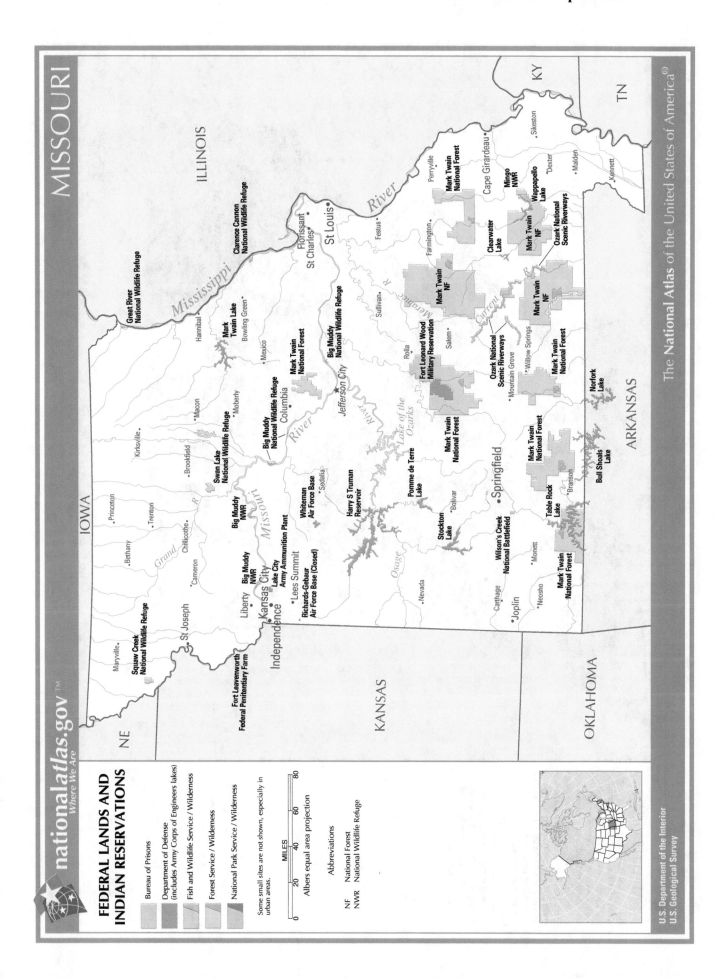

MISSOURI

nationalatlas.gov™
Where We Are

FEDERAL LANDS AND INDIAN RESERVATIONS

Bureau of Prisons

Department of Defense
(includes Army Corps of Engineers lakes)

Fish and Wildlife Service / Wilderness

Forest Service / Wilderness

National Park Service / Wilderness

Some small sites are not shown, especially in urban areas.

MILES

0   20   40   60   80

Albers equal area projection

Abbreviations

NF   National Forest
NWR   National Wildlife Refuge

U.S. Department of the Interior
U.S. Geological Survey

The **National Atlas** of the United States of America®

IOWA

NE

ILLINOIS

KANSAS

OKLAHOMA

ARKANSAS

TN

KY

Squaw Creek National Wildlife Refuge

Maryville

St Joseph

Fort Leavenworth Federal Penitentiary Farm

Liberty

Kansas City

Independence

Lake City Army Ammunition Plant

Lees Summit

Richards-Gebaur Air Force Base (Closed)

Big Muddy NWR

Big Muddy NWR

Cameron

Princeton

Bethany

Trenton

Chillicothe

Brookfield

Kirksville

Macon

Moberly

Columbia

Big Muddy National Wildlife Refuge

Swan Lake National Wildlife Refuge

Grand R.

Missouri R.

Sedalia

Whiteman Air Force Base

Pomme de Terre Lake

Harry S Truman Reservoir

Stockton Lake

Osage River

Nevada

Bolivar

Springfield

Wilson's Creek National Battlefield

Monett

Carthage

Joplin

Neosho

Mark Twain National Forest

Mark Twain National Forest

Table Rock Lake

Branson

Bull Shoals Lake

Norfork Lake

Mark Twain National Forest

Mark Twain National Forest

Mark Twain NF

Mark Twain NF

Ozark National Scenic Riverways

Ozark National Scenic Riverways

Willow Springs

Mountain Grove

Fort Leonard Wood Military Reservation

Salem

Rolla

Sullivan

Lake of the Ozarks

Jefferson City

Mexico

Bowling Green

Hannibal

Mark Twain Lake

Great River National Wildlife Refuge

Mississippi River

Clarence Cannon National Wildlife Refuge

St Charles

Florissant

St Louis

Festus

Mississippi River

Meramec R.

Current R.

Farmington

Perryville

Cape Girardeau

Clearwater Lake

Mingo NWR

Wappapello Lake

Mark Twain National Forest

Dexter

Malden

Sikeston

Kennett

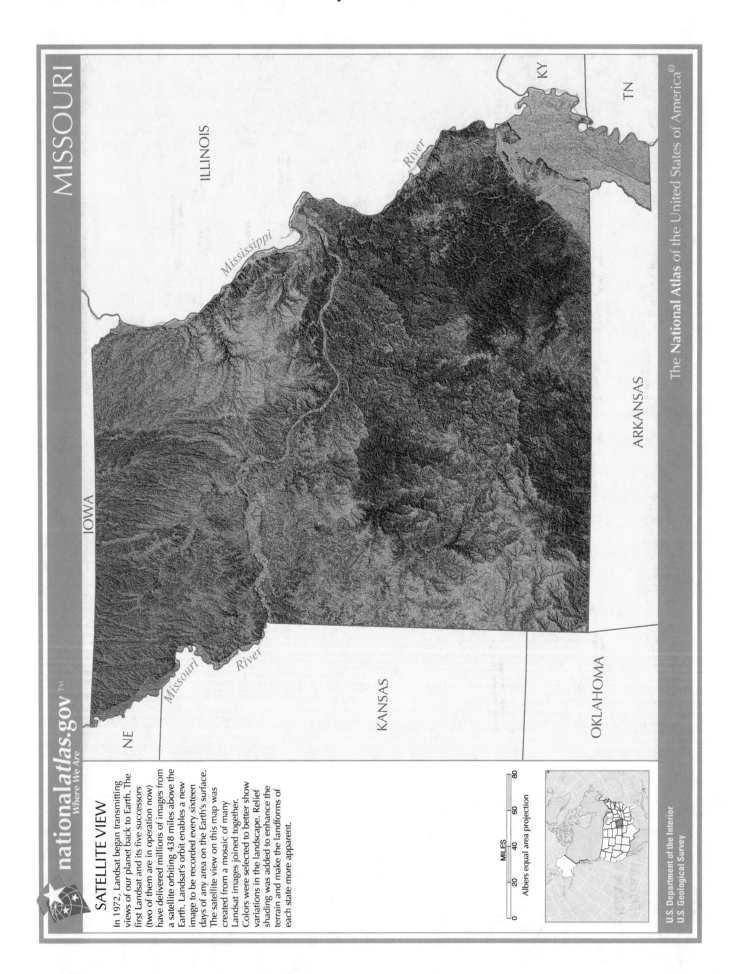

MISSOURI

nationalatlas.gov™
Where We Are

SATELLITE VIEW

In 1972, Landsat began transmitting views of our planet back to Earth. The first Landsat and its five successors (two of them are in operation now) have delivered millions of images from a satellite orbiting 438 miles above the Earth. Landsat's orbit enables a new image to be recorded every sixteen days of any area on the Earth's surface. The satellite view on this map was created from a mosaic of many Landsat images joined together. Colors were selected to better show variations in the landscape. Relief shading was added to enhance the terrain and make the landforms of each state more apparent.

IOWA

ILLINOIS

KY

TN

Mississippi

River

Missouri River

NE

KANSAS

ARKANSAS

OKLAHOMA

MILES
0   20   40   60   80
Albers equal area projection

U.S. Department of the Interior
U.S. Geological Survey

The **National Atlas** of the United States of America®

Montana

Topic	Value	Time Period
Total Surface Area (acres)	94,110,000	2007
Land	93,070,600	2007
Federal Land	27,092,000	2007
Owned	460,712	FY 2009
Leased	35,545	FY 2009
Otherwise Managed	702	FY 2009
National Forest	17,083,000	September 2006
National Wilderness	3,443,407	October 2011
Non-Federal Land, Developed	1,047,000	2007
Non-Federal Land, Rural	64,931,600	2007
Water	1,039,400	2007
National Natural Landmarks	10	December 2010
National Historic Landmarks	25	December 2010
National Register of Historic Places	1,084	December 2010
National Parks	8	December 2010
Visitors to National Parks	4,584,011	2010
Historic Places Documented by the National Park Service	425	December 2010
Archeological Sites in National Parks	891	December 2010
Threatened and Endangered Species in National Parks	7	December 2010
Economic Benefit from National Park Tourism (dollars)	269,523,000	2009
Conservation Reserve Program (acres)	2,510,678	October 2011
Land and Water Conservation Fund Grants (dollars)	37,340,899	Since 1965
Historic Preservation Grants (dollars)	21,144,662	2010
Community Conservation and Recreation Projects	27	Since 1987
Federal Acres Transferred for Local Parks and Recreation	120	Since 1948
Crude Petroleum Production (millions of barrels)	24	2010
Crude Oil Proved Reserves (millions of barrels)	343	2009
Natural Gas Reserves (billions of cubic feet)	976	2009
Natural Gas Liquid Reserves (millions of barrels)	11	2008
Natural Gas Marketed Production (billions of cubic feet)	98	2009
Coal Reserves (millions of short tons)	119,017	2009

Sources: U.S. Department of the Interior, National Park Service, State Profiles, December 2010; United States Department of Agriculture, Natural Resources Conservation Service, 2007 National Resources Inventory; U.S. General Services Administration, Federal Real Property Council, FY 2009 Federal Real Property Report, September 2010; University of Montana, www.wilderness.net; U.S. Department of Agriculture, Farm Services Agency, Conservation Reserve Program, October 2011; U.S Census Bureau, 2012 Statistical Abstract of the United States

Montana Energy Overview and Analysis

Quick Facts

- Montana accounts for about 4 percent of total U.S. coal production and delivers coal to markets in more than 15 States.
- The Williston Basin covers eastern Montana (as well as western North Dakota) and contains three of the Nation's 100 largest oil fields, two of which are in Montana.
- Montana is a major hydroelectric power producer.
- Six of Montana's 10 largest generating plants run on hydroelectric power.

Analysis

Resources and Consumption

Montana is rich in fossil fuel resources and renewable energy potential. Its geologic basins hold more than one-fourth of the Nation's estimated recoverable coal reserves. Montana's eastern basins also hold large deposits of oil and gas. Rivers flowing from Montana's Rocky Mountains offer substantial hydroelectric power resources. Considerable wind energy potential is found throughout the State.

Montana's population and total energy demand are low. However, the State economy is energy intensive and per capita energy consumption is relatively high. The industrial sector, which includes the energy-intensive mining industry, dominates State energy consumption.

Petroleum

Montana typically accounts for nearly 2 percent of U.S. crude oil production. Production is concentrated in the Williston Basin, which covers eastern Montana and western North Dakota and contains three of the Nation's 100 largest oil fields, two of which are in Montana. Several pipelines carry Williston production south to Wyoming and east to Midwest markets. In addition, a new extension to the Keystone XL Pipeline has been proposed that would pass through Montana as it transfers crude oil from Canada to markets in Texas and on the Gulf Coast. Refineries near Billings supply regional markets with petroleum products, using crude oil brought in primarily from Wyoming and Alberta, Canada. During the winter months, Montana requires oxygenated motor gasoline in the Missoula area but allows the use of conventional motor gasoline in the rest of the State.

Natural Gas

Montana produces minor quantities of natural gas, and consumes only about three-fifths of this production and ships the remainder of its natural gas output to out-of-State markets. Several natural gas pipeline systems pass through the State, transporting Canadian supplies to Midwest markets. About three-fifths of Montana households use natural gas as their primary energy source for home heating.

Coal, Electricity, and Renewables

Montana typically accounts for roughly 4 percent of total U.S. coal production. The majority of Montana's output is produced from several large surface mines in the Powder River Basin, which straddles the border between Montana and Wyoming. Just over one-fourth of Montana's coal production is used for State electricity generation; Montana delivers the remainder to markets in more than 15 States. Minnesota and Michigan are the largest recipients of Montana coal.

Accounting for nearly two-thirds of State electricity generation, coal-fired power plants dominate the Montana electricity market. Hydroelectric power accounts for most of the remainder. Montana is a major hydroelectric power producer, and six of the State's 10 largest generating plants run on hydroelectric power. The State has also initiated programs to expand and enhance hydroelectric power capacity. There are several operational wind farm projects in central Montana, just east of the Rockies. High-voltage transmission lines connect Montana to other western electric power grids, allowing Montana to export large amounts of electricity to neighboring States.

In April 2005, Montana adopted a renewable portfolio standard that requires 15 percent of the State's energy to come from renewable sources by 2015.

Source: U.S. Energy Information Administration, October 2009

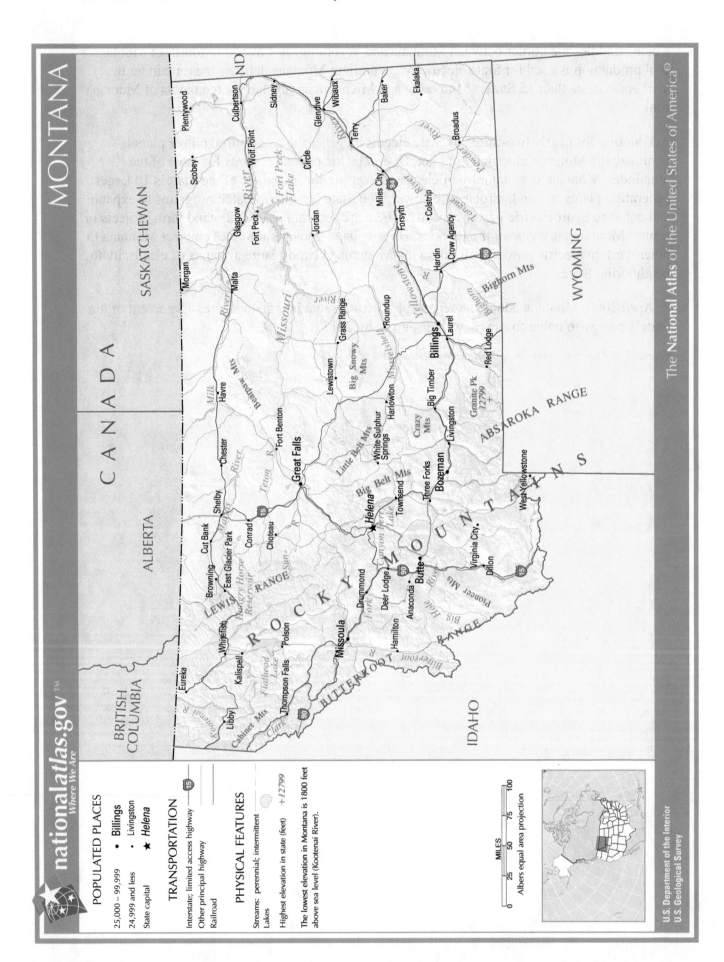

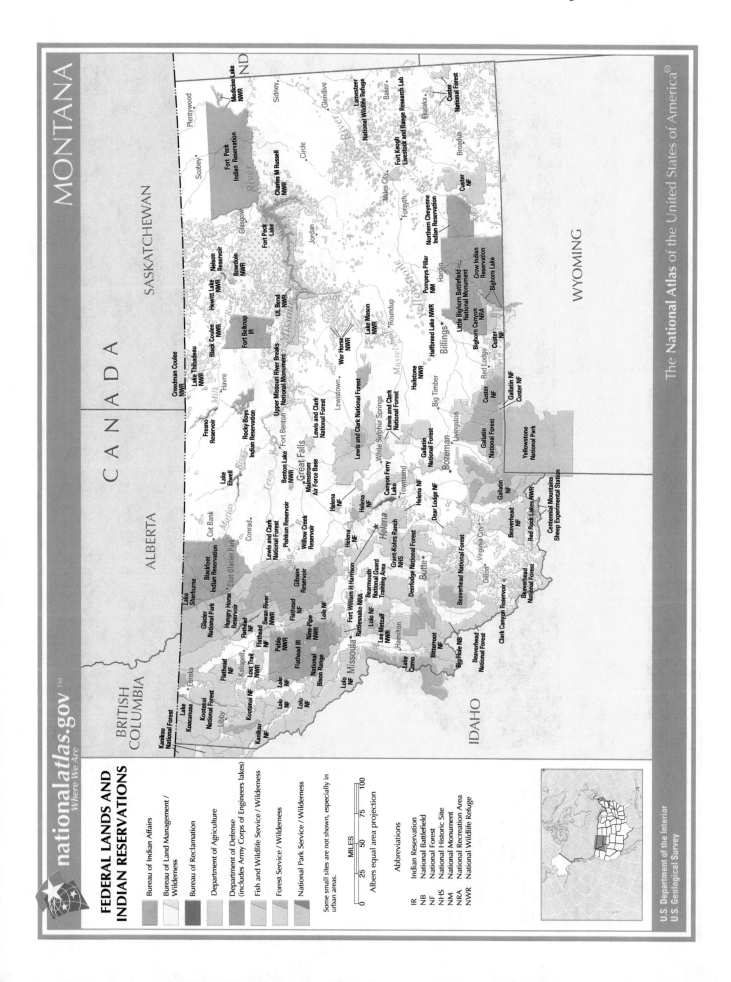

nationalatlas.gov™
Where We Are

FEDERAL LANDS AND INDIAN RESERVATIONS

Bureau of Indian Affairs

Bureau of Land Management / Wilderness

Bureau of Reclamation

Department of Agriculture

Department of Defense
(includes Army Corps of Engineers lakes)

Fish and Wildlife Service / Wilderness

Forest Service / Wilderness

National Park Service / Wilderness

Some small sites are not shown, especially in urban areas.

MILES

0   25   50   75   100

Albers equal area projection

Abbreviations

IR   Indian Reservation
NB   National Battlefield
NF   National Forest
NHS   National Historic Site
NM   National Monument
NRA   National Recreation Area
NWR   National Wildlife Refuge

U.S. Department of the Interior
U.S. Geological Survey

CANADA

SASKATCHEWAN

ALBERTA

BRITISH COLUMBIA

IDAHO

WYOMING

ND

Plentywood

Medicine Lake NWR

Scobey

Fort Peck Indian Reservation

Sidney

River

Glendive

Circle

Lanesteer National Wildlife Refuge

Baker

Ekalaka

Custer National Forest

Miles City

Broadus

Fort Keogh Livestock and Range Research Lab

Forsyth

Custer NF

Northern Cheyenne Indian Reservation

Jordan

Glasgow

Fort Peck Lake

Nelson Reservoir

Hewitt Lake NWR

Bowdoin NWR

UL Bend NWR

Charles M Russell NWR

Fresno Reservoir

Lake Thibadeau NWR

Black Coulee NWR

Fort Belknap IR

Creedman Coulee NWR

Havre

Upper Missouri River Breaks National Monument

Fort Benton

Lake Mason NWR

War Horse NWR

Lewistown

Roundup

Pompeys Pillar NM

Little Bighorn Battlefield National Monument

Hardin

Crow Indian Reservation

Bighorn Lake

Halfbreed Lake NWR

Hailstone NWR

Big Timber

Billings

Bighorn Canyon NRA

Custer NF

Red Lodge

Custer NF

Gallatin NF

Yellowstone National Park

Livingston

Bozeman

Gallatin National Forest

Lewis and Clark National Forest

White Sulphur Springs

Lewis and Clark National Forest

Gallatin National Forest

Canyon Ferry Lake

Townsend

Helena NF

Helena NF

Helena NF

Helena

Grant-Kohrs Ranch NHS

Deerlodge National Forest

Deer Lodge NF

Butte

Gallatin NF

Beaverhead NF

Red Rock Lakes NWR

Centennial Mountains Sheep Experimental Station

Virginia City

Beaverhead National Forest

Dillon

Clark Canyon Reservoir

Beaverhead National Forest

Great Falls

Malmstrom Air Force Base

Benton Lake NWR

Rocky Boys Indian Reservation

Teton River

Lewis and Clark National Forest

Pishkun Reservoir

Willow Creek Reservoir

Gibson Reservoir

Helena NF

Fort William H Harrison

Bearmouth National Guard Training Area

Rattlesnake NRA

Lolo NF

Missoula

Hamilton

Lee Metcalf NWR

Lolo NF

Bitterroot NF

Lake Como

Big Hole NB

Lolo NF

National Bison Range

Nine-Pipe NWR

Flathead NF

Lolo NF

Cut Bank

Conrad

Marias River

Lake Elwell

Blackfeet Indian Reservation

East Glacier Park

Glacier National Park

Lake Sherburne

Hungry Horse Reservoir

Flathead Reservoir

Swan River NWR

Flathead NF

Pablo IR

Flathead IR

Kalispell

Flathead NF

Lost Trail NWR

Flathead Lake

Lolo NF

Kootenai NF

Lolo NF

Eureka

Lake Koocanusa

Kootenai National Forest

Libby

Kaniksu NF

Kaniksu National Forest

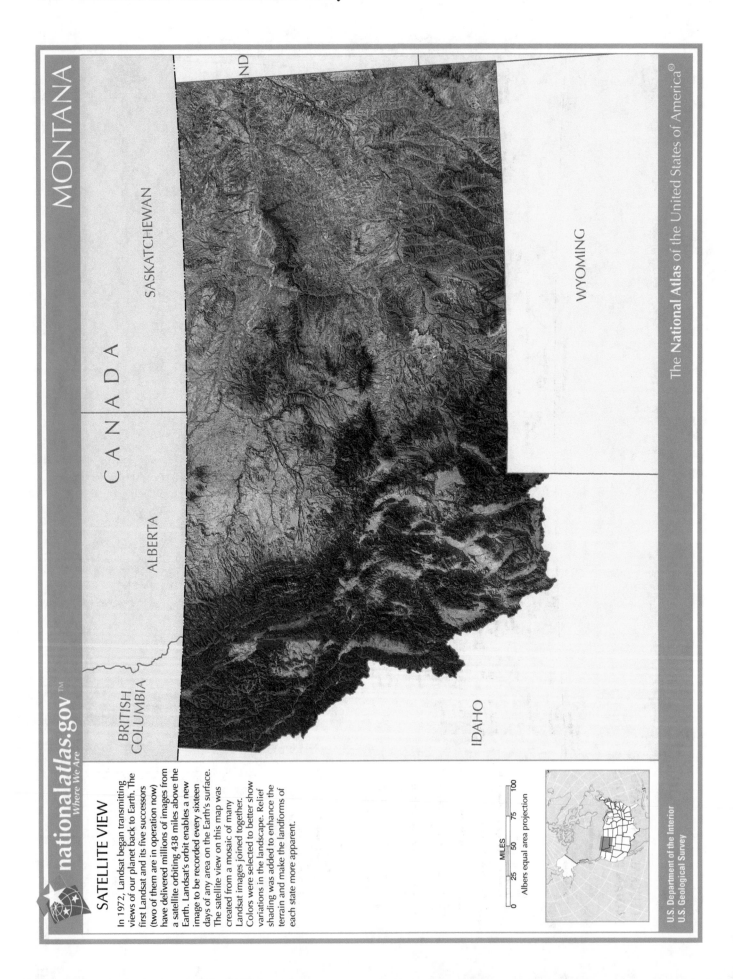

MONTANA

nationalatlas.gov™
Where We Are

SATELLITE VIEW

In 1972, Landsat began transmitting views of our planet back to Earth. The first Landsat and its five successors (two of them are in operation now) have delivered millions of images from a satellite orbiting 438 miles above the Earth. Landsat's orbit enables a new image to be recorded every sixteen days of any area on the Earth's surface. The satellite view on this map was created from a mosaic of many Landsat images joined together. Colors were selected to better show variations in the landscape. Relief shading was added to enhance the terrain and make the landforms of each state more apparent.

CANADA

SASKATCHEWAN

ALBERTA

BRITISH COLUMBIA

ND

WYOMING

IDAHO

MILES
0   25   50   75   100
Albers equal area projection

U.S. Department of the Interior
U.S. Geological Survey

The **National Atlas** of the United States of America®

Nebraska

Topic	Value	Time Period
Total Surface Area (acres)	49,509,600	2007
Land	49,033,400	2007
Federal Land	647,600	2007
Owned	176,025	FY 2009
Leased	6,296	FY 2009
Otherwise Managed	234	FY 2009
National Forest	352,000	September 2006
National Wilderness	12,429	October 2011
Non-Federal Land, Developed	1,156,500	2007
Non-Federal Land, Rural	47,229,300	2007
Water	476,200	2007
National Natural Landmarks	5	December 2010
National Historic Landmarks	20	December 2010
National Register of Historic Places	1,016	December 2010
National Parks	5	December 2010
Visitors to National Parks	290,323	2010
Historic Places Documented by the National Park Service	112	December 2010
Archeological Sites in National Parks	160	December 2010
Threatened and Endangered Species in National Parks	5	December 2010
Economic Benefit from National Park Tourism (dollars)	8,763,000	2009
Conservation Reserve Program (acres)	1,005,750	October 2011
Land and Water Conservation Fund Grants (dollars)	44,324,768	Since 1965
Historic Preservation Grants (dollars)	16,970,269	2010
Community Conservation and Recreation Projects	47	Since 1987
Federal Acres Transferred for Local Parks and Recreation	1,152	Since 1948
Crude Petroleum Production (millions of barrels)	2	2010
Crude Oil Proved Reserves (millions of barrels)	9	2009
Natural Gas Reserves (billions of cubic feet)	Not Available	2009
Natural Gas Liquid Reserves (millions of barrels)	Not Available	2008
Natural Gas Marketed Production (billions of cubic feet)	3	2009
Coal Reserves (millions of short tons)	Not Available	2009

Sources: U.S. Department of the Interior, National Park Service, State Profiles, December 2010; United States Department of Agriculture, Natural Resources Conservation Service, 2007 National Resources Inventory; U.S. General Services Administration, Federal Real Property Council, FY 2009 Federal Real Property Report, September 2010; University of Montana, www.wilderness.net; U.S. Department of Agriculture, Farm Services Agency, Conservation Reserve Program, October 2011; U.S Census Bureau, 2012 Statistical Abstract of the United States

Nebraska Energy Overview and Analysis

Quick Facts

- Nebraska is among the Nation's top producers of corn-based ethanol.
- Nebraska is one of the few States that allow the use of conventional motor gasoline statewide.
- Most of Nebraska's small oil reserves are located in the western half of the State.
- Nebraska recently opened its first biodiesel facility, which has a capacity of 5 million gallons per year.

Analysis

Resources and Consumption

Nebraska has small oil reserves concentrated in the Denver and Anadarko basins in the western part of the State. The north-central and southwestern parts of the State have wind power potential. Nebraska's high-yield corn crop allows the State to be among the leading producers of ethanol in the Nation. Nebraska's total energy consumption is low, commensurate with the State's population. The industrial sector leads State energy demand, and the transportation and residential sectors are also important energy consumers.

Petroleum

Nebraska has minor crude oil production. The Platte crude oil pipeline from Wyoming passes though southern Nebraska on its way to larger markets in the U.S. Midwest. A network of petroleum product pipelines connects Nebraska markets to refining centers in nearby States. A 2,148 mile pipeline is currently under construction and once completed in 2010, will transport crude oil from Alberta, Canada through eastern Nebraska to other Midwest markets.

A national leader in corn production, Nebraska is also among the Nation's top producers of corn-based ethanol, and numerous ethanol plants are concentrated in the central and eastern parts of the State. The State is considering the use of other feedstocks, including soybean or other vegetable oils, in the expansion of its biofuels program. The State recently opened its first biodiesel facility, with the capacity to produce 5 million gallons of biodiesel per year by refining crude soybean oil. The State's ethanol production is largely for use in other States, as Nebraska is one of the few States in the Nation that allow the statewide use of conventional motor gasoline. (Most States require the use of specific gasoline blends in non-attainment areas due to air-quality considerations.)

Natural Gas

Nebraska's consumption of natural gas is low, and the State relies on interstate transfers to meet virtually all of that demand. Natural gas is supplied from Rocky Mountain-, Texas-, and Oklahoma panhandle-area producers via pipelines entering the State via Kansas, Colorado, and Wyoming. Nebraska ships over three-fifths of the natural gas it receives to Iowa, Missouri, and South Dakota. The industrial sector is the State's leading consumer, followed by the residential sector. Over two-thirds of Nebraska households use natural gas as their primary fuel for home heating.

Coal, Electricity, and Renewables

Coal-fired power plants supply two-thirds of Nebraska's electricity generation market, nuclear power supplies just under three-tenths, and hydroelectric power supplies most of the remainder. Nebraska receives virtually all of its coal by rail from Wyoming. Nebraska's two nuclear power plants are located along the Missouri River on the State's eastern border. Nebraska also has several small hydroelectric dams along the Platte River and produces a minor amount of energy from wind power.

Source: U.S. Energy Information Administration, October 2009

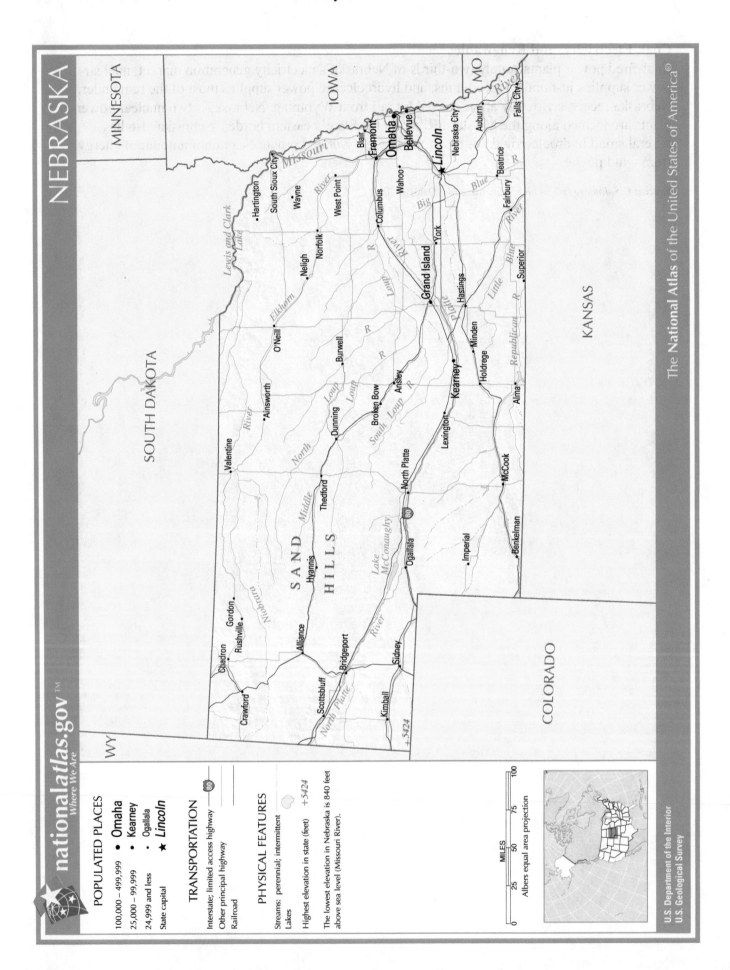

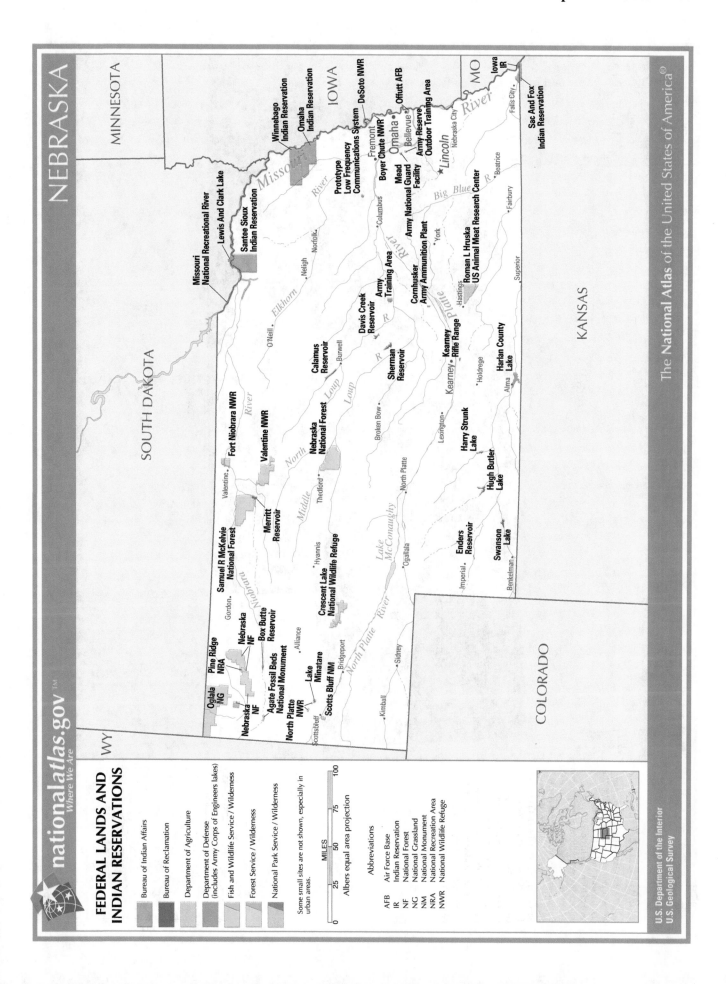

nationalatlas.gov™
Where We Are

FEDERAL LANDS AND INDIAN RESERVATIONS

Bureau of Indian Affairs

Bureau of Reclamation

Department of Agriculture

Department of Defense
(includes Army Corps of Engineers lakes)

Fish and Wildlife Service / Wilderness

Forest Service / Wilderness

National Park Service / Wilderness

Some small sites are not shown, especially in urban areas.

MILES
0   25   50   75   100

Albers equal area projection

Abbreviations

AFB   Air Force Base
IR   Indian Reservation
NF   National Forest
NG   National Grassland
NM   National Monument
NRA   National Recreation Area
NWR   National Wildlife Refuge

U.S. Department of the Interior
U.S. Geological Survey

NEBRASKA

MINNESOTA

SOUTH DAKOTA

WY

IOWA

MO

KANSAS

COLORADO

Winnebago Indian Reservation

Omaha Indian Reservation

DeSoto NWR

Offutt AFB

Army Reserve Outdoor Training Area

Iowa IR

Sac And Fox Indian Reservation

Falls City

Nebraska City

Missouri National Recreational River

Lewis And Clark Lake

Santee Sioux Indian Reservation

Missouri River

River

Prototype Low Frequency Communications System

Boyer Chute NWR

Fremont

Mead

Omaha

Bellevue

Army National Guard Facility

Lincoln

Cornhusker Army Ammunition Plant

Roman L Hruska US Animal Meat Research Center

Columbus

York

Big Blue R

Beatrice

Fairbury

Superior

Norfolk

Neligh

Elkhorn

O'Neill

Army Training Area

Davis Creek Reservoir

Calamus Reservoir

Burwell

Sherman Reservoir

Platte River

Hastings

Kearney

Kearney Rifle Range

Harlan County Lake

Holdrege

Alma

Lexington

Loup

North Loup

Middle Loup

Fort Niobrara NWR

Valentine NWR

Nebraska National Forest

Thedford

Valentine

Merritt Reservoir

Hyannis

Crescent Lake National Wildlife Refuge

Broken Bow

North Platte

Lake McConaughy

Ogallala

Harry Strunk Lake

Hugh Butler Lake

Enders Reservoir

Swanson Lake

Imperial

Benkelman

Samuel R McKelvie National Forest

Gordon

Niobrara River

Pine Ridge NRA

Nebraska NF

Box Butte Reservoir

Alliance

Oglala NG

Nebraska NF

Agate Fossil Beds National Monument

North Platte NWR

Lake Minatare

Scotts Bluff NM

Bridgeport

North Platte River

Scottsbluff

Sidney

Kimball

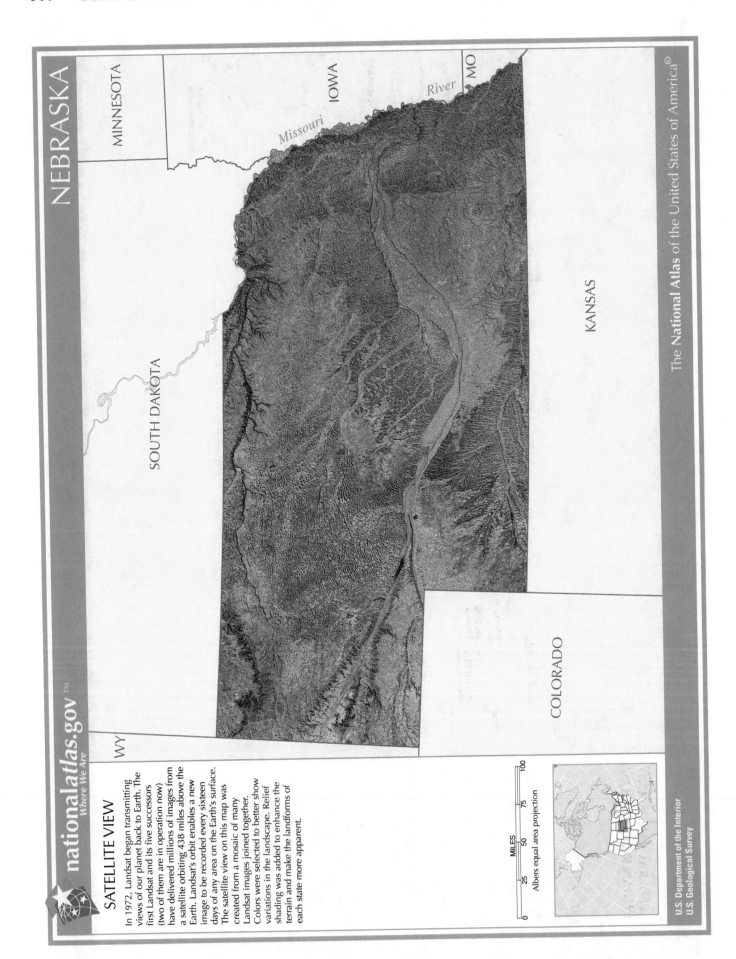

NEBRASKA

MINNESOTA

IOWA

MO

Missouri

River

SOUTH DAKOTA

KANSAS

COLORADO

WY

nationalatlas.gov ™
Where We Are

SATELLITE VIEW

In 1972, Landsat began transmitting views of our planet back to Earth. The first Landsat and its five successors (two of them are in operation now) have delivered millions of images from a satellite orbiting 438 miles above the Earth. Landsat's orbit enables a new image to be recorded every sixteen days of any area on the Earth's surface. The satellite view on this map was created from a mosaic of many Landsat images joined together. Colors were selected to better show variations in the landscape. Relief shading was added to enhance the terrain and make the landforms of each state more apparent.

MILES

0   25   50   75   100

Albers equal area projection

The **National Atlas** of the United States of America ®

U.S. Department of the Interior
U.S. Geological Survey

Nevada

Topic	Value	Time Period
Total Surface Area (acres)	70,763,100	2007
Land	70,332,000	2007
Federal Land	59,868,900	2007
Owned	2,013,950	FY 2009
Leased	1,602	FY 2009
Otherwise Managed	4,180	FY 2009
National Forest	5,746,000	September 2006
National Wilderness	3,371,425	October 2011
Non-Federal Land, Developed	582,900	2007
Non-Federal Land, Rural	9,880,200	2007
Water	431,100	2007
National Natural Landmarks	6	December 2010
National Historic Landmarks	7	December 2010
National Register of Historic Places	364	December 2010
National Parks	3	December 2010
Visitors to National Parks	5,399,439	2010
Historic Places Documented by the National Park Service	327	December 2010
Archeological Sites in National Parks	779	December 2010
Threatened and Endangered Species in National Parks	11	December 2010
Economic Benefit from National Park Tourism (dollars)	173,140,000	2009
Conservation Reserve Program (acres)	Not Available	October 2011
Land and Water Conservation Fund Grants (dollars)	40,375,689	Since 1965
Historic Preservation Grants (dollars)	18,115,304	2010
Community Conservation and Recreation Projects	41	Since 1987
Federal Acres Transferred for Local Parks and Recreation	431	Since 1948
Crude Petroleum Production (millions of barrels)	Not Available	2010
Crude Oil Proved Reserves (millions of barrels)	Not Available	2009
Natural Gas Reserves (billions of cubic feet)	Not Available	2009
Natural Gas Liquid Reserves (millions of barrels)	Not Available	2008
Natural Gas Marketed Production (billions of cubic feet)	Not Available	2009
Coal Reserves (millions of short tons)	Not Available	2009

Sources: U.S. Department of the Interior, National Park Service, State Profiles, December 2010; United States Department of Agriculture, Natural Resources Conservation Service, 2007 National Resources Inventory; U.S. General Services Administration, Federal Real Property Council, FY 2009 Federal Real Property Report, September 2010; University of Montana, www.wilderness.net; U.S. Department of Agriculture, Farm Services Agency, Conservation Reserve Program, October 2011; U.S Census Bureau, 2012 Statistical Abstract of the United States

Nevada Energy Overview and Analysis

Quick Facts

- Nevada has large geothermal resources and is second only to California in the generation of electricity from geothermal energy.
- Though total State petroleum consumption is low, Nevada's jet fuel consumption is disproportionately high due in large part to demand from airports in Las Vegas and Reno and from two air bases.
- The State's largest power generating plant, the Mohave Generating Station, which was fueled primarily with coal, was shut down at the end of 2005 for failing to install agreed-upon pollution-control equipment.
- Nevada has become a substantial producer of solar energy.

Analysis

Resources and Consumption

Nevada is rich in renewable energy potential but has few fossil energy resources. Nevada leads the Nation in geothermal and solar power potential and much of the State is suitable for wind power development. The Colorado River, which forms Nevada's southern border, is a powerful hydroelectric power resource. Nevada's population and total energy consumption are low and the State's economy is not energy intensive. Due in part to the Las Vegas tourism industry, the transportation sector is the leading energy-consuming sector in the State.

Petroleum

Nevada has one small crude oil refinery that produces primarily asphalt and diesel fuel. The State relies on California refineries for nearly all its transportation fuels and three petroleum product pipelines transport supply from California refining centers to the Las Vegas and Reno fuel markets. A new 400-mile pipeline has been proposed to connect Salt Lake City refineries to southern Nevada consumers. The UNEV Pipeline is expected to be completed by the end of 2010 and would help accommodate the growing population of the Las Vegas region, one of the fastest growing metropolitan areas in the Nation. Although total petroleum consumption is low, Nevada's jet fuel consumption is disproportionately high due to demand from airports in Las Vegas and Reno and from two military air installations. The Las Vegas metropolitan area requires the year-round use of a cleaner burning gasoline (CBG) blend, which has low volatility and contains oxygenates, and both the Las Vegas and Reno metropolitan areas require the use of oxygenated motor gasoline during the winter months.

Natural Gas

Natural gas in Nevada is used overwhelmingly for electricity generation, and over one-half of Nevada households use natural gas as their primary energy source for home heating. Interstate pipelines supply Nevada with natural gas from Utah and other neighboring Rocky Mountain States. The largest of these lines, the Kern River Gas Transmission pipeline from Wyoming, supplies the Las Vegas area as it passes through southern Nevada on the way to markets in southern California. Nevada ships almost 70 percent of the natural gas it receives to California.

Coal, Electricity, and Renewables

Natural gas-fired power plants supply over one-half of the electricity generated in Nevada, while coal-fired power plants supply nearly two-fifths. Hydroelectric and geothermal power plants supply most of the remainder and Nevada is one of the few States that generate electricity from geothermal resources. Nevada has also become a substantial producer of solar energy. Arizona and Utah are Nevada's primary coal suppliers.

Until 2006, Nevada's largest operating power plant was the Mohave Generating Station, which supplied power to southern California until it was shut down at the end of 2005 for failure to install pollution control equipment. The coal supply for this plant was mixed with water and transported from mines in northwestern Arizona through a 275-mile pipeline-the only pipeline coal delivery system in the world. The State's largest operating power plant is now the Chuck Lenzie Generating Station, a natural gas-fueled plant that utilizes North America's largest air cooled condenser system and a water clarifier system that recycles about 75 percent of the used water. These technologies allow the Lenzie Station to use only 2.2 percent of the water required by a conventional coal plant per megawatt of electricity generated.

The State's second largest operating power plant is the hydroelectric Hoover Dam on the Colorado River, which supplies markets in southern California, in addition to those in Nevada and Arizona. Built in less than 5 years during the Great Depression, the Hoover Dam stands today as a world-renowned structure and a National Historic Landmark.

Several high-voltage transmission lines currently connect Nevada to other western electricity grids, and Nevada hopes to increase electricity sales to California in the near future. In April 2005, four western State governors agreed to develop a 1,300-mile high-capacity power line from Wyoming to California that would allow as much as 12 thousand megawatts of electricity to flow from the energy-rich Rocky Mountain region to high-demand markets in California. A feasibility study was released in 2007 that supports the development of this transmission line project and a second phase development study is currently underway. Nevada may use that line to deliver electricity produced from an expanding renewable power portfolio, which includes geothermal, wind, and solar power projects. Currently, several geothermal power-generating facilities operate in the northwestern part of Nevada. Although over one-third of Nevada households use electricity as their main energy source for home heating, the State's overall electricity demand is low.

In June 2009, Nevada established a new renewable portfolio standard (RPS) that requires 25 percent of the State's electricity come from renewable sources by 2025, with at least 6 percent coming from solar energy sources by 2016.

Source: U.S. Energy Information Administration, October 2009

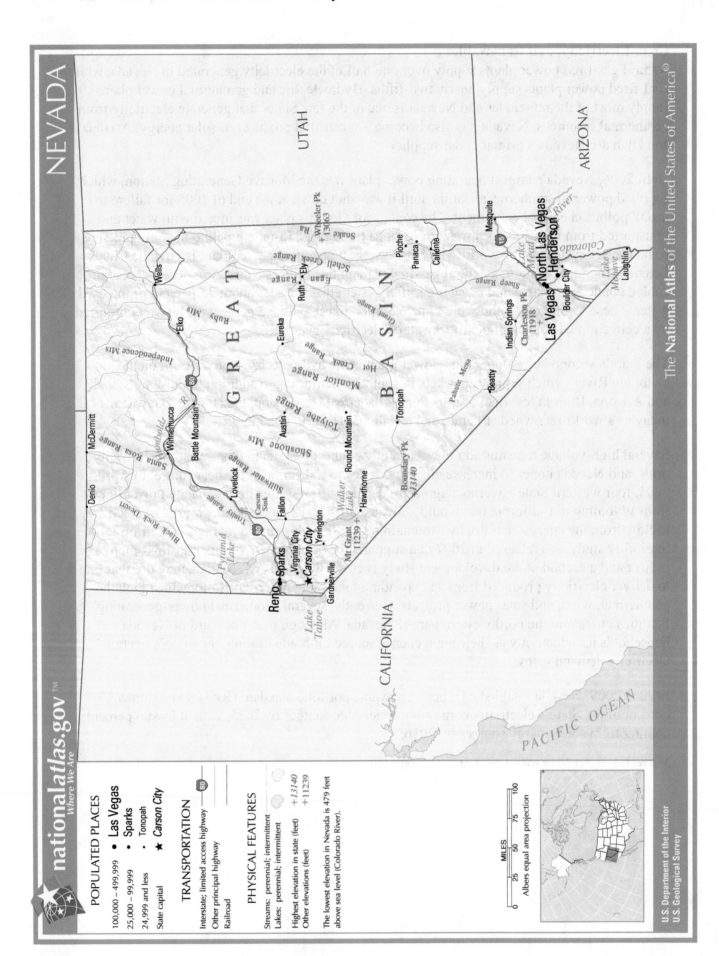

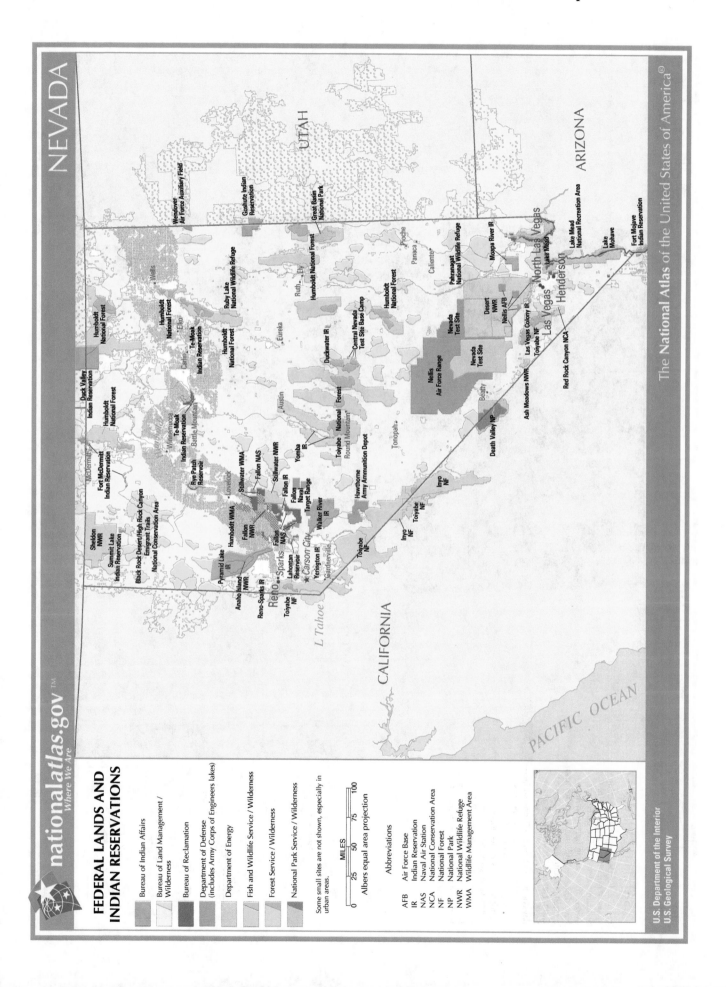

FEDERAL LANDS AND INDIAN RESERVATIONS

Bureau of Indian Affairs

Bureau of Land Management / Wilderness

Bureau of Reclamation

Department of Defense (includes Army Corps of Engineers lakes)

Department of Energy

Fish and Wildlife Service / Wilderness

Forest Service / Wilderness

National Park Service / Wilderness

Some small sites are not shown, especially in urban areas.

MILES

0   25   50   75   100

Albers equal area projection

Abbreviations

AFB   Air Force Base
IR   Indian Reservation
NAS   Naval Air Station
NCA   National Conservation Area
NF   National Forest
NP   National Park
NWR   National Wildlife Refuge
WMA   Wildlife Management Area

nationalatlas.gov™
Where We Are

NEVADA

The National Atlas of the United States of America®

U.S. Department of the Interior
U.S. Geological Survey

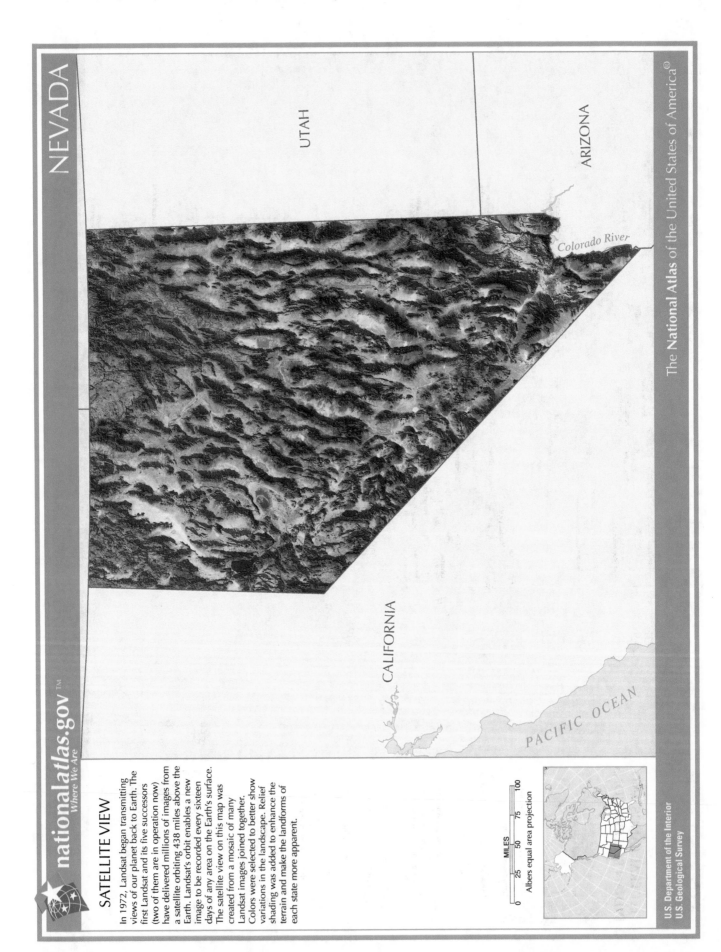

NEVADA

UTAH

ARIZONA

Colorado River

CALIFORNIA

PACIFIC OCEAN

The National Atlas of the United States of America®

nationalatlas.gov™
Where We Are

SATELLITE VIEW

In 1972, Landsat began transmitting views of our planet back to Earth. The first Landsat and its five successors (two of them are in operation now) have delivered millions of images from a satellite orbiting 438 miles above the Earth. Landsat's orbit enables a new image to be recorded every sixteen days of any area on the Earth's surface. The satellite view on this map was created from a mosaic of many Landsat images joined together. Colors were selected to better show variations in the landscape. Relief shading was added to enhance the terrain and make the landforms of each state more apparent.

MILES
0   25   50   75   100
Albers equal area projection

U.S. Department of the Interior
U.S. Geological Survey

New Hampshire

Topic	Value	Time Period
Total Surface Area (acres)	5,941,000	2007
Land	5,704,800	2007
Federal Land	763,200	2007
Owned	21,898	FY 2009
Leased	370	FY 2009
Otherwise Managed	400	FY 2009
National Forest	736,000	September 2006
National Wilderness	138,418	October 2011
Non-Federal Land, Developed	695,500	2007
Non-Federal Land, Rural	4,246,100	2007
Water	236,200	2007
National Natural Landmarks	11	December 2010
National Historic Landmarks	22	December 2010
National Register of Historic Places	726	December 2010
National Parks	2	December 2010
Visitors to National Parks	30,941	2010
Historic Places Documented by the National Park Service	278	December 2010
Archeological Sites in National Parks	20	December 2010
Threatened and Endangered Species in National Parks	1	December 2010
Economic Benefit from National Park Tourism (dollars)	1,176,000	2009
Conservation Reserve Program (acres)	13	October 2011
Land and Water Conservation Fund Grants (dollars)	36,699,617	Since 1965
Historic Preservation Grants (dollars)	17,201,029	2010
Community Conservation and Recreation Projects	66	Since 1987
Federal Acres Transferred for Local Parks and Recreation	184	Since 1948
Crude Petroleum Production (millions of barrels)	Not Available	2010
Crude Oil Proved Reserves (millions of barrels)	Not Available	2009
Natural Gas Reserves (billions of cubic feet)	Not Available	2009
Natural Gas Liquid Reserves (millions of barrels)	Not Available	2008
Natural Gas Marketed Production (billions of cubic feet)	Not Available	2009
Coal Reserves (millions of short tons)	Not Available	2009

Sources: *U.S. Department of the Interior, National Park Service, State Profiles, December 2010; United States Department of Agriculture, Natural Resources Conservation Service, 2007 National Resources Inventory; U.S. General Services Administration, Federal Real Property Council, FY 2009 Federal Real Property Report, September 2010; University of Montana, www.wilderness.net; U.S. Department of Agriculture, Farm Services Agency, Conservation Reserve Program, October 2011; U.S Census Bureau, 2012 Statistical Abstract of the United States*

New Hampshire Energy Overview and Analysis

Quick Facts

- The Seabrook nuclear power plant, located near Portsmouth, is the largest single nuclear reactor in New England.
- More than one-half of New Hampshire households use fuel oil for winter heating.
- The transportation and residential sectors are New Hampshire's largest energy consumers.
- New Hampshire's total energy consumption and per capita energy consumption are among the lowest in the Nation.
- In May 2007, New Hampshire adopted a renewable portfolio standard that requires 25 percent of the State's electricity to be generated from renewable sources by 2025.

Analysis

Resources and Consumption

New Hampshire has no fossil fuel reserves but has substantial renewable energy potential. The Appalachian Mountains, which cover much of western New Hampshire, offer wind power potential, and several waterways, including the Connecticut and Merrimack river basins, are hydroelectric power resources. In addition, dense forests in northern and southern New Hampshire offer potential fuel wood for electricity generation. New Hampshire is not an energy-intensive State; both total energy consumption and per capita energy consumption are among the lowest in the Nation. The transportation and residential sectors are New Hampshire's largest energy consumers.

Petroleum

Portsmouth, on New Hampshire's Atlantic coast, receives petroleum product shipments from other States and from abroad. Residential per capita petroleum consumption is high in New Hampshire due to widespread use of fuel oil for home heating during the long, cold winters. New Hampshire households are among the most petroleum-dependent in the Nation, as more than one-half of New Hampshire homes use fuel oil as their primary energy source for home heating. The State requires reformulated motor gasoline blended with ethanol in the populated areas in southeastern New Hampshire.

New Hampshire, along with much of the U.S. Northeast, is vulnerable to distillate fuel oil shortages and price spikes during the winter months. In January and February 2000, distillate fuel oil prices rose sharply when extreme winter weather increased demand unexpectedly and hindered the arrival of new supply, as frozen rivers and high winds slowed the docking and unloading of barges and tankers. In July 2000, in order to reduce the risk of future shortages, the President directed the U.S. Department of Energy to establish the Northeast Heating Oil Reserve. The Reserve gives Northeast consumers adequate supplies for about 10 days, the time required for ships to carry heating oil from the Gulf of Mexico to New York Harbor. The Reserve's storage terminals are located in Perth Amboy, New Jersey, and Groton and New Haven, Connecticut.

Natural Gas

Although New Hampshire's total natural gas consumption is low compared to other States, demand has grown rapidly in recent years, particularly for use in electricity generation. The majority of the gas is supplied by pipelines entering the State from Maine and Canada. New Hampshire ships about one-half of the natural gas it receives to Massachusetts.

Coal, Electricity, and Renewables

New Hampshire's net electricity generation is among the lowest in the Nation. Before 2003, the Seabrook nuclear power plant near Portsmouth provided more than one-half of State generation. Since then, however, that dominance has slipped as two new natural gas-fired power plants have come online. As in other New England States, the growing use of natural gas in New Hampshire's power industry has been driven by natural gas's lower emission levels compared with other fossil fuels and the ease of siting new natural gas-fired power plants. Natural gas-fired generation now accounts for about one-quarter of the State's power production. New Hampshire's residential electricity use is low compared with the national average, in part because demand for air-conditioning is low during the generally mild summer months and because few households use electricity as their primary energy source for home heating.

New Hampshire also produces electricity from renewable energy sources, including hydroelectric power, fuel wood, landfill gas, and municipal solid waste. Ten percent of New Hampshire's electricity generation is derived from these renewable sources. In May 2007, New Hampshire adopted a renewable portfolio standard that requires 25 percent of the State's electricity to be generated from renewable sources by 2025.

Source: U.S. Energy Information Administration, October 2009

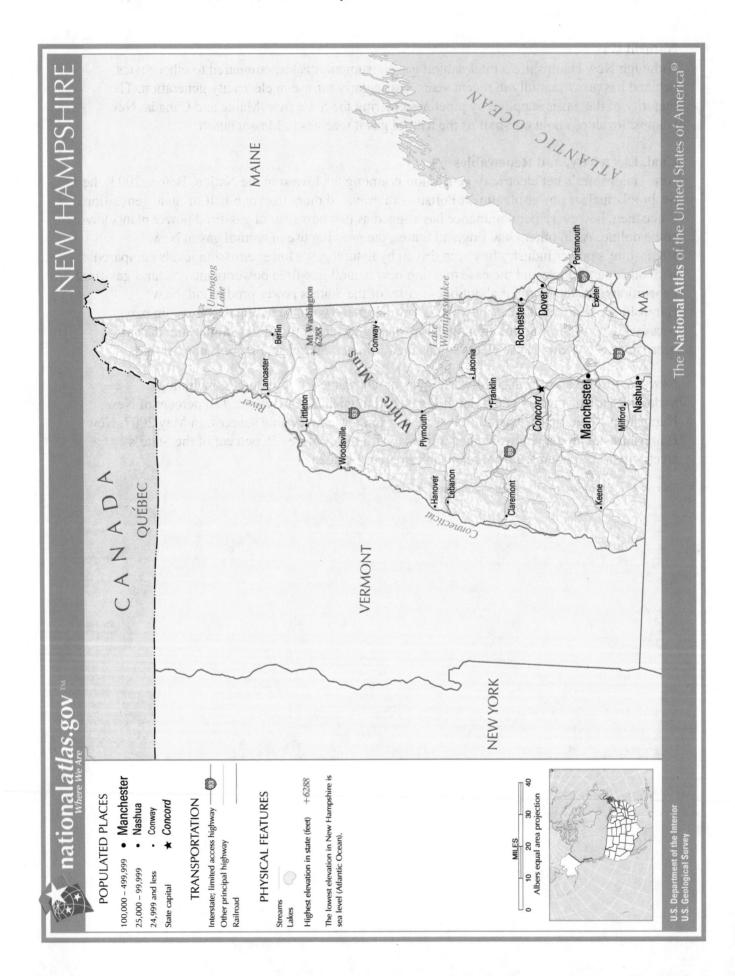

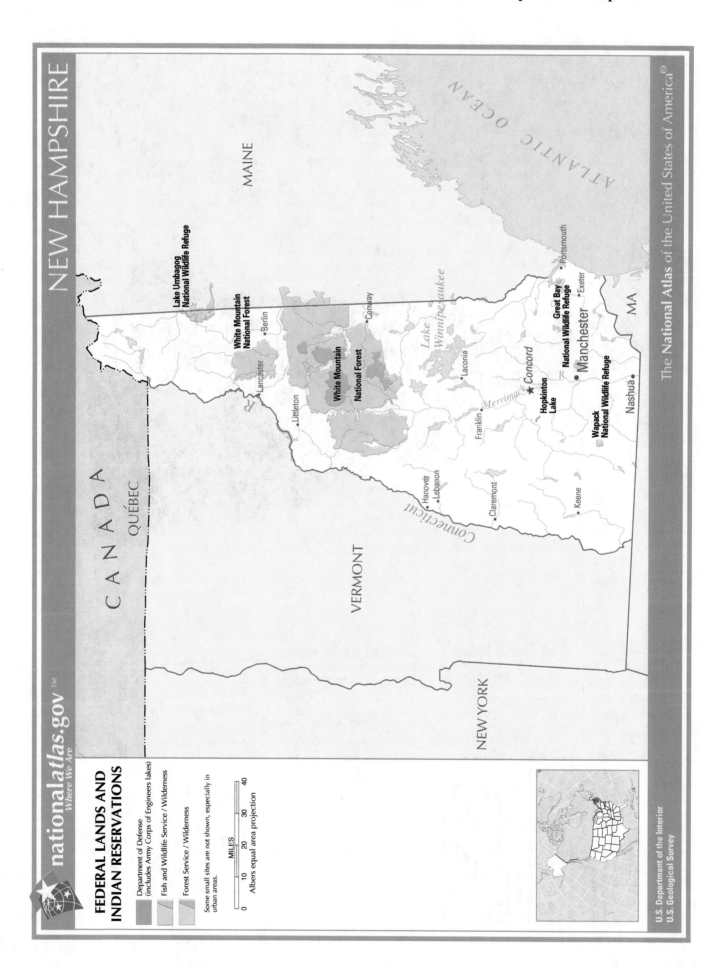

NEW HAMPSHIRE

nationalatlas.gov™
Where We Are

**FEDERAL LANDS AND
INDIAN RESERVATIONS**

Department of Defense
(includes Army Corps of Engineers lakes)

Fish and Wildlife Service / Wilderness

Forest Service / Wilderness

Some small sites are not shown, especially in
urban areas.

MILES
0   10   20   30   40
Albers equal area projection

The National Atlas of the United States of America®

U.S. Department of the Interior
U.S. Geological Survey

CANADA
QUÉBEC

MAINE

ATLANTIC OCEAN

VERMONT

NEW YORK

MA

Lake Umbagog
National Wildlife Refuge

White Mountain
National Forest

Berlin

Lancaster

Littleton

White Mountain
National Forest

Conway

Lake Winnipesaukee

Laconia

Franklin

Concord

Hopkinton
Lake

Merrimack

Hanover

Lebanon

Claremont

Keene

Nashua

Manchester

Great Bay
National Wildlife Refuge

Portsmouth

Exeter

Wapack
National Wildlife Refuge

Connecticut

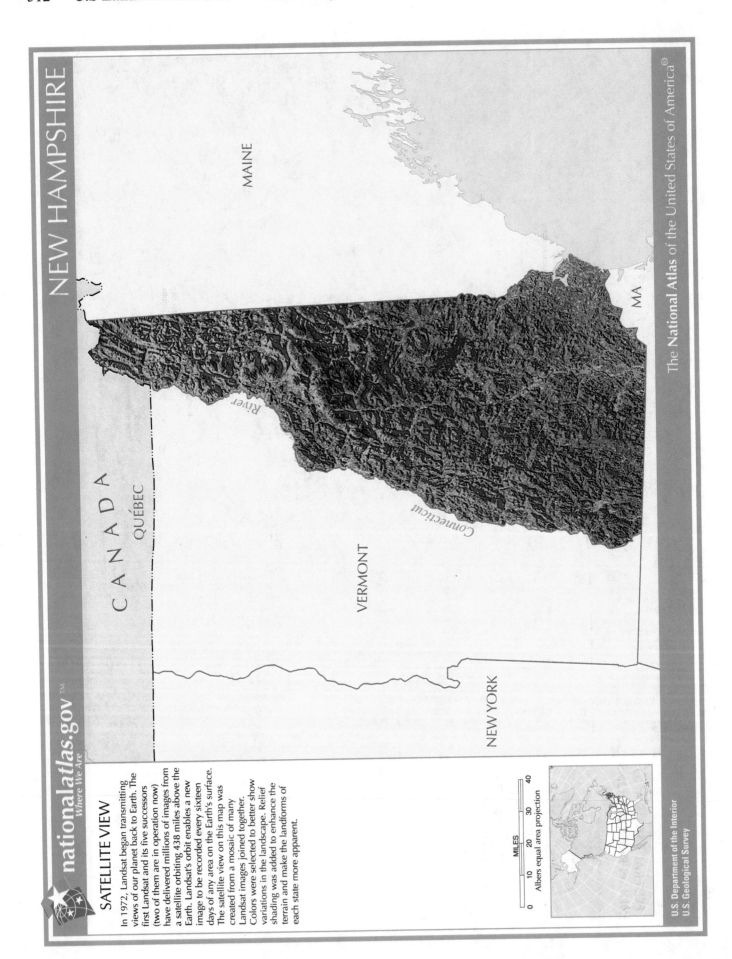

NEW HAMPSHIRE

nationalatlas.gov™
Where We Are

The *National Atlas* of the United States of America®

SATELLITE VIEW

In 1972, Landsat began transmitting
views of our planet back to Earth. The
first Landsat and its five successors
(two of them are in operation now)
have delivered millions of images from
a satellite orbiting 438 miles above the
Earth. Landsat's orbit enables a new
image to be recorded every sixteen
days of any area on the Earth's surface.
The satellite view on this map was
created from a mosaic of many
Landsat images joined together.
Colors were selected to better show
variations in the landscape. Relief
shading was added to enhance the
terrain and make the landforms of
each state more apparent.

CANADA

QUÉBEC

MAINE

River

Connecticut

VERMONT

MA

NEW YORK

MILES
0   10   20   30   40
Albers equal area projection

U.S. Department of the Interior
U.S. Geological Survey

New Jersey

Topic	Value	Time Period
Total Surface Area (acres)	5,215,600	2007
Land	4,689,600	2007
Federal Land	148,300	2007
Owned	87,684	FY 2009
Leased	1,478	FY 2009
Otherwise Managed	697	FY 2009
National Forest	0	September 2006
National Wilderness	10,341	October 2011
Non-Federal Land, Developed	1,849,300	2007
Non-Federal Land, Rural	2,692,000	2007
Water	526,000	2007
National Natural Landmarks	11	December 2010
National Historic Landmarks	55	December 2010
National Register of Historic Places	1,613	December 2010
National Parks	8	December 2010
Visitors to National Parks	5,858,443	2010
Historic Places Documented by the National Park Service	1,575	December 2010
Archeological Sites in National Parks	410	December 2010
Threatened and Endangered Species in National Parks	12	December 2010
Economic Benefit from National Park Tourism (dollars)	94,657,000	2009
Conservation Reserve Program (acres)	2,356	October 2011
Land and Water Conservation Fund Grants (dollars)	119,179,924	Since 1965
Historic Preservation Grants (dollars)	23,131,412	2010
Community Conservation and Recreation Projects	41	Since 1987
Federal Acres Transferred for Local Parks and Recreation	2,164	Since 1948
Crude Petroleum Production (millions of barrels)	Not Available	2010
Crude Oil Proved Reserves (millions of barrels)	Not Available	2009
Natural Gas Reserves (billions of cubic feet)	Not Available	2009
Natural Gas Liquid Reserves (millions of barrels)	Not Available	2008
Natural Gas Marketed Production (billions of cubic feet)	Not Available	2009
Coal Reserves (millions of short tons)	Not Available	2009

Sources: *U.S. Department of the Interior, National Park Service, State Profiles, December 2010; United States Department of Agriculture, Natural Resources Conservation Service, 2007 National Resources Inventory; U.S. General Services Administration, Federal Real Property Council, FY 2009 Federal Real Property Report, September 2010; University of Montana, www.wilderness.net; U.S. Department of Agriculture, Farm Services Agency, Conservation Reserve Program, October 2011; U.S Census Bureau, 2012 Statistical Abstract of the United States*

New Jersey Energy Overview and Analysis

Quick Facts

- The New York Harbor area between New York and New Jersey has a petroleum bulk terminal storage capacity of over 75 million barrels (much of which is in New Jersey), making it the largest petroleum product hub in the United States.
- The largest of the three U.S. Northeast Heating Oil Reserve sites is located in Perth Amboy, New Jersey.
- New Jersey's Oyster Creek nuclear reactor, which first came online in 1969, is the oldest operating nuclear plant in the United States.
- Nuclear power dominates New Jersey's electricity market, typically supplying more than one-half of State generation.
- The transportation sector leads energy consumption in New Jersey, where the average commute time is among the longest in the Nation.
- A 350-megawatt offshore wind farm was approved by the New Jersey Board of Public Utilities and will consist of 96 wind turbines arranged in a rectangular grid 16 to 20 miles off the coast of Cape May and Atlantic counties, pending completion of the permitting process.

Analysis

Resources and Consumption

New Jersey has no fossil fuel reserves, but it does have high wind power potential located onshore and offshore along its Atlantic coast. Many New Jersey residents live in the greater metropolitan areas of New York City and Philadelphia and work out-of-State in those cities. Due in part to this dynamic, the average commute times for New Jersey workers are among the longest in the Nation, and the transportation sector leads State energy consumption. Residential and commercial energy demand is also high. New Jersey's industrial energy consumption ranks near the National average, although the energy-intensive chemical manufacturing and petroleum refining industries are well represented in the State.

Petroleum

New Jersey is a major petroleum refining State and distribution center for petroleum products for the high-demand Northeast States. The State's six oil refineries, clustered along the Delaware River near Philadelphia and in the New York Harbor area, process crude oil mostly imported from overseas. New Jersey is connected to major petroleum product pipeline systems. The Buckeye Pipeline system branches through much of the Midwest and Northeast, while the Colonial Pipeline system pumps supplies from the Gulf Coast through the South and across the Eastern Seaboard before terminating in the New York Harbor area. New Jersey also receives petroleum product imports by tanker and barge principally from Canada, the Caribbean, South America, and Europe.

Located in both New York and New Jersey, New York Harbor acts as a central distribution center for the region, and many of the petroleum products delivered to the Harbor are later redistributed to smaller ports along the Hudson River where they supply local demand. The New

York Harbor area has a petroleum bulk terminal storage capacity of over 75 million barrels, making it the largest and most important petroleum product hub in the Northeast.

New Jersey is one of a handful of States that requires the statewide use of reformulated motor gasoline blended with ethanol, and the New York Harbor area is the primary Northeast distribution hub for ethanol supplies. A large ethanol storage facility in Sewaren receives ethanol rail shipments from the Midwest and marine imports from Brazil and the Caribbean and then redistributes these supplies to markets throughout the Northeast.

New Jersey, along with much of the Northeast, is vulnerable to distillate fuel oil shortages and price spikes during winter months due to high demand for home heating. Nearly one-fifth of New Jersey households use fuel oil as their primary energy source for home heating. In January and February 2000, distillate fuel oil prices rose sharply when extreme winter weather increased demand unexpectedly and hindered the arrival of new supply, as frozen rivers and high winds slowed the docking and unloading of barges and tankers. In July 2000, in order to reduce the risk of future shortages, the President directed the U.S. Department of Energy to establish the Northeast Heating Oil Reserve. The Reserve gives Northeast consumers adequate supplies for about 10 days, the time required for ships to carry heating oil from the Gulf of Mexico to New York Harbor. The Reserve's storage terminals are located in Perth Amboy, New Jersey, and Groton and New Haven, Connecticut. The storage terminal located at Perth Amboy is the largest of the three, with a capacity of almost 1 million barrels.

Natural Gas

New Jersey receives natural gas supplies through several natural gas pipeline systems that enter the State from Pennsylvania, and then delivers over one-half of these receipts to New York. Natural gas in New Jersey is used primarily by the residential sector, as roughly two-thirds of New Jersey households use natural gas as their primary energy source for home heating. To help meet demand in the Philadelphia metropolitan area, a liquefied natural gas (LNG) facility has been approved by the Federal Energy Regulatory Commission in Logan Township, New Jersey. If constructed, the plant would have the capacity to import up to 1.2 billion cubic feet of LNG per day from overseas.

Coal, Electricity, and Renewables

Nuclear power dominates New Jersey's electricity market, typically supplying more than one-half of State generation. New Jersey has three nuclear power plants, including the Oyster Creek Nuclear Generating Station, which came online in 1969 and is the oldest operating nuclear plant in the Nation. Natural gas- and coal-fired power plants supply most of New Jersey's remaining electricity generation. New Jersey's coal-fired plants burn coal received by rail and barge primarily from West Virginia, Pennsylvania, and Virginia. Although it contributes only minimally to net generation, New Jersey is a major producer of electricity from landfill gas and municipal solid waste.

In April 2006, the New Jersey Board of Public Utilities approved regulations that expanded the State's renewable portfolio standard, requiring utilities to generate 22.5 percent of their electricity from renewable sources by 2021, with solar sources generating at least 2 percent of this standard. In October 2008, Garden State Offshore Energy was approved by the New Jersey Board of Public Utilities as the developer of a 350-megawatt wind farm off New Jersey's coast and will evaluate the project's environmental impacts and wind resource quality as well as begin the permitting process at both the State and Federal levels. The proposed project consists of 96 wind turbines arranged in a rectangular grid 16 to 20 miles off the coast of Cape May and Atlantic counties.

Source: U.S. Energy Information Administration, October 2009

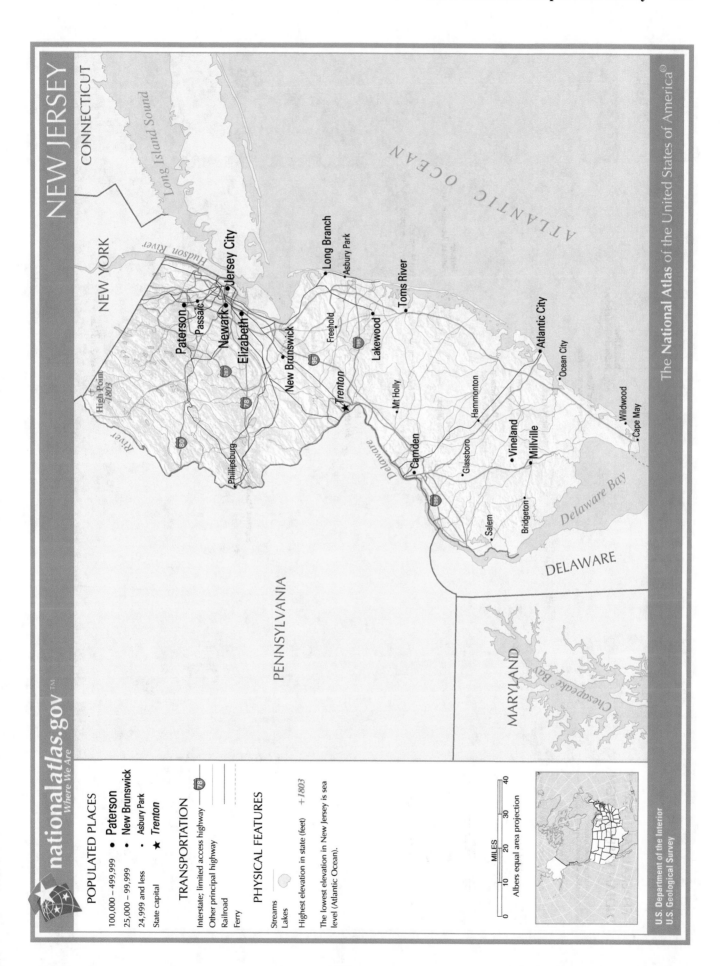

NEW JERSEY

CONNECTICUT

Long Island Sound

ATLANTIC OCEAN

NEW YORK

Hudson River

High Point
+1803

River

NEW YORK

Paterson
Passaic
Newark
Elizabeth
Jersey City

Long Branch
Asbury Park

Freehold

Toms River

New Brunswick

95

Trenton

Lakewood

Phillipsburg

78

80

Mt Holly

Hammonton

Camden

Atlantic City

Ocean City

Delaware

Vineland
Millville

Glassboro

Bridgeton

Salem

Wildwood
Cape May

Delaware Bay

PENNSYLVANIA

DELAWARE

MARYLAND

Chesapeake Bay

nationalatlas.gov ™
Where We Are

POPULATED PLACES

100,000 – 499,999   ● **Paterson**

25,000 – 99,999   ● **New Brunswick**

24,999 and less   · Asbury Park

State capital   ★ *Trenton*

TRANSPORTATION

Interstate; limited access highway   (78)

Other principal highway

Railroad

Ferry

PHYSICAL FEATURES

Streams

Lakes

Highest elevation in state (feet)   +1803

The lowest elevation in New Jersey is sea level (Atlantic Ocean).

MILES
0   10   20   30   40
Albers equal area projection

U.S. Department of the Interior
U.S. Geological Survey

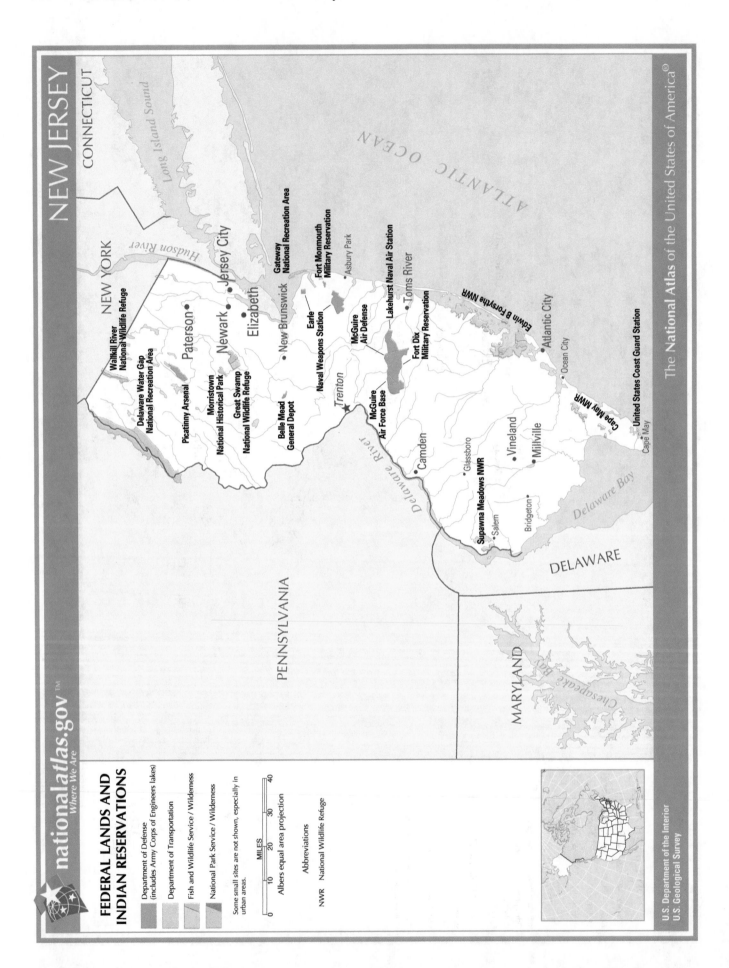

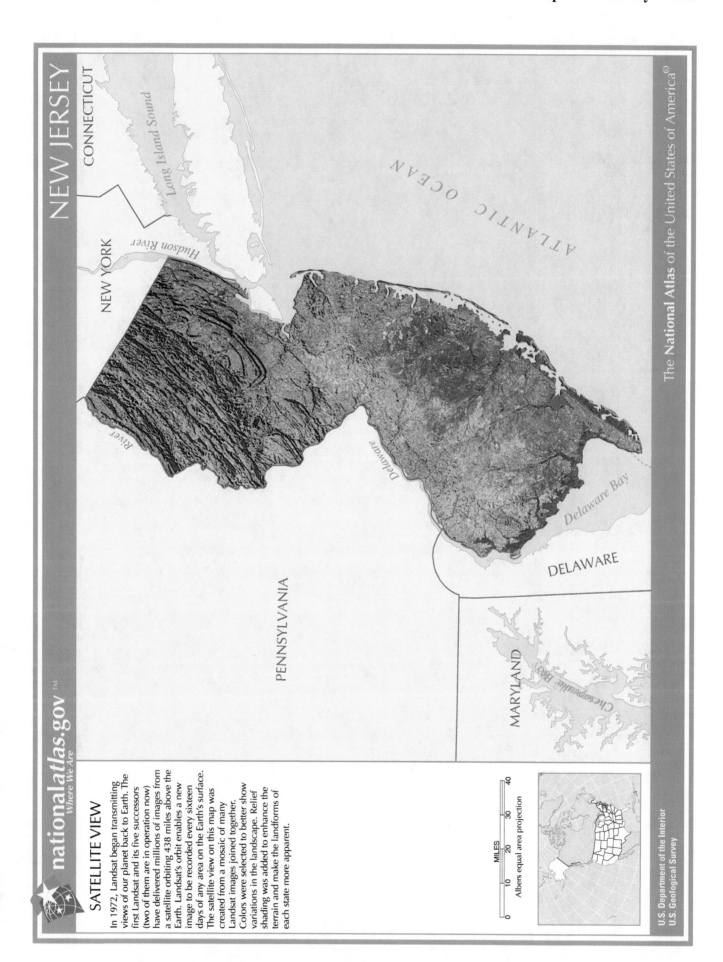

NEW JERSEY

nationalatlas.gov ™
Where We Are

SATELLITE VIEW

In 1972, Landsat began transmitting views of our planet back to Earth. The first Landsat and its five successors (two of them are in operation now) have delivered millions of images from a satellite orbiting 438 miles above the Earth. Landsat's orbit enables a new image to be recorded every sixteen days of any area on the Earth's surface. The satellite view on this map was created from a mosaic of many Landsat images joined together. Colors were selected to better show variations in the landscape. Relief shading was added to enhance the terrain and make the landforms of each state more apparent.

CONNECTICUT

Long Island Sound

NEW YORK

Hudson River

ATLANTIC OCEAN

River

PENNSYLVANIA

Delaware

Delaware Bay

DELAWARE

MARYLAND

Chesapeake Bay

MILES

0   10   20   30   40

Albers equal area projection

U.S. Department of the Interior
U.S. Geological Survey

The **National Atlas** of the United States of America®

New Mexico

Topic	Value	Time Period
Total Surface Area (acres)	77,823,300	2007
Land	77,670,200	2007
Federal Land	26,448,500	2007
Owned	3,830,417	FY 2009
Leased	30,644	FY 2009
Otherwise Managed	1,125	FY 2009
National Forest	9,418,000	September 2006
National Wilderness	1,650,596	October 2011
Non-Federal Land, Developed	1,261,900	2007
Non-Federal Land, Rural	49,959,800	2007
Water	153,100	2007
National Natural Landmarks	12	December 2010
National Historic Landmarks	44	December 2010
National Register of Historic Places	1,085	December 2010
National Parks	13	December 2010
Visitors to National Parks	1,657,550	2010
Historic Places Documented by the National Park Service	266	December 2010
Archeological Sites in National Parks	8,694	December 2010
Threatened and Endangered Species in National Parks	12	December 2010
Economic Benefit from National Park Tourism (dollars)	62,474,000	2009
Conservation Reserve Program (acres)	420,076	October 2011
Land and Water Conservation Fund Grants (dollars)	40,936,429	Since 1965
Historic Preservation Grants (dollars)	24,280,611	2010
Community Conservation and Recreation Projects	48	Since 1987
Federal Acres Transferred for Local Parks and Recreation	1,800	Since 1948
Crude Petroleum Production (millions of barrels)	62	2010
Crude Oil Proved Reserves (millions of barrels)	700	2009
Natural Gas Reserves (billions of cubic feet)	15,598	2009
Natural Gas Liquid Reserves (millions of barrels)	804	2008
Natural Gas Marketed Production (billions of cubic feet)	1,383	2009
Coal Reserves (millions of short tons)	11,984	2009

Sources: U.S. Department of the Interior, National Park Service, State Profiles, December 2010; United States Department of Agriculture, Natural Resources Conservation Service, 2007 National Resources Inventory; U.S. General Services Administration, Federal Real Property Council, FY 2009 Federal Real Property Report, September 2010; University of Montana, www.wilderness.net; U.S. Department of Agriculture, Farm Services Agency, Conservation Reserve Program, October 2011; U.S Census Bureau, 2012 Statistical Abstract of the United States

New Mexico Energy Overview and Analysis

Quick Facts

- New Mexico is a leading U.S. producer of crude oil and natural gas.
- New Mexico natural gas production accounts for close to one-tenth of the U.S. total.
- The San Juan Basin located in New Mexico and Colorado contains the Nation's largest field of proved natural gas reserves.
- New Mexico rivals Colorado and Wyoming as the Nation's top coalbed methane producer, and approximately one-third of all natural gas produced in New Mexico is coalbed methane.
- The Blanco Hub, located in the San Juan Basin, is a major transportation point for Rocky Mountain natural gas supplies heading to West Coast markets.
- New Mexico's Permian Basin holds three of the 100 largest oil fields in the United States.

Analysis

Resources and Consumption

New Mexico is rich in fossil fuel and renewable energy resources. Major oil and gas deposits are located in the Permian Basin in southeast New Mexico and in the San Juan Basin in the northwest. The San Juan Basin Gas Area, which extends into Colorado, is the largest field of proved natural gas reserves in the United States. New Mexico's Permian Basin contains three of the 100 largest oil fields in the United States. The northwest corner of the State also contains major coal deposits. Much of New Mexico's geologically active Rocky Mountain region holds geothermal power potential, and pockets of the State are suitable for wind power development. New Mexico possesses some of the Nation's highest potential for solar energy and New Mexico's southern deserts offer the State's most concentrated solar power potential. Although rich in energy resources, New Mexico has low energy demand due in large part to its small population. The transportation and industrial sectors lead State energy consumption.

Petroleum

New Mexico's crude oil production is substantial, and State crude oil output is typically just over 3 percent of the U.S. total. Production, which has been relatively steady since a steep decline through most of the 1970s, occurs in the Permian and San Juan basins. The Permian Basin, most of which lies in west Texas, is one of the most productive areas in the United States. New Mexico has three oil refineries, and several petroleum product pipelines connect the refineries to State and area markets. New Mexico requires the wintertime use of oxygenated motor gasoline to reduce carbon monoxide emissions in the Albuquerque metropolitan area. Ethanol, which is blended with gasoline to increase its oxygen content, is produced from corn and grain milo at New Mexico's only ethanol plant in Portales.

Natural Gas

New Mexico is one of the top natural gas-producing States in the Nation, and its output accounts for close to one-tenth of U.S. production. New Mexico produces natural gas in its Permian and San Juan basins. Although natural gas production declined through much of the 1980s, output increased sharply during the 1990s due in large part to the rapid development of coalbed methane production (the production of unconventional natural gas from coal seams). Today, coalbed methane accounts for about one-third of New Mexico's natural gas production. The San Juan Basin, which straddles the Colorado-New Mexico border, is the leading coalbed methane-producing region in the United States. New Mexico rivals Colorado and Wyoming as the Nation's leading coalbed methane producer and is responsible for around one-fourth of all coalbed methane produced in the United States. Although coalbed methane production from the San Juan Basin has declined since the late 1990s, new production is under development in the Raton Basin in the northeastern part of the State.

Although more than two-thirds of New Mexico's households use natural gas as their primary energy source for home heating, State natural gas consumption is low. Less than one-tenth of New Mexico's natural gas is used in the State. New Mexico delivers natural gas via pipeline to consumption markets in Arizona and to market centers in West Texas that supply the Midwest. New Mexico's Blanco Hub, located in the San Juan basin, is a major gathering point for Rocky Mountain natural gas supplies heading to West Coast markets.

Coal, Electricity, and Renewables

A substantial amount of coal is produced in New Mexico. Most of New Mexico's coal mines are clustered in the San Juan Basin. About three-fifths of New Mexican coal is used within the State; the remainder is delivered by rail primarily to electricity generators in Arizona. Coal-fired power plants dominate the New Mexico electricity market and supply over four-fifths of the State's electricity generation. Natural gas-fired plants supply most of the remainder. Just over one-tenth of New Mexico households use electricity as their main energy source for home heating.

A proposed solar thermal power plant in southwestern New Mexico, located 10 miles outside of El Paso, Texas, is scheduled for completion by the summer of 2011. This plant is part of an effort to place 500 megawatts of solar power in California and the southwestern United States. New Mexico also produces a small amount of energy from wind resources. In March 2007, New Mexico adopted a renewable portfolio standard that requires 20 percent of an electric utility's power to come from renewable energy sources by 2020.

Source: U.S. Energy Information Administration, October 2009

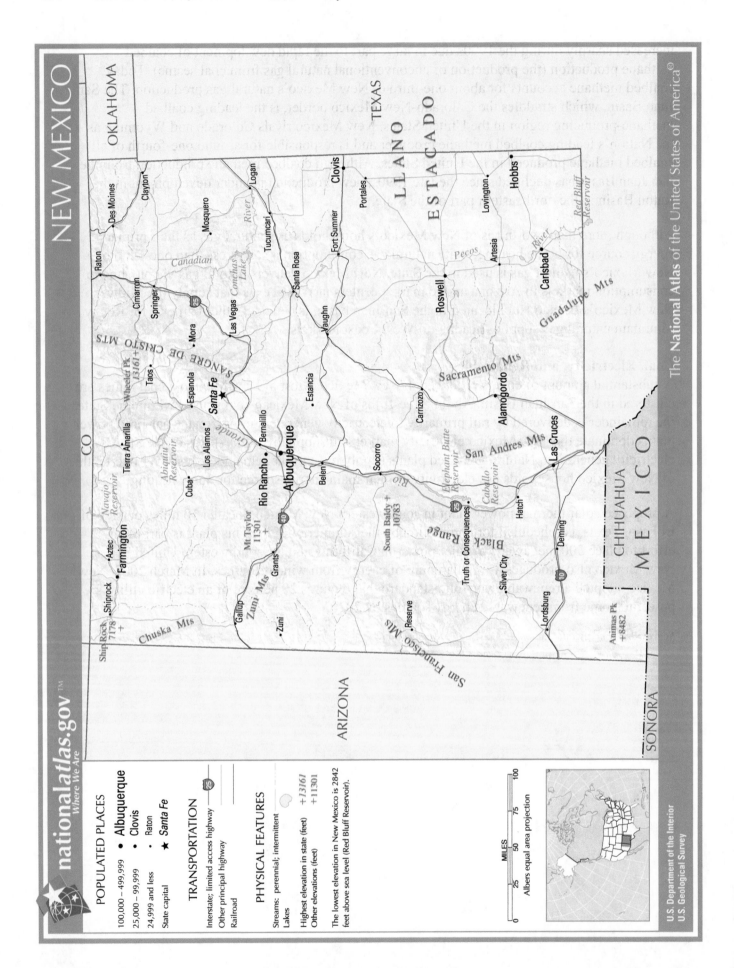

NEW MEXICO

nationalatlas.gov™
Where We Are

POPULATED PLACES

100,000 – 499,999   ● Albuquerque
25,000 – 99,999   ● Clovis
24,999 and less   · Raton
State capital   ★ Santa Fe

TRANSPORTATION

Interstate; limited access highway
Other principal highway
Railroad

PHYSICAL FEATURES

Streams: perennial; intermittent
Lakes
Highest elevation in state (feet)   +13161
Other elevations (feet)   +11301

The lowest elevation in New Mexico is 2842
feet above sea level (Red Bluff Reservoir).

MILES
0   25   50   75   100

Albers equal area projection

U.S. Department of the Interior
U.S. Geological Survey

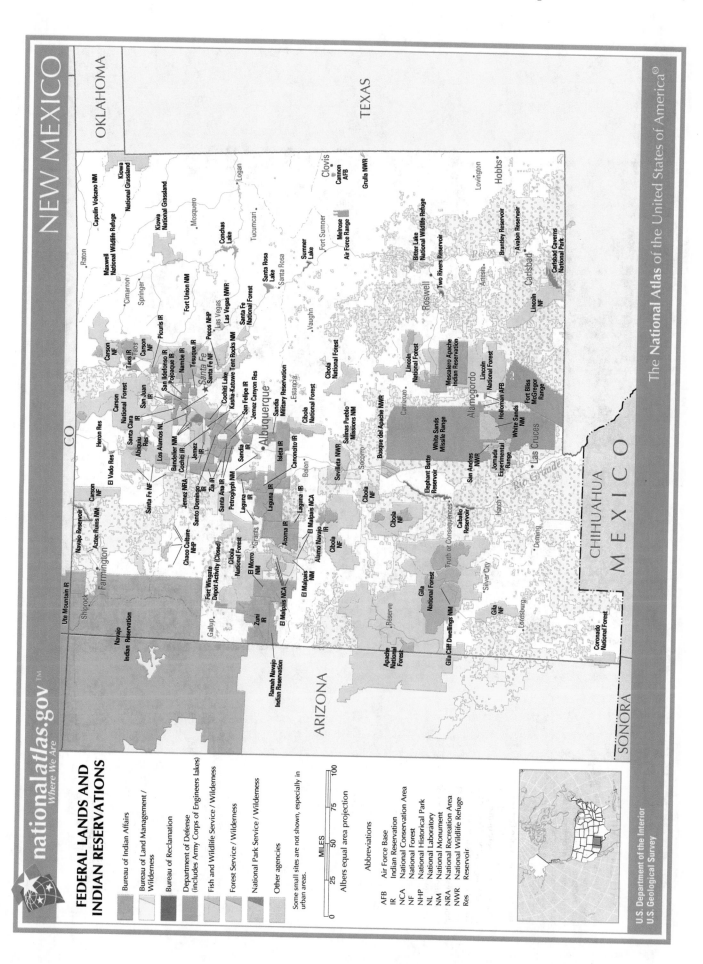

FEDERAL LANDS AND INDIAN RESERVATIONS

nationalatlas.gov™
Where We Are

Legend:
- Bureau of Indian Affairs
- Bureau of Land Management / Wilderness
- Bureau of Reclamation
- Department of Defense (includes Army Corps of Engineers lakes)
- Fish and Wildlife Service / Wilderness
- Forest Service / Wilderness
- National Park Service / Wilderness
- Other agencies

Some small sites are not shown, especially in urban areas.

MILES
0   25   50   75   100
Albers equal area projection

Abbreviations
- AFB   Air Force Base
- IR   Indian Reservation
- NCA   National Conservation Area
- NF   National Forest
- NHP   National Historical Park
- NL   National Laboratory
- NM   National Monument
- NRA   National Recreation Area
- NWR   National Wildlife Refuge
- Res   Reservoir

U.S. Department of the Interior
U.S. Geological Survey

The **National Atlas** of the United States of America®

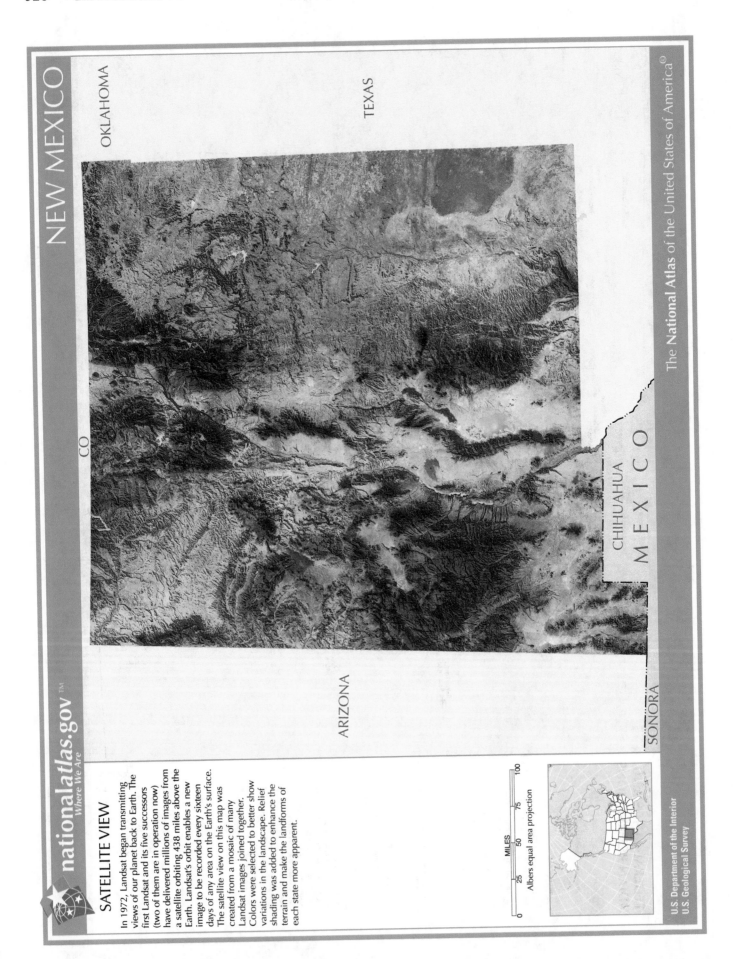

NEW MEXICO
Where We Are
nationalatlas.gov ™

The **National Atlas** of the United States of America ®

OKLAHOMA

TEXAS

CO

ARIZONA

SONORA

CHIHUAHUA
MEXICO

SATELLITE VIEW

In 1972, Landsat began transmitting views of our planet back to Earth. The first Landsat and its five successors (two of them are in operation now) have delivered millions of images from a satellite orbiting 438 miles above the Earth. Landsat's orbit enables a new image to be recorded every sixteen days of any area on the Earth's surface. The satellite view on this map was created from a mosaic of many Landsat images joined together. Colors were selected to better show variations in the landscape. Relief shading was added to enhance the terrain and make the landforms of each state more apparent.

MILES
0   25   50   75   100
Albers equal area projection

U.S. Department of the Interior
U.S. Geological Survey

New York

Topic	Value	Time Period
Total Surface Area (acres)	31,360,800	2007
Land	30,070,900	2007
Federal Land	205,300	2007
Owned	164,132	FY 2009
Leased	2,378	FY 2009
Otherwise Managed	2,482	FY 2009
National Forest	16,000	September 2006
National Wilderness	1,380	October 2011
Non-Federal Land, Developed	3,793,900	2007
Non-Federal Land, Rural	26,071,700	2007
Water	1,289,900	2007
National Natural Landmarks	27	December 2010
National Historic Landmarks	261	December 2010
National Register of Historic Places	5,318	December 2010
National Parks	22	December 2010
Visitors to National Parks	17,506,355	2010
Historic Places Documented by the National Park Service	1,931	December 2010
Archeological Sites in National Parks	266	December 2010
Threatened and Endangered Species in National Parks	14	December 2010
Economic Benefit from National Park Tourism (dollars)	340,054,000	2009
Conservation Reserve Program (acres)	51,654	October 2011
Land and Water Conservation Fund Grants (dollars)	232,947,093	Since 1965
Historic Preservation Grants (dollars)	60,761,211	2010
Community Conservation and Recreation Projects	80	Since 1987
Federal Acres Transferred for Local Parks and Recreation	5,952	Since 1948
Crude Petroleum Production (millions of barrels)	Not Available	2010
Crude Oil Proved Reserves (millions of barrels)	Not Available	2009
Natural Gas Reserves (billions of cubic feet)	196	2009
Natural Gas Liquid Reserves (millions of barrels)	Not Available	2008
Natural Gas Marketed Production (billions of cubic feet)	45	2009
Coal Reserves (millions of short tons)	Not Available	2009

Sources: *U.S. Department of the Interior, National Park Service, State Profiles, December 2010; United States Department of Agriculture, Natural Resources Conservation Service, 2007 National Resources Inventory; U.S. General Services Administration, Federal Real Property Council, FY 2009 Federal Real Property Report, September 2010; University of Montana, www.wilderness.net; U.S. Department of Agriculture, Farm Services Agency, Conservation Reserve Program, October 2011; U.S Census Bureau, 2012 Statistical Abstract of the United States*

New York Energy Overview and Analysis

Quick Facts

- The New York Harbor area between New York and New Jersey has a petroleum bulk terminal storage capacity of over 75 million barrels, making it the largest petroleum product hub in the Northeast.
- New York produces more hydroelectric power than any other State east of the Rocky Mountains.
- The 2,353-megawatt Robert Moses Niagara plant, harnessing power from the Niagara River, is one of the largest hydroelectric facilities in the world.
- Per capita energy consumption in New York is among the lowest in the Nation due in part to its widely used mass transportation systems.
- During the Northeast Blackout of August 2003, almost the entire State lost power and all four of New York's nuclear plants were shut down.
- A proposed pipeline could transport up to 10 million gallons of ethanol per day from production facilities in the Midwest to terminals in the Northeast, including New York Harbor.

Analysis

Resources and Consumption

New York has minor reserves of oil and conventional natural gas, found primarily in the far western part of the State near Lake Erie. The Marcellus shale formation, which contains unconventional shale gas, extends into the lower portion of the State.

Although New York's fossil fuel resources are limited, the State possesses considerable renewable energy potential. Several powerful rivers, including the Niagara and the Hudson, provide New York with some of the greatest hydropower resources in the Nation, and New York's Catskill and Adirondack mountains offer substantial wind power potential. In addition, parts of New York are densely forested, allowing for potential fuelwood harvesting.

Although New York's total energy consumption is among the highest in the United States, energy intensity and per capita energy consumption are among the lowest, due in part to the region's widely used mass transportation systems. The commercial and residential sectors lead State energy demand, while the transportation sector is also a major consumer.

Petroleum

New York's petroleum products are supplied by refineries located in New Jersey and Pennsylvania, the Colonial Pipeline system from the Gulf Coast, and foreign imports that principally originate in Canada, the Caribbean, South America, North Africa, and Europe. Located in both New York and New Jersey, the New York Harbor area has a petroleum bulk terminal storage capacity of over 75 million barrels, making it the largest and most important petroleum product hub in the high-demand Northeast.

New York Harbor acts as a central distribution center for the region, and many of the petroleum products delivered to the Harbor are redistributed to smaller ports where they supply local demand. In particular, the Hudson River, which meets the Atlantic Ocean in New York Harbor, provides a major inland water route for petroleum product barges supplying eastern New York and parts of western New England. On the other side of the State, western New York product markets are primarily supplied from Canada at the Port of Buffalo, and via the Buckeye and Sunoco pipeline systems from Pennsylvania and the Midwest. The TEPPCO pipeline system from the Gulf Coast delivers mostly propane to upstate markets.

As in many northeastern urban areas, New York City and the surrounding metropolitan areas require reformulated gasoline blended with ethanol, and the New York Harbor area is the primary Northeast distribution hub for ethanol supplies. Ports located on the New Jersey side of New York Harbor receive ethanol rail shipments from the Midwest and marine imports from Brazil and the Caribbean, and then redistribute these supplies to markets throughout the Northeast. Another large ethanol storage facility serving the Northeast is located in Albany, New York. A proposed pipeline would transport up to 10 million gallons of ethanol per day from production facilities in Iowa, Illinois, Minnesota, and South Dakota to terminals in Pittsburgh, Philadelphia, and the New York Harbor.

New York, along with much of the Northeast, is vulnerable to distillate fuel oil shortages and price spikes during the winter months due to high demand for home heating. One-third of New York households use fuel oil as their primary energy source for home heating. In January and February 2000, distillate fuel oil prices in the Northeast rose sharply when extreme winter weather increased demand unexpectedly and hindered the arrival of new supply, as frozen rivers and high winds slowed the docking and unloading of barges and tankers. In July 2000, in order to reduce the risk of future shortages, the President directed the U.S. Department of Energy to establish the Northeast Heating Oil Reserve. The Reserve gives Northeast consumers adequate supplies for about 10 days, the time required for ships to carry heating oil from the Gulf of Mexico to New York Harbor. The Reserve's storage terminals are located at Perth Amboy, New Jersey, and Groton and New Haven, Connecticut.

Natural Gas

Although western New York produces a small amount of natural gas, the vast majority of New York's natural gas supply is brought in via pipeline from other States and Canada. The Transcontinental and Tennessee Gas Transmission pipelines from the Gulf Coast and the Iroquois pipeline from Canada link up with local gas distribution networks that supply the New York City metropolitan area and Long Island. Numerous other gas transmission systems branch in from Pennsylvania and Canada to feed other parts of the State.

New York has moderate natural gas storage capacity, developed principally from depleted natural gas fields in the Appalachian Basin in western New York. These storage sites, along with those in Pennsylvania, Ohio, and West Virginia, are important for supplying the Northeast region, particularly during the peak demand winter season. New York's residential, commercial, and electric power sectors all consume large amounts of natural gas. To meet New York and Connecticut's growing demand for natural gas, particularly for electric power generation, an offshore liquefied natural gas (LNG) import terminal with a capacity of 2 billion cubic feet per day has been proposed in Federal waters on the Outer Continental Shelf south of Long Island, 25 miles away from New York Harbor.

Coal, Electricity, and Renewables

Unlike many States, New York does not rely heavily on any one fuel for electricity generation. Nuclear power from New York's four nuclear plants and natural gas are the leading generation fuels, each typically accounting for about three-tenths of State generation. Hydroelectricity, coal, and petroleum each account for a substantial share of the power generated in the State, as well. New York also imports electricity from neighboring States and Canada.

The average New York household consumes about one-half the electricity of the average U.S. household, largely because few use electricity as their primary energy source for home heating and because demand for air-conditioning is low during the typically mild summer months.

Various failures led to major electricity outages affecting New York in 1965, 1977, and 2003. The August 2003 blackout was the most severe blackout in North American history, affecting an estimated 55 million people in the U.S. Northeast and eastern Canada. For safety reasons, nuclear power plants are required by Federal law to shut down if back-up power systems fail, and all four of New York's nuclear power plants were forced offline. As a result, almost the entire State lost power during the incident.

New York is a major hydroelectric power producer, and its hydroelectric generation is the highest of any State east of the Rocky Mountains. When New York's Robert Moses Niagara plant opened near the Niagara River in 1961, it was the largest hydroelectric generation facility in the world. Today, the 2,353-megawatt power plant is still New York's largest electricity generator. Nonhydroelectric renewable energy sources contribute only minimally to the State's power grid, although New York is one of the Nation's top generators of electricity from municipal solid waste and landfill gas. As of 2008, New York ranked among the top 10 States in photovoltaic solar power capacity and had become a substantial producer of wind energy by doubling its wind energy capacity between 2006 and 2008. In September 2004, the New York Public Service Commission adopted a renewable portfolio standard requiring 24 percent of the State's electricity to be generated from renewable sources by 2013.

Source: U.S. Energy Information Administration, October 2009

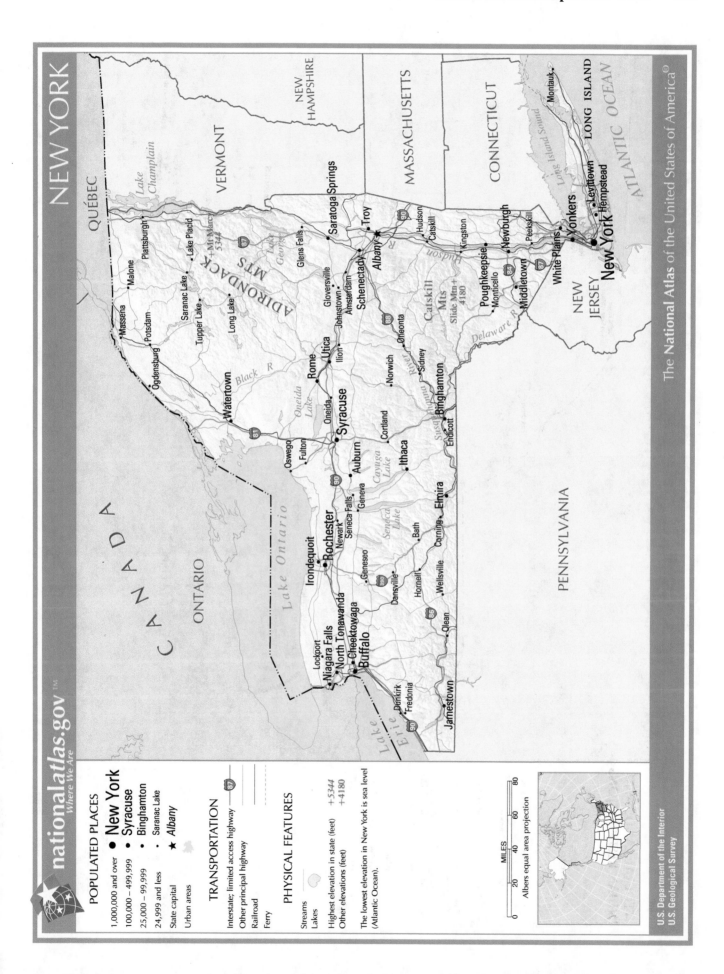

NEW YORK

nationalatlas.gov ™
Where We Are

The **National Atlas** of the United States of America®

U.S. Department of the Interior
U.S. Geological Survey

POPULATED PLACES

1,000,000 and over	● **New York**
100,000 – 499,999	● Syracuse
25,000 – 99,999	● Binghamton
24,999 and less	· Saranac Lake
State capital	★ *Albany*
Urban areas	

TRANSPORTATION

Interstate; limited access highway
Other principal highway
Railroad
Ferry

PHYSICAL FEATURES

Streams
Lakes
Highest elevation in state (feet)   +5344
Other elevations (feet)   +4180

The lowest elevation in New York is sea level (Atlantic Ocean).

MILES
0   20   40   60   80
Albers equal area projection

QUÉBEC

CANADA

ONTARIO

NEW HAMPSHIRE

VERMONT

Lake Champlain

Lake George

MASSACHUSETTS

CONNECTICUT

Long Island Sound

LONG ISLAND

ATLANTIC OCEAN

Montauk

NEW JERSEY

PENNSYLVANIA

Lake Ontario

Lake Erie

ADIRONDACK MTS

+Mt Marcy 5344

Catskill Mts

Slide Mtn +4180

Delaware R

Hudson R

Susquehanna River

Black R

Oneida Lake

Cayuga Lake

Seneca Lake

Massena
Malone
Plattsburgh
Potsdam
Ogdensburg
Saranac Lake
Lake Placid
Tupper Lake
Long Lake
Watertown
Oswego
Fulton
Rome
Utica
Ilion
Oneida
Syracuse
Auburn
Seneca Falls
Geneva
Newark
Rochester
Irondequoit
Geneseo
Dansville
Hornell
Wellsville
Olean
Bath
Corning
Elmira
Cortland
Ithaca
Norwich
Sidney
Oneonta
Binghamton
Endicott
Jamestown
Fredonia
Dunkirk
Buffalo
Cheektowaga
North Tonawanda
Niagara Falls
Lockport
Gloversville
Johnstown
Amsterdam
Schenectady
Albany
Troy
Saratoga Springs
Glens Falls
Hudson
Catskill
Kingston
Monticello
Middletown
Poughkeepsie
Newburgh
Peekskill
White Plains
Yonkers
New York
New Rochelle
Hempstead
Levittown

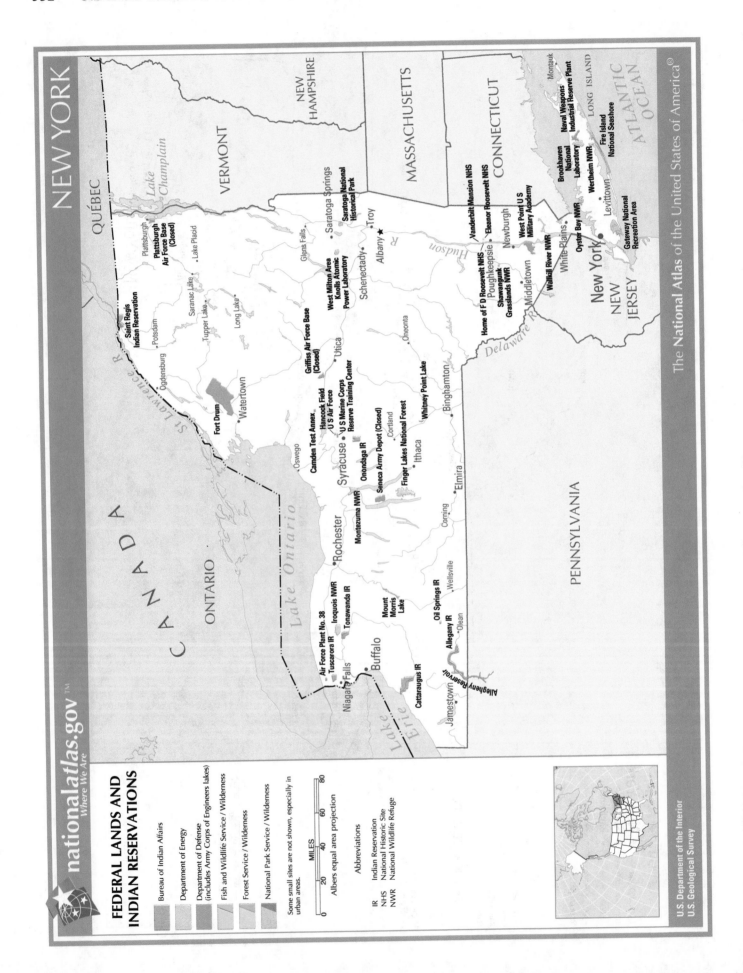

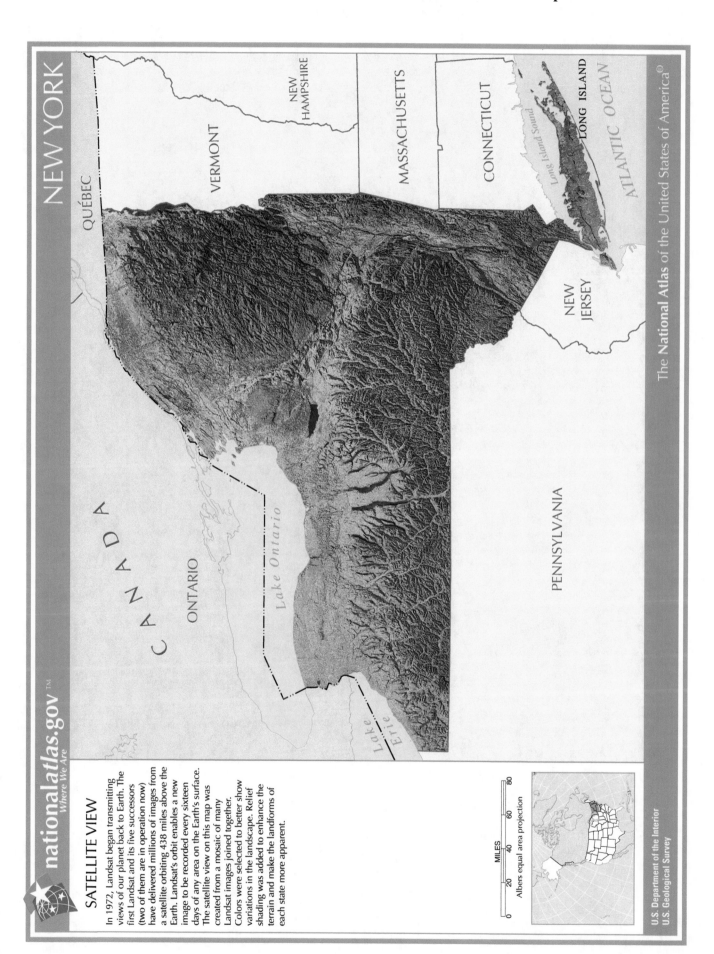

NEW YORK

nationalatlas.gov™
Where We Are

SATELLITE VIEW

In 1972, Landsat began transmitting views of our planet back to Earth. The first Landsat and its five successors (two of them are in operation now) have delivered millions of images from a satellite orbiting 438 miles above the Earth. Landsat's orbit enables a new image to be recorded every sixteen days of any area on the Earth's surface. The satellite view on this map was created from a mosaic of many Landsat images joined together. Colors were selected to better show variations in the landscape. Relief shading was added to enhance the terrain and make the landforms of each state more apparent.

QUÉBEC

C A N A D A

ONTARIO

Lake Ontario

Lake Erie

VERMONT

NEW HAMPSHIRE

MASSACHUSETTS

CONNECTICUT

Long Island Sound

LONG ISLAND

NEW JERSEY

PENNSYLVANIA

ATLANTIC OCEAN

The **National Atlas** of the United States of America®

MILES
0   20   40   60   80
Albers equal area projection

U.S. Department of the Interior
U.S. Geological Survey

North Carolina

Topic	Value	Time Period
Total Surface Area (acres)	33,709,300	2007
Land	30,926,000	2007
Federal Land	2,507,500	2007
Owned	484,587	FY 2009
Leased	9,449	FY 2009
Otherwise Managed	5,573	FY 2009
National Forest	1,256,000	September 2006
National Wilderness	111,419	October 2011
Non-Federal Land, Developed	4,796,700	2007
Non-Federal Land, Rural	23,621,800	2007
Water	2,783,300	2007
National Natural Landmarks	13	December 2010
National Historic Landmarks	38	December 2010
National Register of Historic Places	2,742	December 2010
National Parks	10	December 2010
Visitors to National Parks	17,093,464	2010
Historic Places Documented by the National Park Service	499	December 2010
Archeological Sites in National Parks	530	December 2010
Threatened and Endangered Species in National Parks	24	December 2010
Economic Benefit from National Park Tourism (dollars)	707,241,000	2009
Conservation Reserve Program (acres)	111,380	October 2011
Land and Water Conservation Fund Grants (dollars)	78,780,372	Since 1965
Historic Preservation Grants (dollars)	32,425,677	2010
Community Conservation and Recreation Projects	35	Since 1987
Federal Acres Transferred for Local Parks and Recreation	234	Since 1948
Crude Petroleum Production (millions of barrels)	Not Available	2010
Crude Oil Proved Reserves (millions of barrels)	Not Available	2009
Natural Gas Reserves (billions of cubic feet)	Not Available	2009
Natural Gas Liquid Reserves (millions of barrels)	Not Available	2008
Natural Gas Marketed Production (billions of cubic feet)	Not Available	2009
Coal Reserves (millions of short tons)	Not Available	2009

Sources: U.S. Department of the Interior, National Park Service, State Profiles, December 2010; United States Department of Agriculture, Natural Resources Conservation Service, 2007 National Resources Inventory; U.S. General Services Administration, Federal Real Property Council, FY 2009 Federal Real Property Report, September 2010; University of Montana, www.wilderness.net; U.S. Department of Agriculture, Farm Services Agency, Conservation Reserve Program, October 2011; U.S Census Bureau, 2012 Statistical Abstract of the United States

North Carolina Energy Overview and Analysis

Quick Facts

- North Carolina is one of the top nuclear power producers in the United States.
- The Dixie Pipeline, a major supplier of propane to the Southeast, terminates in Apex, North Carolina, where a terminal and above-ground storage tanks are located.
- North Carolina's electricity consumption is among the highest in the Nation.
- North Carolina ranks among the top 10 States in wind power capacity and several rivers in western and central North Carolina provide hydroelectric power.

Analysis

Resources and Consumption

North Carolina energy resources include several rivers in western and central North Carolina that provide substantial hydropower, and high wind power potential off the State's Atlantic Coast. North Carolina's transportation sector leads State energy consumption by a small margin, followed closely by the residential, industrial, and commercial sectors. North Carolina is a leader in the energy-intensive chemical manufacturing industry.

Petroleum

North Carolina acquires all of its petroleum products from other States and from abroad. The Colonial and Plantation pipelines from the Gulf Coast supply the State with petroleum products. The Dixie Pipeline, a major supplier of propane to the Southeast, terminates in Apex, North Carolina, where a terminal and above-ground storage tanks are located. Tankers from other States and other countries deliver petroleum products to the ports of Wilmington and Morehead City.

Natural Gas

The majority of North Carolina's natural gas is supplied by the Transcontinental Gas Pipeline Co. as the pipeline traverses the State en route from the Gulf Coast to major population centers in the Northeast. The industrial sector is the leading natural gas-consuming sector, although consumption by residential and commercial users is also substantial. Approximately one-fourth of North Carolina households use natural gas as their main source of energy for home heating.

Coal, Electricity, and Renewables

North Carolina's electricity production is high. Coal-fired power plants typically account for about three-fifths of the State's electricity generation, and nuclear power typically accounts for about one-third. Hydroelectric and natural gas-fired power plants produce most of the remainder. North Carolina's coal-fired power plants burn coal shipped primarily by rail from West Virginia and Kentucky. With three nuclear power plants, North Carolina is a major nuclear power producer. Hydroelectric power plants located along several rivers in central and western North Carolina produce substantial amounts of electricity. North Carolina's electricity consumption is among the highest in the Nation. As is typical in the South, more than one-half of North Carolina households use electricity as their main energy source for home heating.

North Carolina possesses about 5 percent of the Nation's net summer capacity for wood energy production and ranks among the top 10 States with the highest net summer capacity for wind power. In August 2007, North Carolina adopted a renewable energy and energy efficiency portfolio standard requiring electric utilities to meet 12.5 percent of retail electricity demand through renewable energy or energy efficiency measures by 2021. Electric membership corporations and municipalities that sell electric power within the State must meet a 10-percent standard by 2018.

Source: *U.S. Energy Information Administration, October 2009*

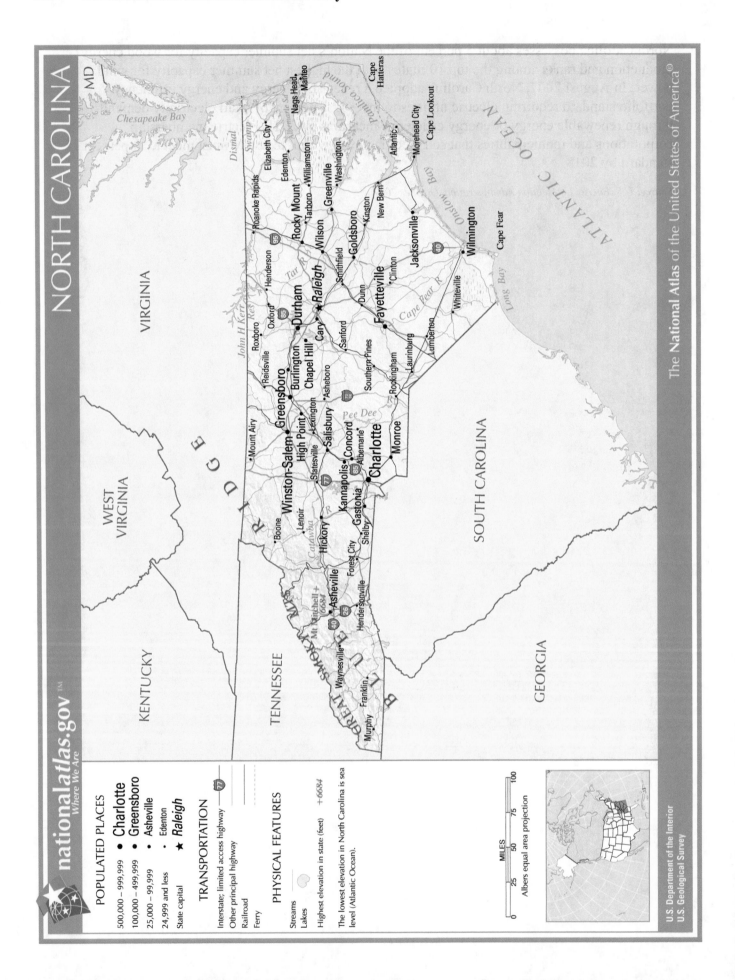

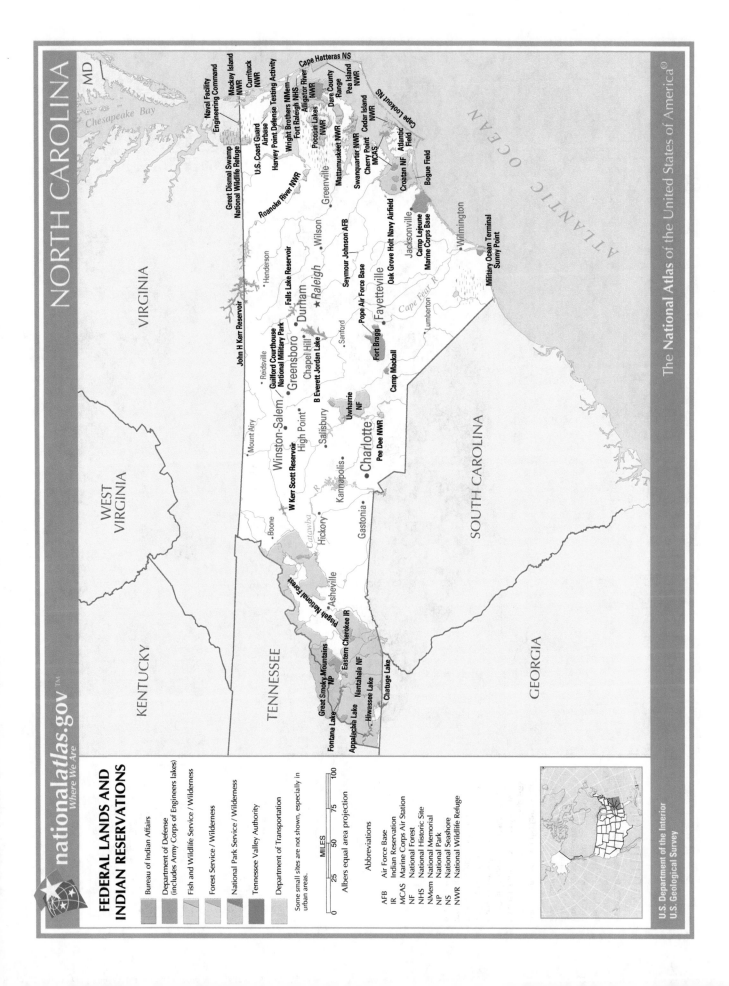

NORTH CAROLINA

nationalatlas.gov™
Where We Are

FEDERAL LANDS AND INDIAN RESERVATIONS

Bureau of Indian Affairs

Department of Defense
(includes Army Corps of Engineers lakes)

Fish and Wildlife Service / Wilderness

Forest Service / Wilderness

National Park Service / Wilderness

Tennessee Valley Authority

Department of Transportation

Some small sites are not shown, especially in urban areas.

MILES

0   25   50   75   100

Albers equal area projection

Abbreviations

AFB   Air Force Base
IR   Indian Reservation
MCAS   Marine Corps Air Station
NF   National Forest
NHS   National Historic Site
NMem   National Memorial
NP   National Park
NS   National Seashore
NWR   National Wildlife Refuge

The **National Atlas** of the United States of America®

U.S. Department of the Interior
U.S. Geological Survey

MD
VIRGINIA
Chesapeake Bay
Naval Facility Engineering Command
Mackay Island NWR
Currituck NWR
Harvey Point Defense Testing Activity
Cape Hatteras NS
U.S. Coast Guard Airbase
Wright Brothers NMem
Fort Raleigh NHS
Alligator River NWR
Dare County Range
Pea Island NWR
Great Dismal Swamp National Wildlife Refuge
Pocosin Lakes NWR
Cape Lookout NS
Roanoke River NWR
Mattamuskeet NWR
Cedar Island NWR
Swanquarter NWR
Cherry Point MCAS
Atlantic Field
Croatan NF
Bogue Field
Greenville
Wilson
Henderson
Seymour Johnson AFB
John H Kerr Reservoir
Falls Lake Reservoir
Reidsville
Durham
Raleigh
Oak Grove Holt Navy Airfield
Jacksonville
Camp Lejeune Marine Corps Base
Wilmington
Military Ocean Terminal Sunny Point
Guilford Courthouse National Military Park
Greensboro
Chapel Hill
B Everett Jordan Lake
Sanford
Pope Air Force Base
Fayetteville
Winston-Salem
High Point
Salisbury
Mount Airy
Fort Bragg
Camp Mackall
Cape Fear R
Lumberton
Uwharrie NF
Pee Dee NWR
Charlotte
Kannapolis
Boone
W Kerr Scott Reservoir
Hickory
Gastonia
Catawba R
Asheville
Pisgah National Forest
Eastern Cherokee IR
Great Smoky Mountains NP
Nantahala NF
Chatuge Lake
Hiwassee Lake
Appalachia Lake
Fontana Lake
KENTUCKY
WEST VIRGINIA
TENNESSEE
SOUTH CAROLINA
GEORGIA
ATLANTIC OCEAN

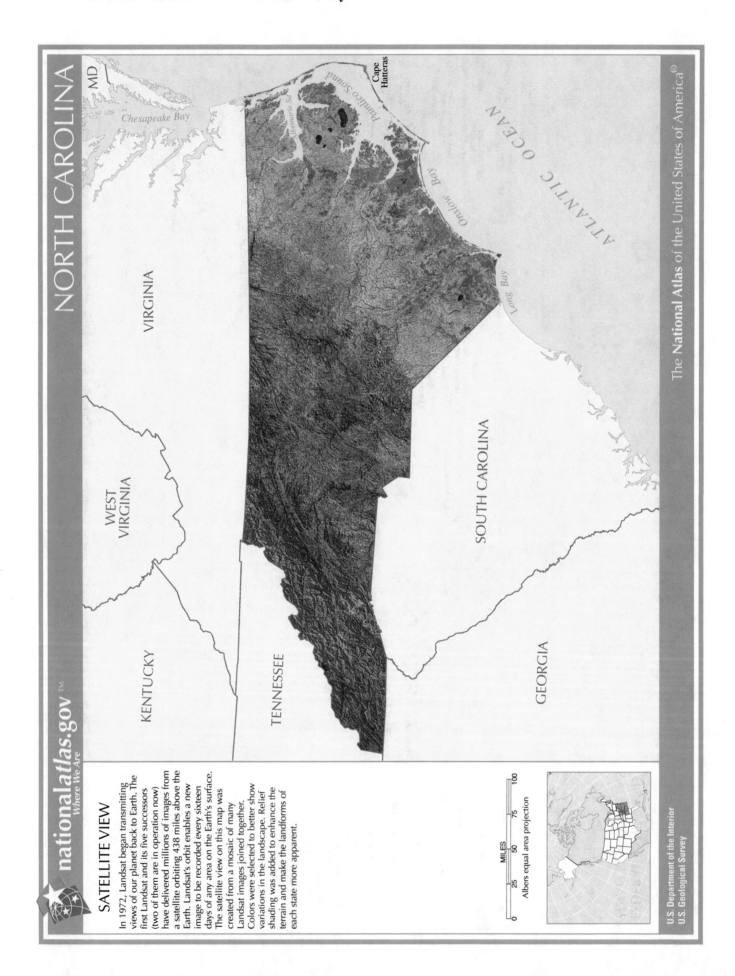

NORTH CAROLINA

SATELLITE VIEW

In 1972, Landsat began transmitting views of our planet back to Earth. The first Landsat and its five successors (two of them are in operation now) have delivered millions of images from a satellite orbiting 438 miles above the Earth. Landsat's orbit enables a new image to be recorded every sixteen days of any area on the Earth's surface. The satellite view on this map was created from a mosaic of many Landsat images joined together. Colors were selected to better show variations in the landscape. Relief shading was added to enhance the terrain and make the landforms of each state more apparent.

nationalatlas.gov ™
Where We Are

MD
Chesapeake Bay
VIRGINIA
WEST VIRGINIA
KENTUCKY
TENNESSEE
Albemarle Sound
Pamlico Sound
Cape Hatteras
Onslow Bay
Long Bay
ATLANTIC OCEAN
SOUTH CAROLINA
GEORGIA

MILES
0   25   50   75   100
Albers equal area projection

U.S. Department of the Interior
U.S. Geological Survey

The **National Atlas** of the United States of America®

North Dakota

Topic	Value	Time Period
Total Surface Area (acres)	45,250,700	2007
Land	44,162,100	2007
Federal Land	1,784,800	2007
Owned	612,888	FY 2009
Leased	5,362	FY 2009
Otherwise Managed	11,919	FY 2009
National Forest	1,106,000	September 2006
National Wilderness	39,652	October 2011
Non-Federal Land, Developed	973,200	2007
Non-Federal Land, Rural	41,404,100	2007
Water	1,088,600	2007
National Natural Landmarks	4	December 2010
National Historic Landmarks	5	December 2010
National Register of Historic Places	420	December 2010
National Parks	3	December 2010
Visitors to National Parks	659,927	2010
Historic Places Documented by the National Park Service	126	December 2010
Archeological Sites in National Parks	387	December 2010
Threatened and Endangered Species in National Parks	4	December 2010
Economic Benefit from National Park Tourism (dollars)	27,545,000	2009
Conservation Reserve Program (acres)	2,381,437	October 2011
Land and Water Conservation Fund Grants (dollars)	34,860,107	Since 1965
Historic Preservation Grants (dollars)	14,171,499	2010
Community Conservation and Recreation Projects	6	Since 1987
Federal Acres Transferred for Local Parks and Recreation	155	Since 1948
Crude Petroleum Production (millions of barrels)	112	2010
Crude Oil Proved Reserves (millions of barrels)	1,046	2009
Natural Gas Reserves (billions of cubic feet)	1,079	2009
Natural Gas Liquid Reserves (millions of barrels)	55	2008
Natural Gas Marketed Production (billions of cubic feet)	59	2009
Coal Reserves (millions of short tons)	8,903	2009

Sources: *U.S. Department of the Interior, National Park Service, State Profiles, December 2010; United States Department of Agriculture, Natural Resources Conservation Service, 2007 National Resources Inventory; U.S. General Services Administration, Federal Real Property Council, FY 2009 Federal Real Property Report, September 2010; University of Montana, www.wilderness.net; U.S. Department of Agriculture, Farm Services Agency, Conservation Reserve Program, October 2011; U.S Census Bureau, 2012 Statistical Abstract of the United States*

North Dakota Energy Overview and Analysis

Quick Facts

- North Dakota accounts for about 2 percent of total U.S. crude oil production.
- Due partly to high heating demand in winter, North Dakota's per capita energy consumption is among the highest in the Nation.
- Nearly all of the electricity generated in North Dakota is produced by coal-fired power plants.
- North Dakota is one of the few States that allow the statewide use of conventional motor gasoline.
- North Dakota is a substantial producer of wind energy and leads the Nation in potential wind power capacity.

Analysis

Resources and Consumption

North Dakota has considerable fossil fuel reserves. Coal is extracted from large surface mines in central North Dakota. Substantial crude oil and natural gas reserves are located in the Williston Basin, in the western part of the State. Although a low population largely accounts for the State's low total energy consumption, North Dakota's per capita energy consumption ranks among the highest in the Nation, in large part due to high demand for heating during the cold winters and an energy-intensive economy. Industry accounts for nearly one-half of the State's total energy consumption.

Petroleum

North Dakota is a substantial crude oil-producing State with an output typically equal to over 2 percent of total U.S. production. The State is also an entrance point for Canadian crude oil transported via pipeline to U.S. Midwest refining markets. An additional 2,148-mile pipeline is currently under construction and once completed in 2010, will transport crude oil from Alberta, Canada through eastern North Dakota to markets in the Midwest. A small petroleum refinery near Bismarck refines crude oil extracted from the Williston Basin, which covers eastern Montana and the western Dakotas, as well as a small amount of Canadian crude. The refinery produces transportation fuels primarily for the northern Great Plains States and the Twin Cities area. A small new refinery has been proposed on the Fort Berthold Indian reservation in western North Dakota. If constructed, it would be the first new crude oil refinery in the United States in decades.

North Dakota has six ethanol plants, four of which are currently producing ethanol, giving the State substantial ethanol production capacity. North Dakota is a moderate consumer of ethanol in blended motor gasoline, although it is one of the few States in the Nation that allow the statewide use of conventional motor gasoline. (Most States require the use of specific gasoline blends in non-attainment areas due to air-quality considerations.)

Natural Gas

North Dakota typically accounts for roughly 1 percent of the Nation's natural gas production. The majority of the State's supply is transported via major pipelines originating in Montana and western Canada on their way to U.S. Midwest consumption markets via South Dakota and Minnesota. North Dakota has the distinction of being one of only three States that produce synthetic natural gas . The largest source of synthetic gas in the United States is the Great Plains Synfuels Plant in Beulah, North Dakota, which annually produces more than 54 billion cubic feet of gas from coal. Overall State use of natural gas is low, with the industrial sector leading State consumption. Over two-fifths of the households in North Dakota use natural gas as their primary source of energy for home heating.

Coal, Electricity, and Renewables

Electricity generation and demand are both low in North Dakota, commensurate with the State's population. Coal-fired plants provide nearly all of North Dakota's electricity generation. Most of the coal used for power generation is supplied by several large surface mines in the central part of the State. State coal production is substantial, and North Dakota brings in only small amounts of coal from other States. Hydroelectric dams account for most of the State's non-coal electricity. The Garrison Dam, located about 75 miles northwest of Bismarck, is North Dakota's fifth largest plant in electricity generation capability. North Dakota is a substantial producer of wind energy, with over 20 operational wind power projects, and leads the Nation in potential for wind power. Nearly three-tenths of North Dakota households use electricity as their primary energy source for home heating.

In March 2007, North Dakota adopted a voluntary renewable portfolio objective that aims to have one-tenth of electricity generated from renewable sources by 2015.

Source: U.S. Energy Information Administration, October 2009

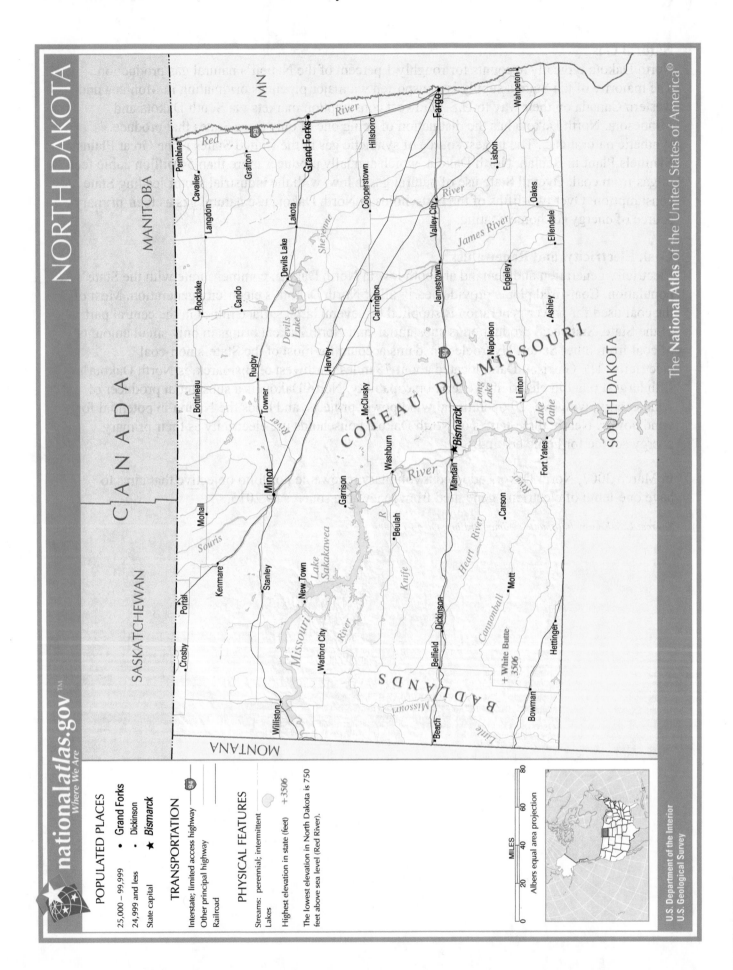

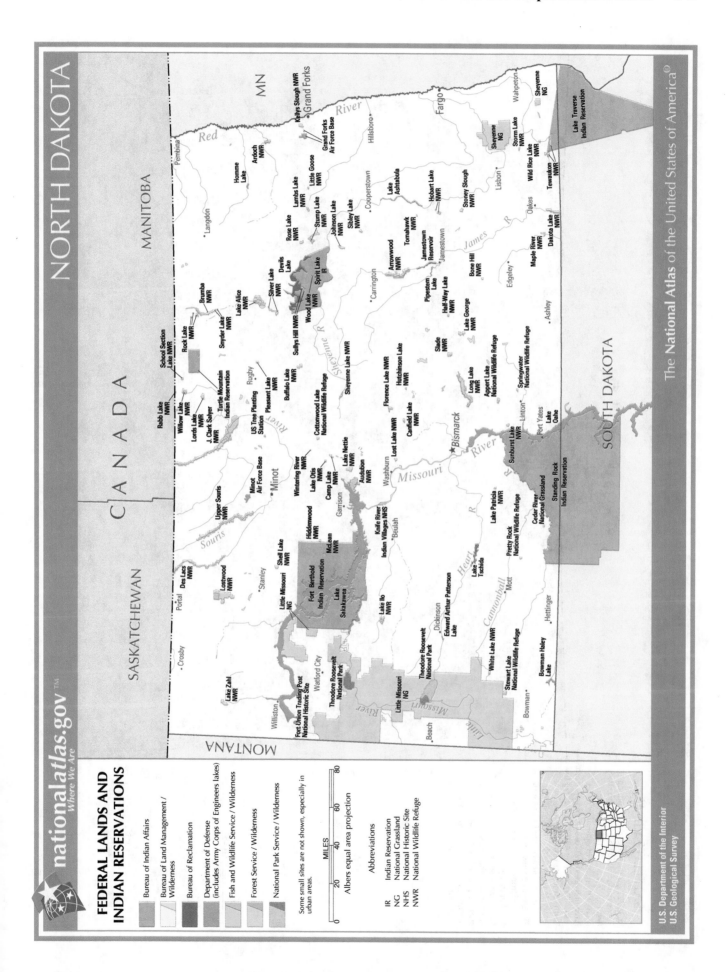

NORTH DAKOTA

nationalatlas.gov™
Where We Are

FEDERAL LANDS AND INDIAN RESERVATIONS

Bureau of Indian Affairs

Bureau of Land Management / Wilderness

Bureau of Reclamation

Department of Defense (includes Army Corps of Engineers lakes)

Fish and Wildlife Service / Wilderness

Forest Service / Wilderness

National Park Service / Wilderness

Some small sites are not shown, especially in urban areas.

MILES
0   20   40   60   80
Albers equal area projection

Abbreviations

IR   Indian Reservation
NG   National Grassland
NHS   National Historic Site
NWR   National Wildlife Refuge

The **National Atlas** of the United States of America®

U.S. Department of the Interior
U.S. Geological Survey

CANADA
SASKATCHEWAN
MANITOBA
MONTANA
SOUTH DAKOTA
MN

Pembina
Langdon
Crosby
Portal
Des Lacs
NWR
Lostwood
NWR
Stanley
Williston
Watford City
Fort Union Trading Post
National Historic Site
Lake Zahl
NWR
Upper Souris
NWR
Minot
Air Force Base
Minot
Souris
Shell Lake
NWR
Little Missouri NG
Fort Berthold
Indian Reservation
Lake
Sakakawea
Theodore Roosevelt
National Park
Little Missouri NG
Beach
Bowman
Bowman Haley
Lake
Stewart Lake
National Wildlife Refuge
White Lake NWR
Theodore Roosevelt
National Park
Edward Arthur Patterson
Lake
Dickinson
Hettinger
Mott
Pretty Rock
National Wildlife Refuge
Cedar River
National Grassland
Lake
Tschida
Lake
Patricia
NWR
Standing Rock
Indian Reservation
Sunburst Lake
NWR
Fort Yates
Lake
Oahe
Linton
Bismarck
Washburn
Beulah
Garrison
Knife River
Indian Villages NHS
Lake Ilo
NWR
Lake Nettie
NWR
Audubon
NWR
Lake Otis
NWR
Camp Lake
NWR
Wintering River
NWR
Hiddenwood
NWR
McLean
NWR
Rabb Lake
NWR
Willow Lake
NWR
Lords Lake
NWR
J. Clark Salyer
NWR
School Section
Lake NWR
Rock Lake
NWR
Brumba
NWR
Snyder Lake
NWR
Lake Alice
NWR
Turtle Mountain
Indian Reservation
Rugby
US Tree Planting
Station
Pleasant Lake
NWR
Buffalo Lake
NWR
Silver Lake
NWR
Devils
Lake
Sullys Hill NWR
Wood Lake
NWR
Spirit Lake
IR
Homme
Lake
Ardoch
NWR
Grand Forks
Air Force Base
Grand Forks
Kellys Slough NWR
Red
River
Hillsboro
Rose Lake
NWR
Lambs Lake
NWR
Little Goose
NWR
Stump Lake
NWR
Johnson Lake
NWR
Sibley Lake
NWR
Cottonwood Lake
National Wildlife Refuge
Sheyenne Lake NWR
Cooperstown
Carrington
Florence Lake NWR
Hutchinson Lake
NWR
Canfield Lake
NWR
Lost Lake NWR
Slade
NWR
Arrowwood
NWR
Jamestown
Reservoir
Jamestown
Lake Ashtabula
Hobart Lake
NWR
Bone Hill
NWR
Stoney Slough
NWR
Tomahawk
NWR
Pipestem
Lake
Half-Way Lake
NWR
Lake George
NWR
Long Lake
NWR
Appert Lake
National Wildlife Refuge
Springwater
National Wildlife Refuge
Edgeley
Ashley
Oakes
Lisbon
Maple River
NWR
Dakota Lake
NWR
Tewaukon
NWR
Wild Rice Lake
NWR
Storm Lake
NWR
Wahpeton
Sheyenne
NG
Fargo
Lake Traverse
Indian Reservation
Sheyenne
River
James
R
Missouri
River
Heart
R
Cannonball
Little
Missouri
River
Sheyenne
R

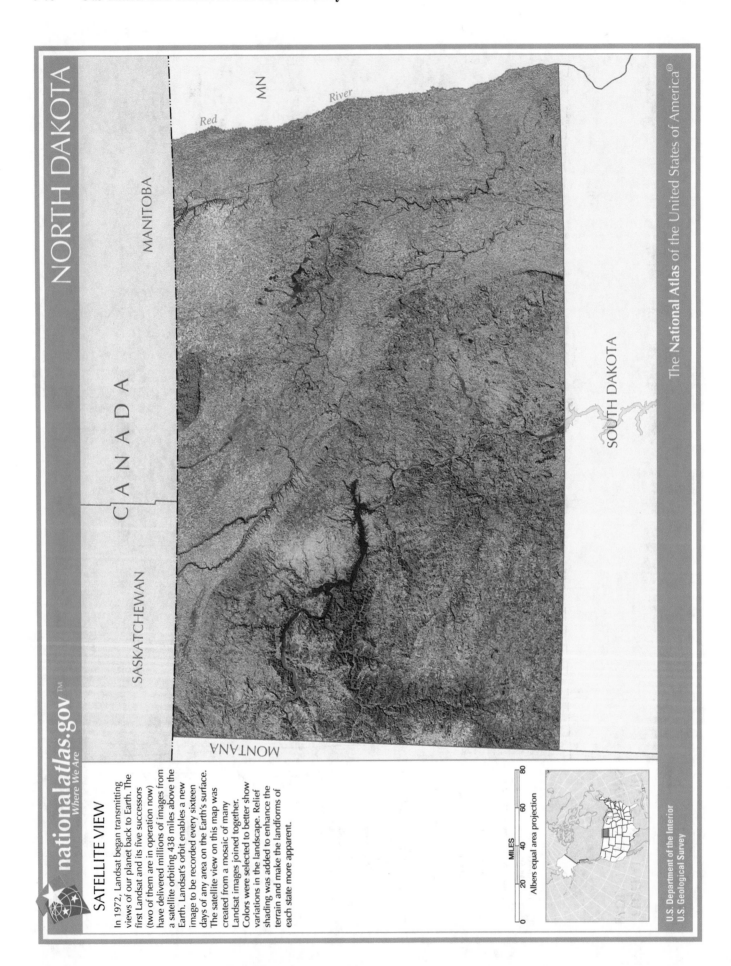

NORTH DAKOTA

nationalatlas.gov ™
Where We Are

The **National Atlas** of the United States of America®

CANADA

SASKATCHEWAN

MANITOBA

MONTANA

SOUTH DAKOTA

MN

Red   River

SATELLITE VIEW

In 1972, Landsat began transmitting views of our planet back to Earth. The first Landsat and its five successors (two of them are in operation now) have delivered millions of images from a satellite orbiting 438 miles above the Earth. Landsat's orbit enables a new image to be recorded every sixteen days of any area on the Earth's surface. The satellite view on this map was created from a mosaic of many Landsat images joined together. Colors were selected to better show variations in the landscape. Relief shading was added to enhance the terrain and make the landforms of each state more apparent.

MILES

20   40   60   80

Albers equal area projection

U.S. Department of the Interior
U.S. Geological Survey

Ohio

Topic	Value	Time Period
Total Surface Area (acres)	26,444,800	2007
Land	26,036,300	2007
Federal Land	373,300	2007
Owned	142,320	FY 2009
Leased	3,724	FY 2009
Otherwise Managed	1,031	FY 2009
National Forest	241,000	September 2006
National Wilderness	77	October 2011
Non-Federal Land, Developed	4,140,300	2007
Non-Federal Land, Rural	21,522,700	2007
Water	408,500	2007
National Natural Landmarks	23	December 2010
National Historic Landmarks	69	December 2010
National Register of Historic Places	3,792	December 2010
National Parks	7	December 2010
Visitors to National Parks	2,738,275	2010
Historic Places Documented by the National Park Service	882	December 2010
Archeological Sites in National Parks	239	December 2010
Threatened and Endangered Species in National Parks	3	December 2010
Economic Benefit from National Park Tourism (dollars)	56,716,000	2009
Conservation Reserve Program (acres)	336,761	October 2011
Land and Water Conservation Fund Grants (dollars)	145,656,016	Since 1965
Historic Preservation Grants (dollars)	39,848,941	2010
Community Conservation and Recreation Projects	51	Since 1987
Federal Acres Transferred for Local Parks and Recreation	2,373	Since 1948
Crude Petroleum Production (millions of barrels)	6	2010
Crude Oil Proved Reserves (millions of barrels)	38	2009
Natural Gas Reserves (billions of cubic feet)	896	2009
Natural Gas Liquid Reserves (millions of barrels)	Not Available	2008
Natural Gas Marketed Production (billions of cubic feet)	89	2009
Coal Reserves (millions of short tons)	23,127	2009

Sources: *U.S. Department of the Interior, National Park Service, State Profiles, December 2010; United States Department of Agriculture, Natural Resources Conservation Service, 2007 National Resources Inventory; U.S. General Services Administration, Federal Real Property Council, FY 2009 Federal Real Property Report, September 2010; University of Montana, www.wilderness.net; U.S. Department of Agriculture, Farm Services Agency, Conservation Reserve Program, October 2011; U.S Census Bureau, 2012 Statistical Abstract of the United States*

Ohio Energy Overview and Analysis

Quick Facts

- Energy consumption in Ohio's industrial sector ranks among the highest in the Nation.
- Ohio has the second-highest refining capacity in the Midwest.
- The completion of a pipeline from the Rocky Mountains could increase Ohio's total natural gas supply in the near future.
- In August 2003, a transmission failure in Ohio led to the largest blackout in North American history, affecting over 50 million people.
- Coal typically fuels close to nine-tenths of net electricity generation in Ohio.

Analysis

Resources and Consumption

Ohio is rich in coal and offshore wind energy potential but has relatively few other energy resources. The Appalachian Basin, which crosses the eastern part of the State, holds considerable reserves of coal and small deposits of oil and conventional natural gas. The Basin's Marcellus shale formation also contains unconventional shale gas. Winds offshore in Lake Erie reach the highest energy potential classification. With a large population and a heavily industrial economy, Ohio is among the top States in total energy consumption. The industrial sector dominates energy consumption, largely due to several energy-intensive industries, including chemicals, glass, metal casting, and steel.

Petroleum

Although Ohio's crude oil production is minor, the State has the second-highest refining capacity in the Midwest. Nearly all of Ohio's crude oil output is derived from stripper wells (wells producing fewer than 10 barrels per day) in the eastern part of the State. Ohio's four refineries primarily depend on crude oil delivered by pipeline from the Gulf Coast and through an oil transportation hub in central Illinois. Ohio has a large network of product pipelines that connect its refineries to markets in Ohio and adjacent States. Ohio's total petroleum demand is high, and Ohioans consume large amounts of motor gasoline and distillate fuel. Ohio allows the use of conventional motor gasoline throughout most of the State, but requires gasoline to be formulated to reduce emissions that contribute to ozone formation in the area surrounding Cincinnati adjacent to the southwest border with Kentucky. Ohio has substantial ethanol production. The additive is frequently blended with the State's motor gasoline, making Ohio's share of U.S. ethanol consumption significantly higher than its share of production.

Natural Gas

Ohio produces a small amount of natural gas. Most of its supply is brought in via several major interstate pipelines from western Canada and the Gulf Coast region. Ohio has major natural gas storage capacity, in depleted oil or natural gas reservoirs, that is used to meet peak demand during the winter. Total supply and consumption have slightly declined in recent years, although the construction of a natural gas pipeline from Colorado could reverse that trend in the near future. The eastern leg of the Rockies Express Pipeline is expected to be completed by late 2009 and to terminate in Monroe County, Ohio, near the border with West Virginia. Recent assessments also indicate that there may be significant potential for future coalbed methane production in the State. Ohio natural gas consumption is high, led by the residential and industrial sectors. Nearly seven-tenths of Ohio households use natural gas as their primary source of energy for home heating.

Coal, Electricity, and Renewables

Although Ohio is a moderate producer of coal, it is a substantial consumer - Ohio ranks fourth in the United States in coal consumption. Ohio's coal mines, concentrated in the Appalachian basin in the eastern part of the State, typically supply less than one-third of State coal consumption. The remaining coal is brought in primarily by railcar and river barge from West Virginia, Wyoming, Kentucky, and Pennsylvania. Although large amounts of coal are used by industry, its primary use is for electricity generation and coal fuels close to nine-tenths of Ohio's total generation. Two nuclear plants located along Lake Erie supply most of the remainder of the State's generation.

Although it is one of the Nation's top generators of electricity, Ohio is also among the major importers of electricity. Ohio's total electricity consumption is high due primarily to the State's energy-intensive industrial sector, which accounts for more than one-third of the State's electricity consumption. The residential sector consumes around one-fourth of the State's electricity, with nearly one-fifth of Ohio households relying on electricity as their primary source of energy for home heating. In August 2003, a transmission failure in northeastern Ohio led to the largest blackout in North American history, affecting an estimated 50 million people in the northeastern United States and Canada. Over half a million Ohio homes and businesses lost power during the incident.

Ohio established an alternative energy portfolio standard in 2008, mandating that at least 25 percent of all electricity sold in the State come from alternative energy resources by 2025. At least half of this electricity must be generated in Ohio itself. Renewable sources such as wind, solar, hydroelectric power, geothermal, and biomass must account for at least half of the standard, or 12.5 percent of electricity sold. The other half of the standard can be met through alternative energy resources like third-generation nuclear power plants, fuel cells, energy-efficiency programs, and clean coal technology that can control or prevent carbon dioxide emissions.

Source: U.S. Energy Information Administration, October 2009

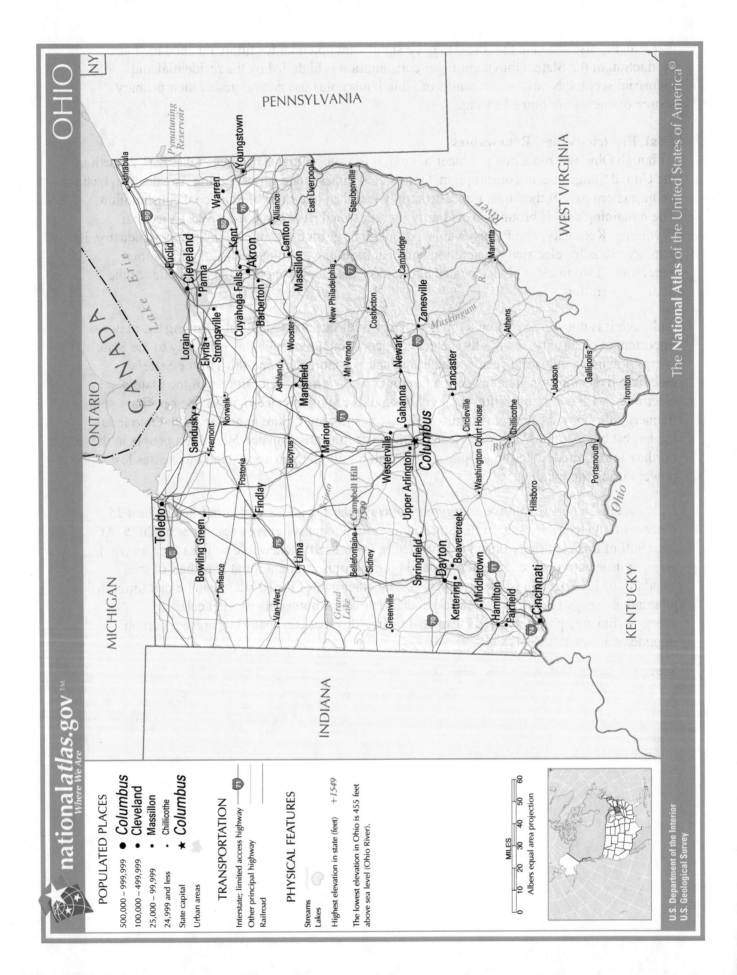

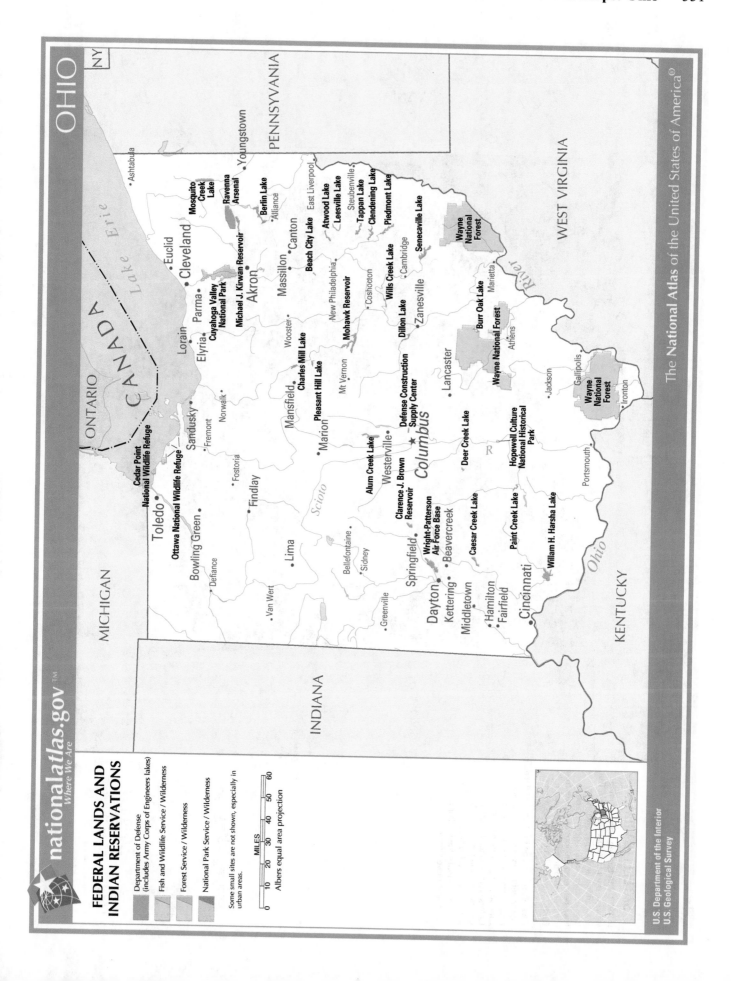

OHIO

**FEDERAL LANDS AND
INDIAN RESERVATIONS**

Department of Defense
(includes Army Corps of Engineers lakes)

Fish and Wildlife Service / Wilderness

Forest Service / Wilderness

National Park Service / Wilderness

Some small sites are not shown, especially in
urban areas.

MILES
0   10   20   30   40   50   60

Albers equal area projection

The *National Atlas* of the United States of America®

MICHIGAN

ONTARIO

CANADA

Lake Erie

NY

PENNSYVANIA

WEST VIRGINIA

INDIANA

KENTUCKY

Ashtabula

Youngstown

Euclid

Cleveland

Parma

Lorain

Elyria

Sandusky

Fremont

Norwalk

Cedar Point
National Wildlife Refuge

Ottawa National Wildlife Refuge

Toledo

Bowling Green

Defiance

Findlay

Fostoria

Lima

Van Wert

Bellefontaine

Sidney

Greenville

Mosquito
Creek
Lake

Ravenna
Arsenal

Berlin Lake

Alliance

Canton

Massillon

Akron

Michael J. Kirwan Reservoir

Cuyahoga Valley
National Park

Beach City Lake

Atwood Lake

Leesville Lake

Tappan Lake

Clendening Lake

Piedmont Lake

Steubenville

East Liverpool

New Philadelphia

Coshocton

Wooster

Mt Vernon

Mansfield

Marion

Charles Mill Lake

Pleasant Hill Lake

Mohawk Reservoir

Wills Creek Lake

Cambridge

Senecaville Lake

Zanesville

Dillon Lake

Lancaster

Defense Construction
Supply Center

Columbus

Westerville

Alum Creek Lake

Clarence J. Brown
Reservoir

Springfield

Wright-Patterson
Air Force Base

Beavercreek

Dayton

Kettering

Middletown

Hamilton

Fairfield

Cincinnati

Caesar Creek Lake

Deer Creek Lake

Paint Creek Lake

Willam H. Harsha Lake

Hopewell Culture
National Historical
Park

Jackson

Gallipolis

Ironton

Portsmouth

Athens

Wayne National Forest

Burr Oak Lake

Marietta

Wayne
National
Forest

Wayne
National
Forest

Scioto

Ohio

River

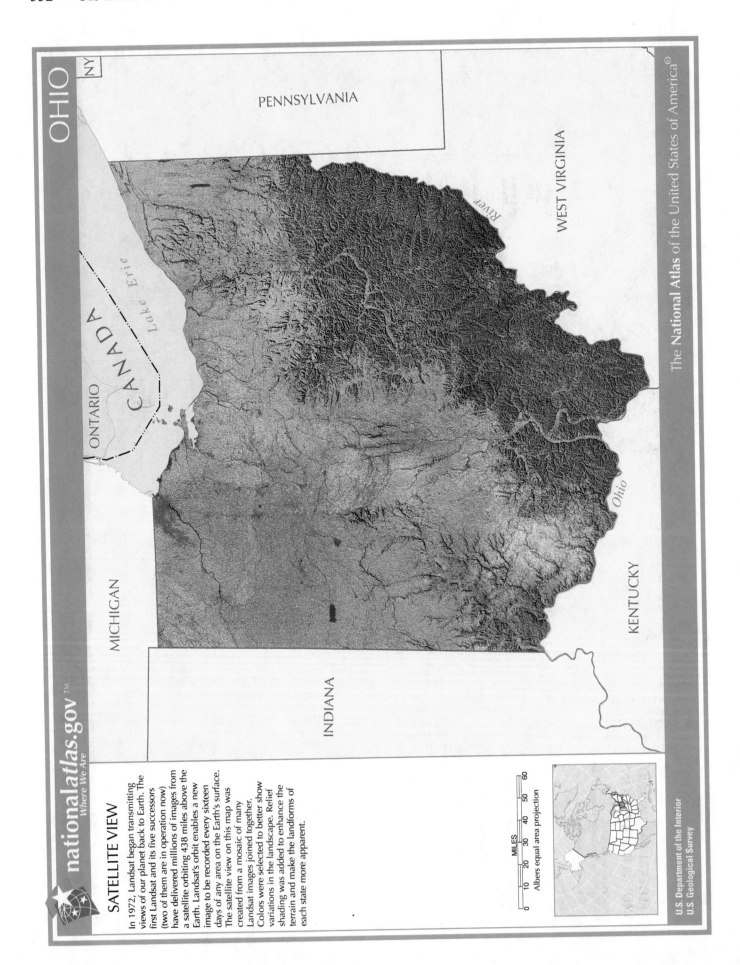

OHIO

NY

PENNSYLVANIA

CANADA

ONTARIO

Lake Erie

MICHIGAN

WEST VIRGINIA

River

Ohio

KENTUCKY

INDIANA

nationalatlas.gov™
Where We Are

The National Atlas of the United States of America®

SATELLITE VIEW

In 1972, Landsat began transmitting views of our planet back to Earth. The first Landsat and its five successors (two of them are in operation now) have delivered millions of images from a satellite orbiting 438 miles above the Earth. Landsat's orbit enables a new image to be recorded every sixteen days of any area on the Earth's surface. The satellite view on this map was created from a mosaic of many Landsat images joined together. Colors were selected to better show variations in the landscape. Relief shading was added to enhance the terrain and make the landforms of each state more apparent.

MILES

0   10   20   30   40   50   60

Albers equal area projection

U.S. Department of the Interior
U.S. Geological Survey

Oklahoma

Topic	Value	Time Period
Total Surface Area (acres)	44,738,100	2007
Land	43,649,400	2007
Federal Land	1,148,300	2007
Owned	1,080,354	FY 2009
Leased	5,509	FY 2009
Otherwise Managed	1,533	FY 2009
National Forest	461,000	September 2006
National Wilderness	23,113	October 2011
Non-Federal Land, Developed	2,056,800	2007
Non-Federal Land, Rural	40,444,300	2007
Water	1,088,700	2007
National Natural Landmarks	3	December 2010
National Historic Landmarks	20	December 2010
National Register of Historic Places	1,188	December 2010
National Parks	3	December 2010
Visitors to National Parks	1,266,189	2010
Historic Places Documented by the National Park Service	107	December 2010
Archeological Sites in National Parks	79	December 2010
Threatened and Endangered Species in National Parks	0	December 2010
Economic Benefit from National Park Tourism (dollars)	12,670,000	2009
Conservation Reserve Program (acres)	829,338	October 2011
Land and Water Conservation Fund Grants (dollars)	55,414,720	Since 1965
Historic Preservation Grants (dollars)	20,374,369	2010
Community Conservation and Recreation Projects	20	Since 1987
Federal Acres Transferred for Local Parks and Recreation	1,965	Since 1948
Crude Petroleum Production (millions of barrels)	68	2010
Crude Oil Proved Reserves (millions of barrels)	622	2009
Natural Gas Reserves (billions of cubic feet)	22,769	2009
Natural Gas Liquid Reserves (millions of barrels)	1,034	2008
Natural Gas Marketed Production (billions of cubic feet)	1,858	2009
Coal Reserves (millions of short tons)	1,545	2009

Sources: *U.S. Department of the Interior, National Park Service, State Profiles, December 2010; United States Department of Agriculture, Natural Resources Conservation Service, 2007 National Resources Inventory; U.S. General Services Administration, Federal Real Property Council, FY 2009 Federal Real Property Report, September 2010; University of Montana, www.wilderness.net; U.S. Department of Agriculture, Farm Services Agency, Conservation Reserve Program, October 2011; U.S Census Bureau, 2012 Statistical Abstract of the United States*

Oklahoma Energy Overview and Analysis

Quick Facts

- Oklahoma is one of the top natural gas-producing States in the Nation.
- More than a dozen of the 100 largest natural gas fields in the country are found in Oklahoma.
- Oklahoma has five petroleum refineries with a combined capacity of roughly 3 percent of the total U.S. distillation capacity.
- Cushing, Oklahoma, is the designated delivery point for NYMEX crude oil futures contracts.
- The Oklahoma State Legislature created the Commission on Marginally Producing Oil and Gas Wells in 1992 to keep State production decline to a minimum.

Analysis

Resources and Consumption

Oklahoma is rich in energy resources. Many of the largest oil and gas fields in the country are found in the Anadarko, Arkoma, and Ardmore geologic basins and their associated shelves and platforms. Small coal deposits are also found in the Arkoma Basin and the Cherokee Platform, both in eastern Oklahoma. Oklahoma's fossil fuel reserves make up part of the Mid-Continent Oil Region, a vast fossil fuel-producing region extending from Nebraska to south Texas and flanked by the Mississippi River and the Rocky Mountains. Oklahoma also has hydroelectric potential in several river basins, as well as wind and solar potential, primarily in the western portion of the State. The industrial sector is the leading energy-consuming sector in the State. Due in part to the energy-intensive oil and gas industry, Oklahoma's per capita energy consumption ranks highly.

Historically, Oklahoma's economy has been heavily dependent on the oil and gas industry. Several oil and gas exploration and production booms in the 20th century spurred rapid and sustained economic development in much of the State. Although the Oklahoma oil and gas industry has been in steady decline since the mid-1980s, the industry remains a considerable source of employment and revenue, in part because, in 1992, the Oklahoma State Legislature created the Commission on Marginally Producing Oil and Gas Wells to keep the decline in production to a minimum. The intent of the Commission is to help operators sustain production from marginally producing wells, which, in recent years, have accounted for over three-fourths of Oklahoma oil production and about one-tenth of the State's natural gas production. High prices for oil and gas also have slowed the decline.

Petroleum

Oklahoma produces a substantial amount of oil, with annual production typically accounting for more than 3 percent of total U.S. production in recent years. Crude oil wells and gathering pipeline systems are concentrated in central Oklahoma, although drilling activity also takes place in the panhandle. Two of the 100 largest oil fields in the United States are found in Oklahoma.

The city of Cushing, in central Oklahoma, is a major crude oil trading hub that connects Gulf Coast producers to Midwest refining markets. In addition to Oklahoma crude oil, the Cushing hub receives supply from several major pipelines that originate in Texas. Traditionally, the Cushing Hub has pushed Gulf Coast and Mid-Continent crude oil supply north to Midwest refining markets. However, production from those regions is in decline, and an underused crude oil pipeline system has been reversed to deliver rapidly expanding heavy crude oil supply - produced in Alberta, Canada, and pumped to Chicago via the Enbridge and Lakehead Pipeline systems - to Cushing, where it can access Gulf Coast refining markets. Cushing is the designated delivery point for NYMEX crude oil futures contracts.

Crude oil supplies from Cushing that are not delivered to the Midwest are fed to Oklahoma's five refineries, which have a combined distillation capacity of over 500 thousand barrels per day - roughly 3 percent of the total U.S. refining capacity. Several petroleum product pipelines connect those refineries to consumption markets in Oklahoma and nearby States. One of the largest of these, the Explorer Pipeline, originates on the Texas coast and receives products from Oklahoma refineries before continuing on to supply Midwest markets.

Natural Gas

Oklahoma is one of the top natural gas producers in the United States and production typically accounts for almost one-tenth of the U.S. total. More than a dozen of the 100 largest natural gas fields in the country are found in Oklahoma, and proven reserves of conventional natural gas have been increasing in recent years. Oklahoma also has large reserves of coalbed methane in the Arkoma Basin and the Cherokee Platform in the eastern part of the State. Extraction of those resources has grown in recent years.

Most natural gas in Oklahoma is consumed by the electricity generation and industrial sectors. About three-fifths of Oklahoma households use natural gas as their primary energy source for home heating. Nevertheless, only about one-third of Oklahoma's natural gas output is consumed within the State. The remaining supply is sent via pipeline to neighboring States, the majority to Kansas, including the natural gas trading hubs in Texas and Kansas. Almost 90 percent of the natural gas that enters the State arrives via pipelines from Texas and Colorado.

Coal, Electricity, and Renewables

Coal- and natural gas-fired power plants dominate electric power production in Oklahoma. Nearly all of the State's coal is supplied by railcar from Wyoming. Oklahoma produces a substantial amount of energy from wind resources, and other renewable energy resources - hydroelectric dams and, to a limited extent, wood and wood-waste - also contribute about 7 percent of the electricity to the Oklahoma power grid. Just over one-fourth of Oklahoma households rely on electricity as their primary energy source for home heating.

Source: U.S. Energy Information Administration, October 2009

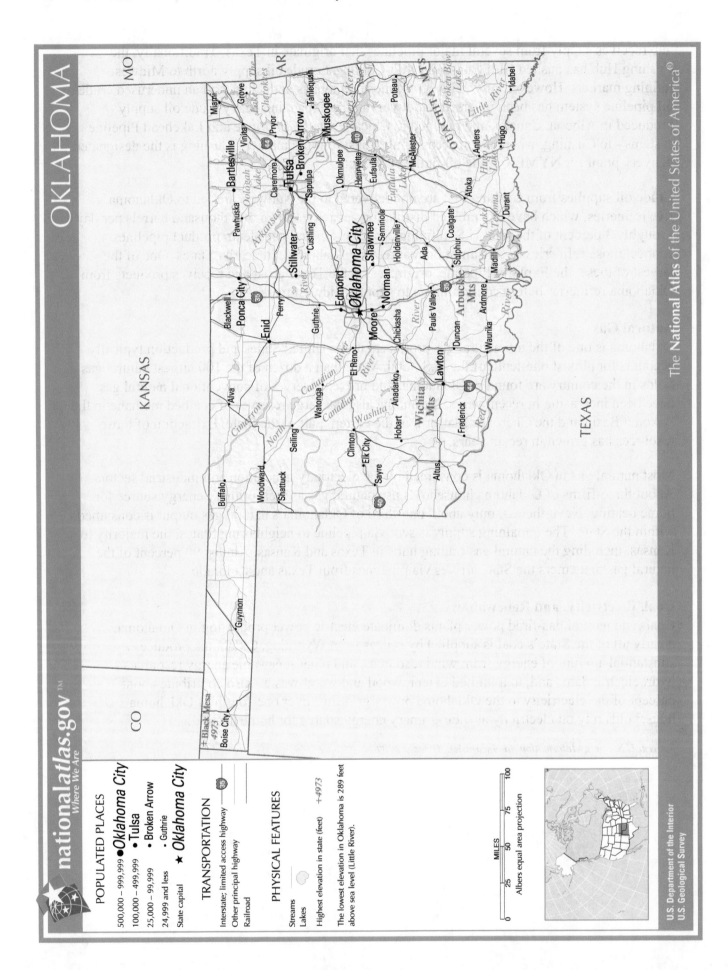

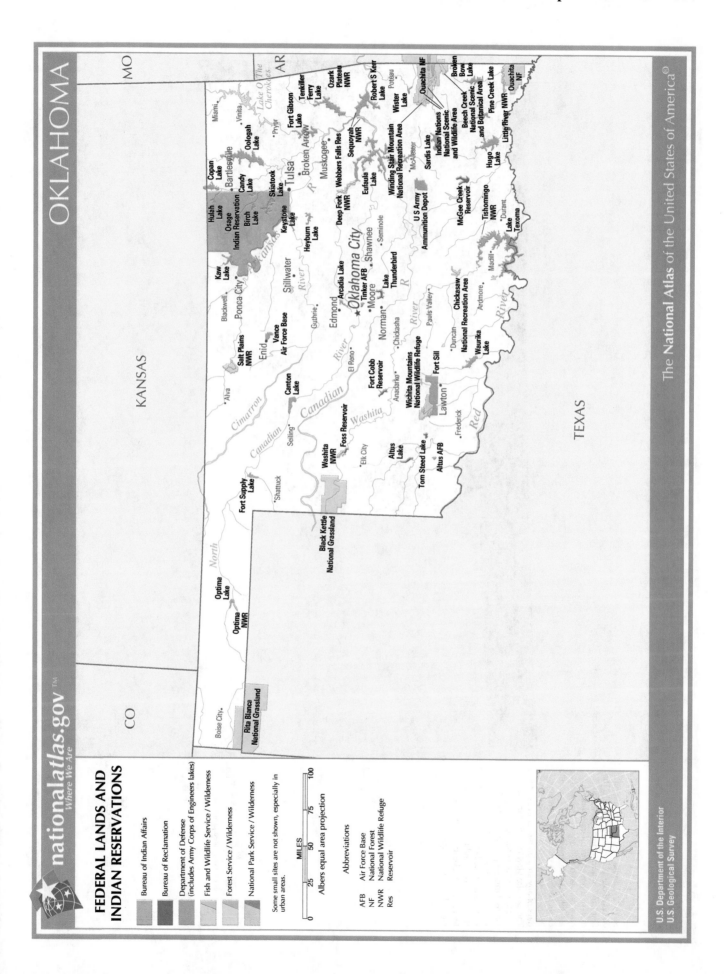

OKLAHOMA

nationalatlas.gov ™
Where We Are

**FEDERAL LANDS AND
INDIAN RESERVATIONS**

Bureau of Indian Affairs

Bureau of Reclamation

Department of Defense
(includes Army Corps of Engineers lakes)

Fish and Wildlife Service / Wilderness

Forest Service / Wilderness

National Park Service / Wilderness

Some small sites are not shown, especially in
urban areas.

MILES
0   25   50   75   100

Albers equal area projection

Abbreviations

AFB   Air Force Base
NF   National Forest
NWR   National Wildlife Refuge
Res   Reservoir

MO

AR

KANSAS

CO

TEXAS

The **National Atlas** of the United States of America®

U.S. Department of the Interior
U.S. Geological Survey

Lake O' The Cherokees

Miami

Vinita

Pryor

Copan Lake

Hulah Lake

Bartlesville

Osage Indian Reservation

Candy Lake

Oologah Lake

Skiatook Lake

Tenkiller Ferry Lake

Ozark Plateau NWR

Fort Gibson Lake

Robert S Kerr Lake

Poteau

Broken Arrow

Tulsa

Keystone Lake

Birch Lake

Muskogee

Webbers Falls Res

Sequoyah NWR

Wister Lake

Broken Bow Lake

Ouachita NF

Kansas River

Kaw Lake

Blackwell

Ponca City

Stillwater

Heyburn Lake

Deep Fork NWR

Eufaula Lake

Winding Stair Mountain National Recreation Area

McAlester

Beech Creek National Scenic and Botanical Area

Pine Creek Lake

Indian Nations National Scenic and Wildlife Area

Sardis Lake

Little River NWR

Ouachita NF

Salt Plains NWR

Enid

Vance Air Force Base

Guthrie

Edmond

Arcadia Lake

Oklahoma City

Tinker AFB

Moore

Norman

Thunderbird Lake

Shawnee

Seminole

U S Army Ammunition Depot

McGee Creek Reservoir

Tishomingo NWR

Durant

Hugo Lake

Alva

Canton Lake

El Reno

Fort Cobb Reservoir

Chickasha

Anadarko

Pauls Valley

Chickasaw National Recreation Area

Lake Texoma

Madill

Seling

Canadian River

Washita

Washita NWR

Foss Reservoir

Elk City

Wichita Mountains National Wildlife Refuge

Fort Sill

Lawton

Duncan

Waurika Lake

Ardmore

Shattuck

Fort Supply Lake

North Canadian

Altus Lake

Tom Steed Lake

Altus AFB

Frederick

Red River

Black Kettle National Grassland

Optima Lake

Optima NWR

Boise City

Rita Blanca National Grassland

Cimarron River

Canadian River

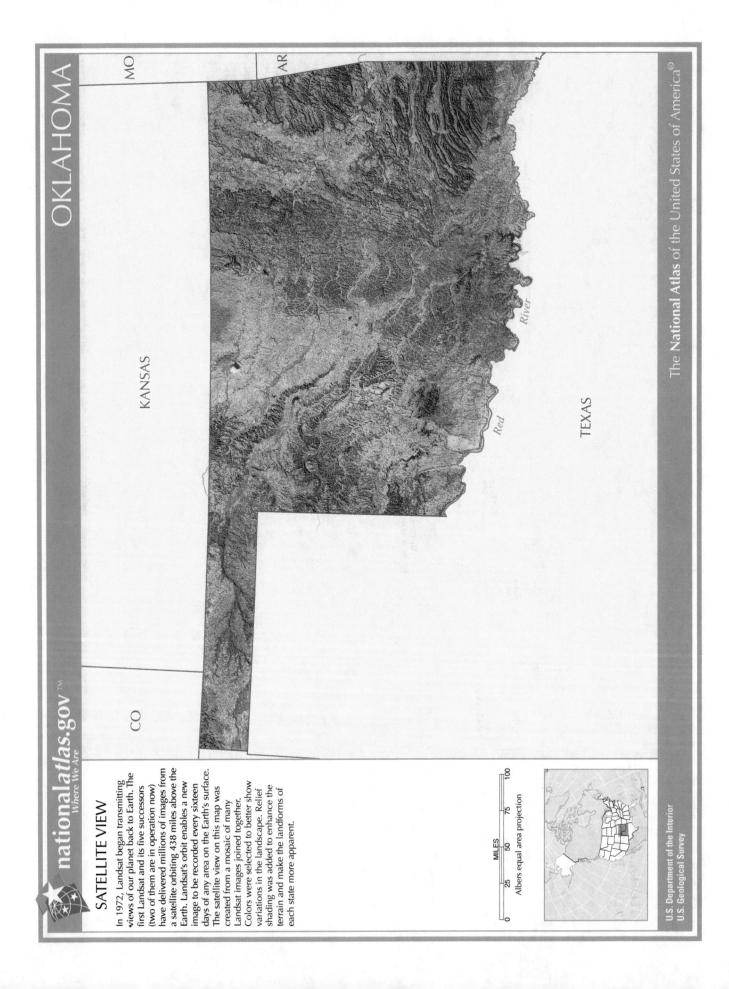

nationalatlas.gov™
Where We Are

OKLAHOMA

MO

AR

KANSAS

CO

TEXAS

Red   *River*

SATELLITE VIEW

In 1972, Landsat began transmitting views of our planet back to Earth. The first Landsat and its five successors (two of them are in operation now) have delivered millions of images from a satellite orbiting 438 miles above the Earth. Landsat's orbit enables a new image to be recorded every sixteen days of any area on the Earth's surface. The satellite view on this map was created from a mosaic of many Landsat images joined together. Colors were selected to better show variations in the landscape. Relief shading was added to enhance the terrain and make the landforms of each state more apparent.

MILES

0   25   50   75   100

Albers equal area projection

U.S. Department of the Interior
U.S. Geological Survey

The **National Atlas** of the United States of America®

Oregon

Topic	Value	Time Period
Total Surface Area (acres)	62,161,000	2007
Land	61,334,200	2007
Federal Land	31,260,400	2007
Owned	329,961	FY 2009
Leased	1,486	FY 2009
Otherwise Managed	282,512	FY 2009
National Forest	15,688,000	September 2006
National Wilderness	2,474,435	October 2011
Non-Federal Land, Developed	1,389,600	2007
Non-Federal Land, Rural	28,684,200	2007
Water	826,800	2007
National Natural Landmarks	7	December 2010
National Historic Landmarks	16	December 2010
National Register of Historic Places	1,912	December 2010
National Parks	5	December 2010
Visitors to National Parks	888,358	2010
Historic Places Documented by the National Park Service	485	December 2010
Archeological Sites in National Parks	148	December 2010
Threatened and Endangered Species in National Parks	12	December 2010
Economic Benefit from National Park Tourism (dollars)	51,375,000	2009
Conservation Reserve Program (acres)	546,649	October 2011
Land and Water Conservation Fund Grants (dollars)	57,983,273	Since 1965
Historic Preservation Grants (dollars)	20,645,477	2010
Community Conservation and Recreation Projects	84	Since 1987
Federal Acres Transferred for Local Parks and Recreation	3,492	Since 1948
Crude Petroleum Production (millions of barrels)	Not Available	2010
Crude Oil Proved Reserves (millions of barrels)	Not Available	2009
Natural Gas Reserves (billions of cubic feet)	Not Available	2009
Natural Gas Liquid Reserves (millions of barrels)	Not Available	2008
Natural Gas Marketed Production (billions of cubic feet)	Not Available	2009
Coal Reserves (millions of short tons)	Not Available	2009

Sources: U.S. Department of the Interior, National Park Service, State Profiles, December 2010; United States Department of Agriculture, Natural Resources Conservation Service, 2007 National Resources Inventory; U.S. General Services Administration, Federal Real Property Council, FY 2009 Federal Real Property Report, September 2010; University of Montana, www.wilderness.net; U.S. Department of Agriculture, Farm Services Agency, Conservation Reserve Program, October 2011; U.S Census Bureau, 2012 Statistical Abstract of the United States

Oregon Energy Overview and Analysis

Quick Facts

- Oregon is one of the Nation's leading generators of hydroelectric power, which accounts for nearly two-thirds of State electricity generation.
- Major transmission lines connect Oregon's electricity grid to California and Washington State, allowing for large interstate energy transfers.
- A liquefied natural gas (LNG) import facility has been approved along the northwest coast in Bradwood while two others have been proposed along Oregon's northwest and southwest coast to help meet demand for natural gas.
- The geologically active basin and range country in southern and eastern Oregon, as well as the Cascade Mountains in western Oregon, are promising sites for geothermal energy development.

Analysis

Resources and Consumption

Oregon has few conventional energy resources but is rich in renewable energy potential. The Columbia River in the north and several smaller waterways flowing from the Cascade Mountains give Oregon some of the highest hydroelectric power potential in the United States. Much of the State has considerable wind power potential. The geologically active basin and range country in southern and eastern Oregon, as well as the Cascades in western Oregon, are promising sites for geothermal energy development, with the potential for generating as much as 2,200 MW of electric power. Oregon's total energy consumption is moderate although the State is a leader in the energy-intensive forest products industry. The transportation sector is the leading energy-consuming sector in Oregon, followed closely by the industrial and residential sectors.

Petroleum

Oregon's only refinery, which is located in the Portland area and primarily produced asphalt and vacuum gas oil, was shut down in December 2008. The State receives petroleum-based transportation and heating fuels from Washington State and northern California. Tanker trucks from California supply southern Oregon, while ships and barges deliver additional product from San Francisco to the Portland area. The use of oxygenated motor gasoline is required throughout the entire State.

Natural Gas

Oregon receives its natural gas supply by pipeline from Canada and the Rocky Mountain States. The Northwest Pipeline Corp. system supplies the Portland area and western markets, while the Gas Transmission Northwest system line serves the east. Although Oregon has two market hubs along the Gas Transmission Northwest line, they primarily serve California markets. In Oregon, natural gas is principally used for electricity generation, with the industrial and residential sectors, respectively, as the next largest consumers. Over one-third of Oregon households use natural gas as their primary energy source for home heating. A liquefied natural gas (LNG) import facility has been approved by the Federal Energy Regulatory Commission along Oregon's northwest coast in Bradwood. Two additional LNG import facilities have been proposed along Oregon's northwest and southwest coast to help meet natural gas demand in the Pacific Northwest, northern California, and northern Nevada regions.

Coal, Electricity, and Renewables

Hydroelectric power dominates the electricity market in Oregon, providing nearly two-thirds of the power generated in the State. Oregon's four largest electricity generation facilities, all located on the Columbia River, are hydroelectric plants. Smaller hydroelectric plants generate power along several rivers flowing from the Cascade Mountains. Natural gas-fired power plants are located along major gas transmission lines and supply about one-quarter of the electricity market. The Boardman plant in the north central part of the State is Oregon's lone coal plant and supplies most of the rest of Oregon's electricity needs. Oregon also imports electricity from coal-fired plants in Utah, Wyoming, and Montana.

Major transmission lines connect Oregon's electricity grid to California and Washington State, allowing for large interstate energy transfers. One of these transmission systems is the Western Interconnection, which runs from British Columbia and Alberta in Canada through Washington, Oregon, and southern California to the northern part of Baja California, Mexico. The system, also known as the Pacific Intertie, is the largest single electricity transmission program in the United States and covers all or part of 14 states. Although the Pacific Intertie was originally designed to transmit electricity south during California's peak summer demand season, flow is sometimes reversed overnight and has occasionally been reversed during periods of reduced hydroelectric generation in the Northwest. Nearly one-half of Oregon households use electricity as their main source of energy for home heating.

Oregon utilizes several renewable energy sources and is one of the leading hydroelectric power producers in the Nation. The State is a major producer of wind energy, generating about 4 percent of the Nation's total. Oregon also generates some electricity from wood and wood waste, and produces smaller amounts of electricity from landfill gas. In June 2007, Oregon adopted a renewable energy portfolio standard requiring the State's largest utilities to meet 25 percent of their electric load with new renewable energy sources by 2025.

Source: U.S. Energy Information Administration, October 2009

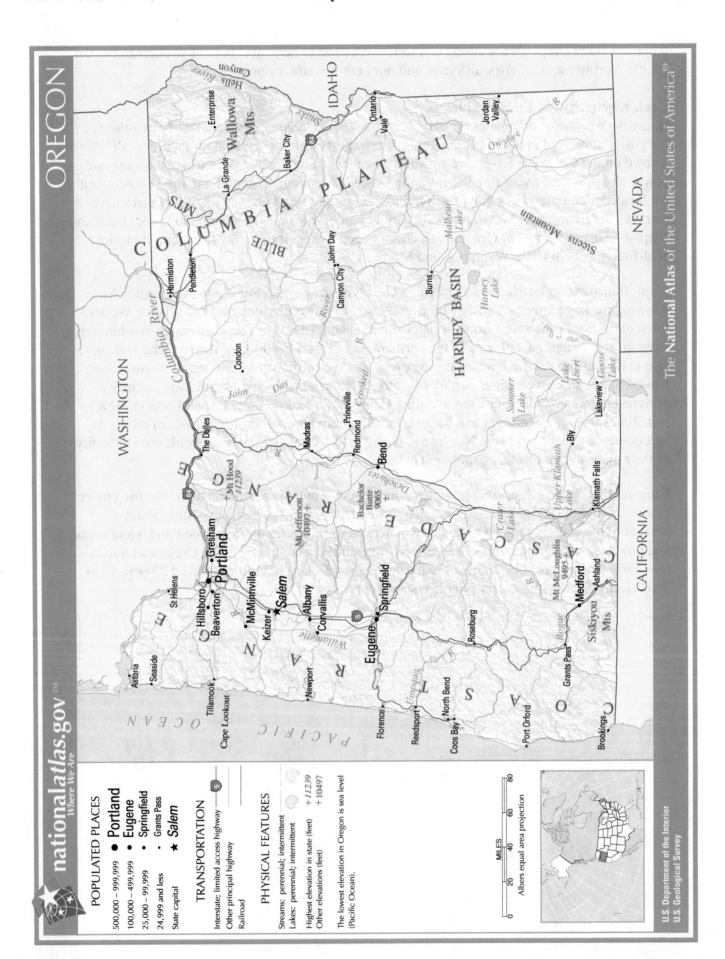

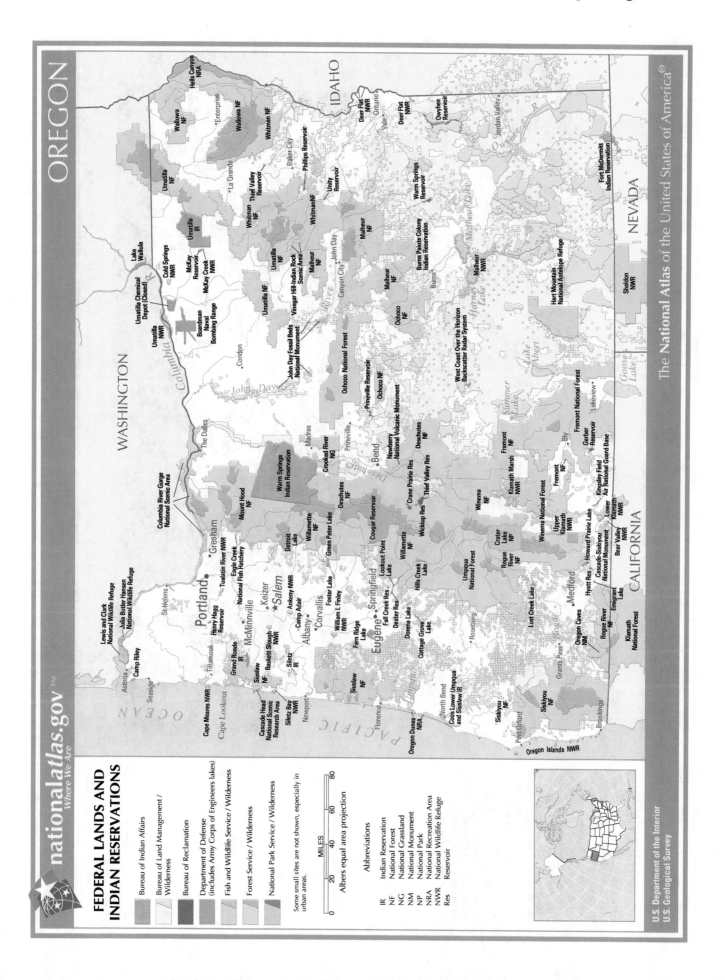

OREGON

nationalatlas.gov™
Where We Are

FEDERAL LANDS AND INDIAN RESERVATIONS

Bureau of Indian Affairs

Bureau of Land Management / Wilderness

Bureau of Reclamation

Department of Defense (includes Army Corps of Engineers lakes)

Fish and Wildlife Service / Wilderness

Forest Service / Wilderness

National Park Service / Wilderness

Some small sites are not shown, especially in urban areas.

MILES
0   20   40   60   80

Albers equal area projection

Abbreviations

IR   Indian Reservation
NF   National Forest
NG   National Grassland
NM   National Monument
NP   National Park
NRA   National Recreation Area
NWR   National Wildlife Refuge
Res   Reservoir

U.S. Department of the Interior
U.S. Geological Survey

The **National Atlas** of the United States of America®

OREGON

IDAHO

Snake *River*

WASHINGTON

Columbia *River*

NEVADA

The **National Atlas** of the United States of America®

CALIFORNIA

Goose Lake

P A C I F I C   O C E A N

nationalatlas.gov ™
Where We Are

SATELLITE VIEW

In 1972, Landsat began transmitting
views of our planet back to Earth. The
first Landsat and its five successors
(two of them are in operation now)
have delivered millions of images from
a satellite orbiting 438 miles above the
Earth. Landsat's orbit enables a new
image to be recorded every sixteen
days of any area on the Earth's surface.
The satellite view on this map was
created from a mosaic of many
Landsat images joined together.
Colors were selected to better show
variations in the landscape. Relief
shading was added to enhance the
terrain and make the landforms of
each state more apparent.

MILES
0   20   40   60   80
Albers equal area projection

U.S. Department of the Interior
U.S. Geological Survey

Pennsylvania

Topic	Value	Time Period
Total Surface Area (acres)	28,995,200	2007
Land	28,514,400	2007
Federal Land	724,300	2007
Owned	156,380	FY 2009
Leased	35,659	FY 2009
Otherwise Managed	1,423	FY 2009
National Forest	513,000	September 2006
National Wilderness	9,002	October 2011
Non-Federal Land, Developed	4,360,700	2007
Non-Federal Land, Rural	23,429,400	2007
Water	480,800	2007
National Natural Landmarks	27	December 2010
National Historic Landmarks	161	December 2010
National Register of Historic Places	3,268	December 2010
National Parks	18	December 2010
Visitors to National Parks	8,970,475	2010
Historic Places Documented by the National Park Service	3,724	December 2010
Archeological Sites in National Parks	1,000	December 2010
Threatened and Endangered Species in National Parks	4	December 2010
Economic Benefit from National Park Tourism (dollars)	295,605,000	2009
Conservation Reserve Program (acres)	203,656	October 2011
Land and Water Conservation Fund Grants (dollars)	162,163,928	Since 1965
Historic Preservation Grants (dollars)	52,341,882	2010
Community Conservation and Recreation Projects	136	Since 1987
Federal Acres Transferred for Local Parks and Recreation	9,683	Since 1948
Crude Petroleum Production (millions of barrels)	3	2010
Crude Oil Proved Reserves (millions of barrels)	10	2009
Natural Gas Reserves (billions of cubic feet)	6,985	2009
Natural Gas Liquid Reserves (millions of barrels)	Not Available	2008
Natural Gas Marketed Production (billions of cubic feet)	274	2009
Coal Reserves (millions of short tons)	26,998	2009

Sources: U.S. Department of the Interior, National Park Service, State Profiles, December 2010; United States Department of Agriculture, Natural Resources Conservation Service, 2007 National Resources Inventory; U.S. General Services Administration, Federal Real Property Council, FY 2009 Federal Real Property Report, September 2010; University of Montana, www.wilderness.net; U.S. Department of Agriculture, Farm Services Agency, Conservation Reserve Program, October 2011; U.S Census Bureau, 2012 Statistical Abstract of the United States

Pennsylvania Energy Overview and Analysis

Quick Facts

- The first commercial U.S. nuclear power plant came online in 1957 in Shippingport; today, Pennsylvania ranks second in the Nation in nuclear power generating capacity.
- Pennsylvania is a major coal-producing State and sells about one-half of its coal output to other States throughout the East Coast and Midwest.
- Pennsylvania is the leading petroleum-refining State in the Northeast.
- The Drake Well in Titusville, Pennsylvania, was the world's first commercial oil well, and western Pennsylvania was the site of the world's first oil boom.

Analysis

Resources and Consumption

Pennsylvania is rich in fossil fuels. The Appalachian Basin, which covers most of the State, holds substantial reserves of coal and minor reserves of conventional natural gas. The Basin's Marcellus shale region, an area of increased activity in recent years, is estimated to contain potentially large reserves of unconventional shale gas.

Renewable energy resources are also abundant. The Susquehanna River and several smaller river basins offer considerable hydropower resources, and the Appalachian and Allegheny mountain ranges are areas of high wind power potential, as are areas both onshore and offshore along Pennsylvania's short Lake Erie shoreline.

The industrial sector is Pennsylvania's leading energy-consuming sector, due in part to energy-intensive industries including aluminum production, chemical manufacturing, glass making, petroleum refining, forest product manufacturing, and steel production.

Petroleum

Pennsylvania is the leading petroleum-refining State in the Northeast. Although Pennsylvania is credited with drilling the first commercial oil well in 1859, the State's current production is minimal, with output derived primarily from stripper wells that produce less than 10 barrels per day. Pennsylvania's large-scale petroleum refineries are located along the Delaware River near Philadelphia and process primarily foreign crude oil shipped from overseas. These refineries supply regional Northeast markets. In addition to local Pennsylvania and New Jersey refineries, Pennsylvania receives propane via the TEPPCO pipeline from the Gulf Coast and by rail from other States and Canada. To reduce emissions of smog-forming pollutants, motorists in the heavily populated areas of southeastern Pennsylvania, including Philadelphia, are required to use reformulated motor gasoline blended with ethanol. The Pittsburgh area requires 7.8 RVP gasoline, a fuel specially blended to reduce emissions that contribute to ozone formation.

Pennsylvania, along with much of the U.S. Northeast, is vulnerable to distillate fuel oil shortages and price spikes during winter months, due to high demand for home heating. More than one-fifth of Pennsylvania households rely on fuel oil as their primary energy source for home heating. In January and February 2000, distillate fuel oil prices rose sharply when extreme winter weather increased demand unexpectedly and hindered the arrival of new supply, as frozen rivers and high winds slowed the docking and unloading of barges and tankers. In July 2000, in order to reduce the risk of future shortages, the President directed the U.S. Department of Energy to establish the Northeast Heating Oil Reserve. The Reserve gives Northeast consumers adequate supplies for about 10 days, the time required for ships to carry heating oil from the Gulf of Mexico to New York Harbor. The Reserve's storage terminals are located in Perth Amboy, New Jersey, and Groton and New Haven, Connecticut.

Natural Gas

Although minor, Pennsylvania's natural gas production has grown in recent years. The State's Marcellus shale region, in particular, has experienced markedly increased new development over the past few years. However, compared to Pennsylvania's total natural gas production, shale gas production remains minimal.

Pennsylvania remains dependent on several major interstate pipelines, most of which originate in the Gulf Coast region, to meet the majority of State demand. Two proposed projects could increase natural gas supply to Pennsylvania: an eastern expansion of the Rockies Express Pipeline system, which is expected to be completed in 2009 and a liquefied natural gas (LNG) terminal in Logan Township, New Jersey, just across the Delaware River from Philadelphia, that has been approved by the Federal Energy Regulatory Commission (FERC) but for which construction has not begun. Pennsylvania delivers over three-fifths of its natural gas receipts to New Jersey.

Pennsylvania's natural gas storage capacity is among the highest in the Nation, which allows the State to store the fuel during the summer when national demand is typically low, and quickly ramp up delivery during the winter months when markets across the Nation require greater volumes of natural gas to meet their home heating needs. Natural gas is used in Pennsylvania primarily for residential and industrial use, although its use for electricity generation has grown rapidly in recent years.

Coal, Electricity, and Renewables

Pennsylvania is a major coal-producing State. Northeastern Pennsylvania's coal region holds the Nation's largest remaining reserves of anthracite coal, a type of coal that burns cleanly with little soot. It is used primarily as a domestic fuel in either hand-fired stoves or automatic stoker furnaces. Although Pennsylvania supplies virtually all of the Nation's anthracite, most of the State's coal production consists of bituminous coal mined in the western part of the State, where several of the Nation's largest underground coal mines are located. Enlow Fork Mine is the largest underground coal mine in the United States.

Large volumes of coal are moved both into and out of Pennsylvania, mostly by railcar, river barge, and truck. Pennsylvania transports close to one-half of its coal production to other States throughout the East Coast and Midwest. Pennsylvania coal demand is high, and it is one of the top coal-consuming States in the Nation. Pennsylvania's coal dominates the State's power generation market, typically accounting for more than one-half of net electricity production.

Pennsylvania's electricity markets also rely substantially on nuclear power, and the State ranks second in the Nation after Illinois in nuclear generating capacity. Pennsylvania's five operating nuclear plants have supplied slightly more than one-third of State electricity generation in recent years. Nuclear power has been an important fuel for electricity generation in Pennsylvania since 1957, when the first commercial U.S. nuclear power plant came online in Shippingport. The Shippingport plant was shut down and decommissioned in 1982 after 25 years of service. Pennsylvania's nuclear power industry has experienced problems in the past. In 1979, an accident led to a partial meltdown at the Three Mile Island nuclear plant and became the most serious accident in U.S. nuclear power plant operating history, changing the U.S. nuclear industry and leading to sweeping changes at the Nuclear Regulatory Commission.

Pennsylvania is one of the top electricity-producing States in the Nation and electricity production exceeds State demand. Pennsylvania is among the largest users of municipal solid waste and landfill gas for electricity generation and produces substantial hydroelectric power. The State also produces a small amount of energy from wind. In December 2004, Pennsylvania adopted an alternative energy portfolio standard that requires electric distribution companies and generators in the State to supply 18.5 percent of Pennsylvania's electricity from alternative energy sources by 2020.

Source: U.S. Energy Information Administration, October 2009

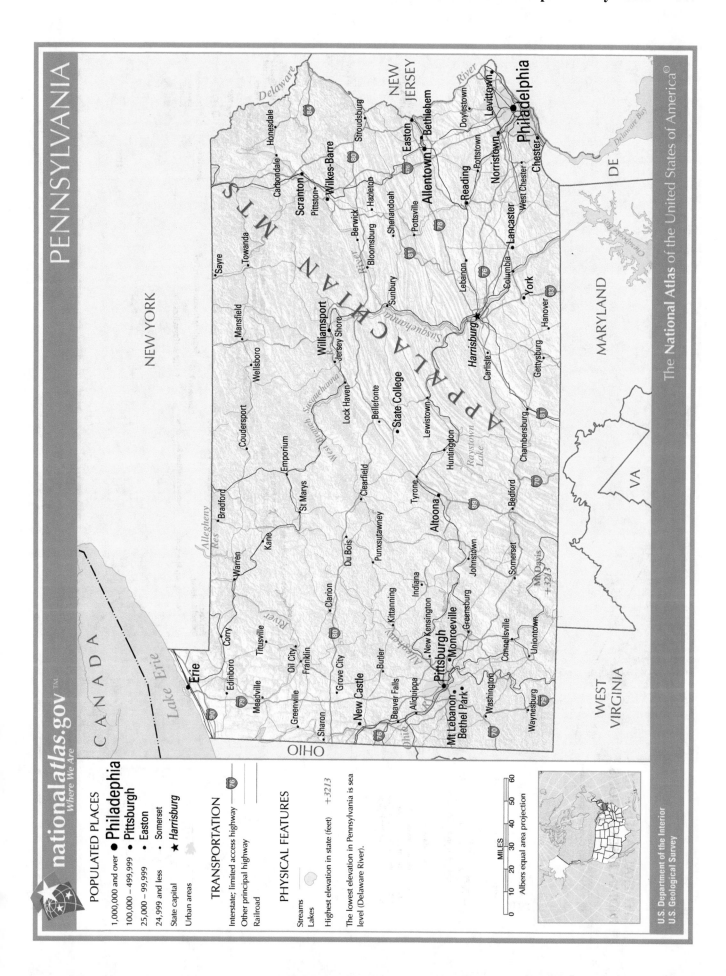

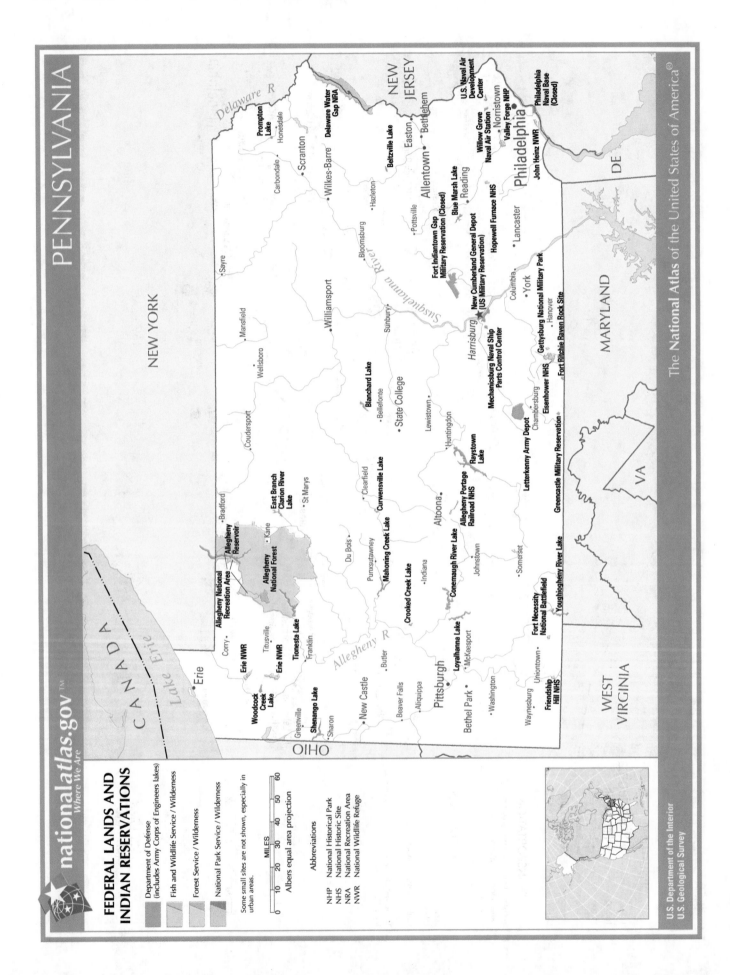

PENNSYLVANIA

nationalatlas.gov™
Where We Are

FEDERAL LANDS AND INDIAN RESERVATIONS

Department of Defense
(includes Army Corps of Engineers lakes)

Fish and Wildlife Service / Wilderness

Forest Service / Wilderness

National Park Service / Wilderness

Some small sites are not shown, especially in urban areas.

Abbreviations

NHP   National Historical Park
NHS   National Historic Site
NRA   National Recreation Area
NWR   National Wildlife Refuge

MILES

0   10   20   30   40   50   60

Albers equal area projection

U.S. Department of the Interior
U.S. Geological Survey

The National Atlas of the United States of America®

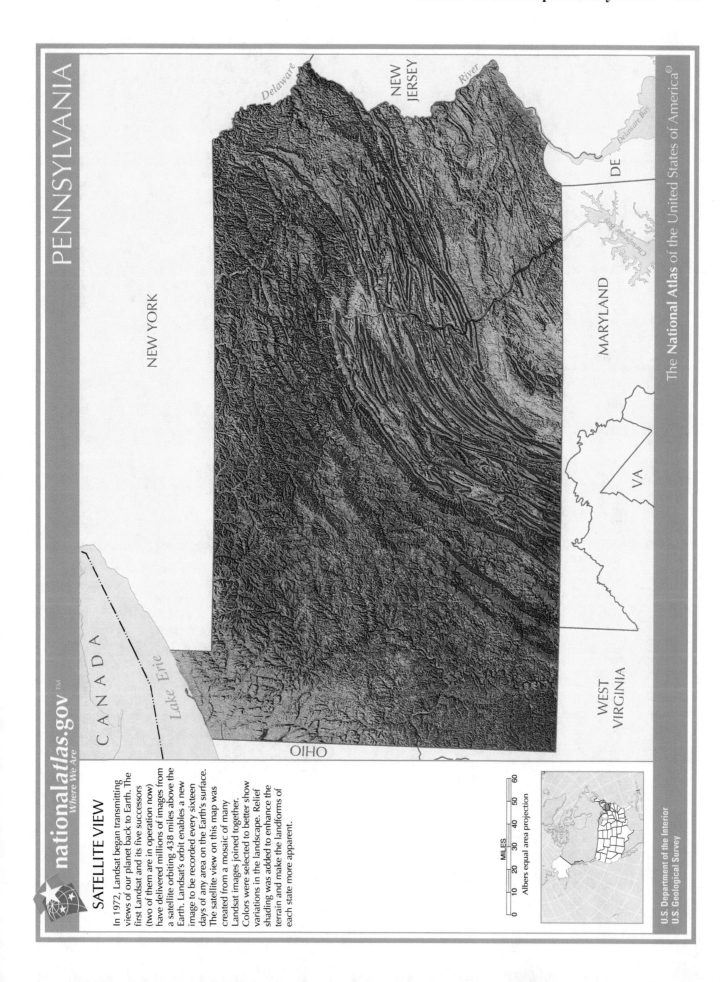

PENNSYLVANIA

nationalatlas.gov™
Where We Are

SATELLITE VIEW

In 1972, Landsat began transmitting views of our planet back to Earth. The first Landsat and its five successors (two of them are in operation now) have delivered millions of images from a satellite orbiting 438 miles above the Earth. Landsat's orbit enables a new image to be recorded every sixteen days of any area on the Earth's surface. The satellite view on this map was created from a mosaic of many Landsat images joined together. Colors were selected to better show variations in the landscape. Relief shading was added to enhance the terrain and make the landforms of each state more apparent.

CANADA

Lake Erie

NEW YORK

OHIO

Delaware

NEW JERSEY

River

Delaware Bay

DE

MARYLAND

VA

WEST VIRGINIA

Chesapeake Bay

The **National Atlas** of the United States of America®

MILES
0 10 20 30 40 50 60
Albers equal area projection

U.S. Department of the Interior
U.S. Geological Survey

Rhode Island

Topic	Value	Time Period
Total Surface Area (acres)	813,300	2007
Land	662,000	2007
Federal Land	3,500	2007
Owned	3,011	FY 2009
Leased	412	FY 2009
Otherwise Managed	82	FY 2009
National Forest	0	September 2006
National Wilderness	0	October 2011
Non-Federal Land, Developed	232,200	2007
Non-Federal Land, Rural	426,300	2007
Water	151,300	2007
National Natural Landmarks	1	December 2010
National Historic Landmarks	44	December 2010
National Register of Historic Places	753	December 2010
National Parks	1	December 2010
Visitors to National Parks	51,559	2010
Historic Places Documented by the National Park Service	464	December 2010
Archeological Sites in National Parks	39	December 2010
Threatened and Endangered Species in National Parks	0	December 2010
Economic Benefit from National Park Tourism (dollars)	2,936,000	2009
Conservation Reserve Program (acres)	Not Available	October 2011
Land and Water Conservation Fund Grants (dollars)	39,643,701	Since 1965
Historic Preservation Grants (dollars)	26,603,140	2010
Community Conservation and Recreation Projects	21	Since 1987
Federal Acres Transferred for Local Parks and Recreation	1,986	Since 1948
Crude Petroleum Production (millions of barrels)	Not Available	2010
Crude Oil Proved Reserves (millions of barrels)	Not Available	2009
Natural Gas Reserves (billions of cubic feet)	Not Available	2009
Natural Gas Liquid Reserves (millions of barrels)	Not Available	2008
Natural Gas Marketed Production (billions of cubic feet)	Not Available	2009
Coal Reserves (millions of short tons)	Not Available	2009

Sources: U.S. Department of the Interior, National Park Service, State Profiles, December 2010; United States Department of Agriculture, Natural Resources Conservation Service, 2007 National Resources Inventory; U.S. General Services Administration, Federal Real Property Council, FY 2009 Federal Real Property Report, September 2010; University of Montana, www.wilderness.net; U.S. Department of Agriculture, Farm Services Agency, Conservation Reserve Program, October 2011; U.S Census Bureau, 2012 Statistical Abstract of the United States

Rhode Island Energy Overview and Analysis

Quick Facts

- Rhode Island has the lowest per capita energy consumption in the Nation.
- Natural gas fuels almost all of Rhode Island's electricity generation.
- Rhode Island is one of the few States that require the statewide use of reformulated motor gasoline blended with ethanol.
- A 2007 study commissioned by the State determined that 15 percent of Rhode Island's electricity needs could be met by offshore wind energy.

Analysis

Resources and Consumption

Rhode Island's energy resources include fuelwood in the south and wind power on and near Block Island, off the State's Atlantic Coast. The Rhode Island economy is one of the least energy intensive in the Nation, and the State typically ranks last, just behind New York, in per capita energy consumption. Industrial energy consumption is low, and the residential sector is Rhode Island's leading energy consumer.

Petroleum

Rhode Island's Port of Providence is a key petroleum products hub for the New England area. Almost all of the transportation and heating fuel products consumed in Rhode Island, eastern Connecticut, and parts of Massachusetts are supplied via marine shipments through this port. A small-capacity petroleum product pipeline runs from Providence to central Massachusetts. Rhode Island is one of a handful of States that require the statewide use of reformulated motor gasoline blended with ethanol.

Rhode Island, along with much of the U.S. Northeast, is vulnerable to distillate fuel oil shortages and price spikes during the winter months due to high demand, as about two-fifths of Rhode Island households use fuel oil as their primary energy source for home heating. In January and February 2000, distillate fuel oil prices rose sharply in the Northeast when extreme winter weather increased demand unexpectedly and hindered the arrival of new supply, as frozen rivers and high winds slowed the docking and unloading of barges and tankers. In July 2000, in order to reduce the risk of future shortages, the President directed the U.S. Department of Energy to establish the Northeast Heating Oil Reserve. The Reserve gives Northeast consumers adequate supplies for about 10 days, the time required for ships to carry heating oil from the Gulf of Mexico to New York Harbor. The Reserve's storage terminals are located in Perth Amboy, New Jersey, and Groton and New Haven, Connecticut.

Natural Gas

Electric power generators and the residential sector are the State's largest natural gas consumers. The State's natural gas is supplied by pipelines from production areas in the U.S. Gulf Coast, and from natural gas storage sites in the Appalachian Basin region, which includes parts of New York, Pennsylvania, and Ohio. The majority of the gas is supplied by pipelines entering the State from Connecticut. Rhode Island ships over half of the natural gas it receives to Massachusetts.

Like other New England States, Rhode Island has no natural gas storage sites and must rely on the Appalachian Basin storage capacity to supply peak winter demand.

Coal, Electricity, and Renewables

Natural gas fuels almost all of Rhode Island's electricity generation. Rhode Island residential electricity use is low compared with the national average, in part because demand for air-conditioning is low during the mild summer months and relatively few households rely on electricity as their main energy source for home heating. Just over 2 percent of Rhode Island's total electricity is generated with renewable sources, including hydroelectric power, municipal solid waste, and landfill gas. Rhode Island has potential wind energy generation from offshore wind farms. A 2007 state-sponsored study identified 10 suitable areas for wind farm development and determined that at least 15 percent of Rhode Island's electricity needs could be met by offshore wind energy generation. A law signed in June 2009 may result in one of the first offshore wind farms in the Nation, off Block Island, by enabling the purchase of long-term renewable energy contracts by the utility National Grid. In June 2005, Rhode Island adopted a renewable portfolio standard that requires State electricity retailers to obtain at least 3 percent of State-sold electricity from renewable sources by December 31, 2006. The requirement for renewable energy purchases could potentially rise to 17 percent by 2020.

Source: U.S. Energy Information Administration, October 2009

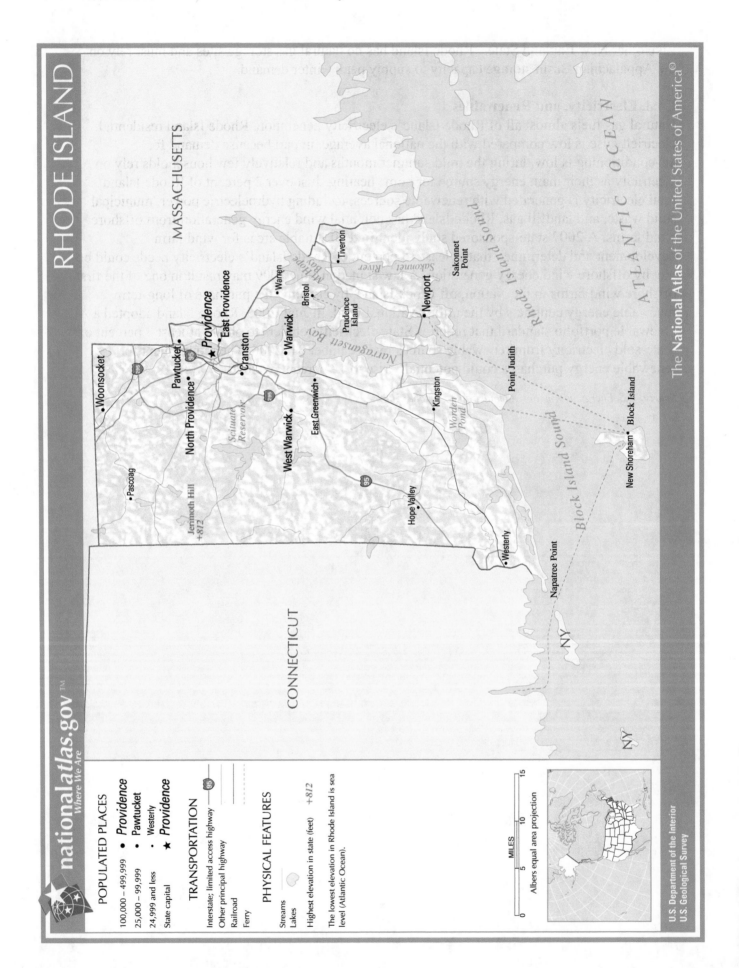

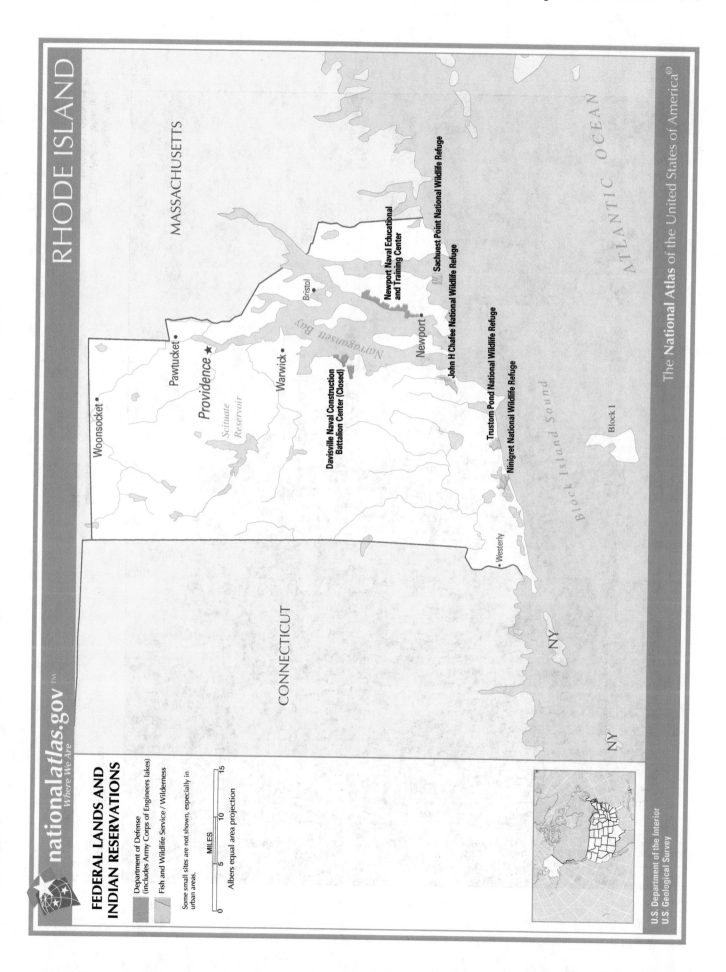

RHODE ISLAND

nationalatlas.gov™
Where We Are

**FEDERAL LANDS AND
INDIAN RESERVATIONS**

Department of Defense
(includes Army Corps of Engineers lakes)

Fish and Wildlife Service / Wilderness

Some small sites are not shown, especially in
urban areas.

MILES
0   5   10   15
Albers equal area projection

MASSACHUSETTS

CONNECTICUT

Woonsocket

Pawtucket

Providence

Warwick

Scituate
Reservoir

Bristol

Narragansett Bay

Davisville Naval Construction
Battalion Center (Closed)

Newport Naval Educational
and Training Center

Newport

Sachuest Point National Wildlife Refuge

John H Chafee National Wildlife Refuge

Trustom Pond National Wildlife Refuge

Ninigret National Wildlife Refuge

Westerly

Block Island Sound

Block I

NY

NY

ATLANTIC OCEAN

The **National Atlas** of the United States of America®

U.S. Department of the Interior
U.S. Geological Survey

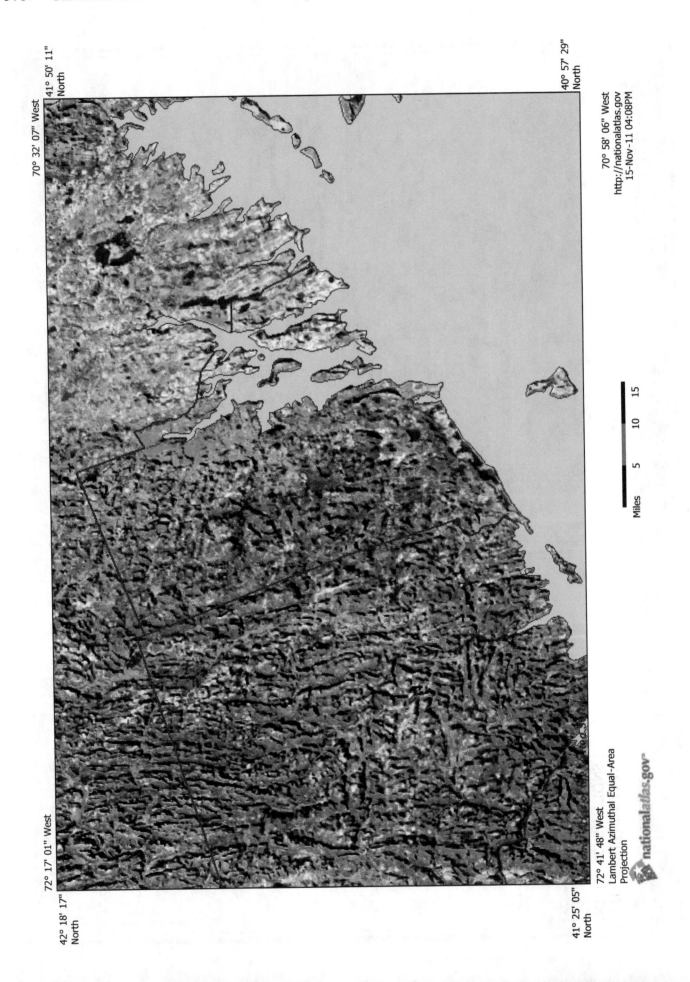

South Carolina

Topic	Value	Time Period
Total Surface Area (acres)	19,939,300	2007
Land	19,127,700	2007
Federal Land	1,036,200	2007
Owned	457,938	FY 2009
Leased	3,611	FY 2009
Otherwise Managed	721	FY 2009
National Forest	631,000	September 2006
National Wilderness	60,681	October 2011
Non-Federal Land, Developed	2,672,600	2007
Non-Federal Land, Rural	15,418,900	2007
Water	811,600	2007
National Natural Landmarks	6	December 2010
National Historic Landmarks	76	December 2010
National Register of Historic Places	1,457	December 2010
National Parks	6	December 2010
Visitors to National Parks	1,529,172	2010
Historic Places Documented by the National Park Service	1,144	December 2010
Archeological Sites in National Parks	83	December 2010
Threatened and Endangered Species in National Parks	7	December 2010
Economic Benefit from National Park Tourism (dollars)	40,265,000	2009
Conservation Reserve Program (acres)	144,221	October 2011
Land and Water Conservation Fund Grants (dollars)	58,966,737	Since 1965
Historic Preservation Grants (dollars)	28,583,499	2010
Community Conservation and Recreation Projects	22	Since 1987
Federal Acres Transferred for Local Parks and Recreation	7,830	Since 1948
Crude Petroleum Production (millions of barrels)	Not Available	2010
Crude Oil Proved Reserves (millions of barrels)	Not Available	2009
Natural Gas Reserves (billions of cubic feet)	Not Available	2009
Natural Gas Liquid Reserves (millions of barrels)	Not Available	2008
Natural Gas Marketed Production (billions of cubic feet)	Not Available	2009
Coal Reserves (millions of short tons)	Not Available	2009

Sources: *U.S. Department of the Interior, National Park Service, State Profiles, December 2010; United States Department of Agriculture, Natural Resources Conservation Service, 2007 National Resources Inventory; U.S. General Services Administration, Federal Real Property Council, FY 2009 Federal Real Property Report, September 2010; University of Montana, www.wilderness.net; U.S. Department of Agriculture, Farm Services Agency, Conservation Reserve Program, October 2011; U.S Census Bureau, 2012 Statistical Abstract of the United States*

South Carolina Energy Overview and Analysis

Quick Facts

- South Carolina's four nuclear power plants typically supply more than one-half of the State's electricity generation.
- South Carolina receives most of its coal from Kentucky.
- Industry is the State's largest energy-consuming sector and accounts for nearly two-fifths of total energy consumption.
- Two new nuclear reactors could come online in South Carolina by 2016, if licensing and construction go as planned.
- Per capita electricity use in South Carolina is higher than the nationwide average, due in part to high air-conditioning demand during the hot summer months and the widespread use of electricity for home heating in winter.
- South Carolina has adopted energy standards for public buildings and other energy-reduction goals that together are meant to reduce energy use by 20 percent from 2000 levels by July 1, 2020.

Analysis

Resources and Consumption

South Carolina's only substantial energy resource is its system of rivers and lakes, which provides for substantial hydroelectric power generation. South Carolina's industrial sector accounts for nearly two-fifths of State energy consumption.

Petroleum

South Carolina receives petroleum product shipments at the Port of Charleston and via the Colonial and Plantation pipelines from the Gulf Coast. The Dixie Pipeline, also originating in the Gulf Coast, supplies the State's propane demand. South Carolina's total petroleum consumption is near the national median, and South Carolina is one of the few States that allow the statewide use of conventional motor gasoline. (Most States require the use of specific gasoline blends in non-attainment areas due to air-quality considerations.)

Natural Gas

South Carolina's natural gas supply is transported from the Gulf Coast by two major interstate pipeline systems. The State receives substantial amounts of natural gas on a net basis; however, over four-fifths of this supply is delivered to North Carolina on its way to markets in the Northeast. Although approximately one-fourth of households in South Carolina use natural gas as their main energy source for home heating, winters are generally mild and overall demand is relatively low.

Coal, Electricity, and Renewables

Nuclear power accounts for more than one-half of South Carolina's electricity generation. With four active nuclear power plants, South Carolina is among the top nuclear power producers in United States. Two new nuclear reactors could come online in South Carolina by 2016 if licensing and construction go as planned. Coal fuels about two-fifths of net electricity generation. South Carolina has no coal mines, and coal-fired power plants rely on supplies shipped from Kentucky, and, to a lesser extent, Pennsylvania, West Virginia, and Tennessee. South Carolina produces substantial hydroelectric power from facilities located in several river and lake basins. Per capita electricity consumption in South Carolina is among the highest in the United States, due to high industrial use, high demand for air-conditioning during the hot summer months, and the widespread use of electricity for home heating during the typically mild winter months. More than three-fifths of South Carolina households use electricity as their primary energy source for home heating.

While South Carolina does not have a renewable portfolio standard, the State adopted energy standards for public buildings that require major facility projects in the State to be constructed to high energy efficiency standards The State has also established a goal of reducing energy use by 20 percent from 2000 levels by July 1, 2020.

Source: U.S. Energy Information Administration, October 2009

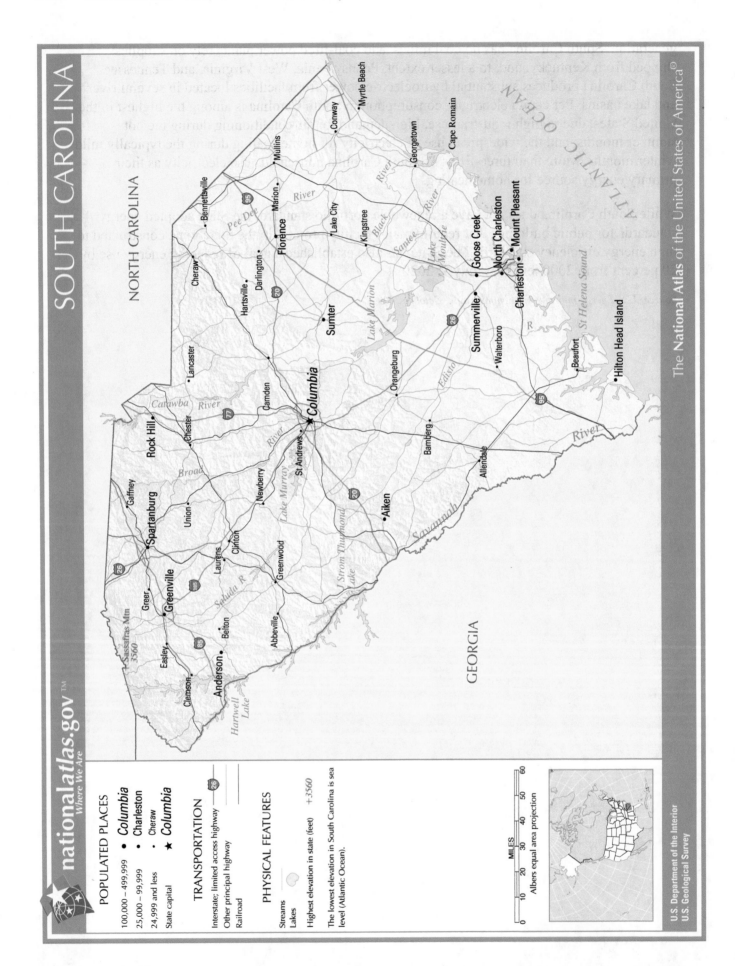

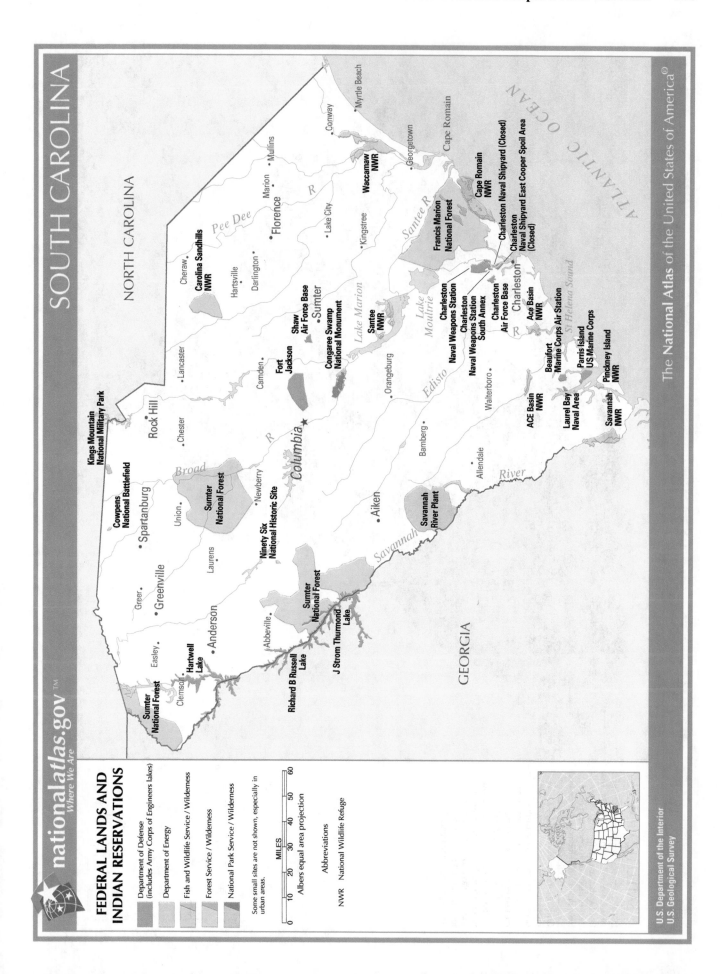

SOUTH CAROLINA

NORTH CAROLINA

GEORGIA

ATLANTIC OCEAN

The National Atlas of the United States of America ®

nationalatlas.gov ™
Where We Are

FEDERAL LANDS AND INDIAN RESERVATIONS

Department of Defense
(includes Army Corps of Engineers lakes)

Department of Energy

Fish and Wildlife Service / Wilderness

Forest Service / Wilderness

National Park Service / Wilderness

Some small sites are not shown, especially in urban areas.

MILES
0 10 20 30 40 50 60
Albers equal area projection

Abbreviations

NWR National Wildlife Refuge

U.S. Department of the Interior
U.S. Geological Survey

Myrtle Beach
Conway
Cape Romain
Georgetown
Cape Romain NWR
Charleston Naval Shipyard (Closed)
Charleston Naval Shipyard East Cooper Spoil Area
Charleston Naval Shipyard (Closed)
Mullins
Marion
Florence
Pee Dee
R
Lake City
Kingstree
Santee R
Francis Marion National Forest
Charleston Naval Weapons Station
Charleston Naval Weapons Station South Annex
Charleston Air Force Base
Charleston
Ace Basin NWR
St Helena Sound
Cheraw
Carolina Sandhills NWR
Hartsville
Darlington
Lake Marion
Santee NWR
Lake Moultrie
Beaufort Marine Corps Air Station
Parris Island US Marine Corps
Pinckney Island NWR
Shaw Air Force Base
Sumter
Congaree Swamp National Monument
Orangeburg
Edisto
Lancaster
Camden
Fort Jackson
R
Columbia
Walterboro
ACE Basin NWR
Laurel Bay Naval Area
Savannah NWR
Kings Mountain National Military Park
Rock Hill
Chester
Bamberg
Allendale
River
Cowpens National Battlefield
Spartanburg
Broad
Union
Sumter National Forest
Newberry
Ninety Six National Historic Site
Laurens
Aiken
Savannah River Plant
Savannah
Greer
Greenville
Anderson
Easley
Clemson
Hartwell Lake
Abbeville
Sumter National Forest
Richard B Russell Lake
J Strom Thurmond Lake
Sumter National Forest

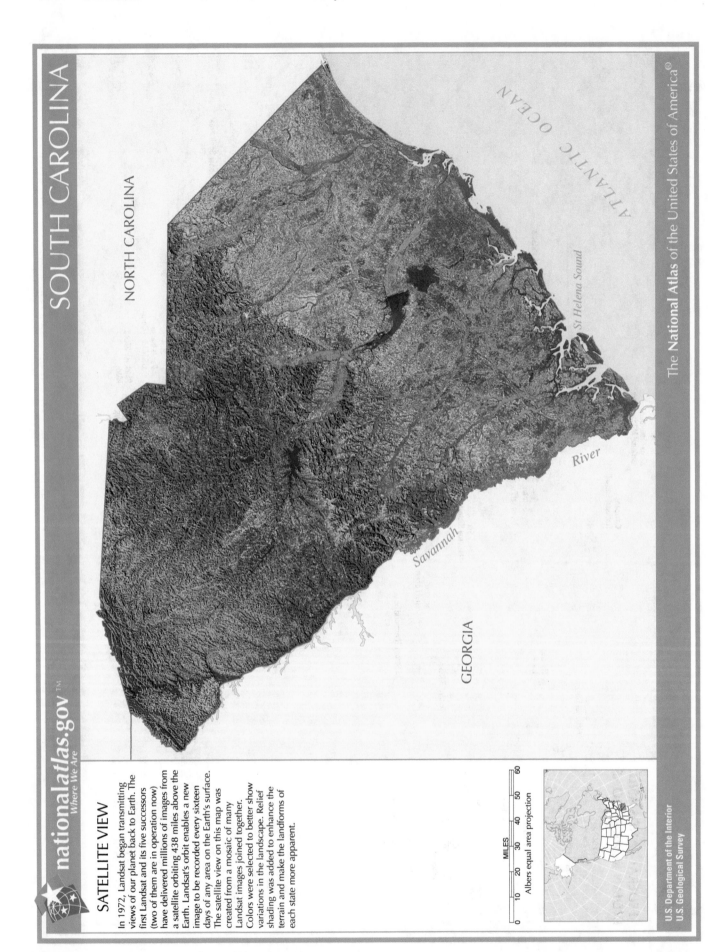

SOUTH CAROLINA

nationalatlas.gov™
Where We Are

SATELLITE VIEW

In 1972, Landsat began transmitting views of our planet back to Earth. The first Landsat and its five successors (two of them are in operation now) have delivered millions of images from a satellite orbiting 438 miles above the Earth. Landsat's orbit enables a new image to be recorded every sixteen days of any area on the Earth's surface. The satellite view on this map was created from a mosaic of many Landsat images joined together. Colors were selected to better show variations in the landscape. Relief shading was added to enhance the terrain and make the landforms of each state more apparent.

NORTH CAROLINA

ATLANTIC OCEAN

The **National Atlas** of the United States of America©

St Helena Sound

River

Savannah

GEORGIA

MILES

0   10   20   30   40   50   60

Albers equal area projection

U.S. Department of the Interior
U.S. Geological Survey

South Dakota

Topic	Value	Time Period
Total Surface Area (acres)	49,358,000	2007
Land	48,478,600	2007
Federal Land	3,112,200	2007
Owned	548,264	FY 2009
Leased	5,719	FY 2009
Otherwise Managed	2,676	FY 2009
National Forest	2,017,000	September 2006
National Wilderness	77,570	October 2011
Non-Federal Land, Developed	962,800	2007
Non-Federal Land, Rural	44,403,600	2007
Water	879,400	2007
National Natural Landmarks	13	December 2010
National Historic Landmarks	15	December 2010
National Register of Historic Places	1,274	December 2010
National Parks	6	December 2010
Visitors to National Parks	4,199,267	2010
Historic Places Documented by the National Park Service	81	December 2010
Archeological Sites in National Parks	396	December 2010
Threatened and Endangered Species in National Parks	7	December 2010
Economic Benefit from National Park Tourism (dollars)	141,846,000	2009
Conservation Reserve Program (acres)	1,097,799	October 2011
Land and Water Conservation Fund Grants (dollars)	36,284,157	Since 1965
Historic Preservation Grants (dollars)	19,192,380	2010
Community Conservation and Recreation Projects	12	Since 1987
Federal Acres Transferred for Local Parks and Recreation	201	Since 1948
Crude Petroleum Production (millions of barrels)	Not Available	2010
Crude Oil Proved Reserves (millions of barrels)	Not Available	2009
Natural Gas Reserves (billions of cubic feet)	Not Available	2009
Natural Gas Liquid Reserves (millions of barrels)	Not Available	2008
Natural Gas Marketed Production (billions of cubic feet)	Not Available	2009
Coal Reserves (millions of short tons)	Not Available	2009

Sources: *U.S. Department of the Interior, National Park Service, State Profiles, December 2010; United States Department of Agriculture, Natural Resources Conservation Service, 2007 National Resources Inventory; U.S. General Services Administration, Federal Real Property Council, FY 2009 Federal Real Property Report, September 2010; University of Montana, www.wilderness.net; U.S. Department of Agriculture, Farm Services Agency, Conservation Reserve Program, October 2011; U.S Census Bureau, 2012 Statistical Abstract of the United States*

South Dakota Energy Overview and Analysis

Quick Facts

- South Dakota is among the Nation's leading producers of ethanol.
- South Dakota consumes more electricity generated from hydroelectric power than from any other source.
- South Dakota has high geothermal and wind power potential.
- South Dakota is one of the few States that allow the statewide use of conventional motor gasoline.

Analysis

Resources and Consumption

South Dakota has few fossil fuel reserves but has substantial renewable energy potential. Small crude oil and natural gas reserves are concentrated in the western corners of the State. South Dakota's renewable energy potential includes flat open areas for wind power, the Missouri River for hydroelectric power, corn produced in the eastern part of the State for ethanol production, and geothermal resources located in the south-central part of the State. As one of the least-populated States, South Dakota has low energy demand.

Petroleum

South Dakota has minimal crude oil production and no refineries. Several petroleum product and liquefied petroleum gas (LPG) pipelines supply South Dakota from neighboring States. Over two-tenths of South Dakota households use LPG as their primary fuel for home heating. South Dakota is one of the few States in the Nation that allow the statewide use of conventional motor gasoline. (Most States require the use of specific gasoline blends in non-attainment areas due to air-quality considerations.) As a leading corn producer, South Dakota is one of the Nation's leading producers of ethanol, which is currently produced at several large plants in the eastern part of the State. Additional ethanol plants are under construction.

Natural Gas

South Dakota's natural gas consumption is very low. The State is supplied via pipelines from producers in Canada and Texas and ships over 90 percent of the natural gas it receives to Minnesota on the way to other Midwest markets. Nearly one-half of South Dakota households use natural gas as their primary fuel for home heating.

Coal, Electricity, and Renewables

Electricity in South Dakota is generated primarily by hydroelectric and coal-fired power plants. Hydroelectric power typically supplies about one-half of the electricity consumed in the State, and three of the State's five largest electricity generation plants are hydroelectric. South Dakota relies on shipments of coal from Wyoming to meet its coal demand. The majority of the State's nonhydroelectric and non-coal electricity is generated from natural gas and wind. Per capita electricity use in South Dakota is near the average for the United States, and about two-tenths of the State's households use electricity as their primary energy source for home heating.

South Dakota offers incentives, such as property tax exemptions, to encourage expansion of renewable sources for electricity generation within the State. In February 2008, South Dakota adopted a voluntary renewable Portfolio objective that aims to have 10 percent of all electricity generation come from renewable sources by 2015.

Source: U.S. Energy Information Administration, October 2009

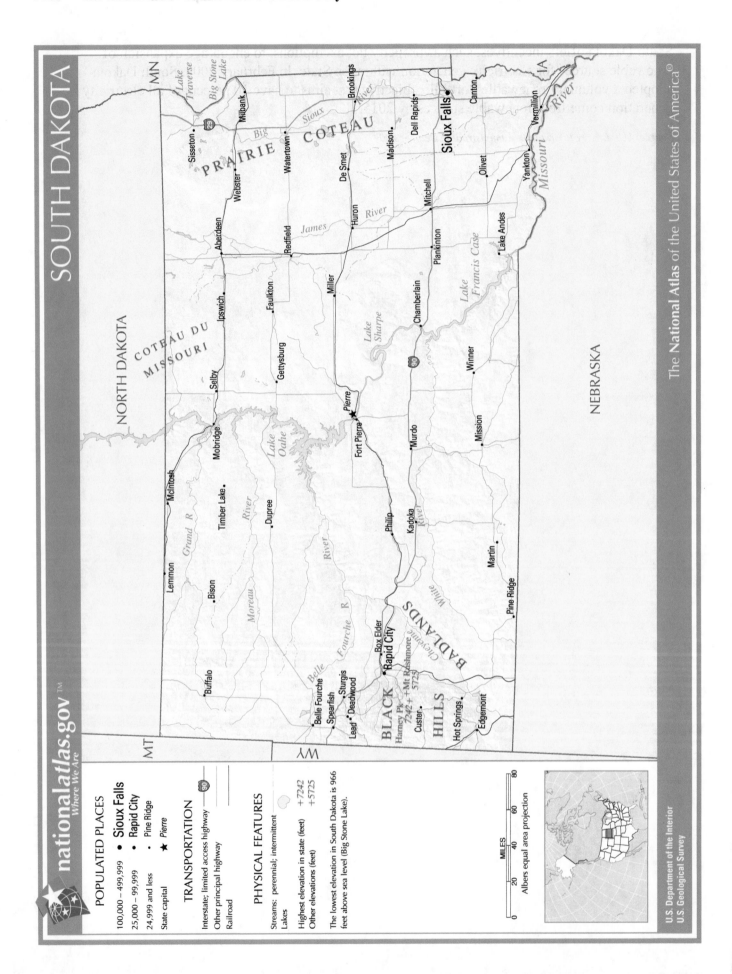

SOUTH DAKOTA

nationalatlas.gov ™
Where We Are

POPULATED PLACES

100,000 – 499,999   ● Sioux Falls
25,000 – 99,999   ● Rapid City
24,999 and less   ● Pine Ridge
State capital   ★ Pierre

TRANSPORTATION

Interstate; limited access highway   90
Other principal highway
Railroad

PHYSICAL FEATURES

Streams: perennial; intermittent
Lakes
Highest elevation in state (feet)   +7242
Other elevations (feet)   +5725

The lowest elevation in South Dakota is 966
feet above sea level (Big Stone Lake).

MILES
0   20   40   60   80
Albers equal area projection

U.S. Department of the Interior
U.S. Geological Survey

The National Atlas of the United States of America®

NORTH DAKOTA

NEBRASKA

MN
IA
MT
WY

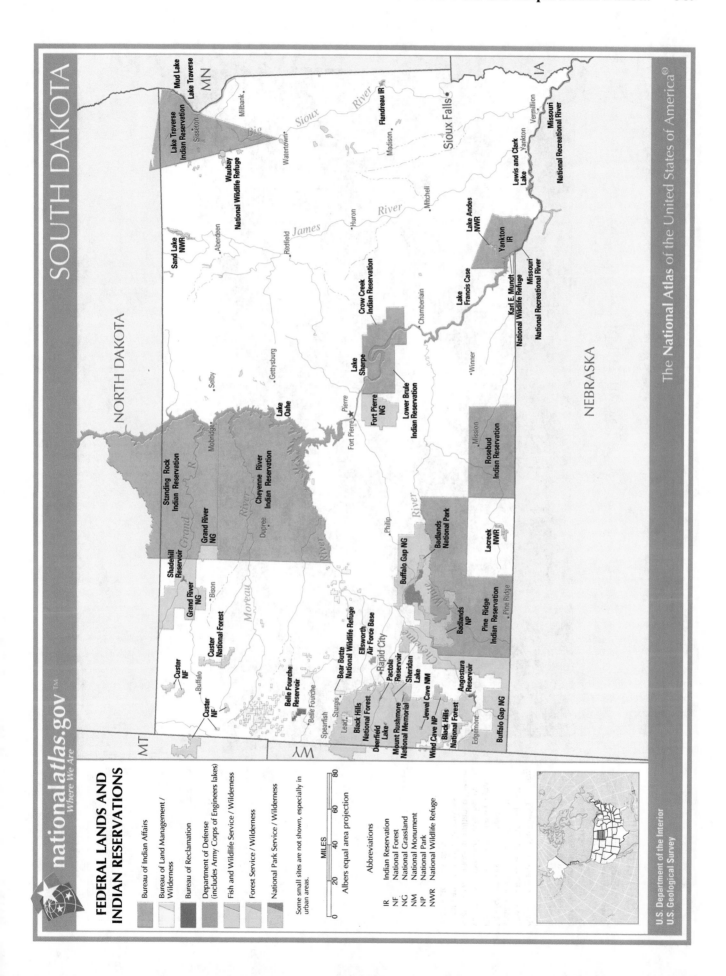

SOUTH DAKOTA

nationalatlas.gov ™
Where We Are

FEDERAL LANDS AND INDIAN RESERVATIONS

Bureau of Indian Affairs

Bureau of Land Management / Wilderness

Bureau of Reclamation

Department of Defense (includes Army Corps of Engineers lakes)

Fish and Wildlife Service / Wilderness

Forest Service / Wilderness

National Park Service / Wilderness

Some small sites are not shown, especially in urban areas.

MILES

0   20   40   60   80

Albers equal area projection

Abbreviations

IR   Indian Reservation
NF   National Forest
NG   National Grassland
NM   National Monument
NP   National Park
NWR   National Wildlife Refuge

The *National Atlas* of the United States of America®

U.S. Department of the Interior
U.S. Geological Survey

MN
IA
NORTH DAKOTA
NEBRASKA
MT
WY

Mud Lake
Lake Traverse
Lake Traverse Indian Reservation
Milbank
Sisseton
Flandreau IR
Big Sioux River
Watertown
Madison
Sioux Falls
Vermillion
Missouri National Recreational River
Waubay National Wildlife Refuge
Sand Lake NWR
Aberdeen
Redfield
James River
Huron
Mitchell
Lewis and Clark Lake
Yankton
Lake Andes NWR
Yankton IR
Missouri National Recreational River
Karl E. Mundt National Wildlife Refuge
Selby
Gettysburg
Crow Creek Indian Reservation
Lake Sharpe
Lake Francis Case
Chamberlain
Winner
Mobridge
Lake Oahe
Standing Rock Indian Reservation
Grand River NG
Grand River
Pierre
Fort Pierre
Fort Pierre NG
Lower Brule Indian Reservation
Mission
Rosebud Indian Reservation
Dupree
Cheyenne River Indian Reservation
Philip
Lacreek NWR
Shadehill Reservoir
Bison
Buffalo
Moreau River
Grand River NG
Custer National Forest
Custer NF
Custer NF
Belle Fourche Reservoir
Belle Fourche
Spearfish
Sturgis
Lead
Deadwood
Bear Butte National Wildlife Refuge
Ellsworth Air Force Base
Rapid City
Pactola Reservoir
Sheridan Lake
Black Hills National Forest
Deerfield Lake
Mount Rushmore National Memorial
Jewel Cave NM
Wind Cave NP
Black Hills National Forest
Edgemont
Angostura Reservoir
Buffalo Gap NG
Buffalo Gap NG
Badlands National Park
Badlands NP
Pine Ridge Indian Reservation
Pine Ridge
Cheyenne River
White River

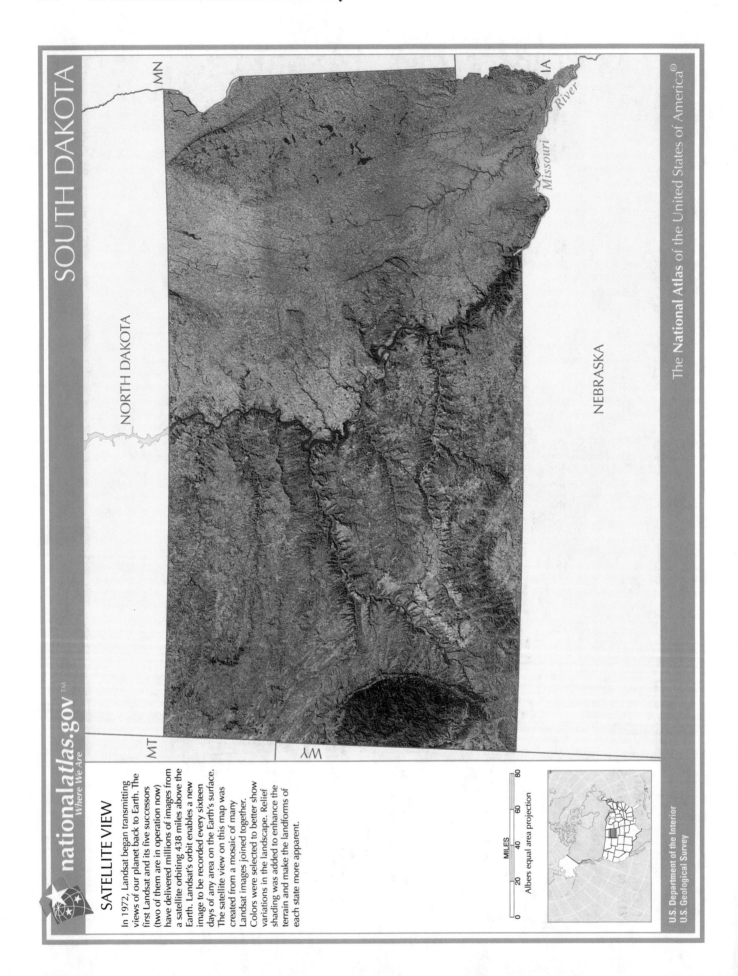

SOUTH DAKOTA

nationalatlas.gov™
Where We Are

SATELLITE VIEW

In 1972, Landsat began transmitting views of our planet back to Earth. The first Landsat and its five successors (two of them are in operation now) have delivered millions of images from a satellite orbiting 438 miles above the Earth. Landsat's orbit enables a new image to be recorded every sixteen days of any area on the Earth's surface. The satellite view on this map was created from a mosaic of many Landsat images joined together. Colors were selected to better show variations in the landscape. Relief shading was added to enhance the terrain and make the landforms of each state more apparent.

The **National Atlas** of the United States of America®

NORTH DAKOTA

NEBRASKA

MN

MT

WY

IA

Missouri River

MILES

0   20   40   60   80

Albers equal area projection

U.S. Department of the Interior
U.S. Geological Survey

Tennessee

Topic	Value	Time Period
Total Surface Area (acres)	26,973,600	2007
Land	26,182,800	2007
Federal Land	1,302,600	2007
Owned	368,954	FY 2009
Leased	3,146	FY 2009
Otherwise Managed	1,521	FY 2009
National Forest	718,000	September 2006
National Wilderness	66,349	October 2011
Non-Federal Land, Developed	3,038,300	2007
Non-Federal Land, Rural	21,841,900	2007
Water	790,800	2007
National Natural Landmarks	13	December 2010
National Historic Landmarks	29	December 2010
National Register of Historic Places	1,996	December 2010
National Parks	12	December 2010
Visitors to National Parks	7,898,557	2010
Historic Places Documented by the National Park Service	348	December 2010
Archeological Sites in National Parks	1,405	December 2010
Threatened and Endangered Species in National Parks	39	December 2010
Economic Benefit from National Park Tourism (dollars)	501,305,000	2009
Conservation Reserve Program (acres)	191,574	October 2011
Land and Water Conservation Fund Grants (dollars)	71,358,348	Since 1965
Historic Preservation Grants (dollars)	27,845,608	2010
Community Conservation and Recreation Projects	43	Since 1987
Federal Acres Transferred for Local Parks and Recreation	3,309	Since 1948
Crude Petroleum Production (millions of barrels)	Not Available	2010
Crude Oil Proved Reserves (millions of barrels)	Not Available	2009
Natural Gas Reserves (billions of cubic feet)	Not Available	2009
Natural Gas Liquid Reserves (millions of barrels)	Not Available	2008
Natural Gas Marketed Production (billions of cubic feet)	Not Available	2009
Coal Reserves (millions of short tons)	759	2009

Sources: U.S. Department of the Interior, National Park Service, State Profiles, December 2010; United States Department of Agriculture, Natural Resources Conservation Service, 2007 National Resources Inventory; U.S. General Services Administration, Federal Real Property Council, FY 2009 Federal Real Property Report, September 2010; University of Montana, www.wilderness.net; U.S. Department of Agriculture, Farm Services Agency, Conservation Reserve Program, October 2011; U.S Census Bureau, 2012 Statistical Abstract of the United States

Tennessee Energy Overview and Analysis

Quick Facts

- The federally administered Tennessee Valley Authority (TVA) owns over 90 percent of Tennessee's electricity generation capacity.
- A 100-million-gallon-per-year ethanol plant near Obion, Tennessee began production in late 2008, bringing Tennessee's total ethanol operating production capacity to 167 million gallons per year.
- Tennessee is one of the top hydroelectricity-generating States east of the Rocky Mountains.
- The single-unit Watts Bar Nuclear Plant began commercial operation in 1996 and was the last new nuclear reactor to be brought online in the United States.

Analysis

Resources and Consumption
The Tennessee and Cumberland river systems, originating in the Appalachian Mountains, provide Tennessee with major hydroelectric power potential. Tennessee also has minor coal reserves in the Appalachian Basin in the eastern part of the State. Tennessee ranks among the top 20 States in terms of both absolute and per capita energy consumption. The industrial sector leads State energy demand.

Petroleum
Tennessee's crude oil production is minor. The State's only refinery, located in Memphis, receives crude oil supply via the Capline pipeline, which originates in the Gulf Coast region and passes through western Tennessee on its way to Midwest refining markets. Tennessee receives petroleum products by pipeline from several systems, including branches of the Colonial and Plantation pipelines. Several waterways, including the Mississippi River, also provide important transportation routes for interstate petroleum product shipments. Tennessee has two operating ethanol plants and has the second-highest ethanol production in the South behind Texas.

Natural Gas
Several major natural gas pipelines from the Gulf Coast supply Tennessee as they pass through the State on the way to Northeast and Midwest markets. Industry is Tennessee's largest natural gas-consuming sector and accounts for more than two-fifths of State demand. Over one-third of Tennessee households use natural gas as their primary home-heating fuel.

Coal, Electricity, and Renewables
Coal-fired power plants typically generate over one-half of the electricity produced in Tennessee; nuclear and hydroelectric power supply most of the remainder. Tennessee's coal production is minor, and the State's coal-fired power plants rely on coal delivered primarily by railroad and river barge from other States. Tennessee receives most of its coal from Wyoming, Illinois, Colorado, Kentucky, West Virginia, and Virginia. Tennessee is a major nuclear power producer, with two nuclear power plants in the southeastern part of the State near Chattanooga. The single-unit Watts Bar plant, which began commercial operation in 1996, was the last new

nuclear reactor to come online in the United States. With numerous hydroelectric power plants located on the Tennessee and Cumberland river systems, Tennessee is one of the top hydroelectric power producers east of the Rocky Mountains. Hydroelectric power typically provides Tennessee with over 8 percent of its total electricity production, while other renewable sources including wood, wood waste, and wind contribute minimally. The federally administered Tennessee Valley Authority (TVA) owns over 90 percent of the State's electricity generation capacity. Tennessee electricity consumption is high and the State leads the Nation in per capita residential electricity consumption. More than one-half of Tennessee households use electricity as their primary source of energy for home heating.

Source: U.S. Energy Information Administration, October 2009

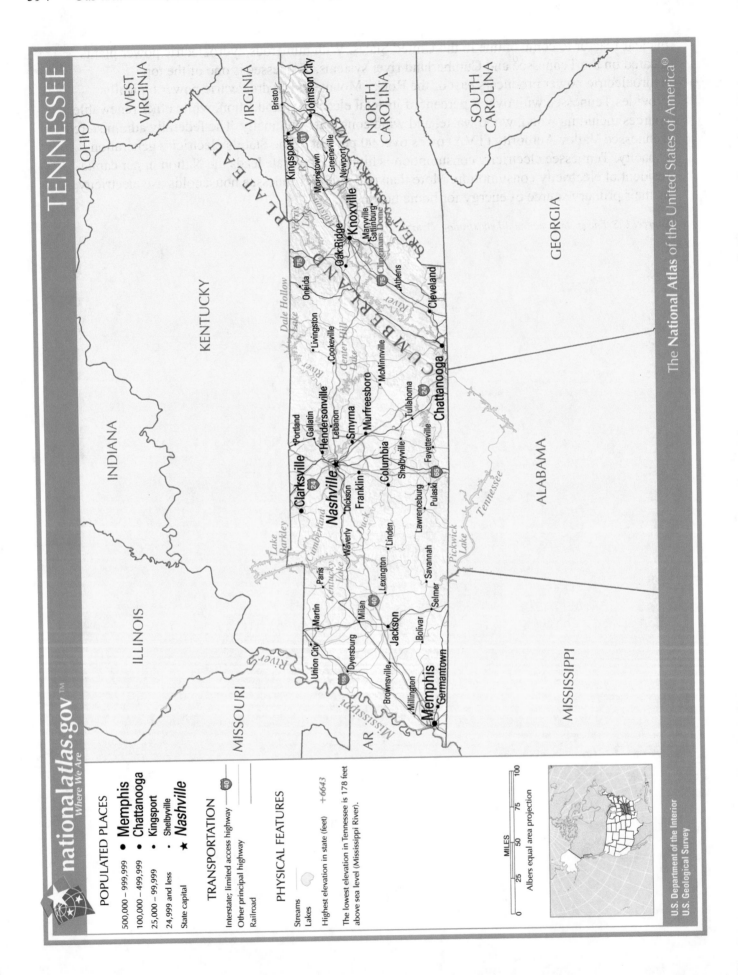

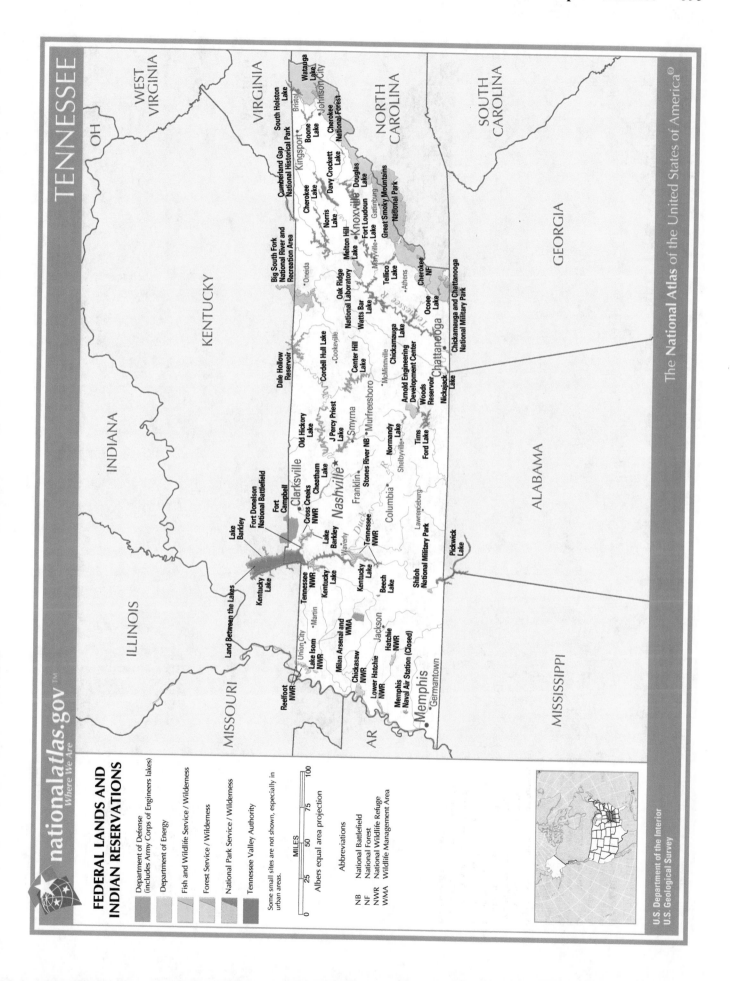

TENNESSEE

nationalatlas.gov™
Where We Are

FEDERAL LANDS AND
INDIAN RESERVATIONS

Department of Defense
(includes Army Corps of Engineers lakes)

Department of Energy

Fish and Wildlife Service / Wilderness

Forest Service / Wilderness

National Park Service / Wilderness

Tennessee Valley Authority

Some small sites are not shown, especially in
urban areas.

MILES
0   25   50   75   100

Albers equal area projection

Abbreviations

NB   National Battlefield
NF   National Forest
NWR   National Wildlife Refuge
WMA   Wildlife Management Area

The National Atlas of the United States of America®

U.S. Department of the Interior
U.S. Geological Survey

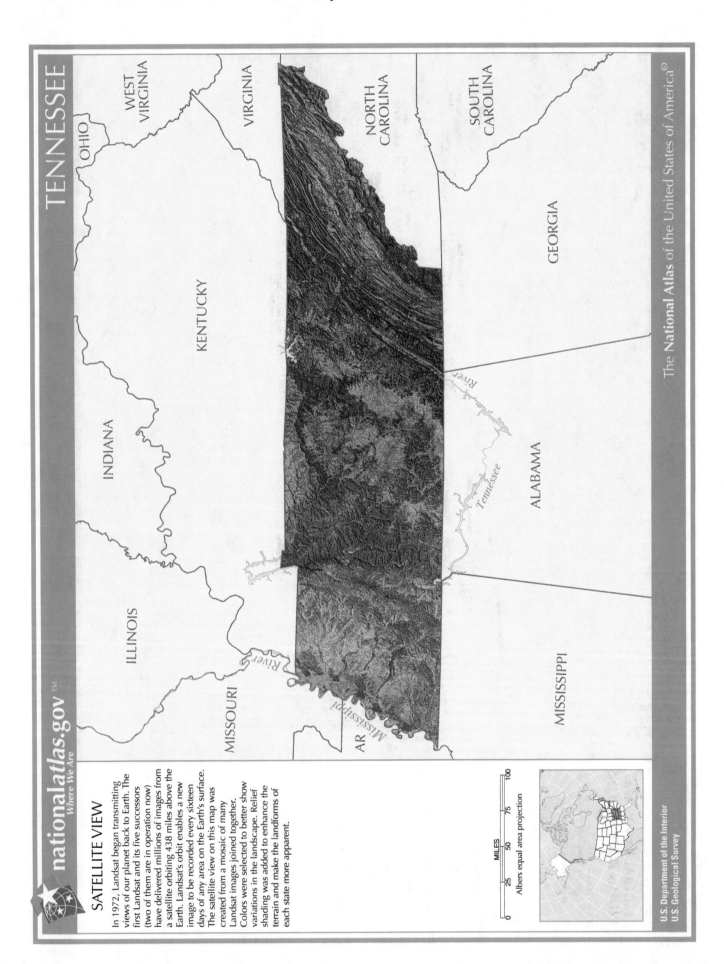

TENNESSEE

nationalatlas.gov™
Where We Are

SATELLITE VIEW

In 1972, Landsat began transmitting views of our planet back to Earth. The first Landsat and its five successors (two of them are in operation now) have delivered millions of images from a satellite orbiting 438 miles above the Earth. Landsat's orbit enables a new image to be recorded every sixteen days of any area on the Earth's surface. The satellite view on this map was created from a mosaic of many Landsat images joined together. Colors were selected to better show variations in the landscape. Relief shading was added to enhance the terrain and make the landforms of each state more apparent.

MILES
0   25   50   75   100

Albers equal area projection

U.S. Department of the Interior
U.S. Geological Survey

The National Atlas of the United States of America®

Texas

Topic	Value	Time Period
Total Surface Area (acres)	171,051,900	2007
Land	166,925,800	2007
Federal Land	2,909,900	2007
Owned	1,644,525	FY 2009
Leased	20,075	FY 2009
Otherwise Managed	13,691	FY 2009
National Forest	755,000	September 2006
National Wilderness	85,333	October 2011
Non-Federal Land, Developed	8,515,700	2007
Non-Federal Land, Rural	155,500,200	2007
Water	4,126,100	2007
National Natural Landmarks	20	December 2010
National Historic Landmarks	46	December 2010
National Register of Historic Places	3,086	December 2010
National Parks	13	December 2010
Visitors to National Parks	5,495,156	2010
Historic Places Documented by the National Park Service	856	December 2010
Archeological Sites in National Parks	3,634	December 2010
Threatened and Endangered Species in National Parks	28	December 2010
Economic Benefit from National Park Tourism (dollars)	247,074,000	2009
Conservation Reserve Program (acres)	3,362,690	October 2011
Land and Water Conservation Fund Grants (dollars)	174,083,496	Since 1965
Historic Preservation Grants (dollars)	39,221,885	2010
Community Conservation and Recreation Projects	97	Since 1987
Federal Acres Transferred for Local Parks and Recreation	8,080	Since 1948
Crude Petroleum Production (millions of barrels)	417	2010
Crude Oil Proved Reserves (millions of barrels)	5,006	2009
Natural Gas Reserves (billions of cubic feet)	80,424	2009
Natural Gas Liquid Reserves (millions of barrels)	3,560	2008
Natural Gas Marketed Production (billions of cubic feet)	6,819	2009
Coal Reserves (millions of short tons)	12,183	2009

Sources: U.S. Department of the Interior, National Park Service, State Profiles, December 2010; United States Department of Agriculture, Natural Resources Conservation Service, 2007 National Resources Inventory; U.S. General Services Administration, Federal Real Property Council, FY 2009 Federal Real Property Report, September 2010; University of Montana, www.wilderness.net; U.S. Department of Agriculture, Farm Services Agency, Conservation Reserve Program, October 2011; U.S Census Bureau, 2012 Statistical Abstract of the United States

Texas Energy Overview and Analysis

Quick Facts

- Texas is the leading crude oil-producing State in the Nation (excluding Federal offshore areas, which produce more than any single State).
- The State's signature type of crude oil, known as West Texas Intermediate (WTI), remains the major benchmark of crude oil in the Americas.
- Texas's 27 petroleum refineries can process more than 4.7 million barrels of crude oil per day, and they account for more than one-fourth of total U.S. refining capacity.
- Approximately three-tenths of total U.S. natural gas production occurs in Texas, making it the Nation's leading natural gas producer.
- Texas also leads the Nation in wind-powered generation capacity; there are over 2,000 wind turbines in West Texas alone.
- Texas produces and consumes more electricity than any other State, and per capita residential use is significantly higher than the national average.

Analysis

Resources and Consumption

Texas leads the Nation in fossil fuel reserves and in nonhydroelectric renewable energy potential. Texas crude oil reserves represent almost one-fourth of the U.S. total, and Texas natural gas reserves account for over three-tenths of the U.S. total. Although Texas's oil reserves are found in several geologic basins throughout the State, the largest remaining reserves are concentrated in the Permian Basin of West Texas, which contains more than 20 of the Nation's top 100 oil fields. Similarly, deposits of natural gas are found in abundance in several Texas production basins, with the largest fields heavily concentrated in the East Texas Basin in the northeastern part of the State. Texas's fossil fuel reserves also include substantial deposits of lignite coal, found in narrow bands in the Gulf Coast region, and bituminous coal, found in north central and southwestern Texas.

Texas is also rich in renewable energy potential, including wind, solar, and biomass resources. Wind resource areas in the Texas Panhandle, along the Gulf Coast south of Galveston, and in the mountain passes and ridgetops of the Trans-Pecos offer Texas some of the greatest wind power potential in the United States. Solar power potential is also among the highest in the Nation, with high levels of direct solar radiation suitable to support large-scale solar power plants concentrated in West Texas. Due to its large agricultural and forestry sectors, Texas has an abundance of biomass energy resources. Although Texas is not known as a major hydroelectric power State, substantial untapped potential exists in several river basins, including the Colorado River of Texas and the Lower Red.

Due to its large population and an energy-intensive economy, Texas leads the Nation in energy consumption, accounting for more than one-tenth of total U.S. energy use. Energy-intensive industries in Texas include aluminum, chemicals, forest products, glass, and petroleum refining.

Petroleum

Texas leads the United States in both crude oil production and refining capacity. (Louisiana surpasses Texas as the leading U.S. oil producer when production from the Louisiana section of the federally administered Outer Continental Shelf is included in its State production total). The State's first major oil boom began in 1901 with the discovery of the Spindle Top oil field in the upper Gulf Coast basin. Since then, major discoveries have been made in East Texas, West Texas, and offshore in the Gulf of Mexico. Texas oil production increased until 1972, when it peaked at more than 3.4 million barrels per day. Afterward, production declined rapidly, and in recent years Texas crude oil output has fallen to less than one-third of its 1972 peak.

Although Texas oil production is in decline, the State's signature type of crude oil, known as West Texas Intermediate (WTI), remains the major benchmark of crude oil in the Americas. Because of its light consistency and low-sulfur content, the quality of WTI is considered to be high, and it yields a large fraction of gasoline when refined. Most WTI crude oil is sent via pipeline to Midwest refining centers, although much of this crude oil is also refined in the Gulf Coast region.

Texas's 27 petroleum refineries can process more than 4.7 million barrels of crude oil per day, and they account for more than one-fourth of total U.S. refining capacity. Most of the State's refineries are clustered near major ports along the Gulf Coast, including Houston, Port Arthur, and Corpus Christi. These coastal refineries have access to local Texas production, foreign imports, and oil produced offshore in the Gulf of Mexico, as well as the U.S. Government's Strategic Petroleum Reserve, which operates two large storage facilities in Bryan Mound and Big Hill, Texas. Many of Texas's refineries are sophisticated facilities that use additional refining processes beyond simple distillation to yield a larger quantity of lighter, higher-value products, such as gasoline. Because of this downstream capability, Texas refineries often process a wide variety of crude oil types from around the world, including heavier, lower-value varieties.

Refineries in the Houston area, including the Nation's largest refinery in Baytown, make up the largest refining center in the United States. Refined-product pipelines spread out from Houston across the country, allowing Texas petroleum products to reach virtually every major consumption market east of the Rocky Mountains. This network includes the Colonial Pipeline system, which is the largest petroleum product pipeline system in the United States and is vital for supplying markets throughout the South and East Coast.

Texas's total petroleum consumption is the highest in the Nation, and the State leads the country in consumption of asphalt and road oil, aviation gasoline, distillate fuel oil, liquefied petroleum gases (LPG), and lubricants. Texas LPG use is greater than the LPG consumption of all other States combined, due primarily to the State's active petrochemical industry, which is the largest in the United States. Four separate motor gasoline blends are required in different parts the State to meet its diverse air quality needs, including the reformulated motor gasoline blended with ethanol that is required in the metropolitan areas of Houston and Dallas-Forth Worth. The agriculture-rich Texas Panhandle has several corn- and milo-based ethanol plants that are operational or under construction.

Natural Gas

Texas is the Nation's leading natural gas producer, accounting for approximately three-tenths of total U.S. natural gas production. In the early days of Texas oil production, natural gas found with oil was largely considered a nuisance and was often flared (burned off) at the wellhead. Although some Texas cities and towns located near oil fields began using natural gas for energy, it was not until the State banned flaring after World War II that oil producers began to find new markets for natural gas. Two pipelines that once carried crude oil to the East Coast were converted to carry natural gas and a new natural gas pipeline to California was built, setting the stage for strong natural gas production growth in the 1950s and 60s. Texas natural gas production reached its peak in 1972 at more than 9.6 billion cubic feet of annual production. Output declined steadily to less than three-fifths of that level by 2005, but has subsequently increased to approximately four-fifths of the 1972 peak production level.

Today, an expansive network of interstate natural gas pipelines extends from Texas, reaching consumption markets from coast to coast, including those in California, the Midwest, the East Coast, and New England. Natural gas is also supplied to Texas via pipelines entering the State from New Mexico, Oklahoma, and Mexico. Texas has 7 natural gas market hubs located in both East and West Texas, more than any other State, and its natural gas storage capacity is among the highest in the Nation. A majority of the State's 34 active storage facilities are depleted oil and gas fields converted for storage use, and the others were developed in salt dome formations. These facilities allow Texas to store its natural gas production during the summer when national demand is typically low and to ramp up delivery quickly during the winter months when markets across the country require greater volumes of natural gas to meet their home heating needs. However, due to the growing use of natural gas for electricity generation in the United States, Texas has occasionally withdrawn natural gas from storage during the summer months to help meet peak electricity demand for air-conditioning use.

Texas consumes more natural gas than any other State and accounts for nearly one-fifth of total U.S. natural gas consumption. Texas natural gas demand is dominated by the industrial and electric power sectors, which together account for more than four-fifths of State use. Because Texas demand is high, and because the State's natural gas infrastructure is well connected to consumption markets throughout the country, several liquefied natural gas (LNG) import terminals have been proposed along the Gulf Coast in Texas. The State's first LNG terminal became operational in April 2008 with a capacity of 1.5 billion cubic feet of natural gas per day. Another LNG terminal in Sabine, Texas is currently under construction and several other terminals have recently been approved for construction.

Coal, Electricity, and Renewables

Natural gas-fired power plants typically account for about one-half of the electricity produced in Texas and coal-fired plants account for much of the remaining generation. Although Texas produces a substantial amount of coal from its 11 surface mines, including five of the 50 largest in the United States, the State relies on rail deliveries of subbituminous coal from Wyoming for the majority of its supply. Nearly all of the coal mined in Texas is lignite, the lowest grade of coal, and all of it is consumed in the State, mostly in arrangements where a single utility operates both the mine and an adjacent coal-fired power plant. Although lower in energy content than other varieties of coal, lignite coal is also low in sulfur, an important consideration in the State's efforts to lower emissions. Texas consumes more coal than any other State and its emissions of carbon dioxide and sulfur dioxide are among the highest the Nation.

Texas is a major nuclear power generating State. Two nuclear plants, Comanche Peak and South Texas Project, typically account for about one-tenth of the State's electric power production. Until the recent capacity increase of the number 2 reactor at Palo Verde in Arizona, the two South Texas Project nuclear reactors were the largest in the Nation.

Although renewable energy sources contribute minimally to the Texas power grid, Texas leads the Nation in wind-powered generation capacity, and substantial new wind generation capacity is under construction. Texas became the country's largest wind energy producer in 2006 when it surpassed California, Currently, there are over 2,000 wind turbines in West Texas alone, and the numbers continue to increase as development costs drop and wind turbine technology improves. In 2007, Texas became the first State to reach the milestone of one gigawatt of wind capacity installed in a single year. At 736 MW, the Horse Hollow Wind Energy Center in central Texas is the largest wind power facility in the world.

Texas produces and consumes more electricity than any other State. Despite large net interstate electricity imports in some areas, the Texas Interconnect power grid is largely isolated from the integrated power systems serving the eastern and western United States, and most areas of Texas have little ability to export or import electricity to and from other States. Texas per capita residential use of electricity is significantly higher than the national average, due to high demand for electric air-conditioning during the hot summer months and the widespread use of electricity as the primary energy source for home heating during the typically mild winter months.

In August 2005, Texas adopted a law requiring 5,880 megawatts of new renewable generation be built by 2015, representing about 5 percent of the State's total 2005 electricity demand. The new law also set a target for 10,000 megawatts of renewable generation by 2025, with 500 megawatts from non-wind generation sources.

Source: U.S. Energy Information Administration, October 2009

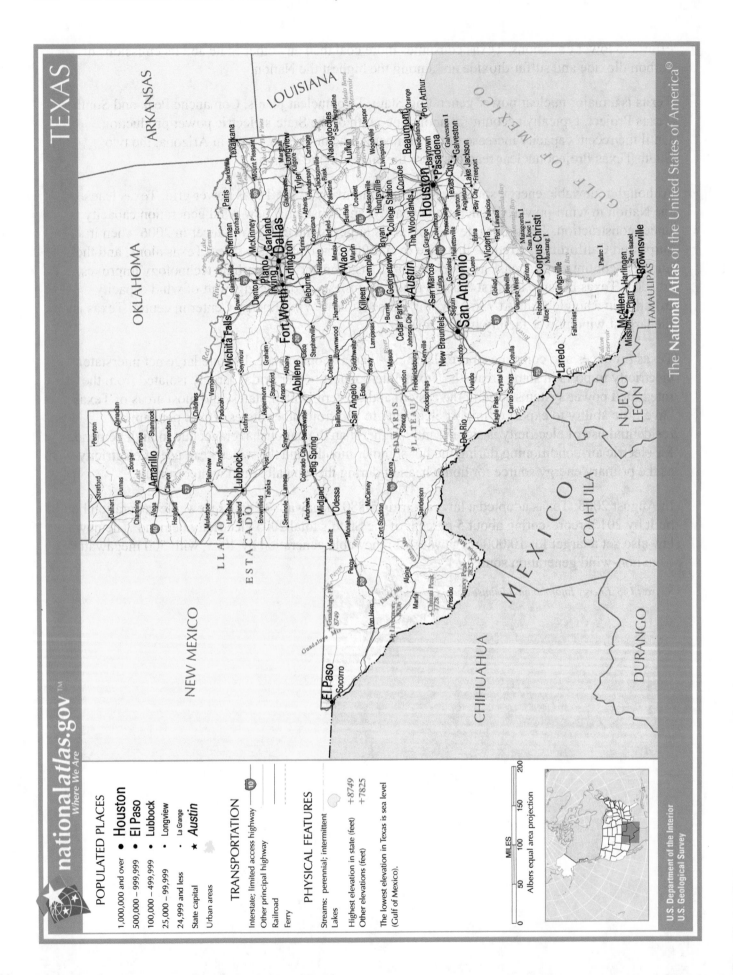

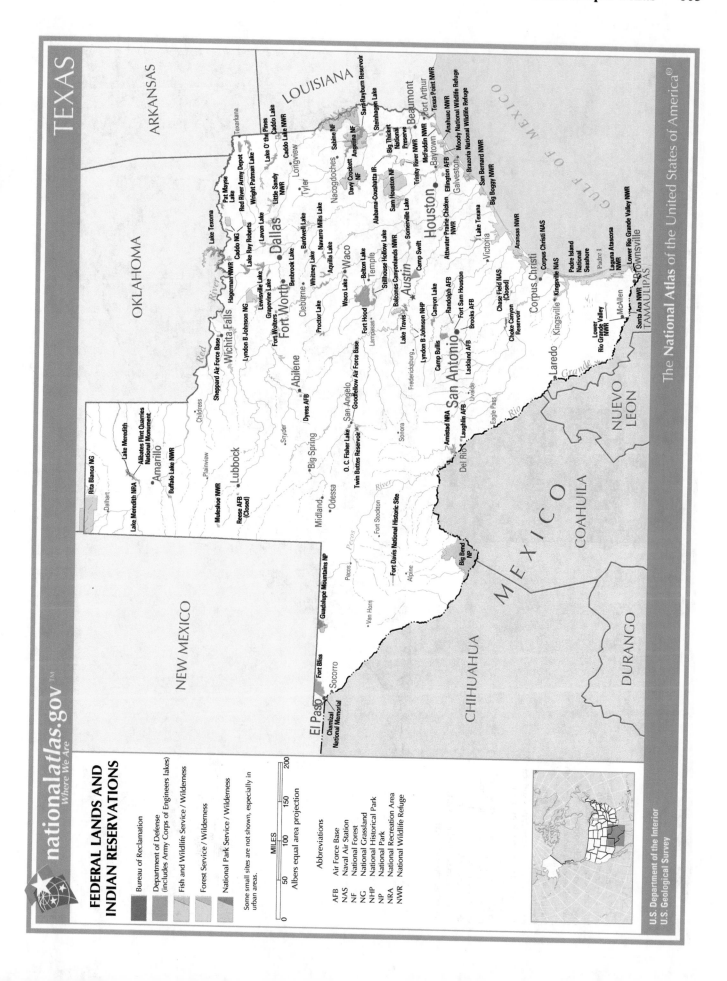

TEXAS

nationalatlas.gov™
Where We Are

**FEDERAL LANDS AND
INDIAN RESERVATIONS**

Bureau of Reclamation

Department of Defense
(includes Army Corps of Engineers lakes)

Fish and Wildlife Service / Wilderness

Forest Service / Wilderness

National Park Service / Wilderness

Some small sites are not shown, especially in
urban areas.

MILES
0   50   100   150   200

Albers equal area projection

Abbreviations

AFB   Air Force Base
NAS   Naval Air Station
NF   National Forest
NG   National Grassland
NHP   National Historical Park
NP   National Park
NRA   National Recreation Area
NWR   National Wildlife Refuge

U.S. Department of the Interior
U.S. Geological Survey

The **National Atlas** of the United States of America®

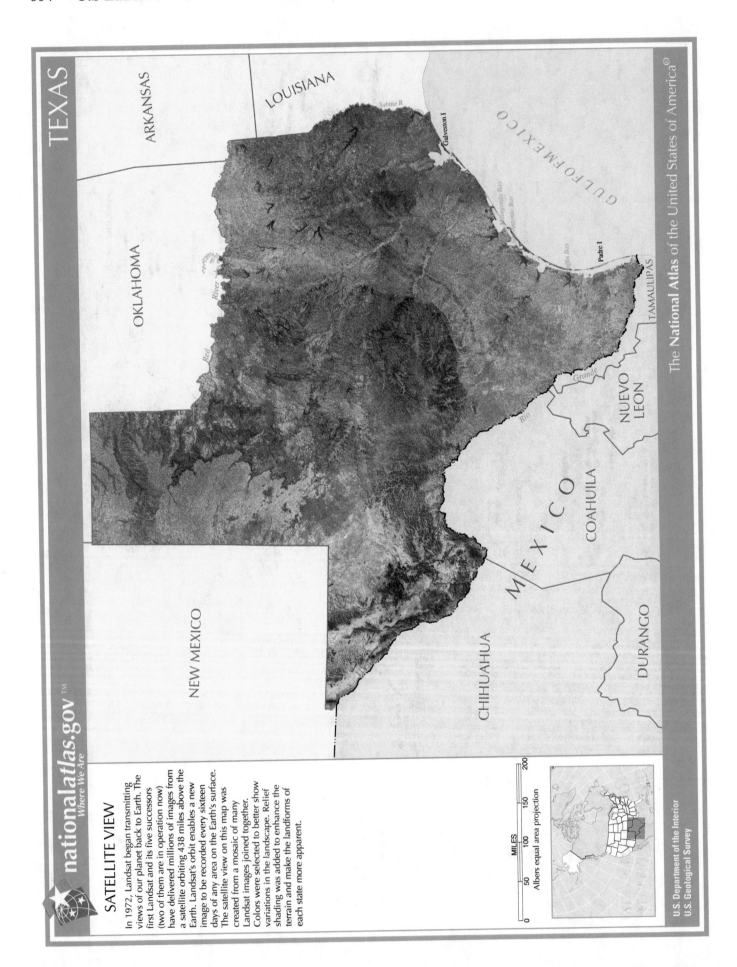

SATELLITE VIEW

In 1972, Landsat began transmitting views of our planet back to Earth. The first Landsat and its five successors (two of them are in operation now) have delivered millions of images from a satellite orbiting 438 miles above the Earth. Landsat's orbit enables a new image to be recorded every sixteen days of any area on the Earth's surface. The satellite view on this map was created from a mosaic of many Landsat images joined together. Colors were selected to better show variations in the landscape. Relief shading was added to enhance the terrain and make the landforms of each state more apparent.

nationalatlas.gov ™
Where We Are

TEXAS

The **National Atlas** of the United States of America®

U.S. Department of the Interior
U.S. Geological Survey

MILES
0   50   100   150   200
Albers equal area projection

Utah

Topic	Value	Time Period
Total Surface Area (acres)	54,338,900	2007
Land	52,538,200	2007
Federal Land	34,278,800	2007
Owned	2,434,773	FY 2009
Leased	19,924	FY 2009
Otherwise Managed	3,097	FY 2009
National Forest	8,207,000	September 2006
National Wilderness	1,160,300	October 2011
Non-Federal Land, Developed	744,600	2007
Non-Federal Land, Rural	17,514,800	2007
Water	1,800,700	2007
National Natural Landmarks	4	December 2010
National Historic Landmarks	13	December 2010
National Register of Historic Places	1,453	December 2010
National Parks	13	December 2010
Visitors to National Parks	8,975,525	2010
Historic Places Documented by the National Park Service	642	December 2010
Archeological Sites in National Parks	6,428	December 2010
Threatened and Endangered Species in National Parks	23	December 2010
Economic Benefit from National Park Tourism (dollars)	565,592,000	2009
Conservation Reserve Program (acres)	179,011	October 2011
Land and Water Conservation Fund Grants (dollars)	48,180,040	Since 1965
Historic Preservation Grants (dollars)	21,344,571	2010
Community Conservation and Recreation Projects	48	Since 1987
Federal Acres Transferred for Local Parks and Recreation	2,765	Since 1948
Crude Petroleum Production (millions of barrels)	24	2010
Crude Oil Proved Reserves (millions of barrels)	398	2009
Natural Gas Reserves (billions of cubic feet)	7,257	2009
Natural Gas Liquid Reserves (millions of barrels)	116	2008
Natural Gas Marketed Production (billions of cubic feet)	444	2009
Coal Reserves (millions of short tons)	5,203	2009

Sources: *U.S. Department of the Interior, National Park Service, State Profiles, December 2010; United States Department of Agriculture, Natural Resources Conservation Service, 2007 National Resources Inventory; U.S. General Services Administration, Federal Real Property Council, FY 2009 Federal Real Property Report, September 2010; University of Montana, www.wilderness.net; U.S. Department of Agriculture, Farm Services Agency, Conservation Reserve Program, October 2011; U.S Census Bureau, 2012 Statistical Abstract of the United States*

Utah Energy Overview and Analysis

Quick Facts

- Utah contains four of the Nation's 100 largest oil fields and two of its 100 largest natural gas fields.
- More than four-fifths of Utah households use natural gas for home heating.
- Coalbed methane accounts for nearly one-fifth of Utah's natural gas production.
- Utah is one of the few States with electricity generation from geothermal power sources.
- Utah has enormous deposits of oil shale rock, known as marlstone, which can be converted into crude oil.

Analysis

Resources and Consumption

Utah has substantial fossil energy resources. Three major basins in the eastern part of the State contain coal, natural gas, and oil reserves, including four of the nation's 100 largest oil fields and two of its 100 largest natural gas fields. Utah also has substantial renewable energy potential; areas with geothermal, wind, and solar power potential cover much of the State. Utah's population is low, as is its total energy consumption. The transportation and industrial sectors lead State energy demand.

Petroleum

Utah typically accounts for approximately 1 percent of U.S. crude oil production. Drilling operations and oil wells are concentrated in the Uinta and Paradox basins in eastern Utah. The State's five refineries, located in the Salt Lake City area, process crude oil from Utah and other Mountain States. The Frontier Pipeline also supplies those refineries with crude oil imports from Canada. Petroleum products are delivered to the Salt Lake City area from refineries in Wyoming and Montana via the Pioneer Pipeline, and another pipeline, operated by Chevron, flows out of Salt Lake City refining centers to supply markets in Idaho, eastern Oregon, and eastern Washington State. Another pipeline, the UNEV, has been proposed in order to help accommodate the growing population and petroleum demand in southern Utah. The new 400-mile pipeline is scheduled for completion by the end of 2010 and would connect Salt Lake City refineries to the southern Utah area on its way to southern Nevada. Total petroleum consumption in the State is low. Utah requires the use of a motor gasoline blend with low volatility in the Salt Lake City and Provo/Orem areas; the rest of the State uses conventional motor gasoline.

Although its proven crude oil reserves only account for just over 1 percent of the U.S. total, Utah has enormous deposits of oil shale rock, known as marlstone, which can be converted into crude oil through a process called destructive distillation. The Green River Formation, a group of basins in Colorado, Wyoming, and Utah, holds the largest known oil shale deposits in the world. Utah's oil shale deposits are concentrated in the Uinta Basin in the east-central part of the State. Utah's oil shale resources are smaller than those found in Colorado and Wyoming, but much of the State's high-grade deposits are located close to the surface in thick seams. Although this natural resource holds tremendous promise, oil shale development remains speculative and faces several major obstacles involving technological feasibility, economic viability, resource ownership, and environmental considerations.

Natural Gas

Utah's natural gas production, concentrated in the Uinta Basin, typically accounts for nearly 2 percent of U.S. output. Coalbed methane (unconventional natural gas produced from coal seams) accounts for nearly one-fifth of Utah's natural gas production. Although more than four-fifths of its households use natural gas as their primary energy source for home heating, Utah consumes only about one-half of its own production. The remainder is shipped to other States including Nevada, Idaho, Wyoming, and Colorado. Utah is also part of the transportation corridor for shipping gas from Opal Hub in Wyoming through the Salt Lake City area to markets in Southern California via the Kern River Gas Transmission Pipeline.

Coal, Electricity, and Renewables

Utah typically accounts for more than 2 percent of U.S. coal production. More than two-thirds of Utah's coal production is consumed for electricity generation within the State; the remainder is shipped by rail primarily to Nevada and California.

Although natural gas-fired and hydroelectric generators also contribute, coal-fired power plants dominate electricity generation in Utah and supply almost the entire market. With two operational geothermal facilities, Utah is one of the few States with electricity generation from geothermal power sources, although that source contributes minimally to State supply. Utah electricity demand is low, and approximately one-tenth of Utah households use electricity as their primary energy source for home heating.

In April 2005, four western State governors agreed to develop a 1,300-mile high-capacity power line from Wyoming to California that would allow as much as 12 thousand megawatts of electricity to flow from the energy-rich Rocky Mountain region to high-demand markets in California. A feasibility study was released in 2007 that supports the development of this transmission line project and a second phase development study is currently underway.

In March 2008, Utah adopted a voluntary renewable portfolio goal that encourages utilities to produce 20 percent of their energy from renewable sources by 2025. The goal requires that utilities pursue cost-effective renewable energy.

Source: U.S. Energy Information Administration, October 2009

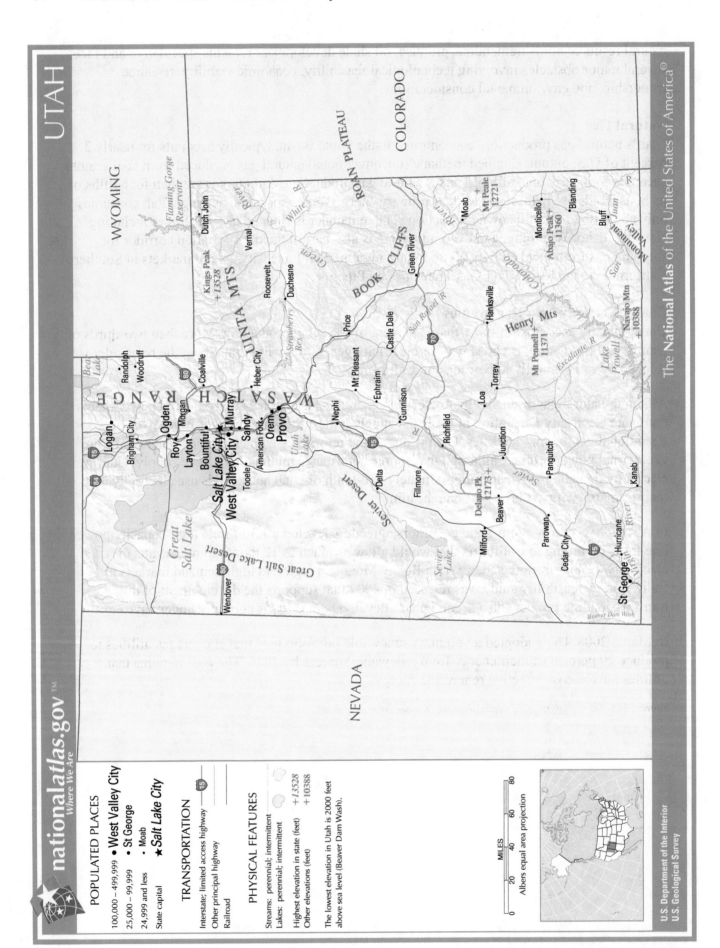

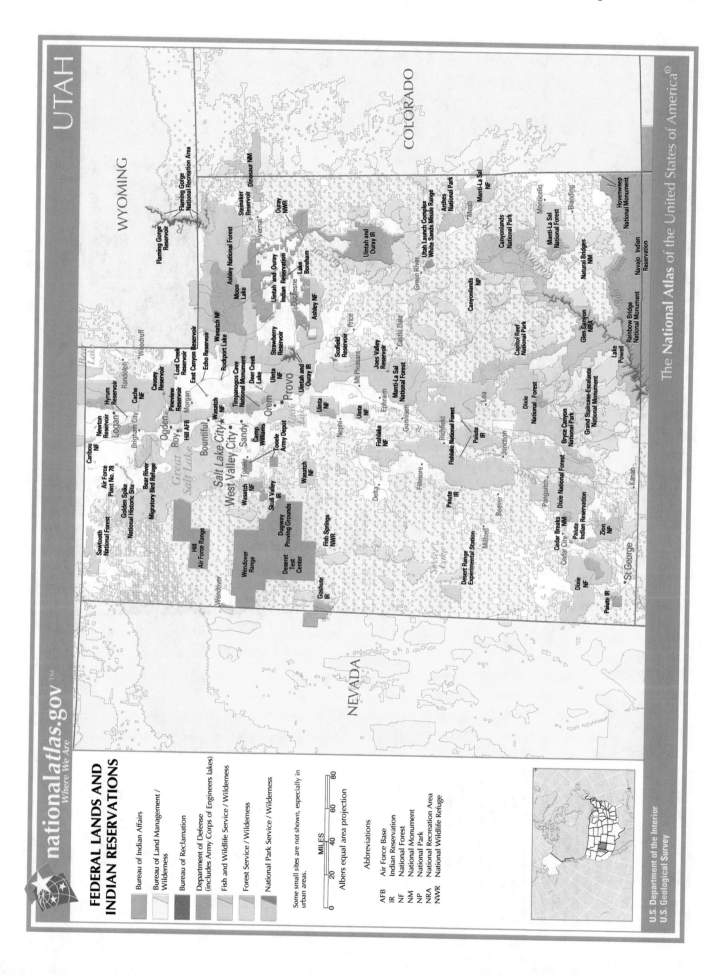

UTAH

nationalatlas.gov™
Where We Are

**FEDERAL LANDS AND
INDIAN RESERVATIONS**

Bureau of Indian Affairs

Bureau of Land Management /
Wilderness

Bureau of Reclamation

Department of Defense
(includes Army Corps of Engineers lakes)

Fish and Wildlife Service / Wilderness

Forest Service / Wilderness

National Park Service / Wilderness

Some small sites are not shown, especially in
urban areas.

MILES
0   20   40   60   80

Albers equal area projection

Abbreviations

AFB   Air Force Base
IR   Indian Reservation
NF   National Forest
NM   National Monument
NP   National Park
NRA   National Recreation Area
NWR   National Wildlife Refuge

U.S. Department of the Interior
U.S. Geological Survey

The **National Atlas** of the United States of America®

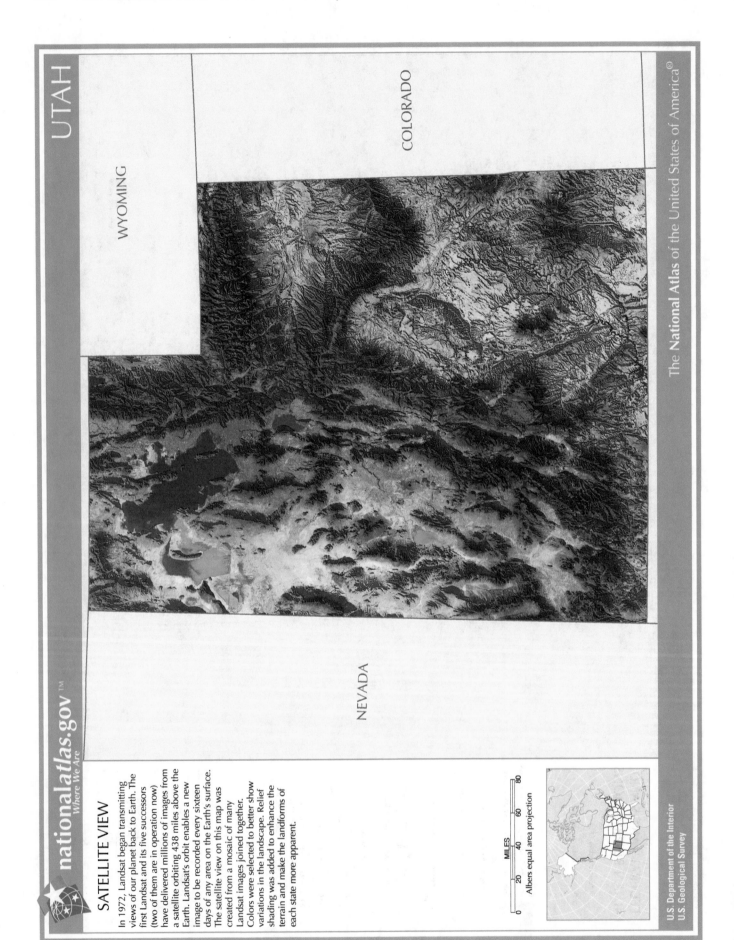

UTAH

WYOMING

NEVADA

COLORADO

nationalatlas.gov™
Where We Are

SATELLITE VIEW

In 1972, Landsat began transmitting views of our planet back to Earth. The first Landsat and its five successors (two of them are in operation now) have delivered millions of images from a satellite orbiting 438 miles above the Earth. Landsat's orbit enables a new image to be recorded every sixteen days of any area on the Earth's surface. The satellite view on this map was created from a mosaic of many Landsat images joined together. Colors were selected to better show variations in the landscape. Relief shading was added to enhance the terrain and make the landforms of each state more apparent.

MILES
0   20   40   60   80

Albers equal area projection

U.S. Department of the Interior
U.S. Geological Survey

The **National Atlas** of the United States of America®

Vermont

Topic	Value	Time Period
Total Surface Area (acres)	6,153,600	2007
Land	5,891,700	2007
Federal Land	422,600	2007
Owned	18,066	FY 2009
Leased	412	FY 2009
Otherwise Managed	175	FY 2009
National Forest	400,000	September 2006
National Wilderness	100,870	October 2011
Non-Federal Land, Developed	393,200	2007
Non-Federal Land, Rural	5,075,900	2007
Water	261,900	2007
National Natural Landmarks	12	December 2010
National Historic Landmarks	17	December 2010
National Register of Historic Places	800	December 2010
National Parks	2	December 2010
Visitors to National Parks	31,209	2010
Historic Places Documented by the National Park Service	146	December 2010
Archeological Sites in National Parks	19	December 2010
Threatened and Endangered Species in National Parks	0	December 2010
Economic Benefit from National Park Tourism (dollars)	1,395,000	2009
Conservation Reserve Program (acres)	2,871	October 2011
Land and Water Conservation Fund Grants (dollars)	33,004,602	Since 1965
Historic Preservation Grants (dollars)	21,362,234	2010
Community Conservation and Recreation Projects	57	Since 1987
Federal Acres Transferred for Local Parks and Recreation	180	Since 1948
Crude Petroleum Production (millions of barrels)	Not Available	2010
Crude Oil Proved Reserves (millions of barrels)	Not Available	2009
Natural Gas Reserves (billions of cubic feet)	Not Available	2009
Natural Gas Liquid Reserves (millions of barrels)	Not Available	2008
Natural Gas Marketed Production (billions of cubic feet)	Not Available	2009
Coal Reserves (millions of short tons)	Not Available	2009

Sources: U.S. Department of the Interior, National Park Service, State Profiles, December 2010; United States Department of Agriculture, Natural Resources Conservation Service, 2007 National Resources Inventory; U.S. General Services Administration, Federal Real Property Council, FY 2009 Federal Real Property Report, September 2010; University of Montana, www.wilderness.net; U.S. Department of Agriculture, Farm Services Agency, Conservation Reserve Program, October 2011; U.S Census Bureau, 2012 Statistical Abstract of the United States

Vermont Energy Overview and Analysis

Quick Facts

- Total energy consumption in Vermont is the lowest of any State in the Nation.
- Nuclear power accounts for about three-fourths of the electricity generated within Vermont, a higher share than in any other State.
- Vermont is one of only two States in the Nation with no coal-fired power plants.
- Vermont's hills and mountains cover most of the State and offer wind power potential, while dense forests in the State's northeast offer biomass resources for home heating and electricity generation.
- In March 2008, Vermont adopted a renewable energy goal to produce 25 percent of the energy consumed in the State from renewable sources, in particular from the State's farms and forests, by 2025.

Analysis

Resources and Consumption

Vermont has no fossil fuel resources but does have minor renewable energy potential. The Connecticut River, which defines the State's eastern border with New Hampshire, and Lake Champlain, along the western border with New York, offer hydroelectric power resources. Vermont's hills and mountains cover most of the State and offer wind power potential, while dense forests in the State's northeast offer biomass resources for home heating and wood-fired electricity generation. Vermont's total energy consumption is the lowest in the Nation, and per capita energy consumption is among the lowest. The transportation and residential sectors are the State's leading energy consumers.

Petroleum

Vermont ranks last among the 50 States in petroleum product demand and receives supply from neighboring States and Canada. Because it has no air quality non-attainment areas, Vermont allows the statewide use of conventional motor gasoline. (Most States require the use of special fuel blends in non-attainment areas.)

Vermont, along with much of the U.S. Northeast, is vulnerable to distillate fuel oil shortages and price spikes during the winter months due to high demand for home heating. Nearly three-fifths of Vermont households use fuel oil as their primary energy source for home heating. In January and February 2000, distillate fuel oil prices in the Northeast rose sharply when extreme winter weather increased demand unexpectedly and hindered the arrival of new supply, as frozen rivers and high winds slowed the docking and unloading of barges and tankers. In July 2000, in order to reduce the risk of future shortages, the President directed the U.S. Department of Energy to establish the Northeast Heating Oil Reserve. The Reserve gives Northeast consumers adequate supplies for about 10 days, the time required for ships to carry heating oil from the Gulf of Mexico to New York Harbor. The Reserve's storage terminals are located in Perth Amboy, New Jersey, and Groton and New Haven, Connecticut.

Natural Gas

With the exception of Hawaii, Vermont has the lowest natural gas consumption in the United States. Supply is imported primarily for residential use through a small-capacity pipeline from Canada.

Coal, Electricity, and Renewables

Vermont is one of only two States in the Nation with no coal-fired power plants; the other is Rhode Island. Vermont generates a higher percentage of its electricity from nuclear power than any other State. The Vermont Yankee nuclear plant typically accounts for about three-fourths of total electricity generation.

Most of Vermont's remaining generation is produced from renewable energy sources, largely from hydroelectric power and fuel wood. Vermont's numerous small-scale hydroelectric power projects typically account for about one-fifth of State electricity production. Nonhydroelectric renewable energy sources, including wood, wood waste, and wind, account for between 5 and 10 percent of State electricity production. In March 2008, Vermont adopted a renewable energy goal to produce 25 percent of the energy consumed in the State from renewable sources, in particular from the State's farms and forests, by 2025.

Vermont's per capita residential electricity use is low compared with the rest of the Nation, in part because demand for air-conditioning is minimal during the mild summer months and only a small share of households use electricity for home heating.

Source: U.S. Energy Information Administration, October 2009

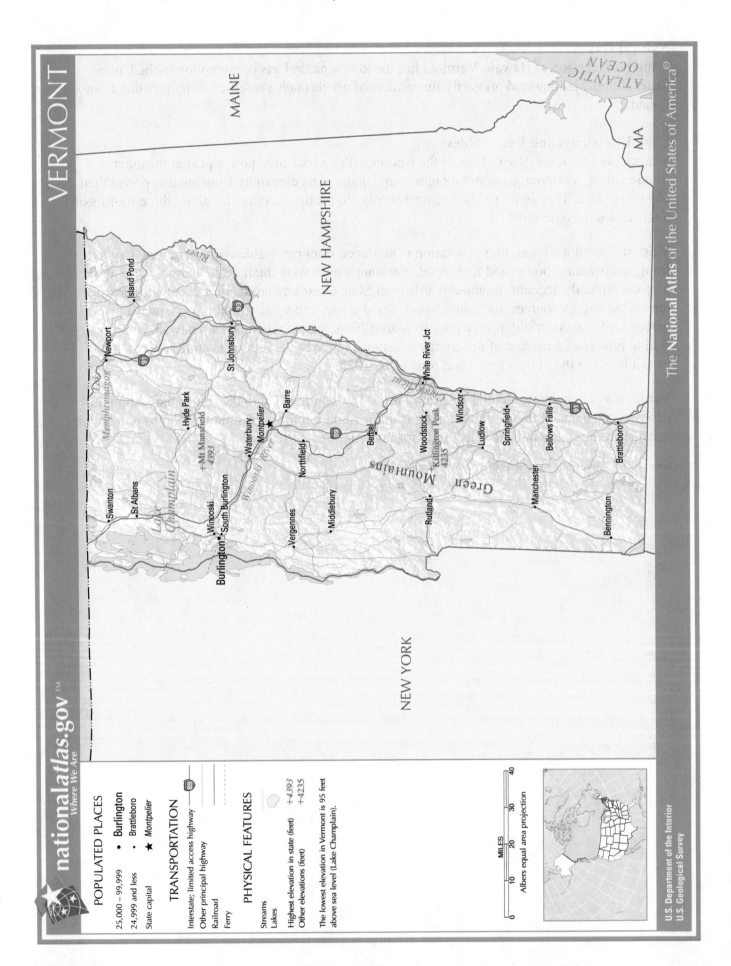

VERMONT

MAINE

ATLANTIC OCEAN

MA

NEW HAMPSHIRE

NEW YORK

River

Island Pond

93

Newport

St Johnsbury

57

Memphremagog

Hyde Park

Barre

Mt Mansfield
4393

Waterbury   Montpelier

Winooski River

89

Bethel

White River Jct

Connecticut

Windsor

Woodstock

Killington Peak
4235

Ludlow

Springfield

91

Swanton

St Albans

Lake Champlain

Winooski
South Burlington

Burlington

Northfield

Vergennes

Middlebury

Green

Mountains

Rutland

Manchester

Bellows Falls

Brattleboro

Bennington

nationalatlas.gov ™
Where We Are

POPULATED PLACES

25,000 – 99,999   ● **Burlington**

24,999 and less   • Brattleboro

State capital   ★ *Montpelier*

TRANSPORTATION

Interstate; limited access highway ── 89

Other principal highway ────

Railroad ┤┤┤┤

Ferry ‑ ‑ ‑ ‑

PHYSICAL FEATURES

Streams

Lakes

Highest elevation in state (feet)   +4393

Other elevations (feet)   +4235

The lowest elevation in Vermont is 95 feet
above sea level (Lake Champlain).

MILES

0   10   20   30   40

Albers equal area projection

The **National Atlas** of the United States of America ©

U.S. Department of the Interior
U.S. Geological Survey

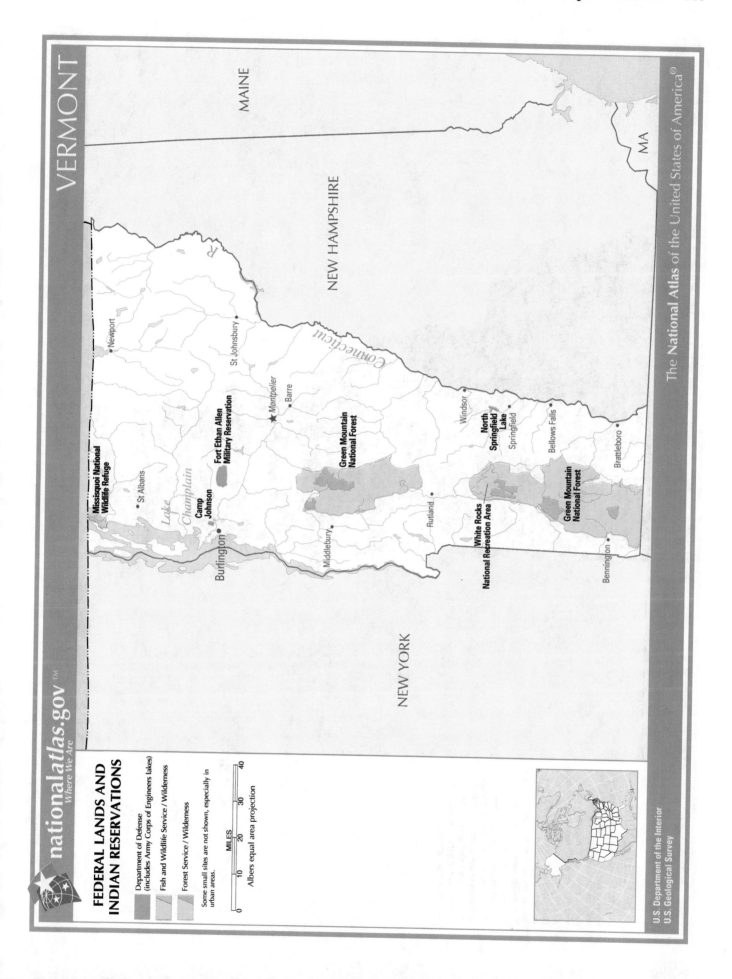

U.S. Department of the Interior
U.S. Geological Survey

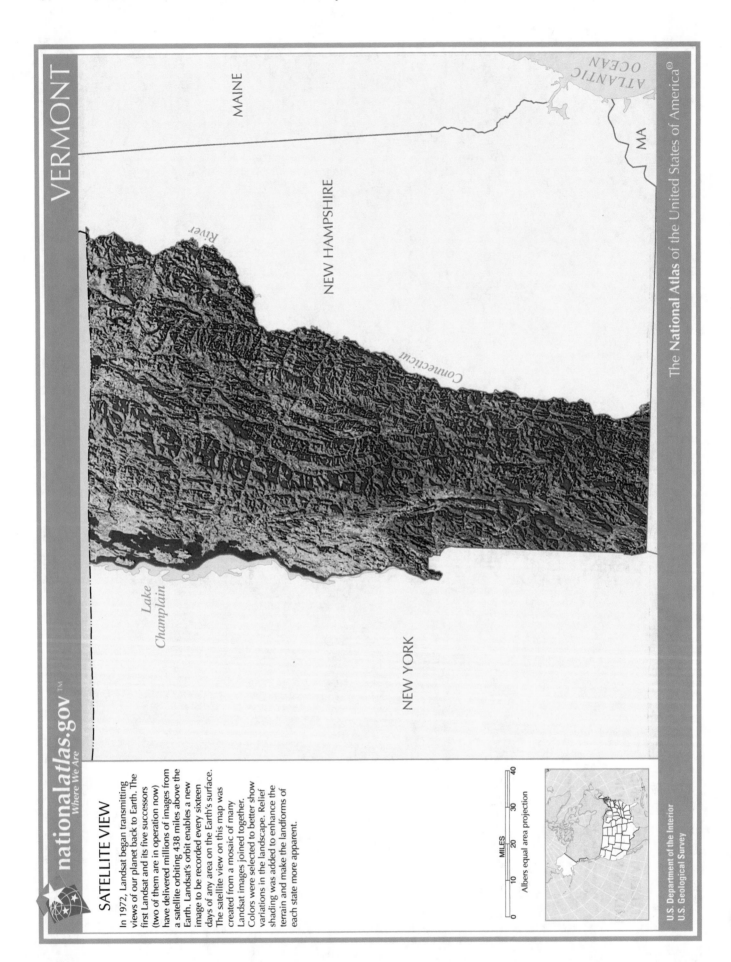

VERMONT

nationalatlas.gov™
Where We Are

MAINE

NEW HAMPSHIRE

Connecticut

River

Lake
Champlain

NEW YORK

MA

ATLANTIC
OCEAN

The **National Atlas** of the United States of America®

SATELLITE VIEW

In 1972, Landsat began transmitting views of our planet back to Earth. The first Landsat and its five successors (two of them are in operation now) have delivered millions of images from a satellite orbiting 438 miles above the Earth. Landsat's orbit enables a new image to be recorded every sixteen days of any area on the Earth's surface. The satellite view on this map was created from a mosaic of many Landsat images joined together. Colors were selected to better show variations in the landscape. Relief shading was added to enhance the terrain and make the landforms of each state more apparent.

MILES
0   10   20   30   40

Albers equal area projection

U.S. Department of the Interior
U.S. Geological Survey

Virginia

Topic	Value	Time Period
Total Surface Area (acres)	27,087,100	2007
Land	25,144,000	2007
Federal Land	2,646,400	2007
Owned	412,858	FY 2009
Leased	3,187	FY 2009
Otherwise Managed	523	FY 2009
National Forest	1,664,000	September 2006
National Wilderness	214,904	October 2011
Non-Federal Land, Developed	3,101,200	2007
Non-Federal Land, Rural	19,396,400	2007
Water	1,943,100	2007
National Natural Landmarks	10	December 2010
National Historic Landmarks	119	December 2010
National Register of Historic Places	2,797	December 2010
National Parks	21	December 2010
Visitors to National Parks	22,708,338	2010
Historic Places Documented by the National Park Service	1,899	December 2010
Archeological Sites in National Parks	1,501	December 2010
Threatened and Endangered Species in National Parks	19	December 2010
Economic Benefit from National Park Tourism (dollars)	493,128,000	2009
Conservation Reserve Program (acres)	61,509	October 2011
Land and Water Conservation Fund Grants (dollars)	82,784,757	Since 1965
Historic Preservation Grants (dollars)	55,070,645	2010
Community Conservation and Recreation Projects	97	Since 1987
Federal Acres Transferred for Local Parks and Recreation	5,630	Since 1948
Crude Petroleum Production (millions of barrels)	Not Available	2010
Crude Oil Proved Reserves (millions of barrels)	Not Available	2009
Natural Gas Reserves (billions of cubic feet)	3,091	2009
Natural Gas Liquid Reserves (millions of barrels)	Not Available	2008
Natural Gas Marketed Production (billions of cubic feet)	Not Available	2009
Coal Reserves (millions of short tons)	1,519	2009

Sources: *U.S. Department of the Interior, National Park Service, State Profiles, December 2010; United States Department of Agriculture, Natural Resources Conservation Service, 2007 National Resources Inventory; U.S. General Services Administration, Federal Real Property Council, FY 2009 Federal Real Property Report, September 2010; University of Montana, www.wilderness.net; U.S. Department of Agriculture, Farm Services Agency, Conservation Reserve Program, October 2011; U.S Census Bureau, 2012 Statistical Abstract of the United States*

Virginia Energy Overview and Analysis

Quick Facts

- Virginia accounts for nearly 10 percent of U.S. coal production east of the Mississippi River.
- Virginia's only petroleum refinery, in Yorktown, processes foreign crude oil delivered by barge via the Chesapeake Bay.
- Virginia has two nuclear power plants, which typically provide about one-third of the electricity generated within the State.
- Two of Virginia's coalbed methane fields are among the top 100 natural gas fields in the United States.
- Virginia established a voluntary renewable portfolio goal that encourages utilities to generate 12 percent of base-year 2007 sales from renewable sources by 2022.

Analysis

Resources and Consumption

Virginia has minor natural gas and coal reserves, nearly all of which are found in the Central Appalachian Basin in the southwestern part of the State. In addition, resource assessments show that substantial oil and gas reserves could underlie the land beneath Virginia's offshore waters, which are part of the federally administered Mid-Atlantic Outer Continental Shelf (OCS). Congressional and Presidential moratoria prohibiting energy development in that offshore area were established in 1990 and expired in 2008. High wind power potential exists off of Virginia's Atlantic coast and in the Chesapeake Bay. Virginia's energy demand is distributed fairly evenly among the sectors of the economy, with transportation leading the others by a small margin.

Petroleum

Virginia's only petroleum refinery, in Yorktown, processes foreign crude oil delivered by barge via the Chesapeake Bay. The Yorktown refinery primarily supplies regional markets. Petroleum products are also delivered to Virginia at the Port of Norfolk and via the Colonial and Plantation pipelines from the Gulf Coast. Virginia's total petroleum consumption is high. Reformulated motor gasoline blended with ethanol is required in the northern Virginia suburbs of Washington, D.C., and in the metropolitan areas of Richmond and Norfolk-Hampton Roads.

Natural Gas

Virginia's natural gas production is minor but enough to supply about one-third of State demand. Virginia produces both conventional natural gas and coalbed methane in the Central Appalachian Basin, which covers the State's western panhandle. Most of Virginia's natural gas production comes from coalbed methane fields, two of which are among the 100 largest natural gas fields in the United States. As with most States on the East Coast, the majority of Virginia's natural gas supply is delivered from the Gulf Coast region via several major interstate natural gas pipelines. The State ships over four-fifths of its natural gas receipts to Maryland and the District of Columbia en route to other markets in the Northeast. Virginia's natural gas consumption is distributed relatively evenly among the residential, commercial, industrial, and electricity generation sectors. About one-third of households in Virginia use natural gas as their primary energy source for home heating.

Coal, Electricity, and Renewables

Virginia accounts for more than 5 percent of U.S. coal production east of the Mississippi River. Production takes place at surface and underground mines in the Central Appalachian Basin. Large volumes of coal move through Virginia by rail, including production from Kentucky and West Virginia. Virginia's coal is shipped to nearly half of the States in the Nation; the primary recipients are Georgia and Tennessee. Most coal consumed in Virginia is used for electricity generation.

Coal-fired power plants typically account for nearly one-half of the State's electricity generation. Two nuclear power plants account for about one-third of the State's generation, and natural gas- and petroleum-fired power plants account for much of the rest. Close to one-half of households in Virginia use electricity as their primary energy source for home heating. Wood and wood waste provide Virginia with about 2.5 percent of its total electricity production, while other renewable sources, such as hydroelectric power, municipal solid waste, and landfill gas, contribute minimally. In April 2007, Virginia established a voluntary renewable portfolio goal that encourages utilities to generate 12 percent of base-year 2007 sales from renewable sources by 2022.

Source: U.S. Energy Information Administration, October 2009

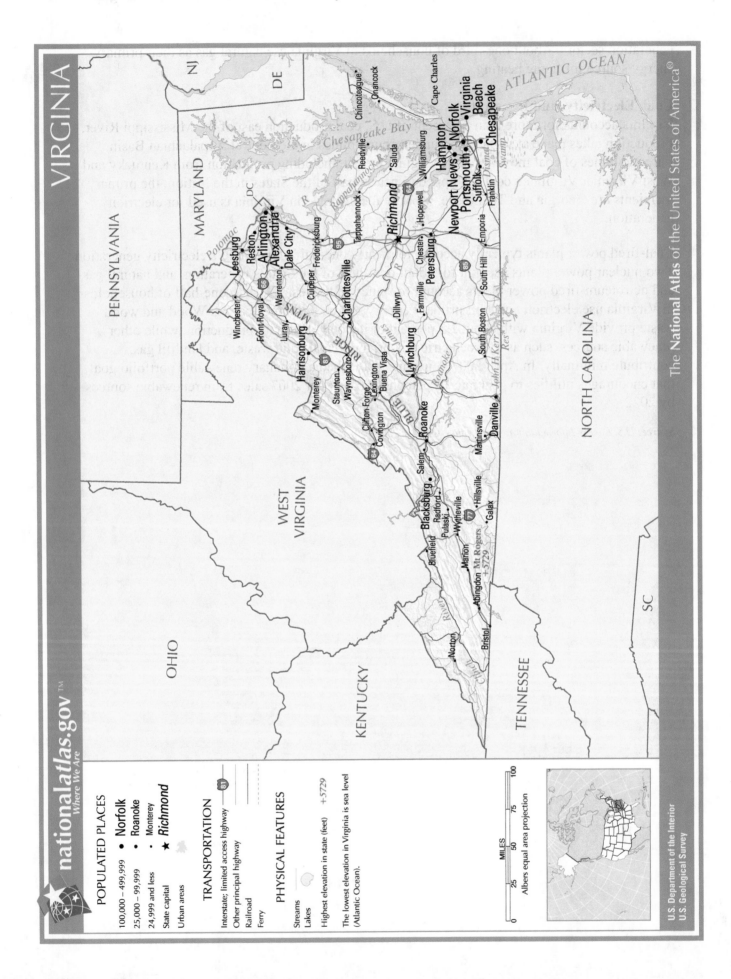

U.S. Department of the Interior
U.S. Geological Survey

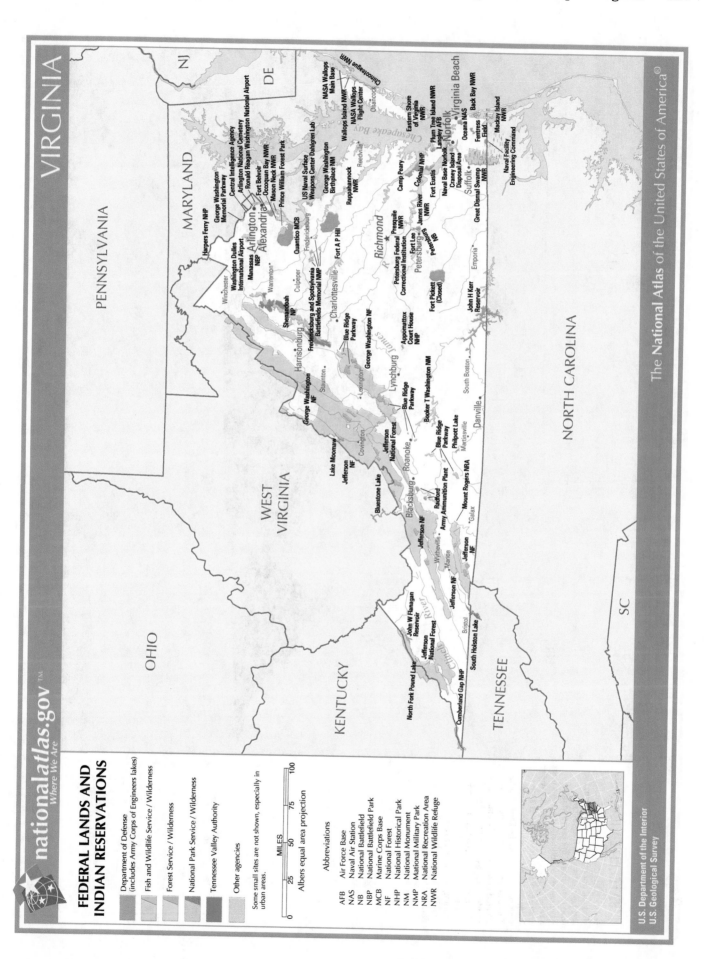

nationalatlas.gov™
Where We Are

FEDERAL LANDS AND INDIAN RESERVATIONS

Department of Defense
(includes Army Corps of Engineers lakes)

Fish and Wildlife Service / Wilderness

Forest Service / Wilderness

National Park Service / Wilderness

Tennessee Valley Authority

Other agencies

Some small sites are not shown, especially in
urban areas.

MILES
0   25   50   75   100

Albers equal area projection

Abbreviations

AFB	Air Force Base
NAS	Naval Air Station
NB	National Battlefield
NBP	National Battlefield Park
MCB	Marine Corps Base
NF	National Forest
NHP	National Historical Park
NM	National Monument
NMP	National Military Park
NRA	National Recreation Area
NWR	National Wildlife Refuge

VIRGINIA

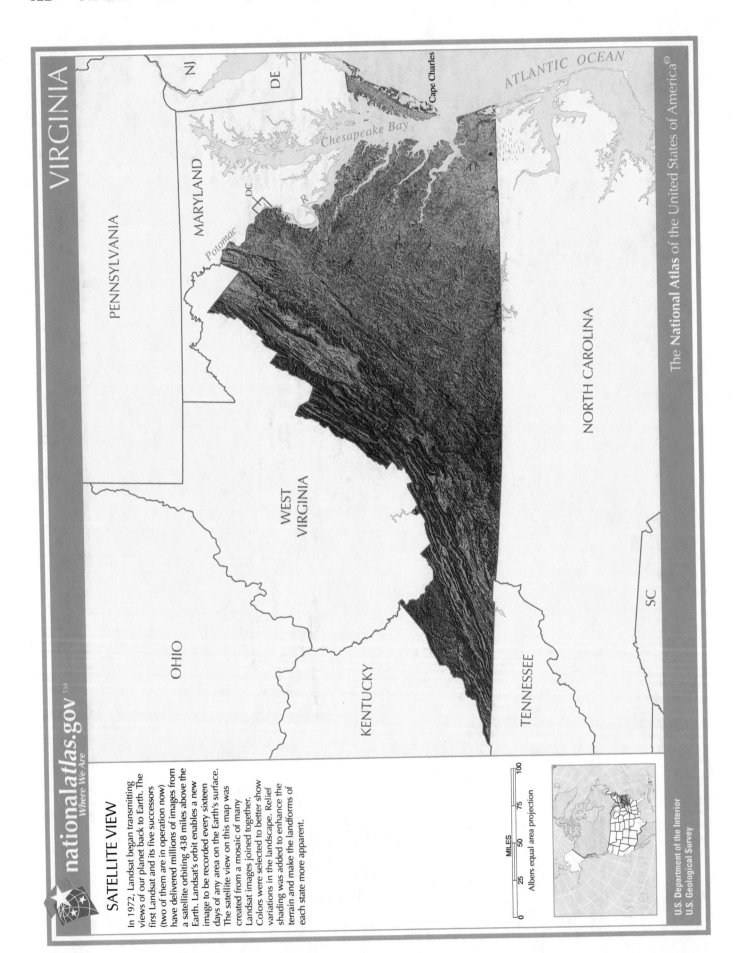

VIRGINIA

nationalatlas.gov ™
Where We Are

SATELLITE VIEW

In 1972, Landsat began transmitting views of our planet back to Earth. The first Landsat and its five successors (two of them are in operation now) have delivered millions of images from a satellite orbiting 438 miles above the Earth. Landsat's orbit enables a new image to be recorded every sixteen days of any area on the Earth's surface. The satellite view on this map was created from a mosaic of many Landsat images joined together. Colors were selected to better show variations in the landscape. Relief shading was added to enhance the terrain and make the landforms of each state more apparent.

PENNSYLVANIA

NJ

DE

MARYLAND

DC

Potomac

Chesapeake Bay

Cape Charles

ATLANTIC OCEAN

R

OHIO

WEST VIRGINIA

KENTUCKY

TENNESSEE

NORTH CAROLINA

SC

MILES
0   25   50   75   100

Albers equal area projection

The National Atlas of the United States of America ®

U.S. Department of the Interior
U.S. Geological Survey

Washington

Topic	Value	Time Period
Total Surface Area (acres)	44,035,300	2007
Land	42,491,300	2007
Federal Land	11,923,500	2007
Owned	1,332,765	FY 2009
Leased	163,342	FY 2009
Otherwise Managed	498	FY 2009
National Forest	9,289,000	September 2006
National Wilderness	4,462,493	October 2011
Non-Federal Land, Developed	2,464,500	2007
Non-Federal Land, Rural	28,103,300	2007
Water	1,544,000	2007
National Natural Landmarks	17	December 2010
National Historic Landmarks	24	December 2010
National Register of Historic Places	1,440	December 2010
National Parks	13	December 2010
Visitors to National Parks	7,281,785	2010
Historic Places Documented by the National Park Service	763	December 2010
Archeological Sites in National Parks	913	December 2010
Threatened and Endangered Species in National Parks	19	December 2010
Economic Benefit from National Park Tourism (dollars)	247,832,000	2009
Conservation Reserve Program (acres)	1,461,969	October 2011
Land and Water Conservation Fund Grants (dollars)	70,282,953	Since 1965
Historic Preservation Grants (dollars)	26,749,740	2010
Community Conservation and Recreation Projects	101	Since 1987
Federal Acres Transferred for Local Parks and Recreation	9,858	Since 1948
Crude Petroleum Production (millions of barrels)	Not Available	2010
Crude Oil Proved Reserves (millions of barrels)	Not Available	2009
Natural Gas Reserves (billions of cubic feet)	Not Available	2009
Natural Gas Liquid Reserves (millions of barrels)	Not Available	2008
Natural Gas Marketed Production (billions of cubic feet)	Not Available	2009
Coal Reserves (millions of short tons)	1,340	2009

Sources: U.S. Department of the Interior, National Park Service, State Profiles, December 2010; United States Department of Agriculture, Natural Resources Conservation Service, 2007 National Resources Inventory; U.S. General Services Administration, Federal Real Property Council, FY 2009 Federal Real Property Report, September 2010; University of Montana, www.wilderness.net; U.S. Department of Agriculture, Farm Services Agency, Conservation Reserve Program, October 2011; U.S Census Bureau, 2012 Statistical Abstract of the United States

Washington Energy Overview and Analysis

Quick Facts

- Washington is the leading hydroelectric power producer in the Nation. Hydroelectric power accounts for nearly three-fourths of State electricity generation.
- The Grand Coulee hydroelectric power plant on the Columbia River is the highest capacity electric plant in the United States.
- With five refineries, Washington is a principal refining center for the Pacific Northwest.
- State jet fuel consumption is among the highest in the Nation, due in part to several large Air Force and Navy installations.
- Washington is a major producer of energy from wind, wood, and wood waste.

Analysis

Resources and Consumption

Washington has few fossil fuel resources but has tremendous renewable power potential. The Columbia and Snake Rivers are immense hydroelectric power resources. The State's western forests offer fuel wood resources, and large areas of the State are conducive to wind and geothermal power development. The high-temperature geothermal areas found in Washington have the potential to produce up to 300 MW of electric power. Transportation is the leading energy-consuming sector in the State, followed by the industrial and residential sectors. Washington is a leader in the energy-intensive forest products industry and is the site of several large U.S. military bases.

Petroleum

Although Washington has no indigenous crude oil production, it is a principal refining center serving Pacific Northwest markets. Five refineries receive crude oil supply primarily by tanker from Alaska. However, because Alaskan production is in decline, Washington's refineries are becoming increasingly dependent on crude oil imports from Canada and other countries. The Trans Mountain Pipeline from Alberta supplies more than one-tenth of Washington's crude oil. Washington's total petroleum demand is high. Jet fuel consumption is among the highest in the Nation, due in part to several large Air Force and Navy installations. The use of oxygenated motor gasoline is required throughout the State.

Natural Gas

Washington relies heavily on natural gas produced in Canada and transported by pipeline to U.S. markets. The Sumas Center, in Canada near the border between Washington and British Columbia, is the principal natural gas trading and transportation hub for the U.S. Northwest. The Northwest Pipeline Corp. system supplies markets in western Washington and Oregon, and the Gas Transmission Northwest line supplies the eastern part of the two States. The residential sector leads Washington's natural gas consumption, followed closely by the industrial and electric power generating sectors. Roughly one-third of Washington households use natural gas as their primary energy source for home heating.

Coal, Electricity, and Renewables

Washington has one large coal-fired plant located near the State's only coal mine in the southwest. The mine was closed in November 2006, and Washington currently imports coal from Wyoming and Montana. The State's only nuclear plant, the Columbia Generating Station, is located near the Columbia River in the south-central part of the State, and generates nearly one-tenth of the State's electricity. Washington is a major net electricity exporter, supplying electricity to the Canadian power grid and to U.S. markets as far away as California. The State transmits large amounts of cheaply produced hydroelectric power via the Western Interconnection, which runs from British Columbia and Alberta, Canada through Washington and Oregon to southern California and the northern part of Baja California, Mexico. The system, also known as the Pacific Intertie, is the largest single electricity transmission program in the United States and covers all or part of 14 states. Although the Pacific Intertie was originally designed to transmit electricity south during California's peak summer demand season, flow is sometimes reversed overnight and has occasionally been reversed during periods of reduced hydroelectric generation in the Northwest.

Typically accounting for close to three-fourths of State electricity generation, hydroelectric power dominates the electricity market in Washington. Coal-fired, natural gas-fired, and nuclear power plants account for roughly equal shares of the remaining generation. Washington is the leading hydroelectric power producer in the Nation, typically generating about twice that of the next leading State. Eight of the State's 10 largest power plants produce hydroelectricity, primarily from the Columbia and Snake Rivers. The 7,079-megawatt Grand Coulee hydroelectric facility, located on the Columbia River, is the largest generating plant in the United States. Grand Coulee's generation capacity is almost twice that of Arizona's Palo Verde nuclear plant, the second-ranked U.S. electric plant.

Nonhydroelectric renewable energy sources currently contribute about 3 percent of Washington's total electricity generation. Washington is a major producer of wind energy and in 2008 ranked fifth in the U.S. in wind capacity. Washington is also a substantial producer of energy from wood and wood waste, accounting for approximately 3 percent of U.S. production. In November 2006, Washington adopted a renewable energy standard that requires all utilities serving at least 25,000 people to produce 15 percent of their energy from renewable sources by 2020.

Source: U.S. Energy Information Administration, October 2009

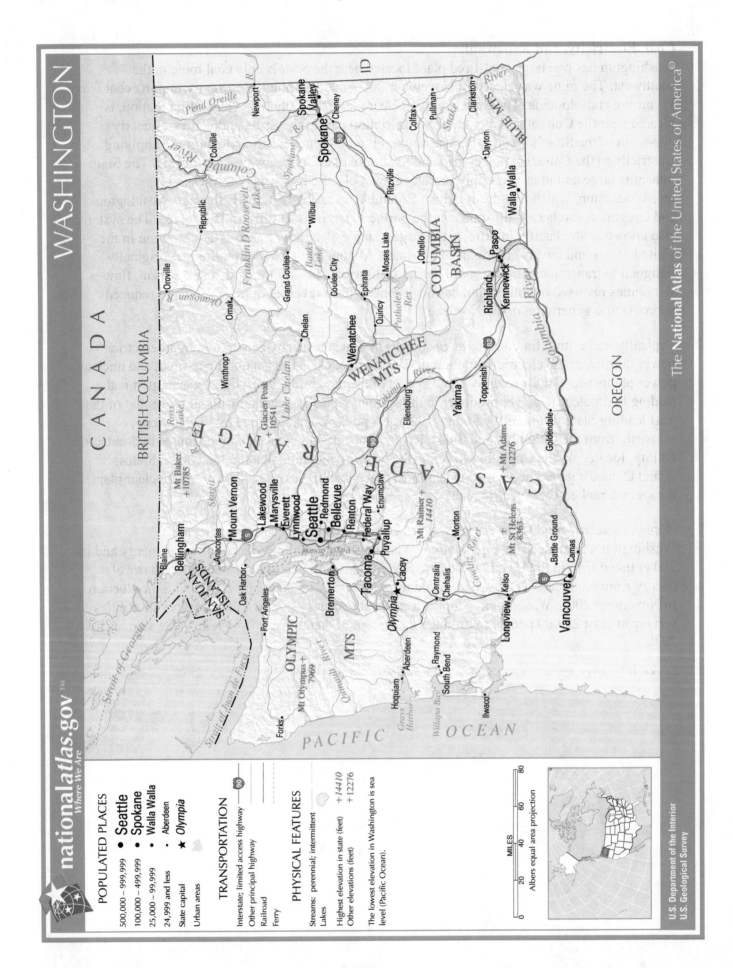

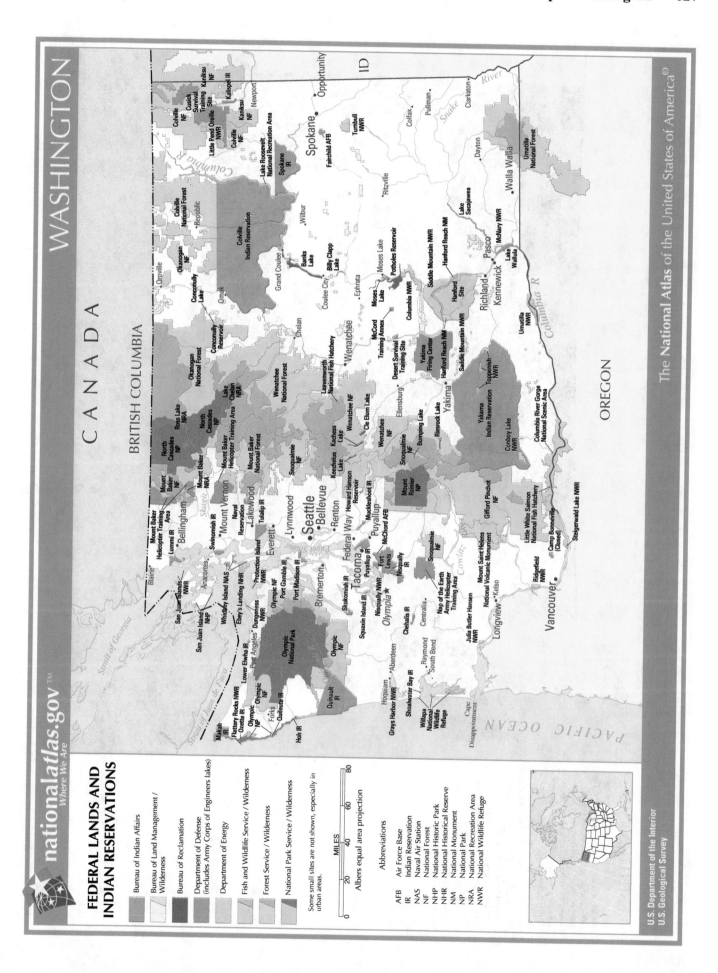

FEDERAL LANDS AND INDIAN RESERVATIONS

Bureau of Indian Affairs

Bureau of Land Management / Wilderness

Bureau of Reclamation

Department of Defense (includes Army Corps of Engineers lakes)

Department of Energy

Fish and Wildlife Service / Wilderness

Forest Service / Wilderness

National Park Service / Wilderness

Some small sites are not shown, especially in urban areas.

MILES

0   20   40   60   80

Albers equal area projection

Abbreviations

AFB   Air Force Base
IR   Indian Reservation
NAS   Naval Air Station
NF   National Forest
NHP   National Historical Park
NHR   National Historical Reserve
NM   National Monument
NP   National Park
NRA   National Recreation Area
NWR   National Wildlife Refuge

U.S. Department of the Interior
U.S. Geological Survey

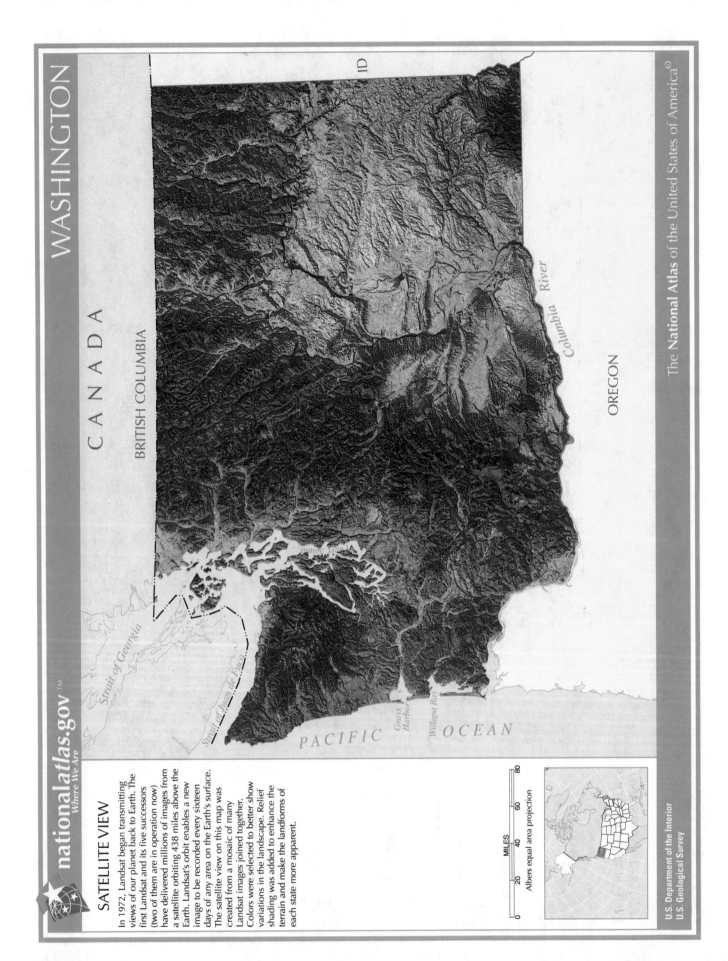

WASHINGTON
Where We Are

nationalatlas.gov™
Where We Are

SATELLITE VIEW

In 1972, Landsat began transmitting views of our planet back to Earth. The first Landsat and its five successors (two of them are in operation now) have delivered millions of images from a satellite orbiting 438 miles above the Earth. Landsat's orbit enables a new image to be recorded every sixteen days of any area on the Earth's surface. The satellite view on this map was created from a mosaic of many Landsat images joined together. Colors were selected to better show variations in the landscape. Relief shading was added to enhance the terrain and make the landforms of each state more apparent.

CANADA

BRITISH COLUMBIA

Strait of Georgia

Strait of Juan de Fuca

PACIFIC   OCEAN

Grays Harbor

Willapa Bay

ID

Columbia River

OREGON

The **National Atlas** of the United States of America®

MILES

0   20   40   60   80

Albers equal area projection

U.S. Department of the Interior
U.S. Geological Survey

West Virginia

Topic	Value	Time Period
Total Surface Area (acres)	15,508,200	2007
Land	15,327,600	2007
Federal Land	1,211,900	2007
Owned	149,582	FY 2009
Leased	4,105	FY 2009
Otherwise Managed	2,708	FY 2009
National Forest	1,044,000	September 2006
National Wilderness	118,810	October 2011
Non-Federal Land, Developed	1,151,600	2007
Non-Federal Land, Rural	12,964,100	2007
Water	180,600	2007
National Natural Landmarks	13	December 2010
National Historic Landmarks	16	December 2010
National Register of Historic Places	996	December 2010
National Parks	6	December 2010
Visitors to National Parks	1,811,722	2010
Historic Places Documented by the National Park Service	501	December 2010
Archeological Sites in National Parks	379	December 2010
Threatened and Endangered Species in National Parks	8	December 2010
Economic Benefit from National Park Tourism (dollars)	57,779,000	2009
Conservation Reserve Program (acres)	6,072	October 2011
Land and Water Conservation Fund Grants (dollars)	44,627,320	Since 1965
Historic Preservation Grants (dollars)	22,478,602	2010
Community Conservation and Recreation Projects	64	Since 1987
Federal Acres Transferred for Local Parks and Recreation	531	Since 1948
Crude Petroleum Production (millions of barrels)	2	2010
Crude Oil Proved Reserves (millions of barrels)	19	2009
Natural Gas Reserves (billions of cubic feet)	5,946	2009
Natural Gas Liquid Reserves (millions of barrels)	100	2008
Natural Gas Marketed Production (billions of cubic feet)	264	2009
Coal Reserves (millions of short tons)	31,955	2009

Sources: U.S. Department of the Interior, National Park Service, State Profiles, December 2010; United States Department of Agriculture, Natural Resources Conservation Service, 2007 National Resources Inventory; U.S. General Services Administration, Federal Real Property Council, FY 2009 Federal Real Property Report, September 2010; University of Montana, www.wilderness.net; U.S. Department of Agriculture, Farm Services Agency, Conservation Reserve Program, October 2011; U.S Census Bureau, 2012 Statistical Abstract of the United States

West Virginia Energy Overview and Analysis

Quick Facts

- West Virginia is the largest coal producer east of the Mississippi River and accounts for more than one-tenth of total U.S. coal production.
- West Virginia leads the Nation in coal production from underground mines, which account for over one-half of State production.
- West Virginia's recoverable coal reserves at producing mines are the second largest in the Nation after Wyoming.
- Coal-fired plants account for nearly all of the electricity generated in West Virginia.
- West Virginia ranks second in the Nation in interstate sales of electricity.

Analysis

Resources and Consumption

West Virginia has more estimated recoverable coal reserves at producing mines than any other State except Wyoming. Coal deposits are located in the Central and Northern Appalachian Basins, which underlie all but the eastern edge of the State. These basins also hold smaller conventional natural gas and crude oil reserves. Unconventional shale gas can also be found within the Appalachian Basin's Marcellus shale formation. Several rivers flowing from the Appalachian Mountains offer hydroelectric power resources. The industrial sector dominates West Virginia energy consumption, and per capita energy use is high.

Petroleum

West Virginia's annual crude oil production is minimal, typically accounting for less than 1 percent of total U.S. output. Much of the State's crude oil output is derived from stripper wells (wells producing less than 10 barrels of oil per day). West Virginia's only refinery, located in Newell in the far north of the State's panhandle, processes the majority of the crude oil produced in the State and the Appalachian Basin. The Newell refinery specializes primarily in lubricants and process oils but also produces motor gasoline and diesel fuel. No petroleum product pipelines serve West Virginia markets, and the State relies on barge deliveries to meet demand. The Ohio River, on the State's western border, serves as a major petroleum product transportation route. West Virginia is one of the few States that allow the statewide use of conventional motor gasoline. (Most States require the use of specific gasoline blends in non-attainment areas due to air-quality considerations.)

Natural Gas

Although the State's natural gas production is minimal, West Virginia's Marcellus shale region has experienced markedly increased new development over the past few years. However, compared to the State's total natural gas production, shale gas production remains a small percentage. West Virginia's underground natural gas storage capacity, including more than 30 facilities developed in depleted oil and gas fields, accounts for about 6 percent of the U.S. total. Because of this storage capacity, the State is an important supplier to the Northeast region during the winter months when natural gas demand peaks. The industrial sector is West Virginia's leading consumer of natural gas, accounting for almost 30 percent of the State's natural gas consumption. Nearly one-half of West Virginia households use natural gas as their main source of energy for home heating.

Coal, Electricity, and Renewables

West Virginia is the top coal-producing State east of the Mississippi River, and its output is second in the Nation after Wyoming. State production accounts for nearly one-third of U.S. production east of the Mississippi River and over one-tenth of total U.S. coal production. Although all West Virginia coal is bituminous, coal sulfur content varies across the State. Coal produced in southern West Virginia is low in sulfur, while coal produced in northern West Virginia is high in sulfur. West Virginia leads the Nation in coal production from underground mines, which account for about 55 percent of State production. Large shipments of coal move in and out of the State primarily by rail and barge. West Virginia delivers coal to more than 25 States, most of which are on the East Coast and in the Midwest. Over 90 percent of the coal consumed in West Virginia is used for electricity generation, while the rest is mostly consumed in industrial and coke plants.

Coal-fired plants account for nearly all of West Virginia's electricity generation. Several small hydroelectric facilities account for most of the remaining power production. West Virginia electricity production is high, and, although more than one-third of West Virginia households use electricity as their primary source for home heating, State electricity consumption is low. West Virginia ranks second in the Nation after Pennsylvania in net interstate electricity exports. West Virginia does not have a renewable portfolio standard. However, the State has adopted a net metering policy to credit customers' utility bills for electricity they provide to the grid generated from renewable sources.

Source: U.S. Energy Information Administration, October 2009

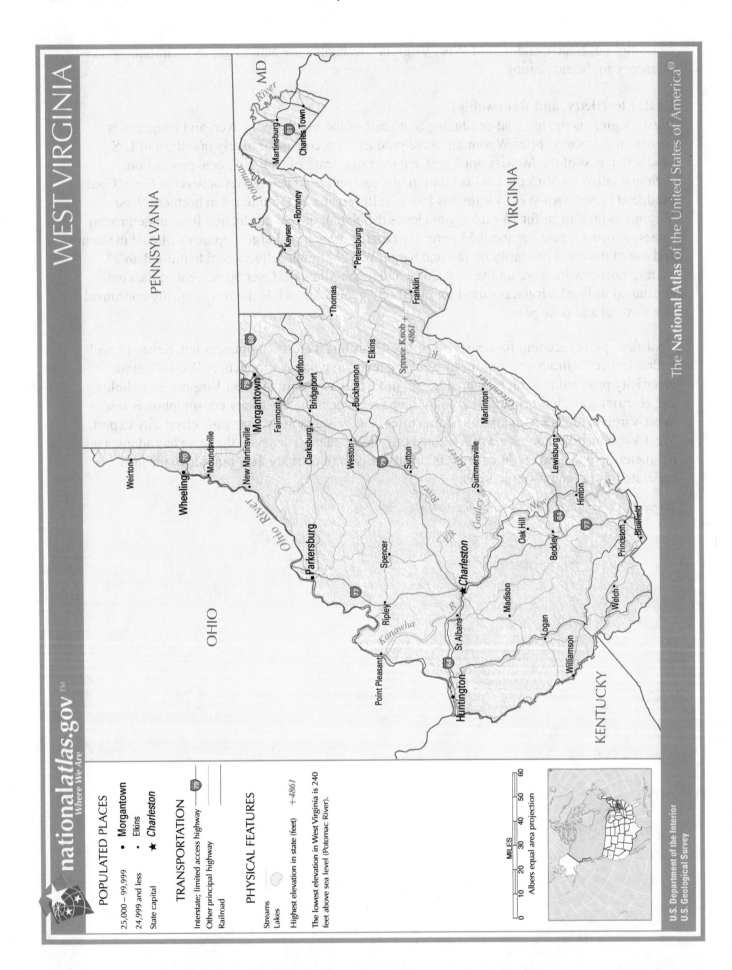

WEST VIRGINIA

nationalatlas.gov™
Where We Are

POPULATED PLACES

25,000 – 99,999   • Morgantown
24,999 and less   • Elkins
State capital   ★ *Charleston*

TRANSPORTATION

Interstate; limited access highway
Other principal highway
Railroad

PHYSICAL FEATURES

Streams
Lakes
Highest elevation in state (feet)   +4861

The lowest elevation in West Virginia is 240
feet above sea level (Potomac River).

MILES
0 10 20 30 40 50 60
Albers equal area projection

U.S. Department of the Interior
U.S. Geological Survey

PENNSYLVANIA

MD

VIRGINIA

OHIO

KENTUCKY

Spruce Knob +4861

Weirton
Wheeling
Moundsville
New Martinsville
Morgantown
Fairmont
Grafton
Bridgeport
Clarksburg
Buckhannon
Weston
Elkins
Thomas
Parkersburg
Spencer
Ripley
Point Pleasant
Huntington
St Albans
Charleston
Madison
Sutton
Summersville
Marlinton
Oak Hill
Beckley
Logan
Williamson
Welch
Princeton
Bluefield
Hinton
Lewisburg
Franklin
Petersburg
Keyser
Romney
Martinsburg
Charles Town

Potomac River
Ohio River
Kanawha River
Elk River
Gauley River
New River
Greenbrier River

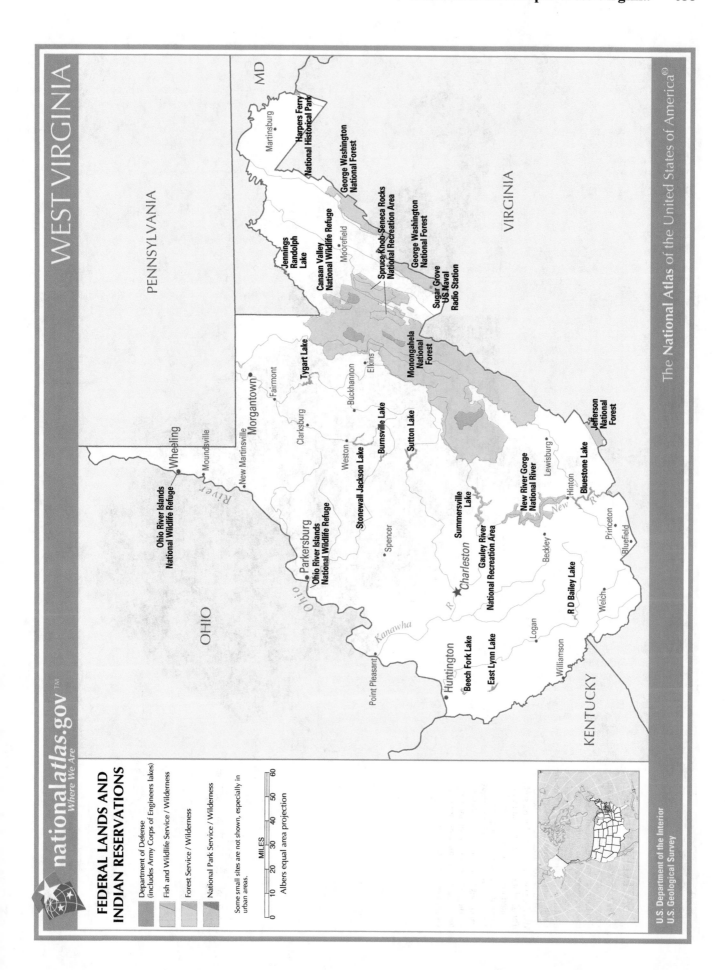

WEST VIRGINIA

nationalatlas.gov™
Where We Are

**FEDERAL LANDS AND
INDIAN RESERVATIONS**

Department of Defense
(includes Army Corps of Engineers lakes)

Fish and Wildlife Service / Wilderness

Forest Service / Wilderness

National Park Service / Wilderness

Some small sites are not shown, especially in
urban areas.

MILES

0   10   20   30   40   50   60

Albers equal area projection

The National Atlas of the United States of America©

U.S. Department of the Interior
U.S. Geological Survey

PENNSYLVANIA

OHIO

MD

VIRGINIA

KENTUCKY

Martinsburg

Harpers Ferry
National Historical Park

George Washington
National Forest

Jennings
Randolph
Lake

Canaan Valley
National Wildlife Refuge

Moorefield

Spruce Knob-Seneca Rocks
National Recreation Area

George Washington
National Forest

Sugar Grove
US Naval
Radio Station

Monongahela
National Forest

Tygart Lake

Fairmont

Elkins

Buckhannon

Morgantown

Wheeling

Moundsville

New Martinsville

Clarksburg

Weston

Burnsville Lake

Sutton Lake

Jefferson
National
Forest

Bluestone Lake

Lewisburg

Hinton

New River Gorge
National River

New River

Ohio River Islands
National Wildlife Refuge

Parkersburg

Ohio River Islands
National Wildlife Refuge

Stonewall Jackson Lake

Spencer

Charleston

Summersville
Lake

Gauley River
National Recreation Area

Princeton

Bluefield

Beckley

R D Bailey Lake

Welch

Logan

Kanawha

Huntington

Beech Fork Lake

East Lynn Lake

Williamson

Point Pleasant

Ohio River

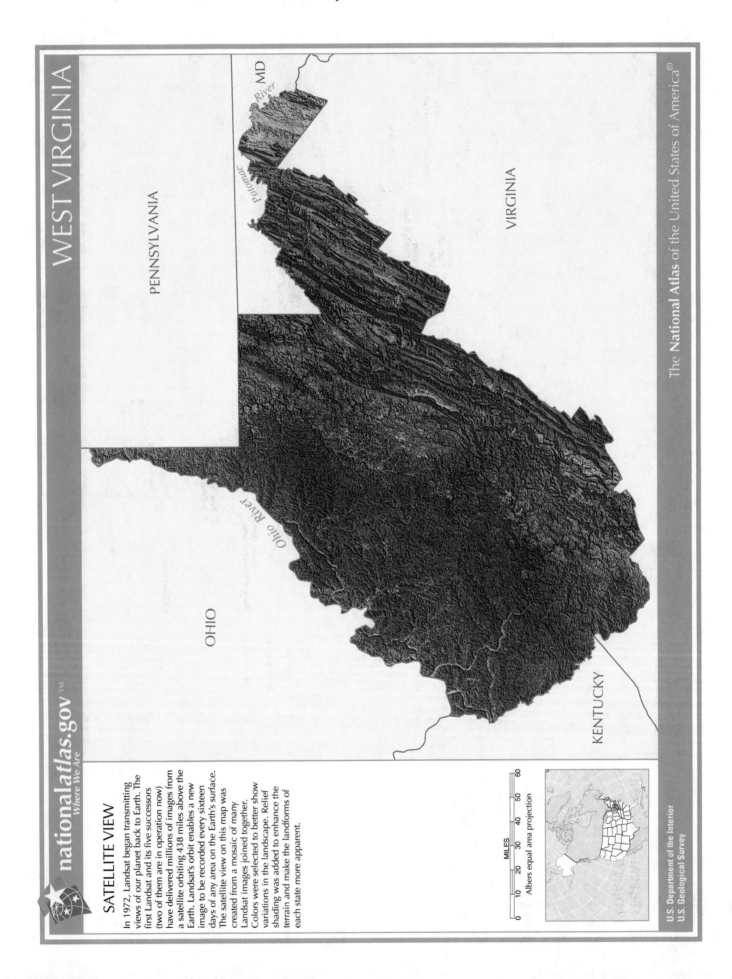

WEST VIRGINIA

nationalatlas.gov ™
Where We Are

SATELLITE VIEW

In 1972, Landsat began transmitting views of our planet back to Earth. The first Landsat and its five successors (two of them are in operation now) have delivered millions of images from a satellite orbiting 438 miles above the Earth. Landsat's orbit enables a new image to be recorded every sixteen days of any area on the Earth's surface. The satellite view on this map was created from a mosaic of many Landsat images joined together. Colors were selected to better show variations in the landscape. Relief shading was added to enhance the terrain and make the landforms of each state more apparent.

PENNSYLVANIA

MD

Potomac River

Ohio River

OHIO

VIRGINIA

KENTUCKY

MILES

0   10   20   30   40   50   60

Albers equal area projection

U.S. Department of the Interior
U.S. Geological Survey

The **National Atlas** of the United States of America®

Wisconsin

Topic	Value	Time Period
Total Surface Area (acres)	35,920,000	2007
Land	34,627,800	2007
Federal Land	1,845,300	2007
Owned	90,621	FY 2009
Leased	16,215	FY 2009
Otherwise Managed	3,856	FY 2009
National Forest	1,534,000	September 2006
National Wilderness	79,943	October 2011
Non-Federal Land, Developed	2,724,900	2007
Non-Federal Land, Rural	30,057,600	2007
Water	1,292,200	2007
National Natural Landmarks	18	December 2010
National Historic Landmarks	40	December 2010
National Register of Historic Places	2,214	December 2010
National Parks	2	December 2010
Visitors to National Parks	251,145	2010
Historic Places Documented by the National Park Service	679	December 2010
Archeological Sites in National Parks	264	December 2010
Threatened and Endangered Species in National Parks	6	December 2010
Economic Benefit from National Park Tourism (dollars)	25,044,000	2009
Conservation Reserve Program (acres)	372,765	October 2011
Land and Water Conservation Fund Grants (dollars)	74,743,616	Since 1965
Historic Preservation Grants (dollars)	26,510,468	2010
Community Conservation and Recreation Projects	66	Since 1987
Federal Acres Transferred for Local Parks and Recreation	2,806	Since 1948
Crude Petroleum Production (millions of barrels)	Not Available	2010
Crude Oil Proved Reserves (millions of barrels)	Not Available	2009
Natural Gas Reserves (billions of cubic feet)	Not Available	2009
Natural Gas Liquid Reserves (millions of barrels)	Not Available	2008
Natural Gas Marketed Production (billions of cubic feet)	Not Available	2009
Coal Reserves (millions of short tons)	Not Available	2009

Sources: U.S. Department of the Interior, National Park Service, State Profiles, December 2010; United States Department of Agriculture, Natural Resources Conservation Service, 2007 National Resources Inventory; U.S. General Services Administration, Federal Real Property Council, FY 2009 Federal Real Property Report, September 2010; University of Montana, www.wilderness.net; U.S. Department of Agriculture, Farm Services Agency, Conservation Reserve Program, October 2011; U.S Census Bureau, 2012 Statistical Abstract of the United States

Wisconsin Energy Overview and Analysis

Quick Facts
- Wisconsin produces ethanol at several plants in the central and southern portions of the State.
- The Unit 1 reactor at the Point Beach nuclear plant is one of the oldest operating reactors in the United States.
- Coal dominates electricity generation in Wisconsin, fueling about two-thirds of the State's power plants.
- Energy-intensive industries in Wisconsin include forest products and metal casting, and Wisconsin's industrial sector is the largest energy-consuming sector in the State.

Analysis

Resources and Consumption

Wisconsin has some renewable energy resources but lacks more conventional fossil fuel resources. Several rivers that cross the State provide hydroelectric power potential, and the State's high corn production allows Wisconsin to produce substantial amounts of ethanol. Wisconsin's population and energy consumption are about average among U.S. States. The industrial sector leads total State energy consumption. Energy-intensive industries in Wisconsin include forest products and metal casting.

Petroleum

Wisconsin has one small refinery on Lake Superior. It receives crude oil supply from the Lakehead Pipeline System, which originates in western Canada and delivers crude to eastern Ontario and throughout the Great Lakes region. Refineries in the metropolitan areas of Chicago and Minneapolis provide petroleum products for most of Wisconsin's market. The southeastern corner of Wisconsin requires the use of reformulated motor gasoline blended with ethanol. Wisconsin produces a substantial amount of ethanol at several ethanol plants in the southern and central portions of the State.

Natural Gas

Natural gas markets in Wisconsin receive supplies primarily from Louisiana, Texas, Oklahoma, and Kansas, with the remaining gas coming from Canadian sources. The ANR Pipeline, Northern Natural Gas Co., Viking Gas Transmission Co., the Natural Gas Pipeline Co. of America, and Guardian Pipeline, all of which run through a major hub in Joliet, Illinois, provide most of the natural gas supplied to Wisconsin. The Great Lakes Gas Transmission Company pipeline transports natural gas from Canada across Minnesota, Wisconsin, and Michigan and delivers most of the gas back to Canada at the Michigan/Ontario border. Wisconsin's residential and industrial sectors lead the State's natural gas consumption. Natural gas dominates the home heating market, as roughly two-thirds of Wisconsin households use natural gas as their primary fuel for home heating.

Coal, Electricity, and Renewables

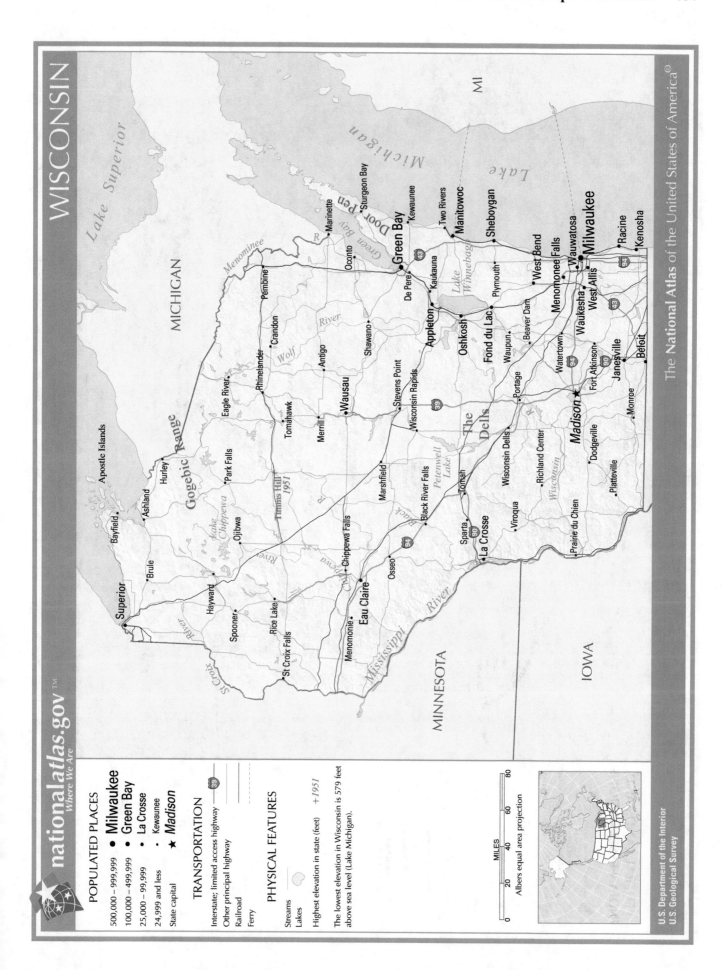

nationalatlas.gov™
Where We Are

WISCONSIN

POPULATED PLACES

500,000 – 999,999   ● **Milwaukee**
100,000 – 499,999   ● **Green Bay**
25,000 – 99,999   ● La Crosse
24,999 and less   · Kewaunee
State capital   ★ *Madison*

TRANSPORTATION

Interstate; limited access highway   ⬡39
Other principal highway
Railroad
Ferry

PHYSICAL FEATURES

Streams
Lakes
Highest elevation in state (feet)   +1951

The lowest elevation in Wisconsin is 579 feet
above sea level (Lake Michigan).

MILES
0   20   40   60   80
Albers equal area projection

U.S. Department of the Interior
U.S. Geological Survey

The **National Atlas** of the United States of America®

MICHIGAN

Lake Superior

Apostle Islands
Bayfield
Brule
Superior
Hayward
Spooner
Rice Lake
St Croix Falls
Menomonie
Eau Claire
Osseo
Chippewa Falls
Ojibwa
Park Falls
Hurley
Ashland

Gogebic Range

Lake Chippewa

Timms Hill
1951

Eagle River
Rhinelander
Tomahawk
Merrill
Crandon
Pembine

Wolf River

Antigo
Shawano
Wausau
Stevens Point
Wisconsin Rapids
Marshfield
Black River Falls
Sparta
La Crosse
Tomah
Viroqua
Prairie du Chien

Menominee R

Marinette
Oconto

Green Bay

Door Pen

Sturgeon Bay
Kewaunee
Two Rivers
Manitowoc
Sheboygan

Green Bay
De Pere
Kaukauna
Appleton
Oshkosh

Lake Winnebago

Fond du Lac
Plymouth
Waupun
Beaver Dam
West Bend

The Dells

Wisconsin Dells
Richland Center
Dodgeville
Platteville

Madison
Watertown
Portage
Fort Atkinson
Janesville
Monroe
Beloit

Menomonee Falls
Wauwatosa
Milwaukee
West Allis
Waukesha
Racine
Kenosha

Lake Michigan

MI

MINNESOTA

IOWA

Mississippi River

St Croix River

Chippewa R

Black R

Wisconsin R

Petenwell Lake

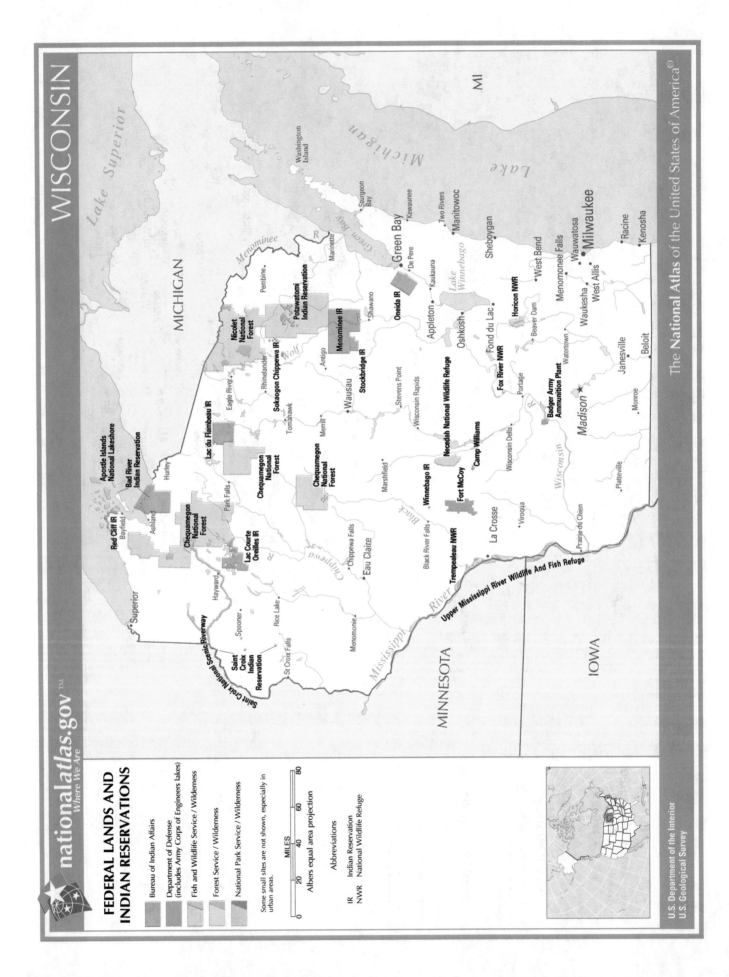

WISCONSIN

MICHIGAN

MI

Lake Superior

Lake Michigan

Washington Island

Sturgeon Bay

Menominee R

Green Bay

Kewaunee

Two Rivers

Manitowoc

Marinette

Pembine

De Pere

Sheboygan

Kaukauna

Oneida IR

Potawatomi Indian Reservation

Nicolet National Forest

Shawano

Lake Winnebago

Appleton

West Bend

Menomonee Falls

Menominee IR

Antigo

Stockbridge IR

Oshkosh

Fond du Lac

Horicon NWR

Wauwatosa

Milwaukee

West Allis

Rhinelander

Sokaogon Chippewa IR

Wolf

Wausau

Stevens Point

Fox River NWR

Beaver Dam

Waukesha

Racine

Kenosha

Eagle River

Lac du Flambeau IR

Merrill

Tomahawk

Wisconsin Rapids

Portage

Badger Army Ammunition Plant

Watertown

Janesville

Beloit

Necedah National Wildlife Refuge

Camp Williams

Madison

Monroe

Chequamegon National Forest

Park Falls

Chequamegon National Forest

Marshfield

Winnebago IR

Fort McCoy

Wisconsin Dells

Wisconsin

Platteville

Apostle Islands National Lakeshore

Bad River Indian Reservation

Hurley

Ashland

Bayfield

Red Cliff IR

Chippewa Falls

Eau Claire

Black River Falls

Viroqua

La Crosse

Trempealeau NWR

Prairie du Chien

Lac Courte Oreilles IR

Hayward

Rice Lake

Black

Upper Mississippi River Wildlife And Fish Refuge

Superior

Spooner

Saint Croix National Scenic Riverway

Saint Croix Indian Reservation

Menomonie

St Croix Falls

Chippewa

Mississippi River

MINNESOTA

IOWA

FEDERAL LANDS AND INDIAN RESERVATIONS

Bureau of Indian Affairs

Department of Defense (includes Army Corps of Engineers lakes)

Fish and Wildlife Service / Wilderness

Forest Service / Wilderness

National Park Service / Wilderness

Some small sites are not shown, especially in urban areas.

MILES

0   20   40   60   80

Albers equal area projection

Abbreviations

IR   Indian Reservation
NWR   National Wildlife Refuge

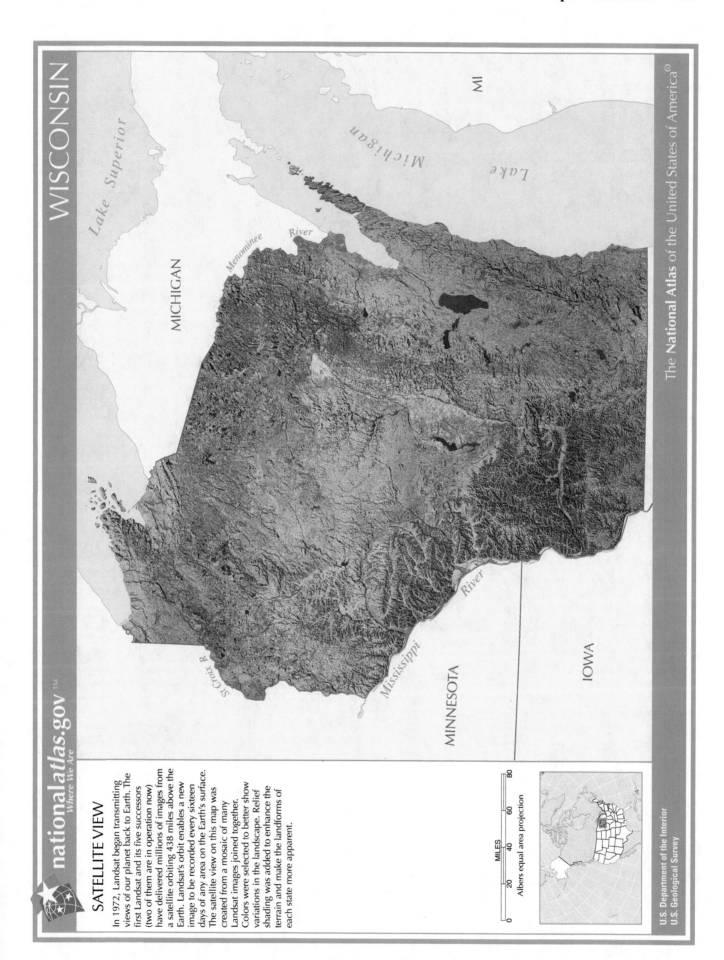

WISCONSIN

SATELLITE VIEW

In 1972, Landsat began transmitting views of our planet back to Earth. The first Landsat and its five successors (two of them are in operation now) have delivered millions of images from a satellite orbiting 438 miles above the Earth. Landsat's orbit enables a new image to be recorded every sixteen days of any area on the Earth's surface. The satellite view on this map was created from a mosaic of many Landsat images joined together. Colors were selected to better show variations in the landscape. Relief shading was added to enhance the terrain and make the landforms of each state more apparent.

MILES

0   20   40   60   80

Albers equal area projection

U.S. Department of the Interior
U.S. Geological Survey

The **National Atlas** of the United States of America®

Lake Superior

MICHIGAN

Menominee River

Lake Michigan

MI

St Croix R

Mississippi River

River

MINNESOTA

IOWA

Wyoming

Topic	Value	Time Period
Total Surface Area (acres)	62,602,800	2007
Land	62,161,700	2007
Federal Land	28,748,000	2007
Owned	984,024	FY 2009
Leased	4,689	FY 2009
Otherwise Managed	61,544	FY 2009
National Forest	9,242,000	September 2006
National Wilderness	3,111,232	October 2011
Non-Federal Land, Developed	681,100	2007
Non-Federal Land, Rural	32,732,600	2007
Water	441,100	2007
National Natural Landmarks	6	December 2010
National Historic Landmarks	24	December 2010
National Register of Historic Places	512	December 2010
National Parks	7	December 2010
Visitors to National Parks	6,307,997	2010
Historic Places Documented by the National Park Service	481	December 2010
Archeological Sites in National Parks	2,042	December 2010
Threatened and Endangered Species in National Parks	5	December 2010
Economic Benefit from National Park Tourism (dollars)	570,480,000	2009
Conservation Reserve Program (acres)	215,797	October 2011
Land and Water Conservation Fund Grants (dollars)	33,849,595	Since 1965
Historic Preservation Grants (dollars)	17,857,718	2010
Community Conservation and Recreation Projects	13	Since 1987
Federal Acres Transferred for Local Parks and Recreation	793	Since 1948
Crude Petroleum Production (millions of barrels)	52	2010
Crude Oil Proved Reserves (millions of barrels)	583	2009
Natural Gas Reserves (billions of cubic feet)	35,283	2009
Natural Gas Liquid Reserves (millions of barrels)	1,121	2008
Natural Gas Marketed Production (billions of cubic feet)	2,335	2009
Coal Reserves (millions of short tons)	61,563	2009

Sources: *U.S. Department of the Interior, National Park Service, State Profiles, December 2010; United States Department of Agriculture, Natural Resources Conservation Service, 2007 National Resources Inventory; U.S. General Services Administration, Federal Real Property Council, FY 2009 Federal Real Property Report, September 2010; University of Montana, www.wilderness.net; U.S. Department of Agriculture, Farm Services Agency, Conservation Reserve Program, October 2011; U.S Census Bureau, 2012 Statistical Abstract of the United States*

Wyoming Energy Overview and Analysis

Quick Facts

- The Powder River Basin, most of which lies in northeastern Wyoming, is the largest coal-producing region in the Nation, accounting for approximately 40 percent of all coal mined in the United States.
- More than 30 States receive coal from Wyoming, and several Midwestern and Southern States are highly or entirely dependent on Wyoming's coal supply.
- Wyoming is one of the top natural gas-producing States in the Nation.
- Wyoming produces a substantial amount of wind-generated electricity and the Southern Wyoming Corridor is one of the most favorable locations for wind power development in the Nation.
- The Governors of four Western States are pursuing a 1,300-mile high-capacity power line that would allow Wyoming and other Rocky Mountain States to transmit as much as 12 thousand megawatts of electricity to California.

Analysis

Resources and Consumption

Wyoming's geologic basins contain some of the largest fossil fuel deposits in the United States. Wyoming's estimated recoverable coal reserves are second only to Montana's, its dry natural gas reserves are second only to those in Texas, and its crude oil reserves are substantial. Wyoming has over a dozen of the Nation's largest oil and gas fields, including the Pinedale and Jonah natural gas fields, which rank among the top 10 in the Nation.

Wyoming also has substantial wind power potential. The Southern Wyoming Corridor, where a gap in the Rocky Mountains channels strong winds across the plains, is ideally suited for wind power development. Wind power resources also exist in the northwestern part of the State. Although Wyoming's aggregate energy demand is low, per capita energy consumption is the second highest in the Nation due to an energy-intensive economy that is dependent on fossil fuel extraction, processing, and transportation. The industrial sector, which includes Wyoming's mining, oil, and gas industries, is the State's leading consumer of energy.

Petroleum

Wyoming typically accounts for nearly 3 percent of U.S. oil production. The State is a transportation crossroads for Canadian crude oil imports and local Rocky Mountain production flowing to U.S. Midwest and Mountain markets. The State has five oil refineries, located in the southern and eastern parts of the State. Wyoming's total petroleum consumption is low, and refineries deliver much of their product to markets in neighboring States. Wyoming is one of the few States in the Nation that allow the statewide use of conventional motor gasoline. (Most States require the use of specific gasoline blends in non-attainment areas due to air-quality considerations.)

Although its proven crude oil reserves account for only about 3 percent of the U.S. total, Wyoming has enormous deposits of oil shale rock, known as marlstone, which can be converted into crude oil through a process called destructive distillation. The Green River Formation, a group of basins in Colorado, Wyoming, and Utah, contains the largest known oil shale deposits in the world. Wyoming's oil shale deposits, concentrated in the Green River and Washakie Basins in the southwestern part of the State, contain an estimated 300 billion barrels of oil, equal to about one-fourth of the world's proven oil reserves. Although this natural resource holds tremendous promise, oil shale development remains speculative and faces several major obstacles involving technological feasibility, economic viability, resource ownership, and environmental considerations. Wyoming's oil shale deposits are less favorable for commercial extraction than those in Utah and Colorado because they are generally situated in thinner, less continuous layers.

Natural Gas

Wyoming is one of the top natural gas-producing States in the Nation and typically accounts for almost one-tenth of U.S. natural gas production. Drilling activities take place throughout the State, but most of Wyoming's production comes from fields in the Greater Green River Basin.

Recovery of coalbed methane (unconventional natural gas produced from coal seams) from the Powder River Basin has grown rapidly since the late 1990s and now accounts for over one-fifth of State natural gas production. Wyoming is the second leading coalbed methane producer in the United States, behind only Colorado. The full potential of Powder River Basin coalbed methane resources has not been tapped due to the basin's few pipelines and rugged terrain. The Bureau of Land Management approved new drilling in the basin in 2003, which may encourage increased production from that area.

Unlike other major U.S. natural gas-producing regions, Wyoming's natural gas production is expanding. State consumption is low and Wyoming generally consumes less than one-tenth of the natural gas it produces. Major pipeline systems deliver the majority of Wyoming's supply to markets in the Midwest and California, and natural gas producers have recently completed construction on a new pipeline to ease transportation constraints and help move Wyoming's increasing output to the Midwest. The new system, known as the Rockies Express Pipeline, originates in northwestern Colorado and adds supply in Wyoming's Greater Green River Basin for delivery to Midwest markets.

Coal, Electricity, and Renewables

The Powder River Basin in northeastern Wyoming is the largest coal-producing region in the Nation, accounting for nearly two-fifths of all coal mined in the United States. Powder River Basin coal seams are thick and facilitate surface mining, making extraction easy and efficient. As a result, the price of Powder River Basin coal at the mine mouth is less than that of coal produced elsewhere in the Nation. Powder River Basin coal also has lower sulfur content than other coal varieties, making it attractive for electricity generators that must comply with strict emission standards.

More than thirty States receive coal from Wyoming, and several Midwestern and Southern States are highly or entirely dependent on Wyoming supply. Two railroads, operating the Powder River Basin Joint Line, move coal out of the Powder River Basin. In May 2005, three train derailments severely damaged the Joint Line, causing the railroads to curtail promised deliveries to electric utilities in several States. The affected utilities were forced to either buy more expensive coal supplies from other sources or reduce coal use by using other, more expensive fuels. A second railroad line serving the Powder River Basin has been proposed to provide an alternative coal transportation route and alleviate bottlenecks on the Joint Line.

Coal-fired power plants dominate Wyoming electricity generation. Small hydroelectric facilities also contribute to the electric power grid and Wyoming has become a substantial producer of wind energy. Although most of Wyoming's wind power facilities are in the southeastern part of the State, its largest wind facility is situated in the southwest corner of the State. State electricity demand is low, and Wyoming exports electricity to neighboring States. Electricity transfers may reach as far as California in the future. In April 2005, four western State governors agreed to develop a 1,300-mile high-capacity power line from Wyoming to California that would allow as much as 12 thousand megawatts of electricity to flow from the energy-rich Rocky Mountain region to high-demand markets in California. A feasibility study was released in 2007 that supports the development of this transmission line project and a second phase development study is currently underway.

Source: U.S. Energy Information Administration, October 2009

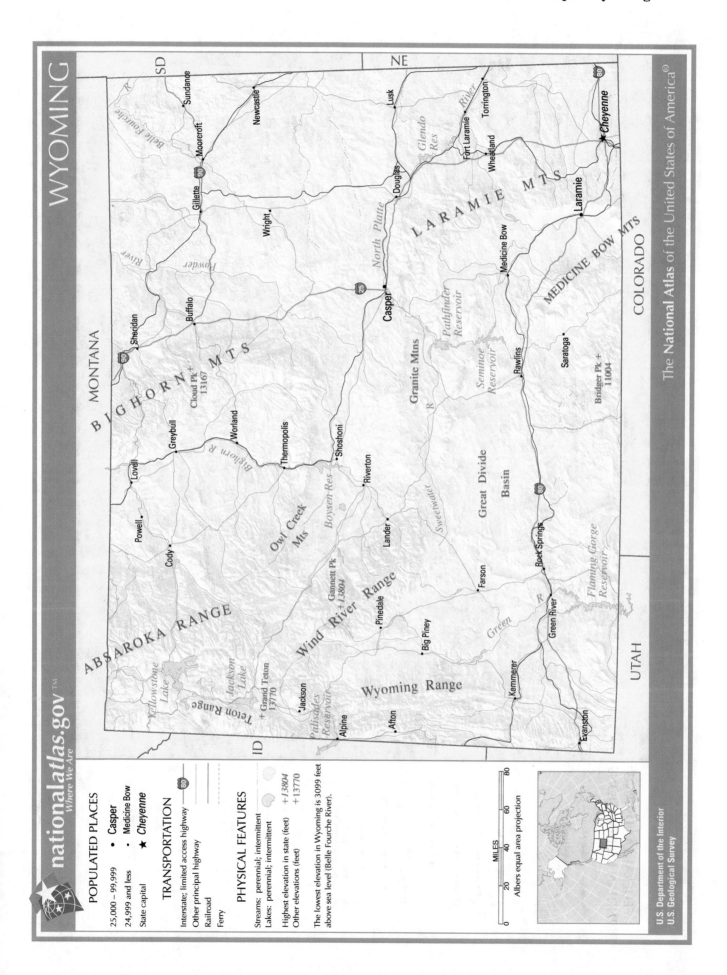

U.S. Department of the Interior
U.S. Geological Survey

The National Atlas of the United States of America®

WYOMING

nationalatlas.gov ™
Where We Are

POPULATED PLACES

25,000 – 99,999   • Casper
24,999 and less   · Medicine Bow
State capital   ★ *Cheyenne*

TRANSPORTATION

Interstate; limited access highway ──[80]──
Other principal highway
Railroad
Ferry

PHYSICAL FEATURES

Streams: perennial; intermittent
Lakes: perennial; intermittent
Highest elevation in state (feet)   +13804
Other elevations (feet)   +13770

The lowest elevation in Wyoming is 3099 feet above sea level (Belle Fourche River).

MILES
0   20   40   60   80

Albers equal area projection

MONTANA

SD

NE

ID

UTAH

COLORADO

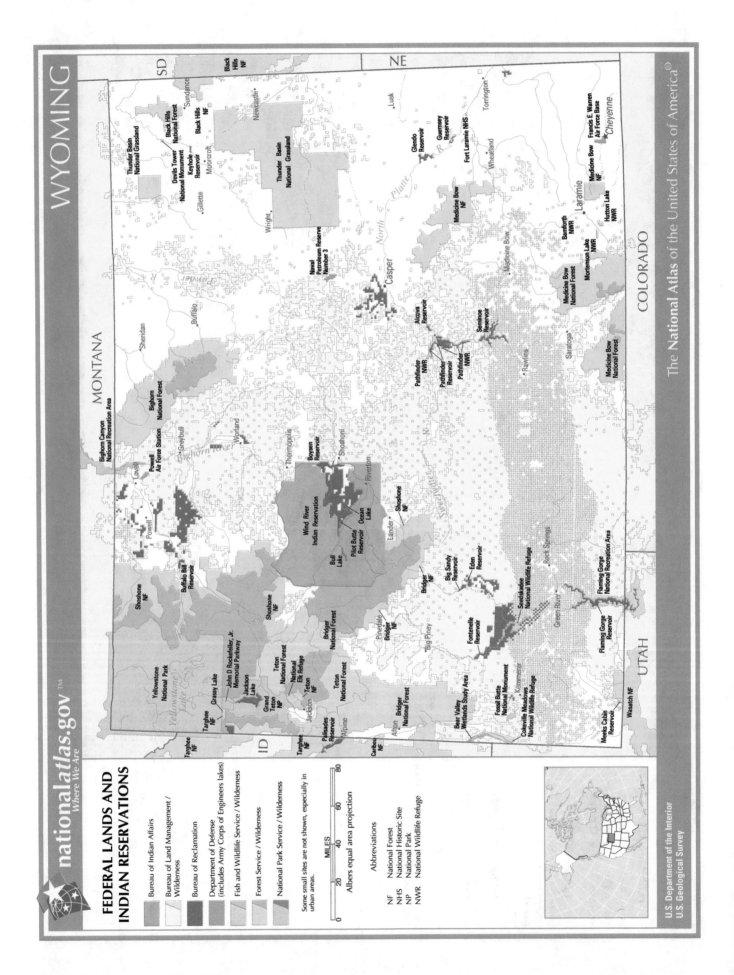

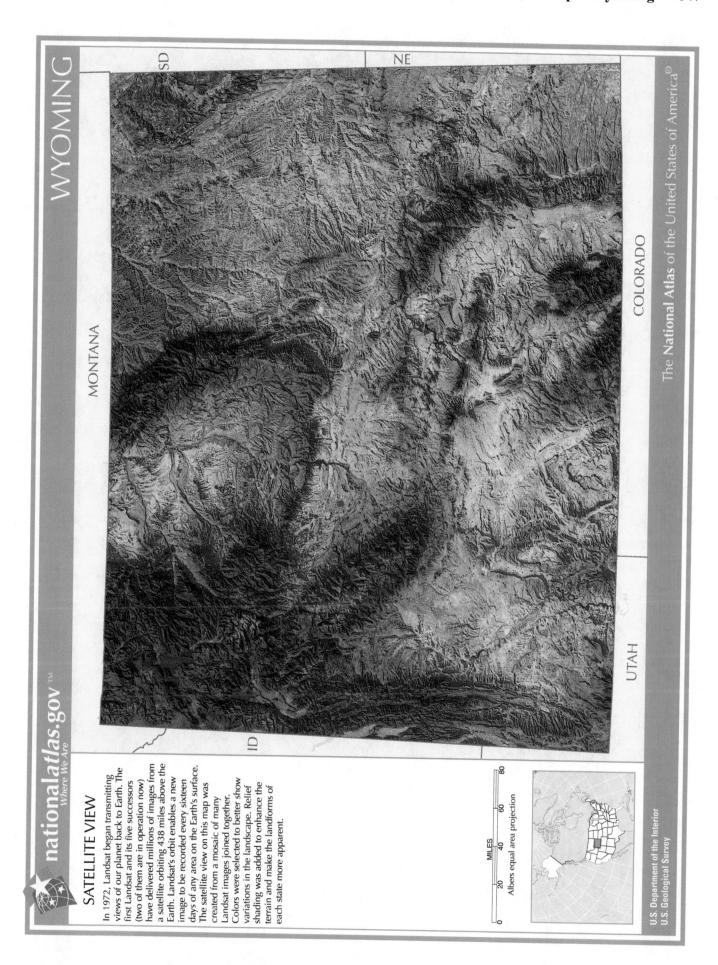

WYOMING

nationalatlas.gov™
Where We Are

SATELLITE VIEW

In 1972, Landsat began transmitting views of our planet back to Earth. The first Landsat and its five successors (two of them are in operation now) have delivered millions of images from a satellite orbiting 438 miles above the Earth. Landsat's orbit enables a new image to be recorded every sixteen days of any area on the Earth's surface. The satellite view on this map was created from a mosaic of many Landsat images joined together. Colors were selected to better show variations in the landscape. Relief shading was added to enhance the terrain and make the landforms of each state more apparent.

MONTANA

SD

NE

ID

UTAH

COLORADO

The **National Atlas** of the United States of America©

MILES

0   20   40   60   80

Albers equal area projection

U.S. Department of the Interior
U.S. Geological Survey

National Data, Maps and Rankings

This section begins with a chart of information that is significant to the nation's land and natural resources. Like the state charts in the previous section, it provides 31 pieces of data, including the total acres of land and water, and how much of that is federal land, either owned, leased, national forest or wilderness. This chart also gives the nation's total number of national landmarks and parks, acres in conservation programs, plus quantities of energy resources—oil, gas and coal. The Glossary on page 883 gives helpful definitions for many terms used throughout this book. Additional definitions, specifically relevant to this section, include:

- National Forest – land managed by the National Forest Service.

- National Wilderness – area of undeveloped federal land retaining its primeval character and influence, without permanent improvement or human habitation.

- National Natural Landmark – area that offers a best known example of a natural region's characteristic biotic or geologic features, including land or water communities, landforms, geological features, habitats of native species, or fossil evidence of the development of life on earth.

- Archeological Sites in National Parks – a site that contains objects of antiquity or cultural value relating to history or prehistory that warrant special protection.

- Conservation Reserve Program – a cost-share and rental payment program that encourages farmers to convert highly erodible cropland to vegetative cover.

- Land and Water Conservation Fund Grants – provides funds for the acquisition of land and water for recreation and the protection of national natural treasures in the form of parks and protected forest and wildlife areas.

Following the chart, are ten full-color maps that provide a visual understanding of the nation's federal land, under the management of various federal agencies, including the Bureau of Land Management, Bureau of Reclamation, Department of Defense, Fish and Wildlife Service, Forest Service, National Park Service, Department of the Interior, and Indian lands and reservations.

The Ranking Tables that follow the maps rank all 31 data points, by state, from top to bottom. You will see, for example, that while Texas has the most land of all the states, it falls 17th in federal land. New York has the most National Historic Landmarks and the most places on the National Register of Historic Places, and Pennsylvania has the most Historic Places Documented by the National Park Service, while South Dakota has the least. Further, Montana has the most coal reserves, with Texas at the top and Wisconsin at the bottom of the list for petroleum, crude oil and gas reserves.

United States

Topic	Value	Time Period
Total Surface Area[1] (acres)	1,937,664,200	2007
Land[1]	1,886,846,900	2007
Federal Land[1]	401,936,900	2007
Owned	36,306,584	FY 2009
Leased	835,796	FY 2009
Otherwise Managed	1,904,644	FY 2009
National Forest	206,379,000	September 2006
National Wilderness	109,502,960	October 2011
Non-Federal Land, Developed[1]	111,251,200	2007
Non-Federal Land, Rural[1]	1,373,658,800	2007
Water[1]	50,817,300	2007
National Natural Landmarks	569	December 2010
National Historic Landmarks	2,458	December 2010
National Register of Historic Places	85,871	December 2010
National Parks	444	December 2010
Visitors to National Parks	279,337,866	2010
Historic Places Documented by the National Park Service	39,500	December 2010
Archeological Sites in National Parks	71,192	December 2010
Threatened and Endangered Species in National Parks	725	December 2010
Economic Benefit from National Park Tourism (dollars)	10,627,746,000	2009
Conservation Reserve Program[2] (acres)	29,562,573	October 2011
Land and Water Conservation Fund Grants (dollars)	3,824,947,595	Since 1965
Historic Preservation Grants (dollars)	1,384,176,830	2010
Community Conservation and Recreation Projects	2,524	Since 1987
Federal Acres Transferred for Local Parks and Recreation	164,635	Since 1948
Crude Petroleum Production[3] (millions of barrels)	2,012	2010
Crude Oil Proved Reserves[3] (millions of barrels)	20,682	2009
Natural Gas Reserves[3] (billions of cubic feet)	272,509	2009
Natural Gas Liquid Reserves[3] (millions of barrels)	9,275	2008
Natural Gas Marketed Production[3,4] (billions of cubic feet)	21,604	2009
Coal Reserves[3] (millions of short tons)	486,102	2009

Note: All figures were calculated by totaling available state figures except if noted otherwise; (1) figures do not include Alaska, Hawaii and District of Columbia; (2) figures do not include Arizona, District of Columbia, Nevada and Rhode Island; (3) figures include Federal offshore and state data not shown separately; (4) excludes nonhydrocarbon gases
Sources: U.S. Department of the Interior, National Park Service, State Profiles, December 2010; United States Department of Agriculture, Natural Resources Conservation Service, 2007 National Resources Inventory; U.S. General Services Administration, Federal Real Property Council, FY 2009 Federal Real Property Report, September 2010; University of Montana, www.wilderness.net; U.S. Department of Agriculture, Farm Services Agency, Conservation Reserve Program, October 2011; U.S Census Bureau, 2012 Statistical Abstract of the United States

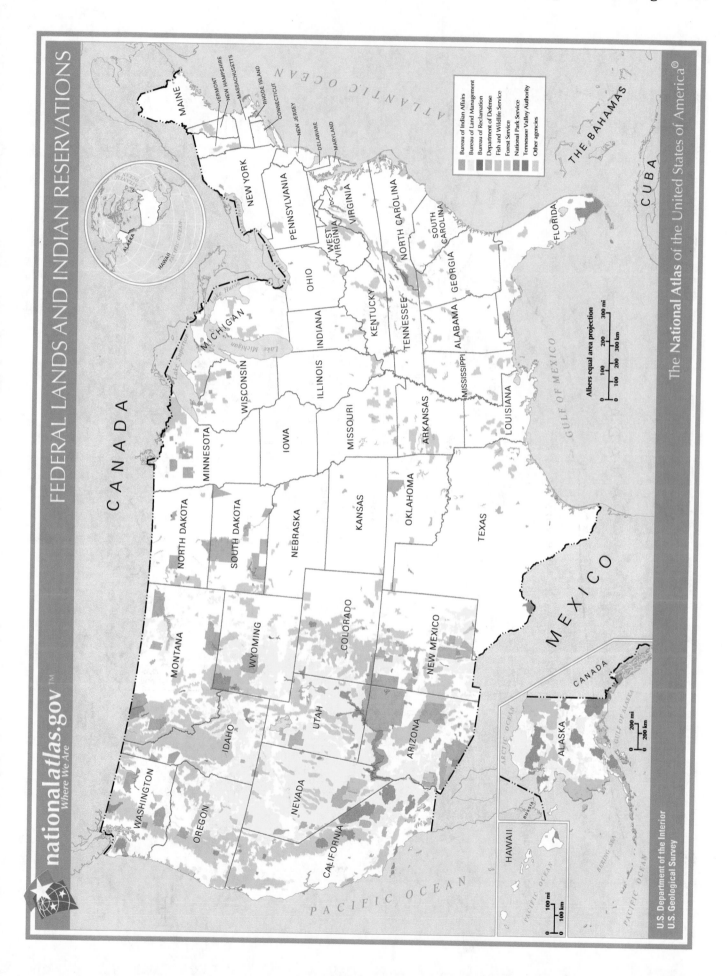

FEDERAL LANDS AND INDIAN RESERVATIONS

nationalatlas.gov™
Where We Are

Bureau of Indian Affairs
Bureau of Land Management
Bureau of Reclamation
Department of Defense
Fish and Wildlife Service
Forest Service
National Park Service
Tennessee Valley Authority
Other agencies

Albers equal area projection

The **National Atlas** of the United States of America©

U.S. Department of the Interior
U.S. Geological Survey

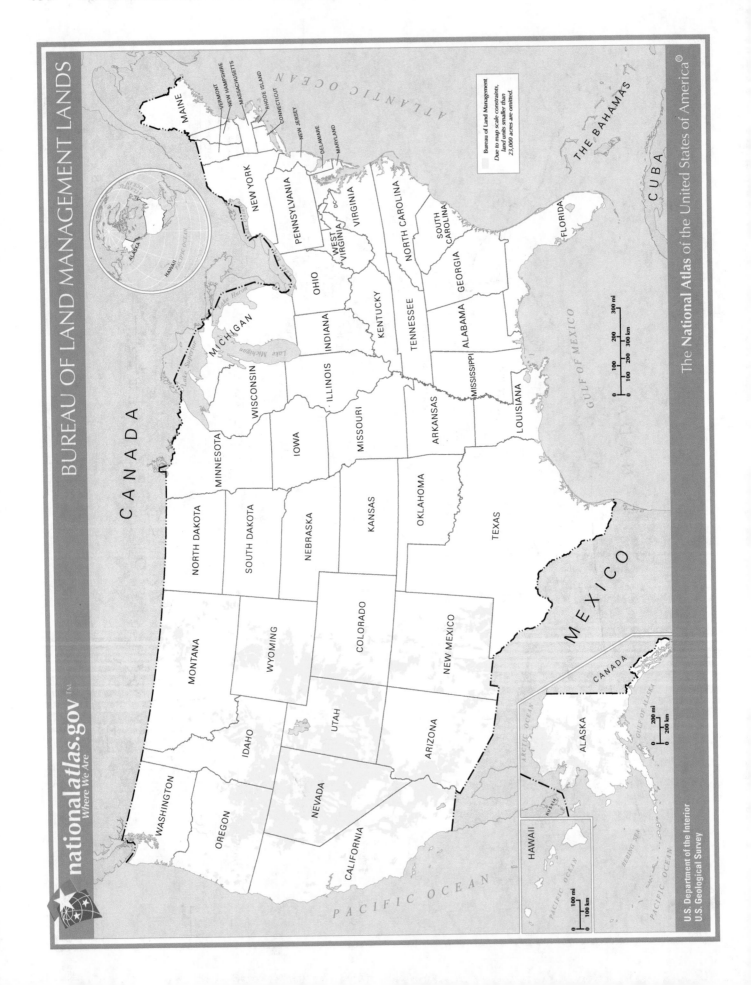

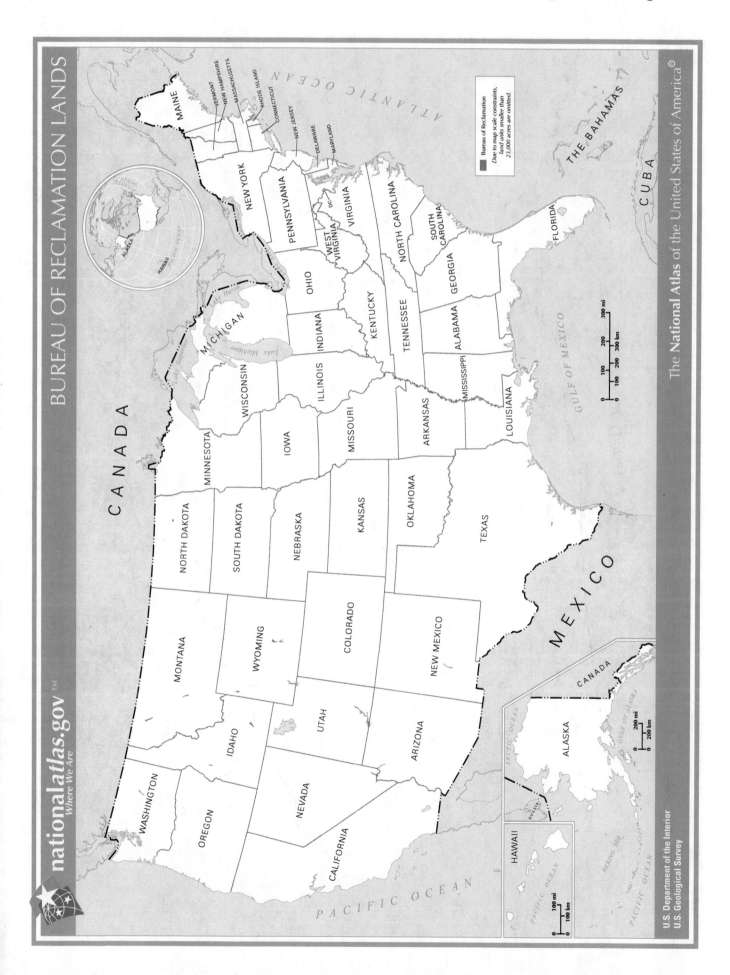

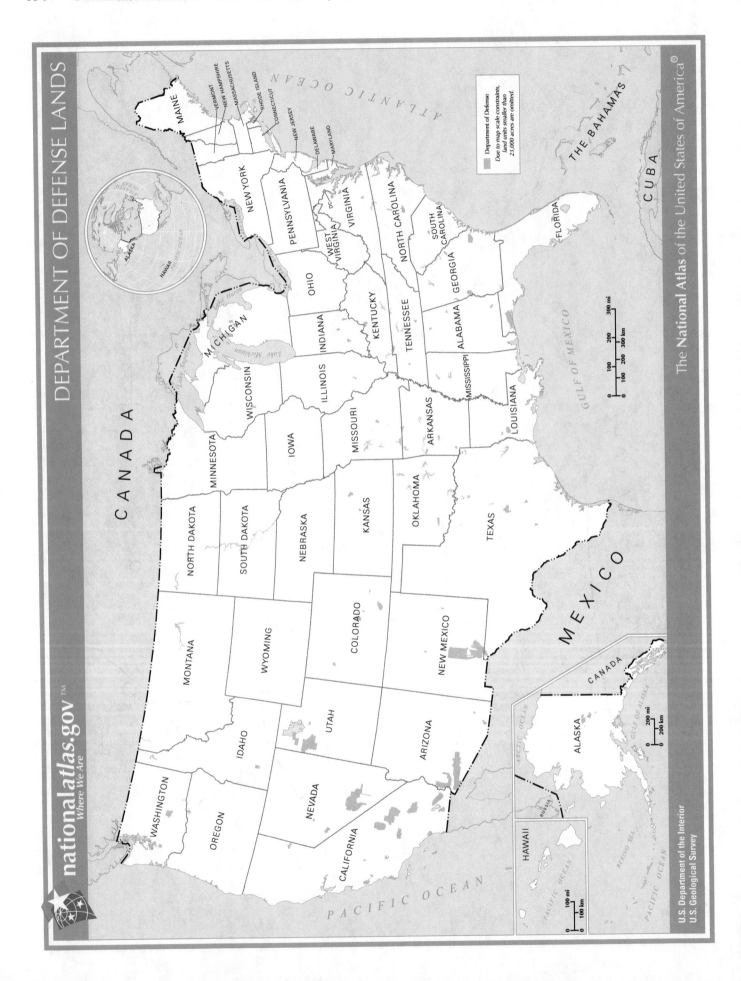

The **National Atlas** of the United States of America®

U.S. Department of the Interior
U.S. Geological Survey

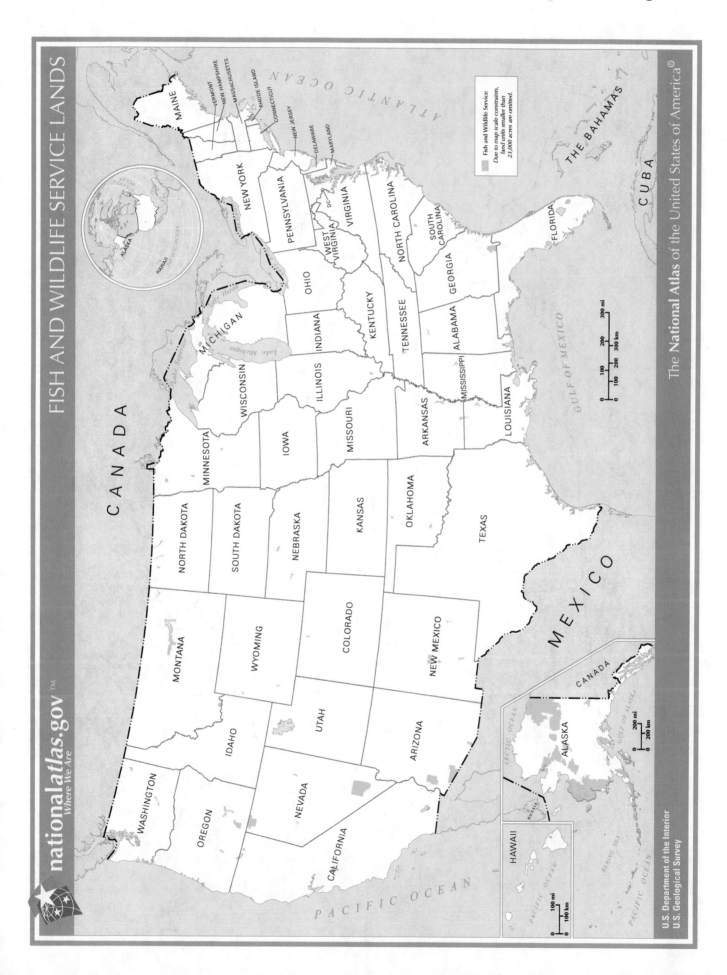

FISH AND WILDLIFE SERVICE LANDS

Fish and Wildlife Service

Due to map scale constraints,
land units smaller than
23,000 acres are omitted.

nationalatlas.gov™
Where We Are

The **National Atlas** of the United States of America©

U.S. Department of the Interior
U.S. Geological Survey

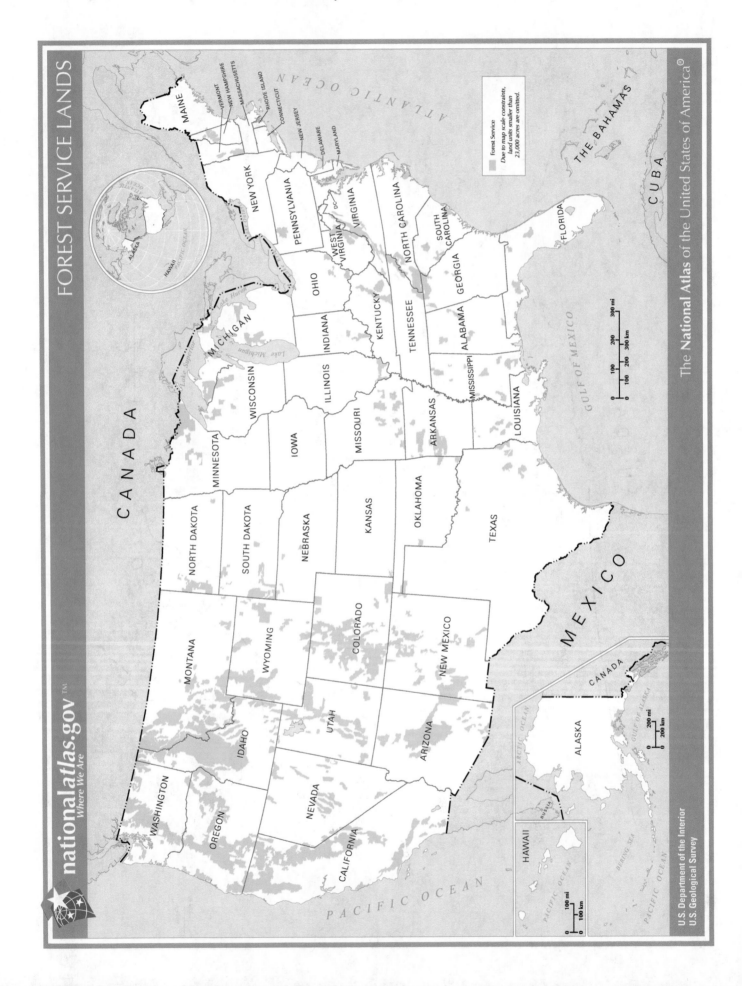

FOREST SERVICE LANDS

nationalatlas.gov™
Where We Are

The *National Atlas* of the United States of America®

U.S. Department of the Interior
U.S. Geological Survey

Forest Service

Due to map scale constraints, land units smaller than 23,000 acres are omitted.

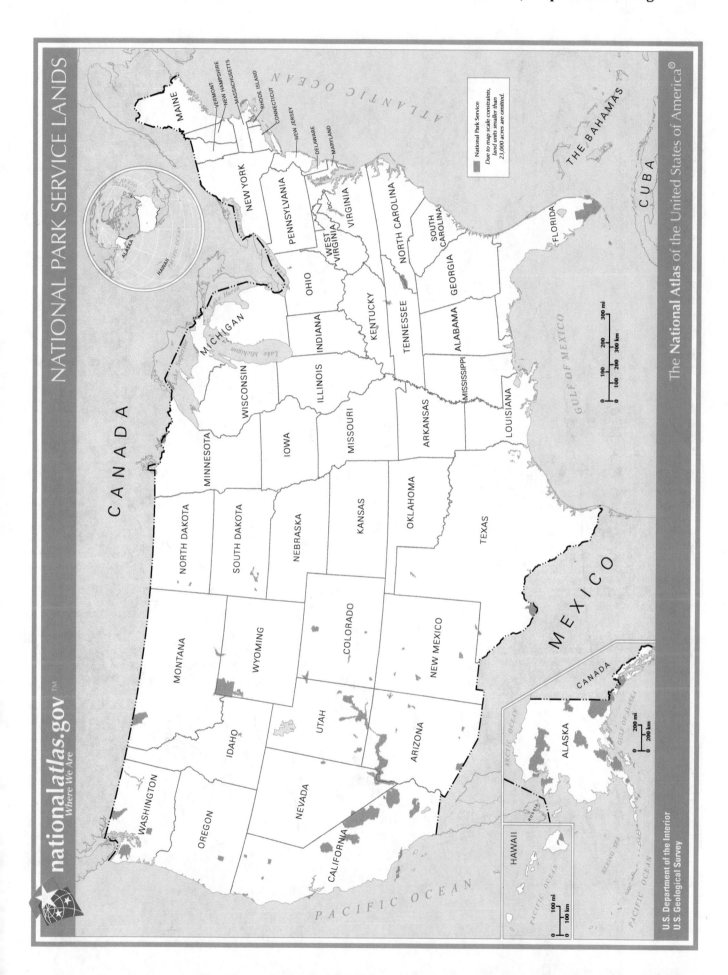

National Park Service

Due to map scale constraints,
land units smaller than
23,000 acres are omitted.

NATIONAL PARK SERVICE LANDS

nationalatlas.gov ™
Where We Are

The **National Atlas** of the United States of America ®

U.S. Department of the Interior
U.S. Geological Survey

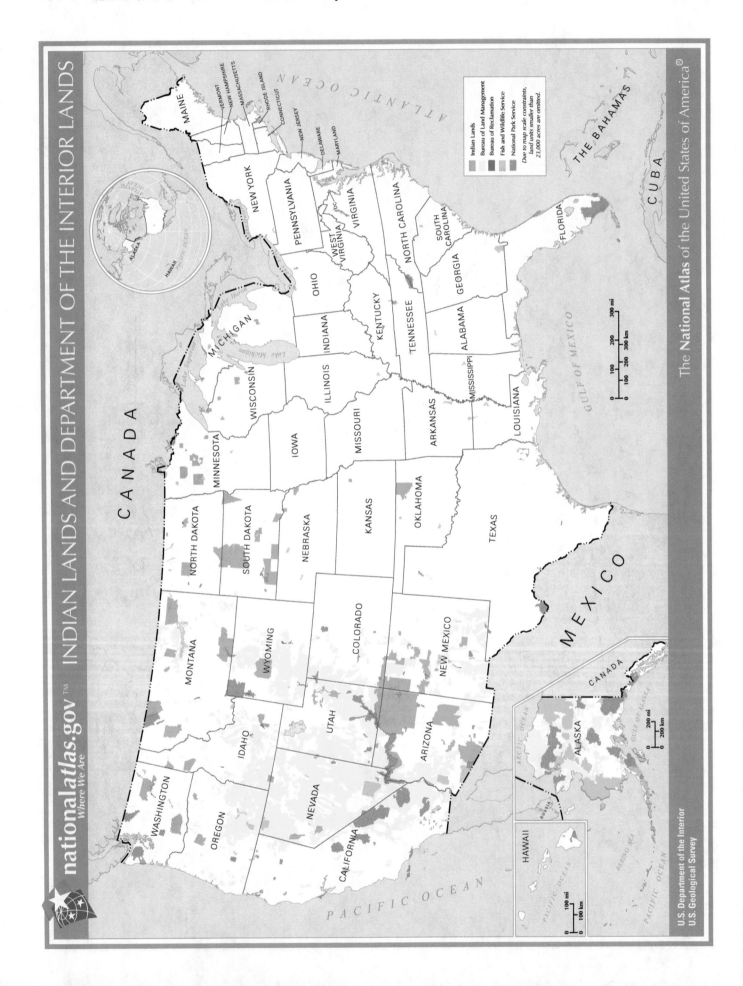

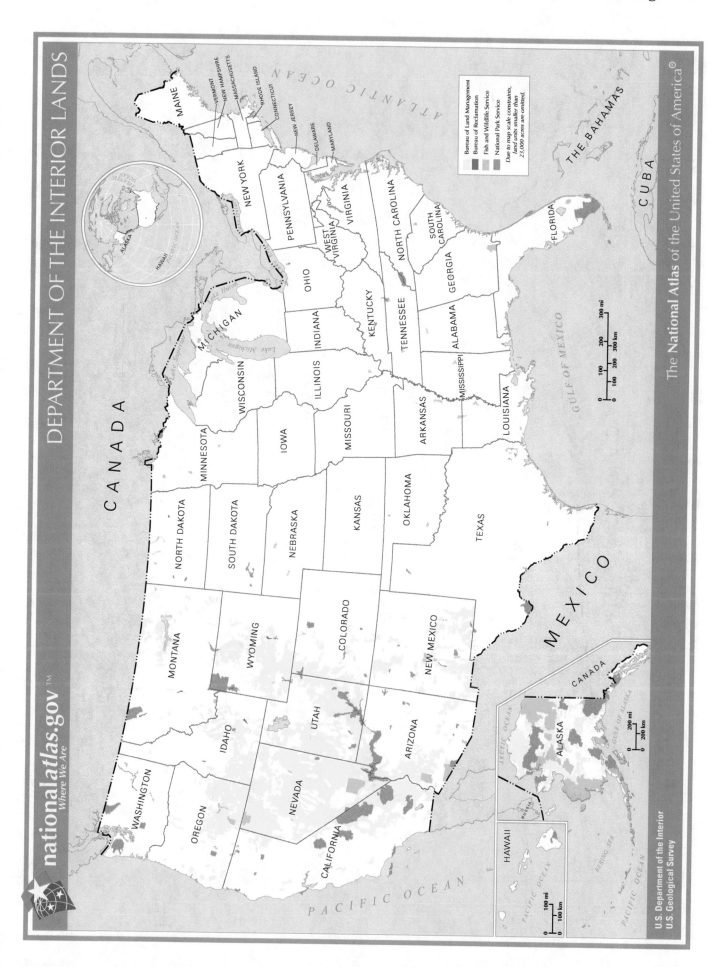

DEPARTMENT OF THE INTERIOR LANDS

nationalatlas.gov™
Where We Are

CANADA

MEXICO

ATLANTIC OCEAN

PACIFIC OCEAN

GULF OF MEXICO

THE BAHAMAS

CUBA

The **National Atlas** of the United States of America®

MAINE
VERMONT
NEW HAMPSHIRE
MASSACHUSETTS
RHODE ISLAND
CONNECTICUT
NEW JERSEY
DELAWARE
MARYLAND
NEW YORK
PENNSYLVANIA
WEST VIRGINIA
VIRGINIA
DC
OHIO
INDIANA
MICHIGAN
WISCONSIN
ILLINOIS
KENTUCKY
TENNESSEE
NORTH CAROLINA
SOUTH CAROLINA
GEORGIA
ALABAMA
MISSISSIPPI
FLORIDA
MINNESOTA
IOWA
MISSOURI
ARKANSAS
LOUISIANA
NORTH DAKOTA
SOUTH DAKOTA
NEBRASKA
KANSAS
OKLAHOMA
TEXAS
MONTANA
WYOMING
COLORADO
NEW MEXICO
IDAHO
UTAH
ARIZONA
WASHINGTON
OREGON
NEVADA
CALIFORNIA

Lake Superior
Lake Michigan
Lake Huron

Bureau of Land Management
Bureau of Reclamation
Fish and Wildlife Service
National Park Service

Due to map scale constraints, land units smaller than 23,000 acres are omitted.

ALASKA
HAWAII
ARCTIC OCEAN
PACIFIC OCEAN
CANADA
RUSSIA
BERING SEA
GULF OF ALASKA

300 mi
300 km

200 mi
200 km

100 mi
100 km

U.S. Department of the Interior
U.S. Geological Survey

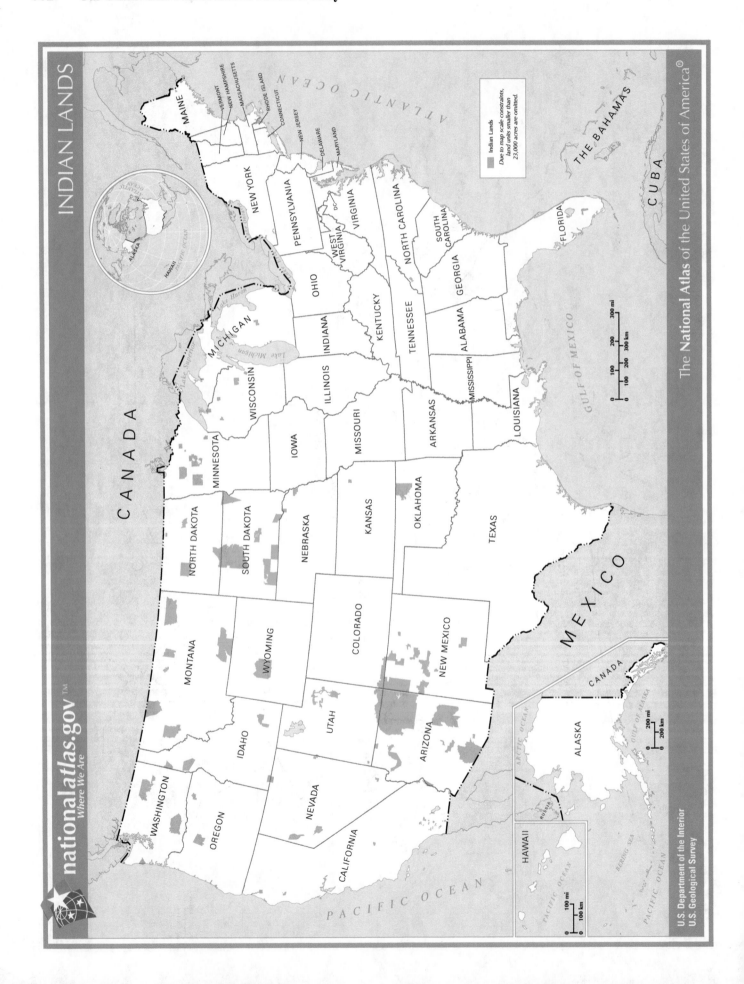

Total Surface Area	
State	Acres
Texas	171,051,900
California	101,510,200
Montana	94,110,000
New Mexico	77,823,300
Arizona	72,964,400
Nevada	70,763,100
Colorado	66,624,500
Wyoming	62,602,800
Oregon	62,161,000
Utah	54,338,900
Minnesota	54,009,900
Idaho	53,487,500
Kansas	52,660,800
Nebraska	49,509,600
South Dakota	49,358,000
North Dakota	45,250,700
Oklahoma	44,738,100
Missouri	44,613,900
Washington	44,035,300
Georgia	37,740,500
Florida	37,533,700
Michigan	37,349,200
Illinois	36,058,700
Iowa	36,016,500
Wisconsin	35,920,000
Arkansas	34,036,900
North Carolina	33,709,300
Alabama	33,423,800
Louisiana	31,376,800
New York	31,360,800
Mississippi	30,527,300
Pennsylvania	28,995,200
Virginia	27,087,100
Tennessee	26,973,600
Ohio	26,444,800
Kentucky	25,863,400
Indiana	23,158,400
Maine	20,966,200
South Carolina	19,939,300
West Virginia	15,508,200
Maryland	7,869,900
Vermont	6,153,600
New Hampshire	5,941,000
Massachusetts	5,339,000
New Jersey	5,215,600
Connecticut	3,194,700
Delaware	1,533,500
Rhode Island	813,300
Alaska	Not Available
District of Columbia	Not Available
Hawaii	Not Available

Time Period: 2007

Total Land Area	
State	Acres
Texas	166,925,800
California	99,635,300
Montana	93,070,600
New Mexico	77,670,200
Arizona	72,774,700
Nevada	70,332,000
Colorado	66,292,400
Wyoming	62,161,700
Oregon	61,334,200
Idaho	52,929,900
Utah	52,538,200
Kansas	52,106,400
Minnesota	50,865,000
Nebraska	49,033,400
South Dakota	48,478,600
North Dakota	44,162,100
Missouri	43,747,600
Oklahoma	43,649,400
Washington	42,491,300
Georgia	36,681,200
Michigan	36,228,400
Iowa	35,530,600
Illinois	35,326,200
Wisconsin	34,627,800
Florida	34,400,100
Arkansas	33,134,800
Alabama	32,133,700
North Carolina	30,926,000
New York	30,070,900
Mississippi	29,637,400
Pennsylvania	28,514,400
Louisiana	27,452,600
Tennessee	26,182,800
Ohio	26,036,300
Kentucky	25,232,500
Virginia	25,144,000
Indiana	22,785,300
Maine	19,709,600
South Carolina	19,127,700
West Virginia	15,327,600
Maryland	6,208,300
Vermont	5,891,700
New Hampshire	5,704,800
Massachusetts	4,972,400
New Jersey	4,689,600
Connecticut	3,066,100
Delaware	1,243,300
Rhode Island	662,000
Alaska	Not Available
District of Columbia	Not Available
Hawaii	Not Available

Time Period: 2007

Federal Land	
State	Acres
Nevada	59,868,900
California	46,639,000
Utah	34,278,800
Idaho	33,563,300
Oregon	31,260,400
Arizona	30,426,200
Wyoming	28,748,000
Montana	27,092,000
New Mexico	26,448,500
Colorado	23,796,900
Washington	11,923,500
Florida	3,784,200
Minnesota	3,336,100
Michigan	3,273,600
South Dakota	3,112,200
Arkansas	3,104,200
Texas	2,909,900
Virginia	2,646,400
North Carolina	2,507,500
Georgia	2,124,000
Missouri	1,919,400
Wisconsin	1,845,300
Mississippi	1,794,800
North Dakota	1,784,800
Louisiana	1,310,000
Tennessee	1,302,600
Kentucky	1,295,400
West Virginia	1,211,900
Oklahoma	1,148,300
South Carolina	1,036,200
Alabama	997,900
New Hampshire	763,200
Pennsylvania	724,300
Nebraska	647,600
Kansas	504,000
Illinois	491,100
Indiana	472,400
Vermont	422,600
Ohio	373,300
Maine	207,200
New York	205,300
Iowa	172,400
Maryland	168,900
New Jersey	148,300
Massachusetts	97,100
Delaware	31,000
Connecticut	14,500
Rhode Island	3,500
Alaska	Not Available
District of Columbia	Not Available
Hawaii	Not Available

Time Period: 2007

Federal Land: Owned	
State	Acres
California	4,537,255
Arizona	3,993,434
New Mexico	3,830,417
Utah	2,434,773
Nevada	2,013,950
Alaska	1,782,622
Texas	1,644,525
Washington	1,332,765
Oklahoma	1,080,354
Wyoming	984,024
Georgia	974,375
Idaho	916,725
Colorado	819,789
Florida	802,079
Arkansas	621,732
North Dakota	612,888
Kansas	605,202
Missouri	585,879
South Dakota	548,264
Kentucky	532,573
Mississippi	523,633
North Carolina	484,587
Montana	460,712
South Carolina	457,938
Virginia	412,858
Tennessee	368,954
Oregon	329,961
Louisiana	248,416
Indiana	239,808
Iowa	225,630
Illinois	221,650
Alabama	194,917
Hawaii	178,192
Nebraska	176,025
New York	164,132
Pennsylvania	156,380
West Virginia	149,582
Ohio	142,320
Maryland	125,613
Wisconsin	90,621
New Jersey	87,684
Massachusetts	57,888
Minnesota	40,345
Maine	25,148
New Hampshire	21,898
Michigan	21,357
Vermont	18,066
Delaware	11,711
Connecticut	9,277
District of Columbia	4,645
Rhode Island	3,011

Time Period: FY 2009

Federal Land: Leased	
State	Acres
Alabama	185,547
Washington	163,342
Hawaii	55,811
Colorado	37,324
Arizona	37,151
Pennsylvania	35,659
Montana	35,545
New Mexico	30,644
Massachusetts	23,119
Texas	20,075
Utah	19,924
Wisconsin	16,215
Kansas	15,932
Alaska	14,900
Idaho	11,998
California	11,807
North Carolina	9,449
Michigan	8,381
Georgia	6,569
Louisiana	6,348
Nebraska	6,296
Florida	6,280
South Dakota	5,719
Minnesota	5,578
Oklahoma	5,509
North Dakota	5,362
Mississippi	5,127
Wyoming	4,689
Maine	4,606
West Virginia	4,105
Illinois	3,797
Ohio	3,724
South Carolina	3,611
Virginia	3,187
Tennessee	3,146
Missouri	2,541
Arkansas	2,420
New York	2,378
Nevada	1,602
Iowa	1,536
Oregon	1,486
New Jersey	1,478
Kentucky	1,472
Indiana	1,071
Maryland	1,024
Connecticut	858
Rhode Island	412
Vermont	412
New Hampshire	370
Delaware	198
District of Columbia	62

Time Period: FY 2009

Federal Land: Otherwise Managed	
State	Acres
Maine	722,198
Oregon	282,512
Idaho	196,143
Michigan	147,351
Mississippi	132,785
Florida	87,841
Wyoming	61,544
Minnesota	54,457
Alaska	46,413
Arkansas	33,208
Louisiana	31,614
Texas	13,691
Kentucky	13,493
North Dakota	11,919
California	7,414
Missouri	6,704
Illinois	6,002
North Carolina	5,573
Nevada	4,180
Wisconsin	3,856
Utah	3,097
West Virginia	2,708
Iowa	2,689
South Dakota	2,676
New York	2,482
Connecticut	2,342
Maryland	2,280
Indiana	1,603
Oklahoma	1,533
Tennessee	1,521
Pennsylvania	1,423
Alabama	1,215
New Mexico	1,125
Hawaii	1,035
Ohio	1,031
Massachusetts	831
Georgia	808
South Carolina	721
Montana	702
New Jersey	697
Arizona	687
Virginia	523
Washington	498
New Hampshire	400
Kansas	324
Nebraska	234
Delaware	205
Vermont	175
Colorado	89
Rhode Island	82
District of Columbia	10

Time Period: FY 2009

National Forest	
State	Acres
Alaska	21,956,000
California	20,822,000
Idaho	20,465,000
Montana	17,083,000
Oregon	15,688,000
Missouri	14,923,000
Colorado	14,521,000
Arizona	11,265,000
New Mexico	9,418,000
Washington	9,289,000
Wyoming	9,242,000
Utah	8,207,000
Nevada	5,746,000
Michigan	2,876,000
Minnesota	2,842,000
Arkansas	2,599,000
South Dakota	2,017,000
Virginia	1,664,000
Wisconsin	1,534,000
North Carolina	1,256,000
Florida	1,176,000
Mississippi	1,174,000
North Dakota	1,106,000
West Virginia	1,044,000
Georgia	867,000
Kentucky	814,000
Texas	755,000
New Hampshire	736,000
Tennessee	718,000
Alabama	670,000
South Carolina	631,000
Louisiana	604,000
Pennsylvania	513,000
Oklahoma	461,000
Vermont	400,000
Nebraska	352,000
Illinois	298,000
Ohio	241,000
Indiana	203,000
Kansas	108,000
Maine	54,000
Connecticut	24,000
New York	16,000
Hawaii	1,000
Delaware	0
District of Columbia	0
Iowa	0
Maryland	0
Massachusetts	0
New Jersey	0
Rhode Island	0

Time Period: September 2006

National Wilderness	
State	Acres
Alaska	57,425,910
California	14,982,645
Arizona	4,529,613
Idaho	4,522,717
Washington	4,462,493
Colorado	3,700,148
Montana	3,443,407
Nevada	3,371,425
Wyoming	3,111,232
Oregon	2,474,435
New Mexico	1,650,596
Florida	1,422,247
Utah	1,160,300
Minnesota	816,267
Georgia	486,530
Michigan	258,596
Virginia	214,904
Hawaii	155,509
Arkansas	153,655
New Hampshire	138,418
West Virginia	118,810
North Carolina	111,419
Vermont	100,870
Texas	85,333
Wisconsin	79,943
South Dakota	77,570
Missouri	71,849
Tennessee	66,349
South Carolina	60,681
Alabama	41,367
North Dakota	39,652
Illinois	32,113
Oklahoma	23,113
Maine	18,625
Kentucky	18,132
Louisiana	17,025
Indiana	12,463
Nebraska	12,429
New Jersey	10,341
Mississippi	10,126
Pennsylvania	9,002
Massachusetts	3,244
New York	1,380
Ohio	77
Connecticut	0
Delaware	0
District of Columbia	0
Iowa	0
Kansas	0
Maryland	0
Rhode Island	0

Time Period: October 2011

Non-Federal Land: Developed			Non-Federal Land: Rural			Total Water Area			National Natural Landmarks	
State	**Acres**		**State**	**Acres**		**State**	**Acres**		**State**	**Number**
Texas	8,515,700		Texas	155,500,200		Texas	4,126,100		California	35
California	6,173,800		Montana	64,931,600		Louisiana	3,924,200		Indiana	30
Florida	5,515,200		New Mexico	49,959,800		Minnesota	3,144,900		New York	27
North Carolina	4,796,700		Kansas	49,506,700		Florida	3,133,600		Pennsylvania	27
Georgia	4,639,900		Nebraska	47,229,300		North Carolina	2,783,300		Ohio	23
Pennsylvania	4,360,700		California	46,822,500		Virginia	1,943,100		Texas	20
Michigan	4,227,600		Minnesota	45,133,700		California	1,874,900		Florida	18
Ohio	4,140,300		South Dakota	44,403,600		Utah	1,800,700		Illinois	18
New York	3,793,900		North Dakota	41,404,100		Maryland	1,661,600		Wisconsin	18
Illinois	3,383,300		Colorado	40,561,200		Washington	1,544,000		Washington	17
Virginia	3,101,200		Oklahoma	40,444,300		Wisconsin	1,292,200		Alaska	16
Tennessee	3,038,300		Arizona	40,342,300		Alabama	1,290,100		Missouri	16
Alabama	2,942,900		Missouri	38,896,700		New York	1,289,900		Maine	14
Missouri	2,931,500		Iowa	33,465,900		Maine	1,256,600		North Carolina	13
Wisconsin	2,724,900		Wyoming	32,732,600		Michigan	1,120,800		South Dakota	13
South Carolina	2,672,600		Illinois	31,451,800		Oklahoma	1,088,700		Tennessee	13
Washington	2,464,500		Wisconsin	30,057,600		North Dakota	1,088,600		West Virginia	13
Indiana	2,446,000		Georgia	29,917,300		Georgia	1,059,300		Colorado	12
Minnesota	2,395,200		Michigan	28,727,200		Montana	1,039,400		Michigan	12
Kansas	2,095,700		Oregon	28,684,200		Arkansas	902,100		New Mexico	12
Kentucky	2,093,100		Arkansas	28,221,300		Mississippi	889,900		Vermont	12
Oklahoma	2,056,800		Alabama	28,192,900		South Dakota	879,400		Idaho	11
Arizona	2,006,200		Washington	28,103,300		Missouri	866,300		Massachusetts	11
Colorado	1,934,300		New York	26,071,700		Oregon	826,800		New Hampshire	11
Iowa	1,892,300		Mississippi	26,030,700		South Carolina	811,600		New Jersey	11
Louisiana	1,862,800		Florida	25,100,700		Tennessee	790,800		Georgia	10
New Jersey	1,849,300		Louisiana	24,279,800		Illinois	732,500		Montana	10
Mississippi	1,811,900		North Carolina	23,621,800		Kentucky	630,900		Virginia	10
Arkansas	1,809,300		Pennsylvania	23,429,400		Idaho	557,600		Arizona	9
Massachusetts	1,716,400		Kentucky	21,844,000		Kansas	554,400		Connecticut	8
Maryland	1,496,700		Tennessee	21,841,900		New Jersey	526,000		Minnesota	8
Oregon	1,389,600		Ohio	21,522,700		Iowa	485,900		Alabama	7
New Mexico	1,261,900		Indiana	19,866,900		Pennsylvania	480,800		Hawaii	7
Nebraska	1,156,500		Virginia	19,396,400		Nebraska	476,200		Iowa	7
West Virginia	1,151,600		Maine	18,651,300		Wyoming	441,100		Kentucky	7
Connecticut	1,051,600		Idaho	18,459,300		Nevada	431,100		Oregon	7
Montana	1,047,000		Utah	17,514,800		Ohio	408,500		Maryland	6
North Dakota	973,200		South Carolina	15,418,900		Indiana	373,100		Nevada	6
South Dakota	962,800		West Virginia	12,964,100		Massachusetts	366,600		South Carolina	6
Idaho	907,300		Nevada	9,880,200		Colorado	332,100		Wyoming	6
Maine	851,100		Vermont	5,075,900		Delaware	290,200		Arkansas	5
Utah	744,600		Maryland	4,542,700		Vermont	261,900		Kansas	5
New Hampshire	695,500		New Hampshire	4,246,100		New Hampshire	236,200		Mississippi	5
Wyoming	681,100		Massachusetts	3,158,900		Arizona	189,700		Nebraska	5
Nevada	582,900		New Jersey	2,692,000		West Virginia	180,600		North Dakota	4
Vermont	393,200		Connecticut	2,000,000		New Mexico	153,100		Utah	4
Delaware	280,100		Delaware	932,200		Rhode Island	151,300		Oklahoma	3
Rhode Island	232,200		Rhode Island	426,300		Connecticut	128,600		Rhode Island	1
Alaska	Not Available		Alaska	Not Available		Alaska	Not Available		Delaware	0
District of Columbia	Not Available		District of Columbia	Not Available		District of Columbia	Not Available		District of Columbia	0
Hawaii	Not Available		Hawaii	Not Available		Hawaii	Not Available		Louisiana	0

Time Period: 2007   *Time Period: 2007*   *Time Period: 2007*   *Time Period: December 2010*

National Historic Landmarks	
State	Number
New York	261
Massachusetts	185
Pennsylvania	161
California	138
Virginia	119
Illinois	85
South Carolina	76
District of Columbia	74
Maryland	71
Ohio	69
Connecticut	60
New Jersey	55
Louisiana	53
Alaska	49
Georgia	48
Texas	46
New Mexico	44
Rhode Island	44
Florida	42
Arizona	41
Maine	41
Wisconsin	40
Mississippi	39
North Carolina	38
Indiana	37
Missouri	37
Alabama	36
Michigan	34
Hawaii	33
Kentucky	30
Tennessee	29
Montana	25
Iowa	24
Washington	24
Wyoming	24
Kansas	23
Minnesota	23
New Hampshire	22
Colorado	21
Nebraska	20
Oklahoma	20
Vermont	17
Arkansas	16
Oregon	16
West Virginia	16
South Dakota	15
Utah	13
Delaware	12
Nevada	7
North Dakota	5
Idaho	Not Available

Time Period: December 2010

National Register of Historic Places	
State	Number
New York	5,318
Massachusetts	4,161
Ohio	3,792
Kentucky	3,296
Pennsylvania	3,268
Texas	3,086
Virginia	2,797
North Carolina	2,742
Arkansas	2,514
California	2,479
Wisconsin	2,214
Iowa	2,142
Missouri	2,082
Georgia	2,040
Tennessee	1,996
Oregon	1,912
Michigan	1,759
Indiana	1,716
Illinois	1,715
Florida	1,619
New Jersey	1,613
Minnesota	1,592
Connecticut	1,552
Maine	1,540
Maryland	1,496
South Carolina	1,457
Utah	1,453
Washington	1,440
Colorado	1,400
Arizona	1,362
Louisiana	1,346
Mississippi	1,334
South Dakota	1,274
Alabama	1,239
Kansas	1,233
Oklahoma	1,188
New Mexico	1,085
Montana	1,084
Idaho	1,016
Nebraska	1,016
West Virginia	996
Vermont	800
Rhode Island	753
New Hampshire	726
Delaware	681
District of Columbia	516
Wyoming	512
North Dakota	420
Alaska	410
Nevada	364
Hawaii	325

Time Period: December 2010

National Parks	
State	Number
California	25
Alaska	23
Arizona	22
District of Columbia	22
New York	22
Virginia	21
Pennsylvania	18
Maryland	16
Massachusetts	15
Colorado	13
New Mexico	13
Texas	13
Utah	13
Washington	13
Tennessee	12
Florida	11
Georgia	11
North Carolina	10
Mississippi	8
Montana	8
New Jersey	8
Alabama	7
Arkansas	7
Hawaii	7
Idaho	7
Ohio	7
Wyoming	7
Missouri	6
South Carolina	6
South Dakota	6
West Virginia	6
Kansas	5
Louisiana	5
Michigan	5
Minnesota	5
Nebraska	5
Oregon	5
Kentucky	4
Indiana	3
Maine	3
Nevada	3
North Dakota	3
Oklahoma	3
Connecticut	2
Iowa	2
New Hampshire	2
Vermont	2
Wisconsin	2
Illinois	1
Rhode Island	1
Delaware	0

Time Period: December 2010

Visitors to National Parks	
State	Number
California	34,915,676
District of Columbia	33,140,005
Virginia	22,708,338
New York	17,506,355
North Carolina	17,093,464
Arizona	10,546,150
Massachusetts	9,913,501
Florida	9,222,981
Utah	8,975,525
Pennsylvania	8,970,475
Tennessee	7,898,557
Washington	7,281,785
Georgia	6,776,556
Mississippi	6,588,026
Wyoming	6,307,997
New Jersey	5,858,443
Colorado	5,635,307
Texas	5,495,156
Nevada	5,399,439
Montana	4,584,011
Hawaii	4,493,123
South Dakota	4,199,267
Missouri	4,140,544
Maryland	3,541,570
Arkansas	3,125,664
Ohio	2,738,275
Maine	2,504,208
Indiana	2,395,485
Alaska	2,274,843
West Virginia	1,811,722
Kentucky	1,797,894
Michigan	1,796,006
New Mexico	1,657,550
South Carolina	1,529,172
Oklahoma	1,266,189
Oregon	888,358
Alabama	781,550
North Dakota	659,927
Minnesota	540,195
Idaho	530,977
Louisiana	496,329
Illinois	354,125
Nebraska	290,323
Wisconsin	251,145
Iowa	222,295
Kansas	100,361
Rhode Island	51,559
Vermont	31,209
New Hampshire	30,941
Connecticut	19,313
Delaware	0

Time Period: 2010

Historic Places Documented by the National Park Service	
State	**Number**
Pennsylvania	3,724
California	3,310
New York	1,931
Virginia	1,899
Massachusetts	1,629
New Jersey	1,575
Maryland	1,572
Missouri	1,341
Alabama	1,229
South Carolina	1,144
District of Columbia	996
Illinois	926
Georgia	920
Ohio	882
Colorado	881
Texas	856
Hawaii	807
Washington	763
Wisconsin	679
Utah	642
Connecticut	637
Michigan	622
Louisiana	597
Minnesota	562
Florida	557
Arizona	537
Alaska	516
West Virginia	501
North Carolina	499
Oregon	485
Wyoming	481
Iowa	480
Rhode Island	464
Indiana	447
Montana	425
Kentucky	400
Delaware	390
Idaho	367
Tennessee	348
Mississippi	339
Maine	331
Nevada	327
New Hampshire	278
New Mexico	266
Kansas	205
Arkansas	161
Vermont	146
North Dakota	126
Nebraska	112
Oklahoma	107
South Dakota	81

Time Period: December 2010

Archeological Sites in National Parks	
State	**Number**
Arizona	10,999
California	9,261
New Mexico	8,694
Colorado	6,767
Utah	6,428
Alaska	4,539
Texas	3,634
Wyoming	2,042
Kentucky	1,581
Virginia	1,501
Tennessee	1,405
Hawaii	1,388
Florida	1,116
Pennsylvania	1,000
Washington	913
Montana	891
Nevada	779
Arkansas	710
Maryland	581
Missouri	530
North Carolina	530
Minnesota	508
Massachusetts	440
Michigan	433
New Jersey	410
South Dakota	396
North Dakota	387
West Virginia	379
Georgia	297
New York	266
Wisconsin	264
Mississippi	239
Ohio	239
Alabama	223
Maine	204
Indiana	199
Nebraska	160
District of Columbia	149
Oregon	148
Idaho	105
Louisiana	90
South Carolina	83
Oklahoma	79
Iowa	77
Rhode Island	39
Kansas	21
New Hampshire	20
Illinois	19
Vermont	19
Connecticut	10
Delaware	0

Time Period: December 2010

Threatened and Endangered Species in National Parks	
State	**Number**
California	99
Hawaii	89
Florida	54
Tennessee	39
Arizona	32
Texas	28
Kentucky	27
North Carolina	24
Utah	23
Mississippi	22
Georgia	20
Virginia	19
Washington	19
Alabama	15
New York	14
Colorado	13
Maryland	12
New Jersey	12
New Mexico	12
Oregon	12
Massachusetts	11
Nevada	11
Alaska	8
Idaho	8
West Virginia	8
Montana	7
South Carolina	7
South Dakota	7
Arkansas	6
Indiana	6
Minnesota	6
Missouri	6
Wisconsin	6
District of Columbia	5
Michigan	5
Nebraska	5
Wyoming	5
Iowa	4
North Dakota	4
Pennsylvania	4
Louisiana	3
Ohio	3
Kansas	2
Maine	2
New Hampshire	1
Connecticut	0
Delaware	0
Illinois	0
Oklahoma	0
Rhode Island	0
Vermont	0

Time Period: December 2010

Economic Benefit from National Park Tourism	
State	**Dollars**
California	1,054,833,000
District of Columbia	966,189,000
North Carolina	707,241,000
Arizona	659,180,000
Wyoming	570,480,000
Utah	565,592,000
Florida	552,809,000
Tennessee	501,305,000
Virginia	493,128,000
Massachusetts	384,992,000
New York	340,054,000
Colorado	336,956,000
Pennsylvania	295,605,000
Montana	269,523,000
Washington	247,832,000
Texas	247,074,000
Hawaii	222,157,000
Alaska	216,224,000
Georgia	199,024,000
Nevada	173,140,000
Maine	159,106,000
Maryland	155,549,000
Missouri	142,684,000
South Dakota	141,846,000
Arkansas	129,498,000
Michigan	124,132,000
New Jersey	94,657,000
Kentucky	76,593,000
Mississippi	76,254,000
New Mexico	62,474,000
West Virginia	57,779,000
Ohio	56,716,000
Oregon	51,375,000
Indiana	51,232,000
South Carolina	40,265,000
Minnesota	27,990,000
North Dakota	27,545,000
Wisconsin	25,044,000
Illinois	23,166,000
Louisiana	19,869,000
Alabama	18,781,000
Idaho	17,952,000
Oklahoma	12,670,000
Iowa	11,494,000
Nebraska	8,763,000
Kansas	4,337,000
Rhode Island	2,936,000
Vermont	1,395,000
New Hampshire	1,176,000
Connecticut	1,130,000
Delaware	0

Time Period: 2009

Conservation Reserve Program	
State	Acres
Texas	3,362,690
Kansas	2,536,321
Montana	2,510,678
North Dakota	2,381,437
Colorado	2,160,890
Iowa	1,656,057
Minnesota	1,558,423
Washington	1,461,969
Missouri	1,294,005
South Dakota	1,097,799
Illinois	1,024,409
Nebraska	1,005,750
Oklahoma	829,338
Mississippi	827,191
Idaho	646,391
Oregon	546,649
New Mexico	420,076
Wisconsin	372,765
Alabama	361,053
Ohio	336,761
Kentucky	335,167
Louisiana	324,938
Georgia	315,213
Indiana	277,609
Arkansas	248,740
Michigan	222,370
Wyoming	215,797
Pennsylvania	203,656
Tennessee	191,574
Utah	179,011
South Carolina	144,221
North Carolina	111,380
California	108,870
Maryland	76,955
Virginia	61,509
Florida	51,993
New York	51,654
Alaska	19,007
Maine	13,573
Delaware	6,721
West Virginia	6,072
Vermont	2,871
New Jersey	2,356
Hawaii	490
Connecticut	151
New Hampshire	13
Massachusetts	10
Arizona	Not Available
District of Columbia	Not Available
Nevada	Not Available
Rhode Island	Not Available

Time Period: October 2011

Land and Water Conservation Fund Grants	
State	Dollars
California	287,823,890
New York	232,947,093
Texas	174,083,496
Pennsylvania	162,163,928
Illinois	155,159,737
Ohio	145,656,016
Florida	128,772,261
Michigan	128,032,310
New Jersey	119,179,924
Massachusetts	97,519,236
Missouri	83,944,170
Indiana	83,729,854
Virginia	82,784,757
Georgia	81,455,120
North Carolina	78,780,372
Maryland	78,414,087
Wisconsin	74,743,616
Tennessee	71,358,348
Louisiana	70,723,303
Minnesota	70,412,569
Washington	70,282,953
Alabama	63,927,462
Connecticut	63,407,882
Colorado	59,060,399
South Carolina	58,966,737
Kentucky	58,728,074
Arizona	58,531,701
Oregon	57,983,273
Oklahoma	55,414,720
Iowa	54,145,208
Kansas	50,383,110
Utah	48,180,040
Arkansas	48,121,617
Mississippi	46,678,810
West Virginia	44,627,320
Nebraska	44,324,768
New Mexico	40,936,429
Maine	40,472,779
Nevada	40,375,689
Rhode Island	39,643,701
Idaho	38,699,925
Hawaii	38,308,514
Montana	37,340,899
New Hampshire	36,699,617
South Dakota	36,284,157
Delaware	35,989,038
North Dakota	34,860,107
Wyoming	33,849,595
Alaska	33,609,258
Vermont	33,004,602
District of Columbia	14,425,124

Time Period: Since 1965

Historic Preservation Grants	
State	Dollars
New York	60,761,211
Virginia	55,070,645
Pennsylvania	52,341,882
California	46,667,855
Massachusetts	42,037,690
Ohio	39,848,941
Texas	39,221,885
Maryland	35,077,169
Kentucky	34,033,765
North Carolina	32,425,677
Georgia	32,149,564
Alabama	31,160,393
Florida	31,077,920
Michigan	28,956,082
South Carolina	28,583,499
Illinois	28,315,736
Tennessee	27,845,608
Missouri	27,475,484
Washington	26,749,740
Rhode Island	26,603,140
Wisconsin	26,510,468
Arkansas	26,415,983
Minnesota	26,388,433
Colorado	25,910,178
Mississippi	25,587,829
Connecticut	24,951,043
District of Columbia	24,785,473
Louisiana	24,563,495
Iowa	24,473,390
New Mexico	24,280,611
New Jersey	23,131,412
West Virginia	22,478,602
Alaska	22,289,153
Vermont	21,362,234
Utah	21,344,571
Montana	21,144,662
Arizona	21,112,060
Indiana	20,764,490
Oregon	20,645,477
Oklahoma	20,374,369
South Dakota	19,192,380
Idaho	18,717,254
Nevada	18,115,304
Maine	18,087,441
Wyoming	17,857,718
Delaware	17,775,495
New Hampshire	17,201,029
Nebraska	16,970,269
Kansas	16,253,023
Hawaii	14,917,599
North Dakota	14,171,499

Time Period: 2010

Community Conservation and Recreation Projects	
State	Number
California	153
Pennsylvania	136
Washington	101
Texas	97
Virginia	97
Oregon	84
Alaska	80
New York	80
Maryland	74
Maine	72
New Hampshire	66
Wisconsin	66
Colorado	64
West Virginia	64
Michigan	60
Minnesota	58
Illinois	57
Vermont	57
Arizona	55
Massachusetts	54
Ohio	51
New Mexico	48
Utah	48
Nebraska	47
Florida	46
Iowa	43
Tennessee	43
Georgia	41
Indiana	41
Nevada	41
New Jersey	41
Missouri	40
Connecticut	39
Louisiana	36
North Carolina	35
Idaho	32
Hawaii	29
Montana	27
Mississippi	25
Alabama	24
Kentucky	24
South Carolina	22
Rhode Island	21
Oklahoma	20
Delaware	16
Arkansas	13
District of Columbia	13
Wyoming	13
Kansas	12
South Dakota	12
North Dakota	6

Time Period: Since 1987

Federal Acres Transferred for Local Parks and Recreation	
State	Acres
California	13,816
Indiana	12,521
Florida	12,061
Washington	9,858
Pennsylvania	9,683
Texas	8,080
South Carolina	7,830
Kentucky	7,498
Massachusetts	6,781
New York	5,952
Virginia	5,630
Illinois	5,059
Michigan	4,499
Missouri	4,133
Alabama	4,073
Georgia	3,617
Oregon	3,492
Tennessee	3,309
Colorado	3,014
Idaho	2,915
Wisconsin	2,806
Utah	2,765
Delaware	2,394
Ohio	2,373
New Jersey	2,164
Rhode Island	1,986
Oklahoma	1,965
New Mexico	1,800
Maryland	1,513
Nebraska	1,152
Louisiana	1,125
Kansas	899
Iowa	889
Arkansas	852
Mississippi	800
Arizona	794
Wyoming	793
West Virginia	531
Minnesota	508
Nevada	431
Hawaii	364
Connecticut	297
Maine	273
Alaska	266
North Carolina	234
South Dakota	201
New Hampshire	184
Vermont	180
North Dakota	155
Montana	120
District of Columbia	0

Time Period: Since 1948

Crude Petroleum Production	
State	Mil. Barrels
Texas	417
Alaska	219
California	204
North Dakota	112
Oklahoma	68
Louisiana	67
New Mexico	62
Wyoming	52
Kansas	40
Colorado	26
Mississippi	24
Montana	24
Utah	24
Illinois	9
Alabama	7
Michigan	7
Arkansas	6
Ohio	6
Kentucky	3
Pennsylvania	3
Florida	2
Indiana	2
Nebraska	2
West Virginia	2
Arizona	Not Available
Connecticut	Not Available
Delaware	Not Available
District of Columbia	Not Available
Georgia	Not Available
Hawaii	Not Available
Idaho	Not Available
Iowa	Not Available
Maine	Not Available
Maryland	Not Available
Massachusetts	Not Available
Minnesota	Not Available
Missouri	Not Available
Nevada	Not Available
New Hampshire	Not Available
New Jersey	Not Available
New York	Not Available
North Carolina	Not Available
Oregon	Not Available
Rhode Island	Not Available
South Carolina	Not Available
South Dakota	Not Available
Tennessee	Not Available
Vermont	Not Available
Virginia	Not Available
Washington	Not Available
Wisconsin	Not Available

Time Period: 2010

Crude Oil Proved Reserves	
State	Mil. Barrels
Texas	5,006
Alaska	3,566
California	2,835
North Dakota	1,046
New Mexico	700
Oklahoma	622
Wyoming	583
Utah	398
Louisiana	370
Montana	343
Colorado	279
Kansas	259
Mississippi	244
Illinois	66
Ohio	38
Alabama	37
Michigan	33
Arkansas	28
Kentucky	20
West Virginia	19
Pennsylvania	10
Florida	9
Nebraska	9
Indiana	8
Arizona	Not Available
Connecticut	Not Available
Delaware	Not Available
District of Columbia	Not Available
Georgia	Not Available
Hawaii	Not Available
Idaho	Not Available
Iowa	Not Available
Maine	Not Available
Maryland	Not Available
Massachusetts	Not Available
Minnesota	Not Available
Missouri	Not Available
Nevada	Not Available
New Hampshire	Not Available
New Jersey	Not Available
New York	Not Available
North Carolina	Not Available
Oregon	Not Available
Rhode Island	Not Available
South Carolina	Not Available
South Dakota	Not Available
Tennessee	Not Available
Vermont	Not Available
Virginia	Not Available
Washington	Not Available
Wisconsin	Not Available

Time Period: 2009

Natural Gas Reserves	
State	Bil. Cu. Ft.
Texas	80,424
Wyoming	35,283
Colorado	23,058
Oklahoma	22,769
Louisiana	20,688
New Mexico	15,598
Arkansas	10,869
Alaska	9,101
Utah	7,257
Pennsylvania	6,985
West Virginia	5,946
Kansas	3,279
Virginia	3,091
Alabama	2,871
Kentucky	2,782
California	2,773
Michigan	2,763
North Dakota	1,079
Montana	976
Mississippi	917
Ohio	896
New York	196
Florida	7
Arizona	Not Available
Connecticut	Not Available
Delaware	Not Available
District of Columbia	Not Available
Georgia	Not Available
Hawaii	Not Available
Idaho	Not Available
Illinois	Not Available
Indiana	Not Available
Iowa	Not Available
Maine	Not Available
Maryland	Not Available
Massachusetts	Not Available
Minnesota	Not Available
Missouri	Not Available
Nebraska	Not Available
Nevada	Not Available
New Hampshire	Not Available
New Jersey	Not Available
North Carolina	Not Available
Oregon	Not Available
Rhode Island	Not Available
South Carolina	Not Available
South Dakota	Not Available
Tennessee	Not Available
Vermont	Not Available
Washington	Not Available
Wisconsin	Not Available

Time Period: 2009

Natural Gas Liquid Reserves	
State	Mil. Barrels
Texas	3,560
Wyoming	1,121
Oklahoma	1,034
New Mexico	804
Colorado	716
Alaska	312
Louisiana	300
Kansas	181
Utah	116
California	113
Alabama	106
Kentucky	100
West Virginia	100
Michigan	62
North Dakota	55
Montana	11
Mississippi	9
Arkansas	2
Florida	0
Arizona	Not Available
Connecticut	Not Available
Delaware	Not Available
District of Columbia	Not Available
Georgia	Not Available
Hawaii	Not Available
Idaho	Not Available
Illinois	Not Available
Indiana	Not Available
Iowa	Not Available
Maine	Not Available
Maryland	Not Available
Massachusetts	Not Available
Minnesota	Not Available
Missouri	Not Available
Nebraska	Not Available
Nevada	Not Available
New Hampshire	Not Available
New Jersey	Not Available
New York	Not Available
North Carolina	Not Available
Ohio	Not Available
Oregon	Not Available
Pennsylvania	Not Available
Rhode Island	Not Available
South Carolina	Not Available
South Dakota	Not Available
Tennessee	Not Available
Vermont	Not Available
Virginia	Not Available
Washington	Not Available
Wisconsin	Not Available

Time Period: 2008

Natural Gas Marketed Production	
State	Bil. Cu. Ft.
Texas	6,819
Wyoming	2,335
Oklahoma	1,858
Louisiana	1,549
Colorado	1,499
New Mexico	1,383
Arkansas	680
Utah	444
Alaska	397
Kansas	354
California	277
Pennsylvania	274
West Virginia	264
Alabama	236
Michigan	154
Kentucky	113
Montana	98
Ohio	89
Mississippi	88
North Dakota	59
New York	45
Indiana	5
Nebraska	3
Illinois	1
Florida	0
Arizona	Not Available
Connecticut	Not Available
Delaware	Not Available
District of Columbia	Not Available
Georgia	Not Available
Hawaii	Not Available
Idaho	Not Available
Iowa	Not Available
Maine	Not Available
Maryland	Not Available
Massachusetts	Not Available
Minnesota	Not Available
Missouri	Not Available
Nevada	Not Available
New Hampshire	Not Available
New Jersey	Not Available
North Carolina	Not Available
Oregon	Not Available
Rhode Island	Not Available
South Carolina	Not Available
South Dakota	Not Available
Tennessee	Not Available
Vermont	Not Available
Virginia	Not Available
Washington	Not Available
Wisconsin	Not Available

Time Period: 2009

Coal Reserves	
State	Mil. Sh. Tons
Montana	119,017
Illinois	104,222
Wyoming	61,563
West Virginia	31,955
Kentucky	29,234
Pennsylvania	26,998
Ohio	23,127
Colorado	15,981
Texas	12,183
New Mexico	11,984
Indiana	9,271
North Dakota	8,903
Alaska	6,102
Missouri	5,988
Utah	5,203
Alabama	4,074
Iowa	2,189
Oklahoma	1,545
Virginia	1,519
Washington	1,340
Kansas	971
Tennessee	759
Maryland	623
Arkansas	416
Arizona	Not Available
California	Not Available
Connecticut	Not Available
Delaware	Not Available
District of Columbia	Not Available
Florida	Not Available
Georgia	Not Available
Hawaii	Not Available
Idaho	Not Available
Louisiana	Not Available
Maine	Not Available
Massachusetts	Not Available
Michigan	Not Available
Minnesota	Not Available
Mississippi	Not Available
Nebraska	Not Available
Nevada	Not Available
New Hampshire	Not Available
New Jersey	Not Available
New York	Not Available
North Carolina	Not Available
Oregon	Not Available
Rhode Island	Not Available
South Carolina	Not Available
South Dakota	Not Available
Vermont	Not Available
Wisconsin	Not Available

Time Period: 2009

Department of the Interior

1849 C Street, NW
Washington, DC 20240
202-208-3100
www.doi.gov
Email: feedback@ois.doi.gov
Secretary of the Interior: Ken Salazar
Deputy Secretary: David J. Hayes

The U.S. Department of the Interior protects America's natural resources and heritage, and honors its cultures and tribal communities. The DOI is managed by Ken Salazar, the Deputy Secretary, five Assistant Secretaries, and eight Bureau Directors. All of its Presidential appointees are confirmed by the Senate and have experience managing federal and state agencies, and/or non-profit associations; several appointees also have significant private sector experience.

In order to forge solutions to the nation's natural resource challenges, the DOI works closely with state, local, tribal and insular governments.

Promoting coordinated, mutual efforts among many levels help the government pool resources, share expertise, and eliminate duplication.

The Department of the Interior manages the following agencies, which are fully described below: National Park Service; Bureau of Indian Affairs; Bureau of Land Management; U.S. Geological Survey; and the Office of Insular Affairs.

National Park Service

1849 C Street, NW
Washington, DC 20240
202-208-3818
www.nps.gov
Director: Jon Jarvis

Since 1916, the National Park Service (NPS), through its seven regional offices listed below, has been entrusted with the care of the nation's national parks. With the help of volunteers, archeologists, architects, curators, historians, and

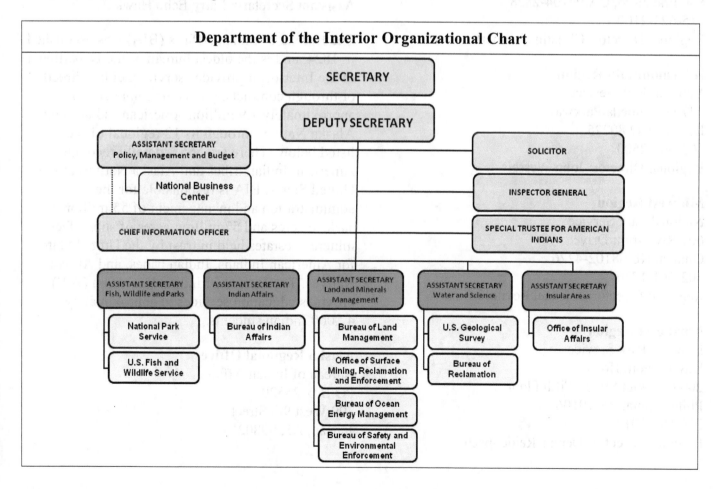

Department of the Interior Organizational Chart

other cultural resource professionals, the NPS safeguards the nearly 400 national parks that preserves, protects, and shares the history of this land and its people with more than 275 million visitors every year.

In addition, the National Park Service is part of a national preservation partnership working with American Indian Tribes, states, local governments, nonprofit organizations, historic property owners, and others who believe in the importance and preservation of America's shared heritage.

Alaska Region
National Park Service
240 West 5th Avenue, Suite 114
Anchorage, AK 99501
907-644-3510
Regional Director: Sue Masica

Pacific West Region
National Park Service
333 Bush Street, Suite 500
San Francisco, CA 94104-2828
415-623-2100
Regional Director: Christine Lehnertz

Intermountain Region
National Park Service
12795 Alameda Parkway
Denver, CO 80225
303-969-2500
Regional Director: John Wessels

Midwest Region
National Park Service
601 Riverfront Drive
Omaha, NE 68102-4226
402-661-1736
Regional Director: Michael Reynolds

Northeast Region
National Park Service
U.S. Custom House
200 Chestnut Street, Fifth Floor
Philadelphia, PA 19106
215-597-7013
Regional Director: Dennis Reidenbach

National Capital Region
National Park Service
1100 Ohio Drive, SW
Washington D.C. 20242
202-619-7000
Regional Director: Steve Whitesell

Southeast Region
National Park Service
100 Alabama Street, SW
1924 Building
Atlanta, GA 30303
404-507-5600
Regional Director: David Vela

Bureau of Indian Affairs
MS-4606
1849 C Street, NW
Washington, DC 20240
202-208-5116
800-246-8101
Fax: 202-208-6334
www.bia.gov
Assistant Secretary: Larry Echo Hawk

The Bureau of Indian Affairs (BIA) was establshed in 1824, and is the oldest bureau of the Department of the Interior. It provides services, either directly or through contracts, grants, or compacts, to approximately 1.9 million American Indians and Alaska Natives through its 12 regional offices, listed below. There are 565 federally recognized American Indian tribes and Alaska Natives in the United States. BIA is responsible for the administration and management of 55 million surface acres and 57 million acres of subsurface minerals, estates held in trust by the United States for American Indians, Indian tribes, and Alaska Natives. The Bureau of Indian Education (BIE) provides education services to approximately 42,000 Indian students.

Alaska Regional Office
Bureau of Indian Affairs
PO Box 25520
709 West 9th Street
Juneau, AK 99802

907-586-7177
Fax: 907-586-7252
Regional Director: Eugene Virden
Deputy Regional Director, Trust Services: Rose
Brady

Eastern Regional Office
Bureau of Indian Affairs
545 Marriott Drive, Suite 700
Nashville, TN 37214
615-564-6700
Fax: 615-564-6701
Regional Director: Franklin Keel
Deputy regional Director, Trust Services: Robert
Impson

Eastern Oklahoma Regional Office
Mailing Address:
Bureau of Indian Affairs
P.O. Box 8002
Muskogee, OK 74401-6201
Physical Address:
Bureau of Indian Affairs
3100 W. Peak Boulevard
Muskogee, OK 74401
918-781-4600
Fax: 918-781-4604
Regional Director: Jeanette Hanna
Deputy Regional Director - Indian Services: Karen
Ketcher

Great Plains Regional Office
Bureau of Indian Affairs
115 4th Avenue Southeast
Aberdeen, SD 57401
605-226-7343
Fax: 605-226-7446
Regional Director: Weldon B. Loudermilk
Deputy Regional Director, Trust Services: Timothy
L. LaPointe

Midwest Regional Office
Bureau of Indian Affairs
Department of the Interior
Bishop Henry Whipple Federal Building
One Federal Drive, Room 550
Ft. Snelling, MN 55111-4007

612-713-4400
Fax: 612-713-4401
Regional Director: Diane Rosen
Acting Deputy Regional Director - Indian Services:
Stuart Mani

Navajo Regional Office
Mailing Address:
Bureau of Indian Affairs
P.O. Box 1060
Gallup, NM 87305
Physical Address:
Bureau of Indian Affairs
301 West Hill Street
Gallup, NM 87301
505-863-8314
Fax: 505-863-8324
Regional Director: Omar Bradley
Deputy Regional Director - Trust Services: Sharon
A. Pinto

Northwest Regional Office
Bureau of Indian Affairs
911 Northeast 11th Avenue
Portland, Oregon 97232-4169
503-231-6702
Fax: 503-231-2201
Regional Director: Stanley M. Speaks
Deputy Regional Directory, Indian Services: Scott
Akin

Pacific Regional Office
Bureau of Indian Affairs
2800 Cottage Way
Sacramento, CA 95825
916-978-6000
Fax: 916-978-6099
Regional Director: Amy Dutschike
Deputy Regional Director, Indian Services: Dale
risling

Rocky Mountain Regional Office
Bureau of Indian Affairs
316 N 26th Street
Billings, MT 59101
406-247-7943
Fax: 406-247-7976

Regional Director: Edward F. Parisian
Deputy Regional Director - Trust Services: Gordon Jackson

Southern Plains Regional Office

Bureau of Indian Affairs
WCD Office Complex
P.O. Box 368
Anadarko, OK 73005
405-247-6673
Fax: 405-247-5611
Regional Director: Dan Deerinwater
Deputy Regional Director, Indian Services: Terry Bruner

Southwest Regional Office

Bureau of Indian Affairs
1001 Indian School Road, NW
Albuquerque, NM 87104
505-563-3103
Fax: 505-563-3101
Regional Director: Bill Walker
Deputy Regional Director, Indian Services and Trust Services: Ryan Riley

Western Regional Office

Bureau of Indian Affairs
2600 N. Central Avenue, 4th Floor Mailroom
Phoenix, AZ 85004-3050
602-379-6600
Fax: 602-379-4413
Regional Director: Bryan Bowker
Deputy Regional Director, Indian Services: Matt Crain

Bureau of Land Management

1849 C Street NW, Rm. 5665
Washington DC 20240
202-208-3801
Fax: 202-208-5242
www.blm.gov
E-mail: Director@blm.gov
Director: Bob Abbey
Deputy Director (Operations): Mike Pool

The Bureau of Land Management (BLM) has one of the most challenging and complex missions of any federal agency. Its goal is to sustain the health, diversity, and productivity of public lands for the use and enjoyment of present and future generations. The BLM offers some of the most exciting and unique opportunities to enhance the quality of life for all citizens through the balanced stewardship of the National System of Public Lands, and its 12 regional offices, listed below.

Alaska State Office

Bureau of Land Management
222 West 7th Avenue
Anchorage, AK 99513
907-271-5960
Fax: 907-271-3684
TTY/1-800-877-8339
State Director: Bud C. Cribley
Associate State Director: Julia Dougan
www.blm.gov/ak/st/en.html
Email: AK_AKSO_Public_Room@blm.gov

Alaska is known for its scenic beauty as well as for its natural, cultural and historical resources. Its Tangle Lakes Archaeological District covers 266,660 acres of scenic wildlands and is home to over 600 prehistoric archaeology sites. The district is one of the most culturally and historically significant areas in the United States and was listed on the National Register of Historic Places in 1971.

BLM Alaska plans for oil and gas exploration and development in the National Petroleum Reserve in Alaska, a 23-million-acre block of mostly arctic tundra on the state's North Slope. The agency monitors oil and gas activities to ensure the environment is protected and habitats for wildlife and waterfowl populations remain healthy. Alaska also contains undetermined amounts of gas hydrates and crude oil, and the BLM works with federal, state, and Native corporations to assess these resources. The agency's Rural Energy Program also partners with these entities to explore the availability of coal bed natural gas deposits near rural villages far from the road system.

Conveyance of federal land into state and private ownership is a major program for BLM Alaska.

When its analysis, adjudication, outreach, survey, and conveyance work is complete, more than 150 million acres (approximately 42 percent of the state's land) will have been transferred out of federal ownership.

Arizona State Office
Bureau of Land Management
One North Central Avenue, Suite 800
Phoenix, AZ 85004
602-417-9200
Fax: 602-417-9556
Acting State Director: Ray Suazo
Acting Associate State Director: Joanie Losacco
www.blm.gov/az/st/en.html
Email: ASOWEB_AZ@blm.gov

BLM public land resources in Arizona range from open range lands to endangered species, from national historic sites to national monuments. Vegetation across the state includes woodlands, wetlands, and riparian areas in which a wide variety of wildlife can thrive, including more than 800 vertebrate species. Public lands provide habitat for both hardy, big game animals, as well as 54 threatened and endangered species.

These lands and their habitats not only support the modern day environment, but also include historical Mammoth kill sites, remains of a Spanish fort, and Native American petroglyphs. More than 10,500 cultural sites have been recorded on BLM-managed public lands in Arizona and five areas have been designated as national monuments: Agua Fria, Grand Canyon-Parashant, Ironwood Forest, Sonoran Desert, and Vermilion Cliffs. BLM Arizona also manages three national conservation areas (Gila Box Riparian, San Pedro Riparian, and Las Cienegas) and protects 47 wilderness areas totaling 1.4 million acres.

The BLM cares for two wild horse herds totaling approximately 215 head in Arizona, and the nation's largest wild burro populations crisscross Arizona's public lands in 10 herd areas.

California State Office
Bureau of Land Management

2800 Cottage Way, Suite W-1623
Sacramento, CA 95825
916-978-4400
Fax: 916-978-4416
TDD/1-916-978-4419
State Director: Jim Kenna
Acting Associate State Director: Peter Ditton
www.blm.gov/ca/st/en.html
Email: jkenna@blm.gov

In addition to its diverse population and features, California enjoys a rich variety of natural resources. About 800 wildlife species can be found on California public lands, including 26 animal species and 12 plant species that are listed as threatened or endangered under the Endangered Species Act. California is also home to wild horses and burros and leads the BLM's western states in annual adoptions of these animals. Additionally, thousands of historical sites are found on California public lands, and the BLM coordinates with more than 100 tribes throughout the state to study and protect these resources.

Many of California's varied and unique landscapes are part of the BLM's National Landscape Conservation System (NLCS). The BLM manages three national monuments in California: the Santa Rosa and San Jacinto; the Carrizo; and the California Coastal. California's other specially designated areas include the Headwaters Forest Reserve, Piedras Blancas Outstanding Natural Area which was designated in 2008, and other conservation areas, wilderness, preserves, national trails, and wild and scenic rivers.

Colorado State Office
Bureau of Land Management
2850 Youngfield Street
Lakewood, CO 80215
303-239-3600
Fax: 303-239-3933
State Director: Helen Hankins
Associate State Director: John Mehlhoff
www.blm.gov/co/st/en.html
Email: hhankins@blm.gov

BLM lands in Colorado serve as important areas for conservation programs. As the number of plant and animal species listed as threatened or endangered on public lands under the Endangered Species Act grows, public lands provide essential habitat for endangered plants and animals, and the BLM's policies ensure that these key habitat areas are protected.

BLM Colorado has four wild horse Herd Management Areas (HMAs) throughout the state: the Little Bookcliffs; Spring Creek Basin; Sand Wash Basin; and East Douglas/Piceance. The BLM manages wild horse and burro populations and offers excess animals to the public for adoption throughout the year.

Public lands managed by BLM Colorado encompass numerous prehistoric sites, some dating from 12,000 years ago, and several nationally significant historic sites that represent mining, transportation, and western settlement.

Eastern States State Office

Bureau of Land Management
7450 Boston Boulevard
Springfield, VA 22153
703-440-1600
Fax: 703-440-1701
Acting State Director: Dr. John Lyon
Associate State Director: Marie Stewart
www.blm.gov/es/st/en.html
Email: es_general_web@blm.gov

BLM Eastern States is a 31-state region. Cooperative management agreements with state and local governments allow it to provide key recreation sites at such public land treasures as the Meadowood Special Recreation Management Area in Virginia, Lake Vermilion Islands in Minnesota, scenic beaches in Florida, historic lighthouses within the Great Lakes area and along the Florida Coast, and an oasis of green space in Maryland near Washington, DC. BLM Eastern States is also home to the Jupiter Inlet Outstanding Natural Area in Florida, a unit of the National Landscape Conservation System, which was designated in 2008.

On average, BLM Eastern States is able to find good homes for about 1,200 wild horses and burros each year through adoptions, a fostering program, and temporary site adoptions throughout the East.

BLM Eastern States provides for lighthouse transfers (there are eight lighthouse properties located on BLM land), land disposal, title dispute resolution, and many other realty actions.

BLM Eastern States also manages recreation, cultural resources, and fish and wildlife habitat at sites in Florida, Alabama, Maryland, Minnesota, Wisconsin, and Virginia. The BLM plays a major role in monitoring sensitive species and habitat restoration.

Idaho State Office

Bureau of Land Management
1387 S. Vinnell Way
Boise, ID 83709
208-373-4000
Fax: 208-373-3899
State Director: Steven Ellis
Associate State Director: Peter Ditton
www.blm.gov/id/st/en.html
Email: id_so_information@blm.gov

Idaho's abundant rivers and lakes and sagebrush-covered range lands provide habitat for a diversity of wildlife. Idaho provides food and cover for sage-grouse, mule deer, and elk; a spawning place for salmon; and a stopover for thousands of migrating water birds. About 800 pairs of falcons, eagles, hawks, and owls mate and raise their young in the Snake River Birds of Prey area each spring.

The public lands in Idaho are also rich in cultural history. Remains of railroads and ranching and mining operations are still visible today and wild horses and burros roam Idaho's range lands, reminders of the history of the West.

Montana State Office
Bureau of Land Management
5001 Southgate Drive
Billings, MT 59101
406-896-5000
Fax: 406-896-5299
State Director: Jamie Connell
Associate State Director: Kate Kitchell
www.blm.gov/mt/st/en.html
Email: MT_SO_Information@blm.gov

The public lands in Montana and the Dakotas provide important habitat for around 600 species of fish and wildlife. They contain 2,500 miles of rivers and streams as well as important riparian areas that help improve water quality. They provide forest products ranging from Christmas trees to commercial timber and a renewable source of forage for domestic livestock that helps maintain a rural economy and lifestyle that, for many, epitomizes the region's character.

Some of the nation's largest coal deposits lie beneath the eastern Montana and western North Dakota prairies. While the coal itself is a key source of energy, significant quantities of what is known as coal bed natural gas are trapped in the coal seams, especially in Montana's Powder River Basin.

In south-central Montana, the rugged Pryor Mountain National Wild Horse Range covers about 40,000 acres and is home to Montana's only free-roaming wild horses, reputed to be of Spanish ancestry. The Pryor range was the first to be designated in the United States.

Nevada State Office
Bureau of Land Management
1340 Financial Boulevard
Reno, NV 89502
775-861-6400
Fax: 775-861-6601
State Director: Amy Lueders
Acting Associate State Director: Rex McKnight
www.blm.gov/nv/st/en.html
Email: nvsoweb@blm.gov

Nevada supports a biologically diverse population of animals, plants, and habitats, despite an average of less than 10 inches of rainfall annually Mule deer, elk, and bighorn sheep are scattered throughout the state. Tens of thousands of migratory birds rely on sparse lakes, rivers, and ponds. Protecting riparian habitat along small creeks that flow down canyons is critical to the survival of many of the native fishes.

More than half of the nation's free-roaming wild horses and burros are in Nevada—about 12,995 animals in 102 herd management areas covering 16 million acres. The BLM prepares excess animals for adoption in Nevada other states.

The BLM's first National Conservation Area (NCA), Red Rock Canyon in Nevada, has long been considered one of the Bureau's crown jewels, as both an international climbing destination and an environmental education program for schools in nearby Las Vegas. The Black Rock Desert NCA in northwestern Nevada is host to the BLM's largest permitted recreation event—Burning Man—with more than 50,000 participants. Sloan Canyon, which is also near Las Vegas, is a stunning repository of petroglyphs.

Among the states with BLM-managed public lands, Nevada ranks second (behind California) in acreage designated as wilderness. BLM Nevada manages 45 wilderness areas totaling more than 2 million acres. Forty-four of these wilderness areas have been designated since 2002.

New Mexico State Office
Bureau of Land Management
P.O. Box 27115
Santa Fe, NM 87502-0115
301 Dinosaur Trail
Santa Fe, NM 87508
505-954-2000
Fax: 505-954-2115
Acting State Director: Jesse Juen
Acting Associate State Director: Tony Herrell
www.blm.gov/nm/st/en.html
Email: nm_comments@nm.blm.gov

A diversity of wildlife can be found in New Mexico, and BLM New Mexico is focusing on restoring habitat and reintroducing native species into the wild. In July 2007, The Peregrine Fund, BLM, U.S. Fish and Wildlife Service, White Sands Missile Range, and New Mexico State Land Office released aplomado falcons south of Socorro. The effort will continue on public lands until a viable, self-sustaining population is established. The BLM, working with the New Mexico Department of Game and Fish and the Taos Pueblo, augmented a population of Rocky Mountain bighorn sheep in the Rio Grande Gorge north of Espanola in the first release of the sheep on BLM land in New Mexico. Working closely with the Department of Game and Fish, the BLM spends $500,000 annually in Sikes Act funding to enhance wildlife habitat throughout the state, benefiting the state-endangered desert bighorn sheep and a variety of game species.

Public lands in New Mexico are home to irreplaceable cultural and historical artifacts, fossils, and geological and biological resources. In fiscal year 2007, BLM New Mexico hosted a heritage tourism workshop that brought in state and federal agency experts from around the Southwest to develop strategic plans for heritage tourism opportunities on public lands. The BLM also certified 10 non-federally owned sites as components of El Camino Real de Tierra Adentro National Historic Trail.

The BLM manages a variety of units within the National Landscape Conservation System—a national conservation area, a national monument, three national scenic and historic trails, and four wilderness areas, including the Ojito Wilderness, designated in October 2006. Completing, maintaining, and protecting the Continental Divide National Scenic Trail is a statewide priority. The 3,100-mile trial will connect nationally significant cultural and natural treasures.

The BLM holds wild horse and burro adoptions to ensure a healthy population of these animals on public lands. In 2007, the Mustang Heritage Foundation worked with the BLM to create an

Extreme Mustang Makeover competition held in Fort Worth, Texas, now an annual event.

Oregon State Office

Bureau of Land Management
P.O. Box 2965
Portland, OR 97208
333 S.W. 1st Avenue
Portland, OR 97204
503-808-6001
Fax: 503-808-6308
State Director: Ed Shepard
Associate State Director: Michael Mottice
www.blm.gov/or/st/en.html
Email: BLM_OR_SO_Land_Office_Mail@blm.gov

The Cascade Mountain Range separates the distinct eastern and western lands of the Pacific Northwest. Western Oregon's rainforests, wetlands, rivers, and coastal beaches on BLM lands form a distinctive checkerboard ownership pattern as designated under the Oregon and California Lands Act of 1937 (O&C Lands Act) and are managed as timberlands. The O&C lands offer rich habitat for fish and wildlife; a variety of forest products such as timber, ferns, mushrooms, and bear grass; and an abundance of recreational opportunities.

East of the Cascade Mountain Range, the public lands consist of high desert terrain covered with juniper, sagebrush, and prairie grasses. Wild horses, elk, birds, other wildlife, and livestock find shelter and forage here. The unique Kiger mustangs run free at Steens Mountain Cooperative Management and Protection Area in southeast Oregon, a unit of the BLM's National Landscape Conservation System.

Interpretive facilities throughout Oregon and Washington help travelers understand and appreciate the BLM's cultural and natural resources, including The National Historic Oregon Trail Interpretive Center. Public lands in Oregon and Washington are a primary source of timber and wood products, and BLM's grazing program focuses on retaining healthy and productive landscapes. Interest in renewable energy (geothermal, wind, and biomass) on Oregon and Washington public lands continues to increase.

Across Oregon and Washington, 488 recreation sites received over 8.3 million visits from bicyclists, backpackers, hunters, photographers, rafters, and avid adventurers. The BLM offers camping, hiking, and picnic sites, and the popularity of geocaching-high-tech outdoor treasure hunting-has grown rapidly in recent years.

Utah State Office
Bureau of Land Management
P.O. Box 45155
Salt Lake City, Utah 84145-0155
440 West 200 South, Suite 500
Salt Lake City, UT 84101
801-539-4001
Fax: 801-539-4237
State Director: Juan Palma
Acting Associate State Director: Shelley Smith
www.blm.gov/ut/st/en/html
Email: Public_Room_UT_State_Office@blm.gov

In Utah, more than 2,543 wild horses roam freely within 20 Herd Management Areas, and 195 wild burros roam in two of those areas. The areas range from 32,000 to 256,000 acres, and animal populations vary from 25 to more than 400. Horses and burros available for adoption can be viewed at holding facilities in Herriman and Delta, Utah. A partnership between BLM Utah and the Central Utah Correctional Facility in Gunnison, Utah, gives prison inmates the opportunity to care for excess wild horses, readying them for adoption.

The Grand Staircase-Escalante National Monument (GSENM) in Utah contains one of the highest concentrations of dinosaur fossils found anywhere in the world, and numerous species have been discovered since GSENM's creation in 1996. In July 2007, while searching for a dinosaur nesting site, a GSENM paleontologist and two Geological Society of America interns came across a trail of bone fragments belonging to a "super" crocodile, a 30 plus foot long animal with a 4-foot long head. Utah's Cleveland-Lloyd Dinosaur Quarry is home to one of the most impressive collections of dinosaur fossils worldwide. More than 12,000 bones have been excavated from the quarry, with many of these bones on exhibit in about 65 museums worldwide.

Wyoming State Office
Bureau of Land Management
5353 Yellowstone Road
Cheyenne, WY 82009
307-775-6256
Fax: 307-775-6129
State Director: Don Simpson
Associate State Director: Ruth Welch
www.blm.gov/wy/st/en.html
Email: wycopywork@blm.gov

Wyoming sits between the northwestern Great Plains, Rocky Mountain, and Great Basin regions, and is also home to nearly 2 million acres of wetlands that are important to the state's ecosystem. About 34,739 of these wetland acres are located on BLM public lands. Additionally, 4,497 miles of streams and associated riparian habitat on public lands provide water, food, or shelter for 90 percent of the state's wildlife species. Two of Wyoming's threatened plant species, the Ute lady's tresses and Colorado butterfly plant, rely on riparian habitat for survival. Riparian habitats, along with other landscape characteristics, permit Wyoming to boast the largest single desert elk herd and the largest single-state populations of both sage-grouse and pronghorn antelope.

Prior to the arrival of western culture, several Native American ribes existed in what is now Wyoming. Today, Wyoming offers opportunities to tour and view original wagon ruts along the historic trails in landscapes that remain much as they were in the 19th century. BLM Wyoming manages more miles of the Oregon, California, Mormon Pioneer, and Pony Express National Historic Trails than any other western state. The BLM focuses on maintaining these national treasures to keep this significant piece of American history alive, and in 2002, opened the National

Historic Trails Interpretive Center in partnership with the City of Casper.

Wyoming also maintains a large population of wild horses and burros, mainly found in southwest Wyoming near Rock Springs and Rawlins; these animals roam public lands and are protected under the Wild Free Roaming Horses and Burros Act of 1971. The estimated 4,000 wild horses in Wyoming are continually monitored by the BLM.

U.S. Geological Survey

USGS National Center
12201 Sunrise Valley Drive
Reston, VA 20192, USA
703-648-5953
888-275-8747
www.usgs.gov/ask/
Director: Marcia McNutt
Deputy Director: Suzette Kimball
Regional Executive: David Ross

The U. S. Geological Survey (USGS) is a science organization that provides impartial information on the health of the country's ecosystems and environment, the natural hazards that threaten it, the natural resources we rely on, the impacts of climate and land-use change, and the core science systems that help provide timely, relevant, and useable information. Its four regional offices are listed below.

Denver Federal Center (Colorado)

U.S. Geological Survey
Box 25046 Denver Federal Center
Denver, CO 80225, USA
303-236-5900
updike@usgs.gov
Regional Executive: Randall Updike

Menlo Park (California)

U.S. Geological Survey
345 Middlefield Road
Menlo Park, CA 94025, USA
650-853-8300
jkeay@usgs.gov
Regional Executive: Jeff Keay

Rolla (Missouri)

U.S. Geological Survey
1400 Independence Road
Rolla, MO 65401, USA
573-308-3500
methridge@usgs.gov
Regional Executive: Max Ethridge

Office of Insular Affairs

U.S. Department of the Interior
Office of Insular Affairs
1849 C Street, N.W.
Washington, DC 20240
202-208-6816
Fax: 202-219-1989
www.doi.gov/oia/
Assistant Secretary: Anthony M. Babauta
Director: Nikolao Pula

The U.S. Department of the Interior's Office of Insular Affairs coordinates federal policy in the territories of American Samoa, Guam, the U.S. Virgin Islands and the Commonwealth of the Northern Mariana Islands. The office also administers U.S. federal assistance to the Freely Associated States of the Federated States of Micronesia, the Republic of the Marshall Islands and the Republic of Palau under the Compacts of Free Association.

Industry Resources for Land and Natural Resources

With current, comprehensive coverage of the industries that support the researcher of U.S. land and natural resources, this section includes 1,354 listings. The listings are arranged first by industry—Agriculture; Environment and Conservation; Fishing; Lumber and Wood; Mining; Paper and Allied Products; Petroleum and Allied Products; and Water Supply—and then by resource type—Associations, Newsletters, Magazines & Journals, Trade Shows and Directories & Databases. Each listing includes name, address, phone, fax, web site, email, key contacts and a brief description.

Agriculture

Associations

Agribusiness Council

PO Box 5565
Washington, DC   20016

202-296-4563
FAX 202-887-9178
E-Mail: info@agribusinesscouncil.org
Home Page:
www.agribusinesscouncil.org

Nicholas E Hollis, President

Private, nonprofit/tax-exempt, membership organization dedicated to strengthening U.S. agro-industrial
competitiveness through programs
which highlight international trade and
development potentials.
Founded in 1967

Agricultural Communicators of Tomorrow

1008 McCarty Hall
P.O. Box 110180
Gainesville, FL   32611-0180

352-392-1971
FAX 352-392-9589
Home Page: www.ifas.ufl.edu

Dr Jimmy G Cheek, VP

A national organization of college students professionally interested in communications related to agriculture, food,
natural resources and allied fields.
Founded in 1970

Agricultural Education National

6060 FFA Drive
PO Box 68960
Indianapolis, IN   46268

317-802-6060
E-Mail: membership@ffa.org
Home Page: www.ffa.org

Dr Larry Case, CEO
Dr Steve Brown, Executive Secretary

The organization's mission is to prepare
students for successful careers and a life-
time of informed choices in the global
agriculture, food, fiber and natural resources systems.
507M Members
Founded in 1928

Agricultural Research Institute

40 W Gude Drive
Suite 101
Rockville, MD   20814-3998

301-294-5303
FAX 301-294-9006
Home Page: www.amwa.org

Michelle Hogan, Executive Director
Laurie Glimcher, President
Susan Swian, VP

One hundred and twenty-five member
institutions concerned with environmental issues, pest control, agricultural meteorology, biotechnology, food irradiation,
agricultural policy, research and development, food safety, technology transfer
and remote sensing.

Agriculture Council of America

11020 King St
Suite 205
Overland Park, KS   66210-1201

913-491-1895
FAX 913-491-6502
E-Mail: info@agday.org
Home Page: www.agday.org
Social Media: *Facebook*

Jennifer Pickett, President
Dr John Bonner, Secretary/Treasurer

The ACA is an organization uniquely
composed of leaders in the agriculture,
food and fiber communities dedicated to
increasing the public awareness of agriculture's vital role in our society.
75 Members
Founded in 1973

American Agricultural Economics Association

555 E Wells Street
Suite 1100
Milwaukee, WI   53202-6600

414-918-3190
FAX 414-276-3349
E-Mail: info@aaea.org
Home Page: www.aaea.org
Social Media: *Facebook*

Otto C Doering III, President
Yvonne C Bennett, Executive Director

The professional association for agricultural economists and related fields.
3000 Members
Founded in 1910
Mailing list available for rent

American Agricultural Law Association

127 Young Rd
Kelso, WA   98626

360-200-5699
FAX 360-423-2287
E-Mail: roberta@aglaw-assn.org
Home Page: www.aglaw-assn.org

Robert Achenbach, Executive Director
Roger A McEowen, President

Association devoted to education about
agricultural law.
600 Members
Founded in 1980

American Agriculture Movement

AAM National Secretary
Rural Route 1
Box 135J
Memphis, MO   63555-9766

660-465-2200
E-Mail: lynnkirk@nemr.net
Home Page: www.aaminc.org

Larry Matlack, President
Arthur Chaney, Executive Vice President
John Willis, Vice President
Anna Kirkpatrick, Secretary
Wayne Allen, Vice President of Political
Action

This farmer-created organization has
farmers themselves as leaders, speakers
and organizers, empowering farmers to
be self advocate for themselves and and
agriculture industry.
Founded in 1977

American Angus Association

3201 Frederick Ave
St Joseph, MO   64506-2997

816-383-5100
FAX 816-233-9703
E-Mail: angus@angus.org
Home Page: www.angus.org

Bryce Schumann, CEO
Bill Davis, VP

Dedicated to serve the beef industry and
provide the best beef quality.
36000 Members
Founded in 1873

American Beekeeping Federation

3525 Piedmont Rd NE
Bldg 5 Suite 300
Atlanta, GA   30305-1509

404-760-2875
FAX 404-240-0998

E-Mail: info@abfnet.org
Home Page: www.abfnet.org

Robin Dahlen, Executive Director
Zac Browning, President
David Mendes, VP

A organization that includes honey producers, packers, suppliers and shippers of honey products.
1200 Members
Founded in 1943

American Brahman Breeders Association

3003 S Loop W
Suite 520
Houston, TX   77054-1375

713-349-0854
FAX 713-349-9795
E-Mail: abba@brahman.org
Home Page: www.brahman.org
Social Media: *Facebook*

Chris Shivers, Executive VP
Theresa Dominguez, Membership & Promo Items

American Brahman Breeders is a beef crossbreeding organization that plays a significant role in the agricultural and food industries.
Founded in 1924

American Cranberry Growers Association

Po Box 423
Chatsworth, NJ   08019-0423

609-268-0641
FAX 609-268-9232
E-Mail: crangrowers@hotmail.com
Home Page: www.njcranberries.org

Stephen V. Lee IV, President

Committed to preserving and enhancing the vitality of the cranberry industry regarding environmental issues, research to advance cranberry cultivation, and identifying other issues important to cranberry growers.

American Dairy Science Association

2441 Village Green Pl
Champaign, IL   61822-7676

217-356-5146
FAX 217-398-4119
E-Mail: adsa@assochq.org
Home Page: www.adsa.org

Donald C Beitz, President
Philld C Tongz, VP

Peter Studney, Executive Director
William R Aimutis, Treasurer

Organization that provides leadership and support to dairy farmers and the industry at large.
3000 Members
Founded in 1898
Mailing list available for rent

American Farm Bureau Federation

600 Maryland Ave SW
Suite 1000W
Washington, DC   20024-2555

202-484-3600
FAX 202-484-3604
E-Mail: bstallman@fb.org
Home Page: www.fb.org
Social Media: *Facebook, Twitter, YouTube*

Bob Stallman, President
Julie Anna Potts, Executive Vice President & Treasure
Jean Bennis, Executive Assistant

An organization that helps support and bring together agricultural communities across the country.
3M Members
Founded in 1919

American Forage and Grassland Council

PO Box 867
Berea, KY   40403

800-944-2342
FAX 859-623-8694
E-Mail: info@afgc.org
Home Page: www.afgc.org
Social Media: *Facebook*

Michael Bandy, Executive Director
Howard Straub, VP
Ed Rayburn, Secretary/Treasurer

International organization whose objective is to promote the profitable production and sustainable utilization of quality forage and grasslands.
2700 Members

American Guernsey Association

1224 Alton Darby Creek Rd.
Suite G
Columbus, OH   43228

614-864-2409
FAX 614-864-5614

E-Mail: infon@usguernsey.com
Home Page: www.usguernsey.com

Seth Johnson, Executive Secretary-Treasurer
Brian Schnebly, Programs Coordinator
Ida Albert, Records Director

Promotes programs and services to the dairy industry worldwide.
900 Members
Founded in 1877

American Hereford Association

PO Box 014059
Kansas City, MO   64101

816-842-3757
FAX 816-842-6931
E-Mail: aha@hereford.org
Home Page: www.hereford.org
Social Media: *Facebook*

Craig Huffhines, Executive VP

Association for people in the Hereford cattle industry.

American Jersey Cattle Association

6486 E Main Street
Reynoldsburg, OH   43068

614-861-3636
FAX 614-861-8040
Home Page: www.usjersey.com

Associtin for the support and improvement of the Jersey cattle industry.
540 Members
Founded in 1868

American Livestock Breeds Convervancy

PO Box 477
Pittsboro, NC   27312

919-542-5704
FAX 919-545-0022
Home Page: www.albc-usa.org
Social Media: *Facebook, Blogger*

Charles Bassett, Executive Director

Ensuring the future of agriculture through genetic conservation and the promotion of endangered breeds of livestock and poultry. A nonprofit membership organization working to protect over 180 breeds of livestock and poultry from extinction.

American Phytopathological Society

3340 Pilot Knob Road
Saint Paul, MN   55121-2097

651-454-7250
800-328-7560
FAX 651-454-0766
E-Mail: aps@scisoc.org
Home Page: www.apsnet.org
Social Media: *Facebook, Twitter, LinkedIn, YouTube*

Steve Nelson, APS Executive VP
Amy Hope, VP of Operations
Barbary Mock, VP of Finance

Scientific organization dedicated to the study and control of plant diseases.
4500 Members
Founded in 1908

American Seed Trade Association

1701 Duke Street
Suite 275
Alexandria, VA   22314-2878

703-837-8140
FAX 703-837-9365
Home Page: www.amseed.com

Andy Lavigna, CEO

Supports companies involved in seed production and distribution, plant breeding and related industries in North America.
850 Members
Founded in 1883

American Sheep Industry Association

9785 Maroon Circle
Suite 360
Englewood, CO   80112

303-771-3500
FAX 303-771-8200
Home Page: www.sheepusa.org
Social Media: *Facebook, Twitter*

Margaret Hinson, President
Peter Orwick, Executive Director
Rita Kourlis Samuelson, Wool Marketing Director

A federation of state associations dedicated to the welfare and profitability of the sheep industry.
8000+ Members
Founded in 1865

American Society for Horticultural Science

1018 Duke Street
Alexandria, VA   22314

703-836-4606
FAX 703-836-2024
E-Mail: webmaster@ashs.org
Home Page: www.ashs.org

Michael Neff, Executive Director

A cornerstone of research and education in horticulture and an agent for active promotion of horticultural science.
1200 Members
ISSN: 0018-5345
Founded in 1903

American Society of Agricultural Consultants

N78W14573 Appleton Ave
Suite 287
Menomonee Falls, WI   53051

262-253-6902
FAX 262-253-6903
E-Mail: cmerry@country-marketing.com
Home Page: www.agconsultants.org
Social Media: *Facebook*

Paige Gilligan, President
Peggy Raisanen, President-Elect
Gary Wagner, VP/Secretary

An association representing the full range of agricultural consultants which serves as an information, resource, and networking base for its members.
181 Members
Founded in 1963

American Society of Agricultural and Biological Engineers

2950 Niles Rd
St Joseph, MI   49085-8607

269-429-0300
800-371-2723
FAX 269-429-3852
E-Mail: hq@asabe.org
Home Page: www.asabe.org
Social Media: *Facebook, Twitter, YouTube*

Darrin Drollinger, Executive Director
Donna Hull, Publication Director

Supports its membership of agricultural engineers and biological engineers.
8500 Members
Founded in 1907

American Society of Agronomy

5585 Guilford Road
Madison, WI   53711-1086

608-273-8080
FAX 608-273-2021
E-Mail: headquarters@agronomy.org
Home Page: www.agronomy.org
Social Media: *Facebook, Twitter, LinkedIn*

Ellen E Bergfeld, Executive VP
Luther Smith, Executive Director
Michela Cobb, Director Financial Services
Audrey Jankowski, Analyst/Programmer
Ian Popkewitz, Director IT/Operations

Advances the acquisition and dissemination of scientific knowledge concerning the nature, use improvement and interrelationships of plants, soils, water and environment. Promotes effective research, facilitates technology transfer, and fosters high ethical standards of education and advancements in the field.
11000 Members
Founded in 1907

American Society of Animal Science

2441 Village Green Pl
Champaign, IL   61822-7676

217-356-9050
FAX 217-398-4119
E-Mail: asas@assochq.org
Home Page: www.asas.org
Social Media: *Facebook, Twitter, RSS*

Meghan Wulster-Radcli, Executive Director
Louise Adams, Managing Editor
Lorena Nicholas, Communications Director

A professional organization for animal scientists designed to help members provide effective leadership through research, extension, teaching and service for the dynamic and rapidly changing livestock and meat industries.
ISSN: 0021-8812
Founded in 1908

American Society of Consulting Arborists

9707 Key West Ave
Suite 100
Rockville, MD   20850-3992

301-947-0483
FAX 301-990-9771
E-Mail: asca@mgmtsol.com

Home Page: www.asca-consultants.org
Social Media: *Facebook, LinkedIn*

Beth Palys, Executive Director

Supports consulting arborists as authoritative experts on trees, as they serve property owners, municipalities, attorneys, insurance professionals and others on tree disease, placement, preservation, environmental issues and dispute resolution.

American Society of Farm Managers and Rural Appraisers

950 S Cherry St
Suite 508
Denver, CO   80246-2664

303-758-3513
FAX 303-758-0190
E-Mail:
nhardiman@agri-associations.org
Home Page: www.asfmra.org
Social Media: *Facebook, Twitter, LinkedIn*

Nancy Hardiman, Director Education
Brian Stockman, Executive VP
Debe L Alvarez, Manager
Education/Faculty

Promoste the professions of rural appraisal, real property review appraisal and farm management.
2300 Members
Founded in 1929
Mailing list available for rent

American Soybean Association

12125 Woodcrest Executive
Suite 100
Creve Coeur, MO   63141-5009

314-576-1770
800-688-7692
FAX 314-576-2786
Home Page: www.soygrowers.com
Social Media: *Facebook, Twitter, LinkedIn*

Steve Censky, CEO
Alan Kemper, President
Steve Williams, First VP
Rob Joslin, Chairman

The primary focus of the association is policy development and implementation and improved profitibility for the US soybean farmer.
22000 Members
Founded in 1920

American Sugar Alliance

2111 Wilson Blvd
Suite 600
Arlington, VA   22201-3051

703-351-5055
FAX 703-351-6698
E-Mail: info@sugaralliance.org
Home Page: www.sugaralliance.org

James Johnson, President
Jack Roney, Director Economics/Policy Analysis
Luther Markwart, Executive Vice President
Carolyn Cheney, Vice President

National coalition of cane, beet and corn farmers, processors, suppliers, workers and others dedicated to preserving a strong domestic sweetener industry.
Founded in 1983

Animal Agriculture Alliance

PO Box 9522
Arlington, VA   22209

703-562-5160
FAX 703-524-1921
E-Mail: info@animalagalliance.org
Home Page: www.animalagalliance.org
Social Media: *Facebook, Twitter*

Kay Johnson, Executive VP
Sarah Hubbart, Communications Coordinator

The Animal Agricultural Alliance's mission, as an education foundation, is to support and promote animal agricultural practices that provide for farm animal well-being through sound science and public education.
3000 Members
Founded in 1987

Aquatic Plant Management Society

PO Box 821265
Vicksburg, MS   39182-1265

FAX 601-634-5502
E-Mail: dpetty@ndrsite.com
Home Page: www.apms.org
Social Media: *Facebook, LinkedIn*

Linda Nelson, President
Terry Goldsby, VP
Sherry Whitaker, Treasurer
Jeff Schardt, Secretary
Greg Aguillard, Director

Individuals and companies interested in supporting the control of water plants that hinder recreation or navigation.
Founded in 1961

Association for Arid Lands Studies

601 Indiana Avenue
PO Box 45004
Lubbock, TX   79409-5004

806-742-2974
FAX 806-742-1286
E-Mail: gay.riggan@ttu.edu
Home Page: www.iaff.ttu.edu

Tibor Nagy, VP
Dr. A C Correa, International Director/ICASALS

Promotes the interdisciplinary study of arid and semi-arid environments and the human relationship to these environments from an international perspective.
200 Members
Founded in 1966

Association for Communication Excellence i n Agriculture

59 College Road
Taylor Hall
Durham, NH   03824

855-657-9544
866-941-3048
FAX 603-862-1585
E-Mail: info@aceweb.org
Home Page: www.aceweb.org

Frankie Gould, President
Robert Casler, VP
Holly Young, Interim Executive Director

Focuses on advancing the public's knowledge and understanding of agriculture, natural resources and life and human sciences.
Founded in 1970

Association for Communications Excellence

Mowry Road, Building 116
PO Box 110811
Gainesville, FL   32611

352-392-9588
FAX 352-392-8583
E-Mail: ace@ifas.ufl.edu
Home Page: www.aceweb.org

Amanda Aubuchon, ACE Coordinator

International association of communicators and information technologists that disseminates knowledge about agricul-

ture, natural resources and life and human sciences worldwide.
600 Members
Founded in 1970

Association of American Seed Control Officials

Utah Department of Agriculture
350 N Redwood Road
PO Box 146500
Salt Lake City, UT   84114-6500

801-848-8543
FAX 801-538-7189
E-Mail: stburningham@utah.gov
Home Page: www.seedcontrol.org

G Richard Wilson, Director
Gary G Peterson, Commissioner
Dr. Stanford Young, Secretary/Treasurer

Officials of government agencies at state and federal levels engaged in the regulation and distribution of seeds.
Founded in 1949

Bio-Dynamic Farming and Gardening Association

25844 Butler Road
Junction City, OR   97448

541-998-0105
888-516-7797
FAX 541-998-0106
E-Mail: info@biodynamics.com
Home Page: www.biodynamics.com
Social Media: *Facebook*

Restoring the soil to a balanced living condition through the application and use of crude organic matter known as stabilized humus. Crop rotation, correct composting and proper intercropping can all contribute to a healthier biodynamic yield.

Cape Cod Cranberry Institute

1 Carver Square Boulevard
PO Box 97
Carver, MA   02330

508-866-7878
FAX 508-866-4220
E-Mail: cinews@earthlink.net
Home Page: www.cranberries.org
Social Media: *Facebook*

Jere Downing, Executive Director
Mike Bartling, Vice Chair
David McCarthy, Secretary/Treasurer

Promotes the success of US and Canadian cranberry growers through health,

agricultural and environmental stewardship research and education.
Founded in 1951

Committee on Organic and Sustainable Agric ulture

5585 Guilford Road
Madison, WI   53711

608-273-8080
FAX 608-273-2021
Home Page: www.cosagroup.org

Supports its members and divisions interested in sustainable and organic agriculture and develops recommendations on ways to better serve members interested in this endeavor.

Communicating for Agriculture

112 E Lincoln Avenue
P.O. Box 677
Fergus Falls, MN   56538-2217

218-739-3241
FAX 218-739-3832
E-Mail: info@cabenefits.org
Home Page: www.cabenefits.org

Milt Smedsrud, CEO

Strives to promote health, well-being and advancement of people in agriculture and agribusiness.
40M Members
Founded in 1972

Community Alliance with Family Farmers

36355 Russell Boulevard
P.O. Box 363
Davis, CA   95617

530-756-8518
800-892-3832
FAX 530-756-7857
E-Mail: judith@fullbellyfarm.com
Home Page: www.caff.org
Social Media: *Facebook, Twitter, YouTube*

Judith Redmond, President
George Davis, VP
Diane Del Signore, Secretary
David Visher, Treasurer

Mission is to build a movement of rural and urban people to foster family-scale agriculture that cares for the land, sustains local economies and promotes social justice.
Cost: $47.95
Founded in 1978

Corn Refiners Association

1701 Pennsylvania Ave NW
Suite 950
Washington, DC   20006-5806

202-331-1634
FAX 202-331-2054
E-Mail: aerickson@corn.org
Home Page: www.corn.org

Audrae Erickson, President
Thomas D Malkoski, Vice Chairman of the Board
J Patrick Mohan, Treasurer

Supports carbohydrate research programs through grants to colleges, government laboratories and private research centers.
8 Members
Founded in 1913

Council for Agricultural Science and Technology

4420 West Lincoln Way
Ames, IA   50014-3447

515-292-2125
FAX 515-292-4512
E-Mail: cast@cast-science.org
Home Page: www.cast-science.org
Social Media: *, Twitter, LinkedIn, YouTube*

John Bonner, Executive VP
Donna Freeman, Director Membership/Marketing

Assembles, interpets and communicates science based information regionally, nationally and internationally on food, fiber, agriculture, natural resources, and related societal and environmental issues.
2000+ Members
Founded in 1972

Crop Science Society of America

677 S Segoe Rd
Madison, WI   53711-1086

608-273-8086
FAX 608-273-2021
E-Mail: headquarters@crops.org
Home Page: www.agronomy.org

Ellen Bergsfeld, VP
Susan G Chapman, Director/Member Services
Paul Kamps, Development Officer
Ian Popkewitz, Director IT & Operations
Luther Smith, Exec VP/Executive Dir Certification

Seeks to advance research, extension, and teaching of all basic and applied phases of the crop sciences.
4700 Members
Founded in 1955

Ecological Farming Association

2901 Park Avenue
Suite D-2
Soquel, CA   95073

831-763-2111
FAX 831-763-2112
E-Mail: info@eco-farm.org
Home Page: www.eco-farm.org
Social Media: , *Twitter, RSS*

Kristin Rosenow, Executive Director
Ken Dickerson, President
Thomas Wittman, VP/Secretary
Arty Mangan, Treasurer

A nonprofit educational organization that seeks to promote agricultural practices that are ecologically sound, economically viable and socially just.
2M Members
Founded in 1980

Farm Foundation

1301 W 22nd St
Suite 615
Oak Brook, IL   60523-6817

630-571-9393
FAX 630-571-9580
Home Page: www.farmfoundation.org

Neil Corklin, President
Steve Halbrook, VP
Mary M Thompson, Communications Director

A publicly supported nonprofit organization working to improve the economic health and social well-being of US agriculture, the food system and rural people by helping private and public sector decision makers identify and understand forces that will shape the future.

Foundation for Agronomic Research

107 S State St
Suite 300
Monticello, IL   61856-1968

217-762-2074
E-Mail: hreetz@farmresearch.com
Home Page: www.farmresearch.com

Harold Reetz, President

Helps facilitate development and implementation of science-based research and education programs in applied crop and soil management.
Founded in 1980

Fresh Produce Association of the Americas

590 East Frontage Road
PO Box 848
Nogales, AZ   85628

520-287-2707
FAX 520-287-2948
E-Mail: info@freshfrommexico.com
Home Page: www.fpaota.org

Lee Frank, President
Alicia Bon Martin, Vice Chair
Allison Moore, Communications Director
Jose Luis Obregon, Deputy Director
Martha Rascon, Public Affairs Director

Represents more than 125 member companies involved in growing, harvesting, marketing and importing of Mexican produce entering the US at Nogales, Arizona.
125+ Members
Founded in 1944

Herb Growing and Marketing Network

PO Box 245
Silver Spring, PA   17575-0245

717-393-3295
FAX 717-393-9261
E-Mail: herbworld@aol.com
Home Page: www.herbworld.com

Maureen Rogers, Director

Trade association for the herb industry.
Cost: $48.00
2000 Members
Founded in 1990

Holstein Association USA

1 Holstein Place
PO Box 808
Brattleboro, VT   05302-0808

802-254-4551
800-965-5200
FAX 802-254-8251
E-Mail: info@holstein.com
Home Page: www.holsteinusa.com

John Meyer, CEO
Lisa Perrin, Marketing

Dairy cattle breed association with a membership base of people with strong interests in breeding, raising and milking Holstein cattle.
30000 Members
Founded in 1885

Horticultural Crop and Sciences Center

Ohio State University
1680 Madison Avenue
Wooster, OH   44691-4114

330-263-3700
FAX 330-263-3658

More than 750 individuals and institutions in 72 countries involved in the research or application of soil tillage and related subjects.

International Agricultural Aviation Association

PO Box 1607
Mount Vernon, WA   98273-1607

360-734-9757
FAX 360-336-2506

Members are pilots and aircraft owners licensed by the FAA as agricultural aviators (crop dusters).
4859 Members
Founded in 1978

International Association of Operative Millers

10100 West 87th Street
Suite 306
Overland Park, KS   66212

913-338-3377
FAX 913-338-3553
E-Mail: info@iaom.info
Home Page: www.iaom.info
Social Media: *Facebook, Twitter, LinkedIn*

Joe Woodward, President
Melinda Farris, Executive VP
Joel Hoffa, Treasurer
Aaron Black, VP

An international organization, comprised of flour millers, cereal grain and seed processors and allied trades representatives and companies devoted to the advancement of technology in the flour milling and cereal grain processing industries.
1500 Members
Founded in 1896

International Maple Syrup Institute

5014 Route Seven
Ferrisburgh, VT   05456

802-877-2250
FAX 802-877-6659
E-Mail: larry.myott@uvm.edu
Home Page:
www.internationalmaplesyrupinstitute.com

Lynn Reynolds, Executive Manager
Luc Lussier, General Manager/CEO
Robert Montambault, Director Quality
Yves Gosselin, Director Human
Ressources
Lise Belleville, Executive Secretary

The mission of the organization is to
promote the use of pure maple syrup and
protect the integrity of the product while
encouraging cooperation among all persons or groups involved in any aspect of
the maple industry.
15M Members
Founded in 1975

Irrigation Association

6540 Arlington Blvd
Falls Church, VA   22042-6638

703-536-7080
FAX 703-536-7019
E-Mail: info@irrigation.org
Home Page: www.irrigation.org

Deborah Hamlin, Executive Director
Denise Stone, Meetings Director

Promotes education and use of irrigation
in many areas of agriculture.
1600 Members
Founded in 1949

Irrigation Foundation Faculty Academy

6540 Arlington Blvd
Falls Church, VA   22042-6638

703-536-7080
FAX 703-536-7019
E-Mail: info@irrigation.org
Home Page: www.irrigation.org

Deborah Hamlin, Executive Director
Denise Stone, Meetings Director

Promotes education and use of irrigation
in many areas of agriculture.
1600 Members
Founded in 1949

Mid-South Grain Inspection

1390 Channel Avenue
Memphis, TN   38114

901-942-3216
FAX 901-774-9651
E-Mail: mphsgrain@aol.com

Tim Adams, Agency Manager

Established to provide a liaison between
the Federal Grain Inspection Service and
designated agencies. Annual meeting
held in January.
60 Members
Founded in 1980

National Alliance of Independent Crop Consultants

349 E Nolley Dr
Collierville, TN   38017-3538

901-861-0511
FAX 901-861-0512
E-Mail: jonesnaicc@aol.com
Home Page: www.naicc.org

Allison Jones, Executive VP
Shannon Gomes, Secretary

Represents individual crop consultants
and contract researchers.
500+ Members
Founded in 1978

National Association of Animal Breeders

PO Box 1033
Columbia, MO   65205-1033

573-445-4406
FAX 573-446-2279
E-Mail: naab-css@naab-css.org
Home Page: www.naab-css.org

Gordon Doak, President
Jere Mitchell, Technical Director

Trade association for the artificial insemination of beef & dairy cattle industry.
20 Members
Founded in 1946

National Association of County Agricultural Agents

6584 W Duroc Road
Maroa, IL   61756

217-794-3700
FAX 217-794-5901
E-Mail: exec-dir@nacaa.com
Home Page: www.nacaa.com
Social Media: *Facebook, Twitter*

Rick Gibson, President

Geared toward Extension educators and
other professionals who work in agriculture, horticulture, forestry and natural resources, 4-H youth development,
community development, administration,
aquaculture and Sea Grant, and related
disciplines.
3850 Members
Founded in 1917
*Mailing list available for rent: 3500
names at $500 per M*

National Association of State Departments of Agriculture

1156 15th St NW
Suite 1020
Washington, DC   20005-1711

202-296-9680
FAX 202-296-9686
E-Mail: nasda@nasda.org
Home Page: www.nasda.org
Social Media: *Facebook, Twitter*

Stephen Haterius, Executive Director
Roger Johnson, President
Ron Sparks, President-Elect
Michael Scuse, Vice President

Represents the state departments of agriculture in the development, implementation and communication of sound public
policy and programs which support and
promote the American agricultural industry, while protecting consumers and
the environment.
Founded in 1915

National Association of Wheat Growers

415 2nd Street NE
Washington, DC   20002-4993

202-547-7800
FAX 202-546-2638
E-Mail: wheatworld@wheatworld.org
Home Page: www.wheatworld.org
Social Media: *Facebook, Twitter,
YouTube*

David Cleavinger, First Vice President
Karl Scronce, Second Vice President
Dana Peterson, CEO
Melissa George Kessler, Director of
Communications

Nonprofit partnership of US wheat
growers, by combining their strengths,
voices and ideas are working to ensure a
better future for themselves, their industry and the general public.
Founded in 1950

National Bison Association

8690 Wolff Court
200
Westminster, CO   80234

303-292-2833
FAX 303-845-9081
E-Mail: david@bisoncentral.com
Home Page: www.bisoncentral.com

Dave Carter, Executive Director
Jim Matheson, Assistant Director

Formed to promote the production, marketing and preservation of bison.
2400 Members
Founded in 1995

National Cattlemen's Beef Association

9110 E. Nichols Ave. #300
Centennial, CO   80112

303-694-0305
Home Page: www.beef.org

Dave Benino, Executive Director
Andy Groseta, Vice President

Membership organization of 35,000 cattlemen.
23000 Members
Founded in 1898

National Cooperative Business Association

1401 New York Ave NW
Suite 1100
Washington, DC   20005-2160

202-638-6222
FAX 202-638-1374
E-Mail: ncba@ncba.coop
Home Page: www.ncba.coop

Paul Hazen, President
Judy Bennett, Executive Secretary

Leading US organization strengthening the cooperative form of business to empower people and improve quality of life worldwide. To make cooperatives a strong, distinct and unified sector, recognized by the American public. Our member co-ops operate in the areas including, agricultural supply and marketing, children, energy, food distribution, healthcare and housing.
1800 Members
Founded in 1916

National Cotton Council of America

7193 Goodlett Farms Parkway
Cordova, TN   38016

901-274-9030
FAX 901-725-0510
Home Page: www.cotton.org

Mark Lange, President/CEO
A. John Maguire, Senior Vice President

Membership consists of approximately 300 delegates named by cotton interests in the cotton-producing states.
35 Members

National Cottonseed Products Association

866 Willow Tree Circle
Cordova, TN   38018-6376

901-682-0800
FAX 901-682-2856
E-Mail: info@cottonseed.com
Home Page: www.cottonseed.com

Ben Morgan, Executive VP
Bobby Crum, Vice President

National association of cottonseed products.
200 Members
Founded in 1929

National Council of Agricultural Employers

8233 Old Courthouse Road
Suite 200
Vienna, VA   22182

703-790-9039
E-Mail: matt@ncaeonline.org
Home Page: www.ncaeonline.org

Frank Gasperini, Executive VP
Jason Rios, Administration Manager

Members are growers and producers who employ agricultural laborers, as well as processors and organizations related to the agriculture business.
250 Members
Founded in 1964

National Dairy Herd Improvement Association

421 S Nine Mound Round
PO Box 930399
Verona, WI   53593-0399

608-848-6455
FAX 608-848-7675

E-Mail: info@dhia.org
Home Page: www.dhia.org

Jay Mattison, CEO
Dan Sheldon, President
Lee Maassen, VP

The objective is to promote accuracy, credibility and uniformity of DHI records. To represent the DHI system on issues involving other National and International organizations
65M Members

National Farmers Organization

Po Box 2508
Ames, IA   50010-2508

515-292-2000
FAX 515-292-7106
E-Mail: nfo@nfo.org
Home Page: www.nfo.org
Social Media: *Facebook, YouTube*

Paul Olson, President
Pete Lorenz, Regional Director
Perry Gainer, Communications Director

Advocates collective bargaining through contract marketing by farmers.
30M Members
Founded in 1955

National Farmers Union

20 F Street NW
Suite 300
Washington, DC   20001

202-554-1600
800-347-1961
FAX 202-554-1654
E-Mail: dave.frederickson@nfu.org
Home Page: www.nfu.org
Social Media: *Facebook, Twitter, YouTube*

Roger Johnson, President
Claudia Svarstad, Vice President
Jeff Knudson, VP of Operations
Chandler Goule, VP of Government Relations

Promotes educational, cooperative and legislative activities of farm families in 26 states.
25000 Members
Founded in 1902

National Fisheries Institute

7918 Jones Branch Dr
Suite 700
Mc Lean, VA   22102-3319

703-752-8880
FAX 703-752-7583

E-Mail: contact@nfi.org
Home Page: www.aboutseafood.com
Social Media: *Facebook, Twitter*

John Connely, President
Gavin Gibbons, Director, Media
Relations

A non-profit organization dedicated to
education about seafood safety,
sustainability, and nutrition.
241 Members
Founded in 1945

National Grain and Feed Association

1250 I St NW
Suite 1003
Washington, DC   20005-3939

202-289-0873
FAX 202-289-5388
E-Mail: ngfa@ngfa.org
Home Page: www.ngfa.org

Kendell Keith, President
Ronald D Olson, Chairman
Tom Coyle, Second Vice Chair
Randall Gordon, Vice President

NGFA is the national trade association of
grain elevators, feed and feed ingredient
manufacturers, grain and oilseed processors, exporters, livestock and poultry
integrators, and firms providing products
and services to the industry.
Founded in 1896

National Grange

1616 H St NW
Suite 10
Washington, DC   20006-4999

202-628-3507
888-447-2643
FAX 202-347-1091
E-Mail: bsteel@nationalgrange.org
Home Page: www.nationalgrange.org

Ed Luttrell, President
Jennifer Dugent, Communications
Manager
Leroy Watson, Legislative Director
Cindy Greer, Director Youth\Young
Adult
DoriAnn Gedris, Marketing Director

Promotes general welfare and agriculture
through local organizations. Presides
over the advancement and promotion of
the farming and agriculture industry.
300k Members
Founded in 1960

National Grape Cooperative

2 South Portage Street
Westfield, NY   14787-1400

716-326-5200
FAX 716-326-5494
E-Mail: nationalinfo@welchs.com
Home Page: www.nationalgrape.com

Joseph C Falcone, President and
Director
Brent Roggie, General Manager, COO,
& Treasurer
Michael Perda, Financial and
Accounting Officer

Focus on delivering grapes of outstanding quality. The investment of our
grower/owners in stringent quality growing and harvesting standards, viticultural
research, and aggressively funding new
product development, manufacturing and
marketing programs of Welch's - the Cooperative has enjoyed a long history of
industry leadership and growth.
1282 Members

National Hay Association

151 Treasure Island Cswy. #2
St. Petersburg, FL   33706-4734

727-367-9702
800-707-0014
FAX 727-367-9608
E-Mail: darthay@yahoo.com
Home Page: www.nationalhay.org

Ron Bradtmueller, President
Gary Smith, First VP
Richard Larsen, Second VP
Rollie Bernth, Director
Don Kieffer, Executive Director

NHA is the trade group that represents
the interests of the hay industry throughout the United States and internationally.
750 Members
Founded in 1895

National Onion Association

822 7th St
Suite 510
Greeley, CO   80631-3941

970-353-5895
FAX 970-353-5897
E-Mail: kreddin@onions-usa.org
Home Page: www.onions-usa.org
Social Media: *, Twitter*

Wayne Mininger, Executive VP

Represents interests of US onion producers. Informational lobbying and generic
promotional headquarters for fresh dry

bulb onion growers. Provides connections for networking and education
exchange.
550 Members
Founded in 1913
*Mailing list available for rent: 600
names*

National Pork Producers Council

122 C Street NW
Suite 875
Washington, DC   20001

202-347-3600
800-937-7675
FAX 202-347-5265
E-Mail: warnerd@nppc.org
Home Page: www.nppc.org
Social Media: *Facebook, Twitter*

Don Butler, President
Sam Carney, President-Elect
Doug Wolf, Vice President
Neil Dierks, CEO

Established as the National Swine Growers Council, NPPC assumed its present
name in 1967 and is now a federation of
45 state associations.
44 Members

National Potato Council

1300 L St NW
Suite 910
Washington, DC   20005-4107

202-682-9456
FAX 202-682-0333
E-Mail:
spudinfo@nationalpotatocouncil.org
Home Page:
www.nationalpotatocouncil.org

John Keeling, Executive VP/CEO
Hollee Stubblebine, Director Industry
Communications
Keith Masser, President
Jim Wysocki, VP Finance
Dan Elmore, VP Grower/Public
Relations

Represents US potato growers on federal
legislative and regulatory issues.
45000 Members
Founded in 1948

National Young Farmer Educational Association

PO Box 20326
Montgomery, AL   36120

334-213-3276
888-332-2668
FAX 334-213-0421

E-Mail: natloffice@nyfea.org
Home Page: www.nyfea.org
Social Media: *Facebook, Twitter, Flickr*

C.J. Fleenor, President
Gordon Stone, Executive Vice President
Carol Corman, President Elect

To promote the personal and professional growth of all people involved in agriculture.

North American Millers' Association

600 Maryland Ave SW
Suite 825 W
Washington, DC   20024

202-484-2200
FAX 202-488-7416
E-Mail: generalinfo@namamillers.org
Home Page: www.namamillers.org

Betsy Faga, President
James Bair, VP

Trade association representing the wheat, corn, oat and rye milling industry. NAMA members operate one hundred and seventy mills in thirty-eight states and Canada. Their aggregate production of more than one hundred and sixty million pounds per day is approximately ninety-five percent of the industry capacity in the U.S.
45 Members
Founded in 1902

Organic Crop Improvement Association

1340 North Cotner Blvd
Lincoln, NE   68505

402-477-2323
FAX 402-477-4325
E-Mail: info@ocia.org
Home Page: www.ocia.org

Jeff See, Executive Director

OCIA International is a farmer owned international program of certification, which adheres to strict organic standards, who has thousands of farmers and processors in North, Central and South America and Asia.
3500 Members
Founded in 1985
Mailing list available for rent: 3500 names at $50 per M

Organic Seed Alliance

PO Box 772
Port Townsend, WA   98368

360-385-7192
FAX 360-385-7455
E-Mail: info@seedalliance.org
Home Page: www.seedalliance.org
Social Media: *Facebook, Twitter*

Dan Hobbs, Executive Director
Matthew Dillon, Executive Director

Supports the ethical development and stewardship of the genetic resources of agricultural seed.
Founded in 1975

Professional Farmers of America

1818 Market Street 31st Floor
Philadelphia, PA   19103

800-772-0023
E-Mail: editors@profarmer.com
Home Page: www.profarmer.com
Social Media: *, Twitter*

Sue King, Contact

Provides farmers with marketing strategies and market-trend data, as well as seminars and home study courses.
25M Members
Founded in 1973

Santa Gertrudis Breeders International

PO Box 1257
Kingsville, TX   78364-1257

361-592-9357
FAX 361-592-8572
Home Page: www.santagertrudis.com

Ervin Kaatz, Executive Director

America's first beef breed developed in 1918 and recognized in 1940 by the USDA. The breed is known for efficient growth, solid red color, hardiness, good disposition and being adaptable to many environments.

Society of American Foresters

5400 Grosvenor Ln
Bethesda, MD   20814-2198

301-897-8720
FAX 301-897-3690
E-Mail: safweb@safnet.org
Home Page: www.safnet.org
Social Media: *Facebook, Twitter, LinkedIn*

Michael T Goergen Jr, Executive VP/CFO

Brittany Brumby, Assistant to the CEO/Council
Amy Ziadi, Information Technology Manager
Larry D Burner CPA, Sr Director Finance

Provides access to information and networking opportunities to prepare members for the challenges and the changes that face natural resource professionals.
Founded in 1900

Society of Commercial Seed Technologists

101 E State Street
Suite 214
Ithaca, NY   14850-1257

607-256-3313
FAX 607-270-1638
E-Mail: scst@twcny.rr.com
Home Page: www.seedtechnology.net

Brent Reschly, President
Neal Foster, Vice President
Anita Hall, Executive Director

Professionals involved in the testing and analysis of seeds, including research, production and handling based on botanical and agricultural sciences.
250 Members
Founded in 1922

Southern Cotton Ginners Association

874 Cotton Gin Pl
Memphis, TN   38106-2588

901-947-3104
FAX 901-947-3103
E-Mail: carmen.griffin@southerncottonginners.org
Home Page: www.southerncottonginners.org
Social Media: *Facebook*

Tim Price, Executive VP
Will Wade, President/Tennessee
Richard Kelly, VP
Allen Espey, VP/Tennessee

Operates in a five state area as an information center covering safety and governmental regulations. Serves its members by providing safety, training and regulatory representation. Sponsors certification programs and hosts the industry's leading trade show, The Mid-South Farm & Gin Show.
700 Members
Founded in 1950

USA Rice Federation

USA Rice Federation
4301 N Fairfax Drive
Suite 425
Arlington, VA   22203

703-226-2300
FAX 703-236-2301
E-Mail: riceinfo@usarice.com
Home Page: www.usarice.com
Social Media: *Facebook, Twitter, LinkedIn, YouTube*

Jamie Warshaw, Chairman

The global advocate for all segments of the U.S. rice industry with a mission to promote and protect the interests of producers, millers, merchants and allied businesses. USA Rice is made up of the USA Rice Grower's Assoc, USA Rice Millers' Assoc, USA Rice Council, and the USA Rice Merchants' Association.

United Fresh Fruit and Vegetable Association

1901 Pennsylvania Ave NW
Suite 1100
Washington, DC   20006-3412

202-303-3400
FAX 202-303-3433
E-Mail: united@unitedfresh.org
Home Page: www.uffva.org
Social Media: *Facebook, Twitter, YouTube*

Thomas E Stenzel, CEO
Nicholas J Tompkins, Chair
Robert A Grimm, Executive Committee
Daniel G Vache, Secretary/Treasurer

Equipment, supplies, cartons, packaging machinery, computers, sorting and sizing equipment, harvesting equipment, film wrap manufacturing and commodity organizations.
1000+ Members
Founded in 1904

United Producers

8351 North High Street
Suite 250
Columbus, OH   43235-1440

614-890-6666
800-456-3276
FAX 614-890-4776
Home Page: www.uproducers.com
Social Media: *Facebook, LinkedIn*

A cooperative marketing organization owned by farmers and ranchers in the United States' corn belt, midwest and southeast.
36000 Members
Frequency: Annual Meetings
Founded in 1962

United States Animal Health Association

4221 Mitchell Ave.
St Joseph, MO   64508

816-671-1144
FAX 816-671-1201
E-Mail: usaha@usaha.org
Home Page: www.usaha.org

Benjamin Richey, Executive Director
Kelly Janicek, Executive Assistant

Seeks to prevent, control and eliminate livestock diseases.
1400 Members
Founded in 1897

United States Canola Association

600 Pennsylvania Ave SE
Suite 320
Washington, DC   20003-6300

202-969-8113
FAX 202-969-7036
E-Mail: info@uscanola.com
Home Page: www.uscanola.com

John Gordley, Executive Director
Dale Thorenson, Assistant Director
Angela Dansby, Communications Director

USCA members are producers and processors of canola and grapeseed.
Founded in 1989

United States Grains Council

1400 K St NW
Suite 1200
Washington, DC   20005-2449

202-789-0789
FAX 202-898-0522
E-Mail: grains@grains.org
Home Page: www.grains.org

Kenneth Hobbie, President
Michael T Callahan, Director International Operations
Cheri Johnson, Manager Communications
Valerie Smiley, Manager Membership
Andrew Pepito, Director Finance/Administration

Motivated by the grain sorghum, barley and corn producer associations and representatives of the agricultural community. Provides commodity export market development.
175 Members
Founded in 1960

Veal Quality Assurance Program & Veal Issu es Management Program

PO Box 148
Meshoppen, PA   18630

717-823-6995
E-Mail: info@vealfarm.com
Home Page: www.vealfarm.com

Members include veal producers and processors.
1300 Members
Founded in 1984

Walnut Council

1011 N 725 W
West Lafayette, IN   47906-9431

765-583-3501
FAX 765-583-3512
E-Mail: walnutcouncil@walnutcouncil.org
Home Page: www.walnutcouncil.org

Liz Jackson, Executive Director
Larry R Frye, VP
William Hoover, Treasurer

Assisting in the technical transfer of forest research to field applications, helping build and maintain better markets for wood products and nut crops, and promoting sustainable forest management, conservation, reforestation, and utilization of American black walnut and other high quality fine hardwoods.
1000 Members
Founded in 1970

Western United States Agricultural Trade Association

4601 NE 77th Avenue
Suite 200
Vancouver, WA   98662-2697

360-693-3373
FAX 360-693-3464
Home Page: www.wusata.org

Andy Anderson, Executive Director
Eliza Lane, Outreach Coordinator

A nonprofit organization that promotes the export of food and agricultural products from the Western region of the US Comprised of 13 state funded agricultural promotion agencies.

Wild Blueberry Association of North America

PO Box 100
Old Town, ME   04468

207-570-3535
FAX 207-581-3499
E-Mail: wildblueberries@gwi.net
Home Page: www.wildblueberries.com
Social Media: *Facebook, Twitter*

Jerel Kim Higgins, President
Sue Till, Marketing Manager

Represents processors and growers of wild blueberries in Eastern Canada and Maine. The Association is focused on the generic promotion of wild blueberries around the world. It offers promotional materials, joint funding, product development, assistance, seminars, newsletters, supplier lists and ongoing support to users of wild blueberries in all retail, manufacturing, foodservice and bakery trade segments.
Founded in 1981

Newsletters

AAM Newsletter

American Agriculture Movement
24800 Sage Creek Road
Scenic, SD   57780

605-993-6201
FAX 605-993-6185
E-Mail: jjobgen@hotmail.com
Home Page: www.aaminc.org

Larry Matlack, President
Arthur Chaney, Executive Vice President
John Willis, Vice President
Anna Kirkpatrick, Secretary
Wayne Allen, Vice President of Political Action

The creation of the AAM has provided a farmer-created, farmer-built organization within which farmers themselves have been the leaders, speakers and organizers; empowering farmers as they had not been in the past, to speak for and advocate for themselves. Updates about events, news, articles and letters to the editor.
Founded in 1977

ALBC News

American Livestock Breeds
Conservancy
PO Box 477
Pittsboro, NC   27312

919-542-5704
FAX 919-545-0022
Home Page: www.albc-usa.org

Charles Bassett, Executive Director

Provides in-depth information about current ALBC activities, breed information, member updates, and more.
Frequency: Bi-Monthly

ARClight

National Agri-Marketing Association
11020 King St
Suite 205
Overland Park, KS   66210-1201

913-491-6500
FAX 913-491-6502
E-Mail: agrimktg@nama.org
Home Page: www.nama.org

Jennifer Pickett, CEO
Vicki Henrickson, Vice President

Agricultural Relations Council - a national association with members involved in agricultural public relations. Electronic newsletter of interest to association members.

ASA Today

American Soybean Association
12125 Woodcrest Executive
Suite 100
Creve Coeur, MO   63141-5009

314-576-1770
800-688-7692
FAX 314-576-2786
E-Mail: bcallanan@soy.org
Home Page: www.soygrowers.com

Steve Censky, CEO
Cassandra Schlef, Communications Coordiniator

For members only
Frequency: Weekly

ASAC News

American Society of Agricultural
Consultants
N78W14573 Appleton Ave
#287
Menomonee Falls, WI   53051

262-253-6902
FAX 262-253-6903
E-Mail:

cmerry@countryside-marketing.com
Home Page: www.agconsultants.org
Frequency: Quarterly
Founded in 1963

Agri Times Northwest

PO Box 1626
Pendleton, OR   97801

541-276-6202
FAX 541-278-4778
E-Mail: editor@agritimesnw.com
Home Page: www.agritimesnw.com

Sterling Allen, Publisher
Jim Eardley, Editor

Contains news stories and columns pertaining to rural life and agri-business, designed to keep farmers and ranchers up to date with agriculture in their backyard.
Cost: $20.00
Frequency: 2x/Month
Founded in 1981

Agricultural Law Update

American Agricultural Law Association
PO Box 835
Brownsville, OR   97327

541-466-5444
FAX 541-466-3311
E-Mail: lindamccormick@gotsky.com
Home Page: www.aglaw-assn.org

Linda Grim McCormick, Editor

Articles written about environmental and agricultural issues.

Agweek

Grand Forks Herald
PO Box 6008
Grand Forks, ND   58206-6008

701-780-1236
FAX 701-780-1211
E-Mail: kdeats@gfherald.com
Home Page: www.gfherald.com

Kim Deats, Editor
Michael Jacobs, Publisher

Features classifieds, weather information, farming, ranch news and opinion for the Upper Midwest
Cost: $32.00
80 Pages
Frequency: Weekly
Printed in on newsprint stock

Alliance Link Newsletter

Animal Agriculture Alliance
PO Box 9522
Arlington, VA   22209

703-562-5160
FAX 703-524-1921
E-Mail: info@animalagalliance.org
Home Page: www.animalagalliance.org

Kay Johnson, Executive VP
Sarah Hubbart, Communications
Coordinator

Helps members and industry stake-
holders stay informed about the key issues impacting animal agriculture
Frequency: Monthly

American Agriculturist

Farm Progress Companies
255 38th Ave
Suite P
St Charles, IL   60174-5410

630-797-8289
800-441-1410
E-Mail: circhelp@farmprogress.com
Home Page: www.farmprogress.com

Agricultural magazine serving New York
farmers and agri-businesses.
Cost: $26.95
Frequency: Monthly

American Beekeeping Federation Newsletter

American Beekeeping Federation
3525 Piedmont Rd NE
Bldg 5 Suite 300
Atlanta, GA   30305-1509

404-760-2875
FAX 404-240-0998
E-Mail: info@abfnet.org
Home Page: www.abfnet.org

Raymond Payne, President

Newsletter for members of the American
Beekeeping Federation.
Cost: $35.00
24 Pages
Circulation: 1750
Founded in 1943
Printed in on newsprint stock

American Dairy Science Newsletter

American Dairy Science Association
2441 Village Green Pl
Champaign, IL   61822-7676

217-356-5146
FAX 217-398-4119

E-Mail: adsa@assochq.org
Home Page: www.adsa.org

Gary W Rogers, Editor

Aquatic Plant News

Aquatic Plant Management Society
PO Box 821265
Vicksburg, MS   39182-1265

FAX 601-634-5502
E-Mail: dpetty@ndrsite.com
Home Page: www.apms.org
Social Media: *Facebook, LinkedIn*

Linda Nelson, President
Terry Goldsby, VP
Sherry Whitaker, Treasurer

Aquatic Plant News is produced 3 times
each year, and is distributed primarily by
email.
Frequency: 3x/Year
Founded in 1961

Association of American Seed Control Officials Bulletin

Utah Department of Agriculture
350 N Redwood Road
PO Box 146500
Salt Lake City, UT   84114-6500

801-848-8543
FAX 801-538-7189
E-Mail: stburningham@utah.gov
Home Page: www.ag.utah.gov

Stephen T Burningham, Control Officer
Leonard Blachham, Commissioner
Jed Christenson, Marketing

Seed laws in the United States and Can-
ada.
Frequency: Annual+
Circulation: 5000

Bison Connection

National Bison Association
8690 Wolff Ct
200
Westminster, CO   80031

303-292-2833
FAX 303-845-9081
E-Mail: marilyn@bisoncentral.com
Home Page: www.bisoncentral.com

Marilyn Wentz, Editor

Informs member of association activities
as well as industry news, opportunities
and events.
Frequency: Monthly

CSA News

5585 Guilford Road
Madison, WI   53711-1086

608-273-8080
FAX 608-273-2021
E-Mail: headquarters@agronomy.org
Home Page: www.agronomy.org
Social Media: *Facebook, Twitter,
LinkedIn*

Ellen E Bergfeld, Executive VP
Luther Smith, Executive Director
Michela Cobb, Director Financial
Services
Audrey Jankowski, Analyst/Programmer
Ian Popkewitz, Director IT/Operations

The official magazine for members of
the American Society of Agronomy,
Crop Science Society of America, and
Soil Science Society of America.
11000 Members
Founded in 1907

Chaff Newsletter

American Association of Grain
Inspection
PO Box 26426
Kansas City, MO   64196

816-569-4020
FAX 816-221-8189
E-Mail: info@aagiwa.org
Home Page: www.aagiwa.org

Welcomes member information about
new products, business changes, personnel changes and other items that may be
of interest to AAGIWA members.
Frequency: Monthly

Council for Agricultural Science and Technology Newsletter

Council For Agricultural Science and
Technology
4420 Lincoln Way
Ames, IA   50014-3447

515-292-2125
E-Mail: info@cast-science.org
Home Page: www.cast-science.org

John Bonner, Executive VP

Identifies food, fiber, environmental and
other agricultural issues for all stake
holders, including legislators, policy
makers and the public.
Frequency: Quarterly
Circulation: 4000
Founded in 1972
Printed in 2 colors

Country World Newspaper

Echo Publishing Company
401 Church St
Sulphur Springs, TX   75482-2681

903-885-0861
800-245-2149
FAX 903-885-8768
E-Mail: scott@ssecho.com
Home Page:
www.countryworldnews.com

Scott Key, President
Kari Arnold, Editor

A newspaper offering agricultural information to farmers, ranchers, dairyfarmers, and agribusinesses.
Frequency: Weekly
Founded in 1981

Daily Advocate

Brown Publishing
428 S Broadway St
Greenville, OH   45331-220

937-548-3151
FAX 937-548-3913
E-Mail: info@brownpublishing.com
Home Page: www.brownpublishing.com

David W Compton, Publisher
Christina Chalmers, Editor

Farming interests, grain, livestock. Sections on senior citizens, farmers, builders, religion, sports, as well as special sections on agriculture and home improvement.
Cost: $31.20
Frequency: Daily
Circulation: 110,053
Founded in 1920

Decision Support Systems for Agrotechnology Transfer

ICASA
2440 Campus Road
PO Box 527
Honolulu, HI   96822

808-956-2713
FAX 808-956-2711
E-Mail: icasa@icasanet.org
Home Page: www.icasa.net

Systems analysis and crop simulation models for agrotechnology transfers and risk assessment. Reference guides and models for maize, wheat, rice, sorghum, millet, barley, soybean, peanut and potato are included. Linked to GIS

sofeware.
Cost: $495.00
Frequency: Annual
Circulation: 2,500
ISBN: 1-886684-00-6
Printed in 2 colors on matte stock

Doane's Agricultural Report

Doane Agricultural Services
77 Westport Plz
Suite 250
St Louis, MO   63146-3121

314-569-2700
866-647-0918
FAX 314-569-1083
Home Page: www.doane.com

Ken Morrison, Manager

Provides information to US farmers and agricultural professionals. Doane keeps you up to date on factors affecting your farm program benefits and production costs too.
Frequency: Weekly

FMRA News

950 S Cherry St
Suite 508
Denver, CO   80246-2664

303-758-3513
FAX 303-758-0190
E-Mail:
nhardiman@agri-associations.org
Home Page: www.asfmra.org
Social Media: Facebook, Twitter, LinkedIn

Nancy Hardiman, Director Education
Brian Stockman, Executive VP
Debe L Alvarez, Manager
Education/Faculty

Current information relative to the industry and educational offerings. Also keeps members informed about government legislation, career opportunities, activities and news withing the American Society and provides regular membership updates.
2300 Members
Frequency: Bi-Monthly
Founded in 1929
Mailing list available for rent

Forestry Source

Society of American Foresters
5400 Grosvenor Ln
Bethesda, MD   20814-2198

301-897-8720
866-897-8720

FAX 301-897-3690
E-Mail: safweb@safnet.org
Home Page: www.safnet.org

Joe Smith, Editor

Offers the latest information on national forestry trends, the latest developments in forestry policy at the federal, state, and local levels, the newest advances in forestry-related research and technology, and up-to-date information about SAF programs and activities
Cost: $35.00
Frequency: Monthly
Founded in 1990
Printed in 4 colors on newsprint stock

Global Dairy Update

6437 Collamer Road
East Syracuse, NY   13057-1031

315-703-7979
800-334-1904
FAX 315-703-7988
E-Mail: dgarno@dairybusiness.com
Home Page: www.dairybusiness.com

Focuses on dairy developments throughout the world.
Cost: $197.00
4 Pages
Frequency: Monthly
Founded in 1904
Printed in 2 colors on newsprint stock

Hay There

National Hay Association
151 107th Ave
Suite 2
Treasure Island, FL   33706-4734

727-367-9702
800-707-0014
FAX 727-367-9608
Home Page: www.nationalhay.org

Don Kieffer, Executive Director

Production and marketing information for members. Accepts advertising.
Frequency: Monthly
Founded in 1895
Printed in one color on glossy stock

Holstein Association News

Holstein Association
PO Box 808
Brattleboro, VT   05302-0808

802-254-4551
800-952-5200
FAX 802-254-8251

E-Mail: info@holstein.com
Home Page: www.holsteinusa.com

John Meyer, CEO
Tom A Nunes, President
Beth Patchen, Communication Specialist

Bimonthly newsletter provides active customers with information on the association programs and services and how to intergrate them into their dairy operations.
15 Pages
Founded in 1953
Printed in 4 colors on glossy stock

Irrigation Association E-Times

Irrigation Association
6540 Arlington Blvd
Falls Church, VA   22042-6638

703-536-7080
FAX 703-536-7019
E-Mail: info@irrigation.org
Home Page: www.irrigation.org

Deborah Hamlin, Executive Director
Denise Stone, Meetings Director
Kate Baumann, Membership
Coordinator
Rebecca Bayless, Finance Director
Marsha Cram, MBA, Foundation &
Membership Manager

Reports on federal and state policies and legislation that affect the irrigation industy. Status updates on industry initiatives, and information on the latest association events, programs, services and awards.
1600 Members
Frequency: Monthly
Founded in 1949

Irrigation Foundation E-Newsletter

Irrigation Association
6540 Arlington Blvd
Falls Church, VA   22042-6638

703-536-7080
FAX 703-536-7019
E-Mail: info@irrigation.org
Home Page: www.irrigation.org

Deborah Hamlin, Executive Director
Denise Stone, Meetings Director
Kate Baumann, Membership
Coordinator
Rebecca Bayless, Finance Director
Marsha Cram, MBA, Foundation &
Membership Manager

Published on a quarterly basis, this e-newsletter provides updates on Foundation activities and accomplishments.
1600 Members
Frequency: Quarterly
Founded in 1949

Journal of Dairy Science

American Dairy Science Association
2441 Village Green Pl
Champaign, IL   61822-7676

217-356-5146
FAX 217-398-4119
E-Mail: adsa@assochq.org
Home Page: www.adsa.org

Gary W Rogers, Editor

Dairy research journal.

NAMA Newsletter

North American Millers' Association
600 Maryland Ave SW
Suite 825 W
Washington, DC   20024

202-484-2200
FAX 202-488-7416
E-Mail: generalinfo@namamillers.org
Home Page: www.namamillers.org

Betsy Faga, President
James Bair, VP

Trade association representing the wheat, corn, oat and rye milling industry. NAMA members operate one hundred and seventy mills in thrirty-eight states and Canada. Their aggregate production of more than one hundred and sixty million pounds per day is approximately ninety-five percent of the industry capacity in the U.S.
Frequency: Monthly
Circulation: 250

NASDA News

1156 15th St NW
Suite 1020
Washington, DC   20005-1711

202-296-9680
FAX 202-296-9686
E-Mail: nasda@nasda.org
Home Page: www.nasda.org
Social Media: *Facebook, Twitter*

Stephen Haterius, Executive Director
Roger Johnson, President
Ron Sparks, President-Elect
Michael Scuse, Vice President

Represents the state departments of agriculture in the development, implementa-

tion and communication of sound public policy and programs which support and promote the American agricultural industry, while protecting consumers and the environment.
Founded in 1915

National Cottonseed Products Association Newsletter

National Cottonseed Products
Association
866 Willow Tree Cir
Cordova, TN   38018-6376

901-682-0800
FAX 901-682-2856
E-Mail: info@cottonseed.com
Home Page: www.cottonseed.com

Ben Morgan, Executive VP
Bobby Crum, Vice President

Current events.
Founded in 1897

National Honey Report

Federal Market News Service
1400 Independence Avenue SW
STOP 0238
Washington, DC   20250

202-720-2175
FAX 202-720-0547
Home Page:
www.ams.usda.gov/mnreports/fvmhoney
.pdf

Billy Cox, Director
Becky Unkenholz, Deputy Director
Joan Shaffer, Senior Public Affairs
Specialist

Current honey market information and colony conditions in the United States and other countries.
16 Pages
Frequency: Monthly

National Onion Association Newsletter

National Onion Association
822 7th St #
Suite 510
Greeley, CO   80631-3941

970-353-5895
FAX 970-353-5897
E-Mail: wmininger@onions-usa.org
Home Page: www.onions-usa.org

Wayne Mininger, Executive VP
Kim Redtin, Publisher

Newsletter published by and only for the National Onion Association.
Frequency: Monthly
Circulation: 600
Founded in 1913
Mailing list available for rent: 600 names

National Young Farmer Educational News

PO Box 15160
Alexandria, VA   22309-0160

888-332-2668
FAX 800-366-6556
Home Page: www.ffa.org

Wayne Sprick, Publisher

Tabloid which receives articles and information from state associations, as well as information from the National Association.
12 Pages
Frequency: TriAnnual
Circulation: 45,000
Founded in 1928

News of the Association of Official Seed Analysts

Association of Official Seed Analysts (AOSA)
101 East State Street
#214
Ithaca, NY   14850

607-256-3313
FAX 607-273-1638
E-Mail: aosa.office@twcny.rr.com
Home Page: www.aosaseed.com

Michael Stahr, President
Dan Curry, Vice President

News items, technical reports, rules changes for testing seeds, surveys, identification and tax news, legislative updates and updates on the Association and publications in progress.
Cost: $20.00
Frequency: TriAnnual
Circulation: 500
Printed in one color on matte stock

No-Till Farmer

Lessiter Publications
225 Regency Court
Suite 200
Brookfield, WI   53045

262-782-4480
800-645-8455
FAX 262-782-1252

E-Mail: info@lesspub.com
Home Page: www.no-tillfarmer.com

Frank Lessiter, Owner
Mike Lessiter, Executive VP
Erin Weileber, Marketing
Stacy Johnson, Circulation Manager

Management information for farmers interested in conservation tillage.
Cost: $37.95
Frequency: Monthly
Circulation: 8000
ISSN: 0091-9993
Founded in 1972
Printed in 2 colors on glossy stock

North American Millers' Association Newsletter

600 Maryland Ave SW
Suite 825 W
Washington, DC   20024

202-484-2200
FAX 202-488-7416
E-Mail: generalinfo@namamillers.org
Home Page: www.namamillers.org

Betsy Faga, President
James Bair, VP

Trade association representing the wheat, corn, oat and rye milling industry. NAMA members operate one hundred and seventy mills in thrirty-eight states and Canada. Their aggregate production of more than one hundred and sixty million pounds per day is approximately ninety-five percent of the industry capacity in the U.S.
45 Members
Founded in 1902

OCIA Communicator Newletter

1340 North Cotner Boulevard
Lincoln, NE   68505-1838

402-477-2323
FAX 402-477-4325
E-Mail: info@ocia.org
Home Page: www.ocia.org

Jeff See, Executive Director
Patricia Saldania,
Marketing/Communications

A quarterly newsletter published by the Organic Crop Improvement Association International (OCIA).
Cost: $50.00
Frequency: Quarterly
Circulation: 300
Mailing list available for rent: 3500 names at $50 per M

Organic Report

Organic Trade Association
60 Wells Street
PO Box 547
Greenfield, MA   01301

413-774-7511
FAX 413-774-6432
E-Mail: info@ota.com
Home Page: www.ota.com

Dan Pratt, Directory Coordinator
Phil Margolis, CEO/President

Targets an audience of manufacturers, growers, retailers, importers, distributors, and consultants in the organic food and fiber industry.
Frequency: Monthly
Circulation: 2500
Printed in 2 colors on matte stock

Pro Farmer

Farm Journal Media
1550 N Northwest HW
Suite 403
Park Ridge, IL   60068

215-578-8900
800-320-7992
FAX 215-568-6782
E-Mail: rmurray@farmjournal.com
Home Page:
www.farmjournalmedia.com

Andy Weber, Chief Executive Officer
Steve Custer, Executive Vice President
Jeff Pence, President, Electronic Media
Chuck Roth, Senior Vice President

Farm market news, analysis and management advice.
Cost: $159.00
8 Pages
Frequency: Weekly
Founded in 1973

SI Report

Salt Institute
700 N Fairfax Street
Suite 600
Alexandria, VA   22314-2040

703-549-4648
FAX 703-548-2194
E-Mail: info@saltinstitute.org
Home Page: www.saltinstitute.org

Richard L Hanneman, President

A monthly e-newsletter published by the Salt Institute.
Frequency: Monthly
Founded in 1914
Printed in on glossy stock

Salt & Trace Mineral Newsletter

Salt Institute
700 N Fairfax Street
Suite 600
Alexandria, VA   22314-2085

703-549-4648
FAX 703-548-2194
E-Mail: info@saltinstitute.org
Home Page: www.saltinstitute.org

Richard L Hanneman, President

Information on animal nutrition.
Frequency: Quarterly
Founded in 1914
Printed in on glossy stock

Seed News

PO Box 772
Port Townsend, WA   98368

360-385-7192
FAX 360-385-7455
E-Mail: info@seedalliance.org
Home Page: www.seedalliance.org

Dan Hobbs, Executive Director

Information covering events, seminars
and meetings.
Cost: $8.00
8 Pages

USA Rice Daily

USA Rice Federation
4301 N Fairfax Drive
Suite 425
Arlington, VA   22203

703-226-2300
FAX 703-236-2301
E-Mail: riceinfo@usarice.com
Home Page: www.usarice.com

Jamie Warshaw, Chairman

The latest news on issues and activities
for the U.S. rice industry.

Webster Agricultural Letter

Webster Communications Corporation
1530 Key Blvd
Suite 401W
Arlington, VA   22209-1531

703-525-4512
FAX 703-852-3534
E-Mail: editor@agletter.com
Home Page: www.agletter.com

James C Webster, Owner

Agricultural politics and policy issues.
Cost: $397.00
6 Pages
Frequency: Fortnightly

ISSN: 1073-4813
Founded in 1980
Printed in one color on matte stock

Weekly Livestock Reporter

PO Box 7655
Fort Worth, TX   76111-0655

817-831-3147
FAX 817-831-3117
E-Mail: service@weeklylivestock.com
Home Page: www.weeklylivestock.com

Ted Gouldy, Publisher
Phil Stoll, CEO/President
Mickey Schwarz, Circulation Manager

Offers comprehensive weekly informa-
tion for cattle farmers and livestock agri-
cultural professionals.
Cost: $18.00
Frequency: Weekly
Circulation: 10000
Founded in 1897

Magazines & Journals

Agribusiness Council Magazine

PO Box 5565
Washington, DC   20036

202-296-4563
FAX 202-887-9178
E-Mail: info@agribusinesscouncil.org
Home Page:
www.agribusinesscouncil.org

Council news, information and calendar.
Frequency: Monthly
Founded in 1967

Agricultural Research Magazine

Agricultural Research Service
5601 Sunnyside Avenue
Beltsville, MD   20705-5130

301-504-1651
FAX 301-504-1641
E-Mail: rsowers@ars.usda.gov
Home Page: www.ars.usda.gov/is/ar

Robert Sowers, Editor
Sue Kendall, Associate Editor

U.S. Department of Agriculture's sci-
ence magazine.
Cost: $50.00
27 Pages
Frequency: Monthly
Circulation: 44000
Founded in 1954

Agronomy Journal

5585 Guilford Road
Madison, WI   53711-1086

608-273-8080
FAX 608-273-2021
E-Mail: headquarters@agronomy.org
Home Page: www.agronomy.org
Social Media: *Facebook, Twitter,
LinkedIn*

Ellen E Bergfeld, Executive VP
Luther Smith, Executive Director
Michela Cobb, Director Financial
Services
Audrey Jankowski, Analyst/Programmer
Ian Popkewitz, Director IT/Operations

Journal of agriculture and natural resource sciences. Articles convey original
research in soil science, crop science,
agroclimatology, agronomic modeling,
production agriculture, instrumentation,
and more.
11000 Members
Founded in 1907

American Agriculturist

Farm Progress Companies
255 38th Avenue
Suite P
Saint Charles, IL   60174-5410

630-462-2224
800-441-1410
E-Mail: jvogel@farmprogress.com
Home Page: www.farmprogress.com

John Vogel, Editor
Willie Vogt, Corporate Editorial Director
Dan Crummett, Executive Editor

Serves Northeast producers with information to help them maximize their productivity and profitability. Each issue is
packed with information, ideas, news
and analysis.
Cost: $26.95
Frequency: Monthly
Founded in 1842

American Bee Journal

Dadant and Sons
51 S 2nd St
Hamilton, IL   62341-1397

217-847-3324
888-922-1293
FAX 217-847-3660
E-Mail: editor@americanbeejournal.com
Home Page:

www.americanbeejournal.com
Social Media: *Facebook, Twitter*

Tim C Dadant, President
Marta Menn, Advertising
Dianne Behnke, Publisher
Joe Graham, Editor

Read by commercial and hobby
beekeepers and entomologists.
Cost: $22.95
80 Pages
Frequency: Monthly
Circulation: 11000
ISSN: 0002-7626
Founded in 1861
Printed in 4 colors on glossy stock

American Fruit Grower

Meister Media Worldwide
37733 Euclid Ave
Willoughby, OH   44094-5992

440-942-2000
800-572-7740
FAX 440-942-0662
E-Mail: afg.circ@meistermedia.com
Home Page: www.meistermedia.com

Gary Fitzgerald, President
Frank Giles, Editor
Frank Maxcy, Publisher

Specialized production and marketing
information and industry-wide support
for fruit growers.
Cost: $19.95
66 Pages
Frequency: Monthly
Circulation: 14000
Founded in 1880

American Small Farm Magazine

1867 N Galena Road
Sunbury, OH   43074

740-200-7030
FAX 740-200-7033
E-Mail: sales@smallfarm.com
Home Page: www.smallfarm.com

Andy Stevens, Editor
Marti Smith, Director of Sales
Ryan Mumm, Creative Director

Published for the owner/operator of
farms from 5 to 300 acres. Focuses on
production agriculture including alternative and sustainable farming ideas and
technology, case studies, small farm lifestyle and tradition.
Cost: $18.00
Frequency: Monthly
Circulation: 62,444

ISSN: 1064-7473
Founded in 1992

American Vegetable Grower

Meister Media Worldwide
37733 Euclid Ave
Willoughby, OH   44094-5992

440-942-2000
800-572-7740
FAX 440-975-3447
Home Page:
www.growingproduce.com/americanveg
etablegrower/

Gary Fitzgerald, President
Rosemary Gordon, Editor
Jo Monahan, Publisher

American Vegetable Grower magazine
provides insight on field, greenhouse
and organic production, marketing, and
new varieties and products.
Cost: $19.95
Frequency: Monthly
Circulation: 26000
Founded in 1908

Animal & Dairy News

American Dairy Science Association
2441 Village Green Pl
Champaign, IL   61822-7676

217-356-5146
FAX 217-398-4119
E-Mail: adsa@assochq.org
Home Page: www.adsa.org

Donald C Beitz, President
Philld C Tongz, VP
Peter Studney, Executive Director
William R Aimutis, Treasurer

A Publication of ADSA
3000 Members
Founded in 1898
Mailing list available for rent

Beef Today

Farm Journal Media
1818 Market Street
31st Floor
Philadelphia, PA   19103-3654

215-578-8900
800-331-9310
FAX 215-568-6782
E-Mail: jstruyk@farmjournal.com
Home Page: www.beeftoday.com

Andy Weber, Chief Executive Officer
Steve Custer, Executive Vice President
Jeff Pence, President, Electronic Media
Chuck Roth, Senior Vice President

This is the only nationwide publication
that currently serves beef producers of
all sizes-large and small. It delivers the
tools cattlemen need to make sustainable
and profitable choices to transition their
herd to the next generation. Topics include genetics, animal health, business
planning, pasture management, wildlife
management and market analysis.
Frequency: Weekly
Founded in 1973

Biodynamics Journal

PO Box 944
East Troy, WE   53120-0944

541-998-0105
888-516-7797
FAX 541-998-0106
E-Mail: info@biodynamics.com
Home Page: www.biodynamics.com
Social Media: *Facebook*

Provides a thoughtful collection of original articles centered on a theme of interest to the biodynamic community.
Recent themes have included urban agriculture, biodynamic community, earth
healing, raw milk, and the biodynamic
preparations.

CALF News Magazine Ltd.

1531 Kensington Boulevard
Garden city, KS   67846

620-276-7844
800-888-0368
FAX 719-495-9204
E-Mail: wilsoncattle@cornhusker.net
Home Page: www.calfnews.com

Betty Jo Gigot, Editor/Publisher
Patti Wilson, Sales Manager
Larisa Willrett, Circulation Manager

This magazine brings its readers industry
news in a creative and original way.
Each issue includes in-depth stories on
current events and cattlemen, along with
columns from regular columnists.
Cost: $33.00
Frequency: Monthly
Circulation: 7000
Founded in 1963

Capital Press

Press Publishing Company
1400 Broadway NE
PO Box 2048
Salem, OR   97308-2048

503-364-4431
800-882-6789

FAX 503-370-4383
E-Mail: news@capitalpress.com
Home Page: www.capitalpress.com

Carl Sampson, Managing Editor
Elaine Shein, Executive Editor
Michael O'Brien, General Manager

For the agricultural and forest community of the Pacific Northwest.
Cost: $44.00
60 Pages
Frequency: Weekly
Circulation: 37000
Founded in 1928
Printed in 4 colors on newsprint stock

Carrot Country

Columbia Publishing
8405 Ahtanum Rd
Yakima, WA   98903-9432

509-248-2452
800-900-2452
FAX 509-248-4056
E-Mail:
dbrent@columbiapublications.com
Home Page: www.carrotcountry.com

Brent Clement, Editor/Publisher
Mike Stoker, Publisher

Includes information on carrot production, grower and shipper feature stories, carrot research, new varieties, market reports, spot reports on overseas production and marketing and other key issues and trends of interest to US and Canadian carrot growers.
Cost: $10.00
Frequency: Quarterly
Circulation: 2500
ISSN: 1071-6653
Founded in 1993
Printed in 4 colors on glossy stock

Cattleman

Texas & Southwestern Cattle Raisers
Association
1301 W 7th St
Fort Worth, TX   76102-2604

817-332-7064
800-242-7820
FAX 817-332-8523
E-Mail:
lionel@thecattlemanmagazine.com
Home Page: www.texascattleraisers.org

Eldon White, Executive VP
Lionel Chambers, Editor
Anita Braddock, Marketing
Sherrie Caraway, Circulation Manager
Matt Brockman, Manager

Full overview of information for the cattle producer in Texas and Oklahoma.
Cost: $25.00
130 Pages
Frequency: Monthly
Circulation: 16000
Founded in 1877
Printed in 4 colors on glossy stock

Choices

Agricultural & Applied Economics
Association
555 E Wells Street
Suite 1100
Milwaukee, WI   53202

414-918-3190
FAX 414-276-3349
E-Mail: info@aaea.org
Home Page: www.choicesmagazine.org

Walter J Armbruster, Editor
James Novak, Associate Editor

Provides current coverage regarding economic implications of food, farm, resource, or rural community issues directed toward a broad audience. Publishes thematic groupings of papers and individual papers.
Frequency: Quarterly
ISSN: 0886-5558
Founded in 1910
Printed in 4 colors on glossy stock

Citrus & Vegetable Magazine

Vance Publishing
400 Knightsbridge Pkwy
Lincolnshire, IL   60069

847-634-2600
FAX 847-634-4379
E-Mail: info@vancepublishing.com
Home Page: www.vancepublishing.com

William C Vance, Chairman
Peggy Walker, President

Devlivers profitable production and management strategies to commercial citrus and vegetable growers in Florida.
Cost: $45.00
Frequency: Monthly
Circulation: 12004
Founded in 1937
Printed in 4 colors on glossy stock

Citrus Industry

Associated Publications Corporation
5053 NW Hwy 225-A
Ocala, FL   34482

352-671-1909
FAX 352-671-1364

E-Mail: office@southeastagent.com
Home Page: www.citrusindustry.net

Gary Cooper, Publisher
Ernie Neff, Editor
Robin Loftin, Marketing

News, facts and data of interest to citrus growers, processors and shippers.
Cost: $24.00
64 Pages
Frequency: 6 issues per year
Circulation: 9851
Founded in 1920
Printed in 4 colors on glossy stock

Cotton Farming

One Grower Publishing, LLC
Collierville, TN   38117-5710

901-853-5067
FAX 901-853-2197
Home Page: www.cottonfarming.com

Mike Rolfs, President
Lia Guthrie, Publisher
Tommy Horton, Editor

For commercial cotton growers across the United States Cotton Belt.
52 Pages
Frequency: Monthly
Circulation: 36,297
Founded in 1993
Printed in 4 colors on glossy stock

County Agents

National Association of County
Agricultural Agents
6584 W Duroc Road
Maroa, IL   61756

217-794-3700
FAX 217-794-5901
E-Mail: exec-dir@nacaa.com
Home Page: www.nacaa.com

Rick Gibson, President

Members receive professional improvement, news of association activities, shared education efforts from other states and reports from NACAA leadership and member states.
Cost: $10.00
Circulation: 5000
Founded in 1916
Mailing list available for rent: 3850 names at $125 per M
Printed in 4 colors on matte stock

Cranberries Magazine

Cranberries Magazine
PO Box 190
Rochester, MA   02770-190

508-763-8080
FAX 508-763-4141
E-Mail: cranberries@comcast.net

Carolyn Gilmore, Editor/Publisher

Containing up-to-date news, technical
articles, new product information,
grower profiles, economic data and other
related features regarding the cranberry
industry. Accepts advertising.
Cost: $25.00
28 Pages
Frequency: Monthly
Circulation: 850
Founded in 1936

Dairy Herd Management

Vance Publishing
400 Knightsbridge Parkway
Lincolnshire, IL   60069

847-634-2600
FAX 847-634-4379
E-Mail: info@vancepublishing.com
Home Page: www.vancepublishing.com

William C Vance, Chairman
Peggy Walker, President

Helps top dairy producers prepare for
and adapt to the different management
skills needed in this increasingly evolving industry
Cost: $60.00
Frequency: Monthly
Circulation: 61638

Dairy Today

Farm Journal
30 S 15th Street
Suite 900
Philadelphia, PA   19102-4803

215-578-8900
800-320-7992
E-Mail: dcrisafulli@farmjournal.com
Home Page: www.farmjournal.com

Charlene Finck, Editor
Katie Humphreys, Managing Editor
Beth Snyder, Art Director
Sara Schafer, Business & Crops Online
Editor

Award-winning editorial covers the
broad spectrum of production, nutrition
and marketing information. It serves
dairy producers who milk 40+ cows or

are members of the Dairy Herd Improve-
ment Association.
Frequency: Monthly
Circulation: 124421
Founded in 1989

Down to Earth

DowElanco/Dow AgroSciences
9330 Zionsville Rd
Indianapolis, IN   46268-1053

317-337-3000
FAX 800-905-7326
Home Page: www.drovers.com

Antonio Galindez, CEO

Offers international reviews of agricultural research and practice.
32 Pages
Frequency: Quarterly

Drovers

Vance Publishing
400 Knightsbridge Parkway
Lincolnshire, IL   60069

847-634-2600
FAX 847-634-4379
E-Mail: info@vancepublishing.com
Home Page: www.vancepublishing.com

William C Vance, Chairman
Peggy Walker, President

Recognized as the beef industry leader
for more than 130 years, valued for its
management, production and marketing
information.
Cost: $60.00
Frequency: Monthly
Circulation: 91715
Founded in 1873

Eastern DairyBusiness

DairyBusiness Communications
6437 Collamer Road
East Syracuse, NY   13057-1031

315-703-7979
800-334-1904
FAX 315-703-7988
E-Mail: bbaker@dairyline.com
Home Page: www.dairybusiness.com

Joel P Hastings, Editor
John Montandon, President & Co-CEO
Debbie Morneau, Marketing Coordinator

Reports on milk production and prices,
quotes on hay and feed markets, animal
health and nutrition, and the newest innovations in dairying technology, specifically tailored to the Eastern parts of the

United States
Cost: $49.95
67 Pages
Frequency: Monthly
Circulation: 14000
ISSN: 1528-4360
Founded in 1904
Printed in 4 colors on glossy stock

Egg Industry

WATT Publishing Company
303 N Main Street
Suite 500
Rockford, IL   61101

815-966-5400
FAX 815-966-6416
E-Mail: tokeefe@wattnet.net
Home Page: www.wattnet.com

James Watt, Chairman/CEO
Greg Watt, President/COO
Terrance O'Keefe, Editor

Regarded as the standard for information
on current issues, trends, production
practices, processing, personalities and
emerging technology. A pivotal source
of news, data and information for deci-
sion-makers in the buying centers of
companies producing eggs and fur-
ther-processed products.
Cost: $36.00
Frequency: Monthly
Circulation: 2500

Executive Guide to World Poultry Trends

WATT Publishing Company
303 N Main Street
Suite 500
Rockford, IL   61101

815-966-5400
FAX 815-966-6416
Home Page: www.wattnet.com

James Watt, Chairman/CEO
Greg Watt, President/COO
Jeff Swanson, Publishing Director

Offers detailed analysis on a coun-
try-by-country and market-by-market
basis.

FFA New Horizons

National FFA Organization
6060 FFA Drive
Indianapolis, IN   46268

317-802-4235
800-772-0939

E-Mail: newhorizons@ffa.org
Home Page: www.ffanewhorizons.org

Jessy Yancey, Association Editor
Christina Carden, Associate Production
Director
Julie Woodard, FFA Publications
Manager

The official member magazine of the
FFA is published bimonthly and mailed
to more than 525,000 readers. Each issue
contains information about agricultural
education, career possibilities, chapter
and individual accomplishments and
news on FFA. Now available online.
100 Pages
ISSN: 1069-806x
Founded in 1928
Printed in 4 colors

Farm Chemicals International

Meister Media Worldwide
37733 Euclid Ave
Willoughby, OH 44094-5992

440-942-2000
800-572-7740
FAX 440-975-3447
E-Mail: fci.circ@meistermedia.com
Home Page:
www.farmchemicalsinternational.com

Gary Fitzgerald, President
Frank Giles, Editor

Information on production, marketing
and application of crop protection chemicals and fertilizers.
Circulation: 8000
Founded in 1986

Farm Journal

30 S 15th Street
Suite 900
Philadelphia, PA 19102-4803

215-557-8900
800-523-1538
FAX 215-568-4436
E-Mail: scuster@farmjournal.com
Home Page:
www.farmjournalmedia.com

Andrew J Weber Jr, CEO/President
Crain Freiberg, Editor
Steve Custer, Publisher

Published for operators and owners of
commercial farms and ranches. Provides
timely, useful marketing and management information to help them produce
more efficiently, buy more wisely, sell
their products at the highest possible
prices, and retain as much of their in-

come as possible.
Cost: $24.75
182 Pages
Frequency: Monthly
Circulation: 443,529
Founded in 1878

Farm Reporter

Meridian Star
814 22nd Avenue
PO Box 1591
Meridian, MS   39302

601-693-1551
FAX 601-485-1210

Reports on every phase of farming including timber, cattle, poultry and all
growing crops.
Cost: $2.00
Frequency: Monthly

Farm Talk

Farm Talk
1801 S Highway 59
PO Box 601
Parsons, KS   67357-4900

620-421-9450
800-356-8255
FAX 620-421-9473
E-Mail: farmtalk@terraworld.net
Home Page:
www.farmtalknewspaper.com

Mark Parker, Publisher
Ted Gum, Manager

Agriculture for Eastern Kansas, Western
Missouri, Northeast Oklahoma and
Northwest Arkansas.
Cost: $30.00
60 Pages
Frequency: Weekly
Circulation: 10000
Founded in 1974

Farm World (Farm Week)

Mayhill Publications
27 N Jefferson Street
PO Box 90
Knightstown, IN   46148-1242

317-326-2235
800-876-5133
FAX 765-345-3398
E-Mail:
webmaster@mayhill-publications.com
Home Page:
www.mayhill-publications.com/

Dave Blower Jr, Editor
Richard Lewis, Publisher
Diana Scott, Marketing Manager

Agriculture, farming, and related areas
in Indiana, Ohio and Kentucky. Accepts
advertising.
Cost: $28.50
84 Pages
Frequency: Monthly

Farm and Dairy

Lyle Printing and Publishing Company
185 E State Street
PO Box 38
Salem, OH   44460

330-337-3419
800-837-3419
FAX 330-337-9550
E-Mail: farmanddairy@aol.com
Home Page: www.farmanddairy.com

Scot Darling, Chief Executive Officer,
Publisher
Susan Crowell, Editor
Billy Sekely, Advertising Manager
Howard Marsh, Circulation Manager

Briefs of research reports from experi-
ment stations in agriculture, success sto-
ries concerning farmers of Ohio,
Pennsylvania and West Virginia, sale
and livestock market reports, auctions
and more. Accepts advertising.
Cost: $ 28.00
132 Pages
Circulation: 33500
ISSN: 0014-7826
Founded in 1914
Printed in 4 colors on n stock

Farmers Digest

Heartland Communications
1003 Central Avenue
PO Box 1115
Fort Dodge, IA   50501-1115

515-955-1600
800-247-2000
FAX 515-574-2182
E-Mail: fd@farmersdigest.com
Home Page: www.agdeal.com

Sandra J Simonsoa, Group Publisher
Melanie Filloon, Subscription
Coordinator

Straightforwarded, commonsense articles on every aspect of farming and
ranching edited with one goal in mind -
to make you a better farmer or rancher.
Cost: $19.95
100 Pages
Frequency: 10 per year
ISSN: 0046-3337

Founded in 1941
Printed in 4 colors on matte stock

Farmers' Advance

Camden Publications
331 E Bell Street
PO Box 130
Camden, MI   49232

517-368-0365
800-222-6336
FAX 517-368-5131
E-Mail: transfer@ca.homecomm.net
Home Page: www.farmersadvance.com/

Deb Fink, Circulation Coordinator
Julia Hite, Printing & Production
Manager
Kurt Greenhoe, Sales Manager

Farming technology magazine.
Cost: $25.00
Frequency: Weekly
Circulation: 17500

Food & Fiber Letter

Sparks Companies
6862 Elm St
Suite 350
Mc Lean, VA   22101-3867

703-848-4700
FAX 703-893-7371
E-Mail: editor@scipubs.com
Home Page: www.sparksco.com

Robert R Sparks Jr, Partner

Legislative updates, news and informa-
tion on agricultural policy, environment
and conservation industry.
Cost: $473.90
Frequency: Weekly
Printed in 2 colors on matte stock

Forest Science

5400 Grosvenor Ln
Bethesda, MD   20814-2198

301-897-8720
FAX 301-897-3690
E-Mail: safweb@safnet.org
Home Page: www.safnet.org
Social Media: *Facebook, Twitter,*
LinkedIn

Michael T Goergen Jr, Executive
VP/CFO
Brittany Brumby, Assistant to the
CEO/Council
Amy Ziadi, Information Technology
Manager
Larry D Burner CPA, Sr Director
Finance

Provides access to information and networking opportunities to prepare members for the challenges and the changes
that face natural resource professionals.
Founded in 1900

Game Bird Breeders, Agiculturists, Zoologists and Conservationists

Game Bird Breeders
1155 W 4700 S
Salt Lake City, UT   84123

George Allen, Editor

Articles on how to keep and breed all
types of game birds.
Cost: $18.00
45 Pages
Frequency: Monthly
Founded in 1974

Grain Journal

Country Journal Publishing Company
3065 Pershing Court
Decatur, IL   62526

217-877-9660
800-728-7511
FAX 217-877-6647
E-Mail: mark@grainnet.com
Home Page: www.grainnet.com

Mark Avery, Publisher
Ed Zdrojewski, Editor

A bi-monthly magazine for grain/feed
operators
Cost: $40.00
Frequency: Bi-Monthly
Circulation: 14,419
ISSN: 0274-7138
Founded in 1972
Mailing list available for rent: 10,000
names at $600 per M

Grape Grower

Western Agricultural Publishing
Company
4969 E Clinton Way
Suite 104
Fresno, CA   93727

559-252-7000
FAX 559-252-7387
E-Mail: westag@psnw.com
Home Page: www.westagpubco.com

Paul Baltimore, Co Publisher
Jim Baltimore, Co Publisher
Randy Bailey, Editor
Robert Fujimoto, Assistant Editor

The West's most widely read authority
on the cultivation of table grapes, raising
grapes and wine grapes. All aspects of
production are covered with the most
current university, government and private research.
Cost: $19.95
Frequency: Monthly
Circulation: 11,276

Grower

Vance Publishing
400 Knightsbridge Parkway
Lincolnshire, IL   60069

847-634-2600
FAX 847-634-4379
E-Mail: info@vancepublishing.com
Home Page: www.vancepublishing.com

William C Vance, Chairman
Peggy Walker, President

Positioned as the key source of profitable production and management strategies to commercial producers who
control 90% of the U.S. fruit and vegetable market.
Cost: $45.00
Frequency: Monthly
Circulation: 22,004
Founded in 1937

Guernsey Breeders' Journal

Purebred Publishing Inc
7616 Slate Ridge Blvd
Reynoldsburg, OH   43068-3126

614-575-4620
FAX 614-864-5614
Home Page: www.usguernsey.com

Seth Johnson, Manager

The journal discusses breeder stories,
management trends and events in the
Guernsey industry.
Cost: $20.00

Gulf Coast Cattleman

EC Larkin
11201 Morning Ct
San Antonio, TX   78213-1300

210-344-8300
FAX 210-344-4258
E-Mail: info@gulfcoastcattleman.com
Home Page: www.gulfcoastpub.com

E C Larkin Jr, President
Joan Dover, Circulation
M'Lys Lloyd, Managing Editor

Services commercial cattlemen along the
Gulf Coast states with industry news,

management and herd health related articles.
Cost: $15.00
64 Pages
Frequency: Monthly
Circulation: 16000
ISSN: 0017-5552
Founded in 1935
Printed in 4 colors on glossy stock

Hereford World

American Hereford Association
PO Box 014059
Kansas City, MO   64101-59

816-218-2250
FAX 816-842-6931
E-Mail: hworld@hereford.org
Home Page: www.hereford.org

Craig Huffhines, Executive VP
Mary Ellen Hummel, Executive
Assistant

Trade magazine for breeders of registered Polled Hereford cattle.
Frequency: Monthly
Circulation: 9500
Founded in 1742

High Country News

High Country Foundation
119 Grand Avenue
PO Box 1090
Paonia, CO   81428

970-527-4898
1 8-0 9-5 11
FAX 970-527-4897
E-Mail: circulation@hcn.org
Home Page: www.hcn.org

Paul Larmer, Executive Director
Greg Hanscom, Editor
Gretchen Nicholoff, Circulation
Manager

Covers environmental and public lands
issues.
Cost: $32.00
Circulation: 23000
Founded in 1970

High Plains Journal/Midwest Ag Journal

High Plains Publishing Company
1500 E Wyatt Earp Boulevard
PO Box 760
Dodge City, KS   67801

620-227-1834
800-452-7171
FAX 620-227-7173

E-Mail: journal@hpj.com
Home Page: www.hpj.com

Duane Ross, Publisher
Holly Martin, Editor
Todd Fuller, Director of Consumer Mark
Jeff Keeten, Circulation Manager

Farming news for the central states.
Cost: $46.00
Frequency: Weekly
Circulation: 50000
Printed in 4 colors on glossy stock

Hog Producer

Farm Progress
6200 Aurora Avenue
Suite 609 E
Urbandale, IA   50322-2838

515-278-6693
FAX 515-278-7797
E-Mail: jotte@farmprogress.com
Home Page: www.farmprogress.com

Sara Wyant, Publisher
John Otte, Editor

Management publication to help pork
producers in the production, housing,
genetics, health care and marketing of
hogs.
Frequency: Bi-Monthly
Circulation: 119,700

Holstein Pulse

Holstein Association USA
PO Box 808
Brattleboro, VT   05302-0808

802-254-4551
800-965-5200
FAX 802-254-8251
E-Mail: info@holstein.com
Home Page: www.holsteinusa.com

John Meyer, CEO
Lisa Perrin, Marketing

Frequency: Quarterly
Circulation: 19000

Holstein World

Dairy Business Communications
6437 Collamer Road
East Syracuse, NY   13057

315-703-7979
800-334-1904
FAX 315-703-7988
Home Page: www.holsteinworld.com

Joel P Hastings, Publisher/Editor
Janice Barrett, Associate Editor

Showcases breeders who own America's
genetically superior cattle. Elite group of

progressive dairymen who have income,
herd size, and milk production considerably above the national averages.
Cost: $38.95
123 Pages
Frequency: Monthly
Circulation: 12000
ISSN: 0199-4239
Founded in 1904
Printed in 4 colors on glossy stock

HortScience

American Society for Horticultural
Science
113 S West St
Suite 200
Alexandria, VA   22314-2851

703-836-4606
FAX 703-836-2024
E-Mail: webmaster@ashs.org
Home Page: www.ashs.org

Michael Neff, Executive Director
Nancy Hubbell, Managing Editor

HortScience is a bimonthly journal concentrating on significant research, education, extension findings, and methods.
Cost: $55.00
160 Pages
Frequency: Monthly
Circulation: 2500
ISSN: 0018-5345
Founded in 1903
*Mailing list available for rent: 2500
names at $100 per M*

Invasive Plant Science and Management Journal

P.O.Box 7065
Lawrence, KS   66044-7065

785-429-9622
800-627-0629
FAX 785-843-1274
E-Mail: wssa@allenpress.com
Home Page: www.wssa.net

Dale Shaner, President
Jeff Derr, VP
Tom Mueller, Secretary
Dave Gealy, Treasurer
Michael Foley, Director Publications

Promotes research, education and extension outreach activities related to weeds,
provides science-based information to
the public and policy makers; and fosters
awarenes of weeds and their impacts on
managed and natural ecosystems.
2000 Members
Founded in 1956

Jojoba Happenings

John S Turner Public Relations
805 N 4th Avenue
Unit 404
Phoenix, AZ   85003-1304

FAX 602-252-5722

John Turner, Publisher
Ken Lucas, Editor

Jojoba farming. Accepts advertising.
8 Pages
Frequency: Bi-Monthly

Journal of Agricultural & Food Chemistry

American Chemical Society
1155 16th St NW
Washington, DC   20036-4892

202-872-4600
800-227-9919
FAX 202-872-4615
E-Mail: jafc@ucdavis.edu
Home Page: www.pubs.acs.org

Madeleine Jacobs, CEO
John W Finley, Associate Editor
Elizabeth Waters, Associate Editor

Research results in pesticides, fertilizers, agricultural and food processing chemistry.
Cost: $146.00
Frequency: Monthly
Circulation: 159000
Founded in 1856

Journal of Animal Science

American Society of Animal Science
2441 Village Green Pl
Champaign, IL   61822-7676

217-356-9050
FAX 217-398-4119
E-Mail: asas@assochq.org
Home Page: www.asas.org

Meghan Wulster-Radcli, Executive Director
Amy Kemp, Editorial Manager
Judy McClughen, Administrator Assistant
Mike Galyean, Editor-in-Chief

For professional researchers in the Animal Science field.
Cost: $110.00
Frequency: Monthly
Circulation: 3000
ISSN: 0021-8812
Founded in 1908
Printed in on glossy stock

Journal of Applied Communications

Association for Communications Excellence
Mowry Road, Building 116
PO Box 110811
Gainesville, FL   32611

352-392-9588
FAX 352-392-8583
E-Mail: ace@ifas.ufl.edu
Home Page: www.aceweb.org

Mark Tucker, Executive Editor
Amanda Aubuchon, Managing Editor

A referred journal offering professional development for educational communicators who emphasize agriculture, natural resources, and life and human sciences.
Frequency: Quarterly
ISSN: 1051-0834

Journal of Aquatic Plant Management

PO Box 821265
Vicksburg, MS   39182-1265

FAX 601-634-5502
E-Mail: dpetty@ndrsite.com
Home Page: www.apms.org
Social Media: *Facebook, LinkedIn*

Linda Nelson, President
Terry Goldsby, VP
Sherry Whitaker, Treasurer
Jeff Schardt, Secretary
Robert J. Richardson, Editor

A publication of the Aquatic Plant Management Society, Inc.
Founded in 1961

Journal of Dairy Science

American Dairy Science Association
2441 Village Green Pl
Champaign, IL   61822-7676

217-356-5146
FAX 217-398-4119
E-Mail: adsa@assochq.org
Home Page: www.adsa.org

Donald C Beitz, President
Philld C Tongz, VP
Peter Studney, Executive Director
William R Aimutis, Treasurer

Official Journal of the American Dairy Science Association
3000 Members
Founded in 1898
Mailing list available for rent

Journal of Environmental Quality

5585 Guilford Road
Madison, WI   53711-1086

608-273-8080
FAX 608-273-2021
E-Mail: headquarters@agronomy.org
Home Page: www.agronomy.org
Social Media: *Facebook, Twitter, LinkedIn*

Ellen E Bergfeld, Executive VP
Luther Smith, Executive Director
Michela Cobb, Director Financial Services
Audrey Jankowski, Analyst/Programmer
Ian Popkewitz, Director IT/Operations

Published by ASA, CSSA, and SSSA. Papers are grouped by subject matter and cover water, soil, and atmospheric research as it relates to agriculture and the environment.
11000 Members
Founded in 1907

Journal of Forestry

Society of American Foresters
5400 Grosvenor Ln
Bethesda, MD   20814-2198

301-897-8720
FAX 301-897-3690
E-Mail: wallsm@safnet.org
Home Page: www.safnet.org

Michael T Goergen Jr, Executive VP/CEO
Matthew Walls, Publications Dir/Managing Editor

To advance the profession of forestry by keeping professionals informed about significant developments and ideas in the many facets of forestry: economics, education and communication, entomology and pathology, fire, forest ecology, geospatial technologies, history, international forestry, measurements, policy, recreation, silviculture, social sciences, soils and hydrology, urband and community forestry, utilization and engineering, and wildlife management.
Cost: $85.00
Frequency: 8 Times
ISSN: 0022-1201
Founded in 1902
Printed in 4 colors on glossy stock

Journal of Natural Resources & Life Sciences Education

5585 Guilford Road
Madison, WI 53711-1086

608-273-8080
FAX 608-273-2021
E-Mail: headquarters@agronomy.org
Home Page: www.agronomy.org
Social Media: *Facebook, Twitter, LinkedIn*

Ellen E Bergfeld, Executive VP
Luther Smith, Executive Director
Michela Cobb, Director Financial
Services
Audrey Jankowski, Analyst/Programmer
Ian Popkewitz, Director IT/Operations

Today's educators look here for the latest teaching ideas in the life sciences, natural resources, and agriculture.
11000 Members
Founded in 1907

Journal of Soil and Water Conservation

Soil and Water Conservation Society
945 SW Ankeny Rd
Ankeny, IA 50023-9764

515-289-2331
800-843-7645
FAX 515-289-1227
E-Mail: pubs@swcs.org
Home Page: www.swcs.org

Oksana Gieseman, Director of
Publications

The JSWC is a multidisciplinary journal of natural resource conservation research, practice, policy, and perspectives. The journal has two sections: the A Section containing various departments and features and the Research Section containing peer-reviewed research papers.
Cost: $99.00
Frequency: Bimonthly
Circulation: 2000
ISSN: 0022-4561
Founded in 1945

Journal of Sustainable Agriculture

Taylor & Francis Group LLC
325 Chestnut St
Suite 800
Philadelphia, PA 19106-2614

215-625-8900
800-354-1420
FAX 215-625-2940
E-Mail:

haworthorders@taylorandfrancis.com
Home Page: www.taylorandfrancis.com

Kevin Bradley, President

Focuses on new and unique systems in which resource usage and environmental protection are kept in balance with the needs of productivity, profits, and incentives that are necessary for the agricultural marketplace. It increases professional and public awareness and gains support for these necessary changes in our agricultural industry.
Frequency: 8x/Year

Journal of Vegetable Science

Taylor & Francis Group LLC
325 Chestnut St
Suite 800
Philadelphia, PA 19106-2614

215-625-8900
800-354-1420
FAX 215-625-2940
E-Mail:
haworthorders@taylorandfrancis.com
Home Page: www.taylorandfrancis.com

Kevin Bradley, President

Features innovative articles on all aspects of vegetable production, including growth regulation, pest management, sustainable production, harvesting, handling, storage, shipping and final consumption.

Land

Free Press Company
418 S 2nd Street
PO Box 3169
Mankato, MN 56001

507-344-6395
800-657-4665
E-Mail: theland@the-land.com
Home Page: www.the-land.com

Kevin Schulz, Editor
Lynnae Schrader, Assistant Editor
Kim Henrickson, Advertising Manager
Ken Lingen, Manager

Agricultural news
Cost: $20.00
48 Pages
Frequency: Weekly
Circulation: 40000
ISSN: 0279-1633
Founded in 1976
Printed in 4 colors on newsprint stock

MidAmerican Farmer Grower

MidAmerica Farm Publications
19 N Main Street
PO Box 323
Perryville, MO 63775

573-547-2244
877-486-6997
FAX 573-547-5663
E-Mail: publisher@mafg.net
Home Page: www.mafg.net

John M LaRose, CEO/Publisher
Barbara Galeski, Editor
Jack Thompson II, Marketing

Offers farming news for the middle states.
Cost: $19.00
Frequency: Weekly

Midwest DairyBusiness

DairyBusiness Communications
6437 Collamer Road
East Syracuse, NY 13057-1031

315-703-7979
1 8-0 3-4 19
FAX 315-703-7988
E-Mail: cbryant@dairybusiness.com
Home Page:
www.dairybusiness.com/midwest

Dave Natzke, Editorial Director
Joel P Hastings, Publisher
JoDee Sattler, Associate Editor

Business resource for successful milk producers. Only business-oriented dairy publication exclusively for the large herd, Midwest milk producer.
Cost: $45.00
43 Pages
Frequency: Monthly
Circulation: 27500
ISSN: 1087-7096
Founded in 1904
Printed in 4 colors on glossy stock

Milling Journal

3065 Pershing Court
Decatur, IL 62526

217-877-9660
800-728-7511
FAX 217-877-6647
E-Mail: ed@grainnet.com
Home Page: www.grainnet.com

Mark Avery, Publisher
Arvin Donley, Editor
Jody Sexton, Production Manager

Mailed to all active AOM members in the US, Canada, and internationally, in-

cluding wheat flour/corn mills and corn/oilseed processors in US and Canada.
Frequency: Quarterly
Circulation: 1224

Mushroom News

American Mushroom Institute
1284 Gap Newport Pike
Suite 2
Avondale, PA   19311-9503

610-268-7483
FAX 610-268-8015
E-Mail: ami@mwmlaw.com
Home Page:
www.americanmushroom.org

For growers and scientists in the mushroom production.
Cost: $275.00
Frequency: Monthly
Founded in 1955

National Farmers Union News

National Farmers Union
11900 E Cornell Ave
Aurora, CO   80014-6201

303-368-7300
800-347-1961
FAX 303-368-1390
E-Mail: info@nfu.org
Home Page: www.nfu.org

Dave Frederickson, President
Rae Price, Editor

Grass roots structure in which policy positions are initiated locally. The goal is to sustain and strengthen family farm and ranch agriculture.
Cost: $10.00
Frequency: Monthly
Circulation: 250000
Founded in 1902

National Hog Farmer

7900 International Dr
Suite 300
Minneapolis, MN   55425-2562

952-851-4710
FAX 952-851-4601
E-Mail:
dpmiller@primediabusiness.com
Home Page:
www.nationalhogfarmer.com

Dale Miller, Manager
Steve May, Publisher
John Frinch, President
Robert Moraczewski, Senior Vice

President
Susan Rowland, Marketing Manager

Offers production information for hog farming business managers.
Cost: $35.00
Frequency: Monthly
Circulation: 31000
Founded in 1956
Mailing list available for rent: 84M names
Printed in 4 colors on glossy stock

National Wheat Growers Journal

National Association of Wheat Growers
415 2nd St NE
Suite 300
Washington, DC   20002-4993

202-547-7800
FAX 202-546-2638
E-Mail: wheatworld@wheatworld.org
Home Page: www.wheatworld.org
Social Media: *Facebook, Twitter*

David Cleavinger, Publisher
Karl Scronce, Second Vice President
Dana Peterson, Second Vice President
Melissa George Kessler, Director of Communications

Information for wheat growers.
Founded in 1950

Northeast DairyBusiness

DairyBusiness Communications
6437 Collamer Road
East Syracuse, NY   13057-1031

315-703-7979
800-334-1904
FAX 315-703-7988
E-Mail: webmastr@dairybusiness.com
Home Page:
www.dairybusiness.com/northeast

Eleanor Jacobs, Editor
Susan Harlow, Managing Editor
Joel Hasting, CEO/Publisher
Sue Miller, Circulation Manager

Business resource for successful milk producers. Devoted exclusively to the business and dairy management needs of milk producers in the 12 northeastern states.
Cost: $3.00
51 Pages
Frequency: Monthly
Circulation: 17500
ISSN: 1523-7095
Founded in 1904
Printed in 4 colors on glossy stock

Nut Grower

Western Agricultural Publishing Company
4969 E Clinton Way
Suite 119
Fresno, CA   93727-1549

559-252-7000
FAX 559-252-7387
E-Mail: westag@psnw.com
Home Page: www.westagpubco.com

Paul Baltimore, Co Publisher
Jim Baltimore, Co Publisher
Randy Bailey, Editor
Robert Fujimoto, Assistant Editor

Covers production topics, the latest in research developments, and crop news on almonds, walnuts, pistachios, pecans and chestnuts.
Cost: $19.95
Frequency: Monthly
Circulation: 11,993

Onion World

Columbia Publishing
8405 Ahtanum Rd
Yakima, WA   98903-9432

509-248-2452
800-900-2452
FAX 509-248-4056
Home Page: www.onionworld.net

Brent Clement, Editor
Mike Stoker, Publisher

Includes information on onion production and marketing, grower and shipper feature stories, onion research, from herbicide and pesticide studies to promising new varieties, martket reports, feedback from major onion meetings and conventions, spot reports on overseas production and marketing, and other key issues and trends of interest to US and Canadian onion growers.
Cost: $16.00
32 Pages
Circulation: 6500
Founded in 1984
Printed in 4 colors on glossy stock

Organic WORLD

Loft Publishing
3939 Leary Way NW
Seattle, WA   98107-5043

206-632-2767
FAX 206-632-7055

Covers the news of organic gardening.
Cost: $15.00
Frequency: Quarterly

Pacific Farmer-Stockman

999 W Riverside
PO Box 2160
Spokane, WA   99201

509-595-5385
800-624-6618
FAX 509-459-5102
Home Page:
www.farmerstockmaninsurance.com

Michael R Craigen, General Manager
Tracy Sikes, Sales Manager

Offers farming news and information for
farmers and herdsmen located in the Pacific states.

Peanut Farmer

Specialized Agricultural Publications
5808 Faringdon Place
Suite 200
Raleigh, NC   27609

919-872-5040
FAX 919-876-6531
E-Mail: publisher@peanutfarmer.com
Home Page: www.peanutfarmer.com

Dayton H Matlick, Chairman
Mary Evans, Publisher/Sales Director
Mary Ann Rood, Editor

Offers peanut farmers profitable meth-
ods of raising, marketing and promoting
peanuts, plus key related issues.
Cost: $15.00
24 Pages
Frequency: Monthly January-July
Circulation: 18,500
Founded in 1965
Printed in 4 colors on glossy stock

Peanut Grower

Vance Publishing
10901 W 84th Ter
Suite 200
Lenexa, KS   66214-1631

913-438-5721
FAX 913-438-0697
E-Mail: mweeks@vancepublishing.com
Home Page: www.vancepublishing.com

Cliff Becker, VP
William C Vance, CEO

Written for the US peanut farmers. Covers disease, weed and insect control, legislation, farm equipment, marketing and
new research.
Circulation: 17700

Pig International

WATT Publishing Company
303 N Main Street
Suite 500
Rockford, IL   61101

815-966-5400
FAX 815-966-6416
E-Mail: rabbott@wattnet.net
Home Page: www.wattnet.com

James Watt, Chairman/CEO
Greg Watt, President/COO
Roger Abbott, Editor

Covers nutrition, animal health issues,
feed procurement, and how producers
can be profitable in the world pork
market.
Frequency: Monthly
Circulation: 17604
ISSN: 0191-8834
Founded in 1971
Mailing list available for rent
Printed in 4 colors on glossy stock

Plant Disease

American Phytopathological Society
3340 Pilot Know Road
Saint Paul, MN   55121-2097

651-454-7250
800-328-7560
FAX 651-454-0766
E-Mail: aps@scisoc.org
Home Page: www.apsnet.org

Amy Hope, Director of Operations

Frequency: Monthly
Circulation: 1200
ISSN: 0191-2917

Pork

Vance Publishing
400 Knightsbridge Parkway
Lincolnshire, IL   60069

847-634-2600
FAX 847-634-4379
E-Mail: info@vancepublishing.com
Home Page: www.vancepublishing.com

William C Vance, Chairman
Peggy Walker, President

Delivers practical, how-to information
on production management, business
techniques, industry trends and market
analysis to the pork industry.
Cost: $50.00
Frequency: Monthly
Circulation: 15874
Mailing list available for rent

Pork Report

PO Box 10383
Clive, IA   50325

515-223-6186
FAX 515-223-2646

Charles Harness, Publisher

Hog farming news and information.

Potato Country

Columbia Publishing
8405 Ahtanum Rd
Yakima, WA   98903-9432

509-248-2452
800-900-2452
FAX 509-248-4056
Home Page: www.potatocountry.com

Brent Clement, Editor/Publisher
Mike Stoker, Publisher

Edited for potato growers and allied industry people throughout the Western
fall-production states. Editorial material
covers production, seed, disease fore-
cast, equipment, fertilizer, irrigation,
pest/weed management, crop reports and
annual buyers guide.
Cost: $18.00
32 Pages
Frequency: Daily
Circulation: 7500
ISSN: 0886-4780
Founded in 1993
Printed in 4 colors on glossy stock

Potato Grower

Harris Publishing Company
360 B Street
Idaho Falls, ID   83402

208-524-4217
FAX 208-522-5241
E-Mail: jason@potatogrower.com
Home Page: www.potatogrower.com

Jason Harris, Publisher
Gary Rawlings, Editor

Current news on growing potatoes, mar-
ket trends, technology.
Cost: $20.95
48 Pages
Frequency: Monthly
Founded in 1971
Printed in on glossy stock

Poultry Digest

WATT Publishing Company
122 S Wesley Ave
Mt Morris, IL   61054-1451

815-734-7937
FAX 815-734-4201
E-Mail: olentine@wattmm.com
Home Page: www.wattnet.com

Jim W Watt, Chairman/CEO
Charles G Olentine Jr PhD,
VP/Publisher
Clay Schreiber, Publisher
Jim Wessel, Circulation Director

A magazine serving the production side
of the entire poultry industry.
Cost: $15.00
Frequency: Monthly
Circulation: 19000

Poultry International

WATT Publishing Company
303 N Main Street
Suite 500
Rockford, IL   61101

815-966-5400
FAX 815-966-6416
E-Mail: mclements@wattnet.net
Home Page: www.wattnet.com

James Watt, Chairman/CEO
Greg Watt, President/COO
Mark Clements, Editor

Viewed by commercial poultry integra-
tors as the leading international source
of news, data and information for their
businesses.
68 Pages
Frequency: Monthly
Circulation: 20,000
ISSN: 0032-5767
Founded in 1962
Printed in 4 colors

Poultry Times

Poultry & Egg News
345 Green Street NW
PO Box 1338
Gainesville, GA   30503

770-536-2476
FAX 770-532-4894
Home Page: www.poultrytimes.net
Social Media: *Facebook*

Christopher Hill, Publisher/Editor
David Strickland, Editor
Barbara Olejnik, Associate Editor
Dinah Winfree, National Sales
Representative

Stacy Louis, National Sales
Representative

The only newspaper in the poultry in-
dustry. We deliver the most up to date
news in teh poultry industry.
Cost: $22.00
Frequency: 26 X a year
Circulation: 13000
Founded in 1954

Poultry USA

WATT Publishing Company
303 N Main Street
Suite 500
Rockford, IL   61101

815-966-5400
FAX 815-966-6416
Home Page: www.wattnet.com

James Watt, Chairman/CEO
Greg Watt, President/COO
Jeff Swanson, Publishing Director

The only resource focused on the entire
integrated poultry market, delivering relevant and timely information to industry
professionals across the entire poultry
supply chain - from farm to table.
Frequency: Monthly

Prairie Farmer

Prairie Farm Dairy
300 E Washington St
PO Box 348
Pana, IL   62557-1239

217-562-3956
FAX 217-877-9695
Home Page: www.prairiefarms.com

James R Smith, Manager
Mike Wilson, Editor

Agricultural news.

Progressive Farmer

2100 Lakeshore Drive
Birmingham, AL   35209-6721

205-445-6000
FAX 205-445-6422
E-Mail: bruce_thomas@timeinc.com
Home Page:
www.progressivefarmer.com

Bruce Thomas, Publisher
Jack Odle, Editor
Allen Vaughan, Business Manager

Farming news with regional focus on the
midwest, midsouth and southwest.
Cost: $18.00
106 Pages
Frequency: 6 issues/Year

Circulation: 610000
ISSN: 0033-0760
Founded in 1886

RF Design

RFD News
131 E Main Street
Bellevue, OH   44811-1449

419-483-7410
FAX 419-483-3737

Barry LeCerf, Publisher

Comprehensive source of rural agricultural news and information for farmers
and the general public.
Frequency: Weekly

Rice Farming

Vance Publishing
400 Knightsbridge Pkwy
Lincolnshire, IL   60069-3628

847-634-2600
800-888-9784
FAX 847-634-4379
E-Mail: vlboyd@worldnet.att.net
Home Page: www.vancepublishing.com

Peggy Walker, President
William Vance, Chairman
Judy Riggs, Director
Vicky Boyd, Editor

Profitable production strategies for com-
mercial rice growers.
Cost: $25.00
Frequency: Monthly
Circulation: 13000
Founded in 1937
Printed in 4 colors on glossy stock

Rice Journal

Specialized Agricultural Publications
3000 Highwoods Boulevard
Suite 300
Raleigh, NC   27604-1029

919-878-0540
FAX 919-876-6531
E-Mail: publisher@ricejournal.com
Home Page: www.ricejournal.com

Dayton H Matlick, President
Mary Evans, Publisher

Offers rice growers profitable methods
of producing, marketing and promoting
rice, plus key related issues.
Cost: $15.00
24 Pages
Circulation: 11600
Founded in 1897
Printed in 4 colors on glossy stock

Santa Gertrudis USA

Caballo Rojo Publishing
PO Box 1257
Kingsville, TX   78364-1257

361-592-9357
FAX 361-592-8572
Home Page: www.santagertrudis.com

Ervin Kaatz, Executive Director

America's First Beef Breed developed in
1918 at the famous King Ranch in
Texas. Recognized in 1940 by the
USDA. Famous for raid and efficient
growth, solid red color, hardiness and
good disposition. They are adaptable to
many environments and are present
throughout the US and in other
countries.

Seed Industry Journal

Freiberg Publishing Company
2701 Minnetonka Dr
PO Box 7
Cedar Falls, IA   50613-1531

319-553-0642
FAX 319-277-3783
Home Page: www.care4elders.com

Bill Freiberg, Owner
Carol Cutler, Editor

International seed industry news.

Seed Today

Grain Journal Publishing Company
3065 Pershing Ct
Decatur, IL   62526-1564

217-877-9660
800-728-7511
FAX 217-877-6647
E-Mail: ed@grainnet.com
Home Page: www.grainnet.com

Mark Avery, Publisher
Joe Funk, Editor
Kay Merryfield, Circulation
Administrator
Ayanna Green, Manager

Information for individuals related to
seeds.
Frequency: Quarterly
Circulation: 4000
Founded in 1978

Seed World

Scranton Gillette Communications
380 E Northwest Highway
Suite 200
Des Plaines, IL   60016-2282

847-298-6622
FAX 847-390-0408
E-Mail: sweditor@sgcmail.com
Home Page: www.seedworld.com

E S Gillette, Publisher
Angela Dansby, Editor

Seed marketers.
Cost: $30.00
48 Pages
Frequency: Monthly
Circulation: 5000
ISSN: 0037-0797
Founded in 1915

Self Employed Country

Communicating for Agriculture & The
Self Employed
112 E Lincoln Ave
Fergus Falls, MN   56537-2217

218-739-3241
800-432-3276
FAX 218-739-3832
Home Page:
www.selfemployedcountry.org

Milt Smedsrud, Owner
Jerry Barney, Production Manager

For members of Communicating for Agriculture, including legislation relating to
CA activities, exchange program activities, rural seniors news, health and insurance material, feature stories and
columns.
Cost: $6.00
Frequency: Quarterly
Founded in 1985

Shorthorn Country

Durham Management Company
5830 S 142nd St
Siote A
Omaha, NE   68137-2894

402-827-8003
FAX 402-827-8006
E-Mail: durham@beefshorthornusa.com
Home Page:
www.durhamstaffingsolutions.com

Machael Durham, President
Tracy Duncan, Editor
Peggy Gilliland, Circulation Manager

Magazine published for cattle producers
who breed and sell registered Shorthorn

and Polled Shorthorn cattle.
Cost: $24.00
Circulation: 3000
ISSN: 0149-9319
Founded in 1956

Soil Science

Lippincott Williams & Wilkins
351 W Camden St
Baltimore, MD   21201-2436

410-949-8000
800-638-6423
FAX 410-528-4414
E-Mail: soilscience@rutgers.edu
Home Page: www.lww.com

J Arnold Anthony, Operations

Covers investigations in environmental
soils.
Cost: $205.00
Frequency: Monthly
Circulation: 2800
ISSN: 0038-075X

Soil Science of America Journal

Soil Science Society of America
677 S Segoe Rd
Madison, WI   53711-1086

608-273-8095
FAX 608-273-2021
E-Mail: headquarters@soils.org
Home Page: www.soils.org

Ellen Bergfeld, CEO

For those involved in research, teaching
and extension activities in physics,
chemistry, mineralogy, microbiology,
soil fertility and plant nutrition
Cost: $600.00
Circulation: 4000
Founded in 1961

Southeast Farm Press

166 N Gay St
Auburn, AL   36830-4800

334-826-7451
FAX 212-745-0121
E-Mail: phollis@farmpress.com
Home Page: southeastfarmpress.com

Greg Frey, Publisher
Paul Hollis, Editor
Darrah Parker, Director of Marketing

Offers farming news for the southeastern
states.
Frequency: Weekly
Circulation: 47,700
Founded in 1989

Southeastern Peanut Farmer

Southern Peanut Farmer's Federation
110 E 4th Street
Po Box 706
Tifton, GA   31794

229-386-3470
FAX 229-386-3501
E-Mail: info@gapeanuts.com
Home Page: www.gapeanuts.com

Joy Carter, Editor

Offers information to peanut farmers.
Cost: $25.00
20 Pages
Frequency: Monthly
Circulation: 8400
ISSN: 0038-3694
Founded in 1961
Printed in 4 colors on glossy stock

Southwest Farm Press

Farm Press Publications
2104 Harvell Circle
Bellevue, NE   68005

402-505-7173
866-505-7173
FAX 402-293-0741
E-Mail: sscs@pbsub.com
Home Page: southwestfarmpress.com

Greg Frey, Publisher
Ron Smith, Editor
Hembree Brandon, Editorial Director
Forrest Laws, Executive Editor
Darrah Parker, Marketing Manager

Farming news.
Cost: $40.00
Frequency: Fortnightly
Circulation: 33,100
Founded in 1974

Soybean South

6263 Poplar Avenue
Suite 540
Memphis, TN   38119-4736

901-385-0595
FAX 901-767-4026

John Sowell, Publisher
Jeff Kehl, Circulation Director

Profitable prediction strategies for soybean farmers.
Frequency: 5 per year
Printed in 4 colors on glossy stock

Speedy Bee

American Beekeeping Federation
3525 Piedmont Road NE
Bldg 5 Suite 300
Atlanta, GA   30305-1509

404-760-2875
FAX 404-240-0998
E-Mail: info@abfnet.org
Home Page: www.abfnet.org

Troy Fore, Publisher/Editor

Honey and beekeeping industry news.
Cost: $17.95
16 Pages
Frequency: Monthly
Circulation: 1500
ISSN: 0190-6798
Founded in 1972
Printed in on newsprint stock

Spudman Magazine

Great American Publishing
Po Box 128
Suite A
Sparta, MI   49345-0128

616-887-9008
FAX 616-887-2666
Home Page: www.spudman.com

Matt McCallum, Owner
Kimberly Warren, Managing Editor
Erica Bernard, Circulation Manager

Information for potato farming and marketing.
Circulation: 15500
Printed in on glossy stock

Successful Farming

Meredith Corporation
1716 Locust St
Des Moines, IA   50309-3023

515-284-3000
800-678-2659
FAX 515-284-3563
E-Mail: tom.davis@meredith.com
Home Page: www.meredith.com

Stephen M Lacy, CEO
Sandy Williams, Production Manager
William Kerr, CEO
Tom Davis, Publisher

U.S. commerical farmers, ranchers and those employed in those operations or a directly related occupation.
Cost: $15.95
Frequency: Monthly
Circulation: 442000
Founded in 1902
Mailing list available for rent: 500M

names at $75 per M
Printed in 4 colors on glossy stock

Sugar: The Sugar Producer Magazine

Harris Publishing Company
360 B Street
Idaho Falls, ID   83402

208-524-4217
800-638-0135
FAX 208-522-5241
E-Mail:
customerservice@harrypublishing.com
Home Page: www.sugarproducer.com

Jason Harris, Publisher
David FairBourn, Editor
Rob Erickson, Marketing
Eula Endecott, Circulation Manager

Sugar beet industry information.
Cost: $15.95
Frequency: Monthly
Circulation: 16000
Founded in 1975

Sugarbeet Grower

Sugar Publications
503 Broadway
Fargo, ND   58102-4416

701-476-2111
FAX 701-476-2182
E-Mail: sugar@kayesprinting.com
Home Page: www.sugarpub.com

Provides news and feature articles pertaining to sugarbeet production practices, research, legislation and marketing, along with profiles of industry leaders and outstanding producers. Primary audience is United States and Canadian sugarbeet growers.
Cost: $12.00
Circulation: 11,336
Founded in 1963

Sunflower and Grain Marketing Magazine

Sunflower World Publishers
3307 Northland Drive
Suite 130
Austin, TX   78731-4964

512-407-3434
FAX 512-323-5118

Ed R Allen, Editor

Offers news and information on the sunflower and grain industries.
Cost: $1.00
Circulation: 15,000

Super Hay Today Magazine

Mt Adams Publishing and Design
14161 Fort Road
White Swan, DC 98552-9786

509-848-2706
800-554-0860
FAX 509-848-3896
E-Mail: hortexponw@aol.com
Home Page: www.hortexponw.com

Vee Graves, Editor
Julie LaForge, Advertising Manager

Swine Practitioner

10901 W 84th Terrace
Suite 200
Lenexa, KS 66214-1649

913-438-8700
800-255-5113
FAX 913-438-0695
E-Mail:
bnewham@vancepublishing.com
Home Page: www.vancepublishing.com

Kristal Arnold, Editor
Kevin Murphy, Sales/Marketing
Manager
Bill Newham, Publishing Director
Cliff Becker, Group Publisher

Offers technical information, primarily
on swine health and related production
areas, to veterinarians and related industry professionals.
Frequency: Monthly
Circulation: 4800
Mailing list available for rent

The Forestry Source

5400 Grosvenor Ln
Bethesda, MD 20814-2198

301-897-8720
FAX 301-897-3690
E-Mail: safweb@safnet.org
Home Page: www.safnet.org
Social Media: *Facebook, Twitter,
LinkedIn*

Michael T Goergen Jr, Executive
VP/CFO
Brittany Brumby, Assistant to the
CEO/Council
Amy Ziadi, Information Technology
Manager
Larry D Burner CPA, Sr Director
Finance

Provides access to information and networking opportunities to prepare members for the challenges and the changes
that face natural resource professionals.
Founded in 1900

Today's Farmer

MFA
201 Ray Young Dr
Columbia, MO 65201-3599

573-874-5111
FAX 573-876-5521
E-Mail: hr@mfa-inc.com
Home Page: www.mfa-inc.com

William Streeter, CEO
J Brian Griffith, VP

Management and marketing news.
Cost: $12.00
Founded in 1914

Tomato Country

Columbia Publishing
8405 Ahtanum Rd
Yakima, WA 98903-9432

509-248-2452
800-900-2452
FAX 509-248-4056
Home Page: www.tomatomagazine.com

Brent Clement, Editor/Publisher
Mike Stoker, Publisher

Includes information on tomato production and marketing, grower and shipper
feature stories, tomato research, from
herbicide and pesticide studies to new
varieties, market reports, feedback from
major tomato meetings and conventions,
along with other key issues and points of
interest for USA and Canada tomato
growers.

Top Producer

Farm Journal Media
1818 Market Street
31st Floor
Philadelphia, PA 19103-3654

215-578-8900
800-320-7992
FAX 215-568-6782
E-Mail: topproducer@farmjournal.com
Home Page:
www.topproducer-online.com

Andy Weber, Chief Executive Officer
Steve Custer, Executive Vice President
Jeff Pence, President, Electronic Media
Chuck Roth, Senior Vice President

Top Producer is the premier magazine
devoted to the business of farming. The
focus on industry leaders, entrepreneurs
and innovators in agriculture make this

magazine the authoritative business re-
source for commercial farm operators.
Frequency: Weekly
Founded in 1973

Tree Farmer Magazine, the Guide to Sustaining America's Family Forests

American Forest Foundation
1111 19th St NW
Suite 780
Washington, DC 20036

202-463-2700
FAX 202-463-2785
E-Mail: info@forestfoundation.org
Home Page: www.forestfoundation.org

Tom Martin, President & CEO
Brigitte Johnson APR, Director
Communications, Editor

The official magazine of ATFS, this periodical provides practical, how-to and
hands-on information and techniques,
and services to help private fore landowners to become better stewards, save
money and time, and add to the enjoyment of their land.

Tree Fruit

Western Agricultural Publishing
Company
4969 E Clinton Way
Suite 104
Fresno, CA 93727-1546

559-252-7000
FAX 559-252-7387
E-Mail: westag@psnw.com
Home Page: www.westagpubco.com

Paul Baltimore, Co Publisher
Jim Baltimore, Co Publisher
Randy Bailey, Editor
Robert Fujimoto, Assistant Editor

For tree fruit growers in California.
Cost: $19.95
Frequency: 8 per year
Circulation: 7,470

Valley Potato Grower

420 Business Highway 2
PO Box 301
East Grand Forks, MN 56721

218-773-7783
FAX 218-773-6227
E-Mail: vpgsales@nppga.org
Home Page: www.nppga.org

Todd Phelph, CEO
Duane Maatz, Executive Director

Information on potato farming.
Circulation: 10616
Founded in 1946

Vegetable Growers News

Great American Publishing
75 Applewood Drive Suite A
PO Box 128
Sparta, MI   49345

616-887-9008
FAX 616-887-2666
Home Page:
www.vegetablegrowersnews.com

Matt McCallum, Executive Publisher
Brenda Bradford, Advertising
Kimberly Warren, Managing Editor
Erica Bernard, Circulation Department

Market and marketing news.
Cost: $12.00
Frequency: Monthly

Vegetables

Western Agricultural Publishing
Company
4969 E Clinton Way
#104
Fresno, CA   93727-1549

559-252-7000
FAX 559-252-7387
E-Mail: westag@psnw.com
Home Page: www.westagpubco.com

Paul Baltimore, Co Publisher
Jim Baltimore, Co Publisher
Randy Bailey, Editor
Robert Fujimoto, Assistant Editor

The definitive source for information on
all aspects of western vegetable production.
Frequency: Monthly

WD Hoard and Sons Company

PO Box 801
Fort Atkinson, WI   53538-0801

920-563-5551
FAX 920-563-7298
E-Mail: hoards@hoards.com
Home Page: www.hoards.com
Social Media: *Facebook, Twitter*

Brian V Knox, CEO
Gary L Vorpahl, Director Marketing

News aimed at the dairy farmer.
Cost: $18.00
5000 Members
Frequency: 20x/Year
Circulation: 63317

Founded in 1885
Printed in 4 colors on glossy stock

Western DairyBusiness

DairyBusiness Communications
6437 Collamer Road
East Syracuse, NY   13057-1031

315-703-7979
800-334-1904
FAX 315-703-7988
E-Mail: bbaker@dairyline.com
Home Page: www.dairybusiness.com

Joel P Hastings, Editor
John Montandon, President & Co-CEO
Debbie Morneau, Marketing Coordinator

Business resource for successful milk
producers. Covers 13 Western states.
Provides information and news that is
helpful in the daily operations of dairy-
men.
Cost: $49.95
67 Pages
Frequency: Monthly
Circulation: 14000
ISSN: 1528-4360
Founded in 1904
Printed in 4 colors on glossy stock

Western Farm Press

Penton Media
249 W 17th Street
New York, NY   10011

212-204-4200
E-Mail: hbrandon@farmpress.com
Home Page: westernfarmpress.com

Greg Frey, VP
Hembree Brandon, Editorial Director
Harry Cline, Editor

Provides growers and agribusiness with
in-depth coverage of the region's major
crops plus the legislative, environmental
and regulatory issues that affect their
businesses.

Western Fruit Grower

Meister Media Worldwide
37733 Euclid Ave
Willoughby, OH   44094-5992

440-942-2000
800-572-7740
FAX 440-975-3447
E-Mail: rljones@meistermedia.com
Home Page: www.meisternet.com

Gary Fitzgerald, President
John Monahan, Publisher
Richard Jones, Editor

Edited for commercial growers of decid-
uous crops, citrus fruit and nut grape
crops in the Western US.
Cost: $19.95
66 Pages
Frequency: Monthly
Circulation: 36000
Founded in 1933

Western Livestock Journal

Crow Publications
7355 E Orchard Road
Suite 300
Greenwood Village, CO   80111

303-722-7600
800-850-2769
FAX 303-722-0155
E-Mail: editorial@wlj.net
Home Page: www.wlj.net

Pete Crow, Publisher

Offers its readers the best coverage of
timely, necessary news and information
that affects the livestock industry, partic-
ularly cattle.
Cost: $45.00
Frequency: Weekly
Circulation: 30000+
Founded in 1922

Wheat Grower

National Association of Wheat Growers
415 2nd St NE
Suite 300
Washington, DC   20002-4993

202-547-7800
FAX 202-546-2638
E-Mail: wheatworld@wheatworld.org
Home Page: www.wheatworld.org
Social Media: *Facebook, Twitter*

David Cleavinger, First VP
Karl Scronce, Second Vice President
Dana Peterson, CEO
Melissa George Kessler, Director of
Communications

Offers valuable information for wheat
farmers.
Cost: $100.00
Frequency: Weekly
Circulation: 30000
Founded in 1950

Trade Shows

AAEA Symposia
555 E Wells Street
Suite 1100
Milwaukee, WI 53202-6600

414-918-3190
FAX 414-276-3349
E-Mail: info@aaea.org
Home Page: www.aaea.org

Otto C Doering III, President
Yvonne C Bennett, Executive Director

Providing a platform for research on the economics related to the role of consumers' food environments on their choices and health outcomes. The conference is aimed at providing insights into the influence of the food environment on the quality, price, and availability of food, associatec health or environmental impacts, and to uncover the impact of policies aimed at influencing the food production and choice.
3000 Members
Frequency: Annual
Founded in 1910
Mailing list available for rent

AAFCO Meeting
Association of American Feed Control Officers
PO Box 478
Oxford, IN 47971

765-385-1029
FAX 765-385-1032
E-Mail: sharon@aafco.org
Home Page: www.aafco.org

Sharon Krebs, Assistant
Secretary/Treasurer

Frequency: July/August

AATA Annual Conference
Animal Transportation Association
12100 Sunset Hills Road
Cuite 130
Reston, VA 20190

703-437-4377
FAX 703-435-4390
E-Mail: info@aata-animaltransport.org
Home Page:
www.aata-animaltransport.org

Robin Turner, Association Director
Lisa Schoppa, AATA President
Erik Liebegott, President-Elect
Chris Santarelli, Secretary/Treasurer

An international association promoting the humane handling and transportation of animals. 10-15 booths.
150 Attendees
Frequency: Annual

AAW Annual Convention
American Agri-Women
11404 Appleton Road
Croton, OH 41303

740-893-2624
FAX 740-893-4003
E-Mail:
president@americanangriwomen.org
Home Page:
www.americanagriwomen.org

Marcie Williams, President
Chris Wilson, VP/Resoultions & Vital Issues
Arlene Kovash, VP/Communications
Pamela Sweeten, VP/Education
Cheryl Day, Secretary

Tradeshow consisting of products of interest to women in agribusiness, farms and ranches.
350 Attendees
Frequency: November
Founded in 1974

AEM Annual Conference
Association of Equipment Manufacturers
6737 W Washington St
Suite 2400
Milwaukee, WI 53214-5650

414-272-0943
866-236-0442
FAX 414-272-1170
E-Mail: info@aem.org
Home Page: www.aem.org

Dennis Slater, President

Frequency: November

AFIA Expo
American Feed Industry Association
2101 Wilson Boulevard
Suite 916
Arlington, VA 22201

703-524-0810
FAX 703-524-1921
E-Mail: afia@afia.org
Home Page: www.afia.org

Joel Newman, President/CEO
Richard Sellers, VP
Anne Keller, Communications Director
Donald E Orr, Chairman

Exhibits feed and ingredient suppliers as well as equipment manufacturers.
3000 Attendees
Frequency: September
Founded in 1909

ALBC Conference
American Livestock Breeds Conservancy
PO Box 477
Pittsboro, NC 27312

919-542-5704
FAX 919-545-0022
Home Page: www.albc-usa.org

Charles Bassett, Executive Director

An educational opportunity where members can share their knowledge with other members by sharing posters at the annual conference, subtting articles to the newsletter and more.
Frequency: Annual

AMSA Reciprocal Meat Conference
American Meat Science Association
2441 Village Green Place
Champaign, IL 61822

217-356-5370
800-517-AMSA
FAX 888-205-5834
FAX 217-356-5370
E-Mail: information@meatscience.org
Home Page: www.meatscience.org\rmc

Thomas Powell, Executive Director
Diedrea Mabry, Program Director
Kathy Ruff, Meetings & Member Svcs Director

RMC is the annual meeting for AMSA, featuring an interactive program tailored to bring attendees the very best and inspiring educational experience. Attendees are professionals in academia, government and industry, as well as students in the meat, food and animal science fields.

AOSA/SCST Annual Meeting-Association of Official Seed Analysts
PMB #411
101 East State Street
Suite 214
Ithaca, NY 14850

607-256-3313
FAX 607-273-1638

E-Mail: aosa.office@twcny.rr.com
Home Page: www.aosaseed.com

Ellen Chirco, President
Wayne Guerke, VP
Dan Curry, Secretary/Treasurer
Aaron Palmer, Certificate/Analysist
Larry Nees, Membership

Seed testing and laboratory equipment, supplies and services; workshops and discussions.
Frequency: June

ARA Conference & Expo

1156 15th St NW
Suite 500
Washington, DC   20005-1745

202-457-0825
FAX 202-457-0864
E-Mail: info@aradc.org
Home Page: www.aradc.org

Jack Eberstacher, CEO
Jon Nienas, Secretary/Treasurer
Stacy Mayuga, Marketing Director

Advocates in the ag retail and distribution industry.
Frequency: Annual
Founded in 1993

ARBA National Convention

American Rabbit Breeders Association
8 Westport Court
Bloomington, IL   61704

309-664-7500
FAX 309-664-0941
E-Mail: arbamail@aol.com
Home Page: www.arba.net

Curt Rock, President
Paul Reichert, Vice-President
Bobbi Coats, Secretary
Dennis Roloff, Treasurer

Seminar, banquet, luncheon and 1500 rabbit breeders exhibits.
3000 Attendees
Frequency: Annual/April
Founded in 1910

ASA-CSSA-SSSA International Annual Meeting

American Society of Agronomy
677 S Segoe Road
Madison, WI   53711-1086

608-273-8080
FAX 608-273-2021

E-Mail: pscullion@agronomy.org
Home Page: www.agronomy.org

Marcus M Alley, ASA President
Francis J Pierceld, ASA President-Elect
Patricia Scullion, Exhibits Manager

Society members are dedicated to the conservation and wise use of natural resources to produce food, feed and fiber crops while maintaining and improving the environment. Annual meeting and exhibits of agricultural equipment, supplies and services.
Frequency: Annual/Fall

ASABE Annual International Meeting

American Society of Agricultural & Bio-Engineers
2950 Niles Road
Saint Joseph, MI   49085-9659

269-429-0300
800-371-2723
FAX 269-429-3852
Home Page: www.asabe.org

Melissa Moore, Exec VP/Meetings & Conference Dir
Donna Hull, Publication Director

A forum to expand awareness of industry trends, promote and acknowledge innovations in design and technology, and provide opportunities for professional development. Networking, trade show, technical workshops and presentations, specialty sessions, and career fair.
Frequency: June
Founded in 1907

ASAS-ADSA Annual Meeting

American Society of Animal Science
2441 Village Green Place
Champaign, IL   61822

217-356-9050
FAX 217-398-4119
E-Mail: asas@assochq.org
Home Page: www.asas.org

Terry D Etherton, President
Normand St Pierre, Treasurer
Mary M Beck, Director
Lorena K Nicholas,
Conventions/Communications

Professional organization for animal scientists designed to help members provide effective leadership through research, extension, teaching and service for the dynamic and rapidly changing livestock and meat industries. Containing 45 booths. Always a joint meeting

with ADSA, and usually with one or more of these organizations: CSAS, AMPA, WSASAS, and PSA.
2000 Attendees
Frequency: July
Founded in 1908

ASCA Annual Conference

American Society of Consulting Arborists
9707 Key West Ave
Suite 100
Rockville, MD   20850-3992

301-947-0483
FAX 301-990-9771
E-Mail: asca@mgmtsol.com
Home Page: www.asca-consultants.org

Beth Palys, Executive Director

Recognized as a high quality, in depth conference with cutting edge speakers. Combining the best forum for discussion of current and relevant arboricultural issues, as well as consulting practice management issues and key consulting topics such as the role of the expert witness, risk assessment and tree appraisal
300 Attendees
Frequency: November/December

ASEV National Conference

American Society for Enology and Vinticulture
PO Box 1855
Davis, CA   95617-1855

530-753-3142
FAX 530-753-3318
E-Mail: society@asev.org
Home Page: www.asev.org

Lyndie Boulton, Executive Director
Stephanie Bree, Event/Tradeshow Coordinator

Frequency: Annual/June
Founded in 1950

ASFMRA Annual Meeting

American Socitey of Farm Mgrs & Rural Appraisers
950 S Cherry Street
Suite 508
Denver, CO   80246-2664

303-758-3513
FAX 303-758-0190
E-Mail: meetings@asfmra.org
Home Page: www.asfmra.org

Cheryl L Cooley, IT Manager
Brain Stockman, Executive VP
Sally Quinn, Director

Finance/Administration
Debe L Alvarez, Education Manager

Twenty-five exhibits of agricultural
equipment, supplies and services; educational seminars and program sessions.
Cost: $1.00
375 Attendees
Frequency: November

ASHS Annual Conference
American Society for Horticultural
Science
113 SW Street
Suite 200
Alexandria, VA 22314-2851

703-836-4606
FAX 703-836-2024
E-Mail: webmaster@ashs.org
Home Page: www.ashs.org

Fred T Davies, President
Jeanine Davis, Extension Division,
VP-Elect
Robert Mikkelson, Industry Division,
VP-Elect
Penelope Perkins-Veazie, ASHS
Meber-at-Large
John R Clark, Chair

Frequency: Annual/August

AVMA Annual Convention
American Veterinary Medical
Association
1931 N Meacham Road
Suite 100
Schaumburg, IL 60173

847-036-6142
FAX 847-925-1329
E-Mail: avmaininfo@avma.org
Home Page: www.avma.org

Larry Corry DVM, 2009-10 President
Larry Kornegay DVM, 2009-10
President-Elect

Seminar and more than 300 exhibits of
products, materials, equipment, data, and
services for veterinary medicine. Education and hands-on labs, exhibit hall,
charitable events and networking
10000 Attendees
Frequency: Annual/July

Agri News Farm Show
Agri News
18 1st Avenue SE
Rochester, MN 55904-6118

507-857-7707
800-533-1727
FAX 507-281-7436

E-Mail: rallen@agrinew.com
Home Page: www.agrinew.com

John Losness, Publisher
Rosie Allen, Advertsising Manager
Mychal Wilmes, Managing Editor

Annual show of 123 exhibitors of farming equipment, supplies and services.
7,500 Attendees
Frequency: March

Agricultural Retailers Association Convention and Expo
Agricultural Retailers Association
1156 15th Street
Suite 302
Washington, DC 20005

202-570-0825
800-535-6272
FAX 314-567-6808
E-Mail: kelly@aradc.org
Home Page: www.aradc.org

Kelly Jones, Conference Registrar

Annual show of 120 manufacturers, suppliers and distributors of agricultural
chemicals and fertilizers. Seminar, conference and banquet.
1200 Attendees
Frequency: December
Founded in 1993

Allied Social Sciences Association Annual Meeting
555 E Wells Street
Suite 1100
Milwaukee, WI 53202-6600

414-918-3190
FAX 414-276-3349
E-Mail: info@aaea.org
Home Page: www.aaea.org

Otto C Doering III, President
Yvonne C Bennett, Executive Director

The professional association for agricul-
tural economists and related fields.
3000 Members
Frequency: Annual
Founded in 1910
Mailing list available for rent

America Trades Produce Conference
590 East Frontage Road
PO Box 848
Nogales, AZ 85628

520-287-2707
FAX 520-287-2948

E-Mail: info@freshfrommexico.com
Home Page: www.fpaota.org

Lee Frank, President
Alicia Bon Martin, Vice Chair
Allison Moore, Communications
Director
Jose Luis Obregon, Deputy Director
Martha Rascon, Public Affairs Director

Represents more than 125 member companies involved in growing, harvesting,
marketing and importing of mexican
produce entering the US at Nogales,
Arizona.
125+ Members
Founded in 1944

American Farriers Association Annual Convention Marketplace
American Farriers Association
4059 Iron Works Parkway
Suite 1
Lexington, KY 40511

859-233-7411
FAX 859-231-7862
E-Mail: farriers@americanfarriers.org
Home Page: www.americanfarriers.org

Craig Trnka, President
Bob Earle, VP
Walt Taylor, Secretary
Jeff Ridley, Representative/Board of
Directors
Bryan J Quinsey, Executive Director

One-hundred and seventy exhibits of
equipment and supplies for farriers, seminar, banquet, luncheon and tours.
1500 Attendees
Frequency: Annual/February
Founded in 1971

American Livestock Breeds Convervancy ALBC Conference
PO Box 477
Pittsboro, NC 27312

919-542-5704
FAX 919-545-0022
Home Page: www.albc-usa.org
Social Media: *Facebook, Blogger*

Charles Bassett, Executive Director

Ensuring the future of agriculture
through genetic conservation and the
promotion of endangered breeds of livestock and poultry. A nonprofit membership organization working to protect
over 180 breeds of livestock and poultry
from extinction.

American Seed Trade Association Annual Conference

1701 Duke Street
Suite 275
Alexandria, VA   22314-2878

703-837-8140
FAX 703-837-9365
Home Page: www.amseed.com

Andy Lavigna, CEO

Producers of seeds for planting purposes. Consists of companies involved in seed production and distribution, plant breeding and related industries in North America.
850 Members
Founded in 1883

Annual Agricultural Law Symposium

PO Box 835
Brownsville, OR   97327

541-466-5444
FAX 541-466-3311
E-Mail: roberta@aglaw-assn.org
Home Page: www.aglaw-assn.org

Robert Achenbach, Executive Director
Roger A McEowen, President

Association devoted to education about agricultural law.
600 Members
Founded in 1980

Annual Board of Delegates Meeting

1400 K St NW
Suite 1200
Washington, DC   20005-2449

202-789-0789
FAX 202-898-0522
E-Mail: grains@grains.org
Home Page: www.grains.org

Kenneth Hobbie, President
Michael T Callahan, Director
International Operations
Cheri Johnson, Manager
Communications
Valerie Smiley, Manager Membership
Andrew Pepito, Director
Finance/Administration

Motivated by the grain sorghum, barley and corn producer associations and representatives of the agricultural community. Provides commodity export market development.
175 Members
Founded in 1960

Annual Convention of the American Assoc. of Bovine Practitioners

American Association of Bovine
Practicioners
Box 1755
Rome, GA   30162-1755

706-232-2220
FAX 706-232-2232
E-Mail: aabphq@aabp.org
Home Page: www.aabp.org

Roger Saltman, President
Brian J Gerloff, Vice President
Brian K Reed, Treasurer
M Gatz Riddell, Executive Vice President
Brittani Rogers, Member Services

130 exhibits of pharmaceutical and biological manufacturers, equipment and agricultural companies, computer programs and supplies.
1905 Attendees
Frequency: Annual/September
Founded in 1967

Annual Meeting and Professional Improvement Conferences (AM/PIC)

6584 W Duroc Road
Maroa, IL   61756

217-794-3700
FAX 217-794-5901
E-Mail: exec-dir@nacaa.com
Home Page: www.nacaa.com
Social Media: *Facebook, Twitter*

Rick Gibson, President

Hundreds of NACAA members from all over the country, every one relates to the same challenges faced every day on the job. Networking with other professional organizations.
3850 Members
Founded in 1917
Mailing list available for rent: 3500 names at $500 per M

Aquatic Plant Management Society Annual Meeting

Aquatic Plant Management Society
PO Box 821265
Vicksburg, MS   39182-1265

FAX 601-634-5502
E-Mail: dpetty@ndrsite.com

Home Page: www.apms.org
Social Media: *Facebook, LinkedIn*

Tyler Koschnick, President
Mike Netherland, VP
Sherry Whitaker, Treasurer
Jeff Schardt, Secretary
Craig Aguillard, Director

An international organization of educators, scientists, commercial pesticide applicators, administrators and individuals interested in aquatic plant species and plant management.
Founded in 1961

Beltwide Cotton Conference

National Cotton Council of America
1918 North Parkway
Memphis, TN   38112-5000

901-274-9030
FAX 901-725-0510
Home Page: www.cotton.org

Mark Lange, President/CEO
A. John Maguire, Senior Vice President

Offers a forum for agricultural professionals.
Frequency: January

Beltwide Cotton Conferences

7193 Goodlett Farms Parkway
Cordova, TN   38016

901-274-9030
FAX 901-725-0510
Home Page: www.cotton.org

Mark Lange, President/CEO
A. John Maguire, Senior Vice President

Membership consists of approximately 300 delegates named by cotton interests in the cotton-producing states.
35 Members

Breeders of the Carolinas Field Day

PO Box 1257
Kingsville, TX   78364-1257

361-592-9357
FAX 361-592-8572
Home Page: www.santagertrudis.com

Ervin Kaatz, Executive Director

America's First Beef Breed developed in 1918 at the famous King Ranch in Texas. Recognized in 1940 by the USDA. Famous for raid and efficient growth, solid red color, hardiness and good disposition. They are adaptable to many environments and are present throughout the US and in other countries.

COSA Annual Meeting

Committee on Organic and Sustainable Agriculture
677 S Segoe Road
Madison, WI   53711

608-273-8080
FAX 608-273-2020
Home Page: www.cosagroup.org

COSA is a committee of the Tri-Societies for agronomy. The annual committee meeting is held in conjunction with the ASA-CSSA-SSSA Annual Meeting.
Frequency: Annual/Fall

CPMA Convention

590 East Frontage Road
PO Box 848
Nogales, AZ   85628

520-287-2707
FAX 520-287-2948
E-Mail: info@freshfrommexico.com
Home Page: www.fpaota.org

Lee Frank, President
Alicia Bon Martin, Vice Chair
Allison Moore, Communications Director
Jose Luis Obregon, Deputy Director
Martha Rascon, Public Affairs Director

Represents more than 125 member companies involved in growing, harvesting, marketing and importing of mexican produce entering the US at Nogales, Arizona.
125+ Members
Founded in 1944

Citrus Expo

Southeast AgNet Publications/Citrus Industry Mag
5053 NW Hwy 225-A
Ocala, FL   34482

352-671-1909
FAX 352-671-1364
E-Mail: citrusexpo@southeastagent.com
Home Page: www.citrusindustry.net

Maryann Holland, Show Manager

Citrus Trade Show with seminars, containing 150 exhibits. Complimentary attendance and lunch are provided to bona-fide grove owners & managers, citrus production managers, professional crop advisors, association execs & board

members, government & legislative officials and the citrus research community
1500 Attendees
Frequency: August
Founded in 1992

Commodity Classic

Commodity Classic: ASA, NWGA, NCGA, NSP
632 Cepi Drive
Chesterfield, MO   63005-6397

636-733-9004
FAX 636-733-9005
E-Mail: corninfo@ncga.com
Home Page:
www.commodityclassic.com

Dave Burmeister, Registration Information
Kristi Burmeister, Exhibitor Information
Susan Powers, Media/Press Information
Beth Musgrove, General Information
Peggy Findley, Sponsorship Information

550 booths of equipment, seed and chemicals. Lecture series, classes, entertainment, awards, annual meetings of several agri-organziations/associations, and the trade show.
4000 Attendees
Frequency: February

Eastern Milk Producers Cooperative Annual Meeting

1985 Isaac Newton Square West
Reston, VA   20190-5094

703-742-6800
FAX 703-742-7459
Home Page: www.mdvamilk.com

Known for being a leader in the dairy industry, the Eastern Milk Producers Cooperative has an 85-plus year reputation for integrity, service and high quality products.
ISSN: west-

EcoFarm Conference

2901 Park Avenue
Suite D-2
Soquel, CA   95073

831-763-2111
FAX 831-763-2112
E-Mail: info@eco-farm.org
Home Page: www.eco-farm.org
Social Media: , *Twitter, RSS*

Kristin Rosenow, Executive Director
Ken Dickerson, President
Thomas Wittman, VP/Secretary
Arty Mangan, Treasurer

A nonprofit educational organization that seeks to promote agricultural practices that are ecologically sound, economically viable and socially just.
2M Members
Founded in 1980

Farm Bureau Showcase

American Farm Bureau Federation
1850 Howard Avenue
Suite C
Elk Grove, IL   60007

224-656-6600
FAX 847-685-8696
Home Page: www.fb.org

Bob Stallman, President

Two-hundred plus booths featuring exhibits of agricultural equipment, supplies and services.
6-8M Attendees
Frequency: January

Farm Progress Show

Farm Progress Companies
255 38th Avenue
Suite P
St Charles, IL   60174-5410

630-462-2224
800-441-1410
E-Mail: mjungmann@farmprogress.com
Home Page:
www.farmprogressshow.com

Matt Jungman, National Shows Manager

Annual farm show of 400 exhibitors representing various types of agricultural products and services for farmers and agribusiness, including small operations to top producers.
Frequency: August/September

Farm Science Review

Ohio State University
590 Woody Hayes Drive
232 Ag Engineering Building
Columbus, OH   43210-1057

614-926-6691
800-644-6377
FAX 614-292-9448
E-Mail: gamble.18@osu.edu
Home Page: fsr.osu.edu

Chuck Gamble, Manager
Mattk Sullivan, Assistant Manager
Suzanne Steel, Media Coordinator

Annual show of 600 exhibitors of agricultural equipment, supplies and services.
140M Attendees
Frequency: September

Fresh Summit International Convention & Expo

1500 Casho Mill Road
PO Box 6036
Newark, DE   19714-6036

302-738-7100
FAX 302-731-2409
E-Mail: pma@pma.com
Home Page: www.pma.com
Social Media: *Facebook, Twitter, Flickr, YouTube, Xchange*

Bryan Silbermann, President
Lorna Christie, VP/Industry Products & Services
Julie Stewart, Director Communications
Nancy Tucker, VP Global Business Development
Rayne Yori, VP Finance

PMA brings together leaders from around the world and from every segment of the supply chain. Participants throughout the global fresh produce and floral supply chains come together as a community to learn, network, build relationships, and do business.
2400+ Members
Founded in 1949

Government Affairs Conference

USA Rice Federation
4301 N Fairfax Drive
Suite 425
Arlington, VA   22203

703-226-2300
FAX 703-236-2301
E-Mail: riceinfo@usarice.com
Home Page: www.usarice.com

Jamie Warshaw, Chairman

Discuss issues and activities for the U.S. rice industry, legislation, training, and seminars.
Frequency: Annual

Grape Grower Magazine Farm Show

Western Agricultural Publishing Company
4974 E Clinton Way
Suite 123
Fresno, CA   93727-1520

559-261-0396
FAX 559-252-7387
Home Page: www.westagpubco.com

Phill Rhoads, Manager

Seminars, exhibits and prizes for grape growers. Contianing 80 booths and exhibits.
1000 Attendees
Frequency: March/November

Green Industry Conference - GIC

Professional Lawncare Network, Inc (PLANET)
950 Herndon Parkway
Suite 450
Herndon, VA   20170

703-736-9666
800-395-2522
FAX 703-736-9668
E-Mail: info@gie-expo.com
Home Page: www.landcarenetwork.or/cmc/gic.html

Held in conjunction with the GIE+EXPO, the conference offers leadership series, workshops, educational opportunities, events, and new member orientation.
Frequency: Annual

GrowerExpo

Ball Publishing
335 N River Street
PO Box 9
Batavia, IL   60510-0009

630-208-9080
800-456-5380
FAX 630-208-9350
E-Mail: info@ballpublishing.com

Diane Blazek, President

A trade show devoted to horticulture and floriculture production and marketing. 200 booths.
2M Attendees
Frequency: January

Hawkeye Farm Show

Midwest Shows
PO Box 737
Austin, MN   55912

507-437-7969
FAX 507-437-7752
Home Page: www.farmshowsusa.com

Penny Swank, Show Manager

18000 Attendees
Frequency: March

Holstein Association USA Regional Meeting

1 Holstein Place
PO Box 808
Brattleboro, VT   05302-0808

802-254-4551
800-965-5200
FAX 802-254-8251
E-Mail: info@holstein.com
Home Page: www.holsteinusa.com

John Meyer, CEO
Lisa Perrin, Marketing

Dairy cattle breed association with a membership base of people with strong interests in breeding, raising and milking Holstein cattle.
30000 Members
Founded in 1885

IAOM Conferences and Expos

International Association of Operative Millers
10100 West 87th Street
Suite 306
Overland Park, KS   66212

913-338-3377
FAX 913-338-3553
E-Mail: info@iaom.info
Home Page: www.aomillers.org
Social Media: *Facebook, LinkedIn*

Bart Hahlweg, President
Joe Woodard, Executive VP
Aaron Black, Treasurer

Premier educational events for grain milling and seed processing professionals. The annual events gather milling and allied trade professionals from around the world for several days of education, networking and fellowship.
Frequency: May
Founded in 1896

International Feed Expo

American Feed Industry Association
2101 Wilson Blvd
Suite 916
Arlington, VA 22201-3047

703-524-0810
FAX 703-524-1921
E-Mail: afia@afia.org
Home Page: www.afia.org
Social Media: *Facebook, Twitter, LinkedIn*

Joel Newman, President
Richard Sellers, VP
Donald E Orr, Chairman
Anne Keller, Communications Director

Organization devoted to representing companies in the animal feed industry and its suppliers.
690 Members
Founded in 1909

Irrigation Show

Irrigation Association
6540 Arlington Blvd
Falls Church, VA 22042-6638

703-536-7080
FAX 703-536-7019
E-Mail: info@irrigation.org
Home Page: www.irrigation.org

Deborah Hamlin, Executive Director
Denise Stone, Meetings Director
Kate Baumann, Membership Coordinator
Rebecca Bayless, Finance Director
Marsha Cram, MBA, Foundation & Membership Manager

The Irrigation Show is the industry's one-stop event. Discover innovations on the show floor and in technical sessions, make connections with industry experts, business partners, and peers and build expertise with targeted education and certification.
1600 Members
3.5M Attendees
Frequency: November
Founded in 1949

Kentucky Grazing Conference

151 Treasure Island Cswy. #2
St. Petersburg, FL 33706-4734

727-367-9702
800-707-0014
FAX 727-367-9608

E-Mail: darthay@yahoo.com
Home Page: www.nationalhay.org

Ron Bradtmueller, President
Gary Smith, First VP
Richard Larsen, Second VP
Rollie Bernth, Director
Don Kieffer, Executive Director

NHA is the trade group that represents the interests of the hay industry throughout the United States and internationally.
750 Members
Founded in 1895

Legislative Action Conference

122 C Street NW
Suite 875
Washington, DC 20001

202-347-3600
800-937-7675
FAX 202-347-5265
E-Mail: warnerd@nppc.org
Home Page: www.nppc.org
Social Media: *Facebook, Twitter*

Don Butler, President
Sam Carney, President-Elect
Doug Wolf, Vice President
Neil Dierks, CEO

National Pork Producers Council hosts a legislative action conference twice a year for pork producers from around the nation to learn about, discuss and lobby on agriculture legislation important to the U.S. pork industry.
44 Members

Legislative Conference

6540 Arlington Blvd
Falls Church, VA 22042-6638

703-536-7080
FAX 703-536-7019
E-Mail: info@irrigation.org
Home Page: www.irrigation.org

Deborah Hamlin, Executive Director
Denise Stone, Meetings Director

Promotes education and use of irrigation in many areas of agriculture.
1600 Members
Founded in 1949

Mid-America Farm Show

Salina Area Chamber of Commerce
120 W Ash Street
PO Box 586
Salina, KS 67401

785-827-9301
FAX 785-827-9758

E-Mail: chamber@informatics.net
Home Page: www.salinakansas.org

Don Weiser, Show Manager

Annual show of 325 exhibitors of agricultural equipment, supplies and services, including irrigation equipment, fertilizer, farm implements, hybrid seed, agricultural chemicals, tractors, feed, farrowing crates and equipment, silos and bins, storage equipment and farm buildings.
13M Attendees
Frequency: March
Founded in 1911

Mid-America Horticulture Trade Show

Mid Am Trade Show
1000 N Rand Road
Suite 214
Wauconda, IL 60084

847-526-2010
FAX 847-526-3993
E-Mail: mail@midam.org
Home Page: www.midam.org

Rand A Baldwin CAE, Managing Director
Suzanne Spohr, Show Manager

Mid-Am is a green-industry event featuring more than 650 leading suppliers offering countless products, equipment, and services for the horticulture industry. Mid-Am also offers a variety of educational seminars featuring the best and the brightest in the horticultural and business communities to help keep you informed of the latest trends.
Frequency: Annualy

Mid-West Ag Expo

Midwest Equipment Dealers Association
5330 Wall Street
Suite 100
Madison, WI 53718

608-240-4700
FAX 608-240-2069
E-Mail: gmanke@medaassn.com
Home Page: www.meda-online.com

Gary Manke, Executive VP
Dale Gaugert, Membership Service Representative
Michael Hedge, President
Jerry Deblaey, Vice President

Annual show of 300 exhibitors of farm machinery, including tractors, field equipment, minimum tillage, no-till harvesting equipment and farm supplies,

lawn, garden and outdoor power equipment, irrigation equipment, farmstead mechanization equipment and dairy equipment.
18M Attendees
Frequency: March

Midwest Agri Industries Expo

Illinois Fertilizer & Chemical Association
130 W Dixie Highway
PO Box 186
Saint Anne, IL   60964-0186

815-939-1566
800-892-7122
FAX 815-427-6573

Jean Trobec, President

Annual show of 130 manufacturers, suppliers and distributors of agricultural chemical and fertilizer application equipment, supplies and services.
2500 Attendees
Frequency: August, Danville

Midwest Farm Show

North Country Enterprises
5330 Wall St
Suite 100
Madison, WI   53718

608-240-4700
FAX 608-240-2069
E-Mail: meda@medaassn.com
Home Page: medaassn.com

Bill Henry, President

250 booths. Top farm show exhibiting dairy and Wisconsin's tillage equipment, feed and seed.
175 Members
11M+ Attendees
Frequency: January

NCTA Convention & Trade Show

National Christmas Tree Association
16020 Swingley Ridge Rd
Suite 300
Chesterfield, MO   63017-6030

636-449-5070
FAX 636-449-5051
E-Mail: info@realchristmastrees.org
Home Page: www.realchristmastrees.org

Steve Drake, CEO
Pam Helmsing, Executive Director
Becky Rasmussen, Assistant Director
Rick Dungey, PR/Marketing Director

Draws christmas tree growers, retailers and suppliers from around the world for

education, contests, networking and the trade show.
500 Attendees
Frequency: Annual/August

NDHIA Annual Meeting

National Dairy Herd Improvement Association
421 S Nine Mound Round
PO Box 930399
Verona, WI   53593-0399

608-848-6455
FAX 608-848-7675
E-Mail: info@dhia.org
Home Page: www.dhia.org

Jay Mattison, CEO
Dan Sheldon, President
Lee Maassen, VP
Cost: $250.00

250 Attendees

NHA Annual Convention

National Hay Association
102 Treasure Island Causeway
St Petersburg, FL   33706

727-367-9702
800-707-0014
FAX 727-367-9608
E-Mail: darthay@yahoo.com
Home Page: www.nationalhay.org

Ron Tombaugh, President
Gary Smith, First VP
Richard Larsen, Second VP
Rollie Bernth, Director
Don Kieffer, Executive Director

National Alliance of Independent Crop Consultants Annual Meeting

349 E Nolley Dr
Collierville, TN   38017-3538

901-861-0511
FAX 901-861-0512
E-Mail: jonesnaicc@aol.com
Home Page: www.naicc.org

Allison Jones, Executive VP
Shannon Gomes, Secretary

Represents individual crop consultants and contract researchers.
500+ Members
Founded in 1978

National Association of Agricultural Educators (NAAE) Convention

300 Garrigus Building
University of Kentucky
Lexington, KY   40545

859-257-2224
800-509-0204
FAX 859-323-3919
E-Mail: jay_jackman@ffa.org
Home Page: www.naae.org

Greg Curlin, President
Ken Couture, President-elect
Jay Jackman PhD, CAE, Executive Director
Alissa Smith, Associate Executive Director
Julie Fritsch, Com. and Marketing Coordinator

A federation of 50 affiliated state vocational agricultural teacher associations.
7600 Members
Founded in 1948

National Association of County Agricultural Agents Conference

National Association of County Agricultural Agents
6584 W Duroc Road
Maroa, IL   61756

217-794-3700
FAX 217-794-5901
E-Mail: exec-dir@nacaa.com
Home Page: www.nacaa.com

Rick Gibson, President

Annual conference and exhibits for county agricultural agents and extension workers.

National Association of Wheat Growers Convention

National Association of Wheat Growers
415 2nd St NE
Suite 300
Washington, DC   20002-4993

202-547-7800
FAX 202-546-2638
E-Mail: wheatworld@wheatworld.org
Home Page: www.wheatworld.org
Social Media: *Facebook, Twitter*

David Cleavinger, First Vice President
Karl Scronce, Second Vice President
Dana Peterson, CEO
Melissa George Kessler, Director of Communications

Convention and trade show for the wheat, corn, soybean and sorghum industries.
Frequency: February
Founded in 1950

National Cotton Council Annual Meeting

7193 Goodlett Farms Parkway
Cordova, TN 38016

901-274-9030
FAX 901-725-0510
Home Page: www.cotton.org

Mark Lange, President/CEO
A. John Maguire, Senior Vice President

Membership consists of approximately 300 delegates named by cotton interests in the cotton-producing states.
35 Members

National No-Tillage Conference

No-Till Farmer
225 Regency Court, PO Box 624
Suite 200
Brookfield, WI 53008-0624

262-782-4480
800-645-8455
FAX 262-782-1252
E-Mail: info@lesspub.com
Home Page: www.no-tillfarmer.com

Mike Lessitor, Executive VP
Alice Musser, Conference Manager

Conference held for America's leading most innovative no-till farmers.
Frequency: January

National Orange Show Fair

National Orange Show
689 South E Street
San Bernardino, CA 92408

909-888-6788
FAX 909-889-7666
Home Page:
http://nationalorageshow.com

Five days of entertainment, art, exhibits, music, food and rides celebrating and educating the community on the California orange.
80000 Attendees
Frequency: May
Founded in 1889

National Potato Council Annual Meeting

1300 L St NW
Suite 910
Washington, DC 20005-4107

202-682-9456
FAX 202-682-0333
E-Mail:
spudinfo@nationalpotatocouncil.org
Home Page:
www.nationalpotatocouncil.org
Social Media: , *Twitter*

John Keeling, Executive VP/CEO
Hollee Stubblebine, Director Industry Communications
Keith Masser, President
Jim Wysocki, VP Finance
Dan Elmore, VP Grower/Public Relations

Connect with other grower leaders from across the country on shaping national public policy impacting potato production and distribution. Such issues as keeping potatoes in schools, finalizing free trade agreements, and gearing up for the next Farm Bill will be reviewed and strategies will be developed.
45000 Members
Founded in 1948

National Potato Council's Annual Meeting

National Potato Council
1300 L Street
Suite 910
Washington, DC 20005

202-682-9456
E-Mail:
spudinfo@nationalpotatocouncil.org
Home Page:
www.nationalpotatocouncil.org

John Keeling, CEO
Holly Stubblebine, Communications Director

Annual meeting and exhibits of potato growing equipment, supplies and services.

New England Grows

New England Grows
415 Summer Street
Boston, MA 07115

617-954-2000
FAX 617-954-2125

E-Mail: info@mccahome.com
Home Page: www.negrows.org

Jon Ciffolilo, President
M Virginia Wood, Executive Director
Diane Zinck, Exhibit Sales Coordinator
Aley Botelho, Registration Manager
Owen Regan, Director of Operations

One of the largest and most visited horticulture and green industry events in North America, this event is known for its progressive educational conference and world-class trade show.
13000 Attendees
Frequency: February

North American Beekeeping Conference

American Beekeeping Federation
3525 Piedmont Road NE
Bldg 5 Suite 300
Atlanta, GA 30305-1509

404-760-2875
FAX 404-240-0998
E-Mail: info@abfnet.org
Home Page: www.abfnet.org

Zac Browning, President
David Mendes, VP

Experts talks and discussions about beekeeping hot topics; exhibits and introduction of new products; and workshops. Regsitraion varies, but starts at $75 for the 1st day.
1500 Attendees
Frequency: January
Founded in 1943

North American International Livestock Exposition

Kentucky Fair and Exposition Center
937 Phillips Lane
PO Box 37130
Louisville, KY 40209-7130

502-367-5000
FAX 502-367-5139
E-Mail: ellenaderson@mail.state.ky.us
Home Page: www.livestockexpo.org

Debbie Burda, Booking/Events
Ellen Anderson, Event Contact

Purebred livestock show with more than 20,000 entries in eight major divisions: dairy cattle, dairy goats, llamas, quarter horses, draft horses, market swine, beef cattle, sheep. Held at Kentucky Fair and Exposition Center in Louisville, Kentucky.
Frequency: November

Northwest Agricultural Show

Northwest Agricultural Show
4672 Drift Creek Road SE
Sublimity, OR   97385

503-769-7120
FAX 503-769-3549
E-Mail: info@nwagshow.com
Home Page: www.nwagshow.com

The goal of the NW Ag Show is to educate the ag industry in the very latest equipment, pesticides, business practices and more, and is held in conjunction iwht educational seminars provided by the three NW horticultural Congress partners. The event features educational seminars, certification sessions, Society meetings, and over 200 exhibitors of agricultural equipment from across the country.
Cost: $6.00
26M Attendees
Frequency: Annual/Winter

Nut Grower Magazine Farm Show

Western Agricultural Publishing Company
4974 E Clinton Way
Suite 123
Fresno, CA   93727-1520

559-252-7000
FAX 559-252-7387

Phill Rhoads, Manager

Productions seminars, guest speakers, prizes and exhibits for nut growers. Containing 80 booths and exhibits.
1000 Attendees
Frequency: March

Nut Grower Magazine Harvest Show

Western Agricultural Publishing Company
4974 E Clinton Way
Suite 123
Fresno, CA   93727-1520

559-261-0396
FAX 559-252-7387

Phill Rhoads, Manager

Productions seminars, guest speakers, prizes and exhibits for nut growers. Containing 80 booths and exhibits.
1000 Attendees
Frequency: November

Organic Seed Growers Conference

PO Box 772
Port Townsend, WA   98368

360-385-7192
FAX 360-385-7455
E-Mail: info@seedalliance.org
Home Page: www.seedalliance.org
Social Media: *Facebook, Twitter*

Dan Hobbs, Executive Director
Matthew Dillon, Executive Director

Supports the ethical development and stewardship of the genetic resources of agricultural seed.
Founded in 1975

Organic Stone Fruit Jubilee

2901 Park Avenue
Suite D-2
Soquel, CA   95073

831-763-2111
FAX 831-763-2112
E-Mail: info@eco-farm.org
Home Page: www.eco-farm.org
Social Media: *, Twitter, RSS*

Kristin Rosenow, Executive Director
Ken Dickerson, President
Thomas Wittman, VP/Secretary
Arty Mangan, Treasurer

A nonprofit educational organization that seeks to promote agricultural practices that are ecologically sound, economically viable and socially just.
2M Members
Founded in 1980

Ozark Fall Farmfest

Ozark Empire Fair
3001 North Grant Street
PO Box 630
Springfield, MO   65308

417-833-2660
FAX 417-833-3769
Home Page: www.ozarkempirefair.com

Pat Lloyd, Manager

Annual show of 700 exhibitors with about 600 booths of agricultural products and services, including livestock.
40M Attendees
Frequency: October

PMA Convention & Exposition

Produce Marketing Association
1500 Casho Mill Road
Newark, DE   19711-3547

302-738-7100
FAX 302-731-2409

E-Mail: pma@pma.com
Home Page: www.pma.com

Janet Erickson, Chairman
Bryan Silbermann, President
Dave Corsi, Retail Chairman
Gene Harris, Food Service Chairman

A trade association of companies engaged in the marketing of fresh and safe produce and floral products. Show will inlcude 600 exhibitors with 1,600 booths.
16000 Attendees
Frequency: October
Founded in 1949

Potato Expo

1300 L St NW
Suite 910
Washington, DC   20005-4107

202-682-9456
FAX 202-682-0333
E-Mail:
spudinfo@nationalpotatocouncil.org
Home Page:
www.nationalpotatocouncil.org
Social Media: *, Twitter*

John Keeling, Executive VP/CEO
Hollee Stubblebine, Director Industry Communications
Keith Masser, President
Jim Wysocki, VP Finance
Dan Elmore, VP Grower/Public Relations

Largest conference and tradeshow for the potato industry held in North America. Offers educational programming covering the top issues facing the potato industry, provides networking opportunities with key decision makers and showcases the latest products and services for potato production and distribution.
45000 Members
Founded in 1948

Prairie Farmer Farm Progress Show

Farm Progress Publishers
1301 E Mound Road
Decatur, IL   62526-9394

217-877-9070
FAX 217-877-9695

Sherry Stout, Editor
Jeffrey Smith, Advertising

One of the largest farm shows in the country.

Pro Farmer Midwest Crop Tour

1818 Market Street 31st Floor
Philadelphia, PA   19103

800-772-0023
E-Mail: editors@profarmer.com
Home Page: www.profarmer.com
Social Media: , *Twitter*

Sue King, Contact

Join the Pro Farmer editors at these seminars to discuss commodity markets, world economy, farm policy, land prices and more.
25M Members
Founded in 1973

Produce for Better Health Annual Meeting

590 East Frontage Road
PO Box 848
Nogales, AZ   85628

520-287-2707
FAX 520-287-2948
E-Mail: info@freshfrommexico.com
Home Page: www.fpaota.org

Lee Frank, President
Alicia Bon Martin, Vice Chair
Allison Moore, Communications Director
Jose Luis Obregon, Deputy Director
Martha Rascon, Public Affairs Director

Represents more than 125 member companies involved in growing, harvesting, marketing and importing of mexican produce entering the US at Nogales, Arizona.
125+ Members
Founded in 1944

Profit Briefing Professional Farmers of America

1818 Market Street 31st Floor
Philadelphia, PA   19103

800-772-0023
E-Mail: editors@profarmer.com
Home Page: www.profarmer.com
Social Media: , *Twitter*

Sue King, Contact

Join the Pro Farmer editors at these seminars to discuss commodity markets, world economy, farm policy, land prices and more.
25M Members
Founded in 1973

SAF National Convention

5400 Grosvenor Ln
Bethesda, MD   20814-2198

301-897-8720
FAX 301-897-3690
E-Mail: safweb@safnet.org
Home Page: www.safnet.org

Michael T Goergen Jr, Executive VP/CFO
Brittany Brumby, Assistant to the CEO/Council
Amy Ziadi, Information Technology Manager
Larry D Burner CPA, Sr Director Finance

Provides access to information and networking opportunities to prepare members for the challenges and the changes that face natural resource professionals.
Founded in 1900

SBS Conference & Exhibition

Society for Biomolecular Sciences
36 Tamarack Ave
Suite 348
Danbury, CT   06811

203-743-1336
FAX 203-748-7557
E-Mail: email@sbsonline.org
Home Page: www.sbsonline.org

Laura Edgar, Education/Meetings Director

Scientists, innovators, researchers and industry analysts from around the world will converge to learn about the latest trends and basic and applied research that are transforming the way new pharmaceuticals are developed.
2000 Attendees
Frequency: Annual

Santa Gertrudis Breeders International Annual Meeting

PO Box 1257
Kingsville, TX   78364-1257

361-592-9357
FAX 361-592-8572
Home Page: www.santagertrudis.com

Ervin Kaatz, Executive Director

America's First Beef Breed developed in 1918 at the famous King Ranch in Texas. Recognized in 1940 by the USDA. Famous for raid and efficient growth, solid red color, hardiness and good disposition. They are adaptable to many environments and are present

throughout the US and in other countries.

Soil and Water Conservation Society Annual International Conference

Soil and Water Conservation Society
945 SW Ankeny Road
Ankeny, IA   50021-9764

515-289-2331
800-843-7645
FAX 515-289-1227
E-Mail: swsc@swsc.org
Home Page: www.swsc.org

Craig A Cox, Executive VP

Explores ways to improve the linkages among conservation science, policy and application at local, national, and international scales. The conference will provide participants an opportunity to teach skills, learn techniques, compare successes, and improve understanding.
1200 Attendees
Frequency: Annual

Southern Farm Show

590 Woody Hayes Drive
Room 232
Columbus, OH   43210

614-292-4278
FAX 614-292-9448
E-Mail: gamble.19@osu.edu
Home Page: www.farmshows.org

Doug Wagner, President
Dennis Alford, 1st Vice President
Chip Blalock, 2nd Vice President
Chuck Gamble, Secretary-Treasurer

Members are agriculture trade show sponsors and suppliers of services to these shows. Provides members with education, communication and evaluation. Provides the best possible marketing showcase for exhibitors and related products to the farmer/rancher/producer customer.
37 Members
Founded in 1972

State Masters Conference

1616 H St NW
Suite 10
Washington, DC   20006-4999

202-628-3507
888-447-2643
FAX 202-347-1091

E-Mail: bsteel@nationalgrange.org
Home Page: www.nationalgrange.org

Ed Luttrell, President
Jennifer Dugent, Communications
Manager
Leroy Watson, Legislative Director
Cindy Greer, Director Youth\Young
Adult
DoriAnn Gedris, Marketing Director

Promotes general welfare and agriculture
through local organizations. Presides
over the advancement and promotion of
the farming and agriculture industry.
300k Members
Founded in 1960

Sunbelt Agricultural Exposition

Sunbelt Ag Expo
290-G Harper Boulevard
Moultrie, GA   31788-2157

229-985-1968
FAX 229-890-8518
E-Mail: info@sunbeltexpo.com
Home Page: www.sunbeltexpo.com

Chip Blalock, Executive Director
Gina McDonald, Director of Marketing
& PR
Michael Williams, Expo Farm Manager
Amy Willis, Communications Specialist
Wendell Brown, Exhibitor Coord. &
Special Events

Over 1,200 exhibitors showing the latest
agricultural technology in products and
equipment plus harvesting and tillage
demonstrations in the field. Largest
farm show in North America's premier
farm show.
200M Attendees
Frequency: Oct

Sustainable Foods Summit

1340 North Cotner Blvd
Lincoln, NE   68505

402-477-2323
FAX 402-477-4325
E-Mail: info@ocia.org
Home Page: www.ocia.org

Jeff See, Executive Director

OCIA International is a farmer owned
international program of certification,
which adheres to strict organic standards. It currently certifies thousands of
farmers and processors in North, Central
and South America and Asia. OCIA International is IFOAM accredited and adheres to the USDA ISO Guide 65, Japan
Agriculture Standards and the Quebec

Accreditation Council. OCIA has also
been accredited from the USDA National Organic Program and Costa Rica
Ministry of Agriculture.
3500 Members
Founded in 1985
Mailing list available for rent: 3500
names at $50 per M

Sweetener Symposium

2111 Wilson Blvd
Suite 600
Arlington, VA   22201-3051

703-351-5055
FAX 703-351-6698
E-Mail: info@sugaralliance.org
Home Page: www.sugaralliance.org

James Johnson, President
Jack Roney, Director Economics/Policy
Analysis
Luther Markwart, Executive Vice
President
Carolyn Cheney, Vice President

Covering a broad range of timely issues
affecting the industry.
Founded in 1983

The Heartland Festival

2901 Park Avenue
Suite D-2
Soquel, CA   95073

831-763-2111
FAX 831-763-2112
E-Mail: info@eco-farm.org
Home Page: www.eco-farm.org
Social Media: , *Twitter, RSS*

Kristin Rosenow, Executive Director
Ken Dickerson, President
Thomas Wittman, VP/Secretary
Arty Mangan, Treasurer

A nonprofit educational organization that
seeks to promote agricultural practices
that are ecologically sound, economically viable and socially just.
2M Members
Founded in 1980

Tree Fruit Expo

Western Agricultural Publishing
Company
4974 E Clinton Way
Suite 123
Fresno, CA   93727-1520

559-252-7000
FAX 559-252-7387

Phill Rhoads, Manager

Productions seminars, dessert contest,
guest speakers, prizes and exhibits for
tree fruit growers. Containing 80 booths
and exhibits.
1000 Attendees
Frequency: October

USA Rice Outlook Conference

USA Rice Federation
4301 N Fairfax Drive
Suite 425
Arlington, VA   22203

703-226-2300
FAX 703-236-2301
E-Mail: riceinfo@usarice.com
Home Page: www.usarice.com

Jamie Warshaw, Chairman
Jeannette Davis, Conference Contact

Discuss issues and activities for the U.S.
rice industry, legislation, training, and
seminars.
Frequency: Annual

USHSLA Annual Convention

United States Hide, Skin & Leather
Association
1150 Connecticut Avenue, NW
12th Floor
Washington, DC   20036

202-587-4244
E-Mail: abray@meatami.com
Home Page: www.ushsla.org

John Reddington, President
Susan Hogan, Manager

Represents the hide, skin and leather industries. Members range from small
family-owned businesses to large corporations.
Frequency: Annual

United Fresh Convention

590 East Frontage Road
PO Box 848
Nogales, AZ   85628

520-287-2707
FAX 520-287-2948
E-Mail: info@freshfrommexico.com
Home Page: www.fpaota.org

Lee Frank, President
Alicia Bon Martin, Vice Chair
Allison Moore, Communications
Director
Jose Luis Obregon, Deputy Director
Martha Rascon, Public Affairs Director

Represents more than 125 member companies involved in growing, harvesting,

marketing and importing of mexican produce entering the US at Nogales, Arizona.
125+ Members
Founded in 1944

United Fresh Fruit and Vegetable Association Annual Convention

United Fresh Fruit & Vegetable Association
1901 Pennsylvania Avenue NW
Suite 1100
Washington, DC   20006

202-624-4989
FAX 202-303-3433
E-Mail: united@uffva.org
Home Page: www.uffva.org

Thomas Stenzel, CEO
Mark Overbay, Manager Communications

30000 Attendees

Walnut Council Annual Meeting

1011 N 725 W
West Lafayette, IN   47906-9431

765-583-3501
FAX 765-583-3512
E-Mail: walnutcouncil@walnutcouncil.org
Home Page: www.walnutcouncil.org

Liz Jackson, Executive Director
Larry R Frye, VP
William Hoover, Treasurer

Inviting scientists with the latest research on hardwood forestry, black walnut in particular, to present.
1000 Members
Founded in 1970

Walnut Council Conference

Walnut Council
1011 North 725 West
West Lafayette, IN   47906-9431

765-583-3501
FAX 765-583-3512
Home Page: www.walnutcouncil.org

R Daniel Schmokey, President
Larry R Frye, VP
Liz Jackson, Executive Director
Robert D Burke, Legislative Committee
Keith Wolste, Nut Culture Committee

Annual conference and exhibits of equipment, supplies and services for walnut growing.
Frequency: July
Founded in 1970

Washington Public Policy Conference

1901 Pennsylvania Ave NW
Suite 1100
Washington, DC   20006-3412

202-303-3400
FAX 202-303-3433
E-Mail: united@unitedfresh.org
Home Page: www.uffva.org
Social Media: *Facebook, Twitter, YouTube*

Thomas E Stenzel, CEO
Nicholas J Tompkins, Chair
Robert A Grimm, Executive Committee
Daniel G Vache, Secretary/Treasurer

Equipment, supplies, cartons, packaging machinery, computers, sorting and sizing equipment, harvesting equipment, film wrap manufacturing and commodity organizations.
1000+ Members
Founded in 1904

Water Conference

6540 Arlington Blvd
Falls Church, VA   22042-6638

703-536-7080
FAX 703-536-7019
E-Mail: info@irrigation.org
Home Page: www.irrigation.org

Deborah Hamlin, Executive Director
Denise Stone, Meetings Director

Promotes education and use of irrigation in many areas of agriculture.
1600 Members
Founded in 1949

Western Farm Show

Investment Recovery Association
638 W 39th Street
Kansas City, MO   64111

816-561-5323
800-728-2272
FAX 816-561-1991

Annual show of 700 manufacturers, suppliers and distributors of equipment, supplies and services relating to the agricultural industry.
35M Attendees
Frequency: February
Founded in 1962

Western Growers Association Annual Convention

590 East Frontage Road
PO Box 848
Nogales, AZ   85628

520-287-2707
FAX 520-287-2948
E-Mail: info@freshfrommexico.com
Home Page: www.fpaota.org

Lee Frank, President
Alicia Bon Martin, Vice Chair
Allison Moore, Communications Director
Jose Luis Obregon, Deputy Director
Martha Rascon, Public Affairs Director

Represents more than 125 member companies involved in growing, harvesting, marketing and importing of mexican produce entering the US at Nogales, Arizona.
125+ Members
Founded in 1944

Wheat Conference

415 2nd Street NE
Washington, DC   20002-4993

202-547-7800
FAX 202-546-2638
E-Mail: wheatworld@wheatworld.org
Home Page: www.wheatworld.org
Social Media: *Facebook, Twitter, YouTube*

David Cleavinger, First Vice President
Karl Scronce, Second Vice President
Dana Peterson, CEO
Melissa George Kessler, Director of Communications

Nonprofit partnership of US wheat growers, by combining their strengths, voices and ideas are working to ensure a better future for themselves, their industry and the general public.
Founded in 1950

Wheat Industry Conference

415 2nd Street NE
Washington, DC   20002-4993

202-547-7800
FAX 202-546-2638
E-Mail: wheatworld@wheatworld.org
Home Page: www.wheatworld.org
Social Media: *Facebook, Twitter, YouTube*

David Cleavinger, First Vice President
Karl Scronce, Second Vice President
Dana Peterson, CEO

Melissa George Kessler, Director of Communications

Nonprofit partnership of US wheat growers, by combining their strengths, voices and ideas are working to ensure a better future for themselves, their industry and the general public.
Founded in 1950

World Dairy Expo

151 Treasure Island Cswy. #2
St. Petersburg, FL   33706-4734

727-367-9702
800-707-0014
FAX 727-367-9608
E-Mail: darthay@yahoo.com
Home Page: www.nationalhay.org

Ron Bradtmueller, President
Gary Smith, First VP
Richard Larsen, Second VP
Rollie Bernth, Director
Don Kieffer, Executive Director

NHA is the trade group that represents the interests of the hay industry throughout the United States and internationally.
750 Members
Founded in 1895

World Pork Expo

122 C Street NW
Suite 875
Washington, DC   20001

202-347-3600
800-937-7675
FAX 202-347-5265
E-Mail: warnerd@nppc.org
Home Page: www.nppc.org
Social Media: *Facebook, Twitter*

Don Butler, President
Sam Carney, President-Elect
Doug Wolf, Vice President
Neil Dierks, CEO

The world's largest pork-specific trade show featuring business seminars, hundreds of exhibitors, breed shows and sales, and plenty of food and entertainment for everyone.
44 Members

Directories & Databases

ARI Network

Ari Network Services
10850 W Park Pl
Suite 900
Milwaukee, WI   53224-3636

414-973-4300
800-558-9044
FAX 414-973-4619
E-Mail: info@airnet.com
Home Page: www.arinet.com

Roy W Olivier, Chief Executive Officer
Timothy Sherlock, Chief Financial Officer
John C Bray, VP, New Market Division
Jeffrey E Horn, VP, North American Sales
Michael E McGurk, VP, Technology Operations

Offers current information on agricultural business, financial and weather information as well as statistical information for farmers.
Frequency: Numeric

Ag Ed Network

ARI Network Services
10850 W Park Pl
Suite 900
Milwaukee, WI   53224-3636

414-973-4300
800-558-9044
FAX 414-973-4619
E-Mail: info@arinet.com
Home Page: www.arinet.com

Roy W Olivier, Chief Executive Officer
John C Bray, New Market Development

Offers access to more than 1500 educational agriculture lessons covering farm business management and farm production.
Frequency: Full-text

Agricultural Research Institute: Membership Directory

Agricultural Research Institute
9650 Rockville Pike
Bethesda, MD   20814-3998

301-530-7122
FAX 301-571-1816
E-Mail: ari@nal.usda.gov

Richard A Herrett, Executive Director

125 member institutions; also lists study panels and committees interested in en-

vironmental issues, pest control, agricultural meteorology, biotechnology, food irradiation, agricultural policy, research and development, food safety, technology transfer and remote sensing.
Cost: $50.00
Frequency: Annual

American Meat Science Association Directory of Members

American Meat Science Association
2441 Village Green Place
Champaign, IL   61822

217-356-5370
800-517-AMSA
FAX 888-205-5834
FAX 217-356-5370
E-Mail: information@meatscience.org
Home Page: www.meatscience.org

Keith Belk, President, Executive Committee
Randy Huffman, President-Elect
Thomas Powell, Executive Director
Kathy Ruff, Meetings & Member Svcs Director

Directory for American Meat Science members only.
Cost: $20.00
230 Pages
Frequency: Biennial

American Society of Consulting Arborists: Membership Directory

American Society of Consulting Arborists
9707 Key West Ave
Suite 130
Rockville, MD   20850-3992

301-947-0483
FAX 301-990-9771
E-Mail: asca@mgmtsol.com
Home Page: www.asca-consultants.org

Beth Palys, Executive Director
Steve Campano, President
Robert Delmore Jr, Director

About 270 persons specializing in the growth and care of urban shade and ornamental trees; includes expert witnesses and monetary appraisals.
Frequency: Annual March

Crop Protection Reference

Vance Communications Corporation
315 W 106th St
Suite 504
New York, NY   10025-3473

212-932-1727
800-839-2420
FAX 646-733-6010
E-Mail: cpp@cppress.com
Home Page: www.greenbook.net

Hilda Vazquez, Director Marketing,
Sales

A single comprehensive source of
up-to-date label information of crop protection products marketed in the United
States by basic manufacturers and formulators. Extensive product indexing
helps to locate products by: brand name,
manufacturer crop site, mode of action,
disease, insect, week, product category,
common name, tank mix.
Cost: $50.00
Frequency: Annual

Directory for Small-Scale Agriculture

US Department of Agriculture
Secretary oF Agriculture
Whitten Building/Room 200A
Washington, DC   20250-0001

202-012-2000

Offers information on persons involved
with projects and activities relating to
small-scale agriculture.
Cost: $5.50
119 Pages

Grain & Milling Annual

Sosland Publishing Company
4800 Main St
Suite 100
Kansas City, MO   64112-2513

816-756-1000
FAX 816-756-0494
E-Mail: web@sosland.com
Home Page: www.sosland.com

Gordon Davidson, President

Offers a list of milling companies, mills,
grain companies and cooperatives.
Cost: $115.00
Frequency: Annual
Circulation: 6,000
ISSN: 1098-4615

Guernsey Breeders' Journal: Convention Directory Issue

Purebred Publishing Inc
7616 Slate Ridge Blvd
Reynoldsburg, OH   43068-3126

614-575-4620
FAX 614-864-5614
E-Mail: sjohnson@usguernsey.com
Home Page: www.usguernsey.com

Seth Johnson, Manager
Dale Jensen, President
Tom Ripley, VP

A convention directory offering a list of
officers and national members of the
American Guernsey Cattle Association.
Cost: $20.00
Frequency: 10 per year

Hort Expo Northwest

Mt Adams Publishing and Design
14161 Fort Road
White Swan, WA   98952-9786

509-848-2706
800-554-0860
FAX 509-848-3896
E-Mail: hortexponw@aol.com
Home Page: www.hortexponw.com

Vee Graves, Editor
Julie LaForge, Advertising Manager

The directory is mailed to subscribers
and is also available complimentary at
horticulture shows in the Northwest.
32 Pages
Frequency: Annually
Circulation: 8,700
Founded in 1989
Printed in 4 colors on glossy stock

Industrial Economic Information

Global Insight
800 Baldwin Tower
Eddystone, PA   19022

610-490-4000
800-933-3374
FAX 610-490-2557
E-Mail: info@globalinsight.com
Home Page: www.globalinsight.com

Joseph E Kasputys,
Chair/President/CEO
Pricella Trumbull, Chief Operations
Officer
Vicki Van Mater, VP
Kenneth J McGill, Product Management

Global Insight's unique perspective provides the most comprehensive economic

and financial coverage of countries, regions and industries from any source.

International Green Front Report

Friends of the Trees Society
PO Bo 253
Twisp, WA   98856

509-997-9200
FAX 509-997-4812
E-Mail: friendsofthetree@yahoo.com
Home Page: www.friendsofthetrees.net

Michael Pilarski, Director

Organizations and periodicals concerned
with sustainable forestry and agriculture
and related fields.
Cost: $7.00
192 Pages
Frequency: Irregular
Circulation: 8,000
Founded in 1978

International Soil Tillage Research Organization

International Soil Tillage Research
1680 Madison Avenue
Wooster, OH   44691-4114

330-263-3700
FAX 330-263-3658

A Franzluebbers, Editor-in-Chief

More than 750 individuals and institutions in 72 countries involved in the research or application of soil tilage and
related subjects.
Cost: $100.00
Frequency: 10 per year

Journal of the American Society of Farm Managers and Rural Appraisers

ASFMRA
950 S Cherry St
Suite 508
Denver, CO   80246-2664

303-758-3513
FAX 303-758-0190
E-Mail: asfmra@agri-associations.org
Home Page: www.asfmra.org

Cheryl L Cooley, Manager
Communications/PR

Frequency: Annually
Mailing list available for rent: 2500
names at $1M per M

Landscape & Irrigation: Product Source Guide

Adams Business Media
147 W 35th St
New York, NY   10001-2110

212-566-7600
FAX 212-370-0736
E-Mail: info@admmail.com
Home Page: www.acgresources.com

Len Adams, CEO
Nick Ferrari, Executive Vice President
John Holden, Senior VP
Claudia Flowers, VP/Business Development
Steve Ennen, Director Communications

Offers information on suppliers, distributors and manufacturers serving the professional agriculture and landscaping community.
Cost: $6.00
Circulation: 37,000

NASDA Directory

National Association of State Dept of Agriculture
1156 15th St NW
Suite 1020
Washington, DC   20005-1711

202-296-9680
FAX 202-296-9686
E-Mail: nasda@nasda.org
Home Page: www.nasda.org

Stephen Haterius, Executive Director
Richard Kirchoff, Executive VP/CEO

Top agricultural officials in 50 states and four territories.
Cost: $100.00
Frequency: Annual

National Agri-Marketing Association Directory

11020 King St
Suite 205
Overland Park, KS   66210-1201

913-491-6500
FAX 913-491-6502
E-Mail: agrimktg@nama.org
Home Page: www.nama.org

Jennifer Pickett, CEO
Vicki Henrickson, Vice President

Orginated as the Chicago Area Agricultural Advertising Association with 39 charter members. In 1963 the name was changed to the National Agricultural Advertising and Marketing Association and the present name was assumed in 1973.
Cost: $150.00
2500 Pages
Frequency: Annual Spring
Founded in 1956

National Organic Directory

Community Alliance with Family Farmers
36355 Russell Boulevard
PO Box 363
Davis, CA   95617-0363

530-756-8518
800-892-3832
FAX 530-756-7857
E-Mail: nod@caff.org
Home Page: www.caff.org

Judith Redmond, President
George Davis, VP
Pete Price, Secretary
Poppy Davis, Treasurer
Leland Swendon, Executive Director

Wriiten for all sectors of the booming organic food and fiber industry. Offers international listing with full contact information and extensive, cross-referenced index. Also provides regulatory updates, essays by industry leaders and other ressources.
Cost: $47.95
400 Pages
Frequency: Annual
Circulation: 2,500
ISBN: 1-891894-04-8
Founded in 1983

Organic Pages Online North American Resource Directory

Organic Trade Association
60 Wells Street
PO Box 547
Greenfield, MA   01301

413-774-7511
FAX 413-774-6432
E-Mail: info@ota.com
Home Page: www.ota.com

Katherine DiMatteo, Executive Director
Holly Givens, Communications Director
David Gagnon, Director Operations
Lisa Murray, Sales Manager
Linda Lutz, Membership Manager

Provides over 1,300 listings by company name, brand name, business type, supply chain, product and service.
Printed in 2 colors

Professional Workers in State Agricultural Experiment Stations

US Department of Agriculture
200 Independence Ave SW
Whitten Bldg/Room 200A
Washington, DC   20201-0007

202-690-7650
FAX 202-512-2250
Home Page: www.access.gpo.gov

Mike Johanns, Secretary of Agriculture

This directory offers information on academic and research personnel in all agricultural, forestry, aquaculture and home economics industries.
Cost: $15.00
289 Pages
Frequency: Annual
Founded in 1963

US Agriculture

Global Insight
800 Baldwin Tower Boulevard
Eddystone, PA   19022-1368

610-490-4000
FAX 610-490-2770
E-Mail: info@globalinsight.com
Home Page: www.globalinsight.com

Harry Baumes, Manager

This large database offers information on US macroeconomic farm crop and related agricultural data.

USAHA Report of the Annual Meeting

United States Animal Health Association
4221 Mitchelle Ave.
St Joseph, MO   64507

816-671-1144
FAX 816-671-1201
E-Mail: usaha@usaha.org
Home Page: www.usaha.org

Benjamin Richey, Executive Director
Kelly Janicek, Executive Assistant

Held in conjunction with the American Association of Veterinary Laboratory Diagnosticians. (AAVLD)
Founded in 1897

Who's Who International
WATT Publishing Company
303 N Main Street
Suite 500
Rockford, IL 61101

815-966-5400
FAX 815-966-6416
Home Page: www.wattnet.com

James Watt, Chairman/CEO
Greg Watt, President/COO
Jeff Swanson, Publishing Director

Contains a detailed statistical section of key contacts in the industry. Includes industry phone book, genetic hatcheries and products, company directories, poultry marketers by city and state, refrigerated warehouses and federal agencies and associations.
310 Pages

Who's Who in the Egg & Poultry Industry in the US and Canada
WATT Publishing Company
303 N Main Street
Suite 500
Rockford, IL 61101

815-966-5400
FAX 815-966-6416
Home Page: www.wattnet.com

James Watt, Chairman/CEO
Greg Watt, President/CEO
Jeff Swanson, Publishing Director

Contains a detailed statistical section of key contacts in the industry. Includes industry phone book, genetic hatcheries and products, company directories, poultry marketers by city and state, refrigerated warehouses and federal agencies and associations.
Cost: $105.00
Frequency: Annual
ISSN: 0510-4130

World Databases in Agriculture
National Register Publishing
890 Mountain Avenue
Suite 300
New Providence, NJ 07974

800-473-7020
FAX 908-673-1189
E-Mail:
nrpeditorial@marquiswhoswho.com
Home Page:
www.nationalregisterpub.com

Eileen Fanning, Managing Editor

Agricultural information on databases, including CD-ROM, magnetic tape, diskette, online, fax or databroadcast worldwide.

Environment & Conservation

Associations

Earth Island Institute

2150 Allston Way
Suite 460
Berkeley, CA   94704-1375

510-859-9100
FAX 510-859-9091
E-Mail: arch@earthisland.org
Home Page: www.earthisland.org
Social Media: *Facebook, Twitter, YouTube*

Martha Davis, President
Kenneth Brower, Vice President
Michael Hathaway, Vice President
Jennifer Snyder, Secretary
Alex Giedt, Treasurer

Seeks to prevent destruction of environment and sponsors fund drives and activist projects to protect wildlife.
33M Members
Founded in 1985

Earth Regeneration Society

1442A Walnut Street
#57
Berkeley, CA   94709-1405

510-527-9716
FAX 510-559-8410
E-Mail:
alden@earthregenerationsociety.org
Home Page:
www.earthregenerationsociety.org

Alden Bryant, President
Cynthia Johnson, Secretary
Glen A. Frendel, Executive Director

Organized to develop and study scientific and practical solutions to environmental issues.

Earth Society Foundation

238 East 58th Street
Suite 2400
New York, NY   10022

212-832-3659
800-3EA-THDA
E-Mail: earthsociety1@hotmail.com
Home Page:

www.earthsocietyfoundation.org
Social Media: *Facebook*

Monica Getz, Chairperson
Stan Cohen, President
Tom Dowd, VP

News of interest in environmental and sociological issues. Purpose is to promote Earth Day and the Earth Trustee agenda; Every individual and institution should seek choices in ecology, economics, and ethics that will eliminate pollution, poverty, and violence.

Ecological Farming Association

2901 Park Avenue
Suite D-2
Soquel, CA   95073

831-763-2111
FAX 831-763-2112
E-Mail: info@eco-farm.org
Home Page: www.eco-farm.org
Social Media: *Facebook, Twitter*

Thomas Wittman, President
Lisa Bunin, Vice President
Jeremiah Ridenour, Executive Committee

Supports organic farmers, farm suppliers and consultants, produce handlers, researchers, extension, agents, and students involved in the ecological farming industry.
800 Members
Founded in 1986

Ecological and Toxicological Association of Dyes

1850 M St NW
Suite 700
Washington, DC   20036-5810

202-721-4154
FAX 202-296-8120
Home Page: www.etad.com

Jill Aker, President

Represents the interests of manufacturers and formulators of dyes in the region with regard to environmental and health hazards in the manufacture, processing, shipment, use and disposal of thier products.
Founded in 1982

Environmental & Energy Study Institute

122 C Street NW
Suite 630
Washington, DC   20001

202-628-1400
FAX 202-628-1825
E-Mail: eesi@eesi.org
Home Page: www.eesi.org
Social Media: *Facebook, Twitter, YouTube*

Jared Blum, Board Chair
Shelley Fidler, Board Treasurer
Richard L. Ottinger, Board Chair Emeritus

A non-profit organization dedicated to promoting environmentally sustainable societies.
Founded in 1984

Environmental Assessment Association

810 N. Farrell Drive
PO Box 879
Palm Springs, CA   92263

760-327-5284
877-810-5643
FAX 760-327-5631
E-Mail: info@eaa-assoc.org
Home Page: www.eaa-assoc.org
Social Media: *, LinkedIn*

Robert Johnson, Executive Director

Supports all those involved in environmental assessment, including training and education, publications, conferences and research resources.

Environmental Business Association

991 Broadway
Suite 207
Albany, NY   12204

518-432-6400
FAX 518-432-1383
E-Mail: info@eba-nys.org
Home Page: www.eba-nys.org

Suzanne Maloney, Executive Director
Deidre Murphy, Program Director

EBA members represent all segments of the environmental industry—consultants, labaoratories, remediation companies, disposal firms, recyclers and technology innovators. EBA facilitates arrangements and information exchange among members to develop business opportunities. Services include sponsoring

seminars, monthly meetings, industry trends, changes in technology and legislation.
Founded in 1989

Environmental Compliance Institute

165 Sherwood Ave
Farmingdale, NY 11735

631-414-7757
FAX 631-843-6331
E-Mail: pbany@c2g.us
Home Page: www.c2g.us

Attorneys and corporations interested in environmental law and federal regulations governing waste disposal and other matters related to the environment.

Environmental Design Research Association

1760 Old Meadow Road
Suite 500
McLean, VA 22102

703-506-2895
FAX 703-506-3266
E-Mail: edra@telepath.com
Home Page: www.edra.org
Social Media: *Facebook, Twitter, LinkedIn*

Nick Watkins, Chair
Mallika Bose, Chair-Elect
Vikki Chanse, Secretary
Shauna Mallory-Hill, Treasurer
Kate O'Donnell, Executive Director(ex-officio)

Is to advance the art and science of environmental design research, to improve understanding of the interrelationships between people and their built and natural surroundings, and to help create environments responsive to human needs. EDRA members are designers and other professionals with an interest in environmental design research.
700 Members
Founded in 1968

Environmental Industry Association

4301 Connecticut Ave Nw
Suite 300
Washington, DC 20008-2304

202-244-4700
800-424-2869
FAX 202-966-4824
E-Mail: wa@envasns.org

Home Page: www.envasns.org
Social Media: *Facebook*

Bruce Parker, President

Supports all those involved with technology of recycling, resource recovery and sanitary landfills. Publishes magazine.

Environmental Information Association

6935 Wisconsin Ave
Suite 306
Chevy Chase, MD 20815-6112

301-961-4999
888-343-4342
FAX 301-961-3094
E-Mail: info@eia-usa.org
Home Page: www.eia-usa.org

Dana Hudson, President
Mike Schrum, President Elect
Kevin Cannan, Vice President
Joy Finch, Secretary
Chris Gates, Treasurer

Nonprofit organization dedicated to providing environmental information to individuals, members and industry. Disseminates information on the abatement of asbestos and lead-based paint, indoor air quality, safety and health issues, analytical issues and environmental site assessments.

Environmental Law Institute

2000 L St NW
Suite 620
Washington, DC 20036-4919

202-939-3800
800-433-5120
FAX 202-939-3868
E-Mail: law@eli.org
Home Page: www.eli.org

John Cruden, President
Martin Dickinson, VP Development
Chandra Middleton, Director Associates Programs
Melodie DeMulling, Director, Associates Programs

Supports all those involved in environmental issues from a legal perspective, fostering the exchange of ideas and solutions for pressing environmental issues.

Environmental Protection Agency

Ariel Rios Building
1200 Pennsylvania Avenue NW
Washington, DC 20460

202-272-0167
E-Mail: zachariasiewicz.robert@epa.gov
Home Page: www.epa.gov
Social Media: *Facebook, Twitter, YouTube*

Bob Zachariasiewicz, Acting Director

Federal agency concerned with maintaining land, air and water quality.
18000 Members
Founded in 1970

Federation of Environmental Technologists

W175 N11081 Stonewood Dr.
Ste 203
Germantown, WI 53022-4771

262-437-1700
FAX 262-437-1702
E-Mail: info@fetinc.org
Home Page: www.fetinc.org

Dan Brady, Board Chair
Mark Steinberg, President
Dave Seitz, Vice President
Anthony Montemurro, Treasurer
Jeffrey Nettesheim, Secretary

FET assists members in interpretation of and compliance with environmental regulations.
700 Members
Founded in 1981

Forest History Society

701 William Vickers Ave
Durham, NC 27701-3162

919-682-9319
FAX 919-682-2349
E-Mail: recluce2@duke.edu
Home Page: www.foresthistory.org
Social Media: *Facebook, Twitter*

L. Michael Kelly, Chairman
Robert Healy, Co-Vice Chairman
Mark Wilde, Co-Vice Chairman
Henry I. Barclay III, Treasurer
Steven Anderson, Secretary & President

Nonprofit, educational institution that explores the history of the environment, forestry and conservation.
2000 Members
Founded in 1946

Forestry, Conservation Communications Association

PO Box 162655
Miami, FL 33116-2655

717-338-1505
FAX 717-334-5656
E-Mail: ed@fcca-usa.org
Home Page: www.fcca.info

Lloyd M. Mitchell, President
Roy Mott, Vice President
John McIntosh, Secretary/Treasurer
Ralph Haller, Executive Director

Association for manufacturers or suppliers of forestry and conservation communications equipment, systems and procedures.

Friends of the Trees Society

PO Box 826
Tonasket, WA 98855

509-486-4056
E-Mail: friendsofthetrees@yahoo.com
Home Page: www.friendsofthetrees.net

Michael Pilarski, Director

Nonprofit organization helping tree lovers worldwide.
Founded in 1978

Great Lakes United

4380 Main St
Amherst, NY 14226-3592

716-886-0142
FAX 716-204-9521
E-Mail: glu@glu.org
Home Page: www.glu.org

Catherine Gillespie, President
Julie O'Leary, VP
Robert Miller, Treasurer

An international, environmental coaltion working to preserve and protect the Great Lakes and St. Lawrence River. Memberships are as follows: $100 organizational members, $25 organizational members w/bugdets below $15,000, $25 individuals, and $50 family members.
1.1M Members
Founded in 1982

Greenpeace USA

702 H St NW
Suite 300
Washington, DC 20001-3876

202-737-2336
FAX 202-462-4507
E-Mail: goa@wdc.greenpeace.org
Home Page: www.greenpeaceusa.org
Social Media: *Facebook*

John Passacantando, CEO
Ellen McPeake, COO

Leading independent campaigning organization that uses non-violent direct action and creative communication to expose global environmental problems and to promote solutions that are essential to a green and peaceful future.
2.5M Members
Founded in 1971

Hazardous Materials Information Resource S ystem

One Church Street
Suite 200
Rockville, MD 20850

301-577-1842
FAX 301-738-2330

CAPT Michael J. Macinski, Commanding Officer
CAPT Robert W. Farr, Executive Officer
HMCM Robert E. Searles, II, Command Master Chief

The Hazardous Materials Information Resource System is a Department of Defense (DOD) automated system developed and maintained by the Defense Logistics Agency. HMIRS is the central repository for Material Safety Data Sheets (MSDS) for the United States Government military services and civil agencies.

Institute for Environmental Auditing

St. Nicholas House 70 Newport
Lincoln LN1 3DP

152-540-90
E-Mail: info@iema.net
Home Page: www.iema.net

Jam Chimel, Chief Executive
Matrin Baxter, Executive Director
Allison Hall, Marketing Director
Claire Lea, Director of Membership Services
Bea Walshaw, Operations Manager

A professional organization of environmental auditors.
100 Members

Institute for World Resource Research

PO Box 50303
Palo Alto, CA 94303-0303

630-910-1551
FAX 630-910-1561
Home Page: www.globalwarming.net

BJ Jefferson, Advertising/Sales

Supports those involved in all phases of developments in forestry and reforestation of northern nations including the US, Canada, Russia, Sweden, Finland, Norway, China, Japan and others. Its goal is to increase the worldwide understanding of the ecological and economic roles of the northern forest regions of the world.

Institute of Environmental Sciences and Technology

5005 Newport Drive
Suite 506
Rolling Meadows, IL 60008-3841

847-255-1561
FAX 847-255-1699
E-Mail: iest@iest.org
Home Page: www.iest.org
Social Media: *Facebook, Twitter, LinkedIn*

Julie Kendrick, Executive Director
Robert Burrows, Director Communications Services
Corrie Roesslein, Director Programs/Administration

Is an international professional society that serves members and the industries they represent through education and the development of recommended practices and standards.
1600 Members
Founded in 1953

Institute of Gas Technology

1700 S Mount Prospect Rd
Des Plaines, IL 60018-1804

847-768-0664
FAX 847-768-0669
E-Mail: gtiadmin@gastechnology.org
Home Page: www.gastechnology.org
Social Media: *Facebook, Twitter, LinkedIn, YouTube*

David Carroll, President & CEO
Ronald Snedic, Vice President/Corporate Devel.
Paul Chromek, General Counsel & Secretary

Supports all those involved in the gas industry worldwide, including energy industry production, consumption, reserves, imports and prices.

Institute of Scrap Recycling Industries

1615 L St NW
Suite 600
Washington, DC   20036-5664

202-662-8500
FAX 202-626-0900
E-Mail: isri@isri.org
Home Page: www.isri.org

John Sacco, Chairman
Jerry I. Simms, Chair Elect
Douglas Kramer, Vice Chair
Mark R. Lewon, Secretary Treasurer

Supports all those involved in the scrap processing and recycling industry.
165 Members
1987 Attendees

International Association for Energy Economics

28790 Chagrin Blvd
Suite 350
Cleveland, OH   44122-4642

216-464-5365
FAX 216-464-2737
E-Mail: iaee@iaee.org
Home Page: www.iaee.org
Social Media: *Facebook, LinkedIn*

Mine Yucel, President
Lars Bergman, President-Elect
David L. Williams, Executive Director

Association for those involved in energy economics including publications, consultants, energy database software.
3400 Members
Founded in 1977

International Association of Wildland Fire

1418 Washburn Street
Missoula, MT   59801

406-531-8264
888-440-4293
E-Mail: iawf@iawfonline.org
Home Page: www.iawfonline.org
Social Media: *Facebook, Twitter*

Chuck Bushey, President
Kris Johnson, VP
Mikel Robinson, Executive Director
Kevin Ryan, Secretary
Daniel Bailey, Treasurer

IWAF members are academics and professionals with an interest in wildland fires.
800 Members
Founded in 1990

International Ecotourism Society

PO Box 96503 #34145
Washington, DC   20090-6503

202-506-5033
FAX 202-789-7279
E-Mail: info@ecotourism.org
Home Page: www.ecotourism.org
Social Media: *Facebook, Twitter, YouTube*

Kelly Bricker, Chair
Tony Charters, Vice Chair
Neal Inamdar, Director Finance/Administration

Society members include park managers, tour operators, conservation professionals, and others with an interest in the development of ecology-centered tourism.
900 Members
Founded in 1990

International Lead Zinc Research Organization

1822 NC Highway 54 East
Suite 120
Durham, NC   27713

919-361-4647
FAX 919-361-1957
E-Mail: rputnam@ilzro.org
Home Page: www.ilzro.org

Stephen Wilkinson, President
Frank Goodwin, VP Materials Sciences
Scott Mooneyham, Treasurer
Rob Putnam, Director Communications

ILZRO members are miners and refiners of lead and zinc. Trade association of the lead and zinc industry worldwide. Focus on research and development to detect new uses for the metals and refine existing uses.
Founded in 1958

International Society for Ecological Economics

15 River Street
#204
Boston, MA   02108

703-790-1745
FAX 703-790-2672
E-Mail: secretariat@ecoeco.org

Home Page: www.ecoeco.org
Social Media: *Facebook, Twitter*

John Gowdy, President
Bina Agarwal, President-Elect
Anne Aitken, Treasurer

Members are researchers, academics, and other professionals who study the impact of economic models and policies on the environment.
750 Members
Founded in 1989

Isaak Walton League

707 Conservation Lane
Gaithersburg, MD   20878

301-548-0150
800-453-5463
FAX 301-548-0146
E-Mail: general@iwla.org
Home Page: www.iwla.org
Social Media: *Facebook, Twitter*

Jim A. Madsen, President
Robert Chapman, Vice President
Marj Striegel, Secretary
Walter Lynn Jr., Treasurer

Protects America's outdoors through education, community-based conservation, and promoting outdoor recreation.
37000 Members
Founded in 1922

Marine Technology Society

1100 H St., Nw
Suite LL-100
Washington, DC   20005

202-717-8705
FAX 202-347-4302
E-Mail: membership@mtsociety.org
Home Page: www.mtsociety.org
Social Media: *Facebook, Twitter, LinkedIn*

Jerry Boatman, President
Drew Michel, President-Elect
Jerry Wilson, VP of Industry and Technology
Jill Zande, VP of Education and Research
Justin Manley, VP of Gov. & Public Affairs

Addresses coastal zone management, marine, mineral and energy resources, marine environmental protection, and ocean engineering issues.
2M Members
Founded in 1963

Midwest for Environmental Science and Public Policy

1845 N Farwell Avenue
Suite 100
Milwaukee, WI   53202

414-271-7280
FAX 414-273-7293
E-Mail: mcespp@mcespp.org
Home Page: www.mcespp.org

Patrice Ann Morrow, Chair
Jeffery A Foran, President/CEO

For citizens concerned with environmental protection.

NORA: Association of Responsible Recyclers

5965 Amber Ridge Rd
Haymarket, VA   20169-2623

703-753-4277
FAX 703-753-2445
E-Mail: sparker@noranews.org
Home Page: www.noranews.org

Chris Ricci, President
Brandon Velek, Executive Vice President
Bill Hinton, Vice President
Don Littlefield, Vice President, Finance

Is a trade association representing the interests of companies in the United States engaged in the safe recycling of used oil, antifreeze, waste water and oil filters.
Founded in 1984

National Association for Environmental Management

1612 K St NW
Suite 1102
Washington, DC   20006-2830

202-986-6616
800-391-6236
FAX 202-530-4408
E-Mail: programs@naem.org
Home Page: www.naem.org
Social Media: *Facebook, Twitter, LinkedIn*

Kelvin Roth, President
Stephen Evanoff, 1st Vice President
Debbie Hammond, 2nd Vice President
Frank Macielak, Secretary and Treasurer

Dedicated to advancing the profession of environmental management and supports the professional corporate and facility environmental manager.
1000+ Members
Founded in 1990

National Association for PET Containers

Po Box 1327
Sonoma, CA   95476

707-996-4207
FAX 707-935-1998
E-Mail: information@napcor.com
Home Page: www.napcor.com
Social Media: *Facebook*

Dennis Sabourin, Executive Director
Kate Eagles, Communications
Don Kneass, Director
Sandi Childs, Director

National association for the PET plastic industry. Promotes the use of PET plastic packaging and facilitates the recycling of PET containers.
Frequency: Bi-Monthly
Founded in 1987

National Association of Environmental Professionals

PO Box 460
Collingswood, NJ   08108

856-283-7816
FAX 856-210-1619
E-Mail:
naep@bowermanagementservices.com
Home Page: www.naep.org
Social Media: *Facebook, LinkedIn*

Paul Looney, President
Harold Draper, Vice President
Joseph F. Musil Jr., Treasurer
Robert P. Morris Jr., Secretary

Our mission is to be the interdisciplinary organization dedicated to developing the highest standards of ethics and proficiency in the environmental professions. Our members are public and private sector professionals who promote excellence in decision-making in light of the environmental, social, and economic impacts of those decisions.

National Association of Local Government Environmental Professionals

1333 New Hampshire Ave NW
Second Floor
Washington, DC   20036-1532

202-879-4014
FAX 202-393-2866
E-Mail: nalgep@spiegelmcd.com

Home Page: www.nalgep.org
Social Media: *Facebook*

Is a national organization representing local government professionals responsible for environmental compliance and the development of local environmental policy. NALGEP brings together local environmental officials to share information on practices, conduct policy projects, promote environmental training and education, and communicate the view of local officials on national environmental issues.
150 Members
Founded in 1993

National Audubon Society

225 Varick Street
New York, NY   10014

212-979-3000
E-Mail: webmaster@audubon.org
Home Page: www.audubon.org
Social Media: *Facebook, Twitter, YouTube*

Conserves and restores natural ecosystems, focusing on birds, other wildlife, and thier habitats for the benefit of humanity and the earth's biological diversity.
50000 Members
Founded in 1992

National Center for Appropriate Technology

3040 Continental Drive
PO Box 3838
Butte, MT   59702

406-494-4572
800-275-6228
FAX 406-494-2905
E-Mail: info@ncat.org
Home Page: www.ncat.org
Social Media: *Facebook, Twitter, LinkedIn*

Gene Brady, Chairman
Randall Chapman, Vice Chairman
George Ortiz, Chairman Emeritus
Jeannie Jertson, Secretary
Brian Castelli, Treasurer

Their mission is to help people by championing small-scale, local, and sustainable solutions to reduce poverty, promote healthy communities, and protect natural resources. Every day, they help individuals find solutions that will insure that children and grandchildren inherit a world with cleaner air and wa-

ter, efficient and renewable energy production, and healthy foods grown with sustainable techniques.
Founded in 1976

National Conference of Local Environmental Health Administrators

1010 South Third Street
Dayton, WA 99328

509-382-2181
FAX 360-382-2942
E-Mail:
David_Riggs@co.columbia.wa.us
Home Page: www.ncleha.org

A professional association for supervisors, administrators and managers of environmental health programs in local agencies.

National Environmental Balancing Bureau

8575 Grovemont Cir
Gaithersburg, MD 20877-4121

301-977-3698
866-497-4447
FAX 301-977-9589
E-Mail: karen@nebb.org
Home Page: www.nebb.org

Neil J. Marshall, President
Stanley J. Fleischer, President-Elect
Bob Linder, Vice President
James Huber, Treasurer

NEBB is an international certification assocaition for firms that deliver high performance building systems. Members perform testing, adjusting and balancing (TAB) of heating, ventilating and air-conditioning systems, commission and retro-commission building systems commissioning, execute sound and vibration testing, and test and certify lab fume hoods and electronic and bio clean rooms. NEBB holds the highest standards in certification.
Founded in 1971

National Environmental Development Association

One Thomas Circle NW
10th Floor
Washington, DC 20006

202-332-2933
FAX 202-530-0659

Phil Clapp, President
Steve Hellem, Executive Director

NEDA members are companies and other organizations concerned with balancing environmental and economic interests to obtain both a clean environment and a strong economy.
Founded in 1973

National Environmental, Safety and Health Training Association

2700 N. Central Avenue
Suite 900
Phoenix, AZ 85004-1147

602-956-6099
FAX 602-956-6399
E-Mail: neshta@neshta.org
Home Page: www.neshta.org

A non-profit educational society for environmental, safety, health and other technical training and adult education professionals. Mission is to promote trainer competency through trainer skills training, continuing education, voluntary certification, peer networking and the adoption of national and international training and trainer standards.
Founded in 1977

National Institutes for Water Resources

47 Harkness Road
Pelham, MA 10002

413-253-5686
FAX 413-253-1309
E-Mail: tracy@uidaho.edu
Home Page: niwr.net

Jeffery Allen, President
Reagan Waskom, President-Elect
John Tracy, Secretary-Treasurer

NIWRD represents 54 state and territorial Water Research Institutes and Centers in collective activities to implement the provisions of the Water Resources Act of 1984, and subsequesnt federal legislation. NIWR networks these separate institutes into a coordinated unit, represented by 8 regional groupings, and facilitates the response of the Water Research Institutes and its membership to other mutual concerns and interests in water resources.
54 Members
Founded in 1974

National Registry of Environmental Professionals

PO Box 2099
Glenview, IL 60025

847-724-6631
FAX 847-724-4223
E-Mail: nrep@nrep.org
Home Page: www.nrep.org
Social Media: *Facebook, Twitter, LinkedIn, YouTube*

Richard A Young, PhD, Executive Director
Edward Beck, PhD, Senior Director
Carol Schellinger, Director

To promote legal and professional recognition of individuals possessing education, training and experience as environmental managers, engineers, technologists, scientists and technicians-and to consolidate that recognition in one centralized source-so that the public, government, employers and insurers can justify the importance and acceptance of such individuals to carry out operations and management of environmental activities.
17000 Members
Founded in 1983
Mailing list available for rent

National Society of Environmental Consultants

PO Box 12528
San Antonio, TX 78212-0528

210-271-0781
800-486-3676
FAX 210-225-8450

Supports all activities of environmental consultants.
600 Members
Founded in 1992

National Solid Wastes Management Association

4301 Connecticut Ave NW
Suite 300
Washington, DC 20008-2304

202-244-4700
800-424-2869
FAX 202-966-4824
E-Mail: wa@envasns.org
Home Page: www.envasns.org
Social Media: *Facebook, Twitter, YouTube*

Bruce Parker, President
Chaz Miller, Director, State Programs
David Biderman, General Counsel &

Director, Safety
Christine Hutcherson, Director, Member Services
Alice Jacobsohn, Director, Education

Supports all those involved in the environment industry, especially the handling, transportation and disposal of infectious wastes.

National Wildlife Federation

11100 Wildlife Center Dr
Reston, VA   20190-5362

703-438-6000
FAX 703-438-3570
Home Page: www.nwf.org

Mark Van Putten, CEO

Encourages management of natural resources. Gives financial aid to local groups and graduate studies. Conducts guided nature trail tours, produces programs and sponsors competitions.
4.5MM Members
Founded in 1936

National Woodland Owners Association

374 Maple Ave E
Suite 310
Vienna, VA   22180-4718

703-255-2300
800-470-8733
E-Mail: argow@nwoa.net
Home Page: www.nationalforestry.net

Keith A Argow, President
Bert Udell, Executive Committee Chair
Gerald A Rose, Midwest Regional VP

Provides timely information about forestry and forest practices with news from Washington,DC and state capitals. Written for non-industrial land owners. Includes state landowner association news.
39M Members
Founded in 1983

Natural Renewable Energy Laboratory

United States Department of Energy
1617 Cole Blvd
Lakewood, CO   80401-3305

303-275-3000
866-294-8886
FAX 303-275-4222
E-Mail: admin@millionsolarroofs.com
Home Page: www.millionsolarroofs.com

Dan Arvizu, Manager

Created by the Solar Energy Research, Development and Demonstration Act of 1974, which authorized a federal program aimed at developing solar energy as a viable source of the nation's future energy needs. As a primary federal laboratory for solar energy research, SERI conducts and coordinates solar research, technology development and testing functions as developed by the US Department of Energy.
Founded in 1977

Natural Resources Defense Council

40 W 20th St
New York, NY   10011-4231

212-727-2700
FAX 212-727-1773
E-Mail: nrdcinfo@nrdc.org
Home Page: www.nrdc.org
Social Media: *Facebook, Twitter, YouTube*

Frances Beinecke, President
Daniel R. Tishman, Chair
Frederick A.O. Schwarz Jr., Chair Emeritus
Adam Albright, Vice Chair
Patricia Bauman, Vice Chair

Dedicated to the wise management of natural resources through research, public education and the development of effective public policies.
50000 Members
Founded in 1970

North American Association for Environmental Education

2000 P Street NW
Suite 540
Washington, DC   20036

202-419-0412
FAX 202-419-0415
E-Mail: info@naaee.org
Home Page: www.naaee.org
Social Media: *Facebook*

Brian Day, Executive Director
Bridget Chisholm, Conference Manager
Sue Bumpous, Communications Manager

Purpose is to assist and support the work of individuals and groups engaged in environmental education, research and service.
1500 Members
Founded in 1971

North American Chapter - International Society for Ecological Modelling

550 M Ritchie Highway
PMB 255
Severna Park, MD   21146

Home Page: www.isemna.org

Sven E. Jorgensen, President
Tarzan Legovic, Secretary-General
David A. Mauriello, Treasurer

Promotes the international exchange of general knowledge, ideas and scientific results in the area of the application of systems analysis and simulation to ecology, environmental science and natural resource management using mathematical and computer modelling of ecological systems.
150 Members
Founded in 1983

North American Lake Management Society

4513 Vernon Boulevard, Suite 100
PO Box 5443
Madison, WI   53705-443

608-233-2836
FAX 608-233-3186
E-Mail: info@nalms.org
Home Page: www.nalms.org
Social Media: *Facebook, LinkedIn*

Bev Clark, President
Al Sosiak, President-Elect
Reesa Evans, Secretary
Linda Green, Treasurer

Members are academics, lake managers and others interested in furthering the understanding of lake ecology. The North American Lake Management Society's mission is to forge partnerships among citizens, scientists and professionals to foster the management and protection of lakes and reservoirs for today and tomorrow. Please call for rate information.
1700 Members
Founded in 1980

Northeast Sustainable Energy Association

50 Miles St
Greenfield, MA   01301-3255

413-774-6051
FAX 413-774-6053
E-Mail: nesea@nesea.org
Home Page: www.nesea.org

Social Media: *Facebook, Twitter, LinkedIn*

David Barclay, Executive Director
Sonia Hamel, Vice Chair
Daniel Sagan, Secretary
Michael Skelly, Treasurer

The nation's leading regional membership organization focused on promoting the understanding, development and adoption of energy conservation and non-polluting, renewable energy technologies.
1802 Members
Founded in 1974
Mailing list available for rent

Organic Seed Alliance

PO Box 772
Port Townsend, WA 98368-0772

360-385-7192
FAX 425-385-7455
E-Mail: info@seedalliance.org
Home Page: www.seedalliance.org
Social Media: *Facebook, Twitter*

Stephen Harris, President
Tony Kleese, Secretary
Zea Sonnabend, Treasurer

Organic Seed Alliance suppports the ethical development and stewardship of the genetic resources of agricultural seed.
25M Members
Founded in 1975

Plant Growth Regulation Society of America

Rhone-Poulenc, Ag Company
1018 Duke Street
Alexandria, VA 22314

703-836-4606
FAX 706-883-8215
E-Mail: dmancini@ashs.org
Social Media: *Facebook, Twitter*

Dr Eric A Curry, President
Dr Louise Ferguson, VP
Dr Ed Stover, Secretary

Functions as a nonprofit educational and scientific organization.
325 Members
Founded in 1973

Rachel Carson Council

PO Box 10779
Silver Springs, MD 20914

301-593-7507
E-Mail: rccouncil@aol.com

Home Page: rachelcarsoncouncil.org
Social Media: *, Twitter*

Diana Post, Executive Director
David B McGrath, Treasurer
Dr Diana Post, Secretary

Library and clearinghouse on pesticide toxicity, lower risk alternatives for pest control, and Rachel Carson. Produces publications and sponsors conventions/meetings on these topics, issues newsletter. Nonprofit.
Founded in 1965

Renewable Fuels Association

425 Third Street, SW
Suite 1150
Washington, DC 20024

202-289-3835
FAX 202-289-7519
E-Mail: info@ethanolrfa.org
Home Page: www.ethanolrfa.org
Social Media: *Facebook, Twitter*

Chuck Woodside, Chairman
Neill McKinstray, Vice Chairman
Randall Doyal, Treasurer
Walter Wendland, Secretary

Members are companies and individuals involved in the production and use of ethanol.
55 Members
Founded in 1981

Renewable Natural Resources Foundation

5430 Grosvenor Ln
Bethesda, MD 20814-2193

301-493-9101
FAX 301-493-6148
E-Mail: info@rnrf.org
Home Page: www.rnrf.org

Howard N. Rosen, Chairman
Richard A. Engberg, Vice-Chairman
Robert D. Day, Executive Director

A consortium of professional and scientific societies whose members are concerned with the advancement of research, education, scientific practice and policy formulation for the conservation, replenishment and use of the earth's renewable natural resources.
14 Members
Founded in 1972

Resource Policy Institute

1525 Selby Avenue
Ste. 304
Los Angeles, CA 90024-5796

310-470-9711

Dr Arthur Purcell, Director/Founder

Education, and consulting research group concerned with environmental policies, technologies, and management strategies..
Founded in 1975

Safe Buildings Alliance

Metropolitan Square
655 15th Street NW
Suite 1200
Washington, DC 20005-5701

202-879-5120
FAX 202-638-2103
Home Page: sba.lfpc.org

An association of building products companies that formerly manufactured asbestos-containing materials for building construction. Its main focus is to provide public information on issues relating to asbestos in building. SBA promotes a reasonable, safe response to the problem of asbestos in buildings, including the development of uniform, objective Federal and State standards for asbestos identification and abatement, nonremoval alternatives and the regulation of inspectors.
Founded in 1984

Sagamore Institute of the Adirondacks Inc

Great Camp Sagamore
PO Box 40
Raquette Lake, NY 13436-0040

315-354-5311
FAX 315-354-5851
E-Mail: info@greatcampsagamore.org
Home Page:
www.greatcampsagamore.org
Social Media: *Facebook, YouTube*

Beverly Bridge, Executive Director

Non-profit 501c3 National Historic Landmark, former retreat of the Vanderbilts, offering educational programs on history, ecology and culture of the Adirondack Park.

Silicones Environmental Health and Safety

2325 Dulles Corner Boulevard
Suite 500
Herndon, VA   20171

703-788-6570
FAX 703-788-6545
E-Mail: sehsc@sehsc.com
Home Page: www.sehsc.com

Karluss Thomas, Executive Director

A not-for-profit trade association comprised of North American silicone chemical producers and importers.
6 Members
Founded in 1971

Society for Ecological Restoration International

1017 O Street NW
Washington, DC   20001

202-299-9518
FAX 270-626-5485
E-Mail: info@ser.org
Home Page: www.ser.org
Social Media: *Facebook*

Steve Whisenant, Chair
Cara R. Nelson, Vice Chair
Mary Travaglini, Treasurer
Alan Unwin, Secretary

SER members are academics, scientists, environmental consultants, government agencies and others with an interest in ecological restoration.
2300 Members
Founded in 1988

Society for Environmental Geochemistry and Health

4698 S Forrest Avenue
Springfield, MO   65810

417-851-1166
FAX 417-881-6920
E-Mail: DRBGWIXSON@aol.com
Home Page: www.segh.net

Prof. Xiangdong Li, President
Prof. Andrew Hursthouse, European Chair
Kyoung-Woong Kim, Asia/Pacific Chair
Anthea Brown, Membership Secretary/Treasurer
Malcolm Brown, Secretary

To promote a multi-disciplinary approach to research in fields of geochemistry and health to facilitate and expand communication among scientists within these disciplines and to advance knowledge in the area.
400 Members
Founded in 1971

Society for Human Ecology

College of the Atlantic
105 Eden Street
Bar Harbor, ME   04609-0180

207-288-5015
FAX 207-288-3780
E-Mail: carter@coa.edu
Home Page:
www.societyforhumanecology.org
Social Media: *Facebook, Twitter*

Zachary Smith, President
Rob Dyball, Vice President
Lee Cerveny, Second Vice President
Chiho Watanabe, Third Vice President-International
Rob Lilieholm, Treasurer

SHE members are academics, scientists, health professionals and others with an interest in studying the interrelationship of man's actions and his environment.
150 Members
Founded in 1981

Society for Occupational and Environmental Health

111 North Bridge Road
#21-01 Peninsula Plaza
Singapore   179098

Home Page: www.oehs.org.sg

Gregory Chan, President
Ang Boon Tian, Vice President
Kam Wai Kuen, Honorary Secretary
Kenneth Choy, Honorary Treasurer

Members include physicians, hygienists, economists, laboratory scientists, academicians, labor and industry representatives, or anyone interested in occupational and/or environmental health. Serves as a forum for the presentation of scientific data and the exchange of information among members; sponsors conferences and meetings which address specific problem areas and policy questions.
300 Members
Founded in 1972

Society of Environmental Toxicology and Chemistry

1013 N 12th Ave
Pensacola, FL   32501-3306

850-437-1901
FAX 850-469-9778
E-Mail: setac@setac.org
Home Page: www.setac.org
Social Media: *Facebook, Twitter, LinkedIn*

Paul van den Brink, President
Tim Canfield, Vice President
Fred Heimbach, Treasurer

Is a professional society established to promote the use of multidisciplinary approaches to solving problems of the impact of chemicals and technology on the environment. SETA members are professionals in the fields of chemistry, toxicology, biology, ecology, atmospheric sciences, health sciences, earth sciences, and environmental engineering.
4000 Members
Founded in 1979

Society of Exploration Geophysicists

8801 South Yale
Suite 500
Tulsa, OK   74137-3575

918-497-5500
FAX 918-497-5557
E-Mail: web@seg.org
Home Page: www.seg.org
Social Media: *Facebook, Twitter, LinkedIn*

Mary Fleming, Executive Director
Vladimir Grechka, Editor

The Society of Exploration Geophysicists/SEG is a not-for-profit organization that promotes the science of geophysics and the education of applied geophysicists. SEG fosters the expert and ethical practice of geophysics in the exploration and development of natural resources, in characterizing the near surface, and in mitigating earth hazards.
Founded in 1930

Soil and Plant Analysis Council

347 North Shores Circle
Windsor, CO 80550

970-686-5702
E-Mail: rmiller@lamar.colostate.edu
Home Page: www.spcouncil.com

Rigas Karamanos, President
Robert Miller, Secretary/ Treasurer
Rao Mylavarapu, Vice President

Supports all those involved in the analysis of soil and plants.

Soil and Water Conservation Society

945 SW Ankeny Rd
Ankeny, IA 50023-9764

515-289-2331
800-843-7645
FAX 515-289-1227
E-Mail: swcs@swcs.org
Home Page: www.swcs.org

Bill Boyer, President
Dan Towery, Vice-President
Clark Gantzer, Secretary
Jerry Pearce, Treasurer

SWCS is a nonprofit scientific and educational organization that serves as an advocate for conservation professionals and for science-based conservation practice, programs, and policy.
5000+ Members
Founded in 1943

Solar Energy Research Institute

United States Department of Energy
1617 Cole Boulevard
Golden, CO 80401-3305

303-275-4700
FAX 303-275-4788

Created by the Solar Energy Research, Development and Demonstration Act of 1974, which authorized a federal program aimed at developing solar energy as a viable source of the Nation's future energy needs. As a primary Federal laboratory for solar energy research, SERI conducts and coordinates solar research, technology development and testing functions as developed by the US Department of Energy.
Founded in 1977

Steel Recycling Institute

680 Andersen Drive
Pittsburgh, PA 15220-2700

412-922-2772
800-876-7274
FAX 412-922-3213
Home Page: www.recycle-steel.org
Social Media: *Facebook, Twitter, YouTube*

William H Heenan Jr, President

Promotes steel recycling and works to forge a coalition of steelmakers, can manufacturers, legislators, government officials, solid waste managers, business and consumer groups.
Founded in 1988

Student Conservation Association

689 River Road
PO Box 550
Charlestown, NH 03603-0550

603-543-1700
FAX 603-543-1828
E-Mail: jcota@thesca.org
Home Page: www.sca-inc.org
Social Media: *Facebook, Twitter, YouTube*

Dale Penny, President and CEO
Valerie Bailey, Vice President

To build the next generation of conservation leaders and inspire lifelong stewardship of our environment and communities by engaging young people in hands-on service to the land.
35000 Members
Founded in 1957

Surfaces in Biomaterials Foundation

1000 Westgate Drive
Suite 252
St Paul, MN 55114-8679

651-290-6267
FAX 651-290-2266
E-Mail: memberservices@surfaces.org
Home Page: www.surfaces.org
Social Media: *, LinkedIn*

Andy Shelp, Executive Director
Ashley Crunstedt, Events/Meetings Planner
Janey Duntley, Web Coor/Newsletter Managing Editor

Dedicated to exploring creative solutions to technical challenges at the BioInterface by fostering education and multidisciplinary cooperation among industrial, academic, clinical and regulatory communities.
250 Members

The Indoor Air Institute

2548 Empire Grade
Santa Cruz, CA 95060

831-426-0148
FAX 831-426-6522
E-Mail: info@IndAir.org
Home Page: indair.org

Hal Levin, President
William Fisk, Vice President
William Nazaroff, Vice President

Supports all those involved with indoor air quality and climate with training, education, resource materials and an annual conference.

The Nature Conservancy

4245 North Fairfax Drive
Suite 100
Arlington, VA 22203-1606

703-841-5300
Home Page: www.nature.org
Social Media: *Facebook, Twitter*

Teresa Beck, Co-Chairman of the Board
Steven A. Denning, Co-Chairman of the Board
Mark R. Tercek, President and CEO
Gordon Crawford, Vice Chair
Roberto Hernandez Ramirez, Vice Chair

The leading conservation organization working around the world to protect ecologically important lands and waters for nature and people. Addresses the most pressing conservation threats at the largest scale.
Founded in 1984

United Association of Used Oil Services

318 Newman Road
Sebring, FL 33870-6702

941-655-3880
800-877-4356

Established to be an effective presence in dealing with regulations and to provide a network for those with an interest in the collection and proper disposition of used lubricating oils.
Founded in 1987

Water Environment Federation

601 Wythe St
Alexandria, VA 22314-1994

703-684-2400
800-666-0206
FAX 703-684-2492
E-Mail: thardwick@wef.org
Home Page: www.wef.org
Social Media: *Facebook, Twitter*

Matt Bond, President
Cordell Samuels, President-Elect
Sandra Ralston, Vice President
Chris Browning, Treasurer
Jeff Eger, Secretary and Executive Director

Supports those involved in issues that affect the international water environment.
79 Members
ISSN: 1044-9943
Founded in 1928

Water Quality Association

4151 Naperville Rd
Lisle, IL 60532-3696

630-505-0160
FAX 630-505-9637
E-Mail: info@wqa.org
Home Page: www.wqa.org
Social Media: *Facebook, Twitter, YouTube*

Peter Censky, Executive Director

An international, nonprofit trade association representing retail/dealers and manufacturer/suppliers in the point of use/entry water quality improvement industry. Membership benefits and services include technical and scientific information, educational seminars and home correspondence course books, professional certification and discount services.
2.5M Members
Founded in 1974

Wilderness Society

1615 M St NW
Washington, DC 20036-3258

202-833-2300
800-843-9453
FAX 202-429-3958
E-Mail: member@tws.org
Home Page: www.wilderness.org
Social Media: *Facebook, Twitter*

Douglas W. Walker, Chair
Molly McUsic, Vice Chair
William J. Cronon, Vice Chair

Marcia Kunstel, Secretary
Kevin Luzak, Treasurer

Establishes the land ethic as a basic element of the American culture and educates people on the importance of wilderness preservation and land protection.
200M Members
Founded in 1935
Mailing list available for rent: 178000 names at $90 per M

Wildlife Conservation Society

2300 Southern Boulevard
Bronx, NY 10460

718-220-5100
FAX 718-584-2625
E-Mail: membership@wcs.org
Home Page: www.wcs.org
Social Media: *Facebook, YouTube*

Ward W. Woods, Chair
Edith McBean, Vice Chair
Gordon B. Pattee, Vice Chair
Brian J. Heidtke, Treasurer
Andrew H. Tisch, Secretary

Supports all those involved in the conservation of wildlife, especially the most rare and endangered species.

Wildlife Habitat Council

8737 Colesville Road
Suite 800
Silver Spring, MD 20910

301-588-8994
FAX 301-588-4629
E-Mail: whc@wildlifehc.org
Home Page: www.wildlifehc.org
Social Media: *Facebook, YouTube*

Greg Cekander, Chairman
Lawrence A Selzer, Vice Chairman
Kevin Butt, Secretary-Treasurer

Supports corporate, government and conservation leaders from around the globe involved in environmental stewardship.
120+ Members
Founded in 1988

Wildlife Management Institute

4426 VT Route 215N
Cabot, VT 05647

802-563-2087
FAX 802-563-2157
E-Mail: wmisw@together.net

Home Page:
www.wildlifemanagementinstitute.org

Richard E McCabe, Executive VP
Scot J Williamson, VP
Carol J Peddicord, Finance Manager
Robert L Byrne, Wildlife Program Coordinator
Ronald R Helinski, Conservation Policy Specialist

Supports all those involved with the challenges of modern conservation.

Wildlife Society

5410 Grosvenor Ln
Suite 200
Bethesda, MD 20814-2144

301-897-9770
FAX 301-530-2471
E-Mail: tws@wildlife.org
Home Page: www.wildlife.org
Social Media: *Facebook, Twitter, LinkedIn*

Michael Hutchins, Executive Director
Laura Bies, Director, Government Affairs
Jane Jorgensen, Office and Finance Manager
Yanin Walker, Operations Manager

Supports all those involved in wildlife conservation, including wildlife artists, environmental consultants, conservation groups, scientific associations and natural resource companies, industry groups and government agencies.
9000 Members
Founded in 1937

Women's Council on Energy and the Environment

PO Box 33211
Washington, DC 20033-0211

202-997-4512
FAX 202-478-2098
Home Page: www.wcee.org
Social Media: *Facebook, Twitter*

Ronke Luke, President
Mary Brosnan-Sell, Secretary
Robin Cantor, Vice President
Alice Grabowski, Treasurer
Joyce Chandran, Executive Director

Supports women involved in the environmental community with education, research, new trend information and several publications.

World Society for the Protection of Animals

Lincoln Plaza
89 South Street #201
Boston, MA 02111

800-883-9772
FAX 617-737-4404
Home Page: www.wspa-usa.org
Social Media: *Facebook, Twitter, YouTube*

Robert S. Cummings, President
John Bowen, Secretary
Carter Luke, Treasurer

International animal protection news reports. Lobbies for effective animal welfare laws and provides educational material.
12 Members

World Wildlife Fund

1250 24th Street, NW
PO Box 97180
Washington, DC 20090-7180

202-293-4800
FAX 202-293-9211
E-Mail: archer@wwfus.org
Home Page: www.worldwildlife.org
Social Media: *Facebook, Twitter, YouTube*

Carter Roberts, President
Lawrence H. Linden, Chairman
Neville Isdell, Vice-Chair
Pamela Matson, Vice-Chair
Brenda S. Davis, Treasurer

Supports all those involved in maintaining wildlife and their environment. Monitors human development, and seeks to influence public opinion and policy makers in favor of ecologically sound practices.
4M Members
Founded in 1961

Newsletters

AEESP Newsletter

AEESP
2303 Naples Court
Champaign, IL 61822

217-398-6969
FAX 217-355-9232
Home Page: www.aeesp.org

Joanne Fetzner, Business Secretary

Official newsletter of the Association of Environmental Engineering and Science

Professors. Topics cover the scope and diversity of challenges faced in environmental engineering and science.
Frequency: Quarterly

AERE Newsletter

Association of Environmental and Resource
1616 P St Nw
Suite 400
Washington, DC 20036-1434

202-328-5157
FAX 202-939-3460
E-Mail: voigt@rff.org
Home Page: www.aere.org

Marilyn Voigt, Executive Secretary
Ralph Metts, President

Includes policy essays, meeting announcements, calls for papers, new publications, research reports, position announcements and other information of interest to AERE members and environmental economists in general.
Frequency: Semi-Annual

AIH Bulletin

American Institute of Hydrology
1230 Lincoln Drive
Carbondale, IL 62901

618-453-7809
E-Mail: aih@engr.siu.edu
Home Page: www.aihydrology.org

Cathy Lipsett, Owner
Cathryn Seaburn, Manager

Newsletter for the American Institute of Hydrology, providing information designed to improve professional skills and abilities of its members, the professional community and the public at large.
Frequency: Quarterly

ASMR Newsletter

American Society of Mining and Reclamation
3134 Montavesta Road
Lexington, KY 40502

859-335-6529
E-Mail: asmr@insightbb.com
Home Page: www.ca.uky.edu/assmr

Richard I Barnhisel, Executive Secretary

Promotes the advancement of basic and applied reclamation science.
Frequency: 10/year

ATTRAnews

National Center for Appropriate Technology
3040 Continental Drive
PO Box 3838
Butte, MT 59702

406-494-4572
800-275-6228
FAX 406-494-2905
E-Mail: info@ncat.org
Home Page: www.ncat.org
Social Media: *Facebook, Twitter, LinkedIn*

Eugene Brady, Chairman
Kathleen Hadley, Executive Director

ATTRAnews brings you up to date on the latest developments in sustainable agriculture, what's happening at the USDA and with Sustainable Agriculture Working Groups around the country. ATTRAnews features events and opportunities in sustainable agriculture, information on funding and financing, and it keeps you current on programs and policies that can affect your future.
Frequency: 6x/Year
Founded in 1976

Advisor

Great Lakes Commission
2805 S Industrial Hwy
Suite 100
Ann Arbor, MI 48104-6791

734-971-9135
FAX 734-971-9150
E-Mail: glc@great-lakes.net
Home Page: www.glc.org

Tim Eder, Executive Director
Cook Havtrkamp, Author

Covers economic and environmental issues of the Great Lakes region with a special focus on activities of the Great Lakes Commission.
12 Pages
Frequency: Quarterly
Founded in 1955
Printed in one color on matte stock

Air Water Pollution Report's Environment Week

Business Publishers
8737 Colesville Road
Suite 1100
Silver Spring, MD 20910-3928

301-876-6300
800-274-6737
FAX 301-589-8493

E-Mail: custserv@bpinews.com
Home Page: www.bpinews.com

Leonard A Eiserer, Publisher
Beth Early, Operations Director
David Goeller, Editor

Provides a balanced, insightful update on the week's most important environmental news from Washington, D.C.
Cost: $595.00
Frequency: Weekly
Founded in 1963

Annual Research Program Report

National Institutes for Water Resources

Home Page: niwr.net

Paul Joseph Godfrey, PhD, Executive Director

Frequency: Annual

Aquatic Plant News

Aquatic Plant Management Society
PO Box 821265
Vicksburg, MS 39182-1265

FAX 601-634-5502
E-Mail: dpetty@ndrsite.com
Home Page: www.apms.org
Social Media: *Facebook, LinkedIn*

Linda Nelson, President
Terry Goldsby, VP
Sherry Whitaker, Treasurer

Aquatic Plant News is produced 3 times each year, and is distributed primarily by email.
Frequency: 3x/Year
Founded in 1961

Asbestos & Lead Abatement Report

Business Publishers
8737 Colesville Road
Suite 1100
Silver Spring, MD 20910-3928

301-876-6300
800-274-6737
FAX 301-589-8493
E-Mail: custserv@bpinews.com
Home Page: www.bpinews.com

Leonard Eiserer, Publisher

Contains articles on regulation compliance, environmental trends, and business opportunities.
Cost: $382.00
Frequency: Monthly
Founded in 1963

BNA's Environmental Compliance Bulletin

Bureau of National Affairs
1801 S Bell St
Arlington, VA   22202-4501

703-341-3000
800-372-1033
FAX 800-253-0332
E-Mail: customercare@bna.com
Home Page: www.bnabooks.com

Paul N Wojcik, CEO
Gregory C McCaffery, President

Water and air pollution, waste management and regulatory updates, as well as a summary of selected regulatory actions and a list of key environmental compliance dates.
Cost: $649.00
Frequency: Annual+
Founded in 1929

Bulletins

World Research Foundation
41 Bell Rock Plaza
Sedona, AZ   86351-8804

928-284-3300
FAX 928-284-3530
E-Mail: info@wrf.org
Home Page: www.wrf.org

Steven A Ross, President

Updates on recent research including topics involving health information pertinent to the World Research Foundation.
Frequency: Quarterly

Business and the Environment

Cutter Information Corporation
37 Broadway
Suite 1
Arlington, MA   02474-5500

781-648-1950
800-888-8939
FAX 617-648-8707
Home Page: www.homeenergy.org
Social Media: *, Twitter, Flickr*

Karen Fine Coburn, Publisher
Kathleen Victory, Editor

Environmental investment trends, deals and market developments.
Cost: $497.00
Frequency: Monthly

CCHEST Newsletter

Council on Certification of Health, Environmental
2301 W. Bradley Avenue
Champaign, IL   61821

217-359-9263
FAX 217-359-0055
E-Mail: cchest@cchest.org
Home Page: www.cchest.org
Social Media: *Facebook, Twitter, LinkedIn*

Margaret M. Carroll, President
Carl W. Heinlein, Vice President
Emory E. Knowles III, Treasurer

Keeps members up to date on events, OSHA news and the latest safety courses.
Frequency: Annual
Mailing list available for rent: 20,000 names

Clean Water Report

Business Publishers Inc.
8737 Colesville Road
Suite 1100
Silver Spring, MD   20910-3928

301-589-5103
800-274-6737
FAX 301-589-8493
E-Mail: custserv@bpinews.com
Home Page: www.bpinews.com

Follows the latest news from the EPA, Congress, the states, the courts, and private industry. A key information source for environmental professionals, covering the important issues of ground and drinking water, wastewater treatment, wetlands, drought, coastal protection, non-point source pollution, agrichemical contamination and more.
8 Pages

Composting News

McEntee Media Corporation
9815 Hazelwood Ave
Strongsville, OH   44149-2305

440-238-6603
FAX 440-238-6712
E-Mail: ken@recycle.cc
Home Page: www.recycle.cc

Ken Mc Entee, Owner

The latest in composting, wood waste recycling and organics management in a

monthly newsletter.
Cost: $83.00
Frequency: Monthly
Circulation: 2000
Founded in 1990

Conservation Commission News
New Hampshire Association of
Conservation Comm.
54 Portsmouth Street
Concord, NH   03301-5486

603-224-7867

Marjory Swope, Publisher

Encourage conservation and appropriate
use of New Hampshire's natural resources by providing assistance to New
Hampshire's municipal conservation
commissions and by facilitating communication among commissions and between commissions and other public and
private agencies involved in conservation.
Cost: $5.00
8 Pages
Frequency: Quarterly
Circulation: 1,650
Printed in one color on matte stock

Conservogram
Soil and Water Conservation Society
945 SW Ankeny Rd
Ankeny, IA   50023-9723

515-289-2331
800-843-7645
FAX 515-289-1227
E-Mail: pubs@swcs.org
Home Page: www.swcs.org

Craig Cox, President
Deb Happe, Editor

The professional conservationist's newsletter, Conservogram is produced for
members of the Soil and Water Conservation Society.
Frequency: Monthly
Founded in 1943

Convention Proceedings
Society for Human Ecology
College of the Atlantic
105 Eden Street
Bar Harbor, ME   04609-0180

207-288-5015
FAX 207-288-3780
E-Mail: carter@ecology.coa.edu

Home Page:
www.societyforhumanecology.org

Barbara Carter, Assistant to Executive
Director

Frequency: 1/18 months

Daily Environment Report
Bureau of National Affairs
1801 S Bell St
Arlington, VA   22202-4501

703-341-3000
800-372-1033
FAX 800-253-0332
E-Mail: customercare@bna.com
Home Page: www.bnabooks.com

Paul N Wojcik, CEO
Gregory C McCaffery, President

A 40-page daily report providing comprehensive, in-depth coverage of national and international environmental
news. Each issue contains summaries of
the top news stories, articles, and
in-brief items, and a journal of meetings,
agency activities, hearings and legal proceedings. Coverage includes air and water pollution, hazardous substances, and
hazardous waste, solid waste, oil spills,
gas drilling, pollution prevention, impact
statements and budget matters.
Cost: $ 3537.00
40 Pages
Frequency: Daily
ISSN: 1060-2976

Defense Cleanup
Business Publishers
2222 Sedwick Dr
Suite 101
Durham, NC   27713

800-274-6737
FAX 800-508-2592
E-Mail: custserv@bpinews.com
Home Page: www.bpinews.com

Covers the lates news and analysis of defense cleanup activity, including base
remediation and closure, contract
awards, and site cleanups.
Cost: $627.00
8 Pages
Frequency: Weekly
Printed in on matte stock

Digital Traveler
International Ecotourism Society
733 15th Street NW
Suite 1000
Washington, DC   20005

202-547-9203
FAX 202-387-7915
E-Mail: ecomail@ecotourism.org
Home Page: www.ecotourism.org

Martha Honey, Executive Director
Amos Bien, Director International
Programs
Neal Inamdar, Director
Finance/Administration

Regular updates about TIES work and
programs.
Frequency: Monthly

E&P Environment
Pasha Publications
1616 N Fort Myer Dr
Suite 1000
Arlington, VA   22209-3107

703-528-1244
800-424-2908
FAX 703-528-1253
E-Mail: epenvr@pasha.com
Home Page: www.newsletteraccess.com

Harry Baisden, Group Publisher
Jerry Grisham, Editor

Reports on environmental regulations,
advances in technology and litigation
aimed specifically at the exploration and
production segments of the oil and gas
industry.
Cost: $395.00

E-Scrap News
Resource Recycling
PO Box 42270
Portland, OR   97242-270

503-233-1305
FAX 503-233-1356
E-Mail: info@resource-recycling.com
Home Page:
www.resource-recycling.com

Jerry Powell, Publisher/Editor
Andrew Santosusso, Managing Editor
Betsy Loncar, Circulation Director

Monthly newsletter covering all aspects
of recovering, recycling, and managing
electronics scrap. Coverage includes
market prices and trends, collection
events, product stewardship develop-

ments and global trends.
Cost: $99.00
6 Pages
Frequency: Monthly
Circulation: 1000
ISSN: 1536-3856
Founded in 1983
*Mailing list available for rent: 40,000
names at $100 per M*
Printed in 2 colors on matte stock

ECOMOD Newsletter

International Society for Ecological
Modelling
University of California, Animal
Sciences Dept
One Shields Avenue
Davis, CA   95616-8521

530-752-5362
FAX 530-752-0175
Home Page: www.isemna.org

Wolfgang Pittroff, Secretary-General

Information on conferences, workshops
and symposia that promote the systems
philosophy in ecological research and
teaching. Members frequently contribute
articles.
Frequency: Quarterly

EH&S Software News Online

Donley Technology
PO Box 152
Colonial Beach, VA   22443-152

804-224-9427
800-201-1595
FAX 804-224-7958
Home Page: www.ehssoftwarenews.com

John Donley, Editor

Reports on news and upgraded software
products, database, and on-line systems
from commercial developers and government resources.
Cost: $125.00
Founded in 1988

EMS Newsletter

Environmental Mutagen Society
1821 Michael Faraday Drive
Suite 300
Reston, VA   20190

703-438-8220
FAX 703-438-3113
E-Mail: emshq@ems-us.org
Home Page: www.ems-us.org

Kathleen Hill, Editor
Barbara Parsons, Editor
Cathy Klein, Editor

Current scientific research, policies, and
guidelines for the causes and consequences of damage to the genome and
epigenome.
Frequency: Bi-Annual

Environment Reporter

Bureau of National Affairs
1801 S Bell St
Arlington, VA   22202-4501

703-341-3000
800-372-1033
FAX 800-253-0332
E-Mail: customercare@bna.com
Home Page: www.bnabooks.com

Paul N Wojcik, CEO
Gregory C McCaffery, President

A weekly notification and reference service covering the full-spectrum of legislative, administrative, judicial, industrial
and technological developments affecting pollution control and environmental
protection.
Cost: $3776.00
Frequency: Weekly
ISSN: 0013-9211
Founded in 1929

Environmental Health Letter

Business Publishers
2222 Sedwick Dr
Suite 101
Durham, NC   27713

800-223-8720
FAX 800-508-2592
E-Mail: custserv@bpinews.com
Home Page: www.bpinews.com

Comprehensive coverage of the latest
policies and ground-breaking research
that explores the potential links between
environmental factors and human health.
Cost: $567.00
8 Pages
Frequency: Monthly
Founded in 1963
Mailing list available for rent
Printed in 2 colors on matte stock

Environmental Health Newsletter

International Lead Zinc Research
Organization
2525 Meridian Parkway, Suite 100
PO Box 12036
Durham, NC   27713

919-361-4647
FAX 919-361-1957

E-Mail: jhendric@ilzro.org
Home Page: www.ilzro.org

Stephen Wilkinson, President
Frank Goodwin, VP Materials Sciences
Scott Mooneyham, Treasurer
Rob Putnam, Director Communications

Information on environmental health sciences, use of technology, rules, and public education.
Frequency: Quarterly

Environmental Policy Alert

Inside Washington Publishers
1919 S Eads St
Suite 201
Arlington, VA   22202-3028

703-418-3981
800-424-9068
FAX 703-416-8543
E-Mail: iwp@sprintmail.com
Home Page: www.iwpnews.com

Alan Sosenko, Owner

Adresses the legislative news and provides reports on the federal environmental policy process.
Cost: $560.00
Founded in 1980

Environmental Problems & Remediation

InfoTeam
PO Box 15640
Plantation, FL   33318-5640

954-473-9560
FAX 954-473-0544
E-Mail: infoteamma@aol.com

Merton Allen, Editor

Concerned with environmental problems
and effects, the methods and approaches
for mitigation and remediation. Covers
air pollution; surface and ground water
pollution; wastewater; soil contamination; waste recycling; medical wastes;
landfills and waste sites; stack gases;
combustion and incineration; earth
warming and more.
Cost: $289.00
Frequency: Monthly

Environmental Regulation

State Capitals Newsletters
PO Box 7376
Alexandria, VA   22307-7376

703-768-9600
FAX 703-768-9690

E-Mail: newsletters@statecapitals.com
Home Page: www.statecapitals.com

Keyes Walworth, Publisher
Ellen Klein, Editor
Cost: $245.00

Frequency: Weekly
ISSN: 1061-9682

Environmental Regulation: From the State Capitals

Wakeman Walworth
PO Box 7376
Alexandria, VA   22307-7376

703-768-9600
FAX 703-768-9690
E-Mail: newsletters@statecapitals.com
Home Page:
www.statecapitals.com/environreg.html

Keyes Walworth, Publisher

Keeps individuals informed on state programs regarding brownfields, air and water pollution, MTBE, beach renourishment, land management, green space laws, biotech restrictions, livestock regulation, forest control, wilderness preservation, urban sprawl, solid waste, recycling, hazardous wastes, radioactive waste, acid rain, sewage disposal, pesticide policies, environmental insurance protection, water quality, groundwater protection, wetlands .
Cost: $245.00
8 Pages
Frequency: Weekly
Printed in one color on matte stock

Environmental Regulatory Advisor

JJ Keller
3003 W Breezewood Lane
Neenah, WI   54956-368

920-722-2848
800-327-6868
FAX 800-727-7516
E-Mail: sales@jjkeller.com
Home Page: www.jjkeller.com

Webb Shaw, Editor
Robert Keller, CEO

Covers developments at the EPA.
Cost: $90.00
12 Pages
Frequency: Monthly
ISSN: 1056-3164
Founded in 1953

Environotes Newsletter

Federation of Environmental
Technologists
PO Box 624
Slinger, WI   53086-0624

414-540-0070
FAX 262-644-7106
E-Mail: info@fetinc.org
Home Page: www.fetinc.org

Triese Haase, Administrator

Educating and Developing Excellence in Environmental Professionals
Frequency: Monthly

Fibre Market News

GIE Media
4012 Bridge Avenue
Cleveland, OH   44113-3320

216-961-4130
800-456-0707
FAX 216-961-0364

Richard Foster, Publisher
Daniel Sandoval, Editor

Covers the international paper recycling industry. Trends, markets, expansions, economics covered in an in-depth fashion. Also have weekly fax update covering late-breaking news.
Cost: $115.00
16 Pages
Frequency: BiWeekly

Forest History Society

Forest History Society
701 William Vickers Ave
Durham, NC   27701-3162

919-682-9319
FAX 919-682-2349
E-Mail: recluce2@duke.edu
Home Page: www.foresthistory.org

Steven Anderson, President
R Scott Wallinger, Chairman
Yvan Hardy, Co-Vice Chairman
Mark Wilde, Co Vice-Chairman

Nonprofit educational institution that explores the history of the environment, forestry and conservation.

Forestry Notes

National Association of Conservation
Districts
509 Capitol Ct. NE
Washington, DC   20002-4937

202-547-6223
FAX 202-547-6450

E-Mail: krysta-harden@nacdnet.org
Home Page: www.nacdnet.org

Krysta Harden, CEO
Bob Cordova, Second Vice President

Highlights forestry issues of importance to districts and to showcase district-related forestry projects and success stories. Funded through a cooperative agreement between NACD and the U.S. Forest Service.
Cost: $35.00
12 Pages
Frequency: Monthly
Circulation: 25000
Founded in 1937

Global Environmental Change Report

Aspen Publishers
76 Ninth Avenue
7th Floor
New York, NY   10011

212-771-0600
800-638-8437
Home Page: www.aspenpublishers.com

Mark Dorman, CEO
Gustavo Dobles, VP Operations

News and analysis of policy, science and industry developments in the areas of global warming and acid rain.
Cost: $447.00
Frequency: BiWeekly

HazTECH News

Haztech News
14120 Huckleberry Lane
Silver Spring, MD   20906

301-871-3289
FAX 301-460-5859
E-Mail: HazTECH@ix.netcom.com

Cathy Dombrowski, Editor/Publisher

Describes technologies for hazardous waste management, site remediation, industrial wastewater treatment and VOC control.
Cost: $385.00
8 Pages
Frequency: Bi-Weekly
Printed in one color

Hazardous Materials Intelligence Report

World Information Systems
PO Box 535
Cambridge, MA   02238-535

617-492-3312
FAX 617-492-3312
Home Page:
members.aol.com/socejp/hmir.html

Richard S Golob, Publisher
Roger B Wilson Jr, Editor

Provides news analysis on environmental business, hazardous materials, waste management, pollution prevention and control. Covers regulations, legislation and court decisions, new technology, contract opportunities and awards and conference notices.
Cost: $375.00
Frequency: Weekly
Circulation: 50000

Hazardous Materials Transportation

Bureau of National Affairs
1801 S Bell St
Arlington, VA   22202-4501

703-341-3000
800-372-1033
E-Mail: customercare@bna.com
Home Page: www.bnabooks.com

Gregory C McCaffery, President
Paul N Wojcik, Chairman

A two-binder service containing the full-text of rules and regulations governing shipment of hazardous material by rail, air, ship, highway and pipeline, including DOT's Hazardous Materials Tables and EPA's rules for its hazardous waste tracking system.
Cost: $933.00
Frequency: Monthly

Hazardous Waste Business

McGraw Hill
3333 Walnut Street
Boulder, CO   80301

720-485-5000
800-424-2908
FAX 720-548-5701
E-Mail:
customer.service@mcgrawhill.com
Home Page: www.mcgraw-hill.com/

Kevin Hamilton, Publisher
James Keener, Manager
Karen Cleale, Marketing Manager

Focuses on the control and cleanup of hazardous wastes.
Cost: $675.00
8 Pages
Founded in 1996

Hazardous Waste News

Business Publishers
2222 Sedwick Dr
Suite 101
Durham, NC   27713

800-223-8720
FAX 800-508-2592
E-Mail: custserv@bpinews.com
Home Page: www.bpinews.com

Comprehensive federal, state and local coverage of legislation and regulation affecting all aspects of the hazardous waste industry including Superfund, Resource Conservation and Recovery Act, US EPA, incineration, land disposal and more.
Cost: $597.00
8 Pages
Frequency: Weekly
Mailing list available for rent
Printed in 2 colors

Hazardous Waste Report

Aspen Publishers
7201 McKinney Cir
Frederick, MD   21704-8356

301-698-7100
800-638-8437
FAX 212-597-0335
E-Mail: paul.gibson@aspenpubl.com
Home Page: www.aspenpublishers.com

Paul Gibson, Publisher
Sally Almeria, Editor
Bruce Becker, CEO/President
Tom Ceodi, Marketing

Provides information on industry news.
Cost: $875.00
8 Pages
Founded in 1958

Health Facts and Fears.com

American Council on Science and Health
1995 Broadway
2nd Floor
New York, NY   10023-5882

212-362-7044
FAX 212-362-4919

E-Mail: acsh@acsh.org
Home Page: www.acsh.org

Dr Elizabeth Whelan, President
Jeff Stier, Associate Director

Daily e-mail blast on the latest public health news and junk science scares.
Frequency: Weekly

IALR Newsletter

3134 Montavesta Road
Lexington, KY   40502

859-335-6529
E-Mail: asmr@insightbb.com
Home Page: www.ca.uky.edu/assmr

Richard I Barnhisel, Executive Secretary

Depends on news items contributed by its membership, as well as other individuals concerned with land reclamation.
Frequency: Annual

IES Quarterly Newsletter

International Ecotourism Society
733 15th Street NW
Suite 1000
Washington, DC   20005

202-547-9203
FAX 202-387-7915
E-Mail: ecomail@ecotourism.org
Home Page: www.ecotourism.org

Martha Honey, Executive Director
Amos Bien, Director International Programs
Neal Inamdar, Director Finance/Administration

Offering information on advocacy uniting communities, conservation, and sustainable travel.
Frequency: Quarterly

Industrial Health & Hazards Update

InfoTeam
PO Box 15640
Plantation, FL   33318-5640

954-473-9560
FAX 954-473-0544
E-Mail: infoteamma@aol.com

Merton Allen, Editor

Covers occupational safety, health, hazards, and disease, mitigatioin and control of hazardous situations; waste recycling and treatment; environmental pollution and control; product safety and liability; fires and explosions; plant and computer security,; air pollution; surface and

ground water; wastewater; soil gases; combustion and incineration; earth warming; ozone layer depletion; electromagnetic radiation; toxic materials; and many other related topics.
Frequency: Monthly

Infectious Wastes News
National Solid Wastes Management Association
4301 Connecticut Ave Nw
Suite 300
Washington, DC   20008-2304

202-966-4701
FAX 202-966-4818
E-Mail: wa@envasns.org
Home Page: www.envasns.org

Bruce Parker, President

A publication by the Environmental industry association geared toward providing readers with timely news and information about the handling, transportation and disposal of infectious wastes.
Frequency: BiWeekly

Integrated Environmental Assessment and Management
Society of Environmental Toxicology and Chemistry
1013 N 12th Ave
Pensacola, FL   32501-3306

850-437-1901
FAX 850-469-9778
E-Mail: rparrish@setac.org
Home Page: www.edwardjones.com

Rodney Parrish, Executive Director

Focuses on the application of science in environmental decision-making, regulation, and management, including aspects of policy and law, and the development of scientifically sound approaches to environmental problem solving.
Frequency: Quarterly

Integrated Waste Management
1801 S Bell Street
Arlington, VA   22202

212-512-3916
800-372-1033
FAX 212-512-2723
Home Page: www.bna.com

Gregory C McCaffery, President
Paul N Wojcik, Chairman

Articles geared toward integration of solid waste management.
Cost: $745.00
8 Pages
Frequency: BiWeekly

Interface Newsletter
Society for Environmental Geochemistry and Health
4698 S Forrest Avenue
Springfield, MO   65810

417-885-1166
FAX 417-881-6920
E-Mail: drbgwixson@wixson.com
Home Page: www.segh.net

Bobby Wixson, Director Membership

International Environment Reporter
Bureau of National Affairs
1801 S Bell St
Arlington, VA   22202-4501

703-341-3000
800-372-1033
FAX 800-253-0332
E-Mail: customercare@bna.com
Home Page: www.bnabooks.com

Gregory C McCaffrey, President
Paul N Wojcik, Chairman

A four-binder information and reference service covering international environmental law and developing policy in the major industrial nations.
Cost: $2555.00

Marine Conservation News
Center for Marine Conservation
2029 K Street
Washington, NW   20006

202-750-0574
800-519-1541
FAX 202-872-0619
E-Mail: cmc@dccmc.org
Home Page: www.cmc-ocean.org

Rose Bierce, Publisher
Roger Rufe, President
Stephanie Drea, VP Commun
Matt Schatzle, VP Membership & Development
Wanda Cantrell, Manager

Updates members of CMC on the organization projects and activities.
24 Pages
Frequency: Quarterly
Circulation: 100000
Printed in 2 colors on matte stock

Matrix Newsletter
AEHS Foundation Inc.
150 Fearing Street
Suite 21
Amherst, MA   01002

413-549-5170
888-540-2347
E-Mail: info@aehsfoundation.org
Home Page: www.aehsfoundation.org

Paul T Kostecki, PhD, Executive Director

Frequency: Bi-Annual

McCoy's Hazardous Waste Regulatory Update Service
McCoy & Associates
25107 Genesee Trail Road
Suite 200
Golden, CO   80228-4173

303-526-2674
FAX 303-526-5471
E-Mail: info@mccoyseminars.com
Home Page: www.mccoyseminars.com/contact.cfm

Offers a complete text of the federal hazardous waste regulations, summaries, interpretations and indexes.
Cost: $350.00
Frequency: Quarterly
Founded in 1983

McCoy's Regulatory Analysis Service
McCoy & Associates
25107 Genesee Trail Road
Golden, CO   80401-5708

303-526-2674
FAX 303-526-5471
E-Mail: info@mccoyseminars.com
Home Page: www.mccoyseminars.com

Provides timely, in-depth analyses of hazardous waste regulations within 10 working days after their publication in the Federal Register.
Cost: $550.00
Founded in 1983

Meeting Proceedings
American Society of Mining and Reclamation
3134 Montavesta Road
Lexington, KY   40502

859-335-6529
Home Page: www.asmr.org

Richard I Barnhisel, Executive Secretary

Frequency: Annual

Monographs

North American Association for
Environmental
2000 P St Nw
Suite 540
Washington, DC   20036-6921

202-419-0412
FAX 202-419-0415
E-Mail: emai@naaee.org
Home Page: www.naaee.org

Brian Day, Executive Director

Frequency: 1-3/year

Montana Green Power Update

National Center for Appropriate
Technology
3040 Continental Drive
PO Box 3838
Butte, MT   59702

406-494-4572
800-275-6228
FAX 406-494-2905
E-Mail: info@ncat.org
Home Page: www.ncat.org
Social Media: *Facebook, Twitter,
LinkedIn*

Eugene Brady, Chairman
Kathleen Hadley, Executive Director

This free monthly electronic newsletter
contains the latest success stories in renewable energy development in the state
of Montana, hot tips, information on financing and tax incentives, upcoming
events, and links to stories from regional
and national sources as featured on the
Montana Green Power web site.
Frequency: Monthly
Founded in 1976

NAESCO Newsletter

NAESCO
1615 M St NW
Suite 800
Washington, DC   20036-3213

202-822-0950
FAX 202-822-0955
Home Page: www.naesco.org

Terry E Singer, Executive Editor
Michael Hamilton, Marketing Manager
Mary Lee Berger-Hughes, Publisher

Targets energy service companies, electric and gas utilities amd other energy
providers. Highlights industry news and
features energy conservation.
Circulation: 200
Founded in 1985

NORA News

NORA: an Association of Responsible
Recyclers
5965 Amber Ridge Rd
Haymarket, VA   20169-2623

703-753-4277
FAX 703-753-2445
E-Mail: sparker@noranews.org
Home Page: www.noranews.org

Scott Parker, Executive Director

Frequency: Quarterly

Nature's Voice

National Resources Defense Council
40 W 20th St
New York, NY   10011-4231

212-727-2700
FAX 212-727-1773
E-Mail: nrdcinfo@nrdc.org
Home Page: www.nrdc.org
Social Media: *Facebook, Twitter,
YouTube*

Frances Beinecke, President
Daniel R. Tishman, Chair
Frederick A.O. Schwarz Jr., Chair
Emeritus
Adam Albright, Vice Chair
Patricia Bauman, Vice Chair

Environmental news and activism, using
law, science and the support of more
than 1 million members and online activists to protect the plante's wildlife and
wild places and to ensure a healthy environment for all living things.
50000 Members
Founded in 1970

Networker

National Center for Appropriate
Technology
3040 Continental Drive
PO Box 3838
Butte, MT   59702

406-494-4572
800-275-6228
FAX 406-494-2905
E-Mail: info@ncat.org
Home Page: www.ncat.org
Social Media: *Facebook, Twitter,
LinkedIn*

Eugene Brady, Chairman
Kathleen Hadley, Executive Director

The newsletter is compiled by the
LIHEAP Clearinghouse, and NCAT project. Stories highlight state energy assis-

tance program and low-income energy
news.
Frequency: Quarterly
Founded in 1976

News Flash

National Association of Local
Government
1333 New Hampshire Ave Nw
Suite 400
Washington, DC   20036-1532

202-887-4107
FAX 202-393-2866
E-Mail: nalgep@spiegelmcd.com
Home Page: www.nalgep.org

Kenneth E Brown, Executive Director
David Dickson, Projects Manager

Brings together noteworthy funding opportunities, conferences, legislative
tracking on climate change and highlights projects completed on the federal
or local level.
Frequency: Bi-Weekly

Noise Regulation Report

Business Publishers
2222 Sedwick Dr
Suite 101
Durham, NC   27713

800-223-8720
FAX 800-508-2592
E-Mail: custserv@bpinews.com
Home Page: www.bpinews.com

Exclusive coverage of airport, highway,
occupational and open space noise, noise
control and mitigation issues.
Cost: $511.00
10 Pages
Frequency: 12 per year
Printed in on matte stock

Nuclear Monitor

Nuclear Information & Resource
Services
1424 16th Street NW
Suite 404
Washington, DC   20036-2239

202-328-0002
FAX 202-462-2183
E-Mail: nirsnet@nirs.org
Home Page: www.nirs.org
Social Media: *, Twitter, YouTube*

Michael Mariotte, Editor
Linda Gunder, Media Manager

NIRS and WISE merged the Nuclear
Monitor and WISE News Communique
into a new Nuclear Monitor. Now avail-

able as an international edition.
Cost: $250.00
12 Pages
Frequency: 18 issues per y
Circulation: 1200
Founded in 1978
Printed in one color on matte stock

Nuclear Waste News

Business Publishers
2222 Sedwick Dr
Suite 101
Durham, NC   27713

800-223-8720
FAX 800-508-2592
E-Mail: custserv@bpinews.com
Home Page: www.bpinews.com

Worldwide coverage of the nuclear
waste management industry including
waste generation, packaging, transport,
processing and disposal.
Cost: $697.00
10 Pages
Frequency: 25 per year
Mailing list available for rent
Printed in 2 colors on matte stock

Outdoor News Bulletin

Wildlife Management Institute
4426 VT Route 215N
Cabot, VT   05647

802-563-2087
FAX 802-563-2157
E-Mail: wmisw@together.net
Home Page:
www.wildlifemanagementinstitute.org

Richard E McCabe, Executive VP
Scot J Williamson, VP
Carol J Peddicord, Finance Manager
Robert L Byrne, Wildlife Program
Coordinator
Ronald R Helinski, Conservation Policy
Specialist

Reports on select, significant issues, circumstances and other information that
bear on the professional management of
wildlife and related natural resources.

Proceedings

Institute of Environmental Sciences and
Technology
5005 Newport Drive
Suite 506
Rolling Meadows, IL   60008-3841

847-255-1561
FAX 847-255-1699

E-Mail: iest@iest.org
Home Page: www.iest.org

Julie Kendrick, Executive Director
Robert Burrows, Director
Communications Services
Corrie Roesslein, Director
Programs/Administration
Frequency: Annual

Proceedings of Annual Meetings

Environmental Design Research
Association
PO Box 7146
Edmond, OK   73083-7146

405-330-4863
FAX 405-330-4150
E-Mail: edra@telepath.com
Home Page: www.edra.org

Janet Singer, Executive Director

Document collection includes pdfs of
full papers that have appeared in the annual EDRA conference proceedings.
Frequency: Annual

Questions and Answers About the Use and Handling of Dyes

ETAD North America
1850 M St Nw
Suite 700
Washington, DC   20036-5810

202-721-4100
FAX 202-296-8120
Home Page: www.etad.com

Jill Aker, President

RCRA Land Disposal Restrictions: A Guide to Compliance

McCoy & Associates
13701 W Jewell Avenue
Suite 202
Lakewood, CO   80228-4173

303-870-0835
FAX 303-989-7917

Drew McCoy, Publisher
Deborah McCoy, President

Land disposal restrictions for hazardous
waste.
300 Pages
Frequency: Annual

RESTORE

Society for Ecological Restoration
1017 O Street NW
Washington, DC   20001

202-299-9518
FAX 270-626-5485
E-Mail: info@ser.org
Home Page: www.ser.org

Steve Whisenant, Chair
Cara R. Nelson, Vice Chair
Mary Travaglini, Treasurer
Alan Unwin, Secretary

Weekly e-bulletin. Contains articles of
interest to people in the field of restoration ecology, and is an indispensable
way to keep up with what's happening in
the world of ecological restoration,
rounding up all the latest, breaking news
from around the world on a wide variety
of restoration-related issues. Available in
electronic form only.
Frequency: Semi-Annual

Reclamation Matters

American Society of Mining and
Reclamation
3134 Montevesta Road
Lexington, KY   40502-3548

859-351-9032
FAX 859-335-6529
E-Mail: asmr@insightbb.com
Home Page: www.asmr.us

Eddie Bearden, President
Bruce Buchanen, President Elect
Richard Barnhisel, Executive Secretary

Newsletter of the ASMR. Free to members or $10/year.
500 Members
Founded in 1983

Recycling Markets

NV Business Publishers Corporation
43 Main St
Avon By the Sea, NJ   07717-1051

732-502-0500
FAX 732-502-9606
E-Mail: nvrecycle@aol.com
Home Page: www.nvpublications.com

Ted Vilardi, Owner
Anna Dutko, Managing Editor
Tom Vilardi, President/Publisher
Ted Vilardi Jr., Co-Publisher

Contains profiles on recycling mills, as
well as large users and generators of recycled materials for the broker, dealers
and processors of paper stock, scrap

metal, plastics and glass.
Cost: $180.00
Frequency: Weekly
Circulation: 3315
Printed in 4 colors on newsprint stock

Resource Development Newsletter

University of Tennessee
PO Box 1071
Knoxville, TN   37996-1071

865-974-1000
FAX 865-974-7448
E-Mail: rpdavis@utk.edu

Alan Barefield, Publisher

Community development information.
4 Pages
Frequency: Quarterly
Circulation: 2000
Founded in 1794
Printed in one color on matte stock

Resource Recovery Report

PO Box 3356
Warrenton, VA   20188-1956

540-347-4500
800-627-8913
FAX 540-349-4540
E-Mail: rrr@coordgrp.com
Home Page: www.coordgrp.com

Richard Will, Production Manager

Covers all alternatives to landfills, i.e.,
recycling, energy recovery, composting
in North America, Government, industry, associations, universities, etc. are included.
Cost: $227.00
12 Pages
Frequency: Monthly
Mailing list available for rent: 12M
names
Printed in one color on matte stock

Reuse/Recycle Newsletter

Technomic Publishing Company
2455 Teller Road
Thousand Oaks, CA   91320

800-818-7243
FAX 800-583-2665
E-Mail: aflannery@techpub.com
Home Page: rrn.sagepub.com/

Amy Flannery, Marketing Manager
Susan Selke, Editor

Provides news and information on important developments in both industrial
and municipal recycling, and focuses on

large-scale post-consumer, post-commer-
cial, and post-industrial waste recycling.
8 Pages
Frequency: Monthly
ISSN: 0048-7457
Founded in 1965
Printed in 2 colors

SER News Newsletter

Society for Ecological Restoration
285 W 18th Street #1
Phoenix, AZ   85701

520-622-5485
FAX 520-622-5491
E-Mail: info@ser.org
Home Page: www.ser.org

Mary Kay C LeFevour, Executive
Director
Jane Cripps, Membership
Julie St John, Communications

Frequency: Quarterly

SOEH Letter

Society for Occupational and
Environmental Health
6728 Old McLean Village Dr
Mc Lean, VA   22101-3906

703-556-9222
FAX 703-556-8729
E-Mail: soeh@degnon.org
Home Page: www.soeh.org

George K Degnon CAE, Executive
Director

Frequency: Quarterly

Salt & Highway Deicing

Salt Institute
700 N Fairfax St
Suite 600
Alexandria, VA   22314-2085

703-549-4648
FAX 703-548-2194
E-Mail: info@saltinstitute.org
Home Page: www.saltinstitute.org

Richard L Hanneman, President

A quarterly e-newsletter published by
the Salt Institute that focuses on high-
way uses of salt.
Frequency: Quarterly
Circulation: 77000
Founded in 1914
Printed in on glossy stock

Salt and Trace Minerals Newsletter

Salt Institute
700 N Fairfax St
Suite 600
Alexandria, VA   22314-2085

703-549-4648
FAX 703-548-2194
E-Mail: info@saltinstitute.org
Home Page: www.saltinstitute.org

Richard L Hanneman, President

E-Newsletter containing information on
animal nutrition.
Frequency: Quarterly
Circulation: 77000
Founded in 1914
Printed in on glossy stock

State Recycling Laws Update

Raymond Communications
PO Box 4311
Silver Spring, MD   20914-4311

301-879-0628
E-Mail: circulation@raymond.com
Home Page: www.raymond.com

Lorah utter, Editor
Bruce Popka, VP
Allyn Weet, Circulation Manager

Contains analysis and reports, provides
coverage of recycling legislation affecting business, as well as the outlook on
future legislation across the states and
Canada. Also publishes special reports
on related topics, for example, Transportation Packaging and the Environment.
Cost: $367.00
Frequency: Monthly
Circulation: 200
Founded in 1991

Superfund Week

Business Publishers Inc.
951 Pershing Drive
Silver Spring, MD   20910-3928

301-587-6300
FAX 301-587-1081
E-Mail: custserv@bpinews.com
Home Page: www.bpinews.com

Harry Baisden, Group Publisher
Michael Hopps, Editor

Reporting the most recent developments
in Congress, the EPA, and other government offices affecting hazardous waste
investigations and cleanups in the federal Superfund and RCRA programs.
Contains progress reports on specific

cleanup sites in federal and state programs.
Cost: $525.00
Frequency: Weekly
Founded in 1963

SurFACTS in Biomaterials

Surfaces in Biomaterials Foundation
1000 Westgate Drive
Suite 252
St Paul, MN   55114-8679

651-290-7487
FAX 651-290-2266
E-Mail: memberservices@surfaces.org
Home Page: www.surfaces.org

Steven Goodman, Executive Editor
Janeyy Duntley, Managing Editor

Dedicated to exploring creative solutions to technical challenges at the BioInterface by fostering education and multidisciplinary cooperation among industrial, academic, clinical and regulatory communities.
Frequency: Bimonthly

The Current

Women's Council on Energy and the Environment
PO Box 33211
Washington, DC   20033-0211

202-997-4512
FAX 202-478-2098
Home Page: www.wcee.org
Social Media: *Facebook, Twitter*

Ronke Luke, President
Mary Brosnan-Sell, Secretary
Robin Cantor, Vice President
Alice Grabowski, Treasurer
Joyce Chandran, Executive Director

Keeps members up to date on energy and environmental issues to foster the professional development.

The Dirt

Land and Water
Po Box 1197
Fort Dodge, IA   50501-1197

515-576-3191
FAX 515-576-2606
E-Mail: landandwater@dodgenet.com
Home Page: www.landandwater.com
Social Media: *Facebook*

Amy Dencklau, Publisher
Shanza Dencklau, Assistant Editor
Rasch M. Kenneth, President

eNewsletter including information relating to the erosion control and water management industry such as: feature stories, industry news, conferences, expert tips and video clips, new products and more. Striving to keep readers up-to-date on all current happenings and relevant information beyond the pages of Land and Water Magazine.
Cost: $20.00
72 Pages
Circulation: 20000
Founded in 1959
Mailing list available for rent: 20M names
Printed in 4 colors on glossy stock

The Resource

National Association of Conservation Districts
509 Capitol Ct. NE
Washington, DC   20002-4937

202-547-6223
FAX 202-547-6450
E-Mail: krysta-harden@nacdnet.org
Home Page: www.nacdnet.org

Krysta Harden, CEO
Bob Cordova, Second Vice President

NACD's print publication provides in depth coverage of the association's recent activities and features columns by the NACD CEO and President, in addition to guest and partnership columns.
Cost: $35.00
12 Pages
Frequency: Monthly
Circulation: 25000
Founded in 1937

The Soil Plant Analyst

Soil and Plant Analysis Council
347 North Shores Circle
Windsor, CO   80550

970-686-5702
E-Mail: rmiller@lamar.colostate.edu
Home Page: www.spcouncil.com/

Rigas Karamanos, President
Robert Miller, Secretary/Treasurer
Rao Mylavarapu, Vice President

Quarterly newsletter dedicated to the Agricultural Laboratory Industry.
Cost: $80.00
Circulation: 250

Underwater Letter

Callahan Publications
PO Box 1173
Mc Lean, VA   22101-1173

703-356-1925
FAX 703-356-9614
Home Page: www.newsletteraccess.com

Vincent F Callahan Jr, Editor

A non-technical report for businessmen and others who want to share in the nation's mushrooming underwater-related budget. The Letter provides vital contracting, marketing and development data in military, civilian government, private industry, and academic ocean-related programs. With a reorienting of priorities for federal budgets, including increased emphasis on new energy sources, the oceans offer a vast potential for thousands of companies and institutions in the underwater field.
Cost: $190.00
Frequency: Bi-monthly
Printed in one color

Washington Environmental Protection Report

Callahan Publications
PO Box 1173
Mc Lean, VA   22101-1173

703-356-1925
FAX 703-356-9614
E-Mail: sue@newsletteraccess.com
Home Page: www.newsletteraccess.com

Vincent Callahan, Editor

Twice-monthly letter on contracting opportunities, legislation, research and development, and rules and regulations for the nation's environmental programs. The war on pollution, in all its forms, is coming to the forefront of federal priorities and could be the answer to the many economic problems facing America.
Cost: $190.00
8 Pages
Frequency: Bi-monthly
Founded in 1990
Printed in one color

Waste Handling Equipment News

Lee Publications
6113 Strate Highway 5
PO Box 121
Palatine Bridge, NY   13428

518-673-3237
800-218-5586
FAX 518-673-2381

E-Mail: mstanley@leepub.com
Home Page: www.wastehandling.com

Fred Lee, Publisher
Matt Stanley, Sales Manager
Holly Rieser, Editor

Addresses equipment needs of owners and operating managers involved in construction demolition, asphalt/concrete recycling, wood waste recycling, scrap metal recycling and composting. Every issue features editorial on new equipment, equipment adaptations, site stories, and news focused on our targeted segment of the recycling industry.
Frequency: Monthly
Circulation: 14000
Founded in 1993
Printed in on newsprint stock

Waste News

Crain Communications
1155 Gratiot Ave.
Detroit, MI   48207-2997

313-446-6000
E-Mail: info@wastenews.com
Home Page: www.crain.com

Keith Crain, Chairman
Rance Crain, President
Mary Kay Crain, Treasurer/Assistant Secretary
Merrilee P. Crain, Secretary/Assistant Treasurer

Trade publication covering the solid waste industry.
Frequency: Bi-Weekly
Circulation: 52838
Founded in 1995

Waste Recovery Report

Icon: Information Concepts
211 S 45th St
Philadelphia, PA   19104-2995

215-349-6500
FAX 215-349-6502
E-Mail: wasterec@aol.com
Home Page: www.wrr.icodat.com

Alan Krigman, Publisher/Editor

Contains information on waste-to-energy, recycling, composting and other technologies.
Cost: $60.00
6 Pages
Frequency: Monthly
Circulation: 500
ISSN: 0889-0072
Founded in 1975

Weather & Climate Report

Nautilus Press
1056 National Press Building
Washington, DC   20045-2001

202-347-6643

John R Botzum, Editor

Reports on federal actions which impact weather, climate research and global changes in climate.
Frequency: Monthly

Weekly Harvest

National Center for Appropriate Technology
3040 Continental Drive
PO Box 3838
Butte, MT   59702

406-494-4572
800-275-6228
FAX 406-494-2905
E-Mail: info@ncat.org
Home Page: www.ncat.org
Social Media: *Facebook, Twitter, LinkedIn*

Eugene Brady, Chairman
Kathleen Hadley, Executive Director

This e-newsletter is a Web digest of sustainable agriculture news, resources, events and funding opportunities gleaned from the Internet and featured on the website.
Frequency: Weekly
Founded in 1976

Wind Energy Smart Brief

American Wind Energy Association
1501 M Street NW
Suite 1000
Washington, DC   20005

202-383-2500
FAX 202-383-2505
E-Mail: windmail@awea.org
Home Page: www.smartbrief.com/awea

Denise Bode, CEO

This newsletter delivers quickly digestible summaries of the day's wind energy-related stories from across the media, as well as links to those stories.
Frequency: Weekly

Wind Energy Weekly

American Wind Energy Association
1501 M Street NW
Suite 1000
Washington, DC   20005

202-383-2500
FAX 202-383-2505
E-Mail: windmail@awea.org
Home Page: www.awea.org

Denise Bode, CEO

Packed with detailed and up-to-date information on the world of wind energy that simply can't be obtained elsewhere. If you have a professional interest in wind energy, or need to keep up with wind energy development news or late-breaking legislative, economic, and environmental developments affecting wind, a subscription is a must.
Frequency: Weekly

Woodland Report

National Woodland Owners Association
374 Maple Ave E
Suite 310
Vienna, VA   22180-4718

703-255-2300
800-470-8033
Home Page: www.nationalforestry.net

Keith A Argow, President

Provides timely information about forestry and forest practices with news from Washington, DC and state capitals. Written for non-industrial, private woodland owners. Includes state landowner association news.
Cost: $15.00
2 Pages
Frequency: 8 per year
Circulation: 2,200
Printed in one color on matte stock

World Research News

World Research Foundation
41 Bell Rock Plaza
Sedona, AZ   86351-8804

928-284-3300
FAX 928-284-3530
E-Mail: laverne@wrf.org
Home Page: www.wrf.org

LaVerne Boeckman, Co-Founder
Steven Ross, Co-Founder

Health information that is collected, categorized and disseminated in an independent and unbiased manner. Including allopathic medicine alongside comple-

mentary and alternative medicine... ancient and traditional techniques and healing therapies as well as the latest medical technology.
Frequency: Quarterly

World Wildlife Fund: Focus

World Wildlife
PO Box 97180
Washington, DC 20090-7180

202-293-4800
FAX 202-293-9211
E-Mail: archer@wwfus.org
Home Page: www.worldwildlife.org

Kathryn S Fuller, CEO
Jennifer Seeger, Editor

WWF projects are highlighted around the world in 450 national parks and nature reserves, with emphasis on coverage of programs and activities in the US.
8 Pages
Frequency: Monthly
Founded in 1960

eNotes

National Association of Conservation Districts
509 Capitol Ct. NE
Washington, DC 20002-4937

202-547-6223
FAX 202-547-6450
E-Mail: krysta-harden@nacdnet.org
Home Page: www.nacdnet.org

Krysta Harden, CEO
Bob Cordova, Second Vice President

NACD's weekly news briefs.
Cost: $35.00
12 Pages
Frequency: Monthly
Circulation: 25000
Founded in 1937

Magazines & Journals

ASEH News

American Society for Environmental History
119 Pine Street
Suite 301
Seattle, WA 98101

206-343-0226
FAX 206-343-0249

E-Mail: mighetto@hrassoc.com
Home Page: www.aseh.net

Lisa Mighetto, Acting Executive Director

Frequency: Quarterly

Aerosol Science and Technology (AS&T)

American Association for Aerosol Research
15000 Commerce Parkway
Suite C
Mount Laurel, NJ 08054

856-439-9080
FAX 856-439-0525
E-Mail: info@aaar.org
Home Page: www.aaar.org

Peter McMurry, Editor-In-Chief
Tami C Bond, Editor
Warren H Finlay, Editor

AS&T is the offficial journal of AAAR. It publishes the results of theoretical and experimental investigations into aerosol phenomena and closely related material as well as high-quality reports on fundamental and applied topics.
Cost: $1214.00

Alternative Energy

PWG
205 S Beverly Drive
#208
Beverly Hills, CA 90212-3827

310-273-3486

Irwin Stambler, Publisher
Ahmad Taleban, President

Reports on future economic and technological trends.
Cost: $95.00
12 Pages
Frequency: Monthly
Printed in 2 colors on matte stock

Alternative Energy Retailer

Zackin Publications
PO Box 2180
Waterbury, CT 06722-2180

203-755-0158
800-325-6745
FAX 203-755-3480
E-Mail: info@aer-online.com
Home Page: www.aer-online.com

Michael Griffin, Editor
Jeanette Laliberte, Subscription
Andrew Wold, Associate Publisher

Paul Zackin, Publisher
June Han, Marketing Manager

Covers solid fuel burning, marketing, technology, and sales.
Cost: $32.00
Frequency: Monthly
Circulation: 10,000
Founded in 1970

American Environmental Laboratory

International Scientific Communications
30 Controls Drive
PO Box 870
Shelton, CT 06484-0870

203-926-9300
E-Mail: webmaster@iscpubs.com
Home Page: www.iscpubs.com

Brian Howard, Editor
Robert G Sweeny, Publisher

Laboratory activities, new equipment, and analysis and collection of samples are the main topics.
Cost: $282.42
Frequency: Monthly
Circulation: 185000

American Forests

Po Box 2000
Suite 800
Washington, DC 20013-2000

202-737-1944
FAX 202-955-4588
E-Mail: info@amfor.org
Home Page: www.americanforests.org

Deborah Gangloff, Executive Director

A publication that offers our members the best in conservation news. Articles include different perspectives on current environmental issues, stories on wildlife restoration projects, updates on forest management practices, and ways to engage the conservation movement in your community.
Cost: $25.00
Frequency: Quarterly
Founded in 1875

American Public Works Association

2345 Grand Blvd
Suite 700
Kansas City, MO 64108-2625

816-472-6100
800-848-2792
FAX 816-472-1610

E-Mail: ddancy@apwa.net
Home Page: www.apwa.net

Kaye Sullivan, Executive Director
David Dancy, Director Of Marketing
Kevin Clark, Editor

International educational and professional association of public agencies, private sector companies, and individuals dedicated to providing high quality public works goods and services. APWA provides a forum in which public works professionals competency, increase the performance of their agencies and companies, and bring important public works-related topics to public attention in local, state, and federal areas. Mailing list for members only.
Cost: $100.00
40 Pages
Frequency: Monthly
Circulation: 27000
ISSN: 0092-4873
Founded in 1933

American Waste Digest

Charles G Moody
226 King St
Pottstown, PA   19464-9105

610-326-9480
800-442-4215
FAX 610-326-9752
E-Mail: awd@americanwastedigest.com
Home Page:
www.americanwastedigest.com

Carasue Moody, Publisher
Shannon Costa, Circulation Manager
J. Robert Tagert, Sales Manager

Provides reviews on new products, profiles on sucessful waste removal businesses, and provides discussion on legislation on municipal regulations on recycling.
Cost: $24.00
86 Pages
Frequency: Monthly
Circulation: 33000
Printed in 4 colors on glossy stock

Annual Review

International Lead Zinc Research Organization
2525 Meridian Parkway, Suite 100
PO Box 12036
Durham, NC   27713-2036

919-361-4647
FAX 919-361-1957

E-Mail: jhendirc@ilzro.org
Home Page: www.ilzro.org

Stephen Wilkinson, President
Frank Goodwin, VP Materials Sciences
Scott Mooneyham, Treasurer
Rob Putnam, Director Communications

Frequency: Annual

Archives of Environmental Health

Society for Occupational and Environmental Health
111 North Bridge Road #21-01
Peninsula Plaza
Singapore   179098

703-556-9222
FAX 703-556-8729
Home Page: www.oehs.org

Laura Degnon, Manager

Publishing new research based on the most rigorous methods and discussion to put this work in perspective for public health, public policy, and sustainability, the Archives addresses such topics of current concern as health significance of chemical exposure, toxic waste, new and old energy technologies, industrial processes, and the environmental causation of disease.
Frequency: Bi-Monthly

Bio-Mineral Times

Allen C Forter & Son
3450 W Central Avenue
#328
Toledo, OH   43606-1418

419-535-6374
FAX 419-535-7008
E-Mail: nviroint@aol.com
Home Page: www.nviro.com

Bonnie Hunter, Publisher

Issues focus on environmental legislation efforts, regulation compliance, and finding answers to the mechanics and practical applications of the distribution and management of biosolids derived products.
Frequency: Quarterly
Circulation: 25,000

C&D Recycler

Gie Publishing
4012 Bridge Avenue
Cleveland, OH   44113

216-961-4130
800-456-0707
FAX 216-961-0364

E-Mail: btaylor@gie.net
Home Page: www.recyclingtoday.com

Bryan Tailor, Editor
Jim Keefe, Publisher
Helen Duerr, Production Manager
Cost: $17.00

Frequency: Monthly
Circulation: 7000
Founded in 1963

Code of Professional Practice

National Registry of Environmental Professionals
PO Box 2099
Glenview, IL   60025

847-724-6631
FAX 847-724-4223
E-Mail: nrep@nrep.org
Home Page: www.nrep.org

Richard A Young, PhD, Executive Director
Edward Beck, PhD, Senior Director
Carol Schellinger, Director

Frequency: Annual

Design Research News

Environmental Design Research Association
PO Box 7146
Edmond, OK   73083-7146

405-330-4863
FAX 405-330-4150
E-Mail: erda@telepath.com
Home Page: www.edra.org

Janet Singer, Executive Director

Frequency: Quarterly

E/Environmental Magazine

28 Knight St
Norwalk, CT   06851-4719

203-854-5559
800-967-6572
FAX 203-866-0602
E-Mail: info@emagazine.com
Home Page: www.emagazine.com

Jim Motavalli, Editor
Karen Soucy, Associate Publisher
Doug Moss, Publisher & Executive Dir

Providing information about environmental issues and sharing ideas and resources so that readers can live more sustainable lives and connect with ongoing efforts for change. Covers everything environmental, from big issues like climate change, renewable energy and toxins and health, to the topics that di-

rectly impact our readers' daily lives; how to eat right and stay healthy, where to invest responsibly and how to save energy at home.
Cost: $19.95
Circulation: 185,000
Founded in 1988

ECON: Environmental Contractor

Duane Publishing
51 Park St
Dorchester, MA   02122-2643

617-282-4885
FAX 617-282-0320
E-Mail: info@decmagazine.com
Home Page: www.rubblemakers.com

Herb Duane, Owner

Information and news of the environment.
Cost: $35.00
90 Pages
Frequency: Monthly
Founded in 1986

EM, Air & Waste Management Environmental Managers

Air & Waste Management Association
420 Fort Duquesne Blvd.
Pittsburgh, PA   15222-1420

412-232-3444
800-270-3444
FAX 412-232-3450
E-Mail: info@awma.org
Home Page: www.awma.org

Adrian Carolla, Executive Director
Edith M. Ardiente, President

A magazine that contains sections of Washington and Canadian reports, a calendar of events, government affairs, news focus, campus research, business briefs, district control news, professional development programs, professional services and other issues facing the environmental professionals.
Frequency: Monthly
Circulation: 15000
Founded in 1901

Ecological Economics Journal

International Society for Ecological Economics
1313 Dolley Madison Boulevard
Suite 402
McLean, VA   22101

703-790-1745
FAX 703-790-2672

E-Mail: iseemembership@burkinc.com
Home Page:
www.ecologicaleconomics.org

Heide Scheiter-Rohland, Director Membership

Concerned with extending and integrating the study and management of nature's household(ecology) and humankind's household(economics). Specific research areas covered include; valuation of natural resources, ecologically integrated technology, implications of thermodynamics for economics and ecology, renewable resource management and conservation, gene pool inventory and management, alternative principles for valuing natural wealth, and more.
Frequency: Monthly

Ecological Restoration

Society for Ecological Restoration
1017 O Street NW
Washington, DC   20001

202-299-9518
FAX 270-626-5485
E-Mail: info@ser.org
Home Page: www.ser.org

Steve Whisenant, Chair
Cara R. Nelson, Vice Chair
Mary Travaglini, Treasurer
Alan Unwin, Secretary

Features articles on a broad range of topics including technical, biological and social aspects of restoring landscapes, as well as emerging professional issues, the role of education, evolving theories of post-modern humans and their environment, land-use policy, the science of collaboration, and more. Peer-reviewed feature articles, short restoration notes, and book reviews as well as abstracts of pertinent work published elsewhere. Available in print and online.
Frequency: Semi-Annual

Ecology

Johnson Publishing Company
820 S Michigan Ave
Chicago, IL   60605-2191

312-322-9200
FAX 312-322-0918

Linda Johnson-Rice, CEO

News on the environment and conservation industries.
Cost: $16.00

Ecosphere

Forum International
91 Gregory Lane
Suite 21
Pleasant Hill, CA   94523

925-671-2900
800-252-4475
FAX 925-671-2993
E-Mail: fti@foruminternational.com
Home Page:
www.foruminternational.com

Dr. Nicolas Hetzer, Production Manager
J McCormack, Circulation Director

Accepts advertising.
Cost: $12.00
16 Pages
Frequency: Quarterly
Circulation: 36000
ISSN: 0046-1237
Founded in 1956

El Digest: Hazardous Waste Marketplace

Environmental Information
PO Box 390266
Minneapolis, MN   55439

952-831-2473
FAX 952-831-6550
E-Mail: ei@enviro-information.com
Home Page: www.envirobiz.com

Cary Perket, President

Focused on serving the market information needs of the commercial hazardous waste management sector. Included those involved in recycling and re-use, energy recovery, waste treatment, and waste disposal. Provides compilations and analysis of the commercial markets for hazardous waste energy recovery, fuel blending, incineration, landfill and solvent recovery. Also undertakes special reports on chemical distributors, RCRA metal recyclers and wastewater treatment.
ISSN: 1042-251X
Founded in 1983
Printed in 2 colors

Energy Engineering

Association of Energy Engineers
4025 Pleasantdale Rd
Suite 420
Atlanta, GA   30340-4264

770-447-5083
FAX 770-446-3969

E-Mail: info@aeecenter.org
Home Page: www.aeecenter.org

Albert Thumann, Executive Director
Ruth Whitlock, Executive Admin
Albert Thumann, Executive Director
Ruth Marie, Managing Editor

Engineering solutions to cost efficiency
problems and mechanical contractors
who design, specify, install, maintain,
and purchase non-residential heating,
ventilating, air conditioning and refriger-
ation equipment and components.
Circulation: 8000
Founded in 1976

Environ: A Magazine for Ecologic Living and Health

Environ
1616 Seventeenth Street
Suite 468
Denver, CO   80202

303-285-5543
FAX 303-628-5597
Home Page: www.environcorp.com

Suzanne Randegger, Publisher/Editor
Ed Randegger, Co-Publisher/Ad
Director
John Haasbeek, Senior Manager

Designed to keep health and ecology
conscious readers aware of circumstances hazardous to human health, and
provide alternatives - practical, political,
and global. Coverage of environmental
legislation, ecologic food-growing practices and certification, geographically
and climatically safe and hazardous locations, and a view of today's health
problems with active solutions. Supported by screened advertisers.
Cost: $15.00
40 Pages
Frequency: Quarterly

Environment

Helen Dwight Reid Educational
Foundation
1319 18th Street NW
Washington, DC   20036-1802

202-296-6267
FAX 202-296-5149
E-Mail: brichman@heldref.org
Home Page: www.heldref.org

Douglas Kirkpatrick, Publisher
Barbara Richman, Editor
Fred Huber, Circulation Manager
Emily Tawlowski, Marketing Manager
Steve Hellem, Executive Director

Analyzes the problems, places, and people where environment and development
come together, illuminating concerns
from the local to the global. Articles and
commentaries from researchers and
practitioners who provide a broad range
of international perspectives. Also features in-depth reviews of major policy
reports, conferences, and environmental
education initiatives, as well as guides to
the best Web sites, journal articles, and
books.
Cost: $51.00
Frequency: Monthly
Circulation: 11,408
Founded in 1956

Environmental Business Journal

Environmental Business International
4452 Park Boulevard Suite 306
PO Box 371769
San Diego, CA   92116-1769

619-295-7685
FAX 619-295-5743
E-Mail: ebi@ebiusa.com
Home Page: www.ebiusa.com

Grant Ferrier, Publisher
Dan Johnson, Manager

An overview piece, segment analysis by
country, profiles of domestic and foreign
firms, financial data on listed environmental companies in the region, the latest developments on government
initiatives and regulations, company
news and projects are included in the
features of this publications.
Cost: $495.00
Founded in 1988
Printed in 2 colors

Environmental Communicator

North American Association for
Environmental
2000 P St NW
Suite 540
Washington, DC   20036-6921

202-419-0412
FAX 202-419-0415
E-Mail: email@naaee.org
Home Page: www.naaee.org

Brian Day, Executive Director

A publication of the North American Association for EE. Feature articles, association news, affiliate news, op-ed pieces,
announcements on new EE resources,

available jobs, and future events and
opportunities.
Frequency: Bi-Monthly

Environmental Engineering Science

Mary Ann Liebert
140 Huguenot St
New Rochelle, NY   10801-5215

914-740-2100
FAX 914-740-2101
E-Mail: info@liebertpub.com
Home Page: www.liebertpub.com

Mary A Liebert, Owner
Dumpnico Grosso, Editor-in-Chief
Stephanie Paul, Production Editor
Lisa Cohen, Associate Editors

Publishing studies of innovative solutions to problems in air, wter, and land
contamination and waste disposal. Features applications of environmental engineering and scientific discoveries, policy
issues, environmental economics, and
sustainable development.
Cost: $330.00
Frequency: Monthly
Circulation: 1800
ISSN: 1092-8758
Founded in 1980

Environmental Geochemistry and Health

Society for Environmental Geochemistry
and Health
4698 S Forrest Avenue
Springfield, MO   65810

417-885-1166
FAX 417-881-6920
E-Mail: drbgwixson@wixson.com
Home Page: www.segh.net

Bobby Wixson, Director Membership

Publishes original research papers, short
communications, reviews and topical
special issues across the broad field of
environmental geochemistry. Coverage
includes papers that directly link health
and the environment.
Frequency: Quarterly

Environmental History (EH)

UW Interdisciplinary Arts and Sciences
Program
1900 Commerce Street
Tacoma, WA   98402

206-343-0226
FAX 206-343-0249

E-Mail: director@aseh.net
Home Page: www.aseh.net

John McNeill, President
Gregg Mitman, Vice President/ President
Elect
Ellen Stroud, Secretary
Mark Madison, Treasurer

The world's leading scholarly journal in
environmental history. Brings together
scholars, scientists, and practitioners
from a wide array of disciplines to explore changing relationships between
humans and the environment over time.
1200 Members
Founded in 1976

Environmental Management Report

McGraw Hill
PO Box 182604
Columbus, OH   43272

614-304-4000
FAX 614-759-3749
E-Mail:
customer.service@mcgraw-hill.com
Home Page: www.mcgraw-hill.com

Paul Scicchitano, Executive Editor
Harold McGraw III, President/CEO

Emphasises the interest and needs of the
companies and individuals involved in
site assessments, regulations, and environmental auditing.
Cost: $195.00
Frequency: Monthly
Founded in 1902

Environmental Practice

National Association of Environmental
Professional
PO Box 2086
Bowie, MD   20718-2086

888-251-9902
FAX 301-860-1141
E-Mail: office@naep.org
Home Page: www.naep.org

John Perkins, Editor

Incorporates original research articles,
news of issues and of the NAEP, and
opinion pieces. Of interest to private
consultants, academics, and professionals in federal, state, local, and tribal governments, as well as in corporations and
non-governmental organizations. Reports on historic and contemporary environmental issues that help inform current
practices.
Frequency: Quarterly

Environmental Protection

Stevens Publishing Corporation
5151 Belt Line Rd
10th Floor
Dallas, TX   75254-7507

972-687-6700
FAX 972-687-6767
E-Mail:
aneville@stevenspublishing.com
Home Page: www.eponline.com

Craig S Stevens, President
Dana Cornett, President/COO
Randy Dye, Publisher
Sherleen Mahoney, Editor
Margaret Perry, Circulation Director

The comprehensive online information
resource for environmental professionals.
Circulation: 63000
Founded in 1925

Environmental Regulation & Permitting

John Wiley & Sons
111 River St
Hoboken, NJ   07030-5790

201-748-6000
800-825-7550
FAX 201-748-6088
E-Mail: info@wiley.com
Home Page: www.wiley.com

William J Pesce, CEO
Richard M Hochhauser, CEO

Furnishes practical information on work-
able solutions to winning permits that
both society and the industry will ap-
prove.
Cost: $170.00
Frequency: Quarterly
Circulation: 1800
Founded in 1807

Environmental Science and Technology

American Chemical Society
1155 16th St Nw
Washington, DC   20036-4892

202-872-4600
800-227-5558
FAX 202-872-4615
E-Mail: service@acs.org
Home Page: www.acs.org

Madeleine Jacobs, CEO/Executive
Director

Publishes news and research in diverse
areas of environmental science and engi-

neering.
Cost: $156.00
110 Pages
Frequency: Monthly
Circulation: 13000
Founded in 1966

Environmental Times

Environmental Assessment Association
1224 N Nokomis NE
Alexandria, MN   56308

320-763-4320
E-Mail: info@eaa-assoc.org
Home Page: www.iami.org/eaa.html

Robert Johnson, Executive Director

This publications contents contain environment conferences and expos, industry
trends, federal regulations related to the
environment and industry assessments.
Cost: $19.95
24 Pages
Circulation: 7000
Founded in 1972
Printed in 4 colors on newsprint stock

Environmental Toxicology and Chemistry

Society of Environmental Toxicology
and Chemistry
1013 N 12th Ave
Pensacola, FL   32501-3306

850-437-1901
FAX 850-469-9778
E-Mail: rparrish@setac.org
Home Page: www.edwardjones.com

Chad Stacy, Manager

Dedicated to furthering scientific knowledge and disseminating information on
environmental toxicology and chemistry,
including the application of these sciences to risk management. Provides a forum for professionals in academia,
business, and government.

Environmental and Molecular Mutagenesis

Environmental Mutagen Society
1821 Michael Faraday Drive
Suite 300
Reston, VA   20190

703-438-8220
FAX 703-438-3113
E-Mail: emshq@ems-us.org
Home Page: www.ems-us.org

Publishes original research articles on
environmental mutangenesis. Manu-

scripts published in the six general areas of mechanisms of mutagenesis, genomics, DNA damage, replication, recombination and repair, public health, and DNA technology.
Frequency: 8/year

ExecutiveBrief

Synthetic Organic Chemical
Manufacturers Assn
1850 M St Nw
Suite 700
Washington, DC   20036-5803

202-721-4100
FAX 202-296-8120
E-Mail: info@socma.org
Home Page: www.socma.org

Joseph Acker, President
Vivian Diko, Executive Assistant &
CEO
Charlene Patterson, Editor

Provides quality content on software development, outsourcing, project and risk management.

Fisheries

American Fisheries Society
5410 Grosvenor Ln
Suite 110
Bethesda, MD   20814-2199

301-897-8616
FAX 301-897-8096
E-Mail: main@fisheries.org
Home Page: www.fisheries.org

Gus Rassam, Executive Director
Charles Moseley, Journals Manager

Peer reviewed articles that address contemporary issues and problems, techniques, philosophies and other areas of interest to the general fisheries profession. Monthly features include letters, meeting notices, book listings and reviews, environmental essays and organization profiles.
Cost: $76.00
50 Pages
Frequency: Monthly
Founded in 1870
Mailing list available for rent: 8500 names at $250 per M

Food Protection Trends

International Association for Food
Protection
6200 Aurora Ave
Suite 200W
Urbandale, IA   50322-2864

515-276-3344
800-369-6337
FAX 515-276-8655
E-Mail: info@foodprotection.org
Home Page: www.foodprotection.org

David W Tharp, Executive Director
Vickie Lewandowski, VP
Isabel Walls, Secretary

Each issue contains articles on applied research, applications of current technology and general interest subjects for food safety professionals. Regular features include industry and association news, and industy-related products section and a calendar of meetings, seminars and workshops. Updates of government regulations and sanitary design are also featured.
Cost: $227.00
Frequency: Monthly
Circulation: 9000
ISBN: 0-362028-X -
Founded in 1911
Mailing list available for rent
Printed in 4 colors on glossy stock

Hauler

Hauler Magazine
166 S Main Street
PO Box 508
New Hope, PA   18938

800-220-6029
800-220-6029
FAX 215-862-3455
E-Mail: mag@thehauler.com
Home Page: www.thehauler.com

Thomas N Smith, Publisher/Editor
Barbara Gibney, Circulation Manager
Leslie T Smith, Marketing Director

Dedicated to the refuse and solid waste industry. It is the acknowledged leader in the new and used refuse truck and equipment marketplace, and now lists hundreds of new and used trash trucks, trailers, containers, services, plus parts and accessories from the best suppliers in the industry.
Cost: $12.00
Frequency: Monthly
Circulation: 18630
Founded in 1978

Hazard Technology

EIS International
1401 Rockville Pike
Suite 500
Rockville, MD   20852-1436

800-999-5009
FAX 301-738-1026

James W Morentz PhD, Publisher
Leslie Atkin, Managing Editor

Application of technology to the field of emergency and environmental management to save lives and protect property.
Frequency: Quarterly
Circulation: 50,000
Founded in 1990

Hazardous Management

Ecolog
1450 Don Mills Road
Don Mills, Ontario   M3B-2X7

416-442-2292
888-702-1111
FAX 416-442-2204
Home Page: www.hazmatmag.com

Lynda Reilly, Publisher

The latest environmental regulations and programs as well as the evolving technology and equipment needed to achieve compliance.
Cost: $39.50
Frequency: Bi-Monthly
Circulation: 16,000
ISSN: 0843-9303
Founded in 1989
Mailing list available for rentat $250 per M
Printed in 4 colors on glossy stock

Hazardous Materials Control

Hazardous Materials Control Resources
Institute
7237 Hanover Highway
Greenbelt, MD   20770

301-577-1842
FAX 301-220-3870

Patricia Segato, Managing Editor
Victoria Mellin, Advertising Coordinator

Accepts advertising.
Cost: $18.00
64 Pages
Frequency: Bi-Monthly
Founded in 1988

Hazardous Waste Consultant

Aspen Publishers
8400 east cresent parkway
6 floor greenwood village
Lakewood, CO   80111

720-528-4270
800-638-8437
FAX 212-597-0335

A unique approach to hazardous waste issues. It is written by engineers and regulatory specialists who have an extensive background in the field and understand the problems that industry, consultants, and regulators face.
Cost: $475.00

Hazmat World

Advanstar Communications
641 Lexington Ave
8th Floor
New York, NY   10022-4503

212-951-6600
FAX 212-951-6793
E-Mail: info@advanstar.com
Home Page: www.advanstar.com

Joseph Loggia, CEO

Business and news publication edited for the environmental world.
Cost: $30.00
100 Pages
Frequency: Monthly
Founded in 1988

Human Ecology Review

Society for Human Ecology
College of the Atlantic
105 Eden Street
Bar Harbor, ME   04609-0180

207-288-5015
FAX 207-288-3780
E-Mail: carter@ecology.coa.edu
Home Page:
www.societyforhumanecology.org

Barbara Carter, Assistant to Executive Director

Publishes peer-reviewed research and theory on the interaction between humans and the environment and other links between culture and nature, essays and applications relevant to human ecology, book reviews, and relevant commentary, announcements, and awards.
Frequency: Semi-Annual

Hydrological Science and Technology

American Institute Of Hydrology
300 Village Green Circle
Suite 201
Smyrna, GA   30080

770-269-9388
E-Mail: aihydro@aol.com
Home Page: www.aihydro.org

Cathy Lipsett, Owner
Cathryn Seaburn, Manager

Peer-reviewed international journal covering research and practical studies on hydrological science, technology, water resources and related topics including water, air and soil pollution and hazardous waste issues. Communicating ideas, findings, methods, techniques and summaries of interesting projects or investigations in the area of hydrology.
Frequency: Quarterly

IEEE Power and Energy Magazine

IEEE
PO Box 1331
Piscataway, NJ   08855

732-981-0061
FAX 732-981-9667
E-Mail: custome-service@ieee.org
Home Page: www.ieee.org

Mel Olken, Editor
Susan Schneiderman, Business Development

Dedicated to disseminating information on all matters of interest to electric power engineers and other professionals involved in the electric power industry. Feature articles focus on advanced concepts, technologies, and practices associated with all aspects of electric power from a technical perspective in synergy with nontechnical areas such as business, environmental, and social concerns.
Cost: $260.00
82 Pages
Frequency: Monthly
Circulation: 23000
ISSN: 1540-7977
Founded in 2003
Mailing list available for rent
Printed in on glossy stock

Industrial Wastewater

Water Environment Federation
601 Wythe St
Alexandria, VA   22314-1994

800-666-0206
FAX 703-684-2492
E-Mail: thardwick@wef.org
Home Page: www.wef.org
Social Media: Facebook, Twitter

Matt Bond, President
Cordell Samuels, President-Elect
Sandra Ralston, Vice President
Chris Browning, Treasurer
Jeff Eger, Secretary and Executive Director

Discusses relevant regulatory and legal issues, provides examples of real-world treatment options, and offers suggestions on minimizing waste and preventing pollution.
79 Members
ISSN: 1044-9943
Founded in 1928

Inside EPA

Inside Washington Publishers
1919 S Eads St
Arlington, VA   22202-3028

703-418-3981
800-424-9068
FAX 703-416-8543
E-Mail: iwp@iwpnews.com
Home Page: www.iwpnews.com

Alan Sosenko, Owner

Gives timely information on all facets of waste, water, air, and other environmental regulatory programs.
Frequency: Weekly
Founded in 1980

International Dredging Review

PO Box 1487
Fort Collins, CO   80522-1487

970-416-1903
FAX 970-416-1878
E-Mail: editor@dredgemag.com
Home Page: www.dredgemag.com

Judith Powers, Publisher
Julia Leach, Production Manager

Targeted to dredging company executives, project managers and dredge crew members, suppliers and service people such as pump manufacturers, hydrographic surveyors, consulting engineers,

etc.
Cost: $85.00
Frequency: Monthly
Circulation: 3300
ISSN: 0737-8181
Founded in 1967

International Environmental Systems Update

CEEM
10521 Braddock Road
Fairfax, VA   22030-3223

703-250-5900
800-745-5565
FAX 703-250-5313
E-Mail: jleonard@qsuonline.com
Home Page: www.qsuonline.com

Paul Scicchitano, Publisher
Suzanne Leonard, Senior Editor

Provides information covering the emerging environmental issues that affect business and industry around the globe including competitive advantages, global updates, strategies, management systems and company profiles.
Cost: $ 390.00
24 Pages
Frequency: Monthly
Circulation: 50000
ISSN: 1079-0837
Founded in 1994
Mailing list available for rent
Printed in 2 colors on matte stock

International Journal of Phytoremediation

AEHS Foundation Inc.
150 Fearing Street
Amherst, MA   01002

413-549-5170
888-540-2347
E-Mail: info@aehs.com
Home Page: www.aehsfoundation.org

Paul T Kostecki, PhD, Executive Director

Devoted to the publication of current laboratory and field research describing the use of plant systems to remediate contaminated environments. Designed to link professionals in the many environmental disciplines involved in the development, application, management, and regulation of emerging phytoremediation technologies.
600 Members
Frequency: Quarterly
Founded in 1989

International Journal of Wildland Fire

International Association of Wildland Fire
1418 Washburn Street
Missoula, MT   59801

406-531-8264
888-440-4293
E-Mail: info@awfonline.org
Home Page: www.iawfonline.org
Social Media: *Facebook, Twitter*

Sacha Dick, Programs Manager

Online journal publishing new and significant papers that advance basic and applied research concerning wildland fire. Aims to publish quality papers on a broad range of wildland fire issues, and has an international perspective, since wildland fire plays a major social, economic, and ecological role around the globe.
Frequency: Quarterly

Journal of Air & Waste Management Association

Air & Waste Management Association
420 Fort Duquesne Blvd.
Pittsburgh, PA   15222-1435

412-232-3444
800-270-3444
FAX 412-232-3450
E-Mail: info@awma.org
Home Page: www.awma.org
Social Media: *Facebook, Twitter, LinkedIn*

Andy Knopes, Production Manager/Editor
Richard Sherr, Execetive Director
Jeffry Muffat, President
Merlyn L. Hough, President Elect
Mike Kelly, Secretary

Intended to serve those occupationally involved in air pollution control and waste management through the publication of timely and reliable information. Descriptions of contemporary advances in air quality and waste management science and technology for use in improving environmental protection.
Cost: $330.00
Frequency: Monthly
Circulation: 3500
ISSN: 1047-3289
Founded in 1907

Journal of Environmental Economics and Management

Association of Environmental and Resource
1616 P St Nw
Suite 400
Washington, DC   20036-1434

919-515-4672
FAX 919-515-1824
E-Mail: jeem.editor@ncsu.edu
Home Page: www.aere.org

Daniel J. Phaneuf, Managing Editor

Devoted to the publication of theoretical and empirical papers concerned with the linkage between economic systems and environmental and natural resources systems. The top journal in natural resources and environmental economics, it concentrates on the management and/or social control of the economy in its relationship with the management and use of natural resources and the natural environment.
Frequency: Bi-Monthly

Journal of Environmental Education

Heldref Publications
325 Chestnut Street
Suite 800
Philadelphia, PA   19106

202-296-6267
FAX 202-296-5149
E-Mail: jee@heldref.org
Home Page: www.heldref.org

James Denton, Executive Director
J. Heldref, Editor

Details how best to present environmental issues and how to evaluate programs already in place for primary through university level and adult students. Publishes material that advances the instruction, theory, methods, and practice of environmental education and communication. Subject areas include the sciences, social sciences, and humanities.
Cost: $58.00
Frequency: Quarterly
Circulation: 1250
Founded in 1970

Journal of Environmental Engineering

American Society of Civil Engineers
1801 Alexander Bell Dr
Reston, VA 20191-4382

800-548-2723
703-295-6300
FAX 703-295-6222
E-Mail: member@asce.org
Home Page: www.asce.org

D Wayne Klotz, President
M. Kathy Banks, Editor

Emphasizes on the implementaion of effective and safe methods for handling, transporting, and treating waste materials.
Cost: $308.00
Frequency: Monthly
Circulation: 2,500
Founded in 1852

Journal of Environmental Geochemistry and Health

Society for Environmental Geochemistry & Health
4698 S Forrest Avenue
Springfield, MO 65810

417-851-1166
FAX 417-881-6920
E-Mail: DRBGWIXSON@aol.com
Home Page: www.segh.net

Prof. Xiangdong Li, President
Prof. Andrew Hursthouse, European Chair
Kyoung-Woong Kim, Asia/Pacific Chair
Anthea Brown, Membership Secretary/Treasurer
Malcolm Brown, Secretary

Publishes original research papers, research notes and reviews across the broad field of environmental geochemistry.
400 Members
Founded in 1971

Journal of Environmental Health

National Environmental Health Association
720 S Colorado Blvd
Suite 1000-N
Denver, CO 80246-1926

303-756-9090
FAX 303-691-9490
E-Mail: staff@neha.org
Home Page: www.neha.org

Social Media: *Facebook, Twitter, LinkedIn*

Nelson Fabian, Executive Director
Kristen Ruby, Content Editor
Jill Cruickshank, Marketing/Sales Manager

A practical journal containing information on a variety of environmental health issues.
Cost: $90.00
5000 Members
70 Pages
Frequency: 10 per year
Circulation: 20,000
ISSN: 0022-0892
Founded in 1937
Printed in 4 colors on glossy stock

Journal of Environmental Quality

American Society of Agronomy
5585 Guilford Rd.
Madison, WI 53711-1086

608-273-8080
FAX 608-273-2021
E-Mail:
headquarters@sciencesocieties.org
Home Page: www.agronomy.org
Social Media: *Facebook, Twitter, LinkedIn*

Newell Kitchen, President
Kenneth Barbarick, President-Elect

Papers are grouped by subject matter and cover water, soil, and atmospheric research as it relates to agriculture and the environment.
10000 Members
Founded in 1907

Journal of Natural Resources & Life Sciences Education

American Society of Agronomy
5585 Guilford Rd.
Madison, WI 53711-1086

608-273-8080
FAX 608-273-2021
E-Mail:
headquarters@sciencesocieties.org
Home Page: www.agronomy.org
Social Media: *Facebook, Twitter, LinkedIn*

Newell Kitchen, President
Kenneth Barbarick, President-Elect

Today's educators look here for the latest teaching ideas in the life sciences, natural resources, and agriculture.
10000 Members
Founded in 1907

Journal of Soil and Water Conservation

Soil and Water Conservation Society
945 SW Ankeny Rd
Ankeny, IA 50023-9764

515-289-2331
800-843-7645
FAX 515-289-1227
E-Mail: pubs@swcs.org
Home Page: www.swcs.org

Oksana Gieseman, Director of Publications

The JSWC is a multidisciplinary journal of natural resource conservation research, practice, policy, and perspectives. The journal has two sections: the A Section containing various departments and features and the Research Section containing peer-reviewed research papers.
Cost: $99.00
Frequency: Bimonthly
Circulation: 2000
ISSN: 0022-4561
Founded in 1945

Journal of Wildlife Management

Wildlife Society
5410 Grosvenor Ln
Suite 200
Bethesda, MD 20814-2197

301-897-9770
FAX 301-530-2471
E-Mail: tws@wildlife.org
Home Page: www.wildlife.org
Social Media: *Facebook, Twitter, LinkedIn*

Michael Hutchins, Executive Director

One of the world's leading scientific journals covering wildlife science, management and conservation.
Founded in 1937

Journal of the Air Pollution Control Association

Air Pollution Control Association
1 Gateway Center 3rd Floor
420 Fort Duquesne Blvd.
Pittsburgh, PA 15222-1435

412-232-3444
800-270-3444
FAX 412-232-3450
E-Mail: info@awma.org
Home Page: www.awma.org/

Social Media: *Facebook, Twitter, LinkedIn*

Tim Keener, Technical Editor-in-Chief
George Hidy, Co-Editor
Jeffrey Brook, Associate Editor

A comprehensive journal offering information to the environment and conservation industry.
Cost: $95.00
Frequency: Monthly
Circulation: 700
Founded in 1907

Journal of the Institute of Environmental Sciences and Technology

Institute of Environmental Sciences and Technology
2340 South Arlington Heights Road
Suite 100
Arlington Heights, IL   60005-4516

847-981-0100
FAX 847-981-4130
E-Mail: information@iest.org
Home Page: www.iest.org

Julie Kendrick, Executive Director
Robert Burrows, Director Communications Services
Corrie Roesslein, Director Programs/Administration

Contains technical articles and reports on simulation, testing, modeling, control, current research, and the teaching of the enrionmental sciences and technologies. The content covers contamination control, environmental laboratory and field-testing and evaluation, reliability assessment and evaluation methods, environmental instrumentation and measurements, envrionmental effects, environmental and safety standards, computer applications, and many other topics.
Frequency: Annual

Lake & Reservoir Management

North American Lake Management Society
PO Box 5443
Madison, WI   53705

608-233-2836
FAX 608-233-3186
E-Mail: info@nalms.org
Home Page: www.nalms.org

Social Media: *Facebook, LinkedIn, Flickr*

Bev Clark, President
Reesa Evans, Secretary

Publishes original studies relevant to lake and reservoir management. Papers address the management of lakes and reservoirs, their watersheds and tributaries, along with limnology and ecology needed for sound supervision of these systems.
Frequency: Quarterly

LakeLine Magazine

North American Lake Management Society
PO Box 5443
Madison, WI   53705-443

608-233-2836
FAX 608-233-3186
E-Mail: info@nalms.org
Home Page: www.nalms.org

Bev Clark, President
Reesa Evans, Secretary
Linda Green, Treasurer

Contains news, commentary and articles on topics affecting lakes, reservoirs and watersheds. Organized around a theme, like control of invasive species or resolving recreational conflicts, each issue becomes a valued resource for lake users and advocates.
Frequency: Quarterly

Land and Water Magazine

Land and Water
Po Box 1197
Fort Dodge, IA   50501-1197

515-576-3191
FAX 515-576-2606
E-Mail: landandwater@dodgenet.com
Home Page: www.landandwater.com
Social Media: *Facebook*

Amy Dencklau, Publisher
Shanza Dencklau, Assistant Editor
Rasch M. Kenneth, President

Edited for contractors, engineers, architects, government officials and those working in the field of natural resource management and restoration from idea stage through project completion and maintenance.
Cost: $20.00
72 Pages
Circulation: 20000
Founded in 1959
Mailing list available for rent: 20M

names
Printed in 4 colors on glossy stock

NETAnews

National Environmental, Safety and Health Training
2700 N. Central Avenue
Suite 900
Phoenix, AZ   85004-1147

602-956-6099
FAX 602-956-6399
E-Mail: info@neshta.org
Home Page: www.neshta.org

Charles L Richardson, Executive Director
Joan J Jennings, Manager Association Services
Suzanne Lanctot, Manager Certification/Membership

Frequency: Quarterly

Natural Resources & Environment

American Bar Association
321 N Clark St
Chicago, IL   60654-7598

312-988-5000
800-285-2221
FAX 312-988-5280
E-Mail: askaba@abanet.org
Home Page: www.abanet.org
Social Media: *Facebook, Twitter*

Lori Lyons, Staff Editor
Christine LeBel, Executive Editor

Practical magazine on the latest developments in the field of natural resources law for the ABA Section of Environment, Energy, and Resources.
Cost: $80.00
64 Pages
Frequency: Quarterly
ISSN: 0822-3812
Printed in 4 colors

North American Elk: Ecology & Management

Wildlife Management Institute
1146 19th St NW
Suite 700
Washington, DC   20036-3727

202-973-7710
FAX 202-785-1348
Home Page:
www.wildlifemanagementinstitute.org

Dale E Toweill, Editor

Northeast Sun

NE Sustainable Energy Association
50 Miles St
Greenfield, MA   01301-3255

413-774-6051
FAX 413-774-6053
E-Mail: nesea@nesea.org
Home Page: www.nesea.org

David Barclay, Executive Director
Paul Horowitz, Chairman

Includes articles by leading authorities on sustainable energy practices, energy efficiency and renewable energy.
Frequency: Quarterly
Circulation: 5000
Founded in 1974

Outdoor America

Isaak Walton League
707 Conservation Lane
Gaithersburg, MD   20878

301-548-0150
FAX 301-548-0146
E-Mail: general@iwla.org
Home Page: www.iwla.org

David Hoskins, Executive Director

Entertaining and educational articles about the conservation work of IWLA members. Also provides in-depth coverage of broader conservation issues such as national energy policy, urban sprawl, and wetland loss.
Cost: $36.00
Frequency: Quarterly
Circulation: 37000
ISSN: 0021-3314

Phytopathology

American Phytopatholgical Society
3340 Pilot Knob Road
Saint Paul, MN   55121-2097

651-454-7250
800-328-7560
FAX 651-454-0766
E-Mail: aps@scisoc.org
Home Page: www.apsnet.org

Greg Grahek, Director of Marketing

The premier international journal for publication of articles on fundamental research that advances understanding of the nature of plant diseases, the agents that cause them, their spread, the losses they cause, and measures that can be used to control them.
Frequency: Monthly
Circulation: 1200

ISSN: 0031-949X
Printed in 4 colors

Plant Disease

American Phytopathlogical Society
3340 Pilot Know Road
Saint Paul, MN   55121-2097

651-454-7250
800-328-7560
FAX 651-454-0766
E-Mail: aps@scisoc.org
Home Page: www.apsnet.org

Greg Grahek, Director of Marketing

Leading international journal for rapid reporting of research on new diseases, epidemics, and methods of disease control. Covers basic and applied research, which focuses on practical aspects of disease diagnosis and treatment.The popular Disease Notes section contains brief and timely reports of new diseases, new disease outbreaks, new hosts, and pertinent new observations of plant diseases and pathogens worldwide.
Frequency: Monthly
Circulation: 1200
ISSN: 0191-2917

Plastics Recycling Update

Resource Recycling
PO Box 42270
Portland, OR   97242-270

503-233-1305
FAX 503-233-1356
E-Mail: pru@resource-recycling.com
Home Page:
www.resource-recycling.com

Jerry Powell, Publisher

The only magazine in North America focusing exclusively on polymer recovery efforts. A superb source for marketing recycling equipment and services and offers an excellent means of sourcing new suppliers of recovered plastics. The authority in plastic recycling market analysis, coverage of the latest legislation, industry news and views, and technical specs on the latest equipment.
Cost: $59.00
6 Pages
Frequency: Monthly
Circulation: 1000
ISSN: 1052-4908
Founded in 1981
Mailing list available for rent: 40,000 names at $100 per M
Printed in one color on matte stock

Pollution Engineering

Business News Publishing Company
2401 W Big Beaver Rd
Suite 700
Troy, MI   48084-3333

248-362-3700
FAX 248-362-0317
E-Mail: Roy@PollutionEngineering.com
Home Page: www.bnpmedia.com
Social Media: *Facebook, Twitter*

Mitchell Henderson, CEO
Roy Bigham, Managing Editor
Seth Fisher, Products Editor

Providing must read information for today's Engineers and Consulting Engineers in Pollution Control for; Air, Wastewater, and Remediation Hazardous Solid Waste. Up-to-date information on regulatory requirements, coverage of economic benefits of environmental control techniques, and up-to-date information on innovative and cost-effective environmental equipment, products, technology and services.
Frequency: Monthly
ISSN: 0032-3640
Founded in 1969

Pollution Equipment News

Rimbach Publishing
8650 Babcock Blvd
Suite 1
Pittsburgh, PA   15237-5010

412-364-5366
800-245-3182
FAX 412-369-9720
E-Mail: info@rimbach.com
Home Page: www.rimbach.com
Social Media: *Facebook, Twitter*

Norberta Rimbach, President
Karen Galante, Circulation Manager
Paul Henderson, VP of Sales and Marketing

Provides information to those responsible for selecting products and services for air, water, wastewater and hazardous waste pollution abatement.
Frequency: Bi-Annually
Circulation: 91000
Founded in 1968

Pollution Prevention Northwest

US EPA
Ariel Rios Building
1200 Pennsylvania Avenue NW
Washington, DC   20460

202-272-0167
E-Mail: zachariasiewicz.robert@epa.gov
Home Page: www.epa.gov

Bob Zachariasiewicz, Acting Director

Articles include recent information on source reduction and sustainable technologies in industry, transportation, consumer, agriculture, energy, and the international sector.
Frequency: Monthly
Circulation: 12000
Founded in 1970

Popular Science

2 Park Ave
9th Floor
New York, NY   10016-5614

212-779-5000
FAX 212-986-2656
E-Mail: letters@popsci.com
Home Page: www.popsci.com

Greg Hano, Publisher
Robert Novick, General Manager

A leading source of science and technology news, with insightful commentary on the new innovations, and even scientific takes on the hottest Hollywood stories.
Cost: $48.00
Frequency: Monthly
Founded in 1964

Pumper

COLE Publishing
PO Box 220
Three Lakes, WI   54562-220

715-546-3346
FAX 715-546-3786
E-Mail: cole@pumper.com
Home Page: www.pumper.com
Social Media: Facebook, Twitter, YouTube

Ted Rulseh, Editor
Jeff Bruss, President

Emphasis on companies, individuals and industry events while focusing on customer service, environmental issues and employment trends.
Cost: $16.00
Frequency: Monthly
Circulation: 20,740
Founded in 1978

R&D Focus

International Lead Zinc Research Organization
2525 Meridian Parkway, Suite 100
PO Box 12036
Durham, NC   27713-2036

919-361-4647
FAX 919-361-1957
E-Mail: jhendric@ilzro.org
Home Page: www.ilzro.org

Stephen Wilkinson, President
Frank Goodwin, VP Materials Sciences
Scott Mooneyham, Treasurer
Rob Putnam, Director Communications

Frequency: Quarterly

Radwaste Solutions

American Nuclear Society
555 N Kensington Ave
La Grange Park, IL   60526-5592

708-352-6611
800-323-044
FAX 708-352-0499
E-Mail: advertising@ans.org
Home Page: www.ans.org/advertising

Jack Tuohy, Executive Director
Sarah Wells, Editor
Harry Bradley, Executive Director
Gloria Naurocki, Membership & Marketing
Mary Beth Gardner, Scientific Publications

The magazine of radioactive waste management and facility remediation. Serving the nuclear waste management and cleanup business segments of the industry. Also included are articles on radwaste management programs and practices outside the US, as well as guest editorials and letters to the editor, shorter thought-pieces, and articles on recent academic/technical advances detailing their immediate or planned practical applications.
Cost: $455.00
Frequency: Fortnightly
Circulation: 2000
Founded in 1954
Printed in on matte stock

Recycling Laws International

Raymond Communications
P.O.Box 4311
Silver Spring, MD   20914-4311

301-345-4237
FAX 301-345-4768
E-Mail: circulation@raymond.com
Home Page: www.raymond.com

Lorah Utter, Editor
Allyn Sweet, Circulation Manager
Michele Raymond, President

Covers recycling, takeback, green labeling policy for business in 35 countries. Also contains a country page document that is updated annually.
Cost: $485.00
200 Pages
Circulation: 150
Founded in 1991

Recycling Product News

Baum Publications
2323 Boundary Road
#201
Vancouver, BC   0

604-291-9900
FAX 604-291-1906
E-Mail: webadmin@baumpub.com
Home Page: www.baumpub.com

Engelbert J Baum, Publisher
Keith Barker, Editor

Published for the recycling center operators and other waste mangers, articles discuss technology and new products.
Circulation: 14000

Recycling Today

GIE Media
4020 Kinross Lakes Parkway
Suite 201
Richfield, OH   44286

330-523-5400
800-456-0707
FAX 330-659-0823
E-Mail: info@recyclingtoday.com
Home Page: www.recyclingtoday.com/
Social Media: Facebook, Twitter

James R Keefe, Group Publisher
Brian Taylor, Editor
Richard Foster, CEO
Debbie Kean, Manager

Published for the secondary commodity processing/recycling market.
Cost: $30.00
Frequency: Monthly
Circulation: 15000

Renewable Resources Journal

Renewable Natural Resources
Foundation
5430 Grosvenor Ln
Suite 220
Bethesda, MD   20814-2193

301-493-9101
FAX 301-493-6148
E-Mail: info@rnrf.org
Home Page: www.rnrf.org

Robert D Day, Executive Director
Ryan M Colker, Programs Director
Chandru Krishna, Circulation

Provides information of general interest
concerning public policy issues related
to natural resources management. Comprised of contributed and solicited articles on a wide range of natural resource
issues, news items about RNRF's members, notices of significant meetings, editorials, and commentaries.
Cost: $25.00
32 Pages
Frequency: Quarterly
Circulation: 1800
ISSN: 0738-6532
Founded in 1975
Printed in 2 colors on matte stock

Resource Recycling

Resource Recycling
PO Box 42270
Portland, OR   97242-270

503-233-1305
FAX 503-233-1356
E-Mail: info@resource-recycling.co
Home Page:
www.resource-recycling.com

Jerry Powell, Editor/Publisher
Rick Downing, Advertising Director

The nation's leading recycling and composting magazine. This monthly journal
focuses on efforts in the US and Canada
to recover materials from homes and
businesses for recycling. Accepts advertising.
Cost: $52.00
64 Pages
Frequency: Monthly
Circulation: 14000+
ISSN: 0744-4710
Founded in 1982
Printed in 4 colors on glossy stock

Restoration Ecology Journal

Society for Ecological Restoration
International
1017 O Street NW
Washington, DC   20001

202-299-9518
FAX 270-626-5485
E-Mail: info@ser.org
Home Page: www.ser.org
Social Media: *Facebook*

Steve Whisenant, Chair
Cara R. Nelson, Vice Chair
Mary Travaglini, Treasurer
Alan Unwin, Secretary

Primary emphases are: research on restoration and ecological principles that help
explain restoration processes, descriptions of techniques that the authors have
pioneered and that are likely to be of use
to other practicing restorationists,
desriptions of setbacks and surprises encountered during restoration and the lessons learnt, analytical opinions, and
reviews of articles that summarize literature on specialized aspects of
restoration.
2300 Members
Frequency: Bi-Monthly
Founded in 1988

Risk Policy Report

Inside Washington Publishers
1919 S Eads St
Suite 1400
Arlington, VA   22202-3028

703-418-3981
FAX 703-415-8543
E-Mail: iwp@sprintmail.com
Home Page: www.iwpnews.com

Alan Sosenko, Owner
David Clarke, Editor

Contains analysis, great perspectives, in-
dustry news, policymaking profiles and a
calendar of events.
Cost: $295.00
Frequency: Monthly
Founded in 1980

SETAC Globe

Society of Environmental Toxicology
and Chemistry
1013 N 12th Ave
Pensacola, FL   32501-3306

850-437-1901
FAX 850-469-9778

E-Mail: rparrish@setac.org
Home Page: www.edwardjones.com

Chad Stacy, Manager
Greg Schifer, Manager

Stay up to date on the latest firm news,
and learn about the companies followed
with Edward Jones.
Frequency: Bi-Monthly

Shore & Beach

American Shore and Beach Preservation
Association
5460 Beaujolais Lane
Fort Myers, FL   33919

239-489-2616
FAX 239-362-9771
E-Mail: exdir@asbpa.org
Home Page: www.asbpa.org
Social Media: *Facebook, Twitter*

Harry Simmons, President
Kate Gooderham, Executive Director
Nicole Elko, Secretary
Russell Boudreau, VP
Brad Pickel, Treasurer

Information and articles regarding management of shores and beaches.
1M Members
Founded in 1926

Soil & Groundwater Cleanup Magazine

AEHS Foundation Inc.
150 Fearing Street
Suite 21
Amherst, MA   01002

413-549-5170
888-540-2347
E-Mail: info@aehs.com
Home Page: www.aehs.com

Paul T Kostecki, PhD, Executive
Director

Frequency: Bi-Monthly

Soil and Sediment Contamination

AEHS Foundation Inc.
150 Fearing Street
Suite 21
Amherst, MA   01002

413-549-5170
888-540-2347
E-Mail: info@aehs.com
Home Page: www.aehs.com

Paul T Kostecki, PhD, Executive
Director

Focuses on soil and sediment contamination from; sludges, petroleum, petrochemicals, chlorinated hydrocarbons, pesticides, and lead and other heavy metals. Offers detailed descriptions of all the latest and most efficient offsite and in situ remediation techniques, strategies for assessing health effects and hazards, and tips for dealing with everyday regulatory and legal issues. Assess, mitigate, and solve rural and urban soil contamination problems.
Frequency: Bi-Monthly

Solar Energy

Elsevier Science
655 Avenue of the Americas
PO Box 945
New York, NY   10010-5107

212-633-3800
FAX 212-633-3850
E-Mail: usinfo-f@elseview.com
Home Page: www.elsevier.com

Young Suk Chi, Manager

Devoted exclusively to the science and technology of solar energy applications. Presents information not previously published in journals on any aspect of solar energy research, development, application, measurement or policy.
Frequency: Monthly
Circulation: 6400

Solar Today

American Solar Energy Society
4760 Walnut Street
Suite 106
Boulder, CO   80301-2843

303-443-3130
FAX 303-443-3212
E-Mail: ases@ases.org
Home Page: www.ases.org
Social Media: *Facebook, Twitter, LinkedIn*

Susan Greene, President
Regina Johnson, Editor
Annette Delagrange, Advertising Sales

Provides information, case histories and reviews of a variety of renewable energy technologies, including solar, wind, biomass and geothermal.
Cost: $39.00
90 Pages
Frequency: 9x/Year
Circulation: 7000
ISSN: 1042-0630
Founded in 1987

Solid Waste & Recycling

Southam Environment Group
80 Valleybrook Drive
Toronto, ON   M3B2S9

905-305-6155
888-702-1111
FAX 416-442-2026
E-Mail: gcrittenden@solidwastemag.com
Home Page: www.solidwastemag.com

Brad O'Brien, Publisher
Bibi Khan, Circualtion Manager
Guy Crittenden, Editor-in-Chief

Emphasizes municipal and commercial aspects of collection, handling, transportation, hauling, disposal and treatment of solid waste , including incineration, recycling and landfill technology.
Cost: $29.95
Frequency: Weekly
Circulation: 10000

Solid Waste Report

Business Publishers
2222 Sedwick Dr
Suite 101
Durham, NC   27713

800-223-8720
FAX 800-508-2592
E-Mail: custserv@bpinews.com
Home Page: www.bpinews.com

Comprehensive news and analysis of legislation, regulation and litigation in solid waste management including resource recovery, recycling, collection and disposal. Regularly features international news, state updates and business trends.
Cost: $567.00
Founded in 1963

State Environmental Monitor

Inside Washington Publishers
1919 S Eads St
Suite 1400
Arlington, VA   22202-3028

703-418-3981
800-424-9068
FAX 703-415-8543
E-Mail: service@iwpnews.com
Home Page: www.iwpnews.com

Alan Sosenko, Owner

Contains comperhensive coverage of innovations in state environmental programs and the growth of state authority over environmental regulations.
Cost: $245.00
Frequency: Monthly
Founded in 1980

TIDE

Coastal Conservation Association
6919 Portwest Dr
Suite 100
Houston, TX   77024-8049

713-626-4234
800-201-FISH
FAX 713-626-5852
E-Mail: ccantl@joincca.org
Home Page: www.joincca.org
Social Media: *, Twitter*

David Cummins, President

The official magazine of the CCA.
85000 Members
Founded in 1977

The Leading Edge

Society of Exploration Geophysicists
8801 South Yale
Suite 500
Tulsa, OK   74137-3575

918-497-5500
FAX 918-497-5557
E-Mail: web@seg.org
Home Page: www.seg.org
Social Media: *Facebook, Twitter, LinkedIn*

Mary Fleming, Executive Director
Vladimir Grechka, Editor

A gateway publication, introducing new geophysical theory, instrumentation, and established practices to scientists in a wide range of geoscience disciplines. Most material is presented in a semitechnical manner that minimizes mathematical theory and emphasizes practical application. Also serves as SEG's publication venue for official society business.

Urban Land

Urban Land Institute
1025 Thomas Jefferson NW
Suite 500 W
Washington, DC   20007-5201

202-624-7116
800-321-5011
FAX 202-624-7140

E-Mail: reliance@uli.org
Home Page: www.uli.org

Kristina Kessler, Editor in Chief
Karen Schaar, Managing Editor
Joan Campbell, Manager

Focuses on the information needs of land use and development professionals worldwide, providing them with timely, objective, practical, and accessible articles on a wide variety of subjects related to their professional interests.
Cost: $165.00
Frequency: Monthly
Circulation: 23000
Founded in 1936

Washington Environmental Compliance Update

M Lee Smith Publishers
PO Box 5094
Bentwood, TN   37024-5094

615-737-7517
800-274-6774

F Lee Smith, Publisher
Douglas S Little, Editor

Review of environmental laws.
Cost: $225.00
8 Pages
Frequency: Daily
Mailing list available for rent
Printed in 2 colors on matte stock

Waste Age

Environmental Industry Association
4301 Connecticut Ave NW
Suite 300
Washington, DC   20008-2304

202-244-4700
800-424-2869
FAX 202-966-4824
Home Page:
www.environmentalisteveryday.org
Social Media: *Facebook, Twitter,
YouTube*

Bruce Parker, President
Patricia-Ann Tom, Editor
Laura Magliola, Marketing Manager

Contents focus on new system technologies, recycling, resource recovery and sanitary landfills with regular features on updates in the status of government regulations, new products, guides, company profiles, exclusive survey information, legislative implications and news.
Frequency: Monthly
Circulation: 38000

Waste Age's Recycling Times

Environmental Industry Association
4301 Connecticut Ave NW
Suite 300
Washington, DC   20008-2304

202-244-4700
800-424-2869
FAX 202-966-4824
Home Page: www.wasteage.com

Bruce Parker, President
Wendy Angel, Assistant Editor
Gregg Herring, Group Publisher

Features municipalities, recycling goals and rates, program innovations, waste habits, and new materials being recycled.
Cost: $99.00
Frequency: Monthly
Circulation: 5000

Water & Wastes Digest

Scranton Gillette Communications
3030 W Salt Creek Lane
Suite 201
Arlington Heights, IL   60005-5025

847-391-1000
FAX 847-390-0408
E-Mail: nsimeonova@sgcmail.com
Home Page: www.wwdmag.com
Social Media: *Facebook, Twitter,
LinkedIn*

Neda Simeonova, Editorial Director
Caitlin Cunningham, Managing Editor

Serves readers in the water and/or wastewater industries. These people work for municipalities, in industry, or as engineers. They design, specify, buy, operate and maintain equipment, chemicals, software and wastewater treatment services.
Cost: $40.00
128 Pages
Frequency: Monthly
Circulation: 101000
ISSN: 0043-1181
Founded in 1961

Water Quality Products

Scranton Gillette Communications
3030 W Salt Creek Lane
Suite 201
Arlington Heights, IL   60005

847-391-1000
FAX 847-390-0408
E-Mail: nsimeonova@sgcmail.com

Home Page: www.wqpmag.com
Social Media: *Facebook, Twitter*

Neda Simeonova, Editorial Director
Dennis Martyka, VP/Group Publisher
Kate Cline, Managing Editor

Provides balanced editorial content including developments in water conditioning, filtration and disinfection for residential, commercial and industrial systeme.
Cost: $40.00
68 Pages
Frequency: Monthly
Circulation: 19000
ISSN: 1092-0978
Founded in 1995

Wildfire Magazine

International Association of Wildland Fire
330 N. Wabash Ave
Suite 2300
Fairfax, VA   22033

312-595-1080
FAX 312-595-0295
Home Page: www.wildfiremag.com

Sacha Dick, Programs Manager

Addresses the needs of chiefs and wildland forestry managers by providing a unique international prospective. Each issue focuses on the demand of leaders responsible for managing and controlling wildland fires. Readers are the top decision makers and leaders who have influence over purchasing equipment, supplies and contracted services. Readership includes fire chiefs, governmental agencies, private sector professionals, consultants and contractors.
Frequency: Monthly

Wildlife Conservation Magazine

2300 S Boulevard
Bronx, NY   10460

718-220-5121
800-786-8226
FAX 718-584-2625
E-Mail: magazine@wcs.org
Home Page:
www.wildlifeconservation.org/

Debby Bahler, Editor
Diana Warren, Advertising Director
4teve Sanderson, President

A national nature and science magazine. Contains stunning photography, conservation news and special updates on endangered species. Learn how to help

protect local wildlife, and the secrets of the world's rarest and most mysterious animals.
Cost: $19.95
96 Pages
Circulation: 150000
Founded in 1895

World Resource Review

SUPCON International
International Headquarters 2W381
75th Street
Naperville, IL   60565-9245

630-910-1551
FAX 630-910-1561
E-Mail: syshen@megsinet.net
Home Page: www.globalwarming.net

Dr. Sinyan Shen, Production Manager

For business and government readers, provides expert worldwide reviews of global warming and extreme events in relation to the management of natural, mineral and material resources. Subjects include global warming impacts on agriculture, energy, and infrastructure, monitoring of changes in resources using remote sensing, actions of national and international bodies, global carbon budget, greenhouse budget and more.
Cost: $72.00
Frequency: Quarterly
Circulation: 12000
ISSN: 1042-8011

World Wastes: The Independent Voice

Communication Channels
6151 Powers Ferry Road NW
Atlanta, GA   30339-2959

770-953-4805
FAX 770-618-0348

Bill Wolpin, Editor
Jerrold France, President Argus Business

Reaches individuals and firms engaged in the removal and disposal of solid wastes.
Cost: $48.00
Frequency: Monthly
Circulation: 36,000

World Watch

Worldwatch Institute
1776 Massachusetts Ave Nw #800
Suite 800
Washington, DC   20036-1995

202-452-1999
FAX 202-296-7365

E-Mail: worldwatch@worldwatch.org
Home Page: www.worldwatch.org
Social Media: , *Twitter, YouTube*

Christopher Flavin, President
Tom Prugh, Editor
Lisa Mastny, Senior Editor

Magazine on global environmental issues.
Cost: $27.00
40 Pages
Circulation: 10000
ISSN: 0896-0615
Founded in 1974
Printed in 4 colors on glossy stock

Trade Shows

AAAR Annual Meeting

American Association for Aerosol Research
15000 Commerce Parkway
Suite C
Mount Laurel, NJ   08054

856-439-9080
FAX 856-439-0525
E-Mail: dbright@ahint.com
Home Page: www.aaar.org

Lynn Russell, Program Chair
Melissa Baldwin, Executive Director

Exibits related to aerosol research in areas including industrial process, air pollution, and industrial hygiene. Over 600 professionals attend.
600 Attendees
Frequency: Annual, October

AEESP Annual Meeting

Association of Environmental Engineering and
2303 Naples Court
Champaign, IL   61822

217-398-6969
FAX 217-355-9232
Home Page: www.aeesp.org

Joanne Fetzner, Business Secretary

With the Water Environment Federation
Frequency: Fall

AERE Summer Conference

Association of Environmental and Resource
1616 P Street NW
Suite 600
Washington, DC   20036

202-328-5125
FAX 202-939-3460
E-Mail: voigt@rff.org
Home Page: www.aere.org

Marilyn Voigt, Executive Director

nonprofit international professional association for economists working on the environment and natural resources.
850 Members
350 Attendees
Frequency: January
Founded in 1979

APWA International Public Works Congress & Expo

American Public Works Association
2345 Grand Boulevard
Suite 700
Kansas City, MO   64108-2625

816-472-6100
800-848-2792
FAX 816-472-1610
E-Mail: ddancy@apwa.net
Home Page: www.apwa.net

Peter King, Executive Director
David Dancy, Director Of Marketing

Offers the benefit of a variety of educational sessions, depth of the exhibit program and endless opportunities for networking. The latest cutting-edge technologies, managerial techniques and regulatory trends designed to keep you focused on the right solutions at the right time.
6500 Attendees
Frequency: Annual/September
ISSN: 0092-4873
Founded in 1894

ASEH Annual Meeting

American Society for Environmental History
119 Pine Street
Suite 301
Seattle, WA   98101

206-343-0226
FAX 206-343-0249

E-Mail: mighetto@hrassoc.com
Home Page: www.aseh.net

Lisa Mighetto, Acting Executive
Director

Individuals and groups all over the
world will attend to collaborate on ways
to live better with nature, and to make a
better world for all outside of traditional
political structures and older models of
environmentalism.
Frequency: Spring, Texas

ASFE Fall Meeting

ASFE/The Geoprofessional Business
Association
8811 Colesville Road
Suite G106
Silver Springs, MD   20910

301-565-2733
FAX 301-589-2017
E-Mail: info@asfe.org
Home Page: www.asfe.org

John P Bachner, Executive VP

Providing geotechnical, geologic, environmental, construction materials engineering and testing, and related
professional services information and
education.
Frequency: Annual/Fall

ASFE Spring Meeting

ASFE
8811 Colesville Road
Suite G106
Silver Springs, MD   20910

301-565-2733
FAX 301-589-2017
E-Mail: info@asfe.org
Home Page: www.asfe.org

John P Bachner, Executive VP

Provides geotechnical, geologic, environmental, construction materials engineering and testing, and related
professional services information and
education.
Frequency: Annual/Spring

ASFE Winter Leadership Conference

ASFE/The Geoprofessional Business
Association
8811 Colesville Road
Suite G106
Silver Springs, MD   20910

301-565-2733
FAX 301-589-2014

E-Mail: info@asfe.org
Home Page: www.asfe.org

John Bachner, Executive VP

ASFE's leaders meet to finish priorities
for the current year and determine the direction of ASFE for the coming year.
Frequency: Annual/January

ASFPM Annual Conference

Association of State Floodplain
Managers
2809 Fish Hatchery Road
Suite 204
Madison, WI   53713

608-274-0123
FAX 608-274-0696
E-Mail: memberhelp@floods.org
Home Page: www.floods.org

Larry Larson, Executive Director
Alison Stierli, Member Services
Coordinator

Focus on floodproofing techniques, materials, floodproofing and elevation contractors, current issues and programs,
new federal tax impications and the various means of funding floodproofing projects. implications.
Frequency: Annual

ASFPM Annual National Conference

Association of State Floodplain
Managers
2809 Fish Hatchery Rd
Suite 204
Madison, WI   53713-5020

608-274-0123
FAX 608-274-0696
E-Mail: Larry@floods.org
Home Page: www.floods.org
Social Media: *Facebook*

Sally McConkey, Chair
William Nechamen, Vice Chair
Alan J. Giles, Secretary
John V. Crofts, Treasurer

The national conferences all community,
state and federal floodplain managers
plan to attend. Many of the most important consulting firms and product vendors associated with floodplain
management attend.
6500 Members
Founded in 1977

ASMR Meeting & Conference

American Society of Mining and
Reclamation
3134 Montavesta Road
Lexington, KY   40502

859-335-6529
E-Mail: asmr@insightbb.com
Home Page: www.ca.uky.edu/assmr

Richard I Barnhisel, Executive Secretary

Promoting the advancement of basic and
applied reclamation science through research and technology transfer.
Frequency: June

ASPRS Annual Conference

ASPRS
5410 Grosvenor Lane
Suite 210
Bethesda, MD   20814-2160

301-493-0290
FAX 301-493-0208
E-Mail: asprs@asprs.org
Home Page: www.asprs.org

Dr. Carolyn J. Merry, Ph.D., President
Roberta Lenczowski, VP
Dr. Donald Laurer, Treasurer
James Plasker, Executive Director

One hundred exhibits of mapping,
photogrammetry, environmental management, remote sensing, geographic information, natural resources and much
more.
6000 Members
2000 Attendees
Founded in 1934

Air and Waste Management Association Annual Conference and Exhibition

Air and Waste Management Association
1 Gateway Center
3rd Floor
Pittsburgh, PA   15222-1435

412-652-2458
800-270-3444
FAX 412-232-3450
E-Mail: info@awma.org
Home Page: www.awma.org

Deborah Hilfman, Show Manager
Robert Greenbaum, Exhibit Manager

Environmental professionals from all
sectors of the economy including colleges, universities, natural resource manufacturing and process industries,
consultants, local state, provincial, regional and federal governments, con-

struction, utilities industries. Over 300 exhibits of envirnomental control products.
6000 Attendees

Annual North American Waste-to-Energy Conference

Solid Waste Association of North America - SWANA

800-GOS-WANA
FAX 301-589-7068
Home Page: www.nawtec.org

Co-sponsored by ERC, ASME and SWANA, in partnership with WTERT, the conference and trade show focuses on municipal waste-to-energy operational issues and policy, technology and research initiatives.

Aquatic Plant Management Society Annual Meeting

Aquatic Plant Management Society
PO Box 821265
Vicksburg, MS   39182-1265

FAX 601-634-2398
E-Mail: dpetty@ndrsite.com
Home Page: www.apms.org
Social Media: *Facebook, LinkedIn*

Linda Nelson, President
Terry Goldsby, VP
Sherry Whitaker, Treasurer
Jeff Schardt, Secretary
Greg Aguillard, Director

An international organization of educators, scientists, commercial pesticide applicators, administrators and individuals interested in aquatic plant species and plant management.
Founded in 1961

EBA Annual Meeting

Environmental Business Association
1150 Connecticut Avenue NW
9th Floor
Washington, DC   20036-4129

202-624-4363
FAX 202-828-4130
E-Mail: wbode@bode.com

William H Bode, President

Learn more about the research, development and demonstration activities in fuel cells, hydrogen production delivery and storage technologies.
Frequency: June

EMS Annual Meeting

Environmental Mutagen Society
1821 Michael Faraday Drive
Suite 300
Reston, VA   20190

703-438-8220
FAX 703-438-3113
E-Mail: emshq@ems-us.org
Home Page: www.ems-us.org

Tonia Masson, Executive Director

Environmental Impacts on the Genome and Epigenome; Mechanisms and Risks.
Frequency: Spring

ESTECH Annual Technical Meeting and Exposition of IEST

Institute of Environmental Sciences and Technology
5005 Newport Drive
Suite 506
Rolling Meadows, IL   60008-3841

847-255-1561
FAX 847-255-1699
E-Mail: iest@iest.org
Home Page: www.iest.org

Heather Dvorak, Marketing Associate

IEST's annual technical meeting and exposition presents the finest educational program with tutorials, technical sessions, and working group meeting, as well as displays in the tabletop exhibition for design, test and evaluation.
300 Attendees
Frequency: May

ETAD Annual Meeting

ETAD North America
1850 M Street NW
Suite 700
Washington, DC   20036

202-721-4154
FAX 202-296-8120
Home Page: www.etad.com

Dr C Tucker Helmes, Executive Director

Cooperate with ETAD member companies and value chain for the benefit of health and the environment. Learn more about environmental regulations.
Frequency: Spring

Environmental Business: West

World Information Systems
PO Box 535
Cambridge, MA   02238-0535

FAX 617-492-3312

Richard S Golob, Editor-in-Chief
Roger B Wilson Jr, VP

Attracts business leaders in hazardous waste and other key segments of the environmental industry. The events have earned a reputation as summit meetings of environmental business leaders. Speakers have included presidents of major environmental firms, along with well known consultants, financiers and government officials. The two-and-a-half day programs concentrate exclusively on the business issues facing the rapidly growing environmental industry. 25 booths.
800+ Attendees

Environmental Technology Expo

Association of Energy Engineers
4025 Pleasantdale Road
Suite 420
Atlanta, GA   30340

770-447-5083
FAX 770-446-3969
E-Mail: info@aeecenter.org
Home Page: www.aeecenter.org

Ruth Whitlock, Executive Admin
Jennifer Vendola, Accountant

Annual show and exhibits of air and water pollution contrasts, waste-to-energy services information, asbestos abatement and monitoring instruments and equipment.
Frequency: October

FET Annual Meeting

Federation of Environmental Technologists
W175 N11081 Stonewood Dr
Suite 203
Germantown, WI   53022

262-437-1700
FAX 262-437-1702
E-Mail: info@fetinc.org
Home Page: www.fetinc.org

Triese Haase, Administrator

Attend the program, visit the exhibitions and hear from keynote speakers on relevant environmental topics.
Frequency: March

Global Warming International Conference & Expo

SUPCON International
PO Box 5275
Woodridge, IL   60517-0275

630-910-1551
FAX 630-910-1561
E-Mail: syshen@megsinet.net
Home Page: www.globalwarming.net

Environmental and energy technology, global warming mitigation, journals, publications and software, greenhouse gas measurements, alternative vehicles and alternative energy. Containing 100 booths and exhibits.
2000 Attendees
Frequency: April Boston

GlobalCon Conference & Expo

Association of Energy Engineers
4025 Pleasantdale Rd
Suite 420
Atlanta, GA   30340-4264

770-447-5083
FAX 770-446-3969
E-Mail: info@aeecenter.org
Home Page: www.aeecenter.org
Social Media: *Facebook, Twitter, LinkedIn, YouTube*

Eric A. Woodroof, President
Gary Hogsett, President Elect
Bill Younger, Secretary
Paul Goodman, C.P.A., Treasurer

Designed specifically to facilitate those seeking to expand their knowledge of fast-moving developments in the energy field, explore promising new technologies, compare energy supply options, and learn about innovative and cost-conscious project implementation strategies.
8.2M Members
Founded in 1977

Green Industry Conference - GIC

Professional Lawncare Network, Inc (PLANET)
950 Herndon Parkway
Suite 450
Herndon, VA   20170

703-736-9666
800-395-2522
FAX 703-736-9668
E-Mail: info@gie-expo.com
Home Page:
www.landcarenetwork.or/cmc/gic.html

Held in conjunction with the GIE+EXPO, the conference offers lead-ership series, workshops, educational opportunities, events, and new member orientation.
Frequency: Annual

HydroVision

410 Archibald Street
Kansas City, MO   64111-3001

816-931-1311
FAX 816-931-2015

Leslie Eden, Manager

Focusing on asset management, civil works and dam safety, new development, ocean/ tidal/ stream power, operations and maintenance, policies and regulations, and water resources.
1,600 Attendees
Frequency: July-August

IAWF Annual Meetings

International Association of Wildland Fire
4025 Fair Ridge Drive
Fairfax, VA   22033

785-423-1818
FAX 785-542-3511
E-Mail: info@iawfonline.org
Home Page: www.iawfonline.org
Social Media: *Facebook, Twitter*

Sacha Dick, Programs Manager

Participants represent a wide range of organizations, disciplines, and countries. Conference program includes workshops, invited speakers, oral and poster presentations, panels, and vendor displays.

IEST Annual Meeting

Institute of Environmental Sciences and Technology
5005 Newport Drive
Suite 506
Rolling Meadows, IL   60008-3841

847-255-1561
FAX 847-255-1699
E-Mail: iest@iest.org
Home Page: www.iest.org

Julie Kendrick, Executive Director

Single source of contamination control knowledge for the industry. Participate in exceptional continuing education training courses and interactive working group meetings.
Frequency: Spring

ILZRO Annual Meeting

International Lead Zinc Research Organization
2525 Meridian Parkway, Suite 100
PO Box 12036
Durham, NC   27713-2036

919-361-4647
FAX 919-361-1957
E-Mail: jhenric@ilzro.org
Home Page: www.ilzro.org

Stephen Wilkinson, President
Frank Goodwin, VP Materials Sciences
Scott Mooneyham, Treasurer
Rob Putnam, Director Communications

Focused on new technology and its role in managing risks in the production and use of lead, the drivers for health and environmental legislation and their likely future direction, trends, threats and opportunities in the global lead/zinc market, in particular those arising from the increasing desire for more low emission vehicles. Enabling delegates to meet a wide cross-section of key players in the lead producing and consuming countries.
Frequency: November

ISEE Annual Meetings

International Society for Ecological Economics
15 River Street
#204
Boston, MA   02108

703-790-1745
FAX 703-790-2672
E-Mail: iseemembership@burkinc.com
Home Page:
www.ecologicaleconomics.org
Social Media: *Facebook, Twitter, LinkedIn*

Heide Scheiter-Rohland, Director Membership

Provides an excellent opportunity for members to meet other ecological economists, test their ideas by presenting papers, and participate in the governance of the Society.
Frequency: Summer or Fall

ISEMNA Annual Meeting

International Society for Ecological
Modelling
University of California, Animal
Sciences Dept
One Shields Avenue
Davis, CA 95616-8521

530-752-5362
FAX 530-752-0175
Home Page: www.isemna.org

Wolfgang Pittroff, Secretary-General

Providing a forum for scientists from
around the world to exchange ideas, theories, concepts, methodologies, and results from ecological modelling that
address these important issues.
Frequency: August

International Association for Energy Economics Conference

International Association for Energy
Economics
28790 Chagrin Boulevard
Suite 350
Cleveland, OH 44122-4630

216-464-5365
FAX 216-464-2737
E-Mail: iaee@iaee.org
Home Page: www.iaee.org

David Williams, Executive Director

Semi-annual conference and exhibits relating to energy economics including
publications, consultants, energy database software.
325 Attendees

International Hazardous Materials Response Teams Conference

International Association of Fire Chiefs
4025 Fair Ridge Drive
Fairfax, VA 22033

703-273-0911
FAX 703-273-9363

One of the largest gatherings of hazmat
responders, facilitating new ideas. Dedicated exhibit hours and events, and indoor and outdoor exhibits.

NAAEE Annual Meeting

North American Association for
Environmental
2000 P Street NW
Suite 540
Washington, DC 20036

202-419-0412
FAX 202-419-0415
E-Mail: email@naaee.org
Home Page: www.naaee.org

William H Dent, Jr, Executive Director
Barbara Eager, Conference Coordinator
Paul Werth, Owner

Concurrent sessions, plenary sessions
and networking, as well as workshops,
field experiences and special events.
Frequency: Fall

NAAEE Conference

North American Assoc for
Environmental Education
2000 P Street NW
Suite 540
Washington, DC 20036

202-419-0412
FAX 202-419-0415
E-Mail: info@naaee.org
Home Page: www.naaee.org

Bridget Chisholm, Conference Manager

1200 Attendees
Frequency: Annual

NAEP Annual Meeting

National Association of Environmental
Professional
PO Box 2086
Bowie, MD 20718-2086

301-860-1140
888-251-9902
FAX 301-860-1141
E-Mail: office@naep.org
Home Page: www.naep.org

Sandi Worthman, Administrator

Learn unbiased information on environmental practices.
Frequency: Spring

NALMS Symposium

North American Lake Management
Society
4513 Vernon Boulevard, Suite 100
PO Box 5443
Madison, WI 53705-443

608-233-2836
FAX 608-233-3186

E-Mail: nalms@nalms.org
Home Page: www.nalms.org

Bev Clark, President
Reesa Evans, Secretary
Linda Green, Treasurer

A collection of professional presentations, general workshops and non-stop
discussions on managing lakes and reservoirs. Vendors are present with the latest lake management tools displayed.
Scientific and environmental minds will
offer a variety of relevant topical subject
matter to be covered in breakout educational sessions, and networking opportunities will allow for collaboration with
lake property association members and
other interested parties.
1700 Members
Frequency: Annual/October
Founded in 1980

NEDA Annual Meeting

National Environmental Development
Association
One Thomas Circle NW
10th Floor
Washington, DC 20006

202-878-8800
FAX 202-530-0659

Steve Hellem, Executive Director

Frequency: Washington, DC

NEHA Annual Educational Conference and Exhibition

National Environmental Health
Association
720 S Colorado Boulevard
Suite 970-S
Denver, CO 80246-1925

303-756-9090
FAX 303-691-9490
E-Mail: staff@neha.org
Home Page: www.neha.org

Toni Roland, Conference Coordinator
Kim Brandow, Marketing/Sales Manager

The National Environmental Health Association (NEHA) is a unique organization representing all professionals in
environmental health. NEHA offers credentials, publications, training, Journal
of Environmental Health, and discounts
for members. Each year NEHA conducts
the Annual Educational Conference and
Exhibition, this year it will be at the
Minneapolis Hilton in Minneapolis, MN.
2000 Attendees
Frequency: June-July

NEHA Annual Meeting

National Conference of Local
Environmental Health
c/o NEHA, 720 S Colorado Boulevard
South Tower, Suite 970
Denver, CO   80246-1925

303-756-9090
FAX 303-691-9490
E-Mail: nfabian@neha.org

Nelson E Fabian, Executive Director

Held with the National Environmental
Health Association.
Frequency: June

NESHTA Annual Meetings

National Environmental, Safety and
Health Training
PO Box 10321
Phoenix, AZ   85064-0321

602-956-6099
FAX 602-956-6399
E-Mail: info@neshta.org
Home Page: www.neshta.org

Charles L Richardson, Executive
Director
Joan J Jennings, Manager Association
Services
Suzanne Lanctot, Manager
Certification/Membership

The network for academic, government,
industrial, utility and consulting trainers
and training managers responsible for
protecting public health, workers, and
our physical environment.
Frequency: June

NIWR Annual Conference

National Institutes for Water Resources
47 Harkness Road
Pelham, MA   10002

413-253-5686
FAX 413-253-1309
E-Mail: tracy@uidaho.edu
Home Page: niwr.net

Jeffery Allen, President
Reagan Waskom, President-Elect
John Tracy, Secretary-Treasurer

Water Resource Institute directors and
associate directors are invited to join for
the annual meeting.
54 Members
Founded in 1974

NORA Semi-Annual Meetings

NORA: Association of Responsible
Recyclers
5965 Amber Ridge Road
Haymarket, VA   20169

703-753-4277
FAX 703-753-2445
E-Mail: sparker@noranews.org
Home Page: www.noranews.org

Scott D Parker, Executive Director

The liquid recycling industry's premier
networking and education event.
Frequency: May, November

NREP Annual Meetings

National Registry of Environmental
Professionals
PO Box 2099
Glenview, IL   60025

847-724-6631
FAX 847-724-4223
E-Mail: nrep@nrep.org
Home Page: www.nrep.org

Richard A Young, PhD, Executive
Director

Certification preparatory workshops,
technical papers and special seminars.
1000 Attendees
Frequency: Semi-Annual
Mailing list available for rent

National Coastal Conference

American Shore and Beach Preservation
Association
5460 Beaujolais Lane
Fort Myers, FL   33919

239-489-2616
FAX 239-362-9771
E-Mail: exdir@asbpa.org
Home Page: www.asbpa.org
Social Media: *Facebook, Twitter*

Harry Simmons, President
Kate Gooderham, Executive Director
Nicole Elko, Secretary
Russell Boudreau, VP
Brad Pickel, Treasurer

Federal, state and local coastal policy
and legal issues, shoreline processes and
coastal management, shoreline projects
and global coastal issues are discussed.
1M Members
Founded in 1926

National Environmental Balancing Bureau Meeting

National Environmental Balancing
Bureau
8575 Grovemont Circle
Gaithersburg, MD   20877-4121

301-977-3698
FAX 301-977-9589
Home Page: www.nebb.org

Michael Dolim, VP

Annual meeting and exhibits of testing
and balancing equipment, supplies and
services.

North American Wildlife and Natural Resources Conference

Wildlife Management Institute
1101 14th Street NW
Suite 801
Washington, DC   20005

202-371-1808
FAX 202-408-5059
Home Page:
www.wildlifemanagementinstitute.org

Meeting the challenges of modern conservation. Industry leaders dedicated to
the conservation, enhancement and management of North America's wildlife and
other natural resources.

SEG Annual Meeting

Society of Exploration Geophysicists
PO Box 702740
Tulsa, OK   74170-2740

918-497-5500
FAX 918-497-5557
E-Mail: web@seg.org
Home Page: www.seg.org/index.shtml

Mary Fleming, Executive Director
Vladimir Grechka, Editor

The world's largest oil, energy and mineral exposition showcasing cutting-edge
technology for use in exploration and associated industries. It is the premier
venue for individuals to meet and discuss new geophysical technologies and
their uses.
9300 Attendees
Frequency: October

SEGH Annual Meetings

Society for Environmental Geochemistry and Health
4698 S Forrest Avenue
Springfield, MO   65810

417-885-1166
FAX 417-881-6920
E-Mail: drbgwixson@wixson.com
Home Page: www.segh.net

Bobby Wixson, Director Membership

Environmental determinants of quality of life, including water resources, sediments and soil pollution and climate change, engineered solutions to hazardous waste including treatment of hazardous substances and regulatory solutions and approaches to hazardous substances, and all other environmental quality and human health issues.
Frequency: Summer-Fall

SER Annual Meeting

Society for Ecological Restoration
285 West 18th Street #1
Tucson, AZ   85701

520-622-5485
FAX 520-622-5491
E-Mail: info@ser.org
Home Page: www.ser.org

Mary Kay C LeFevour, Executive Director
Jane Cripps, Membership
Julie St John, Communications

Provides members (and non-members) with the opportunity to exchange ideas and information, participate in activities such as workshops and field trips, reconnect with friends and colleagues, and make new acquaintances.
Frequency: Fall

SER World Conference on Ecological Restoration

Society for Ecological Restoration
1017 O Street NW
Washington, DC   20001

202-299-9518
FAX 270-626-5485
E-Mail: info@ser.org
Home Page: www.ser.org

Steve Whisenant, Chair
Cara R. Nelson, Vice Chair
Mary Travaglini, Treasurer
Alan Unwin, Secretary

Provide members and non-members with the opportunity to exchange ideas and

information, participate in activities such as workshops and field trips, reconnect with friends and colleeagues, and make new acquaintances.
Frequency: Semi-Annual

SETAC Annual Meeting

Society of Environmental Toxicology and Chemistry
1010 N 12th Street
Pensacola, FL   32501-3367

850-469-1500
FAX 850-469-9778
E-Mail: rparrish@setac.org
Home Page: www.setac.org

Rodney Parrish, Executive Director
Greg Schifer, Manager

Information and collaboration on environmental toxicology and chemistry.
Frequency: Fall

SHE Bi-Ennial Meetings

Society for Human Ecology
College of the Atlantic
105 Eden Street
Bar Harbor, ME   04609-0180

207-288-5015
FAX 207-288-3780
E-Mail: carter@ecology.coa.edu
Home Page:
www.societyforhumanecology.org

Zachary Smith, President
Rob Dyball, Vice President
Lee Cerveny, Second Vice President
Chiho Watanabe, Third Vice President

Brings together scholars and practitioners associated with the study and practice of human ecology because of the importance of the disciplines' philosophy and applications in developing mutually beneficial solutions for society and the environment. A platform for sharing knowledge on present status and approaches for sustainable development.

SOCMA Annual Meeting

Synthetic Organic Chemical Manufacturers Assn
1850 M Street NW
Suite 700
Washington, DC   20036

202-721-4100
FAX 202-296-8120
E-Mail: info@socma.com
Home Page: www.socma.com

Joseph Acker, President
Vivian Diko, Executive Assistant &

CEO
Charlene Patterson, Director Human Resources

Industry leaders come together.
Frequency: Early Spring

Smart Energy Summit

Parks Associates
5310 Harvest Hill Road
Suite 235, Lock Box 162
Dallas, TX   75230-5805

972-490-1113
800-727-5711
E-Mail: info@parksassociates.com
Home Page: www.parksassociates.com

Tricia Parks, Founder and CEO
Stuart Sikes, President
Farhan Abid, Research Analyst
Bill Ablondi, Director, Home Systems Research
John Barrett, Director of Research

Smart Energy Summit is an annual three-day event that examines the opportunities and technical business requirements inherent in the consumer programs and advanced systems and services made possible by Smart Grids and Residential Energy Management solutions.
Frequency: Annual
Founded in 1986

Soil and Water Conservation Society Annual International Conference

Soil and Water Conservation Society
945 SW Ankeny Road
Ankeny, IA   50021-9764

515-289-2331
800-843-7645
FAX 515-289-1227
E-Mail: swsc@swsc.org
Home Page: www.swsc.org

Craig A Cox, Executive VP

Explores ways to improve the linkages among conservation science, policy and application at local, national, and international scales. The conference will provide participants an opportunity to teach skills, learn techniques, compare successes, and improve understanding.
1200 Attendees
Frequency: Annual

Take It Back

Raymond Communications
5111 Berwin Road
#115
College Park, MD 20740

301-345-4237
FAX 301-345-4768
E-Mail: michele@raymond.com
Home Page: www.raymond.com

Michele Raymond, Publisher/Editor

The conference brings in the top recycling policy experts from around the world to brief customers. We also have practical sessions with case histories on such issues as packaging design, design for environment in electronics, and lifecycle issues.
150 Attendees
Frequency: March
Founded in 1996

WINDPOWER Conference and Exhibition

American Wind Energy Association (AWEA)
1501 M Street NW
Suite 1000
Washington, DC 20005

202-383-2500
FAX 202-383-2505
E-Mail: windmail@awea.org
Home Page: www.windpowerexpo.org

Denise Bode, Chief Executive Officer
Pam Poisson, Chief Financial Officer
Britt Theismann, Chief Operating Officer
Rob Gramlich, Senior VP, Public Policy
Peter Kelley, VP, Public Affairs

The WINDPOWER Conference & Exhibition is produced by the American Wind Energy Association to provide a venue for the wind industry to network, do business, and solve problems. Recognized as one of the fastest-growing trade shows in the U.S., WINDPOWER includes nearly 1,400 exhibiting companies, thousands of qualified wind energy professionals, engaging educational information and unmatched networking opportunities and special events.
2500 Members
20000 Attendees
Frequency: Annual

Waterpower XIII

HCI Publications
410 Archibald Street
Kansas City, MO 64111-3001

816-931-1311
FAX 816-931-2015
E-Mail: waterpower@hcipub.com
Home Page: www.hcipub.com

Leslie Eden, Manager

The conference offers industry professionals a forum in which to share new ideas and approaches to move hydropower forward as the world's leading source of renewable energy. Containing 120 booths.
1,000 Attendees
Frequency: July-August

West Coast Energy Management Congress(EMC)

Association of Energy Engineers
4025 Pleasantdale Rd
Suite 420
Atlanta, GA 30340-4264

770-447-5083
FAX 770-446-3969
E-Mail: info@aeecenter.org
Home Page: www.aeecenter.org
Social Media: *Facebook, Twitter, LinkedIn, YouTube*

Eric A. Woodroof, President
Gary Hogsett, President Elect
Bill Younger, Secretary
Paul Goodman, C.P.A., Treasurer

The largest energy conference and technology expo held specifically for business, industrial and institutional energy users. Brings together the top experts in all areas of the field to help you set a clear, optimum path to energy efficiency, facility optimization and sustainability, as well as innovation solutions to improve your ROI.
8.2M Members
Founded in 1977

Wildlife Habitat Council Annual Symposium

Wildlife Habitat Council
8737 Colesville Road
Suite 800
Silver Spring, MD 20910

301-588-8994
FAX 301-588-4629

E-Mail: whc@wildlifehc.org
Home Page: www.wildlifehc.org

Bill Howard, President

The annual symposium brings together corporate, government and conservation leaders from around the globe for informative sessions, exhibits and field trips on environmental stewardship.
400 Attendees
Frequency: November

Wildlife Society Annual Conference

Wildlife Society
5410 Grosvenor Lane
Suite 200
Bethesda, MD 20814-2144

301-897-9770
FAX 301-530-2471
E-Mail: tws@wildlife.org
Home Page: www.wildlife.org

Lisa Moll, Program Assistant/Membership

Hear from industry leaders to discuss new and evolving trends and innovations in wildlife management and conservation, learn about the latest research from original research and techniques presented by wildlife professionals, connect with colleagues at the largest gathering of wildlife professionals in North America.
1200 Attendees
Frequency: September
Founded in 1994

World Future Energy Summit

Society of Environmental Journalists
PO Box 2492
Jenkintown, PA 19046

215-884-8174
FAX 215-884-8175
E-Mail: barke@sej.org
Home Page: www.sej.org
Social Media: *Facebook, Twitter*

Carolyn Whetzel, President
Peter Fairley, 1st Vice Pres
Jeff Burnside, 2nd Vice Pres
Don Hopey, Treasurer

World leaders, international policy makers, industry leaders, investors, experts, academia, intellectuals and journalists to find practical and sustainable solutions for today's energy security, climate change challenges and the advancement of clean technology.
Founded in 1990

Directories & Databases

A Guide to Internet Resources

American Assoc for the Advancement of
Science
1200 New York Avenue NW
Washington, DC   20005-3941

202-266-6721
FAX 202-371-9227
E-Mail: membership@aaas.org
Home Page: www.aaas.org

Nathan E Bell, Editor

Free online document provides a starting
point for finding internet resources. Topics include internet resources for math,
science, health, english, software, grants,
shareware, and much more.

ACSH Media Update

American Council on Science and
Health
1995 Broadway
2nd Floor
New York, NY   10023-5882

212-362-7044
FAX 212-362-4919
E-Mail: acsh@acsh.org
Home Page: www.acsh.org

Elizabeth Whelan, President
Jeff Stier, Associate Director

Frequency: Semi-Annual

ASMR Membership Directory

American Society of Mining and
Reclamation
3134 Montavesta Road
Lexington, KY   40502

859-335-6529
E-Mail: asmr@insightbb.com
Home Page: www.ca.uky.edu/assmr

Richard I Barnhisel, Executive Secretary

Frequency: Annual

Aboveground Storage Tank Management and SP CC Guide

ABS Group
PO Box 846304
Dallas, TX   75284-6304

FAX 301-921-0264

Acid Rain

Watts, Franklin
90 Sherman Turnpike
Danbury, CT   06816

203-797-3500
800-621-1115
FAX 203-797-3657

Lists over 4,000 citations, with abstracts,
to the worldwide literature on the
sources of acid rain and its effects on the
environment.
Frequency: Bibliographic

Alternative Energy Network Online

Environmental Information Networks
119 S Fairfax Street
Alexandria, VA   22314-3301

703-548-1202

Reports on news of all energy sources
designed as alternatives to conventional
fossil fuels, including wind, solar and al-
cohol fuels.
Frequency: Full-text

American Recycling Market: Directory/Reference Manual

Recycling Data Management
Corporation
PO Box 577
Ogdensburg, NY   13669-0577

315-785-9072

Offers information, in three volumes, encompassing over 15,000 recycling companies and centers.
Cost: $175.00
1000 Pages
Frequency: Annual
ISSN: 0885-2537

American Solar Energy Society Membership Directory

2400 Central Ave
Suite A
Boulder, CO   80301-2843

303-443-3130
FAX 303-443-3212
E-Mail: ases@ases.org
Home Page: www.ases.org

Bradley D Collins, Executive Director

Offers information on over 2,000 manufacturers, professors, architects, engineers and others in the solar energy
field.

Business and the Environment: A Resource Guide

Island Press
1718 Connecticut Ave NW
Suite 300
Washington, DC   20009-1148

202-232-7933
FAX 202-234-1328
E-Mail: info@islandpress.org
Home Page: www.islandpress.org

Chuck Savitt, President
Allison Pennell, Editor

List of approximately 185 business and
environmental educators working to in-
tegrate environmental issues into management, research, education and
practices.
Cost: $60.00

Canadian Environmental Directory

Grey House Publishing
4919 Route 22
PO Box 56
Amenia, NY   12501

518-789-8700
800-562-2139
FAX 845-373-6390
E-Mail: books@greyhouse.com
Home Page: www.greyhouse.com

Leslie Mackenzie, Publisher
Tannys Williams, Managing Editor

Canada's most complete national listing
of environmental associations and organizations, government regulators and
purchasing groups, product and service
companies, special libraries, and more.
Cost: $315.00
900 Pages
ISBN: 1-592372-24-9
Founded in 1981

Carcinogenicity Information Database of Environmental Substances

Technical Database Services
10 Columbus Circle
New York, NY   10019-1203

212-556-0001
FAX 212-556-0036

This database contains test results on the
carcinogenic and mutagenic effects of
approximately 1000 substances of environmental or health concerns.
Frequency: Numeric

Commercial Guide

Synthetic Organic Chemical
Manufacturers Assn
1850 M St NW
Suite 700
Washington, DC   20036-5803

202-721-4100
FAX 202-296-8120
E-Mail: info@socma.org
Home Page: www.socma.com

Joseph Acker, President
Vivian Diko, Executive Assistant &
CEO
Charlene Patterson, Director Human
Resources

Frequency: Annual

Conservation Directory

National Wildlife Federation
11100 Wildlife Center Dr
Reston, VA   20190-5362

703-438-6000
800-822-9919
FAX 703-438-3570
Home Page: www.nwf.org

Mark Van Putten, CEO

Federal agencies, national and international organizations and state government agencies.
Cost: $20.00
500 Pages
Frequency: Annual

Department of Energy Annual Procurement and Financial Assistance Report

US Department of Energy
1000 Independence Ave SW
Washington, DC   20585-0001

202-586-5000
FAX 202-586-0573
Home Page: www.energy.gov

Mary Lein, Manager

Offers a list of universities, research cen-
ters and laboratories that represent the
Department of Energy.
Frequency: Annual

Directory of Environmental Websites: Online Micro Edition

US Environmental Directories
PO Box 65156
Saint Paul, MN   55165-0156

612-331-6050
Home Page:

www.geocities.com/usenvironmentaldire
ctories
Roger N McGrath, Publisher
John C Brainard, Editor

The Directory is a complete guide to the
environmental movement on the
Internet, provides a concise, practical
listing of over 190 of the major Internet
addresses of the Environmental Movement. A clear, understandable and comprehensive guide to national and
international environmental organizations, directories, networks and services
on the Internet.
Cost: $25.75
48 Pages
ISSN: 1096-3316
Founded in 1998

Directory of International Periodicals & Newsletters on Built Environments

Division of Mineral Resources
PO Box 3667
Charlottesville, VA   22903-0667

434-951-6341
FAX 434-951-6365
Home Page: www.mme.state.va.us

More than 1,400 international periodicals and newsletters that cover architec-
tural design and the building industry,
and the aspects of the environment that
deal with the industry are covered.
Cost: $6.00
29 Pages

EDOCKET

Environmental Protection Agency
1200 Pennsylvania Avenue NW
Mail Code 3213A
Washington, DC   20460

202-260-2090
FAX 202-566-0545
Home Page: www.epa.gov

An electronic public docket and on-line
comment system designed to expand access to documents in EPA's major
dockets.
Frequency: Full-text

EMS Membership Roster

Environmental Mutagen Society
1821 Michael Faraday Drive
Suite 300
Reston, VA   20190

703-438-8220
FAX 703-438-3113

E-Mail: emshq@ems-us.org
Home Page: www.ems-us.org

Tonia Masson, Executive Director

Frequency: Irregular

ETAD Annual Report

ETAD North America
1850 M St NW
Suite 700
Washington, DC   20036-5810

202-721-4100
FAX 202-296-8120
Home Page: www.etad.com

Jill Aker, President

Frequency: Annual

Ecological Farming Conference Participants Directory

Ecological Farming Association
406 Main St
Suite 313
Watsonville, CA   95076-4623

831-763-2111
FAX 831-763-2112
E-Mail: info@eco-farm.org
Home Page: www.eco-farm.org

Kristin Rosenow, Executive Director

About 1,000 organic farmers, farm suppliers and consultants, produce handlers,
researchers, extension, agents, students,
organization representatives, and others
who attended the annual Ecological
Farming conference.
Cost: $5.00

Ecology Abstracts

Cambridge Scientific Abstracts
7200 Wisconsin Ave
Suite 601
Bethesda, MD   20814-4890

301-961-6700
800-843-7751
FAX 301-961-6790
E-Mail: market@csa.com
Home Page: www.csa.com

Andrew M Snyder, President
Theodore Caris, Publisher
Robert Hilton, Editor
Mark Furneaux, VP Marketing
Angela Hitti, Production Manager

This large database updated continuously, offers over 150,000 citations, with
abstracts, to the worldwide literature
available on ecology and the environ-

ment.
Cost: $945.00
Frequency: Monthly

Education for the Earth: A Guide to Top Environmental Studies Programs

Peterson's Guides
202 Carnegie Center
#2123
Princeton, NJ   08540-6239

800-338-3282
FAX 609-869-4531

Colleges and universities that offer programs in environment and conservation are listed.
Cost: $10.95
192 Pages

Educational Communications

Educational Communications
PO Box 351419
Los Angeles, CA   90035-9119

310-559-9160
FAX 310-559-9160
E-Mail: ECNP@aol.com
Home Page: www.ecoprojects.org

Nancy Pearlman, Editor

Directory of over 6,500 environmental organizations worldwide are the focus of this comprehensive directory. Over 400 1/2 hour television shows on the environment. Environmental directions - radio has over 1,500 interviews with ecological experts. Monthly newsletter, TV and radio series about ecological problems and solutions; promotion of ecotourem. Audo/video cassettes available.
Cost: $20.00
244 Pages
Frequency: Annual Paperback
Mailing list available for rent

El Environmental Services Directory

Environmental Information Networks
7301 Ohms Lane
Suite 460
Eding, MN   55439

952-831-2473
FAX 952-831-6550
E-Mail: ei@mr.net
Home Page: www.envirobiz.com

Cary Perket

Waste-handling facilities, transportation and spill response firms, laboratories and the broad scope of environmental services. Online versions are also available.
Cost: $1250.00
Frequency: Biennial
ISSN: 1053-475N
Founded in 1984

Emergency Response Directory for Hazardous Materials Accidents

Odin Press
PO Box 536
New York, NY   10021-0011

212-605-0338

Pamela Lawrence, Editor

Over 1,000 federal, state and local governmental agencies, chemical manufacturers and transporters, hotlines and strike teams, burn care centers, civil defense and disaster centers and other organizations concerned with the containment and cleanup of chemical spills and other hazardous materials accidents.
Cost: $36.00
Frequency: Biennial

Energy

WEFA Group
800 Baldwin Tower Boulevard
Eddystone, PA   19022-1368

610-490-4000
FAX 610-490-2770
E-Mail: info@wefa.com
Home Page: www.wefa.com

Peter McNabb

This database covers energy supply and demand, including weekly rig count and gasoline prices by states; reserves, stocks, production, consumption and trade of petroleum products.

Energy Data Base

Newport Associates
7400 E Orchard Road
Suite 320
Englewood, CO   80111-2528

FAX 303-779-0908

This database covers financial, as well as reserves and production data, for over 450 oil companies in over 20 world regions.
Frequency: Numeric

Energy Engineering: Directory of Software for Energy Managers and Engineers

Fairmont Press
700 Indian Trail Lilburn Rd NW
Lilburn, GA   30047-6862

770-925-9388
FAX 770-381-9865
Home Page: www.fairmontpress.com

Brian Douglas, President

Directory of services and supplies to the industry.
Cost: $15.00
Circulation: 8,500
ISSN: 0199-8895

Energy Science and Technology

US Department of Energy
PO Box 62
Oak Ridge, TN   37831-0062

865-574-1000
FAX 865-576-2865
E-Mail: OSTIWebmaster@osti.gov
Home Page: www.osti.gov

This large database offers over 3 million citations, with abstracts, to literature pertaining to all fields of energy.
Frequency: Bibliographic

Energy Statistics Spreadsheets

Institute of Gas Technology
1700 S Mount Prospect Rd
Des Plaines, IL   60018-1804

847-768-0664
FAX 847-768-0669
E-Mail: gtiadmin@gastechnology.org
Home Page: www.gastechnology.org

Carol L Worster, Manager
Edward Johnston, Managing Director

The coverage of this database encompasses worldwide energy industry statistics, including production, consumption, reserves, imports and prices.

Energy User News: Energy Technology Buyers Guide

Chilton Company
300 Park Ave
Suite 19
New York, NY   10022-7409

212-751-3596
FAX 212-443-7701
Home Page: www.chiltonfunds.com

Richard L Chilton Jr, Owner

A list of about 1,500 manufacturers, dealers and distributors of energy conservation and used equipment.
Cost: $10.00
Frequency: Annual
Circulation: 40,000

Environmental Bibliography
International Academy at Santa Barbara
5385 Hollister Avenue
#210
Santa Barbara, CA   93111

805-683-8889
FAX 805-965-6071
E-Mail: info@iasb.org
Home Page: www.iasb.org

Over 615,000 citations are offered in this database, aimed at scientific, technical and popular periodical literature dealing with the environment.
Cost: $1750.00
Frequency: Bibliographic
ISSN: 1053-1440
Founded in 1972

Environmental Cost Estimating Software Report
Donley Technology
PO Box 152
Colonial Beach, VA   22443-0152

804-224-9427
800-201-1595
FAX 804-224-7958
E-Mail: donleytech@donleytech.com
Home Page: www.donleytech.com

Elizabeth Donley, Editor
John Donley, Editor

Profiles 20 software packages for estimating the cost of environmental projects, including detailed product descriptions, tables comparing system features, and contact information.
Cost: $195.00
162 Pages
ISBN: 1-891682-05-9
Founded in 1996
Printed in on matte stock

Environmental Health & Safety Dictionary
ABS Group
PO Box 846304
Dallas, TX   75284-6304

FAX 301-921-0264

Lydia Simpson, Manager

Environmental Law Handbook
ABS Group
PO Box 846304
Dallas, TX   75284-6304

FAX 301-921-0264

Environmental Protection Agency Headquarters Telephone Directory
Environmental Protection Agency
1200 Pennsylvania Avenue NW
Pittsburgh, PA   15250-7954

412-442-4000
FAX 202-512-2250
Home Page:
www.epa.gov/customerservice/phonebook

Ken Bowman, Executive Director

Directory of services and supplies to the industry.
Cost: $15.00
400 Pages

Environmental Resource Handbook
Grey House Publishing
4919 Route 22
PO Box 56
Amenia, NY   12501

518-789-8700
800-562-2139
FAX 845-373-6390
E-Mail: books@greyhouse.com
Home Page: www.greyhouse.com

Leslie Mackenzie, Publisher
Richard Gottlieb, Editor

The most up-to-date and comprehensive source for Environmental Resources and Statistics. Included is contact information for resource listings in addition to statistics and rankings on hundreds of important topics such as recycling, air and water quality, climate, toxic chemicals and more.
Cost: $155.00
1200 Pages
ISBN: 1-592371-95-7
Founded in 1981

Environmental Statutes
Government Institutes
4 Research Place
Suite 200
Rockville, MD   20850-3226

301-921-2323
FAX 301-921-0264
Home Page: www.govinst.com

Two-volume set. Complete and exact text of the statues and amendments made by Congress concerning environmental law.
Cost: $125.00
1678 Pages
Frequency: Paperback
ISBN: 0-865879-33-8

Fibre Market News: Paper Recycling Markets Directory
Recycling Media Group GIE Publishers
4012 Bridge Avenue
Cleveland, OH   44113-3320

216-961-4130
800-456-0707
FAX 216-961-0364
Home Page: www.giemedia.com

A list of over 2,000 dealers, brokers, packers and graders of paper stock in the United States and Canada.
Cost: $28.00
Frequency: Annual
Circulation: 3,000

Floodplain Management: State & Local Programs
Association of State Floodplain Managers
2809 Fish Hatchery Rd
Suite 204
Fitchburg, WI   53713-5020

608-274-0123
FAX 608-274-0696
E-Mail: asfpm@floods.org
Home Page: www.floods.org

Larry A Larson, Executive Director
Alison Stierli, Member Services Coordinator
Anita Larson, Member Services
Mark Riebau, Project Manager

The most comprehensive source assembled to date, this report summarizes and analyzes various state and local programs and activities.
Cost: $25.00

Geothermal Progress Monitor

Office of Geothermal Technologies
EE-12
1000 Independence Avenue SW
Washington, DC   20585-0001

202-586-1361
FAX 202-586-8185

Allan J Jelacic, Director

Lists of operating, planned and under
construction geothermal electric generating plants; geothermal articles and publications; federal and state government
employees active in geothermal energy
development.
Frequency: Annual

Grey House Safety & Security Directory

Grey House Publishing
4919 Route 22
PO Box 56
Amenia, NY   12501

518-789-8700
800-562-2139
FAX 845-373-6390
E-Mail: books@greyhouse.com
Home Page: www.greyhouse.com

Leslie Mackenzie, Publisher
Richard Gottlieb, Editor
Kristen Thatcher, Production Manager

Comprehensive guide to the safety and
security industry, including articles,
checklists, OSHA regulations and product listings. Focuses on creating and
maintaing a safe and secure enviroment,
and dealing specifically with hazardous
materials, noise and vibration, workplace
preparation and maintenance, electrical
and lighting safety, fire and rescue and
more.
Cost: $165.00
1600 Pages
ISBN: 1-592373-75-5
Founded in 1981

Handling Dyes Safely - A Guide for the Protection of Workers Handling Dyes

ETAD North America
1850 M St NW
Suite 700
Washington, DC   20036-5810

202-721-4100
FAX 202-296-8120
Home Page: www.etad.com

Jill Aker, President

Hazardous Materials Guide

JJ Keller
PO Box 368
Neenah, WI   54957-0368

920-722-2848
800-327-6868
FAX 800-727-7516
E-Mail: sales@jjkeller.com
Home Page: www.jjkeller.com

Webb Shaw, Editor

A complete reference guide of hazardous
materials regulations.

Hazardous Waste Guide

JJ Keller
PO Box 368
Neenah, WI   54957-0368

920-722-2848
800-327-6868
FAX 800-727-7516
E-Mail: sales@jjkeller.com
Home Page: www.jjkeller.com

Webb Shaw, Editor

Contains word-for-word regulations.

Hydro Review: Industry Sourcebook Issue

HCI Publications
410 Archibald St
Kansas City, MO   64111-3288

816-931-1311
FAX 816-931-2015
E-Mail: hci@aol.com
Home Page: www.hcipub.com

Leslie Eden, President

List of over 800 manufacturers and sup-
pliers of products and services to the hy-
droelectric industry in the US and
Canada.
Cost: $20.00
180 Pages
Frequency: Annual December
Circulation: 5000
Founded in 1984
Printed in 4 colors on glossy stock

IES Membership Directory

International Ecotourism Society
733 15th Street NW
Suite 1000
Washington, DC   20005

202-547-9203
FAX 202-387-7915

E-Mail: ecomail@ecotourism.org
Home Page: www.ecotourism.org

Martha Honey, Executive Director
Amos Bien, Director International
Programs
Neal Inamdar, Director
Finance/Administration
Frequency: Annual

International Directory of Human Ecologists

Society for Human Ecology
College of the Atlantic
105 Eden Street
Bar Harbor, ME   04609-0180

207-288-5015
FAX 207-288-3780
E-Mail: carter@ecology.coa.edu
Home Page:
www.societyforhumanecology.org

Barbara Carter, Assistant to Executive
Director

Frequency: Irregular

LEXIS Environmental Law Library

Mead Data Central
9443 Springboro Pike
Dayton, OH   45401

888-223-6337
FAX 518-487-3584
Home Page: www.lexis-nexis.com

Andrew Prozes, CEO

This database contains decisions related
to environmental law from the Supreme
Court and other legislative bodies.
Frequency: Full-text

NIWR Member Directory

National Institutes for Water Resources
47 Harkness Road
Pelham, MA   10002

413-253-5686
FAX 413-253-1309
E-Mail: godfrey@tei.umass.edu
Home Page: snr.unl.edu/NIWR

Paul Joseph Godfrey, PhD, Executive
Director

National Directory of Conservation Land Trusts

Land Trust Alliance
1319 F Street NW
Suite 501
Washington, DC   20004-1106

202-638-4725
FAX 202-638-4730
E-Mail: lta@lta.org
Home Page: www.lta.org

More than 1,200 nonprofit land conservation organizations at the local and regional levels are profiled.
Cost: $12.00
210 Pages
Frequency: Biennial

National Environmental Data Referral Service

US National Environmental Data
Referral Service
1825 Connecticut Avenue NW
Washington, DC   20235-0003

202-606-4089

More than 22,200 data resources that have available data on climatology and meteorology, ecology and pollution, geography, geophysics and geology, hydrology and limnology, oceanography and transmissions from remote sensing satellites.
Frequency: Quarterly

National Organic Directory

Community Alliance with Family
Farmers
PO Box 363
Davis, CA   95617-0363

530-756-8518
800-892-3832
FAX 530-756-7857
E-Mail: nod@caff.org
Home Page: www.caff.org

Wriiten for all sectors of the booming organic food and fiber industry. Offers international listing with full contact information and extensive, cross-referenced index - Also provides regulatory updates, essays by industry leaders and other ressources.
Cost: $47.95
324 Pages
Frequency: Annual
Circulation: 2,500
ISBN: 1-891894-04-8
Founded in 1983

Occupational Safety and Health Law Handbook

ABS Group
PO Box 846304
Dallas, TX   75284-6304

FAX 301-921-0264

POWER

US Department of Energy
Forrestal Building
5H - 021
Washington, DC   20585-0001

202-646-5095
FAX 202-586-1605
E-Mail: roger.meyer@hd.doe.gov
Home Page: www.eren.doe.gov

A large database offering information on all forms of energy, including fossil, nuclear, solar, geothermal and electrical.
Frequency: Bibliographic

Pollution Abstracts

Cambridge Scientific Abstracts
7200 Wisconsin Ave
Suite 601
Bethesda, MD   20814-4890

301-961-6700
FAX 301-961-6790
E-Mail: market@csa.com
Home Page: www.csa.com

Andrew M Snyder, President
Ted Caris, Publisher
Evelyn Beck, Editor
Mark Furneaux, VP Marketing
Angela Hitti, Production Manager

This database offers information on environmental pollution research and related engineering studies.
Cost: $985.00
Frequency: Monthly

Public Citizen Organizations

Public Citizen
215 Pennsylvania Ave SE
Suite 3
Washington, DC   20003-1188

202-544-4985
FAX 202-547-7392
E-Mail: cmep@citizen.org

Bob Ritter, Manager
Patricia Lovera, Organizer
Ronald Taylor, Manager

We provide many publications regarding nuclear safety, nuclear waste, water, food, and energy deregulation.
Frequency: Annual

RCRA Hazardous Wastes Handbook

ABS Group
PO Box 846304
Dallas, TX   75284-6304

FAX 301-921-0264

Recycling Today: Recycling Products & Services Buyers Guide

Recycling Today GIE Publishers
4012 Bridge Avenue
Cleveland, OH   44113-3320

216-961-4130
FAX 216-961-0364

Richard Foster, President
James Keefe, Publisher
Mark Phillips, Editor
Rosalie Slusher, Circulation Director
Jami Childs, Production Manager

Directory of services and supplies to the industry.
Cost: $19.95
Frequency: Annual
Circulation: 22,000

US Environmental Law and Regulations

ABS Group
PO Box 846304
Dallas, TX   75284-6304

FAX 301-921-0264

Using Multiobjective Management to Reduce Flood Losses in Your Watershed

Association of State Floodplain
Managers
2809 Fish Hatchery Rd
Suite 204
Fitchburg, WI   53713-5020

608-274-0123
FAX 608-274-0696
E-Mail: asfpm@floods.org
Home Page: www.floods.org

Larry A Larson, Executive Director
Alison Stierli, Member Services
Coordinator

Introduction to multiobjective management and planning process that helps a community select suitable flood loss reduction measures.
Cost: $15.00

Waste Manifest Software Report
Donley Technology
PO Box 152
Colonial Beach, VA   22443-0152

804-224-9427
800-201-1595
FAX 804-224-7958
E-Mail: donleytech@donleytech.com
Home Page: www.donleytech.com

Elizabeth Donley, Editor

Profiles 30 software packages for solid and hazardous waste management, including detailed product descriptions, tables comparing system features, and contact information.
Cost: $97.50
118 Pages
ISBN: 1-891682-01-6
Founded in 1996
Printed in on matte stock

Water Environment and Technology Buyers Guide/Yearbook
Water Environment Federation
601 Wythe St
Alexandria, VA   22314-1994

703-684-2400
800-666-0206
FAX 703-684-2492
Home Page: www.wef.org

Bill Bertera, Executive Director

Offers listings of the Water Environment Federation and consultant members.
Cost: $28.00
Frequency: Annual
ISSN: 1044-9943

Weather America
Grey House Publishing
4919 Route 22
PO Box 56
Amenia, NY   12501

518-789-8700
800-562-2139
FAX 845-373-6390
E-Mail: books@greyhouse.com
Home Page: www.greyhouse.com

Leslie Mackenzie, Publisher
Richard Gottlieb, Editor

Provides extensive climatological data for over 4,000 places throughout the United States - states, counties, cities, and towns. Included are rankings across the US for precipitation, snowfall, fog, humidity, wind speed and more.
Cost: $175.00
2020 Pages
ISBN: 1-891482-29-7
Founded in 1981

Who's Who in Training
National Environmental, Safety and Health Training
5320 N 16th Street
Suite 114
Phoenix, AZ   85016-3241

602-956-6099
FAX 602-956-6399
E-Mail: info@neshta.org
Home Page: www.neshta.org

Charles L Richardson, Executive Director
Joan J Jennings, Manager Association Services
Suzanne Lanctot, Manager Certification/Membership

Frequency: Annual

Wilderness Preservation: A Reference Handbook
ABC-CLIO
PO Box 1911
Santa Barbara, CA   93116-1911

805-705-9339

Offers a list of agencies and organizations concerned with wilderness preservation.

Wind Energy Conversion Systems
South Dakota Renewable Energy Association
PO Box 491
Pierre, SD   57501-0491

605-224-8641

Offers valuable information for electrical-output wind machine manufacturers.
Cost: $2.00
45 Pages
Frequency: Annual

World Directory of Environmental Organizations
California Institute of Public Affairs
PO Box 189040
Sacramento, CA   95818-9040

916-442-2472
FAX 916-442-2478
E-Mail: info@cipahq.org
Home Page: www.interenvironment.org

Over 2,500 governmental, intergovernmental and United Nations organizations are covered.
Cost: $47.00
232 Pages

Your Financial Institution & the Environment
Environmental Bankers Association
310 King St
Suite 410
Alexandria, VA   22314-3212

703-548-7060
800-966-7475
FAX 703-518-8314
E-Mail: eba@envirobank.org
Home Page: www.envirobank.org

Deborah Shockley, Manager

Frequency: Annual

Your Resource Guide to Environmental Organizations
Smiling Dolphin Press
4 Segura
Irvine, CA   92612-1726

Information is offered, in three separate sections, on non-governmental organizations, federal agencies and state agencies that address environmental concerns.
Cost: $15.95
514 Pages

Fishing

Associations

American Fisheries Society

5410 Grosvenor Ln
Suite 110
Bethesda, MD 20814-2199

301-897-8616
FAX 301-897-8096
E-Mail: main@fisheries.org
Home Page: www.fisheries.org
Social Media: *Facebook, Twitter*

Bill Fisher, President
John Boreman, President-Elect
Bob Hughes, First Vice President
Donna Parrish, Second Vice President

AFS promotes scientific research and enlightened management of resources for optimum use and enjoyment by the public. It also encourages a comprehensive education for fisheries scientists and continuing on-the-job training
Cost: $100.00
8500 Members
Frequency: Membership Fee
Founded in 1870

American Institute of Fishery Research Biologists

205 Blades Road
Havelock, NC 28532

E-Mail: feeshdr@starfishnet.com
Home Page: www.aifrb.org

Richard Beamish, President
Allen Shimada, Treasurer
Kathy Dickson, Secretary

A professional organization founded to promote conservation and proper utilization of fishery resources through application of fishery science and related sciences.
1000 Members
Founded in 1956

American Littoral Society

28 West 9th Road
Broad Channel, NY 11693

718-318-9344
E-Mail: driepe@nyc.rr.com
Home Page: www.alsnyc.org

Eileen Kennedy, Director of Communications/Dev.
Mary Ann Griesbach, Membership Director

Dedicated to the environmental well-being of coastal habitat.
5000+ Members
Frequency: Membership Fee: $30-$35
Founded in 1961

American Shrimp Processors Association

PO Box 4867
Biloxi, MS 39535

228-806-9600
FAX 228-385-2565
E-Mail: director@americanshrimp.org
Home Page: americanshrimp.org

C. David Veal, Executive Director
Andrew Blanchard, President
Mark Leckich, Vice-President
Scott Young, Secretary/ Treasurer

A non-profit trade organization designed to represent U.S. shrimp processors in all aspects of business. Allowing processors and related industries to work together to foster a business and technological climate in which its members can prosper while providing the highest quality product to its customers.
Founded in 1964

Association of Fish and Wildlife Agencies

444 N Capitol St NW
Suite 725
Washington, DC 20001-1553

202-624-7890
FAX 202-624-7891
E-Mail: info@fishwildlife.org
Home Page: www.fishwildlife.org
Social Media: *Facebook, Twitter*

Dr. Jon Gassett, President
Jeff Vonk, Vice President
Dave Chanda, Secretary/Treasurer

The organization that represents all of North America's fish and wildlife agencies that promotes sound management ans conservation, and speaks with a unified voice on important fish and wildlife issues.
Founded in 1902

Association of Zoos and Aquariums

8403 Colesville Rd
Suite 710
Silver Spring, MD 20910-6331

301-562-0777
FAX 301-562-0888
E-Mail: membership@aza.org

Home Page: www.aza.org
Social Media: *Facebook, Twitter*

L. Patricia Simmons, Chair
Tom Schmid, Chair-Elect
Jackie Ogden, PhD, Vice-Chair

A nonprofit organization dedicated to the advancement of accredited zoos and aquariums in the areas of animal care, wildlife conservation, education and science.
200 Members
Founded in 1924

Atlantic States Marine Fisheries Commission

1050 N. Highland St.
Suite 200 A-N
Arlington, VA 22201

703-842-0740
FAX 703-842-0741
E-Mail: tberger@asmfc.org
Home Page: www.asmfc.org

Robert H. Boyles Jr., Chair
Paul Diodati, Vice-Chair
John V. O'Shea, Executive Director

The commission was formed by the fifteen Atlantic coast states. It serves as a deliberative body, coordinating the conservation and management of the states shared near shore fishery resources.
45 Members
Founded in 1942

California Fisheries & Seafood Institute

1521 I St
Sacramento, CA 95814-2016

916-441-5560
FAX 916-446-1063
E-Mail: fishead123@aol.com
Home Page: www.calseafood.net

Bill Dawson, President
Kevin Joyce, Treasurer
Sal Balestrieri, Vice President-Legislative
Don Disraeli, Vice President-Promotion
Steve Foltz, Chairman of the Board

Regional trade organization representing members of the consumer seafood supply industry.
130+ Members
Founded in 1954

Catfish Farmers of America

1100 Highway 82 E
Suite 202
Indianola, MS   38751-2251

662-887-2699
FAX 662-887-6857
Home Page:
www.catfishfarmersofamerica.org

Hugh Warren, President

Represents the largest aquaculture industry in the United States. Represents the interests of farm-raised catfish industry of farmers, processors, feed mills, researchers and supplier industries.
Cost: $40.00
Frequency: Membership Fee
Founded in 1968

Fishing Vessel Owners Association

4005 20th Ave W
Room 232, West Wall Bldg
Seattle, WA   98199-1273

206-284-4720
FAX 206-283-3341
Home Page: www.fvoa.org

Bob Alverson, Executive Director
Carol Batteen, Executive Assistant

Trade association of longline vessel operators which promotes safety at sea, habitat-friendly gear with minimum bycatch and ensures competitive pricing.
Founded in 1914

Garden State Seafood Association

210 W State St
Trenton, NJ   08608-1006

609-394-2828
FAX 609-898-6070
E-Mail: njsha@voicenet.com
Home Page: www.fishingnj.org

Greg DiDomenico, Executive Director
Nils Stolpe, Communications Director

Dedicated to assure that New Jersey's marine resources are managed responsibly and are able to be enjoyed by anglers and seafood consumers for generations.

Great Lakes Fishery Commission

2100 Commonwealth Blvd
Suite 100
Ann Arbor, MI   48105

734-662-3209
FAX 734-741-2010
E-Mail: info@glfc.org

Home Page: www.glfc.org
Social Media: *Facebook, Twitter*

Dr Christopher Goddard, Manager
Mr Bruce Swart, CFO

The commission has two major responsibilities; to develop coordinated programs of research on the Great Lakes and to formulate and implement a program to eradicate or minimize sea lamprey populations in the Great Lakes.
Founded in 1955

Gulf and Caribbean Fisheries Institute (GCCFI)

C/O Florida Fish and Wildlife Conservation
2796 Overseas Highway, Suite 119
Marathon, FL   33050

305-289-2330
FAX 305-289-2334
E-Mail: leroy.creswell@gcfi.org
Home Page: www.gcfi.org
Social Media: *Facebook*

Jim Franks, Chairman
Virdin Brown, Vice-Chairman
LeRoy Creswell, Executive Secretary
Mel Goodwin, PhD, Treasurer
Bob Glazer, Executive Director

Provides information exchange among governmental, non-governmental, academic and commerical users of marine resources in the Gulf and Carribean Region
950 Members
Founded in 1947

Gulf of Mexico Fishery Management Council

2203 N Lois Avenue
Suite 1100
Tampa, FL   33607

813-348-1630
888-833-1844
FAX 813-348-1711
E-Mail: info@gulfcouncil.org
Home Page: www.gulfcouncil.org

Wayne Swingle, Executive Director
Rick Leard, Deputy Executive Director

The council preserves fishery plans which are designed to manage fishery resources from where state waters end out to the 200 mile limit of the Gulf of Mexico.
Founded in 1976

International Institute of Fisheries Economics and Trade

Dept of Agricultural & Resource Economic
Oregon State University
Corvallis, OR   97331-3601

541-737-1416
FAX 541-737-2563
E-Mail: iifet@oregonstate.edu
Home Page:
www.oregonstate.edu/dept/iifet

Ann L Shriver, Executive Director
Dr. Rebecca Metzner, President
Dr. Ralph Townsend, President-Elect

An international group of economists, government managers, private industry members, and others interested in the exchange of research and information on marine resource issues. Founded to promote interaction and exchange between people from all countries and professional disciplines about marine resource economics and trade issues.
Founded in 1982

National Fisheries Institute

7918 Jones Branch Dr
Suite 700
Mc Lean, VA   22102-3319

703-752-8880
FAX 703-752-7583
E-Mail: contact@nfi.org
Home Page: www.aboutseafood.com
Social Media: *Facebook, Twitter*

John Connely, President
Gavin Gibbons, Director, Media Relations

Members are farmers, food processors and food distributors with an interest in aquaculture.
380 Members
Founded in 1946

National Shellfisheries Association

C/O US EPA, Atlantic Ecology Division
27 Tazewell Drive
Narragansett, RI   02880

631-653-6327
FAX 631-653-6327
E-Mail: sectretariat@shellfish.org
Home Page: www.shellfish.org

R. LeRoy Creswell, President
Christopher V. Davis, President-Elect
George E. Flimlin, VP & Program Chair
Marta Gomez-Chiarri, Secretary

An international organization of scientists, management officials and members of industry, all deeply concerned with the biology, ecology, production, economics and management of shellfish resources-clams, oysters, mussels, scallops, snails, shrimp, lobsters, crabs, among many other species of commercial importance.
Cost: $85.00
1000 Members
Frequency: Membership Fee
Founded in 1908

North Carolina Fisheries Association

PO Box 12303
New Bern, NC   28561

252-745-0225
FAX 252-633-9616
E-Mail: peggy@ncfish.org
Home Page: www.ncfish.org

Billy Carl Tillett, Chairman
Sherrill Styron, Vice Chairman
Sean McKeon, President
Janice Smith, Treasurer

Non-profit trade organization created to facilitate the promotion of North Carolina families, heritage and seafood through accessible data about the commercial fishing industry. NCFA lobbies Local, State, and Federal legislators and engages in a wide scope of public awareness projects.
Founded in 1952

Pacific Coast Federation of Fishermen's Associations

Building 991, Marine Drive
Po Box 29370
San Francisco, CA   94129-0370

415-561-5080
FAX 415-561-5464
E-Mail: fish1ifr@aol.com
Home Page: www.pcffa.org

Zeke Grader, Executive Director
Chuck Wise, President

Commercial fishermen's organizations from California to Alaska. Works to prevent and improve the resources of the commercial fishing industry, protect rivers from herbicide and pesticide applications that may threaten salmon populations, maintain activity within the

industry, regain local control over fisheries management.
22 Members
Founded in 1976

Pacific Seafood Processors Association

1900 West Emerson Place
Suite 205
Seattle, WA   98119-1649

206-281-1667
FAX 206-283-2387
E-Mail: nancy@pspafish.net
Home Page: www.pspafish.net

Glenn Reed, President

Trade association to foster a better public understanding of the seafood industry and its value to the regional and national economies.
25 Members
Founded in 1914

Recreational Fishing Alliance

Po Box 3080
New Gretna, NJ   08224

609-404-1060
888-564-6732
FAX 609-294-3812
E-Mail: rfa@joinrfa.org
Home Page: www.joinrfa.org

James Donofrio, Executive Director
Gary Caputi, Corporate Relations Director
Courtney Howell Thompson, Marketing Coordinator/PR

An organization that supports and fights back against federal government state legislatures impose unreasonable restrictions on our ability to enjoy recreational fishing.
Frequency: $35/Membership

Southeastern Fisheries Association

1118-B Thomasville Rd.
Tallahassee, FL   32303-6238

850-224-0612
FAX 850-222-3663
Home Page: seafoodsustainability.us

Robert P Jones, Executive Director

To defend, preserve and enhance the commercial fishing industry in the southeastern United States for present participants as well as future generations through all legal means.
Founded in 1952

West Coast Seafood Processors Association

1618 SW 1st Ave
Suite 318
Portland, OR   97201-5708

503-227-5076
FAX 503-227-0237
E-Mail: seafood@integraonline.com
Home Page: www.wcspa.com

Rod Moore, Executive Director

Serves the needs of the shore-based seafood processors in California, Oregon and Washington, helping them to face and survive economic, environmental and regulatory challenges.
13 Members

Women's Fisheries Network

2442 NW Market Street
#243
Seattle, WA   98107

206-789-1987
FAX 206-789-1987
Home Page: www.fis.com/wfn

Stephanie Madsen, President

Men and women dedicated to education of issues confronting the fishing and seafood industry.
2000 Members
Founded in 1983

Newsletters

Aquaculture North America

Capamara Communications
815 1st Ave
#301
Seattle, WA   98104

250-474-3982
800-936-2266
FAX 250-478-3979
E-Mail: jeremy@capamara.com
Home Page: www.naqua.com

Peter Chetteburgh, Editor-in-Chief
Jeremy Thain, Sales Manager
James Lewis, Production Department

Follows the trends, issues, people and events that have set the pace for the fastest growing agribusiness sector on the continent. Coverage is relevant to all finfish and shellfish species grown in North America plus special reports from

other regions around the world.
Cost: $27.95
Frequency: Bi-monthly
Circulation: 4000
Founded in 1985

Crow's Nest

Casamar Group/Holdings
8082 Firethorn Lane
Las Vegas, NV   89123

702-792-6868
FAX 702-792-6668
E-Mail:
casamarholdings@casamarintl.com
Home Page:
www.casamarintl.com/CrowsNest/Crow
sNest.html

Malu Marigomen, Executive Director

An in-depth report on the status of the
Tuna Industry
Frequency: Monthly

Fishermen's News

PCFFA
Building 991, Marine Drive
Po Box 29370
San Francisco, CA   94129-0370

415-561-5080
FAX 415-561-5464
E-Mail: fish1ifr@aol.com
Home Page: www.pcffa.org

Zeke Grader, Executive Director
Chuck Wise, President

Oldest publication in the west coast
commercial fishing industry. Deals with
resource protection and policy issues of
great importance to the fishing industry,
as well as with critical Congressional issues which affect us all.
22 Members
Founded in 1976

IAFWA Newsletter

Association of Fish and Wildlife
Agencies
444 N Capitol St Nw
Suite 544
Washington, DC   20001-1527

202-624-7890
FAX 202-624-7891
E-Mail: rbrittin@iafwa.org
Home Page: www.iafwa.org

John Boffman, Owner
Rachel Brittin, Public Affairs Director

Provides state fish and wildlife agencies
with legal counsel, national surveys and
information on the fish industry
Frequency: Monthly

Littorally Speaking

American Littoral Society Northeast
Chapter
28 W 9th Rd
Broad Channel, NY   11693-1112

718-318-9344
FAX 718-318-9345
E-Mail: driepe@nyc.rr.com
Home Page: www.alsnyc.org

Don Riepe, Executive Director
Don Riepe, Chapter Director

A digest of environmental concerns

Makin' Waves Quarterly Newsletter

Recreational Fishing Alliance
Po Box 3080
New Gretna, NJ   08224

609-404-1060
888-564-6732
FAX 609-294-3812
E-Mail: rfa@joinrfa.org
Home Page: www.joinrfa.org

James Donofrio, Executive Director
Gary Caputi, Corporate Relations
Director
Courtney Howell Thompson, Marketing
Coordinator/PR

This RFA paper has proven that fish and
fishermen are not the only variables in
the equation of fisheries management.
Frequency: $35/Membership

National Shellfisheries Association Quarterly Newsletter

National Shellfisheries Association
C/O US EPA, Atlantic Ecology Division
27 Tazewell Drive
Narragansett, RI   02880

631-653-6327
FAX 631-653-6327
E-Mail: sectretariat@shellfish.org
Home Page: www.shellfish.org

R. LeRoy Creswell, President
Christopher V. Davis, President-Elect
George E. Flimlin, VP & Program Chair
Marta Gomez-Chiarri, Secretary

An informative newsletter for the shellfish industry, shellfish managers and

shellfish researchers.
Cost: $85.00
1000 Members
Frequency: Membership Fee
Founded in 1908

Wheel Watch

Fishing Vessel Owners Association
4005 20th Ave W
Room 232, West Wall Bldg
Seattle, WA   98199-1273

206-284-4720
FAX 206-283-3341
Home Page: www.fvoa.org

Robert D. Alverson, Manager
Carol M. Batteen, Executive Assistant

Brings you up-to-date with regards to
action of the Halibut Commission, North
Pacific Council, Pacific Council, and
market information.
Frequency: Quarterly

Magazines & Journals

American Seafood Institute Report

American Seafood Institute
25 Fairway Circle
Hope Valley, RI   02832

401-491-9017
FAX 401-491-9024
Home Page: www.americanseafood.org

A trade magazine of the seafood industry.
Frequency: Monthly

Aquaculture North America

Capamara Communications
Po Box 1409
Arden, NC   28704

250-474-3982
877-687-0011
FAX 250-478-3979
Home Page:
aquaculturenorthamerica.com

Gregory J Gallagher, Editor/Publisher
Rebekah Craig, Circulation Manager
Brenda Jo McManama,
Advertising/Sales

Earning the respect of aquaculture industry professionals throughout the world
who hold its trade publications in high

regard.
Cost: $24.00
96 Pages
Frequency: Annually/Summer
Circulation: 5000
ISSN: 0199-1388
Founded in 1968

Fisheries

American Fisheries Society
5410 Grosvenor Ln
Suite 110
Bethesda, MD   20814-2199

301-897-8616
FAX 301-897-8096
E-Mail: main@fisheries.org
Home Page: www.fisheries.org
Social Media: *Facebook, Twitter*

Gus Rassam, Executive Director
Myra Merritt, Office Administrator

Peer reviewed articles that address contemporary issues and problems, techniques, philosophies and other areas of interest to the general fisheries profession. Monthly features include letters, meeting notices, book listings and reviews, environmental essays and organization profiles.
Cost: $106.00
50 Pages
Frequency: Monthly
Circulation: 9800
Founded in 1870
Mailing list available for rent: 8500 names at $250 per M

Journal of Aquatic Animal Health

American Fisheries Society
5410 Grosvenor Ln
Suite 110
Bethesda, MD   20814-2199

301-897-8616
FAX 301-897-8096
E-Mail: main@fisheries.org
Home Page: www.fisheries.org
Social Media: *Facebook, Twitter*

Bill Fisher, President
John Boreman, President-Elect
Bob Hughes, First Vice President
Donna Parrish, Second Vice President

International journal publishing original research on diseases affecting aquatic life, including effects, treatments and

prevention.
Cost: $100.00
8500 Members
Frequency: Membership Fee
Founded in 1870

Marine and Coastal Fisheries: Dynamics, Management, and Ecosystem Science

American Fisheries Society
5410 Grosvenor Ln
Suite 110
Bethesda, MD   20814-2199

301-897-8616
FAX 301-897-8096
E-Mail: main@fisheries.org
Home Page: www.fisheries.org
Social Media: *Facebook, Twitter*

Bill Fisher, President
John Boreman, President-Elect
Bob Hughes, First Vice President
Donna Parrish, Second Vice President

Online publication focusing on marine, coastal, and estuarine fisheries.
Cost: $100.00
8500 Members
Frequency: Membership Fee
Founded in 1870

National Fisherman

Diversified Business Communications
Po Box 7437
Portland, ME   04112-7437

207-842-5600
FAX 207-842-5503
E-Mail: editor@nationalfisherman.com
Home Page:
www.nationalfisherman.com
Social Media: *Facebook, Twitter*

Nancy Hasselback, President/CEO
Lincoln Bedrosian, Senior Editor

Regional coverage of boats, fishing gear, environmental developments, technology, new products, and fishery resource information
Cost: $19.95
Frequency: Monthly
Circulation: 38,000
Founded in 1903

North American Journal of Fisheries Management

American Fisheries Society
5410 Grosvenor Ln
Suite 110
Bethesda, MD   20814-2199

301-897-8616
FAX 301-897-8096
E-Mail: main@fisheries.org
Home Page: www.fisheries.org
Social Media: *Facebook, Twitter*

Bill Fisher, President
John Boreman, President-Elect
Bob Hughes, First Vice President
Donna Parrish, Second Vice President

Promotes communication among managers. Published with a focus on maintenance, enhancement, and allocation of resources.
Cost: $100.00
8500 Members
Frequency: Membership Fee
Founded in 1870

Sea Technology Magazine

Compass Publications, Inc.
1501 Wilson Blvd
Suite 1001
Arlington, VA   22209-2403

703-524-3136
FAX 703-841-0852
E-Mail: oceanbiz@sea-technology.com
Home Page: www.sea-technology.com
Social Media: *, Twitter*

Amos Bussmann, President/Publisher
Joy Carter, Circulation Manager
Chris Knight, Managing Editor

Worldwide information leader for marine/offshore business, science and engineering. Read in more than 110 countries by management, engineers, scientists and technical personnel working in industry, government and education.
Cost: $40.00
Frequency: Monthly
Circulation: 16304
ISSN: 0093-3651
Founded in 1960
Mailing list available for rentat $80 per M
Printed in 4 colors

The Fisherman
326 12th Street
1st Floor
New Westminster, BC   V3M-4H6

604-669-5569
FAX 604-688-1142
E-Mail: fisherman@ufawu.org
Home Page: www.thefisherman.ca
Social Media: *Facebook, Twitter, YouTube*

Sean Griffin, Editor
Suzanne Thomson, Advertising Manager

Covering saltwater and freshwater fishing from Maine through Delaware Bay. Local fishing reports.
Frequency: Monthly
Circulation: 8000

Transactions of the American Fisheries Society
American Fisheries Society
5410 Grosvenor Ln
Suite 110
Bethesda, MD   20814-2199

301-897-8616
FAX 301-897-8096
E-Mail: main@fisheries.org
Home Page: www.fisheries.org

Gus Rassam, Executive Director
Myra Merritt, Office Administrator

The Society's highly regarded international journal of fisheries science features results of basic and applied research in genetics, physiology, biology, ecology, population dynamics, economics, health, culture, and other topics germane to marine and freshwater finfish and shellfish and their respective fisheries and environments
Cost: $43.00
Frequency: Bi-Monthly
ISSN: 0002-8487
Founded in 1872

Underwater Naturalist
American Littoral Society Northeast Chapter
28 W 9th Rd
Broad Channel, NY   11693-1112

718-318-9344
FAX 718-318-9345
E-Mail: driepe@nyc.rr.com
Home Page: www.alsnyc.org

Don Riepe, Executive Director

A publication providing news and analysis of animals and wildlife such as fish
Frequency: Quarterly

Trade Shows

AFS Annual Meeting
American Fisheries Society
5410 Grosvenor Lane
Suite 110
Bethesda, MD   20814

301-897-8616
FAX 301-897-8096
E-Mail: main@fisheries.org
Home Page: www.fisheries.org

Gus Rassam, Executive Director
Myra Merritt, Office Administrator

Held in conjunction with American Institute of Fishery Research Biologists. Explore the interrelation between fish, aquatic habitats and man; highlight challenges facing aquatic resource professionals and the methods that have been employed to resolve conflicts between those that use or have an interest in our aquatic resources.
Cost: $295.00
Frequency: Annual/September

AZA Regional Conference
American Zoo and Aquarium Association
8403 Colesville Road
Suite 710
Silver Spring, MD   20910-3314

301-562-0777
FAX 301-562-0888
Home Page: www.aza.org

Jim Maddy, President
Kris Vehrs, Executive Director
Jill Nicoll, Marketing

Exhibits, workshops and discussions about the industry.
200 Members
Founded in 1924

Annual Fish Baron's Ball
North Carolina Fisheries Association
PO Box 12303
New Bern, NC   28561

252-745-0225
FAX 252-633-9616

E-Mail: peggy@ncfish.org
Home Page: www.ncfish.org

Billy Carl Tillett, Chairman
Sherrill Styron, Vice Chairman
Sean McKeon, President
Janice Smith, Treasurer

Attendees getting together for an evening of great seafood and fun, and participate in the silent auction. Program proceeds go toward Association-related activities.
Founded in 1952

CFA Fish Farming Trade Show
Catfish Farmers of America
1100 Highway 82 E
Suite 202
Indianola, MS   38751

662-887-2699
FAX 662-887-6857
Home Page:
www.catfishfarmersamerica.org

America's largest fish farming equipment expo.
Frequency: February

Catfish Farmers of America Annual Convention & Research Symposium
Catfish Farmers of America
1100 Highway 82 E
Suite 202
Indianola, MS   38751-2251

662-887-2699
FAX 662-887-6857
Home Page:
www.catfishfarmersofamerica.org

Hugh Warren, President

Opportunity to launch new products, meet new buyers, learn emerging trends and access the North American seafood market.
Cost: $40.00
Frequency: Membership Fee
Founded in 1968

IAFWA Annual Meeting
International Association of Fish and Wildlife
444 North Capitol Street NW
Suite 725
Washington, DC   20001

202-624-7890
FAX 202-624-7891

E-Mail: rbrittin@iafwa.org
Home Page: www.fishwildlife.org

Gary T Myers, Executive Director
Cindy Delaney, Meetings Coordinator
Wayne Muhlstein, VP

Providing many opportunities to hear from our nation's wildlife conservation leaders, partners, and management experts. The meeting is our response to the need for national consensus on state-by-state fish and wildlife management issues.
Cost: $300.00
250 Attendees
Frequency: September

IIFET Biennial Conference/Meeting

Int'l Institute of Fisheries Economics and Trade
Dept. of Agricultural and Resources Economics
Oregon State University
Corvallis, OR   97331

541-737-1439
FAX 541-737-2563
E-Mail: Ann.L.Shrivor@oregonstate.edu
Home Page: www.osu.orst.edu/dept/iifet

Ann L Shriver, Executive Director
Kara Keenan, Assistant Executive Director

An important forum for members and others to learn about important research developments in seafood trade, aquaculture, and fisheries management issues. Attended by fisheries social scientists, managers, and industry members from all of the world's fishing areas.
Frequency: July

IIFET Biennial International Conference

IIFET
Dept of Agricultural & Resource Economic
Oregon State University
Corvallis, OR   97331-3601

541-737-1416
FAX 541-737-2563
E-Mail: iifet@oregonstate.edu
Home Page:
www.oregonstate.edu/dept/iifet

Ann L Shriver, Executive Director
Dr. Rebecca Metzner, President
Dr. Ralph Townsend, President-Elect

An important forum for members and others to learn about important research

developments in seafood trade, aquaculture, and fisheries management issues. Attended by fisheries social scientists, managers, and industry members from all of the world's fishing areas. Provides participants with unparalleled opportunities to interact with the world's foremost fisheries economists in both formal and informal settings. Learn more about fishing and aquaculture activities across the globe.
Founded in 1982

IPHC Annual Meeting

Pacific Seafood Processors Association
1900 West Emerson Place
Suite 205
Seattle, WA   98119-1649

206-281-1667
FAX 206-283-2387
E-Mail: nancy@pspafish.net
Home Page: www.pspafish.net

Glenn Reed, President

Annual members meeting to discuss catch limits each year.
25 Members
Founded in 1914

Pacific Marine Expo

Diversified Business Communications
121 Free Street
PO Box 7437
Portland, ME   04112

207-425-5608
FAX 207-842-5509
E-Mail: pme@divcom.com
Home Page:
www.pacificmarineexpo.com

Bob Callahan, Show Director
Heather Palmeter, Show Coordinator

A trade show dedicated to the pacific maritime industry that provides a gathering of marine products and services. With nearly 500 manufacturers and distributors showcasing the latest technologies and thousands of products for all commercial vessels, tugs, barges, boat building, marine construction, passenger vessels, seafood processing plants and more, PME is the best source for all marine business needs.
Cost: $20.00
6,000 Attendees
Frequency: November

Seafood Processing America

Catfish Farmers of America
1100 Highway 82 E
Suite 202
Indianola, MS   38751-2251

662-887-2699
FAX 662-887-6857
Home Page:
www.catfishfarmersofamerica.org

Hugh Warren, President

Opportunity to launch new products, meet new buyers, learn emerging trends and access the North American seafood market.
Cost: $40.00
Frequency: Membership Fee
Founded in 1968

Directories & Databases

AZA Membership Directory

American Zoo and Aquarium Association
8403 Colesville Rd
Suite 710
Silver Spring, MD   20910-6331

301-562-0777
FAX 301-562-0888
Home Page: www.aza.org

Jim Maddy, Executive Director
Kris Vehrs, Executive Director
Jill Nicoll, Marketing

Accredited institutions, professional affiliates, professional fellows, commercial members, related facilities and conservation partners receive one complimentary copy as a membership benefit.
Cost: $50.00
200 Members
Founded in 1924

Angling America Database

Po Box 22567
Alexandria, VA   22304

E-Mail: info@anglingamerica.com
Home Page: www.anglingamerica.com

Stephen Aaron, Director
Austin Ducworth, Director

The most searchable database for fishing charters and guides across America.

IIFET Membership Directory

International Institute of Fisheries
Economics
Dept of Agricultural & Resource
Economic
Oregon State University
Corvallis, OR   97331-3601

541-737-1416
FAX 541-737-2563
E-Mail: iifet@oregonstate.edu
Home Page: www.orst.edu/dept/iifet

Ann L Shriver, Executive Director
Kara Kennan, Assistant Executive
Director

This handbook lists all members with
complete contact information, including
an e-mail directory, plus areas of interest. Regular updates are provided with
the newsletter.
Frequency: Biennial

Who's Who in the Fish Industry

Urner Barry Publications
PO Box 389
Toms River, NJ   08754-0389

732-240-5330
800-932-0617
FAX 732-341-0891
E-Mail: sales@urnerbarry.com
Home Page: www.urnerbarry.com

Jay Bailey, Sales Manager
Janice Brown, Advertising Manager

The source for buying and selling contacts in the North American Seafood Industry. This 2006-2007 edition is fully
updated and verified, boasting over
6,000 listings of seafood companies in
the US and Canada. The directory boasts
detailed information about each company listed such as products handled,
contact names, product forms, product
origin, sales volume, company website
and much more.
Cost: $199.00
800 Pages
Frequency: Softcover
ISSN: 0270-1600

Lumber & Wood

Associations

American Forest Foundation
1111 19th St NW
Suite 780
Washington, DC   20036-3652

202-463-2700
FAX 202-463-2785
E-Mail: info@forestfoundation.org
Home Page: www.forestfoundation.org
Social Media: , *Twitter*

Donna Harman, CEO

Encourages the development of commerical forests and forestry products.
120 Members

American Forests
PO Box 2000
Washington, DC   20013-2000

202-955-4500
Home Page: www.americanforests.org

Deborah Gangloff, Executive Director
Jeff Olson, VP Marketing

Supports all those involved in tree planting and tree care equipment. Hosts annual trade show.

American Wood Protection Association
100 Chase Park S
Suite 116
Birmingham, AL   35244-1800

205-733-4077
FAX 205-733-4075
E-Mail: email@awpa.com
Home Page: www.awpa.com

Colin Mc Cown, Executive VP

Supports all those involved in the field of wood protection.
900 Members
Founded in 1904

Association of Millwork Distributors
10047 Robert Trent Jones Pkwy
Trinity, FL   34655-4649

727-372-3665
800-786-7274
FAX 727-372-2879
Home Page: www.amdweb.com

Rosalie Leone, CEO

Provides leadership, certification, education, promotion, networking and advocacy to, and for, the millwork distribution industry.
1200 Members
Founded in 1935

Forest Industries Telecommunications
1565 Oak St
Eugene, OR   97401-4008

541-485-8441
FAX 541-485-7556
E-Mail: license@landmobile.com
Home Page: www.landmobile.com

Kevin Mc Carthy, President

Organized to assist the forest industry in radio matters before the FCC.
600 Members
Founded in 1947

Forest Products Research Society
2801 Marshall Ct
Madison, WI   53705-2295

608-231-1361
FAX 608-231-2152
E-Mail: info@forestprod.org
Home Page: www.forestprod.org

Carol Lewis, VP

Researches products of American Forests.
Founded in 1947

Great Lakes Timber Professionals Association
3243 Golf Course Road
PO Box 1278
Rhinelander, WI   54501-1278

715-282-5828
FAX 715-282-4941
E-Mail: info@timberpa.com
Home Page: www.timberpa.com

Henry Schienebeck, Executive Director & Editor

Hardwood Utilization Consortium
USDA Forest Service
Southern Research Station
Blacksburg, VA   24061-0503

540-231-5341
FAX 540-231-8868
E-Mail: paraman@vt.edu
Home Page:
www.consortium.forprod.vt.edu

Philip Araman, President

The role is to improve hardwood resource viability through better utilization, technology, markets, cooperative extension and education in the eastern United States.

Intermountain Forest Association
204 E Sherman Avenue
Coeur D'Alene, ID   83814

208-667-4641
FAX 208-664-0557
Home Page: www.intforest.org

Jim Riley, President

Seeks to provide a unified voice for the industry. Promotes a sustained timber yield. Monitors federal legislation.
30 Members
Founded in 1986

National Hardwood Lumber Association
PO Box 34518
Memphis, TN   38184

990-137-7181
E-Mail: www.natlhardwood.org
Home Page: membership@nhla.com

Mark Barford, Executive Director
Trisha Clariana, Executive Secretary

Founded to establish a uniform system of grading rules for the measurement and inspection of hardwood lumber
1600 Members
Founded in 1898

National Wood Tank Institute
PO Box 2755
Philadelphia, PA   19120

215-329-9022
FAX 215-329-1177
E-Mail: woodtanks@aol.com
Home Page: www.woodtank.com

Jack Hillman, Company Contact

To promote the use and to guide the proper construction methods for wooden tanks as per NWTI S-82.

National Wooden Pallet & Container Association
329 S Patrick Street
Alexandria, VA   22314-3501

703-519-6104
FAX 703-519-4720

E-Mail: pjsherry@nepapallet.com
Home Page: www.nwpca.com

Patrick Sherry, VP
William E Biedenbach, President
David Eason, Secretary/Treasurer
Bruce N Scholnick, CEO

Represents manufacturers, recyclers and distributors of pallets, containers and reels.
575 Members
Founded in 1947

Northeastern Loggers Association

3311 State Route 28
PO Box 69
Old Forge, NY   13420-0069

315-369-3078
FAX 315-369-3736
E-Mail: nela@northernlogger.com
Home Page: www.northernlogger.com

Joseph Phaneuf, Executive Director
Eric A Johnson, Editor

Works to improve the industry in the Northeast and educate the public about policies and products of the industry.
2000 Members
Founded in 1952

Northwest Forestry Association

1500 SW 1st Ave
Suite 700
Portland, OR   97201-5837

503-222-9505
FAX 503-222-3255
Home Page: www.nwtrees.org

Tom Partin, President

Promotes forestry throughout the region to assure a permanent industry and stable economy. Works to keep informed on current changes affecting forest products.
70 Members
Founded in 1987

Pacific Lumber Exporters Association

1260 NW Waterhouse Avenue
Suite 150
Beaverton, OR   97006-8114

503-439-6000
FAX 503-439-6330
Home Page: www.lumber-exporters.org

Vicki Onuliak, President
John Quast, VP

Provide forum to discuss trade issues and problems; promote member companies through governmental and other trade association channels.
35 Members
Founded in 1923

Pennsylvania Forest Products Association

545 W Chocolate Ave
Hershey, PA   17033

717-312-1244
FAX 717-312-1335
E-Mail: hlma@hlma.org
Home Page: www.hlma.org

Represents the state's entire forest products industry, including foresters, loggers, sawmills, and value-added processors; maintains a full-time government affairs office and lobbyist; has been resposible for the passage of several pieces of legislation aimed at the protection and enhancement of our industry; responsible for the defeat and amendment of legislation threatning the viability of the forest of the forest products industry; & has been recognized as the voice for the forest industry

Redwood Inspection Service

818 Grayson Road
Suite 201
Pleasant Hill, CA   94523

925-935-1499
888-225-7339
FAX 925-935-1496
E-Mail: info@calredwood.org
Home Page: www.calredwood.org

Christopher Grover, President

Authorized by Department of Commerce to develop and supervise redwood lumber grading.
8 Members
Founded in 1917

Society of American Foresters

5400 Grosvenor Ln
Bethesda, MD   20814-2198

301-897-8720
FAX 301-897-3690
E-Mail: safweb@safnet.org
Home Page: www.safnet.org

Michael T Goergen Jr, Executive VP/CEO
Brittany Brumby, Assistant to the CEO and Council
Amy Ziadi, Information Technology

Manager
Larry D Burner, Sr Director Finance

Provides access to information and networking opportunities to prepare members for the challenges and the changes that face natural resource professionals.
Founded in 1900

Society of Wood Science & Technology

1 Gifford Pinchot Dr
Madison, WI   53726-2366

608-231-9347
FAX 608-231-9592
E-Mail: vicki@swst.org
Home Page: www.swst.org

Victoria Herian, Executive Director
James Funck, President Elect

Promotes policies and procedures which assure the wise use of wood and wood-based products; assures high standards for professional performance of wood scientists and technologists; fosters educational programs at all levels of wood science and technology and further the quality of such programs; represents the profession in public policy development.
450 Members
Founded in 1958

Southern Forest Products Association

2900 Indiana Ave
Kenner, LA   70065-4605

504-443-4464
FAX 504-443-6612
E-Mail: mail@sfpa.org
Home Page: www.sfpa.org

Digges Morgan, President
Richard Wallace, VP Communications
Tami Kessler, Corporate Secretary

The Association and its members are committed to quality, and believe that Southern Pine forest products provide a smart, environmentally friendly way to meet our world's needs for a wide range of building and industrial products.
265 Members
Founded in 1915

Temperate Forest Foundation

Ste 400
10200 SW Greenburg Rd
Portland, OR 97223-5556

503-579-6762
FAX 503-579-0300
E-Mail: office@forestinfo.org
Home Page: www.forestinfo.org

Robert M Owens, Chairman
Lee F Freeman, President & CEO

A tax-exempt, non-profit, public charity. Provides leadership by articulating the current realties, and a positive inspiring vision of the future. Helps people move toward the positive vision of living sustainably.
Founded in 1989

Western Forestry and Conservation

4033 SW Canyon Rd
Portland, OR 97221

503-226-4562
888-722-9416
FAX 503-226-2515
E-Mail: richard@westernforestry.org
Home Page: www.westernforestry.org

Richard Zabel, Executive Director

Offers high-quality continuing education workshops and seminars for professional foresters throughout Oregon, Washington, Idaho, Montana, Northern California and British Columbia.
125 Members
Founded in 1949

Western Wood Products Association

522 Sw 5th Ave
Portland, OR 97204-2190

503-224-3930
FAX 503-224-3934
E-Mail: info@wwpa.org
Home Page: www.wwpa.org

Michael O'Halloran, President
Tom Hanneman, VP/Director
Robert Bernhardt Jr, Director Information Services
Kevin CK Cheung, Director Technical Services
Kevin Binam, Director Economic Services

Represents lumber manufacturers in 12 Western states and Alaska. Provides lumber quality control, technical sup-

port, and business information to supporting mills.
135 Members
Founded in 1964

Woodworking Machinery Industry Association

3313 Paper Mill Rd
Suite 202
Phoenix, MD 21131-1457

410-628-1970
FAX 410-628-1972
E-Mail: info@wmia.org
Home Page: www.wmia.org

William P Miller, VP

Providing the North American wood products industry with technologically advanced woodworking systems available in the global market. A wide range of special programs provide industry awards, safety publications, scholarships and a host of other methods to support industry initiatives and address industry issues.
54 Members
Founded in 1978

Newsletters

American Wood Preservers Association Newsletter

American Wood Preservers Association
12100 Sunset Hills Road
Suite 130
Reston, VA 20190

703-204-0500
800-356-2974
FAX 703-204-4610
E-Mail: info@awpa.org
Home Page: www.awpa.org

John Hall, Publisher

Reports on governmental issues and environmental news.
Cost: $7.50
12 Pages
Frequency: Monthly
Founded in 1921

Forestry Source

Society of American Foresters
5400 Grosvenor Ln
Bethesda, MD 20814-2198

301-897-8720
FAX 301-897-3690

E-Mail: source@safnet.org
Home Page: www.safnet.org

Michael T Goergen Jr, Executive VP/CEO
Joe Smith, Editor

Offers the latest information on national forestry trends, the latest developments in forestry at the federal, state, and local levels, the newest advances in forestry-related research and technology, and up-to-date information about SAF programs and activities.
Cost: $33.00
Frequency: Monthly
Founded in 1900
Printed in 4 colors on newsprint stock

SFPA E-Newsletter

Southern Forest Products Association
2900 Indiana Ave
Kenner, LA 70065-4605

504-443-4464
FAX 504-443-6612
E-Mail: mail@sfpa.org
Home Page: www.sfpa.org

Digges Morgan, President
Richard Wallace, VP Communications
Tami Kessler, Corporate Secretary

The Association and its members are committed to quality, and believe that Southern Pine forest products provide a smart, environmentally friendly way to meet our world's needs for a wide range of building and industrial products.
265 Members
Frequency: Weekly/Online

Magazines & Journals

American Forests

American Forests
PO Box 2000
Washington, DC 20013-2000

202-737-1944
FAX 202-955-4588
E-Mail: mrobbins@amfor.org
Home Page: www.americanforests.org

Deborah Gangloff, Executive Director
Lydia Scalettar, Art Director

Updates on forest management and environmental policy, as well as news on the programs and policies of the American

Forests organization.
Cost: $25.00
Frequency: Quarterly
Circulation: 25000
Founded in 1875

Crow's Forest Industry Journal

CC Crow Publications
3635 N Farragut St
Portland, OR   97217-5954

503-241-7382
FAX 503-646-9971
E-Mail: info@crows.com
Home Page: www.chadcrowe.com

Chad Crowe, President

Focuses on the condition of forests
around the world.
Cost: $75.00
Circulation: 100000
Founded in 1921

Evergreen Magazine

Evergreen Foundations
5000 Cirrus Drive
#201
Medford, OR   97504-3102

541-770-4999
FAX 406-837-1385
Home Page:
www.evergreenmagazine.com

James D Petersen, Publisher

Focuses on issues and events impacting
forestry, forest communities, and the forest product industry. Includes profiles of
industry leaders and advocates.
Frequency: Bi-Monthly
Circulation: 100000

Forest Products Journal

Forest Products Society
2801 Marshall Ct
Madison, WI   53705-2295

608-231-1361
FAX 608-231-2152
E-Mail: info@forestprod.org
Home Page: www.forestprod.org

Carol Lewis, VP

Covers the latest research and technology from every branch of the forest
products industry.
Cost: $155.00
Founded in 1945

Great Lakes TPA Magazine

Great Lakes Timber Professionals
Association
3243 Golf Course Road
PO Box 1278
Rhinelander, WI   54501-1278

715-282-5828
FAX 715-282-4941
E-Mail: info@timberpa.com
Home Page: www.timberpa.com

Henry Schienebeck, Executive Director
& Editor

The magazine provides education and
information on the practice and promotion of sustainable forestry and seeks to
instill a sense of pride and professional-
ism among manufacturers, operators,
transporters, landowners, and foresters.
Cost: $24.00
Frequency: Monthly
Circulation: 2500

Journal of Forestry

Society of American Foresters
5400 Grosvenor Ln
Bethesda, MD   20814-2198

301-897-8720
FAX 301-897-3690
E-Mail: mwalls@safnet.org
Home Page: www.safnet.org

Michael T Goergen Jr, Executive
VP/CEO
Matthew Walls, Publications
Dir/Managing Editor

To advance the profession of forestry by
keeping professionals informed about
significant developments and ideas in
the many facets of forestry: economics,
education and communication, entomology and pathology, fire, forest ecology,
geospatial technologies, history, international forestry, measurments, policy, recreation, silviculture, social sciences,
soils anf hydrology, urban and community forestry, utilization and engineering,
and wildlife management.
Cost: $85.00
Frequency: 8 Times
ISSN: 0022-1201
Founded in 1902
Printed in 4 colors on glossy stock

Lumber Co-Operator

Northeastern Retail Lumber Association
585 N Greenbush Rd
Rensselaer, NY   12144-9615

518-286-1010
800-292-6752
FAX 518-286-1755
E-Mail: rferris@nrla.org
Home Page: www.nrla.org

Rita Ferris, President

Includes the latest industry, legislative
and regulatory news, as well as issues
and trends that most influence the lumber and building materials business.
Readers gain insight into the newest
methods, management techniques, new
product ideas, family owned business
concerns and key industry issues.
Cost: $40.00
100 Pages
Circulation: 5000
Founded in 1894

Northeastern Logger Magazine

Northeastern Loggers' Association
3311 State Route 28
PO Box 69
Old Forge, NY   13420-0069

315-369-3078
FAX 315-369-3736
Home Page: www.northernlogger.com

Joseph Phaneuf, Executive Director
Eric A Johnson, Editor

The Northern Logger & Timber Proces-
sor is the monthly magazine written for
the owners of logging and sawmilling
business in the Northeast and Lake
States region. Each issue contains feature articles, regular columns, news and
advertising, with a mission of providing
readers with tools and information they
need to be successful in the constantly
changing business and regulatory environment.
Cost: $12.00
Frequency: Monthly
Circulation: 12000
ISSN: 0029-3156
Printed in 4 colors on glossy stock

Society of American Foresters

Society of American Foresters
5400 Grosvenor Ln
Bethesda, MD   20814-2198

301-897-8720
FAX 301-897-3690

E-Mail: safeweb@safnet.org
Home Page: www.safnet.org

William Banzhaf, Production Manager
Jeff Glannam, VP Marketing

Monthly newsletter for all those involved in forestry research and technology. Regular editorial features.
ISSN: 1084-5496
Founded in 1900

Timber West Journal

Po Box 610
300 Admiral Way, Suite 208
Edmonds, WA 98020-0610

425-778-3388
866-221-1017
FAX 425-771-3623
E-Mail: timberwest@forestnet.com
Home Page:
www.forestnet.com/timberwest

Sheila Ringdahl, Publisher
Diane Mettler, Managing Editor

Packed with valuable and useful stories on successful mechanized harvesting and wood processing techniques and equipment, special editorial features, plus timely information on legislation, industry news, annual events, and people and products pertinent to America's largest forestry market.

Timber West Magazine

Timber West Publications
300 Admiral Way Suite 208
PO Box 610
Edmonds, WA 98020-610

425-778-3388
866-221-1017
FAX 425-771-3623
E-Mail: timberwest@forestnet.com
Home Page: www.forestnet.com

Sheila Ringdahl, Publisher
Diane Mettler, Managing Editor
James Booth, Marketing

Reports on the logging and lumber industries of the western US.
Cost: $20.00
48 Pages
Circulation: 10500
ISSN: 0192-0642
Founded in 1975
Printed in 4 colors on glossy stock

Timberline

Industrial Reporting
10244 Timber Ridge Dr
Ashland, VA 23005-8135

804-550-0323
FAX 804-550-2181
E-Mail: editor@ireporting.com
Home Page: www.palletenterprise.com

Edward C Brindley Jr, Publisher
Tim Cox, Editor
Laura Seal, Circulation

Highlights sawmill, logging, and pallet interests including environmental issues, new machinery and technologies that impact the industry.
52 Pages
Frequency: Monthly
Circulation: 30000
Founded in 1994
Mailing list available for rent: 28,000 names at $250 per M
Printed in 4 colors on newsprint stock

Tree Farmer Magazine, the Guide to Sustaining America's Family Forests

American Forest Foundation
1111 19th St NW
Suite 780
Washington, DC 20036

202-463-2700
FAX 202-463-2785
E-Mail: info@forestfoundation.org
Home Page: www.forestfoundation.org

Tom Martin, President & CEO
Brigitte Johnson APR, Director
Communications, Editor

The official magazine of ATFS, this periodical provides practical, how-to and hands-on information and techniques, and services to help private fore landowners to become better stewards, save money and time, and add to the enjoyment of their land.

Wood and Fiber Science

Society of Wood Science & Technology
1 Gifford Pinchot Dr
Madison, WI 53726-2366

608-231-9347
FAX 608-231-9592
E-Mail: vicki@swst.org
Home Page: www.swst.org

Victoria Herian, Executive Director
James Funck, President Elect

Publishes papers with both professional and technical content. Original papers of professional concer, or based on research dealing with the science, processing, and manufacture of wood and composite products of wood or wood fiber origin are considered for publication. All papers are peer-reviewed and must be unpublished research not offered for publication elsewhere.
Cost: $250.00
Frequency: Quarterly
Circulation: 950
ISSN: 0735-6161
Founded in 1958

Directories & Databases

Imported Wood: Guide To Applications, Sources and Trends

International Wood Products Association
4214 King St
Alexandria, VA 22302-1555

703-820-6696
FAX 703-820-8550
E-Mail: info@iwpawood.org
Home Page: www.iwpawood.org

Brent McClendon, Executive VP/CAE
Annette Ferri, Member Services
Brigid Shea, Government Affairs

An annual magazine featuring imported woods in applications, sustainable Forest Management issues and listing of IWPA members.
84 Pages
Frequency: Annual
Circulation: 15,000

International Green Front Report

Friends of the Trees
PO Box 1064
Tonasket, WA 98855-1064

FAX 509-485-2705

Michael Pilarski, Editor

Organizations and periodicals concerned with sustainable forestry and agriculture and related fields.
Cost: $7.00
Frequency: Irregular

Mining

Associations

Alabama Surface Mining Commission
PO Box 2390
Jasper, AL   35502

205-221-4130
FAX 205-221-5077
E-Mail: nderocher@asmc.state.al.us
Home Page:
www.surface-mining.state.al.us

Randall Johnson, Director
Nick DeRoche, Permit Manager
Gary Heaton, Engineer
Bill Kitchens, Geologist

Doing its part to balance civilization's demands for natural resources and environmental conservation in the state of Alabama.
26 Members
Founded in 1972

Alaska Miners Association
3305 Arctic Blvd
Suite 105
Anchorage, AK   99503-4575

907-563-9229
FAX 907-563-9225
E-Mail: ama@alaskaminers.org
Home Page: www.alaskaminers.org

Steven Borell, Executive Director

Encourage and support responsible mineral production in Alaska.

American Coal Ash Association
15200 E Girard Ave
Suite 3050
Aurora, CO   80014-3955

720-870-7897
FAX 720-870-7889
E-Mail: info@acaa-usa.org
Home Page: www.acaa-usa.org

Thomas H Adams, Executive Director

To advance the management and use of coal combustion products in ways that are environmentally responsible, technically sound, commercially competitive, and supportive of a sustainable global community
126 Members
Founded in 1968

American Geological Institute
4220 King St
Alexandria, VA   22302-1502

703-379-2480
FAX 703-379-7563
E-Mail: agi@agiweb.org
Home Page: www.agiweb.org

Patrick Leahy, Manager
John Rasanen, Marketing/Outreach

A nonprofit federation of 45 geoscientific and professional associations that represents more than 120,000 geologists, geophysicists, and other earth scientists.
45 Members
Founded in 1948

American Institute of Mining, Metallurgical & Petroleum Engineers
3 Park Ave
New York, NY   10016-5991

212-419-7676
FAX 212-419-7671
E-Mail: aimeny@aimeny.org
Home Page: www.aimeny.org

Nellie E Guernsey, Executive Director

Organized and operated exclusively to advance, record and disseminate significant knowledge of engineering and the arts and sciences involved in the production and use of minerals, metals, energy sources and materials for the benefits of humankind, both directly as AIME and through memeber societies.

American Institute of Professional Geologists
1200 N Washington St.
Suite 285
Thornton, CO   80241-3134

303-412-6205
FAX 303-253-9220
E-Mail: aipg@aipg.org
Home Page: www.aipg.org
Social Media: *Facebook, LinkedIn*

William J Siok, Executive Director
Wendy Davidson, Assistant Director

Founded to certify the credentials of practicing geologists and to advocate on behalf of the profession.
5000 Members
Founded in 1963

American Society of Mining and Reclamation
American Society of Mining and Reclamation
3134 Montevesta Road
Lexington, KY   40502-3548

859-351-9032
FAX 859-335-6529
E-Mail: asmr@insightbb.com
Home Page: www.asmr.us

Dennis Neuman, President
Richard Bamhisel, Executive Secretary

Dissemination of technical information relating to the reclamation of lands disturbed by mineral extraction. Members yearly issue is paid out of proceeding. Membership dues $50 regular $10 students.
500 Members
Founded in 1983

Arizona Mining Association
5150 N 16th Street
Suite B-134
Phoenix, AZ   85016-3900

602-266-4416
FAX 602-230-8413
E-Mail: webmaster@azcu.org
Home Page: www.azcu.org

Sydney Hay, President
June Castelhano, Administrative Assistant

Recognizes the importance of educating Arizona's citizens about the critical role the mining industry plays not only in our state and nation, but also in the world.
Founded in 1965

Asbestos Information Association North America
PO Box 2227
Arlington, VA   22202-9227

703-560-2980
FAX 703-560-2981
E-Mail: aiabjpiggj@aol.com

Bob L Pigg, President

The Asbestos Information Association is the informations arm of U.S. and Canadian asbestos producers and asbestos products manufacturers and provides information on asbestos and health.
Founded in 1971

Association for Mineral Exploration British Columbia

889 W Pender Street
Suite 800
Vancouver, BC V6C-3B2

604-689-5271
FAX 604-681-2363
E-Mail: info@amebc.ca
Home Page: www.amebc.ca

Gavin C Dirom, President/CEO

Supports and promotes the mineral exploration community and related services by disseminating information to the public and governments, thereby assisting in the creation of wealth and jobs through sustainable mineral development.
5400 Members
Founded in 1912

California Mining Association

1107 9th Street
Suite 705
Sacramento, CA 95814

916-447-1977
Home Page: www.calmining.org

Adam Harper, Association Manager
Stephanie Pridmore, Association Administrator

Represents the breadth and depth of California's mining industry including producers of precious metals (such as gold and silver), industrial minerals (including borates, limestone, rare earth elements, clays, gypsum and tungsten) and rock, sand and gravel.

Canadian Institute of Mining, Metallurgy and Petroleum

3400 de Maisonneuve Boulevard W
Suite 855
Montreal, QC H3Z-3B8

514-939-2710
FAX 514-939-2714
E-Mail: cim@cim.org
Home Page: www.cim.org

Russell E Hallbauer, CIM President
Jean Vavrek, CIM Executive Director

The leading technical society of professionals in the Canadian minerals, metals, materials and energy industries.
12000 Members
Founded in 1898

China Clay Producers Association CCPA

113 Arkwright Landing
Macon, GA 31210

478-757-1211
FAX 478-757-1949
E-Mail: info@georgiamining.org
Home Page: www.kaolin.com/

Lee Lemke, Executive VP

The mission of the China Clay Producers Association is to promote the common business interest of producers of china clay and the development of coordinated policies, which assure the industry will continue to provide jobs and contribute to the Georgia economy. In addition, objectives also include informing members of proposed legislation, regulatory actions and other matters affecting the kaolin industry, and to maintain the industry's strong community commitment.
Founded in 1978

Colorado Mining Association

216 16th St
Suite 1250
Denver, CO 80202-5161

303-575-9199
FAX 303-575-9194
E-Mail: colomine@coloradomining.org
Home Page: www.coloradomining.org

Stuart Sanderson, President
James T Cooper, Chairman

Composed of both small and large enterprises engaged in the exploration for, production and refining of, metals, coal, oil shale, and industrial minerals; firms that manufacture and distribute mining and mineral processing equipment and supplies; and other institutions providing services and supplies to the mineral industry.
Founded in 1876

Copper Development Association

260 Madison Ave
16th Floor
New York, NY 10016-2403

212-251-7200
FAX 212-251-7234
Home Page: www.copper.org

Andrew G Kireta, President
Victoria Prather, Manager Communications

Michels Harold, Sr VP Technolagy Services

Promoting the use of copper by communicating the unique attributes that make this sustainable element an essential contributor to the formation of life, to advances in science and technology, and to a higher standard of living worldwide.
Founded in 1963

Desert Research Institute

2215 Raggio Pkwy
Reno, NV 89512-1095

775-673-7300
FAX 775-673-7421
Home Page: www.dri.edu

Stephen G Wells, President

A nonprofit statewide division of the university and community college system of Nevada, DRI pursues a full-time program of basic and applied environmental research on a local, national, and international scale. DRI employees nearly 400 full and part-time staff scientists, technicians, and support personnel.
Founded in 1959

Geological Society of America

Po Box 9140
Boulder, CO 80301-9140

303-357-1019
800-472-1988
FAX 303-357-1070
E-Mail: gsa@geosociety.org
Home Page: www.geosociety.org

Jack Hess, Executive Director
William A Thomas, VP

16000 Members
Founded in 1888

Idaho Mining Association

802 W Bannock St
Suite 301
Boise, ID 83702-5840

208-342-0031
FAX 208-345-4210
E-Mail: ima@idahomining.org
Home Page: www.idahomining.org

Jack Lyman, VP

Founded to further the interests of Idaho's mining industry and minerals production. Mission is to act as the unified voice for its members to ensure the long-term health and well being of Idaho's mining industry.
Founded in 1903

Lead Industries Association

13 Main Street
Sparta, NJ   07871

973-726-5323
FAX 973-726-4484
E-Mail: miller@leadinfo.com
Home Page: www.leadinfo.com

Nonprofit trade association representing the lead industries in the US and abroad. It collects and distributes information about the users of lead products in industry, vehicles, radioactive waste disposal and noise barriers. Its services are availble, generally free of charge, to anyone interested in the uses of lead and lead products.

Lignite Energy Council

1016 E Owens Avenue Suite 200
PO Box 2277
Bismarck, ND   58502-2277

701-258-7117
800-932-7117
FAX 701-258-2755
E-Mail: lec@lignite.com
Home Page: www.lignite.com

John Dwyer, President/CEO
Steve Van Dyke, VP, Communications
Michael Jones, VP, Research & Development
Renee Walz, Dir., Member Services & Education

Regional Trade Association - promotes policies and activities that maintain a viable lignite industry and enhance development of our regions' lignite resources.
355 Members
Founded in 1974

Mine Safety Institue of America

319 Paintersville Road
Hunker, PA   15139

724-925-5150
E-Mail: sikora.lisa@dol.gov
Home Page:
www.miningorganizations.org/msia.htm

Frank Linkous, President
Ronnie Biggerstaff, VP

The objectives of the Mine Safety Institute of America is to provide successful educational programs, safer and healthier working conditions, more productivity in the mining industry, and support of good legislature pertaining to mining.
Founded in 1908

Mine Safety and Health Administration

1100 Wilson Blvd
Arlington, VA   22209-2249

202-693-9400
800-746-1553
FAX 202-693-9401
Home Page: www.msha.gov

David G Dye, Executive Director

Administers the Federal Mine Safety and Health Act of 1977 (Mine Act) and enforces compliance with mandatory safety and health standards as a means to eliminate fatal accidents; to reduce the frequency and severity of nonfatal accidents, to minimize health hazards and to promote mineral processing operations in the US, regardless of size, employees, commodity mined or method of extraction.

Mineral Information Institute

12999 E. Adam Aircraft Circle
Englewood, CO   80112

303-948-4236
FAX 303-948-4265
E-Mail: mii@mii.org
Home Page: www.mii.org

Jaqueline S. Dorr, Manager

Nonprofit organization dedicated to educating youth about the science of minerals and other natural resources and about their importance in our everyday lives.

Mineral Insulation Manufacturers

44 Canal Center Plaza
Suite 310
Alexandria, VA   22314

703-684-0084
FAX 703-684-0427
Home Page: www.naima.org

Howard Deck, Chair
Kenneth Mentzer, President/CEO

Trade association of North American manufacturers of fiberglass, rock wool, and slag wool insulation products.

Mineral and Ecomnomics Management Society

Colorado School Of Mines
Golden, CO   49931

303-273-3150
FAX 906-487-2944

Home Page:
www.minecon.com/index.html

Patricia Dillon, President

The Mineral and Economic Management Society is a not-for-profit organization that provides a professional forum for academic, industrial, private and government specialists interested in mineral economics and materials management.
200 Members
Founded in 1991

Minerals, Metals & Materials Society

184 Thorn Hill Road
Warrendale, PA   15086-7528

724-776-9000
FAX 724-776-3770
E-Mail: tmsgeneral@tms.org
Home Page: www.tms.org

Dedicated to the development and dissemination of the scientific and engineering knowledge bases for materials-centered technologies.

Mining Foundation of the Southwest

PO Box 42317
Tucson, AZ   85733

520-577-7519
FAX 520-577-7073
E-Mail: mfsw@dakotacom.net
Home Page:
www.miningfoundationsw.org

William Dresher, President

Advances the science of mining and related industries by educating members and the public. Annual American Mining Hall of Fame First Saturday in December. A newsletter is published.
92 Members
Founded in 1993

Mining and Metallurgical Society of America

476 Wilson Avenue
Novato, CA   94947-4236

415-897-1380
E-Mail: info@mmsa.net
Home Page: www.mmsa.net

Concerned with the conservation of the nation's mineral resources and the best interest of the mining and metallurgical industries.
340+ Members
Founded in 1908

National Association of State Land Reclamationists

Coal Research Center/Southern Illinois University
Carbondale, IL   62901-4623

618-536-5521
FAX 618-453-7346
E-Mail: aharrington@crc.siu.edu
Home Page: www.crc.siu.edu/nasir.htm

Bruce Ragon, President
Dennis Baker, VP

The National Association of State and Land Reclamationists advocates the use of research, innovative technology and professional discourse to foster the restoration of lands and waters affected by mining related activities.
140 Members
Founded in 1972

National Lime Association

200 N Glebe Rd
Arlington, VA   22203-3728

703-243-5463
FAX 703-243-5489
E-Mail: natlime@lime.org
Home Page: www.lime.org

Arline Seeger, Executive Director
Lisa McFadden, Meetings

Trade association for US and Canadian manufacturers of high calcium quicklime, dolomitic quicklime and hydrated lime, collectively referred to as lime. NLA represents the interests of its members in Washington, provides input on standards and specifications for lime, and funds and manages research on current and new uses for lime.
63 Members
Founded in 1902

National Mining Association

101 Constitution Ave Nw
Suite 500 East
Washington, DC   20001-2133

202-463-2625
FAX 202-463-6152
E-Mail: craulston@nma.org
Home Page: www.nma.org

Craig Naaz, President
Carol L Raulston, Senior VP
Connie Holmes, Executive Director

Membership within the National Mining Association includes corporations involved in all aspects of the mining industry including coal, metal and industrial mineral producers, mineral processors, equipment manufacturers, state associations, bulk transporters, engineering firms, consultants, financial institutions and other companies that supply goods and services to the mining industry.
325 Members
Founded in 1995

National Ocean Industries Association

1120 G St NW
Suite 900
Washington, DC   20005-3801

202-347-6900
FAX 202-347-8650
Home Page: www.noia.org

Tom Fry, President
Jon A Marshall, Vice Chairman

National organization engaged in offshore construction, drilling and petroleum production, geophysical exploration, ship building and repair, deep-sea mining and related activities in the development and use of marine resources.
300 Members
Founded in 1972

National Ready Mixed Concrete Association

900 Spring St
Silver Spring, MD   20910-4015

301-587-1400
FAX 301-585-4219
E-Mail: info@nrmca.org
Home Page: www.nrmca.org

Robert Garbini, President
Deana Angelastro, Executive Administrator

The mission of the National Ready Mixed Concrete Association is to provide exceptional value for our members by responsibly representing and serving the entire ready mixed concrete industry through leadership, promotion, education, and partnering to ensure ready mixed concrete is the building material of choice.
1200 Members
Founded in 1930

National Stone, Sand & Gravel Association

1605 King St
Alexandria, VA   22314-2726

703-525-8788
800-342-1415
FAX 703-525-7782
E-Mail: jwilson@nssga.org
Home Page: www.nssga.org

Joy Wilson, CEO
Dave Thomey, Executive VP/COO

Represents the stone, sand and gravel — or aggregate — industries. Our members account for 90 percent of the crushed stone and 70 percent of the sand and gravel produced annually in the US.
25 Members
Founded in 1916

Nevada Mining Association

9210 Prototype Dr
Suite 200
Reno, NV   89521-2984

775-829-2121
FAX 775-852-2631
E-Mail: amiller@nevadamining.org
Home Page: www.nevadamining.org

Tim Crowley, President
Alexis Miller, Government Affairs/Public Relations
Julanne Kaufman, Education Coordinator
Darcy Lenardson, Newsletter Editor/Website Manager
Jonathan Brown, Regulatory/Environmental Affairs

Represents all aspects of the mining industry. Provides representation for the broad mining industry in public outreach activities such as public relations, media relations, and community relations.

Northwest Mining Association

10 N Post St
Suite 220
Spokane, WA   99201-0722

509-624-1158
FAX 509-623-1241
E-Mail: nwma@nwma.org
Home Page: www.nwma.org

Laura Skaer, Executive Director

Provides liaison between mining, industry and government. Offers short course on current technology.
2000 Members
Founded in 1890

Perlite Institute

4305 North 6th Street
Suite A
Harrisburg, PA 17110

717-238-9723
FAX 717-238-9985
E-Mail: info@perlite.org
Home Page: www.perlite.org

Bill Michalopoulos, President

An international association which establishes product standards and specifications, and which encourages the development of new product uses through research.
183 Members
Founded in 1949

Silver Valley Mining Association

Po Box 1286
Wallace, ID 83872

208-556-1621
E-Mail: info@silverminers.org
Home Page: www.silverminers.org

Dedicated to promoting the Silver Valley of northern Idaho and its mining industry. Informs the public of the history and merits of the region, serving various beneficiary needs of the mining industry, and serving those who work in the industry and the investing public.

Society for Mining, Metallurgy & Exploration

8307 Shaffer Pkwy
Littleton, CO 80127-4102

303-973-9550
800-763-3132
FAX 303-973-3845
E-Mail: sme@smenet.org
Home Page: www.smenet.org

David Kanagy, Executive Director
William Wilkerson Jr, President

Advances the worldwide mining and minerals community through information exchange and professional development.
13000 Members
Founded in 1957

Society of Exploration Geophysicists

PO Box 702740
Tulsa, OK 74170-2740

918-497-5500
FAX 918-497-5557

E-Mail: web@seg.org
Home Page: www.seg.org/index.shtml

Mary Fleming, Executive Director
Vladimir Grechka, Editor

The Society of Exploration Geophysicists/SEG is a not-for-profit organization that promotes the science of geophysics and the education of applied geophysicists. SEG fosters the expert and ethical practice of geophysics in the exploration and development of natural resources, in characterizing the near surface, and in mitigating earth hazards.
Founded in 1930

Society of Mineral Analysts

PO Box 50085
Sparks, NV 89435-0085

562-467-8980
E-Mail: pbraun@sma-online.org

Patrick Brown, Director

The Society of Mineral Analysts is a non-profit organization, whose members are assayers, chemists, laboratory managers, geologists, suppliers and vendors both in and serving the mineral analysis industry.
250 Members
Founded in 1986

Solution Mining Research Institute

105 Apple Valley Circle
Clarks Summit, PA 18411

570-585-8092
E-Mail: smri@solutionmining.org
Home Page: www.solutionmining.org

John O Voight, Executive Director
Carolyn L Diamond, Assistant Executive Director

Members are companies interested in the production of salt brine and solution mining of potash and soda ash, as well as production of slt covers, used for storage of oil, gas, chemicals, compressed air and waste.
100 Members
Founded in 1958

Sorptive Minerals Institute

1155 15th St NW
Suite 500
Washington, DC 20005-2725

202-223-1661
FAX 202-530-0659

E-Mail: lcoogan@navista.net
Home Page: www.sorptive.org

Paul Cicio, President

The Sorptive Minerals Institute represents the absorbent clay industry and is a not-for-profit industry trade association that would serve as the marketing, promotion and research arm of the absorbent clay indsutry with the goal of enhancing long-range growth and profitability.
11 Members
Founded in 1970

State Mine Inspector

1700 W Washington St
Suite 400
Phoenix, AZ 85007-4655

602-542-5971
FAX 602-542-5335
E-Mail: admin@mi.state.az.us
Home Page: www.asmi.az.gov

Joe Hart, Manager
Tim Evans, Senior Deputy Mine Inspector
Hector Lovemore, Deputy Mine Inspector Reclamation
Douglas Martin, Executive Director

330 Members
Founded in 1912

United Mine Workers of America International Union

8315 Lee Hwy
Fairfax, VA 22031-2215

703-208-7200
FAX 703-208-7227
E-Mail: umwa_union@qwest.net
Home Page: www.umwa.org

Cecil E Roberts, President
Daniel J Kane, International Secretary/Treasurer
Phil Smith, Communications Director/Editor
David Kameras, Communications Coordinator

The United Mine Workers of America International Union is an organization with a diverse membership that includes coal miners, clean coal technicians, health care workers, truck drivers, manufacturing workers and public employees throughout the United States and Canada. The Union works to fight for safe

workplaces, good wages and benefits, and fair representation.
120M Members
Founded in 1890

Utah Mining Association
136 S Main St
Suite 709
Salt Lake City, UT 84101-1683

801-364-1874
FAX 801-364-2640
E-Mail: mining@utahmining.org
Home Page: www.utahmining.org

Todd Bingham, President
Terry Maio, Chairman
Marilyn Tuttle, Administrator

Provides its members with full-time professional industry representation before the State Legislature; various government regulatory agencies on the federal, state and local levels; other associations, and business and industry groups. Helps to promote and protect the mining industry.
Founded in 1915

Newsletters

Coal Week International
McGraw Hill
PO Box 182604
Columbus, CO 43272

877-833-5524
800-752-8878
FAX 614-759-3749
E-Mail:
customer.service@mcgraw-hill.com
Home Page: www.mcgraw-hill.com

John Slater, Publisher

Offers information and news to and of the mining industry in North America.
Cost: $467.00
Frequency: Monthly
Founded in 1884

Coaldat Productivity Report
Pasha Publications
1600 Wilson Boulevard
Suite 600
Arlington, VA 22209-2510

703-528-1244
800-424-2908
FAX 703-528-1253

Harry Baisden, Group Publisher
Michael Hopps, Editor
Kathy Thorne, Circulatin Manager

Shows quarterly and year-to-date total coal production in tons, productivity in tons per miner per day, average number of employees for each mine, mining methods used, controlling company, mine location, district number, union affiliation and whether the mine is surface or underground. Both a controlling company and a state/country format are available.
Cost: $545.00
60 Pages
Frequency: Quarterly

Legal Quarterly Digest of Mine Safety and Health Decisions
Legal Publication Services
888 Pittsford Mendon Center Road
Pittsford, NY 14534

585-582-3211
FAX 585-582-2879
E-Mail: MineSafety@aol.com
Home Page: www.minesafety.com

Ellen Smith, Owner/publisher
Melanie Aclander, Editor

Covers legal decisions on health and safety law in the mining industry.
Cost: $525.00
100 Pages
Frequency: Annual+
Founded in 1991

Lignite Energy Council
1016 E Owens Avenue Suite 200
PO Box 2277
Bismarck, ND 58502-2277

701-258-7117
800-932-7117
FAX 701-258-2755
E-Mail: lec@lignite.com
Home Page: www.lignite.com

John Dwyer, President/CEO
Steve Van Dyke, VP, Communications
Michael Jones, VP, Research & Development

Renee Walz, Dir., Member Services & Education

Promotes policies and directs activities that maintain a viable lignite industry and enhance the development of our regions' lignite resources.
355 Members
300 Pages
Circulation: 500
Founded in 1974

Machinery Outlook
Manfredi & Associates
20934 W Lakeview Pkwy
Mundelein, IL 60060-9502

847-949-9080
FAX 847-949-9910
E-Mail: frank@manfredi.com
Home Page:
www.machineryoutlook.com

Frank Manfredi, President

A newsletter about and for the construction and mining machinery industry.
Cost: $365.00
14 Pages
Frequency: Monthly
Founded in 1984
Printed in one color on matte stock

Mine Regulation Reporter
Pasha Publications
1600 Wilson Boulevard
Suite 600
Arlington, VA 22209-2509

703-528-1244
800-424-2908
FAX 703-528-1253

Harry Baisden, Group Publisher
Michael Hopps, Editor
Kathy Thorne, Circulation Manager

The only biweekly newsletter and document service in the US for mine safety and environmental managers and attorneys. It covers mine safety, health and environmental regulations, legislation and court decisions that affect mine operations.
Cost: $785.00
Frequency: BiWeekly

Mining Foundation of the Southwest
PO Box 42317
Tucson, AZ 85733

520-577-7519
FAX 520-577-7073
E-Mail: mfsw@dakotacom.net

Home Page:
www.miningfoundationsw.org

William Dresher, President
Jean Austin, Office Manager

Advances the science of mining and related industries by educating members and the public. Annual American Mining Hall of Fame First Saturday in December.
90 Pages
Founded in 1973

Reclamation Matters

American Society of Mining and Reclamation
3134 Montevesta Road
Lexington, KY   40502-3548

859-351-9032
FAX 859-335-6529
E-Mail: asmr@insightbb.com
Home Page: www.asmr.us

Dennis Neuman, President
Richard Bamhisel, Executive Secretary

Newsletter of the ASMA. Free to members or $10/year.
500 Members
Founded in 1983

Utah Mining Association Newsletter

Utah Mining Association
136 S Main St
Suite 709
Salt Lake City, UT   84101-1683

801-364-1874
FAX 801-364-2640
E-Mail: mining@utahmining.org
Home Page: www.utahmining.org

Todd Bingham, President
Terry Maio, Chairman
Marilyn Tuttle, Admininstrator

Provides updates on the mining industry.

Magazines & Journals

Alaska Miners Association Journal

Alaska Miners Association
3305 Arctic Boulevard
Suite 105
Anchorage, AK   99503-4575

907-563-9229
FAX 907-563-9225

E-Mail: ama@alaskaminers.org
Home Page: www.alaskaminers.org

Steven Borell, Executive Director

CIM Magazine

Canadian Inst of Mining, Metallurgy & Petroleum
3400 de Maisonneuve Boulevard W
Suite 855
Montreal, QC   H3Z-3B8

514-939-2710
FAX 514-939-2714
Home Page: www.cim.org

Dawn Nelley, Publications

Provides important information on mine developments, new technologies, safety, HR, products and services, and business issues.
Frequency: 8x's a Year
Circulation: 11,289

Coal

MacLean Hunter
29 N Wacker Drive
Floor 9
Chicago, IL   60606-3298

312-726-2802
FAX 312-726-4103

Art Sanda, Editor
Elisabeth O'Grady, Executive Director

Articles cover maintenance and production of coal mines.
Cost: $62.50
Frequency: Monthly
Circulation: 22,000
Founded in 1964

Coal Age

Primedia
29 N Wacker Avenue
10th Floor
Chicago, IL   60606

312-726-2802
FAX 312-726-2574
Home Page: www.coalage.com

Peter Johnson, Publisher
Stever P Fiscor, Editor-in-Chief
Ben Fromenthal, Production Manager

Geared primarily toward professionals in the coal mining and processing industries. Coal Age focuses on news, with in-depth features on coal mining operations and changing technologies.
Cost: $49.00
54 Pages
Frequency: Monthly

Circulation: 17900
ISSN: 1040-7820
Founded in 1911
Printed in 4 colors on glossy stock

Coal Journal

PO Box 3068
Pikeville, KY   41502-3068

606-432-0206
FAX 606-432-2162

Terry L May, Publisher

Information concentrating on government regulations, emerging technologies and trade literature, and analyzes governmental actions and their impact on the coal industry.
Frequency: Quarterly
Circulation: 10000

Engineering & Mining Journal

Primedia Publishing
330 N Wabash Avenue
Suite 2300
Chicago, IL   60611

312-595-1080
FAX 312-595-0295
E-Mail: info@mining-media.com
Home Page: www.e-mj.com

Peter Johnson, Publisher
Steve Fiscor, Editor

Serves the field of mining including exploration, development, milling, smelting, refining of metals and nonmetallics
108 Pages
Frequency: Monthly
Circulation: 20589
ISSN: 0095-8948
Founded in 1866
Printed in 4 colors on glossy stock

Geotimes

American Geological Institute
4220 King St
Alexandria, VA   22302-1502

703-379-2480
FAX 703-379-7563
E-Mail: agi@agiweb.org
Home Page: www.agiweb.org

Patrick Leahy, President
John Rasanen, Marketing/Outreach

Nonprofit federation of 40 geoscientific and professional associations that represents more than 100,000 geologists, geophysicsts, and other earth scientists. AGI provides information services to geoscientists, serves as a voice of shared

interests in our profession, plays a major role in strengthening geoscience education, and strives to increase public awareness of the vital role the geosciences play in society's use of resources and interaction with the environment.
Cost: $42.95
40 Pages
Frequency: Monthly
Circulation: 100000
Founded in 1948

Journal of Minerals, Metals & Materials Society

Minerals, Metals & Minerals Society
184 Thorn Hill Road
Warrendale, PA   15086-7514

724-776-9000
800-759-4867
FAX 724-776-3770
E-Mail: tmsgeneral@tms.org
Home Page: www.tms.org

Alexander R Scott, Executive Director
Robert Makowski, Director Communications
James J Robinson, Editor
Stephen Kendall, Publication Manager
Arlene Frances, Advertising Sales Representative

To promote the global science and engineering profession's concerned with minerals, metals and materials. Founded in 1871. Publishes a monthly magazine.
Cost: $131.00
Frequency: Monthly
Circulation: 10000
Founded in 1948

Mine Safety and Health News

Legal Publication Services
888 Pittsford Mendon Center Road
Pittsford, NY   14534

585-582-3211
FAX 585-582-2879
E-Mail: MineSafety@aol.com
Home Page: www.minesafety.com

Ellen Smith, Owner
Melanie Aclander, Editor
Cost: $525.00

Founded in 1991

Miners News

Miners News
9792 W Glen Ellyn Street
PO Box 4965
Boise, ID   83711

800-624-7212
FAX 208-658-4901
E-Mail: minersnews@msn.com
Home Page: www.minersnews.com

Gary White, Publisher
Shirley White, Public Relations

Information on mining history and provides insight into new technology and products used in mining.
Cost: $25.00
Circulation: 6512
ISSN: 0890-6157
Founded in 1985

Mining Record

Mining Record Company
PO Box 1630
Castle Rock, CO   80104-6130

303-888-8871
800-441-4708
FAX 303-663-7823
E-Mail: customerservice@miningrecord.com
Home Page: www.miningrecord.com

Don E Howell, Editor
Dale Howell, Marketing

Has been in continuous publication for 115 years and is recognized as the industry's leading newspaper. Focuses on timely and credible news reporting on exploration, discovery, development, production, joint ventures, acquisitions, operating results, legislation, government reports and metals prices. Its readership is concentrated in the mining industry proper; mining companies and all individuals engaged in large or small mine production.
Cost: $45.00
16 Pages
Frequency: Monthly
Circulation: 5100
ISSN: 0026-5241
Founded in 1889
Printed in on newsprint stock

New Equipment Digest

Penton Media
1300 E 9th St
Suite 316
Cleveland, OH   44114-1503

216-696-7000
FAX 216-696-6662
E-Mail: information@penton.com
Home Page: www.penton.com

Jane Cooper, Marketing
Jennifer Daugherty, Communications Manager
John DiPaola, Group Publisher
Robert F King, Editor
Bobbie Macy, Circulation Manager

Serves the general industrial field which includes manufacturing, processing, engineering services, construction, transportation, mining, public utilities, wholesale distributors, educational services, libraries, and governmental establishments.
Cost: $65.00
Frequency: Monthly
Circulation: 206000
Founded in 1892

North American Mining

Mining Media
1005 Terminal Way
#140
Reno, NV   89502-2179

775-323-1553
FAX 775-323-1553

Dorothy Y Kosich, Editor

Information broken into departments which include environment, finance, government, management, new product news, profiles, safety issues and development technology updates.
Frequency: Bi-Monthly
Circulation: 7000

Pay Dirt

Copper Queen Publishing Company
Copper Queen Plaza
PO Drawer 48
Bisbee, AZ   85603-48

520-432-2244
FAX 520-432-2247
E-Mail: paydirt@thenver.com

Gary Dillard, Editor
Caryl Larkins, CEO
Frank Barco, Publisher
Gruce Rubin, Marketing

Keeps readers informed on current mining developments, changes in policies and decisions by state and federal agencies affecting mining. Accepts advertising.
Cost: $30.00
34 Pages
Frequency: Monthly
Circulation: 2200
ISSN: 0886-0920
Founded in 1938

Skillings Mining Review

WestmorelandFlint
11 E Superior St
Suite 514
Duluth, MN 55802-3015

218-727-1552
FAX 218-733-0463
E-Mail: hollyo@skillings.net
Home Page:
www.westmorelandflint.com

John Hyduke, President
Ivan Hohnstadt, General Manager
Holly Olson, Circulation Manager

Skillings Mining Review covers breaking news about mining companies and their suppliers, dynamics of the global marketplace, technical aspects of mining and processing, people in the industry and their contributions to it. Also production and shipping reports, and the latest news from coal and power industries.
Cost: $69.00
28 Pages
Frequency: Monthly
Circulation: 1500
ISSN: 0037-6329
Founded in 1912
Printed in 4 colors on glossy stock

World Dredging, Mining & Construction

Placer Corporation
PO Box 17479
Irvine, CA 92623-7479

949-474-1120
FAX 949-863-9261
E-Mail: worlddredging@aol.com
Home Page: www.worlddredging.com

MJ Richardson, Publisher
Steve Richardson, Editor
Robert Lindaur, Circulation Manager

International and national news for the dredging.
Cost: $40.00
100 Pages
Frequency: Monthly
Circulation: 3400
ISSN: 1045-0343
Founded in 1965
Printed in 4 colors on glossy stock

World Mining Equipment

13544 Eads Road
Prairieville, LA 70769

225-673-9400
FAX 225-677-8277
E-Mail: info@mining-media.com
Home Page: www.mining-media.com

Steve Fiscor, Editor in chief
Richard Johnson, Publisher
Cost: $29.95

Frequency: Monthly
Circulation: 10,523
Founded in 1866

Trade Shows

ASMA Annual Meeting

American Society of Mining and Reclamation
3134 Montevesta Road
Lexington, KY 40502-3548

859-351-9032
FAX 859-335-6529
E-Mail: asmr@insightbb.com
Home Page: www.asmr.us

Dennis Neuman, President
Richard Bamhisel, Executive Secretary

Approximately 30 exhibitors.
Cost: $300.00
300 Attendees
Frequency: Annual

Alaska Miners Association Convention

Alaska Miners Association
3305 Arctic Boulevard
Suite 105
Anchorage, AK 99503-4575

907-563-9229
FAX 907-563-9225
E-Mail: ama@alaskaminers.org
Home Page: www.alaskaminers.org

Steven Borell, Executive Director

Forty booths supporting businesses of the mining industry and state and federal

agencies involved with regulating the industry.
500 Attendees
Frequency: March

American Conference on Crystal Growth and Epitaxy

American Association for Crystal Growth
25 4th Street
Somerville, NJ 08876

908-575-0649
FAX 908-575-0794
E-Mail: aacg@att.net
Home Page: www.crystalgrowth.org

Laura Bonner, Executive Administrator

Conference registrants and crystallography professionals, scientists and engineers in crystal growth and epitaxy research, theory and manufacturing of crystal.
350+ Attendees
Frequency: July

Arminera

Marketing International
200 N Glebe Road
Suite 900
Arlington, VA 22203

703-527-8000
FAX 703-527-8006
E-Mail: micexpos@aol.com

Seminar, banquet and 400 exhibits of supplies, equipment and services for the mining industry.
8500 Attendees
Frequency: Biennial

MIACON Construction, Mining & Waste Management Show

Finocchiaro Enterprises
2921 Coral Way
Miami, FL 33145-3053

305-441-2865
FAX 305-529-9217
E-Mail: mail@miacon.com
Home Page: www.miacon.com

Michael Finocchiaro, President
Jose Garcia, VP
Justine Finocchiaro, Chief Operations

Annual show of 650 manufacturers, suppliers, distributors and exporters of equipment, machinery, supplies and services for the construction, mining and

waste managment industries. There will be 600 booths.
10M Attendees
Frequency: December
Founded in 1994

MINExpo International

National Mining Association
101 Constitution Avenue NW
Suite 500 E
Washington, DC   20001-2133

202-463-2600
FAX 202-463-2666
E-Mail: craulston@nma.org
Home Page: www.nma.org

Carol Raulston, Communications
Kraig Naasz, President/Ceo

Quadrennial show of nearly 1300 exhibitors covering more than 588,000 square feet that showcases equipment, products and services for mining and processing coal, metals, industrial and agricultural minerals. Exhibitors include manufacturers of equipment, supliers of parts, consultants and providers of mining related services for exploration, mine development, production, processing/preparation, materials handling, environmental remediation, safety and much more.
30000 Attendees

Mineral Exploration Roundup

Assoc for Mineral Exploration British Columbia
889 W Pender Street
Suite 800
Vancouver, BC   V6C 3B2

604-689-4800
FAX 604-682-5733
E-Mail: roundup@amebc.ca
Home Page: www.amebc.ca

Shannon Norris, Conference Director
Simone Hill, Special Events Manager
Morgen Andoff, Conference/Volunteer Coordinator

Brings together individuals and organizations representing all the components of the global mineral exploration and mine development industry in Vancouver, Canada.
Frequency: Annual/January

National Western Mining Conference

Colorado Mining Association
216 16th Street
Suite 1250
Denver, CO   80202

303-575-9199
FAX 303-575-9194
E-Mail: colomine@coloradomining.org
Home Page: www.coloradomining.org

Frequency: Feb Denver

National Western Mining Conference & Exhibition

Colorado Mining Association
216 16th Street
Suite 1250
Denver, CO   80202-5161

303-575-9199
FAX 303-575-9194
E-Mail: colomine@coloradomining.org
Home Page: www.coloradomining.org

Stuart Sanderson, President

Annual show of 90 exhibitors of equipment and support services for the mining industry.
1000 Attendees

Northwest Mining Association Annual Meeting and Exposition

Northwest Mining Association
10 N Post Street
Suite 220
Spokane, WA   99201

509-624-1158
FAX 509-623-1241
E-Mail: nwma@nwma.com
Home Page: www.nwma.com

Pat Nelsen, Operations Director

Annual mining convention in the US. Containing 335 booths, 280 exhibits and more than 20 technical sessions. The second largest annual mining convention in the USA. Founded in 1895.
2.5M Attendees
Frequency: December

Northwest Mining Association Convention

Northwest Mining Association
10 N Post St
Suite 220
Spokane, WA   99201

509-624-1158
FAX 509-623-1241

E-Mail: pheywood@nwma.org
Home Page: www.nwma.org

Pat Heywood, Exhibit Information

Frequency: Dec 4-8 Nevada

Rapid Excavation Tunneling Conference Expo

PO Box 625002
Littleton, CO   80162-5002

303-973-9550

DD Daley, Meeting Manager

75 booths.
1M Attendees
Frequency: June

Society Mining Metallurgy Exploration

8307 Shaffer Parkway
Littleton, CO   80127-4102

303-973-9550
800-763-3132
FAX 303-973-3845
E-Mail: sme@smenet.org
Home Page: www.smenet.org

David Kanagy, Executive Director
William Wilkerson Jr, President

Five hundred booths for mining engineers, geologists and mineral industry professionals.
4M Attendees
Frequency: February

UMA Annual Convention

Utah Mining Association
136 S Main St
Suite 709
Salt Lake City, UT   84101-1683

801-364-1874
FAX 801-364-2640
E-Mail: mining@utahmining.org
Home Page: www.utahmining.org

Todd Bingham, President
Terry Maio, Chairman
Marilyn Tuttle, Admininistrator

Frequency: August

Directories & Databases

Coal Data

National Coal Association
100 Independence Ave, SW
Washington, DC   20585

202-586-8800

Offers important data on the 50 largest
coal mines in the country.
Cost: $50.00

Coal Mine Directory

Primedia
29 N Wacker Drive
10th Floor
Chicago, IL   60606-3203

312-726-2802
800-621-9907
FAX 312-726-2574
Home Page: www.primediabusiness.com

Art Sanda, Editor
Patricia L Yos, Editor

Over 2,000 coal mines are profiled that
are based in the United States and Can-
ada.
Cost: $149.00
Frequency: Annual January
Circulation: 700

DRI Coal Forecast

DRI/McGraw-Hill
24 Hartwell Ave
Lexington, MA   02421-3103

781-860-6060
FAX 781-860-6002
Home Page: www.construction.com

Walt Arvin, President

Offers valuable information on the mining of coal by supply region and producing state; total coal by demand region;
cost and demand by the consumer sector.

Engineering and Mining Journal: Buying Directory Issue

Primedia
29 N Wacker Drive
10th Floor
Chicago, IL   60606

312-726-2802
800-621-9907
FAX 312-726-2574
Home Page: www.primediabusiness.com

Robert Wyllie, Editor

List of manufacturers and suppliers of
mining equipment.
Cost: $35.00
Frequency: Annual November
Circulation: 23,000

Expanded Shale, Clay and Slate Institute Roster of Members

Expanded Shale, Clay and Slate Institute
6877 Hillside Village Cir
Suite 102
Salt Lake City, UT   84121-3363

801-272-7070
FAX 801-272-3377
E-Mail: info@escsi.org
Home Page: www.escsi.org

John Riese, President

About 15 producers by the rotary kiln
method of lightweight aggregates of expanded shales, clays, and slates; international coverage.

Geophysical Directory

Geophysical Directory
PO Box 130508
Houston, TX   77219-0508

713-291-1922
800-929-2462
FAX 713-529-3646
E-Mail: info@geophysicaldirectory.com
Home Page:
www.geophysicaldirectory.com

Claudia LaCalli, Editor
Stewart Schafer, Owner

About 4,500 companies that provide
geophysical equipment, supplies or ser-
vices and mining and petroleum compa-
nies that use geophysical techniques.
Cost: $135.00
400 Pages
Frequency: Annual March
Circulation: 2,000
Founded in 1946
*Mailing list available for rent: 2500
names*
Printed in 4 colors on glossy stock

Iron and Manganese Ore Databook

Metal Bulletin
220 5th Avenue
#Enus-19T
New York, NY   10001-7708

212-136-6202
800-MET-L 25
FAX 212-213-6273

John Bailey, Editor

Iron and manganese ore producers and
traders worldwide.
Cost: $179.00
Frequency: Quadrennial

Keystone Coal Industry Manual

Primedia
29 N Wacker Drive
10th Floor
Chicago, IL   60611

312-726-2802
800-621-9907
FAX 312-726-2574
Home Page: www.primediabusiness.com

Art Sanda, Editor
Patricia L Yos, Editor

Coal companies and mines, coke plants,
coal preparation plants, domestic and ex-
port coal sales companies.
Cost: $260.00
Frequency: Annual January
Circulation: 1,400

Landmen's Directory and Guidebook

American Association of Professional
Landmen
4100 Fossil Creek Boulevard
Fort Worth, TX   76137-2723

817-847-7700
FAX 817-847-7704
E-Mail: aapl@landman.org
Home Page: www.landman.org

Le'ann Callihan, Editor/Publications
Department

About 7,500 member specialists in as-
sembling or disposing of land or rights
required for oil, gas, coal andmineral ex-
ploration and exploitation in the US and
Canada.
Cost: $100.00
Frequency: Annual November
Circulation: 7,500
ISSN: 0272-8370

Minerals Yearbook

US Geological Survey
1730 E Parham Rd
Richmond, VA 23228-2202

804-261-2600
FAX 804-261-2659
E-Mail: dc_va@usgs.gov
Home Page: www.usgs.gov

Charles G Groats, Director

The Minerals Yearbook discusses the performance of the worldwide minerals and materials industry and provides background information to assist in interpreting that performance. Contents of the individual Minerals Yearbook volumes are, Volume I, Metals and Minerals, Volume II, Area Reports:Domestic, and Volume III, Area Reports: International.
200+ Pages
Frequency: Annual
Founded in 1935

Mining Directory

Metal Bulletin
220 5th Avenue
10th Floor
New York, NY 10001-7708

212-213-6202
800-MET-L 25
FAX 212-213-6273
E-Mail: 72610.3721@compuserve.com
Home Page:
www.metbul.com/metbul/mbhome

Don Nelson, Editor

Offers valuable information on mines, mining equipment manufacturers, suppliers of equipment and services to the industry and industry consultants.
Cost: $158.00

Mining Engineering: SME Membership Directory

Society of Mining, Metallurgy & Exploration
8307 Shaffer Pkwy
Littleton, CO 80127-4102

303-973-9550
800-763-3132
FAX 303-973-3845
E-Mail: sme@smenet.org
Home Page: www.smenet.org

David Kanagy, Executive Director
William Wilkerson Jr, President

A list of over 18,000 persons engaged in the location, exploration,treatment and

marketing of all classes of minerals except petroleum.
Cost: $150.00
Frequency: Annual
Circulation: 20,000
ISSN: 0026-5187

National Ocean Industries Association: Directory of Membership

National Ocean Industries Association
1120 G St NW
Suite 900
Washington, DC 20005-3801

202-347-6900
FAX 202-347-8650
Home Page: www.noia.org

Tom Fry, President

Over 300 firms engaged in offshore construction, drilling and petroleum production, geophysical exploration, ship building and repair, deep-sea mining and related activities in the development and use of marine resources.
Frequency: Annual

Pit & Quarry: Reference Manual & Buyers' Guide Issue

Advanstar Communications
641 Lexington Ave
8th Floor
New York, NY 10022-4503

212-951-6600
FAX 212-951-6793
E-Mail: info@advanstar.com
Home Page: www.advanstar.com

Joseph Loggia, CEO

List of approximately 1,000 manufacturers and other suppliers of equipment, products and services to the nonmetallic mining and quarrying industry.
Cost: $25.00
Frequency: Annual, September
Circulation: 25,000

Randol Buyer's Guide

Randol International Limited
18301 W Colfax Avenue
#T-2
Golden, CO 80401-4834

303-526-7618
800-726-3652
FAX 303-278-9229

Hans Von Michaelis, Editor

Approximately 10,000 companies that offer equipment and services used in the

mining industry.
Cost: $35.00
Frequency: Annual
Circulation: 10,000

Randol Mining Directory

Randol International Limited
18301 W Colfax Avenue
#T1B
Golden, CO 80401-4834

303-526-7618
FAX 303-271-0334

Hans Von Michaelis, President
Patti Hamilton, Sales Coordinator

The most comprehensive source of information on all mines in the USA. Used for systematic marketing to mines and exploration companies, statistical research and more, offering 10,000 industry contacts.

Rock Products: Buyer's Guide Issue

Primedia
29 N Wacker Drive
10th Floor
Chicago, IL 60606

312-726-2802
FAX 312-726-2574
Home Page: www.primediabusiness.com

Rick Marley, Editor
Scot Bieda, Publisher
David Pistello, Classified

List of about 1,500 providers worldwide of equipment and services for the non-metallic mineral mining and processing industry.
Cost: $100.00
Frequency: Annual November
Circulation: 23,000

Silver Refiners of the World and their Identifying Ingot Marks

Silver Institute
1112 16th St NW
Suite 240
Washington, DC 20036-4818

202-347-8200
Home Page: www.silverinstitute.org

Over 80 refiners in over 18 countries are profiled.
Cost: $33.00
85 Pages

Western Mining Directory
Howell Publishing Company
1758 Blake St
Denver, CO   80202-1226

303-296-8000
800-441-4748
FAX 303-296-1123
E-Mail: howell@rmi.net

Dave Howell, Owner

Directory of mining companies and
mines nationwide.
Cost: $49.00
Circulation: 5,000
Founded in 1968

**World Aluminum: A Metal
Bulletin Databook**
Metal Bulletin
220 5th Avenue
19th Floor
New York, NY   10001-7781

212-213-6202
FAX 212-213-1870
Home Page: www.metalbulletin.com

Offers information on producers and
traders of aluminum and aluminum al-
loys.
Cost: $247.00
540 Pages
ISSN: 0951-2233

World Mining Equipment
Metal Bulletin
220 5th Avenue
New York, NY   10001

212-213-6202
FAX 212-213-6619
Home Page: www.wme.com

Mike Woof, Editor

Manufacturers of mining equipment.
Cost: $246.00
66 Pages
Circulation: 13M
ISSN: 0746-729X
Printed in 4 colors on glossy stock

Paper & Allied Products

Associations

American Forest & Paper Association
1111 19th St NW
Suite 800
Washington, DC   20036-3652

202-463-2700
FAX 202-463-2785
E-Mail: info@afandpa.org
Home Page: www.afandpa.org

Donna Harman, CEO
Henson Moore, President

To provide significant value to member companies through outstanding performance in those areas that are key to members' success and where an association can be more effective than individual companies.
Founded in 1993

National Council for Air and Stream Improvement
PO Box 12868
New Bern, NC   28561-2868

252-637-4326
FAX 252-637-7111
E-Mail: ryeske@ncasi.org
Home Page: www.ncasi.org

Ronald A Yeske, President
Dedra Barber, Business Manager
Pamela J Bruns, Communications Manager
Carol Dwyer, Executive Secretary
Cathy Emptage, Staff Accountant

Founded by the pulp and paper industry to serve the forest products industry as a center of excellence for providing technical information and scientific research needed to achieve the industry's environmental goals and principals.
Founded in 1943

Paperboard Packaging Council
201 N Union Street
Suite 220
Alexandria, VA   22314

703-836-3300
FAX 703-836-3290
E-Mail:
paperboardpackaging@ppcnet.org
Home Page: www.ppcnet.org

Jerome T Van De Water, President
James Brown, Director Business Services
Steve Smith, Operations Manager

Members are companies making folding cartons. Provides publications and instructional materials on the paper industry and recycling.
92 Members
Founded in 1929

Newsletters

American Forest & Paper Association Report
American Forest & Paper Association
1111 19th St NW
Suite 800
Washington, DC   20036-3652

202-463-2700
FAX 202-463-2785
E-Mail: info@afandpa.org
Home Page: www.afandpa.org

Donna Harman, President & CEO

Covers events of the paper, wood and forest industry. Distribution is limited to association members only.
Cost: $1200.00
4 Pages
Frequency: Weekly
Founded in 1993

Conservatree Greenline
Greenline Publications
PO Box 590780
San Francisco, CA   94159-780

415-386-8646
FAX 415-391-7890
E-Mail: samia@greenlinepub.com
Home Page: www.conservatree.com

Alan Davis, Founder/Publisher
Susan Kinsella, Editor

Reports on efforts and achievements by businesses on the environmental front.
Cost: $59.00
Circulation: 25000
Founded in 1976

Essential Resources, LLC
45 S Park Pl
Suite 330
Morristown, NJ   07960-3924

908-832-6979
FAX 908-832-6970
E-Mail: essresou@na2k.net

Newsletters for plastic, chemical, pharmaceutical, and packaging industries.
5-15 Pages

Magazines & Journals

International Paper Board Industry
Brunton Publications & NV Public
43 Main Street
Avon By The Sea, NJ   07717-1051

732-502-0500
FAX 732-502-9606
E-Mail: jcurley@NVPublications.com
Home Page: www.nvpublications.com

Mike Brunton, Publisher
Jim Curley, Editor-in-Chief
Gail Kalina, Production Manager
Tom Vilardi, President
Dan Brunton, Marketing Manager

Information on corrugated paper and converting industry, encompassing news and production worldwide.
Cost: $60.00
Frequency: Monthly
Circulation: 10021

Journal of Intelligent Materials and Structures
Technomic Publishing Company
PO Box 3535
Lancaster, PA   17601

717-291-5609
800-233-9936
FAX 717-295-4538
E-Mail: aflannery@techpub.com
Home Page: www.techpub.com

Amy Flannery, Marketing

Original papers, describing experimental or theoretical work on all aspects of intelligent materials, systems and structures research. The scope is generally inclusive. Papers related to the science and engineering of intelligent systems are featured, particularly biomimetrics, applied mathematics of phase transitions and material science, neural networks, structural dynamic control, and adaptive

and sensing materials.
Cost: $995.00
80 Pages
Frequency: Monthly
ISSN: 1045-389X
Printed in 2 colors on matte stock

Mill Trade Journal's Recycling Markets

NV Business Publishers Corporation
43 Main St
Avon By the Sea, NJ   07717-1051

732-502-0500
800-962-3001
FAX 732-502-9606
E-Mail:
advertising@NVPublications.com
Home Page: www.nvpublications.com

Ted Vilardi, Owner
Roy Bradbrook, Editor
Jim Curley, Editor-in-Chief
Gail Kalina, Production Manager
Robyn Smith, Executive Publisher

Information on recycling mills paper stock, scrap metal and plastics brokers and dealers used by the municipal governments and private organizations as a basis for letting contracts.
Cost: $130.00
Frequency: Fortnightly
Circulation: 3625
Founded in 1984
Printed in 2 colors on matte stock

Paper Stock Report: News and Trends of the Paper Recycling Markets

McEntee Media Corporation
13727 Holland Road
Brook Park, OH   44142

216-362-7979
FAX 216-362-6553
E-Mail:
mcenteemedia@compuserve.com
Home Page: www.recyle.cc

Ken McEntee, President

Covers news and trends of the scrap paper markets.
Cost: $115.00
Frequency: BiWeekly
Founded in 1990

Paper, Film & Foil Converter

Penton Media Inc
330 N Wabash Ave
Suite 2300
Chicago, IL   60611-7619

312-321-0094
800-458-0479
FAX 312-595-0295
E-Mail: yolanda.simonsis@penton.com
Home Page: www.penton.com

Cameron Bishop, Manager
Scott Bieda, Publisher
Nsenga Byrd Thompson, Marketing Manager

Recognizes experts and experienced staff that assist converters to become more effiecient and profitable in their manufacturing and business practices through newsworthy information on technology; marketing and management trends and products and services.

Recycled Paper News

McEntee Media Corporation
9815 Hazelwood Ave
Strongsville, OH   44149-2305

440-238-6603
FAX 440-238-6712
E-Mail: info@recycle.cc
Home Page: www.recycle.cc

Ken Mc Entee, Owner

Coverage of markets and environmental issues related to recycled paper and evironmentally friendly paper making process.
Cost: $235.00
Frequency: Monthly
Founded in 1990

Trade Shows

International Environmental Conference and Exhibit

Technical Association of the Pulp & Paper Industry
15 Technology Parkway S
Norcross, GA   30092

770-446-1400
800-322-8686
FAX 770-446-6947
E-Mail: webmaster@tappi.org
Home Page: www.tappi.org

Mark McCollister, Chairman
Jeffrey Siegel, Vice Chairman

Fifty booths; pulp and paper environmental control equipment and consultants.
500 Attendees
Frequency: May

National Paper Trade Association Convention Expo

National Paper Trade Association
111 Great Neck Road
Suite 418
Great Neck, NY   11021-5497

516-829-3070
FAX 516-829-3074
E-Mail: bill@goNPTA.com
Home Page: www.gonpta.com

William Frohlich, President

Annual convention of 135 manufacturers, suppliers and distributors of paper products, including packaging materials, health care disposables, industrial and retail packaging supplies, sanitary supplies and computer equipment.
3000 Attendees
Frequency: Annual September
Founded in 1903

Petroleum & Allied Products

Associations

ADSC: The International Association of Foundation Drilling
Pacific Center I
14180 Dallas Parkway Suite 510
Dallas, TX 75254

214-343-2091
FAX 214-343-2384
E-Mail: adsc@adsc-iafd.com
Home Page: www.adsc-iafd.com

Michael D Moore, CEO
Jan Hall, Director of Meetings/MarCom

ADSC seeks to advance technology in the foundation of drilling and anchored earth retention industries. Represents drilled shaft, anchored earth retention, micropile contractors, civil engineers and manufacturing firms world wide.
Founded in 1972

American Association of Petroleum Geologists
PO Box 979
Tulsa, OK 74101-0979

918-584-2555
FAX 918-560-2632
E-Mail: bulletin@aapg.org
Home Page: www.aapg.org

Rick Fritz, Executive Director

Supports those professionals involved in the field of geology as it relates to petroleum, natural gas, and other energy products. Publishes monthly journal of peer-reviewed articles.
30000 Members
Founded in 1917
Mailing list available for rent

American Association of Professional Landmen
4100 Fossil Creek Boulevard
Fort Worth, TX 76137

817-847-7700
FAX 817-847-7704
E-Mail: info@infomine.com
Home Page: www.infomine.com

Andy Robertson, Executive Chairman
Rod Young, CEO
Graham Baldwin, President
Robin Forte, Manager

Supports a four-year college curriculum developed by AAPL. Operates landmen certification programs. Maintains placement service.
7000 Members
Founded in 1955

American Gas Association
400 N Capitol Street NW
Suite 450
Washington, DC 20001

202-824-7000
FAX 202-824-7092
E-Mail: ykorolevich@aga.org
Home Page: www.aga.org

David N Parker, CEO
Kevin Hardardt, CFO/CAO
Ysabel Korolevich, Membership Services

The American Gas Association advocates the interests of its members and their customers, and provides information and services promoting efficient demand and supply growth and operational excellence in the safe, reliable and efficient delivery of natural gas.
Founded in 1918

American Institute of Mining Metallurgical & Petroleum Engineers
8307 Shaffer Parkway
P O Box 270728
Littleton, CO 80127-4012

303-948-4255
FAX 303-948-4260
E-Mail: aime@aimehq.org
Home Page: www.aimehq.org

J Rick Rolater, Executive Director
L Michele Gottwald, Executive Assistant

AIME is and shall be a New York State Nonprofit Corporation organized and operated to advance and disseminate, through the programs of the Member Societies, knowledge of engineering and the arts and sciences involved in the production and use of minerals, metals, energy sources and materials for the benefit of humankind, and to represent AIME and the Member Societies within the larger engineering community.
90000 Members
Founded in 1871

American Petroleum Institute
1220 L St NW
Suite 900
Washington, DC 20005-4070

202-289-2250
FAX 202-682-8232
Home Page: www.api.org

Jack Gerard, CEO

Seeks to maintain cooperation between government and industry, fosters foreign and domestic trade in American petroleum products, conducts research.
500 Members
Founded in 1919

American Public Gas Association
201 Massachusetts Ave NE
Suite C-4
Washington, DC 20002-4957

202-464-0240
FAX 202-464-0246
E-Mail: dnaples@apga.org
Home Page: www.apga.org

Bert Kalisch, President
David Schryver, Exec VP/VP Congressional Affairs

To be an advocate for public-owned natural gas distribution systems, educate and communicate with members to promote safety, awareness, performance and competitiveness.
730 Members
Founded in 1961

Association of Energy Service Companies
Ste 250
14531 Fm 529 Rd
Houston, TX 77095-3528

713-781-0758
800-672-0771
FAX 713-781-7542
E-Mail: pjordan@aesc.net
Home Page: www.aesc.net

Kenny Jordan, Executive Director
Patty Jordan, Publisher/Sales Manager
Angla Fails, Administrative Manager

Professional trade association for well-site service contractors and businesses providing goods and services to well-site contractors. Develops and sells training and safety materials.
600 Members
Founded in 1956

Association of Oil Pipe Lines

1808 Eye St NW
Suite 300
Washington, DC   20006-5423

202-408-7970
FAX 202-408-7983
E-Mail: aopl@aopl.org
Home Page: www.aopl.org

Shirley Neff, President
Steve Kramer, General
Counsel/Secretary

Acts as an information clearinghouse for the public, the media and the pipeline industry; provides coordination and leaderships for the industry's ongoing joint Environmental Safety Initiative; and represents common carrier crude and product petroleum pipleines in Congress, before regulatory agencies, and in the federal courts.
47 Members
Founded in 1947

Coordinating Research Council

3650 Mansell Rd
Suite 140
Alpharetta, GA   30022-3068

678-795-0506
FAX 678-795-0509
E-Mail: jantucker@crcao.com
Home Page: www.crcao.org

Brent Bailey, Executive Director
Christopher Tennant, Deputy Director
Debra Carter, Controller

Coordinates research activities among petroleum and petroleum equipment and transportation industries.
1M Members
Founded in 1942

Council of Petroleum Accountants Societies

3900 East Mexico Avenue
Suite 602
Denver, CO   80210

303-300-1311
877-992-6727
FAX 303-300-3733
E-Mail: NatlOfc@copas.org
Home Page: www.copas.org

Scott Hillman, Executive Director

Members are accountants involved in, or closely related to, the oil and gas industry. Also provides ethical standards for energy accountants and is the certifica-

tion organization for the Accredited Petroleum Accountant program.
3200 Members
Founded in 1961

Domestic Petroleum Council

101 Constitution Avenue NW
Suite 800
Washington, DC   20001-2133

202-742-4300
E-Mail: info@dcpusa.org
Home Page: www.dpcusa.org/

William F Whitsitt, President

To work constructively for sound energy, environmental and related public policies that encourage responsible exploration, development, and production of natural gas and crude oil to meet consumer needs and fuel our economy.
24 Members
Founded in 1975

Energy Security Council

5555 San Felipe Street
Suite 101
Houston, TX   77056

713-296-1893
FAX 713-296-1895
E-Mail: info@energysecuritycouncil.org
Home Page:
www.energysecuritycouncil.org

John J Covert, Executive Director

Founded as Petroleum Industry Security Council and assumed its current name in 1999. Provides support to security professionals and business developers in the energy industry.
450 Members
Founded in 1981

Energy Telecommunications and Electrical Association

5005 W Royal Lane
Suite 116
Irving, TX   75063

972-929-3169
888-503-8700
FAX 972-915-6040
E-Mail: info@entelec.org
Home Page: www.entelec.org
Social Media: , *LinkedIn*

Blaine Siske, Executive Manager
Amanda Prudden, Association Manager
Tiffany Chase, Operations Coordinator

A user association that focuses on communications and control technologies

used by petroleum, natural gas, pipeline and electric utility companies. Primary goal is to provide education for its members.
Founded in 1928

Energy Traffic Association

3303 Main Street Corridor
Houston, TX   77002

713-528-2868
FAX 713-464-0702
E-Mail: russell@energytraffic.org
Home Page: www.energytraffic.org

Russell Powell, Executive Director

The members work in logistics or related company functions for shippers in the energy industry.
100 Members
Founded in 1941

Gas Research Machinery Council

3030 LBJ Freeway
Suite 1300
Dallas, TX   75234

972-620-4024
FAX 972-620-8518
E-Mail: mshort@southerngas.org
Home Page: www.gmrc.org

Marsha Short, VP

Members are companies in the natural gas, oil and petrochemical industries in mechanical and fluid systems design.
75 Members
Founded in 1952

Institute of Gas Technology

1700 S Mount Prospect Rd
Des Plaines, IL   60018-1804

847-768-0664
FAX 847-768-0669
E-Mail: gtiadmin@gastechnology.org
Home Page: www.gastechnology.org

Carol L Worster, Manager
Edward Johnston, Managing Director
David C Carroll, VP Business
Development Division
James E Dunne, VP Administration/CFO

An independent, not-for-profit center for energy and environmental research, development, education and information. Main function is to perform sponsored and in-house research, development and demonstration, provide educational programs and services, and disseminate scientific and technical information.
Founded in 1941

International Association of Drilling Contractors

10370 Richmond Ave
Suite 760
Houston, TX   77042-9687

713-292-1945
FAX 713-292-1946
E-Mail: info@iadc.org
Home Page: www.iadc.org
Social Media: *Facebook, Twitter, LinkedIn*

Lee Hunt, President
Tom Terrell, Senior VP Business Development

Dedicated to enhancing the interests of the oil-and-gas and geothermal drilling and completion industry worldwide
1239 Members
Founded in 1940

International Association of Geophysical

P.O.Box 421275
Houston, TX   77242-1275

713-957-8080
FAX 713-957-0008
E-Mail: iagc@iagc.org
Home Page: www.iagc.org

Chip Gill, President
Criss Rennie, Office Manager

Companies involved in oil exploration.
203 Members
Founded in 1971

International Energy Credit Association

8325 Lantern View Lane
St John, IN   46373

219-365-7313
FAX 219-365-0327
E-Mail: rraichle@ieca.net
Home Page: www.ieca.net

Robert Raichle, Executive VP

Members are credit and financial executives with companies whose product is a petroleum derivative.
800 Members
Founded in 1923

International Oil Scouts Association

PO Box 272949
Houston, TX   77277

512-472-8138
E-Mail: jyoung@newfld.com
Home Page: www.oilscouts.org

Jim Young, President
David Martinez, VP
John Reedy, Treasurer
Bill Morris, Secretary

Compiles statistics on exploration and development wells in the United States. Offers professional development and scholarship programs.
Cost: $75.00
175 Members
Founded in 1924

International Slurry Surfacing Association

3 Church Cir
Annapolis, MD   21401-1933

410-267-0023
FAX 410-267-7546
E-Mail: krissoff@slurry.org
Home Page: www.slurry.org

Mike Krissoff, Executive Director

A non profit association dedicated to the interests, education, and success of slurry surfacing professionals and corporations around the world.
200 Members
Founded in 1963

Interstate Natural Gas Association of America

10 G St NE
Suite 700
Washington, DC   20002-4248

202-216-5900
FAX 202-216-0870
Home Page: www.ingaa.org

Donald Santa, President
Joan Dreskin, VP General Counsel/RA Secretary
Martin Edwards III, VP of Legislative Affairs
Terry D Boss, SVP/Safety/Environment

Trade association of natural gas pipelines in the United States, Canada, Mexico and Europe.
30 Members
Founded in 1944

Interstate Oil and Gas Compact Commission

PO Box 53127
Oklahoma City, OK   73152-3127

405-525-2556
FAX 405-525-3592
E-Mail: iogcc@iogcc.state.ok.us
Home Page:
www.iogcc.oklaosf.state.ok.us

Christine Hansen, Executive Director
Alesha Leemaster, Manager Communications

The members are states that produce oil or gas; associate states support the conservation of America's energy resources. Also establishes rules andguidelines for the proper maintenance of wells.
700 Members
Founded in 1935

Liaison Committee of Cooperating Oil and Gas Association

1718 Columbus Road SW
PO Box 535
Granville, OH   13023-0535

740-587-0444
FAX 740-587-0446
E-Mail: stewart@ooga.org
Home Page:
www.energyconnect.com/liason

Thomas E Stewart, Secretary/Treasurer

Established to facilitate communication among state and regional oil and gas associations.
25 Members
Founded in 1957

Mid-Continent Oil and Gas Association

801 North Blvd
Baton Rouge, LA   70802-5727

225-387-3205
FAX 225-344-5502
E-Mail: e-mail info@lmoga.com
Home Page: www.lmoga.com

Chris John, President

Oil and gas producers and royalty owners.
7.5M Members
Founded in 1917

NLGI

4635 Wyandotte St
Suite 202
Kansas City, MO   64112-1537

816-931-9480
FAX 816-753-5026
E-Mail: nlgi@nlgi.org
Home Page: www.nlgi.org

Kim Bott, Executive Director

Members are companies that manufacture and market all types of lubricating greases, additive or equipment suppliers, and research and educational groups whose interests are primarily technical.
280 Members
Founded in 1933

NORA: An Association of Responsible Recyclers

5965 Amber Ridge Rd
Haymarket, VA   20169-2623

703-753-4277
FAX 703-753-2445
E-Mail: sparker@noranews.org
Home Page: www.noranews.org

Scott Parker, Executive Director

Members are companies that reprocess used antifreeze, wastewater, oil filters, chemicals and companies that provide products or services to the industry.
211 Members
Founded in 1984

National Drilling Association

1545 W 130th Street
Suite A2
Hinckley, OH   44233

330-273-5756
877-632-4748
FAX 216-803-9900
E-Mail: info@nda4u.com
Home Page: www.nda4u.com

Peggy McGee, President
Dan Dunn, VP
Jim Howe, Secretary/Treasurer
Tim Cleary, Board of Directors
R. Alan Garrard, Board of Directors

A non-profit trade association of contractors, manufacturers and affiliated members from the drilling industry representing the geotechnical, environmental and mineral exploration sectors of this industry.
250+ Members
Founded in 1972

National Ocean Industries Association

1120 G St NW
Suite 900
Washington, DC   20005-3801

202-347-6900
FAX 202-347-8650
Home Page: www.noia.org

Tom Fry, President

Represents all facets of the domestic offshore and related industries. Member companies are dedicated to the development of offshore oil and natural gas for the continued growth and security of the US.
300 Members
Founded in 1972

National Petrochemical & Refiners Association

1664 K Street NW
Washington, DC   20006-1654

202-457-0480
FAX 202-457-0486
E-Mail: info@npra.org
Home Page: www.npra.org

Charles Drevna, President
Greg Scott, Executive VP

Association that represents the petrochemical and refining industries, sponsors periodic conferences, and seeks to inform policymakers and the public. Issues include the recycling of used oils and other liquid wastes.
450 Members

National Petroleum Council

1625 K St NW
Suite 600
Washington, DC   20006-1656

202-393-6100
FAX 202-331-8539
E-Mail: info@npc.org
Home Page: www.npc.org

Marshall W Nichols, Executive Director
Lee Raymond, Chair

Self-supporting, federal advisory body to the Secretary of Energy established in 1946 at the request of President Truman.
175 Members
Founded in 1946

National Propane Gas Association

1899 L St NW
Suite 310
Washington, DC   20036-3804

202-466-7200
FAX 202-466-7205
E-Mail: info@npga.org
Home Page: www.npga.org

Richard Roldan, President/CEO
Brian Dunlapford, CFO

Members are producers and distributors of liquified petroleum gas and equipment manufacturers.
3500 Members
Founded in 1931

National Stripper Well Association

1201 15th St NW
Suite 300
Washington, DC   20005-2842

202-857-4722
FAX 202-857-4799
Home Page: www.ipaa.org

Barry Russell, President
Dan Naatz, VP

This operates under the Independent Petroleum Associatin of America, which is an informed voice for the exloration and production segment of the industry It provides economic and statistical information, and develops investment symposia and other opportunities for its memners.
300 Members
Founded in 1934

Natural Gas Supply Association

805 15th St NW
Suite 510
Washington, DC   20005-2276

202-326-9305
FAX 202-326-9330
Home Page: www.ngsa.org

Skip Horvath, President
Pat Jagtiani, VP
Jeff Schrade, Public Relations Director

Represents U.S.-based producers and marketers of natural gas on issues that affect the natural gas industry, including the residential and industrial consumers who rely on the fuel for a myriad of purposes.

Nuclear Energy Institute

1776 Eye St NW
Suite 400
Washington, DC 20006-3700

202-739-8000
FAX 202-785-4019
Home Page: www.nei.org

Marvin S Fertel, CEO

Members are of utilities, manufacturers of electrical generating equipment, researchers, architects, engineers, labor unions, and others interested in the generation of electricity by nuclear power.
370 Members
Founded in 1981

Petroleum Technology Transfer Council

16010 Barkers Point Lane
Suite 220
, TX 77079

281-921-1720
FAX 281-921-1723
E-Mail: hq@pttc.org
Home Page: www.pttc.org

Don Duttlinger, Executive Director
Brian Sim, Chairman
Gene Ames III, Secretary

Fosters the effective transfer of exploration and production technology to US petroleum producers through regional resource centers, workshops, websites, publications, etc.
Founded in 1993

Pipeline Research Council International

1401 Wilson Blvd
Suite 1101
Arlington, VA 22209-2318

703-387-0190
FAX 703-837-0192
E-Mail: gtenely@prci.com
Home Page: www.prci.org

George W Tenley Jr, Manager

Sponsors research on technical issues facing the natural gas transmission industry. Members are companies operating pipeline systems.
24 Members
Founded in 1952

Society of Petroleum Engineers

PO Box 833836
Richardson, TX 75083-3836

972-529-9300
FAX 972-952-9435
E-Mail: spedal@spe.org
Home Page: www.spe.org

Kate Baker, President
Peter Goode, VP Finance
Alex Neyin, Director Africa Region
Ali R Al-Jarwan, Director Middle East Region
Mark Rubin, Executive Director

Supports those professionals involved in the field of exploration, drilling, production, and reservoir management, as well as related manufacturing and service organizations. Publishes monthly magazine.
55000 Members
Founded in 1957

Society of Petroleum Evaluation Engineers

1001 McKinney St
Suite 801
Houston, TX 77002-6417

713-651-1639
FAX 713-951-9659
E-Mail: bkspee@aol.com
Home Page: www.spee.org

B K Buongiorno, Executive Secretary
E Bernard Brauer, President
S Tim Smith, VP

Members are engineers specializing in the fields of petroleum and natural gas properties.
495 Members
Founded in 1962

Society of Petrophysicists and Well Log Analysts

8866 Gulf Fwy
Suite 320
Houston, TX 77017-6531

713-947-8727
FAX 713-947-7181
E-Mail: info@spwla.org
Home Page: www.spwla.org

Vicki J King, Executive Director
Sharon Johnson, Admin Asst

Provides information services to scientists in the petroleum and mineral industries, serves as a voice of shared interests in our profession, plays a major role in strengthening petrophysical education, and strives to increase the awareness of the role petrophysics has in the Oil and Gas Industry and the scientific community.
3300 Members
Founded in 1959

Society of Professional Well Log Analysts

8866 Gulf Freeway
Suite 320
Houston, TX 77017

713-947-8727
FAX 713-947-7181
E-Mail: info@spwla.org
Home Page: www.spwla.org

Vicki J King, Executive Director
Sharon Johnson, Admin Asst

Promotes the evaluation of formations, through well logging techniques, in order to locate gas, oil and other minerals.
2800 Members
Founded in 1959

Solution Mining Research Institute

105 Apple Valley Circle
Clarks Summit, PA 18411

570-585-8092
E-Mail: smri@solutionmining.org
Home Page: www.solutionmining.org

John O Voigt, Executive Director
Carolyn L Diamond, Assistant Executive Director

Members are companies interested in the production of salt brine and solution mining of potash and soda ash, as well as production of salt covers, used for storage of oil, gas, chemicals, compressed air and waste.
100 Members
Founded in 1958

Spill Control Association of America

2105 Laurel Bush Rd
Suite 200
Bel Air, MD 21015

443-640-1085
FAX 443-640-1086
E-Mail: info@scaa-spill.org
Home Page: www.scaa-spill.org

John Parker, President
Ralph Bianchi, VP Manufacturers
Mark Miller, VP Contractors
Michael Sapala, Manager

Members are companies concerned with cleaning up spills of oil and hazardous products and manufacturers of specialized products for spill control.
Founded in 1973

Tubular Exchanger Manufacturers Association

25 North Broadway
Tarrytown, NY 10591

914-332-0040
FAX 914-332-1541
E-Mail: info@tema.org
Home Page: www.tema.org

Richard C Byrne, Secretary

Sets standards for the industry, known as TEMA Standards, which are sold to the chemical processing and petroleum refining industries
18 Members
Founded in 1939

Western States Petroleum Association

1415 L St
Suite 600
Sacramento, CA 95814-3964

916-444-9981
FAX 916-444-5745
Home Page: www.wspa.org

Joe Sparano, President
Catherine Reheis-Boyd, COO
Steven Arita, Senior Environmental Coordinator
Barbara Chichester, Bookkeeper

Trade association that represents the full spectrum of those companies that refine, produce, transport, and market petroleum and petroleum products in six western states: Arizona, California, Oregon, Nevada, Hawaii and Washington.
35 Members
Founded in 1907

Newsletters

Coal and Synfuels Technology

Pasha Publications
1600 Wilson Boulevard
Suite 600
Arlington, VA 22209-2510

703-528-1244
800-424-2908
FAX 703-528-1253

Harry Baisden, Group Publisher
Michael Hopps, Editor

Reports on the US and international advances in clean coal technologies, synthetic fuels and clean air issues.
Cost: $790.00
Frequency: Weekly
Founded in 1985

Cold Water Oil Spills

Cutter Information Corporation
37 Broadway
Suite 1
Arlington, MA 02474-5500

781-648-1950
800-888-8939
FAX 781-648-1950
E-Mail: service@cutter.com
Home Page: www.cutter.com

Kim Leonard, Editor
Karen Coburn, President/CEO

Clean up and control of oil spills in cold and icy waters.
Cost: $175.00
Founded in 1986

Gas Daily

1200 G Street NW
#1000
Washington, DC 20005

202-383-2100
800-752-8878
FAX 202-383-2125
E-Mail: support@platts.com
Home Page: www.gasdaily.com

Mark Davidson, Publisher
Bill Loveless, Manager

Information on spot prices cash markets and regulatory developments for the natural gas industry.
Cost: $2255.00
Frequency: Daily

Gas Storage Report

Pasha Publications
1600 Wilson Boulevard
#600
Arlington, VA 22209-2510

703-528-1244
180- 42- 290
FAX 703-528-7821
E-Mail: gasstor@pasha.com
Home Page: www.pasha.com

Jeff Pruzan, Editor

Detailed charts that list monthly storage activity of all interstate pipelines and covers all phases of the underground storage of natural gas.
Cost: $495.00
Frequency: Monthly

Golob's Oil Pollution Bulletin

World Information Systems
PO Box 535
Cambridge, MA 02238-0535

FAX 617-492-3312

Richard S Golob, Publisher
Roger B Wilson Jr, Editor

Provides news analysis on oil pollution prevention, control and cleanup. Covers oil spills worldwide, regulations, legislation and court decisions, technical reports, new equipment and products, contract opportunities and awards, and conference notices.
Cost: $335.00
Frequency: BiWeekly
Circulation: 20,000

Gulf of Mexico Newsletter

Offshore Data Services
3200 Wilcrest Dr
Suite 170
Houston, TX 77042-3366

832-463-3000
FAX 832-463-3100
E-Mail: editors@offshore-data.com
Home Page: www.ods-petrodata.com

Thomas E Marsh, President
Hannah Hartland, Sales Administrator

Aimed at the supply and service people of the off-shore oil and gas industry in the Gulf of Mexico, covers all significant industry news and events, and summarizes construction and field

development activities.
Cost: $259.00
Frequency: Weekly
Circulation: 2150
Founded in 2002

ILMA Compoundings

Independent Lubricant Manufacturers
Association
400 N Columbus St
Suite 201
Alexandria, VA 22314-2264

703-684-5574
FAX 703-836-8503
E-Mail: ilma@ilma.org
Home Page: www.ilma.org

Celeste Powers, Executive Director
Martha Jolkovski, Director
Publications/Advertising

Focuses on legislative, regulatory, marketing and industry news of concern to independent blenders and compounders of high-quality lubricants. Accepts advertising.
Cost: $150.00
20 Pages
Frequency: Monthly
Circulation: 1800
Founded in 1948

Independent Liquid Terminals Association Newsletter

Independent Liquid Terminals
Association
1444 I St Nw
Suite 400
Washington, DC 20005-6538

202-842-9200
FAX 202-326-8660
E-Mail: info@ilta.org
Home Page: www.ilta.org

E David Doane, President
Gwen Butler, Office Manager

Monthly publication detailing federal, state and local legislative and regulatory action, ILTA response and ILTA events. Geared specifically to bulk liquid terminal owners/operators and establishments supplying equipment, goods and services to the bulk liquid terminaling industry.
8 Pages
Frequency: Monthly
Printed in 2 colors

International Gas Technology Highlights

Institute of Gas Technology
1700 S Mount Prospect Rd
Des Plaines, IL 60018-1804

847-768-0664
FAX 847-768-0669
E-Mail: gtiadmin@gastechnology.org
Home Page: www.gastechnology.org

David Carroll, President/CEO
Edward Johnston, Managing Director

A biweekly newsletter covering international developments in energy with a focus on natural gas.
Cost: $100.00
4 Pages
Circulation: 1600
Founded in 1946
Printed in 2 colors on matte stock

International Oil News

William F Bland
709 Turmeric Ln
Durham, NC 27713-3103

919-544-1717
FAX 919-544-1999
E-Mail: mbs@PetroChemical-News.com
Home Page:
www.petrochemical-news.com/pcn.htm

Susan Kensil, President
Mollie B Sandor, Circulation Director

A weekly report of current news about all areas of the international petroleum industry, exploration, production, processing, transportation and marketing.
Cost: $857.00
Frequency: Weekly
Founded in 1963

International Summary and Review of Oil Spills

Cutter Information Corporation
37 Broadway
Suite 1
Arlington, MA 02474-5500

781-648-1950
FAX 781-648-1950
Home Page: www.cutter.com

Verna Allee, Senior Consultant

International coverage of the gas and oil industry.
Cost: $100.00
Frequency: Monthly
Founded in 1986

LNG Observer

Institute of Gas Technology
1700 S Mount Prospect Rd
Des Plaines, IL 60018-1804

847-768-0664
FAX 847-768-0669
E-Mail: sen@igt.org
Home Page: www.gastechnology.org

David Carroll, President/CEO

A bimonthly publication covering the worldwide liquefied natural gas industry, including political developments, technology, economics, statistics and interviews with industry leaders.
Cost: $395.00
24 Pages
Frequency: Bi-Monthly
Circulation: 2,000
ISBN: 1-053694-9 -

Lundberg Letter

Lundberg Survey
911 Via Alondra
Camarillo, CA 93012-8048

805-383-2400
800-660-4574
FAX 805-383-2424
E-Mail: lsi@lundbergsurvey.com
Home Page: www.lundbergsurvey.com

Trilby Lundberg, President

News on the US gasoline and diesel market. Retail and wholesale prices, market shares, consumption, taxes, station populations and consumer trends.
Cost: $399.00
Founded in 1950

NGI's Daily Gas Price Index

Intelligence Press
PO Box 70587
Washington, DC 20024

202-583-2596
800-427-5747
FAX 202-318-0597
E-Mail:
subscriptions@intelligencepress.com
Home Page: intelligencepress.com

Ellen Beswick, Publisher
Mike Nazzaro, CEO

Gas industry news, reports and statistics.
Cost: $1045.00
Frequency: Daily

Natural Gas Intelligence/Gas Price Index

Intelligence Press
PO Box 70587
Washington, DC   20024

202-583-2596
800-427-5747
FAX 202-318-0597
E-Mail: ellen@intelligencepress.com
Home Page: www.intelligencepress.com

Ellen Beswick, Publisher

Statistics and research for the gas and petroleum industry.
Cost: $1195.00
Frequency: Weekly
Founded in 1981

Natural Gas Week

Energy Intelligence Group
1401 New York Ave Nw
Suite 500
Washington, DC   20005-2102

202-393-5113
FAX 202-393-5115
E-Mail: info@energyintel.com
Home Page: www.accion.org

Maria Otero, President
Mike Sultan, Associate Editor

Economics news covering the gas industry.
Cost: $1860.00
20 Pages
Frequency: Weekly
Founded in 1985
Printed in 2 colors on matte stock

News Fuel & Vehicles Report

Inside Washington Publishers
1919 S Eads St
Suite 201
Arlington, VA   22202-3028

703-418-3981
800-424-9068
FAX 703-416-8543
E-Mail: iwp@iwpnews.com
Home Page: www.iwpnews.com

Latest news, research and reports on alternative fuels and vehicles development aimed toward the program managers, lobbyists, policy makers, and auto, oil and corn chemical industries.
Cost: $985.00
Founded in 1980

Ocean News & Technology

Technology Systems Corporation
PO Box 1096
Palm City, FL   34991-7174

772-221-7720
FAX 772-221-7715
E-Mail: techsystems@sprintmail.com
Home Page: www.ocean-news.com

Dan White, Editor
Sharon White, Circulation Manager

Magazine focusing on the major business areas of the ocean industry. News articles and technology developments are covered in areas including defense, offshore oil, diving, science, environment and marine.
Cost: $45.00
Founded in 1981

Offshore International Newsletter

Offshore Data Services
PO Box 19909
Houston, TX   77224-1909

713-781-7094
FAX 713-781-9594
E-Mail: editors@offshore-data.com
Home Page: www.offshore-data.com

Susanne Pagano, Editor
Thomas E Marsh, Publisher

News and information regrading the offshore oil and gas industry worldwide, while highlighting oil discoveries, licensing arrangements, contract awards, mergers and the market outlook.
Cost: $699.00
Frequency: Weekly
Circulation: 750
Founded in 1973

Offshore Rig Newsletter

Offshore Data Services
3200 Wilcrest Dr
Suite 170
Houston, TX   77042-3366

832-463-3000
FAX 832-463-3100
E-Mail: editors@offhsore-data.com
Home Page: www.ods-petrodata.com

Thomas E Marsh, President
Barry Young, Marketing Director

Emerging markets, accidents, new technology, financing schemes, insurance trends, rig construction, moves, sales, and rates, labor problems, attrition, marketing strategies, and the corporate ac-

tivities of drilling contractors.
Cost: $220.00
Frequency: Monthly
Circulation: 900
Founded in 1973

Oil Daily

Energy Intelligence Group
1401 New York Ave Nw
Suite 500
Washington, DC   20005-2102

202-393-5113
FAX 202-393-5115
E-Mail: info@energyintel.com
Home Page: www.accion.org

Maria Otero, President

Magazine on the petroleum and oil industry, available on line.
Cost: $1880.00
Frequency: Daily
Circulation: 60000
Founded in 1951

Oil Express

United Communications Group
11300 Rockville Pike
Street 1100
Rockville, MD   20852-3030

301-287-2700
FAX 301-816-8945
E-Mail: webmaster@ucg.com
Home Page: www.ucg.com

Benny Dicecca, President

Information for gasoline marketers.
Cost: $447.00
8 Pages
Frequency: Monthly
Founded in 1977

Oil Spill Intelligence Report

Aspen Publishers
111 8th Ave
Suite 700
New York, NY   10011-5207

212-771-0600
800-234-1660
FAX 212-771-0885
E-Mail: newmediainfo@aspenpubl.com
Home Page: www.aspenpublishers.com

Richard Kravits, Executive VP
Gerry Centrowitz,
Marketing/Communications Manager

Provides timely coverage of oil spills worldwide.
Cost: $695.00
6 Pages
Frequency: Weekly
Founded in 1978

Oil Spill United States Law Report

Aspen Publishers
76 Ninth Avenue
7th Floor
New York, NY   10011

212-771-0600
800-638-8437
Home Page: www.aspenpublishers.com

Mark Dorman, CEO
Gustavo Dobles, VP Operations

Professionals who need to stay abreast of US federal and state regulations.
Cost: $7.67
12 Pages
Frequency: Monthly

Oil, Gas and Petrochem Equipment

PennWell Publishing Company
1421 S Sheridan Rd
Tulsa, OK   74112-6619

918-831-9421
800-331-4463
FAX 918-831-9476
E-Mail: headquarters@penwell.com
Home Page: www.pennwell.com

Robert Biolchini, President
Tim L Tobeck, Group Publisher
J B Avants, Publisher & Editor

The petroleum industry's only all new products and services magazine. Each month it announces the newest developments in equipment, products, systems and services for drilling, production, refining, petrochemical manufacturing, pipeline/storage and gas processing.
Cost: $35.00
Frequency: Monthly
Circulation: 32000
Founded in 1955
Mailing list available for rent: 32,000 names
Printed in 4 colors on glossy stock

PTTC Network News

Petroleum Technology Transfer Council
16010 Barkers Point Lane
Suite 220
Houston, TX   77079

281-921-1720
FAX 281-921-1723
E-Mail: hq@pttc.org
Home Page: www.pttc.org

Kristi Lovendahl, Webmaster/Newsletter Editor
Norma Gutierrez, Circulation Director
Donald Duttlinger, Executive Director

16 page newsletter with east to read summaries of new oil and natural gas technologies.
Frequency: Quarterly
Circulation: 17000
Founded in 1994

PetroChemical News

William F Bland
PO Box 16666
Chapel Hill, NC   27516-6666

919-490-0700
FAX 919-490-3002

Susan D Kensil, Editor

A fast, accurate report of significant world petrochemical developments.
Cost: $739.00
4 Pages
Frequency: Weekly

Petroleum Intelligence Weekly

5 E 37th St
Suite 5
New York, NY   10016-2807

212-532-1112
FAX 212-532-4479
E-Mail: info@energyintel.com
Home Page: www.energyintel.com

Tom Wallin, President
Peter Kemp, Editor
Raja W. Sidawi, Chairman
Sarah Miller, Editor-at-Large

News of the oil and gas industries worldwide.
Cost: $3340.00
Frequency: Weekly
Founded in 1961

Platt's Oilgram News

McGraw Hill
3333 Walnut Street
Boulder, CO   80301-2525

720-485-5000
800-752-8878
FAX 720-548-5701
E-Mail: support@platts.com
Home Page: www.platts.com

O Marashian, Publisher
James Keener, Marketing
Harry Sachinsis, President

News of the oil and gas industries worldwide.
Frequency: Daily
Founded in 1888

Public Gas News

American Public Gas Association
201 Massachusetts Ave Ne
Suite C-4
Washington, DC   20002-4957

202-464-0240
FAX 202-464-0246
E-Mail: website@apga.org
Home Page: www.apga.org

Bert Kalisch, President
Bob Beauregard, Marketing

Written for public gas managers to keep them apprised of industry news.
Cost: $50.00
Circulation: 1000
Founded in 1961
Printed in on matte stock

Washington Report

Interstate Natural Gas Association of America
555 13th St Nw
Suite 300W
Washington, DC   20004-1109

202-637-8600
FAX 202-637-8615
Home Page:
www.stonebridge-international.com

Anthony S Harrington, CEO
Samuel Berger, Manager

Natural gas newsletter places a special emphasis on developments that affect the interstate pipeline industry. It covers Congress, the Federal Energy Regulatory Commission and other federal agencies, state and Canadian regulatory boards and company news.

World Gas Intelligence

575 Broadway
New York, NY   10012-3230

212-941-5500
FAX 212-941-5509
Home Page: www.piw.pubs.com

Edward L Morse, Publisher
Jocelyn Strauber, Circulation Director

International coverage of the oil and gas
industry.
Cost: $985.00
Frequency: SemiMonthly
Mailing list available for rent

Magazines & Journals

AAPG Bulletin

American Association of Petroleum
Geologists
PO Box 979
Tulsa, OK   74101-979

918-584-2555
FAX 918-560-2632
E-Mail: bulletin@aapg.org
Home Page: www.aapg.org

Beverly Molyneux, Managing Editor
David Curtiss, CEO/President
Larry Nations, Marketing

Peer reviewed articles that cover major
extent and detailed geologic data. Infor-
mation on petroleum, natural gas, and
other energy products.
Cost: $305.00
Frequency: Monthly
Circulation: 30000
ISSN: 0149-1423
Founded in 1917

AAPG Explorer

American Association of Petroleum
Geologists
1444 S Boulder Avenue
PO Box 979
Tulsa, OK   74101-979

918-584-2555
800-288-7636
FAX 918-560-2665
E-Mail: postmaster@aapg.org
Home Page: www.aapg.org

Patrick J F Gratton, President
Ernest A Mancini, Editor
Brenda Merideth, Advertising Sales
Manage

News for explorationists of oil, gas and
minerals as well as for geologists with

environmental and water well concerns.
Cost: $50.00
Frequency: Monthly
Circulation: 30000
ISBN: 0-195298-6 -
Founded in 1917
Printed in 4 colors on matte stock

American Oil and Gas Reporter

National Publishers Group
PO Box 343
Derby, KS   67037

316-788-6271
800-847-8301
FAX 316-788-7568
E-Mail: reporter@feist.com
Home Page: www.fiest.com

Charlie Cookson, Publisher
Bill Campbell, Managing Editor

The American Oil & Gas Reporter
serves the exploration, drilling and pro-
duction segments of the oil and gas in-
dustry.
Cost: $65.07
Frequency: Monthly
Circulation: 7384
Founded in 1958

BIC - Business & Industry Connection

BIC Alliance
Po Box 3502
Covington, LA   70434

985-893-8692
FAX 985-893-8693
E-Mail: bic@bicalliance.com
Home Page: www.bicalliance.com

Jamie Craig, Editor
Earl Heard, CEO/President
Kathy Dugas, Administrator
Joe Storer, Manager

Information on oil and gas, refining, petrochemical, environmental, construction,
engineering, pulp and paper, state agencies and municipalities business.
Cost: $45.00
Circulation: 75000

Bloomberg Natural Gas Report

Bloomberg Financial Markets
100 Business Park Drive
Princeton, NJ   08542-840

609-279-3000
800-395-9403
FAX 917-369-7000
E-Mail: munis@bloomberg.com

Home Page:
www.bloomberg.com/energy

Michael Bloomberg, Publisher
Ronald Henkoff, Editor

News, interviews, and analysis of topics
of importance to all levels of the natural
gas market.
12 Pages
Frequency: Weekly
Circulation: 1700
Founded in 1980

Butane-Propane News

Butane-Propane News
PO Box 660698
Arcadia, CA   91006

626-357-2168
800-214-4386
FAX 626-303-2854
E-Mail: bpn@bpnews.com
Home Page: www.bpnews.com

Natalie Peal, Publisher
Ann Rey, Editorial Director
Kurt Ruhl, Sales Manager

Petroleum and propane industry news.
Cost: $32.00
56 Pages
Frequency: Monthly
Circulation: 16500
Founded in 1939
Printed in 4 colors on glossy stock

Coal People

Al Skinner Enterprises
PO Box 6247
Charleston, WV   25362-0247

304-342-4129
800-235-5188
FAX 304-343-3124
E-Mail: cpm@newwave.net
Home Page: www.coalpeople.com

A Skinner, Owner
Christina Karawan, Managing Editor
Beth Terranova, Sales Manager
Angela McNealy, Circulation Manager
C K Lane, Senior Vice President

Features special news and product sec-
tions for the coal industry.
Cost: $25.00
60 Pages
Circulation: 11500
Founded in 1976
Printed in 4 colors on glossy stock

Compressor Tech Two

Diesel & Gas Turbine Publications
20855 Watertown Rd
Suite 220
Waukesha, WI   53186-1873

262-754-4100
FAX 262-832-5075
E-Mail: slizdas@dieselpub.com
Home Page: www.dieselspec.com

Michael Osenga, President
Brent Haight, Managing Editor
Kara Kane, Advertising Manager
Christa Johnson, Production Manager
Sheila Lizdas, Circulation Manager

Covers oil and gas exploration, drilling, oilfield contracting, gas and petrochemical pipeline and storage, as well as petrochemical, hydrocarbon and gas processing industries.
Circulation: 12000

Diesel Progress: North American Edition

Diesel & Gas Turbine Publications
20855 Watertown
Suite 220
Waukesha, WI   53186-1873

262-754-4100
800-558-4322
FAX 262-832-5075
E-Mail: mosenga@dieselpub.com
Home Page: www.dieselspec.com

Michael Osenga, President
Sheila Lizdas, Circulation Manager
Lynne Diefenbach, Advertising Manager
Christa Johnson, Production Manager

Geared towards readers interested in state-of-the-art systems technology. Features include new product listings, systems design, research amd product testing as well as systems maintenance and rebuilding.
Frequency: Monthly
Circulation: 26011
Founded in 1969

Drill Bits

National Drilling Association
1545 W 130th St
Suite A2
Hinckley, OH   44233-9121

330-273-5756
877-632-4748
FAX 216-803-9900

E-Mail: info@nda4u.com
Home Page: www.nda4u.com

Peggy McGee, President
Dan Dunn, VP
Jim Howe, Secretary/Treasurer
Tim Cleary, Board of Directors
R. Alan Garrard, Board of Directors

A non-profit trade association of contractors, manufacturers and affiliated members from the drilling industry representing the geotechnical, environmental and mineral exploration sectors of this industry.
250+ Members
Frequency: 2 X/Year
Founded in 1972

Drilling Contractor

International Association of Drilling Contractors
10370 Richmond Ave
Suite 760
Houston, TX   77042-9687

713-292-1945
FAX 713-292-1946
E-Mail: info@iadc.org
Home Page: www.iadc.org

Lee Hunt, President
Tom Terrell, Senior VP Business Development

All drilling, all completing, all the time.
Cost: $50.00
40 Pages
Frequency: 6x/Year
Circulation: 34500
Printed in 4 colors

Energy Markets

Hart Publications
4545 Post Oak Place
#210
Houston, TX   77027

713-993-9320
FAX 713-840-8585

Linda K Rader, Editor
Robert C Jarvis, Publisher

Energy Markets serves the following energy industry business classifications: utilities, municipalities, consultants and financial services, regulators, and other companies allied to or supportive of the energy industry.
Frequency: Monthly
Circulation: 25,751
Founded in 1993

Gas Turbine World

Pequot Publishing
PO Box 447
Southport, CT   36490

203-259-1812
FAX 203-254-3431

Robert Farmer, Editor
Victor Debiasi, Publisher
Janes Janson, Marketing
Peg Walker, Circulation Manager

Serves the electric, utility and non-untility power generation, oil/gas production and processing industries.
Cost: $135.00
Frequency: Weekly
Circulation: 11000
Founded in 1979

Gas Utility Manager

James Informational Media
6301 Gaston Avenue
#541
Dallas, TX   75214-6204

214-827-4630
FAX 847-391-9058
E-Mail: ruth@BetterRoads.com
Home Page: www.betterroads.com

Mike Porcaro, Publisher
Mike Porcaro, CEO/President
Carole Spohr, Marketing Manager
Stacy Stiglic, Circulation Manager
Ruth Stidger, Editor

Federal and international regulations, new supply projects, research and development projects and gas industry news.
Cost: $95.00
40 Pages
Frequency: Annual+
Circulation: 40000
Founded in 1931

Hart's E & P

Hart Publications
1616 S Voss Rd
Suite 1000
Houston, TX   77057-2641

713-993-9320
FAX 713-840-8585
E-Mail: jfisher@hartenergy.com
Home Page: www.hartenergy.com

Rich Eichler, CEO
Joe Fisher, Editor

Technical approaches and improvements related to both offshore and land drilling and extraction of petroleum products, also new product information and per-

sonality profiles.
Cost: $59.00
Frequency: Monthly
Circulation: 25000

Hart's World Refining

Hart Publications
4545 Post Oak Place
Suite 210
Houston, TX   77027-3105

713-993-9320
800-874-2544
FAX 713-840-8585
Home Page: www.hartpub.com

David Coates, Publisher
Jeremy Grunt, Executive Editor
Terry Higgins, Executive Publisher
Robert Gough, Editorial Director
Rich Eichler, President

Covers projects, financing and market
developments, along with feedstock and
product supply, demand, pricing information, technical and regulatory events
associated with the manufacture, supply,
and use of transportation fuels refining
technologies, business strategies and fuel
policy legislation.
Cost: $149.00
Circulation: 15,693
Founded in 1980

Journal of Geophysical Research

American Geophysical Union
2000 Florida Ave Nw
Washington, DC   20009-1231

202-462-6900
800-966-2481
FAX 202-328-0566
E-Mail: service@agu.org
Home Page: www.agu.org

Fred Spilhaus, Executive Director
John Orcutt, Publisher

There are five sections covering soid
earth, oceans, atmosphere, planets, and
space physics.
Cost: $20.00
Frequency: Monthly
Circulation: 10,000
Founded in 1919

Journal of Petroleum Technology

Society of Petroleum Engineers
PO Box 833836
Richardson, TX   75083-3836

972-952-9300
800-456-6863
FAX 972-952-9435

E-Mail: jpt@spe.org
Home Page: www.spe.org

Mark Rubin, Executive Director
Giovanni Paccaloni, President
Paul Thone, Senior Sales Manager

Journal of Petroleum Technology serves
the field of exploration, drilling, production, and reservoir management as well
as related manufacturing and service
organizations.
98 Pages
Frequency: Monthly
Circulation: 51205
Founded in 1949
Printed in 4 colors on glossy stock

NLGI Spokesman

National Lubricating Grease Institute
4635 Wyandotte St
Suite 202
Kansas City, MO   64112-1537

816-931-9480
FAX 816-753-5026
E-Mail: nlgi@nlgi.org
Home Page: www.nlgi.org

Kim Bott, Executive Director
Kim Bott, Administrative Assistant

About 50% of technical or scientific in-
formation amied at the manufacturers,
users and suppliers of lubricating grease.
Cost: $53.00
Frequency: Monthly
Circulation: 2500
Founded in 1933

Natural Gas Fuels

RP Publishing
2696 S Colorado Blvd
Suite 595
Denver, CO   80222-5944

303-863-0521
FAX 303-863-1722
E-Mail: info@rppublishing.com
Home Page: www.rppublishing.com

Frank Rowe, President

Technological advances, marketing strategies, legislative activities, successful
applications, and corporate and government initiatives to promote natural
gas-powered vehicles
Circulation: 7000
Founded in 1992

Oil & Gas Journal

PennWell Publishing Company
1700 West Loop S
#1000
Houston, TX   77027-3005

713-621-9720
FAX 713-963-6285
E-Mail: sales@pennwell.com
Home Page: www.ogjonline.com

Tom T Terrell, Publisher
Tim Sullivant, Manager

Detailed interpreation and information of
the world developments in the oil and
gas industry
Cost: $79.00
Frequency: Weekly
Circulation: 36090
Founded in 1990
Printed in 4 colors on glossy stock

Oil Spill Contingency Planning: A Global Perspective

Aspen Publishers
76 Ninth Avenue
7th Floor
New York, NY   10011

212-771-0600
800-638-8437
Home Page: www.aspenpublishers.com

Mark Dorman, CEO
Gustavo Dobles, VP Operations

Hands-on guidebook to contingency
planning for oil spills.
Cost: $195.00

Petroleo International

Keller International Publishing
Corporation
150 Great Neck Rd
Suite 400
Great Neck, NY   11021-3309

516-829-9722
FAX 516-829-9306
E-Mail: info@kellerpubs.com
Home Page: www.supplychainbrain.com

Victor Prieto, Editor
Sean Noble, Publisher
Steve Kann, Circulation Manager
Jerry Keller, President

Spanish language petroleum/petrochemi-
cal magazine.
100 Pages
Circulation: 10,314
Founded in 1943

SPE Drilling & Completion

Society of Petroleum Engineers
PO Box 833836
Richardson, TX   75083-3836

972-529-9300
800-456-6863
FAX 972-952-9435
E-Mail: spdal@spelink.spe.org
Home Page: www.spe.org

Giovanni Paccaloni, President
Shashana Pearson, Editor
Mary Jane, Circulation Manager
Georgeann Bilich, Publisher

Technical papers selected for the drilling profession reviewed by peers on topics such as casing, instrumentation, bit technology, fluids, measurment, deviation control, telemetry, completion and well control.
Cost: $60.00
Frequency: Quarterly
Circulation: 3588
Founded in 1984

Sea Technology Magazine

Compass Publications, Inc.
1501 Wilson Blvd
Suite 1001
Arlington, VA   22209-2403

703-524-3136
FAX 703-841-0852
E-Mail: oceanbiz@sea-technology.com
Home Page: www.sea-technology.com
Social Media: , *Twitter*

Amos Bussmann, President/Publisher
Joy Carter, Circulation Manager
Chris Knight, Managing Editor

Worldwide information leader for marine/offshore business, science and engineering. Read in more than 110 countries by management, engineers, scientists and technical personnel working in industry, government and education.
Cost: $40.00
Frequency: Monthly
Circulation: 16304
ISSN: 0093-3651
Founded in 1960
Mailing list available for rentat $80 per M
Printed in 4 colors

Society of Professional Well Log Analysts

8866 Gulf Freeway
Suite 320
Houston, TX   77017

713-947-8727
FAX 713-947-7181
E-Mail: info@spwla.org
Home Page: www.spwla.org

Vicki J King, Executive Director
Sharon Johnson, Admin Asst
Julian Singer, VP Publications
Cost: $105.00

Frequency: Annual+
Circulation: 2900
Founded in 1959

Today's Refinery

Chemical Week Associates
110 William St
Suite 11
New York, NY   10038-3910

212-621-4900
FAX 212-621-4800
E-Mail: ltattum@chemweek.com
Home Page: www.chemweek.com

John Rockwell, VP
Joe Minnella, Global Sales Director

Editorials from industry leaders focusing on current problems facing the industry. Highlights on legistation, activity, government regulations,and reports on major industry meetings.
Frequency: Monthly
Circulation: 10,000

Utility & Pipeline Industries

WMO DannHausen Corporation
330 North Wabash
Suite 3201
Chicago, IL   60611

312-628-5870
FAX 312-628-5878
E-Mail: wod@dannhausen.com
Home Page: www.gasindustries.com

Bob Higgins, Publisher
Heidi Liddle, Production Manager
Karen Ebbesmeyer, Circulation Manager
Ruth W. Stidger, Editor-in-Chief
Cory Sekine Pettite, Managing Editor

Market to federal agencies, bureaus, government departments and toll author-

ities. Accepts advertising.
Cost: $20.00
62 Pages
Frequency: Monthly
Circulation: 10680

Washington Report

National Ocean Industries Association
1120 G St Nw
Suite 900
Washington, DC   20005-3801

202-347-6900
FAX 202-347-8650
Home Page: www.noia.org

Tom Fry, President
Franki K Stuntz, Director Administration
Nolty J Thuriot, Director Congressional Affairs

Frequency: Bi-Weekly

Well Servicing

Workover Well Servicing Publications
10200 Richmond Avenue
Suite 275
Houston, TX   77042

713-781-0758
800-692-0771
FAX 713-781-7542
Home Page: www.aesc.net

Kenny Jordan, Executive DIrector
Polly Fisk, Editor
Patty Jordan, Circulation

New products listing and reviews, field reports, and information on companies in the industry. Written and edited for energy service company professionals, and oil & gas operations.
40 Pages
Circulation: 11000
ISSN: 0043-2393
Founded in 1956

World Oil

Gulf Publishing Company
PO Box 2608
Houston, TX   77252

713-529-4301
800-231-6275
FAX 713-520-4433
Home Page: www.gulfpub.com

John D Meador, President/CEO
Ron Higgins, VP Sales/Publisher

Reaches the exploration, drilling, producing, and well servicing segments of

the oil and gas industry.
Cost: $34.00
100 Pages
Frequency: Monthly
Circulation: 36000
ISSN: 0043-8790
Founded in 1916
Printed in 4 colors on glossy stock

Trade Shows

American Association of Petroleum Geologists Annual Convention/Expo

American Association of Petroleum Geologists
PO Box 979
Tulsa, OK   74101-0979

918-584-2555
800-364-2274
FAX 918-560-2684
E-Mail: convene@aapg.org
Home Page: www.aapg.org

Randa Reeder-Briggs, Annual Meeting Manager
Melissa Howerton, Annual Meeting Assistant
Steph Benton, Exhibit Manager
Rick Fritz, Executive Director

Exhibits of instrumentation, equipment, supplies, services and publications for petroleum geologists, geophysicists and engineers.
7000 Attendees
Frequency: Annual/April

American School of Gas Measurement Technology Meeting

PO Box 3991
Houston, TX   77253-3991

903-486-7875
FAX 512-267-9243
Home Page: www.asgmt.com

Seminar, workshop, and tours, plus 95 exhibits of gas measurement, equipment, supplies and services.
600 Attendees
Frequency: Annual
Founded in 1927

Asia Pacific Improved Oil Recovery Conference

Society of Petroleum Engineers-Texas
222 Palisades Creek Drive
PO Box 833836
Richardson, TX   75083-3836

972-952-9300
FAX 972-952-9435
Home Page: www.spe.org

Oil recovery exhibition.

Beaumont Industrial Petrochemical Trade Show

Lobos Services
16016 Perkins Road
Baton Rouge, LA   70810-3631

225-751-5626

Debbie Balough, Show Manager

Informs local industry of the full array of industrial equipment for the chemical industries.
5M Attendees
Frequency: January

Circum-Pacific Council Energy Mineral Resources

5100 Westheimer Road
Houston, TX   77056-5596

713-709-9071
FAX 713-622-5360

Mary Stewart, Show Manager
Napoleon Carcamo, Owner

50 booths.
1.2M Attendees
Frequency: November

Eastern Oil and Gas Equipment Show

Pennsylvania Oil and Gas Association
412 N 2nd Street
Harrisburg, PA   17101-1342

717-939-9551

Stephen Rhoads, Show Manager

175 booths displaying new technologies, products and services relating to the oil and gas industries.
1M Attendees
Frequency: June

Entelec Conference & Expo

Energy Telecommunications and Electrical Assoc
5005 W Royal Lane
Suite 116
Irving, TX   75063

972-929-3169
888-503-8700
FAX 972-915-6040
E-Mail: info@entelec.org
Home Page: www.entelec.org

Blaine Siske, Executive Manager
Susan Joiner, Exhibits Manager

To bring together communications and control technology professionals from the petroleum, natural gas, pipeline, and electric utility companies for three days of quality training, seminars, exhibits and networking.
Frequency: Annual/May

Europe International Offshore Exchange

222 Palisades Creek Drive
Richardson, TX   75080-2040

Donna Anderson, Show Manager

1,100 booths.
21M Attendees
Frequency: September

International Thermal Spray Conference & Exposition

ASM International
9639 Kinsman Road
Materials Park, OH   44073

440-338-5151
800-336-5152
FAX 440-338-4634
E-Mail: natalie.nemec@asminternational.org
Home Page: www.asminternational.org

Natalie Neme, Event Manager
Kelly Thomas, Exposition Account Manager

Global annual event attracting professional interested in thermal spray technology focusing on advances in HVOF, plasma and detonation gun, flame spray and wire arc spray processes, performance of coatings, and future trends.
150 exhibitors.
1000 Attendees
Frequency: Annual/May

Liquified Gas Association Southwest

PO Box 9925
Austin, TX   78766-0925

FAX 512-834-0758

Cheryl Tomanetz, Show Manager

125 booths.
1.8M Attendees
Frequency: September

Liquified Natural Gas

Reed Exhibition Companies
255 Washington Street
Newton, MA   02458-1637

617-584-4900
FAX 617-630-2222

Elizabeth Hitchcock, International Sales

Presentation for the liquefied natural gas
industry.
2.5M Attendees
Frequency: May

Liquified Petroleum Gas Exposition Midwest

4100 Country Club Drive
Jefferson City, MO   65109-0302

573-634-5345
FAX 573-893-2623

Emma Krommel, Show Manager

100 booths of large transport and bobtail
delivery trucks.
1M Attendees
Frequency: June

Midwest Petroleum & Convenience Tradeshow

Illinois Petroleum Marketers Association
PO Box 12020
Springfield, IL   62791-2020

217-544-4609
FAX 217-789-0222

Bill Fleischli, Executive VP, Managing
Editor

Suppliers and manufacturers to petroleum marketing and convenience store
trades, including pumps, computers,
trucks, safety devices, canopies, car
washes and tank testing. 300 booths.
4M Attendees
Frequency: June

National Petro Refiners Association Refinery Petrochemical Plant

1899 L Street NW
Suite 1000
Washington, DC   20036-3810

202-457-0480

Robert Dzuiban, Show Manager
Robert Slaughter, President

A forum for the exchange of technical
information and services to the petroleum industry.
1.3M Attendees
Frequency: May

Offshore Technology Conference

222 Palisades Creek Drive, Richardson
Richardson, TX   75080-2040

972-952-9494
866-229-2386
FAX 972-952-9435
E-Mail: registration@spe.org
Home Page: www.spe.org

Alan Wegener, Show Manager

Consisting of a forum to disseminate
technical information for the advancement of engineering.
30M Attendees
Frequency: May

Oil & Energy Summit and Trade Show

Forum International
1101 Brickell Avenue
Suite 400
Miami, FL   33131-3143

800-926-2202
FAX 305-372-0071
E-Mail: jforum@trianet.net
Home Page:
www.oil-energysummit.com

Jorge Palmero, President
Rafael Yiamonte, VP Marketing

A full week of petroleum and related
products and industries. Includes an international trade show; a summit of secretaries of energy from the Americas and
a series of interdisciplinary seminars dictated by the Energy Institute of the
Americas and the Sarkeys Research
Center. 750 booths.
20M Attendees
Frequency: September

Petroleum Computer Conference

Society of Petroleum Engineers
222 Palisades Creek Drive
Richardson, TX   75080-2040

972-952-9300
FAX 972-952-9435
Home Page: www.spe.org

Annual show of 50 microcomputer manufacturers and suppliers who provide
hardware and software to the petroleum
industry.
650 Attendees

Petroleum Equipment Institute (CONVEX) and Exhibits

Petroleum Equipment Institute
PO Box 2380
Tulsa, OK   74101-2380

918-494-9696
FAX 918-491-9895
E-Mail: cdooley@pei.org
Home Page: www.pei.org

Connie Dooley, Administrative Director
Robert Renkes, Executive VP

Annual show of manufacturers of petroleum marketing equipment. There are
215 exhibiting companies with 675
booths.
4500 Attendees
Frequency: October
Founded in 1951

Society Petro Engineers Annual Meeting

PO Box 833836
Richardson, TX   75083-3836

972-952-9300
FAX 972-952-9435

Lois Woods, Show Manager
Mark Rubin, Executive Director

Conference with exhibits of drilling and
production equipment and materials.
10M Attendees
Frequency: September

Society Petro Engineers Permian Basin Oil Gas Recovery Conference and Expo

PO Box 833836
Richardson, TX   75083-3836

972-952-9300

Susan Bell, Event Manager

70 booths.
400 Attendees
Frequency: March

Society Petro Engineers Petroleum Computer Conference and Expo
PO Box 833836
Richardson, TX   75083-3836

972-952-9300

Georgie Cumiskey, Event Manager

30 booths of microcomputer hardware and software for the petroleum industry.
300 Attendees
Frequency: July

Society Petro Engineers Production Operations Symposium
PO Box 833836
Richardson, TX   75083-3836

972-952-9300

Karen Rodgers, Event Manager
Mark Rubin, Executive Director

70 booths of oil and gas industry related products and services.
1M Attendees
Frequency: March

Society Petro Engineers Rocky Mountain
PO Box 833836
Richardson, TX   75083-3836

972-952-9300

Georgie Cumiskey, Event Manager

60 booths.
300 Attendees
Frequency: April

Society Petro Engineers Western Regional Meeting
PO Box 833836
Richardson, TX   75083-3836

972-952-9300

Lois Woods, Exchange Manager
Mark Rubin, Executive Director

65 booths.
700 Attendees
Frequency: May

Society of Petro Engineers Eastern Regional Meeting
PO Box 833836
Richardson, TX   75083-3836

972-952-9300

Susan Bell, Event Manager
Mark Rubin, Executive Director

Offers a forum for the exchange of ideas between petroleum and gas engineers.
500 Attendees
Frequency: October

Society of Petro Engineers Enhanced Oil Recovery Symposium and Exchange
PO Box 833836
Richardson, TX   75083-3836

972-952-9300

Georgie Cumiskey, Event Manager
Mark Rubin, Executive Director

100 booths.
1.6M Attendees
Frequency: April

Southeast Petro Food Marketing Expo
7300 Glenwood Avenue
Raleigh, NC   27612

919-782-4411
FAX 919-782-4414
E-Mail: ssvinson@ncpma.org
Home Page: www.sepetro.org

Sharon Vinson, Show Manager

550 booths and 400+ exhibitors serving the petroleum and convenience store industries in the southeast.
2,000 Attendees
Frequency: March

Directories & Databases

APILIT
American Petroleum Institute
275 7th Avenue
9th Floor
New York, NY   10001-6708

212-989-9001
FAX 212-366-4298

Over 500,000 citations are offered from 1978, to the literature related to the oil refining and petrochemical industries.
Frequency: Bibliographic

Africa-Middle East Petroleum Directory
PennWell Directories
1700 West Loop S
Suite 1000
Houston, TX   77027-3005

713-621-9720
800-752-9764
FAX 281-499-6310

E-Mail: susana@penwell.com
Home Page:
www.petroleumdirectories.com

Jonelle Moore, Editor
Tim Sullivant, Manager

A directory for: associations, government agencies, drilling, exploration and production of natural gas, petrochemicals, pipeline operators etc.
Cost: $125.00
156 Pages

American Oil and Gas Reporter Directory
Domestic Petroleum Publishers
PO Box 343
Derby, KS   67037-0343

316-788-6271
FAX 316-788-7568
E-Mail: reporter@wichita.fn.net

Bill Campbell, Editor
Charlie Cookson, Publisher

State oil and natural gas regulatory agencies.
Cost: $25.00
Frequency: Annual March
Circulation: 13,540

American Oil and Gas Reporter: American Drilling Rig Directory Issues
National Publishers Group
PO Box 343
Derby, KS   67037-0343

316-788-6271
FAX 316-788-7568
E-Mail: reporter@wichita.fn.net

Bill Campbell, Editor
Charlie Cookson, Publisher

List of contractors engaged in onshore drilling for petroleum and gas.
Cost: $25.00
Frequency: SemiAnnual
Circulation: 13,540

American Oil and Gas Reporter: Directory of Crude Oil Purchasers Issue
Domestic Petroleum Publishers
PO Box 343
Derby, KS   67037-0343

316-788-6271
FAX 316-788-7568
E-Mail: reporter@wichita.fn.net

Bill Campbell, Editor
Charlie Cookson, Publisher

List of companies buying crude oil in the US.
Cost: $25.00
Frequency: Annual July
Circulation: 13,540

Armstrong Oil Directories

Armstrong Oil
Po Box 52106
Amarillo, TX   79159-2106

806-457-9300
FAX 806-457-9301
Home Page: www.armstrongoil.com

Alan Armstrong, Owner

Directory of services and supplies to the industry.
Cost: $53.50
300 Pages
Frequency: Annual

Asia-Pacific Petroleum Directory

PennWell Directories
1700 West Loop S
Suite 1000
Houston, TX   77027-3005

713-621-9720
800-752-9764
FAX 281-499-6310
E-Mail: susana@penwell.com
Home Page:
www.petroleumdirectories.com

Susan Anderson, Editor
Tim Sullivant, Manager

A directory for: suppliers, manufacturers, associations, government agencies, drilling, exploration and production of petroleum.
Cost: $95.00

Association of Energy Service Companies Directory

Association of Energy Service
Companies
6060 N Central Expy
Dallas, TX   75206-5209

214-692-0771
800-692-0771
FAX 214-692-0162
Home Page: www.aesc.net

Patty Jordan, Publisher

About 750 energy service companies and industry suppliers.
Frequency: Bi-Monthly
Circulation: 10,000

Brown's Directory of North American and International Gas Companies

Advanstar Communications
131 W 1st St
Duluth, MN   55802-2065

218-740-7200
FAX 218-723-9122
E-Mail: info@advanstar.com
Home Page: www.advanstar.com

Kent Akervik, Manager

Operating gas companies, brokers and refineries are listed in this comprehensive directory with worldwide coverage.
Cost: $265.00
350 Pages
Frequency: Annual
Circulation: 1,000

Canadian Oil Industry Directory

PennWell Directories
1700 West Loop S
Suite 1000
Houston, TX   77027-3005

713-621-9720
800-752-9764
FAX 281-499-6310
E-Mail: susana@penwell.com
Home Page:
www.petroleumdirectories.com

Susan Anderson, Editor
Tim Sullivant, Manager

A directory for: associations, government agencies, drilling contractors, engineering, construction, exploration, production, petrochemicals, pipeline operators, etc.
Cost: $135.00

Congress Legislative Directory

American Gas Association
1515 Wilson Boulevard
Suite 100
Arlington, VA   22209-2469

703-841-8400

Offers information on members of both houses of the United States Congress, federal government agencies relevant to the natural gas industry.
Cost: $10.00
220 Pages
Frequency: Annual

Contracts for Field Projects & Supporting Research on Enhanced Oil Recovery

US Department of Energy
PO Box 1398
Bartlesville, OK   74005

918-336-0307
FAX 918-337-4418

Herbert A Tiedemann, Editor

Energy Department technical project officers and contractors.
97 Pages
Frequency: Quarterly
Founded in 1997

Crude Oil Analysis Data Bank

PO Box 2565
Bartlesville, OK   74005-2565

918-336-2400

Contains over 9,000 analyses, obtained from the Bureau of Mines, of worldwide crude oil deposits.
Frequency: Full-text

DRI International Oil

DRI/McGraw-Hill
24 Hartwell Ave
Lexington, MA   02421-3103

781-860-6060
FAX 781-860-6002
Home Page: www.construction.com

Walt Arvin, President

This statistical database offers country-specific information on oil and natural gas production, consumption, stocks and imports for members of the International Energy Agency.

DRI Natural Gas Forecast

DRI/McGraw-Hill
24 Hartwell Ave
Lexington, MA   02421-3103

781-860-6060
FAX 781-860-6002
Home Page: www.construction.com

Walt Arvin, President

This time series database contains more than 600 annual forecasts of US oil and natural gas supply, prices and production costs.
Cost: $2500.00
6 Pages
Founded in 1985

DRI World Oil Forecast

DRI/McGraw-Hill
24 Hartwell Ave
Lexington, MA   02421-3103

781-860-6060
FAX 781-860-6002
Home Page: www.construction.com

Walt Arvin, President

This comprehensive look at the oil industry includes information on worldwide crude oil production, supply stocks and consumption.

DRI/Platt's Oil Prices

DRI/McGraw-Hill
24 Hartwell Ave
Lexington, MA   02421-3103

781-860-6060
FAX 781-860-6002
Home Page: www.construction.com

Walt Arvin, President

Database provides weekly, monthly and daily time series of worldwide petroleum product prices.

Dwight's Offshore and Bid Data

Dwight's Energydata
1633 Firman Drive
Suite 100
Richardson, TX   75081-6790

972-783-8002
800-468-3381
FAX 972-783-0058

This large database offers the most current information on bids, lease ownership data, and competitive intelligence data on the petroleum industry.
Frequency: Numeric

Gas and Oil Equipment Directory

Underwriters Laboratories
333 Pfingsten Rd
Northbrook, IL   60062-2096

847-412-0136
877-854-3577
FAX 847-272-8129
E-Mail: cec@us.ul.com
Home Page: www.ul.com

Keith E Williams, CEO
John Drengenberg, Manager Consumer Affairs

Companies that have qualified to use the UL listing mark or classification marking on or in connection with products that have been found to be in compliance with UL's requirements.
Cost: $9.00
Frequency: Annual October

Hart Energy Publishing

4545 Post Oak Place Drive
Suite 210
Houston, TX   77027-3105

713-993-9320
800-874-2544
FAX 713-840-8585
Home Page: www.hartenergy.com

Jeff Miller, Director Marketing
Matt Beltz, Marketing Associate
Rich Eichler, President

Hart Energy Publishing is the worldwide leader in energy industry publishing. With fiver energy magazines, E & P, Oil and Gas investors, Pipeline gas technology, energy markets and world refining. Hart Energy Publishing also has a range of newsletters and centers devoted to the downstream Energy industry.
15 Pages
Frequency: Monthly

International Oil Spill Control Directory

Cutter Information Corporation
37 Broadway
Suite 1
Arlington, MA   02474-5500

781-648-1950
FAX 781-648-1950
Home Page: www.cutter.com

Verna Allee, Senior Consultant

Offers valuable information on more than 1,000 suppliers of more than 3,500 oil spill cleanup, prevention and control products and services.
Cost: $95.00
225 Pages
Frequency: Annual

Member Directory and Oil & Gas Agencies

Interstate Oil and Gas Compact Commission
PO Box 53127
Oklahoma City, OK   73152-3127

405-525-3556
800-822-4015
FAX 405-525-3592

E-Mail: iogcc@iogcc.state.ok.us
Home Page: www.iogcc.state.ok.us

Christine Hansen, Executive Director
Alesha Leemaster, Communications Manager

About 600 state representatives to the commission from 29 oil and gas producing states and seven associate states and committee members from related industries and government agencies.
Cost: $11.00
Frequency: Annual

NOIA Leaders

National Ocean Industries Association
1120 G St NW
Suite 900
Washington, DC   20005-3801

202-347-6900
FAX 202-347-8650
Home Page: www.noia.org

Tom Fry, President
Franki K Stuntz, Director Administration
Nolty J Thuriot, Director Congressional Affairs

Frequency: Annual

Natural Gas Industry Directory

PennWell Directories
1700 West Loop S
Suite 1000
Houston, TX   77027-3005

713-621-9720
800-752-9764
FAX 281-499-6310
E-Mail: susana@penwell.com
Home Page:
www.petroleumdirectories.com

Susan Anderson, Editor
Tim Sullivant, Manager

Major divisions of the natural gas industry worldwide.
Cost: $165.00

Offshore Services and Equipment Directory

Greene Dot
11686 Jocatal Center
San Diego, CA   92127-1147

858-485-0189
FAX 858-485-5139

Renee Garza, Editor

About 5,000 suppliers of equipment and services to the offshore petroleum explo-

ration and production industry world-wide.
Cost: $235.00
Frequency: Annual May
Circulation: 4,000

Oil and Gas Directory

Geophysical Directory
Po Box 130508
Houston, TX   77219-0508

713-529-1922
800-929-2462
FAX 713-529-3646
E-Mail: info@theoilandgasdirectory.com
Home Page:
www.geophysicaldirectory.com

Stewart Schafer, Owner

Valuable information is listed on over 5,000 companies worldwide that are involved in petroleum exploration and drilling.
Cost: $130.00
700 Pages
Frequency: Annual, October
Circulation: 2,000
Founded in 1970

Oil and Gas Field Code Master List

US Energy Information Administration
1000 Independence Av SW
#E1-231
Washington, DC   20585-0001

202-586-8800
FAX 202-586-0727
Home Page: www.eia.doe.gov

John H Weiner, Executive Director

All identified oil and gas fields in the US.
Cost: $27.00
Frequency: Annual December

Permit Data On-Line

Petroleum Information Corporation
PO Box 2612
Denver, CO   80201-2612

303-595-7500
800-645-3282

Oil well drilling permits granted by regional governmental agencies.
Frequency: Weekly

PetroProcess HSE Directory

Atlantic Communications LLC
1635 W Alabama St
Houston, TX   77006-4101

713-831-1768
FAX 713-523-7804
E-Mail: info@oilonline.com
Home Page: www.oilonline.com

Shaun Wymes, President
Rob Garza, Director of Operations
Cost: $79.00

650 Pages
Frequency: Annual
Founded in 1990

Petroleum Equipment Directory

Petroleum Equipment Institute
6514 E 69th St
Tulsa, OK   74133-1729

918-494-9696
FAX 918-491-9895
Home Page: www.pei.org

Robert N Renkes, Executive VP

Member manufacturers, distributors and installers of petroleum marketing equipment worldwide are offered.
Cost: $50.00
395 Pages
Frequency: Annual
Circulation: 3,000

Petroleum Software Directory

PennWell Publishing Company
3050 Post Oak Boulevard
Suite 200
Houston, TX   77056-6570

713-219-9720
800-752-9764
FAX 713-963-6228
E-Mail: susana@pennwell.com

More than 800 companies that produce over 1,800 micro-, mini- and mainframe computer software packages designed for petroleum industry applications.
Cost: $195.00
Frequency: Annual June
Circulation: 1,000

Petroleum Supply Annual

Superintendent of Documents
1000 Independence Ave SW
Washington, DC   20585

202-586-8800
Home Page:

http://www.eia.doe.gov/oil_gas/petroleum/data_publications/petrol

Contains information on the supply and disposition of crude oil and petroleum products. Reflects data collected by the petroleum industry during 1998 through annual and monthly surveys, it is divided in to two volumes. The first volume contains three sections, Summary Statistics, Detailed Statistics, and Refinery Capacity, each with final annual data. Volume 1 cost is $17.00, volume 2 $51.00
175 Pages
Frequency: Annual
Founded in 1999

Pipeline & Gas Journal: Buyer's Guide Issue

Oildom Publishing Company of Texas
PO Box 941669
Houston, TX   77094-8669

281-558-6930
FAX 281-558-7029
Home Page:
www.oildompublishing.com

Jeff Share, Editor

List of over 700 companies supplying products and services used in construction and operation of cross country pipeline and gas distribution systems.
Cost: $75.00
Frequency: May

Pipeline & Gas Journal: Directory of Pipeline Operating Companies

Oildom Publishing Company of Texas
PO Box 941669
Houston, TX   77218-9368

281-558-6930
FAX 281-558-7029
Home Page:
www.oildompublishing.com

Jeff Share, Editor
Oliver Klinger, Editor

List of companies operating oil and gas transmission pipelines worldwide.
Cost: $80.00
Frequency: September
Circulation: 27,000

TULSA Database

Petroleum Abstracts
101 Harwell
Tulsa, OK   74104-3189

918-631-2297
800-247-8678

FAX 918-599-9361
E-Mail: question@tured.pa.utulsa.edu
Home Page: www.pa.utulsa.edu

Contains more than 700,000 citations, with abstracts, to the worldwide literature and patents on the exploration, development and production of petroleum resources.
Frequency: Weekly Updates

US Non-Utility Power Directory on CD-ROM

PennWell Publishing Company
PO Box 1260
Tulsa, OK   74101-1260

918-835-3161
800-752-9764
FAX 918-831-9555

Gockel Delma, Sales

Offers a unique source of information to industry professionals including a listing of over 1,423 plant locations including project names, site addresses, plant types, fuels, installed capacity, power contract information, operating control systems, ownership and more.
Cost: $695.00
Frequency: Annual

US Offshore Oil Company Contact List

Offshore Data Services
PO Box 19909
Houston, TX   77224-1909

713-781-7094
FAX 713-781-9594
E-Mail: editors@offshore-data.com

Marie Sheffer, Editor
Linda Parino, Circulation Director

Approximately 265 oil companies with US offshore leases.
Cost: $135.00
Frequency: Annual
Circulation: 800
ISBN: 1-058587-7 -
Mailing list available for rent

USA Oil Industry Directory

PennWell Publishing Company
3050 Post Oak Boulevard
Suite 200
Houston, TX   77056-6570

713-219-9720
800-752-9764

FAX 713-963-6228
E-Mail: susana@pennwell.com

Laura Bell, Editor
Susan Anderson, Publisher

Over 3,600 independent oil producers, fund companies, petroleum marketing companies, crude oil brokers and integrated oil firms.
Cost: $165.00
Frequency: Annual October
Circulation: 5,000

USA Oilfield Service, Supply and Manufacturers Directory

PennWell Publishing Company
3050 Post Oak Boulevard
Suite 200
Houston, TX   77056-6570

713-219-9720
800-752-9764
FAX 713-963-6228
E-Mail: susana@pennwell.com

Guntis Moritis, Editor

About 3,600 companies that provide oilfield equipment, supplies and services to the oil industry.
Cost: $145.00
Frequency: Annual October
Circulation: 2,500

West Coast Petroleum Industry Directory

Economic Insight
3004 Sw 1st Ave
Portland, OR   97201-4708

503-222-2425
FAX 503-242-2968
E-Mail: info@econ.com
Home Page: www.econ.com

Sam Van Vactor, President

Individuals and companies that refine, buy and sell oil and petroleum products are listed.
Cost: $85.00
204 Pages
Frequency: Quarterly

World Oil-Marine Drilling Rigs

Gulf Publishing Company
3301 Allen Parkway
Houston, TX   77019-1896

713-294-4301

Offers information on over 600 mobile and self-contained drilling rigs including submersibles, drillships and barges.
Cost: $11.00
Frequency: Annual
Circulation: 30,000

Water Supply

Associations

American Recreation Coalition

1225 New York Ave NW
Suite 450
Washington, DC   20005

202-682-9530
FAX 202-682-9529
E-Mail: mmeade@funoutdoors.com
Home Page: www.funoutdoors.com

Derrick Crandall, President
Catherine Ahern, VP
Melinda Meade, Director of
Communications

A non-profit Washington based federation that provides a unified voice for recreation interests to conserve their full and active participation in government policy making on issues such as public land management. ARC works to build public-private partnerships to enhance and protect outdoor recreation opportunities and resources.
100+ Members
Founded in 1979

American Society of Irrigation Consultants

125 Paradise Lane
PO Box 426
Rochester, MA   02770

508-763-8140
FAX 508-763-8102
E-Mail: NormanB@asic.org
Home Page: www.asic.or

Norman F Bartlett, Executive Director
Kathleen A Bartlett, Executive Secretary
Luke Frank, Advertising Director

Promotes education skills on data exchange landscape irrigation. Members are irrigation consultants, suppliers, and manufacturers.
Founded in 1970

Ground Water Protection Council

13308 N Macarthur Blvd
Oklahoma City, OK   73142-3021

405-516-4972
FAX 405-516-4973
E-Mail: dan@gwpc.org
Home Page: www.gwpc.org

Mike Paque, Executive Director
Ben Grunewald, Associate Director

Paul Jehn, Technical Director
Dan Yates, Member Servicess
Coordinator

State ground water and underground injection control agencies whose mission is to promote the protection and conservation of ground water resources for all beneficial uses, recognizing ground water as a component of the ecosystem.
1.75M Members
Founded in 1983

Irrigation Association

6540 Arlington Blvd
Falls Church, VA   22042-6638

703-536-7080
FAX 703-536-7019
E-Mail: webmaster@irrigation.org
Home Page: www.irrigation.org

Deborah Hamlin, Executive Director
Denise Stone, Meetings Director

Members are manufacturers of irrigation systems, with the goal to promote efficient and effective water management and to be the voice of the irrigation industry worldwide.
1600 Members
Founded in 1949

National Drilling Association

1545 W 130th Street
Suite A2
Hinckley, OH   44233

330-273-5756
877-632-4748
FAX 216-803-9900
E-Mail: info@nda4u.com
Home Page: www.nda4u.com

Peggy McGee, President
Dan Dunn, VP
Jim Howe, Secretary/Treasurer
Tim Cleary, Board of Directors
R. Alan Garrard, Board of Directors

A non-profit trade association of contractors, manufacturers and affiliated members from the drilling industry representing the geotechnical, environmental and mineral exploration sectors of this industry.
250+ Members
Founded in 1972

National Institute for Water Resources

University of Massachusetts
Blaisdell House
Amherst, MA   01003

413-545-2842
FAX 413-545-2304
E-Mail: godfrey@tei.umass.edu
Home Page: www.umsu.edu/niwr

Paul Godfrey, Executive Secretary

Offers information on water resource directions across the nation.
54 Members
Founded in 1974

National Onsite Wastewater Recycling

PO Box 1270
Edgewater, MD   21037

410-798-1697
800-966-2942
FAX 410-798-5741
E-Mail: webmaster@nowra.org
Home Page: www.nowra.org

Jerry Stonebridge, President
Brian McQuestion, Secretary/Treasurer
Linda Hanifin Bonner, Ph.D, Executive Director

Dedicated solely to educating and representing members within the onsite and decentralized industry. And also to provide leadership and promote the onsite waste water treatment and recycling through education, training, communication and quality tools to support excellence in performance.
3500 Members
Founded in 1991

National Rural Water Association

2915 S 13th St
Duncan, OK   73533-9086

580-252-0629
FAX 580-255-4476
E-Mail: info@nrwa.org
Home Page: www.nrwa.org

Rob Johnson, CEO

Dedicated to the preservation, as well as the protection of water and other natural resources.
615 Members

National Water Resources Association

3800 Fairfax Dr
Suite 4
Arlington, VA   22203-1703

703-524-1544
FAX 703-524-1548
E-Mail: nwra@nwra.org
Home Page: www.nwra.org

Thomas Donnelly, VP

Dedicated to the wise management and use of the nation's water and land resources.
5M+ Members
Founded in 1932

Soil and Water Conservation Society

945 SW Ankeny Rd
Ankeny, IA   50023-9764

515-289-2331
800-843-7645
FAX 515-289-1227
E-Mail: swcs@swcs.org
Home Page: www.swcs.org

James Guillford, Executive Director
Oksana Gieseman, Director of Publications/Editor
Lisa Manley, Member Services Specialist
Dewayne Johnson, Professional Development Director

SWCS is a nonprofit scientific and educational organization that serves as an advocate for conservation professionals and for science-based conservation practice, programs, and policy.
5000+ Members
Founded in 1943

Submersible Waste Water Pump Association

1866 Sheridan Rd
Suite 201
Highland Park, IL   60035-2545

847-681-1868
FAX 847-681-1869
E-Mail: swpaexdir@tds.net
Home Page: www.swpa.org

Charles Stolberg, Executive Director

Represents and serves the manufacturers of submersible pumps for the municipal and industrial wasterwater applications. Manufacturers of components and accessory items for those products and com-panies providing services to users of those products.
Founded in 1976

Water Environment Federation

601 Wythe St
Alexandria, VA   22314-1994

703-684-2400
800-666-0206
FAX 703-684-2492
Home Page: www.wef.org

Bill Bertera, Executive Director

A technical and educational organization with members from varied disciplines who work toward the vision of preservation and enhancement of the global water environment.
79 Members
Founded in 1928

Water Quality Association

4151 Naperville Rd
Lisle, IL   60532-3696

630-505-0160
FAX 630-505-9637
E-Mail: info@mail.wqa.org
Home Page: www.wqa.org

Peter Censky, Manager
Margit Fotre, Membership/Marketing Director
Laurie Metanchuk, Communications Manager

An international, nonprofit trade association representing retail/dealers and manufacturer/suppliers in the point of use/entry water quality improvement industry. Membership benefits and services include technical and scientific information, educational seminars and home correspondence course books, professional certification and discount services.
2.5M Members
Founded in 1974

Water and Wastewater Equipment Manufacturers Association

PO Box 17402
Washington, DC   20041

703-444-1777
FAX 703-444-1779
E-Mail: info@wwema.org
Home Page: www.wwema.org

Dawn Kristof Champney, President

Represents the interests of companies that manufacture the products that are sold to the portable water and wastewater treatment industries. Also informs, educates and provides leadership on the issues which affect the worldwide water and wastewater equipment industry.
80 Members
Founded in 1908

Newsletters

ARC e-Newsletter

American Recreation Coalition
1225 New York Ave NW
Suite 450
Washington, DC   20005

202-682-9530
FAX 202-682-9529
E-Mail: mmeade@funoutdoors.com
Home Page: www.funoutdoors.com

Derrick Crandall, President
Catherine Ahern, VP
Melinda Meade, Director of Communications

A monthly e-newsletter distributed via e-mail.
Frequency: Monthly, e-Newsletter
Circulation: Variable

Drinking Water and Backflow Prevention

SFA Enterprises
11166 Huron Street
Unit 29
Northglenn, CO   80234-3330

303-510-0979
888-367-3927
FAX 303-452-9776
E-Mail: backflow@dwbp-online.com
Home Page: www.dwbp-online.com

Stuart Asay, Publisher

Accepts advertising.
Cost: $38.00
24 Pages
Frequency: Monthly

Jet News

WaterJet Technology Association/Industrial & Municipal Cleaning Association
906 Olive Street, Suite 1200
Saint Louis, MO   63101-1448

314-241-1445
FAX 314-241-1449

E-Mail: wjta-imca@wjta.org
Home Page: www.wjta.org

George A Savanick PhD, President
Kenneth C Carroll, Association Manager

Provides the latest information on applications, equipment, news from members, new developments, meetings, conferences, and tehnical information.
Frequency: Bi-Monthly
Circulation: 1000

National Association of Regulatory Utility Commisioners

Natl Assoc of Regulatory Utility
Commissioner
1101 Vermont Ave Nw
Suite 200
Washington, DC   20005-3553

202-898-2200
FAX 202-898-2213
E-Mail: admin@naruc.org
Home Page: www.naruc.org

Charles Gray, Executive Director
Diane Munns, Publisher

A national organization that offers valuable information on over 150 consultants and other professionals active in regulated water, sewer and related industries.
Frequency: Monthly
Circulation: 1800
Founded in 1889

National Water Line

National Water Resources Association
3800 Fairfax Dr
Suite 4
Arlington, VA   22203-1703

703-524-1544
FAX 703-524-1548
E-Mail: nrwa@nrwa.org
Home Page: www.nwra.org

Thomas Donnelly, VP

Association news and information.
Frequency: Monthly

US Water News

US Water News
230 Main St
Halstead, KS   67056-1913

316-835-2222
800-251-0046
FAX 316-835-2223
E-Mail: Inquiries@uswaternews.com
Home Page: www.uswaternews.com

Thomas Bell, President/Publisher
Mary DeSana, Editor

Reports news of current events in water resources from across the nation. Accepts advertising.
Cost: $59.00
24 Pages
Frequency: Monthly

Water Newsletter

Water Information Center
1099 18th St
Suite 2600
Denver, CO   80202-1926

303-297-2600
FAX 303-297-2750
Home Page: www.rwolaw.com

Stephen L Waters, Partner

Contents include water supply and waste disposal information, and presents articles on conservation/usage.
Cost: $127.00
Frequency: Monthly
Founded in 1959

Magazines & Journals

APWA Reporter

American Public Works Association
2345 Grand Blvd
Suite 700
Kansas City, MO   64108-2625

816-472-6100
800-848-2792
FAX 816-472-1610
E-Mail: ddancy@apwa.net
Home Page: www.apwa.net

Kaye Sullivan, Executive Director
David Dancy, Marketing Director
Connie Hartline, Publications Manager
Lillie Plowman, Publications/Premiums
Marketing Mgr

Circulation to entire membership of American Public Works Association.
Cost: $100.00
Frequency: Monthly
Circulation: 34000
ISBN: 0-092487-3 -
Founded in 1937
Mailing list available for rent

Bottled Water Reporter

International Bottled Water Association
1700 Diagonal Rd
Suite 650
Alexandria, VA   22314-2870

703-683-5213
800-928-3711

FAX 703-683-4074
E-Mail: ibwainfo@bottledwater.org
Home Page: www.bottledwater.org

Joe Doss, CEO

Provides a vital source of information to bottlers and agencies, consultanats and engineers. Also contains statistical data, marketing and managemant tips and profiles of bottled water operations and supplier companies.
Cost: $ 50.00
Circulation: 3000
Founded in 1958

Cleaner Times

Advantage Publishing Company
1000 Nix Rd
Little Rock, AR   72211-3235

501-280-9111
800-525-7038
FAX 501-280-9233
E-Mail: gpuls@adpub.com
Home Page: www.adpub.com

Charlene Yarbrough, President
Gerry Puls, Circulation
Chuck Prieur, Sales Manager

Application, information, and productivity for persons engaged in the manufacturing, distribution, or the use of high pressure water systems and accessories. The emphasis is on safety, regulatory, which affect the industry as well as cleaning applications.
Cost: $18.00
72 Pages
Frequency: Monthly
Circulation: 10000
ISSN: 1073-9602
Founded in 1989
Printed in 4 colors on glossy stock

Clearwaters

New York Water Environment
Association
525 Plum Street
Suite 102
Syracuse, NY   13204

315-422-7811
FAX 315-422-3851
E-Mail: rdh@nywea.org
Home Page: www.nywea.org

Lois Hickey, Editor
Patricia Cerro-Reehil, Executive
Director

Contains information on pollution control legislation, regulation, and compli-

ance.
Cost: $25.00
Frequency: Quarterly
Circulation: 3000
Founded in 1929

Drill Bits

National Drilling Association
1545 W 130th St
Suite A2
Hinckley, OH   44233-9121

330-273-5756
877-632-4748
FAX 216-803-9900
E-Mail: info@nda4u.com
Home Page: www.nda4u.com

Peggy McGee, President
Dan Dunn, VP
Jim Howe, Secretary/Treasurer
Tim Cleary, Board of Directors
R. Alan Garrard, Board of Directors

A non-profit trade association of contractors, manufacturers and affiliated members from the drilling industry representing the geotechnical, environmental and mineral exploration sectors of this industry.
250+ Members
Frequency: 2x/Year
Founded in 1972

Ground Water

National Ground Water Association
601 Dempsey Rd
Westerville, OH   43081-8978

614-898-7791
800-551-7379
FAX 614-898-7786
E-Mail: customerservice@ngwa.org
Home Page: www.ngwa.org

Paul Humes, VP
Thad Plumley, Publications Director
Shelby Fleck, Advertising
Keviin McKray, Executive Director

Focuses on ground water hydrogeology as a science.
Cost: $395.00
160 Pages
Circulation: 15000
ISSN: 0017-467x
Founded in 1963
Printed in one color

Ground Water Monitoring and Remediation

National Ground Water Association
601 Dempsey Rd
Westerville, OH   43081-8978

614-898-7791
800-551-7379
FAX 614-898-7786
E-Mail: ngwa@ngwa.org
Home Page: www.ngwa.org

Paul Humes, VP
Thad Plumley, Publications Director
Kevin McKray, Executive Director

Contains peer-reviewed papers, product and equipment news, EPA updates, industry news, and a mix of original columns authored by industry leaders.
Cost: $195.00
Frequency: Quarterly
Circulation: 15201
ISSN: 1069-3629
Founded in 1981

Industrial Wastewater

Water Environment Federation
601 Wythe St
Alexandria, VA   22314-1994

703-684-2400
FAX 703-684-2492
Home Page: www.wef.org

Bill Bertera, Executive Director

Provides the information on the practical application of science and technology in the management of water dischages, air emmissions, ground water and soil remediation to the industrial personnel, consultants and other involved in all aspects of management, treatment and disposal of industrial wastewater.
Cost: $129.00
Frequency: Bi-Monthly
Circulation: 35500
ISSN: 1067-5337
Founded in 1928

Journal of Soil and Water Conservation

Soil and Water Conservation Society
945 SW Ankeny Road
Ankeny, IA   50023-9764

515-289-2331
800-843-7645
FAX 515-289-1227

E-Mail: pubs@swcs.org
Home Page: www.swcs.org

Oksana Gieseman, Director of Publications

The JSWC is a multidisciplinary journal of natural resource conservation research, practice, policy, and perspectives. The journal has two sections: the A Section containing various departments and features and the Research Section containing peer-reviewed research papers.
Cost: $99.00
Frequency: Bimonthly
Circulation: 2000
ISSN: 0022-4561
Founded in 1945

Journal of the American Water Resources Association

PO Box 1623
Middleburg, VA   20118-1626

540-687-8390
540-687-8390
FAX 540-687-8395
E-Mail: info@awra.org
Home Page: www.awra.org

Kenneth J Lanfear, Editor
Charlene E Young, Publications Production Director
Billy Journell, Manager

Annual directory offering information on all water resources, technologies, systems and services for the water resources industry.
Cost: $205.00
Frequency: Bi-Monthly
ISSN: 1093-474x
Founded in 1964

Landscape & Irrigation

Adams Business Media
PO Box 17349
Chicago, IL   60617-0349

773-221-4223
FAX 773-374-6270
Home Page: www.adamsbrick.com

Karen Adams, President

National Driller

Business News Publishing Company
1050 IL Route 83
Suite 200
Bensenville, IL   60106

800-223-2194
FAX 248-786-1358
Home Page: www.nationaldriller.com

Linda Moffat, Publisher
Greg Ettling, Editor
Lisa Shroeder, Managing Editor

Provides feature articles, timely and valuable industry information, newly developed products and technologies, and quality marketing and business management advice.
Frequency: Monthly
Mailing list available for rent

Operations Forum

Water Environment Federation
601 Wythe St
Alexandria, VA   22314-1994

703-684-2400
800-666-0206
FAX 703-684-2492
E-Mail: officers@wef.org
Home Page: www.wef.org

Bill Bertera, Executive Director

The emphasis is on process control, plant operations, collection systems and industry news.
Cost: $4995.00
Frequency: Monthly
Circulation: 17005
Founded in 1928

Rural Water Magazine

National Rural Water Association
2915 S 13th St
Duncan, OK   73533-9086

580-252-0629
FAX 580-255-4476
E-Mail: info@nrwa.org
Home Page: www.nrwa.org

Rob Johnson, CEO

Targeted at the operators and board members of rural and small municipal water and wastewater utilities.
56 Pages
Frequency: Quarterly
Circulation: 22800
Founded in 1979

US Water News

US Water News
230 Main St
Halstead, KS   67056-1913

316-835-2222
800-251-0046
FAX 316-835-2223
E-Mail: Inquiries@uswaternews.com
Home Page: www.uswaternews.com

Thomas Bell, President/Publisher

Reports news of current events from across the nation in themunicipal and industrial water and wastewater segments of the water industry.
Cost: $59.00
28 Pages
Frequency: Monthly
Circulation: 20000
Founded in 1984
Printed in on n stock

Water Conditioning and Purification Magazine

Publicom
2800 E Fort Lowell Road
Tucson, AZ   85716

520-323-6144
FAX 520-323-7412
E-Mail: info@wcponline.com
Home Page: www.wcponline.com

Kurt C Peterson, Publisher/Eastern Advertising Exec
Sharon M Peterson, President/Owner
Karen R Smith, Executive Editor
Margo Goldbaum, Circulation Services
Denise M Roberts, Assistant Editor

Comprehensive magazine for all aspects of the water quality improvement industry. Accepts advertising.
Cost: $49.00
100 Pages
Circulation: 20000
ISSN: 1537-1786
Founded in 1959
Mailing list available for rent: 1000 names at $250 per M
Printed in 4 colors on glossy stock

Water Environment & Technology

Water Environment Federation
601 Wythe St
Alexandria, VA   22314-1994

703-684-2400
800-666-0206
FAX 703-684-2492

E-Mail: csc@wef.org
Home Page: www.wef.org

Bill Bertera, Executive Director
Margaret Richards, Editorial Assistant
Tracy Hardwick, Publication Services Manager

Covers a wide range of water quality and municipal wastewater treatment issues, from the design, engineering, and management of domestic wastewater treatment plants to watershed management and wet weather issues.
Cost: $178.00
Frequency: Monthly
Circulation: 27304
Founded in 1928

Water Environment Federation

Water Environment Federation
601 Wythe St
Alexandria, VA   22314-1994

703-684-2400
800-666-0206
FAX 703-684-2492
E-Mail: webfeedback@wef.org
Home Page: www.wef.org

Bill Bertera, Executive Director
David James, Publications Committee

Magazine published monthly for 41,000 members
Cost: $19.00
Founded in 1928

Water Environment Research

Water Environment Federation
601 Wythe St
Alexandria, VA   22314-1994

703-684-2400
FAX 703-684-2492
E-Mail: officers@wef.org
Home Page: www.wef.org

Bill Bertera, Executive Director
Glenn Reinhardt, Foundation Executive Director
Tom Wolfe, Advertising

Research journal reviewed by peers and covering the effects of water pollution and the technology and advances ued for it's control.
Cost: $158.00
Circulation: 9000
Founded in 1928

Water Resources Research

American Geophysical Union
2000 Florida Ave NW
Washington, DC   20009-1231

202-462-6900
800-966-2481
FAX 202-328-0566
E-Mail: service@agu.org
Home Page: www.agu.org

Fred Spilhaus, Executive Director
Karne Blaususs, Circulation Manager

Presents articles on the social, natural, and physical sciences, with emphasis on geochemistry, hydrology, and groundwater transfer technology.
Cost: $1200.00
Frequency: Monthly
Circulation: 4700
Founded in 1919

Water Technology

National Trade Publications
13 Century Hill Drive
Latham, NY   12110

518-783-1281
FAX 518-783-1386
E-Mail: asavino@ntpinc.com
Home Page: www.waternet.com

Humphrey S Tyler, President
Abdul Rehman, Account Executive
Mike Hilts, Publisher
Tom Williams, Senior Editor
Katie Bain, Marketing Manager

Serves the POU/POE water treatment industry. Accepts advertising.
Cost: $39.00
48 Pages
Frequency: Monthly
Circulation: 21000
Founded in 1981
Mailing list available for rent: 20000 names at $125 per M
Printed in 4 colors on glossy stock

Water Well Journal

Ground Water Publishing Company
601 Dempsey Rd
Westerville, OH   43081-8978

614-882-8179
800-551-7379
FAX 614-898-7786
Home Page: www.ngwa.org

Kevin McCray, Executive Director
Jennifer Strawn, Associate Editor
Joanne Grant, Manager

A complete publication of the water supply industry. Covers technical issues related to drilling and pump installation, rig maintenance, business management and professional development, well rehabilitation, water treatment and more.
Cost: $95.00
84 Pages
Frequency: Monthly
Founded in 1948

WaterWorld

PennNet
1421 S Sheridan Road
Tulsa, OK   74112

918-831-9143
FAX 918-831-9415
Home Page: www.pennnet.com

James Laughlin, Editor/Associate Publisher

Gives information about products and services, technology, applications, legislation and regulations to help the water industry pros successfully plan, design, operate and maintain their systems.
Frequency: Monthly
Founded in 1985

World Wastes: the Independent Voice

Communication Channels
6151 Powers Ferry Road NW
Atlanta, GA   30339-2959

770-953-4805
FAX 770-618-0348

Bill Wolpin, Editor
Jerrold France, President Argus Business

Reaches individuals and firms engaged in the removal and disposal of solid wastes.
Cost: $48.00
Frequency: Monthly
Circulation: 36,000

Trade Shows

American Society of Irrigation Consultants Conference

PO Box 426
Byron, CA   94514-0426

925-516-1124
FAX 925-516-1301

Wanda M Sarsfield, Secretary

Irrigation design equipment, supplies, services and seminar.
Frequency: Annual
Founded in 1970

American Water Resources Conference

American Water Resources Association
4 West Federal Street
PO Box 1626
Middleburg, VA   20118-1626

540-687-8390
FAX 540-687-8395
E-Mail: info@awra.org
Home Page: www.awra.org

Terry Meyer, Marketing Coordinator
Ken Reid, Executive VP

Show of water resources science and technology.
Frequency: Annual, November
Founded in 1964

American Water Works Association Annual Conference and Exhibition

6666 W Quincy Avenue
Denver, CO   80235

303-794-7711
800-926-7337
FAX 303-347-0804
Home Page: www.awwa.org

Nilaksh Kothari, President
Jack W. Hoffbuhr, Executive Director

With more than 500 exhibitors, who are a source of knowledge and information for water professionals who work to improve the supply and quality of water in North America and beyond
12000 Attendees
Frequency: Annual, June
Founded in 1881

Chartmaker

American Recreation Coalition
1225 New York Avenue NW
Suite 450
Washington, DC   20005-6405

202-829-9530
FAX 202-662-7424

Derrick Crandall, President

Triennial exhibits relating to the responsible use of US aquatic resources, including issues such as wetlands conservation, boating safety, sportfish research and enhancement and boating access improvements.

Computers in the Water Industry: The Computer Conference

American Water Works Association
6666 W Quincy Avenue
Denver, CO   80235

303-794-7711
800-926-7337
FAX 303-347-0804
Home Page: www.awwa.org

Nilaksh Kothari, President
Jack W. Hoffbuhr, Executive Director

Irrigation Association Annual Meeting

6260 Willow Oaks Corporate Drive
#120
Fairfax, VA   22031

703-573-3551
FAX 800-937-8477

Bob Sears, Executive VP

Four hundred and twenty five booths of the newest in irrigation equipment for the agricultural industry.
3.5M Attendees
Frequency: November

National Ground Water Association Annual Convention and Exposition

National Ground Water Association
601 Dempsey Road
Westerville, OH   43081

614-987-7791
800-551-7379
FAX 614-898-7786
E-Mail: ngwa@ngwa.org
Home Page: www.ngwa.org

Bob Masters, Conference Coordinator
Greg Phelps, Meeting
Planner/Expositions Dir
Kevin McKray, Executive Director

Annual show of 4600 manufacturers, suppliers, distributors, consultants and scientists, and contractors/pump installers.
5,100 Attendees
Frequency: December

National Rural Water Association

2915 S 13th Street
Duncan, OK   73533

580-252-0629
FAX 580-255-4476

E-Mail: info@nrwa.org
Home Page: www.nrwa.org

Larissa M Wood, Publications
Coordinator

100 booths; 300 exhibitors.
1.5M Attendees
Frequency: September

National Water Resources Association Annual Conference

National Water Resources Association
3800 Fairfax Drive
Suite 4
Arlington, VA   22203

703-524-1544
FAX 703-524-1548
E-Mail: nwra@nwra.org
Home Page: www.nwra.org

Norman Semanko, President
Thomas Donnelly, VP

Annual conference and exhibits relating to the development, control, conservation and utilization of water resources in the reclamation states.
700 Attendees
Frequency: November

North American Lake Management Society International Symposium

North American Lake Management
Society
4513 Vernon Boulevard, Suite 103
PO Box 5443
Madison, WI   53705-0443

608-233-2836
FAX 608-233-3186
E-Mail: nalms@nalms.org
Home Page: www.nalms.org

Bev Clark, President

Annual symposium and exhibits related to lake ecology and management.

Soil and Water Conservation Society Annual International Conference

Soil and Water Conservation Society
945 SW Ankeny Road
Ankeny, IA   50021-9764

515-289-2331
800-843-7645
FAX 515-289-1227
E-Mail: swsc@swsc.org
Home Page: www.swsc.org

Craig A Cox, Executive VP

Explores ways to improve the linkages among conservation science, policy and application at local, national, and international scales. The conference will provide participants an opportunity to teach skills, learn techniques, compare successes, and improve understanding.
1200 Attendees
Frequency: Annual

Water Environment Federation

Water Environment Federation
601 Wythe Street
Alexandria, VA   22314-1994

703-684-2400
FAX 703-684-2175

Bill Bertera, Executive Director

Annual show of 650 manufacturers, suppliers and distributors of water treatment equipment, supplies and services.
14M Attendees
Frequency: October, Chicago

Water Quality Association Convention

Water Quality Association
4151 Naperville Road
Suite 100
Lisle, IL   60532-1088

630-505-0160
FAX 630-505-9637
E-Mail: info@wqa.org
Home Page: www.wqa.org

Peter J Censky, Executive Director
Jeannine Collins, CMP,
Convention/Meetings Manager

Annual convention and exhibits of water treatment equipment and related articles.
4,300 Attendees

Directories & Databases

American Water Works Association: Buyers' Guide Issue

American Water Works Association
6666 W Quincy Ave
Denver, CO   80235-3098

303-794-7711
800-926-7337
FAX 303-347-0804
Home Page: www.awwa.org

Andrew Richardson, President
Jack W. Hoffbuhr, Executive Director

Member suppliers and distributors of water supply products and services, con-

tractors for water supply projects and engineering consultants.
Frequency: Annual November
Circulation: 80,000

Directory of Water/Sewer and Related Industries Professionals

National Assn of Regulatory Utility Commissioners
1101 Vermont Ave NW
Suite 200
Washington, DC   20005-3553

202-898-2200
FAX 202-898-2213
E-Mail: admin@naruc.org
Home Page: www.naruc.org

Charles Gray, Executive Director

Offers valuable information on over 150 consultants and other professionals active in regulated water, sewer and related industries.
Cost: $25.00
195 Pages
Frequency: Annual

Ground Water Age: Directory of Manufacture rs

National Trade Publications
13 Century Hill Drive
Latham, NY   12110-2197

518-831-1281
FAX 518-783-1386

Roslyn Scheib Dahl, Editor

List of over 150 companies that provide products and services to the ground water industry.
Cost: $30.00
Frequency: Annual December
Circulation: 13,448

Ground Water Monitoring & Remediation: Buy ers Guide Issue

Ground Water Publishing Company
601 Dempsey Rd
Westerville, OH   43081-8978

614-882-8179
800-332-2104
FAX 614-898-7786
E-Mail: gwpc@ngwa.org
Home Page: www.ngwa.org

Kevin McCray, Executive Director
Thad Plumley, Publications Director

List of companies that provide products used in the ground water monitoring and

remediation industry.
Cost: $15.00
Frequency: Annual
Circulation: 12,382
Founded in 1981

Ground Water Monitoring Review: Consultant & Contract Directory

National Ground Water Association
601 Dempsey Rd
Westerville, OH   43081-8978

614-898-7791
800-332-2104
FAX 614-898-7786
Home Page: www.ngwa.org

Paul Humes, VP
Shelby Fleck, Advertising Manager
Kevin McCray, Executive Director

About 400 consultant and contracting firms engaged in ground water monitoring projects.
Cost: $200.00
Frequency: Annual
Circulation: 17,000

Ground Water On-Line

National Ground Water Association
601 Dempsey Rd
Westerville, OH   43081-8978

614-898-7791
800-554-7379
FAX 614-898-7786
E-Mail: ngwa@ngwa.org
Home Page: www.ngwa.org

Paul Humes, VP

Database offers information on more than 90,000 ground water literature citations, which includes information like key words, abstracts, chemical compounds, biological factors, geographic locations, aquifer names, authors, titles, publication source names and a lot more.
Frequency: Bibliographic

Validated Water Treatment Equipment Directory

Water Quality Association
4151 Naperville Rd
Suite 100
Lisle, IL   60532-3696

630-505-0160
FAX 630-505-9637
Home Page: www.wqa.org

Peter Censky, Manager

Over 700 water treatment products tested by the Water Quality Association and their manufacturers are listed.
Cost: $6.00
Frequency: SemiAnnual

WATERNET

American Water Works Association
6666 W Quincy Ave
Denver, CO   80235-3098

303-794-7711
800-926-7337
FAX 303-347-0804
Home Page: www.awwa.org

Andrew Richardson, President
Jack W. Hoffbuhr, Executive Director

This database contains more than 23,000 citations, with abstracts, to literature on water quality, water utility management, analytical procedures fro water quality testing.
Frequency: Bibliographic

Water Technology: Directory of Manufacturers and Suppliers Issue

National Trade Publications
13 Century Hill Drive
Latham, NY   12110-2197

518-783-1281
FAX 518-783-1386
Home Page: www.ntpmedia.com

Mark Wilson, Editor

List of about 250 manufacturers, distributors and other suppliers of water conditioning and treatment products.
Cost: $21.00
Frequency: Annual December
Circulation: 17,213

Water Treatability

National Ground Water Information Center
6375 Riverside Drive
Dublin, OH   43017-5045

614-717-2770
FAX 614-761-3446

Offers information on treatment technologies for the removal of various containments from water supplies.
Frequency: Full-text

**Water Well Journal: Buyer's
Guide Issue**

National Ground Water Association
601 Dempsey Rd
Westerville, OH   43081-8978

614-898-7791
800-332-2104
FAX 614-898-7786
E-Mail: h20@h20-ngwa.org
Home Page: www.ngwa.org

Paul Humes, VP
Shelby Fleck, Advertising Manager

List of manufacturers, suppliers and
manufacturers' representativess for
equipment, machinery and other products for the water well industry.
Cost: $6.00
Frequency: Annual January
Circulation: 26,000

Appendix 1

Chronology of U.S. Land and National Resource Policy

1787 – Congress enacts the Northwest Ordinance of 1787, authorizing the US government to sell up to 640 acres of land to the highest bidder, at a minimum price of $1 dollar per acre.

1799 – Congress enacts the Federal Timber Purchases Act, under which the U.S. government appropriates $200,000 to purchase timber reserves for the use of the navy.

1827 – Congress enacts the Timber Reservation Act, which authorizes the President to conserve live oaks on federal lands and restrict such lands from sale.

1834 – Congress appropriates $5,000 "to be applied to geological and mineralogical survey and researches," creating the first geological survey.

1849 – Congress creates the Department of the Interior as a Cabinet agency with responsibility over federal and public lands.

1862 – Congress enacts the Homestead Act, which allows pioneers to settle on 160 acres of land, and ultimately own it after working it for five years.

1872 – Congress enacts the General Mining Act of 1872, which gave Congress the oversight over the mining of such minerals as gold, silver, copper, platinum, and other resources.

– Congress enacts the Yellowstone Act of 1872, which sets aside "the tract of land in the Territories of Montana and Wyoming, lying near the headwaters of the Yellowstone River" as a protected area.

1877 – Congress enacts the Desert Land Act, which allows settlers to purchase 640 acres of land and keep it after three years of irrigation.

1878 – Congress enacts the Free Timber Act, allowing settlers in the western states to cut down trees on public lands with mineral reserves.

1886 – The Congress establishes the Division of Forestry as an agency inside of the Department of Agriculture.

1889 – On his last day in office, President Grover Cleveland signs the law establishing the Department of Agriculture as a cabinet-level department.

1890 – Congress enacts the Yosemite National Park Act, which will establish the Yosemite valley in California as a National Park.

1891 – The Forest Reserve Act is enacted by Congress, allowing the President to set aside public lands marked by timber or forest.

1894 – Congress enacts "An Act to Protect the Birds and Other Animals in Yellowstone National Park," also known as the Yellowstone National Park Protection Act.

– Congress enacts the Carey Act, which gives the President of the United States the power to allow the states to sell upwards of one million acres of public land for the use of settlement and irrigation.

1897 – Congress enacts The Forest Management Act, which sets guidelines for the creation and management of forest reserves.

1899 – Congress enacts the Dead and Down Timber Act, which gives the President of the United States the authority to dispose of dead or downed timber on Indian reservations.

– Congress enacts the Rivers and Harbors Act and Refuse Act, which prohibits the dumping of wastes in the nation's harbors, canals, and waterways.

1900 – Congress enacts the Lacey Game and Wild Birds Preservation and Protection Act, which precludes the interstate shipping of wild animals and birds.

1902 – Congress enacts the Alaska Game Act to protect certain game animals in Alaska.

– Congress enacts the Newlands Act, also known as the Reclamation Act, which authorizes the Secretary of the Interior to create irrigation areas for agriculture.

1903 – President Theodore Roosevelt signs an Executive Order creating the Pelican Island National Refuge in Florida, the first such refuge of its kind in the United States.

1906 – Congress enacts the Antiquities Act, also known as American Antiquities Act of the Lacey Antiquities Act, which establishes a program of preserving historic sites in America.

1908 – Congress amends the 1902 Alaska Game Act with the "Act for the Protection of Game in Alaska," laying out a plan of protection areas for animals, how their protection would be administered, and what hunting guidelines if any would be set forth.

1910 – The United States Supreme Court establishes, in *United States v. Grimaud and United States v. Inda*, that only Congress may set penalties for criminal behavior caused on grazing lands, and may not delegate that power to a Cabinet officer or other government employee.

1916 – Congress establishes the National Park Service as an independent agency inside the US Department of the Interior.

1934 – Congress enacts The Taylor Grazing Act, which authorizes the Secretary of the Interior "to establish grazing districts of vacant, unappropriated and unreserved land from any parts of the public domain, excluding Alaska, which are not national forests, parks and monuments, Indian reservations, railroad grant lands, or revested Coos Bay Wagon Road grant lands, and which are valuable chiefly for grazing and raising forage crops."

1935 – Congress enacts the Historic Sites and Buildings Act, an amendment to the Antiquities Act of 1906.

1937 – Congress enacts the Pittman-Robertson Act, which sets an excise tax on firearms and ammunition to be used to acquire wildlife refuges and for wildlife management.

1938 – Congress enacts the Agricultural Adjustment Act, which amended the Soil Conservation Act of 1935, and set as a national policy "of conserving national resources, preventing the wasteful use of soil fertility, and of preserving, maintaining, and rebuilding the farm and ranch land resources in the national interest, (and) to accomplish these (goals) through the encouragement of soil-building and soil-conserving crops and practices."

1940 – Congress enacts the Bald and Golden Eagle Protection Act of 1940 to try to halt the poaching and selling of rare bald and golden eagles.

1946 – Congress creates The Bureau of Land Management (BLM) by merging the General Land Office and the United States Grazing Service under Congressional Reorganization Plan No. 3.

1947 – Congress enacts the Federal Insecticide, Fungicide, and Rodenticide Act.

1948 – Congress enacts the Federal Water Pollution Control Act.

1954 – Congress enacts the Atomic Energy Act.

1955 – Congress enacts the National Air Pollution Control Act, the first such action to deal with air pollution.

1960 – Congress enacts the Multiple-Use Sustained Yield Act.

1962 – Publication of Rachel Carson's landmark work *Silent Spring*, which calls attention to the nation's use of pesticides and gives rise to the modern environmental movement.

    – Congress enacts the Air Quality Act of 1967, amending the Clean Air Act of 1965, to change enforcement mandates to past air pollution legislation.

1963 – Congress enacts the first Clean Air Act, with amendments following in 1965, 1966, 1967, 1969, 1970, 1977, and 1990.

1964 – Congress enacts the Wilderness Act, which establishes the National Wilderness Preservation System.

1965 – Congress enacts three major pieces of pollution and waste legislation: the National Emissions Standards Act, the Motor Vehicle Air Pollution Control Act, and the Solid Waste Disposal Act.

1970 – Congress enacts The Environmental Quality Act of 1970. In amending the Clean Air Act, Congress sets National Ambient Air Quality Standards (NAAQS), New Source Performance Standards (NSPS) Hazardous Air Pollutant standards, and auto emissions tailpipe standards, among others.

1972 – Congress enacts three major pieces of environmental legislation: the Federal Water Pollution Control Amendments (FWPCA) of 1972; the Federal Insecticide, Fungicide, and Rodenticide Act (FIFRA); and the Marine Protection, Research, and Sanctuaries Act of 1972.

1973 – Congress amends the Endangered Species Act of 1966.

1974 – Congress enacts the Safe Drinking Water Act.

1975 – Congress enacts the Hazardous Materials Transportation Act.

1976 – Congress enacts The Resource Conservation and Recovery Act (RCRA) as an amendment to the Solid Waste Disposal Act of 1965 to address the growing problem of municipal and industrial wastes.

    – Congress enacts the Toxic Substances Control Act (TSCA) to address toxic wastes.

1977 – Congress enacts the Surface Mining Control and Reclamation Act.

1978 – Congress enacts the National Energy Conservation Policy Act.

1980 – Congress enacts the Comprehensive Environmental Response, Compensation, and Liability Act (CERCLA), which establishes the "Superfund" of monies to clean up hazardous waste sites across the United States.

– Congress enacts the Alaska National Interest Lands Conservation Act, which sets aside some 97 million acres of formerly private or unused lands in national refuges in Alaska; in addition, 25 rivers are listed as protected, as well as 56 million acres being categorized for the first time as protected wilderness areas.

– Congress also enacts the Fish and Wildlife Conservation Act, which establishes "duck stamps" to be sold to raise funds for wildlife and land preservation.

1982 – Congress enacts the Nuclear Waste Policy Act.

1986 – Congress enacts the Safe Drinking Water Act Amendments of 1986.

– Congress enacts the Superfund Amendments and Reauthorization Act (SARA), amending CERCLA.

1987 – Congress enacts the Water Quality Act, which amends the Federal Water Pollution Control Amendments of 1972.

1990 – Congress enacts the Coastal Wetlands Planning, Protection and Restoration Act, which authorizes the Secretary of the Interior to establish projects in the area of protection, restoration, or enhancement of aquatic and associated ecosystems.

– Congress amends the 1972 Clean Air Act, which establishes new automobile standards, and calls for reductions in the use of chloroflorocarbons (CFCs).

1991 – Congress enacts the Intermodal Surface Transportation Efficiency Act (ISTEA).

1996 – Congress enacts the Mercury-Containing and Rechargeable Battery Management Act, the Food Quality Protection Act, and the Safe Drinking Water Act Amendments of 1996.

2001 – The US Supreme Court, in *Solid Waste Agency of Northern Cook County v. Army Corps of Engineers* holds that provisions of the CWA does not extend to intrastate waters, which it could not consider "navigable."

2002 – Congress enacts the Small Business Liability Relief and Brownfields Revitalization Act to clean up abandoned areas for use for American businesses.

2005 – Congress enacts the Energy Policy Act of 2005.

2009 – The US Supreme Court holds in *Massachusetts v. Environmental Protection Agency* that an EPA ruling that carbon dioxide and other greenhouse gases "endanger both the public health and the public welfare of current and future generations" can go forward under the Clean Air Act.

2011 – *Natural Resources Defense Council and The Sierra Club v. Jackson*

– *American Electric Power Co., Inc., et. al., v. Connecticut.*

Appendix 2

U.S. Land Acts and Laws

Executive Order 1014, 13 March 1903

With this specific order, President Theodore Roosevelt established the Pelican Island Reservation, Volusia County, Florida, creating as a preserve and breeding ground for native birds, and boundaries described in the law.

Executive Order March 14, 1903.

Pelican Island Reservation for birds created.

It is hereby ordered that Pelican Island in Indian River in section nine, township thirty-one south, range thirty-nine east, State of Florida be and it is hereby reserved and set apart for the use of the Department of Agriculture as a preserve and breeding ground for native birds.

Theodore Roosevelt

Executive Order January 26, 1909. [No. 1014]

Pelican Island Reservation for birds, enlarged.

It is ordered that the Pelican Island Reservation, Florida, created by [the] Executive Order of March 13, 1903, for the protection of native birds, be and the same is hereby enlarged so as to include all unreserved mangrove and other islands situated within Sections nine and ten, township thirty-one south, range thirty-nine east, of the Tallahassee Meridian, Florida, as segregated by the broken line shown upon the diagram hereto attached and made a part of this order. It is unlawful for any person to hunt, trap, capture, wilfully disturb, or kill any bird of any kind whatever, or take the eggs of such birds within the limits of this reservation, except under such rules and regulations as may be prescribed by the Secretary of Agriculture. Warning is expressly given to all persons not to commit any of the acts herein enumeratea and which are prohibited by law.

Theodore Roosevelt

Source: Clifford L. Lord, ed., "List and Index of Presidential Executive Orders. Unnumbered Series (1789-1941)" (New York: Books, Inc., 1944), 193; text of Executive Order in US Department of Agriculture, Office of the Solicitor, (Otis H. Gates, comp.), "Laws Applicable to the United States Department of Agriculture" (Washington, D.C.: Government Printing Office, 1913), 210.

Antiquities Act of 1906 (Public Law 59-209)

This legislation, excerpted below, signed into law by President Theodore Roosevelt, as the first time that archaeology became a federal matter. It outlawed the theft of antiquities from federal lands without a permit obtained from a federal agency; otherwise, a fine of up to $500 would be imposed and imprisonment of up to 90 days would be enforced if such a permit was not obtained. The law also established a program of protection for antiquities, through which federal agencies would set aside lands and other sources of antiquities, record scientific findings, and even designate certain archaeological sites as national monuments.

Section 1. Any person who shall appropriate, excavate, injure, or destroy any historic or prehistoric ruin or monument, or any object of antiquity, situated on lands owned or controlled by the Government of the United States, without the permission of the Secretary of the Department of the Government having jurisdiction over the lands on which said antiquities are situated, shall, upon conviction, be fined in a sum of not more than five hundred dollars or be imprisoned for a period of not more than ninety days, or shall suffer both fine and imprisonment, in the discretion of the court.

Proclamation of national monuments, reservation of lands, etc.

Section 2. The President of the United States is authorized, in his discretion, to declare by public proclamation historic landmarks, historic and prehistoric structures, and other objects of historic or scientific interest that are situated upon the lands owned or controlled by the Government of the United States to be national monuments, and may reserve as a part thereof parcels of land, the limits of which in all cases shall be confined to the smallest area compatible with proper care and management of the objects to be protected. When such objects are situated upon a tract covered by a bona fide unperfected claim or held in private ownership, the tract, or so much thereof as may be necessary for the proper care and management of the object, may be relinquished to the Government, and the Secretary of the Interior is hereby authorized to accept the relinquishment of such tracts in [sic] behalf of the Government of the United States.

Permits for excavation, etc.

Section 3. Permits for the examination of ruins, the excavation of archaeological sites, and the gathering of objects of antiquity upon the lands under their respective jurisdictions may be granted by the Secretaries of the Interior, Agriculture, and Army to institutions which they may deem properly qualified to conduct such examination, excavation, or gathering, subject to such rules and regulation as they may prescribe: Provided, That the examinations, excavations, and gatherings are undertaken for the benefit of reputable museums, universities, colleges, or other recognized scientific or educational institutions, with a view to increasing the knowledge of such objects, and that the gatherings shall be made for permanent preservation in public museums.

Rules and regulations

Section 4. The Secretaries of the departments aforesaid shall make and publish from time to time uniform rules and regulations for the purpose of carrying out the provisions of this Act.

The National Park Service Organic Act of 1916 (39 Stat. 535)

Sponsored by Rep. William Kent, Independent of California, and Sen. Reed Smoot, Republican of Utah, the National Park Service Organic Act was established as an agency of the Department of the Interior. It was pushed for years by conservationist Stephen Tyng Mather (1867-1930), an industrialist who was one of the leading environmentalists of the period.

An act to establish a National Park Service, and for other purposes.

Be it enacted by the Senate and House of Representatives of the United States of America in Congress assembled, That there is hereby created in the Department of the Interior a service to be called the National Park Service, which shall be under the charge of a director, who shall be appointed by the Secretary and who shall receive a salary of $4,500 per annum. There shall also be appointed by the Secretary the following assistants and other employees at the salaries designated: One assistant director, at $2,500 per annum, one chief clerk, at $2,000 per annum; one draftsman, at $1,800 per annum; one messenger, at $600 per annum; and, in addition thereto, such other employees as the Secretary of the Interior shall deem necessary: Provided, That not more than $8,100 annually shall be expended for salaries of experts, assistants, and employees within the District of Columbia not herein specifically enumerated unless previously authorized by law. The service thus established shall promote and regulate the use of the Federal areas known as national parks, monuments, and reservations hereinafter specified by such means and measures as conform to the fundamental purpose of the said parks, monuments, and reservations, which purpose is to conserve the scenery and the natural and historic objects and the wild life therein and to provide for the enjoyment of the same in such manner and by such means as will leave them unimpaired for the enjoyment of future generations.

Section 2. That the director shall, under the direction of the Secretary of the Interior, have the supervision, management, and control of the several national parks and national monuments which are now under the jurisdiction of the Department of the Interior, and of the Hot Springs Reservation in the State of Arkansas, and of such other national parks and reservations of like character as may be hereafter created by Congress: Provided, That in the supervision, management, and control of national monuments contiguous to national forests the Secretary of Agriculture may cooperate with said National Park Service to such extent as may be requested by the Secretary of the Interior.

Section 3. That the Secretary of the Interior shall make and publish such rules and regulations as he may deem necessary or proper for the use and management of the parks, monuments, and reservations under the jurisdiction of the National Park Service, and any violations of any of the rules and regulations authorized by this Act shall be punished as provided for in section fifty of the Act entitled "An Act to codify and amend the penal laws of the United States," approved March fourth, nineteen hundred and nine, as amended by section six of the Act of June twenty-fifth, nineteen hundred and ten (Thirty-sixth United States Statutes at Large, page eight hundred and fifty-seven). He may also, upon terms and conditions to be fixed by him, sell or dispose of timber in those cases where in his judgment the cutting of such timber is required in order to control the attacks of insects or diseases or otherwise conserve the scenery or the natural or historic objects in any such park, monument, or reservation. He may also provide in his discretion for the destruction of such animals and of such plant life as may be detrimental to the use of any of said parks, monuments, or reservations. He may also grant privileges, leases, and permits for the use of land for the accommodation of visitors in the various parks, monuments, or other reservations herein provided for, but for periods not exceeding thirty years; and no natural curiosities, wonders, or objects of interest shall be leased, rented, or granted to anyone on such terms as to interfere with free access to them by the public: Provided, however, That the Secretary of the Interior may, under such rules and regulations and on such terms as he may prescribe, grant the privilege to graze live stock within any national park, monument, or reservation herein referred to when in his judgment such use is not detrimental to the primary purpose for which such park, monument, or reservation was created, except that this provision shall not apply to the Yellowstone National Park: And provided further, That the Secretary of the Interior may grant said privileges, leases, and permits and enter into contracts relating to the same with responsible persons, firms, or corporations without advertising and without securing competitive bids: And provided further, That no contract, lease, permit, or privilege granted shall be assigned or transferred by such grantees, permittees, or licensees, without the approval of the Secretary of the Interior first obtained in writing: And provided further, That the Secretary may, in his discretion, authorize such grantees, permittees, or licensees to execute mortgages and issue bonds, shares of stock, and other evidences of interest in or indebtedness upon their rights, properties, and franchises, for the purposes of installing, enlarging or improving plant and equipment and extending facilities for the accommodation of the public within such national parks and monuments.

Section 4. That nothing in this Act contained shall affect or modify the provisions of the Act approved February fifteenth, nineteen hundred and one, entitled "An Act relating to rights of way through certain parks, reservations, and other public lands."

The Migratory Bird Conservation Act of 1929 (45 Stat. 1222)

This legislation, excerpted below, established the Migratory Bird Conservation Commission to set aside areas that had been recommended by the Secretary of the Interior to be protected for migratory birds; these lands would be purchased not with federal funds but with monies from the Migratory Bird Conservation Fund, funded by the sale of so-called Federal Duck stamps and other stamps heralding migratory birds. The law also established a procedure for the reporting by the commission to Congress on its interaction with state officials; it also called for investigations into potential migratory bird area violations.

Migratory Bird Conservation Act

An Act To more effectively meet the obligations of the United States under the migratory bird treaty with Great Britain by lessening the dangers threatening migratory game birds from drainage and other causes by the acquisition of areas of land and of water to furnish In perpetuity reservations for the adequate protection of such birds and authorizing appropriations for the establishment of such areas their maintenance and Improvement and for other purposes.

Be it enacted by the Senate and House of Representatives of the United States of America in Congress assembled, That this act shall be known by the short title of Migratory Bird Conservation Act

Section 2. That a commission to be known as the Migratory Bird Conservation Commission, consisting of the Secretary of Agriculture as chairman, the Secretary of Commerce, the Secretary of the Interior, and two Members of the Senate to be selected by the President of the Senate and two Members of the House of Representatives to be selected by the Speaker, is hereby created and authorized to consider and pass upon any area of land, water, or land and water that may be recommended by the Secretary of Agriculture for purchase or rental under this act and to fix the price or prices at which such area may be purchased or rented and no purchase or rental shall he made of any such area until it has been duly approved for purchase or rental by said commission. Any Member of the House of Representatives who is a member of the commission, if reelected to the succeeding Congress may serve on the commission notwithstanding the expiration of a Congress. Any vacancy on the commission shall be filled in the same manner as the original appointment. The ranking officer of the branch or department of a State to which Is committed the administration of its game laws, or his authorized representative and in a State having no such branch or department, the Governor thereof, or his authorized representative snail be a member ex officio of said commission for the purpose of considering and voting on all questions relating to the acquisition, under this act, of areas in his State.

Section 3. That the commission hereby created shall, through its chairman, annually report In detail to Congress, not later than the first Monday in December, the operations of the commission during the preceding fiscal year.

Section 4. That the Secretary of Agriculture shall recommend no area for purchase or rental under the terms of this act except such as be shall determine Is necessary for the conservation of migratory game birds.

Section 5. That the Secretary of Agriculture is authorized to purchase or rent such areas as have been approved for purchase or rental by the commission at the price or price or fixed by said commission, and to acquire by gift or devise, for use as inviolate sanctuaries for migratory birds, areas which he shall determine to be suitable for such purposes, and to pay the purchase or rental price and expenses incident to the location, examination, and survey of such areas and the acquisition of title thereto, including options when deemed necessary by the Secretary of Agriculture, from moneys to be appropriated hereunder by Congress from time to time: Provided, That no lands acquired, held, or used by the United States for military purposes shall be subject to any of the provisions of this act.

Section 6. That the Secretary of Agriculture may do all things and make all expenditures necessary to secure the safe title in the United States to the areas which may he acquired under this act, but no payment shall be made for any such areas until the title thereto shall be satisfactory to the Attorney General, but the acquisition of such areas by the United States snail in no case be defeated because or rights of way, easements, and reservations which from their nature will in the opinion of the Secretary of Agriculture in no manner interfere with the use of the areas so encumbered for the purposes of this act but such rights of way easements and reservations retained by the grantor or lessor from whom the United States receives title shall be subject to rules and regulations prescribed from time to time by the Secretary of Agriculture or the occupation use operation protection and administration of such areas as inviolate sanctuaries for migratory birds; and it shall be expressed in the deed or lease that the use, occupation, and operation of such rights of way, easements, and reservations shall be subordinate to and subject to such rules and regulations.

The Wilderness Act of 1964 (Public Law 88-577)

Under this landmark act, excerpted below, the National Wilderness Preservation System (NWPS) was established – it created a system in which some 9.1 million acres of wilderness was now set aside as protected federal lands.

An Act To establish a National Wilderness Preservation System for the permanent good of the whole people, and for other purposes.

Be it enacted by the Senate and House of Representatives of the United States of America in Congress assembled,

Short Title

Section 1. This Act may be cited as the "Wilderness Act."

Wilderness System Established – Statement of Policy

Sec. 2. (a) In order to assure that an increasing population, accompanied by expanding settlement and growing mechanization, does not occupy and modify all areas within the United States and its possessions, leaving no lands designated for preservation and protection in their natural condition, it is hereby declared to be the policy of the Congress to secure for the American people of present and future generations the benefits of an enduring resource of wilderness. For this purpose there is hereby established a National Wilderness Preservation System to be composed of federally owned areas designated by Congress as "wilderness areas," and these shall be administered for the use and enjoyment of the American people in such manner as will leave them unimpaired for future use as wilderness, and so as to provide for the protection of these areas, the preservation of their wilderness character, and for the gathering and dissemination of information regarding their use and enjoyment as wilderness; and no Federal lands shall be designated as "wilderness areas" except as provided for in this Act or by a subsequent Act.

(b) The inclusion of an area in the National Wilderness Preservation System notwithstanding, the area shall continue to be managed by the Department and agency having jurisdiction thereover immediately before its inclusion in the National Wilderness Preservation System unless otherwise provided by Act of Congress. No appropriation shall be available for the payment of expenses or salaries for the administration of the National Wilderness Preservation System as a separate unit nor shall any appropriations be available for additional personnel stated as being required solely for the purpose of managing or administering areas solely because they are included within the National Wilderness Preservation System.

Definition of Wilderness

(c) A wilderness, in contrast with those areas where man and his own works dominate the landscape, is hereby recognized as an area where the earth and its community of life are untrammeled by man, where man himself is a visitor who does not remain. An area of wilderness is further defined to mean in this Act an area of undeveloped Federal land retaining its primeval character and influence, without permanent improvements or human habitation, which is protected and managed so as to preserve its natural conditions and which (1) generally appears to have been affected primarily by the forces of nature, with the imprint of man's work substantially unnoticeable; (2) has outstanding opportunities for solitude or a primitive and unconfined type of recreation; (3) has at least five thousand acres of land or is of sufficient size as to make practicable its preservation and use in an unimpaired condition; and (4) may also contain ecological, geological, or other features of scientific, educational, scenic, or historical value.

National Environmental Policy Act of 1969 (Public Law 91-190)

This major legislation, excerpted below, set specific environmental standards and policies and goals for the nation in the coming years, and established the President's Council on Environmental Quality (CEQ). Most importantly, it created a program in which all federal agencies had to conduct environmental impact reports when conducting regular business.

An Act to establish a national policy for the environment, to provide for the establishment of a Council on Environmental Quality, and for other purposes.

Be it enacted by the Senate and House of Representatives of the United States of America in Congress assembled, That this Act may be cited as the "National Environmental Policy Act of 1969."

Purpose

Sec. 2. The purposes of this Act are: To declare a national policy which will encourage productive and enjoyable harmony between man and his environment; to promote efforts which will prevent or eliminate damage to the environment and biosphere and stimulate the health and welfare of man; to enrich the understanding of the ecological systems and natural resources important to the Nation; and to establish a Council on Environmental Quality.

Congressional Declaration of National Environmental Policy

Sec. 101

(a) The Congress, recognizing the profound impact of man's activity on the interrelations of all components of the natural environment, particularly the profound influences of population growth, high-density urbanization, industrial expansion, resource exploitation, and new and expanding technological advances and recognizing further the critical importance of restoring and maintaining environmental quality to the overall welfare and development of man, declares that it is the continuing policy of the Federal Government, in cooperation with State and local governments, and other concerned public and private organizations, to use all practicable means and measures, including financial and technical assistance, in a manner calculated to foster and promote the general welfare, to create and maintain conditions under which man and nature can exist in productive harmony, and fulfill the social, economic, and other requirements of present and future generations of Americans.

(b) In order to carry out the policy set forth in this Act, it is the continuing responsibility of the Federal Government to use all practicable means, consistent with other essential considerations of national policy, to improve and coordinate Federal plans, functions, programs, and resources to the end that the Nation may — fulfill the responsibilities of each generation as trustee of the environment for succeeding generations; assure for all Americans safe, healthful, productive, and aesthetically and culturally pleasing surroundings; attain the widest range of beneficial uses of the environment without degradation, risk to health or safety, or other undesirable and unintended consequences; preserve important historic, cultural, and natural aspects of our national heritage, and maintain, wherever possible, an environment which supports diversity, and variety of individual choice; achieve a balance between population and resource use which will permit high standards of living and a wide sharing of life's amenities; and enhance the quality of renewable resources and approach the maximum attainable recycling of depletable resources.

(c) The Congress recognizes that each person should enjoy a healthful environment and that each person has a responsibility to contribute to the preservation and enhancement of the environment.

Sec. 102

The Congress authorizes and directs that, to the fullest extent possible: (1) the policies, regulations, and public laws of the United States shall be interpreted and administered in accordance with the policies set forth in this Act, and (2) all agencies of the Federal Government shall –

(A) utilize a systematic, interdisciplinary approach which will insure the integrated use of the natural and social sciences and the environmental design arts in planning and in decision making which may have an impact on man's environment;

(B) identify and develop methods and procedures, in consultation with the Council on Environmental Quality established by title II of this Act, which will insure that presently unquantified environmental amenities and values may be given appropriate consideration in decision making along with economic and technical considerations;

(C) include in every recommendation or report on proposals for legislation and other major Federal actions significantly affecting the quality of the human environment, a detailed statement by the responsible official on –

(i) the environmental impact of the proposed action,

(ii) any adverse environmental effects which cannot be avoided should the proposal be implemented,

(iii) alternatives to the proposed action,

(iv) the relationship between local short-term uses of man's environment and the maintenance and enhancement of long-term productivity, and

(v) any irreversible and irretrievable commitments of resources which would be involved in the proposed action should it be implemented.

Prior to making any detailed statement, the responsible Federal official shall consult with and obtain the comments of any Federal agency which has jurisdiction by law or special expertise with respect to any environmental impact involved. Copies of such statement and the comments and views of the appropriate Federal, State, and local agencies, which are authorized to develop and enforce environmental standards, shall be made available to the President, the Council on Environmental Quality and to the public as provided by section 552 of title 5, United States Code, and shall accompany the proposal through the existing agency review processes.

The Clean Air Act of 1970 (Public Law 91-604)

In 1955, Congress enacted the Air Pollution Control Act to address the issue of air pollution in the nation as a whole. The APCA was the first such national legislation to address this issue. However, by 1963 the nation still could not clean the air properly, and Congress was forced to revisit the issue through the passage of the Clean Air Act of 1963. This legislation impacted business, forcing companies to cut emissions from plants and steel mills, although pollution from cars and trucks, a far more dangerous pollutant, was not addressed. Additionally, amendments to the 1963 act were passed in 1965, 1966, 1967, and 1969. All of these amendments authorized the then Secretary of Health, Education and Welfare (now the Secretary of Health and Human Services) to set specific standards for auto and truck emissions, as well as establishing air quality control regions (AQCRs). By 1970, however, the issue of pollution was still important, and Congress enacted the Clean Air Act of 1970 excerpted below. Although considered a "stand-alone" action, nevertheless it was an amendment to the original 1955 act. The 1970 legislation established new federal standards for air quality in cities and towns, specific emission limits for moving and stationary pollution sources, and set certain deadlines for reaching the goals of cleaner air across the nation. Alas, these goals were too ambitious, and Congress had to change the dates for compliance in Clean Air Act amendments in 1977 and 1990.

Congressional findings and declaration of purpose

(a) Findings

The Congress finds—

(1) that the predominant part of the Nation's population is located in its rapidly expanding metropolitan and other urban areas, which generally cross the boundary lines of local jurisdictions and often extend into two or more States;

(2) that the growth in the amount and complexity of air pollution brought about by urbanization, industrial development, and the increasing use of motor vehicles, has resulted in mounting dangers to the public health and welfare, including injury to agricultural crops and livestock, damage to and the deterioration of property, and hazards to air and ground transportation;

(3) that air pollution prevention (that is, the reduction or elimination, through any measures, of the amount of pollutants produced or created at the source) and air pollution control at its source is the primary responsibility of States and local governments; and

(4) that Federal financial assistance and leadership is essential for the development of cooperative Federal, State, regional, and local programs to prevent and control air pollution.

(b) Declaration

The purposes of this subchapter are—

(1) to protect and enhance the quality of the Nation's air resources so as to promote the public health and welfare and the productive capacity of its population;

(2) to initiate and accelerate a national research and development program to achieve the prevention and control of air pollution;

(3) to provide technical and financial assistance to State and local governments in connection with the development and execution of their air pollution prevention and control programs; and

(4) to encourage and assist the development and operation of regional air pollution prevention and control programs.

(c) Pollution prevention

A primary goal of this chapter is to encourage or otherwise promote reasonable Federal, State, and local governmental actions, consistent with the provisions of this chapter, for pollution prevention.

The Clean Water Act of 1972 (Public Law 92-500)

Enacted in 1972, the Federal Water Pollution Control Act (FWPCA), commonly referred to as The Clean Water Act (CWA), was enacted specifically to address the pollution that was infesting America's waters in the late 1960s and early 1970s. Underground water supplies and drinking water appeared threatened nationwide by pollution and chemical contamination. Excerpted below, this legislation, since amended numerous times, established a congressional mandate for providing assistance to the states for water treatment as well as the protection of wetlands.

Congressional findings and declaration of purpose

(a) Findings

The Congress finds—

(a) Restoration and maintenance of chemical, physical and biological integrity of Nation's waters; national goals for achievement of objective

The objective of this chapter is to restore and maintain the chemical, physical, and biological integrity of the Nation's waters. In order to achieve this objective it is hereby declared that, consistent with the provisions of this chapter –

(1) it is the national goal that the discharge of pollutants into the navigable waters be eliminated by 1985;

(2) it is the national goal that wherever attainable, an interim goal of water quality which provides for the protection and propagation of fish, shellfish, and wildlife and provides for recreation in and on the water be achieved by July 1, 1983;

(3) it is the national policy that the discharge of toxic pollutants in toxic amounts be prohibited;

(4) it is the national policy that Federal financial assistance be provided to construct publicly owned waste treatment works;

(5) it is the national policy that areawide waste treatment management planning processes be developed and implemented to assure adequate control of sources of pollutants in each State;

(6) it is the national policy that a major research and demonstration effort be made to develop technology necessary to eliminate the discharge of pollutants into the navigable waters, waters of the contiguous zone, and the oceans; and

(7) it is the national policy that programs for the control of nonpoint sources of pollution be developed and implemented in an expeditious manner so as to enable the goals of this chapter to be met through the control of both point and nonpoint sources of pollution.

(b) Congressional recognition, preservation, and protection of primary responsibilities and rights of States

It is the policy of the Congress to recognize, preserve, and protect the primary responsibilities and rights of States to prevent, reduce, and eliminate pollution, to plan the development and use (including restoration, preservation, and enhancement) of land and water resources, and to consult with the Administrator in the exercise of his authority under this chapter. It is the policy of Congress that the States manage the construction grant program under this chapter and implement the permit programs under sections 1342 and 1344 of this title. It is further the policy of the Congress to support and aid research relating to the prevention, reduction, and elimination of pollution and to provide Federal technical services and financial aid to State and interstate agencies and municipalities in connection with the prevention, reduction, and elimination of pollution.

(c) Congressional policy toward Presidential activities with foreign countries It is further the policy of Congress that the President, acting through the Secretary of State and such national and international organizations as he determines appropriate, shall take such action as may be necessary to insure that to the fullest extent possible all foreign countries shall take meaningful action for the prevention, reduction, and elimination of pollution in their waters and in international waters and for the achievement of goals regarding the elimination of discharge of pollutants and the improvement of water quality to at least the same extent as the United States does under its laws.

(d) Administrator of Environmental Protection Agency to administer chapter Except as otherwise expressly provided in this chapter, the Administrator of the Environmental Protection Agency (hereinafter in this chapter called "Administrator") shall administer this chapter.

(e) Public participation in development, revision, and enforcement of any regulation, etc.

Public participation in the development, revision, and enforcement of any regulation, standard, effluent limitation, plan, or program established by the Administrator or any State under this chapter shall be provided for, encouraged, and assisted by the Administrator and the States. The Administrator, in cooperation with the States, shall develop and publish regulations specifying minimum guidelines for public participation in such processes.

(f) Procedures utilized for implementing chapter It is the national policy that to the maximum extent possible the procedures utilized for implementing this chapter shall encourage the drastic minimization of paperwork and interagency decision procedures, and the best use of available manpower and funds, so as to prevent needless duplication and unnecessary delays at all levels of government.

(g) Authority of States over water

It is the policy of Congress that the authority of each State to allocate quantities of water within its jurisdiction shall not be superseded, abrogated or otherwise impaired by this chapter. It is the further policy of Congress that nothing in this chapter shall be construed to supersede or abrogate rights to quantities of water which have been established by any State. Federal agencies shall co-operate with State and local agencies to develop comprehensive solutions to prevent, reduce and eliminate pollution in concert with programs for managing water resources.

The Federal Land Policy and Management Act of 1976 (Public Law 94-579)

According to The New Mexico Center for Wildlife Law, "This Act . . . governs most uses of the federal public lands, including grazing (and) Act requires the Bureau (of Land Management) to execute its management powers under a land use planning process that is based on multiple use and sustained yield principles. The Act also provides for public land sales, withdrawals, acquisitions and exchanges."

DECLARATION OF POLICY

Sec. 102. [43 U.S.C. 1701] (a) The Congress declares that it is the policy of the United States that–

(1) the public lands be retained in Federal ownership, unless as a result of the land use planning procedure provided for in this Act, it is determined that disposal of a particular parcel will serve the national interest;

(2) the national interest will be best realized if the public lands and their resources are periodically and systematically inventoried and their present and future use is projected through a land use planning process coordinated with other Federal and State planning efforts;

(3) public lands not previously designated for any specific use and all existing classifications of public lands that were effected by executive action or statute before the date of enactment of this Act be reviewed in accordance with the provisions of this Act;

(4) the Congress exercise its constitutional authority to withdraw or otherwise designate or dedicate Federal lands for specified purposes and that Congress delineate the extent to which the Executive may withdraw lands without legislative action;

(5) in administering public land statutes and exercising discretionary authority granted by them, the Secretary be required to establish comprehensive rules and regulations after considering the views of the general public; and to structure adjudication procedures to assure adequate third party participation, objective administrative review of initial decisions, and expeditious decision making;

(6) judicial review of public land adjudication decisions be provided by law;

(7) goals and objectives be established by law as guidelines for public land use planning, and that management be on the basis of multiple use and sustained yield unless otherwise specified by law;

(8) the public lands be managed in a manner that will protect the quality of scientific, scenic, historical, ecological, environmental, air and atmospheric, water resource, and archeological values; that, where appropriate, will preserve and protect certain public

lands in their natural condition; that will provide food and habitat for fish and wildlife and domestic animals; and that will provide for outdoor recreation and human occupancy and use;

(9) the United States receive fair market value of the use of the public lands and their resources unless otherwise provided for by statute;

(10) uniform procedures for any disposal of public land, acquisition of non-Federal land for public purposes, and the exchange of such lands be established by statute, requiring each disposal, acquisition, and exchange to be consistent with the prescribed mission of the department or agency involved, and reserving to the Congress review of disposals in excess of a specified acreage;

(11) regulations and plans for the protection of public land areas of critical environmental concern be promptly developed;

(12) the public lands be managed in a manner which recognizes the Nation's need for domestic sources of minerals, food, timber, and fiber from the public lands including implementation of the Mining and Minerals Policy Act of 1970 (84 Stat. 1876, 30 U.S.C. 21a) as it pertains to the public lands; and

(13) the Federal Government should, on a basis equitable to both the Federal and local taxpayer, provide for payments to compensate States and local governments for burdens created as a result of the immunity of Federal lands from State and local taxation.

(b) The policies of this Act shall become effective only as specific statutory authority for their implementation is enacted by this Act or by subsequent legislation and shall then be construed as supplemental to and not in derogation of the purposes for which public lands are administered under other provisions of law.

DEFINITIONS

Sec. 103. [43 U.S.C. 1702] Without altering in any way the meaning of the following terms as used in any other statute, whether or not such statute is referred to in, or amended by, this Act, as used in this Act–

(a) The term "areas of critical environmental concern" means areas within the public lands where special management attention is required (when such areas are developed or used or where no development is required) to protect and prevent irreparable damage to important historic, cultural, or scenic values, fish and wildlife resources or other natural systems or processes, or to protect life and safety from natural hazards.

(b) The term "holder" means any State or local governmental entity, individual, partnership, corporation, association, or other business entity receiving or using a right-of-way under title V of this Act.

(c) The term "multiple use" means the management of the public lands and their various resource values so that they are utilized in the combination that will best meet the present and future needs of the American people; making the most judicious use of the land for some or all of these resources or related services over areas large enough to provide sufficient latitude for periodic adjustments in use to conform to changing needs and conditions; the use of some land for less than all of the resources; a combination of balanced and diverse resource uses that takes into account the long-term needs of future generations for renewable and nonrenewable resources, including, but not limited to, recreation, range, timber, minerals, watershed, wildlife and fish, and natural scenic, scientific and historical values; and harmonious and coordinated management of the various resources without permanent impairment of the productivity of the land and the quality of the environment with consideration being given to the relative values of the resources and not necessarily to the combination of uses that will give the greatest economic return or the greatest unit output.

(d) The term "public involvement" means the opportunity for participation by affected citizens in rule making, decision making, and planning with respect to the public lands, including public meetings or hearings held at locations near the affected lands, or advisory mechanisms, or such other procedures as may be necessary to provide public comment in a particular instance.

(e) The term "public lands" means any land and interest in land owned by the United States within the several States and administered by the Secretary of the Interior through the Bureau of Land Management, without regard to how the United States acquired ownership, except–

(1) lands located on the Outer Continental Shelf; and

(2) lands held for the benefit of Indians, Aleuts, and Eskimos.

(f) The term "right-of-way" includes an easement, lease, permit, or license to occupy, use, or traverse public lands granted for the purpose listed in title V of this Act.

(g) The term "Secretary," unless specifically designated otherwise, means the Secretary of the Interior.

(h) The term "sustained yield" means the achievement and maintenance in perpetuity of a high-level annual or regular periodic output of the various renewable resources of the public lands consistent with multiple use (i) The term "wilderness" as used in section 603 shall have the same meaning as it does in section 2(c) of the Wilderness Act (78 Stat. 890; 16 U.S.C. 1131–1136).

(j) The term "withdrawal" means withholding an area of Federal land from settlement, sale, location, or entry, under some or all of the general land laws, for the purpose of limiting activities under those laws in order to maintain other public values in the area or reserving the area for a particular public purpose or program; or transferring jurisdiction over an area of Federal land, other than "property" governed by the Federal Property and Administrative Services Act, as amended (40 U.S.C. 472) from one department, bureau or agency to another department, bureau or agency.

(k) An "allotment management plan" means a document prepared in consultation with the lessees or permittees involved, which applies to livestock operations on the public lands or on lands within National Forests in the eleven contiguous Western States and which:

(1) prescribes the manner in, and extent to, which livestock operations will be conducted in order to meet the multiple-use, sustained-yield, economic and other needs and objectives as determined for the lands by the Secretary concerned; and

(2) describes the type, location, ownership, and general specifications for the range improvements to be installed and maintained on the lands to meet the livestock grazing and other objectives of land management; and

(3) contains such other provisions relating to livestock grazing and other objectives found by the Secretary concerned to be consistent with the provisions of this Act and other applicable law.

(1) The term "principal or major uses" includes, and is limited to, domestic livestock grazing, fish and wildlife development and utilization, mineral exploration and production, rights-of-way, outdoor recreation, and timber production.

(m) The term "department" means a unit of the executive branch of the Federal Government which is headed by a member of the President's Cabinet and the term "agency" means a unit of the executive branch of the Federal Government which is not under the jurisdiction of a head of a department.

(n) The term "Bureau" means the Bureau of Land Management.

(o) The term "eleven contiguous Western States" means the States of Arizona, California, Colorado, Idaho, Montana, Nevada, New Mexico, Oregon, Utah, Washington, and Wyoming.

(p) The term "grazing permit and lease" means any document authorizing use of public lands or lands in National Forests in the eleven contiguous Western States for the purpose of grazing domestic livestock.

[The term "sixteen contiguous Western States," where changed by P.L. 95-514, refers to: Arizona, California, Colorado, Idaho, Kansas, Montana, Nebraska, Nevada, New Mexico, North Dakota, Oklahoma, Oregon, South Dakota, Utah, Washington and Wyoming. This term is defined by P.L. 95-514 and found in sections 401(b)(1), 402(a) and 403(a).]

Alaska National Interest Lands Conservation Act of 1980 (Public Law 94-2371)

In 1980, Congress enacted the Alaska National Interest Lands Conservation Act of 1980, also known as ANILCA, which set aside some 100 million acres of lands in the 50th state as federally protected lands. The legislation, excerpted below, expanded the national park system in Alaska by more than 43 million acres, establishing 10 new national parks and expanding three existing parks.

To provide for the designation and conservation of certain public lands in the State of Alaska, including the designation of units of the National Park, National Wildlife Refuge, National Forest, National Wild and Scenic Rivers, and National Wilderness Preservation Systems, and for other purposes.

Section 1. This Act may be cited as the "Alaska National Interest Lands Conservation Act."

Purposes

§101. (a) In order to preserve for the benefit, use, education and inspiration of present and future generations certain lands and waters in the State of Alaska that contain nationally significant natural, scenic, historic, archeological, geological, scientific, wilderness, cultural, recreational, and wildlife values, and units described in the following titles are hereby established.

(b) It is the intent of Congress in this Act to preserve unrivaled scenic and geological values associated with natural landscapes; to provide for the maintenance of sound populations of, and habitat for, wildlife species of inestimable value to the citizens of Alaska and the Nation, including those species dependent on vast relatively undeveloped areas; to preserve in their natural state extensive unaltered arctic tundra, boreal forest, and coastal rainforest ecosystems, to protect the resources related to subsistence needs; to protect and preserve historic and archeological sites, rivers, and lands, and to preserve wilderness resource values and related recreational opportunities including but not limited to hiking, canoeing fishing, and sport hunting, within large arctic and subarctic wildlands and on freeflowing rivers; and to maintain opportunities for scientific research and undisturbed ecosystems.

(c) It is further the intent and purpose of this Act consistent with management of fish and wildlife in accordance with recognized scientific principles and the purposes for which each conservation system unit is established, designated, or expanded by or pursuant to this Act, to provide the opportunity for rural residents engaged in a subsistence way of life to continue to do so.

(d) This Act provides sufficient protection for the national interest in the scenic, natural, cultural and environmental values on the public lands in Alaska, and at the same time provides adequate opportunity for satisfaction of the economic and social needs of the State of Alaska and its people; accordingly, the designation and disposition of the public lands in Alaska pursuant to this Act are found to represent a proper balance between the reservation of national conservation system units and those public lands necessary and appropriate for more intensive use and disposition, and thus Congress believes that the need for future legislation designating new conservation system units, new national conservation areas, or new national recreation areas, has been obviated thereby.

Oil Pollution Act of 1990 (Public Law 101-380)

Congress enacted the Oil Pollution Act of 1990 to establish a system of liabilities for the pollution of the environment by oil companies. Enacted following a series of horrific oil spills, including the Torrey Canyon spill off the coast of the United Kingdom in 1967 and the Exxon Valdez spill in Alaska in 1989, this act was the latest in a series of congressional actions relating to oil pollution. The first was the Oil Pollution Act of 1924 (43 Stat. 604) and the Oil Pollution Act of 1961 (Public Law 87-167). Under the 1990 act, excerpted below, liability for oil spills was placed on the owner or operator of the ship which gave off the discharge, and they were liable for environmental damage, costs of clean-up, repairs to natural resources, and other costs.

An ACT to establish limitations on liability for damages resulting from oil pollution, to establish a fund for the payment of compensation for such damages, and for other purposes.

Be it enacted by the Senate and House of Representatives of the United States of America in Congress assembled,

SECTION 1. SHORT TITLE.

This Act may be cited as the "Oil Pollution Act of 1990".

[...]

DEFINITIONS.

For the purposes of this Act, the term –

(1) "act of God" means an unanticipated grave natural disaster or other natural phenomenon of an exceptional, inevitable, and irresistible character the effects of which could not have been prevented or avoided by the exercise of due care or foresight;

(2) "barrel" means 42 United States gallons at 60 degrees fahrenheit;

(3) "claim" means a request, made in writing for a sum certain, for compensation for damages or removal costs resulting from an incident;

(4) "claimant" means any person or government who presents a claim for compensation under this title;

(5) "damages" means damages specified in section 1002(b) of this Act, and includes the cost of assessing these damages;

(6) "deepwater port" is a facility licensed under the Deepwater Port Act of 1974 (33 U.S.C. 1501–1524);

(7) "discharge" means any emission (other than natural seepage), intentional or unintentional, and includes, but is not limited to, spilling, leaking, pumping, pouring, emitting, emptying, or dumping;

(8) "exclusive economic zone" means the zone established by Presidential Proclamation Numbered 5030, dated March 10, 1983, including the ocean waters of the areas referred to as "eastern special areas" in Article 3(1) of the Agreement between the United States of America and the Union of Soviet Socialist Republics on the Maritime Boundary, signed June 1, 1990;

(9) "facility" means any structure, group of structures, equipment, or device (other than a vessel) which is used for one or more of the following purposes: exploring for, drilling for, producing, storing, handling, transferring, processing, or transporting oil. This term includes any motor vehicle, rolling stock, or pipeline used for one or more of these purposes;

(10) "foreign offshore unit" means a facility which is located, in whole or in part, in the territorial sea or on the continental shelf of a foreign country and which is or was used for one or more of the following purposes: exploring for, drilling for, producing, storing, handling, transferring, processing, or transporting oil produced from the seabed beneath the foreign country's territorial sea or from the foreign country's continental shelf;

(11) "Fund" means the Oil Spill Liability Trust Fund, established by section 9509 of the Internal Revenue Code of 1986 (26 U.S.C. 9509);

(12) "gross ton" has the meaning given that term by the Secretary under part J of title 46, United States Code;

(13) "guarantor" means any person, other than the responsible party, who provides evidence of financial responsibility for a responsible party under this Act;

(14) "incident" means any occurrence or series of occurrences having the same origin, involving one or more vessels, facilities, or any combination thereof, resulting in the discharge or substantial threat of discharge of oil;

(15) "Indian tribe" means any Indian tribe, band, nation, or other organized group or community, but not including any Alaska Native regional or village corporation, which is recognized as eligible for the special programs and services provided by the United States to Indians because of their status as Indians and has governmental authority over lands belonging to or controlled by the tribe...

Appendix 3

Glossary

ACEC (Area of Critical Environmental Concern): Areas where special management is needed to protect important historical, cultural, scenic, and natural areas, or to identify areas hazardous to human life and property.

Acquired lands: Lands in Federal ownership that were obtained by the Government through purchase, condemnation, or gift or by exchange. Acquired lands constitute one category of public lands. (See Public lands.)

Administrative site: A reservation of public lands for use as a site for public buildings, ranger stations, or other administrative facilities.

Administrative State: Bureau of Land Management State Office having administrative jurisdiction. For example, the Montana State Office has administrative jurisdiction for Montana, North Dakota, and South Dakota. See inside back cover for a complete list of State Offices and the respective areas of responsibility for each office.

Allocation of receipts: Determination of moneys paid, or to be paid, to other funds, counties, or States out of receipts collected during the fiscal year reported, as required or specified by law.

ANCSA: Alaska Native Claims Settlement Act of December 18, 1971 (Public Law 92-203, 85 Stat. 688).

Animal unit: A standardized unit of measurement for range livestock that is equivalent to one cow, one horse, five sheep, five goats, or four reindeer, all over 6 months of age.

Application: A formal request for rights to use, or obtain eventual title to, public lands or resources.

Archaeological and historical site: A site that contains objects of antiquity or cultural value relating to history or prehistory that warrant special protection.

AUM (Animal Unit Month): A standardized unit of measurement of the amount of forage necessary for the complete sustenance of one animal unit for a period of 1 month; also, a unit of measurement of grazing privileges that represents the privilege of grazing one animal unit for a period of 1 month.

Big game habitat: Habitat area used by big game animals at some time during their yearly life cycle.

Boating: Motorized boating includes tour boating, power boating, river running (commercial or noncommercial), etc. Nonmotorized boating includes sailing, canoeing, kayaking, and river running (commercial and noncommercial), and activity by other nonmotorized boats, such as rowboats.

Bonus: The cash consideration paid to the United States by the successful bidder for a mineral lease, such payment being made in addition to the rent and royalty obligations specified in the lease.

Cadastral survey: A survey relating to land boundaries and subdivisions made to create units suitable for management or to define the limits of title. The distinguishing features of the cadastral surveys are the establishment of monuments on the ground to define the boundaries of the land and their identification in the records by field notes and plats.

Camping: Includes auto and trailer camping, along with other camping at developed sites, and backcountry camping.

Candidate species: Species designated as candidates for listing as threatened or endangered by the U.S. Fish and Wildlife Service or National Marine Fisheries Service. (See Endangered species and Threatened species.)

Carey Acts: The acts of August 18, 1894 (28 Stat. 372), and March 15, 1910 (36 Stat. 237, 43 U.S.C. Sec. 643), which provide for grants of desert lands to States for disposition to bona fide settlers.

CCF: Hundred cubic feet; 100 units of true volume that measures 1 x 1 x 1 foot or its equivalent. This is the standard unit of measurement for Bureau of Land Management timber sales. It does not include bark or air volume.

Ceded Indian lands: Public lands to which Indian tribal title was relinquished to the United States by the Indians on condition that part or all of the proceeds from their sale or other disposition would be conveyed into the Treasury and held in trust for the Indians.

Certification: The act of final approval of a State selection by the Director of the BLM; the document that passes title to the selected lands to the State; or a document that attests to the truth or authenticity of the papers attached to it.

CFR: Code of Federal Regulations.

Chaining: Vegetation removal that is accomplished by hooking a large anchor chain between two bulldozers; as the dozers move through the vegetation, the vegetation is knocked to the ground. Chaining kills a large percentage of the vegetation, and is often followed a year or two later by burning or seeding.

Color-of-Title Act: The act of December 22, 1928 (43 U.S.C. Sec. 1068), as amended. Under the terms and provisions of this act, a patent may be issued for a parcel of not more than 160 acres of public lands in instances where claim to the lands has been based on a written instrument containing defective evidence of title. The parcel must have been possessed in good faith by a claimant, his ancestors, or grantors for more than 20 years.

Color-of-title entry: A cash entry made by an applicant under the Color-of-Title Act.

Competitive leasing: Refers to leases issued by the United States where there are known minerals (or other resources such as oil and gas) or where inference of probable resources can be drawn from knowledge of the geology of the land. The lands are offered for lease by competitive bidding after publication of the offer of the lands for leasing. The lease is issued to the highest bidder, who is determined at a sale by public auction. (See Leasable minerals and Noncompetitive leasing.)

Concession leases: Long-term authorizations for private parties to possess and use public lands to provide recreation facilities and services for a fixed period; these leases are authorized under 43 CFR 2920 and the Land and Water Conservation Fund Act. Recreation concession leases establish the obligations that the Bureau of Land Management and the concessionaire agree to in providing visitor services necessary for full enjoyment of the public lands or related waters.

Contract fire protection: Fire protection given lands owned, leased, or controlled by the United States and administered by the Bureau of Land Management on which complete fire protection is extended through the use of fire protection forces and facilities contracted for by the Bureau of Land Management.

Crossing permit: An authorization issued for trailing livestock across Federal range for proper and lawful purposes.

Cultural resources: Remains of human activity, occupation, or endeavor that are reflected in districts, sites, structures, buildings, objects, artifacts, ruins, works of art, architecture, and natural features that were of importance in past human events. These resources consist of (1) physical remains, (2) areas where significant human events occurred, even though evidence of the event no longer remains, and (3) the environment immediately surrounding the actual resource.

Desert Land Entry: An entry of irrigable arid agricultural public lands for the purpose of reclamation, irrigation, and cultivation in part.

Disposition: A transaction that leads to the transfer of title of public lands, or resources on or in these lands, from the Federal Government.

Early seral: An ecological condition classification that means that the current vegetation is between zero and 25 percent similar to the potential natural plant community. Early seral describes vegetation that is in "poor" condition.

Eastern States: Includes all states bordering on or east of the Mississippi River.

Emergency fire rehabilitation projects: Any action taken to ameliorate the impacts of a wildfire to the land, including the physical and biological resources. These actions can include exclusion fencing, soil stabilization (such as revegetation), and watershed protection measures. Fire rehabilitation actions are necessary to prevent unacceptable resource degradation, minimize threats to public health and safety, prevent unacceptable off-site damage, and minimize the potential for the recurrence of wildfire.

Endangered species: Any animal or plant species in danger of extinction throughout all or a significant portion of its range. (See Candidate species and Threatened species.)

Entry: An application to acquire title to public lands.

Entry, allowed: An application to acquire title to public lands that has been approved, either as an original entry or as a final entry.

Ephemeral streams: Stream reaches where water flows for only brief periods during storm runoff events.

Exchange: A transaction whereby the Federal Government receives land or interests in land in exchange for other land or interests in land.

Exchange lease (coal): An exchange of coal resources when it is in the public interest to shift the impact of mineral operations from leased lands, or portions of leased lands, to currently unleased lands to preserve public resource or social values, and to carry out congressional directives authorizing coal lease exchanges.

Federal land: All classes of land owned by the Federal Government.

Field examination: An on-the-ground investigation of selected public lands with regard to valuation, land use, application for entry, mineralization, etc.

Fire suppression: Fire control activities concerned with controlling and extinguishing a fire, starting when the fire is discovered.

Fishable stream: A stream that currently supports a sport fishery on public lands. These streams are not necessarily accessible to the public.

Fishing: Includes fishing from the shore and from a boat when the boating is secondary to the fishing activity. Included are warm-water, cold-water, and ice fishing; crabbing; seining; and gigging.

FLPMA: Federal Land Policy and Management Act of October 21, 1976 (Public Law 94-579, 90 Stat. 2743), commonly called the "Organic Act" for the Bureau of Land Management.

Force account fire protection: Fire protection given lands owned, leased, or controlled by the United States and administered by the Bureau of Land Management on which complete fire protection is extended through the use of the protection forces and facilities supervised and operated by the Bureau of Land Management.

Free-use permit: A permit to a governmental agency or nonprofit group to use mineral materials, such as sand and gravel, or other resources at no charge.

GDP (gross domestic product): The total value of all goods and services produced within an economy during a specified period.

Globally Important Bird Areas (IBA): A network of sites and areas in North America identified and protected to maintain naturally occurring bird populations across the ranges of those species. IBAs are important for maintaining critical habitats and ecosystems. This network of areas encompasses lands critical to the conservation of some bird species and may include the best examples of the species' habitat. IBAs help ensure species' survival.

Grazing district: An administrative subdivision of the rangelands under the jurisdiction of the Bureau of Land Management established pursuant to Section 3 of the Taylor Grazing Act to facilitate the management of rangeland resources.

Grazing-fee year: March 1 of a given calendar year through the last day in February of the following year.

Grazing lease: An authorization that permits the grazing of livestock on public lands outside the grazing districts during a specified period (Section 15 of the Taylor Grazing Act).

Grazing lease lands: Lands outside grazing districts that are owned, leased, or otherwise controlled by the United States and administered by the Bureau of Land Management and that are subject to leasing for grazing purposes under the Alaska Grazing Law of March 4, 1927; Section 15 of the Taylor Grazing Act of June 28, 1934; the Oregon Timber Conservation Act of August 28, 1937; or the Reindeer Act of September 1, 1937.

Grazing permit: An authorization that permits the grazing of a specified number and class of livestock on a designated area of grazing district lands during specified seasons each year (Section 3 of the Taylor Grazing Act).

Habitat disking and chaining: Involves use of heavy equipment to remove undesirable vegetation such as juniper trees (chaining) and sagebrush (disking). Usually done to induce the growth of more desirable species.

Hardrock minerals: Locatable minerals that are neither leasable minerals (oil, gas, coal, oil shale, phosphate, sodium, potassium, sulphur, asphalt, or gilsonite) nor salable mineral materials (common variety sand and gravel). Hardrock minerals include, but are not limited to, copper, lead, zinc, magnesium, nickel, tungsten, gold, silver, bentonite, barite, feldspar, fluorspar, and uranium.

Herd Management Areas: Areas established for wild and free-roaming horses and burros through the land use planning process. The Wild Free-Roaming Horses and Burros Act of 1971 requires that wild, free-roaming horses and burros be considered for management where they were found at the time Congress passed the act. The Bureau of Land Management initially identified 264 areas of use as herd areas.

Homestead entry, original: An original entry under the homestead laws; the first homestead entry that was made by an individual; or, a homestead entry that was made pursuant to the first homestead law, the Act of May 20, 1862 (12 Stat. 392) as codified in Sections 2289–2291 of the Revised Statutes. (See Stock raising homestead.)

Hunting: Includes big- and small-game hunting, waterfowl hunting, and trapping.

Indian allotment: An allocation of a parcel of public lands or Indian reservation lands to an Indian for individual use; also, the lands so allocated.

Inholdings: Privately owned or State-owned lands located within the boundary of lands owned by the United States.

Inland water area: Includes permanent inland water surface, such as lakes, ponds, and reservoirs having 40 acres or more of the area; streams, sloughs, estuaries, and canals one-eighth of a statute mile or more in width; deeply indented embayments and sounds, other coastal waters behind or sheltered by headlands, or islands separated by less than 1 nautical mile of water; and islands having less than 40 acres of area.

Lake (or pond): A <u>natural</u> standing body of water.

Lake improvements: Consist of many different techniques to improve water temperature, oxygen content, silt load, etc. This may include the planting of ground cover in the lake watershed and the planting of shade trees.

Lake Todatonten Special Management Area: Congress authorized the creation of the Lake Todatonten Special Management Area—a 37,579-acre parcel of public land in

Interior Alaska for the protection of fish, wildlife, and habitat—in its Omnibus Parks and Public Lands Management Act of 1996 (Public Law 104-333). The area was withdrawn by Public Land Order No. 7372 on December 15, 1998.

Land area: Includes dry land and land temporarily or partly covered by water, such as marshlands, swamps, and river floodplains; streams, sloughs, estuaries, and canals less than one-eighth of a statute mile in width; and lakes, reservoirs, and ponds having less than 40 acres of water-surface area.

Late seral: An ecological condition classification that means that the current vegetation is between 51 and 75 percent similar to the potential natural plant community. Late seral means that the vegetation is in "good" condition.

Leasable minerals: Oil and gas; oil shale; coal; potash; phosphate; sodium; sulfur in Louisiana and New Mexico; gold, silver, and quicksilver in certain private land claims; and silica deposits in certain parts of Nevada.

Lease: An authorization to possess and use public land for a period of time sufficient to amortize capital investments in the land. (See Competitive leasing and Noncompetitive leasing.)

License: An authority granted by the United States to do a particular act or series of acts on public lands without the licensee possessing any estate or interest in the land itself.

LMU (Logical mining unit): An area of land in which the recoverable coal reserves can be developed in an efficient, economical, and orderly manner as a unit with due regard to conservation of coal reserves and other resources. An LMU may consist of one or more Federal coal leases and may include intervening or adjacent lands in which the United States does not own the coal. All lands in an LMU are under the control of one operator or lessee, can be developed as a single operation, and are contiguous. Formation of LMUs was authorized by the Federal Coal Leasing Amendments Act of 1976, which amended the Mineral Leasing Act (30 U.S.C. 181 et seq.).

Locatable minerals: Whatever are recognized as minerals by the standard authorities, whether metallic or other substances, and are found in sufficient quantity and quality to justify their location under the Mining Law of 1872, as amended. (See Hardrock minerals.)

Lode claim: A mining claim located for "veins or lodes of quartz or other rock in place" (30 U.S.C. 23). Lode claims may extend for 1,500 feet along the strike of the vein or lode and to a maximum of 300 feet on either side of the vein or lode.

LU (Land Utilization) project lands: Privately owned submarginal farmlands incapable of producing sufficient income to support the family of a farm owner and purchased under Title III of the Bankhead-Jones Farm Tenant Act of July 22, 1937. These acquired lands became known as "Land Utilization Projects" and were subsequently transferred from the jurisdiction of the U.S. Department of Agriculture to the U.S. Department of the Interior. They are now administered by the Bureau of Land Management.

MBF: Thousand board feet. A board foot is a unit of lumber measurement 1 foot long, 1 foot wide, and 1 inch thick, or its equivalent. It is the standard unit of measurement in the logging and lumber industry by which standing timber is measured and sold and manufactured lumber is merchandised.

Mid seral: An ecological condition classification that means that the current vegetation is between 26 and 50 percent similar to the potential natural plant community. Mid seral describes vegetation that is in "fair" condition.

Mill site: A site located on nonmineral land and used for mining or milling purposes (30 U.S.C. 42). Mill sites are limited to 5 acres and may be located either by metes and bounds or by legal subdivision.

Minerals: Organic and inorganic substances occurring naturally, with characteristics and economic uses that bring them within the purview of mineral laws; substances that may be obtained under applicable laws from public lands by purchase, lease, or preemptive entry.

Mineral materials: Minerals such as common varieties of sand, stone, gravel, pumice, pumicite, and clay that are not obtainable under the mining or leasing laws but that can be obtained under the Materials Act of 1947, as amended.

Mineral permit: A permit that authorizes prospecting for certain leasable minerals on public lands described in the permit.

Mineral reservation: Retention of the mineral estate by the grantor of a property; the grantee or patentee owns the land surface but not the minerals.

Mining claim: A mineral entry and appropriation of public land under the Mining Law of 1872, as amended (30 U.S.C. Sec. 22 et seq.). There are four types of mining claims: lode claims, placer claims, mill sites, and tunnel sites. Only tunnel sites may not be patented. A valid lode or placer claim contains a discovery of a valuable mineral deposit subject to location under the Mining Law of 1872. A valid mill site is one that is being used for the support of a mining or milling operation. A valid tunnel site is one that is being diligently worked and maintained.

Mining claim location: The staking and recordation of a lode or placer claim, mill site, or tunnel site on public land. A valid location is one that is properly located, recorded, and maintained under Section 314 of the Federal Land Policy and Management Act of October 21, 1976, and the mining laws of the State where the claim or site is located.

Multiple use: A combination of balanced and diverse resource uses that takes into account the long-term needs of future generations for renewable and nonrenewable resources, including recreation, range, timber, minerals, watershed, and wildlife and fish, along with natural scenic, scientific, and historical values.

National Back Country Byways: A program developed by the Bureau of Land Management to complement the National Scenic Byway program. Bureau of Land Management's byways show enthusiasts the best the West has to offer—from the breathtaking thunder of waterfalls to geology sculpted by ancient volcanoes, glaciers, and rivers. Back Country Byways vary from narrow, graded roads, passable only during a few months of the year, to two-lane paved highways providing year-round access.

National Conservation Areas: Areas designated by Congress so that present and future generations of Americans can benefit from the conservation, protection, enhancement, use, and management of these areas by enjoying their natural, recreational, cultural, wildlife, aquatic, archaeological, paleontological, historical, educational, or scientific resources and values.

National Historic Trails: Trails established to identify and protect historic routes. They follow as closely as possible the original trails or routes of travel of national historic significance.

National Monument: An area designated to protect objects of scientific and historic interest by public proclamation of the President under the Antiquities Act of 1906, or by Congress for historic landmarks, historic and prehistoric structures, or other objects of historic or scientific interest situated on the public lands. Designation also provides for the management of these features and values.

National Natural Landmarks: Areas having national significance because they represent one of the best known examples of a natural region's characteristic biotic or geologic features. National Natural Landmarks must be located within the boundaries of the United States or on the Continental Shelf and are designated by the Secretary of the Interior. To qualify as a National Natural Landmark, the area must contain an outstanding representative example of the Nation's natural heritage, including terrestrial communities, aquatic communities, landforms, geological features, habitats of native plant and animal species, or fossil evidence of the development of life on earth.

National Outstanding Natural Areas: Protected lands designated either by Congress or administratively by an agency to preserve exceptional, rare, or unusual natural characteristics and to provide for the protection or enhancement of natural, educational, or scientific values. These areas are protected by allowing physical and biological processes to operate, usually without direct human intervention.

National Recreation Area: An area designated by Congress to ensure the conservation and protection of natural, scenic, historic, pastoral, and fish and wildlife values and to provide for the enhancement of recreational values.

National Recreation Trails: Trails established administratively by the Secretary of the Interior to provide for a variety of outdoor recreation uses in or reasonably close to urban areas. They often serve as connecting links between the National Historic Trails and National Scenic Trails.

National Scenic Trails: Trails established by an act of Congress that are intended to provide for maximum outdoor recreation potential and for the conservation and enjoyment of nationally significant scenic, historical, natural, and cultural qualities of the areas through which these trails pass. National Scenic Trails may be located to represent desert, marsh, grassland, mountain, canyon, river, forest, and other areas, as well as land forms that exhibit significant characteristics of the physiographic regions of the Nation.

National Wild and Scenic Rivers: Rivers designated in the National Wild and Scenic Rivers System that are classified in one of three categories, depending on the extent of development and accessibility along each section. In addition to being free flowing, these rivers and their immediate environments must possess at least one outstandingly remarkable value: scenic, recreational, geologic, fish and wildlife, historical, cultural, or other similar values.

NLCS (National Landscape Conservation System): An organized system of Bureau of Land Management lands that have received special designation for their scientific, cultural, educational, ecological, and other values. The NLCS, formally established by Title II of the Omnibus Public Land Management Act of 2009, includes national monuments, national conservation areas, wilderness, wilderness study areas, national wild and scenic rivers, national scenic and historic trails, and other units.

Noncompetitive leasing: Refers to leases issued to qualified applicants for lands not specifically known or presumed to contain mineral or petroleum deposits in quantity. Such leases can be issued on a first-come, first-served basis or through a random drawing procedure. (See Competitive leasing and Leasable minerals.)

Nonconsumptive trips: Wildlife-associated recreation that does not involve fishing, hunting, or trapping. Nonharvesting activities, such as feeding, photographing, and observing fish and other wildlife, picnicking, camping, etc., are nonconsumptive wildlife activities.

Nonexclusive sites: Mineral material disposal areas, such as community pits or common use areas, that are designated, maintained, and managed by the Bureau of Land Management and from which many small disposals are authorized under the Materials Act of 1947, as amended.

Nonoperating revenue: Receipts of a miscellaneous nature, such as incidental receipts from taxes, fines, etc., that are not related specifically to, or received in the process of, conducting the normal and regular business of the Bureau of Land Management as it pertains to the management of public lands and resources.

Nonuse: An authorization issued to an applicant for nonuse of grazing privileges in whole or part; usually issued for one grazing season.

O&C lands: Public lands in Western Oregon that were granted to the Oregon central railroad companies (later the Oregon & California Railroad Company) to aid in the construction of railroads but that were later forfeited and returned to the Federal Government by revestment of title. The term "O&C" lands, as often used, also refers to the reconveyed Coos Bay Military Wagon Road lands, which are public lands in Western Oregon that were once granted to the State of Oregon to aid in the construction of the Coos Bay Military Wagon Road but that were later forfeited and returned to Federal ownership by reconveyance.

Obligations: Payments, and amounts that the Government is obligated to pay, for goods and services received (or contracted for future delivery) made from appropriations during the fiscal year indicated.

Operator: An individual, group, association, or corporation authorized to conduct livestock grazing on public lands.

Original survey: A cadastral survey that creates land boundaries and establishes them for the first time.

Paleontology: A science dealing with the life of past geological periods as known from fossil remains.

Patent: A Government deed; a document that conveys legal title to public lands to the patentee. Public domain lands are patented; acquired lands are deeded by the Government.

Permit: A revocable authorization to use public land for a specified purpose for as long as 3 years.

Placer claim: A mining claim located for "all forms of deposits, excepting veins of quartz or other rock in place" (30 U.S.C. 35). A placer claim must generally be located by legal subdivision in conformance with the public land survey rather than by metes and bounds. A placer claim is limited to 20 acres per individual, although a placer claim may be as high as 160 acres for an association of eight or more persons. Corporations are limited to 20-acre claims.

PLO (Public Land Order): An order affecting, modifying, or canceling a withdrawal or reservation that has been issued by the Secretary of the Interior pursuant to powers of the President delegated to the Secretary by Executive Order 9146 of April 24, 1942, or by Executive Order 9337 of April 24, 1943.

Plugged and abandoned: Refers to new wells that have been drilled to total depth during the reporting period and that did not encounter oil or gas in paying quantities. (Approved plugging and abandonment may or may not have yet occurred.)

Potential natural community: An ecological condition classification that means that the current vegetation is between 76 and 100 percent similar to the potential natural plant community. Potential natural community describes vegetation that is in "excellent" condition.

Prescribed burning: See Prescribed fire projects.

Prescribed fire projects: Includes the Bureau of Land Management's efforts to use fire as a critical natural process to maintain and restore ecosystems, rangelands, and forest lands, and to reduce the hazardous buildup of fuels that may threaten healthy lands and public safety.

Private leases (acquired): Refers to oil and gas leases between private parties that are in existence at the time the Federal Government purchases the mineral estate along with the surface as part of a Federal Government acquisition, for which a Bureau of Land Management serial number is assigned.

Producible and service holes: Wells with one or more producible oil or gas service completions.

Producible completions (oil and gas): Separate completions existing on producible (i.e., physically and mechanically capable of production of oil or gas) or service wells at the end of the reporting period; or, separate completions that are made during the reporting period on newly drilled wells.

Producible leases: Leases that have at least one producible well actually located within the lease, as of the last day of the reporting period; includes producible leases that received allocated production from wells located off the lease and that have no producible wells actually located on the lease, as of the last day of the reporting period.

Protraction diagram: A diagram representing the plan of extension of cadastral surveys over unsurveyed public lands based on computed values for the corner positions.

Public auction: A sale of land through competitive—usually oral—bidding.

Public domain lands: Original public domain lands that have never left Federal ownership; lands in Federal ownership that were obtained by the Government in exchange for public domain lands or for timber on public domain lands; one category of public lands.

Public lands: Any land and interest in land owned by the United States and administered by the Secretary of the Interior through the Bureau of Land Management, without regard to how the United States acquired ownership, except for (1) lands located on the Outer

Continental Shelf, and (2) lands held for the benefit of Indians, Aleuts, and Eskimos. Include Public domain lands and Acquired lands. (See definitions.)

Public Land States: The 30 States that made up the public domain at its greatest extent: Alabama, Alaska, Arizona, Arkansas, California, Colorado, Florida, Idaho, Illinois, Indiana, Iowa, Kansas, Louisiana, Michigan, Minnesota, Mississippi, Missouri, Montana, Nebraska, Nevada, New Mexico, North Dakota, Ohio, Oklahoma, Oregon, South Dakota, Utah, Washington, Wisconsin, and Wyoming.

R&PP (Recreation and Public Purposes Act): Act of June 14, 1926 (44 Stat. 741), as amended, that provides for the purchase or lease of public lands by (a) Federal, State, or local governmental units for any activity that serves the interest of the general public consistent with public policy, or (b) nonprofit organizations if the lands are to be used for recreation purposes in an established or proposed recreation project area.

Receipts: All money received and credited to the proper account as required by law. Does not include collections held by the U.S. Treasury pending future determination of disposition by the Bureau of Land Management.

Reclamation homestead entry: An entry initiated under the act of June 17, 1902 (32 Stat. 338; 43 U.S.C., Sec. 643 et seq.), that provides for the issuance of patents to applicants who settle on and improve agricultural public land parcels not exceeding 160 acres within reclamation projects.

Recreation concession lease: A lease that is a long-term authorization for private parties to possess and use public land to provide recreation facilities and services for a fixed period. These leases are authorized under 43 CFR 2920 and the Land and Water Conservation Fund Act. Recreation concession leases establish the obligations that the Bureau of Land Management and the concessionaire agree to in providing visitor services necessary for full enjoyment of the public lands or related waters.

Recreation visit: A visit to Bureau of Land Management lands and waters by an individual for the purpose of engaging in any activities except those that are part of or incidental to the pursuit of a gainful occupation, whether for a few minutes or a full day.

Reforestation: The reestablishment of forest cover, either naturally or artificially.

Rental: The amount paid periodically (usually annually) by the holder of a lease or right-of-way grant for the right to use land or resources for the purposes set out in the lease or grant.

Research Natural Areas: Special management areas designated either by Congress or by a public or private agency to preserve and protect typical or unusual ecological communities, associations, phenomena, characteristics, or natural features or processes for scientific and educational purposes. They are established and managed to protect ecological processes, conserve biological diversity, and provide opportunities for observation for research and education.

Reserved lands: Federal lands that are dedicated or set aside for a specific public purpose or program and that are, therefore, generally not subject to disposition under the operation of all of the public land laws. (See Revocation and Withdrawal.)

Reservoir: A human-made, standing body of water whose water levels may be controlled.

Resurvey: A cadastral survey to identify and re-mark the boundaries of lands that were established by a prior survey.

Revocation: Generally, an action that cancels a previous official act; specifically, an action that cancels a withdrawal. Revocation is usually done in conjunction with restoration, which opens the public lands.

Right-of-way: A permit or an easement that authorizes the use of lands for certain specified purposes, such as the construction of forest access roads or a gas pipeline.

Riparian areas: Lands adjacent to creeks, streams, and rivers where vegetation is strongly influenced by the presence of water. Excluded are such sites as ephemeral streams or washes that do not exhibit the presence of vegetation dependent on free water in the soil. Riparian areas may constitute less than 1 percent of the land area in the western part of the United States, but they are among the most productive and valuable of all lands.

Salable minerals: Sand, gravel, stone, soil, and other common-variety mineral materials disposed of through sales at not less than their appraised price or through free-use permits (see definition).

Sale of materials: A competitive or noncompetitive sale by contract at not less than the appraised price of materials (timber and mineral) under the Materials Act of 1947, as amended.

Santini-Burton Act: Act of December 23, 1980 (Public Law 96-586, 94 Stat. 3381) that provides for the orderly disposition of Federal lands in Clark County, Nevada, and also provides for the acquisition of environmentally sensitive lands in the Lake Tahoe Basin.

Sawtimber: Logs of sufficient size and quality to be suitable for conversion into lumber or veneer.

Section 3: Lands administered under Section 3 of the Taylor Grazing Act. (See Grazing permit.)

Section 15: Lands administered under Section 15 of the Taylor Grazing Act. (See Grazing lease.)

Service completion or hole: Separate service completions that are for the benefit of oil and gas operations, such as water disposal, salt water disposal, water injection, gas injection, water source, steam injection, or monitoring.

Site-based recreation activities (other than camping, hunting, or nonmotorized travel): Includes sightseeing (the viewing of scenery; natural, historic, and archaeological sites; landscapes; or other features), picnicking, nature study and photography, mountain climbing and caving, gathering and collecting activities (mushrooms, rocks, and flowers), interpretation (guided and unguided touring, talks, and programs), and other environmental education events.

Small game habitat: Habitat area used by small game animals (including upland game species) at some time during their yearly life cycle.

Small tract lease: A parcel of public lands of 5 acres or less that has been found to be chiefly valuable for sale or lease as a home, cabin, camp, recreational, convalescent, or business site under the Act of June 1, 1938.

SNPLMA (Southern Nevada Public Land Management Act): Act approved October 1998 (Public Law 105-263) that provides for the disposal of public land within a specific area in the Las Vegas Valley and creates a special account into which 85 percent of the revenue generated by land sales or exchanges in the Las Vegas Valley is deposited. The remaining 15 percent goes to State and local governments. Revenue in the special account can be used for the acquisition of environmentally sensitive lands in Nevada; capital improvements; development of a multispecies habitat conservation plan in Clark County; and development of parks, trails, and natural areas in Clark County.

Spawning bed development: Consists of efforts made to improve spawning conditions for fish. May include addition of appropriate natural materials, cleaning of gravels, creation of shelter, etc.

Special land use permit: A permit that authorizes the use of public land for a purpose not specifically authorized under other regulation or statute.

Special recreation permit: A permit that authorizes the recreational use of an area and is issued pursuant to the regulations contained in 43 CFR Subpart 8372, and 36 CFR Part 71. Under the Land and Water Conservation Fund Act, implemented by these regulations, special recreation permits are required for all commercial use, for most competitive events, and for the individual, noncommercial use of special areas where permits are required.

Special surveys: Cadastral surveys that involve unusual application of, or departure from, the rectangular system. They often carry out the provisions of a special legislative act and include such work as small tract surveys; townsite surveys; island and omitted land surveys; homestead, homesite, trade and manufacturing site surveys; and also the survey and resurvey of portions of sections. Alaska special surveys are metes and bounds surveys of areas settled on or applied for under certain special land laws applicable to State of Alaska.

State Office: The first-level administrative unit of the Bureau of Land Management field organization. It comprises a geographic area consisting of one or more States.

Stock raising homestead: A homestead not exceeding 640 acres initiated under the Stock Raising Homestead Act of 1916, which provided for the homesteading of lands chiefly valuable for grazing and for raising forage crops. Minerals in these lands were reserved to the United States. The provisions for stock raising homesteads were by implication repealed by the Taylor Grazing Act.

Streambank stabilization: Accomplished for severe cases of erosion that are not natural, to include efforts to reduce streambank movement by adding materials to deflect water, planting vegetation, etc.

Stream with fishery potential: A stream that does not currently support a sport fishery but that could be changed into a fishable stream with management (e.g., stocking, removal of barriers).

Sustained yield: The achievement and maintenance in perpetuity of a high-level annual, or regular periodic, output of the various renewable resources of the public lands consistent with multiple use.

Threatened species: Any animal or plant species likely to become endangered within the foreseeable future throughout all or a part of its range. (See Candidate species and Endangered species.)

Trespass: An unauthorized use of Federal lands or resources.

Tunnel site: A site located for the development of a vein or lode or for the anticipated discovery of previously unknown veins or lodes. The locator of a tunnel site is given the right to all veins cut by the tunnel within 3,000 feet of its portal and to 1,500 feet along the length of each blind vein or lode cut. A tunnel site location lapses if not worked for a period of at least 6 months.

Unlawful enclosures or occupancy: Enclosures of public lands that are made or maintained by any party, association, or corporation without valid claim.

U.S.C.: United States Code.

Vacant public land: Public land that is not reserved, appropriated, or set aside for a specific or designated purpose. Such land is not covered by any non-Federal right or claim other than permits, leases, rights-of-way, and unreported mining claims.

Visitor hour: A unit used to measure duration of recreation use. A visitor hour involves the presence of a person on a recreation area or site for the purpose of engaging in recreation activities for either continuous, intermittent, or simultaneous periods aggregating 60 minutes.

Waterfowl habitat: The total acreage of all wetlands, lakes, ponds, and reservoirs on Bureau of Land Management lands. Uplands used for nesting are not included.

Water sports (other than boating or fishing): Includes swimming, general water play, waterskiing, ski jumping, platter riding, and other similar activities that occur outside a boat.

Wetland improvements: Consist of techniques to restore wetlands to their proper functioning condition. Improvements may consist of establishing vegetation, such as willow, to reduce erosion and improve water retention.

Wetlands: Permanently wet or intermittently flooded areas where the water table (fresh, saline, or brackish) is at, near, or above the soil surface for extended intervals, where hydric wet soil conditions are normally exhibited, and where water depths generally do not exceed 2 meters (about $6\frac{1}{2}$ feet). Marshes, shallows, swamps, muskegs, lake bogs, and wet meadows are examples of wetlands.

Wilderness: An area of undeveloped Federal land retaining its primeval character and influence, without permanent improvement or human habitation, that is protected and managed so as to preserve its natural conditions and that (1) generally appears to have been affected primarily by the forces of nature, with the imprint of human work substantially unnoticeable; (2) has outstanding opportunities for solitude or a primitive and unconfined type of recreation; (3) has at least 5,000 acres of land or is of sufficient size as to make practicable its preservation and use in an unimpaired condition; and (4) may also contain ecological, geological, or other features of scientific, educational, scenic, or historical value.

Wild free-roaming horses and burros: All unbranded and unclaimed horses and burros using public lands as all or part of their habitat.

Winter sports: Include ice skating, skiing (downhill and cross-country), snowboarding, snowshoeing, sledding, snowmobiling, and tobogganing, as well as activities such as snow sculpture and general snow play.

Withdrawal: An action that restricts the disposition of public lands and that holds them for specific public purposes; also, public lands that have been dedicated to public purposes. (See Reserved lands and Revocation.)

Woodlands: Forest lands usually supporting open-grown, widely scattered trees of marginal merchantability and generally more valuable for watershed or wildlife protection purposes than for the production of timber for commercial purposes.

WSA (Wilderness Study Area): An area having the following characteristics: (1) Size—roadless areas of at least 5,000 acres of public lands or of a manageable size; (2) Naturalness—generally appears to have been affected primarily by the forces of natures; and (3) Opportunities—provides outstanding opportunities for solitude or primitive and unconfined types of recreation. The Federal Land Policy and Management Act of 1976 directed the Bureau of Land Management to inventory and study its roadless areas for wilderness characteristics.

Bibliography

BOOKS AND ARTICLES

Adler, Jonathan H., "Fables of the Cuyahoga: Reconstructing a History of Environmental Protection," *Fordham Environmental Law Journal*, XIV (Fall 2002), 89-146.

Allen, David Grayson, "The Olmsted National Historic Site and the Growth of Historic Landscape Preservation" (Lebanon, New Hampshire: Northeastern University Press, 2007).

Anderson, H. Michael, "Reforming National-Forest Policy," *Issues in Science and Technology*, X (Winter 1993-94), 42-43.

Antieau, Chester James, "Our Two Centuries of Law and Life, 1775-1975: The Work of the Supreme Court and the Impact of both Congress and Presidents" (Buffalo, New York: Fred B. Rothman Publications, of William S. Hein & Co., 2001).

Bentley, William R., "Forest Service Timber Sales: A Preliminary Evaluation of Policy Alternatives," *Land Economics*, XXXXIV: 2 (May 1968), 205-18.

Beveridge, Charles E.; and Paul Rocheleau (David Larkin, ed.), "Frederick Law Olmsted: Designing the American Landscape" (New York: Rizzoli, 1995).

Billington, Ray Allen, "Why Some Historians Rarely Write History: A Case Study of Frederick Jackson Turner," *The Mississippi Valley Historical Review*, L: 1 (June 1963), 3-27.

Borman, Michael M., and Douglas E. Johnson, "Evolution of Grazing and Land Tenure Policies on Public Lands," *Rangelands*, XII: 4 (August 1990), 203-06.

Catlin, George, "Letters and Notes on the Manners, Customs, and Condition of the North American Indians. Written During Eight Years' Travel Amongst the Wildest Tribes of Indians in North America" (Philadelphia: Willis P. Hazard; two volumes, 1857).

Cooley, Heather; Juliet Christian-Smith, and Peter H. Gleick, "More with Less: Agricultural Water Conservation and Efficiency in California: A Special Focus on the Delta" (Oakland, California: The Pacific Institute, September 2008).

Cronon, William, "Revisiting the Vanishing Frontier: The Legacy of Frederick Jackson Turner," *The Western Historical Quarterly*, XVIII: 2 (April 1987), 157-76.

Donahue, Debra L., "Western Grazing: The Capture of Grass, Ground, and Government," *Environmental Law*, XXXV (2005), 721-806.

Egleston, Nathaniel H., "Handbook of Tree-Planting; or, Why to Plant, Where to Plant, What to Plant, How to Plant" (New York: D. Appleton, 1884).

Fairfax, Sally K., and Dan Tarlock, "No Water for the Woods: A Critical Analysis of *United States v. New Mexico*," *Idaho Law Review*, XV (1979), 509-54.

Fairfax, Sally K.; and Darla Guenzler, "Conservation Trusts" (Lawrence: University of Kansas Press, 2001).

Faure, Michael, Albert J. Verheij, and Tom vanden Borre, eds., "Shifts in Compensation for Environmental Damage" (New York: SpringerWein, 2007).

George, Rose, "The Big Necessity: The Unmentionable World of Human Waste and Why It Matters" (New York: Macmillan, 2009).

Graf, William L., "Wilderness Preservation and the Sagebrush Rebellions" (Savage, Maryland: Rowman & Littlefield, 1990).

Grossman, Mark, "The ABC-Clio Companion to the Environmental Movement" (Santa Barbara, California: ABC-Clio, 1994).

Hartman, Howard L., A.B. Cummins and I.A. Given, "SME Mining Engineering Handbook" (Littleton, Colorado: Society for Mining, Metallurgy, and Exploration, Inc.; two volumes, 1992).

Hudson, David; Marvin Bergman, & Loren Horton, "The Biographical Dictionary of Iowa" (Iowa City: University of Iowa Press, 2008).

Hutt, Sherry; Caroline M. Blanco, and Ole Varmer, "Heritage Resources Law: Protecting the Archaelogical and Cultural Environment" (New York: John Wiley & Sons for The National Trust for Historic Preservation, 1999).

Ingram, Colin, "The Drinking Water Book: A Complete Guide to Safe Drinking Water" (Berkeley, California: Ten Speed Press, 1991).

Ise, John, "The United States Forest Policy" (New Haven: Yale University Press, 1920).

Kadlec, Robert H.; and Scott D. Wallace, "Treatment Wetlands" (Boca Raton, Florida: CRC Press, 2009).

Kanazawa, Mark T., "Water Subsidies, Water Transfers, And Economic Efficiency," *Contemporary Economic Policy*, XII: 2 (1994), 112-22.

Keele, Denise M.; Robert W. Malmsheimer, Donald W. Floyd, and Jerome E. Perez, "Forest Service Land Management Litigation 1989-2002," *Journal of Forestry*, CIV:4 (June 2006), 196-202.

Kennedy, Bruce A., "Surface Mining" (Littleton, Colorado: Society for Mining, Metallurgy, and Exploration, Inc., 1990).

Klyza, Christopher McGrory, "The United States Army, Natural Resources, and Political Development in the Nineteenth Century," *Polity*, XXXV: 1 (Autumn 2002), 1-28.

Kraft, Michael E.; and Norman J. Vig, eds., "Environmental Policy in the 1990s" (Washington, D.C.: CQ Press, 1997).

Levy, Richard E.; and Robert L. Glicksman, "Judicial Activism and Restraint in the Supreme Court's Environmental Law Decisions," *Vanderbilt Law Review*, 42 (March 1989), 343-431.

Lewis, Scott A., "The Sierra Club Guide to Safe Drinking Water" (San Francisco, California: Sierra Club Books, 1996).

Lipset, Seymour Martin, "American Exceptionalism: A Double-Edge Sword" (New York: W.W. Norton, 1996).

Maclaurin, James; and Kim Sterelny, "What is Biodiversity?" (Chicago: The University of Chicago Press, 2008).

Mathews, Olen Paul; Amy Haak, and Kathryn Toffenetti, "Mining and Wilderness: Incompatible Uses or Justifiable Compromise?" *Environment*, XXVII (April 1985), 12-17, 30-36.

Moore, Jonathan W.; Daniel E. Schindler, Mark D. Scheuerell, Danielle Smith and Jonathan Frodge, "Lake Eutrophication at the Urban Fringe, Seattle Region, US," *Ambio*, XXXII: 1 (February 2003), 13-18.

Morrison, R.S.; and Emilio De Soto, "Mining Rights on the Public Domain: Lode and Placer Claims. Tunnels, Mill Sites and Water Rights. Statutes, Decisions, Forms and Land Office Procedure for Prospectors, Attorneys, Surveyors, and Mining Companies" (Denver, Colorado: The Smith-Brooks Printing Company, 1908).

Muir, John, "The Hetch-Hetchy Valley: A National Question," *American Forestry*, XVI:5 (May 1910), 263-69.

The National Research Council, "Setting Priorities for Drinking Water Contaminants" (Washington, DC: National Academy Press, 1999).

O'Sullivan, John L., "The Great Nation of Futurity," *The United States Magazine and Democratic Review*, VI: XXIII (November 1839), 426-30.

Ranquist, Harold A., "The Winters Doctrine and How It Grew: Federal Reservation of Rights to the Use of Water," Brigham Young University Law Review, III (1975), 639-724.

Rasband, James R., "The Rise of Urban Archipelagoes in the American West: A New Reservation Policy?," *Environmental Law Review*, XXXI:1 (2001), 1-93.

Riebsame, William E., "Ending the Range Wars," *Environment* (May 1996), 4- 9, 27-29.

Roosevelt, Theodore, "Theodore Roosevelt: An Autobiography" (New York: Macmillan, 1913).

Sanger, George P., ed., "By Authority of Congress. The Statutes at Large, Treaties, and Proclamations, of the United States of America. From December 1863, to December 1865. Arranged in Chronological Order and Carefully Collated with the Originals in Washington. With References to the Matter of Each Act and to the Subsequent Acts on the Same Subject. Edited by George P. Sanger, Counsellor at Law" (Boston: Little, Brown, and Company, 1866).

Schacht, Walter H., "Range Management" in David J. Wishart, ed., "Encyclopedia of the Great Plains" (Lincoln: University of Nebraska Press, 2004).

Scheberle, Denise, "Federalism and Environmental Policy: Trust and the Politics of Implementation" (Washington, D.C.: Georgetown University Press, 2004).

Schwartz, Eleanor R., "A Capsule Examination of the Legislative History of the Federal Land Policy and Management Act of 1976," *Arizona Law Review*, XXI (1979), 285-95.

Spicer, John I., "World Issues Today: Biodiversity" (New York: The Rosen Publishing Group, Inc., 2009).

Strong, Douglas Hillman, "Dreamers & Defenders: American Conservationists" (Lincoln: The University of Nebraska Press, 1988).

Sutton, Victoria, "The George W. Bush Administration and the Environment," *Western New England Law Review*, XXV (2003), 221-42.

Weinberg, Marcia, "Water Use Conflicts in the West: Implications of Reforming the Bureau of Reclamation's Water Supply Policies" (Washington, D.C.: Congressional Budget Office, 1997).

Wilson, Edward O., "Nature Revealed: Selected Writings, 1949-2006" (Baltimore: The Johns Hopkins University Press, 2006).

US Government Documents (By Agency)

Bureau of Land Management, "Information Resources Management: Activities and Accomplishments: December 2009" (Washington, D.C.: Government Printing Office, 2009).

Department of the Interior, "Stewardship for America with Integrity and Excellence: US Department of the Interior Annual Performance and Accountability Report: FY 2007 Highlights" (Washington, D.C.: Government Printing Office, 2007).

"Estimated Use of Water in the United States in 2005" (Washington, D.C.: US Geological Survey, 2009).

General Accounting Office, "Endangered Species: Limited Effect of Consultation Requirements on Western Water Projects" (GAO/RCED-87-78) (March 1987).

Government Accountability Office, "Implementation of the Federal Onshore Oil and Gas Leasing Reform Act of 1987: Testimony," 28 September 1989.

Government Accountability Office, "Endangered Species Act: Types and Number of Implementing Actions" (GAO/CED-92-131BR) (May 1992).

Government Accountability Office, "Bureau of Reclamation: Reclamation Law and the Allocation of Construction Costs for Federal Water Projects" (Washington, D.C.: Government Printing Office, 1997).

Government Accountability Office, "Federal Land Management: Use of Stewardship Contracting Is Increasing, but Agencies Could Benefit from Better Strategies" (GAO Report 09-23, November 2008).

US Government Reports, Speeches, and Other Documents

"Army Corps of Engineers: Budget Formulation Process Emphasizes Agency-wide Priorities, but Transparency of Budget Presentation Could Be Improved," US GAO Report 10-453 (April 2010).

"Attachment 4. Prospective Conservation Designation: National Monument Designations Under the Antiquities Act," internal memo, undated, courtesy of The Hill, online at http://thehill.com/images/stories/blogs/antiquitiesdocument.pdf.

"BLM Public Domain Lands: Volume of Timber Offered for Sale Has Declined Substantially Since Fiscal Year 1990," GAO Report 03-615 (June 2003).

Buck, Eugene H., "Magnuson Fishery Conservation and Management Act Reauthorization" (CRS Report for Congress, 4 December 1996).

Buck, Eugene H., et al., "The Endangered Species Act (ESA) and the 111th Congress: Conflicting Values and Difficult Choices" (CRS Report 7-5700 {23 July 2010}).

Chiang, Sie Long, "Public Lands, Onshore Federal and Indian Minerals in Lands of the U.S., Responsibilities of the BLM," Report of the Department of the Interior/Bureau of Land Management, 1 December 2000.

Cody, Betsy A., "Western Water Resource Issues" (CRS Report for Congress, 25 October 2002).

"Endangered Species: Many Factors Affect the Length of Time to Recover Select Species," GAO Report 06-730 (September 2006).

"Endangered Species Act: The U.S. Fish and Wildlife Service Has Incomplete Information about Effects on Listed Species from Section 7 Consultations," GAO Report 09-550 (May 2009).

Gorte, Ross W., "Wilderness: Overview and Statistics" (CRS Report for Congress, 18 March 2005).

_____, Carol Hardy Vincent, and Marc Humphries, "Federal Lands Managed by the Bureau of Land Management (BLM) and the Forest Service (FS): Issues for the 110th Congress" (CRS Report for Congress, 9 May 2008).

Holt, Mark, "Nuclear Energy Policy" (CRS Report for Congress, 10 December 2009).

Humphries, Marc, "Oil and Gas Exploration and Development on Public Lands," CRS Report for Congress (Washington, D.C.: Congressional Research Service, 26 March 2004).

_____, "Mining on Federal Lands: Hardrock Materials" (CRS Report for Congress, 30 April 2008).

Lane, Nic, "The Bureau of Reclamation's Aging Infrastructure" (CRS Report for Congress, 30 April 2008).

Parker, Larry, and Mark Holt, "Nuclear Power: Outlook for New US Reactors" (CRS Report for Congress, 9 March 2007).

Rowley, William D., "The Bureau of Reclamation: Origins and Growth to 1945, Volume I" (Washington, D.C.: US Department of the Interior, Bureau of Reclamation, 2006).

"The Threat of Eco-Terrorism," testimony of James F. Jarboe, Domestic Terrorism Section Chief, Counterterrorism Division, FBI, Before the House Resources Committee, Subcommittee on Forests and Forest Health, 12 February 2002, online at http://www.fbi.gov/congress/congress02/jarboe021202.htm.

Tiemann, Mary, "Safeguarding the Nation's Drinking Water: EPA and Congressional Actions" (CRS Report for Congress, 30 January 2008).

US House of Representatives, "Grazing Management Reform: Hearing before the Subcommittee on National Parks, Forests, and Public Lands of the Committee on Natural Resources, House of Representatives, One Hundred Third Congress, First

Session, on H.R. 1602, to Reform the Management of Grazing on the Public Range Lands, [and] H.R. 643, to Raise Grazing Fees on Public Lands, and For Other Purposes" (Washington, D.C.: US Government Printing Office, 1993).

Wheeler, Christopher H., "Employment Growth in America: Exploring Where Good Jobs Grow," research report of the Federal Reserve Bank of St. Louis, July 2005

OTHER REPORTS

"The Cato Handbook for Policymakers" (Washington, D.C.: The Cato Institute, 2009).

Cavanagh, Sheila M., "National Environmental Policy During the Clinton Years" (Report of the John F. Kennedy School of Government, Harvard University, 28 June 2001).

Committee on Onshore Oil and Gas Leasing, Board on Earth Sciences and Resources, Commission on Physical Sciences, Mathematics, and Resources, the National Research Council, "Land Use Planning and Oil and Gas Leasing on Onshore Federal Lands" (Washington, D.C.: National Academy Press, 1989).

Copeland, Claudia, "Water Quality Initiatives and Agriculture" (CRS Report for Congress, 20 December 2000).

_____, "Pesticide Use and Water Quality: Are the Laws Complementary or in Conflict?" (CRS Report for Congress, 14 June 2007).

_____, et. al., "Federally Supported Water Supply and Wastewater Treatment Programs" (CRS Report for Congress, 15 June 2009).

"Establishment and Modification of National Forest Boundaries and National Grasslands: A Chronological Record, 1891-1996," Report of the Lands Staff, US Department of Agriculture, Forest Service, November 1997.

Hutchins, Wells A., Harold H. Ellis and J. Peter DeBraal, "Water Rights Laws in the Nineteen Western States" (Washington, D.C.: US Department of Agriculture; three volumes, 1971; reprint, Clark, New Jersey: The Lawbook Exchange, Ltd.; three volumes, 2004).

"The Federal Land Policy and Management Act of 1976, As Amended" (a publication of the US Department of the Interior, Bureau of Land Management, and the Office of the Solicitor, Washington, D.C., October 2001).

Hahn, Robert W.; Sheila M. Olmstead, and Robert N. Stavins, "Environmental Regulation During the 1990s: A Retrospective Analysis," a Report of the American Enterprise Institute-Brookings Institute Joint Center for Regulatory Studies (27 January 2003).

Pinchot Institute for Conservation, "Ensuring the Stewardship of the National Wilderness Preservation System: A Report to the USDA Forest Service, Bureau of Land

Management, US Fish & Wildlife Service, National Park Service, [and] US Geological Survey" (Milford, Pennsylvania: Pinchot Institute for Conservation, September 2001).

Walker, Paul K., "Engineers of Independence: A Documentary History of the Army Engineers in the American Revolution, 1775 1783" (Washington, D.C.: Historical Division, U.S. Army Corps of Engineers, 1981).

DISSERTATIONS & THESES

Costello, Philip Paul, "Frederick Jackson Turner Frontier Historian" (Master's thesis, Southern Connecticut State University, 1960).

Forness, Norman Olaf, "The Origins and Early History of the United States Department of the Interior" (Master's thesis, Pennsylvania State University, 1964).

Gallagher, Mary Annette, "John F. Lacey: A Study in Organizational Politics" (Ph.D. dissertation, University of Arizona, 1970).

Handley, William Ross, "The Literary West: Imagining America from Turner to Fitzgerald" (Ph.D. dissertation, University of California, Los Angeles, 1997).

Murray, Scott Fitzgerald, "Civic Virtue and Public Policy: Discerning the Particulars of Reforming the General Mining Law of 1872" (Master of Arts thesis, University of Nevada at Las Vegas, 1997).

Vierling, Ronald, "The New Western Mythology: A Study of Frederick Jackson Turner's Frontier Thesis, its Origins and Relationship to American Thought and Literary Themes" (Master's thesis, University of Wyoming, 1972).

Index